A WNSHAM & JOHN CHURCHILL

A COLLECTION OF VOYAGES AND TRAVELS

1592-1646

A WNSHAM & JOHN CHURCHILL
A COLLECTION OF VOYAGES AND TRAVELS

TRUE TRAVELS AND ADVENTURES INTO EUROPE, ASIA, AFRICA AND AMERICA 1592-1629
CAPT. JOHN SMITH

TWO JOURNALS KEPT BY SEVEN SAILORS IN THE ISLAND OF

ST. MAURICE IN GREENLAND 1633 AND 1634

AN ACCOUNT OF ICELAND AND GREENLAND 1644 AND 1646
LA PEYRERE

THE STRANGE AND DANGEROUS VOYAGE IN THE INTENDED DISCOVERY OF THE NORTH-WEST PASSAGE INTO THE SOUTH SEA 1631 AND 1632
CAPT. THOMAS JAMES

THE HISTORY OF THE LIFE AND ACTION OF CHRISTOPHER COLUMBUS AND HIS DISCOVERY OF THE WEST-INDIES CALLED THE NEW WORLD
BY HIS SON D. FERDINAND COLUMBUS

PYRAMIDOGRAPHIA:
DESCRIPTION OF PYRAMIDS IN EGYPT
AND
A DISCOURSE OF THE ROMAN FOOT AND DENARIUS
MEASURES AND WEIGHTS USED BY THE ANCIENTS
JOHN GREAVES

ACCOUNT OF COCHIN-CHINA
THE TEMPORAL AND SPIRITUAL STATE OF THE KINGDOM
CHRISTOPHER BORRI

A WNSHAM & JOHN CHURCHILL
A COLLECTION OF VOYAGES AND TRAVELS

TRUE TRAVELS AND ADVENTURES INTO
EUROPE, ASIA, AFRICA AND AMERICA 1592-1629
CAPT. JOHN SMITH

TWO JOURNALS KEPT BY SEVEN SAILORS IN THE ISLAND OF
ST. MAURICE IN GREENLAND 1633 AND 1634

AN ACCOUNT OF ICELAND AND GREENLAND 1644 AND 1646
LA PEYRERE

THE STRANGE AND DANGEROUS VOYAGE IN THE INTENDED DISCOVERY OF THE
NORTH-WEST PASSAGE INTO THE SOUTH SEA 1631 AND 1632
CAPT. THOMAS JAMES

THE HISTORY OF THE LIFE AND ACTION OF
CHRISTOPHER COLUMBUS AND HIS DISCOVERY
OF THE WEST-INDIES CALLED THE NEW WORLD
BY HIS SON D. FERDINAND COLUMBUS

PYRAMIDOGRAPHIA:
DESCRIPTION OF PYRAMIDS IN EGYPT
AND
A DISCOURSE OF THE ROMAN FOOT AND DENARIUS
MEASURES AND WEIGHTS USED BY THE ANCIENTS
JOHN GREAVES

ACCOUNT OF COCHIN-CHINA
THE TEMPORAL AND SPIRITUAL STATE OF THE KINGDOM
CHRISTOPHER BORRI

GYAN

Published by

GYAN

Gyan Publishing House
5, Ansari Road
Daryaganj, New Delhi-110002
Phone: 011-47034999, 9811692060
E-mail: books@gyanbooks.com

Distribution Network
gyanbooks.com
India, USA, Canada, UK, Australia, France

ISBN : 978-81-212-4509-8 (HB)
First Published, London, 1732

2nd Impression 2020

Printed at: Gyan Press, Delhi.

The book at your disposal is the edition of an old book originally published long back. The Text quality of this book may not be at par as compared to our other books but many readers approached us to reprint this important book so that it could satiate their hunger. We request all the readers of this book to help us to improve its quality by providing the necessary text of those pages which are not properly visible. Your valuable support in this case will be highly appreciated and acknowledged and our future readers will be benefitted immensely.

A COLLECTION OF Voyages and Travels,

SOME

Now first Printed from *Original Manuscripts*,

OTHERS

Now first Published in ENGLISH.

In Six VOLUMES.

With a General PREFACE, giving an Account of the Progress of NAVIGATION, from its first Beginning.

Illustrated with a great Number of useful Maps and Cuts, Curiously Engraven.

VOL. II.

LONDON:

Printed by Assignment from Messrs. CHURCHILL,

For JOHN WALTHOE, over-against the *Royal-Exchange*, in *Cornhill*; THO. WOTTON, at the *Queen's-Head* and *Three Daggers* over-against St. *Dunstan's* Church, in *Fleet-street*; SAMUEL BIRT, in *Ave-Mary-Lane*, *Ludgate street*; DANIEL BROWNE, at the *Black-Swan*, without *Temple-Bar*; THOMAS OSBORN, in *Gray's-Inn*; JOHN SHUCKBURGH, at the *Sun*, next the *Inner-Temple-Gate*, in *Fleetstreet*; and HENRY LINTOT, at the *Cross-Keys*, against St. *Dunstan's* Church, in *Fleetstreet*. M DCC XXXII.

V. II.

The Effigies of Mr. Jn. Nieuhoff.

Mr. John Nieuhoff's Remarkable
VOYAGES & TRAVELLS into ye
best Provinces of ye West and East Indies.
VOL. II.

A Brasilian

THE
CONTENTS
OF THE
SECOND VOLUME.

Pyrami-

The CONTENTS.

VOYAGES

VOYAGES
AND
TRAVELS
INTO
BRASIL
AND THE
EAST-INDIES.

CONTAINING,

An exact Description of the *DUTCH BRASIL*, and divers Parts of the *EAST-INDIES*; their PROVINCES, CITIES, LIVING CREATURES, and PRODUCTS; the MANNERS, CUSTOMS, HABITS, and RELIGION of the INHABITANTS:

WITH

A particular ACCOUNT of all the remarkable Passages that happened during the Author's stay of nine Years in *BRASIL*; especially in Relation to the REVOLT of the *Portuguese*, and the intestine War carried on there from 1640, to 1649.

AS ALSO

A most ample Description of the most famous City of *BATAVIA* in the *East-Indies*. By Mr. *JOHN NIEUHOFF*.

Both adorned with COPPER PLATES, done after the Life. Translated from the *Dutch* Original.

ADVERTISEMENT to the READER.

IT is about nineteen years since my brother, John Nieuhoff, just before his second voyage into the Indies, presented me with his description of China, and certain draughts he had made during his embassy in that empire, which being afterwards published, were soon after translated into six several languages.

My brother had, before that time, not only been in Brasil, and several other places in those parts, but also since that time, has had the opportunity of travelling through a great part of Asia, till 1671. when returning into Holland, he brought along with him all his papers, observations, and draughts, he had collected during his voyages; which, though much coveted by all curious persons, yet, for some reasons best known to himself, he did not think fit to commit to publick view.

But, after his decease, considering with myself, that such useful collections ought not to be buried in oblivion, I thought fit to publish them for the publick good.

As those things which he relates of the revolt of the Portuguese in Brasil, are extracted verbatim out of the records kept during my brother's abode of nine years in Brasil, under the government of the lords, Henry Hamel, Peter Bas, and Adrian Bullestrate, and authentick letters; so the truth thereof admits not of the least doubt from unbiass'd persons.

The vast countries through which my brother travell'd in his life-time, as Brasil, part of Persia, Malabar, Madura, Coromandel, Amboyna, Ceylon, Malacca, Sumatra, Java, Tagowan, and part of China, besides many islands, could not in the least infect him with that disease, so incident to travellers, to relate fables instead of histories, it having been his constant practice, to adhere most religiously in all his treatises, to the naked truth, without the least disguise.

His last voyage to the isle of Madagascar, where he was lost, I have taken partly out of his own letters, partly out of the journal of captain Reinard Claeson, which he brought along with him from thence.

As to his person, I will only add thus much. He was born at Uffen, in the earldom of Benthem, (where his father, brother, and brother-in-law, were all three Burgomasters) of a good family, the 22[d] of July 1618. He was a comely person, of a good understanding, good humour'd, and agreeable in conversation; a great admirer of poesy, drawing, and musick: As he delighted in travelling, so he was thereby become master of divers languages: In what station he lived during his abode in Brasil, and the East-Indies, will best appear by the two following treatises.

HENRY NIEUHOFF.

Mr. *JOHN NIEUHOFF's* REMARKABLE VOYAGES AND TRAVELS TO *BRASIL.*

1640. IN the year 1640, I entred into the service of the *West-India* company, and on the 24th of *October*, went in the quality of merchant supercargo, aboard the ship called the *Roebuck*, of 28 guns and 130 men, commanded by *Nicholas Selles* of *Durkendam*. We set sail out of the *Texel* the same day, in company of several other vessels bound for *France*, *Spain* and the *Streights*; and pursued our voyage the 28th with a favourable gale through the channel betwixt *France* and *England*.

His departure out of Holland.

A violent storm.

On the 29th we were overtaken with a most violent tempest, which obliged us to take in all our great sails: It continued from morning to night, when the fury of the winds being somewhat allay'd, we found that we had escaped without any considerable damage; but the sea continued very turbulent all that night. The next day following our seamen catch'd a wood snipe, a wild pidgeon, and several other small birds; which were forc'd into the sea by the violence of the storm.

On the 31st we found ourselves under the 45th degree of northern latitude. The next morning being the first of *November*, some of our seamen catch'd a sea-hog by the means of a harpeon: It was so big, that four men could scarce lift it into the ship. It's taste was not very agreeable, but rankish, which was the reason our men did not catch any more of them, though they swam in vast numbers round about our vessel. By sun-set the wind beginning to encrease, we parted from the other ships, bound for *Spain* and the *Streights*, which were not separated from us in the last storm, steering our course south-west. The 2d and 3d it blew very hard, with thunder and lightning, so that we were forc'd to take in all our great sails, and the ship being very leaky ever since the last tempest, to ply the pump with all our might.

Another most violent storm.

The 4th we found ourselves under the 40 deg. 30 min. when about midnight the wind encreased with so much violence, that the air which surrounded us, appearing no otherwise than one continual fire, occasion'd by the lightning, which scarce ever ceas'd all that night. During this calamity we perceived certain small fires or lights fix'd to the mast: They are called *Peaceable's fires* by the seamen. These fires are suppos'd to be certain sulphureous vapours, forc'd by the violence of the winds from the shore into the sea, where being lightned by the violent agitation of the air, they burn till their oily substance be consumed. The seamen look upon them as a good omen, that the storm is going to abate; which prov'd true in effect, the fury of the winds beginning to allay from that

Wild-fire.

that time; and we had the good fortune to discover two leaks near our forecastle, which else might have prov'd of dangerous consequence.

They pass the Barrels. The 5th we pass'd the *Barrels*, under the 39th degree; where according to an antient custom, every one, of what quality or degree soever, that has not passed there before, is obliged to be baptized, or redeem himself from it. He that is to be baptized, has a rope tied round his middle, wherewith he is drawn up to the very top of the bowsprit, and from thence three times successively tumbled into the water. There were some who look'd very blank upon the Matter, but others went cheerfully about it, and for a measure of *Spanish* wine, suffered themselves to be rebaptized for the master and the merchant. But this custom is abolished of late years, by special orders from the governors of the company, to avoid broils and quarrels, which used often to arise upon this occasion.

The 6th, as we were steering our course *S. S. W.* with a fresh gale, we descried two vessels, making all the sail they could towards us, whom we supposed to be *Turkish* pirates (as indeed they proved afterwards) *They discover two* Turkish *vessels.* it was resolved to defend us till the utmost extremity. Accordingly orders were given to clear every thing upon the deck, and to furnish the seamen with musquets, hangers, *Prepare for an engagement.* pikes, and other such like weapons. Every one having taken his station, we put up the bloody flag, and expected their coming under the sound of our trumpets. The master of the ship, being all that time very ill of some wounds he had received formerly, which were now broken up afresh; and the commissary *Francis Zweers*, not being in a condition, by reason of his great age, to remain upon deck, I was fain to undertake the whole management of the ship, and encouraged them to fight bravely for their lives and liberty, ordering them not to fire at all, till they were in their full reach, they being much better mann'd than we.

About noon we saw the *Turks* make up towards us with orange-colour'd flags, which however they soon after changed for the bloody flags, and the biggest of them saluted us with two cannon shot out of his forecastle, without doing us the least harm, *An engagement with two* Turkish *rovers.* but the second time almost shot our foremast in pieces. In the mean while we were come so near to one another, that we sent them a good broadside into their ship, which the *Turks* repay'd us immediately; but it was not long before we observ'd the biggest of the two had received a shot betwixt wind and water, which made her keep at some farther distance, till she had repaired her damage, which gave me opportunity to encourage our people with words, and a good proportion of wine; which they mix'd with some gunpowder, and I, to please them, followed their example.

By this time they returned both to the charge, and saluted us so fiercely with their cannon and small shot, that they took away the roof of our great cabin, and did us some damage in our rigging. I then changed my scimeter for a musquet, and discharged continually upon the enemy, and I found myself sore several weeks after, by the hurt I received from a musquet of one that stood hard by me, which being by a cannon ball forced out of his hands against my body, I fell down stretch'd all along upon the deck, without sense or motion; but having after some time recovered myself, I returned to my post. I then perceived the captain of the biggest *Turkish* ship with a turbant on his head, in the stern, encouraging his men, which made me order those about me, to aim at him with their small shot, which, as I suppose, succeeded according to our hopes, it being not long before we lost sight of him. Notwithstanding this, the heat of the fight encreased on both sides, many broadsides passing betwixt us, accompanied with most dreadful outcries and lamentations of the wounded on both sides. However, the *Turks* durst not attempt to board us; whether it were that they thought us better mann'd than really we were, or that they feared we would set fire to the ship, which we threatned we would, shewing them a match ready for that purpose. They answered us in *Dutch*, that they would not part with us upon those terms; yet was it not long before we saw them make away from us, having received many shots thro' their *The* Turks *leave the fight.* ships; and we with a brisk gale, made all the sail we could to be rid of these unwelcome guests, steering a quite different course, which with the advantage of the darkness of the night, brought us quite out of sight of them by next morning.

We gave thanks to God for his having delivered us from the danger of slavery, and crowning our endeavours with success against an enemy much stronger than us, the biggest of them carrying twenty-four guns, and the other two; whereas we had no more than eighteen, besides that they were much better mann'd than we. After having taken a view of our ship, and found it sound under water, we betook ourselves to repair the damage we had received during the fight; but whilst we were busy in this work, we were on the 7th surprized by so violent a storm, that we were forced to take

1640. take in all our sails. This put us to a great nonplus, but by good fortune the storm blew soon over, when orders were given to give an Allowance of three pounds and a half of bisket *per* week to the seamen, all our other bread being become musty by that time. The 10th we found ourselves under the 39th deg. and 30 min. about 20 leagues off of the *Canary Islands*; here we discovered the pike of *Tenariff*, being two leagues and a half high, and accounted the highest mountain in the world. It may be discovered at 60 leagues distance from the shore. Thus we continued our voyage till the 14th, without any memorable accident, when we passed the tropick of *Cancer*. About noon we were overtaken by another storm, which made us take in most of our great sails, for fear of the worst, but it lasted not long.

This tract of the sea is called by the *Dutch*, the *Kroos Sea*; by the *Portuguese*, *Mar del Aragaco* (or *Largaco*, or *Suargaco*) i. e. *The Sea of Ducks-meat*, because hereabouts, *viz.* from the 18th to the 30th degree, or as some will have it, from the 20th to the 22d and 23d degree of northern latitude, it is found in great quantity, and carried along with the stream: Its leaves are of a pale green colour, like that of parrots, small, thin and carved at the end. It bears berries of the same colour, about the bigness of a pepper corn, that are quite hollow, without any seed within or taste. It is sometimes so closely twisted together, that it stops a ship in its full course; tho' we had the good fortune to pass thro' it without much difficulty, being then about 400 leagues from the coast of *Africk*, where are no islands nor anchorage. It may be pickled with salt and pepper, and used like as we do capers, being accounted a good remedy against the gravel. It is generally found without roots, having only a few thin sprouts, which, as it is supposed, take root in the sandy grounds of the sea; tho' others are of opinion, that it is carried by the violence of the stream from the islands into the sea.

The 18th, one of our ships crew died, who was the next day thrown overboard, at which time I observed, what indeed I had heard often before, that the dead carcasses always float with their heads to the east at sea.

Travado, *what.* The 22d we were overtaken by another tempest, called *Travado*, which with horrible thunder and lightning surprizes the ships so suddenly, that they have scarce leisure to take in their sails, and sometimes returns three times in an hour. We catch'd here abundance of fish, such as *Bonytes* of ten foot long, and *Korets*, and a great *They catch abundance of fish.* lamprey, which we had enough to do to bring aboard; we only took out the brains, being look'd upon as a sovereign remedy against the stone in the bladder, the flesh being of an oily taste. 1640.

The 24th we saw great quantities of small birds about our vessel, and catch'd one not unlike a crane, but somewhat smaller, it being a very fair day.

The 26th, being under the fifth degree, 47 minutes, we were so becalmed that we could not perceive the ship to move, and spent our time in catching of fish, of which we had such plenty, that we chose only the best for our eating; among the rest we met with a fish called the *king's-fish*: For by reason of the impenetrable depth of the sea in this place, the waters are so clear and transparent in still weather, that you may see the fish in vast numbers swimming near two feet deep; so that you need but fasten a crooked nail or any thing else like a hook to a string, and hanging it in the sea, you may catch as many fish as you please. This calm was followed by a most violent storm of rain.

The 30th we found ourselves under the fourth degree, 41 minutes, where we saw abundance of *flying fish*.

The 3d of *December* we came under the first degree, 30 minutes, where we met with millions of fish, and did catch as many as we thought fit: Some we put in salt, others we rubbed in the belly with pepper and salt, and hung them up by the tail in the sun.

The 4th, by break of day, being very clear weather, we saw the island of *St. Paulo*, as it is called by the *Portuguese*, which at a distance represents a sail, which as you approach nearer to it, proves five high rocks. About noon we found ourselves at 53 minutes of northern latitude, taking our course five leagues to the west. Here at several times we catch'd some sea-gulls; those birds make a shew as if they would bite you, but remain unmoveable in the place, till they are caught or kill'd. *They discover the island of* St. Paulo.

The 5th, about eleven a clock we passed the equinoctial line, so that in the afternoon we found ourselves at five minutes southern latitude, where we had but little reason to complain of cold; it being often so calm here, that ships are forced to spend a considerable time in passing this tract. It is extreamly hot here, and great scarcity of good and sweet water, the rain water being not wholesome, but causing the scurvy, by reason of its being corrupted by the violent heat of sun.

About three years after my arrival in *Brasil*, a certan *Portuguese* ship was found adrift under the equinoctial line, without any

1643. any living creature in it, which according to the journal, had been six whole weeks under the line. We had a very good passage, and catched abundance of fish, and among the rest a certain fish called the *Blower*, which swallow a considerable quantity of water in their guts, and then at once spout it forth again. They will follow the ships for a long time.

They pass the Equinoctial Line.

The 8th we passed by the isle called *Ilha Ferdinando* of *Neronha*; it being very serene weather, we saw vast numbers of birds, and whole shoals of flying fish, which were followed by the *Bonytes* and *Korets*.

The Isle of Ferdinando.

The island of *Ferdinando* of *Neronha*, situate under the fourth degree of southern latitude, about fifty leagues from the coast of *Brasil*, was about the year 1630. inhabited by the *Dutch*, but by reason of the vast numbers of rats, which consumed all the fruits of the earth, deserted by them a few years after; it being otherwise a very fruitful island, and abounding with fish, the inhabitants of *Reeief* being used to send their fisherboats thither, which return commonly well freighted with fish. The council of *Brasil* did afterwards send a certain number of negroes thither, under the conduct of one *Gellis Vepant*, to cultivate the ground for their subsistence, who likewise stayed there for some time. About a year and a half after, the council of justice banished several malefactors into that island, who being furnished with necessary instruments for cultivating the ground, were forced to seek for their sustenance there.

The 11th at night we found ourselves under the seventh degree, over against the province of *Goyana*, about twenty leagues on this side of *Olinda*; with break of day we saw the shore of *Brasil*, but kept out at sea till it was broad day.

The 12th it was very foggy, and we kept our course with fair wind and water all along the coast, and arrived before noon safely near the *Recief*, where we cast our anchor at several fathoms depth, after we had spent seven weeks and one day in the voyage.

Their Arrival in Brasil.

After we had returned our thanks to God for his deliverance from the dangers of the sea, and slavery of the *Turks*; I went ashore the same night with the master and commissary in a boat, to notify our happy arrival, and to deliver a letter to count *Maurice*, and the governor of the council. I continued ashore that night, but returned aboard the next day. And,

The 15th the pilots conducted our vessel into the harbour of the *Recief*, where we found twenty-eight vessels and two yachts lying behind the *Water Castel*.

1643. Towards the latter end of *August* 1643, I received orders from the council to sail with the yacht called the *Sea-Hog*, loaden with fullers-earth to the isle of St. *Thomas*, to exchange it for black sugar, this being the chief commodity transported from thence. My voyage proved fortunate enough, not meeting with any sinister accident, except with a violent tempest of thunder, lightning, and rains, and came the 9th of *September* at an anchor there; the cargoe did bear no good price, yet after a stay of fourteen days, I returned with a cargoe of black sugar to *Brasil*, where I arrived the 3d of *October* before the *Recief*, after a voyage of near three months. 1643.

The Island of St Thomas.

The isle of St. *Thomas* is of a circular figure, about thirty-six leagues in compass; the high mountains in the midst of that island are always covered with snow, notwithstanding that in the low grounds, by reason of its situation under the line, it is excessive hot. It is very fertile in black sugar and ginger; the sugar-fields being continually moistned by the melted snow that falls down from the mountains. There were at that time above sixty sugar mills there, but the air is the most unwholsome in the world, no foreigner daring to stay so much as one night ashore, without running the hazard of his life; because by the heat of the sun beams such venomous vapours are drawn from the earth, as are unsupportable to strangers. This fog continues till about ten a clock in the morning, when the same is dispersed, and the air cleared, which made us always stay aboard till after that time. This mist is not observed at sea.

The air here is very hot and moist throughout the year, except in the summer about *June*, when the south-east and south-west winds abate much of the heat of the climate. The vapours drawn up by the sun, occasion certain epidemical intermittent fevers, which carry off the patient in a few days, with excessive pains in the head, and violent torments in the bowels; though some attribute it to the immoderate use of women, and of the juice of *Coco's*. Certain is it, that among a hundred foreigners, scarce ten escape with life, and those seldom live till fifty years of age; though some of the inhabitants, as likewise the negroes (who are all lousy here) live to a great age. Its first inhabitants were *Jews*, banished out of *Portugal*; they are of a very odd complexion. Among the mountains dwell abundance of negroes, who are run away from the *Portuguese*, and make sometimes excursions to the very gates of the city of *Pavaosa*. It is almost next to a miracle, that any people should inhabit so unwholsome a climate; but that the hopes of lucre makes all danger easy.

The city of *Pavaosa*, belonging to this island

1643. island, is situate upon a rivulet; it contains about eight hundred houses, and three churches. This city, as well as the whole island, was 1641, *October* 16, conquered by the admiral *Cornelius Tol*, after a siege of forty days, without any considerable loss; but both he and his lieutenant, as well as several other commanders and many seamen, were swept away by this pestilential air; and of three hundred *Brasilians*, not above sixty escaped with life.

But, before I proceed to give you an account of all the remarkable passages that happened in *Brasil*, since the revolt of the *Portuguese*, and during my stay of eight years there; it will not be amiss to insert a short description of this countrey.

A description of Brasil.

America (or the *West-Indies*) is divided into the *northern* and *southern America*. *Brasil* is part of the last.

The *northern America* borders to the *North* upon the *Terra incognita*, or rather upon *Hudson's Streights*; to the *South* and *West* upon the *South-Sea*, and to the *East* upon the streights of *Panama*, the bay of *Mexico*, or *Nieu Spain*, and the *North-Sea*.

It comprehends the following provinces, *Estotiland* and *Labrador*, *Nieu France*, *Canada*, *Bakalaos*, *Nieu England*, *Virginia*, *Florida*, *Nieu Spain*, the provinces of *Mexico*, *Nieu Mexico*, *Tlaskalla*, *Guaxaka*, *Mechoakana*, *Zakatula*, *Kolim*, *Yukatan*, *Tabasko*, *Nieu Gallicia*, *Nieu Biscay*, *Chiametla*, *Kuliaka*, *Cimalon*, *Nieu Granada*, *Kalifornia*, *Anian*, *Quivira* or *Nieu Albion*, *Konibas*, *Guatemala*, *Sokonusko*, *Chiapa*, *Vera pas*, *Honduras*, *Nikaragua*, *Kostarika*, and *Veragua*.

The *southern America* is a demi-island in form of a pyramid; the basis of which lies to the *North*, the point extends to the streights of *Magellan*, under the 53[d] degree of southern latitude; bordering to the east upon the *Atlantick Ocean*, or *North-Sea*, and to the west upon the *South-Sea*, its whole circuit being of about four thousand *Italian* or one thousand *German* miles. It contains the provinces of *Kastilla d'Or*, *Tierra fierma*, called by the *Portuguese*, *Paria*, *Kumana*, *Karibana*, *Brasil*, *Chika* to the east, to the west *Popayan*, *Peru*, *Chili*, besides several inland provinces.

First Discovery of Brasil.

Brasil was first discovered by *Pedro Alvaro Kapralis*, a *Portuguese*, sometime before *Americus Vesputius*, viz. in the year 1500. He gave it the name of *Santa Cruz*, which was afterwards by the *Portuguese* changed into that of *Brasil*, from the wood of the same name, which is found there in great quantity, and from thence transported into all parts of *Europe*, for the use of the dyers.

1643.

Its Situation.

It is situate in the midst of the *Torrid Zone*, extending to the *Tropick* of *Cancer* and the *Temperate Zone*.

Extent.

Concerning its extent from *north to south*, there is no small difference among the geographers; but according to the best computations, its beginning may be fixed under the second degree and a half of northern latitude, near the river *Para*, and its end under the twenty-fourth degree and a half of southern latitude, to the river *Capibari*, two leagues above the city of St. *Vincent*; so that its whole extent from north to south, comprehends twenty-five degrees, or three hundred seventy-five leagues; some place *Brasil* betwixt the river of *Maranbaen* and *Rio de la Plata*. The extent of *Brasil* from the east (where it borders upon the *North-Sea*) to the west, is not determined hitherto, there being very few who have penetrated so deep into the countrey; tho' its bigness from east to west may be computed to be seven hundred forty-two leagues; there are however some who extend its limits farther to the east, and to the west as far as *Peru* or *Guiana*, which makes an addition of one hundred eighty-eight leagues. Some make the boundaries of *Brasil* to the north the river of the *Amazons*; to the south *Rio de la Plata*; to the east the *North-Sea*, and to the west the mountains of *Peru* or *Guiana*.

Its Division.

Brasil thus limited, is divided by the *Portuguese* into fourteen districts, called by them *Kapitanias*, or Captainships; *viz. Paria*, the first of all towards the north; *Maranhaon*, *Siara*, *Potigi* or *Rio Grande*, *Paraiba*, *Parnambuko*, *Tarmarika* or *Itamarika*, *Seregippo del Rey*, *Quirimune* or *Bahia dos todos los Santos*, *Nhoe-Kombe*, or *os Ilhos*, *Pakata*, or *Porto Securo*, *Rio de Janeiro* or *Nheteroya*, *St. Vincent* and *Espiritu St.*

Whilst part of *Brasil* was in our possession, it might conveniently be divided into the *Dutch* and *Portuguese Brasil*. Each of these captainships is watered by some considerable river or other, besides several others of less note; most of these have very rapid currents in the rainy months, and overflow the adjacent countrey.

The River of St. Francis.

The river of St. *Francis*, the largest and most considerable in those parts, is the common boundary of the captainship of *Parnambuko* and *Bahia dos todos los Santos*, or the *Bay of all Saints*. In some places it is so broad, that a six-pounder can scarce reach over it, and its depth is eight, twelve, and sometimes fifteen yards; but it admits of no Ships of burthen, because its Entrance is choak'd up with sands.

Its first spring is said to arise out of a certain

1643. certain lake, which being augmented by many rivelets out of the mountains of *Peru*, but especially by the rivers of *Rio de la Plata* and *Maranhaon* exonerates it self into the sea. Some of our people went in a shallop near forty leagues up the river, and found it of a good depth and pretty broad. If we may believe the *Portuguese*, there are about fifty leagues from the sea, certain impassable cataracts or water-falls, called by them *Kakocras*; beyond those the river winds to the north, 'till you come to its source in the lake, in which are many pleasant islands, inhabited by the barbarians; as is likewise the shore round about it. They find good store of gold-dust in this lake, but it is none of the best, being carried thither by the many rivulets, which wash the gold-bearing rocks of *Peru*; here is also most excellent salt-petre.

It is observable, that in the summer and and those winter months, when it rains but seldom, this river has more water than in the rain season: The reason alledged for it is, the vast distance from its first source, whether the rains that fall from the mountains must first be convey'd by many rivulets: All the other rivers near the *Receif*, are so empty of water during the summer season, that they are rendred quite unnavigable. But the ridges of mountains which lie not far from the sea-shore, exonerate their waters as well here as in *Peru*, backward to the west, and dividing themselves into two branches; the first runs into the north, and joins with the large and most rapid rivers of *Maranhaon*, and of the *Amazons*; the other with the rivers of St. *Francis de la Plata*, and *Janeiro*. The waters of these rivers being considerably encreased by many rivulets, they exonerate themselves with so much violence into the sea, that the seamen meet often with fresh water at a considerable distance at sea.

The increase of the waters in this river, during the dry season, may likewise be attributed to the vast quantity of snow among the mountains, which being melted by the heat of the sun, occasions the river to transgress its ordinary bounds; which in this point is quite different from other rivers, which commonly in the winter time over-flow their banks.

The Dutch Brasil.

Six of those *captainships* were under the jurisdiction of the *West-India* company, before the *Portuguese* revolted from the *Dutch*, which they had conquer'd with their Swords, *viz.* The *captainship*, (it begins on the south-side) *Seregippe del Rey* of *Parnambuko*, *Itamarika*, unto which belongs *Gauiana*, *Paraiba*, *Potigi* or *Rio Grande* and *Siara* or *Ciara*. The *captainship* of *Maranhaon* was 1644, by special command of the company, left by the *Dutch*. This part of *Brasil* used to be called by the *Portuguese*, the *Northern-Brasil*, as the other remaining in their possession went by the name of *South-Brasil*. 1643.

The six *Dutch captainships* did extend all along the sea coast from north to south, in length about a hundred and sixty or a hundred and eighty leagues; for from *Rio Grande*, to the northern border of *Seregippe del Rey*, is a hundred leagues: The two others, *viz.* that of *Siara* to the north, and *Seregippe del Rey* to the south, make up the rest. Each of these *captainships* contain several other lesser districts, call'd by the *Portuguese Fregesias*, and by us *Fregesien*; as for instance, in *Seregippe del Rey*, are *Pojuka*, *Kameragibi*, *Porto Calvo*, *Serinhaim*, and several others. *Fregasie*, comprehends a certract of ground, composed of divers villages, rivers, hills and vallies, betwixt each of which is commonly a tract of barren hills, of about three or four leagues in length. Most of the *Dutch captainships*, are but indifferently cultivated, because the *Portuguese* used not to manure the ground in those parts, beyond three or four, or at farthest, five leagues distant from the Sea.

The *captainship* of *Seregippe del Rey* is likewise called *Carigi*, from a certain small lake of that name; it is situate in the southern part of *Brasil*, extending about thirty two leagues along the sea coast, bordering on the north side, upon the river of St. *Francis*, by which it is divided from *Parnambuko*; as on the south side it is separated by *Rio Real*, from *Bahia dos todos los Santos*. *Seregippe del Rey*, has among others, a certain *Fregasie*, called *Porto Calvo*, situated betwixt the 9th and the 10th degree of southern latitude; being encompassed on the north-west side by the *Fregasie* of *Serinhaim*, and the small river of *Pirasenunga*, extending to the south as far as the river *Parepuera*, by which it is divided from the *Fregasie* of *Alagoasi*, containing in all about twelve leagues in length near the sea shore, its bounds on the land side reaching to the unpassable woods. Seregippe del Rey

The village of Bon Successo de Porto Cal

In this *Fregasie*, is a village call'd by the *Portuguese*, *Villa de bon successo de Porto Calo*, but was formerly called *Portocano Dos quatros Rios*, it being situate at the confluence of the four rivers, *Maleita*, *Tapamunde*, *Commentabunda* and *Monguaba*. It is built upon a rising ground, about four leagues from the sea shore, and by the *Dutch* strengthened with two forts; the biggest of which was called *Bon Successo*, being built all of stone, surrounded with a good counterscarp, with a large bason for fresh water within. The other fort was called by us, the *New-Church*, being created out of the

ruins

1643. ruins of an old church, called by the *Portuguese*, *Nossa Senhora de Presentacao*. Betwixt both these forts, a third was ordered to be erected by count *Maurice*, upon the banks of the river, but it lying within the reach of musket-shot from the mountains, was not brought to perfection.

The village has two streets, the chief of which runs parallel with the river, from one fort to the other, and is call'd *St. Joseph's-street*; it contain'd no more than three houses of one story high, and about thirty six others cover'd with pantiles, being only built upon the ground. The *Portuguese* have in lieu of their churches, which are demolished, when the fortifications were erected, built themselves another on the other side of the river, where they sometimes hear mass. The village is situate in a most pleasant and wholesome air, being cooled by the continual breezes from the sea, which are not stopp'd by any hills, betwixt them and the shore. In the night time they enjoy the benefit of the land wind, which drives the cool vapours arising from the neighbouring rivers thither: Formerly there was a certain town called *Seregippe del Rey*, somewhat higher up the river, in a very barren place, of a considerable bigness, and well built, with three goodly churches, and a monastery belonging to the *Franciscans*, but without any fortifications. Above this town you see a chapel dedicated to St. *Christopher*, whether the *Roman Catholicks* come on pilgrimage.

This *captainship* was first of all reduced under the obedience of the *Portuguese* or *Spaniards*, by *Christovan de Barros*; who for this his good service, had all the lands betwixt the small lake of *Seregippe* and *St. Francisco*, granted to him, with full power to settle colonies there within a limited time. This drew many of the inhabitants of the *Bay of all Saints* thither; who within a few years after laid the foundations of this town, by erecting four sugar-mills, and building about a hundred houses, with four hundred stables for their cattle. But this town, with all the circumjacent houses, was 1637, the 24th of *December*, laid desolate by our people, the inhabitants retiring to the *Bay of all Saints*. For the *Spanish* general *Benjola* being, 1637, posted with a body of two thousand men near that place, did with ravaging and burning, considerable damage to our colonies, which oblig'd count *Maurice* to dislodge him from thence; but being then sick of an ague, he committed this expedition to the charge of colonel *Schoppe*; for which purpose having gather'd a body of two thousand three hundred men, besides four hundred *Brasilians*, and two hundred and fifty seamen out of the the adjacent Places, near the river of *St. Francis*, *Alagoas*, the *Cape of St. Austin*, out of the *Receif* and *Moribeka*, and given him for his assistant Mr. *John van Giesselen*, a member of the great council, he commanded the *Dutch* admiral *Lichthart*, to cruise with his fleet near the *Bay of all Saints*, thereby to draw the enemy out of his advantageous post to the sea-shoar. The *Spanish* general had no sooner notice of our passing the river, but fearing to be enclosed betwixt us and the fleet, march'd with his body to *Torre Garcie de Avila*, a place about fourteen leagues to the north of the city of *St. Salvador*. 1643.

The *Dutch* general *Schoppe*, hearing of his removal, immediately attack'd the place, which he laid desolate, and returned with incredible swiftness to the south side of the river of *St. Francis*.

Here he intrench'd himself, with an intention to annoy the enemy, by cutting off his provisions, and driving away his cattle; which succeeded so well, that we kill'd above three thousand of their horned beasts, besides what was carried away on the other side of the river; so that what was left by the soldiers, was by the inhabitants carried to the *Bay of all Saints*; from whence it is evident, what vast numbers of cattle this countrey did produce at that time.

The great council took once a resolution to re-people that part of the countrey, and agreed for this purpose with *Nunno Olferdi*, councellor of justice in the *Receif*, who found means to settle several families there: But the council of nineteen disapproving the matter, it was laid aside.

In the year 1641, count *Maurice* reduced this place under the obedience of the *West-India* company, erected a fort there, and surrounded the town *Seregippe del Rey* with a ditch. It lies upon a small river, betwixt *St. Francisco* and *Real*, which however at spring-tide has fourteen foot water or thereabouts. Within the jurisdiction of this *captainship*, is the mountain of *Tabayna*; from whence several sorts of valuable oar was presented to the council of nineteen; but upon proof was found not worth farther looking after.

The captainship *of* Parnambuko.

The *captainship* of *Parnambuko*, is one of the chiefest and biggest of the *Dutch-Brasil*. It extends above sixty leagues along the coast, betwixt the river of *St. Francis*, and the captainship of *Tamarika*. *Parnambuko* properly denotes the entrance of the harbour, which by reason of the many rocks and shelves hidden under water, was called by the *Portuguese*, *Inferno Bokko*, and broken

1643. broken *Parnambuko*, or the *Mouth of Hell.* It is subdivided into eleven lesser districts, inhabited by the *Portuguese*, *viz.* the city of *Olinda*, *Garazu*, *Receif*, *Moribeka*, *St. Anthony*, *Poyuka*, *Serinhaim*, *Consalvi d'Una*, *Porto Calvo*, the *Northern Alagoa*, and the *Southern Alagoa.* Among which *Olinda* and *Garazu* were the chiefest.

Eleven towns and villages of Parnambuko.

Garazu. The town, or rather the village of *Garazu*, lies at some distance from the shoar, over against the Island of *Tamarika*, upon a river of the same name, about five leagues from *Olinda.* It was formerly inhabited by *Portuguese* handicrafts men, but since our taking of *Olinda*, several rich Families settled there; we became masters of the place 1633, in *May.*

Moribeka. *Moribeka* lies deeper into the countrey, more to the south, about five leagues off of the *Receif.*

St. Anthony. *St. Anthony* is about seven or eight leagues distant from the *Receif* to the south, near the *Cape of St. Austin.*

Poyuka. The city of *St. Michael de Poyuka*, lies about ten leagues to the south of the *Receif* upon a river of the same name, which disembogues in the sea, on the south side of the *Cape of St. Austin.* It was formerly a very populous place; and had thirteen sugar-mills.

Serinhaim. The village *Serinhaim*, much about the same distance thence with the former, is a very pleasant place, has twelve sugar-mills, each of which produces six or seven hundred *Aroba's*, an *Aroba* making about twenty seven or twenty eight pound weight.

Gonsalvi d'Una. The village of *Gonsalvi d'Una*, lies twenty leagues from the *Receif*; it has five sugar-mills.

Porto Calvo. The village called *Porto Calvo*, is twenty leagues distant from the *Receif*; it has seven or eight sugar-mills. Here is the castle of *Porocano*, which was not conquer'd by us, till under the government of count *Maurice.*

The towns of the northern and southern *Alagoa's*, are forty leagues from the *Receif.*

Within the district of *Parnambuko*, are two woods, called by the *Portugueses* the *greater* and *lesser Palmairas*, or *Palmtree-Woods.*

The two Palmairas. The *Lesser Palmairas*, which is inhabited by six thousand negroes, lies about twenty leagues above the *Alagoas*, being enclosed with woods near the small lake of *Guagohuhi*, which exonerates it self into the great lake of *Parayba*, six leagues from thence to the north, about four leagues from the lake *Meridai*, to the south of the *Northern Alagoa*, being near that point of land commonly called *Jaragoa.* The village consists of three streets, each near half a league in length. Their huts are made of straw twisted together, one near another, their plantations being behind. They retain something of the religious worship of the *Portuguese*, but have their peculiar priests and judges. Their business is to rob the *Portuguese* of their slaves, who remain in slavery among them, 'till they have redeemed themselves by stealing another: But such slaves as run over to them, are as free as the rest. Their food is dates, beans, meal, barley, sugar-canes, tame-fowl, (of which they have great plenty) and fish, which the lake furnishes them withal. They have twice a year a harvest of barley, which being over, they make merry for a whole Week together. Before sowing time, they light great fires for fourteen days, which may be seen at a great distance. The shortest way from the *Receif* to this *Palmairas*, is along the lake of the *Northern Alago.* 1643.

The greater *Palmairas* is betwixt twenty and thirty leagues distant behind the village of St. *Amar*, near the mountain of *Behe*, being surrounded with a double enclosure. About eight thousand Negroes are said to inhabit the Vallies near the mountains, besides many others, who dwell in lesser numbers of fifty or a hundred, in other places. Their houses lie straggling, they sow and reap among the woods, and have certain caves whither they retreat in case of necessity. They dress their victuals in the day time, and at night tell over their whole number, to see whether any be wanting; if not, they conclude the evening with dancing and beating the drum, which may be heard at a great distance. Then they go to sleep 'till nine or ten a clock the next day. During the dry season, they detach a certain number among them, to steal slaves from the *Portuguese.* The shortest cut to their habitations, is from the *Alagoas* through St. *Amar*, and so cross the plains of *Nhumahu* and *Kororipe*, towards the backside of the mountain of *Warrakaka*, 'till you come to the lake *Paraiba*; along which you pass 'till you reach the mountain *Behe*, from whence you go directly into the vallies. Under the Government of Count *Maurice*, the negroes of this *Palmairas* did considerable mischief, especially to the country people about the *Alagoas*; to repress which, he sent three hundred firelocks, a hundred *Mamelukes*, and seven hundred *Brasilians.*

The Receif, Maurice's *town, and* Anthony Vaez.

The *Receif* is, by reason of its commodious and advantagious situation the strongest *The* Receif.

1643. eſt place of all *Braſil*; beſides that, it is ſtrengthened and defended by ſeveral adjacent Forts: But to give you the moſt commodious view both of the *Receif*, and the ſituation of *Maurice*'s town, it is to be obſerved, that the whole coaſt of *Braſil*, is from one end to the other ſurrounded with a long, thick, and flat ridge of rocks, which in ſome Places is twenty, and in others thirty paces broad: However, there are certain paſſages in this ridge, through which the ſhips approach the ſhoar, and ſome few places, where this ridge is not found at all. Thus a league on this ſide *Rio dolee*, two leagues on the northſide of the city of *Olinda*, there is nothing of this ridge to be found; but begins again near *Poumarelle* or *Soxamardo*, and extends to the iſle of *Itamarika*. Betwixt the ridge and the continent, you may paſs in boats at high water; for at low-tide moſt of thoſe rocks appear above water; tho' the tide never fails to cover the ſame. The rock over-against the *Receif* of *Parnambuko*, is between twenty and thirty paces broad, being not only at ſpring-tides, but at all other tides overflown by the ſea; it is there-abouts very flat, without any prominencies, and extends for a league from ſouth to north. On the north point is an open Paſſage for ſhips to approach the ſhoar, lying five hundred paces further to the north, than the *Receif* it ſelf. It is but narrow, and at ſpring-tide not above twenty two foot deep. 1643.

The ſtone ridge round the coaſt of Braſil.

Betwixt this rocky ridge and the continent, there is a ſandy ridge, or ſmall iſland extended to the ſouth from *Olinda*, a league in length, and about two hundred paces broad. This is by our people commonly called, *The Sandy Receif*, to diſtinguiſh it from *The Stony Receif*.

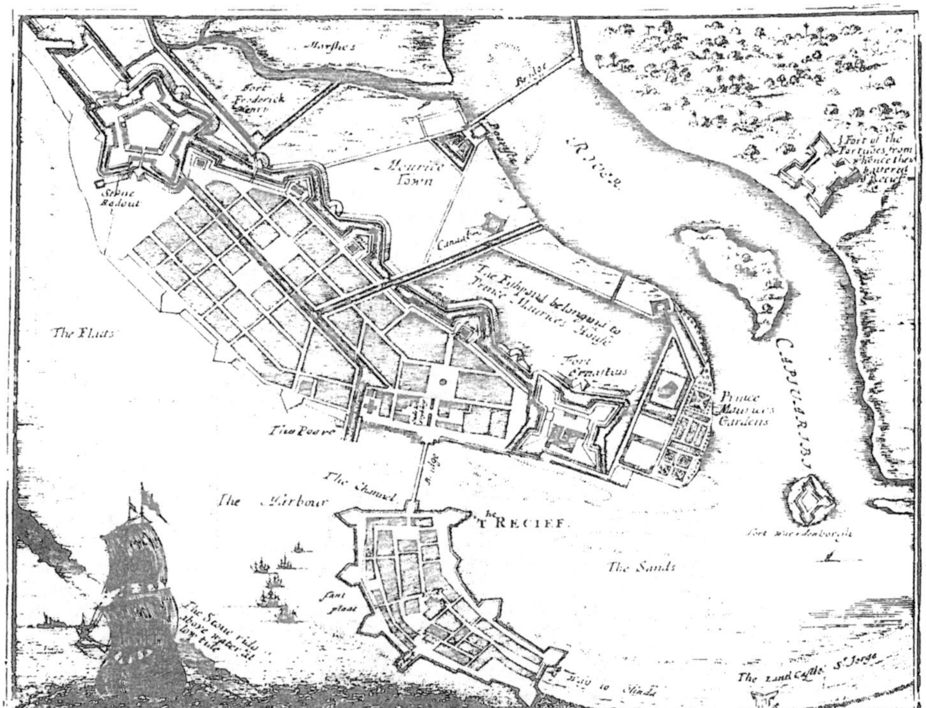

The ſandy Receif.

On the ſouthern point of this little iſland, a league off *Olinda*, the *Portugueſe* had built a village, called *Povoacano*, which ſignifies *peopling*, or elſe *Reciffo*; it was very populous for a conſiderable time, 'till the building of *Maurice*'s town, in the iſland of *Anthony Vaez*. For after *Olinda* was forſaken by its inhabitants, and deſtroy'd by us, many of them, but eſpecially the merchants, ſettled in this *Reciffo*, or the village of *Povoacano*, where they erected magnificent ſtructures. At our firſt arrival, we found no

1643. no more than two hundred houses there, which were afterwards increased to above two thousand, some of which are very goodly edifices. We surrounded it with Pallisadoes on the side of the river *Biberibi*, which at low-water is fordable; and for its better security fortified it with three bulwarks, one towards *Olinda*, the other to the harbour, and the third towards the *Salt River*; upon each of which was raised a good battery with three great cannon. This *Receif* is situate under the 8th degree 20 minutes southern latitude.

The derivation of the word Receif. Some derive the word *Reciffo* from the *Latin*, *recipere* and *receptus* to receive, which after was turned into *Reciffo*, because the ships used to be received betwixt the stony and sandy *Receifs*, to load and unload their goods. Before the building of *Maurice*'s town, we kept here our factories, and all business both of peace and war, was transacted in this place. In the time of the *Portuguese*, all the ships coming out of the sea, did unload on the village of *Povoacano*, or the *Receif*, and the goods were from thence in boats and lighters conveyed up the river *Biberibi*, to the suburbs of *Olinda*.

Before the building of *Maurice*'s town, most of the traffick was in the *Receif*, where all the great merchants had their habitations, and from hence the Sugar was transported into *Holland*. To prevent the frauds in the customs, it was surrounded with pallisadoes, and a goodly hospital was erected for the conveniency of the sick and wounded; and the education of orphans, under the tuition of four governors, and as many governesses.

Upon the uttermost point of the stony *Receif*, on the left side as you enter the harbour out of the sea, is a strong and large castle, built of free-stone, surrounded with a very high wall, upon which are mounted many heavy cannon, with suitable artillery and other provisions. When we took the place, we found nine brass, and twenty two iron pieces of cannon within it; so that it seems both by art and nature impregnable; there being no coming near it on foot, at high-water.

About five leagues higher, upon a branch of the great river, lies a small town of little consequence, called by our people, *The New City*; and upon another branch of the same river, opposite to the former, a village called *Atapuepe*.

The island of Anthony Vaez, *and* Maurice's Town.

The isle of Anthony Vaez. To the south of the *Receif*, opposite to it, lies the isle of *Anthony Vaez*, so called by our People, from its ancient possessor. 1643. It is about half a league in circuit, being divided from the *Receif*, by the *Salt-River*, or *Biberibi*.

On the east-side of this island, count *Maurice* laid the foundation of a city, which, after his own Name, he called *Maurice*'s town or city; the ruines of the churches or monasteries of the city of *Olinda*, furnish'd the materials for the building of it, which were from thence carried to the *Receif*, and so transported to this place. *Maurice's* Town.

On the west-side it is environ'd with a morass; and on the east-side wash'd by the sea, which passes the stony ridge. Besides which, it is on the land-side strengthen'd with an earthen wall, four bulwarks and a large moat.

On that side where the fort of *Ernestus* was, the town lay open, and the houses took up a larger compass than those in the *Receif*; but after the revolt of the *Portuguese*, most of those houses were pulled down, and the place drawn into a more narrow compass, to render it more defensible: Yet was the place well stocked with inhabitants, as well merchants as handicrafts men.

Maurice's town was on each side guarded by a fort. On the south side by the fort called *Frederick Henry*, or the quinquangular fort, from its five bulwarks. This fort was besides this, surrounded by a large ditch and pallisadoes, and strengthened by two hornworks, so that it commanded the whole plain, which at spring-tides used to be overflown by the sea. *The Fort* Frederick Henry.

The second fort *Ernestus*, thus called after *John Ernest*, the brother of count *Maurice*, was four-square, with four bulwarks, with a very large ditch; it commanded the river, the plains, and *Maurice*'s town. Near this last fort was the garden of count *Maurice*, stored with all sorts of trees, brought thither from *Europe* and both the *Indies*. *The Fort* Ernestus.

Upon the north point of the *Stony Receif*, just over against the *Sandy Receif*, lies the beforenamed fort, built all of stone, being about a hundred paces in circumference, provided with a good garrison and twenty pieces of great cannon, though in stormy weather the water flies over it on all sides. It commands the harbour, the land fort, the *Bruin Fort*, and the *Receif*. *The Fort of Stone.*

As the isle of *Antony Vaez* was joined to the continent by a bridge, so it was thought necessary to join the *Receif* with another bridge to the said island, for the conveniency of carriage; the sugar chests being before that time never to be transported to the *Receif*, except at low water, unless the owners would run the hazard of exposing them to the danger of the sea in small boats. Accordingly *The Bridge betwixt the* Receif *and the Island.*

1643. cordingly the great council, with consent of the governor count *Maurice*, agreed with a certain architect for the building of a bridge with stone arches, for the sum of two hundred fifty thousand florins. But after the architect had consumed a prodigious quantity of stone, and raised the structure near to the height of the banks of the river, finding that at low-water there was still eleven foot water, and despairing to be able to accomplish it, left it unfinished. But the council being unwilling to desist, renewed the work, which had already cost a hundred thousand florins; and by means of many trees of forty and fifty foot long, stopped the current till the bridge was brought to perfection, which was done in two months time, and a certain toll imposed upon all passengers, *viz.* for an inhabitant two pence, for a soldier and negroe one penny, for a horse four pence, and a waggon drawn by oxen seven pence.

The harbour. The space betwixt the *Sandy* and *Stony Receif*, is properly the harbour, which at high-water has about thirteen or fourteen foot depth, where the ships ride very safe, being defended from the sea by the stony *Receif.* The passage betwixt the *Sandy Receif* and the continent, is called the *Salt-River*, to distinguish it from the river *Kapivaribi*, which carries sweet water.

The river Kapivaribi. The river *Kapivaribi* has derived its name from a certain kind of river or sea hogs, which used to be found there, and were by the *Brasilians* called *Kapivaribi.* This river arises some leagues to the west, passing by the *Matta*, or the *Wood of Brasil*, *Masyasti*, St. *Lorenzo* and *Real*, where joining with the river *Affogados*, near another river of the same name, disembogues in the sea, near the *Receif.* The river *Kapivaribi* divides itself into two branches; one turns to the south, and passes by the fort *William*, and is called *Affogados*; the other running to the north, retains its former name, continuing its course betwixt the continent and *Maurice*'s town, or the isle of *Anthony Vaez* (into which you may pass over it by a bridge) and so to *Waerdenburgh*, where it joins with the river *Biberibi*, or *Salt-River*, both which are afterwards mixed with the sea. The two branches of this river, surround the river *Biberibi* on the west-side, and to the east the isle of *Anthony Vaez.* Upon that branch of the river called *Affogados*, are abundance of sugar-mills, from whence the *Portuguese* used to convey their sugar-chests, either in boats by the way of the river, or in carts to *Baretta*, and from thence in flat bottomed boats to the *Receif*, and to *Olinda*.

A league to the south of *Maurice*'s Town upon the branch called *Affogados*, is a four-square fort of the same name, otherwise called fort *William*; from whence you may 1633. pass along a dike to the fort *Frederick Henry*, or *Maurice*'s Town. It was a noble *The fort* William. structure, surrounded with high and strong walls, a large ditch and pallisadoes, with six brass cannon: It defended the avenues to the plains.

About half a league from thence, and at the same distance from the continent, lies another fort on the sea shore, called *Baretta:* *The fort* Baretta. This commands the avenues both by sea and land to the cape of *St. Austin*, and the *Receif*.

Upon that part of the island which lies betwixt the rivers *Kapivaribi*, and *Biberibi*, and betwixt the forts of *Ernestus* and the *The garden of count* Maurice. triangular fort of *Waerdenburg*, were the before mentioned gardens of count *Maurice*, stored with all kinds of trees, fruits, flowers and greens, which either *Europe*, *Africk*, or both the *Indies* could afford. There were near seven hundred cocoa-trees of all sizes, some of which were thirty, forty, and fifty foot high; which being transplanted thither, out of the circumjacent countries, bore abundance of fruit the very first year: Above fifty lemon-trees, and eighteen citron-trees, eighty pomgranate-trees, and sixty-six fig-trees, were also to be seen in these gardens.

In the midst of it stood the seat itself, called *Vryburgh*, *The palace of count* Maurice. a noble structure indeed, which as is reported, cost six hundred thousand florins: It had a most admirable prospect, both to the sea and land side, and its two towers were of such a height, that they might be seen six or seven leagues off at sea, and served the seamen for a beacon. In the front of the house was a battery of marble, rising by degrees from the river-side, upon which were mounted ten pieces of cannon for the defence of the river. About two or three rods from the river, were several large basons in the garden, containing very sweet water, notwithstanding the river all round about afforded nothing but salt-water; besides this, there were divers fish-ponds, stocked with all sorts of fish.

His summer seat. At the very foot of the bridge which is built over the river *Kapivaribi*, from *Maurice*'s town to the continent, count *Maurice* had built a very pleasant summer seat, called by the *Portuguese*, *Baavista*, i. e. *A fair Prospect.* It was not only surrounded with very pleasant gardens and fish-ponds, but served likewise as a fort for the defence of the isle of *Anthony Vaez*, and *Maurice*'s Town.

Upon the *Sandy Receif*, opposite to the *Sea*, or *Water Fort*, was a strong fort built *The land fort.* of stone, called by the *Portuguese*, St. *Toris*, our people used to call it the *Land Fort*, to distinguish it from the beforementioned *Water Fort*; it defends the entrance of the har-

bour

1643. bour with thirteen iron pieces of cannon.

About a muſket ſhot thence to the north, lies upon the ſame ſandy *Receif*, a ſmall fort

The fort **Bruin.** with four baſtions, called the fort of *Bruin*; and about a muſket ſhot further to the north, a redoubt, called *Madame de Bruin*: Both theſe forts were built by the *Dutch*.

Near the continent, not far from the ſalt-pits, betwixt the *Sandy Receif*, and the iſle of *Anthony Vaez*, was a triangular fort called

The fort of **Waerdenburgh.** *Waerdenburgh*. It was at firſt a four-ſquare, but afterwards turned by the *Dutch* into a triangular fort, the fourth bulwark being not defenſible, by reaſon of the ground: Thoſe three bulwarks were afterwards changed into as many redoubts, and provided with ſome braſs guns: At high tide it is ſurrounded on all ſides with water.

The City of Olinda.

At a ſmall diſtance from the *Receif*, or *Maurice*'s Town, to the north, is the ruinated city of *Olinda*, once a famous place

Olinda. among the *Portugueſe*; the whole product of *Braſil*, being from thence tranſported by ſea into *Europe*. The beſt part of the city 1643.
was built upon divers hill; towards the ſea, on the ſouth ſide, theſe hills were pretty plain, extending to the ſea-ſhore, which has a very white ſand all along that coaſt: Towards the land ſide, or the north, thoſe hills are more ſteep and craggy, full of thorn-buſhes, intermixed with a few orange-trees. Theſe hills are an additional ſtrength to the place, which beſides this, was guarded by ſeveral baſtions to the land ſide, though by reaſon of the great variety of hills contained in its circuit, it was a difficult taſk to bring the fortifications into a regular form. There is a very fair proſpect from the higher part of the town, both to the ſouth and north, or to the ſea and land ſide, by reaſon of the great quantity of circumjacent trees, which continue green all the year round. You may alſo from thence ſee the iſle of *Anthony Vaez*, and *Maurice*'s town. The point of land near *Olinda*, is called *Tipo* by the inhabitants.

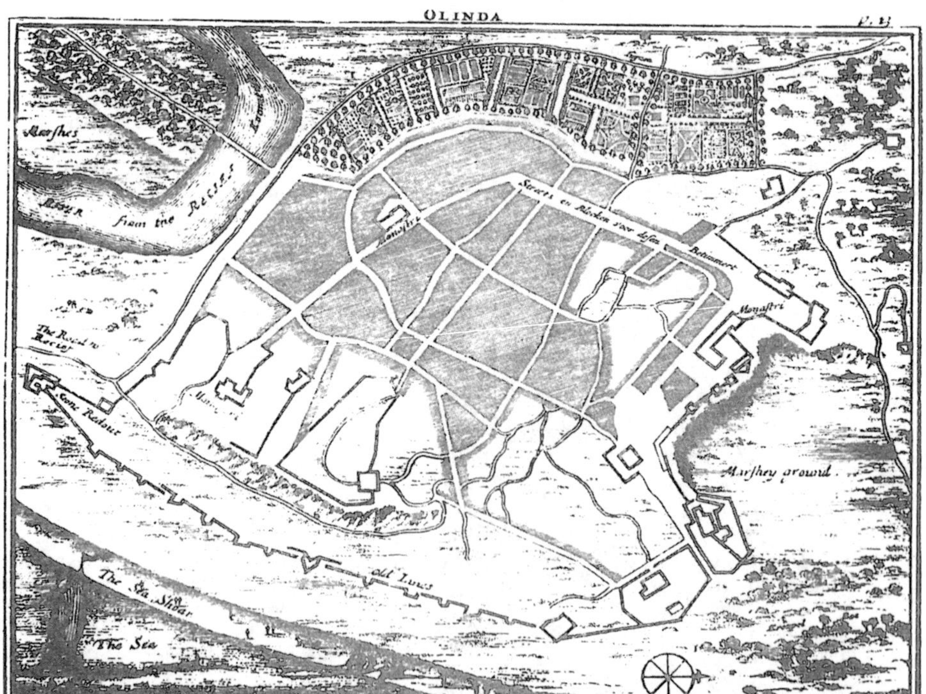

Upon

1643. Upon the highest hill within the place, stood formerly a convent belonging to the *Jesuits*, being a magnificent structure, founded by *Sebastian* king of *Portugal*, who endowed it with considerable revenues. It had a very fair prospect, and might be seen at a good distance at sea. Not far from thence was another Monastery belonging to the *Capucines*; and near the sea-shore, another of the *Dominican* fryars: Besides which, it had two churches, the one called St. *Salvador*, the other St. *Peter*.

It contained above two thousand inhabitants, besides the clergymen and slaves, among whom were two hundred that were accounted very rich. On the foot of the mountain upon which the city of *Olinda* was built, a strong redoubt was erected, which in the year 1645, was by a serjeant betrayed to the *Portuguese* for a sum of money. About a league from the city, near the water-side, were the suburbs, well stored with inhabitants and packhouses; but destitute of fresh water, which they were fain to fetch from beyond the river.

The whole district of *Parnambuko* abounds in divers kinds of fruits and cattle. The vallies afford good pasturage, and the lower grounds near the rivers, great store of sugar-reeds, which are much cultivated hereabouts. The mountains produce richer minerals here, than in the other captainships. During the rainy season the heat is more tolerable here in the day time than the cold nights.

The Cameleon, *or* Indian Salamander, *otherwise called* Gekko.

This creature, which is not only found in *Brasil*, but also in the isle of *Java*, belonging to the *East-Indies*, and which, by our people is called *Gekko*, from its constant cry (like among us that of the *Cuckoe*) is properly an *Indian Salamander*. It is about a foot long, its skin of a pale or sea-green colour, with red spots. The head is not unlike that of a tortoise, with a streight mouth. The eyes are very large, starting out of the head, with long and small eye-apples. The tail is distinguished by several white rings: Its teeth are so sharp as to make an impression even upon steel. Each of its four legs had five crooked claws armed on the end with nails. Its gait is very slow, but wherever it fastens it is not easily removed. It dwells commonly upon rotten trees, or among the ruines of old houses and churches; it oftentimes settles near the bedsteds, which makes sometimes the moors pull down their huts.

Its constant cry is *Gekko*, but before it begins it makes a kind of hissing noise. The sting of this creature is so venomous, that 1643. the wound proves mortal, unless it be immediately burnt with a red hot iron, or cut off. The blood is of a palish colour, resembling poison itself.

The *Javanese* use to dip their arrows in the blood of this creature; and those who deal in poisons among them (an art much esteemed in the island of *Java*, by both sexes) hang it up with a string tied to the tail on the cieling, by which means it being exasperated to the highest pitch, sends forth a yellow liquor out of its mouth, which they gather in small pots set underneath, and afterwards coagulate into a body in the sun. This they continue for several months together, by giving daily food to the creature. It is unquestionably the strongest poison in the world; its urine being of so corrosive a quality, that it not only raises blisters, wherever it touches the skin, but turns the flesh black, and causes a gangrene. The inhabitants of the *East-Indies* say, that the best remedy against this poison is the *Curcumie* root. Such a *Gekko* was got within the body of the wall of the church in the *Receif*, which obliged us to have a great hole made in the said wall, to dislodge it from thence.

The strongest poison in the World.

There are also several sorts of *Serpents* in *Brasil*, such as *Rattle Serpents*, *Double-headed Serpents*, and such like; of which the *Brasilians* enumerate twenty-three, *viz. Boigvacu*, or *Liboya*, *Arabo*, *Bioby*, *Boicininga*, *Boitrapo*, *Boykupekanga*, *Bapoba*, *Kukuruku*, *Kaninana*, *Kurukaki tinga*, *Grinipaijaguara*, *Ibiara*, *Jakapekoaja Ibiboboca*, *Jararaka*, *Manima*, *Vona*, *Tarci...*, *Kakaboya*, *Amorepinima*.

Serpents in Brasil.

We will give you an account of those only that dwell in the houses and woods of *Parnambuko*, passing by the rest, as not so well known among us; and it is observable that though some of the *American* or *Brasilians* serpents exceed those of *Europe* in bigness, they are nevertheless not so poisonous.

The serpent of *Boicininga*, or *Boicinininga*, likewise called *Boiquira* by the *Brasilians*, is by the *Portuguese* called *Kaskeveda* and *Tangedor*, i. e. *a Rattle*, and by our people a *Rattle Serpent*, because it makes a noise with its tail, not unlike a rattle: This serpent is found both upon the highway and in desolate places; it moves with such swiftness, as if it had wings, and is extremely venomous. In the midst it is about the thickness of a man's arm near the elbow, but grows thinner by degrees towards the head and tail. The belly and head is flattish, the last being of the length and breadth of a finger and a half, with very small eyes. It has four peculiar teeth longer than all the rest, white and sharp like a thorn, which it hides sometimes

The Rattle Serpent.

1643. ſometimes within the gums. The ſkin is covered with thick ſcales, thoſe upon the back being ſomewhat higher than the reſt, and of a pale yellowiſh colour, with black edges. The ſides of the body are likewiſe yellowiſh with black ſcales on each ſide; but thoſe upon the belly are larger, four-ſquare, and of a yellow colour. It is three, four, and ſometimes five foot long; has a round tongue ſplit in the middle, with long and ſharp teeth. The tail is compoſed of ſeveral looſe and bony joints, which make ſuch a noiſe that it may be heard at a diſtance. Or rather at the end of the tail, is a long piece conſiſting of ſeveral joints, joined within one another in a moſt peculiar manner, not unlike a chain. Every year there is an addition of one of theſe joints, ſo that you may know the exact age of the ſerpent by their number; nature ſeeming in this point to have favoured mankind, as a warning to avoid this poiſonous creature by this noiſe. One of theſe joints put in the fundament cauſes immediate death; but the ſting of this creature proceeds much ſlower in its operation, for in the beginning a bloody matter iſſues from the wound, afterwards the fleſh turns blue, and the ulcer corrodes the adjacent parts by degrees. 1643.

The moſt ſovereign remedy uſed by the *Braſilians* againſt the poiſon of this and other ſerpents, is the head of the ſame ſerpent that has given the wound, which they bruiſe in a mortar, and in form of a plaiſter apply it to the affected part. They mix it commonly with faſting ſpittle, wherewith they alſo frequently moiſten the wound. If they find the poiſon begins to ſeize the nobler parts, they uſe the *Tiproka* as a cordial, and afterwards give ſtrong ſudorificks. They alſo lay open the wound, and apply cupping-glaſſes, to draw the venom from thence. Or elſe they burn it with a red hot iron.

The ſerpent *Kukuruku* is of an aſh colour, with yellow ſpots within and black ſpeckles without, and has juſt ſuch ſcales as the *Rattle Serpent*. Kukuruku.

The ſerpent *Guaku*, or *Liboya*, is queſtionleſs the biggeſt of all ſerpents; ſome being 18, 24, nay 30 foot long, and of the thickneſs of a man in the middle. The *Portugueſe* call it *Kobre dehado*, or the

Roebuck

1643. *Roebuck serpent*, because it will swallow a whole roebuck or any other deer it meets with; and this is performed by sucking it through the throat, which is pretty narrow, but the belly vastly big. After they have swallowed such a deer, they fall asleep, and so are catch'd. Such a one I saw near *Paraiba*, which was 30 foot long, and as big as a barrel. Some negroes saw it accidentally swallow a roebuck, whereupon thirteen musqueteers were sent out, who shot it, and cut the roebuck out of its belly. It was of a greyish colour, though others are inclining more to the brown. It is not so venomous as the other serpents. The *Negroes* and *Portuguese*, nay even some of the *Dutch* eat the flesh; neither are its stings look'd upon as very infectious, the wound healing often up without any application of remedies; so that it ought not to be reckoned among the number of poisonous serpents, no more than the *Kaninana*, *Mavina* and *Vocia*. This serpent being a very devouring creature, greedy of prey, leaps from amongst the hedges and woods, and standing upright upon its tail, wrestles both with men and wild beasts; sometimes it leaps from the trees upon the traveller, whom it fastens upon, and beats the breath out of his body with its tail.

The Roebuck serpent.

Jararaka. The serpent *Jararaka* is short, seldom exceeding the length of an arm to the elbow. It has certain protuberant veins on the head like the adder, and makes much such a noise. The skin is covered with red and black spots, the rest being of an earth colour. The stings of this creature are as dangerous, and attended with the same symptoms, as those of other serpents. Its body, the head, tail and skin, being before taken away together with the entrails, boil'd in the water of the root of *Jurepeba*, with salt, dill, and such like, is look'd upon as a very good remedy.

Boitrapo. The serpent *Boitrapo*, call'd by the *Portugueze*, *Cobre de Cibo*, is about seven foot in length, of the thickness of a man's arm, feeds upon frogs, and is of an olive colour. It is very venomous, and when it stings, occasions the same symptoms as the serpent *Kukuruku*; nay, the wound is accounted past curing, unless you apply the hot iron.

Ibiara. The adder *Ibiara*, by the *Portuguese* called *Cobra Vega*, or *Cobra de das Cabecas*, i. e. *The Doubleheaded Serpent*, because it appears to have two heads, which however is not so. They are found in great numbers, lurking in holes under ground. They feed upon pismires, are of the thickness of the length of a finger, and a foot and a half long, of a silver colour; nothing is more poisonous than the stings of these creatures, tho' not beyond all hopes of cure, provided the before-mentioned remedies be applied in time. 1643.

The serpent by the *Brasilians* called *Ibiboboka*, the *Portuguese* call *Cobra de Corais*. It is very beautiful, of a snow white colour, speckled with black and red spots, and about two foot long: Its sting is mortal, but kills by degrees. Ibiboboka.

The serpent *Biobi*, called by the *Portuguese Cabro Verde*, or the *Green Serpent*, about three quarters of a yard long, and the thickness of a thumb; of a shining green colour. It lives among houses, and hurts no body, unless when provoked. Its sting is however full of poison, and scarce curable. A certain soldier being wounded by one of these creatures, which lay hidden in a hedge, in his thigh, did for want of proper remedies, die in few hours after: His body swell'd, and turn'd pale blue. Biobi.

The serpent *Kaninana* is yellow on the belly and green on the back; its length is about eight hands, and is look'd upon as the least venomous of all. It feeds upon eggs and birds, and the *Negroes* and *Brasilians* eat the body, after they have cut off the head and tail. Kaninana.

The serpent call'd by the *Brasilians Ibirakoa*, is of several colours, with white, black, and red spots. The sting of this creature is very poisonous, attended with the same symptom as that of *Kukuruku*; for it kills infallibly, unless proper remedies be applied immediately. If the poison has not seised the heart, they boil the flesh of the same serpent with certain roots, and give it the patient in wine. Ibirakoa.

The serpent *Tarciboya* and *Kakaboya*, are amphibious creatures. The first is of a blackish colour, very large, and stings when provoked, but is not very difficult to be cured. The *Kakaboya* is of a yellowish colour, six hands long, and feeds upon tame fowl.

Of the Senembi *or the* Leguan.

Not only in the *Captainship* of *Parnambuko*, but also all over *Brasil* and *America*; as likewise in the Isle of *Java* in the *East-Indies*, are a certain kind of *Land Crocodile*, call'd by the *Brasilians Senembi*, by our people *Leguan*: Some are larger than others, some being three, others four foot long, but seldom exceed five:- They are all over covered with scales, which are somewhat bigger on the back, legs, and beginning of the tail, than on the other parts: The neck is about a finger and a half long, the eyes are black and bright, and the nostrils in the hindermost part of the head. Each jawbone is full of small, black,

1643. black, and ſhort teeth; the tongue is very thick: All along the back from the neck to the tail, are ſmall ſharp teeth of a greeniſh colour; they are biggeſt on the neck, and grow ſmaller and ſmaller towards the tail: Under the throat are likewiſe many of the ſame kind. The whole ſkin is of a delicate green, with black and white ſpots. It has four legs and feet, with five claws armed with very ſharp nails: It can live two or three months without food. Its fleſh is as white as that of a rabbit, and of as good a taſte as that of fowls or rabbits, if it be boil'd or well fry'd with butter. In the head of this creature are certain ſtones, which are an infallible remedy to break and drive the gravel out of the kidneys, given to the quantity of two drams at a time, or carried on ſome part of the body.

There are in *Brazil* lizards both great and ſmall; ſome are green, others greyiſh, and ſome four foot long, with ſparkling eyes. The *Negroes* feed upon ſome of them, whom they kill with blunt arrows; they broil them, after they have ſkin'd them, and eat them without the leaſt harm. Among all thoſe that are found among the thorns and briars, or the ruins of houſes, there is but one kind venomous, which is called *Bibora*. They are like the others, but leſſer, not exceeding the bigneſs of a thumb; they are of an aſh colour, inclining to white; the body and limbs thick and ſwell'd with the poiſon, but the tail ſhort and broad. The wounds given by them are full of a thin ſtinking matter, with blue ſwellings, with a pain near the heart, and in the bowels.

There are alſo certain creatures, called *Thouſand Legs*, as likewiſe *Hundred Legs*, by the natives called *Ambua*, who bend as they crawl along, and are accounted very poiſonous. The firſt are commonly found in the Houſes, and the laſt among the woods, where they not only ſpoil the fruits of the Earth, but alſo plague men and beaſts.

Scorpions. Scorpions, by the *Braſilians* called *Jaaciaiira*, are found here in great numbers, being in ſhape like the *European* ſcorpions, but not ſo peſtiferous, and conſequently the wounds given by them are eaſily cured. They lurk in houſes, behind old ſtools, benches and cheſts. They are exceeding big, no bigger being to be found in any other parts, ſome being five or ſix foot long, and of a conſiderable thickneſs.

There are ſuch prodigious quantities of piſmires in *Braſil*, that for this reaſon, they are called by the *Portugueſe*, *Rey de*
Piſmires. *Braſil*, *i. e.* King of *Braſil*. They eat all that lights in their way, as fruit, fleſh, 1643.
fiſh, and inſects without any harm. There is alſo a certain flying piſmire of a fingers length, with a triangular head, the body being ſeparated into two parts, and faſtned together by a ſmall ſtring. On the head are two ſmall and long horns, their eyes being very ſmall. On the foremoſt part of the body are ſix legs, three joints each, and four thin and tranſparent wings; to wit, two without, and two within; the hindermoſt part is of a bright colour and round, which is eaten by the *Negroes*. They dig into the ground like the moles, and conſume the ſeed.

There is another kind of great piſmires, reſembling a great fly; the whole body of which is about the length of half a finger, and ſeparated into three ſeveral parts. The laſt part reſembling in ſhape and bigneſs a barley corn; the middlemoſt of an oblong figure, with ſix legs, half a finger long, each of which has four joints: The foremoſt part, or the head, is pretty thick, in the ſhape of a heart, with two horns, and as many black crooked teeth: The white of the eyes is inclining to black, the whole compoſition of the head being the two eyes, placed oppoſite to one another, reſembling the figure of a heart. The fore and hindermoſt parts are of a bright red colour.

There is another kind of piſmire, of a bright black colour, with black and rough legs. It is about the length of a finger, with a large fourſquare head, ſtarting black eyes and teeth, and two horns, half a finger longer. The body is alſo ſeparated into three parts. The foremoſt of an oblong figure, not very thick, with ſix legs, each of the length of half a finger; the middlemoſt very ſmall and ſquare, not exceeding the bigneſs of a louſe; the hindermoſt is the biggeſt of the three, of an oval figure, and ſharp on the end. Theſe three parts are faſtned together with a ſingle ſtring, the *Braſilians* call it *Tapijai*.

There is beſides this another piſmire, call'd by the *Braſilians Kupia*, of a cheſnut brown colour; its head being as big as another piſmire, with black eyes, two horns, and two tuſks inſtead of teeth. The whole body is covered with hair; it is divided into two parts; The foremoſt with ſix legs, being ſomewhat leſs than the hindermoſt; at certain ſeaſons it gets four wings, the foremoſt being a little bigger than the hindermoſt, which it loſes again at a certain time.

The *Iron-pig* of *Braſil*, called by the *Braſilians Kuanda*; and by the *Portugueſe Ourico Kachiero*, is of the bigneſs of a large ape, its whole body being covered with ſharp

1643. ſharp ſpikes of three or four fingers long, without any hair. Towards the body thoſe ſpikes are halfways yellowiſh, the remaining part is black, except the points, which are whitiſh, and as ſharp as an awl. When they are vexed, they are able, by a certain contraction of the ſkin, to throw or dart them with ſuch violence, that they wound, nay, ſometimes kill men or beaſts. Their whole body to meaſure from the hindermoſt part of the head to the beginning of the tail, is a foot long, and the tail a foot and five inches in length, which likewiſe has always ſharp ſpikes, the reſt being covered with briſtles like other hogs. The eyes are round, ſtarting and gliſtering like a Carbuncle; about the mouth and noſe are hair of four fingers length, reſembling thoſe of our cats or hares: The feet are like thoſe of apes, but with four fingers only without a thumb, inſtead of which you ſee a place vacant, as if it had been cut away. The four legs are leſs than the hindermoſt, they are likewiſe armed with ſpikes, but not the feet. 1643.

This creature commonly ſleeps in the day time, and roves about by night; it breaths through the noſtrils, is a great lover of fowl, and climbs up the trees, tho' very ſlowly. The fleſh is of no ungrateful taſte, but roaſted and eaten by the Inhabitants. It makes a noiſe *Jii*, like the *Luyaert*.

That four-legg'd creature, by the *Braſilians* called *Ai*, by the *Portugueſe Priguiza*, and by the *Dutch Luyaert* (lazy-back) from its lazy and ſlow pace, becauſe in fifteen days time it ſcarce walks above a ſtones throw. It is about the bigneſs of a middle-ſized fox, its length being a little above a foot, to meaſure from the neck (which is ſcarce three fingers long) to the tail. The fore-legs are ſeven fingers long to the feet, but the hindermoſt about ſix; the head round of three fingers in length: its mouth, which never is without a foam, is round and ſmall, its teeth neither large nor ſharp. The noſe is black, high, and glib, and the eyes ſmall, black and heavy. The body is covered all over with aſh-coloured hair, about two fingers long; which are more inclining to the white towards the back. Round about the neck the

1643. the hair is ſomewhat longer than the reſt. It is a very lazy creature, unable to undergo any fatigues, by reaſon its legs are as it were disjointed in the middle; yet it keeps upon the trees, but moves, or rather creeps along very ſlowly. Its food is the leaves of the trees, it never drinks, and when it rains, hides itſelf. Whereever it faſtens with its paws, it is not eaſily removed; it makes, tho' ſeldom, a noiſe like our cats.

The *Piſmire-Eater*, is thus called, becauſe he feeds upon nothing but piſmires; there are two ſorts, the great and the ſmall: The *Braſilians* call the firſt *Tamanduaï*, and the laſt *Tamanduai-Guacu*. It is a four-legg'd creature, of the bigneſs of a dog, with a round head, long ſnout, ſmall mouth, and no teeth. The tongue is roundiſh, but ſometimes twenty-five inches, nay two foot and a half long. When it feeds, it ſtretches out its tongue upon the dunghills, till the piſmires have ſettled upon it, and then ſwallows them. It has round ears, and a rough tail; is not nimble, but may be taken with the hand in the field. The ſmall one, called *Tamanduai-Guacu*, is of the bigneſs of a *Braſilian* fox, about a foot in length. On the fore-feet it has four crooked claws, two big ones in the middle, and the two leſſer on the ſides. The head is round, yet pointed at one end, a little bent below; with a little black mouth without teeth. The eyes are very ſmall, the ears ſtand upright about a fingers length. Two broad black liſts run along on both ſides of the back; the hairs on the tail are longer than thoſe on the back, the extremity of the tail is without hair, wherewith it faſtens to the branches of the trees. The hairs all over the body are of a pale yellow, hard and bright. Its tongue is round, and about eight fingers long. It is a very ſavage creature, graſps every thing with its paws, and if you hit it with a ſtick, ſits upright like a bear, and takes hold of it with its mouth. It ſleeps all day long, with its head and fore-feet under the neck, and roves about in the night time. As often as it drinks, the water ſpouts forth immediately through the noſtrils. 1643.

They have alſo a kind of ſerpents of about two fathoms long, without legs, with a ſkin of various colours, and four teeth. The tongue is ſplit in the middle, reſembling two arrows, and the poiſon is hid in a bladder in its tail.

The four legg'd creature, called by the *Braſilians*, *Tatu* and *Tatupera*, by the *Spaniards*, *Armadillo*, by the *Portugueſe*, *Encubèrto*, and by the *Dutch*, *Schilt-Verken*, (Shield-Hog) becauſe it is defended with ſcales like as with an armour, reſembles in bigneſs and ſhape our hogs; there are ſeveral ſorts of them. The uppermoſt part of the body, as well as the head and tail, is covered with bony ſhields, compoſed of very fine ſcales. It has on the back ſeven partitions, betwixt each of which appears a dark brown ſkin. The head is altogether like that of a hog, with a ſharp noſe, wherewith they grub under ground; ſmall eyes, which lie deep in the head; a little, but ſharp tongue; dark brown and ſhort ears, without hair or ſcales: The colour of the whole body inclining to red; the tail in its beginning is about four fingers thick, but grows by degrees ſharp and round to the end, like thoſe of our pigs: But the belly, the breaſt, and legs are without any ſcales; but covered with a ſkin not unlike that of a gooſe, and whitiſh hair of a fingers length. It is generally very bulky and fat, living upon maleons and roots, and does conſiderable miſchief in the plantations. It loves to rout under ground, eats rabbets, and the dead carcaſſes of birds, or any other carrion: It drinks much, lives for the moſt part upon the land, yet loves the water and marſhy places. Its fleſh is fit to be eaten. It is catch'd like the doe in *Holland* with the rabbits, by ſending a ſmall dog abroad, who by his barking, gives notice where it lurks under ground, and ſo by digging up the ground it is found and catch'd.

Shield-Hogs.

The

Batts. The batts in *Brasil*, called by the inhabitants *Andirika*, are of the bigness of our crows; they are very fierce, and bite most violently with their sharp teeth. They build their nests in hollow trees and holes.

Wild-geese. The bird called by the *Brasilians*, *Ipekati Apoa*, by the *Portuguese*, *Pata*, is no more than a goose; and for that reason by the *Dutch* called a wild goose. It is of the bigness of one of our geese of about nine months old, and in all other respects resembles them. The belly and under part of the tail, as likewise the neck, is covered with white feathers; but on the back to the neck, on the wings and head, the feathers are black intermixed with some green. There are also some black feathers intermixed with the white ones on the neck and belly. They differ from our geese in this, that they are somewhat bigger; their bills resemble rather those of our ducks, but are black, and turned at the end, and on the top of it grows a broad, round, and black piece of flesh, with white speckles. They are commonly found near the river-side, are very fleshy and well-tasted.

The bird Toukan. The bird by the *Brasilians* called *Toukan*, or large bill, is about the bigness of a wood pigeon. It has a crop about the breast of three or four fingers in compass, of a saffron colour, with high red coloured feathers round the edges, which are yellow on the breast, but black on the back and all the other parts of the body. Its bill is very large, of the length of a palm of a hand, yellow without and red within. It is almost incredible how so small a bird is able to manage so large a bill, but that it is very thin and light.

The bird called by the *Brasilians*, *Kokoi*, is a kind of a crane, very pleasing to the sight, as big as our storks. Their bills are streight and sharp, about six fingers in length, of a yellowish colour inclining to green. The neck is fifteen fingers long, the body ten, the tail five: Their legs are half-ways covered with feathers, about eight fingers in length, the remaining part being six and an half. The neck and throat is white, both sides of the head black, mixt with ash-colour. On the far and undermost part of the neck are most delicious, white, long, and thin feathers, fit for plumes: The wings and tail are of an ash-colour, yet mixt with some white feathers. All along the back you see long and light feathers, like those *The bird* Kokoi.

on

1643. on the necks, but are of an ash-colour: Their flesh is very good, and of a grateful taste. There is another kind of these birds, which is somewhat bigger than a tame duck. Its bill is streight, and sharp at the end, of the length of four fingers and a half, with a double set of teeth both above and below: The head and neck (which is two foot long) resembles the crane, with black eyes enclosed in a gold coloured circle. The body is two foot and a half in length; the tail, which stands even with the extremity of the wings, four fingers. The bill is of an ash colour towards the head, the rest yellow, inclining to green. The head and upper part of the neck are covered with long pale yellowish feathers, intermixt with black. On the back and wings it hath ash coloured feathers inclining to yellow: but the legs and feet are dark grey: The flesh of this bird is eatable, and tastes like that of a crane.

Jabiru-guaku. The bird called by the *Brasilians*, *Jabiru Guaku*, and by the *Dutch*, *Schuur Vogel*, or barn-bird, has no tongue, but a very large bill, near seven foot and a half long; round and crooked towards the end, of a grey colour. On the top of the head is a crown of white and green feathers. The eyes are black, behind each of which are two great concavities instead of ears. The neck is ten fingers in length, one half part of which as well as the head, is not covered with feathers, but with an ash-coloured, whitish, rugged skin. This bird is of the bigness of a Stork, with a short black tail, which stands even with the extremities of the wings. The other part of the neck, and the whole body, is covered with white feathers, and those on the neck very long ones: The wings are likewise white, but mixt with some red. The flesh if boiled, after the skin is taken of, is good food, being very white, but somewhat dry.

Brasil produces incredible quantities of other wild fowl of all sorts, both great and small, some of which live among the woods, others in the water, but are very good food.

Of the best kind are the thrushes, called by them *Bamodi*; Pheasants of divers kinds, called by the *Barbarians*, *Magnagu*, *Jaku*, and *Arakua*.

Mouton is a bird of the bigness of a peacock, but has black feathers, the flesh is very good and tender. Because this countrey is full of fruit trees and woody places, it produces abundance of sparrow-hawks, and other hawks, called by the *Portuguese*, *Guavilon*, and by the *Brasilians*, *Teguata* and *Inage*, which are always at enmity with the chickens and pidgeons.

Among those that live both in the water and upon the land, the wild ducks claim the precedency; some of those are smaller than the *European* ducks, others much exceed them, being as big as a goose. They have also a sort of snipes, called *Jakana-miri* and *Jakana-guaku*. Besides these there are cranes, quails and ostridges, and many others of that kind; the flesh of which is eatable, but not very toothsome. 1643.

The rest of these birds are very greedy after the amber-greese, which is thrown ashore by the boisterous sea, which they devour before the inhabitants can come thither to gather it. They have also abundance of *Parakets*, or small parrots, these never speak; but their parrots are extraordinary fine and large, some of which learn to speak as distinctly as a Man. I have seen some of these parrots express every thing what they heard cried in the streets very plainly; and among the rest I saw one, which if put in a basket upon the floor, would make a dog that belonged to the same house, sit up before the basket, crying out to him, sit up, sit up, you nasty toad. Neither did this parrot leave off calling and crying, till the dog came to sit up before the basket. It was afterwards presented to the queen of *Sweden*.

There is among the rest a certain small bird, no bigger than a joint of a finger, which notwithstanding this, makes a great noise, and is catched with the hands whilst it is sitting among the flowers, from whence it draws its nourishment. As often as you turn this bird, the feathers represent a different colour, which makes the *Brasilian* women fasten then with golden wires to their ears, as we do our-rings. The birds here are never destitute of food, which they always meet with either among the flowers or fruits of the trees, which are never spoiled here during the winter season.

The rivers and lakes of *Brasil*, as well as the neighbouring sea, furnishes them with great store of all sorts of fish, which are accounted so wholsome here, that they are even allowed for those that are troubled with agues. The standing waters near the sea-side, which sometimes are quite dried up, produce abundance of craw-fish, tortoises, shrimps, crabs, oysters, and divers others of this kind, which are all very good food. *Their fish*

There are abundance of fish in *Brasil*, common to the sea and rivers, especially during the rainy season; when a great quantity of the river water being conveyed into the sea, the sweetness of the water allures the fish into the rivers, where meeting with abundance of green weeds (the product of the bottom of the rivers) they never return to the sea.

Among the river fish the chiefest are, the *Duja*, *Prajuba*, and *Akara-Puku*, the last of

1643. of which resembles the best and largest of our perches.

Brasil produces also various kinds of insects, some of which are of four fingers length, and an inch thick. They have likewise silk worms, called by the *Brasilians*, *Isokuku*'s, and their silk, *Isokurenimbo.*

There are also divers sorts of fire-flies, which are likewise found in the *East-Indies*, where we shall give you a further account of them. Besides these, there are many sorts of other flies, hornets, wasps, and bees: some of which produce honey, some none at all. 1643.

Spiders. Among other kinds of spiders there is one of a prodigious bigness, which is always found either in dunghills, or in the concavities of hollow trees: They call it *Nhanduguaka.* These creatures weave cobwebs like other spiders; the skin is rough and black, provided with sharp and long teeth. This creature if provoked wounds with its poisonous sting, which is so small as scarce to be visible, and raises a blueish tumour, which is very painful, and if care be not taken in time, occasions an inflammation, attended with such dangerous symptoms as prove afterwards incureable.

Ballar, *or* Kabitto. Near *Rio St. Francisco* are vast numbers of a certain small insect not unlike our crickets; I have been very curious to get sight of this creature, to satisfy myself as to its shape, and resemblance to others of this kind; but though it makes a very shrill noise, which resembles that of our crickets, I was never able to see any of them; for as soon as you approach they desist, so that you are at a loss which way to look. They sing sometimes for a quarter of an hour without intermission. In the island of *Java* in the *East-Indies* it is commonly heard in the months of *February* and *June.* At last I had the good fortune to get one of these creatures into my hands; by means of a certain *Chinese* woman, after I had often been in search of it, both within and without the city of *Batavia.* The *Javanese* set two of these little creatures a fighting together, and lay money on both sides, as we do at a cock-match.

There are also abundance of ravenous wild beasts in *Brasil*, such as tygers, leopards, *&c.* The tygers are extreamly savage here; they fall upon beasts, and sometimes

1643. times upon men, of whom several were killed by them in my time. A certain *Portuguese* had a sugar-mill very pleasantly situated near a wood, whither we used to go to divert ourselves sometimes. The *Portuguese* sitting one time with four more of his friends in the house, with the windows drawn up for the conveniency of the land air, a dog belonging to the house, who had ventured too far into the adjacent wood, was pursued by a tyger, so that to save his life he leapt into the window to seek for shelter near his master; but the tyger closely pursuing him, leapt also through the window into the room, where the door being shut, he tore two of those there present in pieces before the rest could make their escape, and afterwards went his way.

There is another sort of savage beast in those parts, called by some of our people, *Jan-over-Zee*, or jack beyond sea, which surpasses all others in nimbleness, and tears all to pieces it meets with.

Cattle. *Brasil* has also great plenty of cattle, but the flesh will not keep above twenty-four hours after it is dress'd. The *Dutch* cut off the fat, and cut the lean in thin slices, and dry it in the sun like fish. No butter is to be made here, because the milk turns to curds immediately: the *Dutch* butter is drawn out of a vessel like oil.

Hogs. Their hogs are small and black, but very well tasted, and wholesome; there is another kind of amphibious hogs, by the *Portuguese* called *Kapiverres*, they are very near as black as the others, and good food.

Antes. There is another four legg'd creature in *Brasil*, called by the inhabitants *Taperete*, and by the *Portuguese*, *Antes*; its flesh has the taste of beef, but somewhat finer. It is about the bigness of a calf, but shaped like a hog; it sleeps all day among the woods, and seeks for belly-timber in the night: Its food is grass, sugar-reeds, cabbages, and such like. They have likewise good store of goats, called by them *Pakas*, and *Kotias*, and hares and rabbits, which don't give way in goodness to those of *Europe*. There is also an excellent kind of lizards, called by the inhabitants, *Vuana* and *Teju*, which are accounted a dainty bit.

Fish. The fish in *Brasil* are no less considerable for the supply of our plantations, than the cattle, which are on the coasts of *Brasil*, but especially in *Parnambuko*, where they are found in such plenty, that at one draught they catch sometimes two or three thousand fine fish, in the four or five summer months, for during the rainy season, they catch but few. There are certain districts along the sea coast whither the fish most resort; some of those belong to the inhabitants, the rest to the company, and are farmed at a certain rate *per annum*. The lakes as well as the bays, are stored with an incredible multitude of fish; the first are by the *Portuguese* called *Alagoas*; and the best they produce are the *Sindia*, *Queba*, and *Noja*, all without scales. And though the fish which are catcht in the lakes are not so much esteemed as the river-fish, nevertheless are they not much behind them in goodness, because these lakes are not always standing waters, but intermixt with several rivers. Some of these fish they dry in the sun. The chiefest of this kind are those called by the *Brasilians*, *Kurima Parati*, and by the *Dutch* inhabitants *Herders*. They abound no less in sea-fish of all sorts. The fish called by the *Brasilians*, *Karapantangele*, which is not unlike our perch, has the preference among them. And as the rivers furnish infinite numbers of fish, so they are generally fatter and better tasted than the sea-fish. Those which are catcht in these fisheries near the sea-shore, are for the most part salted, and carried from thence into the countrey, for the use of the sugar-mills, which cause great plenty among them. 1643.

The craw-fish, which are in great quantities near the rivers and in the marshy grounds, serve likewise for food to *Brasilians* and negroes, and some of our people like them tolerably well.

It is further to be observed, that whereas a considerable number of cattle, during the war was run astray out of the parks into the forests and woods beyond the river of *St. Francis*, it was thought convenient by the great council of the company here, to agree with certain persons to catch this cattle, and bring it to the *Receif*, in order to be killed for the use of the inhabitants. The time of the said contract being expired, it was consulted whether the same should be renewed; but it being apparent that there were not enough left to quit cost, the same was laid aside, and this resolution sent to the council of nineteen. For in the mean while the inhabitants near *Rio St. Francisco* and *Rio Grande*, having applied themselves to the breeding of cattle, their parks were so well stockt by this time, that they not only furnished the inhabitants of the *Receif*, but also the sugar-mills, with plenty of meat, which was bought at the rate of three and four pence *per* pound in the countrey; besides that, they provided the garrisons with the same for a twelvemonth, after the store-houses of the *Receif* were emptied; and notwithstanding this, the inhabitants of those parts were not out of debt, when those of *Parnambuko* and *Parayba*, were involved over head and ears; which shews what advantage they reapt from the breeding of cattle; and that if the

1643. the *Dutch Brasil* had continued in peace, those parks might have furnished all the garrisons with meat without impairing their stock for breeding; which, together with the great plenty of fish, are the two main pillars of the state of *Brasil*.

Notwithstanding all which, it is certain that the inhabitants of the *Dutch Brasil* cannot be provided with sufficient maintenance, without a yearly supply from *Europe*, as well eatables as other commodities; as has been found by experience, to the great detriment of the company; after our store-houses were exhausted by the several expeditions against *Angola*, *Meranhaon*, and other places.

Crocodiles. In the rivers and lakes here are also found crocodiles, by the *Brasilians* called *Jakare*, and in the *East-Indies*, *Kaymans*. They are like the *African* crocodiles, but not quite so big, seldom exceeding five foot in length: They lay twenty or thirty eggs bigger than geese eggs, which are eaten by the *Brasilians*, *Portuguese* and *Dutch*, as well as the flesh.

In the seas near the coast of *Brasil*, they meet also sometimes with great lampreys. Before the bridge from the *Receif* to *Maurice-town* was built, one of this kind of a considerable bigness did lurk near that passage, where the boats used to pass over from one side to the other, and snatcht all that fell in his way; both men and dogs that swam sometimes after the boat, into the water: But at a certain time, by the sudden falling of the tide, being got aground with the foremost part of the body, he was with much ado brought ashore.

The district of *Pernambuko* does also abound in various sorts of fruits, as well as all the other parts of *Brasil*, of which we shall say more hereafter.

Upon the captainship of *Pernambuko*, borders to the north the captainship of *Tamarika*, which owes its name to an island of the same name, being the chiefest part of this district, which however extends near thirty-five leagues along the sea coast on the continent.

The island of *Tamarika* lies two leagues to the north of *Pomerello*, in the sea; being parted from the continent by the river *Tamarika*, its most southern point lying under the 7th degree 58m southern latitude. It is from south to north about two leagues long, and its circuit near seven. To the jurisdiction of this isle did also belong *Goyana*, *Kapavaribi*, *Terukupa*, and *Abray* on the continent. Formerly it had but few inhabitants, and scarce any houses, though it is a very pleasant isle, and tolerably fertile, producing brasil-wood, coco nuts, cotton, sugar-reeds, melons, and such like; besides wood for firing, and fresh water for the conveniency of the *Receif*: It abounds likewise in wood both for building of houses and shipping. This island was much infested with wild beasts, which did great mischief to the sugar reeds: This moved *Peter Pas*, director of the captainship of *Itamarika*, to make his application to count *Maurice* and the great council in 1647, to know their pleasure, whether they should dispose of those beasts by contract, to such as would be at the charge of catching of them, or whether they should be taken and killed for the use of the garrisons; but this was rejected by the council, who enjoined the inhabitants not to kill those beasts in the open fields, unless they should break into their plantations, it being for the interest of the company to preserve them in case of a necessity: The damage which from thence might accrue to the sugar reeds, being to be prevented by surrounding their plantations with pales and stakes.

The island is look'd upon as of the greatest consequence to us, it having been proposed by some to transfer the seat of the *Dutch-Brasil* from the *Receif* thither; but the directors of the company did not agree to it, considering that at that time this island was quite desolate; whereas upon the *Receif* were store-houses, magazines, ware-houses, and such like buildings ready to their hands, besides that the place was much more pleasant, fertile, and stronger; and the harbour much more convenient for ships: The river *Tamarika* on the other hand being not navigable, but for small vessels, by reason of the shallowness of the harbour, which was noted for shipwracks. The defect of fresh water in the *Receif*, in which this isle abounds, may be supplied from the river *Biberibi*; besides that, they had several basons with fresh water within the *Receif*, for their present use. During the war with the *Portuguese* we were sensible of the conveniencies we received from this island, by reason of its strength both by art and nature, which might serve as a safe retreat upon all emergencies; besides, that its preservation was absolutely necessary for the *Receif*, which was supplied from thence with fish, and several other other sorts of provisions. *The consequence of this isle.*

Upon the banks of the river at the south entrance of the harbour, we had built a quadrangular fort, called *Orange*. It was provided with a goodly wall, but the ditch was not very deep, and for the most part without water, for which reason it was strenghten'd with pallisadoes. On the north-side we had a hornwork, but much decayed; within the body of the fort was a powder-vault, and other conveniencies for the bedding

1643. bedding of soldiers. Several batteries were raised upon the walls, mounted upon six brass and as many iron great guns. In the island near the entrance of the river, close by a morass full of thorn-bushes, was a small town, most inhabited by soldiers, called by the *Portuguese*, *Nostra Senhora de la Conceptiano*. Upon a hanging rock, just by, was an old redoubt erected by the *Portuguese*, called by the same Names, which together with the whole island, was taken by the *Dutch*, under the command of colonel *Schop* from the *Portuguese*, and the place, after his name, called *Schop's Town*. This fort was afterwards by the *Dutch* closed up on the backside towards the church, so that it afterwards served both for the defence of the town and the harbour, as the *Blockhouse* on the north-side cover'd the gates. There were then eleven pieces of cannon mounted upon it. At the north entrance of the harbour, was another redoubt, which defended that passage on that side, with three iron cannon. One Mr. *Dortmont*, governor of *Itamarika*, found under the before-mention'd rock, in 1645, as he was digging a well, a spring of fresh water, which proved very useful for the garrison, because it could not be cut off by the enemy.

Hanging-rock.

Somewhat higher up the river *Tamarika*, lies an island called *Magioppe*, where are found abundance of *Mandihoka* roots. You may go quite round this island in barks; it having a kind of a harbour on both ends, *viz.* to the south and north, but the first is the best; because there arises from the northern shore of the continent, a shelf, which reaches very close to the island, the channel betwixt both not having above ten or twelve foot water. The only harbour fit for use thereabouts is the south-entrance of the river, which makes *Tamarika* an island, where ships that drew fourteen or fifteen foot water, may pass through; there is no convenient anchorage: That end, where the river returns into the sea, is by the *Dutch* called the northern-entrance, and by the *Portuguese Katuamma*.

The rivers Marafarinha *and* Garassou.

Betwixt *Pomerello* and the river *Tamarika*, a river comes from the continent, fit for barges, called *Marafarinha*; and half a league within the mouth of the river *Tamarika*, another falls likewise from the continent called *Garassou*, but is of little moment. From thence to the north, are several other rivers near the sea-shore, which are navigable with barges, for the conveniency of the sugar-mills, of which there are several thereabouts.

Punto Pedra.

A league and an half further to the north of the north-entrance of *Tamarika*, is a noted point of land called by the *Portuguese*, *Punto Pedra*, surrounded with a *Receif*, betwixt which you may pass with barges and yachts. 1643.

The river Goyana.

A league further to the north from this point, and three leagues to the north-west of *Tamarika*, is the small river *Goyana*, under 7 deg. 46 min. which disembogues in two branches in the bay; at the entrance lies a great rock, where is great store of sea-fowl. Before it lies a great *Receif*, but within are so many shelves that renders the passage very dangerous.

The river Auyay.

About two leagues and a half beyond the river *Goyana*, to the north, is a great river, called *Auyay*, but the entrance is so choak'd up with sands, that there is scarce any passage for barges. This river sends forth several branches into the country, upon one of which to the north, lies the village of *Maurice*, and upon the southern branch the village *Auyay*.

Porto Francisco.

Among others, *Porto Francisco* lies in a creek three long leagues to the north of the river *Auyay*; and five leagues to the north-west of the same river, an unnavigable river called *Grammana*, besides several other rivulets.

Parayba.

About a league and a half to the north-west of the river *Grammana*, is the *Cabo Blanco*, or *White Cape*; and three leagues from thence to the north-west, the cape of *Parayba*, being a long point of land, with a large adjacent bay. The whole coast from *Pomerello* to the cape of *Parayba*, is cover'd with receifs or rocks, which lying for the most part about half a league from the shore, and the water between them being generally very smooth, affords an easy passage to barges, even in tempestuous weather when it is almost impossible for ships to pass without the rocks, by reason of the violence of the current from the northern and the southern winds, which blow there continually.

The Town of Goyana.

Three leagues within the mouth of the river *Goyana* is a town of the same name, where is kept the court of judicature of this *captainship*. There are five or six sugar-mills thereabouts, situated upon the banks of the river, for the more commodious transportation of sugar in barges to *Pernambuko*. This countrey produces likewise brasil-wood, ginger, cotton, and *Indian* nuts; the people called *Petiguaves* inhabit here; tho' this whole tract of land, as far as *Cabo Blanco*, is not very populous, having only a few villages, inhabited by the *Brasilians*.

The isle of *Tamarika* has several landing places on the river-side, the chiefest are: *Os Markos* and *Pedreiros*, where the river is narrowest; *Tapasima* and *Kamboa* of *Domingos Rebeyro*; the great *Makqueira* and

1643. and *Kamboa* of *Conrad Pauli*; in which places the enemy landed in that island. The pass near the north-entrance of *Topowa*, and the island *Taposoka*, where with one single ship you may defend the passage from the rivers *Tujukapape* and *Masserandaku*, as likewise from the sea. For the rest, the shore all along the river being very marshy and full of *Manga* trees, is of a very difficult access. The shore towards the sea-side is very flat, but woody, which together with the sands, that are at some distance in the sea, makes the approach of ships very dangerous on that side. Formerly the court of judicature of the *captainship* was kept in this island, but was afterwards transferred from thence, as we told you before, to the Town of *Goyana* and *Kapivaribi* on the continent, because these places were both more populous, and more sugar-mills were built thereabouts, the ground being much better here than in the Island. In my time there were five judges belonging to this court, three of which lived at *Goyana*, and the other two in the isle of *Itamarika*. However, this court was afterwards likewise removed from *Goyana*. In the year 1641, Mr. *Peter Pas* was director of the *captainship* of *Itamarika* for the *West-India* company, and captain *Sluiter* commander in chief over the soldiers.

Parayba. This *captainship* has derived its name from the capital city, which has borrow'd hers of the river *Parayba*, upon which it is situate. It is one of the most northerly *captainships*, about five leagues distant from the sea. It was formerly in the possession of the *French*, who were 1585, chased from thence and several other harbours, by the *Portuguese* general *Martin Leytan*.

The city Parayba. Five leagues upwards the river *Parayba*, is a city founded by the *Portuguese*, and after *Philip* king of *Spain*, called *Filippen* and *Nossa Senhora de nives*, otherwise *Parayba*, from the river *Parayba*; which name was by the *Dutch*, after they had in *November* 1633, conquered the whole *captainship*, changed into that of *Frederick's Town*, after *Frederick Henry* prince of *Orange*. This city had been but lately built by the *Portuguese*, and had several stately houses with marble pillars, the rest being only of stone. Here is kept the court of judicature of this *captainship*. Before the time of the rebellion of the *Portuguese*, this place was inhabited as well by the *Portuguese* as *Dutch*, being much frequented by the inhabitants of the circumjacent countrey, was used to exchange their sugar for what other commodities they stood in need of, which was afterwards from thence transported to other places.

Within the mouth of the river *Parayba*, were three very considerable forts. One on the south-point, by the *Portuguese* called *Catharine*, but by count *Maurice*, afterwards named *Margaret*, after his Sister. It was defended with five goodly bastions, and a hornwork without. *Fort Margaret.* 1643.

The fort called *St. Antonio*, by the *Portuguese*, was built upon a small island, which by a narrow breach was separated from the north-point. This is only the remainder of a large four square fort, formerly erected by the *Portuguese*, which was afterwards rased by the *Dutch*, part of it having been wash'd away by the river. It is surrounded with pallisadoes and a good ditch, supplied with water from the beforenamed branch of the river: The Walls are very strong, and upon a battery are mounted six iron pieces of cannon. It may be defended by the cannon both from the city of *Parayba*, and from the fort *Margaret*, lying just opposite to it on the south-side, which is the reason it was always but carelesly guarded by the *Portuguese*. *Fort* St. Anthony.

The third fort lies upon a triangular island, called *Restinga*, not far from thence, more upwards the river. It was strengthened with pallisadoes, and upon the batteries were mounted five brass, and as many iron pieces of cannon. *The third fort.*

The *captainship* of *Parayba* is watered and divided by two considerable rivers, *viz.* the *Parayba* and *Mongoapa*, otherwise call'd *St. Domingo*. The great river of *Parayba* lies under the 6th deg. 24 min. four leagues to the north of *Cabo Blanco*, and discharges it self in two branches into the Sea, being separated by a large sand-bank: One is called the northern, and the other the southern entrance. From the last extends a rocky-ridge as far *Cabo Blanco*, and within the river lies a sand-bank quite cross to the fort *Margaret*. This river is very shallow during the summer time, but in the winter season, the waters rise to that height that they overflow all the adjacent countrey, sometimes to the great loss of men and cattle. *The river* Parayba.

Two leagues beyond this river to the north, is a bay which affords a very safe station to the largest ships. It is by the *Portuguese* called *Porto Lucena*, and by the *Dutch* the *Red-Land*, the grounds being red hereabouts. There is very good anchorage here at five and six fathom water, and the country near it affords very good fresh water; which is the reason why the *Dutch* ships bound for *Holland* from the *Receif*, used to stay for one anothers coming in this bay, and to provide themselves with fresh water. Porto Lucena.

1643.

River Mongoapa.

Half a league further to the north, under 6 deg. 34 min. the river *Mongoapa*, or *Mongoanawapy*, exonerates it self into the sea: This river is much larger towards its source than at the mouth; the banks on both sides being full of briers, bushes and *Manga* trees. Before its entrance lies a *Receif*, and at the very mouth two dangerous sand-banks; it has three fathom water at low tide,

About two small leagues to the north of the river *Mongoapa*, is a bay called by the *Portuguese Bahia de Treycano*, or *Treason*, where, at about a league distant from the shore, is eleven or twelve fathom water. Five leagues to the north of this bay, you meet with the river *Barra Conguon* or *Konayo*, which is scarce passable for Yatches. About a league and a half from thence is large bay of about two leagues in length, called *Pernambuko*; and five leagues beyond it to the north, the river *Jan de Sta*, or *Estau*.

The natives of *Parayba* inhabit about seven villages, the chiefest of which is call'd *Pinda Una*, which in 1634, contained about fifteen hundred inhabitants, where each of the others had scarce three hundred; each of these comprehending not above five or six very long buildings, with a great many doors, but very small ones.

The chief commodities of this *captainship* are sugar, brasil-wood, tobacco, hides, cotton, and such like. The sugar-reeds did bear extremely well, because they were transplanted into fresh grounds. Whilst the district of *Parayba* was under our jurisdiction, there were above one and twenty sugar-mills on both sides of the banks of the river, eighteen of which sent away every year four thousand chests of sugar. Near the river-side, the country is low and plain, but not far from thence rises by degrees, and affords a very agreeable variety of hills and vallies. The flat countrey, which is also the most fertile, is distinguish'd into several divisions, some of which have borrow'd their names from small rivers which run thro' them; as for instance, *Gramamma*, *Tapoa*, *Tibery*, *Ingeby*, *Monguappe*, *Increry*, *Kamaratuba*, and several more. All those countries are extremely fertile, occasion'd by the overflowing of the river *Parayba*. Their products are, sugar, barley, turky-wheat, potatoes, ananas, coco-nuts, melons, oranges, citrons, bananas, pakovas, markomas, cucumbers, and all other necessaries for the sustenance of men and beasts. They have here a kind of wild pears, called kajous, which are very juicy and well-tasted; within is a certain bean or small nut, the rind of which is bitter, but the kernel sweet,

Its fertility.

if roasted in the ashes. The pear is very cooling, but the nut has a contrary quality. 1643.

Towards the end of *November* 1634, the *Dutch* undertook the expedition against *Parayba*, their forces being embarked in thirty two ships under the command of colonel *Schoppe*, *Artisjoski*, *Hinderson*, *Stachouwer* and *Carpentier*. The whole fleet was divided into two squadrons; the first consisted of one and twenty ships, in which were nineteen hundred and forty five men, the other of eleven yachts, with four hundred and nine men. *Schoppe* was the first that landed six hundred men, and advanced towards the enemy, who betook themselves to their heels, leaving their arms and cloaths behind them; *Anthony Albuquerque* their general, himself scarce escaping their hands. In the mean while, the rest being likewise got a shore, three companies, under the conduct of *Gasper Ley*, marched directly to the fort of *Margaret*, and intrencht himself near the fort, whilst *Schoppe* kept all along the shore, and *Artisjoski*, posted himself on the right-side, in sight of the garrison: At the same time Mr. *Lichthart* attack'd the fort in the small island *Restinga*, which he took by force, and put the garrison to the sword. By this time *Schoppe* had raised a battery against the fort, from whence he so sorely gall'd the besieged, that their commander *Simon d'Albukirque* surrendred the place. Hereupon the fort of *St. Antonio* was summoned to surrender, *Maglianes* the governor desired three days delay, which being denied, he march'd away secretly by night, leaving the place to *Lichthart*, who found there five great brass pieces, and nineteen iron pieces of cannon.

The Dutch conquer Parayba.

The same night our forces marched towards the city of *Parayba*, being sixteen hundred strong, and having pass'd a small branch of the river called *Tambra Grande*, made themselves masters of it without any opposition: The *Spanish* general *Banjola*, who commanded there with two hundred and fifty men only, having left the place before, and being retired to *Goyana*, after he had either sunk or nail'd up the cannon, set fire to three ships and two warehouses, in which were consumed three thousand chest with sugar. The fort of *St. Catharine* being much decay'd, was order'd by count *Maurice* to be repaired, and the ditch to be enlarged and deepen'd; giving it the name of *Margaret*, after his Sister. The fort of *St. Antonio* was rased, for the greatest part, there being only one bulwark left for the defence of the north-point of the river. The fort *Restingas* was order'd to be surrounded with new pallisadoes

1643. does, and the convent of *Parayba* fortified with a wall and outwork; and the command thereof given to *Elias Harkman*, together with the government of the whole *captainship*.

Potigi, *or* Rio Grande. The *captainship* of *Potigi*, or *Potingi* or *Poteingi*, is otherwise, by the *Portuguese*, called *Rio Grande*, from a river of the same Name: The *Dutch* call it *North-Brasil*, in respect of the more southern *captainships* of *Brasil*. It borders to the south upon *Parayba*, and to the north upon the *captainship* of *Siara*; tho' the *Portuguese* geographers extended its bounds as far as the island *Maranhaon*.

The *French* were once masters of this *captainship*, 'till 1597, they were chased from thence by the *Spanish* commander, *Feliciano Creça de Karvalasho*. It has four divisions, named after so many rivers, that run through them; *viz. Kunhao, Goyana, Mumpobu* and *Potegy*. And tho' this district has been much neglected by the *Portuguese*, yet does it produce plenty of wild-fowl and fish, which are so luscious, that they commonly eat them only with lemon-juice or vinegar, without oil. There is an incredible number of fish in the lake *Goraires*; besides which, abundance of *Farinha* is planted here. This part of the countrey stood us in good stead during the late rebellion of the *Portuguese*, our garrisons in *Parayba*, and other places, being supplied from thence with good store of flesh and fish.

***River* Rio Grande.** Above the river *Rio Grande*, is a town of no great moment, call'd *Amsterdam*; the inhabitants live by planting *Farinha* and *Tobacco*, and fishing. Higher up in the countrey live some *Moradores* or husbandmen, who cultivate the grounds; but on the north-side of *Rio Grande* are but few inhabitants.

The river *Rio Grande, i. e.* the *Great-river*, is so called by the *Portuguese* from its bigness, but by the *Brasilians*, *Potigi* or *Poteingi*. The mouth of this river lies under 50 deg. 42 min. southern latitude, three leagues from *Punto Negro*, coming from the west-side of the continent. It disembogues four leagues above the fort *Keulen*, called by the *Portuguese*, *Tres Reyos*: It bears ships of great burthen; but the river *Kunhao* in the same *captainship* is only navigable with barges and yachts. The bays of this *captainship* are, *Bahia Formosa*, *Punto Negro*, *Ponto de Pipas*, and the *Bay of Martin Tüssen*. The *Bay of Ginapabo* lies beyond *Rio Grande* to the north; and beyond that a river call'd *Guasiavi*, upon which, near the mouth lies the village *Atape Wappa*. Near to the north you meet with the river *Siria Mixui*; and near the village of *Natal*, and the fort of *Tres Reyos*, passes a river called the *Cross-River*, which arises out of a small lake in *Rio Grande*. Over against the same fort, a fresh river falls into the great river, betwixt two land-banks, and not far from thence another salt-water river. 1643.

***The fort* Keulen.** The fort *Keulen* was four-square, built upon a rock or point of a *Receif*, at some distance from the shore, at the mouth of the river *Receif*; being surrounded with water, as oft as it's flowing water, so that at high tide there is no coming at it but with boats. In the midst of this fort is a small chappel, where in 1645, and 1646, our people found a wall about a foot and a half wide on the top, but at the bottom three feet, cut within a rock, which brings fresh supplies of good and sweet water every tide; with an ordinary tide two hundred and twenty five, and at spring-tide about three hundred and fifty quarts; which is more than sufficient for the use of the garrison, in case of siege. The fort is built of a square stone; being towards the shore defended with two half bastions, in form of hornworks. In the year 1646, there was an artillery of twenty nine, as well brass as iron pieces of cannon in the place, and provided with a good under-vault, and convenient lodgments for the soldiers.

***Its conquest by the* Dutch.** This fort was in 1633, taken by the *Dutch*, under the command of *Matthias van Keulen*, one of the governors of the company, who being assisted by several noted captains, *viz. Byma, Kloppenburg, Lichthart, Garstman* and *Mansfelt van Keulen*, set sail thither with eight hundred and eight men, embarked in four ships and seven yachts, and made himself master of it, and the whole captainship at the same time; since which it changed its name *Tres Reyos*, into that of *Keulen*, from the commander in chief of this expedition.

The *Tapoyers* (or mountaineers) use commonly twice a year, especially when the dry season puts them in want of fresh water, to make an inroad into this *captainship*; there being a constant enmity betwixt them and the *Portuguese*. It happen'd in *July* 1645, that these *Tapoyers* being advertised that the *Portuguese* intended to revolt from us, and had actually begun the same in *Pernambuko*, did, under the conduct of one of their leaders, called *Jacob Rabbi*, after several provocations given them by the *Portuguese*, make an incursion into *Kunhao*, where they killed thirty six Persons in a sugar-mill belonging to one *Gonsalvo d'Olivera*. From thence they marched to a certain place, where the *Portuguese* had cast up a line for their defence, which they made themselves masters of, and put the

1643. the *Portuguese* to the sword. The *Brasillians* told us, that this had been done in requital of what had been done to some of those mountaineers by one *Andrew Vidal* in *Serinhaim*, after quarter given them before, of which we shall say more hereafter. Since which time, the *Portuguese* have laid this tract desolate, which the *Dutch* once had a mind to re-people, and to put it in the same condition as the *Portuguese* had possess'd it, but for want of people that design was fain to be laid aside.

Siara.

The *captainship* of *Siara* is one of the most northerly districts of *Brasil*, bordering upon *Maranhaon* to the north upon the river *Siara*. It is of no great extent, its whole compass being not above ten or twelve leagues.

The river Siara.

The river *Siara*, which rises deep in the continent, disembogues about seven leagues and a half to the north of the bay *Mangorypa*, under 3 deg. 40 min. southern latitude.

The native inhabitants of this *captainship*, according to the report of those that have frequently visited it, are very large of stature, with ugly features, long hair and black skin; except the space betwixt the eyes and mouth. They have holes in their ears, which hang downwards upon the shoulders; some make holes in their lips, some in their noses, in which they wear stones as an ornamen . Their food is *Farinha*, wild-fowls, fish and fruit. They drink most water, but make likewise a certain liquor out of *Farinha*; and of late began to be used to drink good store of brandy, tho' it was expresly forbidden to bring it into the villages, to keep them from the excessive use of strong liquors. The countrey produces sugar-reeds, chrystal, cotton, pearls, salt, and several other commodities. Ambergrease is also found on the sea-shore.

The inland part of the countrey was in 1630, governed by one of their own kings, call'd *Algodoi*; in some respect tributary to the *Portuguese*, who had built a fort upon the river *Siara*, and made themselves masters of the whole sea-coast thereabouts; notwithstanding which they were in continual broils with one another, 'till 1638, this fort and the whole countrey was taken by the *Dutch* from the *Portuguese*, in the following manner.

Siara *conquered by the* Dutch.

Count *Maurice* and the council, being sollicited by the natives of that country, to make themselves masters of the *Portuguese* fort on that side, and to deliver them from the oppression they lay under at that time, they offering their assistance, and and giving two young lads of their best families, as pledges of their Fidelity, this expedition was resolved upon. The chief command over the Troops design'd for this exploit, was conferr'd upon colonel *John Garstman*, a man of more than ordinary conduct in martial affairs, tho' as the case then stood, this enterprise was not likely to meet with any considerable difficulties; being assured of the assistance of the *Brasilians*, who bore an old hatred to the *Portuguese*, and were acquainted with the strength and condition both of their forces and places. *Garstman* being provided with ships, men, ammunition, and all other necessaries requisite for such an expedition, set sail towards the river *Siara*; where being met by the *Algodoi*, or king, with white ensigns in token of peace; and having landed his men, two hundred of the natives joined with them. With those he marched directly to the fort, which after a brave resistance from the *Portuguese*, who killed some of his men, he took by storm; and made most of the garrison prisoners, among whom were some commanders of note: They found good store of cannon and artillery in the place. 1643.

The fort Siara.

Since that time, the *Dutch* built a small fort upon the *Siara*, unto which they gave likewise the name of *Siara*, which was provided with a garrison of betwixt thirty and forty soldiers only; not so much for the defence of the countrey, as to maintain a good correspondency with the *Brasilians*, who being very numerous in those parts, might do us considerable service in time of war. It was upon this consideration, that the great council always commanded their officers, sent thither, to cultivate a good understanding with them; and at several times sent them some small presents, which, however proved ineffectual in the end, for in 1644, they attack'd and kill'd several of our men at *Komesay*, (a place about thirty leagues from *Siara*) as we shall hear anon.

For the *Brasilians* being, in 1641, increased to such a number in *Siara*, that the villages thereabouts were not able to contain them without great inconveniency, whereas the district of *Rio Grande* was almost destitute of inhabitants, and consequently not in a condition to oppose an enemy; one *Andrew Uliiss* proposed to the great council, to build a village in *Rio Grande*, for the use of such as intended to settle there out of *Siara*, desiring to be constituted chief of the said village. Count *Maurice* and the great council, being informed of the inclinations of those *Siara*, who were willing to settle in *Rio Grande*, their ancient place of abode, and considering the benefit that was likely to accrue to the company, from the settlement of those *Brasilians*, so near at hand, granted *Uliis*'s request, wishing him to bring thither

1643. thither as many of the *Brasilians* of *Siara* as he thought convenient, for the compass of a village of which he was made chief or captain. Things being thus settled, they chose, with the approbation of our directors, certain chiefs or heads out of the most ancient families of each division, called *Residoor* by the *Portugueze*, and certain judges; as for instance in *Goyana*, *Domingoi*, *Fernandes*, and *Karapeva*; in *Parayba*, *Peter Potty*; and in *Rio Grande*, *Antonio Perapeva*. Notwithstanding all this, the *Brasilians* of *Siara* revolted against the *Dutch* in 1644. surprized the garrison in the fort, which they razed, and killed the commander in chief, *Gideon Morritz*, with the whole garrison, besides all the workmen belonging to the salt-pits near the river *Upanemma*, who were all cut in pieces by these *Barbarians*.

A certain master of a ship, with a captain, lieutenant, and some soldiers, who happened to come ashore in a boat to fetch some fresh provisions, being ignorant of their treachery, were also put to the slaughter, three seamen having the good fortune to escape with their lives into the wood.

Some laid the cause of this rebellion at the door of the *Portuguese* and *Brasilians* of *Maranhaon*, bordering upon them; but if we search into the true source of this evil, it must be attributed to the miscarriage of our own officers, who by their hard usage, had forced the inhabitants to revenge themselves for the injuries received at their hands.

Thus much concerning the *Captainships* of the *Dutch Brasil*; we will in the next place give you an account of all the memorable transactions that happened betwixt the *Dutch* and *Portuguese* in *Brasil* during our stay there; after I have represented to you the excellency and convenient situation of this country, together with the ecclesiastical estate of the *Dutch Brasil*.

The excellency of Brasil.

Brasil is a country excellently well qualified by nature for the producing of all things, which are generally found in the *West-Indies*, under or near the same climate; except, that hitherto no gold or silver mines have been discovered here worth taking notice of. But next to gold and silver, the sugar claims the precedency here before all other commodities. Among all the harbours and places of the *West-Indies*, there is not one that can compare with *Brasil*, either for the product, or conveniency of transportation of sugar; the whole coast of *Brasil* being full of small rivers, which flowing through the adjacent valleys, disembogues in the sea; from whence the sugar-mills built in the valleys reap the benefit of saving vast charges, which else must be bestowed upon labourers and carriages; whereas these rivers drive the mills, serve for the transportation of sugar to other places, and furnish them at an easy rate with what commodities they stand in need of; all which conveniencies, as they are not to be met with in any other place of the *West-Indies*; so, no sugar-mills could be erected there with any prospect of profit. The exportation of sugar from *Brasil* into *Europe* and *Africa*, is likewise performed with much more ease than from any other places in the *West-Indies*; for the situation of *Brasil*, (being the most eastern part of all *America*) is such, as could not be more conveniently contrived by human art or nature for the transportation of so general and agreeable a commodity as sugar, into all the other parts of the world; considering those two excellencies of *Brasil*, together with its vast extent, it is most certain, that, provided it were well peopled, it might command both the *North* and *Æthiopian* seas, and spread its commerce over all parts of the world; nay, it might extend its conquests both to the east and west, or at least establish factories there for the conveniency of traffick. To prove which, it is to be observed: 1643.

That all *East-India* ships, both going and coming, must pass by the coast of *Brasil*; and as those ships in their voyages thither, are often forced to touch upon this coast, so in their return, nothing could be more commodious for them, than to be supplied with fresh provisions here. From *Brasil* you may sail in fourteen days to the *Caribbee* islands, and in the same time, or a little longer, to *Sierra Leona* on the coast of *Guinea*. It is impossible to enter deep into the great south sea, (whereabouts a great part of the terrestrial globe remains as yet undiscovered) unless you take in fresh provisions and firing in *Brasil*, or expose yourself to the greatest hazards imaginable in so long a voyage, as is sufficiently evident from the journals of *Oliver Van North*, *Spilbergen*, *le Maire*, and *John l'Heremite*. And experience has taught us, since Mr. *Brewer's* voyage to *Chili*, how easy the passage is betwixt *Brasil* and the south sea; for he lost not so much as one ship out of four, and very few died in the whole voyage.

Brasil enjoys likewise the advantage of a very wholsome climate; for tho' it lies betwixt the equinoctial line and the *Tropick of Capricorn*, and consequently is subject to burning heats, yet are the same much allayed by the winds, that blow out of the east from the sea, their free passage being

The wholesomeness of its climate.

1643. being not interrupted by any mountains or islands; which is the reason, that in *Brasil* the same distempers are rarely to be met with which reign so frequently in *Angola*, *Guinea*, *St. Thomas*, and several other places, where the east winds cannot afford them the same advantage. A plague is a thing unknown in *Brasil*, in which it excels all other countries; tho' they are not free from continual putrid fevers, caused by the hot and moist air, and the excessive use of raw fruits.

Those that are bound for the coast of *Brasil* ought to have a special regard to the season of the year, which regulates the winds and stream thereabouts; and to be very careful to sail above the harbour whither they are bound; for if they miss and come below it, they lose their aim, and must stay till the next turn of the wind and stream. For it is observable, that on the coast of *Brasil*, the stream runs from *February* till past *July* constantly northernly, during which time there is no passing from the north to the south; but after those months are past the stream turns, and from the beginning of *September* to the latter end of *November*, runs as violently to the south as it did to the north before, and consequently there is no sailing from the north to the south, no more than before from the south to the north. The winds here turn with the stream; and at the beginning of *March* blow south-south-east, and south-east. And like as the stream changes its current till *September*, so the winds continue in the east, and blow till that time out of the east-south-east. For there are but two winds that reign along this coast, *viz.* the south-east and north-east winds; according to which ships must regulate their course here.

The ecclesiastical state of the Dutch Brasil.

The ecclesiastical state of the *Dutch Brasil* was in my time thus ordered:

Before the insurrection of the *Portuguese*, there were to the south of the *Receif* five protestant churches; *viz.* in *Rio* St. *Francisco*, *Porto Calvo*, *Serinhaim*, the Cape St. *Austin*, and St. *Anthony*; though these were seldom altogether provided with ministers, because that some or other of them returned into *Holland*, after their limited time was expired. In the isle *Tamarika* and fort *Orange*, was at that time a minister, one *John Offringo*, who lived formerly in the town of *Schop*, and at the same time preached in the church of *Igarassu*, which was afterwards left by the *Dutch* and possess'd by the *Portuguese*. In *Rio Grande* preached one *John Theodore Polheim*. In *Parayba* were formerly two ministers, whilst the town of *Frederica* was as yet under the *Dutch* jurisdiction, but after the revolt of the *Portuguese* the place was left by the inhabitants, and *Henry Harman* was the only minister in those parts. In the *Receif*, *Maurice*'s town, and the circumjacent forts, which contained about 400 protestants, *Dutch*, *French* and *English*, were three ministers, who preach'd in the *Dutch* tongue; *Nicholas Vogel*, *Peter Ongena*, and *Peter Grib*. Besides these there was a fourth called *Jodocus Astett*, who formerly had been minister of the Cape of *St. Austin*, but now was employed either aboard our fleet, or upon any land expedition. The *French* church here remained without a minister, after the departure of *Joachim Solaer*, so that they were forced to be contented with reading of certain chapters of the bible, and prayers every *Sunday* morning. The *English* minister was one *Samuel Batchelour*, who 1646 return'd likewise to *England*; about which time there were seven *Dutch* ministers in the *Dutch Brasil*. Our religious worship was both in its doctrine and practice regulated exactly according to the prescription of the synod of *Dort*, and peculiar care was taken for the education of the youth, for which purpose the catechism was every *Sunday* in the afternoon explained, both in the *Receif* and *Maurice*'s town. Four times in the year the holy sacrament was administred, those who desired to be partakers of it, being obliged to make their confession before the church-council, or the ministers, who entred their names in a book; and if they came from abroad, published their names to the congregation; and in all other respects the church discipline was carefully observed. The church-council was composed of six church-wardens, besides the minister, these met duly once a week, and if any business of moment happen'd, such as chusing a minister, &c. they called the deacons, who were likewise six in number, to their assistance. Out of the deacons were every month chosen two, who (besides their ordinary business) were to visit the sick and wounded, and to provide for them if necessity required. They also took care of the orphans, to have them instructed in reading and writing. In the same manner the other churches were regulated, with this difference only, that the number of church-wardens and deacons was less, in proportion to the number of their respective congregations. Thus much of the ecclesiastical state.

Their church-council.

Besides those living creatures we have given you a description of before, there are divers sorts of bees in *Brasil*, call'd *Eiruku*'s, which settle upon the trees in a most surprizing manner. They are not unlike

1643. unlike our bees, but somewhat smaller; and swarm chiefly among the woods. The *Brasilians* distinguish them into twelve different kinds; *viz. Amanakay-Miri*, *Amanakay-Veu*, *Aibu*, *Mumbuka*, *Pixuna*, *Urutuetra*, *Tubuna*, *Tujuba*, *Eiruku*, *Eixu*, *Kubiara* and *Kurupireira*; the last of which are in no esteem among them.

The bees *Eiruku* are the largest of all, and produce a very good honey, though it is not commonly used. They make their combs within the hollowness of trees, which the *Brasilians* draw from thence by the means of a hollow pipe. The bees called *Eiku* and *Kopy* are smaller and of a blackish colour; they make holes from without, in the bark of the trees, in the nature of bee-hives; and the comb within is all of white wax; this is now counted the best thing, but is not gathered in the same quantity as the former; besides that these bees sting very furiously. The bees *Thanbuka* are likewise small, of a yellowish colour; they fix their combs on the top of the highest trees, and afford the best honey, which is in great quantities transported from hence to *Europe*, where it is sold very cheap. It is little inferior in goodness to the *European* honey, and of a good substance, transparent and of an agreeable scent. It is accounted very balsamick, corrects the sharp humours in the intestines, and especially in the kidneys, and provokes urine. They make of this honey metheglin, which is very strong, and will keep a great while: You may also make meath with this honey without boiling, only mix'd with some spring water and exposed to the weather.

Balsam. *Brasil* produces likewise several sorts of balsams; the best of which is called by the *Brasilians Kopaiba*, from the trees from whence it comes. *Kopaiba* is a very high wild tree, with an ash-coloured bark, which spreads at the top into many branches. The leaves are about half a foot long, sometimes larger, sometimes lesser, which in the midst of the branches stand opposite to one another, but on the end like other leaves. At the end of the great branches are abundance of lesser sprouts full of leaves, out of which comes forth the blossom, and afterwards berries, not unlike our laurel-berries. They are green at first, but as they ripen turn black and sweet. Within is a round hard stone, the kernel of which is white, but mealy, and not fit to be eaten. The berries ripen in *June*, when the *Brasilians* suck the juice out of them, and throw away the stone and skin. The apes take great delight in this fruit.

The oily and odoriferous balsam, in which this tree abounds, drops every full moon, provided you cut a slit through the bark as deep as to the pith, in such quantity, that in three hours time you may gather above twelve *Mengeln*. But if that does not drop immediately, the slit is made up with wax; and within fourteen days after, they are sure the balsam will come in great quantity. This tree does not grow so plentifully in the captainship of *Pernambuko*, as in the isle *Maranhaon*; from whence this balsam is transported into *Europe*. The balsam is hot in the second degree, of a thick oleaginous and resinous substance. It is very stomachic, and a good remedy against the cholick, occasioned by cold, externally applied to the affected parts; some few drops taken inwardly strengthen the bowels, and stop the overflowing in women, the looseness and involuntary emission of seed in men; against which distempers it likewise is used in clysters or by syringing. Thus far concerning the sole *Dutch Brasil*; we will now proceed to give you an account of what passed during our abode there. 1643. *A Mengeln is near thr quarts.*

New directors sent to Brasil. In the year 1640, Mr. *Henry Hamel*, one of the directors of the *West-India* company for the chamber of *Amsterdam*, and Mr. *Dirck Kodde Vander Burgh* (both persons excellently well qualified for the management of the *Dutch Brasil*, and of great experience in affairs of commerce) were at the request of the council of nineteen, sent to *Brasil*, and arrived there on the 8th of *August*, the two preceeding directors or councellors, *Matthias Van Keulen* and *John Giiseling*, resigned their places to them, and with them the chief management of the *Dutch Brasil*, under the government of *John Maurice* count *Nassau*.

Dutch Brasil. At the time of their arrival in *Brasil*, there were under the jurisdiction of the states the following *Captainships*: *Pernambuko*, *Itamarika* (unto which belongs *Goiana*) *Parayba*, *Rio Grande* and *Siara*, being the northern part of *Brasil*: The southern part, which contained the *Captainships Bahia*, *Ileos*, *Porto securo*, *Spirito Santo*, *Rio Janeiro* and *St. Vincent*, remained under the *Portuguese*, who inhabited the country as far as *Rio de Plate*. Not many months after the island of *Maranhaon* was joined with the *Dutch Brasil*, but the charges we were fain to be at to defend it against the *Portuguese*, those of *Para* and the natives, which over-balancing the profit the company was likely to reap from thence, it was thought most expedient to quit the same; which was done accordingly in the year 1644, or rather to confess the truth, by the combination of the *Portuguese*, those of *Grand Para* and the natives, we were forced to abandon it. Portuguese Brasil.

1643. Before the arrival of those new directors a fleet had been sent to the *Bahia*, to land some men there, and to destroy all with fire and sword; which after they had put in execution, and returned to the *Receif*, the same fleet under the command of admiral *Jol* and *Cornelius Lichthart*, was by special command from the council of nineteen in *Holland* ordered to the *West-Indies*, to lay in wait for the *Spanish* plate fleet of *Terra firma* and new *Spain*; but they returned without doing any thing, 1640 in *December*, having lost four or five ships in this voyage. Colonel *Koin* was much about the same time sent with a body of soldiers into the captainship of *Rio Real*, to bridle the *Portuguese*, by making a diversion in their own territories; but those troops being but indifferently supplied with necessaries in an enemies countrey, and forced to undergo great fatigues; they were so much weakned that it was thought adviseable to recall them out of *Rio Real*, and to assign them quarters of refreshment in the garrisons. Major *Van Brande* had worse success than all the rest, for being sent abroad with a party to fetch in some cattle, was put to the rout, and he himself taken prisoner.

The Dutch *miscarry in their design upon the* Spanish *plate fleet.*

In the mean while that our whole fleet was waiting for the *Spanish* plate fleet on the coast of *America*, and we consequently were not in a condition to undertake any thing at sea; our directors had all the reason in the world to fear, that the *Portuguese* would take this opportunity to revenge their loss, by destroying our sugar-mills, which made them leave no stone unturned to secure the *Dutch Brasil* and its inhabitants, against the attempts of the enemy: And considering that a great part of our security depended on the good inclinations of the *Portuguese* living among us, it was thought convenient to call an assembly of the chiefest *Portuguese* inhabitants of the three captainships of *Pernambuko*, *Itimarika*, and *Parayba*, towards the latter end of *August*, to concert measures how to defend their sugar-mills and fields against the incursions of the enemy.

The most effectual means that could be pitched upon in this assembly were, to provide their forts with good garri sons on the borders, and to secure the sugar-mills, by putting a certain number of soldiers in or near them, for the security of the adjacent fields. This was put in execution accordingly, and the officers had strict charge to keep a watchful eye upon the least motion of the *Portuguese*, notwithstanding which it had not the desired effect; because those *Portuguese* who lived at a considerable distance from us, and near the enemies frontiers, durst not give timely notice of their approach; besides that many among them having a constant hatred to our nation, did favour the enterprizes of those parties that burnt the sugar-fields and plundered the mills, served them sometimes for guides, and had their share in the booty; which obliged our people to be at a constant charge of a strong guard to conduct their goods, and defend them against any sudden attempts. Such an incursion was not long after made by the *Portuguese* into our territories. For in *November* the viceroy, the marquis of *Montelvano* sent two barges full of soldiers to burn our sugar-reeds in the plains, which they effected, but durst not go too far, or attempt any thing against our mills, for fear of the soldiers quartered thereabouts; who could not prevent their burning in the fields, as being done in the night time. The *Dutch* were the greatest losers by it, because they had generally the greatest share in those fields and mills, besides that the *Portuguese* spared those of their own countrey-men; all which brought a great damp upon trade, every one being afraid to venture in any business, where he might lose all his substance in one night, and that perhaps by the hands of a single person, whereby the revenues of the company were greatly impaired, and their charges increased, being forced to maintain twenty or thirty soldiers for the defence of any considerable plantation or sugar-mills; which prevented them from bringing a sufficient body of men into the field, to make head against the enemy. This was the state of the *Dutch Basil* towards the latter end of 1640.

The twenty-second of *December* in the same year, Mr. *Adrian van Bullestraete* arrived at the *Receif* from *Middleburgh*, in the quality of director of *Brasil*, so that now the great council being compleat, the best expedient to obviate all these difficulties, was judged to consist in our fleet; pursuant to this resolution, all our ships were ordered to the *Bahia*, to make the enemy sensible that we were in a condition to be even with them, and thereby to facilitate the negotiation that was in hand, for the surceasing of burning on both sides. The council of nineteen having also sent express orders to cruise with some ships before *Rio Janeiro*, from whence the *Spanish* ships used generally to return into *Spain*, about the month of *May* or *June*, some of the biggest ships were ordered that way to intercept if possible the *Flota*, the rest being left near the *Bahia*. 1643.

The Dutch *ships ordered to the* Bahia.

But whilst our commissioners were treating with the viceroy about the surceasing of burning and plundering, a certain *Portuguese*, *Paulo de Kunha* by name, committed unheard

1643. unheard of cruelties, with murthering, plundering and burning, in the open countrey, which made count *Maurice* write the following letter to the viceroy.

Count Maurice's *letter to the vice-roy.*

Count Maurice's letter to the viceroy.

THE barbarities lately committed by Paulo de Kunha, *with burning, murdering, and plundering in the open countrey, give me great reason to fear, that your last obliging letter was designed for a complement, without any reality. The confidence I had in your excellency's sincerity, made me recal our ships and forces from your territories, to take away all means of offence: But the long stay of our deputies affords great occasion of suspicion, that your intention is only to amuse us; which has obliged me to dispatch a vessel to let them know that in case the treaty is not brought to a conclusion, to return without delay; it being our intention that the said negotiation should not be continued longer. Your excellency will there dismiss them, together with our two hostages, as we are resolved to send back to you* Martin Feirera, *left with us as hostage from your excellency, his companion being dead of late.*

Hereupon, by the mediation of the clergy living under our jurisdiction, but especially by the indefatigable care of *Dirck Kodde Vander Burgh*, who was sent thither for that purpose, the treaty was brought to a happy conclusion in *February* 1641, by virtue of which, all destruction by burning and plundering were to surcease on both sides; which being published by proclamation, the *Portuguese* were ordered to quit our dominions, whereby we reapt this advantage, that now we might turn all our forces where we found it most expedient.

The treaty against burning concluded.

In *June* 1641, count *Maurice* and the great council received advice of the ten years truce concluded betwixt the states of *Holland* and the king of *Portugal*, with all the articles thereunto belonging, which were published by proclamation in all our captainships, and all acts of hostilities ceased on both sides; the *Dutch* living in good understanding with the inhabitants of the *Bahia*, giving them all the demonstrations of friendship, sufficient to convince the *Portuguese* that they had not the least reason to fear any infraction on their side.

The great council being willing to improve this interval of peace for the advancement of traffick, and the benefit of the company, gave all imaginable encouragement, in proportion to the circumstances of time and place, to all the inhabitants of what nation soever, for the cultivating the lands, which had this good effect, that the masters of the sugar-mills rebuilt their mills, and the husbandmen betook themselves with so much eagerness to the cultivating of their sugar-fields, that they borrowed considerable sums, upon a prospect of sure gain, which would over pay their debts; as without question it would have done in a short time, if by the treachery of the *Portuguese* they had not been disappointed in their hopes. The next thing to be taken in hand, was to make such wholesome laws as were thought most expedient for the establishment and increase of commerce, both in the *Receif* and other places, and to improve the domains and other revenues belonging to the company, during this time of truce. 1643.

Trade then began to flourish apace, so that some time after the truce, the merchants and factors sold more commodities than had ever been known either before or since. Many millions were dealt for in a little time, the merchants and factors being contented to sell to those who would pay some money in part, though there were buyers enough who would and could buy for ready cash.

The finances of the company in *Brasil* were in so good a state by the extraordinary care of the great council, that 1640 and 1641, they bought considerable quantities of sugar upon the publick account, which they sent to *Holland*. In the *Receif* and *Maurice Town*, we saw several goodly structures erected by the inhabitants, who lived in great plenty and magnificence, every one looking upon his debts as secure, and having a fair prospect to increase his riches, by the flourishing state of commerce and improvement of the lands.

The flourishing state of Brasil.

But this was of no long continuance, for in the beginning of 1643, things began to appear with a quite different face; for the magazines of the company being exhausted by several expeditions against *Angola*, &c. and having received no supplies in their stead out of *Holland*, as they used to do before, the great council was obliged to make use of what was due to the company, for the payment of the garrisons and other officers, and consequently to force their debtors to prompt payments.

Its decay.

For at the beginning of the government of the new directors, the company had a considerable naval force upon the coast of *Brasil*, their magazines were well provided with provision and ammunition, and they maintained a good number of soldiers. The great council of the *Dutch Brasil* relying upon their strength, did with consent of count *Maurice*, send in 1641, several fleets with soldiers to *Spirito Santo*, *Rio de Janeiro*, the isle of *Maranhaon*, *Angola*, *St. Thomas*, and other places thereabouts, to attack

1643. tack the same, which succeeded according to expectation; but their magazines were greatly exhausted by those expeditions. Besides this, the merchants in *Holland* began to call upon their servants and factors for considerable sums of money, in return of what they had received from them; who being obliged to send all the money they could bring together from their creditors, to their masters in *Holland*; this occasioned great scarcity of ready money, and consequently no small detriment in traffick, which continuing thus from time to time, there arose such a general scarcity of money, as is scarce to be imagined; many of the masters of the sugar-mills, that had no ready money to satisfy their debts at the appointed time, being forced to take up money upon credit, and to pay three or four *per cent per* month, which reduced many of them to such an extremity in a little time, that they were neither able to pay the principal nor interest.

The reason. Upon the arrival of the three new directors, or members of the great council in 1640, *viz. Henry Hamel*, *Kodde*, and *Bullestraete*, they found that the inhabitants, but especially the *Portuguese* of the *Dutch Brasil*, by buying of sugar-mills and plantations, as well as negroes and other commodities, had run themselves much in debt; having bought their negroes not only at three hundred pieces of eight *per* head, but also given most extravagant prices for all other sorts of commodities, and purchasing whole warehouses without making a just account how to be able to pay for them. This was done by the *Portuguese* in hopes of the good success of those great fleets they understood were equipping in *Spain*, to reduce *Brasil* under the king's obedience, which they supposed would free them from all their debts; which the factors not being aware of, and blinded with the prospect of vast profit, sold their goods to the *Portuguese* without reluctancy. But the design of the *Portuguese* vanishing into smoak for that time, they were forced to pay; but new supplies of all sorts of commodities being sent out of *Holland*, they bought on a-fresh, heaping debts upon debts, till failing in their payments, their credit began also to fail with the merchants, who now began to urge for satisfaction of their debts. For the countrey-traders being urged by the factors and merchants, who received those commodities from their correspondents in *Holland*, was obliged to call to an account the *Portuguese* unto whom he had sold the goods. And because the *Portuguese* had not bought those commodities from the *Dutch*, but with an intention never to pay for them, the countrey trader who was obliged to pay the merchants in the *Receif*, saw himself reduced to ruin, the *Portuguese* having not wherewithal to satisfy their debts. 1643.

Thus through the unwariness and mismanagement of those factors, whom the merchants in *Holland* had intrusted with their goods, such a confusion was introduced, as tended to the great detriment of their correspondents in *Holland*. *Great confusion in traffick.* All the business at that time lay among the lawyers, and in the courts of judicature, which considering the chargeableness of law-suits in *Brasil*, tended to their farther ruin; for when they had obtained sentence and execution against the debtors, the greatest difficulty was, how and which way to lay the execution; most of the *Portuguese* sueing for protection from the regency, which if they could not obtain, they lived incognito; especially those who had no lands or effects, or if they had, it was no easy matter to find out where they were. Besides that, if the creditors executed their executions upon the lands, they were forced to be the buyers themselves, and to live in the countrey to manage the lands, a thing altogether inconvenient to the merchants, who had other business upon their hands in the *Receif*. Such as were cast into prison must be maintained there at the charge of the creditor, which in process of time amounted to such a sum, that they themselves were fain to solicite the releasement of their debtors, and to make the best composition with them they could.

Besides these inconveniences, there have happened of late several others, *viz.* a great mortality of the negroes and *Brasilians*, by a certain infectious distemper, incident to the natives, called *Bexigos*, resembling our small-pox in *Europe*. *Mortality among the negroes.* Most of these negroes were bought at the rate of three hundred pieces of eight, and consequently their loss drew after it the ruin of the planters, who also complained much of vermin, and several inundations that had done considerable damage to the sugar-fields. This confusion in traffick introduced no small broils among the inhabitants themselves, who in case of non-payment, threw one another in prison without mercy, and endeavoured to prevent one another by clandestine means, to get in their debts before the rest; offering considerable abatements and rewards to such as would underhand surrender or transport their effects; and those divisions were not a little fomented by some ill minded persons, to the prejudice of the government; many of those, who either by unwariness or other mismanagement lost their debts, laying the fault thereof at the door of the regency and of the courts of justice, vainly imagining that what they had lost by their own neg-

1643. lect or want of care, should be made good by the publick purse; especially if it happened so, that the same persons were indebted to the company as well as private persons, there arise great contests about the preference.

The debts of the company did also increase every day, which at last amounted to some millions: For the directors, which before the year 1640 had the management of affairs in *Brasil*, did sell most of the confiscated estates, sugar-mills, and merchandizes, as well as the negroes bought on account of the company in *Africk*, upon credit, so that their books were filled with debts, but their cash empty of money. The succeeding members of the great council, Mr. *Hamel*, *Bullestraet*, and *Kodde*, did leave no stone unturned to correct this custom, and to sell their commodities for ready money, or otherwise to exchange them for sugars, thereby to ease the company in the great charge they were forced to be at in their several expeditions; and it is certain, that in 1640, 1641, and 1642, they sent such vast cargoes of sugar to *Holland*, that the like had never been known before in *Brasil*. Notwithstanding which, by the vast numbers of negroes that were imported, after our conquest of *Angola*, the company fell more and more in debt, by reason their debtors were very dilatory in their payments. The council of nineteen sent express orders to remedy this evil, by selling the negroes for ready money, or exchanging them for sugar; but this could not be put in practice, because there was no body who would buy upon those conditions, so that the price of the negroes falling daily lower and lower, and these being a great burden to the company, and subject to distempers and mortality, this order was fain to be revoked, unless they would see the negroe trade dwindle away into nothing; for the inhabitants being for the most part such as had bestowed most part of their substance in their sugar-mills, plantations, and negroes, they could not pay ready money, but were forced to deal upon credit, till they could reap the benefit of their labour.

The members of the great council did therefore take all imaginable care to call upon their debtors exactly at the time of their sugar-harvest, and ordered their officers in the countrey to seize upon some of them on account of the company.

From hence arose nothing but law-suits, sentences, executions, and imprisonments: The members of the great council thinking it not below their station, to go sometimes in person into the countrey to promote the payment of the debts owing to the company. But this had a contrary effect, for the merchants and factors began to be extreamly dissatisfied, that the company should seize upon the sugar in the mills, without letting them who were creditors as well as they, have their share in them. This occasioned not only murmurings, but also threats, and complaints to the council of nineteen, where they misrepresented these transactions under the worst colours they could, hoping thereby to deter the officers of the company from doing their duty. The great council having taken the matter into mature deliberation, and fearing, not without reason, that in time it might occasion a general discontent, they left no stone unturned to satisfy the minds of the people; by finding out means to have their debts satisfied. It was proposed by several understanding persons, that the company should undertake to satisfy the debts of private persons, either by way of payment or exchange; in lieu of which the masters of the sugar-mills should surrender to the company every year, the whole product of these mills, till they had satisfied all their debts: And to make the same the more effectual, for the general benefit as well of the company and sugar-mills, as the merchants and factors, it was agreed, that certain articles should be agreed upon for that purpose; the greatest advantage the company pretended to reap by it being, that they should have a fair opportunity of recovering some of their debts, which were given over for lost. These agreements were wonderfully pleasing to the council of nineteen, who in the year 1645, on the 16th of *June*, sent their approbation of a second agreement made with one *George Homo Pinto* (which indeed was of as great consequence as all the other contracts together) to the great council as follows: 1643.

Approbation of the Agreement.

The approbation of the agreement.

Concerning the agreement by you (meaning the council) on the 14th of December *last, made with* George Homo Pinto, *we have had several debates, which we find to have been brought to a conclusion, with the previous advice and approbation of the councellors of justice and of the finances; so that both in respect of the same, and of the great benefit that is likely to accrue thereby to the company, we have thought fit to approve of the said Agreement; recommending to you the execution of it, with the same zeal as you have shewn your conduct and circumspection in the whole management of these contracts.*

That these agreements were by all people, that had any knowledge of those affairs, looked upon as greatly for the interest

1643. rest of the company, is most evident from hence, that several other merchants that were sensible of this advantage, made agreements with their debtors much upon the same terms as the company had done; which that it may be put beyond all doubt, we will give you a copy of one of those agreements, from whence it will plainly appear with how much circumspection the council proceeded in this matter, betwixt the company, the masters of the sugar-mills and their debtors.

The copy of an Agreement.

The copy of an agreement.

MR. Peter John Bas, *and* John van Ratsfield, *councellors of justice of* Brasil, *by special commission from the* West-India *company, and* John van Walbeeck, *assessor of the great council, did appear before us on one side; and* Manuel Fernando Cruz, *Sieur* de Ingenho Tapicura, *in behalf of himself and his heirs; as also* Benjamin de Pina *for ten thousand six hundred gilders;* Isaac de Costa *for thirteen thousand one hundred and eight;* Joseph Abenacar *for four hundred ninety;* Simon de Vale *for three hundred twenty-five;* Gasper Francisco *and* David Brandoa *for eleven hundred thirty-three;* Abraham de Tovaer *for one thousand;* John Parente *for three hundred and fifty;* John Mendonça de Moeribeca *for four thousand three hundred fifty;* James Gabay *for one thousand and fifty;* More de Leon *for six hundred;* Balthazar de Fonseca *for six hundred;* Simon Gomes de Lisboa *for five thousand nine hundred ten;* Bartholomew Rodrigues *for nine hundred; and* Daniel Cardosa *for nine hundred and ten gilders; the whole amounting to forty thousand five hundred twenty-six gilders, being all creditors of the said* Manuel Fernando Cruz, *and for the most part debtors to the company on the other side, who profess and declare to have agreed among themselves, that the beforementioned* Manuel Fernando Cruz, *shall pay to the company the full sum of sixty thousand seven hundred ninety five gilders,* viz. *nineteen thousand two hundred sixty nine gilders upon his own account, being by him owing to the said company, and the remaining sum on the account of his creditors, which proportionably to their respective debts, ought to be discounted for with him by the said company, upon the following conditions.*

I. *That the whole debt is to be satisfied in the three next following years, the first payment to begin in* January 1645, *and if it happen, that in one year a less share be paid than in the other, the whole is to be made good in the last year.*

II. *That no discounts shall be entred in the books of the company, 'till after the payment of the due proportion appointed for each respective term or time.* 1643.

III. *That the creditors of those with whom they have entred into articles of agreement, as well as the debtors of the company, shall not be discharged of their debts in the books of the company, but in case of failure or delay of payment, either of the whole sum or part thereof, all the respective appointed times, shall stand engaged and answerable, each for his respective debt, unless they give other security to the company; but those creditors who have no debts in the books of the company, shall have liberty to transfer other debts, or else to receive their share in two years time, either by assignments or in Negroes; but not in any commodities imported from abroad, or sugar to be exported; provided nevertheless that the articles of agreement be fulfilled, or otherwise the sum be put to their own account immediately, in which case they are to allow eighteen pound* per cent. *and nevertheless be liable to see the agreement put in execution.*

IV. *Those who are entred into articles of agreement shall be obliged to engage both their body and goods for the performance thereof, but especially to deliver an inventory of their personal estates, confirm'd by oath; besides which, they are to give such securities as shall be approved of by the great council; with renouncing the* beneficium ordinis, divisionis & excusationis, *as well for each respective payment at the appointed times, as the whole sum in general.*

V. *These before-mention'd securities are to be persons well-qualified, of good substance, not involv'd in debts, but especially in the company's; and shall be warranted by the magistrates of their respective places of abode.*

VI. *Publick notice is to be given to all persons, who have any bonds, bills, or accounts, or other engagements relating to the personal estates (which shall be named or specified) of such as are entred into those articles, that within the space of three weeks they are to produce the same, or else to be excluded from the benefit thereof, 'till after the expiration of the time mentioned and appointed in the said agreement.*

VII. *That he, who has engaged himself in such an agreement or contract, shall not be permitted to contract new debts, unless with the consent of the great council; otherwise the same to be void and null, of which publick notice shall be given. Neither shall he abalienate any sugars by land as remains, under the penalty of restitution to be made with full interest and charges.*

The

1643. *The creditors shall be obliged to surrender and renounce all their pretensions, engagements and actions to the company; neither shall they lay any claim upon that score of precedence or otherwise.*

Whenever it shall be judged requisite, by the great council, *to send a certain person to the* ingenho *of any person entred into such an agreement, for the better security of their debt, and the receiving and sending away the sugar, allotted to the company, he shall be obliged to find him with victuals and lodgings in his* ingenho; *but the company shall pay him for his pains.*

Pursuant to which, the before named Manuel Fernando Cruz, *with the advice and consent of his before-mentioned creditors, has obliged himself in general, and by these presents, obliges and engages his person and estate, both real and personal, without any reservation or exception; but especially the before-named* Ingenho Tapicura, *with all its appurtenances, according to the inventory thereunto affixed and confirmed by oath; which* Ingenho Tapicura, *he declares to be free from any pre-engagements, with all the grounds, sugar-fields, pasturages, woods, and other things thereunto belonging,* viz. *eight brass* calderns, *ten* tachoos *and ten* parvos, *besides several other copper vessels belonging to the said* ingenho; *twenty slaves belonging to the said* ingenho, *and* Manuel Ferdinando Cruz, *his house and sixty oxen. And for the better performance of this agreement,* Senhor John de Mendose *dwelling at* Moeribeca, *and* Manuel Gomes des Lisboa, *living in* Moquiaxe, *have, after certificates obtained from the magistrates of their respective dwelling-places, engaged themselves, and do by these presents engage themselves as securities for the whole debt, and as debtors for each and every part thereof, promising to indemnify the company of all actions, suits, or other pretensions which may be made against them on the account of any other creditors of the said* Manuel Fernando Cruz, *not mention'd or engaged in this agreement; as likewise, that no sugar shall be surreptitiously convey'd away or abalienated: That in case of non-payment, the company shall be hereby fully empowered to recover their damages with interest and charges, upon their persons and estates; they renouncing by these presents all exceptions,* ordinis, divisionis & excusationis, *as likewise all other pretensions of privileges tending to the invalidity of this contract. The before-named creditors also, in general, and every one of them in particular, declare that they have given in a true account of all their respective pretensions upon the said* Manuel Fernando Cruz, *neither that they do demand any other sum or sums of him, but what have been specified there under their respective names; promising to be well satisfied with what has been stipulated, and, if put in execution accordingly, to renounce all actions or private engagements, discontents or preference in favour of the company; and that in case of non-payment they will be obliged to make good and restore to the said company, not only each particular sum paid at certain limited times, but also the whole, in the same manner, as if the said agreement had never been made betwixt them; leaving it to the discretion of the company, whether they will lay their actions against* Manuel Fernando Cruz *and his securities, or against themselves and their estates; under the condition they were in before the conclusion of this agreement; the benefit of* actionem cessam *being allowed them against the said* Cruz *and his securities, for the recovery of their just debts. In witness and confirmation of which we have granted these our letters, as usual in such cases, sealed with the ordinary seal of the court of justice, and signed by the secretary of the council. Translated in the* Receif, 23[d] September 1644. 1643.

In the same manner all the other contracts were made and penn'd; the contents of which amounted in the whole to two million a hundred and twenty five thousand eight hundred and seven gilders, which were due from the farmers to the masters of the sugar-mills, and from those again to the company.

For what reason these agreements were made

The chief, if not the only reason, why these agreements were resolved upon, was, (as we said before) the intolerable vexations and exactions put upon the masters of the sugar-mills by their creditors, who, unless these masters paid them at the rate of two or three *per cent.* interest *per* month, made immediate seizure of their negroes, oxen, coppers, and other necessaries belonging to the sugar-mills; so that the masters of these sugar-mills being reduced to a necessity of paying such exorbitant exactions, or else to see themselves entirely ruined, began to defend their plantations and mills by force, so that things seemed to tend at that time to a general insurrection, if the same had not been prevented, by entring into those contracts; by which means the masters of the sugar-mills being freed from the oppressions of their creditors, and in lieu thereof now become debtors to the company, and time given them to employ their mills for the payment of their debts, at certain limited times, and that at the rate of one *per cent.* interest *per* month only, all pretensions and occasions of a revolt were thereby removed, at least for that time; the first term of payment being set out for a considerable time.

To

1643. To make this the more evident, these following heads deserve our particular observation: That the company and the merchants, being creditors of the masters of the sugar-mills, endeavouring at the same time to force them to the payment of their debts, by executions. This occasioned from the year 1647 to the time of the making of those contracts, such a confusion, as must needs have tended to the total destruction of the sugar-mills, and consequently of the merchants and company; which induced them to apply themselves to the great council, to find out some means, by way of discount, or otherwise, to put these debts into the company's hands.

The councellors of justice did not at first agree in all points to these proposals, but at their meeting on the 12th of *August* 1644, being better convinced of the matter, and that the company was sufficiently secured and benefited thereby, the next following day did not only approve of the same, but also were of opinion, that some things might be rather mitigated for the Advantage of the masters of mills and their creditors, than not to relieve them at this juncture; so that the conditions were the 10th of *November* 1644, agreed unto with the consent of the councellors of the court of justice and the finances.

Pursuant to these, the great council took care that publick notice should be given of these agreements made betwixt the company and certain private persons, by which every one was forewarned not to sell any thing upon credit to them, without the consent of the great council; and their creditors summoned to make good their debts within three weeks time, or else to be excluded from the benefit of the contract, 'till after the time therein limited was expired. From all which it is sufficiently demonstrable, with how little appearance of truth some have attempted to insinuate, that these contracts were prejudicial to the company, and had given no small occasion to the ensuing revolt of the *Portuguese*; when it is beyond all question, from what has been said before, that these were the only means to prevent those calamities, wherewith the masters of the sugar-mills, and the farmers or countrey planters, were over-whelmed all that time, who were forced to let their mills stand still, and leave the ground uncultivated; all which, as it tended to the utter destruction of the sugar-mills, so the company sustained an irreparable loss, *viz.* thirty eight pounds *per cent.* yearly in *Brasil*, and thirty seven pounds *per cent.* in *Holland*, which being seventy five pound *per cent.* did altogether arise from the use of the sugar-mills.

Besides this, there were not a few of those merchants that were creditors of the sugar-mills, that were considerably indebted to the company, who pleading insolvency, by reason of the non-payment of their debtors; the company would have been considerable losers by them, unless by this way of discounting they had found means to recover those desperate debts. All which moved the great council to make a virtue of necessity, and with the advice of the masters of the sugar-mills and their creditors, and the approbation of the council of nineteen, to enter upon those articles; which could not be in any wise detrimental to the company; tho' some malicious persons have objected against them, that (supposing there had been no revolt) these masters would not in twenty years, nay, perhaps never have been in a condition to wrong the company, what they had laid out upon their account; when it is sufficiently known that the great council never paid one farthing of ready money for them on the account of the company; besides that for the satisfaction of the company, twenty five sugar-mills were engaged, which one with another, affording from two hundred and thirty to two hundred and fifty chests of sugar yearly; if the company had drawn but a hundred and forty or a hundred and fifty chests from each, the same would have amounted to four hundred and twenty thousand gilders; from whence it is evident, that not to include the sugar-mills, their coppers, oxen, and other Instruments thereunto belonging, the sum of two millions one hundred and twenty five thousand eight and sixteen gilders, being the total sum of the debt owing to the company by vertue of these contracts, might have been satisfied without much hazard; the *Portuguese* masters of the sugar-mills, being by this expedient left in the quiet possession of their mills, and eased from the oppressions of their creditors, and our hopes were not a little increased by the industry of the inhabitants of the country, who finding themselves now at ease, applied themselves with so much assiduity to the improvement of their plantations, for the better satisfying of their debts, that in 1645 there was such a fair prospect of a plentiful harvest of sugar, as had not been known in many years before.

Reasons of the revolt of the Portuguese.

But it seems as if the *Portuguese* out of an in-born hatred to our nation, who had conquered them, were resolved not to rest satisfied, 'till by underhand practices and plots they had undermined our government. Add to this, that many of them having involved themselves over head and

1643. and ears in debt, and seeing no way to satisfy their creditors, were become desperate, and more forward to run the hazard of an open revolt (in hopes of assistance from *Portugal*) than to undergo the unavoidable necessities of poverty; which made some of them frankly tell our people afterwards, that in case they were disappointed in their hopes of succours from the *Bahia*, they would seek for aid in *Spain* or *Turkey*.

Towards the latter end of the year 1642, there were rumours spread abroad of a Plot contrived by the *Portuguese* against the state when they were disarmed, and their arms brought into the magazines, which however they got again under some pretence or other afterwards, they living very quietly among us, for fear, as I suppose, of our garrisons, and that they were not then sufficiently assured of succours from the *Babia*. But it will not be amiss to trace the true origin of this revolt.

The 13th *December* 1642, one *John Fernandes Vieira*, alderman of *Maurice*'s-*Town*, appeared in the great council, count *Maurice* being present, where he told them, that he had been informed by certain *Jews*, how he and his father-in-law *Beringel* were suspected in *Holland*, of having sent letters by a son of the said *Beringel* to the king of *Portugal*, tending to the detriment of the state. He did not deny to have sent a letter by the said person to the king of *Portugal*, but containing no more than a recommendation of the said *Beringel*'s person, to help him him to some employment under the king: This he offer'd to prove by his copy, which being produced, there was found nothing material in it, but a congratulation to the king upon his accession to the crown, and a recommendation of the said *Beringel*; *Vieira* further proposed, that he thought it absolutely necessary, for the safety of his estate, to have the *Portuguese* disarmed, as likewise the captains *de Campo*, with those under their jurisdiction, the *Negroes*, *Brasilians*, *Mulatts* and *Mamalukes*.

Suspicion of treachery.

There was also a letter sent by the council of nineteen, dated 1 *June* 1642, to count *Maurice*, containing in substance, that one *John van North*, who had served for fourteen months in the quality of a cadee in *Brasil*, had declared to them at *Amsterdam*, that he had been a servant in a sugar-mill belonging to *John Fernandes Vieira*, where after a stay of two months, he was entreated by *Francisco Beringel Labrador*, to go with his son *Antonio Dandrado Beringel*, as an interpreter to *Holland*, and from thence to *Portugal*; which upon great promises he accepted of, and they set sail on board the Ship called the *Love* from *Brasil* for *Zeeland*, and afterwards from *Ulissimen* went to *Lisbon*. He said, that this *Antonio Dandrado Beringel*, after a familiar conversation of three weeks, had told him that he was sent with a letter sign'd by *John Fernandes Vieira*, *Francisco Beringel*, *Bernardin Karvailho*, *John Biserro* and *Lewis Bras Biserro*, in which they gave to understand to the king of *Portugal*, that they were well provided with men, money and arms, for the reducing *Brasil* under his obedience. The council added, that the king of *Portugal* had made the said *Beringel* a captain, for this piece of service, and that therefore they desired count *Maurice* and the great council to keep a watchful eye over them, being sensible what an aversion the *Portuguese* did bear to the *Dutch*. 1643.

Is encreased by letters from abroad.

At the meeting of the great council of *Brasil*, 16th *February* 1643, count *Maurice* assured them, that he had received intelligence, that some of the chiefest of the *Portuguese* had resolved to surprize our garrisons in the country, at *Moribeca*, *St. Anthony*, and some other places, and to put them to the sword, which was to be put in execution upon one of their saints days, when they used to meet in considerable Numbers. Those who had the chief management of this affair, had their dwelling-places in the *Vargea*, who had proposed to surprize likewise the *Receif*, not questioning that if they could make themselves masters of it, the other garrisons in the country would be easily reduced, and consequently the company not able to subsist long in *Brasil*, without soldiers and traffick.

What resolution taken thereupon.

Hereupon it was taken into deliberation, whether 'twere best to secure the heads of this rebellion immediately, or to delay it 'till a more convenient time, for fear of allarming the whole country by their Imprisonment: The last was resolved upon, because they did not think themselves as yet sufficiently assured of their designs, and did not question, but that by the secret intelligence count *Maurice* was to receive of their transactions, they might prevent them. It was however judged adviseable to draw the garrisons out of the country into the *Receif*, which was strengthened with new pallisadoes, and the old wooden battery repaired; a ship was also ordered with several great chaloops, the first on the sea-side, the others in the river, to defend the avenues of the *Receif* with their cannon. There were likewise divers letters sent by private persons, some without names, to count *Maurice* and the great council

1643. council, confirming the traiterous designs of the *Portuguese*; among others, one Mr. *Van Els* sent a letter to count *Maurice*, dated at *Serinhaim* the 20th of *March* 1643, importing, that he had it from sure hands, that a certain *Mulat*, of the company of *Austin Hardoso*, being asked by certain inhabitants of that *Fregesie*, what business they had thereabouts, had told them, that they had been to carry letters to some persons living near the *Receif*, adding, that in a short time they would see that place taken without any effusion of blood, either of the *Dutch* or *Portuguese*.

In *December* 1643, *Don Michael de Krasto*, *Don Bastian Manduba de Sonho*, and *Don Antonio Ferdinandes*, three ambassadors from the count *Sonho* in *Angola*, arrived in the *Receif*, in the ship call'd the *Arms of Dort*; they had but one servant each, but brought along with them several negroes with golden collars, as a present to count *Maurice*, besides a great number of other Negroes for the company.

Ambassadors from the count of Sonho *admitted to audience.*

Being admitted to audience by count *Maurice* and the great council, they desired in the name of their Master, not to send any assistance to the king of *Congo*, whom they feared would attack them before long, notwithstanding they were at that time both engaged in a war against the *Portuguese*. They received for answer, that the council would write to Mr. *Niewland*, their director there, to interpose his authority and mediation, in order to maintain a good correspondency, and remove all occasion of contest betwixt the king of *Congo* and their master, they being both confederates of the States: The said Earl sent likewise a letter to count *Maurice*, in which he desired leave to buy a chair, a cloak, some ensigns of war, some apparel, and such like things. The great council writ also a letter, as well to the king of *Congo*, as to the count of *Sonho*, exhorting them to peace, and sent them the following presents in the name of the company.

To the King,

A long black velvet cloak, with silver galloons.
A scarf edged with silver lace.
A velvet coat.
And a castor-hat with a silver hatband.

To the Count,

A red velvet elbow-chair, with gold fringes.
A large velvet cloak, with gold and silver galloons.
A scarf with a gold and silver lace. 1643.
A velvet coat.
And a castor-hat with a gold and silver hatband.

They were entertained with all imaginable civility, during their stay here: They were very skillful in playing with the backsword; in the management of which, they made most terrible postures and faces. They understood *latin* very well, and made several learned harangues in the same.

Fresh suspicion of a revolt.

The 13th of *October* 1644, a certain *Jew*, called *Gaspar Francisco de Kunha*, with two others of the chief of the same fraternity, gave notice to the great council, that they had been credibly informed by some *Jews*, who conversed and kept frequent correspondence in the country, that the *Portugueses* were plotting against the *Dutch-Brasil*, telling the council the reasons upon which they founded this suspicion. The council, after having returned thanks to these elders for their care, resolved to leave no stone unturn'd to discover the designs of the *Portuguese*; and having received certain intelligence, that they expected some arms and ammunition to be brought them by sea, they ordered the 12th of *October* 1644, the yacht called *Niewhouse*, with a galliot and a challoop, to cruise along the coast of *Dutch-Brasil*, to observe what vessels did approach the shore.

The 11th of *May* 1644, count *Maurice* left the *Receif*, in order to his return to *Holland*, after he had been eight years governor of the *Dutch-Brasil*. All the citizens and chief inhabitants, both of the *Receif* and *Maurice*'s town, appeared in arms, making a lane from the old town to the water-gate, of whom, as he pass'd by, he took his leave with all imaginable demonstration of kindness. At the gate he mounted on horse-back, and being accompanied by the great council, the councellors of justice and all the military officers, as far as *Olinda*, he there once more took his leave of them in particular, the Sieur *Bullestraet* remaining only with him, being deputed by the regency to conduct him on board the ships design'd for his transportation. They did not set sail from the *Red-Land* 'till the 22d of *May*, with a fleet of thirteen ships, on board of which were a good number of soldiers, leaving only eighteen companies for the defence of the *Dutch-Brasil*. Mr. *Bullestraet* return'd the 26th to the *Receif*.

On the 22d of *April*, not long before the departure of count *Maurice*, the commission from the governors of the *West-India* company, according to a resolution taken at their meeting the first of *July* 1642,

1643. 1642, concerning the government of *Dutch-Brasil*, and dated the 22[d] of *May* 1643, was read in the great council, by which the members thereof were to have the administration of the government 'till further orders. Accordingly count *Maurice* having appointed a day to invest them with the administration of the government, he ordered (with the consent of the said council) an assembly to be called on the 6th of *May*, of the counsellors of justice, of the magistrates, the ecclesiastical council and ministers of *Maurice*'s *Town*; of the commanders in chief both by sea and land, the chief officers of the company, the officers of the militia, and the chief men among the *Jews*.

All these being at the appointed time met in the great hall of the *Stadthuis*, he told them, that since their high and mightinesses the states, his highness the prince of *Orange*, and the council of nineteen, had been pleased to grant him leave, after a stay of eight years among them, in the quality of governor of the *Dutch-Brasil*, to return into *Holland*, he had called them together, to return them thanks for the many services, each in his station, had done to the company; as likewise for the obedience, fidelity and respect they had always shewn to his person; telling them, that from this minute he resign'd the government into the hands of the great council, requiring and desiring them, in the name of the states, the prince of *Orange*, and the council of nineteen, to shew them the same obedience, fidelity and respect they had done before; whereupon count *Maurice* having congratulated the council, and the rest there present done the same, he took his leave of them in the hall, and immediately after in the council-chamber, of the members of the great council, giving them most hearty thanks for their faithful council and assistance upon all occasions, and for the respect and deference they had always shewn to his person; telling them, that since this would be the last time of his appearing in their assembly, he had drawn up a memorial, which might serve them as a guide, for the better administration of the government; and that, if they thought it convenient, he should be ready to discourse with them, and enlarge further upon that subject. The members of the great council returned him their unfeigned thanks, wishing him a happy voyage, and good success in all his undertakings, and recommended themselves and the whole *Dutch-Brasil* to his care hereafter. Before the breaking up of the assembly, it was debated in the presence of count *Maurice*, which of the members should have the precedency there as president, or whether the same should be taken by turns, the same being not determined in their commission: After several arguments *pro* and *con*, it was agreed, that things should remain, in respect of this point, in the same condition as had been usual before, in the absence of count *Maurice*, *viz.* for every one to keep his rank without any priority 'till further orders from the council of nineteen; to wit, first Mr. *Dirk Hamel*, then Mr. *Bullestraete*, Mr. *Kodde Vander Burgh*, &c.

Count Maurice *abdicates the government.*

Takes his leave.

The next thing the great council took in hand, was to inquire more narrowly into the designs of the *Portuguese* against the government; to effect which, it was resolved in *January* 1644, to send *Gilbert de Wit*, councellor of the court of justice, and captain *Dirk Hoogstrate*, then commander in chief in the *Cape of St. Austin*, to *Antonio Telles de Sylva*, then governor of the *Bahia*, with the following instructions, dated the 15th of the same month; to compliment the governor (after the delivery of their credentials) in the name of the great council, with a sincere promise and assurance of friendship, and good neighbourly correspondency. After this, they were to represent to him, that many of the subjects of the *Dutch-Brasil*, after having contracted considerable debts there, both with the company, and other inhabitants, did retire into the *Bahia*; wherefore they desired, that for the promoting of justice, they would either detain those bankrupts in prison, or at least give timely notice of their coming thither, to the *Dutch* government, whereby their subjects might be enabled to prosecute them at law: But their real errant was to be instructed underhand in the following points.

Envoys sent into the Portuguese-Brasil, *and their instructions.*

I. W*Hat forces the* Portuguese *had at that time in the* Bahia, *and the other southern provinces.*

II. *What number of ships.*

III. *What number of ships were expected there out of* Portugal.

IV. *How the negro's trade stood affected, and from what places they were brought thither.*

V. *Whether there was any commerce betwixt them and the inhabitants of* Bonas Aires.

VI. *In what condition their places were thereabouts; of all which they were to give the best account they were able to get, after their*

1643. *their return to the great council; they were also charged by word of mouth, to make diligent enquiry who were the persons that underhand encouraged the so much feared revolt of the* Portuguese *in the* Dutch Brasil, *and what aid or assistance they were to have from them; and to desire the governor not to permit for the future that such of the* Dutch *soldiers as deserted out of the* Receif, *and went by land to the* Bahia, *might from thence be transported into* Portugal, *but be stopt and sent back to the* Receif.

These envoys arrived safely the 8th of *February* 1644 in the *Bahia*, and dropt their anchor towards the evening near the city of *Their arrival at* St. Salvador. *St. Salvador*, and the castle of *St. Antonio*, where two officers came on board them, to enquire from whence they came, and by whom, and to whom they were sent, in order to give an account thereof to the governor *Antonio Telles de Sylva*. The next following day they were complimented in the name of the governor by major *Domingo Delgados*, and captain *David Ventura*, who told them that he intended to send his chaloop with the first opportunity to fetch them ashore. About three a clock in the afternoon, the same officers with three or four more, came with the chaloop to fetch them; and they were no sooner landed but found several horses ready for them to mount upon, which they did, and were conducted up a high hill, all over covered with spectators, to the governor's palace. In the outward hall was a strong guard of soldiers, in the second several ensigns and other inferior officers, in the third apartment they met with nothing but captains and lieutenants, and in the fourth with colonels, general officers, *Are admitted to audience.* some clergymen, and the governor himself; who after having received them at the door, desired them to sit down next to him, upon chairs set for that purpose. The envoys then begun their harangue, in which they told him, that they were extreamly glad to find him in good health at this time, when they were sent by the great council of the *Dutch Brasil*, to assure him of their good inclinations, to maintain a good correspondency and friendship with him, and of their hearty wishes for his majesty's, his own, and the government's prosperity; to preserve which, they were ready to contribute all that lay in their power. Then they told him that they had several things to propose to him, when he should think convenient to receive them; the rest of the discourse run upon mutual complements and news. After which, the envoys were again accompanied by the governor to the door of the apartment, where he ordered the beforementioned *Domingo Delgados* and *David Ventura*, to conduct them to a certain large house finely furnished, in *Bishops-street*, and to entertain them at his charge; which though the envoys refused, alledging it to be contrary to the intentions of their masters, yet were forced to accept of the same, and were very magnificently entertained at supper. 1643.

The next morning about eleven a clock they went again to the palace, and after having desired a second audience, were received in the same manner as before. *Their second audience.* Every one being ordered to withdraw, besides the secretary of the governor; the envoys made their propositions to the last, which they delivered to him in writing in *Portuguese*, recommending the same to his consideration, as tending towards the maintaining a good and firm correspondency betwixt them. To which the governor gave this general answer; *That he should always endeavour to cultivate a good understanding and correspondency with us, pursuant to the strict and reiterated orders he had received for that purpose from the king his master. And that concerning the propositions made by them to him, he would assemble his council of war and justice, and afterwards impart to them his answer.* Then they were by *Domingo Delgados* reconducted to his own house, where they were very well entertained the same day at dinner, and the next by the governor himself.

The 17th they had another audience from the governor, who told them in very obliging terms, *Their third audience.* *that he had consulted the matter with his council, and could give them no other answer but what was contained in this letter*, which he delivered to them, and told them the contents thereof; whereupon our envoys told him, that since thereby a door was left open for rogues and vagabonds, they hoped he would at least order that the names of such as fled to the *Bahia* might be taken notice of, that the great council of the *Dutch Brasil* might not remain quite unsatisfied, whither they were fled; which he promised to do. After some further complements and mutual assurance of friendship, they parted for this time.

The 22d they took their leave of the bishop, and several other persons of note, unto whom they owed any obligations, and last of all of the governor himself, being conducted thither by many persons of quality and officers; they returned him thanks for the civilities and respect he had been pleased to shew them, wishing both him and his *Portuguese* majesty a long and happy reign, and victory against the *Castilians*. The governor returned their complements, and conducted them out of the room, ordering several negroes to attend them down the precipice of the hill, upon which the city is built, with chairs; but the envoys choosing

1643. choosing rather to go on foot, they were in the same chaloop they came in ashore, carried back under the sound of musick on board their yacht. The *Portuguese* officers after having taken their leave, returned to the city, and ours made the best of their way to the *Receif*, where they arrived safely not long after.

Their return to the Receif.

The letter delivered to them by the governor, was as follows.

The Governour's Letter.

The governors letter.

GIlbert de Wit *councellor of your court of Justice, and* Dirk Hoogstraten *commander in chief on the* Cape of St. Austin, *your lordships deputies; whom I received according to their quality and merits, have delivered your letter to me, and proposed such other matters as they were impowered to treat with me about. Though I endeavour nothing so much as to cultivate and maintain in the strictest manner, our neighbourly good correspondency, yet am I constrained at this time frankly to acknowledge, that it is not in my power to give your lordships any more satisfactory answer than this, in hopes that the many proofs you have had of my sincere inclinations, will serve as a plea with your lordships, to assure you, that I shall always be ready in all points depending on my government, to give the same proofs both of obedience and fidelity to the king my master, whose pleasure is, that the truce should be observed inviolably; and of my sincere intentions, and the esteem I have for your lordships friendship, desiring nothing more than that you furnish me with an opportunity of giving real demonstrations of my readiness to serve you; whom I recommend to the protection of God almighty.*

Bahia, Feb. 14. 1645. Signed,

Antonio Telles da Silva.

Concerning the six points mentioned in their secret instructions, they made the following report to the great council.

Report of the envoys to the council.

I. THAT *the* Portuguese *forces in those parts were generally esteemed to be less or more betwixt three and four thousand men, without the* Brasilians *and negroes. But that upon the most exact enquiry they could make, they had found them to be not above three thousand, including the* Brasilians *and negroes, and their garrisons both to the north and south, as far as* Rio Janeiro. *These consisted of five regiments*, viz. *three of* Portuguese, *under the colonels* John Darauge, Martin Soares, *and* N. N. *the fourth of* Brasilians, *under a* Brasilian *colonel*, Antonio Philippo Camarao; *and the fifth of negroes, under the command of negro* Henricio Dyas. *These two last regiments, amounting both not to above three hundred men, were divided in the garrisons to the north, about* Rio Real *on our frontiers; they being the scum and off-casts of all their territories; and consequently not to be quartered near the capital city, there having of late been some broils among them in the garrisons, whither officers were dispatched to compose them. The three* Portuguese *regiments consisting of about two thousand seven hundred men, kept garrison in* St. Salvador, *and the circumjacent forts, except two companies, one of which quartered about* Rio Real, *the other in the island* Morro St. Paulo; *and about one hundred fifty more, which were disposed in the captainships of* Os Ilheos, Porto Seguro *and* Spirito Sancto; *so that the garrisons of* St. Salvador *and the circumjacent forts, consisted in at least two thousand three hundred, each company consisting of one hundred men less or more, all chosen men and well cloathed; four companies mounted the guard every night, one at the palace, at each of the two gates one, and the fourth in the water-forts without the city.* 1643.

II. *Of their naval strength they gave a very slender account, being more considerable in number than force, as consisting only in fifty small vessels and yachts, not in the least fitted for war; neither could they observe the least shew of preparations tending that way; their aim being only to protect their ships bound to the* Portuguese *coasts, against the insults of the* Castilian *and* Denmark *privateers, and the* Turkish *rovers. It was, as they said, upon this account, that, during our stay there, two stout* Portuguese *ships fit for war, manned with six hundred men, and provided with good store of ammunition, arrived in the* Bahia, *under the command of* Salvador Correada-sa, *with orders to go directly from thence to* Rio de Janeiro, *and to fetch all ships ready loaden from thence to the* Bahia, *from whence they were to convoy these as well as such other vessels as they found ready there, to the coast of* Portugal; *for which reason also all the vessels which otherwise used to go according to their own conveniency, were ordered to stay for the said convoy. That news was brought by the said two ships, that the king of* Portugal *had forbid the building of* Caravels *and other such like small vessels, instead of which they were to build ships of better defence against the insults of an enemy at sea. From whence the envoys said they supposed would arise this inconveniency to the* Portuguese, *that the freights and convoy money paid for the commodities transported from* Portugal *to the* Portuguese Brasil, *and for the sugar transported from thence to* Portugal *must encrease, and consequently would not be able to sell the last at the same price the* Dutch *did, considering especially that they must be consi-*

1643. *considerable losers both in their interest and time, where they were forced to tarry for their convoys, whereas they used formerly to make the best of their way home.*

III. *They had observed, that though the inhabitants of the* Bahia *expected the coming of those ships at their first arrival, yet several vessels arrived there, both from the* Portuguese *coast and the islands before the rest.*

IV. *They concluded the negro trade to be very inconsiderable there, they having scarce ever heard it as much as mentioned; but because the price of a good negro did not at that time amount to above three hundred gilders, they supposed them pretty well stockt with them; those which were of late bought there being brought thither from* Cape Verde *and* Arder. *They further reported, that when on wednesday being the 8th of* February, *they entred the* Bahia, *they met two ships of good bulk, carrying about twenty guns each, and well mann'd going out, which upon enquiry were told them to be bound for* Portugal, *but could not learn to what harbour there, which together with some other reasons, made them suspect that they were intended another way, in which we found ourselves not deceived, when on the 22d of* February, *just as they were ready for their departure, they understood from* Mulat Juliana, *and of two monks, that these two ships were sent with men to* Angola, *for the security of the inhabitants of* Masagao, *who being but small in number, were sorely afraid to be set upon by the negroes of the countrey, and having desired the governor's assistance, who ordered those ships and the men to go in the night time, and to endeavour to reach* Masagao *unperceived by any, and without committing any hostilities against the* Dutch. *Whether and how far this might be true, time would shew, but they had all the reason in the world to believe, that it was upon their score of concealing this expedition, as well as some other matters from them, that immediately after arrival (though they were not informed of it till near the time of their departure) that no* Dutch *or* Germans *should appear, as much as in the sight of the envoys, much less discourse with them; which was observed with that strictness that they really imagined there had been no* Dutch *there; but found afterwards that they had been all (how many they knew not) carried on board the* Portuguese *vessels, to prevent their keeping any correspondency with us and our ships crew; to which end also, six centinels were placed in two boats lying near our yacht, during the time of our stay here, under pretence of protecting our vessel, but in effect to prevent any body from coming on board us, pursuant to the orders of the governor.*

V. *That the inhabitants of the* Bahia *and the other* Portuguese *captainships, had not the least commerce at this time with those of* Bonas Aires. *That immediately after the revolution in* Portugal, *those of the* Bahia *had attempted to go thither, but were treated as enemies by them; so that it was their opinion, the place would either soon, or was already totally ruined for want of commerce; all their livelihood consisting in the traffick from the coast of* Brasil *thither; which falling away, no silver could be transported thither from* Peru; *it being not probable that the* Spaniards *would run the hazard of passing along an enemy's coast, when they had a safer way to transport their treasures from the* West-Indies. 1643.

VI. *That they could not get the least certain information concerning the designs carried on betwixt some of the inhabitants of the* Bahia, *and those of the* Dutch Brasil *against the last; besides which they gave them a general relation of what they had been able to learn, concerning the condition of the city of* St. Salvador, *its inhabitants, governour, and some other matters relating to the countrey thereabouts.*

Another revolt of the Portuguese.

The rumours which in 1640 were noised about concerning the treacherous designs of the *Portuguese* inhabitants against us, being for that time vanished into smoak, the same was revived, and their designs began to be discovered in *February* 1645, *viz.* That confiding in the promised succours from *Bahia*, they intended to rise in arms aginst us, looking upon this juncture as the most favourable for their purpose, since count *Maurice* with the greatest part of our fleet, and a good number of soldiers were returned to *Holland*, from whence no fresh supplies were come of late into *Brasil.* The great council not being ignorant of this, were indefatigable in their care, to leave no stone unturned to find out the ring-leaders of this rebellion, so as to charge them effectually with this crime, and find out sufficient cause for their commitment. They sent out several of their officers into the countrey, as spies, to sound the inclinations of the people, and whether they could meet with any one who incited the rest to an insurrection. The like he did on the other side of the river of *St. Francis*, and in *Kamaron*'s camp, whither they had sent certain persons to investigate their designs, and to learn what preparations they made for war, and whether they were intended against *Pernambuko*, but were not able to find out any thing, upon which they could make any sure account. Being nevertheless sensible that those forewarnings were not altogether groundless, and knowing the *Por-*

1643. *tuguese* to be of so haughty a temper (besides the difference in religion) that they would scarce let any opportunity slip of withdrawing themselves from the obedience of their conquerors; they writ the 13th of *February* 1645 the following letter, concerning the designs of the *Portuguese* to the council of nineteen.

A letter from the great council to the West-India *company.*

Most noble and right honourable,

A letter from the great council to the West-India *company.*

During the government of his excellency count Maurice, *there were already several of the inhabitants of this state entred into secret cabals to rise in mutiny against us, in hopes of assistance from the* Bahia; *their business was to insinuate into those that were well affected to them, after their good success in* Maranhaon, *that our forces being considerably weakned by the strong detachments sent to the garrisons of* Angola, St. Thomas, *and others, a fair opportunity was offered them, to withdraw themselves from our obedience, and to enjoy their former liberty under their own king. They were not a little encouraged in their design, imagining the same might be carried on without any great difficulty, when they found that of late we had received no supplies either of meat or other provisions, or of soldiers from* Holland, *whereby the storehouses of the company here being exhausted, the garrisons of the forts were forced to be supplied from time to time with farinha and fresh meats out of the countrey, they judged, if they could once be masters in the field, they must of necessity fall into their hands; as it happened in* 1640 *to the* Spanish *garrisons in* Portugal, *who for the same reason were not in a condition to hold out against the* Portuguese; *being besides that sensible that unless we would too much weaken our garrisons, we had no sufficient number of troops left to appear formidable in the field. These and other such like insinuations have been frequently spread among the* Portuguese, *by those, who finding themselves most uneasy under our government, hoped for a change of their affairs, by changing their masters; which however wrought no considerable effect, as long as his excellency continued in the government, partly because we being forewarned of their designs, kept a watchful eye over all their actions, partly because our sea and land forces being much more considerable at that time than they are now, they had but little prospect of succeeding in their enterprize, which therefore they judged most convenient to defer till after his excellency's departure, which as it was sufficiently known before hand, so they were sensible that thereby our forces both by sea and land must be considerably weakned, and consequently would furnish them with a fairer opportunity of putting their so long rejected design in execution; the more, because that many of the* Portuguese *who relying hitherto upon the authority of count* Maurice, *as the only means to keep the soldiers in awe, being now put in fear of the executions and exorbitancies likely to be committed by the covetous officers and rapacious soldiers, would be forced to join with them against us. After the departure of his excellency for* Holland, *those cabals have instead of divine things encreased every day; they have been very diligent in getting information concerning the strength of all our garrisons, with an intent to carry on their designs before we could be reinforced with supplies of men and provisions from* Holland; *to effect which, they have by messengers sent to the* Bahia, *sollicited for succours of men and arms, of which as it seems they have no small hopes. There is great reason to believe that the journey of* Andrew Vidal *from the* Bahia *hither, in* August *last, undertaken under pretence of taking his leave before his return to* Portugal, *in order to serve the king there, was founded upon no other motive than to inform himself most narrowly concerning the true state of affairs here, in order to give a verbal account thereof in the* Bahia *and afterwards in* Portugal; *as likewise to sound the inclinations of the inhabitants, and to animate such as he found well disposed for his interest, with hopes of speedy succours from the* Bahia; *we have since received secret intelligence that he has been present at several of these cabals. But though they were greatly encouraged with these hopes of good success, by reason of the diminution of our forces and scarcity of provisions, they were not very forward in venturing upon this enterprise, being sensible that their design having taken vent, we made all necessary preparations against them; besides that many of the* Portuguese *inhabitants, being beyond their expectation, well satisfied with the government of the great council, did rather chuse to live quietly and securely, than to engage in so dangerous an enterprise. So that things remained without any considerable alteration at present; and as matters stand now we are not able to find out sufficient cause to satisfy ourselves whether they proceed in the same design. Their chief design as we are credibly informed was laid against the* Receif, *which they intended to surprise, upon a certain day appointed for the sale of negroes, when the inhabitants of the countrey flocking thither in great numbers, they did not doubt but with the assistance of our own negroes, who are for the most part papists, to make themselves, masters of the place, not questioning but if this succeeded, the rest would soon be forced to yield. But in this they were prevented, by the strong guards we took care to post in the* Receif *on those fair days.* 1643.

The

1643. *The chief ringleaders, as they are specified to us, are* John Fernandes Vieira, *and his father-in-law* Francisco Beringel, *with several others, whom we would have committed to prison, if we could have had more certain information against them; but though we left no stone unturned to find out the truth, yet could we not meet with sufficient motives to induce us either to imprison them, or to proceed again to the general disarming of the inhabitants, we having received certain intelligence, that so soon as we should attempt it, we must expect no less than a general insurrection, which considering our own magazines and store-houses were so ill provided, and no sufficient force could be drawn out of the garrison to secure the open countrey, would have drawn after it very ill consequences for our nation, especially those living at some distance from our forts, who thereby, as we had reason to fear, might have been exposed to the danger of being massacred by the* Portuguese. *It is evident from the information given to your lordships in* Holland, *and transmitted to us, that the subjects of the king of* Portugal *themselves are encouraged and animated against us; wherefore it will be absolutely necessary to be very cautious, and to hasten the supplies we have so often requested at your hands. Upon the first information we received, that toward the south of the* Receif *the* Portuguese *intended to land some men or arms, we sent the* 13th *of* October *a yacht, the* Enckhuysen *with another galliot and chaloop to cruise thereabouts, but they returned after some time without being able to discover any such thing. The next intelligence we had was, that a fleet was equipping in the* Bahia, *to transport some forces, for the assistance of our rebellious subjects; to find out the bottom of this design, we thought we could pitch upon no better expedient than to send thither Mr.* Gilbert de Witt *and* Dirk Hoogstraten *with certain instructions; of which we have enlosed the copy, who set sail the* 22th *of the last month. Being further informed that a certain* Portuguese *captain with an ensign and three soldiers have been lately dispatched from the* Bahia *to our captainships, to endeavour to stir up our subjects to rebellion, with assurance of succours from thence; we have employed all necessary means to find them out and get them into our hands. We shall not be wanting in any thing, which according as occasion presents, may contribute to the preservation of this state.*

Receif 13th February, 1645.

The 4th the great council were informed by letter from *Isnac Rasiere* and captain *Blewbeck*, written at *Parayba*, that a rumour was spread thereabouts that *Kamaron* chief commander of the *Brasilians* in the *Bahia*, was on his march from *Sertao* to *Siara*, to join with the *Brasilians* inhabiting thereabouts, to attack with their united forces the inhabitants of the captainship of *Rio Grande.* Whereupon the council sent orders to *Hans Vogel*, governor of *Seregippo del Rey*, to get intelligence and send them speedy word whether *Kamaron* with his camp were still in *Rio Real*; and if not, whither he had taken his march, or whither he intended to take it. They also sent word to the inhabitants of *Parayba*, that they should be very diligent in enquiring after the cause of this rumour, and send them intelligence accordingly. The 15th of *May* they received an answer from *Hans Vogel*, dated the 25th of *April* at *Seregippo del Rey*, wherein he told them that pursuant to their orders he had sent a serjeant with some soldiers to *Kamaron*'s head quarters, about ten leagues from *Seregippo del Rey*, under pretence of looking for some deserters; who after their return reported, that his forces consisting of two hundred *Portuguese* and one thousand two hundred *Brasiians*, were still in the same place, busied for the most part in cultivating some plantations, *Kamaron* himself being then in the *Bahia*, to assist at the solemnity of their easter; from whence they conjectured, that the rumour concerning his march was only a fiction. But two days after the same rumour was renewed by two passengers coming from *Rio St. Francisco*, and being landed by one *John Hoen*, a master of a vessel near *Kandelaria*; but upon a more strict enquiry made by the council, the said master of the vessel declared, that on the eighth of the same month, when he left *Rio de Francisco*, there was no news of *Kamaron*'s march.

The 30th of *May* 1645, a letter without a name was delivered to the great council by one *Abraham Markado* a jew, subscribed only *plus ultra*. This letter being translated out of the *Portuguese* the same night, the contents thereof were, that three unknown persons gave them notice that a good body of troops were come from *Rio Real* into *Parayba*, with an intention to join with a discontented party there, and to surprize the *Dutch* forts; with advice to seize upon the person of *John Fernandes Vieira* their chief ringleader.

The letter is as follows,

A letter of intelligence to the council.

We stand amazed you are so secure, when it is reported that the Matta *of* Parayba *is full of soldiers, come thither lately from* Rio Real, *who consisting in a good number of negroes, mulats, and* Portuguese, *with*

Kamaron

1643. Kamaron *at the head of them, began their march in the month of* March, *expecting now to be joined by other troops, which hitherto were stopt by the overflowing of the rivers. Their aim is to encourage the inhabitants to take up arms, which done, they expect considerable succours from the* Bahia, *both by sea and land, wherewith they pretend to block you up in the* Receif, *intending to fix their camp either at* Olinda, *or in the* Vergea, *and quarter the soldiers in the* Fregesies *thereabouts. They boast that their forces are already considerably encreased by those who are indebted to the company, and other vagabonds, and threatned to massacre all such of your subjects as refuse to join with them. A certain person of note and reputation belonging to the same camp, has given us this information, in order to communicate it to your lordships to be upon your guard, which we do accordingly by these presents. The same person told us, that* John Fernandes Vieira *was the chief ringleader of this insurrection, who maintains the rebellious crew in the* Matta, *as they meet together, till a certain day appointed for their rendezvous, when they are with their joint forces to attack all the* Dutch *forts and out-guards at once. We were also told, that the said* Vieira *does not sleep in his house, and is always upon his guard; to try which, you have no more to do than to send some to take him, with his servants and factors; which if you could do they would be all amazed, and make an open confession, which may be done without the least hazard; for if you miscarry in the attempt, it will nevertheless not redound to your disadvantage. We conjure your lordships to take care of this poor nation, for fear they should be forced to join with the rebels against you. We judge it therefore absolutely necessary to undertake the business without delay, with all imaginable secresy; for if they find themselves discovered, they will begin the game immediately; so that strong guards ought to be put in the outworks, and in the harbours of* Kandelaria *and the* Receif. *We advise your lordships to oblige the inhabitants forthwith to surrender their arms, to order all the masters of the sugar-mills, with their planters, to appear in the* Receif, *especially those of the* Fregesies *of* Vergea, Garassu, St. Lorenzo, St. Amaro, Moribeca, de Cabo, Pojuka, *and* Serinhaim, *with assurance that they shall not be molested for any debts there; and when they are come, to detain them till they see what is further to be done, under pretence of securing them against the attempts of the rebels in the country, by which means you will both secure the government, and oblige many private persons. The same method ought to be used with those of* Parayba, *where they may be detained in the fort, as well as those of* Porto Calvo *in that place. Thus if you can get the chiefest into your hands, the design will dwindle away to nothing. We beseech you not to send away any more soldiers before you have made a full discovery of the rebellion, and provide your forts with good garrisons; whither we would also have all the* Dutch *inhabitants to retire for fear of being massacred. We three being faithful subjects of your lordships, have now satisfied our consciences in proposing your remedy, which consists in the taking of* Vieira, *which must be undertaken with great secrecy and foresight, he being, as it is said, continually upon his guard. Your lordships will be sensible without our advice how much it concerns them, not to divulge to any, from whom they have received this information; and we assure you, that we will not fail to give further intelligence of what we are able to learn by way of letters; and one time or other, we shall make no difficulty to let you know, who these three faithful subjects are. If we had been present, we could have declared no more than we have done in this letter. Your lordships must take effectual care against their attempts without delay, the approaching feast being the time appointed for the putting it in execution. We have sent you immediate notice after it came to our knowledge: We advise you likewise to seize upon* Francisco Beringel, Vieira's *father-in-law, and* Antonio Kavalkanti; *and in short, all the chiefest of the* Vergeas, *and other places.* Signed,

A. Verdade.

Plus Ultra.

Hereupon the great council called *Paul de Linge*, president of the council of justice, vice-admiral *Cornelius Lichthart*, and lieutenant colonel *Garstman*, into their assembly, to consult unanimously what were best to be done at this juncture for the preservation of the *Dutch Brasil*; when by this, as well as several other letters and intelligences, they were forewarned of the approaching danger; and notwithstanding they were much in doubt, whether they ought to make any certain account upon a letter written without a name; yet considering all the circumstances of this, as well as several other informations, it was judged absolutely necessary to provide for the safety of the *Dutch Brasil*, against any attempt of an enemy.

I. By providing all the forts with meal for two months.

II. By giving immediate notice to all commanders of forts to be constantly upon their guard.

III. To write to *John Listry*, chief commander

mander of the *Brasilians*, to keep his people in readiness with their arms in the villages, to be ready to march upon the first orders from the council, we being not in a condition to take the field without them.

IV. To send abroad their spies in all corners, even into the woods, to get intelligence whereabouts the enemies troops are, and to give timely notice of what they are able to learn to the council.

V. It was agreed, to summon *John Fernandes Vieira*, the chief ringleader of the intended rebellion, and his securities, *Francisco Beringel*, *Vieira*'s father-in-law, and *Bernardin Karvalho*, unto the *Receif*, under pretence of making a second agreement with him, which he earnestly desired; by which means they should secure his person, know the whole bottom of the *Portuguese* design, and consequently be the better able to prevent it. A certain broker called *Koin*, who sollicited this agreement for *Vieira*, was prevailed upon to undertake this task, which he might do without the least suspicion; but the *Whitsontide* holidays put some stop to it for the present. With the same care the great council employed all possible means to get the other persons of the *Vergea*, suspected to have a hand in this rebellious design, into their hands, under some pretence or other, they being not likely to be taken by force, because they did not lodge in their mills and houses in the night time, and by day were so strictly upon their guard, that they could not possibly be surprized.

The 31st of *May*, vice-admiral *Lichthart*, and *Henry Haus*, a lieutenant, offered to undertake the delivering of *John Fernandes Vieira* to the council, which they intended to effect, under pretence of giving him a visit, and going a fishing with him in the lake *Lewis Bras Biserra*.

Further advice concerning the insurrection.

The 9th of *July*, the great council received advice by a letter from Mr. *Koin*, governour of *Rio St. Francisco*, dated the 1st of *June*, that *Kamaron*, with a small body was passed the river *St. Francis*; therefore he desired some assistance of men, with suitable ammunition.

The same was confirmed by another letter, dated the 27th of *June*, with advice, that as yet no enemy had appeared within sight of the fort.

Frequent intelligence being likewise sent to the council, that in the *Matta* of *St. Lawrence*, and some other distant places, considerable numbers of soldiers from the *Bahia*, of Mulats and Negroes, were gathering in a body, they sent several small bodies thither, under command of such as were well acquainted with that country, who all unanimously reported, that they could meet with no soldiers, mulats, or any other vagabonds thereabouts.

The 12th of *June*, the director *Moucheron* sent further advice, that he had been credibly informed, by letters dated the 8th of the same month, from *Rio St. Francisco*, that *Kamaron* and *Henrico Dias*, with six companies of *Brasilians*, Mulats, and Negroes, were pass'd the said river; and that just as he was concluding his letter, two inhabitants of the *Algoas* had given him to understand, that some of them had been at their houses for some meal; the copies of which letters he sent to the council, who did now not in the least question, but that their aim was upon the *Dutch Brasil*, especially since they were forewarned by several letters from *St. Antonio*, that the inhabitants thereabouts seem'd to prepare for a revolt.

The Resolution of the council thereupon.

The council finding their project of taking *Vieira* by craft, not to succeed, because he and the securities of his father-in-law, *Francisco Beringel*, and *Bernardino Karvalho*, could not be cajoled into the *Receif*, under pretence of renewing their former contract, and looking upon him as the chief ringleader of this revolt, they ordered *Joachim Denniger*, a lieutenant, with a good number of soldiers, to the mill and house of the said *John Fernandes Vieira*, to bring his person from thence to the *Receif*. Accordingly *Denniger* advanced with his soldiers towards the evening near the mills, which he surrounded, and about midnight unexpectedly entred both the house and mills, making a most strict search throughout all the rooms and corners, but to no purpose. In the morning he withdrew at some distance, but return'd the next night, when after having made another search, but in vain, he was informed by one of his *Turkish* slaves, and some Negroes, that neither *Vieira*, nor his father-in-law *Beringel*, had slept in their houses these last three weeks; that sometimes they came thither on horseback, but after a very short stay went their ways again. *Denniger* likewise search'd the houses of *Antonio Kavalkanti* and *Antonio Biserra*, but to as little purpose as those of the former, being informed by their Negroes, that they had absconded for some weeks before.

In the mean while, the council sent divers parties abroad, under the command of *Hans Katner*, *Slodiniski*, and *Cunraed Hilt*, all which, after their return, agreed in this, that there were no enemies there as yet, especially not in the *Matta*, where they met with no body but those

7 that

1643. that were employed in manuring the grounds.

The great council finding themselves altogether disappointed in their hopes of taking *Vieira*, resolved to secure immediately the persons of *Francisco Beringel*, *Vieira*'s father-in-law; *Bernardino Karvalho*, and his brother *Sebastian Karvalho*, *Lewis Bas*, *Amaro Lopez*, and *John Pessoa*, being persons suspected to have a hand in the conspiracy, inhabiting the *Vergea*. In the more distant provinces were ordered to be seized

In *St. Amaro*, *Antonio de Bulhous*.

In *St. Antonio*; *Amador d'Arouja*; *Pedro Marinho Falcao*; *Antonio del Rasto*.

In *Pojuka*; *Kornero de Morais*; father *Frey Lewis*; and *Francisco Dias del Gado*.

In *Serinhaim*; *John Albuquerq*, son-in-law of *Pero Lopez de Vera*.

In *Porto Calvo*; *Rodrigues de Barros Pimentel*.

In *Iguaraka*; *John Pimenta*.

In *Itamarika*; father *Lawrence d'Alkunha*.

And in *Rio Grande*; *John Lestan Navarro*.

But it being most of all to be feared that the inhabitants of *Parayba*, who were much indebted, would revolt before all the rest, Mr. *Paul de Linge* was sent thither immediately in the quality of director, with full power to act both in that and the *Captainship* of *Rio Grande*, as he should find it most expedient for the company, with express orders to press 100 men out of the ships, with proportionable provisions, immediately after his arrival there, which were to be disposed in the fort of *St. Margaret*, both for its defence, and to keep the inhabitants in due obedience.

Parayba *secured.*

And considering that the scarcity of provisions was one of the main obstacles to be surmounted on our side, which as the case then stood, would more and more increase, unless we could remain masters of the field, from whence we drew most of our provisions, and to over-awe the discontented inhabitants, it was judged requisite, to form a small camp near *S. Lawrence*; and accordingly the two lieutenants *Huykquesloot* and *Hamel* were order'd thither with 35 men each, the first from *Iguaraka*, the last from *Moribeka*, as likewise captain *Wiltschut*, with 50 men more from the *Receif*; *John Listry*, commander in chief of the *Brasilians*, was likewise ordered to join them with all possible speed, 300 *Brasilians* under their own commanders.

A small camp near St. Lawrence.

The same day (being the 12th) after a view was taken of the fortifications of *Moribeka* town, the same were ordered to be repaired, and news being brought, that *John Fernandes Vieira* had been seen in his mill the same night, the council endeavoured with all possible care to have secured his person, but in vain; it being certain, that (according to the depositions made by his steward of the mill, called *St. John*, before the publick notary *Indiik*, in the *Receif*, 21 *Jan.* 1647.) near six months before the breaking out of this insurrection, he had never slept one night in his house: And whenever he happened to be there in the day-time, he remained for the most part in a turret on the top of the house, from whence he could have a prospect at a great distance; if his business called him below, he put some body else there to keep the watch; who, if they saw but two or three persons come that way, gave immediate notice thereof to him; and if any *Dutch* in a body were discovered, he retired instantly into the adjacent woods. He had likewise placed some Negroes at a certain distance from the house, who were to give notice of the approach of any unknown persons that way. 1643.

The 13th *Sebastian Karvalho* and *Antonio de Bulhous*, were brought in prisoners to the *Receif*, the rest who were sensible of their guilt, having escaped their hands; the first being examined the same night by the assessor of the court of justice, Mr. *Walbeek*, concerning the intended conspiracy, gave him the following account by word of mouth.

Sebastian Karvalho *brought in prisoner.*

His Confession.

THAT he was one of those three, who a few days ago, had by way of letter given an account of an intended conspiracy in the Vergea, *to the great council, the ringleader thereof being* John Fernandes Vieira, *who, with the rest of his* Portuguese *accomplices, relied upon the succours promised them from the* Bahia; *with what he had judged most proper for obviating the same. That the whole design of this conspiracy was laid open to him by means of a certain writing, in form of an association, which was delivered to him by a* Portuguese *servant of the said* Vieira, *together with a letter, in which he desired him to subscribe the same, there being no more than two who had subscribed it at that time, viz.* John Fernandes Vieira, *and* Lewis da Costa Sepulpeda. *The contents of this association were, that they promised to rise in arms against this state, and to sacrifice their lives and estates for the recovery of the* Dutch Brasil, *under the obedience of the king of* Portugal. *That indeed he had signed the said association, but given immediate notice thereof to* Ferdinando Vale *and a third person besides; and that he, together with Mr.* Vale, *had*

His confession.

1643. *had cauſed the beforemention'd letter, directed to the great council, to be delivered to* Merkado *the phyſician. That the inſurrection was intended to extend all over* Dutch Braſil, *but that the inhabitants of the* Captainſhip *of* Parayba *were moſt to be feared, as being moſt indebted, and conſequently bearing an ill-will to our government. That their main deſign was to ſurprize one of our forts, on or near the ſea-ſide, whereby they might ſecure themſelves a place to receive ſuccours from the* Bahia; *from whence they expected to be aſſiſted with two men of war, and three or four fregates. That he had ſigned this aſſociation barely out of fear of* Vieira, *who had threatned thoſe that ſhould refuſe with no leſs than death, and had cauſed ſeveral to be murthered upon that account.*

His confeſſion agreeing in all points with what *Ferdinando Vale* had depoſed before, and being all that time ſorely afflicted with the gravel, he was diſpenſed with from any further examination.

The council being by this depoſition of *Karvalho* fully convinced of the treachery of *Vieira* and his adherents, it was reſolved to attempt once more the taking of the ſaid *Vieira*, if perhaps he might as yet lurk ſomewhere or other near the *Receif*, and of his factor *Mor Manuel de Souſa*, engaged in the ſame deſign; as likewiſe of *Antonio Bezerra* and *Amaro Lopez*, both inhabitants of the *Vergea*, but in vain. Thoſe who were ſent upon that errand, bringing back no other ſatisfaction, than that they were not to be met with thereabouts, and that beſides that, *Antonio* and *Manuel Kavalkanti*, *Antonio Bezerra*, *John Peſſoa*, and *Coſmo de Kraſto*, were the ſame day retired out of the *Vergea* to the *Matta*. The ſame day captain *Wiltſchut* was ordered to ſeize the publick notary, *Caſpar Pereira*, dwelling in *St. Lawrence*, who was ſuppoſed to have drawn the beforementioned aſſociation; and it was reſolved to ſend a pardon to *Antonio Kavalkanti*, and *John Pais Kaeral*, who having a great family at home, might thereby be prevailed upon to quit the party of the rebels, whereby we ſhould both weaken that of the enemy, and get a further inſight into their deſigns. *Antonio de Bulhous* being examined at the ſame time, ingenuouſly confeſſed that he had not the leaſt knowledge of the conſpiracy; *Sebaſtian Karvalho* being, notwithſtanding his former confeſſion, detained priſoner upon ſuſpicion till the 4th of *Auguſt*, was, at his requeſt,
Karvalho *diſcharged.* diſmiſſed by the great council, after having given ſufficient proof that he was one of the three who writ the letter concerning the intended conſpiracy to the council.

7

The 14th of *June*, orders were given to all the inhabitants of the *Receif*, and thoſe living upon the back of the river, to ſurround their dwelling places with palliſadoes, under forfeiture of 200 gilders. And to render the companies the more compleat, and expoſe our men to as little danger as might be of being ſurpriſed by the enemy, all the ſafeguards were commanded to be withdrawn by Mr. *Haus*, near the *Receif*, and in *Serinhaim* by captain *Fallo*, who was likewiſe ordered to remove the garriſon of *Huna* to another place of more ſtrength. The better to ſupply the ſcarcity of proviſions in the forts, which for want thereof might be in danger of falling into the enemies hands, orders were diſpatch'd to the chief commanders, to ſeize upon what quantity of *Farinha* (or meal) they ſtood in need of for the uſe of their reſpective garriſons among the inhabitants of the country, which they were to be paid for by the commiſſaries of the company. It was alſo thought neceſſary, that for the greater ſecurity of *Maurice*'s town, the ditches of the fort *Erneſtus* ſhould be made larger, as likewiſe the *Quinqueregular* fort, which was put in execution by *Haus*, as vice-admiral *Lichthart* took care to have two ſpy ſhips poſted, one betwixt the *Quinqueangular* fort and the fort *Bruin*, the other beyond *Baretta*, to prevent any ſurprize on that ſide at low tide; it was alſo reſolved not to let any ſhips or boats go out of the *Receif*, without a paſs from the great council. The major of the city militia was ordered to keep the reſt of his officers with the ſoldiery in readineſs againſt the 17th, to paſs the review, the ſame day being alſo appointed to the garriſon for that purpoſe; ſeveral new commanders were alſo choſen for the militia, inſtead of thoſe that were ready to return into *Holland*. The ſame day *Paul Linge* ſet out on his journey into *Parayba*, being furniſhed with fifteen hundred ſoldiers for neceſſary occaſions; and *Bernardino Karvalho*, who had abſconded for ſome time, had, at his requeſt, leave granted him to come to the *Receif* to anſwer for himſelf.

1643. *The* Receif *ſtrengthened with palliſadoes.*

The fortifications of Maurice *town enlarged.*

The 15th *John Peſſoa*, maſter of the ſugar-mill *Pantello*, one of thoſe that were ordered to be ſecured, deſired leave alſo in a letter to the council, to appear before them, his flight being occaſioned not by his guilt, but only fear, which was granted him, as well as the requeſt of father *Lawrence Alkunha*, upon the ſame account.

On the 16th early in the morning, we received ſecret intelligence, that *Andrew Vidal*, at the head of 1000 *Portugueſe*, and *Kamaron* with *d'Indeos Rondelas*, and *Henry*

ry

1643. *ry Dias* with a body of arm'd Negroes, had posted themselves above *St. Anthony*, near the sugar-mill *Topekura*. The same day *John Karnero de Maris*, and *Francisco Dias del Gado*, both masters of sugar-mills in the district of *Pojuka*, ordered to be apprehended, were brought prisoners to the *Receif*, and *Amador da Rouje*, and *Pero Marinha Falkao*, inhabitants of *St. Anthony*, who had hitherto absconded, did ask permission to come to the *Receif* to answer for themselves, which was easily granted.

Our camp removed to Moribeka. It was then taken into deliberation by the great council, whether, according to the last intelligences received of the enemies designs, it were not most expedient to remove our small camp from *St. Lawrence* to *Moribeka*, which after some debates, was agreed upon accordingly, thereby to secure the passage of the river *Sangea*, and consequently to remain masters of the country as far as the cape of *St. Austin*, from whence both the camp and the *Receif* might conveniently be supplied, both with *Farinha* and cattle; whereas on the contrary, if the enemy should be possessed of it, he might (as had been done in the former wars) cut off all supplies coming from the south to the *Receif*.

Pursuant to this resolution, orders were sent to captain *Wiltschut* to march immediately to *Moribeka*, to expect there the coming of the *Brasilians*, and some further succours: In the mean while, to post himself in the church, and to fortify the same against any sudden attack: And the aldermen of *Maurice*'s town were ordered to buy up the necessary provisions, both of *Farinha* and cattle about *Moribeka*, for their use. A proclamation was also issued, commanding all the inhabitants of *Serinhaim*, *Pojuka*, *St. Antonio*, and *Moribeka*, without any exception, to repair well armed, both horse and foot, with all possible speed to *St. Antonio*, there to list themselves for the defence of the open country, under the command of colonel *Gaspar Vander Ley*, and lieutenant colonel *John Heck*: Those that were not able to maintain themselves at their own charge, being to receive their provision from the company, like other soldiers: The said colonel and lieutenant colonel offering at the same time, to furnish fifteen hundred *Alquera*'s or measures of *Farinha*, for the use of our garrisons, for ready money.

The same day the great council received a letter from *Antonio Kavalkanti*, (unto whom they had lately sent his pardon) in which he protested, that neither he nor the rest of the inhabitants of the *Vergea* were concerned in any cabals against the state, their flight being occasioned only by fear of being imprisoned upon suspicion, raised against them by their enemies. The answer of the council was to this effect, That if he knew himself innocent, he should return to his mill, this being the only means to recover his former reputation. 1643.

The great council having great reason to suspect, that *Kamaron* would endeavour to bring the *Brasilians* under their jurisdiction over to his party, resolved, in order to secure them in their interest, to treat with *Listry*, their commander in chief, to persuade them, to send their wives and children into the isle of *Tamarika*, under pretence of securing them against any attempts of the enemy, to which they might in all probability be exposed in the open villages; but in effect, to keep them as pledges of their fidelity.

The same day the council received secret intelligence from *Antonio d'Olivera*, that the succours sent to the rebels from the *Bahia*, consisted in a considerable number of *Portuguese*, under the the command of the brother of *Kavalkanti*; of four hundred *Brasilians*, under the command of *Kamaron*; three hundred *Indeos Rondelas* from *Sertoa*; and fifty Negroes, under command of *Henry Dias*. *Number of those sent from* Bahia *to the rebels.*

On the same 16th of *June*, Mr. *Slotenitski*, ensign of the guards, was sent abroad to be at the campaigne, with eleven firelocks, and twelve *Brasilians*, who returning the 24th of *June*, gave the following account to the great council. That he took his way from the *Receif* directly to *St. Lawrence*, and from thence directly to the village of *St. Michael*; where being joined by his *Brasilians*, he marched thro' *St. Francisco* to *Kasura*; from thence to *Geyta*, and so further through the *Matta* to *St. Sebastian*, where all the inhabitants had left their houses. At *St. Sebastian* he passed the river *Topikura*, and coming to *John Fernandes Vieira*'s park, met there with good able horses. The Negroes told him, they had orders from their master to fly from before the *Dutch*, but to furnish the *Portuguese* with what they desired. From thence he marched to *Antonio*, and in his way thither did light upon a house belonging likewise to *John Fernandes Vieira*; where he found about fifty or sixty sheep, with good store of poultry, intended for the use of the sick belonging to those rebels, or those come to their assistance from the *Bahia*. They forewarned him not to advance too far, he being likely to meet some troops in the park belonging to the fathers of *St. Bento*; but coming thither found both the *Portuguese* and Negroes fled. From thence he marched to a house belonging to *Michael Fernandes*, who a- *Ensign* Slotenitski *sent abroad, and his account.*

1643. bove three months before had been ordered by *John Fernandes Vieira*, to provide a sufficient quantity of *Farinha* for the use of the succours expected from the *Bahia*; which he lately had transported from thence to *Pedro de Alkunha*, where was the rendezvous of two companies of the rebellious inhabitants, where the said *Michael* expected a good store of cattle, bought up by *Vieira* for their use, according to the information of a Negro, brought by *Slotcnifki* to the *Receif*. Near the park of *Don Pedro d'Alkunha*, he met with the same Mulat who had shot captain *Waldeck*, and with two *Hollanders* who had committed murther, and were never pardoned. *John Fernandes Vieira* had promised to be with them against *Midsummer* day. From thence *Slotenifki* marched directly to *Vna*, and so further to *St. Luce*, but met with no body there except one monk, and so returned to the *Receif*.

On the 17th of *June* it was resolved by the great council, with the consent of the council of justice, to issue a proclamation for a general pardon, except some few ringleaders of the rebellion.

The proclamation was as follows.

A PROCLAMATION *for a general pardon.*

THE great council of Brasil *makes known to every body, whom it may concern, that they being sensible, to their grief, how many of their subjects, having been misled by some of the ringleaders of the rebellion, have left their mills, wives and children for fear, as has been insinuated to them, of being disturbed, plundered, and killed by our stragling parties: We being willing to provide against it, and to contribute as much as in us lies, to the prosperity of our subjects, and their estates, have thought fit to publish their intention, to be, to defend and protect the inhabitants of the open country, against all evil intention'd persons to the utmost of their power. And to reduce those who have left their habitations, to obedience, and prevent their utter destruction, we promise our pardon to all such as shall within five days after sight of this our proclamation, make their personal appearance in the* Receif, *not excepting those who have been actually engaged in the said rebellion (unless they are among the number of the chief ringleaders) provided they leave the rebellious party, and return to their former obedience; and that they shall enjoy the quiet possession of their mills and lands as before, under our protection; under condition however, that they shall be obliged to take a new oath of allegiance to the state. Those on the contrary, who shall persist in their rebellion, or shall assist the rebels under what pretence soever, are hereby declared enemies of the state, who have forfeited their lives and estates, whose persons and estates shall be liable to be prosecuted with fire and sword,* &c. 1643.

This proclamation being immediately translated into the *Portuguese* tongue, was sent in the morning to *St. Antonio* and the *Vergea* to be published there; several copies were also distributed among the friars, in order to publish them from the pulpits, and cause them to be affixed to the church doors.

The 18th, good store of provision and ammunition was sent to the fort *Keulen*, and *Rio Grande*, and the garrisons of both these places forewarned to keep upon their guard. At the same time the proclamation of pardon was sent thither to be published; and *Antonio Parayba*, chief of the *Brasilians* in those parts, was summon'd to keep his *Brasilians* in readiness with their arms, whenever they should be commanded to give proofs of their fidelity to the company.

The 19th of *June*, two inhabitants of *Porto Calvo*, that were landed but the same morning in a small boat on the *Receif*, brought news to the great council, that *Kamaron*, at the head of the *Brasilians*, and *Henry Dias*, with his armed Negroes, consisting in seven companies, had posted themselves in the *Alegoas*, near the sugar-mill *Velho*; that their number was increased since to four or five thousand men, by the conjunction of those who were passed the river *St. Francisco* through the *Matta*, and that they had begun to commit open hostilities; so that now the council had not the least reason to doubt any further of the design of the *Portuguese*. The commander of *Porto Calvo* sent word much to the same purpose, and that he prepared for a vigorous defence. The first effects of this insurrection broke out in the *Open rebellion begun in Pojuka.* district of *Pojuka*, and considering that our whole force there consisted only in 30 men, under *Jacob Flemming*, a lieutenant, orders were sent him to retreat to *St. Antonio*, there to defend themselves with their joint-forces. The first beginning of hostilities was made by those of the *Pojuka*, by seizing upon two boats, all the passengers of which they took prisoners, and slew them afterwards, except one seaman, who had the good fortune to escape. This done, the inhabitants both of the village and the open country, chose for their head *Tabatinga Amador d'Arravio*, whereby they cut off all communication with the cape *Austin* by land, and all about to the south, besides that, the fort on the said cape could

1643. could not, but with great difficulty, be supplied with water from the river.

The 20th of *June*, a *Brasilian* arrived very early in the morning in the *Receif*; his errant to the council was, that he being sent by *John Blaar*, from *Porto Calvo*, with letters to the great council, was set upon by those of *Pojuka*, near *Kamboa*, who took from him the said letters, and kill'd his companion. For the rest he told them, that *Kamaron* was posted in the district of *Porto Calvo*, and that captain *John Blaar* was in the fort. A council being called to consider of the best means to secure the *Dutch-Brasil* against any attempts of the enemy, the first thing that fell in debate was, whether, according to the general advice of those of the inhabitants, who wish'd well to our government, it were not most expedient for our defence, to form a camp to make head against the enemy in the field; who, if once master of the open country, would force the inhabitants to join with him, and cut off our provisions, without which we could not subsist long. The next thing to be taken into consideration was, where to find forces for this camp, the garrisons being so weakly manned, as not to be able to spare any, and the body under captain *Wiltschut* consisting only of one hundred and twenty men, besides the three hundred *Brasilians*, to be joined with him. Considering therefore that the whole force in the *Allegoas*, consisted only of two companies under the command of *Mucheron*, a number not any ways proportionable to the extent of so large a tract of ground; it was judg'd most convenient to make a virtue of necessity, and to draw them from thence to the *Receif*, as indeed they had been ordered before. But their way by land being cut off by the rebels of *Pojuka*, a vessel, which lay ready to go out a crusing, was ordered to *Porto Francisco*, with orders to *Mucheron*, to embark forthwith those forces aboard her, without having any regard to the baggage; but the rest, which could not be put aboard the vessel, should be sent by land to *Rio Francisco*, to reinforce captain *Koin*, for the better defence of that place. Captain *Fallo* was likewise ordered to march with the garrison of *Serinhaim* to *St. Antonio*, it being not likely that the troops in *Serinhaim* should be able to make head there, after the coming of *Kamaron* into *Porto Calvo*, it being an inland country.

A reinforcement sent to Tamarika.

The same day forty new-listed soldiers were sent to *Tamarika*, under command of captain *Peter Seuliin*, master of the sugar-mill *Harlem*; because this island was of the greatest consequence to us; and the garrisons of the fort *Orange*, and the town of *Schop*, consisting each of one company, were very weak, and the armed inhabitants did not amount to above one company more. 1643.

The same day Mr. *Bas* and Mr. *Van de Voerde*, counsellors of the court of justice, were ordered to examine *Gaspar Pereira* the publick notary, concerning his drawing of the instrument of association; as likewise *John Kariero de Maris*, *Francisco Dias Delgado* masters of sugar-mills, in the district of *Pojuka*, and *Sebastian Karvalho*, concerning what they knew of the intended conspiracy.

Second confession of Karvalho.

Karvalho declared a second time, at the house of lieutenant colonel *Haus*, that some days ago (he could not remember exactly which) a certain *Portuguese* servant, whom he knew not, did come to him in the name of *John Fernandes Vieira*, with a letter, in which the said *Vieira* desired him to sign the enclosed writing drawn in form of an association, to take up arms against the government, as soon as they should receive any succours from the *Bahia*; which at that time was subscribed only by *John Fernandes Vieira* and *Lewis da Costa Sepulpeda*; but, as he supposed, was to be carried to most of the inhabitants. He further declared, that he refused to sign the said writing upon the bare letter of *John Fernandes Vieira*, and the hand-writing being unknown to him, he sent both the letter and instrument of association back by the same lad that brought it, with his answer by way of mouth, that he could not subscribe it. Having more maturely weighed the matter, he sent the same evening to his friend *Fernando Vale*, to desire him to give him a meeting the next morning upon the hills of *Garapes*; which being done accordingly, it was agreed among them to give notice of this conspiracy to the great council, in a letter without a name. This letter, with the subscription of *plus ultra*, was writ by *Vale*, and about ten days after given him to read in a bakers house in the *Pont-street*, and afterwards given to *Abraham Merkado* the physician, who delivered it to the great council.

The same day, the 20th of *June*, the great council received a letter from Mr. *Ley* and *Hoek*, dated at *St. Antonio*, importing, that the whole *Fregesie* had taken up arms, and made sixteen or eighteen *Dutch* inhabitants prisoners; that they had fortified the church against those of *Pojuka*, whom they did not question to force from thence, provided they received any succours from the *Receif*. The council having taken the whole matter into serious deliberation, and considering with themselves,

1643. ſelves, that, as the caſe then ſtood, they had no great reaſon to fear any rebellion in the north, in *Parayba* and *Rio Grande*, as long as our fleet remained near the *Red-Land*, and judging it highly neceſſary to bring the rebels in *Pojuka* to reaſon, and by their puniſhment to deter the reſt from attempting the like; they ordered lieutenant colonel *Haus*, with a detachment of a hundred men, to march the next morning to *Moribeka*, there to join with captain *Wiltſchut* and the *Braſilians*, and ſo continue their march to *St. Antonio*; from whence they were with their joint forces to go directly againſt the Rebels of *Pojuka*, to reduce them to obedience; it being otherwiſe to be feared that they would cut off all communication betwixt the *Receif* and the garriſons to the ſouth. This expedition proved ſo ſucceſsful, that the rebels were put to flight, and lieutenant colonel *Haus* made himſelf maſter both of the town and convent, forcing them to quit all the paſſes thereabouts; and forty priſoners were releaſed, whom they had loaded with irons in the ſaid monaſtery. But having received intelligence of the approach of *Kamaron* with his whole Body againſt him, he deſired further ſuccours from the great council to keep the field; but the garriſon of the *Receif* being too much weakened already, they could ſend him no other reinforcement 'till the expected ſuccours ſhould arrive from *Holland*.

Succours ſent to Pojuka.

A faſt.

The 21st, it was reſolved by the great council, to proclaim a general faſt all over *Dutch-Braſil*, to be kept the 28th of *June*, to return thanks to God Almighty for the great mercy ſhewn to them on ſeveral occaſions, but eſpecially of late, in the timely diſcovery of the treacherous deſigns of their enemies, who intended to have ſurpriſed them when they were leaſt aware of them.

Scheme of the Portugueſe *Plot.*

The deſign of this conſpiracy was laid thus by the *Portugueſe*: They intended in the *Whitſuntide* holidays to make ſolemn rejoycings, with feaſting, tournaments, and ſuch like, on occaſion of ſeveral weddings appointed for that purpoſe, unto which were to be invited all the chief men of *Dutch-Braſil*, both civil and military; whom, after they were fluſhed with wine, they intended to murther, in imitation of the *Sicilian veſpers*, or the noted *Pariſian wedding*; not queſtioning but that, when the heads of the *Dutch-Braſil* were cut off, the reſt, when attack'd at once in divers places, would fall an eaſy prey into their hands. But being prevented in this bloody deſign for that time, *Midſummer-day* was pitcht upon, as moſt proper for the execution of it, when the ſhips were departed out of the harbour of the *Receif*. For the *Portugueſe* were not ignorant, that we having received no freſh ſupplies, eſpecially of gun-powder, for a conſiderable time out of *Holland*, our magazines were but very indifferently ſupplied both with ammunition and proviſions; and that conſequently we muſt ſoon be reduced to great extremity, if they were maſters of the field: They knew alſo, that all our ſhips, except two, were ready to ſail with the firſt fair wind, being already fallen down to the *Red-Land*; thus being ſenſible of our weakneſs, the *Portugueſe* propoſed to themſelves no leſs than the conqueſt of the whole *Dutch-Braſil* at one ſtroke. But the whole deſign being diſcovered before *Midſummer-day*, it vaniſh'd into ſmoke, both ſides betaking themſelves to decide the matter by arms. 1643.

Pretences of the Portugueſe.

The *Portugueſe* pretended not ſo much the Allegiance due to their king, as liberty of conſcience; notwithſtanding which, we have all the reaſon in the world to imagine, that this inſurrection was undertaken not only with the knowledge, but alſo at the inſtigation of the court of *Portugal*, and of thoſe of the *Bahia*; it being very improbable, that *Kamaron*, *Henry Dias*, and the reſt of the ring-leaders, ſhould without the approbation of the king of *Portugal*, have attempted to attack us by open force. Beſides this, *Mucheron* declares to have read in a *Portugueſe* commiſſion theſe words: *This revolt and war undertaken for the honour of God, the propagating of the roman catholick faith, for the ſervice of the king and common liberty:* He further adds, that he has heard ſeveral *Portugueſe* ſay, that if they miſcarried in their deſign of chaſing us out of *Braſil*, to deſtroy all with fire and ſword, thereby to bereave us of all future proſpect of receiving any benefit from thoſe lands; which done, they would retire with their wives and children to the *Bahia*, or ſettle in ſome more remote place, where they might be ſecure againſt any attempts of the *Dutch*. There have indeed been ſome, who, conſidering the unſettled eſtate of the king of *Portugal*, and the odd fancy of his reign, have thought it very improbable, he ſhould involve himſelf in a war with us, or have given his conſent to this inſinuation, but the event has ſufficiently contradicted that opinion.

A letter from the heads of the rebels to the council.

The 22[d] of *June* a letter was delivered to the *great council*, ſigned by *John Fernandes Vieira*, *Antonio Kavalkanti*, *John Peſcoa*, *Manuel Kavalkanti*, *Antonio Bezerra* and *Coſmo de Craſto Paſos* in which they complained, that they being a conſiderable time ago accuſed by the *Jews* of a treacherous

1643. rous design against the government, had been great sufferers upon that score; that now they being informed by the same *Jews* that they were in danger of losing all their mills and lands, to be given to certain *Hollanders*, who were sent for, for that purpose, they desired that the time of five days appointed in the last pardon might be prolonged, as being too short for a business of such moment, and that the said pardon might be granted without exception; which they refusing to grant, they did hereby protest before God and all the *Roman* catholic princes, that they thought themselves innocent, and not in the least guilty of all those miseries which might ensue from this refusal hereafter.

The council debates the matter.

The 23[d] in the morning the council was assembled, to consider of the said letter; where after several harangues upon the present state of our affairs and the enemy's design against us, they were divided in their opinions, some being for granting a general pardon, without the least exception, as the case stood with us at present, when we were destitute of sufficient provision, ammunition and men; others maintained, that a letter which contained so many notorious untruths deserved not the least answer; others were of another opinion. Whilst they were thus debating the matter, letters were brought to the council, written by lieutenant colonel *Haus* from *St. Antonio*, that he was ready to attack the rebels of *Pojuka* the next day, not without hopes of good success, so that the council considering of what moment the event of this action was to their affairs, resolv'd to adjourn the said debate 'till the next day, when they hoped to know the issue of the whole enterprise.

The 28th of *June*, *Mucheron* arrived with his two companies in the *Receif*, from the *Allegoas*, where it was resolved to dispose his own company in the *Quinqueregular* fort, of which, as a place of great consequence, he was made commander in chief; the other of captain *William Lambert* was put in the fort *Ernestus*.

Good news out of Parayba.

By letters from *Paul Linge*, governor of *Parayba*, dated the 25th of *June*, we received advice, that the inhabitants thereabouts offered to give him fresh assurance of their fidelity, by taking a new oath of allegiance, and that he did not observe the least motion towards an insurrection.

Jacob Dassine master of the sugar-mill *Supapema*, who had been abroad with a good party, made his report to the council, that he had been at several sugar-mills, where he had met with about two hundred of the enemies troops divided into divers small bodies, composed of *Portuguese*, mulatts and negroes, under the command of *Amador de Araouje*, *Antonio de Crasto*, one *Taborda* and *Henry Dias*. 1643.

The 29th of *June*, by special commission from the council, *Balthasar Vander Voerden* examined *Antonio d'Oliveira*, concerning the design of the *Portuguese* form'd against our government. He declared, that about the beginning of this present *June*, being then at the house of *Sebastian de Karvalho*, together with *Francisco d'Oliveira*, *Bernardin Karvalho*, and the before-named *Sebastian de Karvalho*, a certain *Portuguese* very well known to them all, delivered to him a letter, directed to all the persons there present, with another piece of writing unsealed, which he began to read; but finding the contents to be, that the underwritten persons promised to be, and declare themselves faithful subjects of the king of *Portugal*, and that *John Fernandes Vieira*, *Francisco Beringel*, *Antonio de Sylva*, and several more, whose names he would not look upon, had signed the same, he returned the said writing, and refused to subscribe the same, telling his son at the same time, *You ought rather to suffer your hand to be cut off, than sign this paper*; and so went his way immediately, not any one of all there present having subscribed their names at that time: He protested he knew not the hand-writing. After a more serious consideration, he thought it requisite to make a discovery of it, which he did accordingly within two days after, to *Matthew Reex*, desiring him to give an account of it to the great council; he declared further that the said writing was signed by above one hundred of the inhabitants.

Before-named examination and confession of Antonio Oliveira.

The 30th of *June* one *Digos Lopes Leyte*, who was not long ago taken prisoner by the *Brasilians*, was examined by Mr. *Bullestrate*, *Dortmont* and some other military officers. His confession was, that at the first beginning of the design of the *Portuguese* against this state, they had sent a letter to the governor of the *Bahia*, *Antonio Telles de Silva*, to crave assistance from him, which if he refused, they would seek for aid in *Spain*; and if they did not succeed there, they would rather surrender themselves to the *Turks*, than endure any longer the ill treatment they met with from the *Hollanders*. That nevertheless he had heard many dire imprecations made against *John Fernandes Vieira*; that he deserv'd no less than the gallows, he having raised this rebellion for no other end, than thereby to free himself from the vast debts he owed to the company.

Digos Lopes Leyte *examined.*

The same day it was agreed to send abroad a party of twelve soldiers and eight *Brasilians*, to fetch a good quantity of *Fa-*

1643. *rinha* from *St. Lawrence*, who were put to the rout near that place, ſo that very few eſcaped. At the ſame time the council received the unwelcome news, that ſome of the inhabitants of *Iguaraſu* had taken up arms againſt them.

In the beginning of *July* it was reſolved to draw the fortifications of *Maurice*'s *Town* into a narrower compaſs, and to add a new line with a breaſt-work. This task was performed by the negroes belonging to the inhabitants of *Maurice*'s *Town* and the *Receif*, under the conduct of vice-admiral *Lichthart*, who took care to have the ſame perfected, according to the model drawn by the engineer.

The ſame day advice was brought, that *John Lawrence Frances*, and *John Dias Leyte*, inhabitants of *Iguaraſu*, made it their buſineſs to incite the inhabitants to an inſurrection. Captain *Sluyter* ſent alſo word from *Tamarika*, that about eighty men, and one hundred ten women and children, all *Braſilians* of the villages of *St. Michael* and *Naſſau*, were come into that iſland for ſhelter, and that the *Braſilians* of *Otta* intended to do the like. The magiſtrates and chief *Portugueſe* of *Goyana*, gave the council freſh aſſurances of their fidelity, provided they might in caſe of neceſſity be allowed to retire into the ſaid iſland, which was granted, and thanks given them for their loyalty. The magiſtrates of *Iguaraſu* adviſed, that *Vieira* had cauſed a declaration to be affixed in the ſugar-mills of *Gonſalvo Novo de Lira*, which they had order'd to be torn down, and ſent a copy of it to the council, aſſuring them, that they would take all poſſible care to keep the Inhabitants thereabouts under obedience, tho' they found ſome of them much inclined to a revolt.

Fernandes Vale examined.

At the ſame time *Fernandes Vale* was examined by Mr. *Vander Voerde* and Mr. *Bas*; he declared, that having received a letter from *Sebaſtian de Karvalho*, to meet him the next morning upon the hills *Garapes*, becauſe he had ſomething to communicate to him, concerning no leſs than their eſtates, lives and honour; he without mentioning any thing of it to his wife or brother, went thither on horſe-back, accompanied only by a boy; notwithſtanding he happened at that time to be afflicted with the gravel; there he met *Sebaſtian Karvalho*, with one boy only, who told him, that he having received a letter, with another writing, containing a project of an inſurrection to be undertaken againſt the government, he thought it abſolutely neceſſary, to give notice thereof to the great council; and that he deſired him to write a letter accordingly to the council; he being pretty well verſed in the *Dutch* Tongue. 1643.
That *Vale* ask'd him, whether any body beſides himſelf knew of the matter, unto which he anſwered, that his Brother *Bernardin* did, whoſe opinion was likewiſe to diſcloſe it to the council; hereupon they returning each to their reſpective homes, *Vale* writ a letter in *Portugueſe*, purſuant to the inſtructions he had received from *Karvalho*, for whom the ſaid letter was left to peruſe in a baker's houſe, on a publick fair-day for the ſale of negroes; after which he had ſent the ſaid letter incloſed in another, to Dr. *Markado*, deſiring him to ſee the ſame carefully diſpatch'd to the great council, without mentioning the contents thereof.

The council recal their Ships from the Red-Land.

The great council receiving frequent intelligence, that the *Portugueſe* from the *Bahia* intended to ſend a fleet to the aſſiſtance of the rebels, it was reſolved to ſend orders to the four ſhips, the *Amſterdam*, the *Blackmore*, the *North-Holland*, and *Groningen*, then at anchor near the *Red-Land*, in order to their return to *Holland*, to return forthwith to the *Receif*; the government ſtanding in great need of their aſſiſtance, to prevent the conjuction of the forces from the *Bahia* with the rebels. They received alſo letters from lieutenant colonel *Haus*, dated at *Pojuka* the 26th of *June*, aſſuring them, that he had granted paſſes to above two hundred perſons that were returned to their duty; that two or three of the ring-leaders, excepted in the laſt pardon, ſued for the ſame favour, and that he had cauſed one *Franko Godinho*, one of the chief of the rebels, taken by his people, to be hanged on the gallows he had erected himſelf; that *Amador d'Araouje* being gone from thence with a hundred and fifty men to the *Vergea*, to join with *Vieira*, he expected their orders whether he ſhould follow him, he looking upon it as a faint to draw him from thence. He further told them, that with the *Braſilians* and their wives and children, he was above five hundred ſtrong, and that unleſs they were ſoon ſupplied with proviſions from the *Receif*, they ſhould conſume all the cattle thereabouts.

The great council ſent an anſwer the ſame night to lieutenant colonel *Haus*, requiring him to grant free pardon to all who ſhould deſire it, not excepting the ringleaders themſelves, thereby to weaken *Amador d'Araouje* and his party. That with what forces he could ſpare in *Pojuka*, (after ſufficient proviſion made for the defence of the garriſons, according to their own diſcretion) he ſhould march to the *Receif*, in order to attack *Vieira*, where they need not fear but to be able to ſubſiſt upon what the ſaid *Vieira* had laid up for the uſe of the expected

1643. expected succours from the *Bahia*, and the cattle belonging to the rebels.

But whilst lieutenant colonel *Haus* was employed in securing *Pojuka* against their attempts, those of the *Vergea* strengthned themselves with all possible diligence; to further which, *John Fernandes Vieira* and *Antonio Kavalkanti*, who stiled themselves the heads of this war, did not only affix their declarations round about *Maurice*'s *Town*, and in *Iguarasu*, inciting the inhabitants to rebellion, by promising them considerable succours from the *Bahia*, but their parties also, which they sent frequently abroad, forced those of the open country to take up arms, killing such as refused. The same was practised by *Amador d'Araouje* in *Pojuka*; so, that what with provisions, what with threats and force they got together a considerable body in the *Vergea*, we being not in a capacity to prevent it, because what forces we had were in *Pojuka*.

But judging it absolutely for our interest to stop as much as possible these proceedings, it was resolved to arm some of the lusty young fellows with firelocks, which they were furnished withal by the citizens, (there being none in magazines) and to join with them a detachment of the garrison, besides a hundred *Brasilians*, that were lately arrived under *Peter Potti*.

Captain Blaar *sent abroad with some troops.*

Pursuant to this resolution, captain *John Blaar* received orders to put himself at the head of three hundred men, with whom he was to march with all imaginable secresy from the *Receif*; and by lying in ambush near the passes, to endeavour to intercept some of the enemies Troops, not questioning, but that out of the Prisoners, they should be able to learn where *Vieira* was posted with his main body, and of what strength both he and the succours from the *Bahia* was reputed to be among them. He had strict orders not to molest any of the inhabitants, who were not in arms, but to protect them and their estates, and to receive those who sought for mercy, and bring them into the *Receif*. Orders were also sent to lieutenant colonel *Haus* to march with what forces could possibly be spared out of the garrisons to the south, to the *Vergea*, in order to join with captain *Blaar*, and endeavour to attack the heads of the rebels, which if they could once put to the rout, might be a means to quench the whole fire of rebellion, and to restore peace to the *Dutch-Brasil*.

The first of *July* it was debated in council, whether all such persons as were suspected to have a hand in the conspiracy, ought not to be granted to all that desired it, without exception. The last was resolved upon as conducing most to the quieting of the subjects minds.

The 2d in the evening, the council received advice from captain *Blaar*, that he was posted at *Mongioppe*, with an intention to attack the enemy, wherever he met them. 1643.

The 3d he marched to *Iguarasu*.

The 4th they received letters from lieutenant colonel *Haus*, from *St. Antonio*, importing, that after having left a garrison in *Pojuka* under lieutenant *Flemming*, and one hundred *Brasilians* in *St. Antonio*, he was ready to march to the sugar-mill *Velho*, and from thence to *Moribeka*; where he would expect their further orders.

The condition of Goyana.

At the same time the inhabitants of *Goyana* having fortified themselves in a certain house, belonging to *Listry* their chief magistrate, they desired the council to furnish them with forty musquets, for the use of such among them as were unprovided with arms. Their request was granted, and positive orders sent at the same time to *Servaes Karpentier*, to take this opportunity to disarm all the *Portuguese*, either by fair or foul means; to effect which, he should keep the *Dutch* together in a body as much as possibly he could; his answer was, *he would endeavour to disarm the* Portuguese *by fair means, he wanting power to do it by force.* Besides which, he gave notice in his letter dated the 11th of *July*, that every thing remained quiet hitherto in *Goyana*, but that the *Brasilians*, (contrary to his express orders) claiming a prerogative to be commanded by none but their own officers, pursuant to a decree of the council of nineteen, had in their passages to *Tamarika* plundered several of the *Portuguese* inhabitants.

Most of the rebellious *Portuguese* had left their wives and children in their houses and mills, which as it tended to their no small conveniency, so some of the faithful *Portuguese* inhabitants did propose on the 3d of *July* to the great council, whether it would not be for our interest to oblige those wives and children to quit their houses and mills, and to send them after their husbands. Several reasons were alledged for it.

I. Because the rebels being encumbred with their families, must of necessity make greater consumption of *Farinha*, and other provisions, which would oblige them the sooner to alter their measures, and to change their places.

II. That thereby they would be much disheartened, for fear of a vigorous attack.

III. That they would not be able to march or to change their camp so conveniently as before, or to lurk in unhabitable places.

IV. That by the removal of these women, who served them as spies by the help of

1643. of their negroes, we should take away all opportunity from them, to be informed of our designs.

All which reasons being well weighed, the following proclamation was published.

A Proclamation *for the removal of the rebels wives and children.*

THE *great council of* Brasil, *by the authority of the states general of the* united provinces, *his highness the prince of* Orange, *and the* West-India *company, make known unto every body, that whereas many of those, who have sided with the three head rebels,* John Fernandes Vieira, Antonio Kavalkanti, *and* Amador d'Araouje, *against this state, have left behind them their wives, children and families, which hitherto continue in their former dwelling places; we do by these presents strictly command all the wives and children, whether male or female, whose husbands and fathers are engaged with the rebels, to leave their respective houses within six days after the publication of this proclamation; and to repair to their respective husbands and fathers, or else to incur the penalties due to rebels; it being our resolution not to take the same into our protection; nay, to take away our safe-guards from all such of our subjects as shall be found to harbour or conceal these beforesaid wives, children, and their effects, unless the husbands and fathers of these wives and children shall within the limited time of six days, return to their dwelling-places, and sue for pardon to the council.*

Thus decreed in the assembly of the great council of *Brasil.*

About this time near one thousand *Brasilians*, among whom were three hundred and sixty nine men, the rest women and children, being retired to the isle *Tamarika*, to shelter themselves against the rebellious *Portuguese*, Mr. *Dormont* counsellor of the finances, was sent thither in the beginning of *July*, as supreme director of the territory of *Iguarasu*, to secure that island, which was of so great consequence to the state, in our interest.

The 5th of *July*, a proclamation was issued against the three chief rebels, *John Fernandes Vieira*, *Antonio Kavalkanti*, and *Amador d'Araouje*, declaring their lives and estates to be forfeited, offering a reward for the apprehending of them, as follows.

A proclamation for apprehending the three head rebels.

THE *great council of* Brasil, *by authority of the states general of the* United Provinces, *his highness the prince of* Orange, *and the* West-India *company, send greeting: Be it known by all, that whereas we are fully satisfied that* John Fernandes Vieira, Antonio Kavalkanti, *and* Amador d'Araouje, *setting aside their allegiance, have a considerable time ago entered into a conspiracy against the state, sending their letters throughout several Fregesies of our jurisdiction, to excite our subjects to a revolt; that they have gathered and still are gathering forces to maintain their treacherous designs against this state, forcing our faithful subjects to join with them, threatning with death such as refuse to enter into this rebellion; nay, having caused several, as well* Hollanders *as* Brasilians, *to be murdered upon that score: That they have affixed and published declarations in several places, tending to the disquieting and disturbing the minds of the subjects of this state, with the name and title of governours of this war (whereas they ought to have stiled themselves faithless traitors) covering their villainous designs under the name of the divine majesty, besides many other misdemeanours, whereby they have rendered themselves guilty of high treason. It is for these reasons that we thought it our duty to declare the above named* John Fernandes Vieira, Antonio Kavalkanti, *and* Amador d'Araouje, *and by these presents do declare them enemies of this state, disturbers of the publick peace and our good subjects, rebels and traitors against their lawful magistrates; and to have forfeited all their privileges, rights, lives, and estates; and as such, we grant not only free leave to every one to apprehend or to kill the said* John Fernandes Vieira, Antonio Kavalkanti, Amador d'Araouje, *but also promise a reward of one thousand* Charles's *gilders, to such or such persons as shall do so signal a piece of service to the company, as to apprehend either of those persons, so as they may be brought to justice; and the like reward to any person who shall kill either of the said traitors, besides his pardon for any offence he may have committed before; and if he be a slave, his liberty, together with the reward. We also strictly command by these presents, all the inhabitants of this state, of what quality, degree or nation soever, that they shall not presume to assist the said rebels with arms, provisions, money, men, and ammunition, or harbour, conceal, or advise them in any respect, or keep the least correspondence with them, under pain of being declared traitors, and to be punished as such with the utmost rigour,* &c.

Whilst the great council were thus endeavouring to quench the flame of rebellion, they received frequent intelligence, that besides the succours already come to the rebels from the *Bahia* by land, by way of *Rio St. Francisco*, they expected a considerable fleet from thence; it was resolved

1643. to ſend once more ſome deputies to the governor *Antonio Telles da Silva*, to repreſent to him that *Kamaron* and *Henry Dias* being under his juriſdiction, their entring in an hoſtile manner into the *Dutch Braſil*, could not be interpreted otherwiſe than a breach of the truce concluded betwixt the king of *Portugal* and their high and mightineſſes the ſtates general.

Deputies ſent to the governor of the Bahia. The perſons pitched upon for this purpoſe were *Balthaſar Vander Voerde*, councellor of the court of juſtice, and *Dirk Hoogſtrate*, then commander in chief to the cape of *St. Auſtin*, who being looked upon at that time as a very loyal perſon, was ſent for the 4th of *July*, leaving *Barent Van Ticblenborgh* to command in his abſence. *Francis Krynen Springapple* was appointed their ſecretary, and *Gerrard Dirk Laet*, *Alexander Sylve*, and *Jacob Swearts*, to attend them as gentlemen.

Their inſtructions. Their inſtructions were, to lay open to the governor the true reaſon and occaſion of this inſurrection, and the ringleaders thereof, who would never have dared to attempt it without the hopes of ſuccours, which were ſent them by land through *Rio St. Franciſco*: They were to ſearch into his intentions as near as poſſibly they could, and to deſire him to recal *Kamaron* and *Henry Dias* with their troops out of the *Dutch Braſil*, and to puniſh them according to their deſerts. If they found the governor not inclined to give them due ſatisfaction, by recalling thoſe troops either by publick proclamation, or ſending ſome perſon of authority to bring them back, or by giving them ſome other real demonſtrations of his ſincere intention before their departure, they were to proteſt to, and to declare themſelves innocent of all the damages, murders, and rapines as well againſt the *Hollanders*, as *Portugueſe* and *Braſilians*, already committed or to be committed by thoſe forces. They were to declare to the governor, that they would look upon it as an open breach of peace and act of hoſtility, of which they muſt give an account to their maſters, who, without queſtion would know how to make themſelves amends for the damages ſuſtained; and to proteſt once more, that the *Dutch* declared themſelves innocent of all the miſeries which muſt enſue from their taking up arms for their own defence, after their ſo reaſonable requeſt had been rejected.

Arrive in the Bahia. Accordingly they ſet ſail the 9th of *July* 1645, from the *Receif*, in the ſhip called the *Roebuck*, and coming to an anchor the 17th in the *Bahia*, were in the name of the governor *Antonio Telles da Silva*, complimented aboard their ſhips by ſeveral *Portugueſe* gentlemen, from whom they aſked leave to come aſhore, having ſeveral matters of moment to propoſe to him in the name of the great council of *Braſil*. 1643.

Are admitted to audience. The next day being the 18th of *July*, about noon, lieutenant colonel *Andrew Vidal*, and captain *Pedro Kavalkanti*, with ſome other officers, came in a brigantine to fetch them to the palace; where, after the firſt complements, they delivered their credentials, telling the governor, that out of thoſe he would underſtand that they were ſent to treat with him of certain points, which they were ready to propoſe either now or whenever he ſhould be diſpoſed to receive them. The governor, after the uſual return of complements and peruſal of the credentials, told them, that he was ready to hear them whenever they pleaſed; whereupon they propoſed,

Their propoſitions. That ſome *Portugueſe* ſubjects of their high and mightineſſes the ſtates general of the *United Provinces*, have entred into a cabal, in order to take up arms and attack *Pernambuko*; to effect which, they have by certain letters ſolicited their fellow ſubjects to enter into a rebellion, and provided themſelves with arms, in hopes of ſuccours from abroad. That in the beginning of *May*, *Kamaron* and *Henry Dias* with their *Braſilians* and negroes, and ſome *Portugueſe*, being on their march in an hoſtile manner to *Pernambuko*; *John Fernandes Vieira*, *Antonio Kavalkanti*, and *Amador d'Araouje*, with other *Portngueſe* their accomplices had no ſooner notice of their coming, but they abſconded from their houſes, gathered what forces they could, ſome by force, ſome otherwiſe, publiſhed their declarations, ſtyling themſelves governors of this war for the public liberty; all which they undertook upon hopes of being backt by foreign troops. That through God's mercy their maſters did not want power to protect their faithful ſubjects, and to puniſh the rebels according to their deſerts: But as they could not comprehend what it was that could induce theſe foreign troops to enter their territories in time of peace, in order to aid their rebellious ſubjects againſt them, ſo they were at a ſtand how to deal with them. That the great council as well as all the reſt of the inhabitants, being too well acquainted with his excellency's extraction, exquiſite knowledge in ſtate affairs, and the good neighbourly correſpondency he had always cultivated with our government, than to harbour the leaſt thought that he ſhould give the leaſt encouragement to any of his ſubjects, to aid rebellious ſubjects againſt their ſovereigns: That they were ſenſible he would uſe all poſſible

1643. possible means to prevent it. It was for this reason that they were sent by the great council to give his excellency notice of the hostilities committed by *Kamaron* and *Henry Dias*, desiring that he would be pleased not only to command them not to assist the rebels with their troops, but also to retire out of *Pernambuko* and the other captainships under the *Dutch* jurisdiction; that so the rebels being disappointed of their assistance, might be sooner reduced to their former obedience, and our subjects enjoy the benefit of the truces stipulated betwixt his present majesty of *Portugal*, Don *John* IV. and their high and mightinesses the states general. All which, the great council of *Brasil*, highly recommended to his excellency's consideration, in a letter which was then delivered by the deputies to the governor, which is as follows.

A letter from the great council to the governor of the Bahia.

It is sufficiently known to your excellency with what strictness the truce betwixt his majesty of Portugal *and the high and mighty the states general of the* United Provinces, *has been observed in all its circumstances by the inhabitants of the* Dutch Brasil, *even according to the constitution of those of the* Bahia *and other places, who have of late passed through our captainships; neither have we ever received the least complaints upon that account, either from the king your master, or from your excellency; all which gave us sufficient reason to believe that you would not in the least consent that your subjects should attempt any thing contrary to the said truce. And though some of the* Portuguese *inhabitants, subjects of the states, laying aside their allegiance, have taken up arms and are risen in rebellion against this state, as soon as* Kamaron *and* Henry Dias *at the head of their* Brasilians *and negroes, besides some* Portuguese, *did without licence or the least encouragement from us, enter our territories, contrary to the law of nations, and joining with the rebels, exercised open hostilities against our subjects, not like soldiers but robbers and thieves; yet can we not be persuaded that those troops should have made this attempt by order or consent of his majesty of* Portugal *or your excellency, against us your confederates.*

Thanks be to God we don't want means to bring our revolted subjects to reason, and to destroy those foreign troops; but to shew to all the world how ready we are to fulfil the reiterated command of our masters, to maintain inviolably the truce betwixt his majesty and them; and to remove all sinister interpretations which might be made in foreign courts upon this head, as also to give sufficient opportunity to his majesty of Portugal *and your excellency, to convince the world that you have neither consented to nor abetted this conspiracy; we in the name of their high and mightinesses the states general, his highness the prince of* Orange, *and the governors of the* West-India *company, have sent Mr.* Balthasar Van Voerden, *councellor of the court of justice, and* Dirk Hoogstrate, *commander in chief on the cape of* St. Austin, *as our deputies to you, with full power to propose these points to you, and to desire you forthwith to recall the said* Kamaron, Henry Dias, *and other leaders, with their troops, within a limited time out of our territories, either by publick proclamation, or such other means as your excellency shall think most forcible or expedient, and to punish them according to their deserts; and if they refuse to obey, to declare them open enemies to his majesty; it being impossible for us to conceive, how due satisfaction can be given without it to their high and mightinesses, to the prince of* Orange, *and the* West-India *company, which nevertheless we ought and do expect from your excellency.* 1643.

Subscribed, *Your excellency's*
Well-meaning friends,

On the side stood, Henry Hamel,
A. Van Bullestraten,
From the Receif, P. J. Bas,
July 7, 1640. J. Van Walbeck,
and
Henry de Mucheron.

The governor gave immediate answer to the deputies propositions, that he was so far from sending any succours to the rebels that he had not had the least knowledge of it. That the *Brasilians* and negroes were disbanded by his majesty's order, and that these as well as the *Portuguese* among them, that were come to the assistance of the rebels, could be in no great numbers, consisting (as he supposed) in some vagabonds, or others, who having committed misdemeanours in the *Bahia*, had taken this opportunity to shelter themselves, and flee from punishment, as it frequently happened that such like persons did come to the *Bahia* from *Pernambuko*, which nevertheless had given him not the least suspicion of the councils sincerity. He told them that he was extremely glad to understand the good confidence their masters reposed in him, of maintaining the truce concluded betwixt his majesty of *Portugal* and their high and mightinesses the states general, assuring them

The governor's answer to the deputies.

1643. them that he never should be prevailed upon to act contrary to it, for fear of hazarding his life. And that if he had any such intention, he did not want means to attempt it by the assistance of the *Brasilians*. But that he had never had any thoughts that way, notwithstanding he had been provoked to it by the *Dutch*, who since the truce had taken a *Portuguese* ship and carried it to the *Receif*, which by the bravery of the *Portuguese* was delivered from the *Hollanders*, and they and the ship brought to the *Bahia*; the *Dutch* mariners being dismissed without any punishment. He told them further, that he was not insensible what an opinion their masters entertained of his sincerity; and that he had reason to believe, that they had at this time as they had done before, sent their deputies chiefly to feel his pulse, to enquire into his strengrh, and to dive into his designs. That however, he would communicate the letter to his council, and give them a speedy answer, in order to their return home, pursuant to the request of their masters. Then the governor arising from his seat, the deputies took their leave and returned aboard.

Their second audience. The 19th in the morning they were sent for a shore by a lieutenant, and brought to the house of lieutenant colonel *Pedro Korea de Gama*, where they dined in company of *Andrew Vidal* and *Paulo de Kunha*. Towards the evening they were again conducted to the palace, where the secretary desired them to tarry a minute, because his excellency was busy with closing his letters; after some stay they were introduced to the governor, who told them, that he had understood the contents of the letter, which he found altogether agreeable to the propositions made to him the day before by way of mouth by them, which consisted chiefly in two points.

The governor's second answer. First, the good opinion their masters had of his sincere intention, in maintaining a good correspondency with them, in order to maintain the truce betwixt his majesty and the states general, and the confidence they had of his not being concerned in the rebellion, either by encouraging or assisting the same. Wherefore he desired they would continue in the same sentiments, because he never had made the least infraction of the said truce, neither ever thought of any thing like it, nor suffered any of his subjects to act contrary to it; notwithstanding, said he, the *Hollanders* have broke the same in several respects, *viz.* in their expeditions against *Angola*, *St. Thomas*, and *Marinho*; by the plundering of *Pedro Cesar Mines*, who had been basely used during his imprisonment, 1643. not like a man of quality, being forced to shelter himself among the woods after his escape. They had also taken a *Portuguese* ship in his own harbour. Neither did the inhabitants of *Pernambuko* want reasons of complaint as well as the other captainships; he had understood out of several letters from thence, how the *Jews* were always busy in forging accusations against them, which were taken for truth; and when the *Portuguese* had thereupon absconded themselves out of fear, the *Tapoyers* or mountaineers were armed against them, among the rest they had caused a poor hermit to be hanged. The great council had always given him sufficient proofs of their suspicion, the last embassy being intended to no other purpose (as captain *Hoogstrate* could testify) than to dive into his designs and strength. Thus it was reported and believed, that *Andrew Vidal* and *Paulo Kunha*, with several other officers, were sent by him into *Pernambuko*, though they saw them here before their eyes.

Upon the second point, concerning the troops said to be sent to *Pernambuko*, he gave for answer, that they must be some *Brasilians* and negroes lately disbanded, who were of little account, as we were sensible ourselves: That if a few *Portuguese* were among them, they must be supposed to be criminals who were fled from justice; that he was not unwilling to call them back by proclamation, but feared that he should be but slenderly obeyed, by a sort of people who could not be kept in obedience within his own jurisdiction. That to satisfy our request, and to remove all reasons of complaint, he intended to send his deputies shortly to *Pernambuko*; all which he had more clearly exprest in his letter to the great council, wherewith he would, according to the request of our masters, dispatch us with all imaginable speed.

A reply of the deputies. The deputies replied, that their masters had never entertained any suspicion of his excellency, neither had they given any orders to dive into his designs; but always had a favourable opinion of his firm adherence to the truce, as might be evidenced by Mr. *Andrew Vidal*, who during his stay with them, had liberty to go where he pleased, without any attendance but his own. That what he objected concerning the accusations of the *Jews* was of no moment, the same being never hearkned to, the intended insurrection being discovered by persons of unquestionable credit. That *John Fernandes Vieira*, *Antonio Kavalkanti*, and others their adherents, had always been protected

1643. protected against any false accusations, and had free access to all the counsellors of the court of justice, and those of other colonies, as well as the chiefest among the *Dutch*, so that they had no reason to abscond out of fear for the *Tapoyers*, who never were intended to be employed against them. That they did not know of any hermit that was hanged by them, but remember'd that in an engagement with *Amador d' Araouje*, such a one was shot by the *Brasilians* as he was ringing the bell to give the alarum.

They further told him, that tho' they had no orders to treat with his excellency upon any other points than those that concern the rebellion, they could easily make it out before all the world, that *Angola* and the other places were conquered according to the rules of war, without the least infraction of the truce, it having been expresly stipulated, that the war should continue in those parts till the same was published there. The *Brasilians*, Negroes and *Portuguese* were come in considerable numbers into our territories, not like disbanded soldiers, but well armed, and their coming was not unexpected, but well known to the rebels; but the council was not so much concerned for their number, as to be satisfied under whose authority they had taken up arms against them, that they might deal with them accordingly. But however it was, they desired his excellency to believe, that their masters would be extremely glad to understand his good inclinations, that thereby the effusion of humane blood might be saved; intreating him to send his deputies forthwith with the necessary instructions.

The governor promised to send his deputies soon after their return to *Pernambuko*, telling them, that as he thought himself secure of the good neighbourly correspondency of their masters, so he was resolved to continue in the same on his side. What he had proposed for the rest, had been only by way of discourse, not with an intention to enter into a dispute concerning the legality or illegality of it; tho' it appear'd very odd to him, that they should assist his master at home, and at the same time wage war with him in other parts, under pretence that the peace was not published there; and what had passed with *Pedro Cæsar de Mines* was a thing not justifiable in his understanding.

After the usual compliments he arose from his seat, telling them, that he would send the letter directed to the council to them aboard the next day, and so our deputies returned aboard their ship. The 20th in the morning the secretary of the governour came aboard our vessel, with the governors letter to the council, which he delivered to the deputies, requesting in his master's name, to send him a translation of the letter from the council to the governour out of the *Dutch* into the *Portuguese*, subscribed with their own hands; which they did, and having delivered the same to the secretary, he took his leave and returned ashore.

They take their leave.

1643.

Their return to the Receif.

Our people set sail the same day about noon from the *Bahia* to *Pernambuko*, where they arrived the 28th in the afternoon before the *Receif*, and gave an account the same day of their negotiation to the great council, unto whom they also delivered the letter written by *Antonio Telles da Silva*, and directed to them. The contents of which are as follows.

The governours letter to the council.

The governors letter to the council.

MR. Balthasar Vander Voerden, *counsellor of justice, and captain* Dirk Van Hoogstrate, *commander in chief on the Cape of* St. Austin, *your lordships deputies have delivered your letter to me, in which you are pleased to give me notice of the revolt of some of your subjects against you. I received this news as I ought to do, and should not have been able to receive it without the greatest surprize and discomposure of mind, if I had not been assured in my conscience, that your lordships did not in the least imagine, that this insurrection could derive its source from our government; and, tho' I could upon this occasion enter upon a long recital of the proceedings of my government, tending from its beginning till now, to a sufficient justification, in the eyes of all the world, and of the greatest kings and princes of christendom, that the said good correspondency has been maintained as strictly on our side, as the same is promised in your lordship's letter: But rather than give the least occasion of disgust or difference, by enlarging myself upon those heads, in which your subjects have expresly and manifestly violated the truce concluded and ratified betwixt the king my Master, and the States General of the United Provinces, I will sacrifice the same to the interest of our common neighbourhood, rather than to enter upon a particular account of these miscarriages, in the expedition of* Angola, *at a time when the States General did assist the crown of* Portugal *with their naval force, when our ambassadors residing in the* Receif, *were told, that these troops were not intended to be employed against any of his majesty's harbours, but in the* West-Indies, *tho' at the same time they were embarked for the conquest of* Angola. *The same may be said of the taking of the isle of* St. Thomas, *and the city* Luy de Mapanha, *and the seizing of a* Portuguese

1643. guese *ship upon our coast, loaden with sugar from* Spiritu Sancto. *The commissary* Greening *was dispatch'd hither, under a pretext of buying of* Farinha, *but in effect to sound my inclinations, as he himself confesses, when he says in a certain letter of his,* I was sent thither with this commission, but rather to feel his pulse and try his friendship, than that we were in want. *The unfaithful dealings of the directors of* Angola *in the capitulation with the governor* Pedro Cesar de Mines; *the razing of our fort* Araval *in* Bengo; *the base treatment put upon the said governor, being a person of quality, and a general of his majesty's, are matters altogether inconsistent with the rules of war, nay, with humanity itself, and contrary to the practice not only of the more civilized nations of* Europe, *but also the* Barbarians *themselves. Of the same stamp was the answer given by your council to our ambassador, who urging a cessation of arms in the kingdom of* Angola, *was answered, that the same had no dependency on our jurisdiction, quite contrary to the sincere intentions always observed by me in all our transactions with you; for no sooner did your lordships make complaints to me against one captain* Augustino Condago, *and one* Domingo de Rocha, *who having carried away a barge with sugar, had brought her into the harbour of our city, I sent back the said vessel immediately, and put the captain in prison till he was sent over to his majesty. And that time being informed, that two soldiers living under my jurisdiction, whose names were* John de Campos, *and* Domingo Velho Sigismundo, *had committed some insolencies in your captainship of* Pernambuko, *I caused them to be hanged immediately, looking upon it as a duty not to be dispensed with by me, for the maintaining of our mutual good correspondency: All these beforementioned infractions having never been able to make me forgetful of the reiterated orders of his majesty,* viz. *To improve the effects of the peace and alliances made betwixt him and the States General, to our both sides satisfaction: I must at the same time confess, that looking upon myself as a soldier, (abstracted from the consideration of the interest of the state, and the duty of a subject) I thought I ought not to take tamely so many affronts, and to let slip so many fair opportunities of doing myself justice; much beyond what can be supposed to arise from the conjunction of a few unarmed* Portuguese, *a few discontented Negros, and some rebels, whose protection cannot, as I said before, come in any competition with the several opportunities and provocations pass'd by on our side before, for the common interest; and that consequently our government cannot as much as be conceived to be the hidden cause of this rebellion, as your lordships themselves are pleased to confess;* 1643.
neither would I have entred upon a recital of those particularities, if I had not thought my self obliged both in duty and affection, to give this satisfaction to you. To give you the true account of the absence of Henry Dias, *you must know, that one night he left his guard in* Rio Reael, *and passed over to your side;* Don Antonio Philippo Kamaron, *captain of the* Brasilians, *being sent after him, and not returning, I judged that they were gone towards* Mocambo, *to attack the* Palmairas *of* Rio St. Francisco, *which made me (to avoid all suspicion of being concerned in any thing that might tend to the breach of peace) send two jesuits to persuade them to return, but in vain, they refusing to obey, either for fear of punishment, or that they were already engaged with the rebels, (as I now am apt to believe they were) so that I have heard nothing from them since, except what I have understood out of your lordships letter. The* Portuguese *under your jurisdiction have sent to me the reasons which moved them to this insurrection, imploring my assistance, as subjects of the king my master; they told me, that they stood in fear of being sacrificed to the fury of four hundred* Tapoyers, *sent for that purpose from* Rio Grande; *to avoid which, and dreading your lordships anger, awakened against them by the false accusations of the* Jews, *(the most perfidious and irreconcileable enemies of* Christendom) *had rather chosen to expose themselves to a most miserable flight, leaving behind them their wives and children, than to endure the hardships of a tedious imprisonment. I could scarce have imagin'd, that you could be so far misled by the fictions of a people so much despised by all other nations, as to be persuaded by them, that certain persons were sent from hence into your territories, who have been seen here by your deputies. And tho' I am apt to persuade myself, that some of the* Portuguese *would, as the case now stands, be glad to embrace our protection, it being much more natural to be oppressed by ones own king or prince, than by foreigners: Yet when I seriously reflect upon your lordships proposals made by your deputies,* viz. *to oblige captain* Kamaron *and* Henry Dias, *to return to the* Bahia, *and to use all other proper means to bring the revolted* Portuguese *to reason; when I say, I seriously reflect upon the publick calamities on one side, and how destitute I am of suitable means at present to satisfy your desires, I cannot but be infinitely concerned thereat; being sensible that these captains will not be brought over by persuasions; and wanting means to reduce them to obedience, who have now settled themselves at so great a distance among the woods and forests. But as I am ready to conform*

1643. *myself in all respects to your lordships desires, to convince you of the sincerity of the* Portuguese *nation, which is such, that no opportunity, tho' never so great of promoting their own interest, does ever stand in competition with what they think they owe to their confederates: I am willing to take upon me the office of a mediator, in order to endeavour to appease these troubles by my authority; for which end I intend to send to you with all possible speed, certain persons of known ability, with sufficient instructions and power, to the rebellious to return to their duty; which, if they decline, such measures may be taken as will force them to it; which, as I hope, may serve as the most effectual means to restore tranquillity to your dominions, and to cultivate the good opinion and correspondency betwixt us; which I wish God Almighty will be pleased to continue betwixt these two nations, by a perpetual tye of amity.*

Bahia, July 19, 1645. Signed,

Antonio Telles da Silva.

Mr. *Hoogstrate* at the same time gave a secret verbal account to the great council, that soon after their arrival there, *Andrew Vidal*, captain *Paulo Kunha*, and *John de Sousa* came to them, the last of whom sat himself down near him, (Mr. *Hoogstraten*) enquiring secretly after his uncle *Philip Pays Baretto*, whether he was among the mutineers; to whom he gave for answer, that he was still in his mill. After which, the table-cloth being laid, *Sousa* was invited to stay at dinner with them, which he refused; because, as he said, he was upon the guard: Before dinner was ended *Sousa* came back, and after the table-cloth was taken away, invited Mr. *Hoogstrate* and *Kunha* to smoke a pipe with him in a back room, whither they went, but were followed by the secretary, Mr. *Springapple*. As they passed through a gallery, *Paulo de Kunha* took *Springapple* a little on one side; and in the mean while, *Sousa* told *Hoogstrate* with a loud voice, that he was surprized to hear that his uncle *Philip Pays* had not sided with the rest: Unto which *Hoogstrate* answered, *That he thought he did very wisely to keep himself quiet, because it was likely to turn to no account. That is your opinion,* reply'd *Sousa, but have a little patience; and, because I know you to have always been a friend to the* Portuguese, *I can assure you it will turn to a considerable account. And it is upon this score, I advise you, like a friend, to provide for your own safety and your family. You may rest assured, that if you will engage to do a piece of good service to the king my master, and to the governor, you shall want neither money, sugar-mills, places, nor preferments.* 1643.

Hoogstrate *it tempted by the* Portuguese Sousa.

Mr. *Hoogstrate* appearing somewhat discomposed at this discourse, told him, *That though he was not unwilling to do the king and governor what service he could, he did not know what sort of service he meant.* Unto which, *Sousa* replied, *I am sure you are able to do good service to the king; but then,* says *Hoogstrate, you must tell me how: That I will,* answered *Sousa; are you not governor on the cape of* St. Austin? Unto which Mr. *Hoogstrate* said, *Yes, I am; then,* replied *Sousa, all that is required of you, is, to surrender the said fort, with all its works, into the king's hands, that we may land our men thereabouts: If you will promise to do it, you shall have a very ample reward, and be made commander in chief of our forces.* Mr. *Hoogstrate* gave for answer, *that these were things of such a nature, as were not consistent with his oath and honour.* Their discourse being interrupted at that time by the coming of another person into the gallery, *John Sousa* and *Paulo Kunha* went out another way. Mr. *Hoogstrate* told his secretary, Mr. *Springapple*, with a discomposed look, *What is the meaning of these dogs, do they take me for a traitor?* He was going on to say more, when *Sousa* and *Kunha* returning into the gallery, took him aside, and told him, *That he might be sure every thing should be performed that had been promised him; that if he wanted any money he should have it immediately; and for the rest, they would introduce him alone to the governor, to receive the confirmation of it from his own mouth.* Mr. *Hoogstrate* reply'd, *What you desire is not in my power to perform, if I would never so fain; because I am promised to have a commission of mayor immediately after my return, and then I shall certainly be employed in another place.* During this parley, Mr *Vander Voerde* entred the gallery in company with Mr. *Andrew Vidal*, who entertained him all the while the others were talking together, till *Hoogstrate* taking his opportunity as they were walking together, whispered Mr. *Vander Voerde* in the ear, *I wish I was well rid of them, to talk with you in private, for I know not what their design is; I am afraid they will either kill or detain me here.* Mr. *Vander Voerde* would willingly have made a reply, but could not, by reason *Sousa* and *Kunha*, and *Piedro Korre de Gama*, (the last of which understood *Dutch*) were so near them; so that he thought it the safest way to dissemble, and to pretend as if they had been talking about some indifferent matter. Mr. *Hoogstrate* then told *Sousa*, that he had a great mind to pay a visit to *Donna Katharine de Melo*, mother-in-law

1643. law of *Philip Pays Sousa*; he answered him, that he would ask the governor, who having given his consent, *Hoogstrate* went thitherward with *Sousa*, and at his going out of the gallery, whispered *Vander Voerde* again in the ear, *They have catch'd a mackrel, for I intend to act the hypocrite to the life.* As they were walking along the street to madam *de Melo*'s house, *Sousa* and *Kunha* repeated their former discourse, endeavouring to encourage Mr. *Hoogstrate*, by hopes and promises of great reward, both from the king and governor, with whom they said he should confer in private concerning the point in hand, and that in the following manner.

After their return from madam *de Melo*'s, to the house of *Piedro Korre de Gama*, where *Vander Voerde* expected their coming, *Kunha* was to go privately to the governor, to agree with him, that when Mr. *Vander Voerde*, *Hoogstrate*, *Sousa*, and *Kunha*, should come to speak with him, he should by his secretary, desire them to stay a little while. In the mean while, *Sousa* was to ask Mr. *Hoogstrate* to take a glass of wine with him, and under that pretence bring him to the chamber of the confessor of the governor, where they were to have this private interview. Accordingly, *Paulo de Kunha* went to the governor, whilst *Hoogstrate* and *Sousa* were returning to *Piedro Corre de Gama*'s house; when *Sousa* entertained him with nothing else, but the probability of succeeding in their enterprize against the *Dutch Brasil*, telling him, that the governor stay'd only for the coming of *Salvador Korrea de Saa* and *Benevides*, who were expected with four galleons from *Rio Janeiro*, besides some other ships; and that twenty five hundred men were designed for this expedition, besides those already in arms in *Pernambuko*, who were to be sent from the *Bahia*, and to be landed on the Cape of *St. Austin*; *This is*, said *Sousa*, *the governor's request to you.*

Scarce were they returned to the house of *Piedro Korrea de Gama*, when *Andrew Vidal* came and told them, that the governor was ready to receive them; so they went to the palace, where they were no sooner come within the anti-chamber, but the governor's secretary came to desire them to tarry a little, the governor being busy with closing some letters. So whilst some *Portuguese* were entertaining Mr. *Vander Voerde* near the window, says *Sousa* to Mr. *Hoogstrate*, *Come, shall you and I take a glass of wine in the mean while?* Which Mr. *Springapple*, secretary of the embassy understanding, told him, that he would go along with them; but *Paulo de Kunha*, and some other *Portuguese* taking him aside, kept him in discourse, whilst Mr. *Hoogstrate* was conducted by *Sousa* into the confessor's chamber. 1643.

Mr. Hoogstrate's private interview with the governor.

Within a few minutes after, the governor *Antonio Telles da Silva*, entring the room, saluted Mr. *Hoogstrate* very courteously, and setting himself in a chair near him, order'd the chamber to be lock'd, no body being present besides themselves but *Sousa*. The governor then told Mr. *Hoogstrate*, that he had always taken a particular notice of his character, of his being a friend to the *Portuguese*, that he hoped he would continue in the same opinion, and would not refuse the offer made him by *Don John de Sousa*, in the king's and his name; their intention being not to enter into a war with the *Dutch*, but only to repossess themselves of what of right belonged to the present king of *Portugal*, *Don John* IV. and that if count *Maurice* of *Nassau* had stay'd any longer in this country, he himself would have been instrumental in bringing this matter about. Mr. *Hoogstrate* answered the governor, that he should be glad to understand what it was he could serve him in; *You have*, says he, *understood that from Mr.* Sousa, *and I desire you to turn absolute* Portuguese. Mr. *Hoogstrate* told him it was beyond his power, because immediately after his return, he should be provided with a majors commission, and consequently not be employed in the same place: Unto which the governor reply'd, *You need not question any place of honour or profit among us, but it will perhaps not be convenient to discourse together upon this point at present, for fear Mr.* Vander Voerde *should suspect us: But I intend to send two ambassadors, (of which Mr.* Paulo de Kunha *is to be one) to your government, who shall be empowered to treat with you further upon this account. And*, says he, *giving his hand to Mr.* Hoogstrate, *rest assured in the name of the king my master, that whatever Mr.* Paulo de Kunha *shall promise you will be punctually observed and performed.*

Then the governor took his leave, telling him that he would not detain him any longer, for fear of creating a suspicion in his collegue, and so retired into his own apartment. But Mr. *Hoogstrate* and *John de Sousa* were no sooner return'd from thence, but the governor sent for the said Mr. *Hoogstrate* and his collegue Mr. *Vander Voerden*, to confer with them, concerning their proposals, made in the name of the council of *Dutch Brasil*: As they were walking thither, Mr. *John de Sousa* told again to Mr. *Hoogstrate*, with a low voice, and why are you obliged to accept of the majors

1643. majors commission? It is an easy matter for you to tell them, that you would rather continue governor of the place where you now are; and be satisfy'd that when you come among us, that you will not want any employment fit for a good soldier as you are. Mr. *Hoogstrate* being not a little moved with this discourse, was more desirous to get aboard their vessel, as soon as possible he might, to get an opportunity of communicating the whole matter to Mr. *Vander Voerde*; which he did accordingly, as soon as they were entered the cabin, the door of which he ordered to be lock'd immediately.

The Dutch *debate, whether to employ the* Tapoyers.

In the mean while, *viz.* the 5th of *July*, it was debated in the council of the *Dutch-Brasil*, whether for the security of the country, they should not want the assistance of the *Tapoyers*, under their king *John Duwy*, dwelling in *Rio Grande*; who for that purpose had gathered a good body near *Kunhau*, especially since the *Portuguese* committed all manner of barbarities against the *Dutch*, and had summon'd the *barbarians* called *Rondelas*, from the *Bahia*.

But considering the devastations which must needs ensue upon the march of those barbarous people in the flat countrey, it was thought convenient not to come to any certain resolution upon this point, 'till they had advised with lieutenant colonel *Haus*, to whom a letter was dispatched, immediately upon that account.

On the 7th of *July*, the said Mr. *Haus* sent word to the council, that he intended to march the same day from *Moribeka*, and after being joined with captain *John Blaar*, to attack the enemy at *St. Lawrence*; but by another letter of the 16th, written by captain *Blaar*, they were informed that the rebels continued very strong at *St. Lawrence*, expecting a certain reinforcement from the *Matta*, where they had forced the people to take up arms for them; desiring a succour of fifty men, to drive them from thence. Hereupon the council dispatched messengers both to *Blaar* and *Haus*, ordering them to join their troops, and to rout the rebels near *St. Lawrence*, on which in a great measure depended the preservation of the *Dutch-Brasil*.

Haus *and* Blaar *ordered to join.*

The 7th of the same month the council received also a letter from lieutenant *Flemming*, dated at *Pojuka*, in which he advertised them, that he had received certain intelligence, that *Kamaron* was marching against him, and that two companies were already come to the sugar-mill of *Pikdora*. Hereupon orders were sent him, that if he found himself not in a condition to keep the monastery for want of provisions, he should at the approach of *Kamaron*'s troops retire to *St. Antonio*, the better to make head against the enemy. The same day ensign *Hartstin* marched with a detachment of ninety soldiers and thirty *Brasilians*, of the garrisons of the *Receif* and *Itamarika*, to *Ajama* and *Jegoaribi*, in quest of the rebels, but meeting with none returned about noon, and the same evening directed his march towards *Haus*.

Lieutenant Flemming *ordered to retire to* St. Antonio.

The 8th of *July* the council having received advice from *Haus* that they intended the same day to march from the sugar-mill of *St. John Ferdinando Vieira* to attack the rebels at *St. Lawrence*, if they would abide his coming, it was resolved to send as many forces as possibly they could spare to his relief, considering that the preservation of the whole *Dutch-Brasil* depended on the success of this expedition; and accordingly two companies of foot, of *Mucheron* and *Blaar* were ordered to march thither, not questioning but that before their arrival *Haus* would be join'd by captain *John Blaar*; and in effect the next following day they received advice from Mr. *Haus*, that he was ready to join with the said *Blaar*.

The council sends succours to Haus.

The 10th of *July*, the council gave an account by letters to *Haus*, what intelligence they had received concerning the posture of affairs in *St. Antonio* and *Pojuka*, with orders to send as many firelocks and *Brasilians* as he could possibly spare to their relief, to keep the passage from *St. Antonio* to *Pojuka* and *Serenhaim* open; without which all communication betwixt them and the *Receif* would be cut off by the enemy. Two letters of *John Fernando Vieira* and *Antonio Kavalkanti* were the same day read in council, in which they complained of the severity of the two last proclamations, but were not thought fit to be answered; especially since *Amador d'Araouje* had about the same time retired from the pass of *Pinderama*.

Haus *ordered to send relief to* St. Antonio.

Two days before, *viz.* that the council had received letters from Mr. *Hoek*, dated the 25th of *June*, at *Rio Grande*, intimating that hitherto there had not happened any commotions in those parts, that however he had disarmed the *Portuguese*, and that the *Tapoyers* appeared to be well inclined to the government: Orders were sent him to cultivate a good understanding with the *Tapoyers*, for which purpose they sent some presents to *John Duwy* their king, and that the council approved his disarming of the *Portuguese*. On the same day father *Imanuel*, *Lewis Bras*, *Imanuel Ferdinand de Sa*, *Kaspar de Mendoza*, *Furtado* and *Jeronymo de Rocha*, all *Portuguese* inhabitants of the *Dutch-Brasil* delivered their

1643. their petition to the council, requesting, that the time of six days appointed by the last proclamation, for the wives and children of the revolted *Portuguese*, to leave the countrey, being expired, they might be allowed to stay in their habitations at least, 'till the ways, which at that time were rendred unpassable, by the overflowing of the rivers, were somewhat mended. But considering that the *Portuguese* rebels forced the inhabitants by threats and other unusual methods to take up arms against the government, their request was not granted.

The petition of the Portuguese *refused.*

The 13th of *July* the council were advertised by letters from *Haus*, dated the 12th, that he had passed the river *Kapivaribi*, and marching thro' the *Matta* to the sugar-mills of *Arnao d'Ollanda*, had met with four hundred rebels, who at the approach of his troops were fled to *Moribeka*, with the loss of some of their men, from whence they might without any opposition march to the *Matta* of *Brasil*, and that he was ready to march directly to *St. Lawrence*, where he would expect the further orders of the council. They immediately dispatched their orders to him, to pursue and rout the flying rebels with all possible speed, before they could make head again, which done, he should fix his head quarters, in such a place where he was sure he might be supplied with provisions out of the adjacent countrey; their magazines being so exhausted, as not to be in a condition to supply his troops. *Haus* had already in some measure taken effectual care of this point, having in the mean while sent a reinforcement of one hundred foot, and a company of *Brasilians*, under the command of captain *Tallo*, to Mr. *Ley* governor of *Moribeka* and *St. Antonio*. The council also ordered the governor of the *Cape of St. Austin* to strengthen the fort with pallisadoes; and at the same time received Advice from Mr. *Ley* from *St. Antonio*, that the rebels under *Amador d'Araouje*, and *Pedro Marinha Falkao*, had posted themselves within sight of them, in the new sugar-mill, but as soon as he received the expected succours, he did not question to chase them from thence, *Amador d'Araouje* having in vain attempted to force those of *Pojuka*, to take up arms against the government.

The rebels flee before Haus.

Revolt in Pojuka.

He received also intelligence from Mr. *Carpentier* out of *Goyana*, that things remained in quiet there as yet: But whilst *Haus* was busy in making head against the rebels in the *Vergea*, *Petro Marinho Falkao* having declared himself head of the rebels of *Pojuka*, had gathered a body sufficient to block up the garrison of *St. Antonio*, who had no other supplies of provision, but what they received from the circumjacent countrey; so that the council being sensible of the danger, sent immediately orders to *Haus*, to hasten to the relief of that place; who, accordingly directed his march the same night to the sugar-mill of *Lewis Bras*, leaving captain *Wiltschut* with a company of soldiers, and all the sick, behind at *St. Lawrence*. 1643.

The council received also advice by letters from *Paul de Linge*, dated the 12th of *July* at *Parayba*, that things were as yet quiet thereabouts, but that with much ado he had hitherto kept the *Brasilians*, inhabiting the villages, from plundering the *Portuguese* inhabitants, who were extremely dissatisfied, because some of the *Brasilians* and *Tapoyers*, that had done them considerable mischief, were discharged out of custody. They ordered him to take all possible care to keep both the *Brasilians* and *Dutch* inhabitants, who were both for plundering the *Portuguese*, from doing any mischief to them; for which reason the council sent the following proclamation to be publish'd there.

A PROCLAMATION.

WE the members of the great council, having received frequent complaints, that many of the faithful inhabitants of the countrey, who lately have taken a new oath of allegiance to the government, are plundred and robb'd by the soldiers and volunteers; and being resolved to maintain them in the possession of their estates and goods, have for that reason granted them safeguards, and taken them into our peculiar protection; do hereby forbid all our officers and soldiers, as well as the other inhabitants under our Jurisdiction, to attempt to plunder any of the inhabitants, provided with such safeguards, or to endamage them any otherwise, either in their goods or persons, upon pain of corporeal punishment.

The 15th of *July* in the evening, the council was advertised by Mr. *Ley*, that the rebels had kill'd some soldiers of the garrison of *St. Antonio*, that were sent abroad to fetch some cattle from the sugar-mill *Gurapou*, and had so closely block'd up the place, that no provision could be brought thither; and as they were not provided with necessaries for above a few days longer, they were in the utmost danger of being lost. Lieutenant colonel *Haus* being expected the same evening with his troops at *St. Lawrence*, orders were dispatch'd thither for him to go either in person, or at least to send as many able soldiers as he could bring together, under the

1643. the command of captain *John Blaar*, to the relief of *St. Antonio*, the council being of opinion, that the safety of the *Cape of St. Austin*, and of all the southern provinces, depended on the preservation of this place; for which reason, they also ordered captain *Falho*, who was expected about the same time with a company of soldiers, and as many *Brasilians* at *Moribeka*, to march directly to *St. Antonio*, and to stay there 'till further orders; of all which they sent advice to Mr. *Ley*, and Mr. *Heck*. *Haus* having, pursuant to these orders, directed his march to *St. Antonio*, (notwithstanding the weariness of his soldiers tired by a tedious march) *Pedro Marinho Falkao* had no sooner notice of his approach, but he raised the blockade of *St. Antonio*, and with his body of rebels gathered out of the three districts of *St. Antonio*, *Pojuka* and *Moribeka*, to the number of six hundred, joined with the rebels in the *Vergea* of *Moribeka*.

The blockade of St. Antonio raised.

The 17th of *July* the council were advertised by *Haus* in a letter dated at *Moribeka*, that having received a message from Mr. *Ley* and Mr. *Heck* out of *St. Antonio*, with advice, that in *Puerto de Gallinas*, two boats with ammunition were landed by *Pedro de Kunha*, he had sent thither captain *John Blaar*, and ensign *Hartstein*, with a good Body of his ablest soldiers and *Brasilians*, he himself not being in a condition to follow with the rest, disabled by their late marches; for which reason he had put them into quarters of refreshment in *Moribeka*, where he would expect their further orders, as not judging his presence necessary at the *Receif*, now the enemies were fled before him.

Orders sent J. Haus by the council.

Orders were thereupon dispatch'd to him by the council the 19th of *July*, to keep his head quarters in *Moribeka*, the better to keep a watchful eye over the rebels that were retired into the woods; and to be the nearer at hand to succour either *St. Antonio* or *Pojuka*, for which *Moribeka* lay very convenient; but if the enemy should become too strong for him, he should retreat towards the *Receif*. Advice also was sent him, That *Amador d'Araouje*, *Pedro Marinho Falkao*, *John Pais*, and *Kabral*, were with the rebels they had gathered in *St. Antonio* and *Pojuka*, march'd the day before in the morning from *d'Ingenio Moreno Gardo*, to join their troops with those of *John Fernandes Vieira*.

The council likewise received several letters from *John Hoek*, *Rudolph Baro*, and *James Rabbi*, dated the 5th, 6th and 7th of *July*, concerning the present state of affairs in *Rio Grande*, and that they being threatned with an invasion by *Kamaron* on the south side, and by the *Brasilians* of *Siara* and *Maranhaon* from the north, they had disarmed all the *Portuguese* and laid up their arms in the fort of *Keulen*. They had also by the advice of king *John Duwy*, taken into custody a certain *Portuguese* called *Antonio Vetello*, with his son, being accused by the said king *Duwy* of having had a hand in the murther committed upon the *Dutch* in *Siara*, and in the conspiracy of the rebels. They further complained of the ill practices of the *Portuguese*, who sought by all means possible to oppress the *Dutch* thereabouts; adding withal, that king *Duwy* was ready with his *Tapoyers* to fall upon the *Portuguese*, as soon as he received orders for that purpose, which had made many of the *Portuguese* fly out of *Parayba*. 1643.

About the same time, near one thousand *Brasilians*, *viz.* three hundred and sixty nine men, the rest women and children, being fled for shelter into the isle of *Itamarika*, where they were maintained out of the magazines, it was resolved the 21st of *July* by the council, to send thither Mr. *Listry*, to take effectual care, to ease the company of that burthen, that they might be engaged to provide themselves out of their respective *Aldeas*. Things were as yet quiet about that time in *Itamarika*, *Goyana* and *Parayba*, by the good conduct of Mr. *Paul Vander Linge*, governor of the last. For as soon as the fire of rebellion began to break out in the *Vergea*, *Pojuka*, and in *Olinda*, the council being advertised that they ought to keep a watchful eye over those of *Parayba*, where several were suspected of being conscious of the design, they sent the 13th of *July*, *Paul de Linge*, one of the Assessors in the court of Justice thither, with an ample commission, to endeavour to keep the inhabitants in obedience, and to act for that purpose, as he should find it most conducing to the publick security. He was no sooner arrived there, but he made it his chiefest care to provide the forts with sufficient garrisons, ammunition and provisions, which he took from the ships then lying in the road, behind the *Red-Land*: He further took care to secure all the suspected persons, and summoned the rest to take a new oath of allegiance to the government, which they did accordingly.

The council used the same precaution in the district of *Pojuka*, in the *Vergea*, *Garassu* and *Goyana*, where they obliged such of the inhabitants as had not left their dwelling-places to take a new oath of obedience. But the late succours sent thither from the *Bahia* frustrated all these endeavours.

Propositions made by Mr. Ley to the council.

On the 24th of *July*, Mr. *Ley* came with credentials from *St. Antonio* to the council, unto

1643. unto whom he made the following propositions.

I. That whereas several young and able men, living near *St. Antonio*, had not listed themselves pursuant to the proclamation issued for that purpose, they desired orders might be sent for all those living in the jurisdiction of *Maurice's Town* and *St: Antonio* in the open countrey, to be obliged to take up arms for the defence of the country.

II. To oblige all such young men as were not able to serve as volunteers, at their own charge, to list themselves for soldiers, and to instruct them in martial discipline.

III. That perhaps it might not be unadviseable to draw the garrison out of *Porto Calvo*, to appear the more formidable in the field.

IV. To divide our land forces into two bodies, the better to maintain themselves in the open countrey; whereas now upon the least motion of the enemy, our whole force was obliged to follow them; and that the garrison of *St. Antonio* should be reinforced with such a number, as to be able to send abroad a good party, for the conveniency of fetching the necessary provisions out of the countrey.

After mature deliberation, the council was of opinion as to the

Their resolutions. I. That the young inhabitants of *St. Antonio*, *Pojuka*, and *Moribeka*, ought not to be forced to serve in the fort *St. Antonio*.

II. That they would empower Mr. *Ley* and *Heck*, to take as many of the young men as voluntarily offered themselves into the service for four months, at nine gilders *per* month, and one months advance money.

III. They were absolutely against the leaving of the fort *Porto Calvo*, but that ought to be defended to the utmost.

IV. What concern'd the dividing of their land forces in two bodies, they would advise with colonel *Haus*, but they approved of the proposed reinforcement of the garrison of *St. Antonio*, for reasons by them alledged.

Lieutenant *Haus Vogel*, by his letters dated the 18th and 27th of *July*, at *Seregippo del Rey* advised the council, that he had sent a detachment towards *Kamaron*, who could not get sight either of any *Portuguese* or *Brasilians*, but that they had taken a single *Portuguese*, who was charged with letters to be carried to *Rio St. Francisco*: He told them, that *Kamaron* with some troops was march'd through *Rio St. Francisco* into the captainship of *Seregippo del Rey*; and that three or four small vessels or *caravans*, with some troops under the command of *Andrew Vidal*, were sail'd from the *Babia* to *Maranbaon* and *Siara*. He likewise sent the letters found upon the said *Portuguese* to the council, by which it appear'd, that the first foundation of this revolt had been laid among those of the *Babia*; or at least that they had been made privy to it, and that they had provided these succours. For among others, there was a letter from the bishop of that place, to a certain friar of the *Receif*, in which he told him, that he hoped to be with him before long; whereupon the *Fiscal* was ordered to examine the matter, in order to find out the bottom of this correspondency betwixt these two clergymen. *Certain letters seized and communicated to the council.*

In the mean while the *Tapoyers* of *Rio Grande* (according to Mr. *Linge*'s letter of the 19th of *July*) had murther'd thirty five *Portuguese* in the sugar-mills of *Kunba*, who being of the number of those that had surrendred their arms, pursuant to the proclamation, this caused no small terror among the rest of the *Portuguese* thereabouts, and especially in *Parayba*, where they left their habitations, so that it being to be fear'd they would associate with the rebels, under pretence of self-defence, Mr. *Linge* desired a reinforcement of soldiers to keep the *Tapoyers* in awe. The council therefore commanded Mr. *Astellen* and captain *William Lambert* with his company of foot, besides twenty fusileers, and a detachment of fifty men out of the garrisons of *Parayba* and *Rio Grande*, to take care of the *Tapoyers*, and to conduct them to the *Receif*, *Jacob Rabbi* their commander was ordered to march along with them, and *Rudolph Baro* appointed to provide them quarters upon the road. *The Tapoyers murther thirty five Portuguese.*

Haus having by this time sufficiently refresh'd his troops, writ a letter dated the first of *August* to the council, in which he desired their orders to go in quest of the rebels, and to attack them before they could be reinforced with their expected succours; which being granted him, he attack'd them in *d'Ingenio* of *Balthasar Moreno*, with such success, that he beat them from place to place; 'till on the 3d of *August* they retired to their entrenchment upon a high steep hill, accessible only in one place. Notwithstanding which, he relying upon the bravery of his soldiers, and hoping thereby to put an end to the war, attack'd them vigorously in this advantagious post; but the rebels being superiour to him both in number and in the strength of their camp, his forces were repulsed with the loss of one hundred men, (some say five hundred) among whom was captain *Lor*. After this defeat, *Haus* being sensible that the enemy expected daily a fresh *Haus engages the rebels.* *Is worsted and retires to the Receif.*

2

1643. a fresh reinforcement from the *Bahia*, retired to the *Receif*, where he knew his troops were absolutely necessary for the defence of the place.

Two Portuguese *condemned to death.*

On the first of *August Gonsalvo Kabral de Kalkos*, was by the court of justice condemned to death, having at the instigation of *John Fernandes Vieira*, undertaken to head the rebels in the captainship of *Goyana*. The same fate attending one *Thomas Pais*, an inhabitant of *Tienpio*, who had endeavoured to raise some troops for the said *John Fernandes Vieira*. The same day the great council received advice out of *Serinheim*, (the letters being sent privately in the night time in a small boat down the river to the sea-side) that the rebels began to be very numerous thereabouts, that they were masters of the river, had staved all the boats, and plundred *d'Ingeneo Formosa*, where they carried away the negroes, and kill'd the beasts belonging to the *Dutch*, but spared those of the *Portuguese*. The council being sensible that nothing but force would be able to reduce these rebels to their duty, and that they were from time to time reinforced from the *Bahia*, whereas the *Dutch* troops diminish'd daily, they resolved the first of *August*, to send Mr. *Balthasar Vander Voerden* councellor of justice to *Holland*, to represent to the council of nineteen there, the true state of the affairs of the *Dutch-Brasil*, and to sollicit prompt succours. Accordingly the said Mr. *Vander Voerden* having taken his leave of the council, set sail the next day, with the rest of the ships that lay ready to sail for *Holland*, being instructed with sufficient power and credentials from the council; as follows.

Rebellion in Serinhaim.

Mr. Vander Voerden *sent with a credential into* Holland.

Most noble, honourable, and most prudent lords.

NOtwithstanding the rebels make not the least use of the royal authority, but cover their revolt with the cloak of godly liberty, we were always of opinion, that this rebellion of our* Portuguese *inhabitants has not only been undertaken with the consent of the king of* Portugal, *or at least of his governor of the* Bahia, *but also encouraged and fomented by his authority and conduct. For how can it be supposed that* Kamaron, Henry Dias, *and the other ringleaders, should have dared to attempt to attack us by force of arms without his approbation? It was likewise our constant opinion, (considering the present unsettled state of* Portugal, *and the alliance betwixt that King and the states of* Holland *against* Spain*) that he would be sure never to acknowledge the transactions of the heads of the rebellion, and the succours sent them, to have been done by his authority, lest the breach of faith and all its ill consequences might be one time or other laid at his door, 'till he thought himself sure in the entire conquest of the* Dutch Brasil. *Our guess has since proved more than too true, for* Antonio Telles de la Silva, *governor of the* Bahia *(as is evident from his answer to our letters here inclosed) denies to have had the least knowledge, much less any hand in the contrivance or the conduct of this conspiracy; laying the blame of this insurrection upon their ring-leaders, who refused to obey his orders; and offering to send certain commissioners to appease the fury of the rebels; and in case they should refuse to comply, to force them by the kings authority to lay down their arms. But how little agreeable this offer of putting an end to this rebellion, is to his real intention, is apparent out of the report made by Mr.* Vander Voerden *and captain* Dieterick Hoogstrate, *under-written by their own hands; in which you will find these express words of the governor:* That the *Brasilians* and negroes were disbanded by his majesty of *Portugal*'s particular order. *The abstracts of the several enclosed letters sent from the* Bahia, *and taken from the messenger by our forces in* Seregippo, *will put it beyond all doubt, that several inhabitants of the* Bahia, *and among them the Bishop himself, had already in* May *last some knowledge of the intentions of* John Fernandes Vieira, *and his accomplices; add to this the depositions of captain* Dieterick Hoogstrate *subscribed by himself, concerning the propositions made to him in private, whilst he was managing the company's business there, in the quality of one of our deputies; which as it directly contradicts the governors answer to us, so it unravels the whole secret of his real intentions. And for as much as all these things are sufficient forewarnings to us, that the rebels will be constantly supplied from the* Bahia, *whereas we on the contrary must expect to be weaken'd more and more in every respect, we judged it absolutely necessary and requisite for the service of our state, to send to you the members of the council of nineteen,* Mr. Balthasar Vander Voerden, *councellor in our court of justice, to give you a verbal account of the deplorable state of our affairs here, in a more ample manner, than the same may be express'd in writing, not questioning, but your lordships will thereby be encouraged to send us a speedy and sufficient succour, to re-establish our affairs here, and to deliver your faithful subjects from the imminent dadger that threatens no less than the ruin and loss of their lives and estates, and desiring you to give a favourable reception to the said* Mr. Balthasar Vander Voerden.

Receif *the 2d of* Aug. 1645.

Immediate-

1643. *The Portuguese prepare for the Invasion of the* Dutch-Brasil.

Immediately after the departure of the two beforementioned envoys, Mr. *Vander Voerden* and captain *Hoogstrate* out of the *Bahia*, being the 20th of *July*, the governor *Antonio Telles de Silva*, ordered all the sea and land men that could be got together in haste, to be embark'd in twelve ships ready fitted out for that purpose; with necessary ammunition, arms and provision, for the intended invasion. *Hieronymo Serrao de Payva* had the supreme command over the fleet, as the colonel *Martin*, *Soares Moreno*, and *Andrew Vidal de Nigreiros* had over the land forces, both officers in the service of the king of *Portugal*. The orders given to the admiral by the governor, dated the 20th *July*, contained in substance, that the great council of the *Dutch-Brasil* having notified to him the insurrection of the *Portuguese* inhabitants of *Pernambuko*, he had judged it expedient to equip his fleet, in order to put a speedy stop to those disorders; because he was willing to comply with the said councils request, in respect of the sincere friendship and correspondency betwixt the crown of *Portugal* and them, which he had strict orders from his majesty to observe; whereas it is evident, that the great council of the *Dutch-Brasil* in their letter to *Salvador Korrea de Saa Benavides*, of the 13th of *August* expresly declare, never to have desired any assistance from the governor of the *Bahia*, against the rebellious *Portuguese* inhabitants.

Pretences for this invasion.

Instructions of the Portuguese *Admiral.*

The further Instructions given to the said admiral *Payva* were, that he should directly steer his course from the *Bahia* to *Pernambuko*, keeping about twenty or thirty leagues distance at sea, from the shore; that coming to the tenth degree he should approach the shore, and if he found the wind to blow hard from the south, before he came to the before mentioned height, he should be very careful not to pass beyond the lands point in the night time. After having taken a view of the country, he should, with the advice of his best pilots, endeavour to land his men in the most secure place he could meet with thereabouts, either at *Una*, *Lagamar* or *Tamandare*; being three leagues to the south of the isle of *Alexo*. But if they could not make any of these harbours, they should enter at *Porto Dosser*, *Nambous* or *Lagamar* of *Marakaipe*, lying two leagues to the north of *Alexo*. But if notwithstanding all their endeavours, they also should miss their aim in those places, to make themselves masters of *Porto de Gallinbas*, and to land their men betwixt that place and *Barra Grande*. After they had landed their men, with the necessary ammunition and provisions, he should set sail to the bay of *Pernambuko*, in order to deliver with his own hands the governors letter to the lords of the great council. 1643.

The Portuguese *set sail from the* Bahia.

Accordingly the said fleet set sail towards the latter end of *July* from the *Bahia*, and in few days after arrived in the Bay of *Tamandare*, betwixt the rivers *Olna* and *Formosa*, about four or five leagues beyond *Alevo* and *Serinhaim*. They were no sooner come to an anchor there, but the colonel *Martin Soares Moreno*, and *Andrew Vidal de Nigreiros* landed the 28th of *July* one thousand eight hundred or two thousand landmen, among whom were many reformed officers well appointed, and great store of arms, ammunition, and other necessaries.

Land their men.

The first of *August*, towards evening, three ships with five small vessels appeared in sight of the *Recif*, steering their course to the north, whereupon the council dispatch'd their immediate orders to the two ships, the *Zoutlandia* and the *Zealandia*, to make all the sail they could after them, to observe what course they steer'd, and to prevent their landing of men. About the same time an adviceboat arrived from admiral *Lichthart*, with letters to the council, intimating, that he had seen the said ships, and that he supposed their intent to be, to land some men on the south of the cape of *St. Austin*, for which reason he desired them to send him some ships, and grant him leave to take as many of the garrison of *St. Antonio* as he should judge necessary to attack the enemy; of all which immediate notice was given to the northern parts, to be upon their guard against any sudden surprise.

A false alarum upon the Receif.

But the next following day those ships being got out of sight, several masters of small vessels, that had been near them at sea, reported, that they were heavy freighted ships, which by the strong north winds were forced near the shore, so that it was concluded that they had steered their course towards *Portugal*.

The Portuguese *Fleet sail to* Pernambuko.

Immediately after admiral *Payva* set sail from the bay of *Tamandare*, and meeting with the fleet under the command of admiral *Salvador Korrea de Saa de Benavides*, which was latterly sailed out of the port of *Rio Janeiro*, he returned with him into the said harbour, and on *St. Lawrence*'s day with their joint forces sailed from thence towards the bay of *Pernambuko*.

The first news the council received of it was on the 11th of *August*, by a master of a small vessel called, *John Hoen*, bound for *Seregippo del Rey*, and by commissary *John Barentz*, with advice that they had seen a fleet of twenty eight or thirty ships off of *Una*;

1643. *Una*, or *Rio Formosa*, and that three of them had pursued them, and discharged some of their guns upon them. Much about the same time they received letters from major *Hoogstrate*, from the *Cape of St. Austin*, and the fort *Vander Dussen*, intimating, that *Andrew Vidal*, *Henry Dias* and *Paul de Kunha* were landed at *Una*, and marching to *Serinhaim*, had made themselves masters of the place, where they had given quarter to the *Dutch*, but cut to pieces all the *Brasilians*. The council hereupon took immediate care to send some ammunition and provisions to the said cape, having already, for the better security of that place, ordered Mr. *Ley* and Mr. *Hoek*, two days before, to leave the fort of *St. Antonio*, and to retire with the garrison to the cape of *St. Austin*, before they were enclosed by the enemy. That two ships, the *Deventer* and the *Elias*, which were in the harbour unlading their goods and provisions brought along with them for the service of the company, were ordered to be equipped immediately, in order to join with the other five ships that lay at anchor in the road, *viz.* the *Utrecht*, the *Zealandia*, *Ser Veer*, the *Zoutlandia*, and the *Golden-Doe*. The same Night advice of all what pass'd was sent to colonel *Haus*, with orders to be upon his guard, and to retire with his troops to the sugar-mill belonging to Mr. *Hoek*, or any other convenient place, from whence he might be able to maintain a communication with the *Receif*. Letters were also dispatch'd to Mr. *Dortmont* in *Itamarika*, to Mr. *Carpentier* in *Goyana*, and Mr. *de Linge* in *Parayba*, to advertise them of the enemies arrival.

The council advised the Receif.

They equip some ships.

To supply the want of sea men, many labourers were imprest aboard the ships, as were likewise thirty-five land soldiers of *Moucheron*'s company, who had spoiled their fleet by their last long march; and out of the ship *Elias* were a thousand pounds of gunpowder, and out of the *Douchter* six hundred, sent a shore for the use of the garrison.

Not long after dinner time the enemies fleet, consisting of twenty-eight or thirty ships, appeared in sight of the *Receif*, where they cast anchor to the north of four of our ships and a yacht, which lay in that road; so that the next following night was spent in ballasting the two ships, the *Elias* and *Deventer*, and in fitting them for the sea. The next morning with break of day the *Portuguese* admiral who carried the white flag, sent *Martinho de Rebeira* and *Balthasar de Castilho*, as his deputies aboard the *Dutch* admiral *Cornelius Lichthart*, who brought four letters, *viz.* two from the governor of the *Bahia*, *Antonio Telles de Silva*, the first dated the 21st, and the second the 22d of *July*, the third from the *Portuguese* admiral, *Salvador Korrea de Saa Benavides*, and the fourth from *Jeronymo Sarrao de Pavia*, dated the 12th of *August*; besides another letter from the before-mentioned governor, directed to *John Fernando Vieira*, *Anthony Kavalkanti*, and the other heads of the *Portuguese* rebels. 1643.

Letters sent to the council.

Admiral *Lichthart* carried the said deputies ashore, in order to deliver the letters to the council; which being translated, were read at the meeting of the council the 14th of *August*, as well those of the governor from the 21st, 22d, and 24th of *July*; as from *Salvador Korrea de Saa Benavides*, commodore of the *Portuguese* fleets, and *Jeronymo Sarrao de Pavia*, who had landed *Andrew Vidal* with his men near *Rio Formosa*.

The first letter was as follows.

The first letter.

Pursuant to your lordships letter, and the propositions made in your behalf by your deputies, Mr. Balthasar Vander Voerden *councellor of justice, and* Dieterick Hoogstrate *governour of the* Cape of St. Austin, *in which you requested the recalling of the troops under* Henry Dias; *I being desirous to fulfil my promise, sent to you in my answer by the most effectual means that I could possibly think of, have sent you the two colonels* Martin Soares Moreno, *and* Andrew Vidal de Negreiros *(both persons of unquestionable conduct and prudence) to the captainship of* Pernambuko, *with full power and instructions, to reduce the revolted* Portuguese *to their due obedience, for which reason also I have sent a letter to the said rebels, to exhort them to the remembrance of their duty, and to lay down their arms. Which that it might prove the more effectual, I have sent thither suffitient force, which may be serviceable to your lordships, to reduce those that remain obstinate to reason, and to chase the rebellious troops out of your dominions. I hope that with God's assistance this may prove an effectual means to quench the fire of rebellion, to restore the peace of* Brasil, *and to encrease the good understanding and friendship which has been established betwixt both these nations. We recommend you to God's protection, remaining,*

Bahia, July 21, 1645.

Your lordships affectionate servant,
Antonio Telles de Sylva.

The second letter of the said governor to the council runs thus,

The

1643.

The second letter.

I *Have dispatched my orders to colonel* Jeronymo Sarrao de Pavia, *captain-major of our fleet (which I have sent to your assistance) to deliver these presents to you, immediately after the landing of the forces aboard the said fleet, and to offer in my name all the assistance he is able to give you, pursuant to my command and your lordships request. I am very ready to embrace this opportunity to give you these marks of my zeal for your welfare, especially in contributing what in me lies to the reducing of your revolted subjects to their obedience. Neither do I in the least question, but that by this expedient the flames of an intestine war will be quenched, beyond all hopes of being ever rekindled hereafter; and that I shall have the satisfaction of having been instrumental to answer the expectation of your lordships, pursuant to the proposals made to me upon that account in your behalf. So recommending you to God's protection, I rest*

Bahia, July 22, 1645. *Your lordships affectionate servant,* Antonio Telles de Sylva.

Besides these he sent another letter by *Don Salvador Korrea de Saa Benavides*, admiral of the *Portuguese* fleet, directed to the council of *Dutch Brasil*, as follows,

The third letter.

W*Hilst I was endeavouring to satisfy the request made to me by your ambassadours, and busied in embarking the forces designed for your service, under the command of the two colonels* Martin Soares Moreno *and* Andrew Vidal de Nigreiros, *together with coloiel* Jeronymo de Payva, *captain-major of the forces,* Salvador Korrea de Saa Benavides *admiral of this state, and a member of the council of transmarine affairs, established by authority of the king my master, happened to arrive by God's peculiar direction, with his fleet from* Rio de Janeiro, *in the* Bahia, *in order to conduct them to* Portugal. *But being desirous to redouble my efforts, as well in the conduct of his person as in the strength of his fleet, to render the whole the more serviceable to your lordships, I thought convenient to send the said admiral with the fleet under his command, in conjunction with the rest, to the revolted captainship, not questioning but that by his prudent conduct and authority, he will be very instrumental in restoring the peace in your dominions, according to our utmost wishes; and I live in hopes, that this may serve as real demonstrations of the good understanding and friendship I am willing to cultivate betwixt these two states, both as a just friend and good neighbour. I recommend you to God's protection.* 1643.

Bahia, July 25, 1645. *Your affectionate servant,* Antonio Telles de Sylva.

The chief contents of these letters tended to persuade the great council of the *Dutch Brasil*, that the governor of the *Bahia* had, pursuant to the request made by the deputies of the said council to him, sent certain land forces under the command of the two colonels *Martin Soares Moreno*, and *Andrew Vidal de Nigreiros*, aboard the fleet commanded by *Jeronymo Sarrao de Payva*, in conjunction with the whole fleet of *Rio de Janeiro*, under the conduct of admiral *Korrea*, to assist them both by sea and land, as is evident from the words of the preceding letters: He also requested by his deputies, *viz.* captain *Martinho de Rebeira*, and auditor-general *Balthasar de Kastilho*, that the great council would be pleased to acquaint the king his master with it, in a particular letter from them to his majesty. *The contents of these letters.*

What deserves our particular observation in his letter to *John Fernandes Vieira*, and the rest of the rebels is, that he calls them *the king's subjects, unto whom he has sent this succour for their defence*; yet with this restriction, in order to reduce them by all gentle means to their former obedience to the *Dutch* government. It being evident that the propositions made by our deputies to the governour *Telles* tended to no other purpose than to engage him to recall *Kamaron* and *Dias*, and such others as were come to join with the rebellious *Portuguese*, out of the *Dutch Brasil*, and in case of refusal to declare them rebels and enemies to the king of *Portugal*; but he directly contrary to the intention and request of the said council; had instead of recalling them, sent these forces to their succours; and instead of leaving them to the disposal of the council, had caused them to be landed in a remote place, where the said *Kamaron* and *Dias* were with their forces at that time. Neither was the council ignorant of their intention, in sending a fleet into the road of the *Receif* at this juncture; tending to no other end than to back the revolted rebels in their design, and to encourage the rest to take up arms against them.

The council was fully satisfied as to this point, when they received advice from the cape of *St. Austin*, that the garrison of *Serinhaim* had been forced to surrender to *Andrew Vidal* after his landing thereabouts. Their

1643. Their chief debate then turned upon this point, by what means this fleet might be removed from the road of the *Receif* and our coasts; considering that the whole naval force of the *Dutch* then ready to sail, consisted only in five ships, *viz.* the *Utrecht*, *Zelandia*, *Ter Veere*, *Zoutlandia*, and the *Golden Doe*, not very well manned, and but indifferently provided with ammunition, especially with gunpowder, and few soldiers could be drawn out of the neighbouring garrisons; whereas the *Portuguese* fleet consisted at least in eight or ten stout ships, the admiral being a two-deckt ship, resembling at a distance one of their large galeons, so that the attacking of them appeared to be a hazardous enterprize. After mature deliberation it was unanimously resolved in the said council, to return thanks to the admiral *Salvador Korrea de Saa Benavides*, for the offered succours against the rebels, and to tell him the reasons that obliged us to desire him to retire with his fleet out of our road, as will more at large appear out of the following letter: It was thought convenient to dispatch the said letter immediately, and whilst we staid for his answer, to use all possible diligence in equipping the two beforementioned ships, the *Deventer* and *Elias*; that if the *Portuguese* refused to comply with the councils request, we might be in a condition to attack them, and to drive their fleet from our coast, without which we saw but little probability to make our party good against the rebels, as long as they were backed by constant supplies from the *Bahia*. It was also taken into consideration whether it were not expedient to detain one of the *Portuguese* deputies till such time that *Jeronymo Sarrao de Payva*, should according to the request of the council, come ashore in the *Receif*; but this proposition was rejected, for fear of furnishing the *Portuguese* with a new pretence of staying in our road: Mr. *Gilbert de Wit* and *Henry Moucheron*, both members of the council of justice, being ordered to carry the said letter, they went aboard the *Portuguese* admiral the same evening, unto whom they delivered the following letter to *Salvador Korrea de Saa Benavides*.

A letter from the council to the Portuguese *admiral.*

We understand both out of your lordship's letter and those of the governor Antonio Telles de Sylva, *delivered to us by captain* Martin de Rebeira, *and the auditor-general* Balthasar de Castilho, *as also by the verbal assurances given to us by them in your behalf, that your coming with the fleet into our road is with no other design than to assist us with your authority and council in bringing the rebels to reason, for all which we return our hearty thanks to your lordship. But at the same time we cannot forbear to represent to you, that the coming with so considerable a fleet in this juncture, gives us no small cause of jealousy, not only because we never requested any such assistance, but also by reason that instead of recalling* Kamaron *and* Henry Dias *with their troops, the two colonels* Andrew Vidal *and* Martin Soares Moreno, *have under pretence of reducing the rebels to obedience, landed their men and ammunition without our knowledge, in a far distant place, and consequently for the defence of the revolted* Portuguese; *whereas (pursuant to his excellency the governour's promise to us) this reduction might have been much better obtained by a severe proclamation, to oblige them to return to the* Bahia; *or at least the before-mentioned colonels ought to have made their first addresses to us. These proceedings have, contrary to your lordship's intention, drawn this ill consequence after them, that many of the inhabitants imagining no otherwise than this fleet was intended for the assistance of the revolted* Portuguese, *have also begun to take up arms, in order to join with them; which obliges us to return our thanks to your lordship for the offered succours, desiring you would be pleased with all possible speed to retire with the fleet out of the road; which, as it will undeceive the inhabitants concerning the sinister interpretations of your lordship's intentions, so it will serve as an effectual means to keep them in quiet, which at this juncture will work upon us a singular obligation. What relates to your lordships request to take in fresh water and fuel here, being ill provided with both by reason of your sudden departure from the* Bahia, *we should be very ready to comply with it, were it not for the before alledged reasons, and the badness of the season, which would make it very tedious, which obliges us to beg your excuse for this time upon that account. His excellency* Antonio Telles de Sylva *having told us in his letter that he had ordered* Jeronymo Sarrao de Paiva, *immediately after the landing of the infantry under* Martin Soares Moreno *and* Andrew Vidal, *to give us in person a full account with what power he was instructed by his excellency, we desire your lordship to send the said* Jeronymo Sarrao de Paiva *without delay to us, to confer with him concerning the instruction he has received from his excellency, in relation to the sending and landing of these officers and land forces. For the rest, we refer ourselves to our deputies, councellours in our court of justice here, unto whom we desire your lordship*

1643. *ship to give full credit, proportionable to their own merits and the trust we have reposed in them. God protect your lordship.*

Signed by
Henry Hamel,
A. Van Bullestrate,
P. J. Bas,
J. Van Walbeck,
G. de Wit,
Receif, Aug. 13, 1645. J. Albrecht,
Henry de Moucheron,
J. Van Raesvelt,
and
J. Lichthart.

This letter was pitched upon by the before-mentioned great council, as the best expedient at this juncture, till by the conjunction of the *Deventer* and *Elias*, we might be put in a probability of dislodging them by force, if they refused to retire at the council's request.

The Portuguese *fleet leave the road.* The 14th by break of day we saw the whole *Portuguese* fleet under sail, and for the most part out of sight; and considering that the boats, which carried both ours and the two *Portuguese* deputies, would scarce be able to overtake them, and that our deputies in their return were to give an account to our admiral on board his ship, whether, pursuant to the council's letter, the *Portuguese* admiral had consented to send *Jeronymo Sarrao de Paiva* to the *Receif*, in order to open his instructions to the great council, which they had now all the reason to believe he would not, they dispatched immediate orders to our admiral *Lichthart*, to make all the sail he could with the ships under his command after the *Portuguese*, to observe their motions, and to endeavour to come up with the flag ship, on board of which was the said *Jeronymo Sarrao*, to desire him to return with his ships to the road of the *Receif*, in order to confer with the council in person, concerning his instructions. But after mature deliberation, the whole proceedings of the *Portuguese*, and the letters of the governour of the *Bahia* concerning the pretended reduction of the rebels, being looked upon as meer amusements, orders were sent to our admiral *Lichthart*, to oblige all the *Portuguese* ships he could meet with to strike, and to treat them for the future like enemies.

A letter to the council from Rio Grande. The 28th of *August* the council was advertised by letters dated the 20th, at the fort of *St. Magaret* in *Rio Grande*, from the governour *de Linge*, that twelve of the enemies ships, after having landed some forces near *Tamandare*, were come into the bay of *Traikona*; and that according to the deposition of a certain *Portuguese* prisoner from on board the said fleet, they intended to land likewise some men thereabouts, provided they might be joined by the rebels from the *Matta*; but if they failed to come, they would return to the *Bahia*. Whereupon orders were sent to Mr. *de Linge*, to bring what forces he was able together, either of soldiers, *Tapoyers*, or *Brasilians*, to prevent their landing, and their conjunction with the rebels in that captainship. 1643.

The next thing under debate was, whether it were not convenient to send some ships under the command of admiral *Lichthart* that way, to attack the *Portuguese*; after various consultations, it was agreed to stay till all the ships might be got ready for that service, to supply the want of seamen by good able labourers from the *Receif*, and so to render ourselves as formidable at sea as possible could be.

In the mean while the said admiral *Lichthart* set sail the 1st of *September* with four ships and a yacht only, he himself being in the *Utrecht*, but was forced by stress of weather (in which the *Zelandia* lost a mast) and for fear of the rocks, to come to an anchor not far from the *Portuguese*, who endeavoured to gain the wind of him. Mr. *de Wit* and *Moucheron* returned also with their boat, having not been able, by reason of the violent winds to overtake the *Portuguese*, but had put their deputies on board a small vessel to sail after their fleet. *The* Dutch *admiral sets sail from the* Receif.

The same day the council received letters from Mr. *Hoogstrate*, *Ley*, and *Heck*, from the cape of *St. Austin*, that the enemies had posted themselves in the sugar-mills *Salgado*, *Surhague*, and other places thereabouts; and because the *Portuguese* fleet, which had been seen off of the bay of *Traikona*, appeared again in sight of the *Receif* the same evening, it was thought expedient to order admiral *Lichthart* immediately to go on board the *Utrecht*, and with that and the ship *Ter Veere* and two smaller vessels, to keep a watchful eye over the *Portuguese*: Care was also taken to get the ship the *Overyssel* ready against next day, not questioning that when joined by this and the *Zoutlandia* and *Golden Doe*, which were sent abroad for intelligence, they should be able to cope with the *Portuguese*, or at least to force them out of the road. The next morning early the *Portuguese* fleet might be plainly discovered from the *Receif*, but our admiral was not able to stir by reason of the contrary winds; nevertheless the *Zoutlandia* and the *Ter Veere*, which came from the south a cruising, made all the sail they could to escape

1643. escape the *Portuguese*, which they did, being much the nimbler sailors, and joined our fleet.

The 4th of *September* major *Bayert* and Mr. *Volbergen*, complained to the council, that Mr. *Vierbergen* count *Maurice*'s steward, had made it his business to give it out, that they being impowered to cut down certain trees, and some part of the stabling and gardens, for the better fortifying of the fort *Ernestus*, had transgressed their commission, in cutting down many of the great trees, with an intention, as he said, to ruin the whole plantation; whereas they declared, that they had been very careful in preserving as much as possible could be, all the largest cocoa-trees that stood not in their way; that by these rumours the rage of the populace had been raised to that pitch that they had much ado to appease them, they being for the cutting down not only of all the trees, but also for the pulling down of the whole palace of count *Maurice*; all which they desired to be registered in the publick records, to serve them for a legal defence in due time and place.

In the mean time our admiral *Lichthart* being gone out in pursuit of the *Portuguese* fleet, met with them in the bay of *Tamandare*, consisting of seven ships, three smaller vessels, and four barks, the rest being sent loaden with sugar to *Portugal*. He was not as yet joined by all the ships from the *Receif*; but being resolved not to let slip this opportunity of attacking the enemy, sent the 7th of *September* advice to the great council, that being come in sight of the enemies fleet near the bay of *Tamandare*, consisting in all of eleven vessels, he was resolved to attack them there, desiring them to send as many ships as possible they could immediately. Hereupon it was resolved to join the two ships the *Deventer* and *Elias*, with the *Unicorn* and *Leyden*, then lying ready in the road and bound for *Holland*, and such tenders as were at hand, and to send them forthwith to the admiral *Lichthart*. Pursuant to these resolutions, the whole next following night was spent in manning the said ships, but were the next morning detained for some time by the contrary winds.

The same day orders were given to all the soldiers and inhabitants of the isle called *Antonio Vaez*, to provide themselves with baskets filled with earth; and pallisadoes were planted from the point of the *Receif* next to the river, to the utmost point near the sea-side, and five great guns were planted upon a certain wreck, from whence they could command the sea-shore as far as to the fort of five bastions.

1643. *The* Dutch *fight and worst the* Portuguese *fleet.*

The 8th of *September*, the *Dutch* admiral having ordered the red flag to be put up, boarded the *Portuguese* admiral carrying sixty guns and three hundred men: He behaved himself very valiantly, having posted himself at the entrance of his cabin with a flaming sword in his hand, wherewith he killed three or four, but having received several wounds, was at last forced to yield. The rest of the ships following the example of their admiral, had likewise boarded the *Portuguese* ships; but these seeing the flag taken down from the admiral (a dismal signal of her misfortune) they lost all hopes, and threw themselves headlong into the sea, to escape the fury of the fire and sword; whither being pursued by the *Dutch* in their boats, many perished before they could reach the shore. Above seven hundred *Portuguese* were killed in this action, besides a great number of prisoners, among whom was the admiral himself: Three ships were taken and sent to the *Receif*, the rest were set on fire, being not in a condition to be carried off, because they had cut their cables and were run ashore, where the *Portuguese* had planted some cannon upon batteries, which so annoyed our people, that fearing they might run aground within the reach of the enemies cannon, they set fire to them, and with much ado got their ships clear from among the shelves. After this engagement I returned to the *Receif* to take care of my affairs there, and the admiral sent an express in a fisher-boat, with the following letter to the council of the *Dutch Brasil*.

A letter from the Dutch *admiral to the council.*

No sooner were the ships Leyden, *the yacht and the* Doe, *arrived last night, near the point of* Tamandare, *but pursuant to the result of the council of war, it was resolved to enter the next morning within the bar, which was performed in the following order: First the ship* Utrecht *admiral, second the* Ter Veere, *third the* Zelandia, *fourth the* Overyssel, *fifth the* Zoutlandia, *followed by the* Doe *and* Leyden, *and the yacht, the* Unicorn, *the tenders being ordered to be at hand as occasion should require. Being come within the bar, we found the enemy seven sail strong, besides three small vessels and four barks; and that they had planted several pieces of cannon upon two batteries on the sea shore. We received a very warm salute both from their ships and batteries, and several vollies of small shot; notwithstanding which, the ship the* Utrecht *couragiously laid the* Portuguese *admiral on*

1643. *board, after a short but sharp dispute took the ship and the admiral's flag: To be short, the rest of our ships behaved themselves so well, that soon after they forced the* Portuguese *to quit their ships; God be praised for this victory.* Jeronymo Sarrao de Paiva *the* Portuguese *admiral is our prisoner, and at present in my ship, being sorely wounded, whom I intend to deliver up to your lordships so soon as I shall come to the* Receif; *in the mean while, I intend to send back the* Leyden *and the* Unicorn *to morrow morning, according to your lordships directions. And forasmuch as there is likely to be no more action hereabouts, the enemy having strengthened themselves near the sea-shore, I will with the first opportunity return to the* Receif, *where I hope to give in person a more ample account of the whole action; I recommend your lordships to God's protection. In haste,*

From the ship the Utrecht, *within the bay of* Tamandare, September 9, 1645.

Your lordships servant,

Cornelius Lichthart.

The *Portuguese* admiral *Sarrao de Paiva* in his letter dated the 18th of *September*, gave the following account of his engagement to the two colonels *Martin Soares Moreno* and *Andrew Vidal Negreiros.*

The Portuguese *admiral's letter to* Andrew Vidal.

IT *being the general discourse here in the* Receif, *which is likewise come to my ears, that it is reported by you there, how the* Dutch *admiral* John Cornelius Lichthart, *did before the beginning of the last engagement enter the bay with a white flag, thus surprizing our people, killed many of them in cool blood. I thought myself obliged to acquaint you, that indeed two days before the said engagement, a yacht and a bark with white flags, appeared at the entrance of the bay, at which one of our small vessels and a bark shot three cannon shot. But that day when the admiral entred the said bay, he had put up both the* Dutch *and red flags. Neither is it true what had been said of their killing our men in cool blood, there being not one man slain aboard my ship, but during the heat of the engagement, five or six that had hid themselves below deck having received quarter, and a soldier sorely wounded ordered immediately to be looked after with all care imaginable. Neither was there a stroke given after the yielding of the ship, but every body treated and provided for according to his quality and present necessity. The reason why so few had quarter given them was, because most leapt over-board, the sea men first, and then the soldiers; I being not able with sword in hand to keep them from chusing rather to perish in the sea than to stand it out aboard the ship. Two or three persons of note seeing me sorely wounded, freely gave me quarter, without knowing either my person, or being asked it by me; a convincing argument that they would not have refused the same to all the rest that would have begged quarter. I must confess myself so much obliged to the humanity and generosity of the admiral, that it is not to be exprest in writing. Besides that it is unquestionable that we first shot at them, both from our ships and batteries near the sea-shore. I have given you a true account of the whole matter, of which as I have been an eye witness myself, so I don't question you will give an entire credit to what I have written to you on this account. God protect you for many years.* 1643.

Receif, Sept. 18, 1645. *Jeronymo Sarrao da Paiva.*

Andrew Vidal sent a Letter in answer to this by one of our drummers (sent to the enemy upon some errand) dated the 20th of *September* as follows:

His answer to the admiral's letter.

WE *are sufficiently satisfied by your lordships letter, that instead of being entertained according to your merits, you receive the same ill treatment with the rest of our countreymen; though considering that your case is different from the rest, you ought to have been treated in another manner, your lordship being come without the least intention of waging war against them (which they ought to have made due reflection upon) but only as you were going to convoy some ships homeward, did at their own request, land our forces in that captainship; considering the ill usage and tyrannies our subjects have received at their hands, we are afraid we cannot promise your lordship a much better entertainment; of all which murders committed in cool blood, we have taken so circumstantial an account, that we are sure we shall be able to justify our cause and ourselves, both to the states of the* United Netherlands *and the rest of our allies; for we have fished up many of our* Portuguese *with bullets and stones tied to their legs and necks, some had the good fortune to be saved as they were swimming ashore, but many were burnt alive in the wrecks of the ships, the intention of these gentlemen being without question*

1645. *question, by making so general a slaughter among their fellow christians, to cut off from us all hopes of returning home: of all which they will be obliged to give one day a severe account, both to God almighty and those who shall require satisfaction for it at their hands, it being our constant opinion, that they never will be able to justify their cruelties, and the mischief done to our people, either before God or the king our master. We hope your lordship will rest satisfied in this present condition, and put your trust in God and our king, who are still alive to demand a severe satisfaction from them. God protect your lordship.*

From our quarters at St. John *in the* Vergea, Sept. 29, 1645.
signed
Andrew Vidal de Negreiros.

A certain lieutenant belonging to the enemy, called *Francisco Guomes*, came along with the same drummer, with a letter from the said *Andrew Vidal* directed to the great council, the contents of which were as follows.

Andrew Vidal de Negreiros's *letter to the great council.*

I *Received your lordships letter at* Iguaracu, *wherein you seem to be extremely disgusted at the killing of some* Brasilians, *with their wives, by our soldiers; under pretence that the absolute command over them belongs only to you, which I cannot but be much surprized at, when I consider that your lordships in your proclamation, wherein you command not to give quarter to any* Portuguese *inhabitants (though natural subjects of the king my master) you alledge among other reasons; because they had received their birth and education in this captainship (which however was first conquered by the* Portuguese *kings at the expence of many of their subjects) whereas now you would impose this hardship upon the same inhabitants, to give quarter to those* Brasilians, *who not long ago have been maintained and instructed in the catholick faith, as being their vassals, and consequently not yours, but the king my master's subjects. Your lordships ought to remember, that you are not in possession of this countrey by right of succession, or any other legal pretension, but basely by force of arms. We desire your lordships to take effectual measures concerning the methods to be observed in the carrying on of this war, which we hope will be managed so by your prudence, as that quarter may be allowed to the inhabitants of our nation; if not, I shall be obliged to act as I find it most consistent with my honour, to take satisfaction for these injuries. We desire also to put a stop to the murdering of the women, children, and ancient people, in cool blood, as has been done lately at* Tihicupapo, Rio Grande *and* Parayba. *God protect your lordships.* 1645.

From our quarters at St. John, September 29, 1645.
signed,
Andrew Vidal de Negreiros.

The great council returned with the consent of the members of the court of justice, and colonel *Garsman*, an immediate answer to the said letter, wherewith they sent the said lieutenant in company of the drummer, back the same evening.

An account of their proceeding since their landing.

But we must look back to their proceedings: After *Andrew Vidal de Negreiros* and *Martin Soares Moreno* had landed their men, to the number of eighteen hundred or two thousand, the 28th of *July* 1645, with good store of arms and ammunition, near *Tamandare*, betwixt *Olna* and *Formosa*, they were soon after joined, not only by four companies which had taken their way by land from the *Bahia*, but also by the troops under the command of *Kamaron* and *Henry Dias*, who had hitherto kept *Porto Calvo* blocked up by their forces. From thence they directed their march to the city of *Serinhaim*, and laid siege to the fort in which there was only a garrison of eighty *Dutch* soldiers and sixty *Brasilians*, commanded by *Samuel Lambert* and *Cosmo de Moucheron*. Two days after their arrival near *Serinhaim*, the enemy posted themselves in the *d'Ingenio* of *Daniel Hohn*; about which time *Henry Dias* was seen in *Serinhaim*, notwithstanding the *Portuguese* commanders *Andrew Vidal* and *Moreno* disowned to have any correspondence with them at that time: The said commanders had also sent the captain major *Paulo de Kunha* before to summon the said fort, which he did accordingly by his letter dated the 2d of *August* at the sugar-mill of *James Peres*, and directed to *Samuel Lambert*.

The summons sent to the fort of Serinhaim.

I *Am come to this sugar-mill by special orders from* Martin Soares Moreno *and* Andrew Vidal de Negreiros *our governors, they being very busy at present in landing their men; they have sent me before to prevent all mischief that otherwise might happen betwixt you and us; and if in the mean while you will join your forces with ours, or retire with them to some other place, you may safely do it, I being ready to furnish you with passes for that purpose, the before-mentioned governours being*

1645. *being come with an intention to put a stop to the present insurrection. God protect you.*

From the sugar-mill in St. Antonio, August 2, 1645.

Paulo de Kunha.

Two days after the before-mentioned commanders in chief sent another letter to *Samuel Lambert*, very little different from this.

A second summons from the Portuguese *commanders.*

W*E suppose you not to be acquainted with the intention of our coming, which makes us to be the less surprized at your standing upon your defence. The great council of the* Dutch Brasil *have sent an embassy to our governor general by sea and land,* Antonio Telles da Sylva, *to desire his excellency to make use of his authority and forces to appease the insurrection in this captainship, which request being readily granted, in order to be serviceable to the council, and to free the* Portuguese *from the outrages they suffered in their houses and families, we were sent to land our forces near these sugar-mills of* Rio Formosa; *which having been done accordingly, and ready to march further into the countrey, we thought fit to acquaint you with our intentions, which in all probability may have reacht your ears, the same having been published in several places by our proclamations, of which we send you one, desiring it may be affixed on the church of* Serinhaim. *We desire you therefore to lay by your arms to remove all suspicion; not questioning but that we shall meet with a favourable reception on your side, as we on the other hand shall make it our main endeavours to restore tranquillity among the revolted* Portuguese *by all gentle means that possibly may be used; assuring you at the same time, that in case you refuse to concur with us in this design, you will cause no small displeasure to the great council of the* Dutch Brasil. *God protect you.*

From the sugar-mill of Formosa, August 4, 1645.

Martin Soares Moreno,
Andrew Vidal de Negreiros.

The next following day *Paulo de Kunha* came in person before the place with a body of soldiers and boors, provided with arms from on board the fleet, and after having invested the place, cut off the water of the fountains and rivers from the besieged. In the mean while *Rowland Carpenter* and *Daniel Hohn* had been sent away with passes by the commanders of the *Portuguese* forces, who embarked their heavy cannon on board *Carpenter*'s vessel, in order to carry it up the river *Formosa*. Within five days of the arrival of *Paulo da Kunha*, the whole force of the enemy appeared in sight of *Serinhaim* in battle array, and closely blockt up the fort. The *Dutch* garrison was inconsiderable in proportion of the enemies strength, who had so well guarded all the avenues leading to the place, that they were soon reduced to want all manner of necessaries, especially water. Besides this, many of the circumjacent inhabitants and volunteers went daily over to the enemy, who gave them an account of the condition of the fort; and notwithstanding they had sent several messengers to the *Receif*, they had heard nothing from the council for two months last past; so that being without all hopes of maintaining their post, they judged it more for the interest of the company to preserve the garrison, which might be serviceable in other places, where there was sufficient want of good soldiers, than rashly to expose themselves to the fury of the enemies sword: Accordingly *Samuel Lambert*, *Cosmo de Moucheron*, and *La Montagny*, who commanded in the fort, upon the second summons made by the enemy, entred the 6th of *August* into a capitulation with the *Portuguese*, of which *Moucheron* gave an account in person the 15th of *August* to the council, and delivered it the 20th of *August* to them in writing. 1645.

The fort of Serinhaim *blocked up by, and surrendred to the* Portuguese.

"WE the *Portuguese* commanders make "known to every body that we "were sent into this countrey at the re"quest of the great council of the *Dutch* "*Brasil*, to appease the revolt and trou"bles arisen among the *Portuguese* inhabi"tants. But at our landing here, being "informed that notwithstanding this re"quest and our good intention, the *Dutch* "had murdered many *Portuguese* in cool "blood (it being evident that they had "cut to pieces several *Portuguese*, who "were inticed into a church for that pur"pose) and that they had formed a camp "to oppose us, which ought to be a cau"tion to us, not to leave any strong holds "behind us, whilst we are marching to"wards the *Receif*, we have thought it "necessary to enter into this capitulation, "till such time that we may have the oppor"tunity of concerting new measures with "the great council, of which the articles "are as follows:

I. The commanders *Samuel Lambert* and *Cosmo de Moucheron* shall have leave to march out of the fort and castle, with the garrison, with ensigns displayed, all their arms, matches burning, &c.

II. They

1645. II. They shall be permitted to march along the road with their ensigns, and swords drawn, and shall be safely conducted by one or more captains, who also shall be obliged to provide them carriages and boats, for the transportation of their persons and goods to the *Receif*.

III. The *Portuguese* oblige themselves to restore to *Moucheron* all what has been taken from him, and belonged to him before the siege.

IV. They also oblige themselves to engage the inhabitants of the city as well as those of *Kamara*, to pass by all past injuries either by word or deed; and that such of the *Dutch* as are willing to continue there, shall be maintained in their possessions in the same manner as the *Portuguese* are; and shall enjoy the same privileges, and their own religion, provided they do not preach in publick, and pay due reverence to consecrated places. They shall be at liberty to traffick with the *Portuguese*, and call in their debts as before, neither shall they be obliged to take up arms against the states of the *United Provinces*.

V. The *Dutch* officers shall restore to the *Portuguese* all their *Brasilians*, with their wives and children, as being subjects of king *John* IV. whom God preserve; and what relates to their reception and entertainment, is to be left to the discretion of the chief commanders of the *Portuguese*.

Upon these conditions they shall be obliged to surrender the fort, with every thing thereunto belonging, this afternoon, but are permitted to provide themselves with necessaries for their journey, which they shall have liberty to perform at their own leisure.

signed,
Andrew Vidal de Negreiros,
Alvaro Fregosa d'Albuquerque,
Diogno de Silveira,
Lopes Laurenzo,
Fereiro Betenkor,
Suppolito Abuko de Verkosa,
and
Sebastian de Guimares.

Immediately after the surrender of the fort, *Moucheron* entred into a long discourse with the *Portuguese* commanders, about their proceeding, which he told them were far different from what the governor pretended in his letters, to wit, the appeasing of the revolt of the *Portuguese* inhabitants, according to the request of the *great council*. They answered him with tergiversations, telling him that they would be very careful not to act contrary to the peace establish'd betwixt the king his master and the states general. But it was not long before they began to lord it over the country, by taking such as were in the least suspected to them into custody, and taking an account of those of the *Dutch* that had married *Portuguese* women; nay they erected a court of Justice of their own, and forced *Moucheron* to sell his slaves for the fourth part of what they were worth. They had so little regard to the late articles, that they caused thirty *Brasilians*, part of that garrison, to be tied to the Palisadoes, where they were strangled; the *Portuguese* alledged in their behalf, that they had suffered death for certain crimes they had confessed themselves, tho' it is more probable they were made sacrifices to the discontented *Portuguese* inhabitants, that had made heavy complaints at the *Brasilians*. However, about thirty of them were spared, and bestowed upon the officers to carry their baggage, and their wives given to the inhabitants. The *Portuguese* made *Alvaro Fregoso d'Albuquerque* governor of the city and fort, and made one *Francis de la Tour*, a *French* deserter, captain over forty deserters, who had taken service among them.

Evasions of the Portuguese.

The Portuguese play the Master.

They also raised three companies out of the *Portuguese* boors, or inhabitants, commanded by *Pedro Fregoso*, *Ignatius Ferrere* and *Immanuel de Mello*, which were put into *Serinhaim* for the defence of that place, where they also caused two *Jews* to be baptized, called *Jacquo Franco* and *Isaac Navare*. Most of the *Dutch* who had any possessions or sugar-mills thereabouts had safe-guards allow'd them, so that none, except two, who came to the *Receif*, left that captainship, of which they had sufficient reason to repent afterwards, being very ill treated by the *Portuguese*, as shall be shewn more at large hereafter.

The 15th of *August* in the afternoon, the garrison of *Serinhaim*, consisting of thirty two men (the rest having staid behind) arrived in a bark at the *Receif*; and their commander in chief appear'd the same day before the council, where he gave an account of the reasons that moved him to surrender the place, notwithstanding which he was ordered to be examined by a court-marshal, to answer the same: The ensign who had conducted the garrison to the *Receif*, delivered the same day a letter to the said council, from *Martin Soares Moreno*, and *Andrew Vidal*, dated the 8th of *August*, intimating that they were come into the *Dutch-Brasil*, by special command from the governor of the *Bahia*, and exaspera-

ting

1645. ting the outrages, they ſaid were committed by the *Hollanders* againſt the *Portugueſe*. This letter had another encloſed from the ſaid governor, dated the 30th of *July*, with a proclamation, to be publiſh'd in the captainſhip of *Pernambuko*, whereby all the inhabitants were ſummon'd to appear peremptorily before them, within the ſpace of eight days, to receive their directions for reſtoring tranquility among them. The letter from *Martin Soares Moreno* and *Andrew Vidal* was as follows.

A Letter from the Portugueſe *Commanders to the council.*

WHEN your lordſhips found your ſelves entangled by a dangerous conſpiracy among the Portugueſe *inhabitants of this captainſhip, you made your applications to* Antonio Telles da Sylva, *governor general of* Braſil, *deſiring him to make uſe of the moſt effectual means he could to appeaſe this rebellion. About the ſame time the inhabitants of this countrey by one unanimous voice implored his aid and protection againſt thoſe many affronts, plunderings, murthers and raviſhments of women they groaned under; being reſolved with joint conſent to arm themſelves with ſticks (the uſe of arms being taken away from them by their tyrannical governors) againſt thoſe oppreſſions, and to defend their honour to the laſt gaſp; not queſtioning but that God Almighty would take vengeance for the blood of ſo many innocent people. They repreſented to his excellency, that he was obliged by his ſtation to aſſiſt them in this extremity, as they were his countrymen; but, if that ſhould not be prevailing enough, reaſons of ſtate would induce him, not to force them to deſpair by denying them his aid; which if he did, it ſhould be at the peril of his head, and that he muſt give a ſevere account of it before God Almighty, and others, if they ſhould be conſtrained to beg that from a foreign power, which they could not obtain from their countrymen. The governor having taken all theſe preſſing reaſons into mature conſideration, and in reſpect both of your lordſhips requeſt, and the heavy complaints of the* Portugueſe, *made it his chief care to find out the moſt effectual means (which your lordſhips ſeem'd to leave to his diſcretion) to appeaſe this revolt. Being ſenſible that the revolt of the* Portugueſe *inhabitants had taken deep root among them, and was likely to prove more univerſal againſt your government, he judged it moſt expedient, to ſend hither certain perſons with ſuch forces as he thought might either by their prudence, and, if that fail'd, by force of arms, reſtore the ſo much deſired tranquility. It is upon this account, my lords, we are come to this place, in order to employ all our force and aſſiſtance, according to your requeſt, purſuant to the peace eſtabliſhed betwixt theſe two nations, in regard of which we value not the expences we have been put to upon this occaſion. But we ſcarce had ſet foot aſhore, when our ears and hearts were ſtruck with the doleful outcries of forty innocent catholick* Portugueſe, *murthered in the church of* Rio Formoſo, *whither they were enticed for that purpoſe, by thoſe that were in your ſervice, without the leaſt reſpect of age or ſex, the very babes being by the natives barbarouſly murthered, as they were lying on their mothers breaſts. Neither have the ſighs and groans of many noble maids eſcaped our ears, that were raviſh'd in the* Vergea *and* St. Lawrence, *by the* Braſilians, *not to mention here what barbarities have been committed in* Pojuka, *where is the ſight of many a hermit and innocent babe who were ſlaughter'd in a cave. Neither have they abſtained from holy and conſecrated places; they have cut to pieces the images of the ſaints, and ſtripp'd the queen of heaven, the virgin* Mary, *our bleſſed lady, of all her apparel; things ſo enormous, and never heard of before, enough to create horror and aſtoniſhment in a generous heart. And notwithſtanding your lordſhips had deſired the governor general to interpoſe his authority, you did form a camp, which continues in the field to this day; and we being obliged by our orders to come to you upon the* Receif, *we judged it not convenient to leave any armed power behind us, which in time might prove the occaſion of great inconveniences to us; we ſhall endeavour to ſhew all due reſpect and kindneſs to your ſubjects, and carry the garriſon of* Serinhaim *along with us, 'till matters may be concerted betwixt your lordſhip and us, for the ſervice of god and the ſtate. In the mean while, we moſt earneſtly deſire a ſtop may be put to the outrages committed by your ſoldiers hitherto, to avoid all occaſion of a rupture on your ſide; we proteſt on the other hand, in the name of God and* John IV. *the king our maſter, whom God preſerve, as alſo in the name of the ſtates general, whoſe power God encreaſe, that we deſire nothing ſo much, as the continuation of the late eſtabliſhed peace, which ſhall be the guide of all our actions; of which we have brought along with us an authentick copy, to ſerve us as a ſufficient juſtification by all the princes of* Europe. *And that your lordſhips may be ſatisfied in the reality of it, we have ſent you encloſed a copy of the proclamation publiſhed by us, at our landing in in this captainſhip.* 1645.

God preſerve your lordſhips,

Serinhaim, Aug. 8, 1645. Martin Soares Moreno, Andrew Vidal de Negreiros.

The before-mentioned proclamation runs thus:

Their

1645.

Their PROCLAMATION.

WE the commanders in chief of the Portuguese *forces,* Martin Soares Moreno, *and* Andrew Vidal de Negreiros, *make known to all persons and inhabitants of the captainship of* Pernambuko *that the* great council *of the* Dutch-Brasil, *having by a letter sent to the governor and captain general of* Brasil, *given advice of the revolt arisen among the* Portuguese *of this place; desiring to endeavour the appeasing of this rebellion by his assistance; for which purpose the said governor now having sent us with a sufficent force into this captainship, we command all the* Portuguese, *of what condition and quality soever, to appear peremptorily within eight days after the publication of these presents before us, in order to restore tranquility among them, pursuant to the request of the lords of the council of the* Dutch-Brasil. *We also hereby intreat the said lords, in the most friendly manner that can be, pursuant to the tenour of the strict alliance there is betwixt both these nations, to stop the further persecution of the* Portuguese, *or any other warlike executions; and that if any of their soldiers presume to act contrary to it, they may, upon complaint made thereof to them, be severely punished.*

I Alexes Antunes *have penned this proclamation, and I* Franco Bravo Desembarquador *have approv'd it.*

Martin Soares Moreno,
Andrew Vidal de Negreiros.

The great council resolved to give a short answer to the said letter, and to refute the proclamation by another; and considering, that the origin and cause of all those troubles and misdeameanours were laid at the door of the council, they ordered the two councellors of the court of justice *De Witt* and *Moucheron*, in conjunction with Mr. *Walbeek* assessor in the same court, to answer the same, and thereby to represent to the council of nineteen in *Holland*, that they were occasioned by the rebels and their adherents.

The Portuguese *besiege the* Cape of St. Austin.

In the month of *August* the troops lately come from the *Bahia* marched from *Serinhaim* to *Pojuka*, and so to the *Cape of St. Austin*, where being join'd by the forces under the command of *Kamaron* and *Dias*, and the inhabitants, they resolved (after our men had quitted *Pojuka* and the city *St. Antonio de Cabo*) to attack the fort *Vander Dussen* on the *Cape of St. Austin* from the land side; pursuant to which resolution they posted their troops all along both sides the river.

1645.

Mr. Bullestrate *and admiral* Lichthart *sent to the* Cape of St. Austin.

The council in the mean while being forewarned of the enemies design, had ordered the 2d of *August*, Mr. *Adrian Bullestrate*, one of their own members, and admiral *Lichthart*, to go thither with all speed, and to take effectual care that nothing might be wanting for the defence of the place. They were for that end to take a full view of the fort *Vander Dussen* and all its outworks, and to consider whether the redoubt upon the hill call'd *Nazareth*, and the battery at the entrance of the harbour might be repaired for the better defence of the fort. Accordingly Mr. *Bullestrate* and admiral *Lichthart* left the *Receif* the 5th of *August*, and arrived the same evening in the fort *Vander Dussen*, where having executed their commission, Mr. *Bullestrate* returned the 9th of *August* to the *Receif*, where he gave the following account to the council.

That he left the *Receif* the 5th of *August*, in the morning about nine a clock, and came the same evening to the fort *Vander Dussen* on the *Cape of St. Austin*.

An account of their transactions.

That the 6th of *August*, after forenoon sermon was ended he rid with the admiral, and some other officers, to the hill of the *Cape of St. Austin*; where having taken a view of the harbour, he found the stone-redoubt in a condition to be repaired, without any great charge, the cannon upon the batteries nail'd up, but the works towards the seaside in pretty good order.

That he had ordered a draught to be made, to surround the redoubt with pallisadoes, to raise a battery within it, to build a guard-house, and to widen the ditches: He also had ordered a stone breast-work, (for want of wood) to be made on the backside of the battery, with a row of Pallisadoes, and a guard-house; and that with the first fair weather, they should set on fire all the bushes and brambles on the said hill, and clear the ground round about the church *Nazareth*.

Upon view of the fort *Vander Dussen*, he had commanded the major *Hoogstrate* with all possible speed to put it in a good posture of defence, the admiral having already taken care to have it surrounded with pallisadoes. That on the 7th of *August*, having paid off the garrison, and those belonging to the artillery, he passed through very difficult ways to *St. Antonio*, where he likewise paid off the soldiery, visited the retrenchment, and put every thing in the best order he could.

That he had bargained with certain persons to repair the said redoubt on the hill called *Nazareth*, and the stone breast-work, the building of two guardhouses, and surrounding both the works with pallisadoes

1643. lisadoes, according to his draught, for nine hundred gilders, the whole to be compleated within three weeks time. Here it was he had the first notice of the landing of some forces from the *Bahia*, near *Rio Formosa*, by the same fleet which the week before was seen off of the *Receif*: But not being able to get any sure intelligence, he had sent a messenger to lieutenant *Montangie*, then commander in *Serinhaim*, to give him a true account of the matter, and in what condition he and his garrison were at that time; encouraging him by fair promises, all communication by land being already cut off betwixt them. Here he also listed thirty eight volunteers that offered their service.

That the 8th of *August* he left the said place, and notwithstanding the badness of the weather, rid cross the hills of *Hegendos* to the sea-shore, where meeting with the admiral, they went together up the river *Sangado* with the tide, as far as *Calandaria*, where they staid for some time, and received the news, that in the last encounter betwixt colonel *Haus* and the rebels near that hill, above two hundred of the last, among whom were some officers, were slain, and about forty or fifty on our side. One *Melchior Alvares* came on purpose to tell them, that about three hundred of the revolted inhabitants were inclined to accept of a pardon, which he referred to the council.

That being ready to take horse in order to his return to the *Receif*, a certain soldier of our troops, that had been left behind, complained that he had been stripp'd stark naked by the servants of the ferryman of the river *Sangada*, who had wounded and beat him miserably. *Melchior Alvares* was ordered to take care of his wounds, and captain *Pistor* to go with twenty of his men in quest of these villains; who, coming to the ferry, beset the house, took the ferryman and his three sons prisoners, but the *Mulat*, who had committed the fact, escaped their hands.

That he pursued his journey on horseback towards the *Receif*, notwithstanding the violent rains, and not without great danger pass'd the river the same night near the fort *Æmilia*.

That on the 9th of *August*, he was advertised by some negroes belonging to *Moses Navarre*, whom he had sent with letters to *d'Ingenio Sursacque*, that an ambush had been laid for them near *Candelaria*, but the enemy durst not attack them, their negroes being all such as were taken prisoners, and afterwards made their escape to us.

Major *Hoogstrate* sent advice by his letters on the 13th of *August*, to the council, that the garrison and volunteers of *St. Antonio* being safely arrived on the *Cape of St. Austin*, they were now about two hundred and eighty strong, *viz.* two hundred and seventeen soldiers and gunners, and sixty three volunteers. That immediately after our garrison had left *St. Antonio*, *Kamaron* and *Henry Dias* had posted themselves with their troops in the sugar-mill *Algodais*, near that place, where they expected to be join'd by *Martin Soares* and *Andrew Vidal*'s forces, safely arrived from the *Bahia*. That he expected every day to be besieged, and fear'd nothing so much as want of fresh water, the spring being cut off by the enemy. Hereupon immediate orders were given by the council to send thither thirty barrels of water, some ammunition and provision, and what else should be requisite for a vigorous defence of the place, which was sufficiently provided before with soldiers. The next following day they received intelligence from Major *Hoogstrate*, Mr. *Ley*, and Mr. *Heck*, that the enemies troops had taken post in the sugar-mill *Salgado Zuvistaque* and other circumjacent places. The council rely'd much upon the bravery and fidelity of the offices within the fort, from whom they promised themselves a very vigorous defence, they being all persons who had advanced themselves in their services, and were in expectation of better preferments, *viz.* Major *Hoogstrate*, *Caspar Vander Ley*, formerly a captain of horse, *John Hick*, and *Albert Gerritson Wedda*, an old captain belonging to the company: But their unfaithfulness and covetous temper over-balanced all these considerations; for the said major *Hoogstrate*, commander in chief, with the consent of *Casper Vander Ley*, and *Albert Gerritson Wedda*, treacherously and villanously sold and surrendred the said fort to the *Portuguese* the 23d of *August* for the sum of eighteen thousand gilders, besides some other rewards promised them upon that account. They went over with the whole garrison to the enemy, who made *Hoogstrate* colonel of a *Dutch* regiment, raised out of these and other soldiers of several nations, that had deserted our service. Thus this strong hold was betray'd to the *Portuguese*, by a person who owed his whole fortune to our company.

1645. *Advice from the* Cape of St. Austin.

Martin Soares Moreno gave the following account of the surrender of this fort to the governor *Antonio Telles da Sylva*, in his letter dated from the hill of *Nazareth*, *Aug.* 26, 1645.

1645.

A letter to the governor of the Bahia, *concerning the taking of the* Cape of Puntael.

Sunday the 23[d] of this month, God Almighty, through his mercy, has put us into the possession of the fort of the cape of Puntael, which was besieged by Andrew Vidal de Negreiros: The next day we were rejoyced with the money sent to us by your lordship, and the wine presented to me in particular, part of which I have bestowed upon entertaining some of our friends, who are merry with me at this time.

We have made an excellent bargain; for besides the importance of the place, and its artillery, we have got the very flower of their soldiers; besides that, this will be like a signal to the rest to follow their footsteps.

John Fernand Vieira has raised on saturday last the sum of four thousand ducats for our use, though not without force, but it was very welcome to us at this time, when we were upon striking up the bargain for the better fortifying of this place, the harbour of which is not inferiour to that of the Receif: But I will not trouble your lordship any longer with this point.

Not long after the surrender of the fort, a bark appeared in sight, sent to its relief from the Receif. We sent captain Barreiros with a well arm'd bark out against her, who took her with thirty five men, and good store of gunpowder and bullets, all which will prove very serviceable to us.

I kindly desire your lordship, that in case you send a messenger with this news to his majesty, captain Damian de Lankois may be employed upon that errand, it being very probable, that the king, besides a good present, will reward him with some honourable employment.

Last night we received advice, that the fleet under Jeronymo de Paiva was entred the bay of Tamandare; I am sorely afraid they will be attack'd by the ships sent thither from the Receif, notwithstanding we have desired him several times to come into our road.

Kapivara is gone from that place by land to the Bahia, perhaps he has given him notice that we are masters of the cape; if he thinks fit to bring his fleet to this place, he is safe, if not, it lies at his door. 'Tis discoursed here, that the ship the Bishop is missing, perhaps he has a fancy to convoy Salvador Korrea some part of the way.

I cannot forbear to let your lordship know how much you stand indebted to major Dieterick Hoogstrate, and the rest of the commanders of the fort. We have promised to the first a commandery of Christ. I beg of your lordship to make my promise good to him in his majesty's name, as soon as possible may be, he being a person who will be ready to do us all the further service he can. We have for the present engaged him with some presents of less moment, of which we shall give an account to you hereafter. Captain Vander Ley has likewise deserved well of us, and so have all the rest that had married Portuguese women: It is reported here that he is a person of note in his country: We have likewise promised to him a commandery of Christ, and a yearly pension for one of his sons: We hope your lordship will not refuse to make good our promise, because his sons are born of a Portuguese woman: The name of the eldest being John, and the youngest Caspar Vander Ley. The rest are at present at their habitations, as soon as they return we must engage them with some promises, of which we will give an account to your lordship. They are all of consequence to us, having married Portuguese women. I hope your lordship will be well satisfied with this piece of service, for John Fernand Vieira sometimes brings us more money in an hour, than the conquest of the cape costs us. He is at present in the Vargea among the Barbarians, and we in the fort on the cape, till we have got every thing in readiness. Kapivara is about three days ago gone by land, possibly he may be with you before the bark which carries this letter; I wish it may arrive in safety, and to your lordship a long life for the defence of this state. Signed

Martin Soares Moreno.

Martin Soares Moreno, and *Andrew Vidal de Negreiros*, had in the mean while sent seven or eight letters from the cape of *St. Austin*, dated the 23[d], 30th, and 31st of *August*, and the 2[d] and 6th of *September*, in which they advertised the admiral *Paiva*, that they were in possession of that cape, desiring him by all means to come with his fleet into that harbour. The first of the two last letters was thus written.

Letter from the Portuguese *commanders to admiral* Paiva.

My lord,

We are got now into the possession of the harbour of Nazareth, and that, as the saying is, without casting an anchor; which is the reason we intreat you likewise to come with your fleet hither, where you may careen your ships, and provide yourselves with fresh provisions, men, ammunition, and all other necessaries, till such time we shall mutually agree in what is further to be undertaken for the service of God and his majesty. The enemy has hitherto but one ship of strength at sea, the rest being of no consequence; neither are they for engaging with you at this time, but endeavour to cut off your communication with the sea coast. My lord, you have

1645. *have given so many proofs of your courage before this time, that this retreat will not abate any thing from the fame of your victories: On the other hand, you have to consider, that you are answerable for so many thousand lives of those that are in your fleet; wherefore we desire you once more to come hither with the fleet, and such officers as are under your command, where you will meet with a very kind and comfortable reception. But being sensible that it would be a gross error in us, to urge a matter so evident in itself, any further, to so great a commander as you, we live in hopes of your coming, where we intend, in the house of* Nazareth, *to receive the blessed sacrament, which name we have given to the fort, having among other things found a mass book here, which is of no small service to us.*

God preserve your lordship.

Puntael, *the* 2^d *of* Sept. 1645. *Martin Soares Moreno*, and *Andrew Vidal de Negreiros.*

The contents of the second letter to the same admiral, are as follows:

Y*OUR lordship being already acquainted with our being masters of the* Puntael *(cape) we hope you will take the first opportunity of coming to us; the enemies having two squadrons of ships at sea, with one fireship, to force you from this coast, which has been discovered to us by a letter writ at the* Receif, *and directed to the governor, and taken by us in a bark design'd for the relief of that place, of which we thought fit to give you immediate notice, that you might take your measures according to your wonted prudence. These* Dutch *gentlemen have, by their treacherous dealings, obliged us to have recourse to open force, and we desire your lordship to repay them in their own coin, with fire and sword, as they do to us. If you design to come hither, it must be done speedily, all delay being dangerous at this time. We have a true copy of this letter in our journal to serve for our justification hereafter.*

God preserve your lordship.

Dated in the *Puntael* of the blessed sacrament, *September* the 6th, 1645.

Martin Soares Moreno, and *Andrew Vidal de Negreiros.*

An account of the surrender of the cape of *St. Austin*, and of the further transactions betwixt us and the *Portuguese*, was sent in a letter by *Caspar da Costa d'Abreu*, from the said cape to his friend *Domingos da Kosta*, an inhabitant of the *Bahia*, which runs thus:

I *Wish this letter may find you in good health, as I who am your faithful comrade desire; I am in a tolerable good condition in the* Puntael *of* Nazareth, *which after a siege of twenty days was surrendred to us at an easy rate, because those who commanded within the fort had* Portuguese *wives, and their estates thereabouts. The captain of horse was the most forward of all in surrendering the place they have obtained what conditions they demanded, and a gratuity of four thousand ducats besides. We found in the fort three hundred* Dutch, *of their best troops, and twelve brass pieces of cannon, four of which were four and twenty pounders, and provisions for three months; so that if they had not come with us to a composition, it would have cost us abundance of men, whereas now we have gain'd the place with the loss of one single man, who was kill'd by a random cannon shot. We made ourselves masters of a bark, firing from the* Puntael, *before its surrender, in which was a gentleman with several hundred men that were going to the* Receif. *This gentleman and another of* Serinhaim *(being both magistrates in their respective places) we delivered up to the inhabitants, who soon kill'd them, notwithstanding one was married with a* Portuguese *woman; for they having been heard to say, that they hoped to wash their hands in the blood of the* Portuguese, *the women were so much exasperated against them, that they soon dispatch'd them, according to their desires. The prisoners are for the most part detained at* St. Anthony, *in order to be sent to the* Bahia; *but many among them have taken service with us. We suppose the number of the dead and* Dutch *prisoners amount to near thirteen hundred: We have not seen the squadron under* Salvador Korrea de Saa; *we are afraid some misfortune has befallen him; some of our ships were cruising hereabouts, but within these three or four days none of them have appear'd on this coast. The* Dutch *have a fleet of twelve ships at sea, it is well if they don't venture a brush with us. The* Receif *with all its forts are invested,* Lawrence Karneiro *is at* Porto Calvo; *the* Jews *report, that orders are come to take all the* Dutch *forces out of* Rio Grande, Paraiba *and* St. Francis, *in order to transport them to the* Receif. *There is no great harmony betwixt the* Jews *and* Dutch, *the first pretending that the others intend to sell the country. Four of their head officers, which are our prisoners, are ordered to be sent to the* Bahia, *and among them their master of the artillery. The same day that we were become masters of* Puntael, *a bark arrived there from the* Receif *with orders to keep it to the last extremity; we took the bark with good store of ammunition and provision, worth in all about fifteen hundred ducats.*

Sept. *the* 5th, 1645. *Caspar da Costa d'Abreu.*

From

1645. From this and the following letters, it is apparent, that major *Hoogstrate* had laid the foundation of his treacherous design of betraying the cape of *St. Austin* to the *Portuguese*, long before; to wit, ever since he with Mr. *Balthasar Vander Voorde* was sent to the governor of the *Bahia Antonio Telles de Sylva*. Thus a certain serjeant sold a redoubt near the city of *Olinda* to the enemy for three hundred gilders.

At the beginning of the siege of the cape of *St. Austin*, *Andrew Vidal de Negreiros* sent two letters to major *Hoogstrate*, *Ley* and *Hick*, by one *John Guomes de Mello*, dated the thirteenth of *August*; in the first of which the said *Vidal* complains of the ill treatment and murthers committed upon the *Portuguese* by the *Dutch*; in the second he requests them to declare, pursuant to the promises made by *Hoogstrate* in the *Bahia*, for the king of *Portugal*, and to deliver the fort into their hands.

Two letters from Vidal *to* Hoogstrate.

The first was as follows:

I *Am come this morning to the village of* St. Antonio de Cabo, *in hopes of receiving news from you and captain* Ley. *I give by these presents notice to you, that we are sent hither by order from the governor* Antonio Telles de Sylva, *with no other intention than to appease the troubles lately arisen in this country, pursuant to the request of the council, of which you are a sufficient witness. No sooner were we arrived at* Tamandare, *but we received many informations directly contrary to what we expected to meet with here; viz. That in* Rio Grande *thirty seven inhabitants had been murthered, many virgins deflower'd, and the image of the virgin* Mary *grosly misused by the* Dutch; *things so abominable in themselves, that it is scarce to be imagined so brave a nation should be guilty of such enormities. Whilst I am writing this letter, news is brought me, that the* Dutch *have caused many of the inhabitants of* Goyana *to be murthered, tho' I can scarce give credit to it; for supposing this to be true, we could not avoid giving assistance to these miserable people, tho' they were the most despiseable of all nations, considering they crave our help, and are not only christians, but also subjects of the king our master, whom God preserve. Whilst the council was in expectation of the issues of the intended accommodation, they have surprized and killed many of the inhabitants, which obliges us, to require you in the name of God, of his majesty, his highness and the states general, not to give any occasion for a rupture, but to maintain the late concluded peace to the utmost of your power, as we are ready on our side, to concert all possible measures with the commander in chief of this place, which may tend to the tranquillity of both parties. The bearers hereof are captain* John Guomes de Mello, *and lieutenant* Francis Guomes, *who we desire may be dispatched back with all possible speed.* 1645.

God preserve you for many years.

August 13, 1645. *Andrew Vidal.*

The second letter was written thus:

The second letter.

YOUR *promise made to us in the* Bahia, *and what has since been told by captain* Ley *to* John Fernandes Vieira, *and captain* John Guomes de Mello, *encourages us to proceed in our former design, not questioning but that both you and captain* Ley *will not in the least recede from the engagement you have been pleased to oblige us with, and to tie us to your service. We are come into this country at the head of three thousand chosen men, back'd by two squadrons of men of war well equip'd, one of which has not as yet appear'd on this coast, the other you have seen yourself pass by the other day. I hope this may serve as a means to set the poor miserable inhabitants at liberty; and as both they and we wish for nothing more than to see you embrace our side, that we may not want an opportunity to give you more evident proofs of our respect and affection towards you, so we desire you not to entertain the least sinister suspicion of us; we being ready (for the performance of which we by these presents give you our words) to accomplish in every point, what has been promised to you, by* John Fernandes Vieira, *and* John Guomes de Mello. *And I for my part assure you, that I will not fail to perform and agree to whatever you shall further demand upon this occasion.*

The inhabitants of the place shall be provided with pasports, and protected by us, in the same manner as the commander of Serinhaim, Carpenter, *and some others were; and we expect the same at your hand. And that you may be sure whom to treat with upon this account, we have sent to you* John Guomes de Mello, *who is intrusted with the whole matter; which if you refuse to do, we must take such measures as we shall judge most expedient for us.* In the mean while God preserve you for many years.

St. Antonio de Cabo, Aug. 13, 1645. Your affectionate friend

and servant,

Andrew Vidal de Negreiros.

Major *Hoogstrate*, Mr. *Hick* and *Ley*, sent an answer to this letter immediately, containing

1645. containing in substance, that they were not in the least concerned in the outrages committed by the *Tapoyers* against the *Portuguese*, and seemingly refused to treat with *de Mello*. It runs thus:

His answer to them.

W*E have received your letter sent by* John Guomes de Mello, *out of which we understand, that you are come to* St. Antonio. *We are extremely well satisfied, that the governor* Antonio Telles da Sylva *has undertaken to appease the tumults arisen in these parts, and don't question but that your presence will contribute much towards the accomplishment of it. The affronts and outrages you speak of by the* Tapoyers *and* Dutch *soldiers put upon the inhabitants, as they were committed sorely against our will, so I can assure you, that no body, not so much as the least child, has been suffer'd to be misused upon our accounts, so that these complaints must not be made to us, but ought to be referr'd to the council. The treaty you propose with captain* John Guomes de Mello, *and lieutenant* Francis Guomes, *is beyond our province and power, so that we earnestly desire you not to use any further sollicitations to us upon that account. So we kiss your hands, recommmending you to God's protection.* We rest

Your servants and good friends,

Caspar Vander Ley,
D. Van Hoogstrate.
John Hick.

Hoogstrate *discovers these letters.* Major *Hoogstrate* took care to send these two letters, together with their answer to the council, with repeated assurances of their constant fidelity; whereupon the great council confirm'd *Hoogstrate* in his government, and exhorted *Ley* and *Hick* to persevere in their brave resolution, which they would in due time take care to reward with better preferments. This discovery of the enemies letters being look'd upon as an undeniable proof of Mr. *Hoogstrate*'s sincere intentions, had such an influence upon the generality of the people, that there was scarce any body but what thought himself secure of his fidelity and duty. Nevertheless, as these temptations could not but raise some jealousy in the minds of the council, they thought fit to send colonel *Haus* to the *Receif*, to order him to the Cape of *St. Austin*.

The council in the mean while, being by *Vidal*'s letters to *Hoogstrate* sufficiently convinced, that the intended recalling of the rebellious troops were nothing but amusements, sent immediate orders to their admiral *Lichthart*, that for the future he should treat all the *Portuguese* ships he could meet with as enemies. 1645.

Consultations about drawing all the forces into the Receif. The 15th of *August*, colonel *Haus* being come to the *Receif*, proposed to the council, that he judged it absolutely necessary for the service of the state, that since by the succours come from the *Bahia* to the assistance of the rebels under *Martin Soares Moreno* and *Andrew Vidal*, they were grown very strong and numerous, the troops encamped in the field should be drawn into the *Receif*, because they being besides the *Brasilians*, not above three hundred strong, they might easily be cut off in a place where they could not be seconded from the *Receif*, where they were wanting for the defence of that place, which being the capital of the whole *Dutch Brasil*, would in all likelihood be attack'd with the utmost vigour by the enemy.

Against this opinion many reasons were alledged too.

I. By so doing they must quit all the open country from whence they were now supplied with cattle and meal, which they stood highly in need of, till such time that they could receive new supplies from *Holland*, and that in such a case they must expect the enemy immediately at their gates.

II. That thereby the number of the enemy would be encreased, the inhabitants of the country being freed from the dread of our troops, would join with them against us.

III. That by so doing we must leave the *Tapoyers*, that had taken up arms at our request, and were to be joined by our troops near *Machiape* or *St. Antonio*, to the enemies mercy. To this it was answer'd,

1. That as to the supplies of cattle and meal from the country, they should be in a much better condition to be furnished withal, when their forces could be sent abroad into all circumjacent parts of the country, whereas now they were forced to remain in one certain place. Besides that, we being masters at sea, might embark at any time a certain number of men, and land them where we found it most convenient, which would oblige the enemy, instead of besieging the *Receif*, to divide his forces for the defence of the country. What related to the increase of the enemies forces, by the accession of the *Portuguese* inhabitants of the country, was to be look'd upon as of no great consequence against us; it being more for our interest to see them appear as declared enemies than dissembling friends; it being generally known, that their inclinations were bent for their countrymen, and that notwithstanding all their

1645.

their specious pretences, they miss'd no opportunity of giving intelligence to the enemy of what passed among us; whereas, if they were once declared enemies of the states, we should have a fair opportunity of seizing upon their cattle, provisions, and other moveables, for the use of the *Receif*; which being thus provided, would discourage the enemy from attempting to reduce it by famine.

What was alledged concerning the danger of the *Tapoyers*, was acknowledged to be of no small moment; but considering they had received no news as yet of their motion, it was not judged of such vast consequence as to be put in balance with the welfare of the whole *Dutch Brasil*, which depended in a great measure on the safety of these troops.

After mature deliberation of the whole matter, it was resolved, on the 15th of *August*, by the council, with the approbation of the members of the court of justice, that considering the danger the troops were exposed to, and that on their safety depended the preservation of the *Receif*, they should with all possible speed march thither, and that only fifty men should be left in the house of *de Wit*, under captain *Wiltschut*, in order to command some part of the circumjacent country, and to serve as a retreat for our parties that should be sent abroad to fetch in cattle, and *Farinha*, or meal.

Pursuant to this resolution, colonel *Haus* went thither on horseback the same day, to put it in execution the same evening, if possible he could, or at furthest the next morning. But it seems colonel *Haus* was so neglectful, as to delay the march of these troops not only that afternoon, but also the whole next following day; and instead of retreating towards the *Receif*, tarried in the same sugar-mill, without having the least intelligence of the enemies approach; so that on the 17th of *August*, being surprized by the troops of *Andrew Vidal*, much more numerous than his, before they could betake themselves to their arms they were put to the rout. The council being advertised, that colonel *Haus* with his troops were attacked by the enemy in the sugar-mill of Mr. *de Wit*, they call'd the city militia to their arms, Mr. *Bullestrate* and *de Bas* went to the house *Bavista*; from whence, as being near at hand, they might give the necessary orders, according as they should receive advice from *Haus*: And twelve firelocks were posted in this house for the better security of the bridge cross the river. *Dieterick Hamel*, and the counsellors of justice, took care to look after the *Receif*. Immediately after, word being brought to the council that colonel *Haus* had been overthrown, and was retired to the house of *de Wit* belonging to the sugar-mill, it was consulted, whether by any means they might be able to relieve him; and, tho' by reason of the weakness of the garrison, it was no easy matter to do it; nevertheless, it was resolved, with one hundred volunteers of the inhabitants, and one hundred and fifty soldiers, to attempt his relief. But before this could be put in execution, a certain *Brasilian* that had been present at the whole action, and having, by changing his clothes with a *Portuguese*, found means to escape to the *Receif*, brought the unwelcome news, that colonel *Haus*, with the forces under his command, had surrendred the house belonging to the sugar-mill, and themselves, upon promise of quarters, at discretion.

Colonel Haus *put to the rout.*

Colonel Haus *surrenders at discretion.*

It was generally believed, that this misfortune was chiefly occasioned by colonel *Haus*'s own neglect, who did not, till it was too late, put the soldiers into a posture of defence, which was afterwards confirmed by the deposition of *William Jacobson*, late captain lieutenant of colonel *Haus*'s own company, made before the great council the 6th of *July*, 1646.

A further account of the defeat of colonel Haus *by captain* Jacobson.

It was not till the night before our defeat, that colonel *Haus* received the first intelligences from a prisoner, a *Negro*, that the enemy with a strong body were broken up from *Moribeka*. The next morning, one of our safe-guards brought word to the colonel, that the enemy was passing the river; and soon after, the colonel's groom, who had been to water his master's horse in the said river, came in a full gallop, telling him likewise, that the rebels were passing the river, so that we soon after heard them fire upon our advanced guard, who retired immediately to the main body. Colonel *Haus* did not call the soldiers to their arms, or caused the alarum to be given, until the enemy came within sight of us, and charged our out-guard, when we first began to skirmish with them: But they charging us with their more numerous forces in the front, whilst *Kamaron* with his troops endeavoured to cut off our retreat to the *Receif*, which we were not able to prevent, by reason of the smallness of our number, *Haus* ask'd captain *Wiltschut*, *Blaer* and *Listry*, *What was best to be done? Wiltschut* answered, *You never ask'd our advice before, do what you think best.* Whereupon *Haus* ordered to retreat to the house of Mr. *de Wit*: Captain *Blaer*, who expected no quarter, being on the other hand for fighting our way through to the *Receif*. The house was bravely defended for four

1645. four hours, but at last powder and ball beginning to fail, because half a barrel of gunpowder (which was all they had left) blew up by accident, they surrendred at discretion to *Andrew Vidal*, under condition to have their lives saved, as well for themselves as the *Brasilians* among them; which agreement being signed by *Vidal*, and two or three more of the chief commanders of the *Portuguese*, was delivered to colonel *Haus*. Notwithstanding which, the *Brasilians* were cut to pieces by the inhabitants, with the consent of the *Portuguese* commanders, as soon as we had quitted our post in the house. The *Brasilian* women seeing their husbands murthered before their faces, dash'd most of their childrens brains against the walls, for fear they should fall alive into the hands of the *Portuguese*. All the *Dutch*, about two hundred and fifty strong, among whom were colonel *Haus*, captain *Blaer* and *Listry*, were made prisoners of war, and were for the first four or five days kept in the sugar-mill of *Hacq*, when *John Fernandes Vieira*, and many of the inhabitants sollicited *Andrew Vidal*, to deliver the said prisoners up into their hands, with an intention to kill them, but *Vidal* refused to grant their request, and caused them forthwith to be sent by land to the *Bahia*: They were indifferently well treated in their journey thither; but such as either by reason of sickness, or any other accident, were left behind, fell into the inhabitants hands, who cut them to pieces, and would have done the same with all the rest, had it not been for their convoy. After their arrival in the *Bahia*, an account being taken of their names, they had certain quarters assigned them, and thirty-one pence halfpenny *per* week for their pay, and a measure of meal for every ten days.

They had liberty to walk up and down within the city where they pleased, except colonel *Haus*, captain *Wiltschut*, and *Listry*, who were confined to their lodgings, and durst not, without special leave, talk with any body. Colonel *Haus* was at last sent to *Portugal*, and *Wiltschut* and *Listry*, in *June* 1647, put on board a ship, with two hundred and thirty *Dutch* prisoners; about sixty of our men took service among them there, but they refused the natives of *Holland*.

The enemies being greatly encouraged by these successes, and their strength encreasing daily by the great concourse of the *Portuguese* inhabitants, who in the captainships of *Parayba* and *Goyana*, which hitherto had remained in quiet, and engaged themselves to the government by a new oath of allegiance, now also took up arms against us; so that it was thought convenient to recal our garrisons out of those parts. 1645.

What became of the garrison of the cape of St. Austin.

But to return to the cape of *St. Austin*, after the surrender of which the garrison was carried to *St. Antonio*, where they were forced to deliver up their arms. Among the rest of our prisoners there was *Isaac Zweers* afterwards vice-admiral of *Holland* and *Westfriseland*, *Abraham Van Millingen*, and *John Broeckhusen*, both still living in *Holland*. Major *Hoogstrate* addres'd himself to them, endeavouring to bring them over to the *Portuguese* side, by the allurements of captain, lieutenant, and ensign's places, telling them, that it would now be in his power to promote them to much higher employments; but when he saw them refuse his offer, he swore they should repent it. At the same time he preferr'd three *Dutch* men, to wit, *Winsel Smith*, formerly his lieutenant; *Alexander Boucholt*, and *Claes Claesen*, a native of *Amsterdam*, to captains places; the last of these three being an intimate friend of *Zweers* and *Broekhusen*, told them, and confirmed it by many oaths, that he had taken service among them for no other end, than to get an opportunity of returning to us. They had also liberty given them to walk abroad, but not without a guard to keep a watchful eye over all their actions.

Not long after, the *Portuguese* provider *Mor* sent for *John Broekhusen*, and after the first complements were pass'd, told him, that if he would serve the king of *Portugal* in the quality of commissary-general, he should go along with him to the camp, where he should receive one hundred gilders *per* month, and be welcome to his table besides; and that if he refused his offer, and stay'd behind, he would be in danger of being murthered by the inhabitants. He reply'd, that being engaged by his oath to the company, he could not break it, though with the hazard of his life. *And* (said the providor) *will you chuse rather to serve a company of mob than a king? We are just now upon the point of executing a design which is infallible, and then you will begin to see that the king's cause is the justest, and will be crown'd with success for ever.* Then he gave him a cup with brandy, of which after Mr. *Broekhusen* had taken a good draught, he took his leave, and return'd to his comrades, unto whom he gave an account of what had pass'd betwixt them.

These had in the mean while been inform'd by some *Portuguese*, that this design was upon the isle *Itamarika*, and being certain that the council did not foresee

1645. see this danger, they were contriving all possible means to give them notice of it, but could not pitch upon any person fitly qualified for this undertaking. At last, *Isaac Zweers*, by vast promises of reward, prevailed so far upon a *Dutch* trumpeter, call'd *Martin Stomp*, that he undertook to carry this piece of news in person to the council, and at the same time to request the releasing of the *Dutch* prisoner still remaining at *St. Antonio*. Every thing being agreed upon betwixt them, the trumpeter took his leave of Mr. *Zweers*, and set out on his journey to the *Receif* about midnight, leaving his wife and children behind him. Mr. *Zweers* and Mr. *Broekhusen* appear'd very well satisfied, but nevertheless were in their hearts not a little concerned for the issue of this enterprize.

A Dutch *trumpeter discovers the enemies design upon* Itamarika *to the council.*

They would often call upon the trumpeter's wife to enjoin her silence, and ordered her, that if any enquired after him, to tell them that he was run away from her, in order to take service in the camp in the *Vergea*.

Some days after they met with one *Peter Ritsau*, formerly baker to the garrison of the cape of *St. Austin*; *Broekhusen* having a mind to feel his pulse, and finding him not averse to such a task, he at last with fair words prevail'd upon him to undertake the same journey the trumpeter had done before; that in case he should miscarry, which they much feared he might, the council might nevertheless be advertised of the enemies intended expedition against *Itamarika*. The baker having desired a certificate from them, testifying, that he never had taken service among the *Portuguese*, prepared himself for his journey, which he intended to begin with the first dark night.

A baker sent upon the same errand.

The same night they were forewarn'd of a design against their lives, by a certain *Italian* call'd *Jacomo da Perugalho*, so that *Zweers* and *Broekhusen* guessing, not without reason, that some of the *Portugueze* had got scent of their sending away the trumpeter and baker, thought it not adviseable to stay longer in this place, but to ask leave from colonel *Pedro Marinha Falkabo*, to go to the *Algodais*, where they could not want conveniency to go along with the rest of the prisoners, that were intended to be sent to the *Bahia*, which was readily granted.

In the mean while, the baker having taken the first opportunity to set out on his journey, was met by two *Portuguese* in the sugar-mill *Trapicha*, who having found the beforementioned certificate about him, carried him prisoner to *St. Antonio de Cabo*, where being put to the torture, it made such a noise among the inhabitants, that

Is seized.

they all rise up in arms, protesting, they would not be satisfied till they had fetch'd *Zweers* and *Broekhusen* from the *Algodais*, and cut them to pieces; for which purpose they also obtained seven soldiers from *Pedro Marinha*, and had certainly put it in execution if captain *Ley* had not opposed it; for as good luck would have it, they happened at that time to be in his sugar-mill, and the baker had stood it out bravely, without discovering the matter. The next morning captain *Ley* gave them a visit, telling them what had happened, and says he, to *Broekhusen*, *What is your meaning by this?* but he having no great confidence in *Ley*, denied every thing to the utmost. 1645.

But the 2d of *October* the whole design was likely to have been discovered by the imprudence of the beforementioned trumpeter's wife, who being got drunk, told some of her acquaintance, that her husband was gone to the *Receif*. She was carried a prisoner to the cape of *St. Austin*, where she was miserably tortured, but being a resolute woman, would not confess any thing: It was however major *Hoogstrate*'s advice, that the *Portuguese* ought not to keep the *Dutch* any longer in *Pernambuko*, but that all such as refused to take service among them, ought to be sent to the *Bahia*. Accordingly all the *Dutch* prisoners then about the cape and *St. Anthony*, were sent to the *Algodais*, where every one was ask'd by colonel *Pedro Marinha*, whether they would take service under the king of *Portugal*, and such as would not, should be sent forthwith by land to the *Bahia*, a tedious journey; besides, that they ran the hazard of being murthered by the way. Many took service for fear, but *Zweers* and *Broekhusen* being ask'd again, whether they were not willing to serve the king, they answered, they would rather die than bear arms against their own nation.

The trumpeters journey discovered.

The 5th of *October*, all the prisoners under a convoy, both of soldiers and boors, were carried from the *Algodais* to *Pojuka*. But scarce were they come thither, when *Zweers* was ordered to be sent back to the cape of *St. Austin*, where he was put to the rack, to extort from him a confession concerning the trumpeter's journey to the *Receif*, who, as they supposed, had discovered their design upon *Itamarika*; but not being able to bring him to make the least discovery, they sent him, after an imprisonment of five weeks, to the *Bahia*.

Zweers *tortured.*

In the mean while Mr. *Broekhusen*, with the rest of the *Dutch* prisoners, had been forced to travel day and night till the 28th of *November* 1645, when they came to a castle call'd *Tapuao*, on the sea-shore of the *Bahia*,

The Dutch *prisoners come to the* Bahia.

1645. *Bahia*, about half a league from the city of *St. Salvador*, after a dangerous journey: They were carried in ten boats to the city, on that ſide where it is beſt fortified, the *Portugueſe* being not willing to let them have a ſight of the fortifications on the land ſide, Mr. *Broekhuſen* was by order from the governor *Antonio Telles da Sylva*, made a priſoner in a citizen's houſe, and the ſoldiers diſpoſed into quarters. The next day they heard the drums beat up for volunteers, every one being invited to ſerve the king of *Portugal*, of what nation ſoever, except the *Dutch*.

1646. The next following year, on the 18th of *January* 1646, *Zweers* and *Broekhuſen* intercepted a letter writ by *Hoogſtrate* to *Hondius*, concerning ſeveral tranſactions to be communicated to the governor, of which captain *Ley* having got ſcent, gave immediate notice thereof to the governour the firſt of *February*, who threatned them with no leſs than the gallows, ſent them to a loathſome priſon; with ſtrict orders that no body ſhould be permitted to ſpeak with them, nor that pen, ink, or paper, ſhould be allowed them; nay, whilſt the clerk was ſetting down their names, a captain came and told them from the governor, that they were the traitors who kept correſpondence with the *Dutch* in the *Receif*; and ordered that a centinel ſhould be ſet at the priſon door, to keep the inhabitants from laying violent hands upon them; for as they were carrying to priſon, they made a horrible noiſe, crying, *To the gallows with theſe impoſtors and traitors.* They remained five whole days in this priſon, without any victuals or drink, till being almoſt ſpent with hunger and thirſt, they got leave to write to the governor, repreſenting to him their deplorable condition; who gave immediate orders that victuals ſhould be given them for the future: The *Portugueſe* keeper being afraid, that if they ſhould give them plenty of victuals at firſt, it might turn to the danger of their lives, was ſo cautious, as to ſend them no more than each a piece of bread well dipt in wine at firſt, and after ſome hours, ſuch another, but ſomething bigger, till by degrees their ſtomachs were reſtored to their former digeſtive faculty.

A letter intercepted by Zweers *and* Broekhuſen.

Are committed to priſon.

Suffer for want of victuals.

Are provided with victuals.

The laſt day of *February* the governour gave publick audience (which is done three times every year) for the releaſing of thoſe that are priſoners on the king's account. Upon this occaſion a free acceſs was likewiſe granted to our people to the governor. They paſſed thro' the anti-chamber, lined on both ſides with his guards, into the room of audience, adorned with damaſk hangings of divers colours: Here they found the governor ſitting in an elbow chair, on the right-ſide of which ſtood the royal throne, raiſed four ſteps higher from the ground than the governor's ſeat, which was ſurrounded upon the floor with very fine tapeſtry: Juſt behind him ſtood his ſecretary, and ſome halbardiers; on both ſides ſat ſeveral councellours and lawyers, their heads covered. and behind them the officers of the army, all uncovered. The governor, as ſoon as he ſaw our priſoners, gave them a ſign to come nearer, which they having done accordingly, Mr. *Broekhuſen* upon his knees, ſpoke to him thus: *We ſuppoſe your lordſhip not to be ignorant, that now for a whole month we have been detained in a miſerable priſon; without being conſcious of any crime committed againſt you, unleſs it were, that we have detained the letter your lordſhip knows of; if in this we have committed a fault we beg your lordſhip's pardon.*

Have audience of the governour.

1646.

And (replied the governour) ſuppoſing you had done ſuch a thing in Holland? Upon which *Broekhuſen* anſwered, *That his lordſhip would be pleaſed to remember that it was no more than a private letter, and not directed to his lordſhip*; the governour after having pauſed for a little while, gave immediate order for their diſcharge; from that time they had liberty given them of walking abroad, but were fain to carry themſelves very ſwimmingly, for fear of the inhabitants, who kept a watchful eye over them.

Are diſcharged.

The 7th of *May*, *Iſaac Zweers* and *John Broekhuſen* were carried on board a yacht called the *St. Francis*, in order to be conveyed to the iſle of *Terceira*; and as they were the firſt *Dutch* priſoners that were ſent to that iſland, every body looked upon it no otherwiſe than a pretence to throw them over board after they were come at ſea. Here they met with worſe treatment than before, being forced to ſtand to the pump during the whole voyage, and yet were ready to be ſtarved, notwithſtanding the ſea-men catched more fiſh than they could conſume. At laſt the 28th being arrived in the road near *Terceira*, they ſaw within an hour after a *Dutch* ſhip coming to anchor near them; they called to the ſhip till the maſter ſent ſome of his people aboard them, unto whom they made their complaints, and underſtanding that the maſter was a native of *Niewendam* called *Martin Peter Honing*, they began to be a little chearful, tho' the *Portugueſe* would not allow them to go aboard the *Dutch* ſhip. But the 29th being left alone with the ſteer-man and only one boy in the veſſel, they found means to go in ſpight of their keepers, aboard *Martin Peter Honing*, who promiſed to ſee them delivered. The ſame afternoon *Moor* the governour of this

Are ſent to Terceira.

1646.

this and the adjacent islands, residing in *Terceira* sent for *Zweers* and *Broekhusen*, and told them that he had received a letter from the governour *Antonio Telles da Sylva*, in which he desired him to detain them prisoners in the castle for a twelve month; but that he did not think himself obliged to follow his directions, he having no other dependance but on the king, who being not concerned in this war, his orders were to send all the prisoners brought thither to *Portugal*; that they might rely upon it, and for their present sustenance, till a ship should be ready to go, ordered them nine rix dollars.

And from thence to Portugal.

The 13th of *June* they met with a master of a *French* vessel, who offered to carry them without any reward to *Portugal*, which they willingly accepted of: Here they met with many of their fellow prisoners, who had imagined no otherwise but that the *Portuguese* had thrown them over board. They continued here till the 10th of *September*, when Mr. *Zweers* and *Broekhusen* embarked themselves at *Lisbon* aboard a man of war called the *Prince Henry*, and at last, the 4th of *December*, after a thousand dangers and miseries, which they had sustained since their departure from the *Dutch Brasil*, arrived safely in the *Maese*.

Arrive safely in Holland.

But we must return towards the *Receif*. The unexpected defeat of colonel *Haus*, put all the inhabitants of the *Receif* under a great consternation; but the council left no stone unturned to put the place with all the adjacent forts, in a condition to make a vigorous defence, in case it should be attacked by the enemy; and that every thing might be performed with the best order that could be, *Peter Bas* was constituted commander in chief in the *Receif*. Admiral *Lichthart* was to take care of the batteries, and artillery thereunto belonging; *Henry Moucheron* was made commander in *Maurice's town*; all their thoughts being now bent upon the defence of these places, which before they judged out of danger.

Preparations in the Receif.

The stables and out-houses for the use of the negroes, as likewise the walks and gardens belonging to count *Maurice's* house being no small impediment to the fort *Ernestus*; it being to be feared that under favour of these houses and trees, the enemy might unexpectedly surprize the fort and *Maurice's town*, and the inhabitants earnestly requested the pulling down of those stables, out-houses and trees, and what else might prove dangerous to the place; orders were given to Mr. *Valbergen* and major *Bayert*, commanding in the fort *Ernestus*, to see the same put in execution, with as little damage to the house as possibly could be. The houses near the fort *Bruin* were likewise ordered to be pulled down, and the horn-work belonging to it, to be levelled at the request of the citizens. Many negroes were also employed under the conduct of major *Beck* and the captain of the city militia, to break down all the houses in *Maurice's town*, which lay too near the new retrenchments. All *Portuguese* prisoners were ordered to be distributed in the ships, and several volunteers who had committed many outrages in the countrey, and were detained in custody, were taken into service for three months. A rumour being spread abroad that 18 of the enemy were come into the *Affagados*, a company of citizens were got in readiness to assist them, but it proved not true.

1646.

The same day the ship called the *Orange-tree* arrived near the *Receif*, being come out of the *Maese* the 21st of *May* with thirty-five soldiers for recruits. The watches were so disposed, that in *Maurice's town* Mr. *de Wit* and *Raetfield* (besides the ordinary offices) and in the *Receif* Mr. *Aldrich* and *Valbergen* should go the rounds.

The ship the Orange tree *comes from* Holland.

Balthasar Dortmund, governour of *Itamarika* sent advice to the council the 17th of *August* that *Kavalkanti* was with some troops come to *Iguaraku*, and had summoned the *Brasilians* to join with him in four days, under forfeiture of their lives.

The 19th the citizens presented a petition, shewing the necessity of having the house of count *Maurice* pulled down, as hindring the prospect from the fort *Ernestus*, and if once possessed by the enemy, they might from thence annoy both the fort and the *Receif* itself with their cannon. But the council having advised with Mr. *Walbeck*, admiral *Lichthart*, *Aldrick de Wit*, *Raetfield*, *Moucheron* and *Valbergen*, thought fit not to agree to it for that time, being in hopes that it might be made useful for their defence. Mr. *de Wit* and *Hamel* were commanded to go from hence to each house in *Maurice's town*, and to take an exact account of what negroes were able to bear arms, and to furnish them with musquets and pikes; the same charge was given to admiral *Lichthart*, and captain *Bartholomew Van Collen*, for the *Receif*. All the sick that were in a state of reconvalescency in the castle were likewise ordered to be armed for its defence.

The citizens petition for the pulling down of Maurice's *house.*

Negroes armed.

At the same time an answer was sent to Mr. *Dortmund*, with orders to draw as many *Brasilians* as possibly he could into the isle of *Itamarika*, and to provide himself with as much cattle and meal (farinha) as he was able to get out of the adjacent places; but that if he found himself not in a condition to maintain the whole island, or

Orders sent to Mr. Dortmund.

1646. or the city of *Schop*, he should retire into the fort *Orange*, where he might be supplied by sea, and consequently make a vigorous defence. Mr. *Carpenter* was likewise forewarned to be upon his guard, and to retire in time into the isle of *Itamarika*, with his soldiers and *Brasilians*, if he found the inhabitants ready to take up arms against him.

The 19th at night a party went abroad to get intelligence, but met with no enemy. Some negroes were also sent towards the enemies quarters to know their strength. The same evening the council received a letter by lieutenant *Francis Meades* from *Andrew Vidal*, in which he testified his readiness still to maintain the peace, complaining at the same time of outrages committed by our soldiers, as may be seen out of the following letter.

A letter from Vidal *to the council.*

W*E have sent you advice before by lieutenant* Manuel Antonio, *of our arrival in this captainship, by orders from the governor* Antonio Telles da Sylva, *and at your own request, in order to restore tranquillity here by the most effectual means we could devise. We also did represent to your lordships the many innovations and unaccountable proceedings which had reached our ears, by the lamentable cries of several noble ravished virgins, and the doleful complaints of the inhabitants of* Rio Grande, *where forty persons of note together with a priest, and the other day two more in the* Salinas *were murdered in cool blood. I can scarce mention without horror (and the respect every one ought to have to sacred places forbids me to particularize) the outrages committed against the Images of saints, and especially that of the mother of God, and sacrileges committed by your soldiers: All which considerations, together with that we found you in a warlike condition, with your troops in the field, natural right of self defence established by the constant custom of war did teach us, not to leave an armed power behind our backs, which upon occasion might have proved fatal to us, before we could come to a resolution in conjunction with your lordships, what measures were best to be taken for the re-establishment of that tranquillity which was the only aim of our coming into these parts; according to which we have regulated ourselves in our march towards the* Receif, *till we come to the town of* St. Antonio de Cabo; *where having caused* John Fernandes Vieira *to be taken into custody, under a guard of twelve soldiers, we were surprized at the vast numbers of inhabitants, children, women, and religious men, who to shelter themselves from the outrages and robberies committed against them by captain* Blaer *in the* Vergea, *came to seek for shelter among us. They gave us an account how that the said captain not satisfied with having plundered their houses, had carried away three of the noblest ladies of the countrey, after they had been grievously disgraced before; the inhabitants being exasperated by these violences, did (against our will) leave our camp so suddenly, that whatever haste we made to march after them, we could not overtake them before they were engaged with some of your troops, in the sugar-mill of* Isab. Gonsalves, *which they intended to have set on fire, had it not been for our men, who were forced to interpose betwixt them and your soldiers, to their no small danger and our loss, as being exposed to the vollies of your small shot, which consisted for the most part of bullets cut in pieces and made four square. As the hostilities committed daily against our troops, afford fresh occasions of revolt among the inhabitants, so we cannot but lay before your lordships the late proclamation and ratification of peace betwixt us, protesting now and for ever in the name of God,* John IV. *our king, as also in the name of the states general and all our allies, that your lordships will not let things come to a rupture, and not give us new cause of acting offensively, or to declare war against you. We cannot longer dissemble our opinion, that the reiterated complaints of the inhabitants, may at least in some measure serve for an excuse, if not a justification of the proceedings of* John Fernandes Vieira, *concerning whom we are sufficiently satisfied that his first intentions were only to afford protection to some innocent persons threatned with destruction; which though it was in his power to do, yet did he retire from place to place with his forces, in hopes of avoiding any engagement, till forced thereunto by necessity, he was constrained to repel force by force. We beg of your lordships to take this letter into serious consideration, being of so much consequence, to our both sides safeties; for it seems as if heaven itself were offended at our proceedings. God preserve your lordships.* 1646.

Andrew Vidal de Negreiros.

From de Ingenio of St. John Baptist de Venies, Aug. 19, 1645.

An answer from the council was sent the next following day by the same lieutenant.

The council's answer.

O*UT of our answer to your letter dated at* Serinhaim *the* 8th *of august, you may sufficiently see that the protestations made both by the governour* Antonio Telles da Sylva, *and by yourself, concerning the maintaining of the*

1646. the peace betwixt his majesty of Portugal and the states general of the United Provinces, were never look'd upon by us as sincere, or to be relied upon, since your actions did in no wise agree with your words. The treacherous proposals made to one of our deputies, to betray one of our best strong holds into your hands; the landing of so formidable a force in our territories without any knowledge, under pretence of a misinterpreted sense of our letter to his excellency; the coming with a strong fleet into our road; the taking of the fort of Serinhaim; the slaughter of so many Brasilians our subjects in cool blood; the summons sent to the cape of St. Austin for a surrender, nay the attacking and surprising of our troops, who were forced to keep in the field, for the bridling of our rebellious inhabitants; all these, we say, cannot by any unbiass'd persons be looked upon otherwise, than manifest infractions of the said treaty, and open hostilities. We on our side can without the least contradiction to truth positively declare, that our armament was not in the least intended against his majesty of Portugal, but against the rebels and their adherents; which we were compelled to, when we saw many armed troops to penetrate into our territories cross the river St. Francisco. The surprising of some of our barks in the Salgados; the taking of the house Marecape, and making our safeguards prisoners there, as well as at Cambao, and several other places; the gallows that were erected on purpose to terrify our inhabitants into a compliance with the revolted party; the killing of three of the said inhabitants of Pojuka in cool blood, and the surprising of several of our soldiers and Brasilians sent to St. Lawrence to fetch farinha; the plundering of the houses and shops of several tradesmen in the countrey, with many such like violences committed by the revolted party; and what is the worst, before ever we appeared in arms, but endeavoured by proclamations of pardon and of maintaining them in their possessions, to divert the danger; all these actions, we say, will not admit of any other interpretation but of open hostilities.

How can it be supposed that in the station we are, we could after all those provocations and slights of our kind offers, desist any longer from drawing the sword? Whatever in the mean time has been transacted contrary to the custom of war, has been done without our knowledge and intention, being occasioned by the treacherous dealings of the rebels, and consequently to be looked upon as deserved punishments, rather than the consequences of a just war; besides, that neither his excellency Antonio Telles da Sylva, neither you nor any body else, has any legal power to call us to an account concerning the government or punishment of the subjects of the states general, no more than the king of Portugal is answerable to us for what is transacted upon that account in his kingdom or other dominions. 1646.

Notwithstanding which we would have you not in the least lay the before-mentioned crimes and violencies at our door, we are so far from having encouraged or commanded the Tapoyers to kill the Portuguese inhabitants in Kunhao, that for these several years last past we have endeavoured to prevent it; for having, by the ill treatment they had received from the Portuguese, been exasperated against them, they were for killing most of the inhabitants of that captainship, and had actually put it in execution, had we not interposed our authority, and ordered our garrisons to take them into their particular protection. What you say of ravishing of women, is not only beyond our knowledge, but even beyond whatever we heard of before, having taken all imaginable care to prevent such violences by our proclamation, published for that purpose. It is known to all the world that we afforded our peculiar protection to the women of de Ingenio, of St. Arnout d'Orlanda, and what concerns the taking of the ladies by captain John Blaer, was, as we are informed, done with no other intention, than to exchange them for his wife, or at least to keep them as hostages for her, he having received intelligence that she was very ill treated by you at Serinhaim. The rebels themselves made the first step towards those robberies and rapines that have been committed by our soldiers since; which however cannot come into balance with those cheats, frauds and rapines, wherewith those rebels have defrauded and robbed their creditors of their debts and goods; notwithstanding which we have by granting safeguards and otherwise done all what in us lay to prevent the same.

The late murder upon the person of the Salinhas was committed the 17th of August, without our knowledge, to our great dissatisfaction by the flying Brasilians, who being enraged at the killing of their men, women and children at Serinhaim, without any distinction of age or sex, took this opportunity of revenging themselves. You may easily guess that the papers dispersed by Antonio Kavalkanti at Iguaracu, have also contributed a little to this enterprize.

Of the bullets mentioned by you to have been used in the last encounter, we have more reason to complain than you, it being our constant order not to recede from what is the custom of war in these cases.

The courtesy shewed in saving and receiving our soldiers, we are ready to acknowledge, and to return upon the like occasion, desiring you would send us back your resolution upon this point by the same drummer.

It being evident from what has been alledged, that all the past misfortunes ought to

1645. *be imputed to the rebels, unto whom we endeavoured by all requisite means to restore tranquillity and peace; but they persisting in their rebellious designs, deserve rather condign punishment than the least excuse at your hands. For which reason it is that we protest before God and the whole world, against the proceedings of his excellency* Antonio Telles da Sylva, *and what else has been committed by yourself contrary to the treaty concluded betwixt his majesty of* Portugal *and the states general of the* United Provinces; *not questioning but that upon the receipt of these presents, you will retire with your forces to the* Bahia, *and thereby put an end to the further violation of the said treaty. Thus expecting your answer, we rest, sir,*

Receif. Aug. 20, 1645. *Yours, &c.*

Preparations against the Enemies coming to the Receif.

The same night word being brought that some of the enemies troops were advanced to *Olinda*, notice was given to all the circumjacent forts, to prepare for a vigorous defence, and two batteries ordered to be raised on the back-side of the dwelling-place of the negroes, from whence they might command the avenues to the *Receif* along the river-side. Several volunteers lately come from the flat country, were incorporated into one company under the command of secretary *Hamel*, as captain, and *Jeronymo Holman* their lieutenant: Two advanced guards were placed, one betwixt the fort *Bruin* and the triangular fort; the second betwixt the last and count *Maurice*'s plantation: Part of the bridge of *Boavista* was broken down, to hinder the enemies passage that way; and considering the importance of the triangular fort, a detachment of twenty six soldiers out of several companies was ordered to reinforce the garrison there. The same care was taken for the security of *Maurice*'s *Town*, *Antonio Vaez*, the fort *Ernestus*, the quinquangular fort, and all the rest.

In Maurice's Town *and other forts.*

Major *Bayert* was ordered to have the remaining walls of count *Maurice*'s stables pull'd down, because they hindred the prospect from the fort *Ernestus*; and *Henry Vermeulen* was commanded to employ thirty negroes in clearing the plantation of count *Maurice* and the ditches from all rubbish; and the before-mention'd *Bayert*, ordered to remove the pallisadoes from the said gardens, and to put them round his fort. The engineer *Pisteor* had orders given him to set a row of pallisadoes on that side of the fort of *Ernestus*, where it fronts the before-mention'd gardens, and to extend them five rods into the river. And this fort being not sufficiently stored with heavy cannon, commissary *Sticht* was to carry thither two great pieces, then planted at the bridge-root, and instead of them to place there two culverins; likewise the entrance of the channel of *Maurice*'s *Town* was stopt by a double row of pallisadoes. The members of the council, in conjunction with those of the court of justice, took another view of the suburbs of *Maurice*'s *Town*, to consult whether it were best to maintain or to desert that post, but the resolution thereof was deferr'd 'till the next day. Two great cannons were planted in the *Quinquangular-Fort*, to command the river-side; and in consideration that the hornworks belonging to that fort, required a considerable number of men for their defence, the governor of the fort was ordered to have the same levell'd by his *Brasilians* and soldiers, and one hundred negroes; and the woods betwixt the said fort and the *Afagados*, were ordered to be cut down by the *Brasilians* belonging to the fort, when it was also resolved to draw the fortifications of *Maurice*'s *Town* into a narrower compass, and to repair the walls round the *Receif*; so that by the indefatigable care of the council, all the fortifications both of the *Receif* and the other adjacent places, were put into such a good posture of defence, that the enemy, tho' very strong, durst not attempt any thing thereabouts for that time. Mr. *Dortmund* had drawn near 1400 persons into *Itamarika*, 700 of which being women and children, he desired some supplies of provisions, but for the rest, had put the island in a good posture.

Letters to the council out of Parayba.

Mr. *Linge*, by his letter dated in *Parayba* the 22[d] of *August*, sent advice to the council, that after notice given him of the defeat of colonel *Haus*, he had judged it most convenient to remove the garrison and inhabitants of *Fredericia* into the forts; that however the *Portuguese* were pretty quiet as yet, notwithstanding his whole force consisted not in above four hundred soldiers, one hundred inhabitants, and fifty *Brasilians*, among whom were a good number of sick and maimed men; and that the *Tapoyers* had slain about twelve or fourteen labouring countrymen. Major *Hoogstrate*, *Ley* and *Heck*, had not long before given notice to the council, that they had burnt all the houses, but especially the magazine and church without the fort, for its better defence, and that the enemy had posted themselves on the hill of the cape, and on the southern island.

On the 25th of *August*, upon another review of the fortifications of *Maurice*'s *Town*, the same were ordered to be brought forthwith to perfection.

The same day the council received letters from Mr. *Linge*, by the way of *Itamarika*, dated

1645. dated the 18th and 19th of *August*, in *Parayba*, that *William Barents* had sent him advice from *Kunbao* the 14th of *August*, that he and *Rudolph Bawn* had a troop of *Tapoyers* ready for our service, every thing being very quiet thereabouts; but that the said *Tapoyers* had carried away all the cattle belonging to *Peter Farcharson*, which had occasioned no small scarcity of fresh flesh thereabouts.

It was also judged absolutely necessary by the council, to take into their serious consideration the present condition of the forts in *Rio St. Francisco* and *Seregippo del Rey*, which being provided but with slender garrisons, and all communication cut off betwixt them and the *Receif*, and in great danger of being lost; it was judged absolutely necessary, after the defeat of colonel *Haus*, to endeavour the preservation of them, and consequently of the whole *Dutch-Brasil*, by removing them from thence to the *Receif*.

Consultations about removing several garrisons to the Receif.

To accomplish this with all imaginable security, Mr. *Walbeck* was deputed by the great council to the council of war, to know their opinion, by what means these garrisons, as well as that of *Porto Calvo*, might be with safety brought to the *Receif*, or whether, considering that they would be forced to leave their cannon behind them, they should be ordered to defend themselves to the last extremity, in hopes of receiving speedy succours from *Holland* for their relief.

The council of war, having well weighed the whole matter, unanimously agreed upon the following resolution.

The resolution of the council of war.

THAT *it was their opinion, considering the capital city was in danger for want of a sufficient garrison, the garrisons of the before-mention'd forts, which in all probability could not make any long resistance, ought to be taken from thence with as much ammunition and cannon as could be done, and carried to the* Receif. *But in regard that the fort of* Porto Calvo *lay pretty deep into countrey, where the river was very narrow and shallow, the garrisons of* Rio St. Francisco, *and* Seregippo del Rey, *were to pass that way in order to join them, and that they should bury or break their cannon.*

By order from the council of war, *Aug.* 24, 1645.

Signed,

Kornelis Bayer,	Henry Advocaet.
Albertus Oosterman,	Frederick Pistoor.
L. Van. Harkema,	*capt.* Haelmeister.
John Denning,	Rene de Mouchy.
Samuel Lambartz.	

Accordingly two barks, with the ship *Zelandia*, were ordered for the execution of this enterprize, to *Rio St. Francisco*. 1645.

The last day of *August*, one of the captains of these two barks return'd, and gave an account, that he being advanced into the river of *Rio St. Francisco*, within a league of the said fort, he received so warm a salute of small shot from a *Portuguese* vessel full of firelocks, that he was forced to return, without being able to penetrate any further up the river; that the other bark being discouraged thereat, durst not venture to go to *Seregippo*, but that they thought fit to retreat back with the ship *Zelandia*; he further added, that it would be very difficult to put this design in execution, unless they were provided with some galliots and yachts well armed.

Pursuant to this advice, the council ordered the yacht called the *Sprew*, with three other barks thither, to join with the ship *Zelandia*, for the more effectual execution of this design.

They set sail from the *Receif* the 2d of *September*, captain *William Lambartz* commodore. He return'd with the said yacht, and the *Zelandia*, the first of *October*, to the *Receif*, where he gave the following account of his expedition to the council.

Some ships sent to Rio St. Francisco *under* William Lambartz.

We came the 22d of *September* within a half league of the fort of *St. Maurice*, where we met with a bark, which at the discharge of one of our cannon, sail'd away before us up the river. As we were in pursuit of her, we espied another small vessel, in company of the bark belonging to *John Hoek*, both full of soldiers: We saw the first of these two run ashore, and the soldiers landing, who skirmished with an opsite party for the defence of the vessel: Our yacht under favour of our cannon, boarded the said vessel, with an intention to set it on fire; but finding it loaden with the baggage of our soldiers, fell to plundering first; and soon after espied a boat with a white flag, making all the sail they could towards them: Major *Pappenheim*, late commander of the fort of *Rio St. Francisco*, and Mr. *Hoek*, were in this Boat, being sent by the enemy to let us know, that if we set fire to the vessel, he would cut all the prisoners with their wives and children to pieces, so that we desisted from it. They gave us an account, that the said fort had been forced to surrender three days before, for want of wood and provisions, after a siege of twenty six days: That the *Portuguese* having taken a serjeant with four soldiers of the garrison of *Seregippo*, had killed the soldiers, and sent the serjeant back with a convoy of two hundred men, to fetch the garrison of *Seregippo*, which had

He gives an account of his expedition.

1645. had not above four days provision left, from thence. That about eight days before the surrender of the fort, colonel *Haus*, captain *Listry*, and captain *Wiltschut* pass'd by that way in their journey to the *Bahia*, whither they, pursuant to their capitulation, were to be carried with the rest of the prisoners, and from thence to *Portugal*, and so further to *Holland*, without any other loss except their baggage, being for the rest indifferently well treated. They further added, that the *Portuguese* not long ago detach'd two hundred men to the island of *Melchior Alvares*, in hopes to cut off the retreat of our men, and to prevent their excursions, but came too late, our people being retired before. That the enemy had likewise made themselves masters of the fort *dos Affagados*, where Mr. *Bullestraete* being made a prisoner, was now on his way to the *Bahia*. Captain *Lambartz* hearing this account, thought it his best way to retreat towards the mouth of the river, where having spent two days in refitting his ships, he returned the first of *October* to the *Receif*.

The garrisons of the three forts forced to surrender. The same ill success attended us at *Seregippo* and *Porto Calvo*; for the council having sent a bark with provisions to their relief, the same, contrary to her orders, came to anchor before *Rio St. Francisco*, where being seized by the enemy, the garrison of *Seregippo* being thereby disappointed in their hopes, were forced to surrender after they had spent all their provisions. After this misfortune, there was not the least probability left of saving the garrison of *Porto Calvo*, which lying deep into the countrey, the river was not navigable thereabouts by reason of its narrowness, and that the enemy was master of the field on both sides, so that they were likewise obliged to surrender for want of necessaries. *Are carried to the* Bahia. The garrisons of these three forts, were contrary to their capitulation, (by virtue of which they were to be conducted to the *Receif*) carried prisoners to the *Bahia*; but those that could not follow the rest, by reason of sickness, or otherwise, were cut to pieces by the *Portuguese*.

Many of the soldiers belonging to these as well as other garrisons, and of the troops under colonel *Haus*, dreading the danger of the land-journey to the *Bahia*, did take service among the *Portuguese*; but captain *Nicholas Nicholson* being sent with sixty four of these *Dutch* to prepare an ambush for some of our forces, took this opportunity to join with us, *The* Portuguese *kill all the* Dutch *in their service.* which exasperated the enemy to that degree, that they disarmed all the *Dutch* that had taken service there, and murthered them in cool blood; the like they did with the *Dutch* inhabitants that had staid behind in the country. 1645.

In the mean while the captainship of *Parayba*, through the good conduct of their governor *Paul de Linge*, remained in obedience, at least in outward appearance, 'till the 25th of *August* 1645, when the inhabitants, having received intelligence of the defeat of colonel *Haus*, and the surrender of the *Cape of St. Austin*, and being at the same time encouraged by the succours of five companies, and good store of arms, sent to them by *Vidal* from *Pernambuko*, they began also to take up arms, with an intention to cut off the communication betwixt the garrison in the Monastery of *St. Francisco*, as the inhabitants of *Fredericia*, (a place of no strength) and the forts near the sea shore; but Mr. *Linge* shrewdly suspecting their design, did with consent of *Revolt in* Parayba. the rest of the officers there, order all the citizens with their effects, and the before-mention'd garrison to withdraw within these forts, to prevent their being surprised by the *Portuguese*, and to serve as an additional strength for the defence of the forts; for which reason also the *Brasilians* inhabiting with their families in those parts, were commanded to intrench themselves under the cannon, which served for outworks to them. The enemy finding themselves by the conjunction of these forces, disappointed in their design of making themselves masters of *Parayba* by force, had recourse to their wonted artifice, not questioning, but they might have the same success in purchasing the forts of *Parayba*, as they had had at the *Cape of St. Austin*. To encompass which, they sent in *September* 1645, one *Ferdinand Rodrigo de Bulhaus*, clerk of the court of justice of *Parayba*, with a letter directed to the commander in chief, *Paul Vander Linge*, offering him the sum of 19000 gilders, if he would surrender the said fort into their hands. But this message had not the desired effect, the messenger being by order from Mr. *de Linge* taken into custody and hanged the next day; of which *Their messenger hanged.* he sent notice to the council the 16th of *September*. In the mean while, (according to Mr. *de Linge*'s letter from the 6th of *September*) five companies more of the enemies troops, making in all about three hundred Men, were arrived in *Parayba*, which being join'd by the ablest of the inhabitants, had posted themselves near *Tibery*, where they had published by proclamation, for every one to repair to his sugar-mill, under pain of forfeiting the same.

The Passage betwixt the *Affagados* and the *Quinquangular-Fort*, where the cattle belonging to the *Receif* were kept at pasture, being much infested by the enemies parties, one of which had taken good part of

1645.

of it, a small wooden fort was ordered to be erected in the most convenient post, for the security of the meadows thereabouts.

Sometime before, *viz.* the 26th of *July*, orders were sent from the council to *Servaes Carpenter*, to disarm the inhabitants of *Goyana*, who thereupon petitioned the said council to be excused from surrendering their Arms, considering that thirty seven *Portuguese* of *Kunhao*, who had been disarmed, were murthered by the *Tapoyers*, and that they were daily in fear of the same treatment, 'till they were further removed from their borders. The council answered, that the murther committed upon these *Portuguese* had been done without their knowledge, and contrary to their orders; that in case they persisted in their allegiance, they had nothing to fear from the *Tapoyers*, whilst they were under their protection; neither ought they to imagine that the disarming of them, was done with an intention to leave them a prey to the *Tapoyers*, but for our own security, and to furnish them with a plausible excuse not to join with the rebels, whenever they should be prompted thereunto by them. At the same time they repeated their orders to Mr. *Carpenter*, not to desist from disarming those of *Goyana*, notwithstanding their petition to the contrary, but that he should be very careful, that neither the soldiers, nor *Brasilians* of *Marni* might be burthensome to them. The council also deputed Mr. *Astelle* and captain *William Lambartz*, with letters to *John Duwy* and *Karakara*, the first king, and the second commander in chief of a troop of the *Tapoyers*, with presents to all the rest of their commanders, in order to engage them to join with us, they having complained of their not having been presented, like as *John Duwy* was before; accordingly the said Mr. *Astelle* and captain *William Lambratz* having taken their leave the 28th of *August* of the council, took shipping for *Parayba*, in order to go from thence to *Kunhao* to treat with the *Tapoyers*.

Deputies sent the Tapoyers

The Members of the Court of Justice and the council of war, in conjunction with the magistrates, having represented to the *great council* the absolute necessity of having the houses in *Maurice*'s *Town* pull'd down and laid level with the ground; an order of the said council was publish'd the 29th of *August* by beat of drum, enjoining the inhabitants to pull down such houses, within the space of two days, and in case of failure, every body to be at liberty to break down the same for his use; the house of Mr. *Rechteren* only excepted, which was to be converted into a redoubt, for the defence of the adjacent plain. The same day *John Denninger*, lately lieutenant to colonel *Haus*, succeeded captain *Blaar*, now a prisoner with the enemy, in his command; and many negroes offered to serve the company under a captain of their own choosing.

1645.

The 30th of *August*, captain *William Lambartz*, with part of his forces return'd to the *Receif* from *Parayba*, where he gave the council an account of his negotiation: That not without a great deal of trouble they at last obtained two hundred *Tapoyers* from their king *John Duwy*, who pretended that he dreaded an incursion from one of his neighbours, who in the absence of his troops might perhaps kill him with all his family, and demanded at the same time, that all the *Portuguese* might be killed in *Parayba*. That he marching with these *Tapoyers* into the said captainship of *Parayba*, they actually slew all the *Portuguese* they met with in their way, to the number of one hundred persons, and plunder'd their houses; and as soon as they found him prepared to appease them, one half of them, with what negroes and other booty they had got, returned home; but continuing his march with the rest thro' *Goyana* towards the *Receif*, the *Tapoyers* did no sooner understand, that they were likely to meet with some opposition by the way, but they followed the footsteps of the rest homewards; so that he was forced to retire with all speed to the fort of *St. Margaret* in *Parayba*, from whence he returned by sea to the *Receif*. Hereupon the council dispatched some letters the 16th of *September* for *Rio Grande*, directed to king *John Duwy*, *Jacob Rabbi* and *Rudolf Baro*, exhorting them to join their arms with ours, for our mutual defence, and to chase the *Portuguese* that were on their march thither, from thence.

The successes of their negotiation.

The Tapoyers *desert.*

The 13th of *September* 1645, *Jeronymo Serrao da Paiva*, late admiral of the *Portuguse* fleet, (made prisoners in the late sea engagement in the bay of *Tamandare*) appeared before the council, where being examined concerning the designs of the governor of the *Bahia* in sending a fleet, and landing his forces in the Bay of *Tamandare*, as likewise concerning the fleet under the command of *Salvador Korrea de Saa*, he refused to give any other answer, or to make the least confession, except that he was sent with the said fleet and forces to offer his assistance to appease the revolt arisen among us. He desired also leave to send a letter by a drummer to the colonels *Martin Soares Moreno* and *Andrew Vidal*, about the exchanging of his person, and some other *Portuguese* Prisoners, which was granted.

The captive Portuguese *admiral examined.*

Some

1645. Some of the citizens having conceived a jealousy, as if their pressing circumstances and the need they stood in of present relief, had not been sufficiently represented to the council of nineteen in *Holland*, it was thought fit by the council to communicate the contents of the two last letters to them for their satisfaction.

The 19th of *September*, about noon, our whole fleet retired from the bay of *Tamandare* into the road of the *Receif*, with two men of war, and two small vessels taken from the enemy; where I was arrived long before, having left them, immediately after the engagement. The same night *Servaes Carpenter* who died the day before, was interr'd. The same day the yacht call'd the *Doe*, and one of the small vessels taken from the enemy, and call'd by us the *Receif*, were sent out a crusing to the *Cape of St. Austin*, to prevent the enemies receiving any supplies by sea thereabouts.

The council being sensible that the enemy made it their chiefest endeavour to drive away their cattle, and to prevent them, by strong parties from fetching of wood and fishing, a company of fusileers was order'd to be erected out of other companies, who were to be commanded by captain *Renbagh*, and to serve as a constant guard against the enemy's flying parties. The 21st of *September*, the following proclamation of pardon for such as had taken service with the enemy, was publish'd.

Company of fusileers erected.

A PARDON *publish'd.*

THE great council of the Dutch-Brasil *being made sensible, that many of their subjects being fallen into the enemies hands, have either for fear of being killed or transported, and out of other considerations, taken service among the enemies troops, and considering that most of them have been inveigled by their commanders, and perhaps are in a fair way of repenting of their error, have thought fit, by these presents to grant our pardon to all such as shall return to our service, for all past offences; with our promise, that they shall receive the advantage of the same station they were possess'd of among us before; and such as are willing to return to their native countrey, shall have passports granted them for that purpose; from the benefit of which pardon, are however excepted* Dirck Hoogstrate, *and the other traytors, who being commanders of forts, have treacherously delivered up the same to the enemy.*

By this time the enemy had block'd up all the avenues by land, leading to the *Receif*, in hopes to reduce us by famine, having posted both all the *Portuguese* forces sent to their aid from the *Bahia*, and the rebellious troops, from the city of *Olinda* to the *Baretta*, in the form of a half-moon; and made about half a league from the fort of *Affagados* an entrenchment provided with six pieces of heavy cannon, brought hither from *Porto Calvo*; but durst not attack us by force, knowing we were prepared for their reception. 1645.

Mr. *Dortmund* having by his letters represented to the council, the necessity there was of sending one of their members to provide for the security of *Itamarika*, and to keep the *Brasilians*, (consisting of 1500 men, women and children) by his authority in their duty against the solicitations of *Kamaron*, who left no stone unturn'd to bring them over to his side; they desired Mr. *Bullestrate* to take upon him this province; who accordingly the 23d of *September*, set sail thither in the ship the *Deventer*, and returning the 29th of *September* to the *Receif*, gave the following account to the council.

Mr Bullestrate *sent to* Itamarika.

He arrived about noon at the entrance of the river *Maria Farinha*, where being informed by *John Vos*, master of a bark, that the enemy had twice attack'd the city of *Shoppe*, and continued before it still, he went into a challop, with five or six seamen to the fort *Orange*, but was no sooner espied by the garrison, but they desired him not to come nearer, they being still smartly engaged with the enemy upon the hill, and doubtful of success: Whereupon he sent two seamen, with a letter to Mr. *Dortmund*, who being encouraged by the reward of two reals, brought an answer from him the same night, intimating that the enemy, had been forced to retire.

An account of his proceedings.

The 25th of *August*, by break of day, he went in a challop to the city of *Shoppe*, and finding that the enemy, what with the brave resistance made by the garrison, what with fear of this ship, had abandon'd not only the city, but also the whole island, he ordered the fortifications to be forthwith repaired, and to be put into a good posture of defence.

For the enemy perceiving that it was in vain to attack us upon the *Receif*, sent great part of their forces, embark'd in 8 boats and a bark against *Itamarika*, the 20th of *September*; where having surprized, and vigorously attack'd our forces posted on the hill near the city, (our deserters making the first attack) that they the third time made themselves masters of it, forcing our troops to retreat into their entrenchment of the church.

The Portuguese *attack* Itamarika.

About three days after, *viz.* the 23d, Mr. *Bullestrate*, as we told you, arrived in the ship *Deventer*, to give the necessary orders for the defence of the place; and to keep the *Brasilians* in awe, he brought along with him

1645. him some volunteers chosen from among the citizens, the garrison of the *Receif* being so weak as not to be rendred useless by any further detachments; besides that there were 400 *Brasilians* capable of bearing arms at *Itamarika*. He was charged by the great council, and the members of the council of war, to watch above all things for the defence of the fort *Orange*, which was to be maintained to the last, if they were not able to keep the whole island on the hill.

Mr. *Bullestrate*, after his arrival there, found it absolutely necessary to preserve likewise the city of *Shoppe*, from whence the said fort must be supplied with wood, its situation being such, as that so long as we were masters at sea, we could maintain a correspondence betwixt the said fort and city; for which purpose also, the yacht call'd the *Golden-Doe*, had her station appointed betwixt the fort *Orange* and the hill, to maintain the passage of the river between both. But to return to the siege of the city: The enemy made three vigorous attacks upon the entrenchment on the hill, but was repulsed with the loss of 150 kill'd; tho' a barber, who after the fight deserted them, made their loss amount to 450. *Kamaron* and *Hoogstrate* were wounded, and we had only 15 kill'd and 16 wounded. The *Brasilians* lately transported thither, from the villages of *Goyana*, *Iguaracu*, and other places, behaved themselves to a miracle upon this occasion, tho' it must be allow'd, that the arrival of Mr. *Bullestrate* did not a little cool their courage, which made them abandon the island in the night, betwixt sunday and monday.

Abandon it again.

Further consultations about the safety of Itamarika.

The 2d of *October* the great council entred upon a second debate concerning the preservation of *Itamarika*, they having received certain intelligence, that the enemy had undertaken the last expedition against that island, upon hopes of being seconded therein by certain persons of our party, with whom they kept a secret correspondency; and tho' they were in the dark upon whom in particular to fix the intended treachery, yet did they think it conducing to the safety of that so important place, to remove captain *Sluyter*, with his company from thence, and in their stead to send thither the company commanded by captain *William Lambartz*, and to entrust him with the supreme command of all their forces there, which was put in execution accordingly the next day. The entrenchment round the church and the fort *Orange*, were also ordered to be strengthen'd with pallisadoes; and the first, pursuant to the advice of *Garstman* and *Dortmund*, I ordered to be surrounded with a counterscarp, within the compass of which a company of *Brasilians* were lodged, with their wives and children, and the rest to be employed in the defence of the fort *Orange*; so the redoubt which commanded the place, from which the fort was supplied with water, was ordered to be repaired against a sudden attack, without which the fort could not long subsist, or hold out against an enemy. 1645.

Letters were about the same time delivered to the council, dated the 5th of *October*, by Major *Austin de Magethaes*, sent by *Andrew Vidal*, to treat about the exchange of prisoners; he told them, that since admiral *Serrao de Paiva*, had by two several letters sollicited his releasement, he desired that the same might be exchanged for other soldiers, or be ransomed by *Antonio Telles da Sylva*, governor of the *Bahia*. He desired also that a cartel might be agreed upon for the exchange of the soldiers; and that in the mean while such of the *Portuguese* inhabitants, as were prisoners with us, might be released for reasonable ransom, which was not accepted of by the council.

Vidal *sollicits the exchange of prisoners.*

In the mean while, (pursuant to the letters from the commander in chief of *Rio Grande*, and *John Hoek* of the 6th of *October*) *Jacob Rabbi*, with a small troop of *Tapoyers* and *Brasilians*, in conjunction with 30 *Dutch* inhabitants, made themselves masters of the seat of *John Lestan*, with the slaughter of 15 *Portuguese*. But they had not the same success at *Fernandes Menda*'s house in *Potigi*, which being defended by 50 *Portuguese*, they were repulsed with some loss.

Fifteen Portuguese *killed by the* Tapoyers.

The enemies finding themselves disappointed in their design of gaining *Parayba* by treachery, did again apply all their care to block up all the avenues leading to the *Receif*, in hopes of reducing it by famine. This occasioned many skirmishes, in which the *Brasilians*, who got the greatest part of their provision out of the countrey, did a considerable mischief to the *Portuguese*; who for their greater security built a fort in *Pernambuko* (as they likewise did in the *Vargea* of *Parayba*) near the sugar-mill of *George Huomo Pinto*, but slightly fortified, and not able to hold out against any vigorous attack. In *Rio Grande* the *Tapoyers* plaid the masters over the *Portuguese*; for as we told you before, that according to their custom they entred the said captainship in *July* 1645, when being informed of the rebellion of the *Portuguese* in *Pernambuko*, they out of an inborn hatred to that nation, attacked the 16th of *July* some of them in the sugar-mill of *Kunhao*, and killed every soul of them, the *Dutch* inhabitants thereabouts not being strong enough to prevent it. From thence the *Tapoyers* marched to *Monpobu*, *Goyana*, and

1645. and *Potosi*, places belonging likewise to *Rio Grande*, where finding a body of *Portuguese* entrenched with pallisadoes in the nature of a *Palanka*, they forced them in conjunction with some *Brasilians*, to surrender, under condition that their lives should be saved, provided they did not give any further occasion of disturbance. But some of the *Portuguese* flying afterwards into *Parayba*, the *Tapoyers* looking upon this as a breach of the late treaty, did with the beforementioned *Brasilians* agree to put the rest to the sword wherever they met with them, which they did accordingly, the *Brasilians* exclaiming against the tyranny committed upon thirty or forty of their comrades, who by *Andrew Vidal*'s order, were tied to pallisadoes in *Serinhaim* and strangled, which had this good effect, that *Rio Grande* for that time was entirely purged of the rebellious crew, except some few who escaped their hands. Their estates and cattle were afterwards disposed for the benefit of the company, and others their creditors, which furnished the publick magazines with good store of flesh, at a very seasonable time. The *Portuguese* being sensible that we drew considerable supplies of provisions from that countrey, endeavoured to prevent it by sending several bodies of their troops thither, but were always forced to retire to *Parayba*, whither they carried as much cattle along with them as they could.

The Tapoyers *clear* Rio Grande *of the* Portuguese.

An account of the enemies forces.

According to the deposition of captain *Nicholas Nicholson* (who came over to us the 12th of *November*, as we shall see anon) the four companies of *Dutch* quartered in the *Vargea*, were as follows.

The company of *Nicholas Nicholson*, 63 men, and among them 23 musquets.

The company of *Alexander Buchhalt*, of 43 men, among whom 36 musquets.

The company of captain *Anthony*, who was mortally wounded in a late engagement, consisting of 36 men, and among them 32 musquets.

The company of *John de Witt*, of 40 men, but miserable wretches, and among them only 12 musquets.

Besides these they had two other *Dutch* companies in *Goyana*, one commanded by *George Peterson* of 17 men, all pikes, the other by *La Cour* of 19 men, likewise most pikes. They had also two more in *Parayba*, one under the command of captain *Peter Gendre* of 19 men, most pikes; the second by *Edward Versman* of 20 men, among whom was but one musqueteer: So that the whole number of these eight companies, amounted to no more than 257 men; their colonel was *Hoogstrate*, and *Francis la Tour* late alderman of *Serinhaim*, major, a profest enemy to the *Hollanders*. Most of the *Dutch* prisoners were put under a necessity of taking service with the enemy, being otherwise in danger of being murdered in their way to the *Bahia*, as it happened to 42 prisoners taken at the cape of *St. Austin*, who were all slain in the sugar-mill *Konjau*, near *Serinhaim*. He further declared, that the enemies forces in the *Vergea*, consisted of about 700 men sent from the *Bahia*, divided into nine companies, well armed with musquets and firelocks. That besides these, they had about 100 men, gathered from among the *Portuguese* inhabitants, they having forced all the young men from the south of *Huma*, as far as *St. Lawrence* to take up arms; some being armed with firelocks, others with musquets they had taken from us; they were for the most part mulats, and an undisciplined rabble, commanded by *John Fernand Vieira* as colonel, and *Anthony Dias* (who came from the *Bahia*) their major. Their captains most in esteem among them were, *Simon Mendes*, *Domingos Fagundos*, and *John d'Albuquerque*. *Kamaron* commanded 100 *Brasilians* armed with blunderbusses, and *Dias* 200 negroes (among whom 50 were ours) provided with very good guns; besides some *Tapoyers*. Each soldier had for his daily allowance, a pound of meat, and about a pint of farinha or meal, and 12 gilders *per* month; a captain 120 gilders, an ensign 42, a serjeant 21, and a corporal 15 gilders *per* month. But they only paid the *Dutch* troops with ready money, the account with the *Portuguese* from the *Bahia* being made up but once a year. They were at that time busy in raising of a fort with four small bastions and a powder house, betwixt *Bierbrom*'s sugar-mill and *Casa de Sabrodo*, upon each of which were to be mounted three pieces of cannon, eight pieces having been brought for that purpose from *Porto Calvo*, among which were five of metal. Round about this fort the soldiers from the *Bahia* had their quarters assigned them, except the company commanded by *John de Magehais*, which was quartered in the *Baretta*, with four *Dutch* companies, viz. the *Dutch* that were in the sugar-mill of *Bierbrom*, and those commanded by captain *Peter Kavalkanti*, and *Anthony Jaconio*, and two or three companies of the *Portuguese* come from the *Bahia*, in the sugar-mill *Brito*; the rest being *Portuguese*, *Mulats*, and other idle fellows they had forced to follow them from the south. These were armed for the most part with firelocks and musquets, the rest with pikes, *Andrew Vidal*, *John Fernand Vieira*, and major *Hoogstrate*, were at that time in the *Casa de Sabrodo*; all these consisted not 1645

in

1645. in above 600 men. About the sugar-mill of *John de Mendonce* were quartered three companies, two at the house of *Sebastian Karvalho*, and two more in the sugar-mill of *Mengao*. The rest were posted in the *Salines*, *Baretta*, and the city of *Olinda*. Some of *Kamaron*'s troops were in the sugar-mill of *Van Scholl*, and in the house of *John Kordero de Mendoje*, upon the bank of the river, being their advanced guard; *Henry Dias* with his troops had his post in the house of Mr. *Luffelen*. The redoubts belonging to the city of *Olinda*, were manned only with 17 soldiers.

In *November* the great council received intelligence, both by letters from *Paulo de Linge* out of *Parayba*, as also by several deserters, that the enemy had sent 400 men, 200 of which were soldiers, the rest inhabitants, from *Rio Grande* into *Parayba*, to make themselves masters of the open countrey, or at least to drive away the cattle; whereupon it was resolved, with consent of colonel *Garsman*, to endeavour to hinder the execution of the enemies design.

Captain Nicholas Nicholson *deserts the enemy.*

The 12th of *November*, captain *Nicholas Nicholson*, a native of *Amsterdam*, came, as we told you before, over to us to the *Receif*. He was among other prisoners of the cape of *St. Austin*, carried from thence to *St. Antonio*, where he took service among the *Portuguese*, but with no other intention than to desert them upon the first opportunity; he being intrusted with a captain's commission, to command a company of *Dutch* soldiers forced to list themselves from among the prisoners they had taken, was ordered, at the recommendation of *Hoogstrate*, and *Albert Geuitz Weddo*, with the approbation of *Vidal* and *John Vieira*, to lye in ambush for some of our people in the *Salines*, with a detachment of 60 men, out of the four *Dutch* companies in their service; and four more companies were ordered for a reserve, to assist him upon all occasions. The supreme command of the whole body being committed to him, he approached as near as he could with his *Dutch* to the fort *Bruin*, where he took the opportunity to pass the river by break of day, and to go with them (they being all willing to follow) over to us to the said fort. Captain *Nicholas Nicholson* had the command over the said company confirmed to him by the council, they being all willing to enter into their service: But the enemy had no sooner notice of it, but they disarmed all the *Dutch*, and under pretence of sending them to the *Bahia*, caused them to be murdered by the way, with their wives and children.

The 2d of *November*, the council had received advice from Mr. *Linge* from *Parayba*, that *Andrew Vidal* had entred that captainship with 200 men, and that *Kamaron* had by letters strongly sollicited *Peter Potty*, to desert our service with his *Brasilians*, but had received a smart refusal; the council sent him two pieces of fine linnen cloth as a reward of his fidelity. For it ought to be observed, that the *Portuguese* when they first began to take up arms against the government, did with letters and great promises, tempt the *Regidors* or commanders of the *Brasilians* to join with them, but they were so far from hearkening to them, that they sent all the letters written upon that account, both by *Kamaron* and the rest of the rebellious ringleaders, without opening to the council, thereby to avoid all suspicion of keeping any correspondence with the enemy, *Peter Potty* being a near kinsman of *Kamaron*; and ever since that time they have behaved themselves so well upon all occasions, and have done such considerable mischiefs to the *Portuguese*, by plundering and killing them, wherever they could meet with them, that we had not the least reason to mistrust the sincerity of their intentions.

The Dutch *defeat the* Portuguese.

The said Mr. *Linge* did also send word *November* the 4th, that the enemy had attempted nothing as yet; and from *November* 14, that a party of 300 of our people being joined by some *Brasilians* of *Parayba*, had engaged 800 of the enemies troops, whom after a smart engagement they put to the rout, with the slaughter of a good number of their men. The *Brasilians* being encouraged by this success, did over-run all the flat countrey, and meeting with a good number of *Portuguese*, who were merry-making upon *St. Martin*'s eve in the sugar mill of *Andrew Dias de Tigeireda*, they attackt them so furiously, that after a slender resistance they put them all to the sword, even the son of the said *Tigeireda* himself, and a priest, without giving quarter to any body, except to a very beautiful maiden; who though almost distracted at the death of her father, and some of her other relations, that lay wallowing in their own blood, had such a powerful influence upon the hearts of these *Barbarians*, that they brought her a prisoner safely to the fort of *Parayba*.

The Tapoyers *kill many* Portuguese.

The Dutch *attack the* Portuguese *near* Kunhao *without success.*

The 21st of *November* towards the evening, 360 soldiers (20 of whom were taken from the *Receif*) set sail in small boats to the bay of *Traican*, and continued their march the same night, under the command of lieutenant *Berge*, justice *Hoek*, and the receiver-general of *Pernambuko*, towards *Kunhao*, in order to attack the enemy that were lately come into *Rio Grande* from *Parayba*; but these enemies having got some intel-

1645. intelligence of our designs, were retired from *Kunhao* to a retrenchment among the bogs, which being accessible but in one place, they so warmly saluted our forces that would have forced them from thence, with their shot, that they were obliged to retreat with the loss of some dead and wounded, to the castle of *Keulen*, partly to refresh their men, partly to prevent their penetrating deeper into the council.

The 4th of *December* it was resolved to send the ship the *Overyssel*, and the yacht called the *Sprew*, towards the *Bahia* a cruising, to get intelligence of their naval strength thereabouts, and to endeavour to take some prizes. The 5th of *December* the great council sent for all the commanders of the *Brasilians*, to inform them, that they had received considerable supplies of powder, ball, and all other sorts of ammunition, by the ship called the *Swan*, with letters from *Holland*, that they were equipping a considerable fleet for their relief; at which the *Brasilians* were extremely rejoyced; the *Portuguese* commanders having made it their business to persuade them, that no such thing was expected from *Holland*.

The Brasilian *commanders summoned.*

Advice that all the Dutch *were killed by the* Portuguese.

The same evening a *Brasilian* deserter declared, that all the *Dutch* were killed by the rebellious inhabitants, and their wives and children made slaves. The same thing was confirmed by a negro deserter, concerning captain *Bockholt*; who having taken service with the enemy, and being afterwards suspected by them, had caused him to be murdered, as they had done with all the rest of the *Dutch* in their service, who were slain in their way to the *Babia*.

Four companies of fusiliers erected.

The 7th of *December* it was resolved in council, to erect four companies of fusiliers, the same being found by experience to be more serviceable at this juncture, for which purpose the companies of colonel *Garsman*, captain *Jurian Remberger*, captain *Nicholas Nicholson*, and captain *John Taylor*, were pitched upon before all the rest.

In the same month of *December*, a certain *Portuguese*, *Gasper Gonsalves*, was taken by the *Brasilians* in the island of *Itamarika*, sent on purpose to persuade the *Brasilians*, that the *Dutch* intended to deliver them up to the *Portuguese* for a certain sum of money, and they to retire with their effects into *Holland*, which caused no small commotion among the *Brasilians*, who began to give credit to the relation. And because *Gonsalves* had spread this rumour abroad some time before the arrival of *Caspar Honyhouse* (who the 28th of *August* was appointed commander in chief of the *Brasilians* of *Itamarika* instead of *Listry* taken prisoner by the enemy) he was hardly put to it how to remove this jealousy from among them. 1645.

Jacob Rabbi, pursuant to his letters of the 11th of *December*, was abous the same time preparing to enter 80 leagues further into the countrey towards the *Tapoyers*, to sollicit their assistance: He at last came to *Oyepe*, son-in-law of king *Duwy*, who promised, in case those of *Siara* would send their troops to us, he would endeavour to raise as many of his vassals as he could; but king *Duwy* excused himself under pretence that many of his troops died by sickness in the *Sartan*.

The night before the 27th of *December*, the enemy had by means of a boat, fastned two puppets with fire-works to the ship called the *Swan*; but being discovered as soon as it took fire, was soon quencht without doing any damage to the vessel; which made the ships to be constantly upon their guard for the future.

The Portuguese *endeavour to fire the* Dutch *ships.*

The 30th of *December* two such puppets found by two soldiers in a small boat near the fort *Bruin*, were presented to the council. This boat, which questionless was sent on purpose to fasten these puppets to some ship or other, being discovered by the centinels, the men quitted the boat, leaving the said puppets behind them.

Mr. *de Linge*, by his letters dated the 30th of *December* from the fort *St. Margaret* in *Parayba*, advised, that a certain negro who had deserted the enemies quarter of *St. Andrew* had declared, that the enemy had built two large barks in order to transport 300 men in each, in order to attack *Peter Potty* commander of the *Brasilians* in his entrenchments. That *Kamaron* had been near three weeks in *Parayba*, the enemies troops consisting thereabouts in 16 companies; but that they had many sick among them for want of provisions, and that they had drawn all their forces out of *Rio Grande*.

The 6th of *January* 1646, *Peter Bas* one of the members of the great council, did by order from the said council, set sail with the two ships the *Lichthart* and the *Receif* and a bark called the *Blue-Boar*, towards the captainships of *Parayba* and *Rio Grande*. His instructions were, to consult with Mr. *Linge* commander in chief in *Parayba*, and the rest of the officers there, how to put the intrenchments and other works of the *Brasilians* into a posture of defence. From thence he was to go to *Rio Grande*, there to take an exact account both of the real estates and chattels of such *Portuguese*, as by reason of their being engaged with the rebels, were forfeited to the company; he was also to use his endeavours to have those goods which were upon that account concealed or embezzled, restored for the benefit of the said company. He was also ordered

Mr. Bas's *commission.*

1645. ordered to act in all other respects, but especially in providing for the security of the captainship and the fort, as he found it most consistent with our present interest, and to exhort the inhabitants to remain stedfast in their duty, and not to neglect the cultivating of the grounds and breeding of cattle.

The 12th of *January*, *Peter Dunkerke* arrived from *Parayba*, where he had been a cruising before the *Receif* in the ship *Hamel*; he brought a letter from Mr. *Linge*, dated in the fort *St. Margaret*, the 11th of *January*, who sent also one Mr. *Steinhuisen* to the council, he having deserted the enemy when they began to kill the *Dutch* in their service. This *Steenhuisen* brought advice to the council, that *Kamaron* with 500 well-appointed soldiers, was marched out of *Parayba* into *Rio Grande* to be master of the field there; and consequently to keep our garrisons from being supplied with cattle and farinha from thence. He further added, that the enemy were in want of meat, oil, and other necessaries; but that the inhabitants flattered themselves, that for want of provisions, we should shortly be obliged to surrender our forts into the hands of the *Portuguese*. This being likewise confirmed by Mr. *Linge*'s letter dated the 10th of *January*, a council was called against the 13th of *January*, *Dirk Hamel*, and Mr. *Bullestrate* being present, both members of the great council, besides the assessor *Walbeck*, as likewise lieutenant colonel *Garsman*, Mr. *Raetsfield*, Mr. *de Witt*, *Alrich*, *Volbergen*, and *Sams*, in order to deliberate concerning the present exigency, considering, that in case we should, by the enemies being masters of the field, be bereaved of the supplies of cattle and farinha of *Rio Grande*, at a juncture when *Itamarika* and *Parayba* are closely beset by their troops, it would be next to an impossibility to maintain our selves in the possession of the *Dutch Brasil*, till the arrival of the expected succours from *Hollland*. It was therefore taken into consideration, whether this captainship might be best secured by a powerful diversion, or by endeavouring to drive him from thence. But being sensible that the enemy were so powerful near the *Receif*, *Parayba*, and *Itamarika*, as not to be attack'd in any of these places, without exposing the whole *Dutch Brasil* to an imminent danger, it was resolved, that in order to attempt the relief of the captainship of *Rio Grande*, Mr. *Dortmund* should be ordered to send 60 soldiers under the command of captain *Welling*, and 100 *Brasilians*, in the barks sent him for that purpose, from *Itamarika* to *Rio Grande*: At the same time orders were dispacht to Mr. *Linge*, commander in the fort *St. Margaret* in *Parayba*, to send the same number of soldiers under lieutenant *Bresman*, and of *Brasilians* to *Rio Grande*, to join with the rest that were to rendezvous there. These forces consisting of 120 soldiers and 200 *Brasilians*, set sail the 19th of *January* for *Rio Grande*, and were thought sufficient to oppose the enemies designs on that side.

An account of the enemies designs.

Consultations held hereupon.

Their resolution.

Mr. *Dortmont* and *William Lambartz*, by a letter dated the 15th of *January*, gave notice to the council, that they had sent a body of 60 soldiers and 100 *Brasilians* abroad, as far in the *Aldea* by *Oubus*, and from thence to the sugar-mill *Arraripe*, but did not meet with any enemies in that part of the countrey, tho' they had several guns discharged at them from among the woods; so that they return'd to *Itamarika* by the way of *Tapasima*.

Mr. *Linge* not long after sent advice by his letter dated the 22d of *January*, at the fort of *St. Margaret* in *Parayba* to the council, that *Peter Potty* with 150 *Brasilians* had attack'd the enemy 400 strong in the *Aldea* of *Magrebbe*, and put them to flight with the loss of 20 killed, and many wounded, whereas they lost but one *Brasilian*.

The Portuguese defeated.

The 29th of *January* it was resolved in council, to bring the ships the *Elias*, *Orange-Tree*, *Deventer*, *Omlandia* and the *Swan*, into the road of the *Receif*, to be ready upon all occasions, in case the enemy should again appear at sea.

Mr. *Bas*, pursuant to his letter from the castle of *Keulen* in *Rio Grande*, dated the 23d of *January*, could not, by reason of a tempest, land his forces at *Kunhao*, in order to join them with those under captain *Rhineburgh*; but was forced to land his forces the 14th and 15th near *Peringi*. In the mean while *Kamaron* having found means to break in through the *Matta*, had surprised many of the inhabitants in their *Fazendas*, and kill'd them without distinction of age or sex: He had since posted himself with his forces, consisting of 400 soldiers, as many *Brasilians*, and 80 *Tapoyars*, under the command of *Antonio Jacomo Beserro*, at a house of *Henry Hamme* in *Mompabou*, to cut off the provisions from us. Our forces consisting of about 1000 soldiers, *Brasilians* and *Tapoyars*, march'd the 23d of *January* to a house of *John Lestan Navarre*, to attack the enemy, and to force them to quit the captainship of *Rio Grande*. Besides these *Jacob Rabbi* and the sons of king *Duwy*, were the 19th past, by the fort *Keulen*, at the head of 60 *Tapoyers*, and were daily follow'd by others, that came to our assistance. Mr. *Bas* sollicited also some supplies of provisions, of which they stood in great want, there being above 1500 *Brasilians*

Mr. Bas gives an account of his proceedings.

1643. *Consultations held thereupon.* *silians*, men, women and children, lodged under the castle. He desired also some money, ammunition, linen and silks to present to the *Brasilians* and *Tapoyers*; all which, together with some pieces of red-cloth, was sent him by the council.

According to this advice, it being much to be feared the enemy would scarce stand the brunt in *Rio Grande*, but retire into *Parayba*, it was taken into serious consideration the 29th of *January*, whether it would be adviseable, in case the enemy should be forced by our troops, or voluntarily retreat into *Parayba*, to pursue them thither, and thereby endeavour the recovery likewise of that captainship: But considering that by reason of the weakness of our garrisons, we were not in a condition to send any further succours from the *Receif*, *Itamarika* or *Parayba*, without running a manifest hazard to our troops there; whereas, on the contrary, the enemies did not want opportunity to relieve theirs from the adjacent places of *Parayba*, and that we lived in daily hopes of succours from *Holland*, it was judged the best way, that the welfare of the whole *Dutch-Brasil* ought not to be put to the hazard by such an enterprize as this. *Their result.*

Accordingly orders were sent to Mr. *Bas* and the rest of the commanders of our troops there, to act with all imaginable caution, and rather than expose our men, in following the enemy into *Parayba*, to be contented with the recovery of the captainship of *Rio Grande*.

Colonel Garsman *sent to* Rio Grande. The 30th of *March*, colonel *Garsman* was by special order from the council sent a second time with some Troops to the captainship of *Rio Grande*, to inform himself, whether any troops of the enemy were posted in that captainship, and in what number; his instructions were, that so soon as he had received intelligence of the enemy, he should, with what forces he was able to bring together, endeavour to stop their progress. But if he found himself not strong enough to oppose them, he should send speedy advice thereof to the council, that they might send him speedy succours, and that he was to take all imaginable care not to engage the enemy, before the arrival of the said succours. But if he found the enemy already so strongly entrench'd as to be master of the countrey, without any hopes of forcing them from thence, the defence of the fort *Keulen* should be his chiefest care, as likewise of the *Brasilians*, with their wives and children, and since, in case the said fort of *Keulen* should be in danger of being attack'd by the enemy, it would be of ill consequence, to have these women and children enclosed within the fortifications, for fear of want of provisions, he was strictly ordered to transpo t them in time, to some place of security, such as *Siara*, or the like, where they might be able to subsist, and be secure against any attempt from the enemy. He was ordered also in his return to the *Receif*, to take *en passant* (if it could be done without inconveniency) a view of the fortifications of *Itamarika* and *Parayba*, in order to give an account of their condition to the council. 1645.

But to return to Mr. *Bas*: According to his letters dated the 30th of *January* from the fort *Keulen*, captain *Rhinebergh* had with his body made six several attacks upon the enemy, who was retired from *Mompabou* and *Kunhao* into a bog, without being able to force their entrenchments; we lost about 100 kill'd and wounded in this action, and retreated to the house of *John Leytan* with order to get some cattle, which was very scarce thereabouts, our forces feeding most upon fishes, which they caught by the help of two large nets; 28 of our wounded men were brought to the *Receif*, with advice that notwithstanding this unsuccessful attack on our side, the enemy were retreated into *Parayba*. Mr. *Bas* also sollicited some fresh supplies of men and Ammunition, in order to pursue them into *Parayba*, but the resolution upon this head was deferr'd 'till they should hear further from Mr. *Bas*. The 7th of *February* it was resolved by the council with the approbation of admiral *Lichthart* to equip the *Hollandia* and the *Swan* together with the yachts, the *Flight*, the *Hamel*, *Bullestrate* and *Lichthart* for cruising. By letters from Mr. *Linge*, dated the 11th of *February* at the fort *Margaret* in *Parayba*, the council was advised, how that, according to the deposition of a negro deserter, *Kamaron* was come with all his troops into the city of *Parayba*, with an intention to attack our forts on that side; an answer, with what was thought necessary for this present purpose, was immediately sent back in a bark by the council. By another bark sent by Mr. *Bas* from *Rio Grande*, they were advertised, that he lay still encamped with his troops near the house of *John Lestan*, where with much ado he could get provisions for them, the enemy being still posted at *Momguappe*, and guarding all the avenues into the countrey; that he had sent several spies abroad, to get intelligence concerning the present posture of the enemy. The 17th of *February* the ship the *Swan* and the yacht call'd *Bullestrate* were ordered to go out a cruising; the 18th the yacht the *Flight*, and the 20th the ship *Hollandia* set sail for the same purpose. The ship the *Overyssel* was also

The Dutch *attack the enemy, without success.*

Advice from Mr. Linge.

1645. also ordered to go out, to serve for a spie ship on the coast of *Parayba*.

The 21st of *February* the council received a letter from Mr. *de Linge*, dated the 18th, in the fort of *St. Margaret*, intimating that he had heard nothing since of the enemy. Yet that he wish'd the forces he had sent to *Rio grande* might be returned with all convenient speed, to make use of them for the defence of his forts, in case of an attack.

Parties sent abroad without success.

The 24th of *February* a party under command of captain *Killion Taylor* and captain *Nicholas Nicholson*, were sent abroad towards the island of the *Barette* to get some prisoners, but they return'd the 20th to the *Receif*, having met with no body except with a man, at a considerable distance. Another party which had taken their way towards *Olinda* and *Bracco de St. Jago*, but with the same success, the enemy having only shewn himself at a distance, as they were returning to the fort *Bruin*. The 27th of *February* the enemy appeared with a strong body in the *Salinas*, but being saluted by some cannon-shot from the fort *Bruin*, retired without attempting any thing.

News from Parayba.

In the mean while, according to Mr. *Linge*'s letter, from the 2d of *March*, three barks with soldiers were arrived in *Parayba* from *Rio Grande*, so that the rest, under the command of Mr. *Bas*, being 500 in number, might be hourly expected at the *Receif*. He further advised, that he had seen no enemy of late, but being informed that a considerable body lay encamp'd in a valley near the village of *Magarebbe*, he had ordered thither 120 soldiers, and 100 *Brasilians*, to beat up their Quarters, and to get some prisoners. In effect the 4th of *March*, he, with his troops consisting in 500 Men, arrived from *Rio Grande* at the *Receif*, and the 5th of *March* gave the council an account of his expedition.

Several skirmishes.

The 9th of *March* in the night, the enemy appeared in three bodies near the fort *Prince William*, and gave us several volleys of small shot, but being answered with our cannon retired immediately. The same day a party of 50 men were sent abroad under lieutenant *Mos* to get intelligence; being met by two companies of the enemy, a sharp encounter ensued, our forces retiring without any considerable loss, under the fort *Wardenburgh*, and the enemy retreated at the discharge of some of our cannon. By letters from Mr. *Linge*, dated the 8th of *March* at fort *St. Margaret* in *Parayba*, the council received the unwelcome news that the enemy in *Rio Grande* had by a pretended flight drawn the 5th of *March* lieutenant *John de Vael* with 48 soldiers, who were too eager in the pursuit of them, into an ambush, where they had kill'd 30 of them, tho', according to the report of some deserters that were present at the engagement, not without considerable loss also on their side; *Kamaron*, *Andrew Vidal* and some other *Portuguese* officers of note were also present. About the same time 15 *Brasilians* surprised five men, six women and eight children, in an entrenchment seven leagues above *Iguaracu*, called *Papeku*. 1645.

In the mean while the *Tapoyers*, who according to their custom, come once a year, about midsummer, from among the mountains, some hundreds strong, into the captainship of *Rio Grande*, were, after they had carried away all the horses and mares they could light on, retired to the hills; a thing very fortunate for us, for without it our garrisons would not have been able to subsist there. Provisions growing every day scarcer in the *Receif*, it was agreed the 6th of *March* by the council, to send the *Brasilians* raised in *Rio Grande* with a company of fusileers to *Itamarika*, to ease our magazines of that burthen, whilst they might provide themselves with *farinha* roots in that island. Much about the same time the two majors *Bayert* and *Pistoor*, appear'd before the council, intimating, that being informed that the citizens began to murmur at their staying at home, pretending that they were sufficient to guard the forts; for which purpose, as it was reported admiral *Lichthart* had offered 300 men, they were come on purpose to offer their service, and were ready to take the field with those few forces they had left in the garrison; tho' they at the same time protested, that they were of the same opinion, which had been approved some days before, to wit, that this undertaking, by reason of their small number, would be full of danger, and yet not answer the end of bringing provisions into the *Receif*. Admiral *Lichthart* being thereupon ask'd whether he had made any such offer, he declared not to have spoken any thing like it, his ships being so ill mann'd, that he could spare no men for any other service.

Propositions about the taking of the field.

The night before the 13th of *March*, the enemy appear'd both on the other side of the river and the dike leading to the fort *Bruin*, discharging their musquets and blunderbusses at our centinels, but upon the first salute from the cannon of the fort retired. The same they did near the fort of *Affagados*. The same evening betwixt nine and ten a clock they made an attack upon the wooden fort, built betwixt the *Affagados* and the *Quinquangular-Fort*, for the defence of the plain, which they continued 'till one a clock, cutting down some palisadoes, and bringing great store of dry reeds, in order to set it on fire, but in vain, being

The Portuguese attack a wooden fort near the Receif.

1645. being forced to retreat with the loss of some of their Men; on our side two were kill'd, and four or five wounded, among the last was lieutenant *Casper Ferdinand van Grol*, who received two dangerous wounds. The next morning the broken palisadoes were repaired, and another row ordered to be set beyond the first, and footangles to be laid betwixt both. The 17th of *March* the bark call'd the *Parayba* coming from *Siara*, brought advice, that the *Brasilians* were gone from *Siara* to *Komesi*, having refused to return to *Rio Grande*, for fear they should be call'd to a severe account there for the murther of several inhabitants, committed by them before.

By the same bark Mr. *Linge* sent advice from the 14th of *March*, that the enemy had appeared of late in a considerable body near the northern fort, but was retired now, but whether to *Rio Grande* or *St. Andre*, he was not able to tell. They had spoil'd all the *farinha-root* fields in the *Aldeas Magarebbe*, and thereabouts; so that the *Brasilians* being for the future to be furnished with provisions out of the magazines, he desired a supply of wine and oil: Immediately advice hereof was sent to *Dortmund* commander in chief of *Itamarika*, and some ammunition, besides 1000 gilders in ready money. The same sum was transmitted to Mr. *Linge* in *Parayba*, and a barrel with oatmeal, a pipe of wine, a hogshead with oil, and another fill'd with dry pease, besides good store of ammunition. He was also ordered to send the *Brasilians* back to *Rio Grande* for defence of that captainship, and to get intelligence whether the enemy had directed his march thither, in order to oppose his designs.

In the mean while admiral *Lichthart* (pursuant to his letter of the 21st of *March* to the council) had embark'd some soldiers and *Brasilians* in *Itamarika*, and taking his course to the north-entrance of the river, was got up as far as to the isle of *Tapesco*, from whence they had brought back a great quantity of *farinha* roots, for the use of the *Brasilians* in *Itamarika*, and of the magazines there. *Good store of* farinha *roots brought to* Itamarika.

The 30th of *March* it was resolved, with the approbation of admiral *Lichthart*, to send the following ships a cruising before the *Bahia*; the *Ulissingen*, the *Ter Veer*, and the yachts, the *Greyhound*, the *Heemstede*, *Sprew* and *Bullestrate*; and on the 6th of *April* the *Swan*, the *Zouteland*, the *Flight*, and the yacht the *Lichthart*, were ordered to go a cruising before the *Cape of St. Austin*, and set sail the 10th of *April* accordingly. *Ships sent out a cruising.*

The 31st letters were brought to the council, dated the 25th of *March* in *Rio Grande*, intimating, that *Paulo de Kunha* and *Kamaron* were entred *Kunhao* with 800 men, among whom were 300 musqueteers, to carry away the cattle from thence to *Parayba*. 1645.

But, according to colonel *Garsman*'s letters to the council, upon his arrival, which was the 4th of *April*, the enemy were already retired out of *Rio Grande*, without undertaking any thing against our people, who consisting only in 400 soldiers and 300 *Brasilians* lay encamp'd near the house of *John Lestan*, yet they carried off some cattle. *News from colonel* Garsman.

About the same time they received letters from Mr. *Linge*, that the enemy had made several false alarms near the forts, without attempting any thing. And in effect in *June*, they did not appear any more thereabouts.

In the year 1646, the 5th of *April* in the night, *Jacob Rabbi* was at the instigation of lieutenant colonel *Garsman*, near *Potosi*, about three leagues distant from the castle of the same name, villainously shot with two bullets, as he was going home from one *John Miller*'s house, where he had been entertained that evening in company with colonel *Garsman*. *Rabbi* had a considerable time before (as he had declared to his friends) suspected the treachery of *Garsman*, and was for that reason just upon his departure out of *Rio Grande*, in order to shelter himself among the *Tapoyers*. The council resented this villainy to the highest degree, since, considering that this *Jacob Rabbi* was in great esteem among the *Tapoyers*, and his wife a *Brasilian*, it was to be feared, that this would exasperate both the *Tapoyers* and *Brasilians* against us. So that *Garsman* returning the 19th of *March* to the *Receif*, after he had given an account of his expedition to the council, was by their particular order, the 24th of *March*, taken into custody, and sent on board the *Hollandia*, major *Bayert* being ordered in the mean time to supply his place. This *Jacob Rabbi* a native of *Germany*, had been employ'd by authority of the states general, his highness the prince of *Orange*, and the company, to engage and keep the *Tapoyers* in the interest of our government; in which commission he had acquitted himself so well, that he brought these *Tapoyers* several times, out of the mountains (their habitations) to our assistance. His dwelling-place was in the fort *Keulen* in *Rio Grande*, where he had married a *Brasilian* woman. *Gasper Honyhouse*, commander of the *Brasilians* in *Itamarika*, being slain in the last engagement in that island, Mr. *Vincent van Drillenbergh*, was, at their request, constituted their commander by the council. 1646. Jacob Rabbi *treacherously killed.* Garsman *secured.*

 The

1646.

The 17th of *April*, some papers were delivered to the council, which had been dispersed by the enemy, to debauch our soldiery; in return of which, they sent abroad their summons, upbraiding such of their subjects as were in the enemy's service, with treachery, and exhorting them to return to their duty. It was also agreed to publish a copy of a letter delivered by the *Portuguese* ambassador at the *Hague* to the states general from the king his master; with the answer of the states to the said letter: For since the king of *Portugal* in this letter did disown the war, and the proceedings of *Antonio Telles da Silva*, and his sending of his troops into the *Dutch-Brasil*, they did not question but by this means to open the eyes of the *Portuguese* inhabitants, not to flatter themselves with vain hopes of assistance from *Portugal*; besides, that we were in hopes thereby to sow the seeds of mistrust betwixt them and the *Portuguese* commanders from the *Bahia*.

The 24th of *April*, two *Portuguese* companies commanded by captain *Lawrence Karnero* and *Peter Kavalkanti*, consisting of about 40 men each, marched from the *Vargea* and the city of *Olinda* to *Iguarasu*. They were headed by *Vidal* and *Hoogstrate* in person, who having got intelligence that admiral *Lichthart* and *John Nicholson* were gone to *Itamarika*, to get some *farinba* roots. The 25th of *April*, as they were marching from *Iguarasu*, a certain *German* chirurgeon, named *Christopher Mars*, who was formerly taken prisoner by them, happening to stay somewhat behind, whilst he was pissing, was surprized by one of our parties near *Tapasino*. Upon examination by Mr. *Walbeck*, he declared, that not long ago there were nine companies of the enemies forces quarter'd in the *Baretta*, the city of *Olinda*, and in the mills of *Bierboom* and *Brito*; each company consisting of betwixt 40 or 50 men. That there were five companies more, much of the same strength, posted in the *Salinas*, and *Henry Dias* with 200 mulats and negroes in *Gaspar Cox*'s house, but they had then no forces in the *Vargea*.

One Mars taken prisoner.

His depositions.

That after *Nicholas Nicholson* was come over to us with his troops, *Martin Soares Moreno* had caused 260 *Dutch*, both soldiers and inhabitants, (among whom were six women and two children) to be killed by a company of the country militia, in the woods of *Tabatinga*, betwixt *Sibero* and *Deriba*, in their way to the *Bahia*, besides those killed by his order in other places, amounting in all to 300.

By this time there began to be great scarcity of meat in the *Receif*, notwithstanding which, the garrisons in the outworks, as well as the *Brasilians* in *Itamarika*, with their wives and children, were to be supplied from thence; and the *farinba* roots being either all taken up before by our own people, or else destroy'd by the enemy, in the island *Itamarika*: To supply this pressing necessity, it was resolved by the great council, to send a detachment of 400 men in barks to *St. Lawrence de Praja* or *Tujukapa*, to fetch *mandinka* or farinha-roots from thence. This detachment was composed out of these following troops.

1646.

The Dutch go out for some farinha without success.

Out of captain *Nicholas Nicholson*'s company 9 men.

From the *Quinquangular-fort* 25.

From the *Affagados* 25.

Out of the company of captain *William Lambartz* 50.

Volunteers from *Itamarika* 30.

Brasilians 150.

The 29th of *April* the council was, by letters from *Itamarika*, advertised, that our forces being sent abroad to fetch some *farinha*, had chased the enemy out of two or three entrenchments; but they retiring into another, surrounded with a deep ditch, they were there also with more courage than conduct attack'd by our troops, being forced to retire with the loss of 16 kill'd and 26 wounded, among whom was captain *William Lambartz*: The enemy had likewise not a few kill'd on their side. Mr. *Dortmund*, commander in chief of *Itamarika*, therefore desiring to be supplied with meal, his magazines being quite exhausted, the council sent thither the first of *May*, 20 barrels with meal, two with oatmeal, two with dry pease, besides a pipe of wine and brandy, and 1000 gilders in money, for the use of the *Brasilians*.

The 3d of *May* the council received advice by a letter dated the 2d of *May* from Mr. *Dortmund*, that the enemy had carried away ten Negroes, four belonging to the company, the rest to one Mr. *Seulin*, and four other men from *Itamarika*; and that the *Brasilians* there had been so far debauched by their intreagues, that they retired into a wood, and being twice summon'd to rejoin our troops, had refused so to do. That at last, Mr. *Apprisius*, (Minister of the *Brasilians*) having been sent to reduce them to their duty, either by persuasions or threats, his arguments were so prevailing, that they return'd quietly, alledging for their excuse, that they were forced to fly thither for want of subsistance. Hereupon *Dortmund* desired fresh supplies for his magazines, that a person of authority might be sent thither, and that another company might be put in place of that of captain *Vosterman*, his men being ready to revolt.

Mutiny of the Brasilians appeased.

1646. *Mr.* Bullestrate *sent to* Itamarika.

To remove all these obstacles, it was resolved immediately to dispatch thither Mr. *Bullestrate*, a member of the great council, who was to agree with certain private persons, to provide our garrisons with fish, and to act in every thing there, as he should find it most expedient for the service of the company.

Accordingly Mr. *Bullestrate* set sail the 4th of *May*, in the yacht the *Greyhound*, and arrived the same day in the afternoon in *Itamarika*, where having executed his commission, he return'd the 10th of *May* to the *Receif*, and gave the following account to the council: That he had taken a view of the city of *Schoppe*, and the fort *Orange*, both which he had ordered to be strengthned; as also, to fortify the old brick-house, formerly the *Stadthouse*, with pallisadoes, against any sudden attempt; that he having call'd before him all the commanders of the *Brasilians*, had represented to them that we were in daily expectation of a powerful succour from *Holland*, exhorting them to remain stedfast in their duty, and to keep their soldiers under the best discipline they could; he had also presented their commander with cloth for a suit of clothes, and the rest with some wine and money, which they very thankfully accepted: He had *En Passant* taken a view of the plantations of *Conradt Pauli*, where he had found about 160 cocoa-trees cut down by the *Brasilians*, being forced by famine to feed upon the fruit; the like they had done in several other places; that he had endeavoured to treat with several private persons for a certain quantity of fish to be delivered at the *Receif*, but could meet with none that would accept his offers; they alledging, that most of their negroes being either run away or taken by the enemy, they did catch no more fish but what they could readily sell in the island, without the charge of salt and transportation; that he had likewise proposed to the commander in chief of the *Brasilians*, to give them for the future money instead of meal; and that they were to be furnished with three nets to catch fish for their own use; that the commander promised to propose it to the rest, and gave him some hopes that they would accept of the said offer.

An account of his proceedings.

To supply the present want of provisions, which began to be scarcer and scarcer every day in *Itamarika*, *Parayba*, *Rio Grande*, and the *Receif*, by reason that the expected supplies from *Holland* were not as yet arrived, and we were closely block'd up by land; it was thought fit to give all imaginable encouragement to the fishing trade, for which purpose the two members of the great council, Mr. *Hamel* and Mr. *Bas*, ordered the 7th of *May*, to buy up as much yarn as possible could be got to make fishing nets of, which afterwards stood us in good stead. 1646.

Fishery encouraged.

A certain *Portuguese*, who had committed manslaughter in *Angola*, and was fled from thence to the *Receif*, having accused *John Vieira d Allegoas*, he was by order from the council taken into custody.

John Vieira *accused of treason.*

This *Portuguese* declared, that the said *Vieira* had delivered to him a certain piece of parchment, written in characters, and a box, wherein were several other papers, in order to carry them to the enemy, which parchment and box he produced in the presence of the members of the council. *John Vieira* denying the matter, was put to the rack, but continued resolute in his denial; till at last, the key of these characters being found among his papers, and a certain *Jew* having unciphered these letters, it appear'd, that he had given an account of the whole posture of our affairs to the enemy, with directions how to make themselves masters of the *Receif*: so that finding himself discovered, he confest that he had written and delivered these cyphered papers to the *Portuguese*, and was executed the 29th of *May*.

Is executed.

The magazines being by this time almost exhausted, there being scarce provisions left for a few weeks, it was proposed by the council to the majors, *Beyert* and *Pistoor*, that considering it was not adviseable to exasperate the soldiery at this juncture, by retrenching their allowance of bread and other eatables, whether instead of a pound of meat, they might not be prevailed upon to take six-pence, by this means to preserve that small store of flesh they had left, which these two majors undertook to propose to the soldiers, not without hopes of succeeding in their project, and that nobody might be excepted from bearing his share in the publick calamity, it was ordered that the loaves which used before to weigh a pound and half, should be reduced to one pound weight, and that each citizen and others depending on the company, nay the members of the great council themselves, should have an allowance only of two loaves *per* week; the same was to be given to all seamen, captains, lieutenants and ensigns; but the rest, from the serjeant to the common soldier, should have three pounds of bread allow'd them *per* week.

Orders concerning the allowance of bread.

Mr. *Linge* advised from the 1st of *May*, out of *Paraiba*, that the enemy had not attempted any thing against the forts, and that a party of *Brasilians* was gone abroad towards *Tapoa*, in hopes to take some prisoners. Much about the same time the council received advice, that colonel *Garsman*,

1646. *man*, without orders from the council, had endeavoured by some presents, to draw the *Tapoyers* into *Rio Grande*, under pretence of keeping them at hand, to enter into a confederacy with the new members of the great council that were expected from *Holland*. The council being not a little surprized at this undertaking, since by the coming of the *Tapoyers* into that captainship, they should be disappointed of a considerable part of those supplies they received from thence; they sent word to *Rudolph Barro* to leave no stone unturned to draw the *Tapoyers* by fair means back to their habitations, but that if they would send some of their commanders to the *Receif*, all imaginable satisfaction should be given them concerning the murther of *Jacob Rabbi*; and the more to engage *Barro* to do his utmost, a present of wine, brandy, and some toys, was ordered to be sent him. For as the case then stood, it was absolutely necessary for us to remain masters of *Rio Grande*, till the arrival of the succours from *Holland*; the vast numbers of *Brasilians* that were fled to *Itamarika*, having consumed all sorts of provisions there to that degree, that that island could not only not send any supplies to the *Receif*, but most of the women and children of the *Brasilians* must be supplied out of the magazines there; so that *Rio Grande* was the only place left from whence they received a considerable quantity of *Farinha* and cattle, which in some measure abated the scarcity of provisions in the *Receif*, and by the prudent conduct of the council, was the chief means that the place continued in tolerable good health till the arrival of the succours, which without it, it would in all humane probability have been impossible to be done; and no question but this captainship might for a considerable time after, have furnished the garrisons to the south with necessaries, had it not been for the following accident.

Garsman *summons the* Tapoyers *without orders.*

The consequence of Rio Grande *to the* Dutch.

The expected succours from *Holland* being detained by the winter season and contrary winds, the *Brasilians* of *Gojana*, who with their wives and children had sheltred themselves in *Itamarika*, were reduced to the greatest extremity for want of food; for after they had consumed all what the island could afford for their subsistance, and all the avenues by land being block'd up by the enemy, they had no other supplies but what they received from our magazines: These being now exhausted to such a degree, that each citizen had but one pound of bread allowed him *per* week (which however at that rate would not hold out above fourteen days longer) the council was under an absolute necessity to have it proposed to the *Brasilians*, to retire with their wives and children (in all about 1200) to *Rio Grande*, where they might subsist some time upon what the country afforded. Accordingly they writ to Mr. *Dortmund* the 1st of *May*, and sent Mr. *Walbeck* thither in person, to persuade the *Brasilians* to send at least 500 women and children, with a certain number of their men, to *Siara* and *Rio Grande*, there being at that time in all near 1500 *Brasilians*, men, women and children in that island, among whom were only 500 fit to bear arms, under the command of *Caspar Honyhouse*, who had each scarce a pound of bread allow'd them *per* week. 1646.

Provisions, as I told you before, growing daily scarcer and scarcer, by reason the succours from *Holland* were detained beyond all expectation, by contrary winds; a general council was call'd, where the three numbers of the great council Mr. *Hamel*, Mr. *Bullestrate* and Mr. *Bas*, being present, as likewise admiral *Lichthart*, and the two majors *Beyert* and *Pistoor*, the following points were taken into debate.

Consultations about the scarcity of provisions.

First of all, the sending of the *Brasilians* from *Itamarika* to *Rio Grande*, being look'd upon as unavoidable, immediate orders were given to get the necessary transport vessels ready for that purpose. It was also taken into consideration, whether it were not feasible to gather a sufficient force out of the forts, who in conjunction with the *Brasilians*, might attack some place or other, from whence to provide ourselves with *Farinha*; but to this it was objected by the majors *Beyert* and *Pistoor*, that the garrisons of the forts could not be weakned by any detachment, without running a great hazard; besides that it was a hard matter to pitch upon any place where there was any store of *Farinha*, the enemy having either consumed, spoiled or carried it away before; so that we must expose our men to an apparent danger, without a sure prospect of interest; for, supposing we should be successful, the quantity that might be got, would not be sufficient to maintain our garrisons for any considerable time. It was however agreed to take an exact account of all the garrisons, to see whether upon an occasion something might be undertaken for the service of the state. Accordingly these two majors, *Beyert* and *Pistoor*, having presented a list of these forces the next day to the council, it was concluded that no troops could be spared out of the forts, except it were out of the *Assagados*, but they were but few in number. At the same time it was resolved to send captain *Niger* with his company of *Brasilians* to *Rio Grande*, and the *Omlandia* and *Greyhound* yacht were ordered forthwith to sail

1646. sail to *Itamarika*, to transport the *Brasilians* to *Rio Grande*.

Further debates about the attacking of the enemy. The 30th of *May* the council, the admiral, and two majors, entred into a second debate, whether it were possible to attack the enemy, and in what place: Against which it was alledged, that their chiefest force was at present in the *Vergea*; but supposing it was not, no *Farinha* was to be got there, because they were supply'd with it themselves from far distant places. That the *Farinha* fields nearest to the *Receif* were about *St. Lawrence*, at least five leagues from thence; that the nearest *Farinha* fields to the south were about *St. Antonio* and *Moribeka*, where by reason of the strength of the enemy, and the great distance from us, there was no probability of encompassing our design; and that the *Farinha* fields to the north were likewise at such a distance from the sea-side, as could not in any likelyhood answer our expectation. It was farther taken into consideration, whether some forces might not be spared in *Itamarika*, but it was carried in the negative, because since the *Brasilians* were ready to depart for *Rio Grande*, it was not adviseable to expose the rest of our troops there to a hazard. After serious deliberation, what forces possibly could be raised out of the forts, (their places being in the mean while to be supplied by the inhabitants) it was found that the *Assagados* could furnish about 70 or 80 men, the quinquangular fort, and *Maurice*'s town the same number, and that of *St. Antonio Vaez* about 50. But, considering that the city militia of the *Receif* consisted only of six companies of 70, or at the most 80 men each, and that they were obliged to be upon the guard every night there (the place being without a garrison) if a considerable number of them should be employed in the forts, this must needs expose the capital place, which the enemy chiefly aimed at, to an imminent danger. The seamen being not above 250 in all, could likewise not be employed in that service, unless we could leave our ships quite unmann'd and useless. So that after many arguments on both sides, it was agreed to chuse the securest way, and according to the orders of the council of XIX in *Holland*, to expect the succours from thence with patience, and in the mean while to provide for the security of our forts.

The same day the council received letters from Mr. *Walbeck*, that some of the *Brasilians* of *Itamarika* had deserted, a rumour being spread among them, that we intended to leave them to the mercy of the *Portuguese*, which had put all the rest into a great consternation, but that Mr. *Dortmund* had convinced them to the contrary. 1646. Mr. *Walbeck* and *Dortmund* had in the mean while represented to the *Brasilians*, that they being many in number, and consequently very ill provided for at this juncture, whether it were not best for them to go for some time to *Rio Grande*. They were at first averse to his proposals, for fear of being deserted by us, nevertheless the urgent necessity of providing for their sustenance, and to shew their compliance with the governments orders, were so reconciled with them, as to resolve to go to *Rio Grande*, provided they might be furnished with convenient transport-ships, provisions, and some ammunition for their defence, and fifty men of regular troops. Mr. *Dortmund* having again sollicited for provisions, some were sent (sufficient for fourteen days) immediately, with some gunpowder, bullets, and other ammunition. *The* Brasilians *resolve to leave* Itamarika.

Accordingly above 1200 *Brasilians*, most women and children, whose husbands and fathers had been slain in our service, embark'd aboard the *Omlandia* and some yachts, a pound of salt-cod fish being allow'd to each for the whole voyage without bread. At their arrival in *Rio Grande* they were so emaciated by famine, that they appear'd more like dead carcasses than living bodies, and laid hold of every thing they could meet with to satisfy their greedy stomachs, so that in a little time they consumed all the *Farinha* that was left there.

Mr. *Linge*, by his letters from the 25th of *June* sent advice to the council, that there appear'd no enemy at that time in *Parayba*, but that ten *Tapoyers*, vassals of king *John Duwy*, being come into *Rio Grande*, had shewn themselves extremely dissatisfied at the murther of *Jacob Rabbi*, whereupon it was resolved to reconcile that king to our interest by the following presents:

Presents sent to king John Duwy.

200 gilders in ready money.
1000 Ells of *Osnabrugh* linnen cloth.
100 gallons of *Spanish* wine.
Two casks of brandy.
40 gallons of oil, and a barrel with powdered beef.

The Brasilians *depart from the forts near the* Receif. The *Brasilians* in garrison in the fort, the *Bruin*, the *Quinquangnlar*, and some other forts, being dissatisfied at their being detained there for eight months last past, petitioned the council the 12th of *June*, to be sent back into *Rio Grande*.

The opinion of the two majors being ask'd thereupon, they advised, that considering they did no extraordinary service there they might well be spared; so that it was resolved the 14th of *June* in council, to pay them their arrears, and to send them back

1646. back to *Parayba* and *Rio Grande*, to inhabit their villages as before.

In the *Quinquangular* fort, the company of *Immanuel Barros* was order'd to keep guard instead of the *Brasilians*, who were commanded to depart the 20th of *June*. The 11th, 12th, 13th and 14th of *June*, the enemy shot in the night-time very fiercely against the fort *de Assagados*, a redoubt call'd *Kirk*, and the house *Boavista*.

The 15th of *June* it was proposed to the council by admiral *Lichthart*, and the two majors, *Beyert* and *Pistoor*, to beat up the enemies quarters in the house of *Immanuel Kavalkanti*, and in the *Baretta*, with the following troops.

The company of captain *Killian Taylor*, 40 men.

The company of captain *Nicholas Nicholson*, of 70 men, which were to be joined by captain *de Niger* with 30 men out of the fort *Frederick*, with lieutenant *Mos* from the fort *Ernestus* with 10 men, and lieutenant *Katnar* from the fort *Prince William* with 20 men.

In all 200 men.

About 100 volunteers were supposed to be raised from among the citizens, under the colonel *Walbeck*, and *Immanuel Baros* with his Negroes, consisting in 50 men, these joined with the other 200, would make up a body of 350 men, to be commanded in chief by major *Pistoor*, and to be conducted by sea by admiral *Lichthart* to their landing place, *viz.* the regular troops to the south of the *Baretta*, and the Negroes upon the island on the north-side, from whence they might break thro' the marshes to the *Assagados*, and so further to the house cross the river, where they were to make a false attack, whilst the troops landed at the *Baretta*, assaulted them from before; the admiral, with his transport vessels, to lay ready all this while to receive them, and to secure their retreat upon all occasions. This proposition being approved of by the council, partly to animate our soldiers, partly to get at least some provisions for the sick, it was resolved to be put in execution the next day, but the wind proving contrary, and afterwards the tides being unseasonable for the convenient landing of our men, this project was laid aside, especially when instead of 100 volunteers, scarce 25 offered themselves for this service, notwithstanding the council gave them all imaginable encouragement, by promising them to receive the same treatment as the other servants of the company had, in case they should be wounded or come to some other misfortune.

A project to beat up the enemies quarters.

Is laid aside.

In the mean while, the enemy having been informed by some of our deserters, that by the departure of the *Brasilians* from *Itamarika*, the garrisons there were much weakned, they thought fit to lay hold of this opportunity, to land such a force there, as should be beyond our power to drive from thence. The 15th of *June*, with the break of day they surprized our spy ship there, call'd the *Sprew*, with several barks and boats at the entrance call'd *Passoos*, *(Markers)* they got three prisoners, the rest escaping with the loss of two of their comrades kill'd. 1646.

The ship before *Tapasima* was set on fire by our own people, leaving the galliot, that lay hard by, to the enemy, after they had taken out all her men, who went aboard the yacht call'd the *Golden Doe*, lying before the north entrance. They landed with about 2000 men in chalops and other transport vessels, and *Andrew Vidal* and *John Ferdinand Vieira*, writ the same night the following letter to Mr. *Dortmund*, commander in chief of *Itamarika*, which they sent by a boy they had taken prisoner in the *Sprew*.

The Portuguese land on Itamarika.

Their letter to Mr. Dortmund.

Most honourable and most brave,

YOU are doubtless not unacquainted with the resolution of the inhabitants of this country to retrieve their former liberty; to effect which they neither want power nor any other means; but their chief aim being to encompass their design without effusion of blood, we thought fit to let you know that we are ready to attack you in this island with all our forces, unless you will prevent it by a treaty. For being sensible that you are pass'd all hopes of relief, we were willing to advise you to treat with us, according to the custom of war, used in such cases; that, in case hereafter things should fall out contrary to your expectation by the fury of the conquering sword, you may not lay the fault thereof at our doors; for which reason it is, that we offer to you and the rest of the commanders there, all their arrears due to them from the company. Whereupon we expect your answer to-morrow.

From our head quarter, *June* 15, 1646. — *Andrew Vidal de Negreiros.* *John Ferdinand Vieira.*

The 17th of *June* the council received advice from Mr. *Dortmund* of their landing, desiring prompt succours, without which he would not be in a condition to maintain the island against them. It was therefore taken into debate, whether it were possible for us to bring together such a force, as without much hazard might be able to force the enemy from thence, but 'twas carried in the negative.

For

1646.

Consultations about the relief of Itamarika.

For it was alledged, that without manifest danger, not above 200 soldiers could be taken out of the forts of the *Receif*, which number was not sufficient to attack the enemy, who had already entrench'd himself there, with hopes of success: And, considering that these forces must be transported thither by sea, we wanted ships (there being at that time not above two barks at the *Receif*) both to convoy them thither, and to cut off the communication with the continent to the enemy. Besides, that at least fourteen days provisions were required for this expedition, in case the enemy should stand his ground, which at this juncture was not to be done, unless we would leave the magazines of the *Receif* quite empty; there being then no possibility of attempting its relief, the next thing under consideration was, whether the entrenchments on the hill might be defended or not? Against the maintaining of it was objected; that without fresh supplies of provisions this fort could not hold out a week, especially since the enemy, by cutting off the pipes of the spring that furnished them with fresh water, would soon put them under a necessity of coming to surrender; when it was evident, that they might post themselves betwixt the fort of *Orange* and this hill, and consequently prevent their receiving any supplies from thence.

Whether the fort on the hill was to be defended.

Besides that the hill being of a considerable compass, was the more difficult to be mention'd by our forces, the fort itself being irregular, and but slightly fortified on that side, especially where the old church-wall, making up part of the courtain, would not be proof against the enemies cannon, and consequently expose the whole fort, with the garrison, to the mercy of the enemy: So that it being beyond all dispute in the enemies power to cut off all communication with the fort *Orange*, it was unanimously resolved and ordered, to leave the said entrenchments, and to retire with the garrison, and what provisions and ammunition they had, into the fort *Orange*, before their retreat was stopt by the enemies troops; it being past all doubt, that in case they could maintain themselves in that fort, they could at all times, if they were masters of the field, recover the hill and the whole island.

The council were the more forward in coming to this resolution, because they had received certain information, that the enemy, who knew the importance of the fort *Orange*, had gain'd some of the gunners and volunteers of the fort by presents, who had engaged to assign them a place where it was easiest to be attack'd, whereabouts they were to charge the cannon with gunpowder only, to facilitate their attack: Two of the gunners were hang'd the 23[d] of *June* for this treachery, the rest made their escape to the enemy. For the better preservation therefore of this fort, our people left the entrenchments upon the hill the 21st of *June*, where the enemy posted a strong body of their troops immediately after. The council likewise ordered the yacht the *Heemstede*, to cruise in conjunction with the *Golden Doe*, before the north entrance of the island, to keep open free communication for us with our garrison, and to prevent the enemy from receiving any succours that way; and at the same time some provisions were sent thither for the use of the garrison.

Some gunners turn'd traitors.

1646.

Were hanged.

But whilst things were thus transacting with various fortune, tho' for the most part to our disadvantage, and the so long expected succours from *Holland* not arriving, the want of necessaries encreased more and more every day in the *Receif*, to such a degree, that whatever was found fit for sustenance, either in the publick magazines, or with private persons, was apply'd to the common use; which however amounting to no more than one pound of bread a week for each single person, many died for hunger; their legs beginning to swell first, which was the forerunner of certain death: Cats and dogs, of which we had great quantities, were look'd upon as dainties at that time; and you might see the Negroes digging the half-rotten bones of dead horses out of the ground, and to gnaw them with incredible eagerness; neither was the want of fresh water less insupportable, by reason of the heat of the climate, and the constant use of salt meats, all springs that were dug being brackish. The poor slaves, who had the least share of what was left, look'd so gashly and wild with their eyes and jaws sunk, as appear'd terrible to the most undaunted of men. At last (notwithstanding all the care taken by the council) things came to that pass, that the allowance of one pound of bread *per* week was fain to be taken away from the inhabitants, and allotted the soldiers; who, by the enticements of the *Portuguese* beginning to desert apace, had two pound of bread allow'd them, as long as there was any left; but when all was spent, and no remedy was to be found against this lingring evil, it was proposed by the council, and unanimously resolved, rather to die bravely than to starve, and to fight their way through the enemy. The soldiers were to lead the van, the women, children, sick, and other unable people to keep in the middle, and the members of the great council, with the inhabitants to defend the rear: The *Jews* were

Great famine in the Receif.

1646. were above all the rest in a desperate condition, and therefore resolved rather to die with sword in hand than be burnt alive, which is their doom in *Portugal*.

But when we were just reduced to the last gasp, all horses, cats, dogs, and rats being consumed, and a few quarterns of *Farinha* sold at the rate of betwixt 80 or 90 gilders *per* quartern, which however could not suffice for above two days longer, on the 22[d] of *June*, (a day never to be forgotten) we saw two vessels with *Dutch* colours making all the sail they could towards the *Receif*: They had no sooner cast there anchors, and giving us the signal by the discharge of three guns each, that they came from *Holland*; but you might have read in all our faces the sudden joy we conceived at this relief in our last extremity: There was no body that could stand upon his legs for want of bread, but did crawl to the harbour, where you might hear the cries of the people weeping for joy at a great distance. These two ships, call'd the *Falcon* and *Elizabeth*, were freighted for the chamber of *Amsterdam*, and had left the *Texel* the 26th of *April*; they brought us the welcome news, that we might hourly expect the whole convoy. The captain of the *Elizabeth* told me himself, that having a very fair wind one day, he said to his crew, *I am sure they are in great extremity at the* Receif, *God send us fair wind and weather to relieve them in time*, which happened thus accordingly. The captains were each presented with a golden medal, with the following inscription; *The Falcon and Elizabeth did relieve the* Relief.

The Receif *releived.*

The 23[d] of *June*, Mr. *Bas*, a member of the council was sent to *Itamarika*, to assist in the defence of the fort; by his letters of the 28th he advised, that the enemy continued still in his post on the hill, and that he had sent abroad some spies to get intelligence. The 7th of *July*, the said Mr. *Bas* return'd to the *Receif* with the companies commanded by captain *Blewcock* and *Cunrad Held*, leaving the two companies of *Reinard Sikkema* and *Dignus Bysterman* there in garrison. The enemy had some days before, after having blown up the fort on the hill, and set fire to their camp, left the island, carrying along with them all the cannon, and among them two brass ones. For when they saw that we were reinforced with several ships from *Holland*, they did not think fit to abide there till we should stop their passage back by our vessels; neither were they insensible, that without being masters of the fort *Orange*, they could not promise themselves the possession of the island, the south entrance being commanded by the said fort, and the north passage by our yachts. 1646.

Mr. Bas *sent to* Itamarika.

The Portuguese *leave* Itamarika.

The 29th of *June*, the council received advice from our head quarter at the house of *John Lestan*, in *Rio Grande*, that two sons of king *John Duwy*, with 23 *Tapoyers*, were sent thither by their father, to assure our people of his good inclination and service; but they refused to come into the fort *Keulen*, before they had spoken with *Rudolph Baro*, who had been sent for upon that account. About this time several merchants set out some privateers, but as this could not be done without great charge, and there were but few ships at sea of the *Portuguese*, this turn'd to no great account, and consequently continued not long. A very odd accident happened to me much at the same time: For some of the labourers, who were employed to unload a vessel belonging to the company, were got so drunk, that they had kill'd a man, and hurt several others, by letting a pipe of wine fall upon them: I went thither to prevent any further disorder, but was no sooner entred the ship, when on a sudden I found the silver galoons upon my coat turn black, and myself bereaved of my sight, which however I recovered by degrees in a few days after, the cause of which I attributed to the strong exhalations of the wine, that had been closed up for a considerable time before. Much about the same time a difference arose betwixt the officers of the army and the city militia, about the chief command of the head guard in the *Receif*, which the city officers laid claim to.

An accident happens to the author.

But to return to our so long expected succours.

The reiterated letters from the council of the *Dutch Brasil* to the states general, and the directors of our company, wherein they presented their dangerous condition to them, had had such an influence upon the first, that they advised the directors of the company, to send us a reinforcement of 5 or 6000 men, and a good fleet; for which purpose they sent them 25 companies of their regular troops, and gave leave for the raising as many more, as in all mounted to 4000 land soldiers, besides seamen and volunteers.

This fleet consisting of a good number of brave ships, was ready to set sail in *November* 1645, but by reason of a sudden and hard frost, were detained in the road of *Ulyssingen*, till *February* 1646. One Mr. *Bankert*, admiral of *Zealand*, had the chief command of this fleet, and at the same time the following five gentlemen, who were appointed members of the great council of the *Dutch Brasil*, and were to relieve the old ones, were sent to their stations there; to

A fleet equipt in Holland *for the relief of* Brasil.

1646. to wit *Walter Schonenburgh* president, *Michael Van Goch* Pensionary of *Vlyssingen*, *Simon Van Beaumont* fiscal of the city of *Dort*, *Henry Hacks*, and Mr. *Trowens*, two great merchants of *Amsterdam*, and Mr. *Heremite* a lawyer of *Dort*, their secretary. One *Sigismund Shoppe*, formerly under count *Maurice*, and who had commanded the land forces of *Dutch Brasil*, was now sent in the quality of commander in chief of these forces; he was a most experienced captain, and who always kept a strict discipline among the soldiers.

Never did any fleet sent from *Holland* to *Brasil* meet with so many unfortunate accidents as this, during the six months they were at sea. For within two days after they had left the *Dutch* coast, they were forced to cast anchor in the *Downs* opposite to *Newport*, where they lost two of their ships by stress of weather. After a stay of three days, the winds being somewhat allayed, the squadron under Mr. *Van Goch* set sail again, but was two days after again forced into *St. Helens* in the isle of *Wight*: Three days before their arrival a rich *Dutch* ship, valued at two millions of livres, then lately come from *Brasil*, was lost among the rocks, so that of 300 persons, no more than 30 were saved. Here they were detained by foul weather and contrary winds seven weeks, when another *Dutch* ship coming from *Brasil*, chanced to cast anchor near them, and told them, that their countreymen in the *Receif* were drove to the last extremity; nay, that perhaps the place was surrendered by this time, they having no more than two months provisions left at the time of his departure. Hereupon it was resolved to continue their voyage with the whole fleet, notwithstanding the winds were against them; but on the coast near *Portland* were again overtaken by a violent storm, in which they saw a *Scotch* ship with 200 persons in her perish. The fleet under Mr. *Van Goch* came with much ado to an anchor behind a rock, where they staid till the fierceness of the tempest being allayed, they prosecuted their voyage. But scarce were they got through the channel, just as they were entring the *Spanish* sea, but a difference arose betwixt Mr. *Van Goch* and Mr. *Beaumont* about the flag, the *Zelanders* (in a council of war held for that purpose) allotting the precedency to Mr. *Van Goch*; whereas the *Hollanders* pretended the same to belong to Mr. *Beaumont*; but Mr. *Van Goch* persisting notwithstanding to claim the precedency, Mr. *Beaumont* gave a signal to the *Holland* ships to follow him, and so bid adieu to Mr. *Van Goch*, who after a troublesome and tedious voyage, in which he lost many of his men by sickness, and e- *Some ships arrive from Holland, at the Receif.*

specially by the scurvy, he arrived the 14th of *July* with his ship in the road of the *Receif*, being the first of the five new lords of the council that arrived in the *Dutch Brasil*. The 31st of *July* 1646, the ship the *Bluecock*, and the *Vlyssingen* of *Zealand*, came likewise to an anchor there; in the first came Mr. *Trowens*, and in the last colonel *Sigismund Shoppe*. 1646.

The 6th of *August* the said colonel gave an account to the members of the council, how pursuant to their orders, he was advanced with 450 men as far as the fort of *Olinda*, to discover the countenance of the enemy, and to take some prisoners; that they had made a shew of attacking us, but after some slight skirmishes retired, and with a body of their troops marched thro' *Bracer de St. Jago*, to cut off our retreat; but our people forced them to retreat again with the loss of several of their men killed and wounded; whereas we had but one wounded during the whole action, besides colonel *Shoppe* himself, who received a slight hurt on his leg.

The 8th of *August* the *Arms of Dort*, and in it Mr. *Beaumont*, arrived before the *Receif*, he was conducted the next day with all imaginable respect to the *Receif*.

The 12th late in the evening Mr. *Walter Schonenbergh*, president of the new council, and *Henry Hacks*, arrived in a bark from the north in the *Receif*, where they were received by all the citizens and soldiers in arms; they had been forced to leave their ship called the *Middleburgh*, before the north entrance of *Itamarika*, as likewise the *Dolphin*, loaden with provisions on account of the chamber of *Zealand*, both which were seen the 30th of *July* off of *Olinda*, but being forced back by contrary winds, the last of these two did not come to an anchor near the *Receif* till the 13th of *August*. *More ships arrive from Holland.*

The same day a certain negro deserter coming to the *Receif*, brought information that the enemy intended to erect a fort on the pass of the *Baretta*, to prevent our excursions into the open countrey; whereupon it was resolved, with unanimous consent of Mr. *Schonenbergh* and the whole council, as likewise with the approbation of colonel *Shoppe* and admiral *Lichthart*, to prevent the enemies design by fortifying and maintaining the said pass, as being the only inlett we had left for the recovery of the whole *Dutch Brasil*, all the other passes being so strongly fortified by the enemy, as not to be attempted without great hazard.

Accordingly the said colonel *Shoppe* marched the same night with all the forces he could bring together, ordering the boats laden with materials for the intended fortifications, to follow him the next tide. *Colonel Shoppe marches to the Baretta.*

The

1646. The colonel at his arrival having soon chased the enemy from thence, and possessed himself of the house of the *Baretta*, sent for immediate orders the council, to know whether he should continue in that post all night; who, with the approbation of the new president *Schonenbergh*, dispatcht Mr. *Bullestrate* thither immediately to take a view of it, and to make his report accordingly; he returned the 14th against night, and reported to the council, that he had found the work there very far advanced already, and the fortifications in such a state, that they would soon be in a posture of defence against any attempts from the enemy.

The 13th of *August Rudolph Baro*, who, as we told you, was sent with some presents to *John Duwy* king of the *Tapoyers*, brought a letter from the said king dated the first of *July*, to the council, wherein he thanked them for their presents, and desired they would be pleased to send him some iron weapons, he being then in war with the *Pojuku*'s, and that after he had humbled them, he would march with all his forces against the *Portuguese*.

By this time the president *Walter Schonenbergh*, and the other members of the new great council being arrived at the *Receif*, and having delivered their commissions from their high and mightinesses the states-general, his highness the prince of *Orange*, and the council of XIX. constituting them joint governours of the *Dutch Brasil*, the late members of the said council, to wit, *Henry Hamel*, *Bullestrate*, and *Peter Bas*, ordered all the colleges and other persons of note to be called together, to be present at the installment of the future lords of the council.

The members of the old council surrender the government.

Accordingly all the members of the court of justice, and of the finances, next the magistrates and commissaries of *Maurice's town*, then the ministers and church council, together with the sea and land officers, the heads of the *Jews*, and last of all the factors and book-keepers of the company, being assembled, Mr. *Walbeck* told them in the name of the council, that Mr. *Henry Hamel*, Mr. *Bullestrate*, and *Peter Bas*, had called them together, to lay down in their presence the reins of the government, and to surrender the same to Mr. *Schonenburgh* and the rest of the lords appointed by their high and mightinesses, by his highness the prince of *Orange*, and the council of XIX. for the supreme management of the government of the *Dutch Brasil*; returning them their hearty thanks for the services each in his respective station had done to the government, and for their constant fidelity during these intestine commotions, exhorting them to persevere in the same obedience to the new council; whereupon the new president and other members, having received the congratulations, first of the old council, and then of the other colleges, they from thence forward transacted every thing by their own authority, tho' they in all affairs of moment took the advice of the said members of the old council, during their stay in *Brasil*; for which purpose they desired them the 20th of *August*, to appear every day at eight a-clock at their assembly, and to assist them with their counsel for the better management of the affairs of the company. The 19th of *August* Mr. *Trowens* died late at night. 1646.

A general review.

The 3d of *September* was appointed for a general muster of all the forces in garrison in the forts near the *Receif*. Mr. *Heck* and commissary *Zweers*, were ordered to take a review of those in the fort *Ernestus*, *Wardenburgh* and *Boavista*. Mr. *Beaumont* and *Moucheron* in the fort of *Anthony Vaez* and *Maurice's Town*, Mr. *Van Goch*, *Hamel*, and *Alrich* at the *Receif*, and of those belonging to the artillery. Mr, *Raetsfield* and *Crowvanger* at the *Baretta* and adjacent quarters. Mr. *Volbergin* and commissary *Stricht* in the forts *William* and *Frederick Henry*. Mr. *Bullestrate* and *de Witt* in the fort *Bruin* and the land and sea fort.

The 4th of *September*, a pardon being agreed upon by joint consent of the old and new council, the same was the 6th day sent by a drummer to the enemy, with a letter to the *Portuguese* commanders from the *Bahia*, desiring them to withdraw their forces.

The 10th of *September* being appointed for a review of the militia of the *Receif* and *Maurice's Town*, the same was found to consist of 700 men; they received the thanks of the old council for their faithful services during the present intestine war, and then returned their thanks to them for their prudent management of the government.

The 13th of *September* the letters written by the *Portuguese* colonel the 11th of *September*, in answer to ours of the 6th, were read in the great council, filled with untruths and fictions of their own invention. They pretended that they were prevented by the inhabitants from retiring to the *Bahia*, besides that they wanted transport vessels, their ships being detained in the bay of *Tamandare*, and that they must expect the king's orders for that purpose.

They took also a great deal of pains to magnify their strength. The 12th and 13th of *September* several letters were dispersed abroad by the *Portuguese*, directed to justice *Daems*, to *Matthew Bek*, *Balthasar de Fonseca*, *Duarte Sarayva*, *Caspar Francis da Costa*,

1646. *sta*, being all merchants, and written by *John Fernand Vieira*; in which they again exaggerated their own number, and spoke very despisably of ours, threatening, that in case they should be forced to quit the countrey, they would destroy all with fire and sword, as they had already done in some parts of *Parayba*. The contents of these letters were as follows.

A letter from Vieira *to some merchants in the* Dutch-Brasil.

EXperience has without question convinced you sufficiently of the reasons that moved us to undertake this war, and the success we have met with is an ample testimony that God was pleased to inflict this punishment upon our enemies, for the many outrages committed against the inhabitants of this countrey. This is however in a great measure to be attributed to the general consent of the said inhabitants, who having now forced themselves from the tyrannical yoke of their oppressors, ought to expect from me, who, tho' unworthy, am appointed the chief manager of this war, to be back'd in so brave a resolution. I would not have you be ignorant of our strength, which, in comparison of yours, exceeds all that can be said upon that head; I will only tell you that as by our quitting the captainships of Parayba *and* Goyana, *we are considerably encreased in number, so it is most evident from thence, that the inhabitants chose rather to lose their possessions, than to endure any longer the indignities that were put upon them, which was the true cause of their insurrection, and not (as it is given out among you) because they were unable to satisfy their creditors; because they left more than what would have paid their debts. But if it should happen so, that the said inhabitants should not be able to maintain themselves by force of arms, they are resolved to lay all the other captainships desolate in the same manner.*

Having therefore well weighed the reasons which seem to promise us a good issue of this war, I thought myself obliged as a friend, to advise you that that party is back'd by reason and the unanimous resolution of many thousands; for, I can assure you, we are at least 14000 strong besides the negroes and Tapoyers, *dispersed in several places from* Rio Grande *as far as* Rio St. Francisco. Kamaron *commands 600 musqueteers,* Henry Dias *800 negroes, 200* Minos *and 700* Tapoyers; *and those of the* Sertan *are at our devotion, whenever we are pleased to call for them; but above all the rest we have God on our side. We are not ignorant, that before the arrival of M*r. Sigismund Shoppe *your whole force consisted not in above 600 men, and that the succours come along with him do not amount to above 1200 more; most of which are boys, and the rest either dead or sick. You see I am well acquainted with your strength, having kill'd and taken prisoners about 2600 of your best soldiers, and 500* Brasilians, *besides the wounded that were carried to the* Receif; *when our troops had no other arms than pointed sticks and clubs. These are blessings from heaven, for if we were able to perform these things without powder and ball, what may not be expected from our forces, now they are strengthened with good troops, and provided with sufficient arms and ammunition? All which I confirm to you upon my word, to be nothing but the real truth, and had it not been in respect of those colonels sent from the* Bahia, *and of his majesty of* Portugal, *I had by this time been master of the* Receif, *or some of the forts, or at least I might have done much greater mischeif:* But if matters are not brought to a happy conclusion, I am resolved to act like a desperate man, and not to leave any sugar-mills, cattle or negroes in the countrey, but will rather turn all to ruin and destruction, before we will be compelled to submit again to your obedience. 1645.

As these presents may serve as a warning to you, so, I hope you, and the rest of the merchants will not delay to enter with us into such articles of agreement, as may be most conducing to the preservation of your Possessions; for I would have you call to mind that there are many ingenios (mills) *reduced at present to such a state, as not to be likely to be in a condition to be used these ten years next to come. The* Vargea *is in no better condition than* Parayba *and* Goyana, *and the cattle (without which the mills cannot subsist) destroy'd in most places.*

Colonel Sigismund Shoppe, *I suppose, pretends to keep the field against us, as he did in the last war, but he will find himself egregiously mistaken, because the inhabitants will not be of his side, for if I should hear of one that was, I would cause him to be hanged immediately. You alledge that we are vassals of the company, but when was ever any conquered nation treated thus as we were, worse than the vilest slaves, of which you are sensible as well as we; so that being forced to break our chains, we don't owe you any further obedience. If we had not been in hopes of this opportunity, we would long before have implored the assistance of the king of* Spain *or* France; *and if those had fail'd us, to have had recourse to the* Turks *and* Moors. *I desire you not to throw away this letter, because experience will convince you of the truth of it; and that we shall pursue the same methods here, as we have done in other places; wherefore I would have you not give credit to any body, except to those that come in person from those places; I having told them nothing but the bare truth, which you*

1646. *you will find in effect thus: In the prosecution of this war, I hope you will consider, what is most for your interest, in which I am ready to serve you; for tho' your governors don't direct their letters to me, 'tis I that have the chief management of this war, and under my command the power of the colonels came from the* Bahia, *extending no further, than over those troops they have brought along with them.* A Reyal de bon Jesus September 11 1646.

On the 10th *of this Month, the before-mentioned colonels having sent an answer to a letter directed to them from your council, by one of our captains; several ensnaring questions were ask'd him concerning the present war, which he perhaps not answering according to their expectation, they replied more like drunken cowards than soldiers; if they will be pleased to come out and tell me these things, I will try whether their swords are as nimble as their tongues are, and teach them what respect is due to the messengers of those persons who have the supreme command here. This I write to you at present, but shall not fail in due time to make my words good by the sword, of which your people feel the daily effects as often as they dare to come out of their forts. Pray be not deceived, for* Brasil *is not allotted to you; not questioning but that God will bless our arms, and if we happen to die, we shall lose our lives in the defence of our holy religion and liberty; and all those that have refused to accept of our offers, will pay for it with the loss of their lives, possessions and debts.*

A Reyal, Sept. 12, 1646.

Signed,

John Fernand Vieira.

The 14th of *September* a man of war, call'd the *Ter Veer*, equipped by the chamber of *Zealand*, (aboard of which was colonel *Hinderson*) arrived before the *Receif*, after a voyage of 14 weeks. The 24th of *September* the enemy caused some pamphlets to be dispersed, promising in very haughty terms a general pardon, and a composition of their debts, in case we would leave the island. The 27th of *September* colonel *Shoppe* returned with some troops from *Goyana*, by the way of *Itamarika*; I had not met with any enemy, but had found all the sugar-mills burnt in the first place, but the sugar-reed and farinha fields in a pretty good condition; we received afterwards further information, that the sugar-mills of *Goyana*, were not quite burnt down. The 27th of *October* a conference was held betwixt the old council and Mr. *Van Goch*, unto whom they imparted their advice concerning several matters relating to the state of the *Dutch-Brasil*, and especially to the planting of the *mandioka* or *farinha* roots,

Colonel Shoppe *returns from* Goyana.

A conference betwixt the old council and Mr. Goch.

2

and the killing of cattle, which they advised to be done with great circumspection, *Brasil* being not able to subsist without a considerable number of oxen, which were continually employed in carrying of sugar-reeds, wood and other necessaries to the mills. 1646.

For the planting of *farinha* roots they proposed *Itamarika*, *Rio Grande* and *Parayba*, which countries were thought sufficient to supply their present occasions; provided it were done before the season was elapsed.

In the mean while colonel *Shoppe* having made several, but for the most part, unsuccessful attempts upon the enemy; our forces were thereby so diminished, that we were not in condition to made head against the *Portuguese* near the *Receif*; which made our council take a resolution to endeavour the recovery of *Rio St. Francisco*, the execution of which being committed to the management of colonel *Hinderson*, proved more fortunate for us, he meeting with little resistance thereabouts.

Accordingly the 24th of *October* the following ships; count *Eano* admiral, *Loanda* vice-admiral, the *Arms of Dort* rear-admiral, the *Bluecock*, the *Watchful-Dog*, the *Greyhound*, *Eagle*, the *Star*, *Heemstede* and the *Flight*, with eight barks, set sail under the command of admiral *Lichthart*, and colonel *Hinderson* to the south. The 17th of *November* the council received advice, that our troops under colonel *Hinderson* were safely landed at *Korasippa*, and marching from thence to *Rio St. Francisco* and the fort *St. Maurice* had met with no opposition from the enemy, who had begun to raise the said fort. That they had been seconded by the small vessels, which had followed them up the river, which our forces had passed, and were marched to *Seregippe del Rey*, having left some behind to repair the fort; and that four *Portuguese* had requested their pardon, which was promised them. Whilst our forces were employed thereabouts, I was ordered thither to take care of the necessary provisions (of which there was great plenty) for our troops; having accordingly caused my cargo to be embarked aboard a ship call'd the *Brownfish*, *Francis Frantz* master.

The Dutch *attempt the recovery of* Rio St. Francisco.

I set sail the 24th of *November*. We were carried with a brisk gale as far as the mountains call'd by our people the *Saddle-hills* from their shape, the coast all thereabouts being white sand downs. About half an hour after sun-set we saw our selves off of the Bay of *Tamandare*, and from thence continued our course with a fair wind, which in two days after brought us happily to the entrance of that great river, which is

Mr. Nieuhoff *ordered hither.*

1646. is so broad at the beginning that a six-pounder can scarce reach cross it; it falls with a very soft current into the sea, its waters being low in the winter, but encrease in the summer; perhaps by reason of the snows that are melted by the heat of the sun. About 50 leagues from its mouth is a great cataract or water-fall, surrounded by a great many islands; the sea at its entrance meeting in tempestuous weather with the current, are so boistrous, that they strike terror into the stoutest mariners, and carry away great pieces of the continent along with them. We entered the said river, but were forced to cast anchor immediately after sun-set, for want of an east wind to carry us higher up, which commonly begins to blow thereabouts at three in the morning. The countrey appeared very pleasant on both sides, and we saw abundance of wild beasts near the river-side, and several huts made of straw. We were detained near 24 hours upon a sand-bank, which after we had passed, we came at last to the village called *Penedos*, situate upon a high hill; here we landed with our boats, and found a few houses which were rebuilt by our people, the rest being burnt by the enemy before their flight. In the fort was formerly (in the time of the *Portuguese*) a church, which we turn'd into a magazine; it was surrounded with a goodly wall, the river passing by it on the north-side, where the hill is very steep.

Admiral Lichthart *dies.* The 30th of *November* admiral *Lichthart* was seized with a sudden and violent illness, occasion'd by his drinking too much cold water, after he had over-heated himself before; he was carried into a boat with three soldiers under the command of an officer, lower down the river, but soon after lost his senses, and in my presence expired. The next day his corps being put in a coffin was carried aboard the *Golden-Star*, being conducted by the chief officers there present, and four companies of soldiers to the river-side, who gave three salvo's with their musquets, as did the cannon from the fort and ships, in order to his interment at the *Receif*.

Mr. Nieuhoff *in danger of being drowned.* Towards evening as I was going aboard our ship the boat overturned by the swiftness of the current, and had I not been a good swimmer, I had infallibly been drowned; the master threw out a great cable over-board, by the help of which, and God's mercy I got safely into the ship. The soldiers in the mean while scower'd the countrey, and brought 700 oxen, (of which there was great plenty) and 300 calves into our quarters, having been at pasture in one of the adjacent Islands of the river, under the guard of some soldiers; they were not extraordinary fat, but tolerable good meat.

The soldiers huts were for the most part 1646. planted on the north-side of the hill, which being composed of branches and leaves of *A fire in the soldiers quarters.* trees took fire accidentally the 3d of *December*, with such fury, that in a quarter of an hour the whole quarter was in a flame, notwithstanding that the alarum was given immediately, by the beating of drums and the sounding of trumpets; some soldiers that were then swimming in the river, lost all their cloaths by this accident. It was well it happened by day; for if it had been in the night it would have put us under a great consternation, it being generally reported, that it had been done by treachery.

There was at that time a plentiful crop of tobacco upon the circumjacent fields, but was not quite fit for reaping, which must be done at a certain season, before the low grounds overflow'd. The colonel desired me to provide those who had lost all, with new cloaths, and to deduct it out of their pay; but I told him, that I being only a factor, could not do it without special order from the council, some having but little pay due to them. The 25th of *December* we received intelligence that the enemy began to appear in a considerable body, whereupon the companies of captain *Cousin*, *Schut*, *Gyseling*, *la Montayne*, and of a *Brasilian* captain, call'd *Tomee*, were sent in quest of them, with orders to set their stables on fire, and bring the cattle to our quarters. The next following *Monday* word was brought us, that our troops were so narrowly enclosed by the enemy, that it was feared scarce one of them would escape with life. Whilst we were in a great consternation, not knowing what resolution to take, a *Brasilian* brought us the unwelcome news, that our whole body was routed and dispersed, and captain *Schut*, *Cousin* and *La Montayne*, kill'd upon the spot. He had scarce finish'd his doleful relation before a *German* soldier, who had escaped the fight, by his bleeding wounds and his words gave us a confirmation of what had been told us before, with this addition, that captain *Gyseling*'s lieutenant, *La Montayne*'s ensign, and one *Kilmet*, belonging to captain *Schut*, had fought their way through the enemy, with about 30 soldiers, and would soon be here. This mishap was chiefly attributed to the fool-hardiness of our troops, who contrary to colonel *Hinderson*'s command, having at once discharged all their musquets against the enemy, fell in pell-mell, without any regular order, with sword in hand upon the enemy, which the enemy perceiving, retreated back and drew them into an ambush. Towards night we saw several soldiers miserably wounded with darts come to our quarters, some who had

1646. thrown away their arms, were forced to cast lots for their lives, the misfortune of which fell upon a *Dutchman* and a *Brasilian*, who being tied to a stake to be shot to death, were however pardon'd by the colonel. Captain *Gyseling*'s lieutenant, who came without his arms to the fort, was sent immediately to the *Receif*, where his sword was broke over his head, and he declared incapable of serving the company for the future, notwithstanding he had done them faithful service for seven years last past.

The Dutch *defeated in* Rio St. Francisco.

By this time I was sent for to the *Receif*, so that after having taken my leave of the colonel and Mr. *Dames*, I embarked on board the *Bat* the 16th of *December*, and we were the same evening with a fair wind and stream carried to the mouth of the river. It being a fine moon-light night we catch'd abundance of *Zaggers* as we call them, a fish of a very good taste, and continued our course with a brisk gale: Not far from the rivers mouth we met with four of our ships, who told us they were to fetch provisions, but in case they could not, were to return forthwith to the *Receif*. The 18th we advanced but little, the ships being not out of sight of us, near the rivers mouth, but did catch more fish than we were able to eat. The 20th we were likewise becalmed, and we perceived the moon to be half eclipsed for the space of two hours. The next following day we sailed so near to *St. Antonio*, that we could see them walking along the sea-shore. Towards night we discovered *Porto Calvo*, about 30 leagues from *Rio St. Francisco*. We were often becalmed, but catched abundance of *King's-fish* and *Codds*, and saw fires in many places along the coast. The 24th of *December* we came so near to the cape of *St. Austin* that we discovered five ships and seven row-barges in the harbour; we might have reached some of those that went ashore with our shot, had it not been for the sand-bank which hindred our nearer approach. About noon we came before the *Receif*, but it was so foggy that we could scarce discover the water fort, nevertheless we ventured in, and I got ashore immediately, with an intention to give an account of the state of affairs in *Rio St. Francisco* to Mr. *Schonenburgh*, being conducted thither by colonel *Shoppe*, who happened to meet me immediately after my landing.

Mr. Nieuhoff's *return to the* Receif.

The 27th of *October* the enemy had laid two ambushes in the way to the fort *Prince William*, beyond the redoubt *Kiik*. They did not stir till towards noon, when perceiving a company of our soldiers marching along the dike, they fired so briskly upon them, that they killed 11, wounded 12, and took three prisoners; yet notwithout the loss of some on their side.

The enemy lay an ambush.

In the mean while the *Tapoyers* being much exasperated at the murder of the beforementioned *Jacob Rabbi* their commander, had left our party; the council did what they could to appease them, imprisoned and banished *Garsman* the author of it, and confiscated his estate, notwithstanding which, the *Tapoyers* could not be prevailed upou to join with us as before. 1646.

The Tapoyers *leave our party.*

The 18th of *November* Mr. *Van Goch* entred into a conference with the members of the old council, whether it might not be feasible to embark what forces we were able to spare on board our great ships, and to attempt to make a powerful diversion to the enemy by attacking them in some place or other. But those of the old council having represented to him the danger of this enterprize if it should miscarry, whilst they were blockt up in the *Receif*, the further debate thereof was deferred till the next day. It was then proposed, upon second thoughts, that in case we could bring all our forces together, something of moment might be undertaken without manifest hazard, whereby to oblige the enemy to withdraw his forces from the *Receif*; but Mr. *Van Goch* apprehending no small danger in case we miscarried, they came to no resolution for that time.

Debate concerning an enterprise against the enemy.

It being found by experience that all our promises of pardon had proved ineffectual, it was proposed by Mr. *Van Goch* the first of *December*, whether it were not most expedient to give no quarter for the future; unto which it was answered, that very seldom quarter had been given by us, and few prisoners were taken, and that the enemy had likewise killed most of our people that were fallen into their hands, but they judged it not convenient to refuse quarter to all without distinction, which would induce such of the inhabitants as had remained quiet hitherto, to betake themselves likewise to their arms.

Another about refusing of quarter.

The 23d of *November* we laid an ambush for the enemy near the fort of *Affagados*, who being by some few sent out for that purpose, engaged in a skirmish, and pursuing our men with great eagerness under the cannon of the fort, were set upon by those lying in ambush, who killed and wounded many of them.

The 12th of *December* the corps of the late admiral *Lichthart* was interr'd, one company of the city militia, and two of soldiers appearing in arms upon that occasion, gave him three salvoes with their musquets.

The 30th of *December* the *Eagle* yacht brought letters to the council, dated in *Rio St. Francisco* the 4th of *December*, intimating, that in an island a little above the fort

News from Rio St. Francisco.

1646. fort, one colonel *Rebellia* was arrived with 200 men from the *Bahia*; and that they expected another reinforcement; as well from thence as from the *Vargea*; that our people being sent higher up the river, had attackt some of the enemies troops; but they made their escape to the other side, leaving their arms and clothes behind them.

1647. The 2[d] of *January* 1647, colonel *Shoppe* who had been with 300 fusileers in *Goiana*, returned to the *Receif*, giving an account that he had taken a view of all the rivers thereabouts, but met with noenemy.

Shoppe *returns from* Goiana.

The 5th of *January* the council received an account of the beforementioned action in *Rio St. Francisco*, *viz.* Five companies of our forces being sent to *Orambou*, to beat up the enemies quarters, they met with a body of 100 men, whom they attackt and put to flight; but soon after our forces were attackt by a much stronger body, who put them to the rout, with the loss of 150 men; of our officers one captain was killed, and five taken prisoners, *viz.* captain *Samuel Lambart*, *La Montagne*, *Gerrit Schut*, *Kilian Taylor*, *Daniel Koin*, and three lieutenants, *Joost Koyman*, *Anthony Baliart*, *Jeronymus Hellemen*, and one ensign.

Consultations concerning the state of Parayba.

The 8th of *January* Mr. *Van Goch*, in the name of the new council, advised with those of the old, that it being resolved among them to send for a considerable number of their forces out of *Parayba*, in order to gather a body of troops for some important design, they desired to be informed concerning the present condition of the said captainship; and whether the city of *Parayba* and *St. Andrew* might be defended by a small garrison; whereupon these of the old council replied, that the town of *Fredericia* had no fresh water but what they must fetch at a miles distance, and consequently might be cut off by the enemy; the same thing might be done at the passage leading to the river-side; besides, that there was no fortifications belonging to the place but the monastery, which was of no great consequence, and the *Guarte Domaiges* church, which had been fortified by the enemy in this war. As to *St. Andrew* it was no more than a sugar-mill about four hours distant from the city of *Parayba*, situate upon the bank of the river; that the communication of this place with the fort of *St. Margaret* might easily be cut off by the enemy, as being likewise about four leagues from thence, but it might be relieved from the water-side, and yet not without great difficulty. Mr. *Van Goch* told them he would make his report thereof to the council.

The 12th of *January* the council received advice, that the enemy were with a strong body of troops entred *Parayba*, and advancing very near to the sugar-mill of *St. Andrews*, had in the night time surprised some *Dutch* and *Brasilians*, to the number of 50 men, women and children, of which they had killed some, and ript up the womens bellies. 1647.

The 13th of *January* some pamphlets were again dispersed by the enemy, containing in substance, that since the inhabitants of the *Receif* were now beyond all hopes of further relief, it would be their surest way to come to an accommodation; for they resolved to venture all before they would lay aside their design; but if all failed they would destroy the whole countrey, and so leave it: They exhorted them not to be deceived by the insinuations of those who belonged to the company, and called them rebels; they being no more to be stiled so than the *Dutch* themselves, who had asserted their liberty against *Spain*.

Advice from Parayba.

The 17th of *January* four negroes belonging to one *Isaac de Rassier*, who had been taken prisoners some days before in *Parayba*, came over to us into the *Receif*, and brought advice, that the enemy, after having tarried but a little time in that captainship, where they had killed five *Dutch* men and some *Brasilians*, were retired from thence.

The wooden fort battered.

The 22[d] of *January* early in the morning, the enemy began to batter the wooden fort near the *Baretta*, from a battery on the bank of the south side of the river which he continued the whole day, but desisted at night; the garrison having been reinforced about noon with five companies of soldiers, and some provisions; because Mr. *Hamel*, one of the members of the old council, did represent to Mr. *Van Goch*, that tho' the fort itself was so inconsiderable, as scarce to be worth the trouble of defending it by a good garrison, yet at this juncture, when the enemy had made his first attempt upon it, it would not be adviseable to desert it, for fear of giving encouragement to the enemy to attack the other forts; but that on the contrary, as long as they did meet with a brave resistance here, they would not be so forward to attempt others; especially since we had the conveniency of relieving them with boats at high-water, with low-tide by land by the way of the sandridge; and that we might annoy the enemy with the cannon from our yachts in his trenches, as we had done that day. About the same time a map was ordered to be made, shewing the true situation of the *Receif*, with the turnings and windings of the adjacent rivers and marshes, as far as the *Baretta*, for the better instruction of the council.

Raise the siege.

The 24th of *January* in the morning, news was brought that the enemy had raised the siege

1647. siege of the fort of the *Baretta* the night before, and carried off all their cannon, being sensible that as long as they could be annoyed from the sea-side, and we be able to reinforce them daily with fresh troops, they could promise themselves but slender success: But besides that our people were to struggle against the enemy and famine, they were frequently troubled with desertions, many of our soldiers, nay even to the sergeants and other officers, who begun to despair of our ease, running over to the enemy, even at that time when the before-mentioned ships the *Faulcon* and *Elizabeth* were in sight of the *Receif*.

Now the members of the old council began to prepare in good earnest for their return to *Holland*, they had already in *December* 1646, sollicited Mr. *Schonenburgh* president of the new council, to order some ships to be got ready to transport them thither, and the *Vlyssingen* had been appointed for that purpose; but the same being not as yet returned from crusing, they applied themselves the 25th of *January* 1647, to Mr. *Van Goch*, and told him, that whereas according to their commission, one of them should return after the expiration of three years, they had continued in *Brasil* these six years, Mr. *Kodde* having indeed been ordered to return about that time, but his place not being supplied by another, he died before his departure: That they had for these three years last past, sollicited their return, and had two years ago received promises of being relieved by others; which had not been performed till within these few months, to the great prejudice of themselves and their families: Mr. *Van Goch* promised them to take effectual care to have the ships got ready, and to send for the ship the *Vlyssingen*, in order to their return home. At the time of the accession of the new council to the government, and the departure of *Henry Hamel*, *Adrian Bullestrate*, and *Peter Bas*, late members of the great council, the following forts remained still in the possession of our *West-India* company.

The members of the old council sollicit their return.

A catalogue of the forts in the hands of the Dutch.

The fort *Keulen* at the mouth of *Rio Grande*, provided with 28 brass and one iron cannon.

The redoubt of *St. Antonio*, on the north-side of the river of *Parayba*, with six iron pieces of cannon.

The fort *Restangues* in an island of the same name within the river *Parayba*, with four brass and five iron pieces of cannon.

The fort *Margaret* on the south side of the river *Parayba*, with 14 brass and 24 iron pieces of cannon.

The fort *Orange* in the isle of *Itamarika*, with 6 brass and 7 iron pieces of cannon.

Nossa Senhora de Conceptiano, an old battery upon the hill of *Itamarika*, with two brass and eight iron pieces of cannon. 1647.

The redoubt called *Madame de Bruin*, three iron pieces of cannon.

The fort *Wardenburgh*, alias the *Triangular Fort*, betwixt the *Bruin* and the *Receif*; the first provided with four brass and five iron pieces of cannon; the last with 14 brass guns.

The *Land Fort*, alias *St. John*'s, with 11 iron guns.

The *Water Fort*, at the mouth of the river of the *Receif*, with seven brass guns.

The fort *Ernestus*, with 5 brass and 3 iron pieces of cannon, and the battery with five brass and two iron pieces of cannon.

The *Receif*.

Maurice's Town upon the island of *Anthony Vaez*.

The fort *Frederick Henry*, alias the *Quinquangular Fort*.

The redoubt of stone near this fort.

The redoubt *Kiik*, betwixt the fort *Frederick Henry* and the fort *Prince William*.

The fort *Prince William* upon the river *Affagados*.

The forts then in possession of the *Portuguese*, and taken by them from the *Dutch*, are these;

Seregippo del Rey, *Rio St. Francisco*, and *Porto Calvo*, being reduced by famine, were rased by the *Portuguese*, being sensible that our people could not maintain themselves there without erecting of new ones, which was not to be done without a vast charge. Near the point of *Tamandare*, the place where the *Portuguese* from the *Babia* first of all landed their men; and where afterwards their fleet was beaten by ours, the enemy laid the foundation of a fort for the security of that harbour, where ships of great burden might safely ride at anchor.

Forts in the hands of the Portuguese.

The 23[d] of *January*, Mr. *Beaumont* was sent by the new council to confer with the late members concerning the present condition of *Rio St. Francisco*, and what was best to be done there: They answered him as before, that the fort as it was now, could do but little service, and that therefore it would be worth our consideration, whether the proposals made by them in writing, might not now be put in practice. The said Mr. *Beaumont* further proposed, whether it would not be requisite to erect an earthen redoubt for the defence of the *Baretta*; unto which those of the old council replied, that considering the vast charge and the small benefit which could be expected from it, the same might be more conveniently built in some place or other, to facilitate our passage into the open countrey. *Beaumont* was of opinion, that thereby

A conference about Rio. St. Francisco.

And the Baretta.

1647. by the enemy would be prevented from advancing to the fort *Frederick Henry*; but the old members told him, that notwithstanding we had now a fort on the *Barreta*, we could not hinder the enemies coming upon that island near the fort, unless we would keep a considerable force there for that purpose; that we need not fear their transporting any cannon thither, because their retreat might be cut off at high tide; neither could they from thence do any mischief to the *Receif*, it being evident, that the shot of our biggest cannon in the fort *Frederick William* could not reach the said island. The same evening Mr. *Van Goch* and *Hack*, came to tell the members of the old council, that the *Hollandia* and *Ulyssingen* would be ready in a little time, in order to conduct them to *Holland*, the *Ulyssingen* being ordered forthwith to return from the *Babia*, whither she was sent a cruizing.

The Receif *closely blockt up.* By this time the enemy had block'd us up so closely in the *Receif*, that on the land side we durst scarce look without the gates; and a certain *Portuguese* had prepared us a worse entertainment, having invited all our chief commanders abroad to his daughters wedding, during which time the enemy were to have surprized the city; but this design being timely discovered by some *Portuguese* and *Jews*, miscarried.

The Portuguese *rebuild a fort.* About the 15th of *October*, the *Portuguese* began to rebuild the fort *Bon Jesus*, as it is call'd by them, but by us *Altena*, on the other side of the river. We had some notice of it by deserters, but could not discover the truth of it, because they kept us from advancing that way by their cannon, and the place was surrounded on all sides with woods; but as soon as they had caused them to be cut down, we discovered it both by sight and the roaring of their cannon, which thundring incessantly against the city, caused such a consternation, as is not easy to be express'd, most people sheltring themselves in vaults, to avoid the fury of the enemies cannon. Of this I saw *A miserable spectacle.* a most miserable spectacle in a certain young lady, a niece of the late admiral *Lichthart*, who being come to visit one of her acquaintance, lately married, had both her legs shot off by a cannon bullet, which at the same time kill'd the new married woman upon the spot. At the outcry of these miserable wretches, I ran thither instantly, my house being just by, where I was an eye-witness of their misery, the poor young lady grasping my legs with such an agony, that she could scarce be pull'd off with all the strength I had; it being a most doleful spectacle for me to see the floor covered with the legs and arms of these miserable wretches; the poor young lady died likewise within three days after. It was not 1647. long after that I narrowly escap'd the same misfortune; for whilst I was talking with some of the inhabitants of the city, as I was going the rounds, two of them were kill'd by a cannon bullet, and another had both his hands shot off as he was lighting his pipe. Nay we were forced to remove all the ships out of the harbour for fear of being sunk. Colonel *Shoppe*, in the mean while, had made himself master of and destroyed *Taperika*, 2000 *Portuguese* only having saved themselves by flight; but by the many unsuccessful encounters we had with the *Portuguese*, our forces decreasing daily, whereas theirs encreased, colonel *Shoppe* was ordered to command colonel *Hinderson* to leave *Rio St. Francisco*, and to join him in *Taperika*; but this stood us but in little stead, being not long after obliged to leave likewise *Taperika* for the relief of the *Receif*. All our force consisting of about 1800 men, being now come to the *Receif*, (where they had not provisions for above seven months left) it was several times taken into consideration, what was best to be done at this juncture. Colonel *Shoppe*, with some other officers, were of opinion not to hazard an engagement, our forces being so much inferior to the enemy, but to stay for a more favourable opportunity; but it was carried by the majority to venture a general salley for the relief of the *Receif*, the chief command thereof being given to colonel *Brink*, because colonel *Shoppe* was not as yet cured of his wounds he had received in a late encounter. *A general salley made by the* Dutch. Our forces marched towards evening as far as *Guerapes*, a place fatal to us the year before by the defeat of our people, the fields thereabouts being as yet covered with their bones. The *Portuguese* no sooner perceived us to be upon the march, but they left the fort *Altena*, of which we having got notice, possess'd ourselves of it immediately, and thus drew the thorn out of our foot. But the 16th of *May* prov'd the most fatal of all we had seen for many years before in *Brasil*. For though our forces attack'd the enemy with bravery, and maintained the fight with great obstinacy for some time, yet the enemy, flush'd with their number and late success, with 2500 of their best men, at last forced our men to give way, and afterwards to fly, being pursued by 150 *Portuguese* horse; so that both in the fight and flight, we lost above 1100 *Are routed.* men, among whom were colonel *Brink*, and almost all the rest of our commanders: We lost also 19 colours, and all our cannon and ammunition we had carried along with us. It was not till five days after before leave could be obtained to bury our dead, which

1647. which began to corrupt and ſtink moſt nauſeouſly, by reaſon of the burning heat of the ſun. This was the laſt effort we were likely to make in the field; all our future care being for the preſervation and defence of the *Receif*, unleſs we ſhould be ſupplied with freſh ſuccours from *Holland*; but the ſame arriving but ſlowly, moſt people began to fear, that in caſe God Almighty did not ſend us ſome unexpected relief, we ſhould be at laſt forced to leave that place likewiſe to the mercy of the enemy: The great council laying the fault of our late misfortunes upon the council of war, and theſe again upon them, alledging, that the ſoldiers were ill provided for, and wanted their pay. As for myſelf, being ſenſible that things would be worſe and worſe every day, I thought it the ſafeſt way for me alſo, to deſire a paſſport for my return to *Holland*, which at laſt, with much ado I obtained, and ſo prepared every thing for my voyage. But before I leave *Braſil*, I ought to give you a ſhort account of the products of the ſaid country. 1647.

The captainſhip of *Pernambuko* and *Braſil* in general, being not only well ſtored with cattle, but alſo with ſeveral ſorts of herbs, trees and fruits, we will give you a ſhort view of them, and begin with the *Mandiiba*, and its root, call'd *Mandioka*, unto which the *Braſilians* ſtand chiefly in- Mandioka *root.*

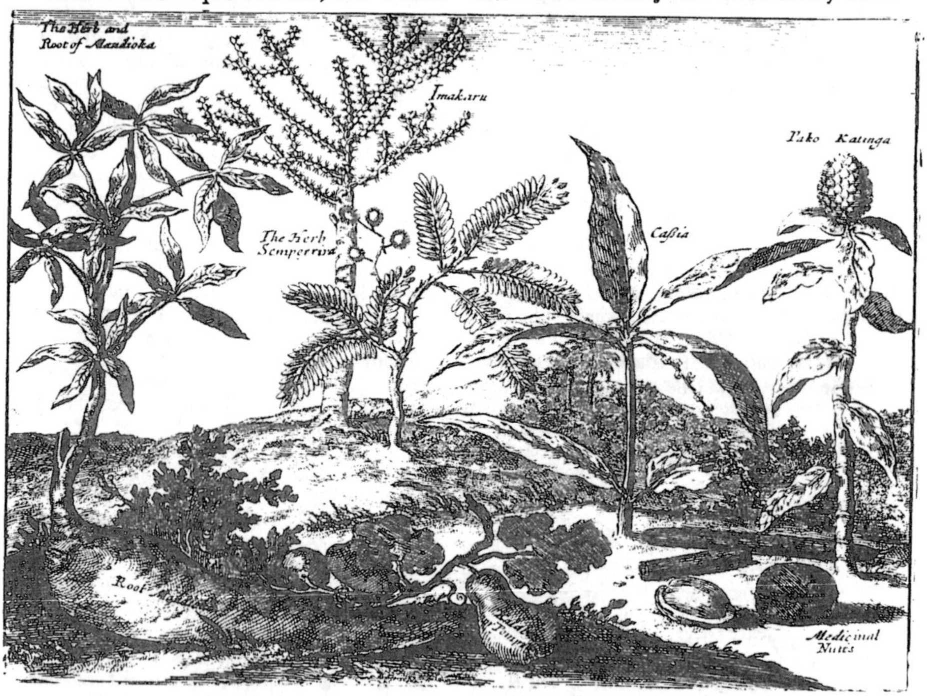

debted for their ſuſtenance. The moſt parts of *America* are ignorant hitherto of wheat or any other grain, inſtead of which nature has furniſhed them with a certain ſhrub, the root of which dried and powdered, and afterwards boil'd and bak'd as we do our bread, is the common food of the inhabitants of *America*. This ſhrub grows in vaſt plenty every where, being by the *Braſilians* called *Maniiba* and *Mandiiba*, and its root *Mandioka*. There are divers kinds of it, diſtinguiſhed by the *Braſilians* by different names, but the root is in general called *Mandioka*. Their leaves are ſmall, green and long, pointed at the end, which grow upon large ſtalks or branches, each of which has five, ſix, or ſeven leaves, growing in a cluſter, reſembling a ſtar, call'd by the *Braſilians Manikoba*. The ſtock or ſtem is diſtinguiſhed by certain knots, not above an inch thick, but generally ſix, ſometimes ſeven foot high, from whence ſprout forth ſeveral branches, which producing again leſſer ſtalks, bear the before-mentioned leaves: It bears a ſmall flower of a pale yellow colour, and of five leaves only, with ſmall ſtalks within, which at laſt turn to ſeed. The root *Mandioka* reſembles our parſnip in ſhape, being two or three foot long, and about a man's arm thick, but grows thinner towards the bottom. Its outward rind reſembles that of a haſel-tree, but

1647. but its substance is white, affording a milky sharp juice, which is pernicious to beasts. This shrub grows in dry, barren and sandy ground, its nature being so averse to moisture, that they are obliged to plant it only in the summer months, where it is most exposed to the sun. For this purpose it is, that the inhabitants cut down the woods on the hills and in the plains, which they burn, and so prepare the ground for the production of this root: These fields are by the *Brasilians* called *Ko*, by the *Portuguese Roza*, or *Chokas*, and by our people *Rossen*. These fields are turn'd up into small round hills like mole-hills; the *Portuguese* call them *Montes de Terra Cavada*, or *Hollowed Hills*; the *Brasilians Kujo*. These hills they make about two foot and a half asunder, each being about three foot in circumference, and half a foot high, that the rain-water may be carried off with the more ease. In each of these hills they commonly plant three small taks of this shrub, of about nine, ten inches, or a foot long, without leaves, notwithstanding which they grow and soon bear fresh leaves, and in time produce new roots, which cannot be transplanted, because no sooner are they taken out of the ground, but they begin to putrify and stink. After these taks have been about ten days in the ground, they begin to bud and produce as many fresh taks as they have knots; each of these taks is about a finger long, from whence sprout forth many lesser ones of a purple colour. The fields must be three or four times a year cleared of the weeds, which grow in great plenty amongst it, and choak it up before it comes to its full growth. The small taks and leaves of these shrubs are mightily infested by the *P*‚*mires*, and likewise coveted by the wild-goats, oxen, horses and sheep, for which reason they are very careful to fence these plantations with stalks and branches of trees: The bees, coneys, and some other *Brasilian* creatures are mighty fond of the root, which takes no harm, tho' the shrub be stript of all the leaves, provided the root itself be not touch'd. This root does not come to its full perfection till a year after the planting of the taks, tho' in case of necessity they may be drawn in six months, but afford but little *Farinha*. Each shrub produces two, three, four, nay sometimes twenty roots, according to the goodness of the ground, and after they are come to full maturity, will keep two or three years under ground; but it is much more safe to take them up at the years end, for else many of them will rot; nay, if the season happens to prove very wet, they must of necessity be drawn tho' they are but half ripe. The root, after it is taken out of the ground, will not keep above three days, but stinks, take what care you can; for which reason they seldom draw more at a time than they can make immediately into *Farinha* or meal. That kind of *Mandioka*, commonly called *Mandibuka*, grows faster and ripens sooner than any other, and affords the best *Farinha*; it thrives best in sandy and hot grounds. But that kind which is most generally used is called *Mandiikparata*, and grows indifferently in all grounds. The *Farinha* is prepared thus: The root after it is taken out of the ground is purged from its outward rind by a knife, and wash'd in fair water: Then the end of the root is held close to a wheel of about four or five foot diameter, which being covered round the edges with a copper or tin plate full of sharp small holes, not unlike a nutmeg-grater, and the wheel being turn'd round continually, grates the said root into small particles, which fall into a trough underneath. The wheel is by the *Brasilians* called *Ibecem Babaca*, and by the *Portuguese Roda de Farinha*, or the flower wheel; the trough the *Brasilians* call *Mukaba*, and the *Portuguese Kobhe de rater Mandiboka*. But the poorer sort are fain to be contented with a hand-grater, called *Tapiti*. The root thus grated is put into a bag, made of the rinds of trees, about four inches wide, called by the *Portuguese Espremendouro de Mandiboka*. This bag with the root is put into a press, and all the juice prest out, (it having a venomous quality) which is by the *Brasilians* called *Maipoera*, or *Munipuera*, and by the *Portuguese Agoa de Mandioka*, i. e. *The water of Mandioka*. The next thing to be done is to beat the root through a sieve, called by the *Brasilians Urupema*; and then to lay it upon a copper plate, or earthen pan, over the fire, and to stir it continually with a wooden spoon or spattle till it be quite dry. This pan or vessel the *Brasilians* call *Vimovipaba*, and the slice *Vipucuitaba*. The *Farinha*, before it is quite dry, is called by the *Brasilians Vitinga*, and by the *Portuguese Farinha Relada*; but when it is compleatly dried and fit for keeping, the *Brasilians* call it *Viata* or *Viccia*, and the *Portuguese Farinha Seca*, or dry meal; or *Farinha de Guerra*, war-meal, because it is most used in time of war. For the more it is dried the better it keeps, but never keeps good above a year, the least moisture being apt to taint it; which is the reason, that both the *Portuguese* and we, in imitation of the *Brasilians*, bake biskets of it upon a grate iron, with hot coals underneath, for the magazines.

How the Farinha *is prepared.*

The juice *Manipuera*, which is press'd

1647. out of the root *Mandioka*, put into a veſſel, gets in two hours time a white ſettlement at the bottom, call'd by the *Braſilians Tipioja*, *Tipiaka*, and *Tipiabika*: This dried, affords a very white meal, called *Tipiocui*, which bak'd into cakes as before, call'd by them *Tipiacika*, taſte as well as wheaten bread. This juice is alſo boil'd to pap, and eaten, and ſerves likewiſe inſtead of ſtarch or paſte. The *Portugueſe* take this pap, mix it with ſugar, rice, and orange flower-water, which they make into a conſerve of a delicious taſte; they call it *Marmelada de Mandiboka*. The juice *Mandiga* or *Manipuera*, is of a ſweetiſh taſte, which is the reaſon the beaſts covet it, but commonly die ſoon after they have drunk of it, it being pernicious, nay mortal, both to man and beaſt. If the juice be kept twice 24 hours it produces worms, called by the *Braſilians Tapucu*; yet it has been found by experience, that this juice loſes its pernicious quality after it has ſtood 24 hours, there being many of *Braſilians* who boil and drink it without any harm. The root *Mandioka* is likewiſe immediately after it is taken out of the ground, ſliced in pieces, and laid in freſh water for four or five days, when it begins to be ſoft, it is called *Puba*, or *Mandiopuba* and *Mandiopubo*. This the wild *Braſilians*, inhabiting the deſerts and woods, roaſt in the aſhes and eat; becauſe it is done without much trouble. The ſame *Mandiopuba*, toaſted before the fire, is called *Kaarima*, which being afterwards beat to powder with a wooden peſtel in a mortar, they call *Kaarimaciu*; of this they make a pap with boiling water, which ſeaſoned with ſome *Braſilian* pepper, or *Nhambi* flowers, affords a very good diſh, eſpecially with the addition of ſome fiſh or meat, when it is called *Minguipitinga* by the *Braſilians*, who look upon it as one of their beſt dainties. It is alſo very wholſome, for this *Kaarima*, and the flower *Tipiaka*, boil'd in orange-flower-water, and ſugar, to the conſiſtency of a ſyrup, affords a very good antidote. They make alſo a kind of ſtarch of the flower called *Kaarima*, which they call *Minguapomonga*; as likewiſe very fine cakes, by mixing it with water, butter, and ſugar. There is a kind of meal prepared from the dregs of the *Mandioka*, or *Mandiopubo* root, thus ſteept in water, call'd by the *Braſilians Vipuba*, and *Viabiruru*, and by the *Portugueſe Farinha Freſca*, or freſh flower, and *Farinha d'Agoa*, or water flower. It is very well taſted, but will not keep above 24 hours. But if you make it up with water into balls or rolls, and let them dry in the ſun, they will keep good for a conſiderable time: Theſe they call *Viapua* and *Miapetika*. The *Tapoyers*, and almoſt all the other *Braſilians* prepare it thus, and afterwards mix it with another meal, called *Viata*, which affords it a more agreeable taſte. 1647.

The *Mandioka* root is likewiſe prepared thus: After it has been cleanſed and cut in thin ſlices, they beat it with a wooden peſtel, and ſqueeze the juice of it out with their hands only, which being dried, they call *Tina* and *Mixakuruba*; another way of preparing the *Mandioka* root is, to cut it into pieces, of about two fingers long, and two inches thick, which without being ſqueezed, is expoſed to the ſun, and afterwards beat to powder in a wooden mortar, call'd by the *Braſilians Tipirati*, by the *Portugueſe Farinha de Mandioka crua*, or the flower of raw *Mandioka*: The pieces before they are beaten to powder are very white, and may be uſed inſtead of chalk. Out of this flower they make very good white bread and biſkets, call'd *Miapeta*, the laſt of which are chiefly uſed in the camp, becauſe they will keep a great while.

Out of the root *Aipimakaxera*, the *Braſilians* boil a certain pleaſant liquor not unlike our whey, call'd by them *Kavimakaxera*. The ſame root, chaw'd and mixed with water, furniſhes them with another liquor they call *Kaon Karazu*. The cakes made from the flower of this root, laid in a caſk with water, till it ferments together, affords them likewiſe a ſort of ſtrong and very good beer.

All theſe different kinds of *Mandioka* roots, if they be eaten freſh prove mortal to mankind, except that call'd *Aipiamakaxera*, which roaſted, may be eaten without danger, and is of a good taſte. But all ſorts of beaſts, both wild and tame ones, don't only feed upon the ſaid roots and leaves, without the leaſt hurt, but alſo grow fat with them, notwithſtanding that the juice of both is mortiferous as well to men as beaſts. The Negroes and *Braſilians* bruiſe the leaves of the *Mandiiba* in a wooden mortar, which being boil'd, they put oil or butter over it, and eat it like as we do our ſpinage; this is ſometimes done by the *Portugueſe*, likewiſe and the *Dutch*, who make a kind of ſallet of the ſame leaves. The *Braſilians* prefer the bread made of the *Mandioka* root before ours, but it is not ſo natural to the *Europeans*, it being, if uſed in a great quantity, pernicious to the nerves and ſtomach, and corrupts the blood. About three buſhels of this meal, (at the rate of two gilders *per* buſhel) will ſuffice a ſtrong labouring man for a whole month, and a piece of ground planted with this root, produces four times the quantity, as if it had been ſown with wheat. There is a certain kind of *Mandioka* root call'd *Pitinga*,

1647. *tinga* by the *Brasilians*, the flower of which cleanses and heals old ulcers. This root is likewise found in the isle of *St. Thomas*, and in those of *Hispaniola*, *Cuba*, and others thereabouts, and in most parts of the continent of *America*; the inhabitants of which call it *Yuka* and *Kassave*, and those of *Mexico Quauhkamoth*, and the bread which is made of the flower, *Kazabis*, *Kazabi*, or *Kakavi*. The *Mandioka* root is originally the natural product of *Brasil*, and from thence transplanted into other parts of *America* and *Africk*. Its flower furnishes all the inhabitants of *Brasil*, as well the *Portuguese* and *Dutch*, as the natives and negroes with bread, which next to wheat is the best of all, so that our soldiers would rather chuse to have their allowance in *Farinha*, than wheaten bread out of the magazines. Since the war in 1645, the price of the *Farinha* was risen to three or four gilders *per* bushel, which, as it tended to the utter destruction of the sugar-mills, so by special orders from the great council of the *Dutch Brasil*, all the inhabitants of the open country were enjoined, under a severe penalty, to plant a certain quantity of *Mandioka* yearly, in proportion to their abilities, by which means the price of the *Farinha* was so considerably abated, that three bushels were sold for two shillings ready money, at the *Receif*, and for less in the country.

Kaaeo or Herba viva. *Brasil* produces a certain herb call'd *Kaaeo* by the *Brasilians*, by the *Europeans* in Latin, *Herba viva*, because it seems to shrink when you touch it, and so it does likewise about sun-set; its seed has been transmitted into *Europe*, where it grows to its full perfection.

Kalabasses. The *Kalabasses* are a kind of pompions, their rind, if dried, being so thick and strong, as to serve for materials for cups, porringers, and such like utensils. But what is most surprizing is, that they always grow of a different shape, some being long, others round, others oval, some thick before, others at the end. They blossom and bear fruit once a month, the blossom being yellow, mix'd with green; the pulp is white at first, but turns to a violet colour; they are of a tolerable pleasant taste, but very unwholesome, by reason they are too astringent.

The tree Imaraku. The tree call'd *Imaraku* by the *Brasilians*, is of a middle size, its trunk round, and its bark grey, covered with small thistles of the same colour. Its branches sprout forth on the top, with broad leaves of an oval figure, edged likewise with small thistles or thorns. There is also another kind of *Imaraku*, much larger than the former, call'd *Kakabu* by the *Brasilians*, and *Kardon* by the *Portuguese*. This sprouts forth first of all in the form of a large octangular leaf, upon which grow crosswise many thorns; this produces other leaves of the same kind, each being three, nay sometimes six foot long, and of the thickness of a man's arm. By degrees the first leaf turns into a woody substance, of a greenish colour, but somewhat spungy; those leaves that grow next to this stem are instead of branches, which produce other leaves. The stem bears only one large white flower, the fruit of which is of an oval figure, and of about twice the bigness of a hens-egg, of a dark brown colour, and fit for use. This tree grows to a great height. There is also another kind of *Imaraku*, being altogether the same with the former in respect of its largeness, blossom and fruit, except that its leaves are of a triangular figure.

Pako Kaatinga. What the *Brasilians* call *Pako Kaatinga*, the *Portuguese* commonly call *Canodo Mato*, or wild reed or canes. The stem or stalk is like that of other canes, about an inch thick, containing a white marrow or pith, of a sweetish taste, on which grow leaves of eight or nine inches long, and three inches broad, shaped like a tongue, smooth and pale green on one, and covered with a white woolly substance on the other side. The fruit of which is not unlike a pine-apple, about ten inches long, growing on the top of the stem; it is divided into several partitions, which opening by degrees, a pale grey flower appears betwixt each, containing underneath twenty or more grains of a black shining seed. The stalk chew'd draws the rheum from the head, and breaks the stone in the bladder. It is look'd upon as an excellent remedy against the involuntary emission of the seed throughout *Brasil*, and cures it in eight days time.

The tree and fruit Kasjou. All over *Brasil*, but especially in the isle of *Itamarika*, grows a certain tree call'd *Kasjui* or *Kasjou*, bearing a fruit of the same name. Its leaves are dark green, broad and round, interspersed with many small veins. It bears two different blossoms and fruits. The white blossom which appears in the lower branches, produces a juicy spungy fruit like an apple, of a very cooling and astringent quality: But the red blossom on the top a kind of chesnut. The *Brasilians* draw no small advantage from this tree; out of the apples they make a very good cyder, call'd by them *Kasjouwy*, which is sourish, but if mix'd with sugar, makes it as pleasant as *Rhenish* wine, and has this excellency, that tho' it soon seizes the head, yet it passes off without any harm. The other fruit they eat like as we do our chesnuts.

Among the products of the *West* and *East*-

1647. *East-Indies* is a tree call'd *Papay*, by the *Javaneses* and *Dutch*, and *Pinoguacu* or *Mamoeira* by the *Americans*; and sometimes intitled with the name of the *Melontree* by our people, by reason of the resemblance of its fruit to our melons. This tree is of two different kinds, to wit, the male and female. It grows and perishes again in a short time; its trunk being so spungy that it may be cut as easy as a cabbage stalk; the leaves it bears are very large and broad, not unlike our vine leaves, growing on long stalks round the top of the tree, and covering the fruit, which hangs in a knot, and is green at the first, but turns yellow at last, resembling in shape a pear, but of the bigness of our small melons, unto which its pulp resembles both in colour and taste, when come to maturity, but whilst they are green, they are boil'd with meat, and give it a tart taste.

Pinoguacu or Papay.

Chili Lada or Brasil *pepper*.

The red pepper, known by the name of *Brasil pepper*, and call'd *Chili Lada* by the *Brasilians*, grows on knotty stalks of about five or six foot high; the rind being a dark green, distinguished with white rings, from whence shoot forth small crooked branches of a hands breadth in length, bearing a small white flower, which produces a green husk, and turns red by degrees as it ripens, with a certain seed within it, being as hot and biting upon the tongue as the common brown pepper, and so does the husk. In the *East-Indies* they preserve it, and call it *Aetzar*, and use it raw in their fish sauces. In *Brasil* they cut two or three of these husks whilst they are green in slices, and mix them with oil and vinegar, or some limon juice, to acuate their appetite, but it is too hot for those that are not used to it, which is allayed by a good quantity of salt. This kind of pepper grows likewise in the *East-Indies*, in the island of *Java*, in *Bengala*, and several other places. I have seen it also in some of our gardens in *Holland*. There is another shrub which grows frequently in the *East-Indies*, not unlike this in shape and bigness, which bears a yellow flower; it is call'd *Halika Kabus* by the *Arabians* or *Alkekengi*, and sufficiently known in these parts. The flower produces a small bladder which contains the fruit and seed, they are not so big as ours. The *Indians* and *Chinese* mix it with a certain fruit call'd by them *Poma d'Oro*, *Tamatas* by the *Portuguese*, and *Melansana* by the *Italians*; they also eat it with *Chili Lada* or *Brasilian* pepper. The *Portuguese* cut the *Poma d'Oro* and the husk of the *Brasilian* pepper in thin slices, which being mix'd with oil and vinegar, they eat as a sallat, and look upon it as a proper remedy to cut the rough flegm of the stomach, a distemper very common in those parts. The *Brasilians*, as well as the *Dutch*, chaw this pepper for the same purpose, but it is very burning upon the tongue. 1647.

Sugar-canes or reeds.

The sugar canes or reeds, call'd by the *Brasilians Viba*, are the product both of the *West* and *East-Indies*, but grow in great plenty throughout all *Brasil*, but especially in the captainship of *Pernambuko*. They are of two different kinds, one bearing small, the other larger leaves. The last, which is accounted the best, sprouts up into a long stem of the thickness of a child's arm, the leaves growing all on the top in a cluster, being of an oval figure, and a dark blue colour. The rind is distinguished by certain joints or knots; the other kind bears small leaves from the top to the bottom. The sugar-canes are propagated from their small sprouts, which being put in the ground like our vines, grow up to the height of twelve foot, if they are planted in good soil, and are kept free from weeds. Six months after they have been planted, a brown seed appears on the top, then it is fit to be cut; for if they stand longer in the ground their juice diminishes, dries up, and turns sour. The juice, if taken immediately after it is drawn, causes a looseness. The low grounds are much more convenient for the planting of sugar-reeds than the hills, especially near the river side, where the banks are often over-flown by the stream. There are a certain kind of winged worms, call'd *Guirapeakoka* by the *Brasilians*, and *Pao de Galinha* by the *Portuguese*, which are great enemies to the sugar-canes, especially in moist grounds, where they gnaw and consume the roots. The sugar, which is the product of these canes, is not procured without a great deal of toil and labour, in which for the most part are employed slaves, under the tuition of certain overseers, appointed by the masters of the sugar-mills, who were for the most part *Portuguese*, the *Dutch* being hitherto not arrived to the utmost perfection in that art. In the captainship of *Pernambuko*, many fine *Ingenho*'s or sugar-mills, with their adjacent plantations were erected for this purpose, amounting in all to above 100 in number, and the labourers, negroes, and other *African* slaves thereunto belonging, to near 40000. The whole yearly product of sugar of the *Dutch Brasil*, is computed to be betwixt 200000 and 250000 chests.

Indigo.

In the year 1642, one *Gillin Venant* brought some indigo seed from the *American* islands into *Brasil*, who having certain lands assigned him near the small river *Mercera*, and being provided with all other conveniencies by the special command of the

1647. the great council, erected several plantations for the producing of *Aniel* or *Indigo:* But it being found by experience, that the pismires consumed most of the leaves, the said Mr. *Venant*, by employing many labourers and negroes, to destroy these pismires with burning and digging, at last so well cleared the ground, that the *Indigo* came to its full perfection, several patterns of which were sent into *Holland*. Mr. *Venant* having made an agreement with Mr. *Christopher Eyershettel* to instruct him in the most necessary points relating to the coagulating the indigo, he was treating with the great council concerning certain grounds for the planting of indigo, so that there was a fair prospect of bringing this design to a considerable perfection here, if the same had not been prevented by the intestine war.

The wild *Aniel*, which grows in *Brasil* in great plenty, has a great resemblance to the true indigo in outward appearance, but affords no good colours. Some pretend to have seen also a kind of wild cochenille in *Brasil*, and the ground would produce good store of cotton, but that the inhabitants draw much more profit from the sugar-plantations.

Drugs. Some ginger is likewise planted in *Brasil*, but not in such quantities as to be transported into other parts, no more than the *Mechoaconna*, *China* and some other medicinal roots; and the *Herba de Cubra* or *Herba de Nossa Senhora*, which is look'd upon as an infallible remedy against the gravel; and the root called *Paquoquanba*, which is the universal medicine of the *Brasilians*. There are also many transplanted hither from other parts, as ginger, tobacco, rice, cotton, turkey-wheat, *Aniel*, or indigo, and the sugar-reeds were first of all transported by the *Portuguese* from the *Canary Islands*. The fruits in daily use among the inhabitants, are *Ananas*, *Bananas*, *Mangaba*, *Akaju*, *Arakou* great and small, *Guajaba*, divers kinds of *Murukuja*, *Ibapiranga*, *Mazaxanduba*, *Akaja*, *Aratiku*, *Guitakori*, *Biringela*, *Mamaon*, *Coco-nuts*, and several sorts of *Indian* figs. The roots chiefly in use, are the *Batatas*, *Nhambi* and *Umbi*, and the *Indian* acorns, call'd *Tembi*, which are of a delicious taste.

Fertility of Brasil. The whole country of *Brasil* is extremely fertile and pleasant, being watered by many rivers and standing waters, most of which arise from the hills, and pass through spacious plains, the last of which are clayey and marshy grounds, (call'd *Vargea*'s by the *Portuguese*) which produce all sorts of fruit: but especially sugar-canes in great plenty. Their meadows and pasture grounds do not appear so pleasant in the summer as in the rainy season, when they are very green; wheat and rye grow soon rank here, which is occasion'd partly by the nature of the soil, partly by the heat of the sun; to prevent which they never let their grounds lie fallow, and manure them with sand instead of dung. The same must be observed with all other foreign seeds here, that require to be kept a considerable time under ground. In *February* and *March* (which is the rainy and winter-season of this climate) they sow their seeds, and that towards evening, not by day time, or about midnight. They take great care not to plant any thing too deep under ground; for whatever is planted beyond the sun-beams, seldom produces any fruit, which our people have learned to their cost. There is a remarkable difference betwixt the seeds and fruits which are produced on the hills, and those of the marshy grounds, as to their time of ripening; tho' the coco and palm-trees are transplanted here without the least regard to their age, bigness, or the season, and grow very well. Most of their own trees and shrubs bear flowers and fruits throughout the whole year, so that at one and the same time, you enjoy the benefit of the spring, summer and winter; the like is observable in the vines, citron, limon, and other trees, brought by the *Portuguese* from *Angola* into *Brasil*, and in several roots pot-herbs, and other fruits, transplanted thither by the *Dutch*. Those who covet ripe-grapes throughout the whole year, do only prune their vines at divers times, which produce a fine grape, and a wine as sweet as molosses. The worst is, that they are much infested by the pismires, which suck all the juice, and leave nothing but the husks to the owners; several other sorts of trees have been transplanted thither from *Holland*, which thrive extremely, and bear very good fruit.

The standing waters of *Brasil* are for the most part covered on the surface with green shrubs and herbs, that they appear rather like land than water, and feed both land and water fowl. At the entrance of most of their rivers, (where you meet with vast quantities of oisters and crabs) the countrey is so overstock'd with a certain kind of a tree call'd *Guaparaba* or *Mangle* by the *Brasilians*, that they render it impassable for travellers. In short, the whole *Brasil* is well stored with trees, shrubs and useful woods, there being scarce a place, either in the vallies or rising grounds, which are clayey, or among the hills, which don't produce something that is useful, and that in such plenty, that the *Portuguese* after their first arrival here, were forced to cut their way through these trees with incredi-

1647. ble pains and charge. The hills furnish also great store of wood, which is of a very good scent, and is used by dyers; as for instance the *Brasil* wood, which is from hence transported into *Europe*.

Brasil wood.

The stem or trunk of this tree is knotty, of a very agreeable scent, and sometimes two or three fathoms thick: Its leaves are dark-green, and small, thorny at the end, and grow on small stalks; the bark, which is about three inches thick, is generally taken from the trunk, before it is fitted for sale: It sprouts from its own root, and produces neither blossom nor fruit. Most of these trees grow about 10 or 12 leagues from the sea-side, where they cut them down, take off the bark, and carry them upon waggons to the sea-shore, from whence they are transported into *Europe* for the use of the dyers chiefly; the *Brasilians* call this tree for its excellency's sake, *Ibirapitanga*. After the *Dutch* had conquered part of *Brasil*, they found great store of this wood ready cut and fitted for use by the *Portuguese*, who sold it to the *Dutch* company; since which time it was cut down promiscuously by the *Portuguese* as well as the *Dutch*, and such vast quantities of it were transported in 1646, and 1647, that the members of the great council of the *Dutch-Brasil*, Mr. *Henry Hamel*, *Bullestrate* and *Codd*, being made sensible of the destructive methods that were made use of in cutting this wood, which must in time have tended to the utter extirpation of these trees, did by their proclamation regulate these abuses. They have another kind of very fine wood in *Brasil*, called by the *Portuguese*, *Pao Santo*, as likewise those call'd *Gitayba*, *Vio Wood*, *Massaranduba*, cedar, and divers others woods fit for cabinet-work. The tree call'd *Tataiba* by the *Portuguese*, the wood of which the *Portuguese* call *Pao Amaretto*, affords a yellow colour for the Dyers. The bark of the tree *Araiba* is of an ash-colour, but boil'd in water gives a red tincture. The tree *Jakauranda*, or *Jaturiba*, or the white-cedar, as well as several other Trees, furnish the inhabitants with materials for building, being very hard and durable. The *Brasilians* make also matches and a kind of hemp out of the bark of some trees.

The Timbo *or* Tipo.

The most barren places of *Brasil* do produce a certain kind of trees without leaves, which they call *Timbo* or *Tibo*; out of these they make hoops, by reason of their flexibility, and the bark serves the ship-carpenters instead of hemp.

Their fuel.

The *Brasilians* light their fires by striking two pieces of wood, of the trees *Karaguata Guacu* and *Imbaiba* together, as we do with our flint-stones and iron. The first is a tree of an admirable nature: Its stem grows 14 or 15 foot high, which being come to its full perfection, bears yellow flowers on the top, and abundance of large long and thick leaves. Out of the stem they make sticks to hang their mattresses on, the leaves afford the fishermen stuff for yarn to make nets of; and out of the leaves issues a certain unctuous liquor, which serves instead of soap. The trees and woods of *Brasil* are never seen to be covered all over with leaves at a time; but whilst some cast their leaves, you see others bring forth new ones; nay, sometimes one tree is half covered with leaves, and bare on the other side. *Brasil* likewise abounds in shrubs and reeds, some of which creep along the grounds, whilst others twist themselves up to the top of the highest trees, which affords a very agreeable spectacle at a distance, and a pleasing shadow to men and beasts, tired with the heat, hunting, or any other exercise. 1647.

Oranges.

Among other fruits, *Brasil* produces very fine oranges of divers kinds; the other vegetables, which besides the *Mandioka* root, serve for the sustenance of the inhabitants, are rice, millet, *Patatas*, *Ananas*, *Bananas*, melons, pompions, water-melons, cucumbers, beans, figs, *Bakovas*, *Marakuja*, *Mangavas*, *Arataku*, *Ape*, cabbages, radish, lettuce, purslain, parsley, chervel, carrots, &c.

The Akaju.

Nothing is so much in request among the *Brasilians*, as the *Akaju*, a kind of wild apple, which furnishes them both with food and drink, being very juicy; so that this tree seems by kind nature to have been planted here for the peculiar comfort of the inhabitants: It spreads its branches round about in a great compass, but does not grow to that height as many other trees in this countrey: Its wood, which is very solid, is very fit for the building of ships, from whence issues a very clear gum in the summer-season. Its leaves, which are red, resemble those of our walnut-trees, especially when they first sprout forth in the spring, but are of a much finer scent, which they never lose but by being distill'd. The blossom is a flower consisting of five small leaves, which grow to the number of about a hundred in one cluster; each of these flowers has a stalk, with a small head in the middle. At their first coming out, which is in *September*, they are very white, but turn soon after to a rose colour; they are very odoriferous, and fill all the circumjacent grounds with their agreeable smell. This tree bears a double fruit, *viz.* an apple, and a chesnut: The apple is of an oval figure, very juicy; its pulp spungy, full of kernels, and of a tartish taste. The juice taints linen with a

 certain

1674. certain colour, such as we call iron-molds, which is never to be taken out, but returns as often as these trees stand in blossoms; it is of a whitish colour after it is first prest out, and tartish, but changes both its colour and taste by fermentation, and becomes very strong. The rind of the apple, which is very thin, is white mixt with red. The chesnut, which grows on the top of the apple in the shape of a lambs kidney, is covered with a thin skin, over which grows a thick ash-colour'd shell, full of a hot, sharp and burning oil, which bites the tongue; To correct which, they roast the chesnut in the ashes, break the shell with a hammer, and eat the pith or kernel, which tastes better than a common chesnut, and will keep good for several years. The *Brasilians* are so fond of this fruit, that they often fight for it; then they encamp among these trees, and remove not 'till they have consumed all thereabouts, unless they are forced thereunto by the enemy. They number the years of their ages by this tree, because it bears fruit but once a year, which ripens towards the latter end of *December* or in *January*, there being none to be found on the trees after *February* in *Pernambubo*. About the time the sun returns back from the tropick of *Capricorn*, it commonly rains in *Brasil*, which the inhabitants call the *rains of Akaju*, for, if the same happens to be moderate, they promise themselves great plenty of this fruit. The chesnuts are hot in the second degree; if eaten raw with wine and salt, they taste like walnuts, but if roasted or preserved with sugar, they are of a delicious taste. The oil which is taken out of the shell, is an excellent remedy against the hair-worm; it is hot in the third and fourth degree, and frequently applied to cancers and other malignant ulcers. The gum, powdered and taken in a convenient vehicle, opens the obstructions of the womb. The juice of the apple furnishes them with good cyder.

Palm-trees. There are many sorts of palm-trees to be met with in *Brasil*, some of which grow wild, some are planted and cultivated by the inhabitants. Among the first the palm-tree call'd *Pindava* by the *Brasilians*, which grows very tall, claims the preference, of which there are whole woods to be seen in the open Countrey. In the more remote and unfrequented places, grows a certain palm-tree called *Karanatham* and *Anabekairi* by the *Brasilians*, and by an *Arabick* word among the *Portuguese*, *Tamar*, or date, which this fruit resembles. The tree grows as high as a common date-tree, its wood is red and very solid, but of no great use. The bark is grey, which from the ground upwards to a certain part of the tree is distinguish'd by

many scales, which are largest at the bottom, and small by degrees, 'till about the 1647 middle of the tree they quite disappear; these scales being nothing else but the remnants of the branches, which fall off by degrees, as the tree grows higher; and continue only towards the top, spread round about the stem, like the *African* date-tree, but much finer. Each of these branches is about two or three foot long, flat on two sides, and cover'd with small thorns, they grow to a vast thickness. At the end of each branch grows one single leaf, which is very large and green, pleated like a fan, and about the middle divided into several other leaves, like those of the common date tree; each of these last is about two foot long. Betwixt those branches, on which grow the leaves, spring forth other branches of four or five foot in length, and these again are full of other white sprouts, which bear flowers, with three pale yellow leaves; these produce a fruit of the bigness of an olive, which is green, bitter and not eatable, but turn black when they ripen, which is in *February*. The *Brasilians* call this fruit *Tirade*, and eat it raw; but our people never took any fancy to it. With the leaves they cover their huts, and make baskets of them. The palm-tree call'd *Pindava* by the *Brasilians*, has instead of the bark a white and rough wooden substance. which contains a spungy sulphurous substance, out of which the *Brasilians* prepare a strong lee. This tree is for the rest but of small use, being rather esteemed for ornaments sake, by reason of its height and fine spreading branches, which however furnish the inhabitants with leaves to cover their hutts, and to make baskets of; the *Portuguese* plant them near their walks and arbours, and round their churches. The leaves of this tree do not hang downwards like those of the coco-tree, but stand upright. Just by these leaves sprout forth certain branches, on which hang bunches of flowers, which produce the fruit, resembling in shape and bigness one of our largest hen-eggs, being sharp at the end, and fasten'd to the bunch on the other like the pine-apple. The outside is of a green yellow colour, inclining to a chesnut; being composed of a hairy substance like that of the coco-nuts, but not near so thick, scarce exceeding in thickness two egg-shells. Under this shell is an insipid saffron yellow pulp, which however is used by the negroes, who eat it with *Farinha*. Within this pulp is a hard nut, of an oval figure, not unlike the coco-nut, of the same thickness, but without holes; it contains a pith or kernel, as white and big as a walnut, but is not near so sweet as the coco-nut; they are eaten both by the natives and strangers, who are furnished with

1647. with them throughout the whole year, and call'd by the *Brasilians Inajamira*, *i. e.* the small coco-nut. The kernels of these nuts furnish them likewise with a white cooling oil, which is used instead of our oil of roses, and when fresh drawn mix'd among their sallets, but when decay'd, in their lamps. The shell affords an oil of the same nature, but not altogether so cooling. Out of the top of the tree flows a fine and odoriferous gum, used here instead of *Gum Arabick*; they also pick a certain pith or marrow out of the top, which has a taste like our walnuts, and when eaten with bread and salt is accounted very nourishing.

Coco-trees.

There also grow coco-trees in *Brasil*, call'd by the natives *Inajaguacuiba*, and the fruit *Inajaguacu*. They are very different from the just now mentioned *Pindava* tree, their trunk or stem being seldom straight, but commonly crooked, sometimes from 7 to 14 foot thick, and 50 foot high; it is without branches, having only 15 or 20 leaves round the top, each of 15 foot long. They have also good store of the common date-trees both male and female. The vast quantity of pismires wherewith *Brasil* abounds, are great enemies to all the products of their grounds, which they endeavour to destroy by fire and water; it is farther to be observed, that some fruits as well as creatures, which are accounted venomous in *Europe*, are commonly eaten in *Brasil*, as on the other hand certain things are poisonous there, which are not in *Europe*. For they have a kind of froggs and some fishes which are extremely poisonous; whereas a certain sort of great pismires and adders, toads, worms and wild rats are eaten by the natives, without any harm.

The food of the Brasilians.

The most universal food of the *Brasilians*, is the flour made of the *Mandioka* root, called by them *Vi*, and *Farinha de Mandioka* by the *Portuguese*, as has been shewn more at large before. They feed also upon the flesh of several wild beasts and birds, crabs, craw-fishes, fruits, herbage; their meat whether boiled or roasted they eat half raw. They boil in earthen pots called *Kamu*, which they make themselves. Their flesh they roast thus; they dig a hole in the ground, the bottom of which they cover with leaves of trees, and upon them lay the meat to be roasted, which being covered with the same leaves, they throw sand or earth upon them. Upon this they light a good fire, which they continue till they think it sufficiently roasted. If they hit it right it eats very well, exceeding in goodness all other roasted meats, they call it *Biaribi*. Their fishes whether roasted or boiled they eat with *Inquitaya*, that is, salt and pepper. They boil their crabs or craw-fishes without salt, and eat them with *Inquitaya*. Small fishes they wrap in leaves, and roast them in the ashes. They take the flour of the *Mandioka* root with their 3 hindermost fingers of the right hand, and so throw it into the mouth; in the same manner they do with beans and such like things; they eat often both day and night, they having no set times for their meals, without the least noise, or any drink, which they reserve till after they have done. They seldom use any spoons, but instead of that their fingers, or some oyster-shell or other serves their turn. The flesh of several wild beasts is much in esteem among the *Brasilians*; as for instance, that of the greater and lesser wild-boars; they have a bunch like a camel on their backs, and are very good food, as well as the flesh of the river pigs, called *Kapiverres* by the *Portuguese*, which is of a very agreeable taste,

Their drink.

The most general and most wholesome liquor used among the *Brasilians*, is their river or fountain water, which by reason of its coolness is a great refreshment to such as are tired by the heat, or the fatigues of other exercises; this is chiefly to be understood of their spring-water, which, though used here in great quantities, never causes any griping in the guts, or other inconveniencies in the bowels, but on the contrary occasions a good appetite, and is soon evacuated by sweating.

The waters of the rivers *Paray* and *Paratybi*, are accounted a good remedy against the stone and gout, which is the reason that many arrive to the age of above 100 years, who drink nothing but those waters, and are never troubled with any of those distempers; for those who are advanced in age are as nice in the different tastes of those waters, as the *Europeans* in their wines; and they look upon those as indiscreet who use the waters without distinction. For, since most of their springs arise among the high eastern hills, they receive no addition either from the snows or any metallic bodies, and being well digested and purged from their dregs by the heat of the sun-beams, they are very clear and wholsome; tho' it must be confess'd that in the winter months some waters, by reason of the rains, are not fine and cool as during the summer-season. The negroes make sometimes a nasty mixture of black sugar and water only, without the least fermentation, which they call *Garapa*; this as it is very cheap, so both men and women sit at it for 24 hours together, spending their time in drinking, singing and dancing, but seldom quarrel, unless they have conceived some jealousy of one another. Sometimes they add to it some leaves of the *Akaju*-tree, which by reason

1647. son of their hot quality make it the more heady. The *Portuguese* and *Dutch* frequently made a kind of sorbette of water, sugar and lemons. Others pour water upon certain herbs, others put a lemon only in water. But besides these, the *Brasilians* know how to make wines or cyder out of several roots and fruits, which they drink at their merry meetings; especially of the *Bakovas*, *Ananas*, *Mangaba*, *Janipaba*, *Karaguata*, &c. For tho' the vines here bear grapes 3 times a year, nevertheless are they not sufficient to furnish them with wine. They make a kind of cyder, called by them *Kooi*, of the apple *Akaju*; these they stamp in a wooden mortar and squeeze the juice out with their hands, which after it is settled they strain; it appears at first like milk, but turns to a pale colour in a few days; its taste is tartish, and apt to seise the head if drunk in any quantity; after some time it turns sour, and makes very good vinegar. The wine or liquor called by the *Brasilians* *Apy*, is made two different ways: First, the slices of the root *Aipimakakara*, a kind of *Mandioka*, are chewed by old women till they are as fluid as a pap, which they call *Karaku*; this they put into a pot, and boil it with a good quantity of water, stirring it continually till they think it fit for expression, which done, they call it *Kaviaraku*, and drink it luke-warm. Or else they take the same root purged and sliced in thin pieces, which they stamp and boil with water as before, which produces a whitish liquor, not unlike our butter-milk or whey; they drink it likewise warm, its taste being agreeable enough; they call it *Kacimakaxera*, tho' both kinds are generally comprehended under the name of *Aipy*. The liquor called *Pakoby* is made out of the fruit of the tree *Pakobete*. What the *Portuguese* call *Vinho da Millo*, is a liquor called *Abaty* by the *Brasilians*, and made of barley or *Turkey* wheat, called *Maiz* by the *Indians*; the liquor *Nandi* has also derived its name from that excellent fruit called *Nana* of *Ananas*, being the strongest of all their wines or cyders. There is another sort of liquor called *Vinho da Batatas* by the *Portuguese* because it is made of the root *Batatas*: The natives call it *Jetici*. Thus the liquors called *Beeutingui* and *Tipiaci* are both made out of the *Farinha* of the *Mandioka* root, *viz.* of the *Beju* and *Tepioja*.

The *Brasilians* are also great admirers of *French* or *Rhenish* brandy, called by them *Kacitata*, and swallow it very greedily as often as they can come at it. They are no less fond of tobacco, the herb of which they call *Petima*, and the leaves *Petimaoba*. After they have dried the leaves in the air, they lay them before the fire, to render them the more fit for cutting. They smoke in pipes made of the shell of the nut *Pindoba*, or of the *Urukuruiba*, *Jocara*, *Aqua*, or such like; to wit, they cut a hole in one end of the shell, take out the kernel, and after they have polished them, put a wooden pipe or a piece of reed in the hole. The *Tapoyers* use very large pipes made of stone, wood or clay, the holes of which are so big that they contain a handful of tobacco at a time. Sometimes the *Brasilians* make use of our *European* pipes, called by them *Amrupetunbuaba*, and *Broken Katunbaba* by the *Portuguese*, and *Katgebouw* by the *Dutch*. Whenever the *Tapoyers*, especially those inhabiting the villages, descended from the *Tapoyers* called *Kariri*, prepare the liquors *Akavi* and *Aipy*, it is done at the same time; then a day being appointed for a general merry meeting, they meet early in the morning at the first house in the village they belong to, where they consume most of the liquor, and make themselves merry with dancing; this done they go to the next house, where they play the same game, and so from house to house, till nothing be left or they can drink no longer. When they find themselves overcharged with liquor, they spew and fall to drinking again, and thus he who can spew and drink most, is accounted the bravest fellow of the company.

On the coast of *Brasil*. *Salt-pits.*

On the north-west coast of *Brasil* are several considerable salt-pits: That near the house called the *Desert*, is about three or four leagues distant from the river *Aguarama*, of which one branch extends to the east, and discharges its water in this salt-pit with a spring-tide, which is here commonly with the new-moon. It is about 550 paces from the sea-shore, and receives no other water but from the river *Aguarama*. There is no bay or harbour near it, but only a flat sandy bottom for about half a league distance from the shore, where you may anchor at three fathom deep. The land-wind which constantly blows on this coast, commonly ceases towards evening, so that the vessels take the opportunity of the night to load salt. This salt-pit produces every month a certain quantity of salt, provided they be careful to shut their sluices as soon as the same is filled with water, for else they are in danger of losing what they had got before, by the next high-tide. To the east of this salt-pit are the famous rocks called *Baxos*, which at low-water may be seen from thence; they extend about three leagues deep in the sea, but don't begin till about a league from the shore, betwixt which and the rocks there is a passage, where you have ten foot depth at low-water. It ebbs here with the lowest tide about eight foot, and a west-

1647. a west-south-west-wind raises the water to the highest.

About five or six leagues to the west of the house called the *Desert*, is the great salt-pit *Karwaratama*, which receiving its water from the sea, and being detained by sluices, produces very good salt in three weeks time. Five leagues further to the west is the river *Maritouva*, the second in rank in those western parts, but has not above twelve foot water at high-tide. On its east point, not above half a league within the mouth, is a very convenient salt-pit: These salt-pits are computed to be manageable with the assistance only of 10 or 12 negroes, 10 christians, and about 30 *Brasilians*, and to afford 2000 tuns of salt *per annum*, which may be transported from thence into the other parts of the *Dutch Brasil* in small barks, during the summer season. About half way betwixt *Rio Grande* and *Siara*, as likewise in *Siara*, near the river *Wapanien*, are likewise several *Salina*'s or salt-pits.

Traffick of Brasil.

The chief traffick of *Brasil* consists in sugar, brasil-wood, and such like; as also in tobacco, hides, preserves, ginger, and cotton, which grows wild here, some indigo was likewise planted there before my departure; but among these, the sugar and brasil-wood are staple commodities. For since the tobacco began to be transported into *Holland* from the *American* islands, the planting of it was neglected in *Brasil*, where labourers wages being excessive high, they could draw much more profit from the sugar, of which, according to computation, betwixt 20000 and 25000 chests were yearly made only in the sugar-mills of the *Dutch Brasil*, if the harvest proves very good.

The peopling of Brasil.

The inhabitants of *Brasil* may at present be divided into free-born subjects and slaves; and these again consist of divers nations, both natives and foreigners. The free inhabitants of *Brasil* were the *Dutch*, *Portuguese*, and *Brasilians*, the last the natives of the countrey. But the *Portuguese* did not only surpass all the rest, at least ten to one in number, during my abode in *Brasil*, but also were in possession of all the sugar-mills and lands, except what was possess'd by a very few *Dutch*, who had applied themselves to sugar-planting, but were for the most part ruined by the intestine war, being forced to leave all behind them in the country: Besides those of the free inhabitants, who made it their business to manure the grounds, there were many merchants, factors, and handicrafts men: The merchants sold their commodities generally with vast profit, and would have questionless been rich men, had they not vented their goods upon credit to the *Portuguese*, who were resolved never to pay them, as the event has sufficiently shewn. The handicrafts men were able to get three, four, five, nay six gilders a day, so that many returned very rich to *Holland*. Those that kept publick houses and chandlers shops were likewise great gainers here, and carried off abundance of ready money. The officers in the company's service whether civil or military, were likewise punctually paid, which made many who had lived in the countrey before the beginning of the civil war, and had served the company before, take service again, who were all entertained according to their respective qualities and former stations.

Free inhabitants of Brasil.

The Jews.

Among the free inhabitants of *Brasil* that were not in the company's service, the *Jews* were the most considerable in number, who had transplanted themselves thither from *Holland*. They had a vast traffick beyond all the rest, they purchased sugar-mills and built stately houses in the *Receif*. They were all traders, which would have been of great consequence to the *Dutch Brasil*, had they kept themselves within the due bounds of traffick,

The slaves of Brasil.

The slaves of *Dutch Brasil* were either negroes or natives of the countrey; the last of which were either bought in *Maranhaon* being prisoners of war, or from the *Tapoyers*, who likewise had made them captives, and otherwise, according to their custom, would have put them to death. For it being resolved immediately, at the first entrance of the *Dutch* in *Brasil*, that none of the natives should be made slaves (except they were either bought from the *Tapoyers* or brought from *Maranhaon*) the *Brasilians* were settled in certain villages to enjoy their own liberty under certain limitations, and permission was given them to assist the *Portuguese* in the management of their mills and grounds, for certain wages appointed for that purpose; by which means many *Alicas* or villages were filled with *Brasilians* in *Parayba* and *Rio Grande*, who during the time of our government enjoyed the sweets of a perfect liberty.

Negroes.

Vast numbers of negroes of divers nations were entertained in the *Receif*, and the open countrey, for the manureing of the ground, and working in the sugar-mills of the *Portuguese*, which could not be done without them, by reason of the extremity of the heat of the climate, and the incredible toils they are fain to undergo; so that in my time near 40000 negroes were employed in the sugar-mills betwixt *Rio Grande* and *St. Francisco*. Most of these negroes are brought hither from the kingdoms of *Congo*, *Angola*, and *Guinea*; a black shining skin, flat nose, thick lips, and short curled hair, is their chief beauty. The lustiest and most

1647. most laborious used in time of good trade, to be sold in *Brasil* for 70, 80, or 100 pieces of eight, nay sometimes for 1400 or 1500 gilders, but these understood something more than ordinary: But when trade began to decay, they were sold for 40 pieces of eight. There was scarce a *Hollander* of any substance but what had several of these slaves. They are most miserably and beastly treated by the *Portuguese*, though at the same time it must be confess'd that it is absolutely necessary they should be kept under a strict discipline; for they are full of rogueries, superstitious to the highest degree, and sorcerers: They would often pretend to tell us what ships were at sea from *Holland* for *Brasil*, tho' they were yet on the other side of the line, and how to recover stolen goods. I remember I happened once to be at a friend's house of mine, when I saw an old negro enter the kitchen, who came thither to cure a negro slave of his illness, which he told us was occasioned by witchcraft. He made the patient rise from his chair, and taking a piece of wood from the fire-hearth, he ordered him to lick three times with his tongue that end which was burning hot with the glowing coals. The same end of the wood he afterwards extinguish'd in a bason of water, and rubb'd the coals in it, till it turn'd as black as ink. This he ordered the sick negro to drink off at a draught, which he did accordingly, and was immediately seized with a slight griping in the guts. This done he rubbed both his sides, and taking hold with his hand of a piece of flesh and fat above the hip, he made an incision there with a knife he pull'd out of his pocket, of two inches deep, out of which he drew a bundle of hair and rags, with a little of the black water that was left he washed the wound, which soon after was healed, and the patient cured. They are very dextrous at swimming and diving, and will fetch a single piece of eight from the bottom of the sea, where it is very deep. They are also excellent fishermen, and get a great deal of money by it. They tie three or four great pieces of wood together, this they manage with one oar, and upon it go a good way into the sea, where they catch great quantities of fish with their hooks, and so return. It happened in my time, that a certain negro, who was very expert in fishing, was sold three times in a little while; this he took so much to heart, that the next time he went thus out a fishing, he tied a stone to his leg and drowned himself. Another negro having conceived a hatred against his master cut his throat, cut out his tongue, and made a house-of-office of his mouth, according to his own confession; he was broke alive upon the wheel, which he endured with an incredible obstinacy. A negro woman was brought to bed in my time of a child, the hair and skin of which were not black, but red. I saw also a young lad born from negro parents, whose skin was white, and his hair and eye-brows the like, but curl'd, with a flat nose like the other negroes. Sometimes I have seen old negroes with long grey beards and hair, which looks very fine. 1647.

The Brasilians. The natives of *Brasil* consist of divers nations, distinguished by their proper names, to wit, the *Tubinambos*, *Tobajaras*, *Petiguaras* and *Tapuijas*, or *Tapuyers*, or *Tapoyers*. The three first use one and the same language, and differ only in the dialect; but the last are subdivided into several nations, differing both in manners and tongue. The *Brasilian* men, which lived among us and the *Portuguese*, are middle-sized, strong and well made, with broad shoulders. They have black eyes, a wide mouth, with black curl'd hair, and a flat nose; the last of which is not natural to them, but the parents, looking upon it as a great beauty, squeeze their childrens noses flat, whilst they are very young. They paint their bodies, and some likewise their faces with divers colours; they have generally no hair about the mouth, tho' some have black beards. Their women are likewise of a middle stature, well limb'd, and not ill-featur'd; they have likewise a black hair, but are not born black, but by the heat of the sun-beams, acquire by degrees a yellow brown colour. The *Brasilians* come soon to maturity, and arrive to a great age, and that without distempers; they also seldom become grey, which is likewise observable in many *European* inhabitants here, who come to the age of 100 or 120 years. This must be chiefly attributed to the temperature of the climate, which is such, that in former times many *Spaniards* that laboured under some lingring distemper, whether in *Spain* or the *East-Indies*, used to come to *Brasil* to partake of the benefit of that excellent air and water; 'tis true, most of the children of foreigners are troubled with lingring sicknesses, so that scarce one in three arrives to a state of manhood; but this must not be attributed to the air, but rather to the bad nourishment. Few cripples or crooked people are to be met with among the *Brasilians*, they being generally very strait and nimble, which is the more admirable, because they never do their children up in swathing cloths, except their feet, looking upon it as unwholsome.

Before the *Dutch* got footing in *Brasil*, the *Portuguese* had made all the natives their slaves, and look'd upon it as the greatest piece

1647. piece of policy quite to extirpate them, which they did so effectually, that whereas about 100 years ago, the captainships of *Rio Grande* alone could raise 100000 fighting men, scarce 300 were to be met with in 1645 and 1646, which had created a mortal hatred in the *Brasilians* against the *Portuguese*; tho' it must also be confess'd, that the late war and some epidemical distempers did sweep away many of the natives. The remainders of them liv'd in certain *Aldens* or villages assigned them for that purpose, where they had their plantations; besides which they served the *Portuguese* in their sugar-mills for a certain monthly pay, which furnished them with clothes and other necessaries. Their huts are made only of wooden stalks, covered with palm-tree leaves. They can't endure the yoke of slavery, nor any toil, especially the *Tapoyers*; they live very quietly among one another, unless they get drunk, when they sometimes sing and dance day and night. Drunkenness is a vice belonging to both sexes here, of which they are so fond, as to be past remedy, tho' this occasions often quarrels and other enormous vices among them. They are likewise much addicted to dancing, which they call *Guau*; they have several ways of dancing, one of which is call'd *Urukapi*; they commonly sing whilst they are dancing. The children divert themselves with divers sorts of games, one is call'd *Kurupirara*, another *Gualbipaie*, and a third *Guaibiquaibibuku*. They will sleep sometimes a whole day and night, and would not stir then if they did not want victuals. Near their hammocks they keep a fire day and night, in the day to dress their victuals, in the night to allay the rawness of the air, which here is colder than in most parts of *Europe*, because day and night is almost of an equal length here throughout the year. 1647.

Their clothing. The inland *Brasilians* of both sexes, go quite naked without the least covering. But those inhabiting nearer to the sea-shore, who converse with the *Dutch* and *Portuguese*, wear only a shirt of linnen or callicoe; tho' in my time, some of the chiefest among them began to take a pride to cloth themselves after the *European* manner. The wife

constantly follows her husband whereever he goes, even in the war. He carries nothing but his arms, but the poor woman is loaden like a mule or sumpter-horse. For besides a great basket which is tied to her back, (call'd by them *Patigua*) she has another upon her head, with all the houshold stuff in it, or a great basket with flower; besides which several other smaller vessels hang on both sides, wherewith they take up water for their drinking. The child is carried in a piece of callicoe, which is fastned

5 to

1647. to her, and hangs down from her right shoulder. It lies there with its legs wide open, one being stretch'd cross the mother's belly, the other over her shoulder. After all this, she carries a parrot or ape in one hand, and leads a dog in a string with the other. Thus they proceed on their journey, without any farther provision except a small quantity of *Farinha*; the hedge or open fields serve instead of inns, which furnish them with necessary food, as the rivers and springs with drink; and so does the tree call'd *Karageata*, which contains always some rain-water within the hollowness of its leaves, to the great relief of travellers, who in some barren places, do often not meet with a river or spring for 12 leagues together. Towards night they hang their hammocks on trees, or else fasten them to stalks neatly; they make a fire to dress their victuals, and against the rain defend themselves with palm-tree leaves. When they are at home, the husband goes commonly in the morning abroad with his bow and arrow, to shoot some wild beast, or catch birds, or else to the sea-side, or next river a fishing, whilst the women are employed in the plantations; some women go abroad with their husbands and carry home the prey. The wild beasts are caught by them in a different manner; some they kill with arrows, others they catch in pits dug for that purpose, and covered with the leaves of trees, under which is hidden some carrion, the scent of which draws them to the pit; this they call *Petaku*. They make also certain wooden traps, and use divers other ways of catching the wild beasts, each of which they distinguish by their proper names. To catch birds they use three sorts of snares or nets, call'd by them *Jukana*; the first sort catches the birds by the feet, this they call *Jukanabiprara*; the second entangles them by the neck, which they call *Jukanajuprara*; the third ensnares their bodies, call'd by them *Jukanapitereba*. They kill the fishes with arrows, or catch them with fishing hooks, their baits being commonly worms, crabs, or some small fishes. They bait the water where they intend to fish, with the leaves of *Japikai*, or with *Timpotiana*, *Tinguy*, or with *Tinguiri*; sometimes with the fruit call'd *Kururuape*, the root *Magui*, or the bark of the tree *Anda*, which make the fish swim on the surface of the water like dead, when they take them with a kind of a sieve, call'd by them *Urupema*, made of cane or reed, which they call *Uruguiboandipia*. Their sea-fish they catch with iron hooks, the bait being some carrion; they go a good way into the sea, only upon three pieces of wood fastened together, which they call *Igapeda*, and the *Portuguese Jangada*; the wood is commonly of the tree *Apiba*. 1647.

Their houshold stuff. The *Brasilians* are not burthened with much houshold-stuff, their hammocks being their chiefest care in this kind; they call them *Ini*, are wrought of cotton like net-work, of about six or seven foot long, and four broad. When they are going to sleep, they fasten them either to two beams of their huts, or else in the open air to two trees; and some distance from the ground, for fear of some obnoxious creatures, and to avoid the pestiferous exhalations of the earth. The *Tapoyers*, call'd *Kariri*, have very large hammocks, of 12 or 14 foot long, which contain four persons at a time. The *Portuguese* women make some very fine hammocks, wrought with divers figures in them. In lieu of dishes and cups they use the *Kalabassek*, cut in the middle, which are painted without with a certain red colour, call'd *Uruku*, and within with black. Their cans, cups and mugs, are likewise *Kalabasses* of divers kinds, call'd *Kuite*, *Jaroba*, and *Kribuka*. One of the biggest of these *Kalabasses* hold 30 or 35 quarts; this the *Brasilians* call *Kuyaba*, but when cut thro' the middle it is called *Kuipeba*. The poorer sort make certain knives they call *Ituque*, of stone, as also of cane, which they call *Taquoaquia*, but the better sort use *Dutch* knives. Their baskets they make of palm-tree leaves, they call them *Patigua*; they have also some made of reed or cane, these are with one general name call'd *Karamemoa*. They make also large broad baskets of reeds and branches twisted together: These they call *Panaku*, and are chiefly used for the carrying of the *Mandioka* root. In their journeys they always make use of the *Patigua*, but the *Panaku* is used by the slaves and negroes in the *Receif* for the conveniency of carriage.

Their weapons. The arms of the *Brasilians* are only bows, arrows, and wooden clubs. Their bows, which they call *Guirapara* and *Virapara*, are made of very hard wood, called *Guirapariba* and *Virapariba*: The bow-strings are made of cotton twisted, and by them call'd *Guirapakuma*; the darts they call *Uba*, and are made of wild cane. The points of these darts are either of wood hardned, or of fish teeth call'd *Jacru*, or of bones or cane well sharpned; some have several points, others but one.

Their way of accounting their age. Being not in the least acquainted with arithmetick, they compute the number of their years and age by the chesnuts which grow on the fruit *Akaju*, which chesnuts they call *Akaguakaya*, as likewise *Akajuti* and *Itamabara*, of which they lay one by every year, this tree producing fruit but once each season, *viz.* in *December* and *Ja-*

nuary;

1647. *nuary*. They begin the computation of their years with the rise of a certain star, call'd by them *Taku*, or the *Rain-star*, which is always there in *May*; they also call the year by the same name.

Their religion. The most barbarous of the *Brasilians* inhabiting the inland countries, scarce know any thing of religion, or an almighty being. They have some knowledge remaining of a general deluge, it being their opinion, that the whole race of mankind were extirpated by a general deluge, except one man and his own sister, who being with child before, they by degrees re-peopled the world. They know not what God is, nay, they have no word expressing the same, unless it be *Tuba*, which signifies as much as something most excellent above the rest; thus they call the thunder *Tubakununga*, *i. e.* a noise made by the supreme excellency, for *Akununga* implies as much as a noise. They are unacquainted with heaven or hell, tho' they have a tradition among them, that the souls don't die with the bodies, but that they are either transplanted into devils or spirits, or else enjoy a great deal of pleasure with dancing and singing in some pleasant fields, which they say are behind the mountains. These fields are enjoyed by all the brave men and women, who have kill'd and eaten many of their enemies; but such as have been idle, and never did any thing of moment, are tortured by the devil, unto whom they give many names, *viz. Anhanga, Jurupari, Kurupari, Taguaiba, Temoti, Taubimama.* They have however some sort of priests among them whose business is to sacrifice, and to foretel things to come; these are especially consulted when they are to undertake a war or journey; they call them *Paye* and *Pey*. They dread spirits to the highest degree; they call them *Kuripira, Taguai, Macachara, Anhanga, Jurupari*, and *Marangigona*, tho' under different significations: For *Kuripari* implies as much as the God of the mind or heart. *Macachara* the God or patron of travellers; *Jurupari* and *Anhanga* signify the devil; *Marangigona* implies as much as the *Manes* or remainders of the soul after death, which are so much dreaded by the *Brasilians*, that some of them upon an imaginary apparition of them, have been struck with sudden death. They don't perform any worship or ceremony to those spirits, except that some pretend to appease their wrath by certain presents they fasten to certain stakes fix'd in the ground for that purpose. Some of the *Brasilians* acknowledge the thunder for the supreme being, others the *Lesser Bear* in the firmament, others some other stars. The *Potiguaras*, a nation among the *Brasilians*, are accounted such sorcerers, that they bewitch their enemies even to death: They call this manner of witchcraft *Anbamombikoab*. The *Brasilians* that lived among the *Portuguese* and *Dutch*, did in some measure follow the christian doctrine, but so coldly, that few, when they come to an advanced age, shew much zeal for it; because the fundamental articles of our faith are not easily imprinted in them, unless in their tender years, and when they are remote from their parents. However several of the *Dutch* ministers, *viz.* Mr. *Doreslaer*, and after him Mr. *Thomas Kemp*, have had good success in converting many of the *Brasilians* in the *Aldeas* or villages where they preached, the last of these two being well versed in the *Brasilian* tongue. Neither were *Dionysius Biscareta*, an honest old *Castilian*, and *Johannes Apricius*, less remiss in performing their duty to instruct these infidels. There were likewise three *Dutch* schoolmasters among them, who taught their young people to read and to write, but these were forced to leave their *Aldeas* or villages during the last intestine commotions raised by the *Portuguese*. 1647.

Their distempers and remedies. Many distempers which are common in *Europe* are unknown in *Brasil*: They use nothing but simple remedies, and laugh at our compositions. They are very dextrous in applying their remedies, especially their antidotes: They draw blood by suction with horn cups, by scarification, or opening a vein; instead of a lancet they use the tooth of a lamprey, call'd by them *Kakaon*, without which no body stirs abroad. So soon as any one of their acquaintance is fallen ill, they all meet, each offering his remedy, which he has found good by his own experience: Then they begin to cut and slice the most musculous parts of the body, either with the thorns of the tree *Karnaiba*, or with fishes teeth, till they have drawn as much blood as they think fit, and for that purpose suck the wounds with their mouths, by which means they pretend to draw all ill humours from the affected part. Vomiting they procure by means of the leaves *Karnaiba*, which being twisted together, they force down the patients throat. When all these pretended remedies prove ineffectual, they proceed to no others; but after some consultation, quite despairing of his recovery, knock him on the head with their clubs, looking upon it more glorious to be thus bravely delivered from their misery, than to expect death till their last gasp. They exercise as much barbarity upon the dead carcasses of their friends as of their enemies; upon the first out of love, against the last out of revenge; for they tear them to pieces with

I their

1647. their teeth, and eat the flesh like a dainty bit.

Their child-bearing. The *Brasilian* women are extremely fruitful, have very easy labours, and rarely miscarry: For no sooner is a woman delivered, but up she gets to the next river, and without any farther help washes herself there: In the mean while the husband keeps the bed for the first 24 hours, and is made as much of as if he had been lately brought to bed. The mothers lament the death of their infants with howling and crying for three or four days.

How they welcome their friends. They receive their friends after a long journey with open arms and tears, and beating their foreheads against their breasts, in remembrance of the misfortunes they have undergone during their absence. Tho' the *Brasilians* were always supposed to be descended from the race of men-eaters, yet by their conversation with us and other nations, many of them have laid aside their barbarity, and are become as affable and civilized as most of the *European* nations.

The Tapoyers. The *Tapoyers* inhabit the inland country of *Brasil* to the west of these countries in the possession of the *Portuguese* and *Dutch*, betwixt *Rio Grande* and the river *Siara*, as far as *Rio St. Francisco*. They are divided into several nations, distinguished both by their language and names: For the *Tapoyers* bordering upon the utmost confines of *Pernambuko*, are called *Kariri*, under their king *Cerioukejou*; the next to them the *Karirivasu*, whose king was *Karapoto*; then the *Kariryou*, and so farther the *Tararyou*; the last of which were best known unto us, *Janduy* or *John Duwy* being their king; tho' some of them lived under the jurisdiction of one *Karakara*. Divers were govern'd by other kings, *viz. Prityaba*, *Arigpaygn*, *Wahasewajug*, *Tsering*, and *Dremenge*. Those under king *John Duwy* inhabit to the west beyond *Rio Grande*, but change their habitations pretty often: About *November*, *December*, and *January*, when the fruit *Kajou* begins to ripen, they come towards the sea-side, because little of it is to be met with in the inland countries. The *Tapoyers* are very tall and strong of body, exceeding both the *Brasilians* and *Dutch* both in strength and tallness by the head and shoulders. They are of a dark brown colour, black hair, which hangs all over their shoulders, they only shaving it on the forehead as far as to the ears. Some are shaved according to the *European* fashion; the rest of their bodies they keep without hair, even without eye-brows. Their kings and great men are distinguished from the vulgar by the hair of their heads and their nails; the first their kings wear shaved in the shape of a crown, and have very long nails on their thumbs; but the king's relations or other officers of note, wear long nails on all their fingers, except their thumbs; for long nails is accounted a peculiar ornament among them. The *Tapoyers* are very strong; prince *Maurice* being one time in a humour to try their strength and skill in fighting with a wild bull, caused one to be brought within his outward court, which was surrounded with pallisadoes, in order to engage two *Tapoyers* appointed for that purpose. There was a great concourse of people to see this spectacle, when on a sudden two *Tapoyers* (the rest with their wives being only spectators) came in stark naked, without any other arms but their bows and arrows. The bull saw them no sooner enter, but he made towards them, who being extremely nimble, avoided the strokes he made at them with great dexterity, and in the mean while so gall'd his flanks with their arrows, that the beast roar'd most terribly, and being all in a foam, set upon them with all his vigour, which they avoided by retiring every foot behind a tree that stood in the middle of the court, and from thence continued to pierce his sides with their darts, till finding the beast begin to languish by the loss of blood, one of the *Tapoyers* got upon his back, and laying hold of his horns, threw him upon the ground, and being seconded by his comrade, they both kill'd the bull, roasted him under ground, with a fire above it, according to their custom, and feasted upon the meat, with the other *Tapoyers* there present.

Their clothing. The *Tapoyers* of both sexes, from the king to the common fellow, go quite naked, only that the men hide their privities, by tying the yard in a little bag or net made of the bark of trees; this they close up with a small ribbon call'd *Takoaynhaa*; when they want to piss they unty it, and are more cautious in exposing their privities, than some of the *Europeans*: In the same manner do the rest of the *Brasilians* inhabiting the inland countries. The women of the *Tapoyers* cover their privities only with a handful of herbs, or a small branch of a tree, with the leaves on them: This they thrust barely under a small cord or rope which is fastned round their middle like girdles: In the same manner they cover their backsides; but so carelessly, that both before and behind, great part of both is exposed to view; they change it every day. The men wear also a kind of garland made of the feathers of the bird *Guara* or *Kaninde*, upon their heads, from which certain feathers of the tail of the bird *Arara*, or *Kamud*, hang down behind upon the back; some only tie

tie a cotton ſtring round their hands, in which ſome red or blue feathers are faſtned behind; this they call *Akanbuaçaba*. They have alſo cloaks made of cotton-thread, and woven like a net; in each of the holes they ſtick a red feather of the bird *Guara*, and intermix them with black, green, and yellow feathers of the birds *Aakukaru*, *Kazinda*, and *Arara*, which lie as cloſe together as fiſh ſcales: There is a kind of cap on the inſide of this cloak, which with the reſt covers the head, ſhoulders, and the body, ſomewhat below the middle, ſo that it is worn both for ornament and conveniencies ſake, it being proof againſt the rain; they call theſe cloaks in their tongue *Guara Abuku*. They alſo faſten certain combs of birds with wild honey to their foreheads, theſe they call *Aguana*.

If their fathers or mothers die, they pull every hair out of their heads; they have holes in their ears ſo big, that you may thruſt a finger into them; in this they wear either a bone of an ape call'd *Nambipaya*, or elſe a piece of wood, wrapt up in cotton-thread. The men have holes in their under lips, in which they wear either a cryſtal, ſmaragd or jaſper, of the bigneſs of a haſel-nut: This ſtone they call *Metara*, and if it be green or blue, *Metarobi*; but they are moſt fond of the green ones: They have alſo holes in their cheeks on each ſide of the mouth; in theſe the married men wear a piece of wood of the bigneſs and thickneſs of a good gooſequill: Sometimes they wear a ſtone in it call'd *Tembekoareta*: In the holes of their noſtrils, ſome have alſo ſuch like ſticks of wood, which they call *Apiyati*: Their bodies are all over painted with a certain juice of brown colour, ſqueezed out of the apple *Janipapa*; this is even uſed among the women and children. Beſides this, they ſtick feathers of divers colours with wild-honey or maſtick to the ſkin of their bodies, which make them appear at a diſtance like large birds; this they call *Akamongui*. Thus they adorn their arms with garlands made of red and yellow feathers of ſeveral birds, call'd *Aguamiranga*; ſometimes they mix corals among them, which they call *Arakoaya*. They make alſo a kind of bracelets of the rind of the fruit *Aguay*; theſe they wear round their legs, and make a noiſe when they are dancing. Their ſhoes are made of the bark *Kuragua*, and call them *Miapakabas*. Some nations of the *Tapoyers* uſe no bows or arrows, but throw their darts with their hands, but the *Kariri* have bows. Their clubs are made of very hard wood, are broad on the top, and full of teeth or bones, well ſharpned

at

1647. at the end. Round the handle they wind a piece of callicoe, or some other stuff, and at the end a bush of feathers of the tail of the bird *Arara*; such another bush is fastned round the middle; they call them *Atirabebe* and *Jatirabebe*. Their trumpets which they call *Kanguenka*, are made of mens bones; but those called *Nhumbugaku*, which are much larger, are of horn; they have also another sort made of cane, called *Meumbrapara*. The *Tapoyers* are not so good soldiers as the rest of the *Brasilians*, for upon any smart encounter they trust to their feet, and run away with incredible swiftness. They neither sow nor plant, not as much as the *Mandioka* root, their common food being fruits, roots, herbs, and wild beasts, and sometimes wild honey, which they take out of the hollow trees. Among all other roots they are extremely fond of a certain kind of wild *Mandioka* root, which rises up to the height of a small tree. Its stem and leaves resemble the other *Mandioka* root, but it is not near so good; the inland *Brasilians* call it *Cuguaçuremia*, but those inhabiting near the sea-shore *Cuaçumandiiba*.

They eat also mens flesh; for if a woman happens to miscarry they eat the child immediately, alledging, that they cannot bestow a better grave upon it than the belly, from whence it came. The *Tapoyers* lead a kind of vagabond life, like some of the *Arabians*, though they always remain within their certain bounds, within the compass of which they change their habitations according to the different seasons of the year; they dwell for the most part among the woods, and live upon hunting, in which perhaps they excel all other nations; for they will shoot a bird flying with their arrows. So soon as a woman has conceived, she abstains from her husband; after she is brought to bed, she goes into the next wood, where she cuts the child's navel-string, with a shell, boils it afterwards with the after-burthen, and eats them both. She washes her self and the child every morning and evening, neither does her husband keep her company, as long as she gives suck, unless he has but one wife. If a woman be discovered to have had an unlawful commerce with another man, her husband turns her away, but if they are catch'd in the act, he may kill them both. The mothers take extraordinary care that the nuptials of their daughters are not consummated 'till after they have had their monthly times, which they give notice of to their physicians, and these to the king, who then gives them license to go to bed with the bridegroom, who pays his acknowledgment to her mother, for the care she has taken of her daughter. 1647. If a young maiden be marriageable, and yet not courted by any, the mother paints her with some red colour about the eyes, and thus carries her to the king, who orders her to sit down near him upon a carpet, and blows the smoak of tobacco in her face. After which he thrusts his yard into the woman's privities, and if any blood comes forth, he licks it up, which is esteem'd a singular honour among them. For the rest of the *Tapoyers*, are the worst of all the other *Brasilians*, being ignorant of any thing that relates to God or religion; neither will they receive any instruction of that kind. They have certain priests or rather sorcerers, who pretend to foretel things to come, and to raise spirits, which they say appear to them in the shape of a fly, or any such like insect: When these spirits disappear, the women make most horrible cries and lamentations, in which consists the main point of their devotion. They avoid night journies, for fear of serpents and other venomous creatures, neither will they set on a journey 'till the dew be dried up by the sun-beams. Several nations of the *Tapoyers*, especially those under king *John Duwy*, liv'd always in a good correspondence with the *Dutch*, unto whom they afforded at divers times considerable assistance; tho' they did not submit to their jurisdiction, but were governed by their own kings. King *John Duwy* had 60 children by 50 wives, tho' sometimes he had not above 14 wives at a time; these *Tapoyers* having a mortal hatred to the *Portuguese*, used to kill them wherever they could meet with them. And thus much may suffice concerning the manners, way of living, cloaths, &c. of the natives of *Brasil*; I will now proceed to give you an account of my voyage back into *Holland*.

Being sensible, as I told you before, that things grew worse and worse every day with us here, I with much ado got leave to depart, and accordingly the 23[d] of *July* 1649 I went aboard the ship call'd the *Union*, mann'd with 80 sailors, under the command of captain *Albert Jants*, a native of *Groningen*. We set sail the same day in company of the *Blue-Eagle*, and a yacht call'd the *Brasilian*. We left the city of *Olinda* to the south-west in the evening; the 25th we were under 3 degrees 6 min. with a north-north-east course, we sail'd that day about 28 leagues. The next day we pass'd the line, with very fair weather and wind; we continued our course without any remarkable accident 'till the 1st of *August*, when about noon we found our selves under 9 deg. 46 min. having sail'd 29 Leagues in the last 24 hours. The same evening we

1649. *The author's return to* Holland.

we saw the first time the north-pole star, after we had pass'd the line. The 2^d of *August* we sail'd 23 leagues with a fresh gale, and found our selves under the 11th deg. 13 min. We continued this our course with a fair wind, 'till the 16th of *August* when we were becalmed, we did not advance above 60 leagues that day, being under the 26 deg. we found it exceeding hot. The 20th of *August* we had but a slender south-east wind, we found our selves under 29 deg. 45 min. we were much troubled with heat, for want of the cool winds, that the knives in the cabin were so hot, that nobody could hold them in his bare hands, nor any one could touch the deck of the ship with his hands or feet. We continued our course thus 'till the 29th, when being under 38 deg. 46 min. we made about eight leagues that day. The 3^d of *September* being under the 40th deg. 18 min. we espied a sail which we found to be a vessel bound for *Virginia*. Towards evening we were forced to stay sometime for the *Brasilian* yacht, she having lost one of her masts. The next following day in the morning we discover'd the island of *Corfu*, whither we directed our course.

The Flemming *islands.*

Corfu and *Floris* are two of the nine islands, the *Dutch* commonly call the *Flemming Islands*. The biggest is *Tercera*, being about 16 leagues in compass. It is very rocky, but fruitful, producing a considerable quantity of oxen, and abounding in canary and other birds. Here is a spring that turns wood into stone, and several hot-springs, in which you may boil an egg. The ground seems to be full of concavities, which is the reason of the many earthquakes here, which over-turn and destroy houses, men and beasts. The island call'd the *Peake* has a rock which reaches to the very clouds, and which as some suppose, may be parallel'd for its height to the peake of the *Canary Island* itself. Betwixt the coast of *Brasil* and the said Islands, the compass bears due south and north. We were gone eight degrees farther to the west, than we intended. About noon we found our selves under 40 deg. and 34 min. We continu'd our course without any remarkable accident, 'till the 16th of *Sept.* when we supposed our selves to be not far from land, which we discovered the same evening to the north north-east of us. The 17th we were becalm'd, and catch'd more fish than we were able to eat. The 18th we discover'd the *Isle of White* to the north of us, whereabouts one of our ships was separated from us; not long after we saw the point of *Dover*. The 19th we pass'd by *Dunkirk* and *Ostend* with a brisk gale, and about noon safely arrived in the road of *Flussingen*. I got imme-

The author arrives at Flussingen.

diately ashore, and after having refreshed my self for five days, I went to *Middleburgh*, where I likewise continued five days. From thence I continued my journey over *Dort*, *Rotterdam*, *Delft* and *Harlem* to the famous city of *Amsterdam*, from whence I undertook this *West-India* voyage 1640. From *Amsterdam* I went to *Zwell*, the birth-place of my father *John Nieuhoff*, and so to *Benthem*, my native countrey, where I met with my parents in good health, after so many fatigues of a tedious voyage; whilst I was at *Benthem* my father died 1651, the 15th of *May*, in the 85th year of his age, being lamented by all, by reason of his good qualifications.

He arrives at Benthem.

Some troublesome people laid the loss of the *Dutch-Brasil* at the door of the members of the great council, *viz. Henry Hamel*, *Adrian Bullestrate* and *Peter Jande Bas*, who left *Brasil* 1647. It was alledged that the before-mentioned contracts made with the *Portuguese* had given them great opportunity of a revolt; for which it was said the said members had received great sums of money; but it being evident that the succeeding members of the great council having taken cognisance of that affair before their departure, *Nov.* 6, 1646, and in *March* 1647, they were fully cleared of these accusations, the same having been transacted by special orders of the council of XIX. in *Holland*; besides, that the revolts which were about the same time in agitation in *Angola*, *Africa*, and the island of *Ceylon* in the *East-Indies*, where no such contracts were made, do sufficiently testify that the foundation of this intestine war was laid in *Portugal*, long before the contracts were set on foot. What is more surprising is, how the *Portuguese*, considering we were pretty well provided with forts and garrisons, durst think of such an attempt; but the reason is plain, for what they wanted in strenghth or otherwise, they were supplied with from the *Bahia*.

What induced the Portuguese *to rebel.*

The motives that induced the *Portuguese* to this revolt, were the recovery of their liberty, the difference of their language and manners from ours; but especially of religion, which our people endeavoured to establish in *Brasil*; these with some other concurring circumstances, such as our present weakness and the disposition the states were in at that time, to be fairly rid of *Brasil*, gave them sufficient encouragement for this attempt. It has been the opinion of some, that the first sparks of this rebellion might soon have been quench'd by seising some of the heads of the *Portuguese* faction; but it being apparent from the records, that nothing was left unattempted upon that account, tho' without

1649. any considerable success, the same cannot be imputed to the neglect of the government; the true reasons of the loss of *Brasil* were the slender garrison, and the inconsiderable number of *Dutch* inhabiting there; nothing being more obvious, than that a conquered country must be maintained, either by a sufficient military force, or strong colonies; the last of which was the constant practice of the ancient *Romans*, who besides this back'd them with good armies to keep the conquered nations in obedience. Another way of establishing themselves in a conquered country, tho' a very barbarous one, was introduced by the *Spaniards* and *Portuguese* in *America*, who by destroying the ancient inhabitants, and planting colonies of their own, saved themselves the charge of keeping many forts and garrisons for their defence. Neither of these was sufficiently observed by the *Dutch*, after their conquest of the *Dutch-Brasil*; for according to their agreement made with the *Portuguese*, the last were left in the entire and quiet possession of all the sugar-mills, plantations, and grounds thereunto belonging, whereby the *Dutch* subjects were in a manner excluded from getting any considerable footing in the open countrey, especially, since such of the sugar-mills as happened to fall into the companies hands, by forfeiture or otherwise, were sold promiscuously to both nations, and commonly at such excessive rates, that the *Dutch* durst seldom venture upon them; the taxes laid upon every thing belonging to the sugar-mills, and upon the sugar itself, being so great, that little profit was to be reap'd from thence, unless the sugar sold at a very dear rate; whereas on the contrary, we ought after the example of the *Spaniards*, to have endeavoured to draw our subjects into *Brasil*, by the granting of considerable immunities of honour and other advantages.

Reasons why Brasil *was not sufficiently peopled by the* Dutch.

The military force of the *Dutch* in *Brasil*, was likewise not duely regarded; for whereas according to a just estimate made in 1641, by count *Maurice*, 7076 men were absolutely requisite to maintain the *Dutch* garrisons there, the states of *Holland* instead of following his directions, did after the conclusion of the ten years truce with *Portugal*, order the great council of the *Dutch-Brasil*, to reduce their forces there to 18 companies of 150 men each; and tho' several remonstrances were made upon that head to the contrary, the truth of which was verified by the event; yet the succours sent from *Holland* arrived so slowly, that after my departute things grew worse and worse every day, and the *Dutch* had lost all their strong holds 1654. For the *Portuguese* began to blow up the *Receif* by sea, with 16 ships, and to besiege it by land 1653, in *December*, with such success, that our people being constrain'd by hunger, and the garrison refusing to fight, were forced to surrender the place with all its circumjacent forts to the enemy; since which time the *Portuguese* have remained in the entire possession of *Brasil*; the same being confirmed to them by the peace made the 6th of *Aug*. 1660, betwixt *Portugal* and the states of the united provinces, in which, among others these following points were agreed upon.

Their want of forces.

Lose all Brasil.

That the crown of *Portugal* shall be obliged to pay to the states the sum of 80 tuns of gold, either in ready money or sugar, tobacco or salt, or else assign the said money upon the *Portuguese* customs.

That the places taken on each side should remain to those, who were then in possession of them.

And that a free trade should be allowed to the *Dutch* in *Portugal*, *Africa* and *Brasil*; without paying any more customs than the native *Portuguese*.

Mr. JOHN NIEUHOFF's REMARKABLE VOYAGES AND TRAVELS TO THE EAST-INDIES.

1653. AFTER a ſhort ſtay in my native country, I reſolved to take a view of the *Eaſt-Indies*, and accordingly embarked at *Amſterdam*, on board the ſhip call'd the *Calf*, carrying 24 guns, under the command of *Cornelius Juſt*. The 23d of *Auguſt* 1653, we ſet ſail from the *Texel*, in company of four ſhips more, *viz.* the *Peace*, the *Lamb*, the *Golden Drake*, and the *Naerden*, ſteering our courſe towards the north of *Ireland*, not thinking it ſafe to paſs thro' the channel of *England*. The 24th we ſteer'd our courſe north by weſt, under 54 deg. 46 min. toward evening we caſt anchor at 13, and in the night found 17 fathom water. We continued the ſame courſe the 25th, under 55 deg. 59 min. 23 fathoms water, and from thence farther till the 29th, under 28 deg. 24 min. Then we took a north-eaſt courſe with a briſk gale. The 30th, with break of day we diſcovered at about 6 leagues diſtance *Hetland*, lying at the northern point of *Scotland*, and found ourſelves about noon under 60 deg. 3 min. latitude, and 18 deg. 49 min. longitude. The 1st of *September* we were under the latitude of 62 deg. 40 min. and 19 deg. 2 min. longitude: We ſteer'd our courſe with a briſk gale to ſouth-weſt by weſt, betwixt the *Fairo* iſlands and *Hetland*. The 4th, being overtaken by a violent ſtorm, we loſt ſight of one of our ſhips call'd the *Lamb*, under 60 deg. 11 min. We continued the ſame courſe till next day, when about noon we diſcovered the iſle of *Kilda*, under 59 deg. at 6 leagues diſtance to the ſouth-weſt of us, the iſland lying to the weſt of *Scotland*. Thus we purſued our voyage for the moſt part with ſtormy weather till the 13th, when we loſt our ſmall ſail at the prow of the ſhip: We found ourſelves about noon under 50 deg. 1 min. the weather continuing very ſtormy, but on the 17th, under 46 deg. 27 min. all our rigging was torn to pieces by a violent ſtorm, in which we got out of ſight of all our company. The 19th we deſcried two ſail which we gueſs'd to be our own, as one of them prov'd afterwards to be the *Lamb*. The 20th we continued our courſe with a briſk wind to the ſouth-weſt, and under 43 deg. 25 min. diſcovered the *Cabo Finis terræ*, or the point of the lands end of *Spain*, at about 5 leagues diſtance as we ſuppoſed. The ſame evening we met with the ſhip the *Lamb*, which as the maſter informs us, had loſt ſight of the ſhip the *Peace*, in the laſt ſtorm, and had her main-maſt and all her ſails brought by the board. Thus we ſailed forward with a ſtrong gale till the 30th, when we found ourſelves under the 30 deg. 20 min. and diſcovered the *African* coaſt about five leagues to the ſouth-weſt of us, with a variable wind. The 2d of

The author's departure to the Eaſt-Indies.

1653. *The iſle of* Kilda.

1653. of *October*, we continued the same course under the 28 deg. 51 min. of latitude, and 57 deg. of longitude; all along the isle of *Lancerotta*, one of the canary islands, we descried a ship, but were not near enough to see what she was. The next day we found ourselves about 40 leagues to the north north-east of the islands *Fretevanture* or *Forterentum*, under 27 deg. 45 min. and sail'd thus in 24 hours, 40 leagues among the *Canary* islands. The 7th a brisk north wind carried us near 20 leagues forwards to the 19 deg. 14 min. In the evening we found but 14 fathoms water, and a small bird settled upon our ship, tho' we judged our selves above 100 leagues from land. The 9th we were under 17 deg. 41 min. and towards evening saw land to the south-west of us. The 10th with break of day we discover'd the isle of *St. Vincent*, one of the salt islands, about five leagues to the south-west; we steering our course south-west, betwixt this island and that of *St. Anthony*. About noon we cast anchor in the bay of *St. Vincent* at four fathom water, in a sandy bottom, and provided ourselves the same day with a whole boat full of fresh water and seven goats; I went in another boat to the isle of *St. Anthony*, to fetch some fresh provisions; but could get none. The 15th our ships crew catch'd 10 tortoises, and those of the *Drake* as many. The 18th I was sent ashore to complement the governor of *St. Vincent*, who received us very kindly, and furnish'd us with an ass to carry us back to the harbour. All this while we catch'd abundance of fish; and the 20th sent some on shoar with some toys, which they exchanged with the inhabitants of *St. Vincent*, for oranges, limons, bekoras and pompions. The same day the ship the *Rose*, bound for *Brasil*, came to an anchor in the same bay. Mr. *Wiltschut* the elder, commander in chief of the land-forces, came on board us, being much surprised to meet with me there. Being by this time provided with as many necessaries as we were able to get, we were ready to set sail, but were detained by contrary winds 'till the 25th. The isle of *St. Vincent* is a rocky and barren island, affording nothing but a little grass for the sustenance of wild goats. It is about five leagues in circuit, under the command of a *Portuguese* governor, who was then a *Mulat*, one born of a christian father and a negro mother. 1653.

The isle of St Vincent.

The inhabitants here are negroes, transplanted hither from several parts to catch wild goats, the skins of which they send to *Portugal*, and the flesh they can't consume they

1653. they throw away. They lead a wretched life without women. All their water is brakish, and of a taste like salt-peter, except what they gather at the foot of the highest rock in bags of goat-skins, which being always covered with clouds on the top, sends a considerable quantity of rain water down to the bottom by small natural channels. The governor's residence is on the other side of the great rock, not far from the sea-shore, near 3 leagues from the harbour. His officers live in hutts cover'd with tortoise-shells, among trees, the shadow of which defends them against the excessive heat of the sun-beams: I went in company of some belonging to our ship, up to the top of the highest rock to take a view of the countrey; my companions stay'd about half way, but I with much a-do got to the top, where I had a full prospect of the island, but lost my hat by the violence of the wind, and was forced to lay upon my belly, for fear of tumbling down the precipice. The inhabitants relate a ridiculous story of a king's daughter turn'd into a serpent here. As I was coming down and met with the rest of my companions in the place where I left them, we saw at some distance a great number of crows, which made us hasten thither, and found them busy in picking the flesh of a living tortoise which was turn'd upon her back; we found above 300 eggs within her, which one of our company kept for his own use, but the flesh was carried on board for the use of the sick.

The island of St. Antony.

The island of *St. Antony* lies at about 3 leagues distance, just opposite to *St. Vincent*. On the foot of the east-point of this island, is a small sandy bay, fit for small vessels only, call'd by the *Portuguese*, *Et Pracaden Siniao*, whereabouts are about 30 hutts inhabited by *Portuguese* and negroes, who sustain themselves most by fruit; of which they had no great store formerly, but of late years they have great plenty, which were transplanted thither by the industry of the *Portuguese*; the isle being full of high barren rocks. The vines bear here twice a year, as well as most other fruit-trees; they abound in wild-fowl of all sorts, but especially in wild-goats. We found the heat so excessive about noon, that it was insupportable: At our first arrival, they refused to supply us with refreshments, but after some time they began to be more pliable, and furnish'd us with what fruits we wanted.

The salt islands.

These islands commonly call'd the *Salt Islands*, being ten in number, are thus call'd from the great quantity of salt they produce, and lies about 160 leagues from the *African* coast, being first discovered by the *Portuguese* 1572, who inhabit there to this day.

We set sail again the 26th with a moderate north-north east wind, and pass'd by the *Ilha Blanco* or *White-island*; so call'd from its *white colour*, being the last of the ten, under 15 deg. 11 min. At first we had a brisk gale, but were soon becalm'd, and advanced very little that day and night. The next following day we had a more prosperous wind, and discovered land the next morning, at about 10 leagues distance, under 14 deg. 16 min. The 3d of *November*, we advanc'd no more than 3 leagues, because the wind slacken'd under the 8 deg. 11 min. Thus we continued our course, but very slowly till the 18th, when we found our selves under 5 deg. being forced much farther to the east than we expected: We were continually afflicted with calms till the 1st of *December*; so that oftentimes we did not make above 3, 4 or 6 leagues a day, and without meeting with any thing remarkable, found our selves under 2 deg. 15 min. The 8th in the morning we pass'd the line, and the next day were under 50 min. southern latitude, and under 355 deg. 10 min. longitude: Here we were overtaken by a violent *Travado* from the east, with violent storms and rains, which much endamaged some of our small sails, being about noon under 1 deg. 37 min. We often saw small black clouds, which in an instant increased prodigiously, and were the certain fore-runners of tempests. For the rest we had favourable wind and weather all this month, and found our selves under 33 deg. 52 min. of southern latitude, and under 358 deg. 36 min. longitude, the sun setting 14 deg. 3 min. north-east; in the mean while our ship's crew began to be much afflicted with the scurvy for want of fresh water. The 1st of *January* we sail'd with a moderate gale under 34 deg. 58. min. about 39 leagues in 24 hours. The 3d we pursued our course east to the north, under 35 deg. 38 min. latitude, and 6 deg. 29 min. longitude: The 6th we continued the same course with a very brisk gale under 35 deg. 4 min. till the 22d, with strong winds and tempestuous weather; when in the morning under 31 deg. 36 min. we discovered land at about 3 leagues distance, to our no small satisfaction; we found 58 fathoms water and a rocky bottom; and in the afternoon 55 fathom sandy ground; we were forced to return deeper in sea, and in the afternoon approached nearer the shoar, but were forc'd to turn back again into the main. The next day about 7 or 8 leagues from the continent, we found a sandy bottom at 80 fathoms depth, and saw abundance of birds; we had very misty weather for some time, during which we lost the *Drake*. The 25th towards evening we got sight again of the 1653.

Drake

1653. *Drake* about 7 or 8 leagues from the shore, under 32 deg. 38 min. without being able to fathom the bottom of the sea. We continued this sailing to and from the shoar till the 28th, but could not make the *Cape of good Hope*, tho' we advanced within a league of the land among the rocks, not without great danger, being then under 32 deg. 58 min. we were therefore oblig'd to choose the main again, to our great dissatisfaction, being so disabled by sickness, and especially the scurvy, that we had scarce hands enough left to manage our ship: Our surgeon was a *German* by birth, a very able person, but never used to the sea before, was so much surprised at it, that he confess'd he never had seen the like, and that few of them would recover; but I told him, that in case we could make the cape, he would find a remarkable alteration in a weeks time, as soon as they touch'd the land, and receiv'd suitable refreshment, which accordingly proved true. The 29th and 30th it was very tempestuous weather, when we lost sight again of the *Drake*; we were forced to keep the open sea 'till the 2d of *February*, when we found our selves under 34 deg. 39 min. southern latitude, and 36 deg. 32 min. longitude. The 3d being overtaken by a storm from the south-east, we were forced to leave the shore again, which continued the next day with such violence that we lost our main-sail. The 4th we pursued our course with a brisk gale under 33 deg. 40 min. when we again discovered land at about 6 or 7 leagues distance. Towards evening we came within a league of *Dassen (Doe Island)* at 60 fathoms depth, but were forced to put to sea again, the shore being all along very rocky here: Thus we made to and from the shore 'till the 8th, when we saw the *Table Mountain* about 9 leagues to the south-west of us, and the isle of *Dassen* 2 or 3 leagues to the N. W. we found hereabouts 30, 36 and 40 fathoms water, about half a league from the shore in a sandy bottom; we did all we could to make the *Robben Island (Rabbet Island)* but being becalm'd, were fain to put to sea again. The 9th we were not above 2 or 3 leagues from the *Table Mountain*, and about noon being favour'd with a brisk S. W. wind got happily into the *Table Bay*, where we cast anchor at five fathoms depth in a sandy bottom. Here we met with the galliot the *Fox*, *John Zymentz* master. Mr. *Rietbeck*, *Dutch* governor of the *Cape of good Hope*, sent us immediately a chaloop with fish on board, and a pilot to conduct us into the harbour. We had lost 8 of our ships crew in this voyage, and had about 40 sick, besides which the rest were so much afflicted with the scurvy, that unless we had received some seasonable refreshments, we could scarce have held it out much longer. I went immediately a-shore in company of the captain *Cornelius Just*, and brought back good store of mustard-leaves which were dress'd for the ship's crew. Much about the same time the fiscal came a-board us, to forbid all commerce with the *Hottentotes* or natives, and to carry a shore, without special leave from the governor; we were also supply'd with more fresh water, which is very good and easy to be got thereabouts. The 12th we saw the ship the *Drake* making the bay, but was forced to cast anchor behind the *Robben Island*, by reason of the violence of the wind; we were then busy in fishing, but the wind blowing hard from the land side, could catch none. The 14th the tempest being somewhat allay'd, we approach'd as near the shore as we could; when we got sight of the top of the *Table Mountain*, which is very often covered with small clouds, a certain presage of tempestuous weather. The same day we went to our former employment of fishing, and catch'd as much in one draught as the chaloop was able to carry, the governor having 14 wheelbarrows full for his share. They were for the most part mullets, which swim in shoals along the shore of this bay. It was not 'till then the *Drake* came into the harbour, having lost 20 of her crew and 50 sick, and the rest being so much disabled by the scurvy, that according to their own confession, if it had lasted thus 14 days longer, they must have left the ship to the mercy of the wind and sea: We were all this while very busy in fishing as often as the weather would permit; but the 19th it blew so hard, that we were forced to make use of all our Anchors. The 22d we spent in providing ourselves with fresh water and fuel, the last of which our carpenters cut down near the banks of the *Salt-River*. The 23d I, in company of some others, went cross the mountain as far as the *Fresh-River*, to see whether we could meet with some wild-fowl, we saw some negroes with about 300 head of cattle, but at the first sight of us they retired. The fields hereabouts were all covered with white lilies and tulips; we saw also abundance of partridges. Being informed that a *Rhinoceros* was fallen into the boggs, the governor *Rietbeck* sent some fusileers thither to kill him, but the musquet ball not being able to penetrate his thick hide, they were forced to cut a hole in it first, and so to shoot it to death; the horn is preserved there to this day, and sometimes used instead of a cup. The 1st of *March* we had very fair weather, notwithstanding which, few of our ship's crew were fond to go on shoar, every

Violent scurvy. *They arrive in the Table Bay.* *The ship the Drake enters the bay.* *They take a view of the country.* *A Rhinoceros kill'd.*

1653. every thing being there at an excessive rate; as for instance, a quartern of *Arack* was sold for six-pence; of brandy for twelve-pence; a water-melon about the bigness of a coco-nut for half a crown. The next day being informed that a whale was got on shoar in the *Salt-River*, the governor and his lady, our master of the ship and I, went thither to see it, it was a very large one; we got upon the back of it, whilst the trumpet sounded merrily, and the negroes were busied in cutting great pieces of the flesh which they buried in the sand in order to eat them. The 6th the governor sent some of his soldiers to the *Hottentots*, to endeavour to exchange some of their cattle for copper, tobacco-pipes and such like baubles, but they retired at first sight. The 9th it was very calm and fair weather, which made most of our crew go on shore to wash their linen, having received orders to be ready to sail the next day; for which reason also good store of cabbage and two sheep were brought a board, a slender provision for such a number of men, but it was impossible to get more for that time. During our stay here, we fetch'd daily two sacks full of cabbage and mustard-leaves, which being boiled with bacon, was served twice a day, this being the best refreshment we were able to get. The *Cape of Good Hope* is situate under 34 deg. 20 min. southern latitude, which jetts out into the sea like a demi-island being to the north joined to the continent by a strait neck of land, with a bay on each side, very convenient for anchorage. The *Table Bay*, which has borrow'd its name from the *Table Mountain*, is about 4 leagues in compass, so that a whole fleet of ships may safely enter, or go out with any wind, except the north-west wind. Near the shore of this bay, upon the banks of the *Fresh-River*, the *Dutch East-India* company has erected a quadrangular fort, call'd the *Good Hope*, well provided with artillery and a good garrison, in which, at this time, Mr. *Rietbeck* was commander in chief; and had his habitation there, with a well-planted garden of about 15 acres round about it. Upon the banks of the *Salt-River* is likewise a small redoubt. Behind the fort of *Good-Hope*, all along the banks of the river, are many fine plantations or gardens, which produce cabbages and such-like herbages, being cultivated by certain *Hollanders* who have settled there, and pay only a small annual acknowledgment to the governor for the use of their grounds, which are for the most part clay, and consequently fruitful, tho' in some parts they are likewise rocky and sandy. Near the sea-shore is great store of small wood, tho' the natives assure us, that deeper in the countrey they have trees of a vast bigness. Their gardens produce likewise olives, oranges, apricocks and peaches; the fields grass and some herbs and flowers; nay, they would bear very good wheat, rye, rice, and barly, were they manur'd as they ought to be. Their field herbs are great and small, some with knotty roots, housleek and some other pot-herbs, besides tulips and white-lilies, &c. They have also here a certain root which the *Hottentots* roast and eat instead of bread, and sometimes make flour of them; some taste like our potatoes or chesnuts, tho' they have others that are much sweeter, not unlike our annisseed. The *Dutch* have planted many thousands of vines on a hill adjacent to the fort, they bear very plentifully, but the wine is of a crab-like tast. The worst of all is, that the winds which arise from the clouds in the mountains, blow in the summer, especially about *July*, with such violence, that they tear up all by the roots, at which time it is very dangerous landing at the cape. For the rest the air is very wholesome here, being always clear, and neither too hot nor too cold. Their winter is in *June* and *July*, when it freezes sometimes, that you may see Ice of the thickness of the back of a large knife. In *October*, *November*, and *December*, there blows always a south wind, which produces a cool air, as the north wind does in *Holland*; and in this season they are troubled with violent rains, which however render their ground very fruitful. 1653.

The Cape of Good Hope.

Table Bay.

The fort.

What creatures are at the Cape.

This countrey likewise abounds in all sorts of wild and tame creatures: They have here birds they call *Pinguwyns*, *Flamingos*, *Antenayas*, *Alkatraces*, *Faysons*, *Gavoytoyns*, *Garagians*, &c. The *Pinguwyns* are short-legged, and may soon be taken, but are not to be forced from their nest without a good stick, because they will bite and defend themselves there to the utmost. They abound also in partridges and pheasants, geese, quails, crows, sparrows of divers kinds, rock-ducks with yellow necks, teal, wood and water snipes, and a kind of demi-ducks; there is also a sort of black birds here of the bigness of a small goose or large duck, call'd by us cormorants, wild peacocks, blue, white and black cranes. The white ones are indifferently large, the black ones of the bigness of our sea-gulls, living for the most part in the marshes; they have a kind of reed-birds with red necks and legs, monkeys, hawks of divers kinds, ravens, magpies and very large ostriches, which can reach with their long necks a man on horse-back. They are gray, and run with their wings spread as swift as a horse; they live upon herbs, but sometimes devour likewise stones, copper and iron. They have

1653. have likewise certain birds not unlike our geese, which lay eggs without yolks, as big as a common goose egg. They are so full, and taste so much like fish, that they are not eatable. Another kind of geese they have somewhat less than ours, tho' their legs are larger, with grey spots all over their bodies; they are not to be tam'd, because they kill any other bird that comes within their reach.

The Pinguwyns. Formerly the sea-shore used to abound with certain birds call'd *Pinguwyns*, both black and white; their skin is very hard, and are of the bigness of an ordinary goose. They live both upon land and in the water; they have a fin on each foot, which makes them swim very swiftly after their prey the small fish, which is the reason their flesh is of a rank taste, and scarce eatable, unless it be seven times boil'd in fresh water, and afterwards fry'd with butter; they make their nest, and lay their legs in hollow places in the sand.

The Flamingos. The *Flamingos* is a very fine bird, resembling a crane, but with a crooked bill. They are pale red, tho' some of their feathers are half white and half black, but the uppermost feathers which cover the rest, are of a rosy colour.

Their oxen are very fat and thick set, with long crooked horns, tho' some have their horns bent back close to the neck; others have no horns at all, they are generally a foot and a half taller than our oxen. Among other creatures they have here those *Sea Cows.* they call *Sea Cows*, being much bulkier than an *European* ox. They are without horns, but have long ears and round eyes, with a short tail, thick legs and feet like an elephant. They have no hair upon their bodies, but prodigious large teeth. They feed upon grass, which they find in the marshes near the lakes, where they duck under water as long as they please, so that they are seldom to be seen or catch'd. The flesh is like other beef, but somewhat coarser; when it is salted, it appears and keeps like the ordinary *Dutch* salted beef.

They have likewise here what they commonly call *Iron Pigs*, with long spikes, which by drawing the skin together, can shoot at those that come too near them with such force, as to wound them mortally. A dead lion was once found here, with such a spike sticking in the breast, which had questionless caused his death. The skin is hung up, and to be seen in the fort to this day. They abound also in hares, wild goats and rabbits; and deeper in the country they have tygers, lions, wolves, leopards, *Rhinoceros*'s, deer, cows, calves and rock-does. They have plenty of sheep, which the inhabitants exchange for copper, tobacco, tobacco-pipes, and such like baubles. They 1653. bear no wool, but hair like our goats; their legs are long, and the tail consists of one long and thick piece of fat, which weighs sometimes 20 pound and above.

On this cape is also a certain creature call'd a *Jackal*, being betwixt a fox and a *The Jackals.* dog, with grey hair; it roars frightfully in the night time, being very greedy after men's flesh, so that it will dig sometimes ten foot deep to come at a dead carcass: It is said to be the most quick-scented of all creatures, and by its scent to discover any carrion that is near at hand to the lion. Among others, they have likewise a certain wild beast in shape and bigness like an elephant, but with two horns on the top of the nose; its tail is likewise like that of an elephant, but has a bush of black hair on the head where it joins to the neck, with two strait and round horns, with short mouse-coloured hair all over the body. On the top of the *Lions Mountain*, (so call'd from its resemblance to a sleeping lion) are great numbers of baboons, which are so unlucky, that they will sometimes with stones, force those who ascend the mountain to turn back. However, most of your ravenous beasts, such as lions, leopards, wolves, jackals and tigers, are but rarely to be met with near the sea-shore, where they are almost rooted out by the inhabitants; a certain reward being set for every one that kills any of these beasts, of which several skins hang up in a gallery of the fort. They have also sea and land tortoises in great quantities, and the woods furnish them with plenty of honey, which the bees hide in the deepest hollowness of the trees. Neither are they without dogs, which are commonly of a red colour, and have short tails.

There is here a certain kind of fish call'd *The* Hottentots *fish.* by the *Dutch* the *Hottentots* fish, because the *Hottentots* are very dextrous in taking them. They are very fine fishes, and taste like our cods. Formerly they used to catch abundance of seols, but now most of their fishes are unknown to us. In the *Table Bay* are also whales in abundance, but they are too lean to afford any considerable quantity of oil. Near the sea-shore you meet with the fish call'd by *Latines Torpedo*, by the *Greeks* *The fish* Torpedo. in the same sense *Naroe*, by the *Spaniards* *Hugia*, and by the *Dutch Krack Fish* or *Lazy Fish*, not because of its laziness in swimming, but of its hidden qualities, which as is reported, consists in this, that when it finds itself in distress, it sends forth a certain juice, which seizes the fishermen with a cramp in all their limbs. The inhabitants here are call'd *Hottentots* by the *Dutch*, *The* Hottentots *and their babits.* by reason of their stammering.

The men here appear for the most part naked,

1653. naked, having only a kind of a cloak made of doe, sheep, or rabbit skins sowed together, hanging from their shoulders down to their buttocks, fastned under the chin with a ribband, with the rough side outward in the summer, and the same turn'd inside in the winter. When they are travelling they wear over this another cloak with the rough side outwards. Their shoes are made of *Rhinoceros* skin without any heels, tied together on the middle of the feet with two leathern straps. In the night time, or in rainy weather, they wear caps of lamb skins with the woolly side inwards. Their privities they cover with a piece of tiger's skin or such like, which is tied behind with two leather strings. In their hair, which is shaved in some places of the head, they twist small copper plates, horns, and pieces of coral. The women wear cloaks of lamb skins like the men, with the rough side inwards, tho' somewhat longer; besides which they cover their bellies and buttocks, as also their privities, with another four-square skin. On their heads they wear caps of doe, sheep, and rabbit skins, tied round about with a broad sheep-skin strap. Their shoes are the same with the men. Such men or women as are rich in cattle, grease not only their bodies and faces, but likewise their cloaks and caps with suet, but the poor wear no cloaks at all; so that greasiness is among them both an ornament and a token of riches. In both ears they wear strings of coral, each weighing commonly four ounces; about their necks copper beads, round the arms they wear an ivory ring, and a strait copper ring about their wrists. When the women go abroad, they commonly have an empty leathern bag hanging down from their shoulders, in which are only some baubles, but if they have a young child it is carried in this bag. They wear stinking guts twisted twice or thrice round their legs for an ornament, or else dried guts, which serve them as a defence against pricking of thorns, and make a rattling noise when they are dancing and merry making. The men wear them likewise about the neck, and hang their tobacco-pipes and other toys in them.

Their arms. The arms chiefly used among the *Hottentots* are javelins, being sticks of 3, 4, or 5 foot long, pointed at the end with a sharp broad piece of iron; these they make themselves, and use them with great dexterity. They have also some bows and arrows, but are as yet quite ignorant of the use of fire arms. When they go abroad they carry this javelin, call'd by them *Assagaye* in one, and an ostrich feather, or a small stick with a wild cat's tail on the end, in the other hand, wherewith they defend themselves against the gnats and other insects.

The *Hottentots* are very nasty and aukward in eating, for they are ignorant of any thing that relates to cookery, but devour raw pieces of flesh or carrion, as greedy as dogs. The guts themselves they swallow down without washing or dressing, after they have only squeezed them a little. For want of carrion they eat dead stinking fish, such as they meet with near the sea-side, mussels and such like. They kill no cattle except it be rendered useless by sickness or age, except it be a sheep against a wedding dinner. The flesh of sea-dogs or rabbits is a dainty with them, which they devour either quite raw without cleansing, or sometimes broil it a little upon coals. They cut and eat the bacon of dead whales which happen to be cast ashore with great eagerness; nay they drink the oil which is drawn from thence by the heat of the sun, like water. Some bury pieces of this bacon in the sand for their future use. However their best and daily food are certain roots, not unlike our large potatoes, which the women dig up near the rivers and in some other places, those they eat either broil'd or boil'd. They are very eager after our wheat or rice bread which is baked there, and willingly exchange it for cattle. 1653. *Their food.*

Their chief drink is water, or milk which their cattle affords them. 'Tis incredible how fond they are of brandy or *Spanish* wine, but a small quantity makes them drunk, when they baul out fearfully, and are very unruly. *Their drink.*

Those inhabitants near the cape are of a brown olive colour, like the *Mulats*, which however is not their natural complection, but acquired by art, for they broil certain herbs with grease, wherewith they besmear their bodies and faces to make them swarthy, it having been found by experience, that a girl, which was carried into the fort immediately after she was born and brought up there, proved of the same complection with the best of our *European* women. They are of opinion, that in case they don't frequently besmear themselves thus from that time of their birth, they shall be subject to the dropsy, a distemper to which many of the *Africans* are most subject, as the *Abyssines* have one thigh swell'd twice as thick as the other. Upon the arrival of our ships on the cape, they get into the cook's room, and with the fat and black of the kettle, besmear their hair and faces to make them shine the better; this being look'd upon as a great piece of beauty among them, tho' it makes them smell very rank, especially if they put grease into the gashes which they make in their skin for that purpose, when you may smell them at 100 yards distance. *Their complection.*

They are generally lean, short and ugly, yet *Their constitution and habit of body.*

1653. yet they have black quick eyes, and very good white teeth. Their noses are somewhat flat, tho' not always, and the lips, especially the uppermost, very thick. Their foreheads are broad but wrinkled, and the hair of the men is curl'd and short like lambs wool, but very nasty and greasy. The women have thicker hair than the men, the last of which pull out all their hair upon their chin. The men have very well made legs, but slender calves, and are so nimble as to be able to out-run a strong bull, and stop him in his full career. The women especially have very fine and small feet, with flat bellies and round buttocks; their hands are very well shaped, but their fingers and nails very long. The mens privities or yards are very large, but have only one stone; for so soon as a male child is born, the mother cuts out the right stone to make it the more fit for running, and afterwards gives it some sea-water and tobacco. The women, especially those that are married, have long breasts which are always bare, and when they are suckling their infants, hang backwards over their shoulders. The inside of the womens privities are so relaxed that they hang out. Their chiefest riches consist in their cattle, which they never kill but when forced thereunto, either by sickness or age of the beast.

Their tongue. They stammer much in their speech, and bluster out their words like a turky-cock; they make use of no letters, neither do they know what writing and reading is; some however have been taught to speak, read and write *Dutch*, which shews them to be apprehensive enough. For the rest of the *Hottentots* are so very stupid, that they are not able to form to themselves the least idea of attacking or defending a strong hold; a house of brick, such as is proof against fire, being as profitable against them as the best fort, for if you enclose them in a house, and only shut their doors and windows fast, they are as safe here as in the strongest prison, having not the least sense to open them for their deliverance, in which they are inferior to beasts, which commonly endeavour to deliver themselves from bondage. Notwithstanding the *Hottentots* are so stupid, and in my judgment, the most wretched nation upon earth, there are some among them that want not cunning, especially if they are brought up to it; an instance of which we saw in our time in two young fellows, who were carried from hence to *Batavia*, where they were instructed in speaking, reading and writing of *Dutch*. One of them was employed as a servant by the general director, *John Maet Zuicker*, and after some time was sent back to the cape to serve as an interpreter there. I met with him at my first return from the *East-Indies*, among the *Hottentots*, and ask'd him whether he would not rather be with us where he lived much better? he told me, he would rather be with his own countrymen. I understood afterwards, that this fellow had proved the occasion of great mischief and differences among the *Hottentots*, and that several had been kill'd in the quarrel on both sides. At last he fell again into the hands of the commander of the cape, who banish'd him to the *Robben Island*, where he died. Theft they punish with a bastinado, and so they do murther, not out of any regard to God Almighty, but for custom's sake. They talk of one *Hunumma*, who has the disposal of rain and fair weather, but they pay no adoration to him.

Their stupidity.

Their marriage. Marriage is in pretty good esteem among them, tho' a man marries as many wives as he pleases. The maid, as soon as she is betrothed, performs the oath of fidelity in the following manner: The mother cuts of the first joint of her daughters little finger, which is tied to her future husband's finger, this they bury, and afterwards kill a cow for their wedding dinner. The maids are distinguish'd from the married women by green twigs which are twisted round their legs; these are taken off at the wedding day, and instead of them the dried guts of the cow kill'd for the wedding dinner put on; these when they dance make a noise, which seems very agreeable to them.

They have something of religion. 'Tis true the *Hottentots* are the most barbarous upon earth; notwithstanding which, I can't agree with those that will not allow of any religious worship among them; it being the opinion of all learned men, that no nation is so barbarous but what has something of religion, be it true or false. For they adore the moon with unusual outcries; and it is not improbable but that they pay the same devotion to the sun, because they follow its course as much as is possible, by changing the pasture of their cattle; for when the sun comes to the tropick of *Capricorn*, it has been observed that they feed their cattle on the south-east side of the rivulet, but when the sun returns to the tropick of *Cancer*, they go to the north-side; if it happens to rain very hard, they shelter themselves in their huts, seem to be fearful, and don't creep out till it be fair weather. Then they begin to be very merry, lifting up their heads and eyes to heaven, which is interpreted by us as a kind of thanksgiving; for when they are asked why they hide themselves during the rain, they answer, that the *Great Captain* being incensed against them, does punish them with this element, which he knows to be contrary to their nature. By this *Great Captain* they question-

1653. less understand the supreme Being; for if you speak to them of God, they are unwilling to hear it, and punish such among them as make use of it; alledging that it is not sufficient to express the glory of the supreme Being. If you talk of the devil they point to the ground Concerning the resurrection, they are of opinion, that those that die near the cape, shall arise again behind the mountains: But perhaps all this they may have learned from the *Portuguese* and *Dutch*. They frequently skirmish with one another, commonly for the conveniency of pastorage, so that sometimes six or seven are left dead upon the spot.

Divers nations of the Hottentots. The *Hottentots* are divided into several nations, known by different names. Those inhabiting near our fort are by the *Dutch* call'd *Capemen*, but in their own tongue *ChourIequa*; they are the most cunning of all the rest, by their frequent commerce with the *Dutch* and other *Europeans*; they live for the most part upon roots, fish and mussels. Somewhat deeper in the country live those commonly call'd *Tobacco Thieves*, because they used to steal the tobacco out of the fields, which is the reason the *Dutch* plant no more tobacco there; in their own tongue they are call'd *Korrochaukon*. There is another sort call'd *Chemakwa*, much more potent and richer than the *Capemen*, yet don't approach in power to the *Cocbukwas*, who living still deeper in the country, are accounted many thousand strong, and have vast herds of cows and sheep; they were then under the jurisdiction of two captains, the first call'd *Odosoy*, the other *Monomana*. The first of these two had married the sister of our interpreter's wife in the fort, and being invited thither by Mr. *Rietbeck*, the governor, he at last, after much enquiry concerning his quality, for fear of demeaning himself, gave him a visit. They rid out together a hunting, when *Odosoy* had the misfortune to be set upon by a fierce lion, who certainly would have torn him to pieces, had not his followers kill'd the lion with their javelins; however he did not escape without being sorely wounded on the neck, the flesh was all torn from one of his shoulder blades, and his face all miserably maul'd: Being judged past recovery, the governor offered him his own surgeon, but he would not accept of him, trusting more to those of his own nation; tho' the skill of these surgeons among the *Hottentots* reaches no farther than to cure a green wound, which they scarce ever perform without leaving a great dent or seam. They carry their remedies about them, and commonly have a parrot or some such creature (not unlike our mountebanks) along with them. Their herbs they keep in tortoise shells, but the roots, claws, teeth, and horns of beasts (these being the ingredients of their physical preparations) are fastned to a string, which they in the same manner as our tooth-drawers hang about the neck. 1653.

There is another nation of the *Hottentots* call'd by the *Dutch Sardiniamen* or *Saldanhas* (from a bay of that name) the natives call them *Krijegoekwa*. Some of the *Hottentots* relate, that to the north-east of those call'd *Kochukas*, there is a potent nation dwelling in stone-houses, that they are not black, and governed by the same laws as we are. Some suppose them to be a people inhabiting the mountains of the moon, but considering they are said to understand gold and silver, and to agree in many other things with the *Europeans*; our people judge them to be a colony of the *Portuguese* that have transplanted themselves thither from *Mozambique*. The *Dutch* have several times attempted to find out a passage thither by land, but without success, having always been forc'd to turn back for want of water. They also talk much of two other nations call'd *Heukumqua* and *Grocman*. The *Hottentots* or inhabitants here are not subject to one head, and what reverence they pay to their captains, is more out of custom than any sense of duty; they have no fix'd habitations, but lead a vagabond life like the antient *Scytes* and *Arabians*, carrying their wives and children along with them. They are not very desirous of gold and silver, unless some few that converse with the *Dutch*, and know the conveniency of buying from them what they stand in need of; for otherwise copper is in the greatest esteem with them. Boats they have none, being extremely fearful of water, and therefore venture seldom farther than to their knees. They are of a very lazy temper; most of their traffick consists in cows and sheep, which they exchange for copper and corals; but after the bargain is struck, they expect an additional present of tobacco, pipes and brandy, which has been introduced among them by foreigners. The seamen do also sometimes swap with them for ostrich feathers, and small tortoise shells call'd *Harego*. It is to be admired how they should make so much account of copper, which they daily tread under their feet, it being certain that very good copper mines are to be found hereabouts. The *Dutch* have at divers times attempted several land journeys into the country; as for instance, in the year 1660, when they discovered two nations, *viz.* the *Illunha* and *Namakkawa*; they supposed to have not been very far from the *Portuguese*, because they thought to have heard a cannon shot at a distance. The inland country swarms with wild fowl, such as wild geese, ducks and teal, but they are so shy as not to

7

1647. to come within reach of a gun, which is the reaſon that the governor's huntſman ſets up ſmall huts of green boughs, from whence he ſhoots them, this being the only way to come at them. Among the mountains are abundance of rocks, and ſome of them contain freſh water in their concavities. Several of our people as they were going one day up the mountains to take a view of the circumjacent country, found a certain rock-ſtone of four fathom long, and one and a half broad, being hollow in the middle, of the depth of a quarter of a yard, where they met with good ſtore of fine freſh water. Here are oſtriches of an extraordinary bigneſs; they are ſo ſwift as to outrun a horſe when they ſet up their wings, and thus by the help of the wind are forced forward, no otherwiſe than a ſhip under ſail. Their large legs and feet are a great addition to them, by the help of which they trot on with ſuch a force and nimbleneſs that like a horſe running down a hill, they are ſcarce to be ſtopt. The ſame way of ſetting up their wings has been obſerved in the tame ſwans. But before we leave this cape, I will give you a ſhort account of the *Lions Mountain*, the *Table Mountain* and *Table Bay*, as likewiſe of the *Robben Iſle*.

The Table Mountain. There are two very high mountains near this cape, *viz.* the *Table Moutain* and the *Lions Mountain.* The firſt is ſo call'd from its flatneſs on the top like a table, being about two leagues high, but ſmall in circumference, and for that reaſon of very difficult acceſs. It is divided from another adjacent mountain, call'd the *Devil's Mountain* by a vaſt cliff. Towards the ſea-ſide it is bare, without any graſs or trees, but on the land-ſide you ſee very agreeable woods, with many tall ſtrait trees fit for building; and towards the foot abundance of leſſer trees for fuel. Among the reſt are a great ſtore of wild almond-trees, but the fruit is very bitter; and if we may believe the *Hottentots*, poiſonous; wild pine-trees are here likewiſe in abundance, they grow very tall, but bear nothing but a huſk.

Table Bay. The *Table Bay* is ſituate under 34 deg. and ſome min. about 5 leagues more to north, this being the moſt ſouthern point of *Africa*. It is a very fine bay, tho' on the ſouth-ſide of the *Robben Iſland* are ſome rocks call'd the *Whale*; a large ſhip may anchor in this bay, from 9 to 7 fathom water, but yachts at 4 or 5 fathom in a good ſandy ground. There is however no truſting to a ſingle anchor, by reaſon of the bluſtring ſouth-eaſt winds which blow often here.

Robben Iſland. At the entrance of the *Table Bay* you ſee the *Robben Iſland*, thus call'd from the vaſt quantity of *Sea Robben (Sea Rabbits)* which are found here. It is not very high, and about two leagues in circumference. In the towns ſome rabbits have been put by the inhabitants which thrive very well. The ground produces a certain herb in great plenty; it has yellow leaves almoſt like cowſlips, which fatten the ſheep exceedingly. 1653.

To the north-eaſt of the *Robben Iſland* lies the *Daſſen Iſland*, under 34 deg. 33 min. It has got its name from the vaſt numbers of *Daſſen (Does)* which formerly were found there, but are of late years much diminiſh'd. It is about a league in compaſs, and produces likewiſe many ſea rabbits and *Pinguwyns*. It is inhabited by four families only with their ſlaves, whoſe chief employment it is to breed pigs and poultry, and to draw oil from the ſea-rabbits, which they ſell to the inhabitants living in and near the fort. Before the bay of *Saldanha* are ſeveral ſmall iſlands, where thoſe of the *Daſſen Iſland* have their liberty of fiſhing and hunting; they catch vaſt quantities of partridges, mullets and other fiſh. The two chief rivers of this cape are the *Salt* and *Freſh Rivers*. Beſides theſe there is another rivulet, which ariſing from among a neighbouring wood, exonerates itſelf in the *Salt River*. It is not above 12 or 14 foot broad, but very deep. Not far from the ſource of this, ariſes another rivulet among the marſhes near the *Wood Bay*. It runs ſouth-eaſt thro' the downs, (which extend as far as *Cabo falſo)* and diſembogues itſelf into the ſea. Daſſen Iſland.

No place in the world is more ſubject to ſtorms than the *Cape of Good Hope*, ſo that it would be impoſſible for ſhips to abide here, had not nature provided againſt theſe inconveniencies by the ſeveral commodious bays that are here. Among thoſe the bay of *Saldanha*, commonly call'd *Sardinia*, is none of the leaſt conſequence, where ſhips may ride ſafely at anchor without the leaſt danger, and were it not for the want of freſh water, it might claim the preference before the *Table Bay* itſelf. The winds blow generally throughout the year very hard here, but eſpecially the ſouth-eaſt wind, which blows from *October* to *April* (call'd the *South-Eaſt Monzon)* and tears ſo terribly thro' the clift, (betwixt the *Table* and the *Devil's Mountain)* that except the country and ground were very ſmooth and hard here, it would be impoſſible for any ſhip to ride it out; from *April* until *October*, the north-weſt wind blows with not much leſs violence, (call'd the *North-Weſt Monzon)* but yet not altogether ſo fierce as the ſouth-eaſt wind, there its violence is more obſervable on the land-ſide of the clift. The main difference betwixt theſe two winds here is, that the ſouth-eaſt wind always produces dry weather, whereas the north-weſt wind brings rains, *The Cape ſubject to ſtorms.*

1653. rains, which are very pernicious to the fruit.

By what signs to discover the nearness of the cape. So soon as you come near the sight of the cape, under the 34 deg. of southern latitude, you meet with certain signs and tokens, by which you may discover whether you are far from land or not. I don't much wonder that some of the ancient authors who have given us an account of the *Indies*, affirm, that when they were at a loss to find out whether they were near land or not, they used to let fly some birds, and according to their flight, to direct their course. Tho' this is out of date now, yet certain it is, that the birds are the best guide as to those who sail to the *East-Indies:* For at a great distance from the cape, whilst you are yet in the open sea, you meet with a peculiar kind of small sea-gulls, which foretel you your approach to this cape. But as these come abroad sometimes above 100 leagues or more at sea, they are but uncertain forerunners, but when you see another kind of large spotted sea-gulls appear, by those that are acquainted in these seas call'd *Cape-Birds*, with speckled wings, you may hope to see land in a very short time, and if you meet with some turtle doves, this puts it beyond all doubt. If you find anchorage at 40 or 50 fathoms depth, in a white sandy ground mix'd with red, you may conclude yourself to be upon the sandridge of the cape *d'Aguillas*, tho' you see no land. If you come to the west of the *Cape of good Hope*, you will find, besides the aforementioned *Cape-Birds*, certain hollow roots growing among the rocks in the sea, the leaves of which swim upon the water; the *Portuguese* call them *Trombas*, and they are to be met with in vast quantities in the *Table Bay*, just under the fort, which the chaloops and boats are very careful to avoid, they being so entangled together, that there is no breaking thro' them with oars: It is likewise found in the seas of *Japan*, and in great esteem among the inhabitants, who make pickles of these leaves, and use them as the *Europeans* do cucumbers, or the *Indians* their *Actsjar*.

The *Hottentots*, a barbarous generation, were so ill-natur'd at that time, that they would not exchange an ox or any other sort of fresh provisions with us, nay they made the spring or places where we used to fetch our fresh water, muddy; we fell rough upon some of them, but they being much stronger than we, pelted us with stones and made us retire; I was at that time with a gun upon the *Table Mountain*, but could not come time enough to their assistance; but the next day several of us went well arm'd to give them another visit, and to fire at them in case they pretended to make any opposition, but they no sooner discovered our arms, but fled with wife, children, and their cattle. 1653.

After we had stay'd there about three days ashore, we set sail the 13th of *March* from the cape, steering our course westward, in hopes to get sight of the ship the *Drake*; but not meeting with her, we chose the open sea, and advanced about 60 leagues from the *Table Bay*, under 34 deg. 20 min. southern latitude. We continued our voyage with pretty good success till the 18th, when about noon we found ourselves under 38 deg. 26 min. southern latitude, and 33 deg. 27 min. longitude. The compass shew'd due south and north. The two next following days proved very rainy and blustring, and the 27th it thundred and lightned very hard, with strong winds and much rain, which ending at last in a violent storm, oblig'd us to take in all our sails, under 39 deg. 20 min. southern latitude. The 1st of *April* we found ourselves far to the north, being forced by the stream, and the weather continued windy and rainy, as it had been ever since the 27th of *March*; we found ourselves then under 39 deg. 21 min. of latitude, and 95 deg. 30 min. of longitude, and had sail'd 36 leagues in the last 24 hours. The same night the winds began to rise to that degree, that we were fain to take in our main sail, which continued to the 3d, when the compass was changed to 15 deg. N. W. The 7th we sail'd 44 leagues with a moderate gale, under 38 deg. 13 min. The rains and strong winds continued till the 13th in the morning, when it began to clear up, and sail'd that day and night 46 leagues under 36 deg. 30 min. latitude, and 98 deg. 42 min. longitude. Then it began to be blustery weather again. The 15th we found the rising of the sun at 24 deg. N. W. this being the first time since the 4th of the last month, by reason of the strong weather. About noon we were under 35 deg. 14 min. of latitude, and 104 deg. 40 min. longitude; having sailed 34 leagues in 24 hours. Towards evening it began to be calm, but continued not long, the winds and rains infesting us by turns, till the 1st of *May*, when we found ourselves under 12 deg. 18 min. latitude, and 124 deg. 46 min. longitude: We then proceeded in our voyage with a good brisk gale till the 3d, when in the night we were overtaken with a violent *Travado* with thunder and lightning, which continued till the next following day. The 6th of *May*, early in the morning, we descried the coast of the isle of *Sumatra*, about 4 or 5 leagues from us, and to the leeward a sail under 5 deg. 22 min. In the night the wind blowing from the land-side, we were forced to take

Their departure from the cape.

They get sight of Sumatra.

1653. take our course to the south. By the 9th we had not advanc'd above 6 or 7 leagues along the coast of Sumatra, being continually pestred with *Travadoes*, thunder and lightning; all our endeavours were to get above the flat point of the streights of *Sunda*. The 12th we had pretty fair wind and weather, and about noon found ourselves under 6 deg. 5 min. In the afternoon we sail'd forward with a moderate gale, within a league and half of the forementioned point to the N. N. E. of us, where we found 16 fathom water. The next day we found ourselves about three leagues from the said point. The 14th we saw the *Imperial Island*, at about three leagues distance, and the next following day discovered to the south-east to east, about 5 or 6 leagues from us the *Princes Islands*, under 60 deg. 45 min. where we were becalm'd all the rest of the day. The 17th we found ourselves under 17 deg. 10 min. about two leagues from these islands, and toward the evening saw the utmost point of land of the isle of *Java*, at 4 or 5 leagues from us; the 18th we were becalm'd again, and the following day advanc'd within two leagues of the point of *Java*; and 2 or 3 leagues of the *Princes Islands*. We endeavoured to have pass'd betwixt them, but were prevented by a *Travado* from the east. The 20th being under 60 deg. 41 min. we were at 6 leagues distance from the said islands, and kept in sight of them the 21st and 22d, with an intent to pass by them on the 23d, but being becalm'd came to an anchor the same night at 30 fathoms depth; the stream did run here very strong to the S. W. The 24th we were directly opposite N. N. E. to the isle of *Java*, and the same evening, a boat with all sorts of refreshments came aboard us from thence, which was very welcome to us, after so tedious a voyage: We came soon after to an anchor at 30 fathoms water, the stream running so strong here, that we were forc'd to remain here this and the next following day; during which time, several other boats with fresh provisions came aboard us. The 26th we set sail again, but by reason of the violence of the stream could not advance far, so that we were forced to cast anchor again, at 25 fathoms depth, where we continued all the next day. The 28th we set up our sails again, but were forced soon after to cast anchor, having the *Iulo* (the isle) *Baly* to the N. E. Great *Pulo modi* to the E. and the lesser *Pulo modi* to the S. of us. Towards evening we set sail again, but whatever we did could not reach the road of the so long wish'd-for city of *Batavia*, being forced to come to an anchor about half a league from the isle of *Rotterdam* at 11 fathoms water. The 30th we put up our sails once more, but with no better success, being oblig'd to cast anchor again, which put us in mind of what befel us lately on the *Cape of good Hope*, where we met with the same ill success before we could double the cape. However, the wind turning fair in the afternoon, we arrived the same afternoon about four a clock, (after a very tedious voyage, in which we had many sick) before the city of *Batavia*, where we cast anchor at four fathoms and a half depth. The next day I went ashore, and took up my lodgings in that famous city, at one Mr. *Gerard Utsens*, till further orders. In the mean time I was very curious in taking an exact view of this city and the circumjacent country: Whilst I tarried at *Batavia*, an embassy was sent from the general director *John Maetzuicker* and the other directors of the *East-India* company, to the *Cham of Tartary*, who some few years before had conquered the most potent empire of *China*, to treat about a free commerce betwixt the two nations, which had several times before been attempted and sought for by the *Dutch*, but was as often refused by the *Chinese*. *Jacob de Keisar* and *Peter de Goyer* being appointed ambassadors, two yachts, *viz.* the *Kaukerk* and *Blocmendael*, man'd with 90 men, and provided with several fine presents for the emperor were got ready for their transport, and I was ordered to go aboard the *Bloemendael* in the quality of steward.

The Imperial Island.

The Princes Islands.

They arrive at Batavia.

The ambassadors embark'd the 14th of *July* 1655, and set sail the same day from the road of *Batavia*. The 4th of *September* they arrived in the city of *Kanton*, and the 4th of *May* 1656, in the city of *Nanking*, and the 16th of *July* at *Peking*. After some stay there, they returned the 21st of *November* to *Nanking*, to *Kanton* the 28th of *February* 1657, and came into the road of *Batavia* the 21st of *March*, where they gave an account of their negotiation to the *Dutch* council of the *Indies*: Of all which I have given you an ample account in my *Chinese* voyage, publish'd first in *Low Dutch*, and since translated into several other languages, and printed at *Amsterdam* for *Jacob Meurs*, with many cuts and draughts of places, living creatures, fruits and other remarkable things.

Mr. Nieuhoff sent to China.

1658. After my return from thence, eight ships were ordered to be equip'd and loaden for *Holland*. viz. the *Pearl*, *Prince William*, the *Orange*, the *Crowned Lion*, *Achilles*, *Malacca*, the *Ulysses* and *Hector*. The command in chief of this fleet was conferred upon Mr. *Koenes*, then first director of the council of the *Indies*, who embark'd aboard the *Pearl* of 700 tuns, man'd with 180 men, and provided with 26 guns. At his request

1658. *He returns from Batavia towards Holland. Arrival at St. Helens.* request I went aboard along with him in the *Pearl*, which carried the flag, in order to my return into *Holland*, tho' my appointed time was not expired here. We set sail the 22[d] of *December*, and the last day of *March* 1658, arrived safely without any remarkable accident, (except that we met with some *Travados*, which soundly tost our ship) at the isle of *St. Helens.*

The isle of *St. Helens*, is situate under 16 deg. 15 min. of southern latitude, at a great distance from the continent, lying at least 350 leagues from *Augusta*, the next place of all. It is very surprising to conceive so small an island at so vast a distance at sea, round about which there is scarce any anchorage, by reason of the vast depth of the seas. It is about seven leagues in circum- 1658. *The isle of St. Helens.*

ference, covered all over with rocky hills, which in a clear day may be seen 14 leagues at sea; the valleys being stor'd with all sorts of trees: So that tho' this island is not very large in its compass, yet it comprehends a large tract of ground by reason of those hills. It has many fine valleys, among which the *Church-Valley* and the *Apple-Valley* are the most remarkable. In the *Church-Valley*, you see to this day the ruins of a chapel, formerly belonging to the *Portuguese*; the whole valleys are planted with lemons, oranges, and pomegranate-trees. At that time the island was destitute of inhabitants, but since the *English* have made a settlement there. After the *Portuguese* left it, a certain hermit, under pretence of devotion, used to kill great numbers of wild goats here, and sell their skins, which the *Portuguese* having got notice of, they removed him from thence. At another time certain negroes with two female slaves were got into the mountains, where they encreased to the number 20, till they at last were likewise forc'd from thence. The valleys are excessive hot, but on the hills it is cool enough: tho' the heat is much tempered by the winds and frequent rain showers, which fall sometimes several times in a day; which, with the heat of the sun-beams, renders the soil very fruitful. It abounds in fine and cool springs, which fall down from the tops of the hills, the water being as clear as crystal, and exonerating itself at last into the sea, it is very pleasant to behold the seamen at their arrival here, to drink, wash and bath themselves in these spring waters. Most of the fruits and beasts which are produced here in great plenty, have been first brought hither by the *Portuguese*;

1658. tuguese; as for instance, orange-trees, (of which you may see whole woods) pomegranate-trees and others, which bear fruit throughout the whole year. Here are likewise, mustard-leaves, parsly, sorrel, purslin, wintercresses and other such-like herbs, which are very good against the scurvy; neither is this island destitute of trees, but such as are not fit for timber, but only for fuel. It abounds likewise in beasts; wild goats are here in vast numbers, but very difficult to be taken, by reason of the many rocks. Tame hogs were brought hither by the *Portuguese*, which have multiply'd to admiration, but are degenerated into wild ones, and are not easy to be kill'd for the aforemention'd reason. Thus it is with the partridges, wild pigeons and peacocks, which are here in vast plenty, but are so shy, that so soon as they see any one approach, they fly from one hill to another cross the valleys, so that you must be an hour before you can come at them again, which when you have done, you are in danger of losing your labour, for they return commonly from whence they came. The only way to catch them, is to go abroad with a good company. It produces no ravenous or poisonous creatures, except large spiders and flies. All about the island you see vast multitudes of sea-gulls, which feed on the fishes in which the sea abounds. Here you meet likewise with several colours fit for dyers, especially with a most excellent red colour, and with very fine white salt, made out of the sea-water by the heat of the sun-beams. By reason of its great distance from the continent, the seas hereabouts are covered with fishes, such as mackarel, carps, &c. They are not to be catch'd with nets by reason of the vast depth, but with a hook, or only an iron nail bent, you may catch as many as you please; craw-fish, crabs, oysters and mussels are likewise to be found in vast quantities near the sea-shore. After we had sufficiently refresh'd our selves here, and provided what necessaries we thought fit, or could get, we left this island the last day of *May*; We continued our former course, and without any remarkable accident, came in sight of *Holland*, and the 6th of *July* 1658 arrived happily at *Amsterdam*. I took up my lodgings at my brother *Henry Nieuhoff's*, whom as well as most of my other friends, I had the good fortune to find in good health. Many of the most curious persons of that place came daily to see me, to take a view of the *Chinese* characters, and other draughts I had brought along with me.

They depart from St. Helens.

Arrive in Holland.

After I had tarried for three months in *Holland*, and dispatch'd my business both here and in *Zeland*, I delivered the journal of my late voyage into *China* to my brother, in order to have it review'd and printed, at the request of several persons of quality; with an intention to take a second voyage to the *East-Indies*, with the first fair opportunity, which was soon after offered me by the directors of the *East-India* company. 5 ships lay then ready for the *East-Indies* under the command of Mr. *Adrian Aelmonde*, *viz.* the *Arnheim*, burthen 500 tuns, with 40 guns and 430 men, *John Tymensz* master; the second the *Pearl* and three yachts; I was ordered aboard the first. We set sail all together from the *Ulic* the 22d of *Dec.* 1658. The ship the *Arnheim* at her entrance into the sea, struck upon the sands and was in some danger of being stav'd, and another ship run foul upon her, by which she lost part of her gallery; but by God's singular mercy, we got clear again the next high tide, and continued our voyage with the rest.

Nieuhoff's *second voyage to the* East-Indies.

The 16th of *March* 1659, we arrived safely at the *Cape of Good Hope*, where we cast our anchor. The 22d, the *Pearl* with the other three yachts came likewise to anchor in the same bay. The first thing we did was to take care of our sick, of which we had not very many, but 12 died in the voyage; we went every day ashore to fetch fresh water, fuel, and what provisions we were able to get; sometimes we catch'd good store of fishes. One day several of us went ashore to shoot some wild fowl; but advancing pretty high up the *Table Mountain*, we unawares espy'd a sleeping lion, at no great distance from us, which made me soon retreat, telling my companions it was dangerous to awake a sleeping lyon, who were glad as well as I, to make the best of their way backwards.

1659. *Arrives at the* Cape of Good-Hope.

After a stay of 14 days at the cape, we set sail again, and with a much more prosperous gale, than I had in my last voyage, arrived safely on the coast of *St. Java*, where just as we got sight of that island, Mr. *Adrian Aelmonde* died, to our great grief; his corps was carried to *Batavia*, where it was honourably interr'd.

He leaves the Cape.

The 18th of *July* 1659, we came to an anchor before the city of *Batavia*, after a voyage of about 7 months; during which, there happen'd scarce any thing worth taking notice of. After I had delivered up the merchandises under my charge, and my accounts: I took a turn to the western coast of *Sumatra*, *viz.* to *Jambe* and *Padane*, which produce abundance of pepper, some gold and salt-peter, and returned the 10th of *December* to *Batavia*.

His arrival at Batavia.

Not long after I was ordered on board the ship *Henrietta Lowisa* bound for *Amboyna*, *Gerard Gerardson* a native of *Flussigen* master,

1659. master, laden with rice and provisions. We set sail from *Batavia* the 23[d] of *Dec.* 1659, and in a month after got among the rocks near the point of *Bimaer*, being forced thither by a whirlpool, which turn'd our ship within the compass of three times the length of the ship, as swift as the nimblest horse could run; we were within a few yards of having been struck against a rock, but had the good fortune to escape without much damage, and after some *Travadoes* at last got into the road of *Amboyna*, not without great difficulty, by reason of the swiftness of the stream there, and cast anchor at 36 fathoms depth. We were very kindly received by Mr. *Jacob Hustard* the governor of *Amboyna*, a man of singular probity and conduct. After the ship was unladen, and I had delivered my cargo, the governor and I resolved to take a tour in the small circumjacent islands. Among the rest we visited the island of *Buero*, where the inhabitants made us heartily welcome after their way, and drank to us merrily in cups made of the leaves of trees.

Goes to Amboyna.

The isle of Bouro or Buero.

The isle of *Bouro* or *Buero*, is situate about 24 leagues off *Amboyna*, being near 30 leagues in compass. The sea, especially on the south side, of a vast depth, from whence the shore rises by degrees, and surrounds the whole island like a steep wall. 1657. The south wind produces both high and low water here. In the island of *Buero* are mountains which reach to the very skies: Near the bay of *Tamahoo* are high mountains of the same name, the blue tops of which penetrate thro' the clouds, and may be seen at 28 leagues distance at sea; tho' it be very difficult to distinguish them from the clouds. The bay of *Tamahoo* is surrounded with these mountains. Hereabouts you see neither houses, huts, nor inhabitants, but only woods and wildernesses. A certain river exonerates itself into this bay, the banks of which are on both sides full of green trees. On the north-east side of the isle *Buero*, in another bay, called the bay of *Kayelle*, which in some places is two leagues broad. The sea-shore of this bay is very pleasant, by reason of the many woods and wildernesses. Here you see great store of green ebony wood-trees, but the wood is somewhat knotty. Within the marshy grounds, adjacent to the middle of the bay, is a whole wood of trees as hard as iron, and of a reddish colour; the *Dutch* call them *Lary* trees.

The Bay of Kayelle.

The constitution of this island.

The island *Buero* is very fertile and abounding in trees near the sea-shore. It produces *Coco* and *Bananas* trees, *Pynany*, green ebony wood-trees, potatoes, beans, *Katjang* (a certain kind of pease) millet or indian-wheat, tobacco, lime-trees, and divers

1659. vers sorts of herbs. In the mountains are civet-cats, and the inhabitants have a peculiar easy way of taking the civet from them, which they sell very cheap. In short, the whole countrey is full of fertile grounds and pleasant woods, and is watered with many fresh water rivers; the worst of all is, that it is much subject to earthquakes.

In the isle of *Buero* lives, among other beasts, a certain strange creature, which by the *Indians* is counted among the number of monsters. It is of the bigness of a large dog, or of a roe-buck, of a dark brown and gray colour, the hair like our gray-hounds; the head and mouth like a hog, with small eyes and ears, the tail curls twice or thrice, and the legs and claws like those of a roe-buck. The flesh is both by the inhabitants and strangers look'd upon as a dainty, and as good as venison. The circumference of its mouth and jaws is as big as a large calf's head, with very strong jaw-bones; on both sides backwards to the throat, are about 12 teeth, but in the fore-part of the undermost jaw-bone, 6 teeth and 2 large ones in the upper part, which are covered by the mouth. From the middle part of the undermost jaw-bone issue forth two large teeth which pierce the mouth. They are a foot long each, about an inch thick, and somewhat crooked like those of the wild boar. Out of the upper jaw-bones spring forth two horns, on each side one, of an inch thick, a quarter of a yard long, smooth like teeth, and turn'd like a hook at the end, which makes it appear at first sight as if it were armed with 4 horns.

On the north-east of the isle of *Buero* are the following villages, *Waiselonga*, *Fogi*, *Wainite*, *Tamahou*, *Palmatte*, *Hokonima*, *Bara*, *Liciela*, *Waisamma*, *Ilat*, and *Romaite*; The eight first of these villages were in 1653, burn'd to the ground by the *Dutch*, with all their boats, the inhabitants having revolted against them. This island is under the jurisdiction of the king of *Tarnate*. In the year 1660, the *Dutch* built a fort with four small bastions, provided with convenient habitations for the use of the garrison in this island, to keep out those of *Makassar*. It was nam'd *Mandarshaa*, after the then king of *Tarnate*. The natives of *Buero* are pursuant to their capitulation made with the *Dutch*, obliged to inhabit round about the bay of *Kayelle*, where they are possess'd of about 14 villages under the *Dutch* protection: Their houses are neatly built of cane, and some have convenient appartments; and for the improvement of the adjacent grounds, are obliged to cut down and burn the trees and woods, and to turn them into fields, gardens and orchards. Before that time, they lived only in wretched huts built along the sea-shore among the woods. They 1659. are very black, and like most of the inhabitants of the other neighbouring islands, almost naked both men and women, having only a piece of stuff to cover their nakedness from the waste down to the knees; but girls and boys till they are twelve years old, go quite naked. A young fellow that has a mind to marry a certain maid, may soon obtain her, by making a small present of eatables, or any other thing of no value to her parents. As soon as a woman is brought to bed, she goes streight to the next river, where she washes both her self and the child, and so returns to her usual employments, in the mean while the husband is attended and made much of in the wife's stead. They bemoan their dead neighbours and friends with lamentable out-crys, but after the corps is buried, they dance, sing, feast and make merry. Their graves are made of brick-work, with stones and clay, to preserve them against the wild-beasts. The common food of the natives is *Zagow*, millet, rice and dry'd fish. They are for the most part mahometans, tho' some retain much of paganism, and adore the crocodiles. In the year 1650, one *Madira* governor for the king of *Ternate* in the isle of *Amboyna*, having taken up arms against the *Dutch* in *Amboyna*, the inhabitants of *Buero*, as well those under the king's as *Dutch* subjection, join'd with *Madira* with so much obstinacy, that they chose rather to die than to leave *Madira*; and in 1652 kill'd four sea men belonging to a vessel call'd the *Goose*, who ventured too far into the woods. Mr. *Arnold Flaming van Outshorn* being, 1652, sent with a strong squadron of ships to *Batavia*, and from thence to *Amboyna* and *Buero*, to bring the inhabitants to reason; having understood their barbarous proceedings, burn'd all their boats, and the before-mention'd villages. The king *Mandarshaa* came along with him in person, having before concluded a peace with the *East-India* company at *Batavia*.

After we had taken a full view of this island, we returned to *Amboyna*, where the governor gave a splendid entertainment to the chiefest officers of the company, and some of the courtiers belonging to the kings of *Amboyna*. After dinner we play'd together, and they seem'd so well satisfied, that it might easily be seen there was a good correspondence betwixt them and the company at that time. In the mean while my ship having been loaden with 16 tuns of cloves and some other commodities, I took my leave from Mr. *Hustard* the governor, and the 3ᵈ of *May* directed my course back towards *Batavia*. Under the government of this Mr. *Hustard* were at that time all the *Molucco*

The author's departure from Amboyna.

1659. *Molucco* islands, whose business it is to keep a strict eye over them, for fear they should export cloves. But before I quite leave the isle of *Amboyna*, I will give you a description of its situation, and what else is worth our observation there.

The isle of Amboyna. The Isle of *Amboyna* or *Amboyno* is by some numbred among the *Molucco* islands, because it produces great store of cloves like the *Molucco* islands. It is situate under 3 deg. southern latitude, about 24 leagues from the isle of *Banda*, and consequently nearer the coast of *Malacca*, than any of the *Molucco* islands. It is 24 leagues in circumference, being divided almost in two parts, by a vast bay or rather gulph. It has a very fine bay where ships may ride safely at anchor near the shore; about two leagues within this bay, is the *Dutch* fort called *Victoria*. It appears like two islands joined together by a neck of land. About 60 or 70 years ago, there were 57 goodly villages or great plantations, inhabited by *Indians* and christians, (some of which were of good strength,) but many of them have been laid desolate, or at least are much decay'd by the intestine wars.

The village Way. Among the rest *Way* was a very fine plantation on the north-side of the island, half a league from the sea-shore, built upon a rock, and defended by a good breast-work; notwithstanding which, it was 1630 surprised by one *Kimelaha*, the inhabitants were christians. Near this village are abundance of clove and *Zague* trees, and all along the sea-shore are several other plantations of less note, all well provided with clove and *Zague* trees. The village of *Way* has this conveniency, that it is well provided with fresh springs, a thing of the utmost consequence in those hot countries.

Noussanive. The village *Noussanive* was situate upon a river on the west-side under the cannon of the fort *Victoria*, being divided into three plantations. The countrey thereabouts abounds in clove-trees; the plantations of which extend as far as to the utmost point of the western cape, and on the other side, as far as *Ayer Kahouba:* The king or captain of this district used to be formerly president of the council of *Amboyna*.

Hittoe. The village of *Hittoe* is very ancient, and built near the sea-side, under the redoubt belonging to the *Dutch* company, being the capital of the whole district of *Hittoe*.

Wawami. *Wawami*, the head village of all, lies above a league from the sea-shore, upon a hill near an *English* mile high, unto which leads but one passage, which in the midst is defended by strong pallisadoes, and the top of the hill (which is of an oval figure) by a stone wall. Betwixt the hill and the fort slides along a pretty river. Formerly this was a noted place of retreat for the inhabitants, who used to shelter them selves here. 1659.

The village *Mousala* is built upon a mountain about a league and a half high, being so strong by nature, as to be counted impregnable; notwithstanding which, it has been reduced by the victorious arms of the *Dutch East-India* company, under whose jurisdiction they now live. Mousala.

The following plantations or villages were in 1630, under the jurisdiction of the *Dutch East-India* company.

The district of *Rossenive* which comprehends *Rossenive*, *Amahoesoe* and *Hattoe*. *Rossenive* had in 1630, one *Andrew Rossenive* for their king or captain; *Amahoesoe* one *Domingos Costa Makkake*, *Poeta* and *Hattoe*, one *Lessemesse*. These villages were better inhabited than most of the rest, the inhabitants making profession of the christian religion, yet not without some mixture of *Mahometanism*, except those of *Amahoesoe*, whose captain was a good christian, and lived much better than the rest; which shews that the chief defect lay in their kings; for *Andrew Rossenive* was none of the best livers, tho' he could very artificially play the hypocrite; he had no wife but many concubines; and tho' he was often admonish'd to marry, he continued obstinate in the same course, which gave great scandal as well to the inhabitants as to the other kings and captains. The common people of this town were always more ready for the service of the company than those of the other villages. For the villages *Rossenive*, *Amahoesoe* and *Hattoe* are obliged to supply and manage one half of the governours *Korrakoren*, (or small vessels of war) as the villages of *Kielang*, *Nakko* and *Hattela* are bound to supply the other half. Rossenive.

Kielang was one of the most considerable villages on the south-side of the mountain of *Laytimor*, not far distant from the sea shore, but of no great strength. Near it are very good springs and great store of clove-trees. Under the district of *Kielang* are the villages of *Kielang*, *Nakko* and *Hattela*. In the year 1630, *Manuel de Silva* was king or captain of *Kielang*, but surrendered the government to his eldest son; he was a very good natur'd honest man, and had the second place in the *Dutch* council. *Anthony Pays* was captain of *Nakko*, and *Anthony Lopes* of *Hattela*, they were all three very good christians. Kielang.

Under the district of *Ema* are the villages *Oekorilla*, *Lewary* and *Routon Lasary*; *Manuel* was captain of *Oekorilla*, *Simau* of *Ema*, and one *Anthony Routon* of *Lasary*. These are obliged to furnish a *Karrakore* of four *Nadjos* for the service of the company. Ema.

They

1659. They are very honeſt and faithful, and profeſs themſelves of the tribe of *Olilymas*, except *Routon Laſary*, which belongs to the tribe of the *Oliſivas*.

Soya. To the diſtrict of *Soya* belong the villages of *Aboeſen*, *Oeritettoe* and *Amantelloe*. Theſe are obliged to find a *Korrakore* of 4 *Nadjos*, are pretty ready in the ſervice, and profeſs all chriſtianity, and ſo does the king with all his *Orangkeys*: They are of the tribe of the *Oliſivas*. *Laurenzo de Sylva* is king of *Soya*, *Anthony Aboeſen* of *Aboeſen*, and *Jeronymo Tebolopoe* of *Oeritettoe*, and *Amantelloe*.

Hative. Under *Hative* belong the villages *Taviery*, *Hokkonaloe* and *Mardykka*; they furniſh *Karrakore* with 4 *Nadjos*. They are good ſoldiers and chriſtians, and their heads come frequently to the communion. Their chief heads are *Laurenzo Marcus* captain of *Hative*. *Pedro Anthonio* of *Taviery*. *Laurence Mendos*, chieftain of *Hokkonaloe* and *Mardykka*. The inhabitants of *Mardykka* are the remnants of the *Portugueſe*, and ſome other ſlaves ſet at liberty: 1630 they conſiſted of 100, or 120 men fit to bear arms, who did conſiderable ſervice to the ſtate of *Amboyna*; they were very good chriſtians and faithful, and furniſh'd an extraordinary *Korrakore* of 4 *Nadjos*; they accounted themſelves to be of the tribe of the *Oliſivas*, their chieftain was then *Anthony de Coſto*.

Halou. To *Halou* belongs the village *Hative-Kiſchilett*, they are pretty well peopled, and chriſtians, and furniſh a *Karrakore* of 4 *Nadjos*; *Diego Paty* was captain of *Halou*, and *Adam Marano* of *Hative-Kiſchilett*.

Pouta. *Pouta* has only two ſmall villages belonging to it, *viz.* *Kapa* and *Chery*; their captains were *Stephen Terſera* of *Pouta*; *Manuel Lopes* of *Kapa*, and *Andrew Pardia* of *Chery*.

Oettomary. The inhabitants of *Oettomary* did revolt three times, but were in 1626 reduced to obedience by the then governor Mr. *Gorkum*, they were then under the tuition of *Don Pedro de Oettomary* their captain, who was a very honeſt perſon, and ever ſince that time they have adhered faithfully to the company. They are generally ſtout ſoldiers and good chriſtians, for they frequent the chriſtian congregations, and add more children to our ſchools than the other villages do. They furniſh a *Korrakore* with 4 *Nadjos*, and are of the *Oliſivas*. The four villages of *Ourien*, *Larik*, *Wakkacſive*, and *Aſſelou* ſtand likewiſe under the juriſdiction of the company; they are all blacks and ſtout fellows, they belong to the *Oliſivas*, and acknowledge *Hittoe* for their captain, yet under the protection of the company. They furniſh a *Korrakore* of 4 *Nadjos*. Thus the two villages of *Alang* and *Lillebay* belong to the company: The inhabitants are chriſtians, except 3 or 4 families at *Alang*. 1659. Of the laſt, one *Salvador* was captain, and of *Lillebay*, *Baſtiaen Kaſtango*. The inhabitants are likewiſe of the tribe of the *Oliſivas*.

Theſe ſix villages are obliged to furniſh the *Dutch Eaſt-India* company with a great quantity of cloves; to wit 300 *Bahar per annum*; vaſt numbers of clove trees having been planted hereabouts, about 1630, which are come to full perfection ſince, and produce vaſt ſtore of fruit. Thus 1636, the planting of clove trees was ſo far encouraged on the ſouth-ſide of this iſland, that each family was obliged to plant, at leaſt, ten trees every year, the ground being very fit hereabouts for this purpoſe; they were alſo not negligent in planting coco and other fruit trees. *Kamariay*, *Seriwawan* and *Kayrato*, are three villages near the ſea-ſhore; the inhabitants are abſolutely devoted to the ſervice of the company, and appear ſometimes with an *Orangay* at the head of them at the fort. They adhere to thoſe of *Mardykka*, and belong to the *Oliſivas*.

Near the point of the bay are four villages, *Quelipapoety*, *Amaſſee*, *Marykque*, and *Savoukque*. The firſt furniſhes a *Korrakore* with 3 *Nadjos*, the three laſt a *Korrakore* of 4 *Nadjos*. In the village of *Amaſſee* lived at that time two young lads, ſons of the *Orangkay*, who formerly had been hoſtages with the *Dutch* governors for ſeven years, but now were got into the government of theſe villages, and ſeem'd well inclin'd to the company's intereſt.

The iſle of *Amboyna* has many high and ſteep mountains, call'd *Gounen* by the natives, which have ſeveral fair villages built on the top, and are irrigated with very clear and freſh-water ſprings. The vallies ſerve for walking-places, by reaſon of the many fine trees that are planted there, as the mountains ſerve the inhabitants for a ſhelter againſt their enemies in time of war, being for the moſt part inacceſſible. There is a certain rock here, call'd the *Elephants Rock*, from its ſhape and bigneſs, from whence iſſues forth a rivulet as clear as cryſtal, which ſlides gently thro' the adjacent verdant plain, whence is a very pleaſant walk up to the rock. *Mountains in Amboyna.*

However the air of *Amboyna* is none of the wholeſomeſt. There rages in this and the reſt of the *Molucco* iſlands, a certain diſtemper, both among the natives and ſtrangers, which by its ſymptoms reſembles altogether the *French* pox (for which reaſon the *Dutch* call it the *Pox of Amboyna*) except that this is communicated without any carnal conjunction. In the face, arms and legs, nay all over the body, appear certain cruſty boils, which *The air of Amboyna.*

1659. which either turn ſchirrous, or if they come to a ſuppuration, a ſlimy, tough but ſharp matter iſſues from thence, reſembling in all its circumſtancee the *French* pox, except that they are not ſo painful, neither corrode the bones. This diſeaſe is attributed to a peculiar conſtitution of the climate and the air, and the exceſſive uſe of ſea-fiſhes, and coco nuts called *Zago*, and of the liquor called *Saguweer*. At firſt this diſtemper is eaſy enough to be cured, but if it takes root, not without great difficulty. They commonly apply the ſame remedies as we do in the *French* pox, in the ſpleen and dropſy: to wit, the decoctions of chica, ſarſaparilla, and guajacum, and purge them ſoundly betwixt whiles.

Its conſtitution. The iſle of *Amboyna* is pretty fertile; it produces millet, tobacco, coco-nuts, potatoes, pinang, oranges, lemons, citrons, ſugar, bamboo canes, and ſeveral other fruits. Some places here afford likewiſe nutmegs, but in no great quantity, neither have they ſo good as thoſe in the iſle of *Banda*, neither do they grow wild here, but the trees are planted in orchards. Neither are they deſtitute of divers ſorts of beaſts, eſpecially roe-bucks and hogs, and have great ſtore of fiſhes; but the chief products of *Amboyna* are cloves, which grow wild here; they are called *Nagalen* (nails) by the *Dutch*, from their ſhape, being flat on the top and ſharp at the end: They call them alſo *Geroffel nagelen*, perhaps from the *Greek Karyophyllon*. In the *Molucco* iſlands they call the cloves *Caampe* or *Chanpe*; in the iſle of *Java Sianeke*, and in *Malacca*, *Synken* or *Thinka*; the *Arabians*, *Perſians*, *Turks*, and moſt of the *Indians*, call them *Kalafur*.

The clove-tree. The clove-tree grows up in form of a pyramid, its branches ſprouting forth cloſe together. This tree is of the bigneſs of our cherry-trees, but in the whole reſembling moſt to a large laurel-tree, the leaves being very near of the ſame ſhape; the bark on the ſtem is of a greyiſh colour like that of the olive-tree. In the midſt of each leaf is a large vein which ſends forth many leſſer branches; theſe leaves grow on long ſtalks, ſometimes ſingle, but for the moſt part in cluſters; thoſe that grow near the extremities of the branches are of a purple colour, but the reſt dark green, if they are rubbed betwixt your hands they ſcent as ſtrong as the cloves themſelves, and ſo do the branches. On the extremities of theſe branches grow certain ſprouts which produce certain buds, and thoſe again flowers, ſometimes 10 or 20 in a knot, which at laſt produce the fruit, which are tough whilſt they are growing, but hard when come to maturity. At firſt they are green, then appear of a pale red colour, as if the trees were covered with ſcarlet, affording a very agreeable ſight to the beholders, becauſe there is often more fruit than leaves on the trees. The bloſſom is white at firſt, not unlike our cherry bloſſom, each leaf of the flower having three ſmall ſtreaks, then they turn green, afterwards red, and laſt of all dark yellow inclining to black. They reſemble in ſhape a nail, with a ſmall hollowneſs in the head, in which remains a thin ſkin which falls off as ſoon as it is touched. The cloves are very hard of ſubſtance; when they ſee more bloſſoms than leaves, they foretel great plenty of fruit; the bloſſoms ſmell much finer and ſtronger in dry than in rainy weather, and the firſt is looked upon as the moſt fruitful, it being common in a dry ſeaſon to ſee more bloſſoms than leaves, though even in ſuch a ſeaſon the clove-trees don't hit always alike, for every third or fourth year it is obſerved that they don't bear ſo plentifully as otherwiſe, juſt as if the tree at that time did remit its vigour ſpent the preceding years. The cloves are gathered once a year, *viz.* from the middle of *September* or beginning of *October* till *February*, this being the beſt ſummer ſeaſon here. Some are gathered, the reſt beat down with canes like flails; but this laſt way is not ſo ſafe as the other, for unleſs they be very careful, they bruiſe the tender ſprigs of the tree, which renders it the leſs fruitful the next following year, tho' the ſeaſon be never ſo good. Before they begin to gather, the ground under the tree is cleared of weeds, that they may not loſe part of the fruit. What cloves are left upon the trees grow very large as they ripen, much bigger than the reſt, but are not ſo fit for uſe. The next following year they drop from the tree, and though they are not ſo aromatick as the others, they are uſed for ſeed, and produce new trees, for which reaſon they are called the mother-cloves; for after they are dropt upon the ground they will take root, and in 8 or 9 years time it will come to the perfection of a good tree, and prove as fruitful as the reſt; but if theſe ſprouts be tranſplanted once in two or three years, they will bear more and better fruit. They ſay the clove-tree will hold good 100 years; the fruit immediately after gathering is dark yellow inclining to black, but if dry'd turns quite black, and if they dip them firſt in ſea-water it preſerves them from being worm eaten. Thus prepared they are laid up in ſtore-houſes and are tranſported to other places, where they are picked and the ſtalks taken from them, which are ſold ſeparately. The *Dutch* call theſe ſtalks *Nagelgruis* (the rubbiſh of cloves) and the *Portugueſe Baſton*. Cloves are hot and dry, of a bitteriſh biting taſte, but eſpecially when they are

CLOVE TREE

1659. are dry'd. They ſeem to conſiſt of a gummous ſulphurous ſubſtance, with a ſtrong drying and attractive quality; as for inſtance, when the *Indians* are to deliver a certain quantity of cloves, they put in the warehouſe, where they are, a tub full of water, which is in a ſhort time attracted by the cloves, to the no ſmall benefit of the ſeller, it being obſervable that the cloves weigh as much the heavier as the water that was put there weighed before. The *Dutch* put this likewiſe often in practice. Some are of opinion that the cloves by their extraordinary drying and attractive quality, draw all the moiſture of the ground round about the tree to that degree that no weeds or graſs can grow there; but this is a vulgar error, the bareneſs of theſe ſpots of ground being not to be attributed to the cloves, but to the owners themſelves who weed and keep them clear, thereby to afford the more nouriſhment to the trees, and not to loſe part of the fruit when they are gathering or beating them from the trees.

'Tis true, the clove-trees are planted for the fruit ſake, neverthleſs the bloſſoms, leaves, ſprigs, nay the gum itſelf that iſſues from the tree, are not deſtitute of an aromatick virtue, and afford very good medicines; the *Indian* and *Portugueſe* women diſtil out of the green cloves and leaves, a water and a ſpirit which is very odoriferous and cephalick; and an excellent remedy againſt the palſy, called by the natives *Beribery*. Againſt the ſame diſtemper they preſerve alſo the cloves with ſugar, and draw an oil both of cloves and leaves. Cloves boiled in milk are accounted a great provocative, they are very cordial, and if chewed take away a ſtinking breath. They make a pickle of the green cloves, which are not ſo hot as the reſt, and provoke the appetite. Perſons of quality put green cloves in vinegar, which is a great ſtrengthener of the ſtomach. The *Indians* call the vinegar *Atzjar*.

Royal clove. There is another kind of cloves but not commonly known, being very ſcarce and dear. The *Indians* call them *Tvinka Papoha*, or curled cloves, tho' they might rather be called ear-cloves, becauſe they ſprout forth like the corn ears. The *Dutch* call them *Royal Cloves*, becauſe they are in ſuch high eſteem among the kings of the *Molucco* iſlands, not ſo much for their excellent taſte and ſcent (in which they ſurpaſs all others) but for their ſcarcity's ſake; for if we may believe them, no more than two ſuch clove-trees are as yet found out, and that in the iſle of *Makjan* only: One of theſe two trees exceeds the other in bigneſs, but both are like the common clove-trees, except that they are much taller, and the cloves bigger and of a different ſhape from the common clove, as may be ſeen by the draught. 1659.

In the iſland of *Ceylon* are likewiſe abundance of wild clove trees, but bear no fruit. It is credibly affirmed that in former times the inhabitants of the *Molucco* iſlands were ignorant as to the uſe of the cloves, till ſome *Chineſe* coming that way found out their goodneſs, and from thence tranſported them to *China*, and ſo farther to the *Indies*, *Perſia*, *Arabia*, and other parts. The iſlands *Ternate*, *Makjan*, *Moſier* and *Batsjan*, did likewiſe in former days abound in clove trees, but purſuant to an agreement made with the kings of the iſlands ſome years ago, the ſame have been rooted out.

In the iſle of *Amboyna* grows likewiſe the wild palm, or *Zagou* tree, otherwiſe called *Papedo*. This tree reſembles the other palm or coco trees, the leaves hanging downwards on the branches, the lowermoſt of which periſh commonly: This tree bears but one fruit, which is of no uſe. The inhabitants make bread of the pith of the young trees; for on the top of the tree grows a certain head like a cabbage, in which is incloſed a certain white flower called *Zagou*, and the bread made of this flower *Zagou manda*. This flower they mix with water, and let it riſe a little, then they put it in earthen pots, put burning coals all round about it, and ſo bake it. This bread, whilſt it is new, taſtes very ſweet, and is of a very agreeable ſcent, but ſoon grows dry, and is brittle and ſhining like glaſs. They alſo mix this *Zagou* with water, and boil it like pap, into which they ſqueeze one or two lemons, and ſo ſtir it about with a ſtick; it is very cooling, and of an agreeable taſte. They eat it with a ſtick, which they put into the pap, and turn it round, till a ſufficient quantity of the pap, which is very glutinous, almoſt like turpentine, adheres to the ſtick, and ſo put it into the mouth. Out of theſe young trees they draw, like out of the coco-trees, a liquor; they cut one of the branches near the top, and in a hole made for that purpoſe, put a piece of hollow *Bamboo* cane, (which in theſe parts are uſed inſtead of tubs, pails and mugs) thro' which in a ſhort time, iſſues forth a great quantity of liquor as ſweet as honey, call'd by the natives *Zagouweer* or *Zagewer*, but is ſomewhat harſher than the liquor drawn from the true coco-tree. *Wild palm-tree called Zagou.*

In the iſle of *Amboyna* they put a certain bitter root, call'd by a general name *Oubat* into this liquor, which preſerves it for ſome time, for elſe this *Zagouweer* turns quickly as ſour as vinegar, and is then uſed for ſuch. They diſtil alſo a certain liquor of it call'd *Arak*. This *Zagouweer* is the

common

1659. common drink, and sold in publick houses for a farthing a glass, but used in great quantity, proves very obnoxious to the nerves, especially whilst you are hot, when it must be taken with great precaution, else it will infallibly cause the gripes in the guts and palsies, call'd by the natives *Beribery*, which leaves a paleness in peoples faces for ever after. Sometimes they can draw 30 quarts of this liquor in 24 hours out of one single tree. In the isle of *Java* there are likewise some of these *Zagou* trees, but the liquor is, as far as I know, not valued at *Batavia*. They draw the liquor out of these trees till they die, and I was told that there was some of these trees in the woods of *Amboyna*, which will give as much liquor in 24 hours, as a man is able to carry away upon his shoulders. Some other islands belong to the isle of *Amboyna*, to wit, the adjacent large country of *Ceram*, the isles of *Manipa*, *Quelang*, and *Amblau*.

Amboyna *under whose jurisdiction.* The isle of *Amboyna* is divided into two parts; one of which is under the jurisdiction of the *Dutch East-India* company; the other under the king of *Ternate*. Unto the company belongs the country of *Laitimor*, where is the fort of *Victoria*, and the wooden fort *Wantrou*, and on the pass of *Bagoale*, the redoubt call'd *Middleburgh*. The three islands *Homa*, *Honomoa*, and *Nausalaut*, which produce great quantities of cloves: The whole coast of *Hittoe* with the redoubts, the *Amsteldam* at *Hila*, the *Rotterdam* at *Larike*, and the *Leoden* at *Hittoe* and *Lamma*; and several small wooden forts at *Ourien*, *Lebelebu*, *Ceit*, and *Way*. Under the king's jurisdiction are the country and coast of *Ceram*, the isles *Amblau*, *Manipa*, *Bonoa*, and some others.

The fort Victoria. The fort *Victoria*, (the staple of the company here) lies five leagues deep in the country, being defended by four bulwarks, a good ditch, and a considerable garrison, with suitable provisions and ammunition. During my stay here, there was a large crocodile in the ditch, which did vast mischief to the wild fowl belonging to Mr. *Hustard* the governor, who took great delight in them. Some soldiers and others were ordered to place themselves whereabouts they supposed the crocodile had his lurking place, but could not meet with it; till at last the crocodile on a sudden leaped towards the secretary of the governor, whom he had certainly devoured, had not the rest that were near at hand, with sticks and half pikes kill'd the beast immediately, which was extraordinary large. Round about the castle live several *Dutch*, *Chinese*, and other nations. Within and without the fort is a church, where divine service is held both in the *Dutch* and *Malacca* tongue.

The men wear large whiskers, but little hair upon their chin; they only cover themselves with a slight piece of stuff round the buttocks and belly. The women tie their hair up in many knots: He that intends to marry a young maid, buys her from her father for money; but if she proves barren, the marriage is null and void: In former ages the natives were a most barbarous people, men-eaters and pagans. Now adays they are for the most part *Mahometans*, the rest are *Christians*, some *Roman Catholicks*, such as were converted by the *Portuguese*, others professing the *Protestant* religion, which was first introduced there in 1647. The *Dutch* have erected schools in all the villages to instruct the youth in reading and writing, and in the fundamentals of the christian religion. The natives are generally brave, but very deceitful and treacherous; they are naturally addicted to laziness, and are so obstinate, that they chuse rather to die than to leave their antient customs. They make use of certain small vessels in time of war. They are very swift in their motion, and managed by *Pagagen* or oars. They call these vessels *Korrakore*, and are shaped like a dragon, the head representing the forecastle, and the tail the stern. They have also some lesser boats call'd *Paros*. Their houses are built of *Bamboe* canes and *Zagou* trees; they sleep likewise in bedsteads made of *Bamboe* canes, or sometimes upon mats only. 1659. *Manners and customs of the* Amboynese.

Their weapons are bows and arrows, half pikes, javelins, scimeters, targets and firelocks, all which they manage with great dexterity, as well as the darts. They have also a kind of hollow pipes, out of which they shoot great numbers of small poison'd arrows; the wounds made with them prove commonly mortal, unless the poison be removed immediately by cutting it out. *Their weapons.*

The women of *Amboyna* are very lascivious, and extremely desirous of the christians; if they find themselves disappointed in their expectation, or that they are left by their gallants, they have a way of infecting them with a certain poison, the operation of which is so slow, that they die a lingring death, neither can they cohabit with any other woman, unless they receive proper antidotes from the same woman that poisoned them. Many *Chinese* live in *Amboyna*, tho' for the most part among the *Mahometans* at *Hittoe*, *Lochoe*, and in *Ceram*. In the year 1636, at the request of king *Hittoe*, three or four *Chinese* were permitted to settle under him, with this limitation however, that they should pay the usual taxes to the *Dutch* receiver-general of *Amboyna*; afterwards one *Chinese* was allow'd to live in each village, to provide them with *Their women.*

I distill'd

1659. distill'd *Arack*. About the year 1636, the slaves belonging to the *Dutch* had got a custom to run away from their masters, and to shelter themselves among the *Mahometans*, but several being punished with death, pursuant to a proclamation published for that purpose, the rest were so terrified thereat, that no such thing was heard of for a great while after. Certain negro christians dwelt likewise in *Amboyna*, commonly call'd *Mardiikers*.

Courts of justic in Amboyna.

There are three courts or councils belonging to the *Dutch* in *Amboyna*; first the court martial, secondly the civil court of justice, and thirdly the great council or council of state.

The court martial used to meet every *Monday* and *Thursday*, composed of the governor, the head factor, and under factor of the company, a captain, a lieutenant, one of the eldest sergeants, and a secretary; these took cognizance of all matters relating to the soldiers and garrisons.

The civil court of judicature was kept in the town, consisting of four officers of the company, of four of the chiefest inhabitants, and of four or five *Orankays* of the council of state; besides which they had two clerks, one a *Dutchman*, and the other a native of *Amboyna*, and two attendants. The head factor in the castle was president here; they took cognizance of, and gave sentence with the governor's approbation, in all civil and criminal cases, neither had the villages any right of exercising of justice without them.

The council of state, or the *Orangkays* of the chamber, who in conjunction with the governor, and his councellors, were to deliberate concerning all publick affairs, such as the equipping of *Korrakoren*, or the management of a war against an enemy, had their seats appointed thus.

Andrea, king of *Rossenive*.
Manuel, the old king of *Kielang*.
Laurentz de Sylva, king of *Soya*.
Simaon Ema, captain of *Ema*.
Laurenzo Marcus, captain of *Hative*.
Diego Pati Halloe, captain of *Halloe*.
Anthony da Costa, captain of the *Mandiikers*.
Don Pedro, captain of *Vettomoery*.
Salvador Paty Alang, captain of *Alang*.
Simon Baguala, captain of *Baguala*.
John Barkabessier, captain of *Way*.
Stephen Tercera, captain of *Pouta*.
Pedro Anthonio, captain of *Tacieri*.
Fernando Latoehalat, captain of *Rossenive*.

How Amboyna *came under* Ternate.

In former ages the island of *Amboyna* was subject to its own kings, till it was reduced under the obedience of the kings of *Ternate*, which according to the relation of the inhabitants happened thus:

Many years ago reign'd a king in *Ternate* call'd *Babou*, son of *Chieroen Diamelou*, who having been the first that introduced *Mahometism* there, was in great esteem with the *Mahometan* priests, who to this day pay a great veneration to his memory. In the mean while, some differences being arisen betwixt the villages of *Warnalete* and *Makatit*, belonging to the district of *Warnoela*, and the last being unable to cope with those of *Warnalete*, they underhand sought for aid by king *Babou*; who having granted their request, sent a good fleet of *Korrakoren*, under the command of his councellor *Samarou*, to the cape of *Saragi*, betwixt *Erang* and *Lissidy*, where they came to an anchor; the inhabitants of *Cambello*, who as well as those of *Erang* and *Lissidy*, had submitted to king *Babou* against those of *Makatit*, advised the inhabitants of *Warnalete* to go to meet *Samarou*, and to purchase his favour by some presents, which being done accordingly, they all attack'd, in conjunction with *Samarou*, those of *Makatit*, and forced them to submission; but *Samarou*, not thus satisfied, reduced all the circumjacent islands under his king's obedience; so that this island owed the loss of its liberty to the intestine divisions of its inhabitants; *Samarou* returning home victorious, was receiv'd with great demonstrations of affection by king *Babou*, who in reward of his service, honour'd his son *Robohongy* with the title and dignity of *Salahakkum* or Stadtholder of these conquer'd countries, having before been dignified with the title of *Kimelaha*, which his successors in the stadtholdership have retained ever since, tho' it be certain, that not *Kimelaha* but *Salahakkum* signifies a stadtholder in their tongue. After the death of *Robohongy*, his eldest son *Adja* succeeded him in the stadtholdership, who was succeeded by his brother *Bassi Frangi*. After him came *Frangi*, who for his treachery was beheaded by *Sabadiin* of *Louhou* his brother's son. *Leliatte*, son to *Bassi Frangi*, then thrusts himself into the government without consent of the king, and following the footsteps of his predecessor, receiv'd the same reward. He was succeeded in the stadtholdership by *Madira*, son of *Sabadiin*, the seventh in order, our company having made use of all their interest with *Hamsia*, king of *Ternate*, to procure him that dignity, in consideration of the singular kindnesses they had received from his father. But they soon found themselves mistaken in their choice; for this *Madira*, of the antient race of the *Tomogolo*'s, of which *Samarou* was the first, rebell'd 1650, against the king, and with the assistance of the inhabitants, made himself master of several strong holds; to wit, *Amblau*

Madira *rebels against the king of* Ternate.

1659. *blau*, *Manipa*, *Lissidy*, *Hatua* the lesser, *Assahoudy*, *Laala* and *Noussatelo*, plunder'd all that oppos'd him, and kill'd about 80 persons belonging to the *Dutch* company. One *John Pays*, captain of *Hatuwe*, *Tawiro* and *Houkonalo*, living near the fort of *Amboyna*, was shrewdly suspected to have had a hand in this conspiracy, which *Simon Kos* (who commanded in the absence of *Arnold Outshorn* at *Amboyna*) having got notice of, secured him in the fort till the arrival of Mr. *Outshorn*, when the war broke out with great violence on both sides.

How the Portuguese *became masters of* Amboyna.

The *Portuguese* made themselves masters of *Amboyna*, 1546, in the following manner: At the time when *Anthony Galvan* was governor of *Ternate*, a great fleet of small vessels belonging to the island of *Java*, *Banda*, *Macassar* and *Amboyna*, was sent to the *Molucco* islands to fetch cloves; *Galvan* being advertis'd thereof, and fearing lest they should by this means spoil the spice trade of the *Portuguese*, armed about 25 *Korrakoren*, with 40 *Portuguese*, and 400 auxiliaries; these, under the command of *Jacob Supi Azevidi*, admiral of the sea *Molukse*, steer'd their course towards *Amboyna*, where meeting with the *Indian* fleet, they attack'd and routed them, taking many of their ships, with good store of great cannon, and a considerable sum of ready money; *Azevedi*, willing to improve this opportunity, landed in *Amboyna*, the inhabitants of which being terrified at their last defeat, did for the most part submit to the *Portuguese*, and receiv'd such laws as they thought fit to prescribe to them; which done, *Azevedi* loaden with glory and spoils, return'd as a conqueror to *Ternate*. After that time, the *Portuguese* used always in their voyages from *Malacca* to the *Molucco* islands, and in their return from thence, to provide themselves with fresh water at *Amboyna*, till 1603, this island was taken by the *Dutch* from the *Portuguese*, who got a vast booty there, tho' the *Dutch* are not very fond of living in *Amboyna*, being a place of no great plenty.

We set sail, as I told you before, the 3[d] of *May* from *Amboyna*, and with a brisk and prosperous gale arriv'd the 29th before *Batavia*.

No sooner was our ship unloaden, but I received orders to go aboard the ship *Achilles*, *John Vander Werven* master, to *Japan*. Every thing being got in readiness for our intended voyage, I took my leave from the directors of the company, and the 28th of *July* set sail with 15 ships more, Mr. *John Vander Laen* being commadore, with orders to sail to *Teywan*, to attack the city *Makao*, (a populous place, and defended by a garrison of 600 men) and to observe *Koxingas*. But scarce were we come within sight of the isle of *Anyam*, when we were overtaken by so terrible a tempest, that I can safely affirm, I never saw the like in my life, and that it is past my skill to express it; the waves rising sometimes to that height, that the very tops of our masts could not be seen, the winds sometimes falling flat upon our ships, and pressing them down flat under the abyss, so that we expected every moment to be swallow'd up by this merciless element, especially when we saw the yacht *Gorkum* (in which was *Francis Lansman*, formerly my companion in our *China* voyage) in a moment perish before our eyes, without the least possibility of saving one man. At last, however thro' God's infinite mercy the fury of the winds began to allay, when with much ado we got with our ships, which were much damag'd by the storm, into the harbour of *Teyvan* the 20th of *September*. The season for our intended voyage to *Japan* being past, as forced against my will to unload my ship here, and the design against *Makao* being laid aside for that time, because *Koxinga* was abroad with a powerful force: We set sail with the whole fleet for the islands call'd *Piskadores*, and came the 3[d] of *October* to an anchor in the *Church-Bay*: Here I received orders to prepare myself for a voyage into *Persia*, aboard the ship the *Leerdam*, loaden with sugar, which I did accordingly. 1659.

A most violent storm.

The islands of Piskadores *or* Pehu.

The islands call'd *Piskadores* or fisher-islands, and by the *Chinese Pehu*, are situate under 23 and 24 deg. northern latitude, about 12 and 13 leagues from the isle of *Teywan*. They have several good harbours, and two commodious bays, where ships may ride safely at anchor at 8 or 9 fathoms water. At the entrance of this bay are the ruins of two antient stone forts, one built by the *Dutch*, the other by the *Chinese*; and betwixt both is another fort. The country thereabouts is not hilly, abounds in grass, yet pretty strong. It contains many populous villages; these islands being all well stor'd with inhabitants, with fat cattle, especially cows, and birds of all sorts, especially with an incredible number of fine large cocks. During the rainy season they gather fresh water in cisterns or ponds, but in dry weather the water is saltish here. The country produces likewise potatoes and many other fruits in abondance, and here are always to be seen great numbers of *Chinese* vessels, which come some for fishing, some for traffick. At the entrance of the *Church-Bay*, stands to the north-side a *Chinese Pagode*, where is very good anchorage, and a convenient place for shelter to those that are bound to *Teywan*, there being no other safe harbour for great ships hereabouts. The

islands

1659. iflands *Piſkadores* are many in number; two are the moſt famous; one call'd the *Piſkadore* or *Fiſher Iſland*, the ſecond *Pehou* or *Pehu*.

The ſouth-eaſt ſide of the *Fiſher Iſland* is ſo bare, that it produces not a tree; to the weſt of it is another ſmall iſland, and the paſſage betwixt both ſo ſhallow, that a yacht is not able to paſs that way. To the ſouth of this lies another iſland, call'd by the *Dutch* the *Troubleſome Iſland*, becauſe there is no anchorage for ſhips here. About a league from thence to the weſt is a rocky iſland, or rather two ſmall rocky iſlands, divided by ſo many rocks, that there is no paſſage or anchorage near them.

Return to Teywan. After we had diſpatch'd our buſineſs here, we ſet ſail again for the iſland of *Teywan*, Mr. *Conject* was at that time governor of this iſle, who having not without reaſon conceiv'd a jealouſy at the vaſt number of ſhips and men, the *Chineſe* had brought together in the river of *Quincheu*, or in the iſle of *Ey* and *Queymuy*, on the coaſt of *China*, I was diſpatch'd thither the 31ſt of *October* with the two yachts the *Graveland* and *Mary*, with expreſs orders, to demand from *Koxinga* whether he was for peace or war, and not to tarry longer than ten days for a categorical anſwer. Nieuhoff *ſent to* Koxinga. I tarried aboard the veſſels to take care of them, whilſt my collegue went to ſpeak with *Koxinga*: Our limited time being near expired, I went aſhore in a boat, ordering our veſſels to be upon their guard. The banks of the river were ſo crouded with people, that I had much ado to paſs thro' them; by good chance I met with a *Chineſe* who underſtood *Portugueſe*, who was ſo complaiſant as to go along with me to the place, where my collegue and his attendants lodg'd; but they being gone abroad to ſee *Koxinga* muſter his forces, I was oblig'd to take the ſame way; we addreſs'd ourſelves to him, deſiring a ſpeedy and poſitive anſwer, the time of our ſtay being expired. Koxinga's *anſwer.* He gave us for anſwer, that being at preſent buſy in muſtering his forces, he would give us his reſolution to-morrow, in a letter directed to the governor of *Teywan*, which he did accordingly: In this letter he told him, that he had not the leaſt thoughts of any war againſt the company, but that he would cultivate a good correſpondence with them. To remove all occaſion of jealouſy, he ſent ſeveral merchant ſhips to *Teywan*, which however did not remove the ſuſpicion they had conceiv'd of him there, eſpecially after we on the 22d of *December* gave a verbal account of his vaſt preparations in the fort of *Teywan*. His letter was as follows.

1659.

KOXINGA's letter.

BEING at a great diſtance from you, I could not but receive your letter with a more than ordinary ſatisfaction, which I peruſed more than once, to inform myſelf the better of your intentions. You mention ſome falſe rumours, but at the ſame time ſeem to give credit to them. In my father Yquam's *time, the* Dutch *poſſeſs'd themſelves of a certain place in the iſle of* Teywan, *with his conſent for the convenience of trade, which I have not in the leaſt interrupted, and therefore judge you to be obliged to me upon that ſcore. I have of late years been ſo deeply involved in a war with the* Tartars, *that I have had no leiſure to trouble my head with an inconſiderable iſland that produces nothing but graſs: It being not my cuſtom to diſcloſe my deſigns, but rather if I aim at the eaſt to point to the weſt; how can you ſuppoſe to be inform'd of them by rumours? The reaſon why ſo few of our ſhips come to that iſland, is, becauſe they cannot trade thither with any profit, the cuſtoms being ſo heavy. It was but this year the* Tartars *made a ſtrong invaſion into the low lands of* China, *in hopes to put an end to the war with one blow, but they were ſo bravely received, that they were forced to retreat with the loſs of* 100 *of their commanders, and a great number of their men; we then retired into the iſlands of* Ey *and* Queymuy, *in hopes to draw them thither, and ſo to catch them in the trap. Concerning your complaints of having been treated in a hoſtile manner in the iſland of* Piſkadores, *if it be really ſo, it has been done without our knowledge. I ſent back an immediate anſwer, together with your preſents, to the letter ſent to me from* Batavia *four years ago; by which I underſtand, that you intended us but a very ſlender ſatisfaction, for the* Joncken *or ſhips, and the loading and money aboard them detained by you, notwithſtanding which, I did not think fit to urge this buſineſs any further, for fear of occaſioning a rupture betwixt us; it ſhall be my endeavour, as ſoon as the* Tartarian *war is brought to a concluſion, to encourage trade as much as poſſible may be, and don't queſtion but you will on the other hand contribute to it, as far as lies in your power.*

Given in the 14th year, the 19th day of the 10th month of the reign of king *Indick*.

After the reading of *Koxinga*'s letter, it was reſolved by the majority of voices not to engage in a war againſt *Koxinga*; moſt being of opinion, that at this juncture he would not undertake any thing againſt the company, tho' the governor Mr. *Conjet* was of a contrary ſentiment, which proved too true afterwards. Thus all the thoughts of war

1659. war being laid aside, the continuation of commerce with him being judged, as indeed it was, to be of more present advantage to the company, all the ships there were ordered to their respective places, and I among the rest, set sail aboard the ship the *Leerdam*, loaden with sugar for *Gamroa* in *Persia*.

The isles of Ey *and* Queymuy.

The before-mentioned islands, *Ey* and *Queymuy*, are high rocky islands; the city of *Eymny* is situate upon a high hill, pretty deep in the countrey, being surrounded with a stone wall, without which you see the ruins of an antient tower, and a *Chinese Pagode* or temple.

The city of *Queymuy* lies upon a river at a pretty distance from the sea, being the capital of the isle from whence it has borrowed its name. It has very large suburbs, which begin on the river side. Not far from thence, deeper into the country, is a strong castle, defended by a very high wall, formerly the residence of *Koxinga*. The country round about is rocky, and not very fertile, except that the valleys afford a little grass for cows; for the rest, the inhabitants feed most upon fish, and some live by traffick.

The Chinese *shelter themselves in these two islands.*

It was not long before the *Chinese*, being forced by the *Tartars* to quit the continent of *China*, and *Koxinga*, strengthned with near 25000 fugitives, and about 500 vessels, they resolved to shelter themselves in the two before-mentioned islands of *Ey* and *Queymuy*, and finding himself in a condition to undertake something against us; he embark'd 20000 of his best men aboard a great number of *Chinese Joncken* or vessels, and the 30th of *May* 1661, appeared within a league of the fort *Zelandia* in the isle of *Teywan*, steering his course directly to the shore, where his countrymen, living in that island, were ready to receive him, with their carts and other necessaries; and soon after, posted a considerable number of his vessels betwixt the fort and the redoubt call'd the *Province*. This put our people under no small consternation, they being not provided either with vessels or forces, to encounter so formidable a power. However captain *Pedel* and *Aldorp*, the first with 240, and the second with 200 men, were sent out to endeavour to prevent the enemies landing, and 4 ships, *viz.* the *Hector*, the *Graveland*, the *Finch*, and the yacht *Mary*, were ordered to fall upon their fleet, which was put in execution immediately. About 60 of the *Chinese Joncken*, each with 2 great guns in the forecastle, came up with our vessels, but were so warmly received, that two of them were sunk, and the rest so much disabled, that they were all glad to retire, except six only, which kept close together, and shot so furiously upon us, that they seem'd all to be on fire; the *Hector* took fire by an accident, and so together with the *Joncken* that lay aboard her, blew up into the air. The other three ships, notwithstanding this fought it out bravely, and killed above a 1000 *Chinese* besides those wounded in the engagement. The yacht *Mary* was also set on fire, but was saved by the indefatigable care and labour of the seamen. On the land-side captain *Pedel*, having divided his forces into two bodies, and exhorted them to stand it out bravely, gave the enemy a very warm salute with his firelocks, which kill'd many of them as they were landing; notwithstanding which, they were so far from giving ground, as we flattered ourselves they would have done, that they sent whole showers of arrows among our people, and at the same time sent a strong detachment to the right, which taking compass round a hill, attack'd us in the flanks, which so terrified our soldiers, that they threw down their arms, and wading thro' the water got into a pilot's boat, and so ashore, leaving the captain with 19 men only, to the mercy of the enemies; upon which, immediate orders were sent to captain *Aldorp* to retire with his forces to the fort; the enemy landed without any farther opposition, and in 4 hours time cut of all communication betwixt the redoubt, the province, and the fort, and betwixt this and the open country; most of the inhabitants afterwards joining with them against us. *Koxinga* being soon informed of our present condition, in very ignominious terms summon'd the fort, threatning to put all to fire and sword if we did not surrender immediately. It was then taken into consideration, whether, considering the enemy had cut off all communication with the redoubt the *Province*, and his great strength, it were not adviseable to treat with *Koxinga*, and to offer the surrender of one of the forts, provided we might preserve a free trade, rather than to lose all; which being agreed upon, and at our request a passport granted for that purpose by *Koxinga*, we sent *Thomas Yperan*, head factor of the fort, and Mr. *Leonardus* the fiscal, as our deputies to him, to salute him in the name of the governor and the council, and to wish him success in all his undertakings, provided they were not intended against the interest of the company. In their letter they told him, that they could have wish'd to have seen him in another posture here, and that they were surprized to find him in arms, without the least declaration of war, that if he had any real cause of being offended, they were ready to give him satisfaction, and to cultivate a good understanding with him. The deputies

Koxinga attacks Teywan.

The Dutch *endeavour to prevent his landing.*

Engagement betwixt the Dutch *and* Chinese.

The Dutch *fly.*

The Chinese *victorious.*

Deputies sent to Koxinga.

1659. ties had express orders, that in case *Koxinga* would not hearken to any accommodation, without the surrender of both the forts, they should treat no farther, and tell him that the company was in a condition to revenge this injury. With these instructions they went the 3[d] of *May* to *Koxinga*'s camp, which was then about 12000 strong, and busy in the siege of the redoubt *Province*. They were armed with three different sorts of weapons; the first with bows and arrows, which they manage with great dexterity; the second with scimeters and targets only, wherewith they cover themselves, and so break in upon an enemy, when they are seconded by their pikemen, whose arms are backswords and pikes of three or four foot long, with broad and sharp irons at the end.

The deputies received into the camp. The deputies were at their first entrance into the camp, received by one of their chief commanders, and conducted into a spacious tent, where they stay'd till *Koxinga* was at leisure to admit them to audience. Whilst they stay'd there, several of the enemies troops march'd by their tent, and as far as they could perceive, the same at several times, to make the greater ostentation of their strength. *Koxinga* was in the mean while employed in combing his black shining hair, a great ornament among the *Chinese*, which done, the deputies were introduced into his tent, which was all hung with blue, he himself seated in an elbow chair, behind a four square table; round about him attended all the chief commanders clad in long robes without arms, and in great silence, with a most awful countenance. On both sides towards the door, his life-guards were placed in very good order. The deputies address'd themselves to him in low *Dutch*, and delivered their letter, which being translated into the *Chinese*, *Koxinga* answered.

KOXINGA's answer.

THat *he was sensible that the good correspondence the* Dutch East-India *company had hitherto cultivated with him, as well as with all the other* Indians *princes, was no longer durable than they found it consistent with their own interest; which always ceased as soon as they found their account in it; that it was contrary to his custom to divulge his thoughts or designs, yet he could not dissemble that it was by reason of the war he was engaged in against the* Tartars, *he had not taken possession of this island, which as it always belonged to the* Chinese, *so it was not injustice that now they stood in need of it themselves, they might retake it from foreigners, who were only settled there by permission. That he was not come there to engage in a war with the* Dutch, *but only to take possession of his own. That he was willing they might take away all that belonged to them, that they might demolish the forts and carry away their cannon; for which purpose he was ready to lend them as many of his ships and men as they wanted, notwithstanding they had so lately attacked him both by sea and land, when he had given them sufficient proofs of his strength.* He told them further, *that they were very proud and haughty in pretending to defend so inconsiderable a fort* (meaning the redoubt the province) *with so small a force against his numerous army, which he threatned to destroy, so as not to leave one stone upon another:* He boasted *that if his forces were united he was able to conquer heaven and earth*; concluding, *that they must take a very short resolution.* 1659.

Our deputies gave for answer, *That since the* Dutch *had left the* Piskadore *islands; this island was surrendred into their hands by contract; but that if he* (Koxinga) *had any pretensions upon the company, they were ready to treat about it, and give him satisfaction.* But after several contests, finding him quite averse to hearken to any accommodation, unless they could surrender all, they departed, protesting that the company would shew their resentments in due time, and so set up the red flag.

Before their departure from the camp they had obtained leave of *Koxinga* to go through the fort the *Province* in their return home; here they found things in a very indifferent posture, and the fort not in a condition to hold out above a week longer, all their powder and ball being spent, there being not enough left to withstand an assault: This, with the weakness of the place, induced the deputies to consent that they might capitulate with the enemy, provided they could get liberty to transfer the garrison into the fort. *The deputies leave the camp. Come into the fort the* Province.

The deputies arrived the same day in the great fort, where having given an account of their transactions, the governour *Conjet* and the rest of the commanders seeing all the communication betwixt them and the redoubt the *Province*, nay with the whole island entirely cut off by the enemy, were at a great loss what to resolve upon at such a juncture as this: After mature deliberation, the only hopes they had left was, to defend the fort *Zelandia* till such time they could be relieved from *Batavia*, which considering the northern *Monzon*, might perhaps take up a whole twelve months time. However it was resolved to defend this fort to the last extremity, notwithstanding the redoubt the *Province* had been forced to surrender, the garrison with all the cannon being fallen into the enemies hands, who had made them prisoners of war. *Arrive at the great fort.* *Resolved to defend this fort to the last.*

To

1659.

They leave the city.

To prepare themſelves for a more vigorous defence, all that were able to bear arms were taken into the fort, and the city ſet on fire, which however could not be executed ſo ſpeedily, but that the enemy preſerved ſome ware and other houſes, by timely quenching the flame, which ſerved them for places of ſhelter. Soon after they began to batter the fort with 28 pieces of cannon, but their cannon as well as their men being expoſed to our ſhot, we plied them ſo warmly with cartrages, and other ſuch like materials, that the ſtreets thereabouts were all covered with the dead carcaſſes of the *Chineſe*, and the reſt were forced to ſhelter themſelves in the by-lanes, leaving their cannon to our mercy, ſome of which were rendered unſerviceable. On the other ſide of the fort 6000 *Chineſe* advanced boldly under our cannon, and attacked our works hand to hand, but were beaten back with great loſs to an adjacent hill; upon which the beſieged made a vigorous ſally, and nailed up all their cannon. It was then propoſed to make a general ſally, but conſidering the diſproportion betwixt us and the enemy, who were advanced under our cannon, it was judged too dangerous, for fear, if we ſhould miſcarry, the enemy might force their way at the ſame time into the fort. The next day the beſieged made another ſally, and carried off a ſix pounder into the fort. The enemy finding all his attacks unſucceſsful, kept the fort cloſe blockt up, and in the mean while made the open countrey feel the effects of his rage; they made all the *Dutch* inhabitants, eſpecially the miniſters and ſchoolmaſters, priſoners, becauſe as they pretended, two certain miniſters had under hand encouraged their pariſhioners to kill all the *Chineſe* living among them, not queſtioning but the reſt would follow their example; but as it commonly happens in things of this nature where many are privy to a deſign, this had been diſcovered by ſome out of fear, or hopes of reward, for which the ringleaders ſuffered a moſt miſerable death, being crucified by the *Chineſe*, and their croſſes erected in their reſpective villages.

The Chineſe *batter the fort.*

The Chineſe *repulſed.*

A Dutch *ſhip taken by the* Chineſe.

Some *Dutch* ſea-men had no better ſucceſs, for 13 of them being taken in a *Dutch* ſhip by a *Chineſe* veſſel near the *Piſkadore* iſlands, theſe were put on board a *Chineſe* veſſel mann'd with 30 men, who were to carry them to *Koxinga*'s camp. So ſoon as the *Dutch* ſea-men came within ſight of the *Dutch* fort, they reſolved to fall upon the *Chineſe* (not above one half of them being above deck at a time) and ſo to carry off the ſhip the next following night; but a *Frenchman* belonging to our ſhips crew, whether out of fear, or hopes to recover his liberty, did betray their deſign to the *Chineſe*, who immediately gave the ſignal to ſome other ſhips near them to come aboard, which being done accordingly, they made them all priſoners, and forthwith ſent them to *Koxinga*'s camp, where they had their noſes, ears, and hands cut off, and in this miſerable condition were ſent into the fort for a terror to the reſt; they were committed to the ſurgeon's care, who performed his part ſo well, that not one of them died.

The Dutch *deſign to carry off a* Chineſe *ſhip.*

1659.

Miſcarry.

Among the reſt of the *Dutch* priſoners taken by the *Chineſe* in the open countrey, was one Mr. *Hambrocock* a miniſter; this man was ſent by *Koxinga* to the governour of the fort, to perſuade him to a ſurrender, upon condition, *viz.* that they ſhould depart ſafely with all that belonged to them and the company; but if he refuſed, he might have a ſufficient occaſion to repent it at leiſure; and that *Koxinga* would revenge himſelf upon the *Dutch* priſoners: With theſe inſtructions Mr. *Hambrocock* came into the caſtle, being forced to leave his wife and children behind him as hoſtages; which being a ſufficient argument to him that in caſe he did not ſucceed in his negotiation, they muſt expect nothing but death at *Koxinga*'s hands, yet was he ſo far from perſuading the garriſon to a ſurrender, that he encouraged them to a brave defence in hopes of relief; and as a farther encouragement, aſſured them that *Koxinga* had loſt many of his beſt ſhips and ſoldiers, and began to be weary of the ſiege, fearing leſt we ſhould hold it out till we received ſuccours from *Batavia*.

A meſſage ſent from Koxinga *to the beſieged.*

Mr. *Hambrocock* having made an end of what he had to propoſe, the council of war left it to his choice, whether he would rather ſtay with them or return to the camp, where he could expect nothing elſe but preſent death, every one entreated him to ſtay; he had two daughters within the caſtle, who hung about his neck overwhelmed in grief and tears, to ſee their father ready to go where they were ſenſible he muſt be ſacrificed to the rage of a mercileſs enemy; he repreſented to them, that having left his wife and two other children as hoſtages in the camp, nothing but preſent death could attend them if he returned not; and ſo untwiſting himſelf from his daughters arms, and exhorting every body to a reſolute defence, he returned to the camp, telling them at parting, that he hoped he might prove ſerviceable to his poor fellow priſoners.

He gave an account to *Koxinga* of his negotiation, and that the beſieged were reſolved not to treat, unleſs they were to remain in poſſeſſion of the caſtle, which was not at all reliſhing to *Koxinga*, who now began to be afraid of an uproar; the inhabitants having ſlain ſeveral of the *Chineſe*,

Koxinga*'s meſſenger returns.*

I

which

1645. which exasperated him to that degree, that having caused industriously a rumour to be spread abroad that the prisoners did under hand encourage the inhabitants of *Formosa* to rebel, he ordered all the *Dutch* male prisoners to be slain, which was done accordingly; some being beheaded, others killed in a more barbarous manner. The dead carcasses after they were stripped quite naked, were to the number of 500, thus buried 50 and 60 in a hole; of all the rest, only the supervisor of the countrey with 25 others, were saved and carried to *China*, tho' they even did not spare the women and children, many of whom were likewise slain, tho' some of the best were preserved for the use of the commanders, and the rest sold to the common soldiers: Happy was she that happened to fall to the lot of an unmarried man, being thereby freed from the importunities of the *Chinese* women, who are very jealous of their husbands. They were however afterwards, pursuant to the capitulation, sent back to *Batavia*. Among the slain were Mr. *Hambrocock*, Mr. *Mus*, and Mr. *Arnold Winshaim*, three ministers, and many schoolmasters, who were all beheaded.

The Dutch *prisoners killed by* Koxinga.

Whilst these things were transacting here, the *Dutch* in *Batavia* had got notice of this invasion by the *Mary* yacht, which in spite of the contrary season had found means to get thither, and to give them an account how matters stood with us. Ten ships were immediately got ready with 700 soldiers aboard them, which set sail in *June* 1661, under the command of *Jacob Kou*, and not long after arrived at the isle of *Formosa*. This unexpected relief as it put the enemy into no small consternation, so it encouraged our men to make a more vigorous defence than ever; and tho' the wind blew very hard, these ships found means to land some men and ammunition; but the winds increasing more and more, were forced to choose the main, to the no small grief of the besieged, and did not return till about a month after; when the ship called the *Urk* being forced upon a rock on the coast of *Formosa*, was split, and her men saved, from whom the enemy having understood our strength, and some other circumstances, they began to be better satisfied, because they had imagined this succour much more formidable than really it was.

Succours sent to Formosa.

However the besieged took a resolution by making a vigorous sally to dislodge the enemy from the city of *Zelandia*, and to destroy their ships. The 16th of *September* was appointed for this enterprise, but whilst some ships were engaged, the wind beginning to slacken, the rest could not come up; our men endeavoured to attack the *Chinese* in their boats, but being exposed to their shot, without being able to do them much harm, ours had the worst on't some of the boats being overset, others sunk, the rest saving themselves by flight. Two of our ships got upon the sands and were both set on fire. In this sea engagement the *Dutch* lost about 130 men, but the enemy a great many more; however this unfortunate action put a stop to the intended sally, and orders were sent to the garrisons of the two northern forts, to withdraw into the castle, the garrison of which was considerably diminished by the many skirmishes, in which the enemy got but little advantage, and lost many of their best men; which put a check for some time to their design, especially when they understood that we had sent all women, children, and other useless persons to *Batavia*, the better to enable us to make a vigorous defence. 1659.

The besieged make a sally.

The Dutch *worsted.*

Much about the same time the governor received letters from the *Tartarian* stadtholder of *Hocksieu*, who requested some ships and forces, to drive the remaining forces of *Koxinga* out of the countrey, promising to come afterwards with his whole power to the relief of *Formosa*. Hereupon *Jacob Kou* was sent thither with five ships well provided with men and ammunition; but being overtaken by a storm, lost all his anchors near the *Piskadores*, which obliged him to send back three of his ships to the island of *Teywan*: With the other two he returned to *Batavia*, where he met with but an indifferent reception.

The Tartars *promise succours.*

The besieged finding themselves by this disaster bereaved of a considerable number of men and ammunition, began to despair of holding it out much longer; so that many deserted, and among the rest a certain serjeant, who gave *Koxinga* not only an account of our weakness, but also encouraged him not to let slip this opportunity to force us to a surrender. *Koxinga* having well weigh'd the matter, attacked us with his whole force more vigorously than ever, and in *January* 1662 raised three batteries, mounted with 28 great cannon, upon the sandy grounds near the fort; the *Dutch* foresaw the danger that must needs ensue from this near approach of the enemy's batteries, and did all that they could, either with cannon or firelocks, to disturb them in their works, but these not hindring, their men continued to batter the walls till they had made a breach; then they made two several attacks, but were as often repulsed with great loss, the ground being all over covered with dead carcasses. This disaster taught them to be more cautious, and so instead of storming, they continued to fire incessantly their guns with such a fury that they laid a whole redoubt level with the ground, 1662.

The Chinese *renew the attack against the fort.*

Are repulsed.

so

1662. so that our men finding it no longer tenible, nailed up the guns, and laid some barrels with gunpowder under it, which blowed up a considerable number of *Chinese* into the air. *Koxinga* himself was in danger of having been among them, had he not been forewarned by the before mentioned serjeant, who told him that it was too dangerous to venture himself in a place so lately left by the enemy. Here *Koxinga* raised a large battery upon a rising ground, from whence he hoped to lay the body of the castle level with the ground. The *Dutch* on their side were not idle to do what possibly could be expected for their defence, with cannon shot, granados and otherwise; they raised their brest-works, and put great packs of linnen and stuffs into the breach; notwithstanding which the enemy played incessantly upon them, and against night had made so large a breach as was judged sufficient to make a general assault. Then it was the besieged began to deliberate what was best to be done in this exigency, whether, since there was no longer abiding in the castle, they should make a sally and force their way to the enemy, or whether they should abide the assault: The most were for a capitulation, there being not the least hopes left of making a sally with any success, and to resist the whole force of the *Chinese* in a place without defence, exposed to the enemies shot, was looked upon no less than to sacrifice themselves to their enemies; these considerations were so prevailing at last, that it was unanimously agreed to capitulate, and to surrender the castle upon articles; this was put in execution immediately, a truce of five days being agreed on for that purpose, at the expiration of which, after great contests it was agreed, *That every thing belonging to the company should be delivered up to* Koxinga. *That all the inhabitants, soldiers and prisoners, should have free liberty to retire to* Batavia *with all their moveables, for which purpose they should be provided with suitable conveniencies.* Thus the besieged after having endured a siege of nine months, with the loss of 1600 men, returned to *Batavia*, where the governour and members of the council of *Formosa*, after all the hazards and incredible fatigues they had been forced to undergo, were put in prison, and their goods confiscated; the governour himself being not long after condemned to a perpetual imprisonment in the isle of *Ey*; but was at the intercession of his highness the prince of *Orange*, and by orders from the directors of the *East-India* company in *Holland* discharged, and returned to his native countrey 1676. Since we have had frequent occasion to speak of the island of *Formosa*, I will give you a short account of it.

The Dutch *defend themselves to the utmost.*

The fort of Zelandia *surrendred.*

The isle of *Formosa* is situated under the 23 deg. 30 min. northern latitude. It is of an oblong figure, being not very broad in proportion to its length, which is 125 leagues. It is full of hills, but intermixed with many fertile vallies; producing great store of grass, and watered by many fine rivers. The countrey produces abundance of rice, but especially sugar, vast quantities of which are exported from thence. Most of the *Indian* fruits are to be seen here, of which more hereafter, as also several sorts of *Dutch* fruits, herbs, and roots, transplanted thither from *Holland*, as peaches, apricots, and such like; cows, oxen, hogs, wild goats, hares, and rabbets, but especially stags are here in great plenty, but the last are somewhat of a lesser size than those of *Europe*, and without horns; the inhabitants catch vast numbers of them meerly for their skins sake, the flesh being not esteem'd here, except their tongues. They have also great store of elks here, which being very strong they use in their carts instead of horses or oxen. One time the master of our ship and I being invited to dinner at his sister's that was married to a native of *Formosa*, they sent us a carr drawn by bufflers; the master of the ship who understood better how to govern the ship than those beasts, would needs supply the carr-mans place, but prickt the bufflers so unmercifully (according to the custom of the countrey) that they run away with us: for some time we kept stedfast in the carr, which overturning at last, threw us at a great distance, but to our great good fortune, without any considerable harm; we walkt the rest of the way on foot, leaving the ordinary carr-man, a native of *Formosa*, to recover the bufflers, which he did at last, and brought them home. Neither do they want partridges, wild pidgeons, and other wild fowl; there are also tygers and bears to be met with, but I never heard of any other ravenous wild beasts here. The mountains are full of brimstone, which questionless occasions so many earthquakes, unto which this isle is much subject. Some are of opinion that these mountains contain likewise gold and silver, some essays of this nature having been made with good success, but it was never attempted to dig for it. This island is destitute of good harbours for great ships, which are forced to ride at anchor in the road of some isles about twelve leagues, from thence. The countrey is very populous, for besides the natives of *Formosa*, above 25000 *Chinese* forced out of *China* by the *Tartars*, have at several times settled themselves here.

1662. *The isle of* Formosa.

The natives of *Formosa*, especially the men, are of an olive colour, fat, strong, well-limbed and nimble, some being able

Nativ. Formo...

1662. to out-run a wild boar or stag; they leap upon the back of them and so cut their throats. The mountainers are of a lesser size. The women are not altogether so large as the men, but very strong bodied, and are cloathed after the same fashion; they have black shining hair, which they tye together in a knot on the top of the head.

Their cloathing. The men throughout the summer appear for the most part quite naked, but those who do not, especially in the winter, wear a kind of silk or callico cloth, which they wrap about their bodies, and button it under the arms; the womens hangs somewhat lower down below the knees. Stuffs made of dogs hair are in great esteem with them. They cut off the dogs hair, like as we do our sheeps wool, spin and weave it afterwards. They are generally very friendly and faithful to the *Europeans*, and don't easily break a contract; they are very apprehensive, and will give a good judgment of matters; many of them were already converted to the christian religion by the industry of the ministers and schoolmasters, which were planted almost in every village, there being no small hopes that the whole island would in a little time have embraced christianity, had not the conquest of *Koxinga* overturned this good design.

Their food. Their bread is made of several roots, but rice is in the greatest esteem; tho' they sow no more than for their own use, and that scarce sufficient. Their drink is here, like all over the *Indies*, water, though they prepare likewise a strong liquor of rice in the following manner: They just parboil the rice and then beat it to a pap, then several old women chew a certain quantity of rice, which they spit out into a vessel, and mix it with the rest, to make it ferment. After they have put it into earthen pots, they pour water upon it, and after they have covered it very well, set it to ferment for two months, till it is well settled and clear, this produces a very strong liquor, which will keep good 20 years, and grow stronger every year. When they go abroad into the fields, they take of this liquor along with them to drink, and the settlement for their food; most of the rice here being consumed in these liquors.

The women manage the ground. Contrary to the custom of most other nations, the women cultivate the grounds here, and manage the rice, sugar, ginger, and other fruits of the earth; the men being employed in nothing but hunting and warlike exploits, unless they be very old, when sometimes they will give a helping hand to the women in the field. At leisure time the women catch crabs, oysters, and shrimps, which they much admire.

The men are mighty eager in hunting. Whole villages join together, and surround a great tract of ground, where they kill all they meet with, and divide it, few of the wild beasts escaping their hands at that time. They also catch wild boars and stags with snares fastned to canes; which the wild beast no sooner touches but one or other of the legs is entangled in the snare, where they kill it immediately. They have also certain cane darts of six foot long, with several bent hooks at the one, and a bell at the other end, this they throw at the stags or other wild creatures, which being fixed in the body they trace it by the sound of the bell till it begins to lose its strength by the loss of blood, and so kill it. 1662. *The men employed in hunting.*

Their houses are but one story high, but very large, built of cane, with many doors looking to all four corners of the winds, and sometimes more; they always raise their houses three or four foot high from the ground, looking upon it otherwise as unwholesome. *Their houses.*

Their houses are adorn'd with painted callico hangings, with wild boars and stags heads; with bows, arrows, clubs, pickaxes, and other warlike instruments, but especially with the skulls and bones of their enemies, which they look upon as the chiefest ornament of their houses: They eat and drink for the most part out of wooden vessels, or such as are made of bamboo-canes, but have some earthen pots to dress their victuals in, and for some other particular uses. *Their utensils.*

This isle has no king or general governor, each village being a kind of a petty common-wealth; their government consists of twelve persons, which must be at least 40 years of age, and are chosen out of the chiefest among them; they continue for life; all their power consists only in consulting what is most expedient for the common good, the result of which is proposed to the assembly of the whole village, who receive it with a great deal of sedateness, and after the breaking up of the assembly they debate among themselves what is best to be done; if they approve of the proposition made to them, it has the force of a law, if not, it is of no consequence. They are also much addicted to follow the directions of their prophetesses or she priests; at a certain season of the year, they are oblig'd to go quite naked for three months, otherwise (say they) we shall want rain. At another certain time they are debarr'd from wearing silk or other fine cloths, or if they do, their council has power to strip them of them, and to tear them to pieces before their faces, unless they redeem them by a certain number of stags-skins, rice or strong liquor. Corporal punishments are unknown *Their government.*

1662.

unknown to them; besides this prerogative of consulting and punishing, they are upon the same level with the rest.

Age in high esteem among them.

Age is the only thing in extraordinary respect among them; this they shew in giving way, either in the streets or at table, to their elders, who are also first served, and speak before the rest.

Their marriage.

The men never marry before they are 50 years of age, but the women as soon as they are marriageable. The natives of *Formosa* don't suffer their hair to grow below their ears, before they come to the state of manhood, when they let it grow as long as it can. If a young man has a mind to marry a certain maid, he sends one of his friends with the ordinary marriage presents, which are commonly a *Chinese* suit of cloths, bracelets of twisted reeds, some broad rings of iron or brass, and such like baubles of an inconsiderable value; if the maid accepts of the presents, the match is made. Whilst they are young they don't dwell together in the same house, which is not allow'd of 'till the husband be 50 years of age. But as soon as the young married man has an inclination to meet with his wife, he comes privately into her hut, which is commonly in the field, and lays himself down in the place where she commonly sleeps, where she comes to him, but is sure to send him away again early in the morning. All the children begot betwixt them, before both the husband and wife be arrived to the age of 37 years, are kill'd; for after the woman is sure she is with child, one of their she priests lays the big bellied woman upon her back, and squeezes her so long with her hands and feet till she miscarries, not without great hazard and pains, which they willingly undergo, because they reckon it a great sin to keep any children, begot before that time, alive, but preserve them carefully afterwards. The mother keeps the infant close by her till it be two years old, when it is sometimes permitted to see the father. Their marriages are as soon dissolv'd as they are contracted, and that upon very slight occasions; but if the husband parts from his wife without any reason, he loses his marriage presents, but in case of adultery, or that the woman is out-rageous, his marriage presents must be restored unto him; the women enjoy the same prerogative, both parties being afterwards at liberty to marry where they please, which sometimes happens twice or thrice a year. They make no great account of fornication, provided it may be done in private, but are very cautious of committing incest.

Justice.

Here are no courts of justice, every one being at liberty to take satisfaction for murther, theft or adultery committed against him. If a man be robb'd, and knows who the thief is, he goes streight to his house and fetches either by fair or foul means as much from thence as he thinks will sufficiently repay his loss, which however occasions great disputes, nay murther. He that has kill'd another flies for it till he has given satisfaction to the deceased's kindred, which consists commonly in some hogs and stags-skins, then he may return unmolested. Adultery, when discovered, is commonly made up with two or three hogs, according to the ability of the cuckold-maker, which done the cuckold lives both with him and his wife in good correspondence. Sometimes one or more villages engage in war against one another, and surprise those that work in the field, whom they kill, and carry their heads and what booty they can get, to their houses; this they often do in the night time; if they have had good success, they rejoyce after their return home, with eating and drinking to great excess. Those who have behaved themselves well in such an expedition, are esteemed before the rest.

Their weapons.

Their weapons are long and broad shields, instead of targets, wherewith they cover their bodies, short and broad scymeters which do great execution, darts pointed with iron; they have also bows and arrows, but use no firelocks. As far as ever I could learn, they have no writings or books; their pagan idolatry is transmitted from the parents to their children by word of mouth; they believe the world to have neither beginning nor end, and that the souls of such as have done well, shall be rewarded hereafter. As soon as they are dead, the friends erect a kind of scaffold before the door of the house, where they place the dead carcass surrounded with small standards; near by they set a vessel with water for the soul to bath it self in, and to wash away all its sins; as for instance, to have brought children into the world before 37 years of age; to have worn rich cloaths in the forbidden season; to have catch'd oysters, crabs and such like insignificant things; but murther, man-slaughter, adultery, fornication, theft, and such like horrid crimes, they look upon as small trespasses only, which may be expiated by a certain quantity of rice, stags-skins and strong liquors.

Religion.

They have several Gods, but adore two in particular; when it thunders they say the great man is angry with his spouse, and for that reason refuses to send them rain, for which reason they adore his spouse; the other they say, is of a malicious nature, and therefore adore him, for fear he should hurt them. They have no other but female priests, they sacrifice pigs, stags and fruits; during which the she priests cry out, and fall

1662. fall into extasies afterwards, with tremblings all over their bodies, as if they were possess'd by an evil spirit, and then they pretend the idol discovers his secrets to them: The standers by, which are for the most part women, in the mean while get drunk with strong liquors. These female priests ascend to the top of their temples, where they expose themselves quite naked, and wash their bodies in the sight of the people. They pretend to foretel good or ill fortune, to banish the devil, and to purge unhallowed places. It was formerly a custom in some certain villages, that if any of the natives lay sick, past all hopes of recovery, they used to tie a rope about his neck, and so pull him up and let him down again, till they had cured his distemper by a certain death. They dry their dead carcasses over a fire, which occasions a nauseous scent, whilst the kindred, relations and friends pass away the time with eating, drinking and dancing for several days together. The dry'd corps is kept two years after, and then buried in the house. This was the ancient government of the isle of *Formosa*, but since the *Dutch East-India* company has got footing there, they have introduced other laws among them, and instead of their councils, constituted one of their chief men as supervisor in every village, who administered justice, and was accountable to the governor of the island. Thus much of *Formosa*, 'tis time to return to our voyage.

The author goes to Malacca.

After we had left *Teywan*, the 11th of *December*, we arrived the 30th of the same month without any remarkable accident, before the city of *Malacca*, where we dropt anchor, and found Mr. *John Tiss* to be chief director there for our *East-India* company.

The countrey and city of Malaga.

The kingdom of *Malacca*, otherwise *Maleja* or *Maleca*, thus called after its capital city, is situate upon the same tract of ground or demi-island, which comprehends the kingdoms of *Martevan*, *Quedam*, *Pera* and some other countries extending it self as far as *Sumatra*, the streights of which border upon it to the west and south, as the kingdoms of *Pan* and *Johor* do to the east. The kingdom of *Malacca* is by some historians taken for the *Golden Chersonese* of *Ptolemy*, tho' at present it is no demi-island. There are some who affirm, that in former ages *Malacca* was join'd by a streight neck of land to the isle of *Sumatra*, instead of which you see now a branch of the ocean, which divides its self into two navigable channels; the first of which is call'd the streights of *Sinkapura*, because it borders on the east side of the cape of that name; the other is call'd the channel of *Saban*, from an island that lies to the west of it. This country extends for about 64 leagues in length, all along the sea-coast, beginning at the island of *Cambilan* or *Zabilan* as far as the isle of *Beitan*, its utmost boundary on that side, or rather it ends in the cape of *Sinkapura*, 20 leagues from *Malacca*. 1662.

Its capital city.

Its capital city is likewise call'd *Malacca*, being the same, in former time call'd *Takola*; it lies under 2 deg. 30 min. of northern latitude, opposite to *Sumatra*, in a bay at the ascent of a hill, on the west-side of the river *Muar* (otherwise call'd *Gaze* and *Tyga* and *Krosant*, or as the *Dutch* express it *Kriisorant*) which having its rise deep in the countrey, divides the castle from the city, and washing its walls, falls with a rapid current into the sea. Cross this river is a strong bridge built of stone, with several arches: This city is very large in compass, being not many years before surrounded with a wall of square stones and bastions, by the *Dutch*. It is very populous, the houses being built very close, tho' it has some very broad and handsome streets, which are planted on both sides with trees. In the midst of the city is a hill with a very fair church dedicated to *St. Paul*, on the top of it, where divine service is perform'd in *Dutch*: The steeple, church and monasteries founded here by the *Portuguese*, are much decay'd. Most of the houses here are built of strong bamboo canes, which are very durable in dry weather, tho' there are also some stone houses here; they are generally not very large, and low, provided with small appartments and slenderly furnish'd.

Malacca *when taken by the* Portuguese.

The city of *Malacca* was in 1610 taken by *Albuquerque* the *Portuguese* general, in the following manner: One *Manuel*, an *Arabian*, or rather *Mahometan*, by birth, being at that time king of *Malacca*, entred into a league with *Albuquerque*, which he soon broke after, putting all the *Portuguese* to the sword. *Albuquerque* soon after appeared before the city, and attack'd it unexpectedly, whilst the king and his courtiers were feasting at the wedding of his daughter; the *Portuguese* set fire to one end of the city, notwithstanding which, the inhabitants defended themselves like desperate men, even the women untiling the houses, and giving what assistance they could for the defence of the place; but at last the *Portuguese* having fought their way thro' the arm'd elephants, they entred the city, forcing the king to fly into the wilderness, where he died. They got a vast booty and above 200000 crowns in money. The *Portuguese* were very careful to fortify the town by a strong castle, and built several fine churches and monasteries; they had

1662. had five parochial churches, and monasteries in great numbers. Among the rest, the jesuits had erected a noble college here, with magnificent appartments; they were very liberal, and received all strangers travelling to those parts. There was a church here dedicated to our lady, where they say *Xaverius* preached often, and performed great miracles. Upon a high hill, within the city, the capuchins had a monastery; whilst the *Roman* catholicks were in possession of it, it was erected into a bishoprick, under the archbishop of *Goa*. Not many years before the *Portuguese* made themselves masters of it, it was no more than a village, but by the *Javanese* made a city.

Malacca *attack'd by the* Dutch.

The *Dutch* admiral *Corielius Matclief* 1605, appeared with 11 ships and 1300 soldiers before the city of *Malacca*, where at that time *Don Furtado de Mendoza*, a brave soldier, was commander in chief: The first thing he did was to sieze upon 4 ships that lay in the road; afterwards he set fire to the suburbs, and batter'd the place for two or three months, which occasioned great famine and mortality within the city. But the *Portuguese*, who were sensible of the importance of this place, sent a considerable fleet from *Goa* to their relief, which engaging with ours, a small fight ensued, in which the *Portuguese* and *Dutch* lost two ships each; at last the *Portuguese* finding the *Dutch* resolved to board them, retired under the castle, but were so closely pursued by *Matclief*, that he ruined their whole fleet, consisting of 16 galleots, 14 galeasses, and 14 smaller vessels, with 3000 men on board them.

The Dutch *take* Malacca.

The king of *Johor* besieged the city of *Malacca* in 1606, with 60000 men, the *Portuguese* having maintained themselves there till 1640, when the *Dutch* after a siege of six months made themselves masters of it; after the *Portuguese* had been in possession of it 130 years. The *Dutch* found here besides a vast booty, a great cannon which carried a shot of 64 pounds weight, since which time the *Dutch* have left no stone unturn'd to stock this city with all sorts of necessaries as well as with inhabitants, both *Dutch* and *Indians*. The origin and progress of *Malacca* is this, described by *Barros* and some other historians.

The origin of Malacca.

The foundation of *Malacca* was laid about 250 years before the arrival of the *Portuguese* in the *Indies*. About that time one *Sangesinga* reign'd in *Sinkapura*, situate under 30 min. of northern latitude, and in the neighbouring countrey of *Java*, one *Paravisa*, who at his death left two sons under the guardianship of his own brother, their uncle; but he having found means to murder the eldest, usurped the throne; at which some of the noble *Javanese* being highly 1662. disgusted, did with *Paramisora*, their late king's youngest son, fly to *Sinkapura*, where they met with a kind reception from *Sangesinga*, but it was not long before *Paramisora*, in combination with his *Javanese*, murder'd *Sangesinga*, and put himself in possession of his kingdom. The king of *Siam* being highly exasperated at the treachery committed against *Sangesinga*, his vassal and son-in-law, forced the *Javanese* to quit the countrey, who being now obliged to seek for a new habitation, settled themselves near the river *Muar*, where they built a strong hold, call'd *Pagopago*; besides the *Javanese*, *Paramisora* was follow'd by 2000 others, such as they call *Cellati*, who live upon fishing and robbing; but tho' they had been very instrumental in resettling him in *Sinkapura*, he did not think fit to receive them within the body of his new built city; which made them settle their colony about three or four leagues from the river *Muar*, not far from whence *Malacca* now lies; where they join'd with the inhabitants, who were half savages; since which time their language is call'd the *Malaga* language. But when they began to be streighten'd for room, some of them settled themselves about a quarter of a league from thence, on a hill call'd *Bitan*, surrounded with a large plain: *Paramisora* being taken with the conveniency and pleasant situation of this place, abandon'd *Pagopago*, and transplanted his colony near this place, which afterwards was call'd *Malacca*, *i. e.* a banish'd person, in memory of the exiled *Javanese*; and in process of time, all the traffick of *Sinkapura* was transferr'd to *Malacca*. *Saquan Dorsa*, son of *Paramisora*, succeeded him in the kingdom, and having submitted himself as a vassal to the king of *Siam*, reduced the whole countrey of *Sinkapura* to the east, as far as *Puto* on the isle of *Zambilan*, which lies west of *Malacca*, a tract of land of forty leagues in length. The successors of *Saquan Dorsa* found means to shake off by degrees the yoke of the king of *Siam*, and to make themselves soveraign kings, especially after they were by the *Persians*, and those of *Surat*, brought over to the mahometan religion. The king of *Siam* 1502, about 9 years before the *Portuguese* became masters of *Siam*, did attack the king of *Malacca* with a fleet of 200 sail, aboard of which were 6000 soldiers, under the conduct of *Laosamava Privan*, his admiral and governor of *Ligoor*, but his fleet was miserably scatter'd by a tempest, and many of his ships fell into the hands of the mahometans by treachery.

The harbour of *Malacca* is one of the finest in all the *Indies*, being navigable at *Its traffick.* all the seasons of the year, a conveniency belong-

1662. belonging scarce to any other in the *Indies.* It it most conveniently situated for traffick, for there you may to this day see vast numbers of merchants ships coming from *Bengal*, *Coromandel*, *Banda*, *Java*, *Sumatra*, *Siam*, and in short from all parts of the *Indies*. Whilst the *Portuguese* were in possession of it, this city was very famous for its traffick and riches in gold, precious stones, and all other rarities of the *Indies*; *Malacca* being the key of the *China* and *Japan* trade, and of the *Malacca* islands and *Sunda*. In short *Malacca* was the richest city in the *Indies*, next to *Goa* and *Ormus*. Before the *Dutch* had made themselves masters of *Malacca*, a ship was sent every year thither from *Portugal*, which setting out a month before their *East-India* fleet, and taking its direct course thither, without staying in any place, except in case of necessity, used to freight there, and return with a richer cargo than any other ship ever did.

Great passage thro' the streights of Malacca.

All the ships that came from the north, *viz.* of *China*, *Japan*, *Siam*, *Cambodia*, *Tonking* and *Manilha*, and are bound for the west, to wit to the coast of *Coromandel*, *Bengale*, and other places thereabouts, as likewise those coming from the west to the north, must pass thro' the streights of *Malacca* or *Sinkapura*, and consequently by *Malacca*, as I told you before. The *Portuguese* used to take 10 *per cent.* custom of all ships passing that way, whereby they got vast riches, but the *Dutch East-India* company has abolish'd this, looking upon it as an unreasonable imposition, and are contented to traffick there. *Malacca* is a countrey producing but very little it self, but must be look'd upon as the staple of the *Indies*, whither all precious commodities are brought from *China*, the *Molucca* and other neighbouring islands, from *Bengal*, *Coromandel*, *Banda*, *Java*, *Sumatra*, *Siam*, *Pegu* and other places. The island of *Sumatra* furnishes them with gold, pepper and other merchandises; from *Ligoor*, *Pera*, *Queda*, *Outjang* and *Salang* they have vast quantities of tin, which is brought up those places by the factors of the company, and sent to *Malacca*, from whence it is transported to the coast of *Coromandel*, to *Bengal*, *Persia* and *Surat*, and sold for ready money. The *Chinese* bring hither vast stores of silk and porcelain, damasks, brocados, sattins, musk, rhubarb, iron, saltpeter, fine silver, pearls great and small, ivory and *China* fans, which they exchange for pepper, frankincense, stuffs of *Camboya*, coral wrought and unwrought, painted callicoes of *Palakatte*, and white callicoes of *Bengal*, cinnabar, quick-silver, and such other drugs as come from *Camboya*. The island of *Java* supplies them with rice, oxen, sheep, stags-flesh and pork; in short, there is such a vast traffick and concourse of merchants here, that from thence probably it got the name of the *Golden Chersonesus* among the ancients; *Malacca* being certainly the richest harbour that can be seen; for formerly, and even to this day, the merchants were so rich here, that they used to compute by no less than by bars of gold, of which a vast quantity is found near the rivers and in the mountains to the west, to wit, on the famous rivers *Kedan*, and *Peren* or *Peragh*. The mahometans living along the coast, used formerly to trade hither with linen and some other commodities, but not so much of late years, neither is the pepper trade so considerable here now, as in former days, since the *Dutch East-India* company have settled their factories on the eastern coast of *Sumatra*, which produces great quantities of pepper. However, ships are sometimes detained here for a considerable time, by reason of the contrary *Monzon* or season winds.

Coin of Malacca.

Formerly they had no other coin but what was made of tin at *Malacca*, being of great weight, but little value; or rather they exchanged their commodities for gold and silver by weight; but now they coin both gold and silver, a piece of eight being worth commonly two gilders 11 stivers. They have two sorts of weights, *viz.* the great and small bar: The great bar consists of 200 *Kattys*, each *Katty* containing 26 *Tayls*, or 38½ ounces *Portuguese* weight, a *Tayl* being a ounce and a half: The small bar comprehends likewise 200 *Kattys*, each *Katty* comprehending 22 *Tayls*. According to the computation of others, a bar of *Malacca* contains 200 *Kattys Aetshyns*, or three *Chinese Pikol* each *Pikol* computed at 122 pound weight, making altogether 366 pound weight. The great bar or weight is made use of when they weigh pepper, cloves, nutmegs, mace, white and red sandals, indigo, allum, eagles-wood and civet; with the lesser weight, quick-silver, copper, leaf-gold, oil of nutmegs, benzoin, camphire and such like commodities. The city of *Malacca* is inhabited by many *Dutch*, but for the most part by *Mestices* and *Kastices*, some *Chinese*, *Pagans* and *Jews*, for the conveniency of traffick.

The Malayars.

The *Malayars* or natives of *Malacca* are tawny, with long black hair, great eyes and flat noses; they deduce their origin from the *Javanese*, but their eyes are quite different, they are for the most part naked, wearing only a piece of stuff wrapt about the middle, with their arms and legs naged. Their only ornament being gold bracelets and earings set with precious stones. The women

Their cloaths.

1662. women wear silk cloaths and short skirts, embroidred with gold and precious stones, some of which are twisted in their locks, which are very long. The women are extravagantly proud here, expecting more reverence than any other *Indian* women. There is also another peculiar sort of men in *Malacca*, called by the *Dutch Kakerlakken* (from a certain monstrous creature in the *Indies* of the same name) who are blind by day, and can only see by night. They can tell money, work, and do any other thing in the dark, which they cannot do by daylight, which they pass away for the most part in sleeping, and seldom rise 'till sunset. In shape and proportion of their limbs, as well as by their complexion, they resemble the *Europeans*, having commonly grey eyes; whereas all the eastern nations have black and dark brown eyes. Their hair is inclining to yellow, and of such a length among the women, that it reaches down to their hipps; their feet are bent inward. The same kind is likewise found in some other places of the *Indies*, and in *Africa*.

Kakerlakken.

The Malaya *tongue.*

The language used at *Malacca* is called the *Malaya* tongue, from the natives of the countrey, being very famous throughout the *East-Indies*. For the general concourse of so many nations, different in their languages, has put them upon a necessity of compiling a certain language, composed of the best and choicest words of all the rest, which therefore is accounted the neatest and most agreeable of the *East-Indies*, which is the reason that not only the neighbouring, but also far distant nations that trade with *Malacca*, are desirous to learn it, and look upon it as a great accomplishment. For the better encouragement of this language, and the benefit of their officers and factors, the *Dutch East-India* company has caused a dictionary both in the *Malaya* and *Dutch* tongues to be publish'd. Most of the *Malayers* are either christians or mahometans, tho' there are likewise some pagans and *Jews* settled at *Malacca*, for the conveniency of commerce. The coast of *Malacca* is a flat or marshy countrey, and consequently not extraordinary wholesome; but deeper in the countrey are many hills and wildernesses, which are plainly discovered at sea. It produces but little for the sustenance of life, except what is brought forth in gardens, and what grows among the mountains, where you meet with some rice and pease; the defect of which is supply'd by vast numbers of small vessels, which come every day from *Bengal* and *Sumatra*, and bring thither rice, and other eatables. However, they are pretty well stored with such fruits as commonly grow in the *Indies*. The fruit *Durions* grow here much better and larger than in any other part of the *Indies*: They have likewise *Ananas*, *Jambos*, *Mangoes*, *Karambolas* and *Papajas*; they have whole woods of cocotrees. Here grows a certain tree call'd the mourning-tree by the *Portuguese*, because its flowers close up in the night-time. Here you may meet also with cinamon trees, but not very many, neither do they approach in goodness to those of *Ceylon*. But of *Kalamback* or *Aloes* wood and *Benzoin* they have great plenty. Here are to be found some *Indian* fruits, peculiar only to this place, but no pears, apples, plums, cheries, or any such like *European* fruits. Oxen, cows, sheep and horses are likewise very scarce here, which are brought thither a great way out of the countrey, and are seldom very fat. Formerly the countrey hereabouts did abound in wild beasts of all sorts, such as tygers, elephants, &c. which were so ravenous, that they used to break in the night-time into the houses of the inhabitants, who for their better security, used to sleep upon trees; but since it has been so well peopled by the *Dutch*, this sort of wild beasts are but seldom heard of. 1662.

Their religion.

The countrey.

Just by *Malacca* is the cape or point of land call'd *Rachado*, and the cape of *Barcelai*, being a very high mountain near a point of land. Not far from *Malacca* is a very large mountain call'd *Madian*, which by reason of the vast quantities of salt-petre it contains within its bowels, 1646, did break out with such a terrible noise and earthquakes, as if the day of judgment was at hand.

Cape Rachado *and* Barcelai.

The mountain Madian.

Sinkapura lies on the most southern point of all *Asia*, about half a degree to the north of the line, and 20 leagues from *Malacca*. This cape has imparted its name to the streights of *Sinkapura*. The country of *Sinkapura* had before *Malacca* was built its own kings, and was the chiefest place of trade on this coast, being much frequented by the *Chinese* merchants, and those of *Camboya*. The mountains near the streights of *Sinkapura* bearing the same name, produce most excellent diamonds. About *Sinkapura* is a certain nation, which with their whole families live always at sea in their small vessels; they are called *Saletes*, live upon fishing, and are subject to the king of *Jor*. About two leagues beyond the streights of *Sinkapura* is the river *Johor*, at the entrance of which you see two mountains, or rather high islands shaped like sugar loaves; one is four times bigger than the other, lying N. N. E. as you enter the river, and the other N. E. On the other side of the river you discover a high hill, tho' the southside of the river is a champain country. There

Sinkapura.

1662. There is 10 fathom water at the mouth of this river.

The isle of Rocks. To the south of *Malacca* is a small isle, of about half a league in compass, by the *Portuguese* call'd *Ilha das Pedras*; or the *Isle of Rocks*, and has very good fresh water.

About half a cannon shot from the city, another small island call'd *Malacca*, and by the *Portuguese Ilha das Naos*, or the *Ship Island*. Two leagues from *Malacca* is a pretty large isle call'd *Sapta*. That vast point or tract of land on which the country of *Malacca* or *Malaya* lies, being the most southern of all the *East-Indies*, comprehends likewise several other kingdoms and cities; to wit, *Patany*, *Pahan*, *Pera*, *Queda*, *Johor* or *Jor*, *Ligoor*; and farther to the north the kingdom and city of *Tanassery*. We will give you a short account of the kingdom of *Johor*, *Putany*, *Ligoor* and *Pahan*.

The kingdom of Jor *or* Johor. The kingdom of *Jor* or *Johor* stands indebted for its name to its capital city, call'd by some *Goer* or *Goera*, and *Joar* or *Goar* or *Gohor*. It is situate at the very streights of *Malacea*, bordering in part upon the kingdom of *Malacca*, and on the other side upon *Pan* or *Pahan*. The antient city of *Johor* or *Jor* (call'd in some maps *Guar*) was very large and magnificently built, but was in 1603 destroyed by the *Portuguese*, who left only a few houses standing, which were immediately inhabited again. The king of *Johor* caused in 1609 another city to be built, somewhat higher up the river above *Johor*; this he call'd *Batusabar*, towards the building of which, the *Dutch* under their admiral *Peter Verkoeven* contributed 3000 pieces of eight, out of the booty they had taken from the *Portuguese* ships coming from *Makao*, near the cape *Rachado*. Most of the chief inhabitants of the old city of *Jor* retired from thence to *Batusabar*; a half day's journey from whence is *Sedalli*, near the sea-side. It is a very fertile country, abounding in lemons, and citrons as big as a man's head, *Bananaes*, *Batataes*, *Ananaes*, and other *Indian* fruits. They have also great store of pepper, cinnamon, buffles, cows, stags, wild boars, and divers sorts of monkeys and birds, besides some sea-monsters.

The disposition of the inhabitants. The inhabitants are naturally brave, but very lascivious, liers, great dissemblers, and proud beyond measure. Their complection is inclining to a light blue, with broad faces, crooked noses, and very black teeth, which they acquire by chewing the weed *Betel*, black teeth being accounted a great ornament among them.

Their clothing. The common people go quite naked, having only a piece of stuff to cover their members, which hangs down to their toes. The rich and better sort wear a kind of jackets made of blue, green or red callicoe, or what colour they please; they are shaped like our shirts, with wide sleeves, are open before; and reach only to their knees. They have also two silken strings of the same colour with the jacket, one serves for a girdle, the other for a head-string. They paint their nails yellow, and the greater quality they pretend to the longer they wear their nails. The richer sort commonly wear a poniard on their side, enriched with precious stones. Their king has many other petty kings, his vassals, under his jurisdiction. The king of *Jor* or *Johor* in 1606 attack'd the city of *Malacca* with 60000 men, which shews him to be a potent prince, and in the taking of the city of *Jor*, the *Portuguese* got 1500 brass pieces of cannon; in 1608, *Ratispont* the then king of *Jor*, being about 30 years of age, came aboard *Dutch* fleet with 30 of his wives, he had three gold chains set with precious stones about his neck, and his poinard was likewise enriched with sapphires and diamonds, valued at 50000 gilders. The inhabitants are one half Mahometans, the other Pagans: 1609, one *John de Paratuan* was king of *Jor*, he was styled the *Great King*, being likewise king of *Malacca*, and *Raya Sybrang*, *i. e.* prince of the other side of the river. In 1611, the king of *Azem* sent back the brother of the king of *Jor*, with a fleet of 36 ships, and a convoy of 2000 men, with abundance of cannon and ammunition, in order to assist in the rebuilding of the city of *Jor*. It was generally reported, that the king of *Azem* having given his sister in marriage to him, did intend to set him upon the throne, instead of his brother, who then reigned.

Linga is an island under the jurisdiction of the king of *Johor*, who has a governor there; it produces abundance of *Zagu*, but no rice; in 1606 it had about 3000 inhabitants. *The isle of* Linga.

The kingdom of *Pan* or *Pahan*, is by the *Portuguese* call'd *Paon*, and by others after the *Arabians Phaan*; it being a custom among the mahometan *Arabians* to pronounce *phe* instead of *p*. To the north it borders upon the kingdom of *Patane*, and adjoins to that of *Johor*, as well as to the streights of *Malacca*. The city of *Pahan* is situate about a league from the sea-shore, being inhabited only by the nobility, the common people dwelling in the suburbs. It is not very large, but surrounded with a wall made of the trunks of trees joined close together, of about four fathoms high, strengthened on each corner with a bastion, but not fill'd with earth. The streets are enclosed on both sides with hedges of reeds, and planted with coco and other trees, resembling rather some gardens adjoining to one another in the suburbs, than a well *The kingdom of* Pan *or* Pahan.

1662. a well regulated city, the houses being generally of reed and straw, only the king's palace is of wood. The river of *Pahan* is very broad, but not navigable by galleys except at high water: The country round about is very low, and produces about 300 bahars of pepper; as likewise *Palo de Aquila* or eagle wood, *Kalamback* wood and camphire, but not so good as that of *Bornee*, gold (but very coarse) nutmegs, mace, *Sapan* wood, diamonds, *Pedro de Porco*, or hogs stones, which are accounted a greater antidote than the bezoar stone. Deeper into the country are abundance of elephants. The inhabitants are the greatest impostors in the world. The king is tributary to the king of *Siam*, but after *Albuquerque* had conquered *Malacca*, he sent his deputies to *Pahan*, to oblige that king to promise fealty to him. At *Pahan* great quantities of baskets are made and sold, they are better than those made in *Java*, but not so good as the *Portuguese*. They also cast great guns here of 3000 pounds weight. The inhabitants are partly mahometans, partly pagans. Their king who reigned in 1612, had married the youngest sister of the queen of *Patane*. The two sisters having not seen one another in 28 years, the queen of *Patane* sent to the king of *Pahan*, to desire leave for her sister, his spouse, to come to see her, which the king refusing, she laid an embargo upon all the ships loaden with rice, and bound from *Siam*, *Campaja*, *Lugor*, and other places to *Pahan*; and immediately sent a fleet of 70 ships, on board of which were 4000 men, with strict orders to bring along with them the queen of *Pahan*, whether the king were willing or not; but it was not long before the king of *Pahan*, with the queen his spouse, and two young children, being forced by famine and a revolt among his subjects to leave the country, came to visit the queen of *Patane*, where they met at first but with a cold reception, not one of all the queen's court giving the king of *Pahan* as much as one visit, but caused all his dogs to be kill'd, he being not able to keep them any longer. Some days after matters began however to look with a better face; for the 1st of *August* the queen of *Patane* invited the king of *Pahan* to a most sumptuous feast, where she diverted him with several *Indian* women dancers. The king of *Pahan* returned not long after with his queen, the sister of the queen of *Patane*, into his country, but carried away with him no presents to make him amends for the charge he had been at, having spent almost all he had. The king of *Pahan* who reigned in 1607. was then about 40 years of age, and his son had married the daughter of the king of *Queda*.

1662. *The kingdom of Patane.* The kingdom of *Patane* or *Patany*, having derived its name from its capital city, borders to the south upon *Pahan*, being situate upon the same eastern coast, to the north upon *Siam* and the kingdom of *Lugor* or *Ligor*; these two kingdoms being incorporated into one. The city of *Patane* is situate under 7 deg. 56 min. of northern latitude, not far from the sea, and surrounded to the land-side by bogs. The harbour is about half a league from the city, which is about half a league in length, and very narrow, fortified with high wooden pallisado's put close together, according to the custom of these countries. The houses are artificially built of wood and canes, and very lightsome. The suburbs are likewise much longer than broad, and are encompass'd on the backside by a pleasant rivulet. The royal palace and court where most persons of quality live, are inviron'd with pallisado-work, in the nature of a *Palanck*; the mahometan church is a stately edifice of brick-work, gilt very richly within, and adorned with pillars, curiously wrought with figures. In the midst close to the wall is the pulpit, carv'd and gilt all over, unto which the priests are only permitted to ascend by four large steps. They have also several temples dedicated to their *Pagan* idols, among which three excel the rest. When the *Dutch* in 1602 settled first here, they saw in one of those temples belonging to the subjects of the king of *Siam*, a gilt statue resembling a man, but of the bigness of a horse, with one hand down and the other upwards. On each side stood a very large dragon gilt, with two stone statues, to wit, a man on the one, and a woman on the other side, with their hands lift up to heaven. The same they saw in the second, with this difference only, that one half of it was only gilt, the other painted red. In the third was one in the same posture, with a gilt streak cross the breast; and behind the altar of the great idol, was another lesser statue resembling a man, with a large horn in the forehead; this idol their priests say, represents the great God.

Temperature of the air. The climate is very temperate and wholesome here, notwithstanding it lies near the line. Their summer begins in *February*, and continues nine months, *viz.* till the end of *October*, during which season they have two different winds, to wit, by day from the sea, and by night from the land-side. In *November*, *December* and *January* is their winter, when it blows and rains so violently from the north-east, that there is no stirring for ships out of the harbour till *February*, when the wind turning to the east the rains cease, and the fair season returns. The

countrey

1662. country of *Patane* is very fruitful, abounding in rice and many other fruits, the chiefest of which are the *Durions*, *Mangestans*, *Ananas*, *Lancrats*, *Ramboutans*, *Pisangs*, pomegranates, oranges, lemons, and a peculiar kind of lemons, call'd *Gibol Lemons*, being transplanted hither from *China*. Each month here produces its peculiar fruits, tho' those of certain months are preferable before the rest. The grounds are plowed with bufflers or oxen, which they sow with rice: They also plant good store of pepper, but cannot sell it so cheap here as in some other parts of the *East-Indies*. The woods and wildernesses are stock'd with wild creatures, such as hares, rabbits, (but not so big as ours) stags, wild boars, tigers, bufflers, elephants, apes, monkeys, geese and ducks, (which lay eggs twice every day) and turtle-doves as finely coloured as the best parrots. The wild hogs do incredible mischief among the rice, which obliges the country-men to watch in the field in the night-time; when they shoot or otherwise kill them, they bury their carcasses under ground; the mahometans (for such those of *Patan* and *Malaya* are) being forbid the use of hogs flesh, neither will they permit any body else to eat it.

How they catch the elephants. The elephants, as I am credibly inform'd, are catch'd in the following manner: They ride on the back of a tame large elephant into the woods, whom they let loose there; as soon as he meets with a wild elephant he engages him, and whilst their snouts are entangled, some come from behind the wild elephant and twist a rope round his hind legs, and so keep him either to render him useful for the wars, or else kill him for his teeths sake, which are in great esteem in *China*.

The sea hereabouts produces great store of craw fish, oysters and tortoises; and the same drugs, metals, and precious stones, that are found in the kingdom of *Pahan*, are likewise to be met with here.

The constitution of the inhabitants. The natives of *Patane* are of an ash-coloured complexion and well shaped, but very proud and conceited; the richer sort never appearing abroad without a great train of servants. They are however very affable and civil in conversation, as well among themselves as to strangers; but they are no soldiers, nor inclined to warlike exercises, courage being none of their talent, but more taken with pleasures than the use of arms. Their clothing is none of the best. The men are extremely addicted to venery, which renders them jealous above measure, their wives and daughters being not permitted to see their nearest and best friends. They have an antient custom since enacted into a law, that to check that enormous vice of sodomy, the men are obliged to wear constantly two or three small bells made of gold, silver or lead, betwixt the prepuce and the glans, or head of the yard. Adultery is a capital crime with them, especially among the great officers and nobles of the kingdom; the father of the person that has committed the crime, or if he be not living, the next of kin is obliged to supply the place of executioner, but the miscreant has the liberty to chuse what kind of death he pleases. Notwithstanding this severe punishment, adultery is very frequent among them, by reason of the extraordinary lasciviousness of the women, who are very desirous, and love to wallow in pleasures. Fornication betwixt two unmarried persons is not look'd upon so much as a trespass. Nothing is more common than if any foreign merchants come to *Patane*, to ask them whether they don't want some women for their conveniency, and there is no want of young handsome women who offer their service, out of whom each may take his choice, and agree with her as he best can, as to what he is to allow her *per* month; which done, she immediately repairs to his lodgings, where in the day time she serves for a chamber-maid, and in the night for a bedfellow; and during this agreement, the man must be as careful to avoid the commerce of other women, as she is on her side, unless he will expose himself to manifest danger. At parting the man pays her her wages, and so they are both free; and if he has a mind to change, he need not look far for one, it being a custom among the nobles here to entertain many female slaves, whom they let out for such a use, and gain great profit by them. For the rest the natives are naturally lazy and idle, living for the most part upon fishing, and some handycraft trades; the best is, that they can be contented with a little, drink scarce any thing but water, and have a natural aversion to strong liquors. Almost all the traffick and other business is in the hands of the *Chinese*, who either themselves or their factors, continually trade betwixt this and the circumjacent countries, such as *Siam*, *Ligor*, *Kamboya*, *Kouchinchina*, *Makassar*, *Pahan*, *Jambi*, *Johor*, *Bantam* and other both inland and maritime places, whither they transport all sorts of *Chinese* commodities from *Patane*, as porcelain pots, pans, kettles, and iron work of all sorts. The chief riches of the natives consist in their lands and slaves, who live upon a small allowance of rice and fish; but the foreign merchants transport thither abundance of rich merchandizes.

From

1662. From *Bengale* and *Malacca* they send clothes to *Patane*; from *Java* sandel wood; from *Borneo* camphire, slaves, wax and bezoar-stones; from *Siam* the inhabitants of *Patane* are furnished with gold, rice, salt and lead; from *Siampa* and *Camboja* with slaves, cotton, *Kalamback*, and the finest aloes-wood; from *China* with white and yellow silk, gauses, damasks, sattins, porcelain, iron and copper; from *Japan* with scimeters, copper, and such like commodities. Many things are also transported hither that are bought up in other places by foreigners; as from *Amboyna* and *Banda*, nutmegs, mace and cloves; from *Timor* sandel-wood; from *Jamby* and *Andragny* pepper, which they

Their traffick.

fetch likewise from *Champor*, *Libor*, *Pahan*, *Mordyllion* and *Ligor*: *Pegu* supplies *Patane* with abundance of precious stones; there are also many things exported from thence by the foreign merchants; those of *Labor* and *Pahan* provide themselves here with rice, salt, oxen, fowls and other eatables; those of *Malacca* transport the bezoar stones; those of *Borneo* iron, steel and copper; the *Siamese* all sorts of clothings and pepper; the *Chinese* pepper, camphire, white and yellow sandel-wood, skins, ivory, bufflers horns, and such like; the *Japanese* stags skins, tin, lead and silk.

The country of *Patane* is much more powerful in shipping than *Johor*, *Pahan*, or any of the circumjacent kingdoms: They are governed by a king, who as well as the king of *Malaya* is tributary to the king of *Siam*; their usual yearly tribute consisting of a flower wrought with gold, some fine cloths, velvets and scarlets; the king's chief counsellors are called *Mentary*.

This kingdom was in 1602 under the government of a queen, after the decease of her husband, she being then but 15 years of age. Her name was *Pratie*, she used to keep constantly within the court among her ladies of honour, of whom she had a great number; she did not allow them to marry, but connived at their amorous intrigues. Wherever she went abroad to take the air, (which indeed happened but very seldom) she was mounted on a very fine elephant, and attended by 2000 nobles and great officers, all clad in her deceased royal spouse's liveries, with his coat of arms upon them. Before they returned, she gave them always a splendid entertainment, and so came with the same cavalcade back to her court. The country of *Patane* is so populous, as to be able to bring 180000 armed men into the field; the city and suburbs of *Patane* alone being able to furnish 10000 men.

Divers languages are in vogue, *viz.* the *Malayan*, *Siamese*, *Patanese* and the *Chinese*; but *Their language.*

1662.

but the firſt is moſt uſed here, as well as in moſt other parts of the *Indies*. The king of *Patane* married his daughter to the eldeſt ſon of the king of *Johor*, (he having ſix in all) who with his youngeſt brother lived at the court of *Patane*; but the youngeſt being engaged in an illegal commerce with his brother's ſpouſe, he kill'd them both, according to the cuſtom of the country, which puniſhes adultery with death; notwithſtanding which, the king of *Patane*, to revenge his daughter's death, cauſed his ſon-in-law, the eldeſt ſon of the king of *Johor* to be ſlain; *John de Paratuan*, and *Regia Sabrang*, two brothers, and both kings of *Johor*, being not without reaſon, highly exaſperated at this proceeding, ſent one *Magat Mangſor Hoch* their ambaſſador, along with admiral *Jacob Heemſkerk*, to ſolicite a powerful aid from the ſtates-general againſt the king of *Patane*, but the ambaſſador dying at ſea put a ſtop to that deſign.

The iſle of Ding Ding.

Having diſpatch'd my buſineſs here, we ſet ſail the next day to a certain iſland call'd *Ding Ding*, abounding in fuel and moſt excellent freſh water. It lies about 30 leagues to the north of *Malacca*, being covered all over with very tall trees, which grow on the hills. We arrived here the 10th of *January* 1661, and immediately after our landing, fell to the cutting down of trees; among the reſt we endeavoured to pick out a certain kind of trees, the wood of which is a pale red, but to our great amazement could meet with none, till at laſt we diſcovered our error, to wit, that the pith only was red, but all the other wood round about it of a different colour. This wood is much valued by the *Indians* for its beauty, of which they make many curious pieces. The freſh water which runs down from the rocks, claims the preference before any in the *Indies*; and this iſle has likewiſe the conveniency of a good bay, where ſhips may ride ſafely at anchor. On the eaſt-ſide it has another bay call'd *Cox Bay*, where we uſed ſometimes to catch as much fiſh at a draught, as our chaloop was able to carry.

Is deſtitute of inhabitants.

It is deſtitute of inhabitants and all ſorts of wild creatures, except wild boars, which ſwim over thither from the continent to feed upon a certain root that grows there, nevertheleſs it abounds in water-fowls more than any other place of the *Indies*: Here is a certain kind of birds call'd by the *Dutch* *Shuies Birds*, being of the bigneſs of a *Storex*, the head being without feathers. Here are alſo great quantities of tortoiſes and oyſters, the laſt of which are often ſeen faſtned to the branches of trees, which hang ſometimes above, ſometimes under water.

The clearneſs of the water having invited us to take a turn at ſwimming, I found ſomething ſticking to one of my legs, which when I look'd upon, I found to be a ſea-apple, and ſtruck it off; but the ſting remaining in the fleſh occaſioned a great inflammation and pain, which was not appeaſed till a conſiderable time after the ſting was taken out.

They leave it.

After we had provided ourſelves with what this place could afford us, we ſet ſail again the 14th of *January*; as we were ſailing the ſame day along the coaſt of *Sumatra*, our trumpeter catch'd a ſtone-bream of about three feet long, which appearing very fine to the eye, we ordered the cook to dreſs it for the table of the cabin. We were all ſo greedy, that when it was brought in, we aſk'd the cook whether he was ſure he had kept none behind, which he took ſo ill, that he anſwered us, whether we look'd upon him as a thief? But it was not long after dinner, before all thoſe that had dined in the cabin, were ſeized with ſuch a giddineſs in their heads, that they were not able to ſit upright; I was the firſt who cry'd out, *We have certainly eat a poiſonous fiſh*; but our ſurgeon having no proper remedies aboard, we ſent our chaloop to the ſhip the *Leerdam*, from whence being furniſhed with vomits, we were by the frequent uſe of them, after a ſickneſs of 14 days reſtored to our former health. During our ſickneſs our beſt diverſion was, that being inform'd how the cook was as ſick as any of us, we were convinced, that notwithſtanding his great pretence of honeſty, our ſuſpicion was not ill grounded, which verified our old proverb, *That the cook is commonly the laſt who dies for want of victuals*: Two cats that had eaten the bones of this fiſh died ſoon after, tho' ſome tobacco-water had been given them to occaſion a vomiting, but none of us died, ſome few however were troubled with a lingring diſtemper afterwards.

A poiſonous ſea bream.

It is not eaſy to imagine what could be the reaſon of this diſaſter, the ſea-bream being otherwiſe a fiſh both toothſome and wholeſome, unleſs we ſuppoſed this bream to have fed upon ſome poiſonous fiſh, ſuch as thoſe call'd by the *Dutch Seaquallan*, which are very poiſonous in thoſe hot countries; for if they touch but your fleſh, they cauſe an immediate inflammation; their fleſh is as ſoft as gelly; they are of the bigneſs of a trencher, or ſomewhat leſſer, have red and purple ſpots on their backs, and eight teats below on their bellies: At certain ſeaſons of the year, the ſeas about *Toutekoriin*, and near other places on the coaſt of *Malabar*, are ſo full of them, that they are obliged to deſiſt from fiſhing. But before we proceed farther in our voyage, it will be requiſite to give you a ſhort account of the iſle of *Sumatra*.

Reaſon of the poiſon of this fiſh.

1662. The large and most potent island of *Sumatra* is by some authors call'd *Somatra*, *Samatra* and *Zamatra*. Its situation is to the south-west just opposite to *Malacca*, about eight leagues from the continent, the great isle of *Java*, lying to the south of it. Its extent is from the 5th degrees of northern latitude, near the gulph of *Bengala*, to the south south-east, to the 7th degree of southern latitude, as far as the streights of *Sunda*, beyond the coast of *Malacca*, comprehending a vast tract of ground of 12 degrees from the south to the north, amounting to 130 leagues. Its whole length is 195 leagues, its breadth 50, and the whole circumference 360.

The isle of Sumatra's *situation.*

This isle was formerly divided by some into four, by others into 10 kingdoms, among which *Pedir*, *Pazem*, *Achem*, *Kampar*, *Menankabo*, *Zunda*, *Andragide* and *Auru* were the chiefest. Some there are who mention no less than 30 petty kingdoms, *viz. Daya*, *Lambry*, *Achem* or *Achen* or *Achin*, *Biar*, *Pedir*, *Lide*, *Pirada*, *Pacem*, *Bara*, *Daru*, *Arkat*, *Irkan*, *Rupat*, *Pury*, *Gaka*, *Kamper*, *Kapokan*, *Andragvery* or *Andragide*, *Jamby*, *Palimbang*, *Tana*, *Malayo*, *Sakampan*, *Tulumbavan*, *Andaloz*, *Piriaman* or *Pryaman*, *Tiko*, or *Tikouw*, *Barros*, *Quinchel*, and *Mankapa*, all which borrowed their names from their respective capital cities; and in antient times were govern'd by their own kings. But in process of time, many of these were swallowed up in the kingdom of *Achin*, the most potent in this island, having under its jurisdiction the kingdoms and cities of *Pedir*, *Pazem*, *Daya*, *Barros*, *Pastaman*, *Pryaman* and *Padang*, and consequently the greatest part of the isle of *Sumatra*, besides the kingdoms of *Queda* and *Pera* on the continent. All the other kingdoms and cities of *Sumatra* were conquered by foreign princes. This the southern parts of *Sumatra*, viz. *Sillabar*, *Dampin*, *Liampon*, *Palimbang*, *Jamby* and some others, acknowledge the king of *Bantam* their sovereign, or else the *Mataram* of *Java* for their protector. Some will have the isle of *Sumatra* to be the same the ancients called *Taprobang*, tho' in my opinion that name belongs more properly to the isle of *Ceylon*.

Is divided in many kingdoms.

Not many years ago one of the chiefest cities of *Sumatra* was *Palimbang* or *Palembang*, situated near the western coast of *Sumatra*, which on 24 *November* 1659, was laid in ashes by the *Dutch* admiral and general *John van der Laen*, because the inhabitants had about two years before surprized by treachery two of their yachts call'd the *Jakkatra* and the *Watchman*, and miserably murthered the whole ships crew; and in the next following year had cut to pieces two other *Dutchmen* that were sent ashore, from aboard the vessels the *Niccoport* and the *Lee dam* (lately come from the *Texel*) to serve as interpreters, their heads being by special order from the *Orangkay*'s put upon lances, and exposed to the view of their comrades that were in the boats. 1662.

The inhabitants of Palimbang *murther some* Dutch.

To revenge so barbarous a murder, a fleet of eleven ships set sail from *Batavia* the 19th of *October* 1659, under command of *John Vander Laen* admiral, and *John Truytsman* vice-admiral, *viz.* the *Orange*, admiral, the *Postilion*, the *Molucco*, the *Arms of Batavia*, and the *Charles*; three galleots, to wit, the *Apple-tree*, the *Hour-glass*, and *Hammebiel*; and the chaloops, the *Crab*, the *Tronk*, and the *Flying Dear*, mann'd with 600 seamen and 700 land soldiers. The 30th they arrived without any remarkable accident in their passage before the river of *Palimbang*, where they met with the yachts the *Bloemendahl*, the *Koukerk*, and the *Cat*, and with the chaloops the *Cony*, and the *Koelong*, that were cruising thereabouts. The same day they got sight of a *Chinese* vessel taking its course towards *Jamby*, which they detained till they had entered the river, and on the 3d of *November* sent her in company of the chaloop the *Tronk* to *Jamby*. They entred the river in the following order. First the *Arms of Batavia*, next the *Postilion*, then the yacht the *Bloemendahl*, aboard of which was the admiral, having left the *Orange* at the entrance of the river; the yacht the *Koukerk* vice-admiral, the yacht the *Cat*, the large chaloop the crab; after these came the three galleots, the *Hour-glass*, the *Apple-tree*, the *Hammebiel*; the ships the *Charles* and the *Molucco*, brought up the rear; the other chaloops were ordered to attack the admiral ship. The 3d and 4th of *November* was spent by the *Dutch* to enter the river, the 9th in the night time they were unexpectedly attacked by some of the inhabitants of *Palimbang*, in which engagement we had four or five wounded, the commanders not being time enough upon their guard. The 10th they were advanced betwixt the isle of *Cambira* and the opposite shore, within sight of the city of *Palimbang*, where they discovered three of the enemies forts; the first called *Bamagangan*, situate on the western point of the river of the isle of *Cambara*, the other two upon its east point, opposite to the other, they were called *Mathapoura* and *Menapoura*. At our first appearance the enemy kept close within their works, which gave us the more encouragement to penetrate higher up the river with our ships. But several large floats, upon which houses filled with combustible matter were built, being laid in the stream, captain *Jurian Paulson* was ordered with some boats and the yacht the *Hour-glass*,

A fleet of Dutch *ships sent to* Palimbang.

They arrive before the river of Palimbang.

Come within sight of the city.

1662. Hour-glass, to take a view of them, to cut their cables, and set them on fire, which being put in execution accordingly, the whole fleet advanced forward in order to attack the fort of *Bamagangan*. But as soon as we came within cannon shot of the fort, the enemy gave us a very warm salute out of his great cannon, from the forts both on the east and western points, tho' without any considerable loss on our side, which gave us sufficient encouragement to fire most furiously upon the first fort, with such success, that we set their magazine of powder on fire, which blew up with it the greatest part of the fort, and all the circumjacent houses; hereupon the yachts the *Bloemendahl*, the *Koukerk*, and the *Cat*, were ordered to anchor within pistol shot from the shore, from whence we so grievously gall'd the enemy, both with our great and small shot, that at last we landed, and made ourselves masters of the fort, where we found 22 iron and brass cannon, which we immediately turned against the enemy to the land side, and continued in arms all the night long, which proved no unnecessary precaution, for the enemy attacked us most furiously not long after, in hopes of regaining the place, but were repulsed most courageously, with the loss of only one man on our side.

But the enemies fire engines.

The fort Bamagangan *attacked.*

Fire engines of the enemy.

Then the enemy sent four or five very large fire engines, being floats of timber with wood on houses filled with combustible matter on the top of them, which took up almost the whole breadth of the river; the yachts the *Bloemendahl*, the *Koukerk*, and the *Cat*, had much ado to escape their fury, being forced to cut their cables; but the *Molucca* yacht had her fore-castle set on fire, and was with much ado saved by the help of many boats that were sent to her assistance, without receiving any considerable damage; so that these fire engines were forced down the river by the current, and soon after vanished into smoak. At the taking of the fort 30 *Javanese* were killed, and among them the old *Quevy*, *Tommagen*, *Nadapen Radia*, with his two sons, who were buried the next day.

The fort Mathapoura *taken.*

The 11th early in the morning we likewise attacked and took the fort *Mathapoura*, where we found only four pieces of cannon, the enemy having thrown four more into the river, which we brought out from thence afterwards; the remaining part of the day was spent in shipping in what artillery and ammunition we had got; eight companies of soldiers were likewise landed the same afternoon in the isle of *Cambara*, to attack the fort there, but to their great amazement found this strong hold left by these cowardly wretches; we found here 12 pieces of cannon, some of which they had likewise thrown into the mud, but were recovered by our people, and carried aboard our vessels, with a small quantity of ammunition. Whilst these things were transacting in sight of the garrison of *Palimbang*, they had found means to set fire to the yacht the *Watchman*, which they burned; and in the evening those that had deserted the fort under favour of a violent rain, did three several times attempt the recovery of it, in which engagement we had two killed and six wounded, and were forced to stand to our arms all the rest of the night. The 12th and 13th were spent in embarking all the cannon and ammunition we had got in the 3 beforementioned forts, which done, it was resolved in a council of war, forthwith to attack the *Chinese* quarter, and so to make ourselves masters of the city before the enemies could recover themselves from the fright they were put in by the loss of their forts: As we were passing by the city we received the same salute we had before from the forts, but without any remarkable harm, or the loss of one of our vessels. 1662.

The isle of Cambara *taken.*

The fortification of Palimbang.

The city of *Palimbang* was fortified with vast trunks of trees put close together, upon which were planted a vast number of great cannon, so that it seemed impossible to be taken by so small a number, being besides this invironed with a deep and miry ditch. We were hard put to it how to find a safe landing place, till at last our admiral having espied at the uttermost point of the fortification a small rivulet, which led up to a place where we perceived very little or none of the enemy's fire, we landed thereabouts with all our forces, and advancing boldly to the very gun-holes of the enemy, they threw their granados through them into the city, which setting the adjacent houses on fire, the enemy were so terrified thereat, that they quitted their post, and thereby gave opportunity to the admiral *Vander Laen*, to Mr. *Truytsman*, and captain *Harman* to break thro' the fortifications into the city by three several ways. Here they met with a brave opposition from the inhabitants, who, according to the custom of these nations, under the sound of their *Amock*, fell courageously upon these three bodies, of whom they killed 18, among which were a lieutenant, an ensign, and a sergeant, but not without a much greater loss on their side; the violent rains obliged the *Dutch* admiral to reconduct his men on board the vessels that night; but the next morning they landed again, and entred the city in the same place, where a doubtful engagement ensued, till the inhabitants being at last forced to give way, were beat out of the place, and retired into the open countrey

Attacked by the Dutch.

And taken.

1662. countrey. The first thing that was sacrificed to the fury of the flames, was the royal palace, after it had been despoiled of all its riches, and a vast train of artillery, which the king and his cowardly subjects left a prey to the *Dutch*, after they had for some time defended themselves, and fought hand to hand against them; but the admiral *Vander Laen* having laid two of their chief or *Quey Nabeys*, dead at his feet, the rest were so terrified thereat, that they sought for their safety in their heels. It is worth taking notice of that these *Indians* seemed to have paid a peculiar reverence to their great cannon, which we found covered with scarlet cloth lined with ramboutins, and so perfumed with incense that the smell thereof stuck a great while after to our fingers. All the artillery and cannon being taken out of the city and from the ramparts, the admiral ordered likewise the fortifications and adjacent houses to be laid in ashes; we found 15 of 21 of our people that were prisoners among them, in the prison on both sides of the royal palace, miserably murdered and mangled by these barbarous wretches, among which was *Jacob de Groot*; one *Dutch* boy only who was not put in irons, had the good fortune to escape their hands by a timely flight, the remaining six they had carried along with them: To revenge as much as possible this barbarity, all that remained of the city, was after the cannon and all the other booty we got were carried aboard our vessels, set on fire and destroyed, the 16th of the same month.

Fifteen Dutchmen *found murthered in the city.*

About the same time the enemy sent one of his before-mentioned fire engines, of a vast bigness, down the river; it consisted of 20 wooden houses erected upon floats of timber, which almost extended from one side to the other. But no sooner had the *Dutch* got sight of this engine, but they sent out their long boats well mann'd, who took care to protect our ships against it, and after it was passed by them, set it on fire in sight of the enemy, which consumed both the engines and a good number of houses standing on the banks of the river. The 17th and 18th our people were still busy in embarking the booty, artillery and cannon, and a day of thanksgiving was appointed to be kept throughout the whole fleet for this victory against the 23d. In the mean while we advanced higher up the river, to try whether we could meet with some vessels or plantations that way, but saw nothing of any moment. Mr. *John Vander Laen* and *John Truytsman* also writ a letter to the *Pangerang* or governour of *Palimbang*, which was dispatched thither the 23d by a *Chinese* prisoner and an old woman.

The enemies fire engine unsuccessful.

John Vander Laen general, and captain *John Truytsman*, commanders in chief of the *Dutch* forces now in the river and the countrey of *Palimbang*, send this letter to the *Pangerang* and all the chief councellours of the countrey of *Palimbang*. 1662.

A letter sent to the Pangerang.

Notwithstanding our last success, we could not but put your highness in mind of the most abominable murder committed by your subjects upon so many innocent persons in the service of the Dutch East-India *company: which barbarous act, tho' it was highly resented by the governour, general, and council of the* Indies *residing at* Batavia, *yet to shew their inclinations to continue in peace with your highness, did at that time for the preventing the effusion of human blood, require and actually demand a reasonable satisfaction for these unheard of barbarities: To accomplish which, they caused certain propositions to be made by* John Truytsman *to your highness, with strict orders to insinuate to your highness all such reasons as might conduce towards the accomplishment of that end, which we don't question would have been sufficiently convincing to your highness, had not your evil councellours misguided you, and thwarted your good intentions. But seeing you slighted these conditions, and were very backward in giving due satisfaction, the great God of heaven and earth being highly displeased at your conduct, did so direct the heart of the beforementioned lord governour and his council, as to have recourse to arms, being the only remedy left them, ordained by God almighty to protect the just cause of their subjects. The great God of heaven having been pleased to bless their undertaking, for the due punishment of your malicious subjects, they are however willing to let your highness know, that the hostilities committed against you and your subjects, were undertaken with no other intention, than to revenge the innocent blood of their subjects, and to procure an honourable and reasonable peace; the said governour and his council being always more inclined to peace than war, if your highness is of the same sentiment we expect to hear from you either by your letter in answer to this, or by your deputies, it being our resolution to tarry for that purpose in your highness's territories, and these presents shall be a sufficient passport to those whom your highness shall be pleased to send to treat with us.* Given aboard the *Bloemendahl* the 20th of *November* 1659.

signed,
John Vander Laen,
John Truytsman.

The 25th our ships went further up the river, and got sometimes sight of three or four lighters, which served for ferry boats; and

The Dutch fleet goes higher up the river.

1662. and some few houses built upon floats of timber; the lighters could not be taken, because they came not within reach of our shot, and afterwards sheltered themselves in the small rivulets among the weeds: The houses were set on fire, and so we returned the 20 before the fort where we lay at anchor till next day. In the mean time *Peter de Goyer* director of the *Dutch* factory of *Jamby*, sent the 11th of *November* from thence by the chaloop the *Tronk*, 75 capons, 100 pullets, and five goats, for the use of Mr. *John Vander Laen*, and the other commanders; this being all he was able to get, all eatables being extreamly scarce thereabouts at that time, because the *Pangerang* of *Adrogory* and the young king of *Johor*, had lately tarried three months, with an attendance of 2000 persons in these parts; and not long ago abundance of cattle and fowls had been killed for the wedding feast of his highness's daughter, who was married to the young *Patuan*. The admiral and captain *Truytsman* received not long after an answer from the *Pangarang* of *Jamby* to their letter dated the 20th of *November*, which being enclosed in another from Mr. *Peter Goyer* dated the 26th, was translated out of the *Malayan*, and runs thus.

This letter is sent from a sincere heart, by the *Pangarang* of *Jamby* to the commanders in chief *John Vander Laen* and *Daman Sittia Bauwa* (meaning captain *Truytsman*) men famous for their prudence and courage.

The Pangerang *having understood that Mr.* John Maetzuicker *governour general of the* Dutch East-Indies, *has sent 18 ships against those of* Palimbang, *has thought fit to declare, that his sentiments agree with the governour's, and that he is ready to approve all without the least contradiction, what shall be undertaken by the said Mr.* John Maetzuicker, *assuring Mr.* John Vander Laen *and* Daman Sittia Bauwa, *that he will stand firm to this as well as to the other promises made by him the* Pangerang *before. Pursuant to this resolution the* Pangerang *did upon the receipt of the letter, send* Zitta Antacca *with some troops to make war upon those of* Palimbang. *The* Pangerang *also forewarns and commands* John Vander Laen *and* Daman Sittia Bauwa *to be upon their guard, because those of* Palimbang *are near at hand; this being all the* Pangerang *commands at this time to* John Vander Laen *and* Daman Sittia Bauwa.

The 27th all the houses that were yet standing near the fort of *Mansapoura* were together with the fort itself, set on fire by special order from the admiral, and the same day we lifted a great piece of ordnance out of the marshes in the isle of *Cambara*. And being sensible that either out of an obstinate temper or out of despair the *Pangerang* of *Palimbang* would scarce send any deputies or answers to ours of the 20th, we resolved to leave that river; and accordingly with the next tide set sail and returned thro' the branch of the river call'd *Banjarmassum* in order to burn all the houses and plantations we should meet with; but having spent 5 days, *viz.* to the 3[d] of *December* in coming down the said river; we met at its entrance with the ship the *Orange*, which joining with the rest, we continued our voyage the 4th, and arrived with the whole fleet and our forces the 9th in the afternoon, in the road of *Batavia*. Our booty consisted chiefly in 75 pieces of great, and 142 lesser cannon, some of which were of iron. We found no pepper here, but great store of rice and *Padie*, all which was consumed by the fury of the flames, as likewise a vast number of small vessels, among which were the king's pleasure boats, of which there was a vast number; some few were carried away by our people, to be kept in remembrance of this action. 1662. *The* Dutch *leave the river.* *Arrive at* Batavia.

The kingdom of Achin. The kingdom of *Achin* is situate in the most northern part of the isle of *Sumatra*. Its capital city bears the same name, being situate in a plain upon a pleasant rivulet, about half a league distant from the sea-shore. The royal place, which lies in the very center of the city, is very large, of an oval figure, surrounded with a ditch, and in some places defended by very large pieces of ordnance; the ditch is guarded by pallisadoes, in which are seven gates. On the left side of the river is a fort to defend its entrance, and several other redoubts are erected in the marshes, round about the city of *Achin*, for its defence. The air seems to be much more wholsome here than in the southern parts of the isle. The houses which are covered with reeds are built upon posts, so that you must enter them by several steps, the reason of which is, that at certain seasons the waters rise to such a height, that the whole city is overflown by it. The chiefest riches of the king of *Achin* consist in gold, jewels and elephants; he entertains a great number of concubines which serve both for his bed and his guards in the antichambers; besides which, he maintains a good number of eunuchs, who attend his person. Four *Sabandars* or nobles have the chief management of the government under the king. This kingdom was in 1663 governed by a queen, who, as it was reported, had an inclination to be married to a *Hollander*; but the council of *Batavia*, for weighty reasons would not consent to the match. The inhabitants of *Achin* were always renowned for their courage and conduct beyond all other neighbouring nations, and have not only extended their conquests

3

1662. quests over the circumjacent countries of *Sumatra*, but also made themselves masters of the kingdoms of *Queda* and *Pera* on the continent of *Malacca*; nay, they frequently have besieged the *Portuguese* in the city of *Malacca*, they having always been declared enemies of that nation.

Sillebar. On the western coast, not above 4 leagues to the south of the line, is within a bay, upon a very large river, a certain place call'd *Sillebar*, being surrounded with craggy mountains and vast woods; tho' the countrey thereabouts is very fertile in pepper; it belongs to the king of *Bantam*. On the same western coast is a very large Bay, the shore of which is all over woody, as the bay of *Sillebar*, is surrounded with mountains; tho' the shore its self is very green and pleasant. Immediately after you come to the bay, you discover a small point of land, behind which lies the town of *Sillebar*.

Tikouw. A few leagues to the south of the line, is likewise the city of *Tikouw*, a place very slightly built, and some leagues from thence to the north, is the town of *Passaman*, at the foot of a high mountain. Passaman.

Barros. *Barros* is also situate on the western coast of *Sumatra*, about a league from the sea-shore, upon a considerable river, betwixt *Passaman* and *Achin*. The countrey hereabouts produces pepper, camphire and benzoin. Hereabouts are likewise *Sinkel*, *Labo*, and *Daya*.

Pedir. *Pedir* lies ten leagues to the east of *Achin*, with a high mountain betwixt both; the countrey, which was formerly a kingdom, is indifferently fruitful of rice and other fruits. Further to the east, on the inward coast of *Sumatra*, are *Pacem*, *Dely*, *Aru*, *Kampar*, *Andripouro*, *Jamby* and *Palimbang*. *Andripouro* is situate under 3 deg. 30 min.

Padang. *Padang* lies on a very pleasant river, whither a considerable number of *Indian* vessels resort. The *Dutch* divide the coast of *Sumatra* into the outward and inward coast. The inward coast is by the *Javanese* call'd the western coast, as the outward coast is the northern coast, where is the kingdom of *Achin*.

Unwholesomeness of the climate of Sumatra. The climate of *Sumatra*, is, by reason of its situation under the line, extremely unwholsome, especially for strangers, and in the rainy season, when scarce a day passes but they are afflicted with sudden showers, storms, thunder and lightnings, which soon after end in a calm. Besides, that the heat of the sun-beams draws up the nauseous vapours of the standing waters, which infect the air, and produce malignant fevers, and other lingring distempers. This is most visible on the western coast of *Sumatra*, and especially in *Tikouw* and *Pryaman*, where the air is equally obnoxious to the inhabitants and foreigners, which makes the *Dutch* inhabiting there, look bloated and very pale. In the *Devil's-Isle*, and near the river *Indapura* the air is so poisonous, that it kills men and beasts as soon as they set foot on shore; and if they happen to escape by returning immediately, they certainly die soon after.

The nature of the isle. The isle of *Sumatra* is full of pleasant woods, craggy high mountains, agreeable valleys, fruitful plains, very fine rivers and large bays affording great store of fish; besides that, the marshes and pools are stock'd with young oak-trees, the bark whereof gives the waters a red tincture. The chief rivers here are, the *Achin*, *Andregiri*, *Jamby*, *Palimbang*, *Manancabo*, *Banjarmassum*, *Sillebar*, *Indapura*, and *Pryaman*, all which have derived their names from their respective adjacent cities, or these from them. The waters of the river *Indapura* are red for two leagues at sea, which proceeds from the great quantity of young oak trees growing in the marshes, the bark of which imparts a red dye to the river; for which reason also the water is very unwholsome to drink. *Its rivers.*

Its soil. The soil produces rice in abundance, and all other sorts of *Indian* fruits, such as *Bananas*, potatoes, coco-nuts, oranges, limons, tamarinds, sugar, honey, ginger, but especially pepper, of which a great quantity is transported from thence into foreign countries. Some years ago many plantations of pepper were destroy'd by the soldiers upon the outward coast of *Sumatra*, which were since replanted, yet in many places cotton-trees have been planted in their stead. The same coast also produces camphire, the most durable of all others, which differs from the *Japonese* camphire in this particular quality, that whereas in this, the scent is in the wood; the camphire of *Sumatra* contains it in its own substance, without imparting the least share thereof to the wood. This island affords likewise white benzoin, *Kalamback* or aloes-wood, eagles-wood, and sandels-wood. The forests here feed divers kinds of wild beasts, *viz.* elephants, bufflers, tygers, staggs, rhinoceroses, wild boars, apes, monkeys and serpents; the rivers, lakes, and ports abundance of fishes; in some you meet with crocodiles. The woods are full of wild fowl of all sorts, and the countrey abounds in tame fowl. They have bats here of an exceeding bigness. It is very remarkable, that the island of *Sumatra* is the only one throughout the *East-Indies*, that has bears. The mountains here afford gold, silver, copper, tin, iron and brimstone. The outward coast of *Sumatra* especially, has very

1662. rich gold mines, but they are neglected for the moſt part. However the queen of *Achin* drew 1000 pounds weight out of one mine, and the *Dutch Eaſt-India* company 300 in the year 1665: They alſo produce Smaragdes, hyacinths and other precious ſtones. On the top of the fiery mountain *Balabam*, is a certain ſpring of ſulphurous liquor like oil; and the like is ſeen in ſeveral other parts of this iſland, to ſweat out of the earth or rocks, not unlike a *Petroleum*: The *Indians* call this liquor *Minjab Tunnah*, *e. i.* earth-oil. This is in ſuch eſteem among the inhabitants, that the king of *Achin* has prohibited the exportation thereof under pain of death; ſo that what is carried away by the *Engliſh* or *Dutch*, is brought on board by ſtealth. It has a very ſtrong ſcent, but not nauſeous; its virtue is extraordinary in curing lameneſs, call'd by the *Indians Beribery*, if the affected parts be only bathed or anointed with it. This iſland has a certain kind of reed, which grows near 300 fathom high, and twiſts its ſelf round the trees. They make hops of it.

Earth-oil.

The language of the inhabitants and their manners. The moſt general language here is the *Malayan*, tho' they uſe likewiſe ſeveral others. They maintain certain ſchools for the young people to be inſtructed in reading and writing. The inhabitants of *Sumatra* are large of ſtature, black and brown of complexion like the *Javaneſe*. The women are well ſhaped, and of a fairiſh complexion, with very white teeth; they make no account of chaſtity, nor look upon it as a diſgrace to expoſe themſelves for money. For the reſt, this nation is extravagantly proud and ill-natured, which ſets ſo high a value upon itſelf, as to deſpiſe all foreigners; they are very treacherous, and make very little account of their faith, if they find it conſiſtent with their intereſt. Every body here is like all the mahometans, does marry as many wives as he is able to keep, one however has the precedency before all the reſt: Women of any quality are ſeldom ſeen to walk along the ſtreets. In the inland countrey lives ſtill the remainder of the ancient men-eaters, call'd *Bataches* or *Batatas*, who not only devour ſtrangers, but likewſe kill their own fathers and brothers, if grown very decrepid, and eat them.

Their diet. Both rich and poor are continually chewing the leaves of *Bethel*, mixt with thyme and *Areka* or *Faufel*. Their bread is made of rice, of which they make alſo a dainty pap, and cakes, and eat them with oil. They feed likewiſe upon fiſh, fleſh and herbs. Their ordinary drink is water; beſides which, they uſe *Arack* diſtill'd of rice and coco-nuts, and palm wine. The inhabitants of *Sumatra* are very moderate in their diet, like all the reſt of the *Indians*. 1662.

Their cloathing. Moſt of the inhabitants, eſpecially the poorer ſort, go naked to the middle, where they have only a piece of ſtuff wrapt about them to cover their privities; both ſexes go without ſhoes or ſtockins. The richer ſort wear a kind of coat of ſilk or callico, after the mahometan faſhion; a linnen cloth wrap'd about their heads two or three times, ſerves them for a cap.

The abſoluteneſs of their kings. They pay a more than ſlaviſh ſubmiſſion and obedience to their kings, not ſo much out of inclination as fear; their princes or governors are ſtiled *Pangerang*.

Their puniſhments. They puniſh the leaſt treſpaſs with great ſeverity, by cutting off their hands and feet. Capital crimes are puniſh'd after the moſt dreadful manner that can be invented. In former ages the kings uſed to ſurrender the miſcreant to the men-eaters, who after they chop'd of their hands, arms and legs, threw pepper upon the trunk of the body and devoured it.

Their Religion. Moſt of the inhabitants living near the ſea-coaſt are mahometans now, whereas formerly, both thoſe inhabiting the ſea-ſhore and the inland countrey were pagans, of which there are ſtill a great number in the countries remote from the ſea.

Traffick of this iſland. The iſle of *Sumatra*, but eſpecially the kingdom of *Achin*, are places of great traffick, whither reſort merchants from all parts of the *Indies*, as the *Chineſe*, *Malayans*, *Javaneſe*, chriſtians and mahometans. There are certain places on the weſtern coaſt of the iſle, which are in confederacy, and under the protection of the *Dutch Eaſt-India* company, unto whom they are obliged to ſell all their pepper and gold at a certain rate. Theſe are *Pryaman*, *Indapoura*, *Padang*, *Tike* and *Barros*. They had alſo ſettled a factory in 1665 at *Andragiry*, but the quantity of pepper and gold to be tranſported from thence was ſo inconſiderable, that it did not turn to account. *Commodities of Sumatra.* The chief commodities of *Sumatra* are, pepper, gold, tin and camphire. The weſtern coaſt affords *Pedro Porcos*, which are ſold at 200 crowns *per* piece. *Jamby* and *Palimbang* are the chiefeſt places for pepper, where the *Engliſh* have likewiſe their factories, and are much eſteemed by that king. The foreigners import commonly pieces of eight, callicoes, *Chineſe* gold, iron wire, ſteel, woollen-cloth, quilts of *Suratte*, ſilks, ſalt and ſuch like commodities, which they exchange for thoſe before-mention'd. Thus much of *Sumatra*.

They continue their voyage. We continu'd our voyage without any remarkable accident, 'till the 3d of *February*, when we paſs'd by *Punte Gale*, and arriv'd the next day at *Colomba*, both cities belong-

1662. belonging to the island of *Ceylon*. Having soon dispatch'd our business here, we set sail again the 9th, and the 12th came within sight of cape *Comorin* and the city of *Koylang*, steering our course along the coast of *Malabar*, where we met with the ship the *Phœnix*, in the road of that city, to load pepper, which done, it join'd with us, to continue its voyage to *Persia*.

Pass by cape Comoirn and Koylang.

Over against the isle of *Baypin* we met with 15 or 16 sail under the command of Mr. *Adrian van der Meyden*, who was sent thither to attack the fortress of *Palipatnam*; we went immediately aboard the *Ulieland*, where we paid our respects to the admiral, who enjoyn'd us, to send all our land and sea men ashore, to assist at the taking of this fortress; which being done accordingly, and the *Dutch* forces marching in good order to the attack, they found, to their great astonishment, that the enemy had deserted the place, and left only one old woman and a boy behind them; thus we became masters of this strong hold, without striking a blow. However our design upon the city of *Cranganor* was laid aside for that time, after we were thoroughly informed concerning its condition, and that we were not sufficiently provided for such an attempt. So we proceeded on our voyage again the next day, and the 5th of *March* pass'd by the bar of *Goa*, where we found several *Dutch* ships under commodore *Roothaes* a crusing, which kept the harbour of *Goa* block'd up. The 6th we came to an anchor in the road of *Wingurla*, where we met several of our men of war, which had been a cruising before *Goa*, and were come hither to refresh themselves: We saw likewise here the *Bantam* yacht, which was sent on purpose hither to carry the queen of *Golconda* to *Mocha*, (a city of *Arabia*, situate on the *Red-Sea*) she being to go from thence to *Medina*, to visit *Mahomet*'s tomb, and to make a present of great value there. Her guards, which had conducted her 80 leagues as far as *Wingurla* consisted of 4000 men, all mounted on fine bright *Persian* horses, well accoutred. They had long coats of mail, on the shoulders of which were imbroider'd serpents-heads in imitation of the ancient *Romans*; they had fine polish'd helmets on their heads, being for the rest arm'd with bows and arrows, and some of them with very long beards. At the head of them rid two trumpeters, who sounded the trumpet by turns. All the persons of quality that attended her, were likewise mounted on very fine horses, with a footman on each side of the horse's head, who held the bridle. The Queen herself and all her ladies, were carried in *Palakins* covered on the top, to keep themselves from being seen by any body; and before them were led several camels cover'd with rich furnitures. On one of these was mounted a kettle-drummer, who with a hammer beat cross-ways, as we do in *Europe*; the drums, of which one hung on each side of the camel, being somewhat sharp at one end like our bee-hives. The commodore *Roothaes* and M. *Santvliet* (director for the *Dutch East-India* company at *Gamron*) were gone to meet and compliment the queen about two leagues from the town; who, whilst she tarried here, dictated several letters in divers languages to her secretaries; she sent soon after to know whether the ships were ready to sail, and being answered they were, she came immediately aboard the yacht, but finding her much less in bulk than the other ships she saw lying at anchor in the road, she was not very well satisfied, till being told by Mr. *Roothaes* and *Santvliet*, that the yacht was most proper for her purpose, by reason of the shallowness of the shore of the red sea, she seem'd to acquiesce in their judgment. Near the sea-side a tent was set up, and from thence a passage covered all over with callico to the chaloop, in which was likewise a tent, as also in the yacht, to prevent her being seen by the ship's crew. She gave a very fine present of gold and diamonds to the commodore Mr. *Roothaes* and Mr. *Santvliet*. The captain of the yacht who carried her to *Mocha*, did not return from thence, but went along with her, being, as we suppose, turn'd mahometan; because the yacht was reconducted by the boatswain. 1662.

Palipatnam.

Pass by Goa.

Come to Wingurla.

The queen of Golconda goes to visit Mahomet's tomb.

Wingurla is no more than a large village, situate on the sea-shore of the kingdom of *Golconda*, under the 15 deg. of northern latitude. The *Dutch East-India* company have built a very fine house here of stone and plaister work, because all ships bound for *Persia*, are obliged to come to an anchor here, to provide themselves with fresh water and fuel, which they buy here at a very low rate, the place scarce affording any thing else.

Wingurla.

After we had left *Wingurla*, we came the 6th of *April* before that famous city of *Persia* call'd *Gamron*, and anchored at six fathoms water. I went ashore the same day to give notice of our arrival, and to make the necessary preparations for unlading our ship, which being done, I apply'd myself to have it laden again with all possible expedition; and our cargo being for the most part gold and silver coin, we might soon have been ready to sail again, had we not been oblig'd to stay for some other commodities till the 2d of *June*, when we set sail again from thence, and Mr. *James Williamson*, director for the company in *Persia*, took

Come to Gamron.

1662. took this opportunity to go along with us to *Batavia*, the time of his stay in *Persia* being expired.

A description of that city. The famous city of *Gamron*, the only sea-haven of *Persia*, is situate on a flat sea-shore, just at the entrance of the *Persian Gulph*, at the foot of a barren sandy mountain, producing neither grass nor trees; it lies betwixt two castles, under the 27 deg. of northern latitude: This city was built out of the ruins of the castle and city of *Ormus*, the destruction of which proved the rise of *Gamron*. It is to the sea-side defended by three stone bastions, on which are mounted good store of iron cannon. But on the land-side it is only surrounded with a stone wall, which is much decay'd, because they fear as it seems nothing from thence. The *Its houses.* houses here which are built after a very antique manner, like most of the *Persian* houses, stand very close together, having each a square turret, which mounts to a considerable height above the whole structure, having on each side several holes for the free passage of the wind and air; in these turrets they sleep every night during the summer season. The best of their houses are built only of loom, which being form'd in four square pieces, and dry'd with the sun, become as hard as stone, and keep out the rains and winds. They whiten them on the outside with lime made of burnt mussel-shells, but their back and out-houses are covered only with the leaves of palm-trees, and are miserable huts, scarce fit to defend the inhabitants from the injuries of the season.

Streets. The streets here are both narrow and short, with many turnings, and are covered by the houses on both sides, which are almost join'd together on the top; notwithstanding which the heat is so excessive here, that they are scarce passable. They are not paved with stones, but only with earth beaten close together, which being continually watered to allay the heat and dust, becomes by degrees as hard as a stone. Both the *English* and *Dutch* have their factories here near one another, each being distinguish'd by their respective flags; the *Dutch* is built close to the water-side, being a goodly structure, and very convenient for the unlading of vessels.

Scarcity of fresh water. The city of *Gamron* affords no fresh water, which must be fetch'd by the slaves in earthen vessels or sheep skins early in the morning (to keep it the cooler) from the mountains, which are near three leagues distant from thence, which makes the fresh water so scarce here, that most people of fashion will rather present you with a cup of wine than water, there being no pools or basons here where any fresh water is to be met with, but during the rainy season. Neither does the countrey produce any thing but palm-trees; notwithstanding which there 1662. is great plenty here of every thing, wherewith they are supplied from *Persia* and other places. The common drink of the inhabitants is water, tho' they also are provided with good *Persian* wines; they are very strong, and of a high red colour, but as sweet as canary wine: It grows about *Schiras* and *Yezd*, and is transported from thence in large flasks and casks. They have also *Arack* distill'd of coco-nuts and rice. They make likewise a mixture of water, lemons and sugar, but if drunk in too great a quantity occasions the bloody flux.

The air of *Gamron* is from the beginning of *May* till *September* more unwholesome *Unwholesomeness of the air.* than in any place of the *East* or *West-Indies* that ever I saw, so that there is no abiding here for foreigners, except in *December*, *January*, *February* and *March*. The natives of any quality being more used to the air, will continue something longer, *viz.* till *May*, when they retire to their countrey houses, which are for the most part built among the mountains, near some river or other, at 10 or 12 leagues from the city: Here they spend merrily what they have got by traffick in the winter, leaving the management of their city houses to their slaves till *October*, the usual time for ships and foreign merchants to come to *Gamron*. The heat which is most excessive here obliges them to sleep upon leather, or with the lower parts of their bodies in water; or in the turrets, which are on the top of their houses; some cool themselves with pouring rose-water down the neck; such ships as are obliged to stay in the port during the summer season, must be covered all over with sails, otherwise the planks would split asunder, the pitch and tar rising up in bubbles as it were a boiling; so that no body dare walk bare-footed upon the deck. Those who venture to continue during the hot season at *Gamron*, commonly get for their pains an ague of a very malicious nature, which if it does not kill, at least seldom quits them, but leaves such relicks behind, as at last brings them to their graves. The cause of this excessive heat seems to me to be the situation of the place, at the foot of a barren mountain facing the south, so that the sun-beams by their refractions against the mountains are redoubled in their strength, especially if it be considered that the wind here during the summer season blows for the most part from the south, and consequently from the same corner, from whence the sun-beams exert their utmost strength. For immediately after *March* is past, the winds turn commonly to the west and south-west, which are sometimes so stifling that they

1662. they kill men and beasts. The *Arabians* call this wind *Elhamudi*, i. e. fish-winds, and the *Persians Badesambour*, because it choaks on a sudden such as it touches. It is very observable, that the dead carcasses of such as are kill'd by it, if touch'd with the hands, are as unctuous as grease or oil, and appear as if they had been dead a month ago. This wind continues here in *May*, *June*, *July* and *August*, as likewise all about *Muassil* over against the old *Nineve*, and near *Bagdat*, but those who are upon the water, even in boats in the river, never feel the effects of this wind, tho' they are quite naked.

Stifling-winds.

Traffick of the inhabitants of Gamron.

Most of the inhabitants of *Gamron* are merchants, who trade to several cities situate upon the branch of the *Euphrates*, such as *Bassora*, *Schiras*, *Ispahan*, *Tauris* and *Smyrna*. Once every year, to wit, in *October*, the caravans, consisting of several thousands of men and beasts, arrive here from the east, *viz.* from *Babylon*, *Turky* and *Persia*, with all sorts of merchandizes loaden upon camels, dromedaries and asses, which they exchange for *East-India* wares. The staple commodities of *Gamron* are cloth of gold, tapestry and pearls, which they take near the island of *Bahrain*, as likewise fruits of all sorts, plumbs, raisins, currans, nuts, dates, oranges, citrons, pomegranates, peaches, &c. They abound likewise in herbs, which are brought thither from other places, especially from the isle of *Kikmis*, not above three leagues from thence. They have also good store of most excellent *Persian* wine, which is brought thither from *Schiras* and *Yezd* in large flasks, pack'd up in casks. They sell also abundance of the best rose-water, which is here in greater plenty than in any other place that ever I saw. There is at certain times such a vast confluence of merchants and ships at *Gamron*, that they want money to buy their commodities; in such cases they write to their correspondents at *Lar*, *Schiras*, *Ispahan* and other *Persian* cities, who if they have ready cash, are sure to buy good bargains at such a juncture. Most of the merchants that resort to *Gamron* are *Persians*, *Armenians* and *Indians*, living in *Persia*. And were it not for the unwholsomeness of the air, abundance more would come from other places, who now stay at home, and rather chuse to buy from the merchants that bring their commodities from *Gamron*.

Disposition of the inhabitants.

The women here, like as in most other eastern countries, are seldom seen abroad, but dwell in separate apartments, where the men live with them for some time, and in the mean while lay aside all other business. The women who expose themselves for money, sit in the evening upon benches at the doors, with lanthorns in their hands, where every man is free to chuse such a one as he likes best. The inhabitants here are generally very brown. The poorer sort go for the most part naked, only with a piece of stuff wrap'd round the middle; in the summer season some appear quite naked, others only in their shirts. The rich clothe themselves very magnificently after the *Persian* fashion, tho' there are yet some few who retain their antient dress with gold, silver, and iron rings on their hands, ears and noses. The common people make use of dates instead of bread or rice; for it is observable, that the ordinary food of the *Indians* all along that coast, from *Basora* to *Sindi* is dates and fish, dry'd in the air. The heads and guts of the fishes they mix with date stones, and boil it altogether with a little salt-water, which they give at night to the cows, after they come out of the field, where they meet with very little herbage. They abound also in hares, sheep, pidgeons and partridges; but as for tame fowl, tho' they have great store of them, they are not much esteem'd, because they have a brackish taste. The sea, especially that of *Solda* and *Sardin*, furnishes them with vast plenty of excellent fishes, and among the rest with very fine oysters, but they are so little regarded by the inhabitants, that if you have a mind to some of them, you must bespeak them of the fishermen on purpose. Preserv'd fruits of all sorts are here in great abundance; the rich merchants, but especially the *Persian* governor, living in great luxury and pomp. 1662.

Their clothing.

Diet.

Sepulchre of an Indian *saint.*

About a league to the east of the city is a famous sepulchre of a *Banyan* saint, buried there some hundred years ago, under a tree call'd *Arvor das Rais*, i. e. root-tree by the *Portuguese*, or *Lul* by the *Persians*, which he planted here sometime before his death. The inhabitants call this tree the *Tree of the Banyans*, either from its first planter, or because the *Banyans* have founded a *Pagod* or *Pagan* temple under it, and a *Caranvansera* or inn for the conveniency of passengers. This tree has spread its branches at a considerable distance round about, and encreases every year to that degree, that its branches, which indeed all descend from one trunk, but by degrees take root again, encompass a space of 550 feet. Under this tree both inhabitants and foreigners shelter themselves against the heat of the sun when they are walking abroad, and entertain one another. Over the sepulchre itself is built a small *Pagode*, in which you see burning lamps hanging day and night under a canopy of silk. The ground all round about is paved with bricks, and adorned with convenient benches and seats neatly kept, where every body is at liberty to take his

Goegÿs of Benjan Saints

8.

Indian faints.

repofe under the agreeable fhadow of this tree. Here the *Indians* come in great numbers to offer their facrifices, efpecially the *Siogs*, call'd by others *Goegys*, *Gioghi*, and *Joeghi*, and *Fakirs* by the *Arabians* and the moors. There are a certain fort of *Banyan* faints (or at leaft pretend to be fuch) belonging to one of the four fects of the *Bramins*, *viz.* the fect of *Cenrawaghi*, of *Samarath*, of *Bifnou*, and the fourth the fect of *Siogs* or *Goegys*. You fee them fitting on the highways with their legs acrofs, as the *Mahometans* do; they never pare their nails; fome have locks of hair hanging down their backs of four or five feet long, others never fhave their heads or beards, which makes them appear more like devils than men. They have no dwelling places of their own, but in the night-time they fleep in the porches of their temples, on dunghills and corners of the ftreets, or perhaps in fome cave or other hole. They always appear naked, having only a piece of cloth wrapt about the middle. The *Indian* women refort to them in great numbers out of devotion, to touch the extremities of their fingers, or to kifs their privy members in a moft humble pofture, which they admit of, without fhewing the leaft fign of fenfibility thereat, for if they fhould do otherwife, they would be look'd upon as unfit for that holy feat. They never caft their eyes upon any body, but draw them in a moft frightful manner upwards, as if they were afflicted with convulfions. They lead a moft fevere and miferable life, conftantly mortifying their bodies by fome ftrange and unnatural penances they lay upon themfelves. Some retire into caves and cellars, where they continue in their devotions fometimes

A fect of Bramins.

The Perfian Shepherds about Gamron

9 or 10 days, without eating or drinking. Some walk both day and night for feveral years together without fitting; and when they intend to fleep, hang themfelves with a rope about their middle to the branch of a tree. Others carry both their arms all their life-time ftrait upright above their heads, fo that in procefs of time they are not able to bend themfelves downwards again. In this pofture they continue day and night throughout the year quite naked, without the leaft fear of being fcorch'd by the fun, or ftung by the gnats, which they won't as much as remove with their hands. Nay they fleep with their arms in the fame pofture, a thing which needs muft be very painful at firft, and at laft makes their arms thus diftorted and bereaved of their ufual nourifhment to hang down behind their backs. There are innumerable forts of other penitents,

1662. tents, some always lifting up their eyes against the sun, others fixing them constantly upon the ground, without ever looking upon or speaking a word to any body living. They besmear their nauseous bodies with ashes, and their greasy hair and faces with sandel-wood and saffron, but especially with cowdung mix'd with ashes; during our stay at *Gamron* we went several times to refresh ourselves under the tree; the common custom is to carry some wine and sweetmeats along with one, and as for dates, almonds, nuts, and other fruits, they are to be sold there.

The governor of Gamron. The *Persian* governor residing at *Gamron* lives in great splendor; the king sends every year certain commissioners thither to take an account of the governor's conduct; he commonly meets them at some distance off the city unarm'd, and if they find him to have transgress'd his commission, they cut off his head; otherwise he is regal'd with a present of clothes, and so they enter the city, where they pass their time together in feasting for some days. The governor of the city did in our time meet the commissioners with some armed bands, and thus conducted them into the city.

Persian *posts.* The posts which go from *Gamron* to *Ispahan* are wonderful expeditious in their journeys; they are appointed by the governor of *Gamron*, after he has made sufficient trial of their nimbleness, which is done by running with the rising of the sun, to an appointed place till sun-set; a certain horseman being appointed to ride along with them, and to take care they don't rest by the way: After they have perform'd this trial, the governor presents them with a suit of clothes and with the title of runners. So soon as any stranger of fashion arrives at *Gamron*, some or other of the inhabitants is ready to offer him his service, to attend him in the quality of a porter, or as a servant to show him the way; they are sure to wait at your lodgings every morning, and follow you all day long wherever you go, for a very slender allowance.

Shepherds near Gamron. I had the curiosity to take a view of the shepherds and their huts, with their flocks of sheep and goats; for which purpose, by the help of my guide, I went some leagues deep into the countrey, where I found them feeding their sheep in a very barren ground; these shepherds, who have no other houshold goods but a slight coat, commonly manage a flock of 500 sheep and goats. Their huts they set up at pleasure in the open fields, they having no certain grounds appointed them, but like the *Arabians* change their places according to the best conveniency of pastorage; and tho' the grounds betwixt the city and the mountains are very barren, yet are the sheep and goats here very good, an evident sign that a small matter is sufficient to feed them. These fields extend from the city to the mountains, which surround them at some distance from thence. They have some sheep of an extraordinary bigness, with two horns on east side of the head. Their he-goats have long curl'd hair, of which they make camlets. Some have such long ears that you may tye them together. *Persia* affords great quantities of tann'd goat and sheep skins. Thus much of *Gamron*. 1662.

A little to the right of the harbour of *Gamron*, you may see the isle of *Ormus*, at the very entrance into the *Persian* gulph, as likewise the islands of *Queixome*, *Kesem* and *Lareck*, of which we will give you a short description.

Some put the island of *Ormus* under 25 deg. 30 min. of latitude, and 22 deg. 45 min. of longitude; others under 26 deg. 4 min. and some others under 27 deg. and 30 min. northern latitude. The isle of *Ormus* is by some taken for the same, which by the antient authors, as *Pliny*, *Pomponius* and *Dionysius*, is call'd *Ogyris*, and by *Ptolemy Vorcchta*; it is situate in the *Persian* gulph, about two leagues distant from the continent of *Persia*, having the province of *Caramania* to the east, *Arabia fœlix* to the south and west, being divided from them only by the streights of *Baharem*, and the continent of *Persia* to the north; it is very near triangular; its largest side which faces the N. N. E. extending from S. E. to the N. W. from the chapel of *St. Lucie* to the point of land where the castle of *Ormus* is, being the nearest to the continent, where formerly the *Portuguese* had a fort call'd *Comoran*, built just opposite to the castle of *Ormus*, which thereabouts is not above a league distant. The second side extends from the same chapel, *viz.* from the S. E. to the S. S. W. as far as the cape *Karu*, and so further to the W. S. W. and the W. and makes the basis of the triangle. The third and smallest side begins at *Karu*, and ends at the before-mentioned castle; it faces the country of *Mogosthan*, a name commonly given to the *Persian* coast on that side, which is about two leagues from the isle. Its whole circuit is about three leagues. *The isle of* Ormus.

The western part of the island extending along the sea-shore, where the mountains end, is call'd *Karu*, where you see a few houses scattered up and down belonging to the moors: At *Turumbake* are a greater number of these houses, but as wretchedly built as the former, except some few formerly belonging to the *Austin* friars, where they used to divert themselves some times. Near to them is a fine fish-pond surrounded- Karu.

1662. ed with very fine trees, and a large ciſtern for rain-water.

Mountain. The whole iſland is divided by a ridge of mountains, extending from the eaſt to the weſt, behind which there is nothing to be ſeen but white and barren hills, producing nothing except very good white ſalt. Among the reſt there is a mountain here called *Kuykaſtaron*, or *the Mountain of the Dead*; on the top of which the *Portugueſe* had built a chapel call'd *our Lady of the Rock*; which chapel is obſerved to riſe higher and higher, becauſe the ſalt, ſaltpetre, and brimſtone, which are contained in the bowels of this mountain, encreaſe daily in quantity. The inhabitants viſit this chapel with a great deal of devotion, unto which they have made a pretty eaſy aſcent by cutting ſteps out of the rock, which otherwiſe is very ſteep. Near the mountain, where the chapel ſtands, is another, which runs upwards in form of a pyramid. Salt-mountain. It is compoſed of one entire maſs of the beſt and whiteſt ſalt that can be ſeen, and appears at a diſtance like a mountain covered with ſnow. Not far from hence is a chapel called *St. Lucy*, built behind the ruines of ſome old towers, where formerly the kings of *Ormus* uſed to keep their brothers priſoners, after they had bereaved them of their eyes. About half ways betwixt this and the city, was another chapel dedicated to *St. Lucy*, with ſome houſes about it, whither the inhabitants of *Ormus* uſed to retire during the ſummer ſeaſon, as likewiſe to ſome others built near the ſea-ſhore of reed only, and covered with palm-tree leaves.

From this chapel to the city is a large plain, where the inhabitants uſed to have their ciſterns to gather and keep rain-water in, which were always locked up; for not only hereabouts, but alſo all over the iſland the ground is brackiſh, which makes the rain-water which is kept in theſe ciſterns much better than what is gathered from the pools or ponds; yet does it not come near in goodneſs to the freſh water that is brought from the continent or the iſle of *Queixome*. The remaining part of this plain is taken up with the graves of the mahometans, pagans, and jews, which are buried here promiſcuouſly without any difference; ſome of theſe tombs are covered with a kind of a chapel, but open on all ſides. Hither you ſee great numbers of mahometan, pagan, and jewiſh women, of all ages and degrees, which come to bring their offerings of eatables in flat ſmall diſhes, to the ſouls of the deceaſed. And ſome of theſe are ſo zealous as to pay their conſtant viſits and devotions to the tombs of ſome of their pious men or ſaints, that are in great reverence among them, and their tombs ſumptuouſly adorned.

1662. Not far from this plain is another extending from the mountains to the city, called by the moors by a peculiar name, *Ardemira*, i. e. *The proſpect over the plain* (in the ſame ſenſe as the *French* ſay *Bellvidere*) where the mahometan courtiers, and other officers of the king uſed to keep their turnaments and running at the ring on horſeback. This plain extends to the weſt as far as the ſea ſhore, the way that leads to *Karu*, from whence the city has the faireſt proſpect. Ardemira

Behind the mountains, being the S. S.W. and the W. S.W. part of the iſland, called *Turumbake*, is the faireſt of all, tho' its compaſs is leſs betwixt the mountains and the ſea than that part beyond the mountains. Here you ſee a countrey ſeat of the old queen of *Ormus*, adorned with walks of palm-trees, and two large ciſterns or baſons, called from the place the *Ponds of Turumbake*, beſides ſeveral leſſer ones. Turumbake.

Their water is the wholeſomeſt and freſheſt of the whole iſland. There is another great baſon belonging to this ſeat, which is continually ſupplied with water out of three adjacent ponds and a ſmall brook; this water is not near ſo ſalt as that which is kept in the ponds more to the E. and N. N. E. where the ſun turns the water into ſolid ſalt. This countrey ſeat was already in a decaying condition 50 or 60 years before my coming here, having only a few apartments left, wherein the king of *Ormus* uſed to lodge during the ſummer ſeaſon; *Turumbake* had at that time not above 15 or 20 huts built of reed cloſe together, like a ſmall village, and covered with palm-tree leaves, after a wretched manner. Moſt of the houſes of this iſland are built after the ſame manner, notwithſtanding which, the inhabitants of *Ormus* retire thither with their families in the ſummer, being taught both by tradition and experience, that the open countrey air is much more wholeſome during the hot ſeaſon, than the city air.

On the north ſide of this iſle lies the city of *Ormus*, which before it was ſubdued by the *Portugueſe* was very populous, foreigners flocking thither daily from *Perſia*, the *Eaſt-Indies* and *Europe* itſelf, for the conveniency of traffick. To be ſhort, the city of *Ormus* was the moſt famous and richeſt trading city of the world, before the *Portugueſe* had found out the paſſage by ſea to the *Eaſt-Indies*, being inhabited and frequented by the *Perſians*, *Arabians*, *Abyſſines*, *Armenians*, *Tartars*, *Turks*, and other mahometans; beſides the *Italians*, *French*, *Dutch*, *Engliſh*, *Poles*, and other *European* nations. It was much inhabited by the *Portugueſe*, but very few *Spaniards*, becauſe the firſt would

1662. would not permit them to go thither by sea, and the *Turks* stop their passage by land, betwixt the *Mediterranean* and the *Persian* gulph; some few dwelt there under the name and protection of some other nations. The natives of *Ormus* are all mahometans, but of different sects, some being called *Kiays*, belonging to the sect of *Hali* son-in-law to *Mahomet*, whose doctrine is followed by the *Persians*; others are called *Suni's*, following the doctrine of *Mahomet*, *Osmar*, and *Osman*, as the *Turks* do; the king himself is of this sect; besides which, divers sorts of pagans, as *Banjans*, *Camboyans*, &c. inhabit here.

The city of Ormus *in the* Portuguese *times.*

The city of *Ormus* whilst under the jurisdiction of the *Portuguese*, and before the *Persians* made themselves masters of it 1619, was a very stately, rich, and magnificent place, of which the inhabitants used to boast, *That if the world were a ring*, Ormus *must be considered as the diamond.* For after the *Portuguese* had conquered this city, they were very careful in adorning it from time to time with most magnificent structures, to such a degree, that all the iron belonging to their windows and doors were gilt; and it was the common opinion in those days, that if they had remained masters of it till now, they would have turned them into massy gold. They had built a stately church upon an eminency, dedicated to the virgin *Mary*, with an adjacent hospital called the *Misericordia*. Next to this was the exchange or custom-house, called by the *Persians Beneckſal*, this was a fine edifice, surrounded with galleries on the out side. They had likewise several monasteries, amongst which those of the *Austin* fryars and *Carmelites* were the chiefest. There is yet to be seen a very high steeple, a most noble piece of architecture, exceeding in magnificence all others of this city; the mahometans call it in the *Arabian* tongue *Alkoran*; on one side of the castle stood formerly a famous *Mosque*, which the *Portuguese* caused to be demolished, as being too near the castle, which proved the occasion of the most inveterate hatred against the *Portuguese*, not only among the moors inhabiting there, but likewise among the *Persians*, their king *Tahamass* or *Tahamas*, grandfather to *Schach Abas*, having been the founder of it.

Under the Persians.

No sooner was this city fallen into the hands of the *Persians*, but she was by them despoiled of her ancient glory, and most of her inhabitants, many of whom were killed in the siege, the rest fled for shelter to some other place. All the churches, houses, and other publick edifices, were laid level with the ground, except some few shops in the *Bazar* or shopkeepers street. The *Dutch* ships which unloaded there, and returned commonly empty from thence, used to make it their practice at that time to ballast their vessels with the finest marble stones, the remnants of the stately structures of this city, and would questionless by degrees have taken all that was left, had not the *Persian* governour there prohibited the exportation of them under a severe penalty. For the *Persians* whose intention was to lay the foundation of the greatness of *Gamron* upon the ruines of *Ormus*, did remove all the best stones from thence, which they made use of in their best buildings at *Gamron*. The fortifications of the city of *Ormus* in the *Portuguese* times, in 1619, were but in a slender posture, the ditch about the castle being filled up with dirt, having scarce 6 foot of water; besides that, it was not spacious enough for the garrison. Their commanders in chief, who were removed from thence every year, had according to the custom of the *Portuguese*, but a slender share of knowledge in martial affairs, the governour at that time being an ancient man, not trained up in the wars, and not provided with experienced engineers and gunners.

The castle of Ormus.

The old four-square castle was built on the utmost northern or north-west point of the land of the isle, where it approaches nearest to the *Persian* shore, two sides of it being washed by the sea, the other two facing the city; betwixt which and the castle is a very fair square of about 300 feet long, from whence you have a fine prospect into the sea. This castle, whilst in the possession of the *Portuguese*, was not very large, being defended only by four bastions, which as well as the cortines, were built with a kind of small flint-stones mixt with mortar and sea-water; so that they were not proof against the thunder of the great cannon. The ditch was likewise very shallow, though it might have been made deeper without any great cost, by reason of the nearness of the sea, which waters it on two sides. In this condition was the castle of *Ormus* under the *Portuguese*, of which the *Portuguese* boasted that it was impregnable. After the *Persians* had made themselves masters of it, they were very careful to repair the old fortifications, and to add some new ones, especially on the point of the ditch, they made a half-moon, the cannon of which commanded the plain and a gallery; since which time they keep it always in a good posture of defence, and maintain a considerable garrison there, under the command of the governour of *Ormus*, who residing for the most part at *Gamron*, appoints a deputy for this place, who has his residence in the palace formerly belonging to the kings of *Ormus*.

5 The

1662. The harbour of this island is a certain bay, made by two points of land that jett out on both sides; upon one of these capes stands the castle, on the other the *Portuguese* had built a church, dedicated to our *Lady of Good-Hope*; but this point turns somewhat nearer towards the city, so that the harbour where the largest vessels, galleys, and smaller vessels used to cast anchor, lies opposite to the north-east part of the city, betwixt the two monasteries built by the *Portuguese*, one of which belonged to the *Carmelites*, the other to the *Austin* fryars. The tide where this bay is deepest rises at high water, near four foot high above the foundations of the houses; notwithstanding which, at low water the shore is dry for above 200 paces; and 150 paces farther the water is not 3 feet high where it is deepest, so that the largest vessels are obliged to cast anchor at 600 paces from the city, and the galleys at 500, which renders this harbour very unsafe, especially if a storm arises from the east, which often forces the ships ashore; nay, this harbour would be much more dangerous, were it not for the nearness of the continent, which covers it on the N. and N. E. side, and the isle of *Queixome*, which lies to the N. N. W. of it, and breaks the violence of the raging waves. Some tell us of two different bays belonging to the isle of *Ormus*, which afford a safe harbour to ships, the one to the east, the other to the west, being divided by a neck of land which jetts out betwixt them a considerable way into the sea.

The harbour.

Scarcity of water.

The whole island is destitute of water, except what some standing pools or ponds afford, which is always brackish, tho' some more than others; some, especially such as are near the sea-side, being tolerably fit for use; for the farther they are from the mountains, the less they participate of the salt. It does sometimes not rain in *Ormus* for three years together; the only springs of fresh water they have being in the royal gardens. *Ferra Gutka* who reigned in 1596 in *Ormus*, found out a spring with fresh water in *Turumbake*. Not far from thence near the sea-side, arises a salt water spring from among the rocks, called by the *Persian* inhabitants *Abdarmon*, i. e. medicinal water, which has a purging quality, and cleanses the bowels from all impurities. Here you see abundance of people drink the waters at a certain season of the year, when they have a mind to be satisfied whether their bowels are thoroughly cleansed, they cut a piece of an orange or citron, and if immediately after they go to stool, they reckon themselves sufficiently purged. 'Tis true, there are three springs here, which all having their rise among the mountains, afford water sufficient for three rivulets, but it is as brackish as the sea water it self. Thus several brooks are to be seen to the S. E. among the mountains which carry a very clear water, but so stockt with salt, that in the summer, when these rivulets are dry'd up, you see vast lumps of salt, which cover the banks on both sides. The vast quantity of salt which is to be met with all over this island, being in some places burnt up and blackned by the violence of the sun-beams, affords a dreadful sight at a distance. They have also a kind of salt clay, out of which they make earthen vessels. 1662.

The whole isle is nothing else but a barren vast lump of salt, which scarce affords either grass or trees, except what is brought forth by force in the royal gardens in the plains, neither does it afford any thing for the sustenance of human life. It has however some few trees in certain places, but bear no fruit except dates, and another small fruit growing on thorn bushes with green leaves; another kind of these thorn bushes they have with a pretty large stem, and small red leaves. In the opening of the rocks you see now and then a large green and well spread tree, notwithstanding several have positively asserted that this isle did produce neither tree, herbs, nor grass. The mountains are full of rock salt, which is very transparent, and contain likewise a considerable quantity of brimstone. In some winters the salt is washed by the rains down from the mountains, which afterwards is again coagulated by the sun, which is the only made use of here, for the rock salt being of too corrosive a nature, does consume the meat instead of preserving it. The *Dutch* transport abundance of salt from hence to the *East-Indies*. The isle also affords a certain kind of white plastering called by the inhabitants *Gueche*, and another that is red of the same kind, but not so good as the white. They have also a certain way of preparing dung for plaister-work, which they perform in the following manner: They take the uppermost part of an old dunghill away, the rest they make up in balls, and let them dry in the sun. This done, they burn them to ashes with fire; the ashes they beat for a considerable time upon an even piece of ground, and immediately after mix it for use, for, if they let the ashes be cold, or keep them only two or three days, they are not fit for their purpose; but this prepared and used keeps the water out of any place for many years. There are scarce any other stones to be met with here but flint-stones, of which the greatest part of the fortifications of the castle are composed. There is also a kind of black

1662. black gliſtering ſand to be found here, which the *Portugueſe* uſed to tranſport from thence to their factories in the *Eaſt-Indies.* No barley or oats is to be ſeen here. Their cattle they feed with a peculiar ſort of peaſe or beans, which they grind, and afterwards ſteep in water, being otherwiſe too hard to digeſt. Of theſe they give a certain quantity every night to their horſes. But in the morning they give to each horſe 2 pounds of black ſugar, mixt with a pound of butter and ſome flour, which they make up into balls; then they waſh the horſes mouth and teeth, becauſe this mixture ſticks very cloſe to their teeth and gums; in the day time they feed them with ſome herbs which they draw out of the ground with roots and all, and cleanſe them very well from all impurities.

Sinking wood. In the bay and all along the coaſt of the iſle of *Ormus*, they fiſh for wood, of which they find great ſtore in the bottom of the ſea, but not very large. This wood is by the violence of the currents of the rivers ariſing from among the mountains of the continent of *Perſia* (which is not above two leagues diſtant from hence) torn off and carried to the ſhore of *Ormus*; a thing moſt ſurpriſing, and contrary to what is obſerved of this kind in other iſlands lying near the continent, or ſome other great iſlands, whither the adjacent rivers force abundance of wood, which however always ſwims on the ſurface of the water, and commonly is found rotten, whereas the wood upon the coaſt ſinks to the bottom, and is not quite rotten, but affords the inhabitants great ſtore of fuel, which has induced ſome to believe that this wood did grow under water.

On the *Perſian* coaſt you meet alſo with certain kind of light porous ſtone under water, not unlike our pumice ſtones; eſpecially near thoſe places where ſubterraneous fires are; which makes theſe ſtones to be always white, in which they differ from the common pumice, which are either blackiſh or grey; they are found here in ſuch prodigious quantities, that they build their houſes of them, becauſe they mix very well with the mortar, by reaſon of their ſpongeous ſubſtance, and very light; and when well cemented with the mortar, reſiſt the violence of the winds, which blow here exceedingly about the change of the ſeaſons, better than any other ſtones. Some are of opinion that theſe ſtones were caſt out by a burning mountain, which ſeems not improbable, there being on the back ſide of a neighbouring mountain found vaſt quantities of theſe ſtones, as black as coals. The reaſon why thoſe on the ſea ſhore are white, ſeems to be becauſe they have for many years, nay, for many ages paſt, been ſcoured by the water of their impurities; the inhabitants call them *Sanchmay*, i. e. *Rock-Fiſh*, becauſe as many as are taken away grow again in a little time, and furniſh them with materials for building. They report that in former ages this iſland did burn for ſeven years together, of which they ſhew the marks to this day; the earth upon the mountains being red, and in the vallies ſpongeous like aſhes or quick lime; beſides that the whole iſland is ſubject to frequent earthquakes. The mountains are all over covered with ſalt, and the grounds are full of ſalt-petre. As often as the wind blows from the ſouth-weſt, there ariſes ſo violent a ſtink of brimſtone from the mountains, as infects the whole air. The heat is more intenſe at *Ormus* than at *Gamron*, for it continues at leaſt five months, *viz.* from *May* till *September*, and ſometimes till the beginning of *December*; in the winter ſeaſon the heat is ſomewhat allayed by the dew which falls all the night long, but in the ſummer the nights are ſo exceſſive hot, that it would be impoſſible for the inhabitants to abide here, if by ſeveral ways they did not aſſwage in ſome meaſure its violence. For on the tops of the houſes they ſet certain wooden veſſels like bathing tubs, big enough to contain two perſons at a time, in theſe they ſit and ſleep all night in the open air with the water up to their necks. The cauſe of this intolerable heat is attributed chiefly to the nature of the ſoil, which is not only ſandy, but full of ſalt-petre, which occaſioning a continual loſs of ſpirits, the inhabitants are forced to repair in ſome meaſure this defect, by continually keeping themſelves in cold water, notwithſtanding it be none of the beſt here; all the water that is brought hither from *Bandel Kongo*, or the iſle of *Queixome*, being taken out of ponds, and conſequently not purified from its dregs for want of motion; which is ſufficiently demonſtrable by its colour which is like milk, and its ſediment which is ſometimes two or three inches thick at the bottom of the veſſel it is kept in. During the violence of the hot ſeaſon you may ſee people of both ſexes and all ages, flock to the city walls; but the *Europeans* ſeldom venture at ſwimming in the ſea, the water being ſo exceſſive ſalt that it excoriates their bodies; but they allay the exceſſive heat of the nights by wetting their quilts and pillows with cold water. It is farther obſervable, that the winds are ſo changeable here, that you may in a quarter of an hours time remarkably feel their different effects; ſome by opening, others by obſtructing the pores of your bodies. During the ſummer ſeaſon the winds blow for the moſt part E. and S. E. or W. S. W. but ſeldom from the 1626.

1662. south, the last of which is not so unwholesome as the rest; and what is more surprising is, that this wind always cools the water contained in any vessels, but not the chambers or rooms where the water is kept.

Their Drink. The drink of the common people is water, those of the better sort drink *Spanish* wine, or *Persian* wines of *Shiras*, but these are very scarce and dear. They distil also a spirit of rice and sugar here, as well as in all other parts of the *Indies*. They have also a certain kind of drink call'd *Tari*, which is drawn from a tree, and as sweet as musk; this is the ordinary liquor sold in publick-houses, who pay a considerable tax for their licenses to the king. This liquor is brought every day to town in casks on horse-back, each horse carrying one on each side.

Origin of the Isle of Ormus. The isle of *Ormus* was in ancient times govern'd by its own kings or princes, descended from the race of these great kings that ruled all over *Arabia*, *Persia* and the adjacent countries. The first famous in their histories, was a certain *Arabian Emir* or prince, call'd *Mahamed Dramku*, of the race of the antient kings that ruled in *Saba*, or *Arabia Fælix*. This prince being extremely desirous to conquer new dominions, extended his conquests to the *Persian Gulph*, where he landed with a great fleet from *Kalayatta*, a city of *Arabia Fælix*, and laid the foundation of a city call'd *Ormus* or *Harmus* on the coast of *Persia*. He left for his successor *Solyman* his son, who was succeeded by the following kings. *Isa* the third in rank, son of *Solyman*; the fourth *Lax Kari* son of *Isa*, who left the court and embraced a private life. The fifth was *Katkobad* his son; the sixth *Isa* II. son to *Katkobad*, the 7th *Mamud* son of *Isa* II. who suspecting *Mir Xabadin Molong* his nephew, made him a prisoner in the castle of *Gati*; from whence he escaped to *Seugon*, and married the daughter of the governor of that castle. The 8th *Xaranta* son of *Mamud*, he engaged in a war against *Molong*, but was slain in an engagement with his enemy.

9th, *Mir Xabadin Molong* was declared king in his stead; his daughter *Sed Alkatum* was married to *Emir*, or prince *Seyfadin Aben Azar*, his brother *Aly*'s son, king of the isle of *Keys*, who dying soon after, his son *Seyfadin* obtained the kingdom of *Keys*. *Mir Xabadin* dying likewise not long afer, his *Vizier Xarcar* made himself master of the kingdom of *Ormus*; and those of *Keys* having at the same time deposed *Seyfadin*, he fled to *Ormus*, where being well received by the inhabitants, he besieged the usurper *Xarcar* in the castle of *Karcan*, whom he kill'd, and thereby became master of the whole kingdom. After *Seyfadin* had well settled his affairs here, he undertook an expedition against those of *Keys*, of whom he kill'd many, and made some of their chief men prisoners. From thence he went to the isle of *Gerun*, (since call'd *Ormus*) where he caused all his prisoners to be slain upon a certain mountain, which from thence was call'd *Kay Kastaron, i. e.* The mountain of the dead. He returned at last victorious to *Ormus*, where he spent the rest of his days in Peace. The 11th was *Xabadin Mamud*, son of *Isa* II. who suceeeded his uncle in the kingdom. The 12th *Emir Roknadin Mamud*, *Xabadin*'s nephew, son of *Hamud*, who was very victorious, and extended his conquests as far as *Safar*, a province of *Arabia Fælix*. He reign'd 35 years, and died 1278.

He was succeeded by his son *Emir Sayfadin Nocerat*, but was soon after forced by *Emir Kodbadin Thabantam* and *Emir Moechzadin Fulad*, or *Pulad*, to fly the kingdom, and to seek for shelter, together with his mother, by sultan *Gebaladin Suraget Mex*, governor of *Kernon*, by whose assistance he was restored to his kingdom: But being a second time vanquish'd, by his brother *Emir Kodbadin* was forced to save himself by flight in a small bark, in the isle of *Queixome*. In the mean while, king *Seyfadin*, who had assisted *Kodbadin*, having caused him to be murthered, the soldiers conceived such a hatred, against this *Seyfadin*, that they instantly recall'd *Emir Sayfadin Nocerat*, chased away *Seyfadin*, and restored him to the throne. Notwithstanding which he was not long after murthered, by his two brothers, *Emir Masaud*, and *Emir Turkonxa*, together with his two sisters, *Bibi Banek*, and *Bibi Neyty*, after he had reign'd 12 years, *viz.* 1290.

Masaud the murtherer of his Brother, succeeded him in his throne, being a very couragious but cruel man, which brought upon him the hatred both of the nobility and common people, of whom he caused many to be killed. This made them implore the assistance of *Emir Bahadin Ayas Seyfin*, formerly a slave only of king *Nocerat*, but now governor of *Kalayatte*, a sea-port of *Arabia-Fælix*; who forced *Masaud* to fly to *Kernon*, and from thence into *Syria*, where he died, after a reign of three years. He was succeeded by *Bahadin Ayas Seyfin*, who caused two brothers of *Masaud* to be beheaded, for endeavouring to restore him to the kingdom.

About that time a great swarm of *Turks*, came out of *Turkestan*, conquered a considerable part of *Persia*, and by their frequent inroads, into the kingdom of *Ormus*, forced the inhabitants to seek for shelter, at

1662. at the command of their king *Azaez*, in the isle of *Queixome*. Whilst they were roving about in the neighbouring seas, to find out a place where to fix their habitations, they happened to light upon a certain island, 2 leagues from *Queixome*, where meeting with a very ancient man, living just on the point of the isle, a fisherman by trade, he advised their king, to settle there. The king approving of his counsel, sent to the king of *Keys*, the proprietor of this, and all the other islands in the *Persian Gulph*, to desire him to sell him the said isle, for a certain sum of money, which being granted, he settled there a colony of his subjects, 1300, and gave it the name of *Ormus*, after his native country. His successors afterwards extended their conquests over a great part of *Arabia* and *Persia*, and over the *Persian* sea, as far as *Basora*; and maintain'd themselves in the possession of it, till this island was conquered by the *Portuguese*. This king died 1312, in the 22 year of his reign.

Some historians give us the following account of this and the succeeding kings of the isle of *Ormus*.

After this king had settled his new colony, he surrendered the government, to *Emir Ayzadin Gordonxa*, son of *Salhor*, and *Bibi Zeineb*, a nephew of the ancient king of *Ormus*, and retiring to *Kalayatte* in *Arabia*, there finish'd his days in peace. *Gordonxa* was engaged in war with the king of *Keys*, because he had intercepted some ships coming from the *East-Indies*, his dominions; *Ormus* he vanquish'd, and forced him to fly his dominions; but the king of *Keys* returning soon after, found means to make *Gordonxa* his prisoner, under pretence of an interview concerning a peace betwixt them; and *Bibi Sultan*, *Gordonxa*'s spouse, committed the administration of the government to *Malek Guaya Hadin Dinar*, son of her husband's brother *Xamxa*; scarce five months were expired, before the king of *Keys* came to *Ormus*, with *Gordonxa* his prisoner, where he was joyfully received by his subjects, except *Dinar*, who being used to rule, would not submit to *Gordonxa*, but forced him to retire to the castle of *Minab*, on the continent of *Persia*. Notwithstanding which, *Dinar* being sensible what affection the people bore to *Gordonxa*, and fearing his return, he thought it his safest way to retreat in time to the kingdom of *Makron*, betwixt *Persia* and the countrey of *Send* or *Ind*. After which *Gordonxa*, once more return'd to his kingdom, where he died 1318.

He was succeeded by his son *Emir Mobaresadin Bararon Xa*, who together with his brother, was by *Emir Xabadin Issuf* his general put in prison; *Issuf* afterwards mounted the throne, but was engaged in a war immediately after, with *Emir Xa Kodbadin*, brother to the imprison'd king: *Dinar* came likewise with a strong flying army, to his assistance, from *Makron*; but finding *Issuf* too strong for them both, he entred into a confederacy with him; and *Issuf* after having caused the imprisoned king, his mother, and one of his brothers to be slain, forced *Kodbadin* to retire to *Kalayatte*, with *Bibi Mariam*, the spouse of *Ayas Ceysin*. But *Kodbadin* afterwards returned unexpectedly to *Ormus*, with a considerable force, and having made *Issuf* his prisoner, he put the crown upon his head, and caused him, his wife and his two sons, to be killed; after which he likewise made himself master of *Keys*. It happen'd that *Kodbadin* being abroad a hunting on the continent, 1345, *Ri d Xur Nosomadin*, in the mean while got himself proclaim'd king of *Gerun* or *Ormus*; but finding most of the inhabitants averse to him, he quitted the countrey. However it was not not long before he return'd with a great power, and having gain'd *Homer Sojadin*, *Kodbadin*'s general, to join with him, he forced *Kodbadin* to fly to *Kalayatte*. He had scarce stay'd here a year, when word was brought him, that *Nosomadin* was dead, and that by his last will, he had enjoined his sons, *Xembe* and *Xady*, to throw themselves at the feet of *Kodbadin*, and to surrender the crown to him; but finding that the two young men, instead of performing their father's will, had seized upon the kingdom; he attack'd them and regained the crown of *Ormus*. He died 1347, in *Nakelstan*, a province of *Mogestan*. 1662.

He was succeeded by *Turonxa* his son, (who writ the lives of the kings his predecessors, both in verse and prose.) He vanquished *Xembe* and *Xady*, and died 1378, after he had reigned 30 years. After him his eldest son *Mazud* obtained the crown of *Ormus*, who was succeeded by *Xabadin*, the second son of *Turonxa*; after whom reign'd *Salgar*, *Turonxa*'s third son. Under his reign, *Sofi Hbalila* conquered all *Persia*, even to the continent, directly opposite to the island of *Gerun*, or *Ormus*, which escaped his hands for want of shipping; but *Salgar* lost all that he was possessed of on the continent. For the rest he reigned in peace, as did his successor *Xauwes*. Him succeeded *Seyfadin*, who reigned 1507, when the *Portuguese*, after they had discovered the passage by sea to the *Indies*, first set footing in the isle of *Ormus*, under the command of *Alfonsus Albuquerque*, the king being then yet in his minority, was under the protection of one *Atar* or *Kogear*, his father's slave, a brave but cunning man,

1662. whose chief aim was to let the young king bear the title of king, but to keep the administration of affairs in his own hands. *Albuquerque* being not ignorant of it, look'd upon this as a favourable opportunity to bring the city of *Ormus*, under the power of *Emanuel*, the then king of *Portugal*, or at least to make it tributary to him, by erecting a fortress near it, by which means he might clear the *Persian* gulph of all the *Turkish* and other Mahometan vessels trading to the *Indies*, and consequently entail that whole trade upon *Portugal*. He was about that time, with six stout men of war well mann'd, cruising in those seas; but thinking it below himself at such a juncture as this to lie privateering at sea, he steer'd his course the 20th of *August* 1507 towards the *Persian* gulph, and passing by the cape *Rosalgat*, came to an anchor before *Kalayatte*, (a noble city, and the first on that coast under the jurisdiction of the kings of *Ormus*) to provide himself with fresh provisions. The inhabitants dreading the name of the *Portuguese*, which was then already become famous throughout the *Indies*, entred into a confederacy with him, upon such conditions as *Albuquerque* was pleased to prescribe them. From thence he set sail for *Kuriatte*, another city belonging to the kings of *Ormus*, on the *Arabian* coast. Here the inhabitants being of a different opinion with those of *Kalayatte* chose rather to defend themselves by force, than to submit to *Albuquerque*, tho' with very ill success. For *Albuquerque* having landing his men, so vigorously attack'd the city, that the garrison after some resistance were forced to leave it to his mercy, which he burnt to the ground, with all their ships he found in the harbour. In the same manner he made himself master of the *Maskate* and *Orfasan*, two strong and well fortified places belonging to the king of *Ormus*; and from thence directly taking his course to *Ormus* it self, the chief aim of this expedition, he sent word to king *Seyfadin* and *Atar* the protector, that *Emanuel* king of *Portugal* having taken a resolution, out of an hereditary hatred to the mahometans, the declared enemies of *Christendom*, to make war against them, which should not end but with the total conquest of either side, he was come to tell them, that if they were ready, according to the example of several other *Asiatick* and *African* kings, to pay his master a certain yearly tribute, he would leave them in the quiet possession of the island, but if they refused to acknowledge the king of *Portugal* for their lord, he was come to denounce them war, which was not to end but with their total total destruction.

The Portuguese *came first into the* Persian *gulph.*

1662. The king being sorely frightned at the last success of the *Portuguese*, and dreading the same fate, thought it his best way to cajole *Albuquerque* with fair words into a belief of his sincere intentions of peace; but at the same time, by the advice of *Atar*, sought to gain time, and to delay his positive answer, till the expected auxiliaries from the continent of *Persia* were arrived. No sooner had he received these supplies but he altered his note, and in plain terms sent word to *Albuquerque*, that the kings of *Ormus* were not used to pay, but to receive tribute from foreigners; that in case the *Portuguese* would be contented with the same privileges of trading other nations enjoy'd there, they should be welcome; but that if they once came to hostilities, they should be convinced to their cost, what difference there was to fight with well appointed *Persians* and *Arabians*, and with an undisciplin'd rabble of *Moors*. By this time *Atar* the protector had got above 20000 men together, part of which he embark'd aboard the merchant vessels then in harbour there, which he posted in a line along the shore, to prevent the enemies landing, whilst he with the men of war put to sea with an intention to attack *Albuquerque* in the rear, so soon as he should be engaged with the merchant men: But *Albuquerque*, instead of attacking the merchant ships, came up with *Atar*'s fleet, and engaged them so furiously, that that in a short time he sunk many of them, and burnt the rest, with a great slaughter of men on the enemies side, whereas the *Portuguese* lost not above ten men during the whole engagement. King *Seyfadin* being sensible that the loss of his fleet must of necessity draw that of the whole island after it, sent immediately his deputies to *Albuquerque* to treat of peace; they were kindly received by the *Portuguese* general, who gave immediate orders, that the fire which had seized by this time upon the merchant ships, should be extinguished immediately, and the next day a peace was concluded betwixt them upon these following conditions.

That *Seyfadin* king of *Ormus*, and all his successors, submit themselves to, and shall acknowledge the king of *Portugal* their protector, and pay him an annual tribute of 15000 *Serafs*.

That *Albuquerque* shall have liberty to pitch upon a place, such as he judges most convenient for the erecting of a fortress, for which purpose he shall be supply'd with ready money, and other necessaries by the said king.

Accordingly *Albuquerque* apply'd himself with all imaginable speed to the building of the fortress, but many of the gentlemen volunteers,

1662. volunteers and other *Portugueſe*, looking upon it as a great hardſhip to ſpend their time here in ſlaviſh drudgery, whilſt they miſs'd their opportunity of getting a rich booty at ſea from the *Mooriſh* ſhips, (the main intent of their voyage) began to murmur, and at laſt, with the conſent of their captains, embark'd themſelves aboard two men of war, and in ſpite of *Albuquerque* return'd to the *Indies*. He was vex'd to to the ſoul to ſee himſelf thus diſappointed in this great deſign, but being forced to comply with neceſſity he follow'd the reſt. But ſome years after he being ſent from the king of *Portugal* in the quality of viceroy of the *Indies*, he did, after the conqueſt of *Goa* and *Malacca*, bring it to perfection in the following manner.

He cauſed 1577, 22 men of war, and a good number of merchant ſhips to be equip'd at *Goa*, and to have it rumour'd abroad, that he intended to go with this fleet to *Aden* (a city at the entrance of the *Redſea*) to prevent thoſe of *Ormus* to conceive any jealouſy of this equipment. But no ſooner was he come to *Maſkate* but he changed his courſe, and ſteer'd directly for *Ormus*, where his arrival cauſed an incredible fear both in the king and people. For *Atar* being dead ſince, and king *Seyfadin* poiſon'd by *Noradin*, governor of the city, his brother *Toro* or *Torunxa* had uſurp'd the kingdom from his children. *Noradin*, who had both by this act, and before heap'd ſo many obligations upon this new king, got thereby the ſole adminiſtration of the government into his own hands, and daily appear'd in publick with a ſtrong guard, conſiſting moſt of his own kinsfolks. Thoſe that bore the chiefeſt rank among theſe were three brothers, among whom was one *Hamades*, *Noradin*'s chief favourite, a man of about 35 years of age, bold, prudent and very ambitious, and reſembling in every reſpect the late deceas'd protector *Atar*. He took effectual care by placing his creatures in all places of truſt, whereby he eſtabliſh'd himſelf in the management of the government, ſo that not only *Noradin*, but alſo *Toro* himſelf durſt not attempt to act contrary to his ſentimens. From hence it was, that tho' the league with *Portugal* had been kept inviolably hitherto, the *Portugueſe* had been civilly receiv'd there, and the yearly tribute punctually paid, yet was the power of *Hamades* ſo prevailing, as to have conſtrained *Toro* to accept of the *Perſian* turbant ſent him by *Iſmael Sophi*, an evident ſign that *Hamades* his inclinations were rather for the *Perſians* than *Portugueſe*. *Albuquerque* being not ignorant of what paſs'd at *Ormus*, reſolved, by delivering king *Toro* from the ſlaviſh ſubmiſſion impoſed upon him by his ſubjects, to confirm him abſolutely in his fidelity and intereſt to the king of *Portugal*; for which purpoſe he ſurrounded the whole iſland with his fleet, to take away from them all hopes of relief, and immediately ſent word to the king, that he was come thither with no other intent than to enter upon a new league betwixt the kings of *Portugal* and *Ormus*. 1662.

King *Toro* being not a little ſurprized at the unexpected appearance of ſo great a fleet, diſpatch'd immediately his deputies to *Albuquerque*, to treat with him concerning the conditions of it; *Albuquerque* demanded, that beſides the annual tribute to be paid to the king of *Portugal*, liberty ſhould be given him to build a fortreſs, and a factory houſe to ſecure the trade of the *Portugueſe*; and king *Toro* being willing enough to grant what he deſired, the league was confirmed by a ſolemn oath on both ſides. But *Hamades*, who ſoon foreſaw that the building of this fortreſs would tend to the no ſmall detriment of his authority, left no ſtone unturn'd to prevent its accompliſhment, which *Albuquerque* being ſoon aware of, he cauſed this ambitious favourite to be kill'd. After his death, the *Portugueſe* meeting with no other obſtacle, the fortreſs was ſoon after brought to perfection; king *Toro* readily furniſhing them with materials and other neceſſaries. The next care of *Albuquerque* was, how to remove all the opportunities of a future revolt among the inhabitants of *Ormus*; for which purpoſe, after having taken the oath of fidelity from king *Toro*, he removed all the great cannon out of the city, and ſent about 30 perſons of the royal family, who had their eyes taken away before, and were maintain'd at the king's charge from thence to *Goa*, where they were to be provided for by certain perſons appointed for that purpoſe by *Emanuel* king of *Portugal*. *Albuquerque* having thus ſettled the affairs of *Ormus* return'd to *Goa*, where he was no ſooner arrived but dy'd. The *Mahometans* call this *Albuquerque Malandy*, becauſe he was born at *Melinde* in *Africa*, call'd by them *Maland*. Albuquerque *dies*.

It was not long before king *Toro* refuſed to pay the uſual tribute to the *Portugueſe*, alledging that they did not defend him againſt the violences committed by *Mokrin* his vaſſal prince, of the iſland of *Baharen*, who hinder'd the ſhips from coming to *Ormus*. *Sequeira*, then governor of the *Indies* for the king of *Portugal*, ſent hereupon ſeven men of war (aboard of which were 400 *Portugueſe* ſoldiers) to the aſſiſtance of king *Toro*, under the command of *Anthony Korrea*, which were join'd by 200 barks of the king's, mann'd with 3000 *Perſians*, under

1662. the conduct of *Xaraf* his admiral. *Mokrin* brought together an army of 12000 men, consisting of three thousand *Arabian* horse, 4000 *Persian* archers; and the rest of *Turkish* firelocks, and some of his own subjects, arm'd only with scimeters and javelins; but being overthrown and slain in battle, the isle of *Baharen* fell into the hands of the king of *Ormus*, who gave it to one *Bardadi*, under condition that he should pay him an annual tribute of 40000 *Serafs*.

By this time *Sequeira* being sufficiently convinced, that the king his master was circumvented in his share of the customs and other taxes, appointed certain *Portuguese* commissioners to have a watchful eye over them, which so exasperated the inhabitants, that king *Toro* in 1521 revolted, and caused all the *Portuguese* at *Ormus*, except such as fled into the fortress, to be kill'd; the same treatment received the *Portuguese* at *Kuriatte*, *Soar*, and in the island of *Baharen*, who were either all slain or imprison'd. Then he attempted the taking of the fortress, but meeting with a brave resistance from the *Portuguese*, and dreading their return with a good fleet, he retired with all his subjects and their effects to the isle of *Queixome*, and set fire to the city of *Ormus*, which burnt four days successively. But not long after *Xaraf*, the chief adviser and promoter of this revolt, having received intelligence of the coming of the *Portuguese* fleet, and fearing to be call'd to a severe account kill'd king *Toro*; and in his stead put *Mamud Scha*, one of the sons of *Seyfadin*, upon the throne. This king being but 13 years of age, made a new league with the *Portuguese*, by virtue of which he was oblig'd to pay an annual tribute of 20000 *Serafs* to the king of *Portugal*: The inhabitants of *Ormus* were to restore to the *Portuguese* all that they had taken from them; in consideration of which, the *Portuguese* were not to intermeddle with their custom-house, or other courts of judicature. In the year 1550, the *Turks* made an inroad into the isle of *Ormus*, and laid it almost desolate. The king who in 1566 reign'd in *Ormus* was call'd *Siasirusia* of *Xasiruxa Gialedin*; and in 1580 reign'd one *Ferraguixa*, who tho' very antient, had a great inclination to marry *Bifatme*, the widow of *Rex Bradadin*, his late governor of *Mogostan*, thereby to be master of her treasure, which was very great; she gave him for answer, *That she would comply with his desires as soon as he had perfected his new gardens at* Tarumbake, *and found out a new spring of fresh water*; both which the king having found means to effect in a short time, he was nevertheless disappointed in his expectation by the crafty widow. He that reign'd in *Ormus* in 1606 was *Xeque*, *i. e.* prince *Ajo*, or as some call him *Ajosia*, *i. e.* king *Ajo*. 1662.

For tho' the *Portuguese* by the conduct of *Albuquerque*, had got into the possession of the island of *Ormus*, ever since 1507, nevertheless the succession of their kings from father to son, was kept inviolable under the protection of the crown of *Portugal*; for no sooner did the king of *Ormus* die, but the inhabitants set another of the royal family, tho' not without the consent of the *Portuguese* governor upon the throne, who was oblig'd to take the oath of fidelity to the king of *Portugal*, after which he was invested with the crown and scepter by the said governor, who conducted him in great pomp to the royal palace, and afterwards gave him all the demonstrations of respect and honour, tho' at the same time he durst not stir from the island without his approbation.

Vast territories belonging to the kings of Ormus.

The antient kings of *Ormus* were masters of vast territories on the continent of *Persia* and *Arabia*; and among the rest of the countries of *Lar* and *Mogostan* in *Persia*, the last of which is commonly call'd the *Persian* coast, and the countrey of *Lar* being a mountainous countrey of very difficult access, serv'd them as a bulwark against the *Persians*. For after these had once taken from the king of *Ormus* the countrey of *Lar*, and what else they were possess'd of on the continent of *Persia*, (whose example was followed by the *Arabians*) the isle of *Ormus* was bereaved of its chief defence, and exposed to the insults of the *Persians*.

How they secur'd the sovereignty.

It was the custom of the antient kings of *Ormus*, in order to secure to themselves the quiet possession of the throne, to confine their next kinsfolks, or such as had any pretensions to the crown, with their wives and children, where they were well entertain'd, and kept till the king thought fit to dispose of them otherwise. They also used to blind their brothers, and others descended of the royal line, because it was a fundamental law amongst them, that no blind man could sway the scepter. It was performed thus; they made a copper bason red hot, which they, immediately after it was taken out of the fire, held frequently close before the eyes of him that was to be bereaved of his eyesight; which without any farther application, had the desired effect, without giving the least blemish to the eyes in outward appearance, which look'd as clear as before. Some will have it to have been done with a red hot iron.

Their riches.

The kings of *Ormus* possessed vast treasures in former ages; the customs they received from all goods exported and import-

1662. ed there, amounting to an immenſe ſum yearly, which empower'd them to extend their conqueſts on the continent of *Perſia* and *Arabia*, which they afterwards loſt again by their own neglect. For whilſt they themſelves were drowned in voluptuouſneſs, they left the ſole management of affairs to their favourites, who encreaſing in pride as they did in riches, at laſt left them nothing but the bare royal name, whilſt they acted in the government at their own pleaſure, diſpoſing of the treaſury and all other matters of moment, as it ſuited beſt with their own intereſt, whereby both the power of the kings and the ſtrength of the kingdom being weakned, they were no longer able to cope as before with their enemies, and at laſt were forced to yield themſelves tributaries to the *Portugueſe*, who were afterwards, *viz.* in 1622, chaſed from thence by the *Perſians*, with the aſſiſtance of the *Engliſh*, under the reign of their king *Schach Abbas*, which happened in the following manner.

The *Portugueſe* at *Ormus* had no ſooner been advertiſed of the taking of the fort of *Queixome* (ſituate upon the point of the iſland of the ſame name;) but they ſent deputies in the name of the king of *Ormus* and of *Goazi* to the *Perſian Chan* of *Schiras*, to come with them to an amicable compoſition, but with ſuch evident marks of fear, that the *Perſians*, who had lately received advice of a powerful incurſion made by the *Uſbeck* and *Nogayan Tartars*, and conſequently would have reſted ſatisfied with the conqueſt of the iſle of *Quiexome*, being ſenſible thereof, reſolved not to let ſlip this opportunity of plundering as it were *en paſſant* the city of *Ormus*. Accordingly the *Chan* of *Schiras*, without tarrying any longer in the iſland of *Queixome*, embark'd about 40000 *Perſians* and *Arabians*, under the conduct of *Emanculibey* his lieutenant, in ſome barks, who coming before the city of *Ormus*, found it deſerted by the *Portugueſe* and moſt of its other inhabitants, but met with a prodigious quantity of merchandiſe, which they either could or would not bring into the caſtle. The *Perſians* ſeeing themſelves thus maſters of the city without ſtriking a blow, and finding that under the protection of the houſes they might open their trenches, without any conſiderable danger from the cannon of the caſtle, fell to work without delay, and ſoon carried them on to the foot of the ditch, which being dry on that ſide, they paſs'd without much oppoſition. Then they attack'd the baſtions of *St. James*, which they undermin'd and made themſelves maſters of it in a few days; the garriſon all this while not making one ſalley, but were forced to ſurrender the place the 3d of *May*, after a ſiege of ten weeks. They conſiſted of 400 men, regular troops, beſides women and children, which were ſome days before ſent to *Maſkate*. The *Engliſh* had the chief hand in making the conditions for this ſurrender, which were,

Conqueſt of Ormus *by the* Perſians.

1662.

That all the ſoldiers ſhould have their lives granted them;

And that all ſuch as were willing ſhould be tranſported to Maſkate, *in two* Engliſh *ſhips appointed for that purpoſe*, which was ſtrictly obſerved by the *Perſians*; they made the king of *Ormus* and *Goazil*, with their families, priſoners, and ſeized upon their whole treaſure, which in pearls and gold amounted to above two millions, beſides a vaſt booty of precious ſtones, and other riches belonging to the inhabitants, and 300 pieces of cannon, all which fell to the *Perſians* ſhare, who loſt a great number of men in the ſiege of this fortreſs. The *Portugueſe*, before they ſurrendered the fort, took care to make all the cannon uſeleſs by nailing of it up. The king of *Ormus*, with ſome other *Arabians* of note were carried priſoners into *Perſia*, together with the beforementioned *Goazil Raia Noradina*. This laſt was a young lord, a ſubject of the king of *Spain*, a very handſome perſon, and well verſed in the *Perſian* and *Arabian* hiſtories. He had at the beginning of the ſiege offered 100000 crowns in ducats and *Xeraſins*, to the *Perſians*, to be tranſported to *Maſkate* or *Goa*; and the unfortunate king of *Ormus*, had likewiſe made an offer of his whole treaſure to the *Portugueſe*, to obtain the ſame favour, which was refuſed by the *Portugueſe*, notwithſtanding they were both vaſſals of the king of *Portugal*, which has given no ſlender cauſe of ſuſpicion to ſome, as if the *Portugueſe* had invited the *Perſians* thither, when they ſued for peace to them in the iſle of *Queixome*. The *Engliſh*, in conſideration of this ſervice, had the moiety of all the cuſtoms and other revenues granted them by the *Perſians*. The chief reaſon of the loſs of the fortreſs of *Ormus*, is attributed to the revolt of the garriſon in the *Portugueſe* fort of *Queixome*, who in ſpight of *Ruy Freira* their governor, ſurrendred it to the *Perſians*. It was alſo alledged, that if the governor of the *Portugueſe* fortreſs of *Ormus*, had, according to the advice of the other commanders, filled the ditch betwixt the city and the fortreſs with water, by opening the ſluices, the *Perſians* would have found it a much harder taſk to have approached ſo near to the baſtion of *St. James*.

Vaſt traffick of Ormus *in former ages.*

Before the *Portugueſe* had diſcovered the paſſage by ſea to the *Indies*, all the *Indian* commodities were brought into *Europe* by the way of *Ormus*, whither they were firſt tranſported

1662. tranſported out of all parts of the *Indies*, and from thence thro' the *Perſian* gulph, and along the river *Euphrates* to *Baſſora*, which city lies upon the confluence of the two great rivers the *Euphrates* and *Tigris*. From *Baſſora* they were by land carried by camels to *Bagdad*, a city upon the *Tigris*. From hence they travelled with their merchandizes in caravans thro' the deſarts of *Syria* to *Aleppo*, being a journey of forty days; and from *Aleppo* to *Tripolis* in *Syria*, bordering upon the mediterranean (only three days journey) from whence they were tranſported by the mediterranean into all parts of *Europe*. From hence it is evident, that *Ormus* in former ages was the ſtaple of all the *Indian* commodities. But ſince the diſcovery of the ſea paſſage to the *Eaſt-Indies* by the *Portugueſe* by the cape of *Good Hope*, this way of tranſporting the *Indian* commodities by land is laid aſide, tho' even to this day, certain *Indian* merchandizes, but eſpecially *Perſian* ſilks, are brought from *Ormus* by land by the caravans, this iſland by reaſon of its ſituation, at the entrance of the *Perſian* gulph, and its two harbours, lying very commodious for traffick and ſhipping from the eaſtern parts of the world. After the city of *Ormus* was fallen into the hands of the *Perſians*, moſt of its traffick and the ſtaple of the *Indian* commodities was from thence transferred to *Gamron*, a city upon the *Perſian* coaſt, built upon the ruins of *Ormus*. We will now proceed to a ſhort deſcription of the iſlands of *Baharen*, *Queixome* and *Keſem*.

The iſle of Baharen. Among a great number of other iſlands in the *Perſian* gulph, and under the juriſdiction of *Perſia*, one of the chief is the iſle of *Baharen*, or *Bahrem*, called by *Strabo* and *Pliny Tilos*, and is by ſome taken to be the ſame iſland, called *Ichara* by *Ptolemy*. It is ſituate in the ſtreights of *Baſſora* or the *Perſian* gulph, betwixt *Baſſora* and the iſle *Gerun*, or *Ormus*, about 60 leagues diſtant from each, near the *Arabian* coaſts, over againſt the harbour of *Katifa*. This iſland abounds in water, but is brackiſh, the beſt of all being found in certain ponds or pools in *Nanyah*, in the midſt of the iſland; next to which that which is taken out of the ſea is in moſt eſteem, which is performed in the following manner.

There are certain ſprings of freſh water ariſing in the bottom of the ſea, at three fathoms and a half deep. Near the city of *Manama*, certain divers go early in the morning in boats, about three muſket ſhot deep in the ſea from the ſhore, and dive to the bottom of the ſea, fill their earthen or leathern veſſels with the water that iſſues from the ſprings, and ſo come up again and return to the ſhore; this they do with a great deal of dexterity and nimbleneſs. 1662. These ſprings are ſuppoſed to have been formerly on the ſhore, not far from the ſea-ſide, which ſince that time have been ſwallowed up by the inundations of the ſea, occaſioned by earthquakes. This iſle is very fertile, abounding in fruits of all ſorts, but eſpecially dates. But all the rice (which together with the dates, is the general food of the inhabitants;) is from the *Indies* tranſported to *Ormus*, and from thence into this iſland, which is famous throughout the *Indies*, by reaſon of the pearl fiſhery here, *Pearl fiſhery.* from whence the king of *Perſia* draws a vaſt revenue yearly, as may be gathered from thence, that after this iſland was fallen into the hands of one *Bardadin*, (who ſucceeded *Anthony Korrea Mokrin*, a vaſſal of the king of *Ormus*) he promiſed to pay a yearly tribute of 40000 *Serafs*. Beſides this, the pearl trade here produces yearly at leaſt 500000 ducats in ready money, not to reckon 100000 ducats more, which are ſhared betwixt the *Perſian* governor and the other officers: For there is a great reſort of merchants to this place, which come hither from all parts of the world to buy up pearls, and to tranſport them to the *Indies* and other places, the beſt and moſt precious pearls in the world being found near this iſland of *Baharen*, and the iſle of *Gionfar* or *Giolfar*, which both in bigneſs and roundneſs, far exceed thoſe found near the other iſlands of *Latif*, *Laſen*, *Barechator*, *Zezirafilhar*, *Alul*, *Seran*, *Dſiud*, *Daas*, *Emergocenon*, *Ancovi*, *Serecho*, *Delmeſialmas*, *Sirbeniaſt*, *Aldane*, *Feſtebruatich*, *Cherizorn*, *Dibei*, *Sarba*, *Agiman*, *Ras*; *Emelgovien*, *Raſagiar*, *Daoin*, *Raſaelchimes*, *Sirkorkor*, *Kaſab*, *Konzar*, *Meſendenderadi*, *Lima*, *Debe*, *Chorf*, *Chelb*, *Sarar*, *Suet*, *Meſtar*, *Garajat*, *Teuji*, *Golaf*, *Furgatile*, *Sam*, *Gameda*, *Bacha* and *Jadi*. All which afford pearls, but they are not exactly round. Near *Maſkate*, about 33 or 34 leagues from *Ormus*, are likewiſe very good pearls to be found.

The pearl fiſhery near *Baharen* begins ſometimes in *June*, but generally in *July*, and continues till the end of *Auguſt*. About 200 barks go abroad together, *viz.* 100 belonging to the iſle of *Baharen*, 50 to *Pilfar* and 50 to *Nibely*; their rendezvous being commonly near *Katar*, a ſea port of *Arabia*, ſix leagues ſouth of *Baharen*. The pearls taken here exceed all the reſt in goodneſs, beauty, and weight, tho' not in bigneſs. They catch them by means of a ſtone, which by its weight is let down 12 or 18 fathom under water. They ſell the pearls by *Karats* and *Abas*, three of which make one *Karat*; and by *Matikals*, or *Mitigals*, each of which contains 42 *Karats*; the ſmall pearls are ſold by *Mitigals*. Beſides this general

1662. fiſhery near *Katar*, which continues for two months, there are ſeveral other particular fiſheries, near *Nibely*, *Baharen*, *Julfar*, *Maſkate*, *Teude*, and *Rozalgate*, in the *Perſian* gulph, which though not of ſo great conſequence as the firſt, yet are commonly greatly beneficial to the owners. As they take up the oyſters they open them, when the pearls drop out. It is generally believed that theſe pearls are progenerated by the *May* dews, during which month the oyſters riſe up to the ſurface of the waters, and opening themſelves, receive a ſmall quantity of dew, which being coagulated, afterwards produces theſe pearls. Certain it is, that if theſe oyſters are opened before *June*, the pearls are ſoft and pliable like pitch. Moſt of the inhabitants of the iſle of *Baharen* are *Arabians*, but the garriſon conſiſts of *Perſians*, under the command of a vizier ſent thither by the king of *Perſia*. Formerly this iſle was under the juriſdiction of the kings of *Ormus*, and in 1602 taken from them by the *Portugueſe*. But when the *Perſian* ſultan of *Xiras* had laid ſiege to the *Portugueſe* fortreſs of *Comoran*, he made himſelf maſter of *Baharen*. The king of *Perſia* alledging that he had not taken it from the *Portugueſe*, but from a vaſſal of the king of *Ormus*, who was his vaſſal; ſo that ever ſince 1602 the *Perſians* have been in poſſeſſion of it.

The iſle of Quiexome Kechmiche. The iſle of *Queixome*, or *Queixume*, or *Quezome*, otherwiſe called *Kechmiche*, and by the inhabitants *Brokt*, lies cloſe to the continent of *Perſia*, being ſeparated from it only by a ſmall branch of the ſea: It has about two leagues in circuit, and is three leagues diſtant from *Ormus*. Its two chief places are *Arbez* and *Homeal*, where the king of *Ormus* at the time when *Albuquerque* firſt appeared hereabouts, had ſtrong garriſons. The other places of note are *Lapht*, the beſt harbours of this iſland, *Darbaga* not far from the *Lapht*, *Chau*, and *Sirmion*, or *Sermion*. It bears plenty of corn, but eſpecially barly, without which the inhabitants of *Ormus*, who are ſupplied from hence with it for their horſes, could ſcarce ſubſiſt there. Here is alſo a moſt excellent ſpring of freſh water; to ſecure which the *Perſians* had erected a fort hard by for fear of the *Portugueſe*, who were then as yet maſters of *Ormus*. If we may believe ſome hiſtorians, this iſland was not inhabited in ancient times; partly by reaſon of the frequent earthquakes that happened there, partly by reaſon of the vaſt numbers of ſerpents and other venomous creatures, which infected both air and ſome trees, ſo as to render the iſland uninhabitable. Among theſe trees is one called *Baxama* or *Baxana*, the fruit of which is ſo poiſonous, that the leaſt taſte of it kills in an inſtant, and its ſhadow is ſo peſtiferous, that it kills thoſe who abide there in leſs than a quarter of an hour. The root of this tree is in ſeveral other parts eſteemed as the greateſt antidote that can be, but here it is mortal, as are its leaves, and fruit called *Rabuzit*. 1662.

The *Portugueſe* in 1622 conquered this iſland from the *Perſians*, and on the point oppoſite to *Ormus* erected a fort, fortified with a wall, and ſurrounded with a broad and deep ditch, but the wall was very ſlight, being ſuſtained from behind only by ſome looſe earth. In ſhort it was a place of no defence, without any great cannon, neither in a condition to bear the weight of them. It had three ponds within its precinct, being chiefly built by the *Portugueſe*, for that purpoſe, becauſe the inhabitants of *Ormus*, were from thence ſupplied with water. Scarce had the *Portugueſe* finiſhed this fort, but the *Perſians* out of the countrey of *Lara* in 1622, beſieged it by land, as the *Engliſh* did at ſea; the *Portugueſe* commander *Ruy Freira de Andreada* defended himſelf bravely for ſome time, and killed many of the *Perſians*, who would have bought it perhaps at a dear rate, had not the *Engliſh* threatned to bring their great cannon againſt it, which obliged the garriſon who were not provided with them, to capitulate, and to ſurrender the fort upon honourable conditions, which were not performed on the enemies ſide. There are ſome others who have given us the following account of the occaſion of this ſiege.

The king of *Perſia* had 1612 taken the iſles of *Queizome* and *Baharen*, and the fortreſſes of *Bandel* and *Mogoſtan* on the continent, from the king of *Ormus*, which he refuſing to reſtore, the king of *Portugal* ſent his expreſs orders to *Ruy Freira*, that in caſe the king of *Perſia* would not reſtore the iſle of *Queixome* and the fortreſs of *Bandel*, he ſhould declare war againſt him, and erect a fort on the point of the iſle of *Queixome*. Accordingly *Ruy Freira de Andreada*, who in the beginning of *June* 1620, came to *Ormus*, cauſed a fort to be built on the point of the ſaid iſland, ſurrounded only with a ſlender wall made of ſtone and clay, or loam, being ſcarce to be compared in ſtrength to ſome private buildings: The *Perſians* with the aſſiſtance of the *Engliſh* having erected a ſmall battery againſt it, did play upon the fort with their cannon, which did ſtrike ſuch a terror into the garriſon that they refuſed to ſtand the brunt any longer, but forced *Ruy Freira* to capitulate. For *Emanchulican* governor of *Schiras* being juſt then come with 5000 men to *Bandel* or *Gamron*, he ſent part of his forces under the command of *Emanculi-*

V. II. Betwixt p. 209, 210.

1662. *bey* to the siege of the fort of *Queixome*; *Ruy Freira*, as I told you, being forced to surrender, had obtained certain conditions from the *English* for himself and the garrison, among which the chiefest was, that the whole garrison as well *Portuguese* as *Arabians* (the last of which were come thither from *Zulfa* upon the coast of *Arabia*, under the command of *Emir Alikamai Zemur Mahomet*, and had done signal services by sallies and otherwise) should be safely conducted to *Maskate*, a city on the coast of *Arabia* belonging to the *Portuguese*; but this was but ill performed by the *Persian* general, who before the *Portuguese* were embarked, caused all the *Arabians* to be beheaded, in spite of the protestations of *Ruy Freira*, who accused the *English* with breach of faith, but these excused themselves, alledging that these *Arabians* having formerly been subjects of the king of *Persia*, it was not in their power to prevent it: No more than 20 out of 250 *Arabians* escaped with life, who were hid by the *English* seamen. The commander in chief of these *Arabians* *Emer Genedin* being brought before the *Persian* general, was by his orders stabbed in his presence by *Xarial* his son-in-law, and then governour of *Mogostan*; but the *Portuguese* garrison consisting of 200 men, were by the *English* instead of conveying them to *Maskate*, set on shore in the isle of *Ormus*, from whence they got safe into the *Portuguese* castle.

The isle of Jarek.

The isle of *Jarek* is situate three leagues from the coasts of *Arabia*, to the south of the isle of *Ormus*, and to the east of the isle of *Kechmeche*. It is destitute of inhabitants, and very small in compass, the *Dutch* who reside on the behalf of the *East-India* company at *Gamron*, have planted there only a garden near a certain pond, whither the wild boars and stags which are here in great numbers, come to drink; they also keep here some tame fowl for their recreation. It is now time we should leave *Gamron* and *Ormus*, and proceed on our voyage.

After we had taken in our lading at *Gamron*, we set sail from thence the 2d of *June*, and with a favourable gale passed along the coast of *Malabar*, towards the isle of *Ceilon*; for before you come to the coast of *Coromandel*, you are obliged to sail round all that vast tract of land. I had letters by me for the governour of *Punto Gale*, a city of *Ceylon*, which I delived to a certain master of a small vessel, without going ashore myself. After we had provided ourselves with fresh water here, that the rendezvous of the *Dutch* ship was appointed to be at *Punto Pedro*, where Mr. *Rijklof van Goens* commanded a body of troops in order to besiege the city of *St. Thomas*, whither we also directed our course. But whilst the great train of artillery was embarking, and the troops ready to go on board for this expedition, we received intelligence that the *Portuguese* had sold the city of *St. Thomas* to the *Jentyves* or *Pagans*, which made us also alter our measures; and I went to *Jafenepatnam* to dispatch my business.

They came to Punto Gale *in* Ceylon.

The city of St. Thomas.

The city of *St. Thomas* is situate under 12 or 13 deg. 30 min. of northern latitude, 26 *German* miles from *Nagapatnam*, one and a half off the river *Ganges* near cape *Komorijn*, and a days journey or five *German* miles to the south of *Paliakatte*, on the coast of *Coromandel*, close to the sea-shore. The city of *St. Thomas* was otherwise called *Kalamina*, and by the natives *Meliapor*, which name the *Portuguese* changed into that of *St. Thomas*, in honour of that apostle, which name it retains to this day, not only among the christians, but also the *Turks* and *Indians*. *Meliapor* signifies in their language as much as a peacock, intimating that as this bird is the most beautiful of all others, so this city did in beauty excel all the rest of the east. Some will have the city of *St. Thomas* or *Meliapor*, to be the same called *Mapura* by *Ptolemy*. This city was quite desolate when the *Portuguese* first came there, who rebuilt it in 1545, since which time it has encreased to that degree, that not many years after she was accounted one of the finest cities in all the *Indies*, both in respect of the magnificence of its building, and the number of rich inhabitants. It is fortified with stone wall, strengthned by several bastions; and had under its jurisdiction above 300 villages and towns. It is one of the richest sea ports of all the *East-Indies*, its situation being in the midst of all the best harbours of those parts, which renders it the more convenient for the *East-India* trade. Whilst this place was in the hands of the *Portuguese*, it was at first incorporated with the diocese of the bishop of *Cochin*, but afterwards erected into a bishopdom, under the jurisdiction of the archbishop of *Goa*. They had a church here dedicated to *St. Francis*, belonging to the *Capuchins*, and two others, one dedicated to *St. John*, the other to the virgin *Mary*, where the *Mahometans* and *Pagans* were instructed and baptized. In the suburbs was the church of *St. Lucy*, and in the city the monastery of *Charity* and *Lazarus*, besides three others. The jesuits, of whom there was a considerable number here, had a goodly college within the city, wherein the children of the *Portuguese* and of the chief *Malabars*, were instructed in the fundamentals of the christian religion. Next to this college was a very large parish inhabited by christians, such as were by the jesuits con-

1662. verted from paganism and mahometanism, of which 120 were baptized in 1604. Here you see also the famous church of *St. Thomas*, this apostle, as the *Portuguese* pretend, being buried here; his sepulchre is shewn to this day on the top of a mountain near a city, over which they have built a small chappel, which may be discovered at some distance at sea. Close to this college upon a pretty high hill is a chappel, which as they say, was *St. Thomas*'s usual sleeping place. The jesuits to shew their reverence to this place, have adorned that part of the chappel where *St. Thomas* used to say his prayers, with gilt iron steps.

St. Thomas's *chappel.*

Here you see also a stone cross, which they say is the same that in the apostles time did fall from heaven; for which reason they have covered it with an arch, as they have done with the adjacent spring, which arising from a rock is covered by another arch resting upon four columns. The whole chappel is likewise adorned with many ornaments, and the wood of the chappel being looked upon as a precious relick, is frequently set in gold and carried away by the devout pilgrims.

We continued our course along the coast till we came to *Negapatnam*, where we were to unload part of our cargo.

Negapatan.

Negapatan or *Nenapatnam* is composed of *Naga*, which in the *Malabar* tongue signifies a serpent, and *Patnam* or *Patan* a city, because round about this place used to be seen a certain kind of very venomous serpents called *Cobros Capellos*, i. e. *Head-serpents*. It is situate under the 9 deg. 45 min. and the adjacent cape under 11 deg. of northern latitude; beyond the rocks of *Romanankir*, over against the isle of *Manar*, just opposite to *Tripalikorin*, three leagues from the city of *Tranguabar*, and about 39 leagues from the cape *Comorin*, at the beginning of the coast of *Bisnagar* and *Coromandel*. This city as well as its castle call'd *Ragu*, acknowledge the *Portuguese* for its founders, the castle being built for their better security against the attempts of the *Naik* or *Neyk*, lord of the circumjacent countrey. They had several goodly churches here, and a very fine monastery belonging to the *Franciscans*, which was maintained at the charge of the chiefest of the inhabitants. There are to this day remaining divers fine churches and other large structures, with spacious apartments and galleries according to the *Portuguese* fashion. Next to the jesuits college stood the church of *Tranguabar*. The city is pretty well fortified with defensible towers, surrounded with a good mote: It is very populous in proportion to its bigness, but most of the inhabitants are of a tawny complexion, being generally either *Mestices*, i. e. such as are born of a *Portuguese* father, and a she blackamoor; or *Kastices*, i. e. such as their fathers were blackamoors and their mothers *Portuguese* women. It is also inhabited by *Banyans* and *Mahometans*, who are the chiefest traders here. 1662.

This city was the 23[d] of *July* 1658, surrendered to the *Dutch* by composition. For Mr. *John Vander Laen* then commander in chief of the *Dutch* forces in those parts, did pursuant to his orders from Mr *Rijklof van Goens* admiral general of the *Dutch* fleet, set sail from *Jafenepatan* in the isle of *Ceylon*, on friday the 19th of *June*, to *Punto Pedro*, where he cast anchor in the evening, and found the yachts *Workum*, the *Morning-star*, *Manaer*, *Waterpass*, *Narsapour*, the galliot the *Amsterdam*, and the chaloop *Japara*, ready to join him; but the *Pidgeon* yacht was run aground, and the *Workum* was fain to stay behind, having lost 3 of her anchors. He took care to provide the fleet immediately with as much meat and other refreshments as the place would afford; and on the 20th was likewise join'd by the yachts the *Goes*, the *Pidgeon*, and the *Workum*; next day Mr. *Lucas Vander Dussen* took a review of the land forces, which consisted of 500 men, divided into 11 companies, besides the sea-men. Mr. *Vander Laen* having summoned all the captains aboard the admiral's ship, where he gave them the necessary directions how every one should behave himself in his post at their arrival before *Negapatan*.

Surrendered to the Dutch.

The 21st of *July* the fleet set sail from *Punto Pedro*, and arrived the 22[d] early in the morning in the road before the city of *Negapatan*, where he met with the yachts the *Pipelen*, the *Naisepour*, and a *Danish* chaloop. Mr. *Vander Laen* ordered to be set up the white flag in the yacht *Vander Goes*, and sent Mr. *Lucas Vander Dussen*, with 3 captains and an interpreter in a chaloop, and credential letters to *Caspar Alphonso de Karvalho*, the *Portuguese* governour of *Negapatan*, and his council, to summon the said city to a surrender upon honourable conditions. About noon Mr. *Vander Dussen* returned; and gave an account to the admiral, that the *Portuguese* governour and his council, refused to admit any of the company, except himself and the interpreter; that he was very civilly received, and admitted to appear before the council, where he had made use of all the arguments he thought might enduce them to surrender, desiring that they would send aboard the admiral their plenipotentiaries to treat about the conditions. They desired time till the next morning to consider of the matter, and that the admiral would be pleased to send another

The Dutch *come before* Negapatan.

Summon the city.

1662. another chaloop to morrow, because the *Jentyves* or natives did stop the passage of their boats at the mouth of the river. Accordingly the 23[d] Mr. *Vander Dussen*, with two ensigns return'd to *Negapatan* in the same chaloop, with a white flag, and brought back from thence *Manuel Karvalho* a jesuit, *Lewis de Quintal Parsire* and *Diego Berisero* two captains, and *Antonio d'Almeyde* a lieutenant, instructed with credentials and full power from the *Portuguese* governor, to treat about the surrender of the city to the *Dutch East-India* company upon reasonable terms. The conditions proposed by them were these; that a church should be allow'd to such *Portuguese* as were willing to remain there, with as many priests as were requisite.

The Portuguese send deputies to treat.

That the inhabitants should have liberty to retire to *Bengal*, and that they might carry along with them all what belong'd to the poor.

Their demands.

After some contests on both sides, it was agreed to surrender the place upon these following conditions.

Conditions agreed upon betwixt them and the Dutch.

That the city of *Negapatan* belonging to his *Portuguese* majesty, should be surrendered on *Wednesday* the 24th of *July*, to the *Dutch East-India* company, with all its territories, cannon, ammunition or arms, as likewise the keys of the magazines and other store-houses thereunto belonging.

That immediately as many soldiers of the *East-India* company shall be admitted into the city, as shall be thought requisite by them and the *Portuguese* governor, for their mutual security; and all merchandizes or what else may belong to the crown of *Portugal*, shall at the same time be delivered without the least fraud.

The *Portuguese* garrison now in the city shall march out with beat of drum, matches lighted and bullets in their mouths, to a certain place to be appointed by the *Dutch* admiral Mr. *Vander Laen*, where they shall be disarm'd, except that the officers even to the ensigns shall have liberty to retain their swords.

All the inhabitants, whether clergy or laymen, married or unmarried, shall be left in the free possession of all their goods, except their arms, as well moveable as unmoveable, houses, gold, silver, merchandizes, slaves of both sexes, till the last day of *October*, of the same year; against which time they shall be provided with convenient shipping, at the charge of the *Dutch East-India* company, in order to carry them to *Goa*, or further to the north, if they please.

The clerymen shall then be at liberty to carry along with them all the church ornaments, or what else belong'd to the exercise of the divine worship, except the bells, as likewise all the moveable goods belonging to them. 1662.

The laymen, soldiers and merchants, may, without the least exception, transport all their moveables, money, gold, silver, jewels, slaves of both sexes, and all their merchandizes, provided the same don't belong to the king of *Portugal*.

The day of their departure being come, the *Portuguese* shall have their swords restored to them.

Gaspar Alfonso de Karvalho the *Portuguese* governor, shall be transported to what place he shall think fit.

Accordingly the 24th about noon, seven companies of *Dutch* soldiers, one of *Bandaneses*, and one of *Laskaryns*, under the *Modlier* of *Negombo*, took possession of the gates of the city, at which time the *Portuguese* drew off from the bastions, and proclamation was made immediately, not to molest, much less rob the inhabitants, under pain of death.

The Dutch *take possession of the City.*

Mr. *Vander Laen* himself was received by the *Portuguese* governor, who was not very well at that time, at the entrance of one of the gates, where he had the keys of all the city gates deliver'd to him. From thence he went to take a view of the bastions, and after having given the necessary orders, he commanded the inhabitants to appear the same afternoon in the court of the *Stadthouse*, in order to be disarmed, pursuant to the last agreement. They were no more than 670 strong, divided into 17 companies, consisting of *Portuguese*, *Mestices* and *Topasses*, being all inhabitants, not in the king of *Portugal*'s pay. Their artillery consisted in 28 brass, and 53 iron pieces of cannon small and great, their ammunition in 8000 pounds of gunpowder, lead, and other things of this nature in proportion; besides which, there were ten large and eight small bells in the town.

Much about the same time the *Dutch* appeared before the city, the *Kapado Negape*, or general of the *Neyk*, or lord of the countrey came to lay siege to it; but understanding that the *Dutch* were got into possession of it, he desired to be admitted into the city to confer with them, concerning the sudden surrender of it. His request being granted, he took a great deal of pains to persuade the *Dutch* that both the city, and all the *Portuguese* ought immediately to be deliver'd to the *Neyk* his master, to make satisfaction for what they stood indebted to him; but this request was civilly refused by Mr. *Vander Laen*, who told him that he was very ready to cultivate a good understanding with the *Neyk* and his subjects, but that both in point of conscience, as he was a christian, and in honour he could not recede

1662. cede from the articles of the surrender. By this time the hour approaching when the inhabitants were to be disarm'd at the stadt-house, he invited the *Kapado* to go along with him, which he courteously accepted of: The inhabitants earnestly intreated Mr. *Vander Laen* to permit them to be transported to *Bengal* instead of *Goa*, unto whom he gave for answer, that he would intercede for them in writing with the *Dutch* admiral general *Vander Goens*. The 25th publication was made by beat of drum, that every one, without any exception of persons or quality, should deliver forthwith all his arms at the stadt-house, unless they would be excluded from the benefit of the capitulation; which was punctually perform'd the next day, which was spent altogether in receiving their arms.

In the mean while the *Neyk*'s army had so inclosed the city, that we began to have some scarcity of provisions; and the *Dutch* living at *Tranguabar*, a *Danish* colony, began to be sorely afraid of being attack'd by *Wardarasje Purmal*, who, as it was given out, was sent for from the countrey of *Tanjaor*, by the *Neyk*, to chastise those of *Tranguabar*; the governor of which, *Esbeck Anderson*, had promised to cruise before the bar of *Negapatan*, with three stout yachts well mann'd, instead of which he had sent only one small chaloop; so that the inhabitants fearing the worst, fled daily with their best moveables into the fort of *Danesburgh*. The 17th the *Kapado Negapa*, sent by the *Neyk* with an *Ola* or letter from *Maniegul*, appeared in the city of *Negapatan*, where he delivered the following letter to Mr. *John Vander Laen*.

A letter from the Neyk *to Mr.* Vander Laen.

THE 16th day of the year Welenby. *I* Assy Para Neyk *send to the* Dutch *commander* Moor *this letter; by which I would have them to understand, that the* Portuguese *inhabitants of* Negapatan *have for these 12 years last past not pay'd their usual taxes, but are run much behind. It is for this reason I sent my army to attack them in the city of* Negapatan, *to demolish its fortifications, and after the inhabitants were reduced under my obedience, to grant them liberty to live as before, under my jurisdiction; having always lived in a good correspondence with the* Dutch East-India *company, I desired their assistance by sea; but now I am credibly informed, that you have made an agreement with the* Portuguese *of* Negapatan, *who have deliver'd the city into your hands, which is very displeasing to us; if you had a mind to maintain a good understanding with us, you ought first to have given us notice of it, and obtained our consent; but now you must surrender the city to us, therefore send one of your deputies to treat with me, and he shall be honourably received, and receive all the satisfaction that may tend to the maintaining a farther good correspondence betwixt us. If you do otherwise, you will have occasion to repent it; but as I know you to be persons of wisdom, I don't question but you will surrender the city to our people; in witness of which I have sent our* Kapado Negapa *with this letter.* 1662.

Unto which Mr. *Vander Laen* sent this answer.

Mr. Vander Laen's *Answer.*

THE Ola *or letter deliver'd to us by your highness's envoy* Negapa, *I received with all imaginable respect, under the discharge of three pieces of ordnance; out of which having fully understood your highness's intentions, I am obliged to tell your highness, that the* Portuguese *having surrendered to us the strong city of* Negapatan, *without making the least opposition, and under certain conditions, agreed on betwixt both parties; we are bound by our duty, as christians, to observe punctually in all respects the said articles, it being unquestionable that without any injustice to your highness, we have power to annoy the* Portuguese, *our enemies, wherever we can meet with them, which makes us live in hopes that the friendship establish'd betwixt your highness and the* East-India *company will not suffer the least detriment upon this account. What has the undertakings of the said company not long ago against the* Portuguese *in the countrey of the* Neyk *of* Madura *and in other neighbouring countries and kingdoms, which were never interpreted to their prejudice, makes us believe that your highness will not be displeased with the advantages obtained by us against the* Portuguese, *which as they tend to no other end than to increase our trade in your highness's dominions, so they must in time turn to your own advantage. In the mean while we have communicated your highness's sentiments, by two several yachts sent for that purpose, to the directors of* Jafenepatan, *from whence we hourly expect an answer, which we don't question will be to your highness's satisfaction.*

In the mean while *Kamerapanijk* the adviser of this siege was fallen in disgrace with the *Neyk*.

The 30th Mr. *Vander Laen* received letters from *Rijklof Goens*, dated the 29th, with the ratification of the capitulation, with orders to send the *Portuguese*, to the number of 150, according to their request, to *Bengal*, where they were likely to do them

1662. the least mischief, and they might soonest rid their hands of them. As to what concerned the difference with the *Neyk*, he advised to endeavour to compose the matter by the means of some presents; but if that would not succeed, to make his forces to retire deeper into the countrey; in the mean time to give all the courteous entertainment to his deputies, and to assure them, that he intended in a few days to be with them in person, to adjust all matters in question betwixt them and his highness; but if he committed any hostilities against the city, to stand upon the defensive, and to protest in writing against his proceedings. In the mean while the *Neyk*'s forces continued in their camp, which extended to the very ditch of the city; and as it increased daily in number, so it occasion'd great scarcity within. The 1st of *August*, Mr. *Vander Laen* was inform'd that the commander in chief of the *Neyk*'s forces before *Negapatan* had received a letter from the *Neyk*, directed to Mr. *Van Goens*; and in the afternoon three persons were sent into the city, to give notice of the said letter and some presents, which they desired might be received with all imaginable demonstrations of respect. In compliance with which Mr. *Vander Laen* commanded immediately captain *Wash* with his company, and the *Modlier* of *Negombo* with his *Laskarths*, to post themselves in good order without the gates of the city, in order to receive the presents with all imaginable respect, under the discharge of three pieces of cannon. They kept their post till evening, without seeing any body, when a certain person belonging to the *Neyk*'s camp came privately to the *Modlier*, and told him in the *Singalese* language (for fear of being understood by others) that there was no *Ola* or letter, nor any presents sent from the *Neyk*, the whole being only a stratagem contriv'd on purpose to draw some of our forces without the gates into an ambush, which they had been disappointed in, by our forces not stirring from the gates, upon which the *Modlier* and captain *Wash* return'd with their troops into the city, and the *Neyk*'s forces retired back into the countrey. This *Neyk* besieged *Negapatan* a second time, 1660, in *September*, but the *Dutch* garrison making a vigorous sally, in which they kill'd 400 of his men, they came to a composition for that time; notwithstanding which, he appeared before it again in the next following year.

The countrey hereabouts bears such great plenty of rice, that abundance of it is transported from hence to other places. But they have great numbers of lewd women and idle fellows here.

Not far from the city is a *Pagode*, with a stone steeple, call'd *Tzina*, the pinacle of which reaches to the very clouds; the inhabitants believe that it was built by the devil, and that in one night. In the suburbs to the north, which are of magnificent houses, there are likewise many *Pagodes* or pagan temples, wherein you see many idols of a terrible aspect, made only of clay. Thus far concerning *Negapatan*. 1662. *The Temple of* Tzina.

From hence we pursued our voyage towards *Paliakatte*, and saw the lofty and most ancient *Pagode*, call'd *Tyripopeliri*, which stands within the precinct of a fort at a little distance from the sea-shore, and of which I had the curiosity to take a full view. It is an ancient structure, the front of which is adorned with many statues artificially cut in stone. It is surrounded by a wall with a gallery on the top of it, over which are placed a great number of large coffins, which rest upon statues of divers figures, some representing a horse, others somewhat else. The walls are made of large blue stones, which are brought thither a vast way out of the countrey, and most artfully joined together. The *Indian Pagodes* or temples seldom have any light but what comes through a hole in the frontispice; notwithstanding which I ventur'd in, and found several lamps burning there; by the light of which I ascended by a pair of stairs of wood, to the top of the temple, from thence to take a view of the circumjacent country. But scarce was I come to the stairs-head, when I saw my self in an instant surrounded by thousands of bats that were striving to get out thro' the hole in the frontispice, so that I was glad to get away from this unwelcome company, which, to avoid the brightness of the sun-beams, shelter themselves by day in these dark lurking holes. *The temple of* Tyripopeliri.

We soon set sail again, and coasted it along the shore, which is flat and sandy here, till the 15th of *June*, when we arrived at *Paliakatte*, where I delivered our whole cargo of gold and silver we had taken in *Persia*, to the director *Lawrence Pit*. *They come to* Paliakatte.

The *Dutch East-India* company has a strong fort here, with four bastions of stone work, call'd *Geldria*, of which they have been possess'd ever since the year 1619. Without the castle is a plantation or town, which to the land-side is defended by an earthen wall, which is but indifferently kept, but the houses within are very close and well built. It is inhabited partly by *Hollanders*, partly by *Jentives* or pagan natives; the last of which live for the most part upon trade with painted and white callicoes and linen. The rice which grows in this countrey in great plenty, is as well as all other *The fort of* Geldria.

1662. other sorts of grains brought weekly to market here. The fort is on one side wash'd by a river, which swells very high in the rainy season, when the merchandizes may be unloaden here by the help of lighters. But in the summer season the river being quite dry'd up, the goods are forc'd to be carried ashore on their backs. This river abounds in fish in the winter-time, most of which die in the summer, which makes the inhabitants catch them before that time, and dry them in the sun, and so transport them to other places. The north *Monzon* begins here in *October*, and holds all the *November* and *December*, with such violence, that the ships can scarce ride in the road. In *January* the *Monzon* changes, and the fair season returns.

As to the city of *Paliakatte*, its inhabitants are for the most part *Mestices* and *Kastices*; *Mestices* are such whose parents were married with foreigners; as for instance, when an *Hollander* marries an *Indian* woman, or an *Indian* man a *Dutch* woman; but the children of the *Mestices* are call'd *Kastices*. Thus many of the natives, especially of the *Thioles* have married *Dutch* women, as on the other hand, several *Hollanders* are married to women of the *Thioles*, from whence is come a numerous off-spring of *Mestices* and *Kastices*. Many *Bramans*, *Banyans* and *Panekayers*, or *Thomists* and *Jews* live here, of great traffick; for every month comes hither the *Kaffila* or caravan of *Agra*. The *Banyans* and *Jews* are the chiefest of all the traders here, this city being a place *Golconda*, *Suratte* and *Cambaia* by land; both *Christians* and *Mahometans* bring to this place their merchandizes from the *Red-Sea*, the *Persian Gulph*, from *Suratte*, *Goa*, *Malabar*, *Sumatra* and *Malacca*. There is great plenty of fish at *Paliakatte*, and a neighbouring country furnishes them with all other sorts of provisions.

They leave Paliakatte. After we had dispatch'd our business here, we pursued our voyage towards the great city of *Masulipatnam*, where we were to load wood and other materials for the building of our fort at *Paliakatte*. We set sail the 20th of *July*, and came to an anchor before *Masulipatnam* the 22d, I went ashore the same evening to take care of our loading, which consisted for the most part in timber and other materials for building, besides some callicoes, which took us up till the 14th of *August*, when we were ready to set sail again. In the mean while I had sufficient leisure to take a full view of the city of *Masulipatnam*. It lies near the sea-shore, upon a branch of the great river *Kisna*, a few leagues from *Negenapatnam*, being surrounded on all sides with water. It is closely built and well peopled, it being the only place of traffick in callicoes, indigo, diamonds, and other precious stones, in the kingdom of *Golconda*. To the land-side, north-west of the city, is a standing pool, over which is built a bridge of 2000 paces long, in the midst of which stands a house for the conveniency of the passengers to repose themselves there. This bridge rests upon very thick posts, which are covered with shells of 12 or 14 feet long, without any leanings on either side. Most of the inhabitants are *Pagans* and merchants. The *Persian Mahometans* have here likewise a mosque built of white stone, after a very antique fashion, in the very center of the city. The houses are all of wood cover'd with pantiles, the king having expresly forbid the building of stone houses, for fear of encouraging his subjects to revolt; who, tho' *Pagans*, wear white callicoe vests and turbants like the *Moors*. They use rice instead of bread, and drink commonly water; they have also great plenty of all sorts of fishes, ducks, geese, and tame and wild fowl. Both the *Dutch* and *English East-India* companies have each a house here, with their respective flags on the top of them. The *Franciscans*, who are all *Portuguese*, have here a Monastery over against the city; on the continent is a village, where the governor has a country-seat, where he diverts himself sometimes.

Arrive at Masulipatnam.

A description of this city.

Its bridge.

The river Kisna. The river of *Kisna* arises very deep in the countrey, and exonerates itself with one branch about five leagues below the city of *Masulipatnam* into the sea, where it is but shallow, but the other turns to *Masulipatnam*, which is much deeper. This river is not join'd to the city by a bridge, but they pass it in boats; it has plenty of fishes, as likewise crocodiles; it swells sometimes to such a heigth during the rainy season, that you may pass in boats thro' the streets of the city, but in the summer season it is so shallow, that near the city it is scarce four foot deep. About half a league to the west is a champaign countrey, and on the east-side the countrey is planted with palm and syry trees, behind which you may discern the tops of the mountains. We left *Masulipatnam*, and the 29th return'd to *Paliakatte*, where meeting with several sorts of commodities that were wanting at *Batavia*, I made all the haste I could to have the ship loaded; but when we were almost ready to depart, the yacht call'd the *Parroket* arrived in the road, with advice, that the ships *the House of Zwieten*, the *Sea Horse*, the *Exchange*, the *Stadthouse of Amsteldam*, the *Rising Sun*, and the *Encreasing Moon* were at sea, being sent from *Holland* with men and all sorts of ammunition, to assist in the expedition against the coast of *Malabar*.

The Dutch lay a design against the coast of Malabar.

1662. *labar.* This soon made us alter our measures, every one having received orders to join the said fleet, so that after we had unladen our ships, we set sail the 10th of *September* for *Colombo*, the general rendezvous of our fleet. We stop'd at *Pedro Punto*, where having provided ourselves with fresh water and fuel, we came to an anchor the 7th of *October* before *Colombo*, where we were employed among the rest to take the great train of artillery aboard of us. The commodore *Roodbacs* in the mean while went out before the rest with seven ships only, ordering the rest to follow him to *Manepara*, one of the seven seaport villages on the coast of *Madure*, where all our ships were to meet, which we did accordingly on the 15th of *November*. Mr. *John vander Werf*, Mr. *Symonson*, and myself, were made not only supervisors, but also treasurers of the whole train of artillery: Being provided with every thing requisite for such an expedition, we set sail from thence, and came with the whole fleet the 7th of *December* to an anchor, about two leagues to the south of the city of *Kolang* or *Koulang*. The remaining part of the day was spent in landing our sol iers and other necessaries, and bringing the ships as close as possible could be to the shore. The 8th we march'd in battle array into the country, and the *Negroes* had thrown up a small redoubt within half a league from the city, from whence they fir'd thick upon our yachts, but without any great loss, yet they ply'd us so warmly near the shore, that we were forced to cut our way thro' the woods to attack them from behind. Immediately all our carpenters were set to work to cut down the bushes and trees, whilst the seamen were employed in levelling the grounds to make way for our artillery. After we were advanced a little way into the wood, we came into a small plain, to the left of which, leading to the sea-side, we saw a stone-house, where we halted a little to take breath, because the seamen had been hard put to it, in drawing the cannon thro' the deep sand along the sea-side. The enemy at the same time kept within his strong hold, but as we advanced farther they charged our vanguard, who were order'd to break in upon them; they bravely stood the first brunt, but afterwards retreated again to their fort. In the mean time our cannon having joined us, we prepar'd for a general attack, which was carried on so vigorously, that the *Negroes* deserted the fort, in hopes of saving themselves by flight, but were most of them either kill'd upon the spot or in the flight. A strong party of them happen'd accidentally to fall in with captain *Polmans* company of firelocks, who were sent thro' the woods to attack the fort from behind; here you might have seen them fight like desperate men, the engagement was very terrible considering the number of men on both sides; at last they were overcome with above 100 kill'd and as many wounded on their side; we had no more than three kill'd, but a great many wounded, who were sent aboard the ships to be taken care of. We found two iron pieces of cannon in this fort, which we nail'd up, and beat the carriages in pieces: After we had placed guards in all convenient posts thereabouts, the soldiers reposed themselves under the shadow of trees; but within two hours after we continued our march to the city of *Kolang*, passing all the way by a great many fine plantations, surrounded on all sides with walls, the road betwixt them being very narrow. As we advanc'd to the city, the enemy fired briskly upon us from a small fort near the water-side, where they had set up the *Portuguese* standard, but perceiving us notwithstanding this to march undaunted towards the walls, their hearts began to fail, and betaking themselves to flight, left the city to our mercy, which we took without the least resistance. All the officers and soldiers, each according to their respective qualities, had their quarters and posts assign'd them; we rested the next day, but every one being animated by the last success in taking so considerable a city without opposition, long'd for action, so that before the morning the whole body being put in battle array without the water-gate, the chief minister of the camp, Mr. *Baldeus*, made a short but very fervent speech, and the commanders exhorted them to fight couragiously for the honour of their countrey and religion; which being joyfully accepted by the soldiers, who promised to hazard all for the service of the company, the drums and trumpets began to sound the march. Mr. *Ysbrand Goskeled* commanded the van, and commodore *Roodhaes* the rear, being both persons of known bravery; Mr. *Riiklof van Goens* commanded the main battle; we carried some field pieces along with us to serve us upon occasion. We were forced to march thro' narrow ways, where scarce four could march a-breast, and finding that the enemy gall'd us from an adjacent small fort, some companies wheel'd to the right, and the rest to the left, whilst the seamen undauntedly approach'd with their scaling ladders, and mounting the walls, took the fort with little resistance. We found here no more than two iron pieces of cannon ready charged; notwithstanding all this they skirmish'd briskly with our foremost troops as they were advancing beyond the fort, but gave way by degrees and retreated 1662.

Their fleet meets at Manepara.

Come before Kolang.

Kolang *taken.*

1662. ed to the royal palace, where they made another halt, and engaged our troops a second time, but with no better success; for being once seiz'd with a panick fear, they soon gave ground, and left the place to our mercy, which we plunder'd and destroy'd. They had however in the mean while attack'd our rear several times, because our heavy cannon could not come up soon enough with us, by reason of the narrowness of the way; the enemy making use of this advantage, attack'd us very furiously, but were bravely repuls'd by the help of our field pieces, which being charged with small shot, were discharged among them with such success, that many of them remained dead upon the spot; and by this means we kept them so long in play, till we received a seasonable reinforcement, when they betook themselves to their heels, and left us absolute masters of the field. In the mean while our troops were advanced to the river, where they made themselves masters of another fort, in which they found 2 brass and 10 iron pieces of cannon. In a certain *Pagode* next to the royal palace, call'd *Matta del Reyne*, we found a great chest with gunpowder, which being set on fire, in an instant blew up and destroy'd this antient structure, covered on the top with brass. Then our troops beat the countrey both to the right and left, burning and destroying all they met with. In an instant we saw whole woods in a flame, the *Bambo* canes making a most terrible noise, and burning like brimstone, a miserable spectacle to the enemy, who from the other side of the river, saw the flame consume in an instant, what had cost them many years labour. *John Piccard* my nephew, a captain lieutenant, and *William van Teylingin* were sent with some chaloops up the river *Arwick*, to pursue the flying enemy on that side, but these took another way; most of them wading thro' the river, where they could not come near them with their chaloops. Mr. *Piccard* then landed his company on the other side, where he set 40 houses on fire, which occasion'd a fresh consternation among the flying enemy. After we had thus ravaged the countrey, we return'd to the before-mention'd *Pagode*, where our troops reposed themselves for a while, and the same evening return'd conquerors to the city of *Koulang*. The 12th, all the ships carpenters were sent for ashore to cut down the trees that stood upon the city walls, and orders were given for breaking down part of it, and to bring it into a narrower compass, which was put in execution immediately. About the same time the natives sent some deputies to sue for peace; by what we were inform'd, that at the time of our arrival there were not above 30 true born *Portuguese* in the city, who fled immediately, and that the *Negroes*, who were near 800 strong, having had some notice of our design near 15 days before, had resolved to kill all the *Hollanders* they met with except a few, whom they intended to preserve to send them aboard their gallies, but the scene was altered; in the mean while we continued with breaking down and removing which had almost proved fatal to the ship the *Sea-Horse*, which happened to take fire, and was in great danger of being burnt by the violence of the flame, had not the seamen quenched the fire.

Cruel design of the Negroes.

By this time it being resolv'd to prosecute the career of our victories, the commodore *Roodhaes* with eight ships sail'd towards the city of *Cranganor*, to block up the entrance of that river, the rest being to follow with all convenient speed. The 19th I went on board the commissary *James Borchorst*, with whom I had some earnest business, but scarce was I come thither, but on a sudden there arose such a tempest, that with much ado I could get ashore again, for the wind arose first from the land-side with most violent rains, but soon after chop'd about with such violence, that it tore roots of trees out of the ground, and untiled abundance of houses. By this sudden change of the wind, our whole fleet consisting of thirty ships great and small, were in no small danger of being shipwrack'd. The ship the *Stadthouse* was driven among the rocks, where having lost her rudder, she gave the signal of being in utmost distress, but no body durst venture to bring her off. The ship the *Achilles* was likewise forced from her anchors among the rocks, but by good fortune happened to cast anchor again, not far from the *Stadthouse*. The ship the *Erasmus* was also got adrift, and was in great danger of running upon the shelves; several of our small craft were beaten to pieces by the sea, and many others much endamaged. The ship the *Stadthouse* continued in great distress all that day and night, striking several times against the rocks, but next morning the fury of the tempest being somewhat appeas'd, we sent out some boats to her assistance, which brought both her and the *Achilles* safe from among the rocks into the open sea. So that at last, thro' God's mercy, all our great ships escap'd the danger of this storm without any considerable damage, except what was in their rigging, which however fell most upon the smaller vessels.

The 24th the garrison of the conquered city of *Koulang*, consisting of 663 men, both soldiers and mariners, under the command of captain *Cox*, and *Henry Walling*, being provided

1662. provided with all necessaries, during our intended stay before *Cranganor*, Mr. *Van Goens* set sail the same day with the ships the *Walnut-tree* and the *Ulieland* towards *Cranganor*, commodore *Gotske* being to follow with the rest; we were in the mean while busy with refitting the ship the *Stadthouse*, and I stay'd ashore with Mr. *Gotske* till such time that the gunpowder of the *Stadthouse* and several other ships, which had got wet in the last storm could be dried again; about the same time we were inform'd, that the negroes had receiv'd a good sum of money to fight against us, but when they perceived we were in earnest, they left the *Portuguese* in the lurch, who as we told you before, left the city of *Koulang* the same afternoon, when we landed. The 29th we set sail in the ship the *Exchange* to follow the fleet; by an express sent us from some of the *Malabars*, we were desired to stay till the next day, which we refus'd, it being not our business to tarry here for matters which might well be deferr'd till another time. The next following day we pass'd by *Kalkoulang*, the governor of which came aboard of us, with a present of fresh provisions, which we accepted. The 31 we coasted it along the shore, where we cast our anchor, because one of our yachts approach'd so near to the shore, that we feared she would run herself into danger, which made us detach 20 soldiers in a boat to her relief, if occasion should require. The 1st of *January* 1662, by break of day we found ourselves within a league of the city of *Cochin*, and soon after sail'd so near the shore, that we could hear the centinels speak. We saw five ships lying in the road, the foremost of which carried *English* colours. The same day about noon we came into the road, at the entrance of the river *Palliport*, and the next day having embark'd our men in boats, and our ammunition with two field pieces in another, we landed them without any opposition, except that the enemy discharg'd some of his great cannon against us from *Cranganor*, but without any loss on our side.

The Dutch *land near* Cranganor.

We had posted our forces in three several places, the better to cut off all correspondency betwixt the enemy and the countrey. The next following day we brought two tuns of rice, and two brass guns ashore, and soon after our whole train of artillery, with all other necessaries requisite for such an undertaking. For some time we had kept the place block'd up both on the land and river side, but now we began to open our trenches with such success, that in a short time we carried them on under the cannon of the city, the garrison being all this while not idle on their side, but endeavouring to hinder our approaching by their continual fire out of their cannon and fire-arms, which they did with such dexterity, that they kill'd many of our men in the trenches; among the rest, a certain soldier had his arm and shoulder shot off at once, notwithstanding which, Mr. *Van Goens* order'd him to be dress'd, which the surgeon did accordingly, who told me at the same time, that since he must infallibly die, he would give him something that might ease his pain; I ask'd the poor wretch how he did, he answered me without any alteration in his countenance, *Pretty well, I don't find myself very ill*, tho' he died in a few hours after. Fourteen days after we had carried our trenches to the body of the place, during which we had several smart skirmishes with the enemy, it was resolv'd to venture a general assault; pursuant to this resolution, I was sent with two servants to confer with commodore *Gotske* and Mr. *Roodhaes*, concerning the most convenient place the assault was to be made in. I was sometimes to wade up to the middle in water, and met with captain lieutenant *Piccard*, who had the advanced guards. He forewarn'd me not to approach too near the city, from whence they fir'd without intermission, but I was forc'd to venture at all, being oblig'd to be with the admiral general again the next morning. I went close under the walls of the place, the centinels ask'd me in *Portuguese*, *who was there?* I answered in the same language, *a friend*, and so escap'd the danger. Mr. *Gotske* and *Roodhaes* had been before inform'd concerning the condition of the place by a certain *Negroe*, and where it might be most conveniently assaulted, of which they having given me a circumstantial account, I return'd forthwith, and was with the admiral by next morning, who thereupon resolv'd to assault the city, and as he left me said, *To morrow the city shall be ours*. So soon as every thing was prepar'd for the intended assault, I went on board the fleet to keep a watchful eye over the ships, which were of the utmost consequence to us all.

Consultations about the assaults.

In the mean time our forces mounted the breach, and assaulted the town with great fury under the favour of the smoak of their cannon and fire arms, which by the wind was forced toward the city; I saw from on board the ships the smoak approach nearer and nearer to the place, which I looked upon as a good omen on our side; the enemies defended themselves with a great deal of bravery for a considerable time, but our men pushing on the assault with the utmost vigour, they were at the last forced to give way, and to leave us masters of the city. Mr. *Polman* and *Shuilenburgh*, two of our captains,

1662.

Cranganor taken by storm.

captains, were dangerously wounded, 80 common soldiers were killed in the assault, and a great many more wounded. The loss of the enemies side was much greater, 200 *Portuguese* being slain during the action, besides a great number of negroes, who were all thrown into the river, and carried back and forwards several times by the tides, a most terrible spectacle to behold. For we found the taking of this place to be another piece of work than that of *Koulang*, and we were upon the point of sounding the retreat, had not the commanders by their own example animated the soldiers to do their utmost; it being almost surprising how with so small a force we were able to attack and conquer so strong a place as this.

Is laid desolate. After the city was plundered it was laid level with the ground, except one stone tower, which standing upon the river, was preserved entire, and a garrison put into it for the security of the river.

A description of this city. This city of *Cranganor* (for there is another on the coast of *Malabar*, nearer to the sea shore) lies about four or five leagues to the north of the city of *Cochin*; being the capital city of a kingdom of the same name, bordering to the north upon *Cochin* and to the south upon *Koulang*. It was very famous among the *Indians*, by reason of its antiquity; being situate upon the banks of a river, about a league from the sea shore, defended by a wall of earth, and a stone breast work; which had seven bastions and the wall of earth three more. At the point near the river is remaining to this day a strong stone tower for the defence of the river, which served instead of a bulwark on that side; on the other point was a small fort which commanded the river, and all ships going out or in. Several goodly stone houses were in this city, and among the rest a church, excelling all the rest; on the opposite side of the river, towards the side of *Cochin*, is the redoubt called *Palliport*, built

The redoubt Palliport. for the better defence of the river; upon a long island called *Baypin* extending to the river of *Gochin*. The royal palace is not far from hence, in a very pleasant countrey; the king then reigning being a prince of great bravery, and well versed in military affairs, in the flower of his age.

After the taking of *Cranganor*, it was concluded by the majority of voices to attack likewise the famous city of *Cochin*, not questioning but that the fame of our late victories would open us likewise a way to the conquest of this place, before the enemies of this could recollect themselves from the fear they were in at that juncture. Accordingly we decamped from thence, and set

Cochin besieged. down before *Cochin*, our forces as in the last siege were again posted in three several places, from whence the attacks were to be carried on against the city; Mr. *Isbrand Gotske* had his post assigned him near the sea shore; Mr. *Roodhaes* upon the bank of the river; and the admiral general's quarter was betwixt both. But the garrison of *Cochin* was not so much frightned as we had flattered ourselves, but made a brave resistance. We did all we could to persuade the negroes that we were not come hither with an intention to hurt them, but the *Portuguese*, our enemies; but in vain, for they all appeared in arms against us, and several times attacked us like madmen, throwing themselves in among our ranks, tho' they were sure to die in the attempt, and thrusting themselves upon our swords and pikes, not like men, but rather like wild boars or enraged bears. Not far from the royal palace was a very large *Pagode*, where the negroes had fortified themselves: Our men, notwithstanding their fury, attacked them in this advantageous post with so undaunted a courage, that they chased them from thence with the loss of 400 negroes, and many more wounded. The old queen would fain have hid herself in a corner on the top of the *Pagode*, but was found out, and brought a prisoner by captain *Henry Rede* into our camp. But after we had spent near two months in the siege, the waters beginning to rise more and more every day, which filled up our trenches to the middle, and our forces by the several losses we had sustained in divers engagements and attacks, and thro' the garrisons we had been obliged to put in the conquered places, being considerably diminished in number, it was thought most expedient to raise the siege for this time, and to return with a greater force against next spring. Accordingly we decamped without any noise, and in one night got all our men, artillery, and ammunition aboard, without being perceived by the enemy, who were not sensible of our departure till next day about noon, as looking upon our motion only as a feint to draw them out of the town into an ambush. But when they found how matters stood, they discharged all their cannon round the walls, unto which we gave no answer for that time, but delayed it till a more convenient opportunity. The next thing the enemy had to do was to slight our works and trenches, which they did immediately, and to cut down all trees and edifices which they had found to be an obstacle to them during the siege, they also took effectual care to have their fortifications repaired and strengthned, as not questioning but that we should give them another visit with the next fair opportunity, in which they found themselves not deceived.

1626.

The siege raised.

After

1662. After the raiſing of the ſiege of *Cochin*, our land forces and ſhips were ordered to ſuch places where their preſence was judged to be moſt neceſſary at the preſent juncture, Mr. *Yſbrand Gotſke* ſailed with a ſquadron of ſhips to *Batavia*, and the reſt ſteered their courſe to other places thereabouts; I went aboard the ſhip the *Exchange*, and paſſed by the city of *Kalkoulang* in my way to *Koulang*, where I was appointed chief director of the company: At the ſame time it was thought convenient to ſtrengthen the fortifications of *Kalkoulang*, and to put a good garriſon into it under captain *Polman* and ſeveral other commanders, till we could diſpoſe our forces in more convenient quarters.

The author comes to Koulang.

I arrived at *Koulang* the 7th of *January*, where I gave immediate orders for the repairing the caſtle, and ſuch houſes as belonged to thoſe that were in the company's ſervice; and ſettling every thing that might tend to the re-eſtabliſhment of traffick with the queen of *Koulang*, and other neighbouring princes, unto whom I was ſent as a deputy, to treat with them concerning the moſt convenient methods, and to enter into a confederacy with them for that purpoſe.

Treaty with the queen of Koulang.

The firſt treaty that was ſet on foot after the taking of the city *Kalkoulang*, was with the queen of *Koulang*, which was ſoon concluded upon theſe conditions; that her palace and great guns ſhould be reſtored to her, for the rebuilding of which, and other damages ſuſtained, ſhe was to have a certain ſum of money to be paid her by the company, whoſe intereſt it was, rather to purchaſe a peace upon reaſonable terms, than be at the charge of a war.

A deſcription of Koulang.

The city of *Kolang*, or *Koulang*, or *Koulon* and *Koylang*, the capital of a kingdom bearing the ſame name, is ſituate upon the ſea ſhore of the coaſt of *Malabar*, under 9 deg. of northern latitude, about 13 *French* leagues (*Linſhot* ſays 24) to the ſouth of *Cochin*. It is fortified with a ſtone wall of 18 or 20 foot high, and 8 baſtions; its ſuburbs which are very large and ſtately, are by the *Portugueſe* called *Colang China*. For *Koulang* is ſeparated into two bodies, one of which is called the *Upper* or *Malabar Koulang*, the other the *Lower Koulang*; in the firſt the king and queen kept their ordinary reſidences; the laſt was formerly in the poſſeſſion of the *Portugueſe*, as lying nearer to the ſea ſide; here the fryars of *St. Paul* and the *Franciſcans* had each a monaſtery, adorned with ſtately chappels and ſteeples. Beſides which there were four other *Portugueſe* churches here, dedicated to as many *Romiſh* ſaints; they had no leſs than ſeven goodly churches, among which was the famous church built many ages ago by the Chriſtians of *St. Thomas*, which was left ſtanding, after we reduc'd the place into a narrower compaſs; in this church is the tomb of a certain great *Portugueſe* captain, who was governor of *Koulang* 60 years. The houſes of the inhabitants were very ſtately and lofty built of freeſtone; among which the ſtadthouſe ſurpaſs'd all the reſt; it was two ſtories high, and had very curious ſtone ſteps on each ſide. But the caſtle, the reſidence of the *Portugueſe* governor, ſurmounted all the reſt in magnificence; this I took up for our own lodgings, it lies very near the ſea-ſide, at one end of the city, being cover'd on the top with coco-leaves, as likewiſe two of its turrets, the third being tiled with pan-tiles. Juſt upon the ſea-ſhore is another four-ſquare tower, where I ſet up the company's flag on the top of a maſt. In the midſt of it is a very lofty edifice, which the *Portugueſe* uſed for a chapel, which I order'd to be made up into divers convenient chambers, and to be fitted for the uſe of the company's officers. This caſtle is the ſtrongeſt the *Portugueſe* ever were maſters of on the coaſt of *Malabar*, being built ſome hundred years ago, by the famous engineer *Hector de la Caſa*. 1662.

This city, as I told you before, was drawn into a leſs compaſs by the *Dutch*, which they fortified on the land-ſide with two half and one whole baſtion. Moſt of the churches and other publick edifices were pull'd down, except the caſtle, *St. Thomas*'s church, and ſome monaſteries, which remain'd ſtanding within the ſaid precinct. Behind moſt of the houſes here are very pleaſant gardens, planted with *Cocoa*, *Mangoes* and other *Indian* fruit trees; and about the city you ſee very fine baſins cut out of the rocks, unto which you aſcend by ſteps. They have alſo ſome ponds with freſh water, their water being elſe for the moſt part brackiſh and full of ſalt-peter. The air is very wholeſome in this countrey, which is low and full of rivers, which afford a convenient paſſage from hence to *Kalkoulang*, *Cochin* and *Cranganor*; and is accounted the beſt both for fruitfulneſs and its pleaſant ſituation in all the *Indies*. This part of the countrey affords abundance of pepper, which twiſts itſelf round the trees; the fruit is gather'd in *January* and *February*. The harbour is very convenient for ſmall veſſels, but not for great ones, becauſe the ſouth wind blows directly upon the ſhore, and forces the waves with great violence thither; they call it *Coydanel*. Near the ſea-ſide you ſee great ſtore of ſtone-like rocks, but they lie looſe upon the ſand, and are frequently waſh'd away by the ſea. About a league to the weſt of *Koulang*, the great river *Eguick* diſembogues into the ſea.

The

1662.

The *Dutch* were once before masters of the city of *Koulang*, till the *Negroes* took the opportunity of murthering captain *Henry Glunning* their governor there, as he was taking a walk without the gates, and afterwards massacred all the *Dutch*; since which time the *Portuguese* got into possession of it. On the side of *Koulang China*, along the sea-shore, the jesuits had built a great village for the *Parvees*, a poor sort of *Malabars* living upon fishing, where the governor of the king of *Travankor* and Prince *Baryette Poele* kept their residence, which are about a mile in circuit, and surrounded with an earth wall, with some points like bastions, on which are mounted good store of great cannon, which command the roads, without which there is scarce any access to them. If we may believe the *Malabars*, the *Maldive* islands, which lie about 60 leagues deep in the sea, just over-against the palace, were formerly part of the continent and torn from thence by the sea; and as a confirmation of their opinion, shew certain rocks betwixt the shore and these islands, upon which they assure us stood at that time a goodly church. The best houses are built along the river-side, with very good gardens, stock'd with all sorts of trees, fruits, flowers and herbs, but especially with citrons, which grow here not on trees, but shrubs; their houses are seldom above two stories high, their stairs within of stone, their rooms above stairs are pav'd with green and yellow four square stones, the ceiling of which is commonly of *Indian* oak, some being finely carved, others painted. They commonly have an arbour or summer-house belonging to each garden, which is commonly near the river-side, where they spend generally their evenings, and divert themselves with angling.

The river Kalchan.

The mouth of the river *Kalchan* or *Mangal*, or *Mangar*, upon which this place is built, is a very large bay, where yachts of 300 tuns may come close to the shore and unload, being 28 feet deep at high water; but of very difficult entrance, if the winds be not favourable, because they blow the waves directly upon the shore. In the midst of this bay you see three vast rocks laying all together in a ridge. During the rainy season this river frequently overflows the neighbouring countrey, and carries away a great deal of the adjacent grounds; these violent rains are occasion'd by the clouds, which gathering among the tops of the mountains, break out into sudden storms and tempests. The countrey is flat and marshy hereabouts, and the air not altogether so wholesome as at *Koulang*.

By this time the season for action drawing near, and every thing being prepar'd for a vigorous expedition, the siege of *Cochin* was resolv'd upon the second time; for which purpose Mr. *Jacob Hustart*, one of the member's of the great council of *India*, with captain *Peter de Pon* and *Henry Van Rode* set sail the 25th of *October* 1662, with 11 ships from *Batavia*, Mr. *Van Goens* being ordered to follow with three more, with all imaginable speed. No sooner had they landed their men, but they began to form their attacks, notwithstanding they found the place much strengthen'd by some additional fortifications, since the last siege, and put them so to it, that the besieged being enclosed on all sides, and beyond all hopes of relief, were forced to capitulate, and to surrender the city, after a siege of three months; after the *Portuguese* had (with the consent of the king of *Cochin*) been in possession of it above 150 years. The *Portuguese* had not long before forc'd *Momadavil*, the lawful king of *Cochin* to leave the city, in whose stead they had set up an aunt of his of the house of *Godarme*; but whilst our forces lay before *Cochin* the dethron'd king stay'd with me at *Koulang*, in order to his solemn coronation after the taking of the place. I had taken all imaginable care to have his room hung with tapestry, and furnish'd with other moveables, the best the place afford; he came often to visit us, being commonly clad in white callicoe, with his hair tied in a knot on the top of his head, rings on his fingers, and a gold chain hanging down before him. He spoke the *Portuguese* and *Malabar* tongues, and was of a pleasant conversation. But scarce a few days were pass'd, when finding himself not very well, he desired to go to the Queen of of *Koulang* for his diversion; which I was very unwilling to grant, being sensible that his person being committed to my care, I might be call'd to an account by his subjects, who much esteem'd him, if any sinister accident should befal him; but at his reiterated instances, and the earnest request of the queen of *Koulang*, who was an excellent good natur'd person, and engag'd her word to bear me harmless, I conducted him thither, but he found no considerable alteration in his health, for when not long after a yacht was sent to *Koulang* on purpose to fetch this prince to the camp before *Cochin*; he was so very weak that he would fain have avoided going thither, but there being positive orders given for his coming, I sent him my *Palakin* or letter, and conducted him with some of our officers aboard, but before he could reach *Cochin*, his sickness encreased to that degree, as to put an end to his life. His brother

1662.

Siege of Cochin.

Is surrender'd.

Momadavil *king of* Cochin.

Dies aboard.

Is succeeded by his brother.

1662. ther, who was aboard the same yacht, being the next heir to the crown, was, after the taking of the city, crowned king of *Cochin*, by the *Dutch*, his crown, which was of gold, having the cypher of the *East-India* company, engraven on one side. He kept his residence not far from *Cochin*, in a place situate in a very pleasant countrey, call'd by the *Dutch Malabar Cochin*, had his guards, musicians, and all other things belonging to a royal court, a cording to the custom of that countrey.

The city of Cochin. The city of *Cochin*, by the *Portuguese* call'd *Cochin*, and generally *Kakochin*, is the capital of a kingdom of the same name, and indeed of the whole coast of *Malabar*. It is situate under 10 deg. of northern latitude, 4 or 5 leagues to the south of *Koulang*, extending along the bank of the great river *Koulang* or *Kolchan*, or *Mangat* or *Mangar*. Some authors make mention of two different *Cochins*, *viz.* the *Old Cochin*, lying about a league and a half from the sea-shore; the *Portuguese* call it *Cochin Dacima*, or *Arabia*, *i. e.* the *Higher Cochin*, because it lies higher up the river; by the *Dutch* it is call'd the *Malabar Cochin*, where the king keeps his residence; being situate upon the banks of a river, and pretty well peopled, and adorn'd with several goodly structures and *Pagodes*, according to the custom of the *Malabars*. The other *Cochin*, call'd commonly the *New Cochin*, is scarce a league distant from the sea, just at the entrance of the same river; it was for many years together in the possession of the *Portuguese*, who had fortified it with a stone wall, and several bulwarks, and beautified it with several fine edifices, churches and monasteries. In the suburbs towards the land-side were several goodly churches, and a little nearer to the sea-shore the monastery of *St. John*. Here the *Austin Fryers*, *Franciscans* and *Jesuits* had likewise their several convents, all magnificently built, with very pleasant gardens and walks, the place being inhabited only by *Portuguese*. But since this city was conquer'd by the *Dutch*, the greatest part of it was laid desolate, and the rest fortified with regular stone, bastions, curtines and a very broad ditch, so that it is now look'd upon as impregnable. Among other steeples, that of *St. Paul* being magnificently built of square stones, exceeded all the rest as well in height as beauty, which is since demolish'd with all the other churches, except one, where divine service is exercised according to the tenets of the reform'd religion. The houses here are cover'd with tiles of about the breadth of a hand, and are fastned to the laths by small hooks. Some make their windows only of a kind of lettice-work, others of canes very artificially twisted together; others make use of large shells in which the pearls grow, these they shave and flatten, and make windows of them, as we do of glass. 1662.

After we thus had made our selves masters of the greatest part of the *Malabar* coast, and had taken all imaginable care, to re-establish the commerce in those parts, it was judg'd necessary for the better obtaining of this end, to enter into strict alliances with the kings and princes of the adjacent countries; for which purpose Mr. *James Hustart*, chief councellor of the *Indies*, of *Ceylon* and the *Malabar* coast, having sent me the necessary instructions and credentials, I provided my self with all things requisite for such a journey, and the 21st of *January* 1664, embark'd aboard a small vessel, with one serjeant, several soldiers, an interpreter, and divers mariners, which carried us up the river, as far as to the city of *Kalkolang*, where we arriv'd safely the next day. So soon as I had provided my self with a convenient lodging, I gave notice of my arrival, by our interpreter to the king, who soon after returned in company of a *Residoor* from the king, to fetch me to court. Accordingly I and Mr. *Willing*, who resided there in the quality of under factor of the *East-India* company, were introduced by the said *Residoor* into the kings presence, whom we found surrounded with a good number of courtiers, that constantly attend his person. After the first ceremonies and compliments, such as are usual in this place, were passed, I surrender'd my credentials to the king, who received them with a great deal of respect and seeming satisfaction. After he had perused them, he gave orders to one of his *Residoors*, one of his chief favourites to treat with me concerning such points as I should propose to him, tending to the maintaining of a good correspondence betwixt us and them, and to make his report to him. This prince had the character of a very sincere person, which appeared both in his countenance and actions; but leaves the chief management of all affairs of moment, to the beforemention'd *Residoor*, who knows how to make his advantage of it. After I had treated with the *Residoor*, as far as my commission would give me leave, I desired to be dismiss'd, under pretence of fetching new instructions, which being granted, I took leave of the king, and with Mr. *Willing* pursu'd my journey to *Porka*; whither I had sent a serjeant with six soldiers before. But at our arrival there, being inform'd that the king of *Porka* was ten days before gone to his palace call'd *Kudda Malair* or *Koramallur*, or *Koromallo*, about ten leagues distance from hence, I

The author sent to treat with divers Malabar Princes.

His audience of the King of Kalkolang.

Departs from thence to Porka.

 resolv'd

1662. resolv'd to go thither. We were forced to go by water through several channels and rivers, the countrey thereabouts being full of both, like the province of *Holland*, which affords scarce any passage by land, but by the dikes, all the rest being rice fields, curiously planted with trees on all sides.

We were forc'd to have our *Mansiool* (vessel) drawn through a narrow sluce, which open'd us the passage into a large lake, which to the north is about two leagues broad; from thence we enter'd into a channel of about a league in length, its entrance is somewhat narrow and so full of flags, that there was scarce room enough to manage our oars. At the end of this channel you see very pleasant rice-fields, which extend to the foot of the mountain, and are stock'd with prodigious quantities of wild and water fouls. The inhabitants hereabouts have a certain way to drain their fields, which makes them bear rice all the year round; so that whilst they are sowing and planting in one field, in another the rice is half ripe, and in another its come to its full maturity, which renders this countrey both very fruitful and populous. The mountains produce some pepper, but in no great quantity. This part betwixt the channel and the mountains is water'd by a very fair and large river, beautified on both sides with many fair houses, gardens and trees, which afford a very agreeable spectacle to those that pass by that way, the houses being all built among small groves. After we had spent several hours in coming up the river, we in the afternoon cast anchor before the court of the king of *Porka*, situate upon the right side of the said river, near a village inhabited by christians of *St. Thomas*, who enjoy great privileges here. As we were passing up the river, not far from the court, we saw a large crocodile sunning himself upon the the sandy bank; I order'd our soldiers to fire at him, which they did, but he escaped under water. This creature was used to set upon the people as they pass'd by that way, and consequently much dreaded by them. The king of *Porka* was at this time rebuilding his palace, in which they say he had already bestow'd 20 years; it was but an odd old fashion'd piece of structure, surrounded with walls of earth and a dry ditch; I sent our interpreter to notify our arrival, and to provide us a lodging, who being return'd, we scarce had set a foot ashore, but the chief *Residoor* of the king came to conduct us to court, where he introduced us into his presence. After the usual compliments I deliver'd him my credentials, which he receiv'd with extraordinary marks of respect, ordering the *Residoor* to entertain me till he had read and consider'd of them. In a little while after he return'd with some of his attendants into the same apartment, where he ask'd me whether I had any other commission to treat with him, and I answering that I had, he declared to me, that his inclications had been always for us, even whilst we appear'd in arms on that coast, though at the same time he was not insensible, that some had endeavour'd to persuade us to the contrary, but that time and opportunity should discover the good sentiments he had for us. He told us farther, that he had caused the flags of the *English* and some other nations to be taken down, and the *Dutch* flag to be set up, for which they threaten'd him with an open war, in his own territories, and refused to quit the countrey, which made them to be look'd upon but with a very indifferent eye by all the neighbouring princes. Having afterwards given him a farther account of the occasion of my coming, he told me that he should be very glad now he was convinc'd of the intentions of the company, which were agreeable to his, to speak with Mr. *Hustart* himself: I return'd for answer, that the company was sensible of his favourable sentiments to them, and had always put a great value upon his person, inviting him at the same time to *Cochin*, to visit Mr. *Hustart*, the last of which he modestly declined, alledging that for several reasons he could not come to *Cochin*, but that if Mr. *Hustart* would come either to *Porka*, or any other place under his jurisdiction, he should be very ready to treat with him concerning such matters as tended to their mutual advantage. The king farther ask'd me, whether I desir'd an account of my negotiation in writing, which I having accepted of, he said it should be sent to my lodgings, and at my departure conducted me in person to the door of his apartment, from whence the *Residoor* carried me to his lodgings, and treated us with all sorts of refreshments, a very welcome entertainment to some of my attendants, who had not met with the like since the beginning of our journey. Towards the evening the *Residoor* brought me the writings, with whom whilst we were taking a view of the court, I had abundance of discourse concerning the intended treaty.

His audience of the king of Porka.

Palace of the king of Porka.

This palace of the king is a four square structure of about 40 paces in the square, in the midst of which is a court, about which the apartments (of which there is a great number) are built; they are all four square, their chief ornaments within being the carving of leaves and other work in all sorts of fine wood; in some of these lodgings you see fine cisterns for the conveniency of bathing; you ascend to them by

1662. by certain broad stone steps, like our grave-stones. In one of these lodgings is a very large bason, surrounded with such stones, which are about 20 feet broad, and a foot and a half thick, which have been brought thither with incredible pains and charges, a great way out of the countrey. The palace it self is cover'd with small tiles of a hand broad, the windows being made either of twisted canes or hells, which transmits the light.

After my return from thence to *Koulang*, I went farther to *Cochin*, to give a verbal account of my transactions to Mr. *Hustart*, who thereupon order'd me to go once more to the court of the king of *Porka*, in order to set matters there upon a sure foundation; accordingly I set out the 3^d^ of *February*, with some of my former attendants from *Cochin* to the king of *Porka*'s court, where within an hour after giving notice of my arrival, one of the king's *Residoors* came to introduce me to the king, whom that time I found in a most magnificent array, (after the *Malabar* fashion) in the midst of his courtiers. After the usual respect paid, I deliver'd to him my credentials, which he having received, he order'd all his attendants and my interpreter among the rest to withdraw, because he had a mind to discourse with me alone in *Portuguese*, which he understood very well. I told him that I was sent on purpose by my masters to his majesty, to assure him of their friendship, and to pay the money stipulated by the last treaty, which sum, though it much exceeded the value of the thing receiv'd, yet notwithstanding all this my masters had thought fit not to recede from what had been promised in their name. The king gave for answer, that it never had been a custom to weigh the pepper at *Cochin*, (which I had desired should be done) and that therefore he hop'd the company would not introduce any novelties in his territories; assuring us withal, that he would be ready to assist the company and their officers upon all occasions, besides several other assurances too tedious to be inserted here. I soon understood his meaning, to wit, that he would not have the pepper trade transferr'd to *Cochin*, which was a matter of no great consequence, so I did not insist any longer upon it, but agreed, that the pepper should be receiv'd and weigh'd at *Porka*; assuring him, that the company had never had the least intention to impair any body's right, as his majesty might easily be convinc'd as well by this as several other transactions and treaties made lately with other kings and princes. The king appeared to be highly satisfied thereat, desiring that a factor might be sent thither forthwith, to buy and receive the pepper; which I having promised to the king, he order'd the *Residoor* to receive the money, and granted me leave to depart.

The author goes a second time to the court of Porka.

Has audience.

The next following day, just as I was ready to depart, a *Residoor* come to my lodgings, which was an old chapel, and presented me, from the king, with several refreshments, according to the custom of the countrey, and knowing this *Residoor* to be a person in great esteem with the king, I requested his favour in behalf of the company, which he promised to do.

Departs from thence.

The king then reigning at *Porka* was a person of 30 years of age, very stately and well made. He was adorn'd with many jewels of diamonds and rubies, which he wore on his hands, arms and ears, according to the *Malabar* fashion. He is a most absolute prince, acknowledging no superior, every foot of the country being his own, and at his disposal. Justice is administred here with extraordinary severity, especially on the account of theft, which makes this crime scarce ever to be heard of here, of which I saw the following instance myself; whilst I was paying the money to the before-mention'd *Residoor*, I was call'd away to the king, and seeing above 50 persons in the same room, I charg'd one of my attendants to take care of the money; the *Residoor* having taken notice of it, laugh'd heartily, and told me, *You need not give yourself that trouble, no body will dare to touch the money, tho' it was untold and unguarded, for we know scarce what thieves are*, which surpriz'd me not a little, knowing that the *Malabars* in general are the errantest thieves in nature.

The king of Porka *and government.*

Theft unknown in Porka.

The kingdom of *Porka* or *Porkah*, otherwise *Perkatti*, has borrow'd its name from its capital city; it borders to the north upon the kingdom of *Cochin*, to the south upon that of *Kalkoulang*, it has *Takken Berkenker* to the north-east, and the sea to the west, being about 12 leagues in length; its capital city is *Porka* or *Porkah*. Another of the chief cities is *Koramallur* or *Koromallo*, situate upon the same river with the cities of *Cochin* and *Koulang*. The kings of *Porka* were in antient times great idolaters, who worship'd at least 900 idols, unto each of which daily sacrifices were offer'd, and visits made them about six or seven a clock in the morning till twelve at noon. It was not till the year 1590, that the *Romish* religion was openly profess'd here with consent of the king. Tho' many years before, the Christians call'd of *St. Thomas* liv'd in these parts. This king granted considerable privileges to the jesuites; such as the building of churches with crosses on the top of them, and the necessary bells, near unto which no

The kingdom of Porka.

Pagodes,

1662. *Pagodes*, *Jewish* synagogues, or *Mahometan* mosques were to be erected; they had also liberty to baptize as many as were willing to embrace the christian religion, all which was punctually observ'd. The king of *Porka* who reign'd 1599, was call'd *Nambrale* or *Numbrane*, which implies as much as the high priest in the *Malabar* tongue. In the year 1640, one *Siam Baatshery Vaubaar* reigned over *Porka*. They claim a superiority over the king of *Cochin*, against whom they waged heavy wars in former ages; but now adays the kings of *Porka* are under the jurisdiction of the *Dutch East-India* company, being forc'd thereunto by their victorious arms; the chief strength of the king of *Porka* consists in his small frigates, of which he has 500, and are made use of, when the fields are overflown with water; formerly the *Portuguese* were masters of the pepper trade here, with the king's consent; but finding that they intended to fortify themselves in several places, he engaged in a war against them, which lasted three whole years. The *Dutch* never came to *Porka* till 1642, under the reign of *Siam Baatshery Vaubaar*, being then not above 24 years old; they were very kindly receiv'd by him, a treaty being concluded betwixt them at that time, by which the *Dutch* had the pepper trade granted to them. This part of the countrey is very fruitful, but unwholesome, most of the inhabitants being afflicted with thick swell'd legs, occasioned by the drinking of brackish water; blindness is also a common distemper here, which by some is ascrib'd to their feeding so much upon hot rice. Most of the inhabitants live by husbandry, tho' during the rainy season, most of the rice fields hereabouts, as well as all along from the cape *Comarin*, as far as *Pokare Biarbar*, lay under water. This countrey produces also a considerable quantity of pepper yearly, which is for the most part bought up by the *English*, who have had a factory here many years ago. Deeper into the countrey live abundance of christians, who were formerly converted by the *Portuguese*, these buy up the pepper in the countrey, which they are oblig'd to deliver to a certain merchant, appointed for that purpose by the king.

The author goes to Marten.

From hence we went to the king of *Marta* or *Marten*, the capital city of the same name, three leagues to the south of *Cochin* upon the same river. I and Mr. *George Henry Willeng*, under factor of *Koulang*, got on horseback early in the morning, and arriv'd at 10 a clock before noon at *Carnopoly*, where we took up our lodgings in a house near the river side, which the *Dutch East-India* company some years before had purchased from the king. It is pretty large, 1662. but not very convenient, being built according to the *Malabar* fashion, with abundance of corners and inlets oddly contriv'd: The gardens are well planted with palm-trees, for the use of the house. I had no sooner given notice of my arrival, but I was sent for to the king. After the usual compliments to be paid to the *Malabar* kings, I deliver'd the following *Ola* (letter) from Mr. *Hustart* to the king.

James Hustart *councellor of the* Indies, *governor and director of the isle of* Ceylon, *and the* Malabar *coasts, sends his* Ola *to the king of* Marten.

Illustrious prince,

Admiral Hustart's *letter to the king*

Nothing could be more welcome to me, than to understand at my first arrival in these parts, that your majesty had always liv'd in a good correspondency with our company. To shew your majesty what an extraordinary value we set upon your friendship, we have sent Mr. John Nieuhoff *captain of* Koulang, *in order to enter with you into a more strict league and friendship. We hope your majesty will give him entire credit, in what he shall propose to you, which I shall be ready to acknowledge upon the like occasions.*

God preserve and give your majesty a long and a happy life.

Cochin
2 *Feb.* 1664. James Hustart.

After which I gave the king a more particular account of my commission, unto which he answer'd, that he would consider of it till the next day; accordingly I was sent for at the appointed time, when I found the king surrounded with a great number of his courtiers, and among the rest some mahometan merchants; he order'd immediately two of them, and one of his captains, who was in great esteem with him, to treat with me concerning the propositions made on behalf of the company; but as I was sufficiently inform'd that most of the mahometan merchants here drove considerable traffick to *Cananor*, to the no small prejudice of our company, I did not think fit to treat with them, if possible I could avoid it, which made me to tell the king, that *I had no commission to treat with the mahometan merchants, but with his majesty; that the company at present offer'd peace to the whole coast of* Malabar, *in which, if his majesty was desirous to be included, and to enjoy the benefit of a flourishing trade, he might himself treat with me, but if not, grant me leave to depart.* The king after a little pausing, desired that my propositions might be drawn up in writing, which I did accordingly: Our demands were,

To

1662. *To forbid the importation of amsion, the peeling of the wild cinamome, and the exportation of pepper.*

These propositions the king order'd to be read aloud in our presence, which the mahometan merchants endeavour'd to oppose with all their might; and the greatest part of the day being spent in messages betwixt the king and us, by the *Residoors*, who gave an exact account of all what pass'd to the king, he gave leave for us to return to our lodgings, and order'd us to attend him again the next day. But early in the morning a certain person of quality, who bears the second rank in that kingdom, came along with the before-mention'd captain, to tell us, that what we desired, was absolutely to the prejudice of the king and kingdom, which I endeavour'd to put out of their heads, by telling them, that we were come with no other intention, than to establish a free commerce with them, as we had done with most of the other *Malabar* kings and princes before, and which would turn to their great advantage; notwithstanding this they were for making several alterations in each point, and five or six messages pass'd betwixt the court and us; at last they ask'd what quantity of pepper we desired yearly? We answer'd them, that it was no matter about the quantity, since we were for buying all. This point was vigorously opposed by the mahometan merchants, who fain would have persuaded the king to reserve part of it for them; but by degrees we overcame all these difficulties, the king having granted us all we demanded, except the peeling of the wild cinnamome, which we did not so much insist upon, being a thing uncertain whether it would quit the cost to the undertakers or not, because it was in the kings power to set what price he pleased upon it.

The kingdom of Marten — The kingdom of *Marta* or *Marten* is very near as big as that of *Kalkolang*, extending to the north as far as *Porka*; to the south it borders upon the *Indian* sea, and to the east it is surrounded by high mountains, and wash'd by the same river, upon which *Cochin* and *Koulang* lie: The capital city is likewise call'd *Marta* or *Marten*. But to the south near the sea-shore is another city call'd by the inhabitants *Panderatoutte*, and *Pesse* by the *Portuguese*; here we built a house by the king's consent, for the conveniency of the pepper trade, which is always weigh'd here. There is another city belonging to this kingdom call'd *Podiogabo* or *Maulikara*. This king possesses some parts of the countrey in common with the king of *Kalkolang*, a thing not usual on this coast, where are so many petty kingdoms, that it requires no small time, to distinguish and know them from on another. The country is well peopled here, abounding in pepper, pease and beans, and the fields near the river-side in rice and salt-pits. The king is a soveraign prince; he that then reign'd being of about 60 years of age, very large of body and a stern countenance; upon his head he wears a bonnet of scarlet cloth lined with callicoe; he keeps constantly 1200 negroes in pay; his residence is at *Carnapoly*, a place surrounded with an earthen wall of 20 foot high, but appeared much decay'd at that time. This kingdom has long ago been inhabited by christians, which however were forced to live there 12 whole years without a church, *viz.* till the year 1581, when the king then reigning, not only gave them liberty to build a church, but also to cut wood in the adjacent forests dedicated to the pagan idols. He also gave permission to his subjects to turn christians, and the jesuits had full power granted them to exercise the church censure, and to inflict it upon those that were baptiz'd by them. The said church was dedicated to St. *Andrew*, because it was finish'd upon that saints day. 1662.

Upon the banks of the same river, where the kingdom of *Marten* lies, is also the kingdom of *Batyma*, with its city call'd *Katyapery*. It is commonly reported in these parts, that the kings of *Batyma* made a law, by which a man was impower'd to kill any woman that should refuse him a kindness.

By this time our negotiation being brought to an entire conclusion, I offer'd the usual presents to the king, which he order'd to be taken by him who bears the second rank in the kingdom, who as well as several others of his courtiers having been very instrumental in promoting the treaty, we thought fit to engage to our party by some small presents. At last we were appointed to attend before the court in the open air, where the king first, and I afterwards sign'd the treaty with our own hands, in the presence of a great multitude of people, that were flock'd thither on purpose to be spectators of this ceremony. This done I took my leave of the king and his chief courtiers, and the same evening went aboard our vessel, which about a league from thence did ride at anchor in the river. — *The author leaves* Marten. A certain lord commanding over the countrey here, a vassal of the king of *Marten*, came on purpose to meet and compliment us and presented us with some fowls, *Pysang* and other refreshments, of whom I likewise took my leave and return'd to *Koulang*, where I arriv'd the 9th of *February*, — *Returns to* Koulang.

Whilst I was negotiating with the king of

1662.

of *Porka*, the king of *Kalkolang* sent for me to his court, where he presented me with a very fine *Brocado* silk gown, made according to the *Indian* fashon, testifying his joy for the good success we had had in our negotiation with his neighbour; I return'd my hearty thanks to the king for this and other favours I had receiv'd at his hands, and went back again to the king of *Porka*.

Is presented by the king of Kalkolang.

But to return to *Koulang*; no sooner was I arrived the 9th of *Feb.* at *Koulang* but the queen of the same name, sent the next day her chief captain to receive the customs and cannon she pretended to be due to her by virtue of the late treaty; I was willing to surrender the cannon, according to our agreement, but could not consent to the other; and in the mean while we were preparing our *Mansio* (vessel) for a voyage to the king of *Travankoor*'s court, the *Residoors* of the king of *Goenree* and *Bariiette Pule* desir'd an interview with me, whom I gave a meeting accordingly in company of Mr. *Cher de Venne*, book-keeper of the *Dutch East-India* company. We saw above 300 negroes all in a body, who with one voice cry'd out for the customs, which made me, after many debates and disputes, tell them, that I would go home, with an intention to return the next day to them, provided they would desist from these things, that were not granted them by the treaty, nor were ever likely to be granted, and so return'd to *Koulang*.

The 12th of *February*, I embark'd at nine a clock in the evening for *Attingen*, where the king of *Travankoor* kept his residence then, being come thither some days before. With break of day we found our selves near the village of *Mappul*, about five leagues to the east of *Koulang*, but not daring to approach the shore with our vessel, we were forced to hire an *Indian* boat, which carried us safely ashore, notwithstanding the violence of the waves that rowled against the shore. We travell'd for about a league along the sea-side, till we came to a large river, which carried us in three hours rowing to the court; here we understood that the king was just then ready to go to *Kalkolang*, I gave immediate notice of my arrival to his majesty, who sent for me by one of his *Residoors*; he met us on the stairs-head, with many of his courtiers; where I presented him with the usual respect, the letter, with some presents, which he receiv'd and caused the letter to be read aloud before all there present, telling me, that he would forthwith let me know his intention, and that in the mean while I might take a walk into the garden of the castle, with some of his *Residoors*; and discourse with them farther in a certain grove, which he pointed at with his fingers. Accordingly I begun to talk more at large, concerning my propositions, with the four *Residoors*, who were for treating with me immediately upon the subject in hand, which I told them I had no orders to do, my business being to treat with the king in person. They having given the king an account of what I said, brought me word, that his majesty, in a matter of such consequence could not take a resolution till next day, desiring me to have patience till then, and presented us with *Pysang* and some other refreshments. On the western-side of the palace is a pleasant house at the foot of a hill, in the midst of a very pleasant grove, from whence there is a prospect into a very fruitful valley full of rice-fields, hedg'd in with palm-trees; this place was assign'd us for our lodgings, our host appearing to be a very honest man, but so mistrustful withal, that when we were going to supper, he refused to let us have dishes or any other utensils; their soldiers being exasperated at this usage, the whole house began to be in an alarum, and I enquiring the reason, could get no other answer from him, than *That the devil and his ill fortune ow'd him a shame, when they brought such lodgers into his house*, desiring us at the same time to look out for another lodging. With much ado I persuaded him, that we were no such fellows as he imagin'd us to be, and so at last with the help of a little money, he let us have what we had occasion for.

Goes to Attingen.

The next day, being the 14th of *Feb.* about eight a clock in the morning the king sent for me to court again by a negro, where we met the before-mention'd four *Residoors* at the gate, ready to receive us, we went together into the garden, where I caused a carpet to be spread under the shadow of some trees, as they did their *Indian* mats; and being seated, the chiefest of the *Residoors* told me, *That his majesty was not a little dissatisfied at our burning the royal palace of* Koulang, *and that he had given him orders to treat of that as well as the other subject with me. That the letter sent to admiral* Hustart *had been written with no other intention, than to treat concerning the pretensions of prince* Gondormo, *and that therefore they would be glad to hear what instructions I had about that matter.* As I thought it not for our purpose to tergiversate in the matter, I told them bluntly, that *Gondormo* might thank himself for his misfortunes; for that when our fleet and forces, about two years ago appear'd near *Cochin*, to attack the *Portuguese* our enemies, the *Dutch* admiral had set up a white flag, to shew his willingness to treat with the queen

Is call'd to court.

Propositions made to him.

His answer.

queen

1662. queen of *Cochin*, which *Gondormo* had not only prevented, but also attack'd our forces, and opposed and still did oppose all our designs tending to the re-establishment of the government of *Cochin* upon its true foundation. I further told them, that, when about two years ago, I had the honour to see his majesty at *Kalikoli*, I assured his majesty that we had conquer'd *Cochin*, and were engaged in an everlasting alliance with *Monta Davila*, their legal sovereign; and that therefore *Gondormo* need not flatter himself with the least hopes of his re-establishment. Of this they gave an account to the king, who soon sent them back with another proposition, to wit, whether he might not be admitted as a second or third person in the kingdom? To make an end at once of this dispute, I ask'd them whether they did acknowledge *Monta Davila* lawful king? They answer'd they did? I demonstrated to them, how unreasonable it was, to demand that one who had set up against his legal sovereign, should be receiv'd in such a station in the same kingdom, and considering the ill consequences which must needs ensue from thence, I told them it was in vain to say a word more of it. This made them insist no more upon the business of *Gondormo*, they only told us, *That we had best be upon our guard*, Gondormo *and his three brothers being resolved to live, and to be buried in the kingdom of* Cochin. I answer'd him carelesly, that I had travelled thro the greatest part of that kingdom; and that I was sure there was room enough for 100000 of them. I assured them farther, that his majesty of *Travankoor*, had been always in great esteem with our company, that they never doubted of his friendship, notwithstanding he seem'd to bear so great a share in *Gondormo*'s business; that I was sent thither on purpose to enter into a more strict league with him, in the same manner as had been done with several other kings his neighbours. Whilst they were debating this matter, an envoy arriv'd from the queen of *Koulang*, with a letter, in which she complain'd, that she had not receiv'd any share of the customs, nor were the cannon restored to her; the *Residoor* ask'd me what the meaning of it was, and whether we would do less than the *Portuguese* had done? I answer'd him, if we should follow the footsteps of the *Portuguese*, we must be guilty likewise of the same enormities, in murthering, plundering, &c. things not customary among us, the intention of our company being to maintain every one in his right, and to establish a free commerce without interruption; and these, said I, are the main contents of my commission, according to which I am to treat with all the kings and princes of the coast of *Malabar*. After several other debates, finding them full of tergiversations, I roundly told them, that I found them very backward in what had been proposed; that for my part, I had done all what I could to procure a peace, but that they seem'd to be rather inclinable to war; and finding them somewhat puzzel'd by their silence, said, that if as yet they could find out any expedient, to compose matters upon reasonable terms, I should be willing to hearken to them, and that, if it was for a yearly present, or a sum of money, once for all, they should have it. The king being inform'd of this resolution, sent me word back, that in a thing of this nature, in which several others besides himself were concerned, he must take some leisure to advise, which done, he would send one of his *Residoors* to *Koulang*, to treat farther of the matter. I insisted upon having all things dispatch'd here, but the *Residoors* telling me, that they durst not urge it any more to the king, for that time, I was fain to acquiesce, and to defer it till our next meeting at *Koulang*, tho' I very well foresaw that this negotiation would meet with no small difficulties, unless something more were granted than had been offer'd hitherto. About the same time the before-mention'd queen, sent me underhand word, that she was very inclinable to a farther treaty, but that it could not be done till the king of *Travankoor* was gone, which as it was no unwelcome news to me, so I desired the *Residoor* whom she sent to me, to use his utmost interest with her majesty to bring it to pass, being sensible that it was the intention of my Masters to live with her in a good correspondence. 1662.

Attingen. The countrey about *Attingen* has hitherto not been describ'd by any that I know; it abounds in pepper, of which a great quantity is brought thither out of the circumjacent parts. The ancient race of the kings of *Travankoor* owed its origine to *Attingen*, but for want of male heirs, one of the princes of *Cochin* was placed in that throne; the king who then reign'd, being descended from the *Cochin* race of *Rammerankoil*, and elected king of *Travankoor*. The ground where the pepper grows, is hereabouts strong and red, which makes the pepper not full so large here, as in the valleys about *Koulang* and *Cochin*. On the descents of the hills you see very pleasant rice-fields, cut out like steps, and water'd from the top by small rivulets. The king and queen's palace are directly opposite to one another, with some rice-fields betwixt them.

The next following day about 10 a clock

1662. clock in the morning, I was call'd to court again, where the king told me in person, that it would be better to reassume the treaty at *Koulang*, which I being fain to be satisfy'd with, I took my leave of his majesty and the *Residoors*, who offer'd me a present from the king, according to the custom of the countrey, which I accepted off, and went directly to the river-side, where we found our boat, and sailing down the river, came just before sun-set to *Maypule*, where I was met by the resident of *Tengepatnam*, whom I had given notice of my coming that way. The next following day, *viz.* the 16th of *February* we reimbark'd our vessels, and steer'd our course by sea to *Koulang*, from whence I immediately dispatch'd our interpreter to *Pule de Margaty*, to inform himself where the queen of *Goenree* at that time kept her court; he return'd the next day with advice, that a month before she was gone deeper into the countrey, to a place call'd *Peretaly*, about four days journey from thence.

Is call'd to court again, and departs from thence.

The kingdom of Travankoor.

The kingdom of *Travankoor* (thus call'd from its capital city) begins at the cape of *Comory* or *Comorin*, and extends all along the sea-coast as far as *Koulang*, comprehending a tract of ground of 20 or 24 leagues in length; the famous village of *Paru*, belonging to the queen of *Singnaty*, being only in the midst. To the east it borders upon the kingdom of *Madure*, and to the west upon the countries of *Peretaly* and *Kotarkery*. It has several considerable villages which are inhabited by the moors, such as *Tengepatnam*, *Kuletture*, *Koritypatnam* and *Allage*. About the year 1544, above 30 villages, inhabited by the *Makaos*, who live for the most part upon fishing, and by the mahometans, were upon this coast. But the chief cities lie deeper in the countrey, which is of a great extent all along the mountains to *Naynar*, near the cape of *Comorin* and toward *Travankoor*, in all 29 great cities and villages. About a league and a half to the north of the cape *Comorin* is the city of *Kotate* or *Kokatti*, a place of great traffick; the populous city of *Simintira* and *Matadavalur*, famous for its bigness, being surrounded by six or seven other towns; *Verrage* is not above a quarter of a league distance from *Kotate* and *Tatikury*, the two most considerable places of the whole countrey. *Kalkolang* is a very large city, being a league and a half long, upon the confines of the *Neyk* of *Madure*. It is situate upon a high hill, 3 leagues from *Tengepatnam*, and 12 from *Koulang*; being on one side strengthen'd by inaccessable mountains, on the other by a wall, the undermost part of which is of stone, the uppermost of brick-work, in all 24 foot high; the royal palace stands at the west end, being surrounded by a stone-wall. On the east-side you see the ruins of an old castle, built on the top of a hill, fortified with a triple wall. The city of *Kalkolang* is the chief residence of the king, who constantly keeps a garrison of 10000 negroes here, to secure it against the *Neyk* of *Madure*, whose power is much dreaded here. It is a very fertile countrey, abounding in pepper, rice and other grains. It also produces wild cinnamome, the best, the whole coast of *Malabar* affords, but it wants several things requisite for the conveniency of life. One of the chiefest rivers which water this countrey, is the river *Mannikorin*, it exonerates itself into the sea, near cape *Comorin*. The king of this countrey is by some stiled the *great king*, because he possesses larger territories than any other of the *Malabar* kings. He is served in great state, and maintains abundance of commanders, whom they call *Mandigals*, and many councellors, call'd *Pullas*. Some ascribe to him a superiority over neighbouring princes, but of this I am convinced to the contrary by my own experience; it is true they reverence him, as a potent king, but pay him no obedience. Others will have him to be a vassal of the king of *Narsinga*. The whole countrey is well stock'd with people, who appear very well cloth'd according to the *Malabar* fashion. 1662.

The 18th of *February*, I set out from *Koulang* in company of Mr. *Siewert Baker*, for the kingdom of *Goenree*. But scarce were we come to *Kaligoli*, but one of the *Residoors* told us, that the queen of *Goenree* was a month ago gone into the countrey, and would not return very quickly, by reason of a certain religious ceremony, she was obliged to perform there, before her return; I desired a guide, because I had something of moment to communicate to the queen, but they excused it, telling me that the ways were so rocky and impassable, that it would be impossible for me to go thither, it being five tedious days journey to the countrey of *Peretaly*, bordering upon the territories of the *Neyk* of *Madure*. Being made sensible that this journey could not be undertaken without great difficulty and charge, I thought it most expedient to leave a letter with the *Residoor*, to be deliver'd to the queen, the contents of which were as follows.

The author goes to Goenree.

His letter to the queen.

THat I was come hither to offer a small present to her majesty, and to enter into a strict and everlasting alliance with her; but tho' I was so unfortunate, as not to meet with

1662. *her majesty, I liv'd however in hopes, that she would not be backward in entering into a general league, which the company had lately concluded with all the* Malabar *princes; to accomplish which as we should be ready to contribute every thing on our side, so we did not question, but that her majesty would be pleased to let us know her sentiments by the bearer of this letter.*

Whilst I tarried here, I understood that the *Residoor* of the king of *Travankoor* was arriv'd the 20th at *Koulang China*, and had notified his arrival by our *Petangatin Thome Bottancho*, desiring to confer with me, concerning certain matters commanded him by the king his master, since my departure from thence. The place appointed for our interview, was the church of the christians of *St. Thomas* in *Koulang China*, where I was present at the appointed hour, but finding them to trifle away the time in altercations and tergiversations; I was ready to mount on horse-back again, in order to return to *Koulang*, which when they perceiv'd, they desired me to stay and give them another meeting, which I agreed to do. At last, after abundance of contests, the following agreement concerning the shares of the customs, the importation of amfion and the exportation of pepper, was made betwixt the *Dutch East-India* company, by their deputy Mr. *John Nieuhoff* on one, and the kings of *Marten*, *Singnaty*, *Goenree*, *Travankoor* and *Barrigetta Pule* on the other side.

Articles of agreement.

I. *NO body shall import, sell or exchange any amfion into these countries, except the* Dutch East-India *company.*

II. *No body, without any exception, shall be permitted to export any pepper or cinamome out of this countrey, or to sell them to any body, except to the said company.*

III. *A certain price was settled, betwixt both parties, and what share each should have in the customs, whereby all former pretensions and exceptions should be annulled.*

February 21, 1664. *Sign'd in the court* Matta del Reyne.

In my return from *Koulang*, in the road leading to *Matta del Reyne*, I found guards posted upon all the cross roads, which made me enquire of *Matta del Pule* chief commander of the negroes, what the meaning of it was, who told me with a sorrowful countenance, that the prince *Barrigetta Pule*, had caused one of the queen's *Residoors* to be slain by his soldiers, who had also laid about 80 houses in ashes, and cut down many palm-trees. That they had been sent to besiege him in his castle, but that at the intercession of the king of *Travankoor's Residoor*, who had promised that the said prince should be call'd to an account by the king his master, they had delay'd the execution of it for three days; but he much fear'd he should scarce withhold them much longer, from taking a direful revenge of him. He was very inquisitive concerning our late transactions with the king of *Marten*, but I excused the matter, telling him only, that I hoped it would be brought to a conclusion, to both sides satisfaction.

Troubles raised by Barrigetta Pule.

The 22d I sent a letter by Mr. *Sebastian Ferdinandi*, our interpreter, to the queen of *Singnaty*, in which I gave her an account of what had been transacted betwixt the *Residoor* of the king of *Travankoor* and my self. In the mean while the king's and prince's soldiers were come to blows, several being kill'd and wounded on both sides: Whereupon the prince finding himself besieged in his castle, sent one of his most trusty servants to desire assistance, and some powder and ball for his master, which I thought fit to refuse, for weighty reasons; for whatever may be the opinion of those who think it a maxim of state to fish in troubled waters, I was too well acquainted with the perfidiousness of the *Malabars*, who make not the least account of faith or leagues, unless they are forced to it, than to put the least confidence in them.

In the mean time the beforementioned *Residoor* of the king of *Travankoor* not appearing at the time and place appointed for the removing of some remaining differences, I sent him the following letter, by *Topaes Nicolaes da Costa*.

The captain of *Koulang* sends this letter with his service, to *Narrano Poly*, *Residoor* of *Travankoor*.

The author's letter to the Residoor *of* Travankoor.

PUrsuant to our mutual agreement, I came to Koulang China, *in order to bring the treaty begun before to a happy conclusion: But your highness did not perform your promise, neither had I the least account since, how the queen of* Singnaty *was likely to relish our transactions. And as the nature of the thing would admit of no delay, I saw my self obliged to send my interpreter to the queen of* Singnaty, *and* Topaes Nicholaes da Costa, *to the* Goenree *and* Barrigetta, *to be inform'd concerning that point. They bring me for answer, that the said queen pretends to the customs without*

1662. *without the least diminution, which is not in my power to agree to. As I am sensible, that I have left nothing unattempted, which might reasonably and honestly be expected from me, for the terminating of these differences, but all in vain, I have nothing left to do, but to protest once for all, according to the strictest rules of justice, in the name of the whole company, against your* Narrano Poly, *and your transactions, and all others who take part with you, that we will, and hereby declare our selves innocent, and guiltless of all the troubles and miseries of a future war.*

Koulang Feb. 26, 1664. John Nieuhoff.

In the mean while I had given an account of the whole matter to Mr. *Hustart*, desiring him to come in person, and to endeavour by his presence to put a happy conclusion to the negotiations. He sent me an answer dated *Cochin* the 24th of *February*, intimating that he had intended to set out from thence within two days after, of which he order'd me to give notice to the king of *Travankoor*, and queen of *Singnaty*, which I did accordingly by an express sent with letters to both their majesty's. The 27th the residoor of *Travankoor* sent me word by *Topaes Nicolaes de Costa*, that he was willing to treat with me once more about the customs, but that no body except the queen must be privy to the matter; for which reason he could cause a quite different rumour to be raised among the people; but considering with my self that the negroes, who are in great esteem here, might get scent of the matter, and that (as the king had told me himself before) several persons in the first rank were concern'd in the customs, I did not look upon this underhand treaty as advantageous for the company; which made me write to the *Residoor*, that I was willing to contribute all what in me lay, towards the composing of the differences betwixt us, provided it could be done in the same nature as with the other *Malabar* princes, who had not refus'd to read the treaties in the presence of their subjects, to shew that their words were altogether consonant to their deeds. I receiv'd an answer the same evening, in which the *Residoor* desired an interview with me in *St. Thomas*'s church the next day. Accordingly I went thither on horse-back with Mr. *James Cher de Venne*. After many contests on both sides, we agreed at last, and the *Residoor* promised to return to morrow to finish the treaty. About this time I receiv'd a letter from the queen of *Singnaty*, in answer to that I had sent her before; as follows.

Another interview with the Residoor *of* Travankoor

The queen of Singnaty*'s letter to the author.* 1662.

I Receiv'd and saw the contents of the letter sent to me from Mr. John Nieuhoff, *captain of* Koulang, *concerning the proposed treaty; I will send word in the Month of* March *to* Kottekkery, *where we will meet together, and I shall be ready to rectify what my plenipotentiaries shall agree to. For which reason I order'd this letter to be written to captain* John Nieuhoff.

The next day the *Residoor* of the king of *Travankoor* came to *Koulang*, who was receiv'd by us with all imaginable respect; he began among other things to renew his former discourse about the prince *Gondormo*, upon which it was agreed to delay the last conclusion of the treaty till the coming of Mr. *Hustart*, who was expected every day at *Koulang*.

The 2d of *March* with break of day, the vice-roy of the king of *Travankoor*, call'd by them *Gorepe*, the chief commander of the negroes, call'd *Matta de Pulo*, and my self, set out for the court of the queen of *Koulang*, which was then kept at *Calliere*. We arriv'd there about two a clock in the afternoon, and as soon as notice was given of our arrival, we were sent for to court, where, after I had deliver'd the presents, and laid the money down for pepper, I was introduced into her majesty's presence. She had a guard of above 700 soldiers about her, all clad after the *Malabar* fashion; the Queen's attirement being no more than a piece of callicoe wrapt round her middle, the upper part of her body appearing for the most part naked, with a piece of callicoe hanging carelesly round her shoulders. Her ears, which were very long, her neck and arms were adorn'd with precious stones, gold rings and bracelets, and her head cover'd with a piece of white callicoe. She was past her middle age, of a brown complexion, with black hair tied in a knot behind, but of a majestick mein, she being a princess who shew'd a great deal of good conduct in the management of her affairs. After I had paid the usual compliments, I shew'd her the proposition, I was to make to her in writing; which she order'd to be read twice, the better to understand the meaning of it, which being done, she ask'd me, whether this treaty comprehended all the rest, and whether they were annull'd by it; unto which I having given her a sufficient answer, she agreed to all our propositions, which were accordingly sign'd immediately. This done, I recommended Mr. *James Cher de Venne*, who was to succeed me at *Koulang*, to her majesty, desiring her to acknowledge

The author goes to the queen of Koulang.

5

Nieuhof's Audience wth ye Queen of Koulang

1662. knowledge him as such, and to continue in a good correspondency with our company, by whom I was order'd to go to *Toutekorin*, which she promised to do. I then desired leave to depart, because I expected Mr. *Hustart* every hour at *Koulang*, which she readily granted, and at the same time took a golden bracelet from her arms, which she presented me as a token of her good inclinations to the company. She order'd one of the *Residoors* to fasten it to my arm, but it being too streight, she caused it to be fitted for me, she having once before, *viz.* when I first gave her notice of Mr. *Hustart's* coming, presented me with another golden bracelet, for which and all other honours, I had received from her majesty, since my residence at *Koulang*, I returned my hearty thanks, desiring her once more not to withdraw her favour from the company.

Returns to Koulang. Thus I return'd to *Koulang*, about two a clock in the night, where I was let in through one of the gates, the admiral *Hustart* being the day before arriv'd there with two ships, the *Erasmus* and the *Niewenhoven* from *Batavia*. The next morning I paid a visit to the admiral at his lodgings, where I gave him an ample account of my negotiations, and other matters relating to our factory here, wherewith he was highly satisfied, and gave me some farther orders about certain matters to be transacted before my departure. 1662.

About the same time the viceroy of the king of *Travankoor* came back to the city of *Koulang*, to compliment the admiral, and to consummate the treaty. *The viceroy of* Travankoor *comes to* Koulang. The admiral sent him afterwards several presents, and let him know, that if the king his master did give any assistance of men or arms to prince *Gondormo* against *Cochin* and the company, he must expect to be treated as an enemy; he return'd for answer, that he was sure his master would not do it, but always maintain a good correspondency with the company, upon which he was dismiss'd, and left *Koulang* the same night, as did the admiral soon after, who set sail for *Cranganor*, leaving the commodore *Bitter* behind him, who with his wife and family was come aboard the ship the *Niewenhoven* to load pepper here. His wife being very desirous to see the queen of *Koulang*, I caus'd her to be carried thither in my *Palankin*; the queen receiv'd her very courteously, being extremely well pleas'd with the sight of a *Dutch* woman; and many of the *Malabars* were so curious as to peep into the *Palankin* to see her; they being no less surpriz'd at the sight of the *Europeans* than we were at them. Commodore *Bitter* having by this time got his full cargo, set sail again for *Batavia*,

1662. *Batavia*, as I did the 11th to the court of *Gonree*, and so to the prince *Baryette Pule*, where I introduced Mr. *Cherde Venne*, who, as I told you before, was to manage the affairs of the company after my departure; they receiv'd him very civilly, and promis'd to maintain an everlasting correspondence with our company. At parting, prince *Baryette Pule* presented me with a golden bracelet curiously wrought, and the viceroy with a silken suit of cloaths, and so I return'd very well satisfied to *Koulang*, where I prepar'd for *Toutekorin*; for within four days after, *viz.* the 12th of *March*, having first surrendred all my accounts, and what also belong'd to the company, and given the best instructions I could to Mr. *James Cherde Venne*, taken my leave of the chiefest officers belonging to the company, I set out for *Toutekorin*, after a stay of two years at *Koulang*, considering that my appointed time was near expiring, and I had settled our traffick at *Koulang* upon a good foot. I could have been very glad to have stay'd the remainder of my time here, for which purpose I sent a letter to *Colomba*, but the chief director of *Toutekorin* being order'd to *Persia* upon some urgent business, I was forc'd to supply his place. And upon this occasion I think it not amiss to give the reader an account of what I have observ'd most remarkable during my stay on the coast of *Malabar*, together with the products, beasts and inhabitants of this countrey.

The author takes his leave of the court of Gonree *and prince* Baryette Pule.

Cape Koulang.

Limits of the coast of Malabar.

The coast of *Malabar* is properly called that tract of ground where the *Malabar* tongue is us'd, beginning 50 leagues to the south below *Goa*, and extending to the south to the cape *Comorin*, under $7\frac{1}{2}$ degree of northern latitude, about 80 leagues along that coast. On the west-side it borders upon the *Indian* sea, and to the east it is surrounded by a ridge of high mountains, which divide it from the coast of *Coromandel*. It is commonly divided into five kingdoms, *viz.* *Cananor*, *Calicut*, *Cranganor*, *Cochin* and *Koulang*, unto which some add the kingdom of *Porka*, *Tanakor* or *Tanor*, *Koulang* and *Travankoor*; not to mention here the petty kingdoms of *Kota*, *Mountingua*, *Badara*, *Chambaya*, *Marta*, *Materte*, and several others among the mountains. It is situate almost in the midst betwixt the line and the tropick of Cancer; which makes the days here excessive hot, notwithstanding which, it is a pleasant, extraordinary fertile and healthful countrey. It is full of very fine springs, pools, rivers and channels, even as far as the mountains, but most towards the sea-side; in which it resembles the province of *Holland*, being scarce passable without boats; tho' most of their rivers are shallow, and consequently unfit for ships of burthen. Here grows great store of the best pepper, exceeding all the rest in goodness; formerly the inhabitants us'd to exchange the pepper with the foreign merchants for silver, gold, amfion and other commodities; but since the *Dutch East-India* company have made themselves masters of the kingdoms of *Cranganor*, *Cochin* and *Koulang*, and forc'd the *Portuguese* from thence, they have by entering into several leagues with the neighbouring princes, got the monopoly of pepper on that coast into their hands, and have so well provided the three before mention'd places with strong fortifications and garrisons, that they are look'd upon as impregnable. Besides this, the countrey of *Malabar* is full of cocoe trees, especially in the marshes, where these trees thrive better than in any other place in the *Indies*, there being some trees here of 95 and more foot high. They drive a considerable trade with the oil and bark of this fruit, neither do they want wood fit for the building of houses and ships. The air is very pure here, and very cold in the night time, during the three months of *January*, *February* and *March*; and when the nights are very foggy, which questionless occasions the cold, the days being excessive hot. The winter begins here in *April*, or at the most in *May*, and ends in *September* or *October*, with thunder, lightnings and storms: This season produces the most fruits, by reason of the warm rains. Then begins the summer season, which continues till *April* or *May* with intolerable heat, and commonly without any rains, which renders the sandy grounds so hot, that they cannot pass over them with their bare feet, but are forced to make use of a certain sort of shoes, call'd by them *Siripous*. Every morning about nine or ten a clock, the land wind blows from the *East*, and immediately after sunset the west wind from the sea, both which contribute much towards the cooling of the air, as well here, as in all other adjacent islands. What is most observable is, that the land wind never reaches above ten leagues in the sea; an observation which has never been known to miss. The seasons here are quite of a different nature from ours, for whilst during the summer months every thing is dried up in the hot climates of *Europe*, here the fruits appear most florid and green, because this is the winter season in *Malabar*, where it rains continually for six months, during which time you not as much as see the least glimpse of the sun, but in the other six months it never rains. During the months of *October*, *November* and *December*, they are much afflicted with dreadful storms. There is another thing which is

Its division.

1662.

Its products.

Its air.

Seasons of the year.

1662. is most surprizing here, that when it is summer on the coast of *Malabar*, it is winter on the coast of *Coromandel*. This is occasioned by the mountains call'd *Gate*, which stop the passage of the winds; for whilst on the east-side of these mountains, which extend all along the coast of *Malabar*, they have great heats and droughts during their summer season, those on the west-side have their winter with violent rains. Thus on the south-side of the cape *Comorin*, they have their summer during *April*, *May*, *June*, *July*, *August* and *September*, whilst at the same time, those on the north-side have their winter, it being very stormy and rainy on one, and fair and calm on the other side at the same time.

Houses. Their ordinary houses are of bamboe canes, cover'd with leaves of coco-trees; some are plaistered with carving, without any cellars, garrets or windows. They never lock up their houses, because their houshold-stuff is not worth stealing, unless they be persons of an eminent rank; their doors are so low, that you cannot enter without stooping, tho' they have also some houses cover'd with lead, copper and tiles, and built otherwise and well fitted up, according to their fashion; their private buildings don't approach in height to ours, they commonly have two or three apartments within one another; within the compass of the middlemost of these apartments is a small square, with some small galleries round about it, which receive the water from the tops of the houses. At the entrance of all their houses, whether rich or poor, are court-yards surrounded with high walls and ditches, and one of strong pallisadoes. These court-yards are for the reception of travellers, who eat, drink and sleep here, with more conveniency than if they were lodged within, being ready at all times to proceed on their journey when the rest of the company goes. Their royal palaces and pagods are commonly built of stone, surrounded with a mud wall, on which are mounted some great cannon. Most of their princely palaces are erected in large ponds or lakes, some having a league and a half in circumference. They have most excellent carvings in wood, with all sorts of images in their houses; their ceiling is of a plain polish'd wood; among the marshes are to be seen many ruins of old houses, which appear to have been built many ages ago. Some tell us, that *Alexander* the great coming into those parts, after he had order'd his admiral to enter by the way of the river *Ganges* the sea, and from thence by the *Euphrates* to *Babylon*, had laid these countries desolate; others ascribe this devastation to *Tamerlane*.

The *Malabars* eat and drink sitting upon the ground, after the *Mahometan* fashion, almost like our taylors. Their cups, dishes and spoons are made of coco-nuts; people of quality have them made of metal. Instead of bread they use nothing but rice; besides which, they feed upon flesh, fish, spices, fruits, milk and eggs. They drink abundance of water, as likewise the juice of the coco-trees; some of which give 30 quarts of this liquor in 24 hours, but if they are drain'd too much, the trees perish. They also distil a spirit call'd *Arack* out of this liquor, but it is not near so good nor wholsome as our brandy. When they drink they don't touch their lips with the cup, but pour the liquor from above into the mouth; some eat neither flesh nor fish, but live purely upon the products of the ground. 1662. *How they eat and drink.*

They use amfion very greedily. They take the quantity or the bigness of a pea, this they either mix with *Arack*, or chew it alone, sometimes till they fall asleep; they pretend that this makes them have very present dreams of the *Elysian* fields and such like. When they are to attack an enemy, they take a good quantity of it, which makes them fall on like enraged wild beasts, and the virtue of the amfion being gone, they don't remember what has past, which shews that it is very obnoxious to the memory. Some have accustomed themselves to use amfion every day, some every two or three days; and before I knew the effects of it, I have been often surpriz'd, that they should be so forgetful in such matters as I had treated with them of before. The queen of *Koulang* asking me once among other things, what was the reason the *Dutch* were more active and perseverant than the *Malabars*, who were generally fickle and unsettled, I laid the fault upon the use of the amfion, telling her withal, that the *Malabars* should imitate the *Dutch*, and drink wines, which used with moderation, did acuate the understanding, made the spirits active, and often discovered the truth. *They use amfion.*

Among these several sects of the *Malabars*, that of the *Brahmans* is most reverenced, and maintains a peculiar manner of living. They are generally very wise, ready, active, modest and charitable, and strict observers of their promises. They betake themselves to divers employments at pleasure; some are soldiers like the natives, and wear the same clothes, except that they are distinguish'd from them by the cord they wear round their middle, and abstain from flesh. Others are priests, whose business it is to offer sacrifices to their idols, no other sect being admitted to that service. *The Brahmans.*

Some

1662. Some alſo encreaſe traffick, and tho' they grow very rich, yet obſerve the ſame rules of living. Some there are among them who addict themſelves to natural philoſophy and other ſciences, but eſpecially to aſtronomy, others to phyſick and pharmacy. They eat neither fleſh nor fiſh, nor any other living creature, and drink nothing but water; nor do they ever eat before they have waſhed and bathed themſelves; which done, they only cover their privy parts, and for the reſt eat naked. They are forbidden to eat any thing but what is prepared by one of their own ſect; which makes them commonly be their own cooks; for they rather chuſe to die than eat any thing touch'd by one of another ſect; whereas all the others are at liberty to eat what is dreſs'd by a *Brahman*. They never (no more than all the other *Malabars*) touch the brim of the cup when they drink, but pour it from above into the mouth. They wear a white turbant upon their heads, red ſhoes, and a callicoe coat, which reaches down to their ankles. Over this they have another large white piece of ſtuff, which they wrap three times round their bodies, which they draw thro' betwixt their thighs, and tie it together behind upon their buttocks in a knot. They wear about the middle a girdle or ſcarf of fine white callicoe, as their turbants are, and over the ſhoulders a piece of colour'd callicoe or ſilk, as the *Europeans* do their cloaks. They alſo have long hair, with pendants in their ears. But that which diſtinguiſhes them from all the other *Malabars*, is a cord of fine cotton thread, which they wear next to their ſkin, and is put about them firſt of all in their temples with a great deal of ceremony, and not without a conſiderable charge, which is the reaſon you cannot do a greater injury to a *Brahman* than to tear this cord, which he is obliged to purchaſe again, if he will paſs for a true *Brahman*; and if any of them is to undergo any corporeal puniſhment, his cord muſt firſt be taken from him, which is likewiſe done if any of them happen to tranſgreſs the rules preſcribed to their ſect. As they paſs along the ſtreets in their white callicoe clothes, they tell ſuch as they meet that they are *Brahmans*, becauſe the cord by which they are chiefly diſtinguiſh'd is worn next to their ſkin, and conſequently not to be ſeen; when they are to take an oath, they lay the hand upon it. The *Brahman* women have holes in their noſes, in which they hang gold and ſilver rings, pearls and precious ſtones, as well as about their legs and in their ears, where they have ſilver and gold plates ſet round with precious ſtones. The wives of the *Negroes*, of the *Moncoris*, and the other *Malabars*, are not permitted to uſe theſe ornaments. They alſo wear bracelets from their wriſts up to their elbows, ſome of gold and ſilver, others of glaſs and tortoiſe-ſhell curiouſly engraven and enamell'd. Theſe women are generally handſome and well-featured, ſome of them being not inferior in complexion to the *Portugueſe* or the brown *Dutch* women. They marry very early, ſometimes before they are quite 7 or 8 years old; for the boys and girls are permitted to ſport together till they come to be in good earneſt; but they take great care not to mix themſelves with another ſect. The men are allow'd to marry twice, tho' no more than one woman at a time. Be they never ſo poor, they will be ſure to keep their rank, and to oblige ſuch as meet them to paſs by with making a bow, in token of their reverence. Thoſe among the *Brahmans* who have liſted themſelves among the *Negroes*, are in the ſame degree with them, except that they obſerve more auſterity. The *Brahmans* are in great eſteem with their kings, who keep ſome of the chiefeſt always near their perſon, to adviſe with them in all matters of moment. Thoſe of the firſt rank among the *Brahmans*, as well as other *Indian* perſons of quality, have commonly a numerous attendance; ſome of whom carry their umbrelloes, others a ſilver baſon full of *Bethel*; others one full of water; ſome are carried in palankins or chairs. 1662.

Feaſt of the Brahmans.

The *Brahmans* have, under pretence of a religious worſhip, introduced a feaſt, which furniſhes them with a certain opportunity of being revenged of their enemies. It is a cuſtom among the the *Malabar* kings once every year, *viz.* at the time of the new-moon in *October*, to remember the bleſſings they ſuppoſe they have received from their Idols, by a ſolemn ſacrifice, which is perform'd by ſetting certain houſes on fire, ſuch as are appointed by the *Brahmans*: This is commonly perform'd in the night time, without the leaſt fore-warning given, ſo that ſometimes not only the houſe, but alſo the inhabitants, with all their goods are burnt, no body daring to quench the flame. This they call *The ſacrifice of fire and blood.*

Several ſorts of Brahmans.

There live many of the *Banjans* of *Cambaya* in *Malabar*; theſe have alſo *Brahmans*, who are in great eſteem among them; the *Brahmans* of *Malabar* are allow'd to frequent their temples. The *Banjans* themſelves lead as auſtere a life as their *Brahmans*, but they are of an inferior degree, nor can they intermarry with them. In the kingdom of *Calicut* is a certain ſort of *Brahmans*, who deſpiſe all images, and live in chaſtity after the 20 or 25th year of age. They

1662. They are ſo averſe to the female ſex that as often as they ſtir abroad, ſome bod cries out aloud before them *Poo*, *Poo*, *i. e.* keep back, keep back, to let the women know they muſt keep out of ſight. Theſe don't wear the cord twiſted of cotton thread, neither do they abſtain (like the other *Brahmans*) from fleſh, fiſh or wine; but to preſerve their chaſtity eat daily a certain quantity of the pulp of the fruit *Karuza*, being taught by experience, that the ſame has a quality of checking the venereal appetite. Neither do they bury their dead bodies like the other *Brahmans*; ſome ſtrew themſelves all over with aſhes, and are encloſed day and night in iron cages, which are ſo ſmall, that they can ſcarce ſit upright in them. Others burn or ſcald certain parts of their bodies, whereby they ſuppoſe to gain the Affections of the common people. Thus far of the *Brahmans*.

Divers ſorts of inhabitants. For the reſt it is to be obſerved, that the inhabitants of the coaſt of *Malabar* may be divided into foreigners and natives; the foreigners are properly thoſe call'd commonly *Malabars*, being a colony of *Arabians*, who have fix'd their habitations there many ages ago, near the ſea-ſide chiefly. The natives are pagans, divided into *Brahmans* or *Bramenis*, *Bramos* or *Bramen*; into the *Nairos* or *Nayros*, and into the common people call'd *Moncoris* or *Pouleas*, and otherwiſe *Parvas*. They are alſo divided into five ſeveral degrees; the firſt are the royal families, among which the houſe of *Gondormo* is one of the moſt illuſtrious; the ſecond is the ſect of the *Brahmans*, or of the prieſts. The third is the military order or nobles, call'd the *Nayros*; the fourth comprehends the merchants, and the fifth the *Parvas* or fiſhermen.

The Nayros. The *Nayros*, as I told you, are deſcended of noble families, and brought up to the war. They appear with a ſhield on their left-arm, which they carry aloft, and with a naked ſword in the right-hand. They are very haughty, and at firſt pretended to diſpute the rank with the *Portugueſe*, which occaſion'd no ſmall diſturbance, 'till the difference was agreed to be decided by a ſingle combat betwixt a *Portugueſe* and a *Nayros*, in which the laſt being worſted, the *Nayros* ever ſince were forced to give way to the *Portugueſe*; but all the other *Malabars* muſt give place to the *Nayros*. They are generally well proportion'd, tho' of a brown or olive colour; they take a ſingular pride in having long ears, which they perform by art; they bore holes thro' the ears of both boys and girls, which they fill up with palm-tree leaves roll'd together; theſe rolls they make bigger and bigger by degrees, 'till the holes are extended to the utmoſt reach the holes 1626. can bear, and hang down to their very breaſts: This is accounted one of their chiefeſt pieces of gallantry, and they adorn them with gold, ſilver and jewels. Tho' the *Nayros* are from their infancy train'd up in arms, and are very bold and brave, they are nevertheleſs very civil and meek in their converſation, according to the cuſtom of that country; notwithſtanding which they are mightily addicted to robbing upon the high-way, and will kill the travellers unawares, unleſs they be well upon their guard. This is the reaſon why the mahometan *Malabars* dwelling in this countrey, whenever they are travelling from one place to another, take one of theſe *Nayros* along with them, who is their conductor for a certain piece of money, to the next place where they take another, and by this means may paſs without any danger thro' a thouſand of *Nayros*, tho' their conductor ſhould be an old decrepit perſon, or only a boy. Theſe *Nayros* are ſtrict obſervers of the times, which are neglected by the common people, for they will not converſe with any of the inferior orders, except the *Brahmans*; nay, if any of the vulgar ſort happen only to touch a *Nayros*, as he paſſes by, he will make his ſervant that carries his meat after him, to throw it down upon the ground; nay, if they do enter their houſes, or only touch the doors and walls, they will not eat there for fear of being defiled. However the *Nayros* are not altogether ſo nice in theſe points, as the *Brahmans*. For the reſt, they are not much inclined to vice, ſodomy and inceſt; nay, the boys and girls, tho' they converſe together daily, and that without cloths, you ſhall ſeldom obſerve in them either in word or action, any thing that ſavours of uncleanneſs. The *Nayros* ſcarce ever laugh, and that not but upon extraordinary occaſions; and if they ſee others laugh they will look downward. Thoſe *Nayros* who are watching at the town gates, and ſerve for conductors to travellers, are the pooreſt of all, yet will they rather follow this employment than a trade, which they look upon below their quality. They apply themſelves from their infancy to the uſe of arms, and frequently fight together with ſwords and targets, which renders them infinitely active at that ſport. They are the beſt wreſtlers in the world, and are very nimble on foot. They attack their enemies quite naked, their privities being only covered. Their arms are bows, arrows, javelins, ſwords and ſhields; theſe are very large, which they uſe with the utmoſt dexterity to cover their bodies. On the hilt of their ſwords they have ſmall plates of metal, which

1662. which makes a noiſe when they are a fighting, and ſerves to animate them. Since the *Portugueſe* and *Dutch* have got footing there, they have alſo learn'd the uſe of fire-arms to that degree, that they will turn right and left, and give a volley of ſhot with the ſame order as the *Europeans* do.

Their marriages. One *Nayros* is not allow'd more than one Wife at a time, but the women in this point have got the ſtart of the men, they being permitted to have three huſbands at once; except that a woman of the ſect of the *Brahmans* that is married to a *Nryros* is not allow'd more than one. Each of theſe three huſbands contribute their ſhare towards the maintenance of this woman and her children, without the leaſt conteſt or jealouſy. As often as any of them comes to viſit her, he leaves his arms at the door, a ſign that neither of the other two muſt come in, for fear of diſturbing the firſt. From hence the poorer ſort reap this benefit, that they have the uſe of a wiſe, yet contribute only the third part towards the maintaining of the family; tho' on the other hand this carries along with it a great inconveniency concerning the inheritance of their children, which they recompenſe in ſome meaſure, by making the ſiſter's children the heirs of their uncles. The *Nayros* employ the common people in the countrey and other drudgeries, but in their houſes they make uſe of none but *Nayros* (or gentlemen) tho' very poor, who are willing to ſerve them for their bread. The vulgar ſort are all clad after the ſame manner, being quite naked except that they have a ſmall girdle round their waſte, on which they hang a piece of callicoe, or perhaps of the bark of a tree, or a few leaves to cover their privities. The women wear a kind of veſtment of callicoe, which reaches down to their knees, and have very long hair; whereas the men are obliged to cut their hair cloſe, except one truſs which they keep on the crown of their head. All the *Malabars* have black teeth, occaſion'd by the continual chewing of the leaves of *Bethel*: Black teeth are in great eſteem among them, becauſe thoſe that don't chaw *Bethel*, are conſidered here as of a mean extraction. The *Malabars* are ſaid to be much addicted to ſorcery, who are able to kill people as they paſs by or at leaſt throw them into a lingring diſtemper. They are extremely covetous, and will venture at any thing for a ſmall gain. The women are generally unchaſte, the young women about 17 or 18, being obliged by cuſtom to diſpoſe of their maidenheads, for no body cares to marry a maiden here, but ſuch as have been beſt beloved, ſooneſt meet with a huſband. The *Malabars* have great ſtore of great artillery, muſkets and pikes; nay, their arms were in more eſteem than thoſe of the *Portugueſe*, only they did not know the art of hardning their armour: They now make very good and ſtrong gun-barrels and gun-powder. The children of the *Nayros* are from the ſeventh year of their age exerciſed in arms, and train'd up to the wars; but every one betakes himſelf to one peculiar kind of arms, it being their opinion, that they cannot excel in the uſe of all. They anoint the limbs of their young children every day with a certain oil, to make their joints pliable; for when they forced to fly, they put their greateſt confidence in the agility of their bodies, and will in an inſtant turn back upon their enemies, and attack them in the rear; beſides, that in their flight they throw their javelins backward with great dexterity, and as ſoon as they have thrown their darts, they know how to ſhelter themſelves behind their ſhields. 1662.

Tho' the *Nayros* in general are very good ſoldiers, yet there is a certain kind among them call'd *Amokos*, who are eſteemed above all the reſt, being a company of ſtout, bold and deſperate bravadoes. They oblige themſelves by moſt direful imprecations againſt themſelves and their families, calling heaven to witneſs, that they will revenge certain injuries done to their friends or patrons, which they certainly purſue with ſo much intrepidity, that they ſtop neither at fire nor ſword, to take vengeance of the death of their maſter, but like mad men run upon the point of their enemies ſwords, which makes them be generally dreaded by all, and makes them to be in great eſteem with their kings, who are accounted the more potent, the greater number they entertain of thoſe *Amokos*; tho' this their fool-hardineſs is chiefly attributed to the exceſſive uſe of the amfion. You ſee the ſtreets of all the towns on the *Malabar* coaſt full of *Nayros*, with their arms always about them, tho' many of them dwell in the countrey, and a good number are kept near the king's perſon. Moſt perſons of quality here maintain ſome of thoſe they call *Janguys*. If a quarrel happens to ariſe betwixt a *Nayros* and another *Malabar*, the king allows the the latter a guard of another *Nayros*, and as long as he ſtays with him, they dare not fight, the firſt aggreſſor being guilty of high-treaſon; for perſons of the chiefeſt rank, if they will be admitted in the number of the *Nayros*, muſt have the king's peculiar leave for it, and are afterwards diſtinguiſh'd by a gold ring they wear on the right arm, or by a buffler's horn. The *Nayroes* frequently hunt the tigers, ſome apply themſelves to philoſophy, but eſpecially *The Amokos.*

A Malabar Man and Wooman 13

1662. pecially astronomy, but never to traffick or any handicraft trade. They eat all sorts of meat, except cows flesh, and are very fond of pork. They go above half naked, with bare heads and feet, having only a large piece of white callicoe wrapt round their middle; which reaches down to their knees, and is drawn thro' betwixt their thighs, and tied together behind above their buttocks. They vear also a red silken scarf, with a fringe of about half a foot long, being half gold and half silk. They let their hair grow very long, without ever cutting it, by which they are distinguish'd from the common people; they have a way of tying it very neatly together in a puff on the crown of their heads. Their shield they carry on the left arm, and their sword in the right hand; some have also a javelin, musket or pike. The *Nayros* women are clothed after the same manner as the men, so that there is not the least distinction to be seen betwixt boys and the girls, till the breasts begin to appear in the last. They are forbid to marry any other person but of the same rank, and but one at a time; and in case a *Nayros* woman should marry another, except a *Nayros*, she instantly forfeits her head; in the same manner, if a *Nayros* should marry a woman of another tribe but a *Nayros*, he is punished with death. This they have provided against, because they would not have their blood mixt with strangers or those of an inferior rank, of which they are so cautious, that they will not as much as suffer any to approach them; for which reason, when they walk abroad, they cry out aloud to the common people, *Popoire*, keep back; for if any of these should touch a *Nayros*, he would certainly ruin him.

The common people of Malabar.

The common people of *Malabar* call'd *Montois* or *Poulias*, or otherwise *Parvas* or *Parivas*, are a wretched sort of slaves; they are blacker and much uglier than the *Nayros*, neither must their ears hang down above three inches at most. They are again of different kinds, for those inhabiting near the sea-shore, are properly call'd *Moncois*; these are all fishermen, and all along the coast of *Malabar* are employed at sea in rowing and otherwise for certain wages. Their wives and daughters perform all manner of drudgery by land, and expose themselves for money to the first man, without the least distinction of quality or religion, without the least fear from their husbands, who are well enough pleased at it. For it is to be known, that there are no common strumpets here, but the wives and daughters of these *Moncois*, and of the *Tivas*, who are handicrafts men; for the rest are obliged to contain themselves within their own tribes. The common people are often put to a great nonplus when they happen to meet a *Nayros* at the corner of a street, when they are fain to stand aside till they are passed by. There is another kind among the vulgar sort, call'd by some *Tivas*, whose employment is to draw the liquor from the coco-trees: The rest are handicraft and husbandmen. But these intermarry with one another, notwithstanding there is some difference in their rank, for the husbandmen claim the first, and the *Tivas* or handicrafts men the second degree, the *Moncois* or fishermen are the last. 1662.

The Parvas.

Those call'd *Parivas* or *Parvas* live in villages near the sea side; some of these live near the coast, and in the isle of *Makar*, where, as well as near *Toutekorin*, betwixt the cape *Comorin* and the isle of *Ceylon*, they live upon pearl fishing; they are a stubborn generation, more addicted to laziness than labour; they live chiefly upon pearl and oyster fishing, being the best divers in the world, unto which they are accustom'd from their first infancy. Whilst the men are abroad at sea, the women and children are employ'd in gathering of pearl dust near the shore. They are a cowardly and deceitful sort of people, lying and deceit being so customary among them, as not to be look'd upon as a sin. They are great admirers of the ecclesiastical laws, it being a strict custom among them, not to punish a crime, if the transgressor confesses it and promises amendment. The *Parvas* were formerly all *Pagans*, but being sorely oppressed by the *Mahometans*, they rebell'd against them, and with the assistance of the *Portuguese*, shook off the yoke, which proved the opportunity of their conversion to the *Romish* religion.

How they were converted to the Roman faith.

For finding themselves daily more and more oppress'd, by the advice of one *John de Cruis* (a native of *Malabar*) they sent their deputies to *Cochin*, to crave assistance against the mahometans, offering at the same time to be baptized. The *Portuguese* receiv'd these *Pantagitini* (being then their magistrates) very courteously promising them immediate succours against their enemies, which had so powerful an influence upon these deputies, that to shew their gratitude, they receiv'd baptism immediately, and took upon them the surname of *De Cruis*, which name is retain'd by many of the *Parvas* to this day. After the *Parvas* had rid their hands of the *Moors*, with the assistance of the *Portuguese*, and got the pearl fishery again into their hands, many thousands of them, at divers times and places, embraced the christian faith; and under the viceroyship of *Stephen Gamma* the *Portuguese*, *viz.* about 1500, above

1662. 20000 *Parvas* received baptism; but for want of good ministers, who understood the *Malabar* tongue (few of the *Portuguese* clergy being willing to settle here) they soon return'd to their pagan superstions, having scarce any thing left among them but the name of christians, till *Francis Xaverius* (who arrived in the *Indies* 1540, and went by the name of the great and holy father) being inform'd by *Michael Vas* of the miserable condition of the *Parvas*, resolv'd to go thither from *Goa*, to re-establish the decay'd state of christianity among the *Parvas*. Accordingly he set out from *Goa* (after a stay of five months there) in the beginning of *October* 1543, in company of *Francis Mansilla*, who was come along with him out of *Portugal*, and two novices of the college of *Goa*, who understood the *Malabar* tongue. After his arrival at the east end of that coast, near the cape *Comorin*, finding that his young interpreters stood him but in little stead, he found out this expedient; he call'd together such of the natives, as he knew to be well versed in the *Portuguese* tongue; among those he chose certain persons, who join'd with those two he had brought along with him from *Goa*, translated the chief articles of the christian faith, the ten commandmets, with a short explication, a general confession of faith, and some other such like necessary matters into the *Malabar* tongue. Then he began to preach to them according to the capacity of his auditors, explaining to them the chief duties of a christian, the glory of heaven, and the punishment of hell, with the reason, why some deserve heaven, and the other hell. He explain'd afterwards to them the sign of the cross, and began to unfold to them the mystery of the holy trinity, of which they had been quite ignorant before, and made such a progress among them, that whereas at his coming thither he found not above 2500 demi-christians, at his going away he left near 40000 good christians behind him. *Xaverius* himself in his letter dated the 12th of *Jan.* 1554, speaks of the vast increase of the christians in those parts, saying thus:

Return to paganism.

Are reconciled to the church by Xaverius.

King, you may guess what a great number of these poor people were reduced back to the flock of Christ from thence, that my arms and hand used to be tired with baptizing, sometimes whole villages at a time. My strength and voice have often failed me, by reason of the frequent repetitions of the articles of faith.

The *Romanists* tell us, that besides these, *Xaverius* converted ten towns betwixt *Bringen* and *Permanel* (and six or seven more near *Bengala* and *Remanankoris.*) This they say he performed by his miracles, by healing the sick, casting out demons, and raising the dead from their graves. He raised a certaing young man, the son of a poor widow, who was choak'd in the mud, from the dead. The same he did to another young man, the son of a person of quality in the city of *Puvicale*, and to a young maid. Another woman in labour, being reduced to the last gasp, he deliver'd without the least pain, as soon as she had received baptism. By his miracles he converted a whole village at once, near *Toutekorin*; so that both christians and pagans used to have their last recourse to him in their sicknesses, many of which he restored by reading the gospel over them; as may be seen more at large in the life of *Xaverius*, of *John de Lucenas*, and other *Roman* authors. 1662.

But whatever success *Xaverius* had in converting the *Parvas* and others to the christian religion, certain it is, that he brought no more than one *Brahman* over to the *Romish* faith, tho' he bestow'd much time and pains in speaking to them. And among the *Parvas* themselves are many to this day, who adhere so deeply to their pagan superstitions, that they make but little account of christianity. However, those that have ever since persevered in the *Romish* faith, are from time to time furnish'd with and instructed by the *Portuguese* priests; who ever since 1685, when we made ourselves masters of *Toutekorin*, lived about a league or two from the town in the countrey, whither they carry their children to be baptized. They are very obstinate in their religion, which extends no farther than the knowledge of the christian faith, our father, the ten commandments and an *Ave Mary*, but they follow blind-fold the directions of the *Portuguese* priests, carry *Pater Nosters* and a rosary constantly about them, and use the sign of the cross on their foreheads and breasts, like as the *Roman* catholicks do. The *Dutch* ministers of the protestant religion, have several times attempted to introduce the reformation into the churches of the *Parvas*, both before and since we were masters of *Toutekorin*, but all in vain; for tho' we caused the word of God to be preached in the *Portuguese* tongue, the *Parvas* durst not venture to come to church for fear of the *Roman* priests living among them. These *Parvas* declared to *Xaverius* and *Michael Jassus*, in those days, that whilst they were yet involv'd in darkness of paganism, the devil used to appear to them in most frightful shapes, so that they durst not stir abroad at night, or go a fishing, unless in great companies. He us'd to enter into the bodies of the living, and declared he would not leave them, till they had erected

1662. temples for him. But since they had embraced the christian religion, the devil never had appear'd either in their houses or vessels, tho' they freely went abroad a fishing without any company. *Xaverius* having exhorted them to persevere in their religion, set out from thence to *Makarara* and the adjacent places, and so further to the isle of *Ceylon*.

The Mahometan Malabars. All the *Mahometan Malabars* are either merchants or pirates; if any foreigners come into the harbours where these pirates lie, they endeavour to engage them into their service; which if they accept of, they maintain them and their families throughout the whole winter; when they are just a going to engage an enemy, they take some *Bethel*, by which they swear to stand by one another; if they take a prize, they ransack the ship, and all the mariners and passengers before they come ashore; the captain and other officers take the best part for themselves, the rest is divided among the crew. These poor wretches endure incredible fatigues and miseries at sea, and tho' they have no head that has any legal authority over them, they seldom fall out or quarrel, a thing scarce to be believ'd among us. Several of the richer sort of the *Malabars* equip certain vessels, with a good number of soldiers and galley slaves, which always keep at sea, except that now and then the captain comes ashore to dispose of the booty, which the merchants buy without any regard, whether they belong to friends or foes, provided they can have a good bargain; the *Mahometan Malabars* knowing no other preference but riches: the merchants are distinguish'd only by their habits; both these and the corsairs being never to be seen without arms; but the merchants wear their hair short, and have a bonnet of red scarlet cloth upon their heads, sometimes with a handkerchief rowl'd about it like a turbant, which they call *Mondu*, and are commonly embroider'd with gold and colour'd silk. They half shave their beard, but without whiskers, wear a silk or callicoe vest, reaching three inches below the middle, and under that a kind of drawers hanging down to the knees. They commonly carry a silk or callicoe handkerchief flourish'd, in which they tie and hide their purses. The corsairs never shave their heads, but wear their hair very long, like the women, which they like the rest of the *Indians*, tie together in a knot, and wear one of these flourish'd and embroider'd handkerchiefs over it; for the rest they go quite naked, except that they wear a silk vestment down to their knees; both the merchants and corsairs have knives with silver hafts, on which hang all sorts of toys, such as tooth-picks and the like, all curiously wrought. 1662.

The corsairs shave their beards, but leave whiskers, which in time grow excessively, that so one may tie them together behind. These, as well as all the *Malabars* use no shoes. Their women are clad like the men, neither do they wear any other ornament upon their heads but their hair, but have pendants in their ears, and rings on their fingers and toes. They wear a slight callicoe coat, reaching only to the middle, and under it a silk or callicoe vestment, from the middle down to their knees; they walk bare-footed like the men. All the *Malabars* are of a middle size, and very hairy upon the breast and other parts of their bodies. The women are very well featured, but small of stature. Their men undergo incredible fatigues at sea, and tho' they are *Mahometans* they use the *Malabar* tongue, and pay allegiance and taxes to the several kings of the *Nayros*, under whom they live, which is commonly near the sea shore. Their priests never meddle with any thing except marriages, and what relates to their temples. They are clad in white, after the *Arabian* manner; besides which, they have a certain kind of religious men call'd *Abedallen*, or *ministers of God*, who vow poverty, and beg in the countrey: You may see sometimes 30 or 40 of them together, tho' they travel not above two or three at a time, and sometimes one alone.

The countrey of *Malabar* was formerly under the subjection of one potent prince, *Sarama Perimal*, who at the persuasion of some *Arabian* merchants that traded thither, having embraced mahometism, became so great a zealot of that religion, that he resolved to leave his kingdom, and to undertake a pilgrimage to *Meccha* and *Medina*, to visit *Mahomet*'s tomb: And having no children, divided before his departure the whole countrey, betwixt his chief favourites and courtiers, to wit, the countrey of *Cananor* to his Esquire; to his sword-bearer, who was his darling favourite, *Calicut*; to his scepter-bearer *Cochin*; and to another *Koulang*, unto which he annexed the title of kingdoms, and gave several other countries to others of his friends. Upon his sword-bearer, who had *Calicut* for his share, he bestowed the title of *Zamory* or *Zamorin*, or emperor, and to have a preheminency above the rest: For *Zamorin* signifies in the *Indian* tongue as much as an emperor, being otherwise express'd by the word *Tambarana*, i. e. *God*, which is the reason that all the other *Malabar* countries follow the religious ceremonies of those of *Calicut*, as being the chiefest kingdom of *Malabar*. *Government of Malabar.*

1662. *Malabar*. From hence it is, that the *Zamorin* claims the preheminence before all the other *Malabar* kings, he having alone the prerogative of coining. The two next in rank were the kings of *Koulang* and *Cananor*; besides which, many other petty princes on the coast of *Malabar* claim the title of kings, tho' they are not really so, nor enjoy the prerogative of coining. The *Zamorin*, or king of *Calicut* lost a considerable share of his lustre, after the coming of the *Portuguese* into those parts, with whose assistance the king of *Cochin* freed himself from all subjection formerly due to the kings of *Calicut*, and soon after arrived to that pitch of greatness, that they thought themselves not in any wise inferior to the *Zamorins*, and waged continual war against them. Nevertheless most of the petty *Malabar* kings, and the *Nayros* are vassals of the *Zamorin*, and never speak of him but with a great deal of reverence, except the king of *Cochin*; and the king of *Koulang* being the most remote of all, pays the *Zamorin* less respect than any of the rest: However, all the kings of *Malabar* are sovereigns in their own dominions. The *Malabar* kings never marry, but maintain a concubine of a noble family, who lives commonly in the same palace; if they happen to disagree, another is taken in her place, tho' they are so modest as seldom to change their bedfellows.

The sons born from these concubines are not regarded as king's children, neither do they succeed in their territories or estates, but are heirs only to their mothers, except what money the kings are pleased to bestow freely upon them, to make them live with the more lustre among other gentlemen: But the king's sisters sons inherit their dominions. These sisters don't marry no more than the kings, but are at liberty to chuse a gallant, such a one as they like best. If they have three or four sons, and two or three daughters, the eldest son succeeds the king his uncle, and the other brother after him. After their decease, the succession goes to the eldest son of the king's second sister, and to his brothers afterwards. After their decease, the sons of the other sisters are the next heirs to the crown, so that the succession descends from the brothers to their sisters sons. If it happens that the king's sisters bear no sons, the chief men of the kingdom elect a king who is next of kin, but for want of such a one, chuse whom they please. When the king's sisters are arrived to age of maturity, *viz.* to their 13 or 14 years, they pitch upon one of the nobility whom they like best; unto whom, after they have made him considerable presents, they send word that he is chosen to get her maiden-head, and to get her with child. The young noble man accosts her the first time with a great deal of respect and ceremony, and after having tied a very fine jewel about her neck, he diverts himself in private for some days with her, and so returns home: If she proves with child, it is well, if not, she commonly chuses some *Brahman* or other to try his strength whether he can get her with child. When a *Malabar* king dies, the corps is burnt three days after. All his subjects, from the next successor to the meanest child, shave themselves from head to foot, leaving no hair, except what is on the eye-brows and eye-lids. They are also obliged to abstain from the use of *Bethel* for the space of 13 days, and if any one should be found to chew *Bethel* during that time, they cut off his lips. During these 13 days they dare eat neither fish nor flesh, and the fishermen are forbidden to fish upon pain of death. Considerable alms are given to the poor out of the king's coffers, and the *Brahmans* are provided with victuals at the publick charge. After the expiration of these 13 days, every one is at liberty to eat what he pleases, except the new king, who is tied to the same rules for a whole year after; during which time, he must neither have the hair of his head or of his body cut, nor pare his nails: He is obliged to say certain prayers every morning, and must eat but once a day. Some time before dinner he bathes himself, which done, he must forbear to cast his eyes upon any body till after he has taken food. Towards the latter end of this mourning year, his next successor in the kingdom, the other princes of the royal blood, and other persons of the chiefest quality attend the new king, and pay their homage to him, in the presence of many thousands; at which time the new king declares his next successor, and the others each in his degree; which done, he confirms the lords there present in their respective places and offices. He that is declared the next successor to any new king, is oblig'd from that time not to appear at court as long as the king lives; but those princes who are to succeed him may continue there. Before the above-mentioned 13 days are expired, the new king has not the least authority in the kingdom, which they take for a general maxim here, to see whether any body else will lay claim to the succession: But, after the expiration of this time, the great men of the kingdom, and chief officers of state, engage the new king by a solemn oath, to maintain the laws made by his predecessor, to pay his debts, and to endeavour the recovery of the territories lost

Burials of the Malabar kings.

1662. under the reigns of his predeceſſors. Whilſt he takes the oath he lays his right hand upon an oil caſk, in which are ſet up many lighted wicks, and with a drawn ſword, which he holds in his left, touches a jewel ſet in gold within the caſk. This done, they ſtrew rice upon his head with a great deal of ceremony, and certain forms of prayers, turning their faces to the ſun. In the ſame manner, all the princes of the blood, and other great men ſwear fealty to the new king. During the firſt 13 days after the king's deceaſe, the ſole adminiſtration of the government is lodged in the lord chancellor, who has alſo the management of the treaſury, without whom the king cannot take or diſpoſe of the publick money, unleſs it be in caſe of the greateſt neceſſity. It is alſo the chancellor who puts the king's mandates in execution. The firſt in rank next to the king are thoſe call'd by them *Kaimales*, then the *Brahmans*, who are in great eſteem in thoſe courts, the king of *Calicut* himſelf being of that ſect, and wearing the twiſted cord. After the *Brahmans* come the *Nayros*, or military order, the true off-ſpring of their ancient nobility; then come the vulgar or common people, call'd *Moukois*, or *Poulias*, or *Parvas*: The king is the only judge here, before whom are brought all ſuch as have committed any crime, or refuſe to pay their debts: In his abſence certain great men of the court determine all affairs of any moment; but if a difference ariſes betwixt two or more *Moukois* or any ſtrangers, he that thinks himſelf aggrieved, makes his complaint to the next *Nayros* he meets, who is obliged to do him juſtice immediately, without receiving any reward, unleſs the plaintiff will voluntarily give him a preſent: This holds in matters of ſmall conſequence, for all matters of moment are decided before the king in perſon. Their ordinary puniſhments are impriſonments, or the loſs of a joint of a limb; if the crime be capital the malefactor is thrown to the elephants. They have no other priſons but what are in the royal palaces. In caſe of any difference betwixt two *Pagans*, when the truth is to be verified by a ſolemn oath, they put one hand into boiling oil, or elſe lay hold of a piece of red hot iron; ſometimes they ſwim croſs a river ſwarming with venomous creatures; it being their opinion, that if they have ſpoke the whole truth, they ſhall not receive any hurt; but the trial with the hot iron is moſt generally received. When the *Malabar* kings or their governors intend to inflict a puniſhment upon the inhabitants of a certain place, they ſurround it with wooden ſtakes like an encloſure, out of which they muſt not ſtir, neither may they buy or ſell, or have the leaſt communication with others, till the ſame be removed again under pain of death. This is ſometimes done alſo before the doors of private perſons. 1662.

A peculiar way of taking an oath.

Their funerals.

All the *Pagans* here, as well *Brahmans* as the *Nayros* and *Moukois*, burn the carcaſſes of their deceaſed friends; tho' this was more univerſally practis'd before the *Portugueſe* and *Dutch* introduced and ſettled the chriſtian religion here. They take peculiar care to provide in their life-time as much fine ſcented wood and other precious drugs as they think requiſite for the burning of their bodies to aſhes, which is afterwards divided among their relations and friends, who preſerve them, and at their feſtivals mix them with water, and paint their faces with them. When a *Brahman* happens to die, his widow is obliged, as a demonſtration of her affection towards her deceas'd huſband, to burn herſelf; this is commonly done under the noiſe of ſeveral muſical inſtruments, to ſuppreſs the doleful outcries of the dying perſon, and in the preſence of their next kindred. However they may excuſe themſelves as to this point if they pleaſe, but then they are branded with infamy, their hair is cut off cloſe, which they muſt not let grow to any length again; they are excluded from the ſociety of other women, nor are allow'd to marry again. Notwithſtanding which, many chuſe rather to diſpenſe with theſe diſadvantages than to burn themſelves. The wives of the *Nayros* are not obliged to this cuſtom, tho' there are not wanting inſtances, that they have thrown themſelves into the flames which conſum'd their huſband's carcaſs; the men are not engaged to mourn for their wives, except that they are forbidden to marry again.

Their marriages.

The marriages of the richer and better ſort are celebrated here with a great deal of ſolemnity; the firſt thing they do after matters are agreed betwixt them, is to repair to the *Pagode* or temple, where the prieſts perform certain ceremonies; after this, the friends and relations of the new married couple, both men and women, lead the bride for 15 days conſecutively to the bridegroom's houſe, where they are entertain'd at his charge; moſt of the women ſinging and playing upon flutes, ſmall drums, and other muſical inſtruments; the bride and bridegroom are placed together very richly attir'd, eſpecially with jewels, to ſuch an exceſs, that they have been computed to amount ſometimes to 200000 crowns. The room is hung with fine ſilk hangings interwoven with gold; and among other things, a plate with *Bethel* offer'd to every one there preſent; nay, even to thoſe that are ſtrangers; towards the

1662. the evening the women reconduct the bride to her houſe. At the expiration of the 15 days, the bride and bridegroom are mounted on an elephant richly accouter'd, ſo as to face one another; the elephant is led by a *Nayros*, and ſurrounded by the friends and relations on foot; thus they are conducted thro' the whole city, and are ſure always to ſtop at the doors of any of their neareſt kinfolks, relations or particular friends, who preſent them with *Bethel*, fruits and ſweet meats, and anoint the head of the elephant with ſweet ſcented waters; they are very careful not to miſs any of their friends houſes, for if any ſuch thing ſhould happen, they would look upon it as a ſignal affront. When they come to the *Pagode* they diſmount, and after they have tarried there for ſome time, return to the bride's houſe, where the marriage is conſummated, each of the gueſts being obliged to preſent the *Nayros* that led the elephant with a coco nut.

They begin their new year in *September*, but have no fix'd day, which they regulate according to the deciſion of the aſtrologers and conjurers, who pretend to find out by their art the very hour which is likely to be the moſt fortunate for the beginning of the year. All thoſe that are above 15 years of age cover their faces that day, for fear of caſting their eyes upon any thing; thus they are led by children to the temple, where uncovering themſelves, they fix their eyes upon what object they find directly before them; if this happen to be an idol (which their temples are full of) they have a peculiar veneration for it, they look upon it as a good omen that the next year will prove proſperous to them.

Their writing. All over *Malabar* they uſe a peculiar language call'd by them *Malkama*. Paper they have none, but inſtead of it write upon the leaves of the wild coco-trees, with an iron pencil or pen; which contain not only their religious ceremonies, but likewiſe the whole ſeries of their moſt antient hiſtories. Theſe leaves they cut all in the ſame ſhape of the breadth of two inches, and two hands length; of theſe they lay together as many as they think fit, and put a ſmall ſtick thro' them on the top; which done, they faſten the ſtick on both ends to the leaves with a pack-thread, which they looſen as often as they have occaſion to peruſe them. Each of theſe leaves is call'd *Ola* by the *Malabars*. They exceed all the *European* writers in ſwiftneſs, which they perform with that dexterity, as to turn their faces frequently from the leaves, and to entertain others with talking whilſt they are writing. The *Malabar* tongue is very difficult to be learn'd, by reaſon of its multitude of words, one and the ſame thing being expreſs'd by different terms; nay, each day throughout the year is diſtinguiſh'd by a peculiar name. Several *Portugueſe* jeſuites have attempted to give us an inſight into the *Malabar* tongue, and among the reſt father *Gaſpar Aquilar*. They have their peculiar letters, which are very ancient, and reſembling the *Syriack* characters. 1662.

The inhabitants of *Malabar*, as we told you before, are either natives, or deſcended from foreigners; the laſt of which being firſt come thither out of *Arabia*, are *Mahometans*, as the natives are *Pagans*. Some are of opinion, that all the kings of *Malabar* follow one and the ſame religion, but that their ſubjects are divided into 18 ſeveral ſects; but, as far as ever I could learn by the moſt exact enquiry I was able to make, all the natives of *Malabar*, as well *Brahmans* as *Nayros* and *Moukois*, perform their religious worſhip in the ſame manner; for they adore their idols, and the ſun, as they riſe in the morning. In their temples you ſee a golden cow, or ſome other image, unto which they pay their devotions; which is the reaſon that neither the *Brahmans*, *Nayros* nor *Moukois* will kill this beaſt, but pay ſuch reverence to it, that they paint the walls of their houſes with its dung mix'd with water; thus, when the king of *Calicut* is to bathe himſelf, fifteen maids with cow-dung in their ſilver baſons, plaiſter the rooms with it thro' which he is to paſs twice aday. Their chief God they call *Parabramma*, with three ſons near him, in remembrance of which the *Brahmans* wear a cord twiſted of three threads on their bare ſkin. They not only worſhip man, but, as I told you, the beaſts alſo, and erected temples for them, exceeding in magnificence thoſe of the ancient *Romans*. There is one temple dedicated to the ape, the gallery of which is ſupported by 700 marble columns. Beſides the cow they pay likewiſe a godly veneration to the elephant, it being their opinion, that the ſouls of men tranſmigrate into thoſe beaſts. They have many books, which contain an account of their religious ceremonies, much reſembling the ancient *Greek* and *Roman* fables. The prieſts and *Brahmans* keep theſe books from the ſight of the vulgar, theſe being their oracles, unto which they have recourſe for their prophecies, to blind theſe poor wretches, as has been confeſs'd by ſome converted *Brahmans*. They make however much more account of religion than the *Nayros*; for they daily provide (at the king's charge) a conſiderable quantity of boil'd rice in their *Their religious worſhip.*

A Malabar Shewing tricks with Serpents. 14

1662. temples, which is diſtributed among the poor, or given to any body elſe that will aſk for it, this being not look'd upon as ignominious among them. They keep continually burning lamps in their temples, and their prophets are almoſt cover'd with bells, which when they dance and make other awkard poſtures make a great noiſe; the *Moukois* have their own temples, which are naſtily kept; they don't frequent them above once a month, *viz.* at the new moon, becauſe they can ſpare no more time from their daily labour: At the entrance, each of them is preſented with ſome aſhes mix'd with water. The *Nayros* go commonly once a day to their temples, where each mutters out a ſhort prayer; theſe temples are diſpoſed throughout the whole countrey, and are moſt frequented at certain days, when they repair thither with a great deal of devotion; ſome for 20 or 30 leagues, for they have their appointed feaſts, but two or three before all the reſt. The chiefeſt is that of the new-years day, when the *Nayros* come to pay their reverence to the king, who receives them ſtanding at a window, and throws a certain quantity of *Bethel* to each, and ſome gold and ſilver among them, as well as the reſt of his ſubjects that appear there.

The *Malabar* kings, *Brahmans* and *Nayros*, pay likewiſe their devotions to ſerpents, which they conſider as evil ſpirits made by God to torment mankind for their ſins. You meet here with certain vagabonds who carry ſerpents in a baſket, with ſome bran for their food, hanging on a ſtick, carried on the ſhoulders of two fellows; ſome of theſe ſerpents are ſix, ſeven or nine foot long, of a graſs green colour, and not above an inch thick; ſome are very large and bulky, with grey ſpots; ſo ſoon as theſe *Malabar* vagabonds begin to play upon a certain inſtrument like a bagpike, the ſerpents ſet themſelves upright upon their tails, twiſt themſelves in a moſt ſurprizing manner, and ſoon after raiſe their fins or briſtles, which are near the head, and fall on with ſuch fury, as if they would tear one another to pieces, to the no ſmall terror of the ſpectators.

The Malleans.

On the tops of the high rocky mountains of *Malabar* (on the foot of which live the chriſtians of *St. Thomas*) dwells a certain nation call'd the *Malleans*, they have a pretty good tillage about 13 or 14 leagues from *Madura* call'd *Priata*. According to the deſcription given us by *Plutarch* and *Curtius*, and the reſemblance of their names, theſe may not unlikely be the ſame mention'd by them as the moſt warlike nation of all the *Indians*, *Alexander* the great having receiv'd a mortal wound as he was attacking one of their cities. Now adays they don't inhabit any cities, towns or villages, but only certain encloſures in the valleys betwixt the rocks; their houſes are built of canes very low, and plaiſter'd up with loom or clay. Some of them live in the woods, theſe make their houſes of wood, which they remove from tree to tree, to ſecure themſelves againſt the elephants and tygers. The firſt they catch in holes cover'd with the branches of trees, with ſome earth on the top; they alſo cultivate the ground, but in a very ſlender manner, tho' their valleys would be very fruitful if they were duly manag'd. They have but one wife at a time, who goes abroad a hunting with them, or wherever they go, whereas the *Pagan Malabars* marry generally ſeveral women. They chiefly differ from the other *Malabars* in their complexion, are juſt and honeſt, good natur'd, charitable, without deceit; for the reſt, courageous, ingenious and cunning; they pretend to converſe with the devils, only out of curioſity to know the event of things; the cuſtom of the other *Malabars* and *Indians*, who hurt others by their ſorceries, being unknown to them. They pay a great deal of deference to the ſepulchres of their anceſtors, and if they happen to be defiled, they look upon it to be an ill omen. Upon their feſtivals they wear a long gown, with a turbant, as the *Mahometans* do; but at other times they go half naked, like as the other *Malabars* do. They have holes in their ears and noſes, in which they hang gold rings and jewels; a cuſtom common alſo to the *Pagan Malabar* women, who look upon this as their chief ornament, eſpecially to wear ſuch things in one of their noſtrils. At their feaſts and feſtivals, the maidens play upon ruſh-pipes and ſmall flutes and drums; theft is a thing unknown among the *Malabars*, every one living in his houſe in a profound ſecurity, with open doors; ſometimes the inhabitants of a whole encloſure transfer their habitations to another. Part of the *Malabars* acknowledge the king of *Turbula*, part the king of *Pugnati Perimal* for their ſuperiors, unto whom they pay ſome yearly tribute, yet with the entire preſervation of their liberty, they being govern'd by their own laws, under captains or judges of their nation, call'd by them *Arley*, each of them has commonly 5000 or 6000 under his diſtrict; beſides which, each encloſure is govern'd by its own judge, call'd *Pandera*, unto whom they pay ſtrict obedience.

Before 1599, when they began firſt to be inſtructed in the *Romiſh* religion, by the aſſiduity of the then archbiſhop of *Goa*, they were all pagans, but ſince that time, a good

1662. a good number of them have embraced christianity; eight of their best men, among whom were three *Pandaras*, with their whole families, first received baptism, who being follow'd by many others, a church dedicated to St. *Michael* was built in the village of *Priata*. Before their conversion they had no temples erected in honour of their idols, neither did they sacrifice with feasting, dancing and such like ceremonies, but each family had its domestick god, unto whom they paid their devotions. They are much more esteem'd among the *Malabars*, than their common people, neither are they look'd upon as unclean by them, no more than the christians of *St. Thomas*, if they happen to touch a *Nayros*; they keep scarce any commerce with the neighbouring nations, even not with the *Thomists* themselves, who live at the foot of the same mountains. Their weapons are the same as the rest of the *Malabars* use, *viz.* a bow and arrows pointed with a broad iron. They use also scimeters or hangers, and a peculiar sort of fire arms, such as are no where else to be seen among the *Malabars*. On the foot of the mountain inhabited by the *Malabars* call'd *Karatkara*, bordering upon the kingdom of *Karanarata*, stands a church belonging to these *Thomists* or christians of *St. Thomas*, dedicated to St. *Austin*, because the inhabitants owe their conversion to certain fryers of that order.

Products of Malabar. *Malabar*, as I told you before, is a countrey abounding in divers sorts of fruits, such as the *Indies* commonly afford, of the choicest of which we will give you a short description here.

Coco-tree. All along the sea-shore of *Malabar*, and the rivers near the sea-side, the *Indian* palm or coco-tree, grows in sandy and brackish grounds; the *Malabars* call it *Tenga*, the *Brahmans Mado*, and in the *Malabar* tongue it is call'd *Kalappa*. Its trunk, which is of an ash colour, rises sometimes to the height of 95 feet; such I have several times measured my self near the city of *Koulang*; it has commonly 16 inches diameter, tho' sometimes it is so thick, as scarce to be grasped by a man; and is of the same thricknes from the bottom to the top; the wood is spongy, and the pith as white as paper. However the trunk does not grow up strait, but is jointed, without any branches, but only on the top, where commonly sprout forth 16 or 18, and in a very large tree sometimes 28, which bear green large leaves like reeds, being about a finger's length broad, and about two foot long. The root of this tree is very small in proportion of its bigness, and does not reach deep under ground, but creeps just under its surface, so that it seems next to a miracle, how these high trees are able to withstand the fury of the winds. The fruit, call'd commonly coco-nuts, after the *Portuguese*, who call them *Coquo* and *Cocoe*, grow at the ends of the branches, about 6, 8, or 10 in a bunch; a bunch weighing sometimes from 60 to 100 pounds weight; each ripe nut exceeds the bigness of a lusty man's head, being of a triangular figure, and cover'd with a double peel; the first is an inch thick, consisting of many threads, extending length-wise round the fruit; the outside is of an ash colour, but inwardly inclining to red; the next peel is hard and brown, which contains the peel. Before they are ripe, they are of a pale yellow colour, and afterwards turn dark green, having at one end a bush of small leaves, resembling our turnep leaves. The pith is white, inclining to yellow, about an inch thick, and to the second peel, the remaining hollowness being fill'd with liquor, and containing according to the bigness of the unripe nut, a pint of liquor, which in the ripe one diminishes by degrees, and encreases the bulk of the peel. This liquor is good to drink, the pith is sweet, and of no ungrateful taste, only a little flat. The blossom, which is not unlike that of the chesnuts, appears at the ends of the branches which produce the fruit, which ripens in three months time. The pith dried, may be kept and transported like chesnuts; if it be powder'd and mixt with sugar and cinnamon, it tastes very well, augments the seed, and is a strong provocative. When the *Nayros* are to gather the nuts, they climb with most wonderful nimbleness to the tops of these high trees, where they cut off as many branches as are ripe, and let them fall down upon the ground. Besides the fruit, this tree affords also a certain liquor, call'd by them *Sury*, and by the *Europeans* palm-wine: When they are to gather this liquor, they only cut off one of its branches, from whence issues the liquor, which falls into a vessel of bamboe, hung under it for that purpose; if they draw too much liquor at a time, the branches turn brown, and the tree produces no more nuts. These trees being planted in a streight line, the *Nayros* lay sticks reaching from one to other, by which means they get to the branches, where they have fasten'd the vessel that receives the liquor. This liquor, whilst fresh is very good to drink, and will inebriate like wine; but if kept in the sun, turns to vinegar in an hours time. But tho' they take never so much care of it, what is gather'd about noon, will turn by night, taste sourish the next day, and turn quite to vinegar the day after that. The liquor which

1662. which diftils from the young trees, is not fo ftrong and fpirituous as that gather'd from the old ones, but the firft affords a greater quantity. After this liquor has been kept 24 hours, they diftil a fpirit of it, with the addition of a fmall quantity of the oil of clove; this is by the *Indians* call'd *Arack*, and by fome *Tula* or *Mype*. Out of this liquor they prepare vinegar, thus: They put the veffels in which the liquor has been gather'd, in lime 15 days, during which time it ferments, cafting grofs fediments to the bottom; the clear is very good vinegar. Out of the fame fugar they make a kind of liquor call'd *Jagra*. They put a fmall quantity of lime in the veffel which contains the liquor, as much as is fufficient to make it turn red; for if you put in too much lime, the liquor turns whiter and whiter, but if you put too little, it does not change its colour. The liquor thus mix'd with a fufficient quantity of lime, muft be boil'd and ftirred continually with a fpoon, till it comes to the confiftency of red fugar; where it is to be obferved, that if there be not lime enough added, it will produce no fugar, but if too much, part of it will fettle to the bottom, which muft be taken out before you can boil it into a fugar. If you intend to make white fugar or *Jayra*, you muft take care to pour the liquor mix'd with the lime out of one pot into another (to feparate the fuperfluous lime) which you muft repeat three times; as for inftance, if your liquor be gather'd in the morning, you muft pour it into another veffel by noon, and repeat the fame a fecond time about two a clock, and a third time before night, and then boil it. What liquor is gather'd in the night-time keeps longer than that gather'd in the day-time. Whilft it is frefh, its tafte is not much unlike our whey, unto which the inhabitants add fome raifins, and make it tafte like *Spanifh* wine. The trunk of the coco-tree is ufed for timber in the building of houfes and fhips, the branches and leaves to write upon and to cover houfes with, as alfo by the basketmakers. Out of the hard fhell of the nuts (fome of which are of a pale, others of a dark brown colour) they make drinking cups and other veffels, which they polifh, and fometimes are edg'd with filver. The hairy fubftance, call'd *Kayer*, is ufed by the rope-makers; thefe ropes don't rot eafily: They alfo make matches of them, which burn very fiercely. In the *Maldive* iflands (where thefe trees are found in vaft quantities) they fometimes equip whole veffels out of the coco-trees; the body of the veffels being made of the trunk of a tree, without any nails or other iron-work; the fail and ropes of the hairy fubftance, the provifions confifting of the liquor and kernels of the coco-nuts, their drinking and other veffels being made of the fhell, and their hammocks, quilts and other implements of the leaves. In fhort, this tree furnifhes the *Indians* upon occafion, with all that is neceffary for their fubfiftence, being very fruitful in marfhy and low grounds, but bears not fo great a quantity of fruit, neither fo big in the mountainous countries. The coco-tree is in its prime from the 25th to the 30th year, and affords the moft fruit and liquor; from the time it begins to bear, the ripe fruits fall off, and others grow continually in their ftead, but when it begins to grow old, the fruit grows leffer and leffer. This tree will continue till it is 100 years old; when the fmall branches and leaves begin to turn yellow, it is an infallible fign of its decay. It is produced out of the kernel of the coco-nut; thefe the *Indians* put into the ground till they begin to fprout, then they make as many holes as they intend to plant trees, and of fuch a depth, that the tops of the leaves don't reach beyond the furface of the ground; then they throw a handful or two of fand (unlefs it be in fandy ground) and half a handful of falt in each hole, upon which they put the kernel, which they cover with the fame ground they had taken out of the hole before, and every other day water them, till they are fure the nuts have taken root. They plant them with the point downwards, out of the oppofite part of which at firft fhoot forth two or three broad leaves, after which comes the right leaves, and foon after the fmall fprouts, which fall off as new ones fucceed, till the tree comes to its full growth. The young tree commonly begins to bear in the fifth year after its planting; great care is taken that the horfeflies don't fpoil the young trees. This is a kind of worm not unlike our hornets, with two fharp horns, but not fo big; this worm gets to the pith of the tree, which he confumes till the tree dies, unlefs he be taken out in time, at which the *Malabars* are very dextrous, and then the tree will recover. It has been obferved that this tree in the third year after its planting, has its branches in their perfection, and from that time the branches begin to fall off. Thofe branches are at that time about five or fix yards long, tho' the ftem on which they grow is not above two foot high, and about a foot in circumference. Every month you fee commonly a new branch come forth, and then the old ones fall off, but in the fummer and dry feafons they fall off more frequently than in rainy weather; thefe branches come to their full growth in

1662. three months. I caused above 4000 coco-trees to be planted near *Koiland*, but most of them came to nothing, being not carefully look'd after by my successors. There are divers kinds of this tree, which are distinguish'd by the fruit, but especially by the watery substance found within the shells of the nuts.

Wild cinnamon trees. *Malabar* produces prodigious quantities of wild cinnamon trees, but the cinnamon is neither in smell nor in goodness comparable to that which grows in the isle of *Ceylon*; this island, and that of *Floris* being the only ones where the true cinnamon grows. The *Portuguese* call this wild cinnamon *Canella de Mato*, *i. e. Wood-Cinamon*, the *Malabars Larva* or *Babona*, as also *Kaunema*, *i. e. Sweet-Wood*, from the word *Kau*, which in their language signifies wood, and *Nema i. e.* sweet, the *Malayans Kais Manis*, the *Zingalese* or inhabitants of *Ceylon Kurudo* or *Kurundo*, and the *Arabians Querfaa* and *Querse*, as also *Kerfak*. Before the *Dutch* got into possession of *Ceylon*, they used to transport this cinnamon, but since that time they make no account of it. The tree is of the bigness of our orange tree, less or more, but not large as the cinnamon trees in *Ceylon*. It has abundance of branches, leaves not unlike the laurel leaves, but broader, of a paler colour, with three distinct veins. The blossom is white, almost without any scent; the fruit not unlike the wild olives, first green, afterwards inclining to red, and when ripe, black shining. It has also a kernel not unlike the wild olive, which is covered with a pulp like the same, out of which issues a kind of green oily liquor, of the same scent as the laurels, biting and bitterish upon the tongue. The rind of this tree (or the cinnamon it self) is thick, without any remarkable taste, tho' the small sprouts or tacks are somewhat bitter, yet don't come near to the cinnamon of the isle of *Ceylon*.

Oil of cinnamon and volatile salt. Out of the rind of the root they prepare a kind of volatile salt, which they call camphire, swimming upon the surface of the water of a yellow colour, clear, strong and well scented, sharp upon the tongue, and very penetrating, being so volatile, that if exposed to the air, it evacuates immediately. This camphire is exceeding white, excelling the common camphire in its scent; the particles of this camphire are insensibly mix'd with the oil, whilst yet warm, immediately after its distillation; but as soon as the oil begins to cool, they adhere to one another in divers shapes, and settle to the bottom. This camphire is very volatile, and so fiery that it takes fire in an instant, and leaves not the least impurity behind, after it is consumed. The oil approaches very near both in smell and taste to the camphire, and is so volatile, that if some of it be dropped upon woollen stuffs, even of the nicest colours, it evaporates immediately, without leaving the least spot behind. It is also very combustible, burning with a white and blue flame; if put upon the fire, it evacuates in a instant, and turns into a white smoak, which is very apt to take fire. This oil mixt with gunpowder, will set it on fire by degrees, yet not till a great part of the oily substance be evacuated. If mix'd with sulphur or salt-peter, or with both, it will take fire immediately and consume the sulphur and salt-peter, remaining without the least alteration. If you put the oil upon the fire, and receive the flame which evaporates from thence, in a thick cloth, a white kind of salt will settle in it, which is the camphire itself. This oil will also in time separate some of those camphirous particles, which falling to the bottom, render the oil more clear and pure. The oil drawn out of the *Malabar* cinnamon, is clear, transparent, yellowish and well scented, swimming upon the water; whereas out of the common cinnamon of *Ceylon*, besides that oil which rises on the top of the water, another is also drawn, which sinks to the bottom. The oil distill'd from the leaves is thin at first, turns yellowish by degrees, and transparent, and of a greenish colour at last, being very sweet, but sharp at last, having something of cinnamon; it sinks to the bottom of the water. 1662.

The oil made out of the rind of the root, with its volatile salt (the camphire) is endow'd with greater virtues. It is a sovereign remedy against all lameness, if applied outwardly, and gives immediate ease in the gout; it may also be taken inwardly with very good success, being a great remedy against malignant fevers, a great sudorifick, expelling the wind, procuring an appetite in the stomach, and consuming the stone both in the kidneys and bladder, and is good in the cough, and many other chronick distempers; to be short, it is the most universal remedy made use of there by the *Dutch* in their hospitals. The camphire is very proficuous in all distempers in the womb, promotes the monthly terms, and is a great sudorifick, being used in all respects like the common camphire. The oil distill'd out of the bark of the tree, is an excellent remedy in all distempers of the stomach, and in the cholick, proceeding from a cold cause; the water of cinnamon is cordial; the oil of the leaves is good against the cholick, if applied outwardly to the belly, and helps lameness. *Its virtues.*

In

1662. In the woods of *Malabar* about *Kananor*, grows a certain shrub in great plenty, call'd *Zua* by the *Malabars*, at *Surate Dekan*, and *Cachora* by the *Canarins*; by the *Arabians* and *Persians Zerumbet*, and *Zeruba* by the *Turks*. If planted or sow'd, it will grow also in many other places. By some it is reckoned a kind of ginger, and not without reason, its leaves resembling those of the ginger, only that they are somewhat larger, as is also the root, which being cut in pieces and dried, is thus transported into foreign parts.

Zua or Zerumbet.

The tree call'd Macre *or* Macer.

On the coast of *Malabar*, in the isle of *St. Cruce*, belonging to the kingdom of *Cochin*, near the river *Manatte*, grows a certain tree call'd *Macre* by the *Brahman* physicians, by the christians there *Makuyre*, and by the *Portuguese Arbore de las Canaras* and *Arbore Sancto*, *i. e.* the *Tree of the Bloody Flux* and *the holy Tree*. The saints of this countrey have this saying of it; *Kura Santea Macre Nistusa garul*: i. e. *Macre was discover'd to mankind for their benefit by the Angels. Galen*, *Dioscorides* and *Pliny* call it *Macer*, and *Avicenna Talisfar*; this tree spreads its branches in a large compass, being bigger than our elm-tree. Its leaves are seven foot long, and two broad, the uppermost side of a pale, and the undermost of a dark green colour. It is generally believ'd, that this tree produces no fruit, but only a kind of seed, of the bigness of a farthing, thin, yellowish, resembling in taste the kernel of an almond or peach-stone, cover'd with a white skin. It is enclosed in a kind of a bladder composed of two different peels. This bladder comes forth in the middle of the leaf, resembling that which in *May* sprouts forth on the elm-trees, except that it is somewhat broader and flatter. The leaf of this bladder is of the bigness of other leaves, but not so much pointed at the end, and narrow towards the stalk, of a deep yellow colour, cover'd with a kind of curl'd down from the stalk to the end. The root of this tree is not unlike that of the *Stone*-palm-tree, with large and thick roots spread at a great distance; the rind of those roots is thick, rough, of an ash-colour without, but white within; containing a juice like milk whilst fresh, but turns yellow; when dry it is very astringent. This tree delights in few but sandy grounds, and kills all other trees or shrubs near it. The rind of the root of this tree is in vast esteem among the *Malabars*, as well as among the *Chinese*, *Javanese*, *Malabars* and all *Bengale*; being look'd upon and made use of in their hospitals, as the most sovereign remedy in the world, against looseness and all manner of bloody fluxes. The *Indian* physicians, as well *Brahmans*, *Canarins*, as *Malabars*, cure with this rind whilst fresh, powder'd and mix'd with butter-milk, the bloody flux; some infuse half an ounce of the rind, dried and powder'd in a quartern of whey for 12 hours, which they give the patient twice a day, *viz.* in the morning and evening, immediately after they give the patient rice to eat, boil'd without salt or butter, and after that a chicken boil'd in the decoction of rice flour. If the distemper be very urgent, they add some *Opium* for the strengthening of the stomach; and to stop vomiting, they mix a little mastich with this rind, and give it in mint water. They tell you that a small quantity of this rind, excels much in virtue a considerable number of the *Myrobolan* rinds, or of *Areka*; nay, they prefer it before the *Koru* of *Malabar* itself. The fruit, or rather seed, expels all sorts of worms, and dissolves the stone in the kidneys, being look'd upon likewise as a great preservative both against the stone and cholick. Besides the tree *Macer*, other trees grow here very different in kind, but agree in virtue with the *Macer* tree. 1662.

The first of these two is by the *Malabars* call'd *Kurodapala*, or *Kuro*, and *Koru* by the *Canariins*, by the *Brahmans Kura*, and by the *Portuguese* the *Malabar* shrub, its use having been first shewn them by the *Malabars*. This tree or shrub is not unlike a small orange tree, especially as to its leaves, except that the vein in the middle of the leaf, out of which come 8 or 9 on both sides, is somewhat thicker. The blossom is yellow, and without the least scent. *Garcias* says this tree is somewhat less than a common crab-tree, its leaves like a peach-tree, with a white blossom. It has a pale green and smooth bark, out of which, if cut with a knife, issues a milk-like juice, more viscous than that which comes forth out of the *Macer* tree, bitterish of taste; the *Malabar* physicians assign it a cooling quality. This tree affords an infallible remedy against all kinds of bloody fluxes, provided the gross ill humours have been purged away before, without which the patient will soon have a relapse. The *Malabars* (according to *Garcias*) prepare a compounded water out of the root, unto which they attribute great virtues against the bloody flux; they take 8 ounces of this root well beaten to powder, and infused in whey, and the liquor of boil'd rice, unto this they add the seeds of pursley, black cummin and coriander, each an ounce and a half; of the *Myrobolan* rind 7 drachms, and fresh butter 2 ounces; this they distil, and mix a quartern of this distill'd water with half a quartern of *Arack*, and give it the patient. They apply this water also in form

The tree Kurodapala.

1662. form of a clyster in the night time, by reason of the excessive heat of the days in those parts. Inwardly they commonly give it twice a day, *viz.* in the morning about six a clock, and in the afternoon about two. Their diet is rice mix'd with fat, and chickens boil'd in the decoction of rice, which they call *Kaaje* in their language, but the use of wine is absolutely forbidden, unless it be in an inveterate bloody flux, to keep up the spirits. Some give only the juice of the shrub whilst green, of which they give a quartern and a half in the morning, and as much in the evening; and to take away the bitterish taste, allow the patient to drink a little whey after it. In case of necessity they mix some *Opium* with it. It is also a good remedy to strengthen the stomach, and to stop vomiting, if taken in mint water, or mix'd with some mastich powder'd. The root taken inwardly with the decoction of rice, or applied outwardly is very good against the piles. The decoction of the leaves, and those of tamarinds, make an excellent fomentation for swell'd legs, held over the hot steam, and a cloth dip'd in the same decoction is with good success applied in the looseness and dropsy.

Pavate *or* Vasa Veli. The third sort of those vegetables which are us'd here against the bloody flux, is call'd by the *Malabars Pavate*, and *Vasa Veli* by the *Brahmans*, and *Canarins*, and *Arbor contra las erysipelas*, i. e. *the Tree against the St. Anthony's Fire.* It is a shrub not above 8 or 9 foot high, with a few branches and leaves, resembling the small leaves of orange-trees before they come to their full growth, green on both sides; the blossom is white and small, the seed round, in bigness like to that of the mastich-tree; dark green at first, which turns black as it ripens. The stem and tacks are of an ash-colour, the root either without scent or taste, except that it is somewhat bitterish.

Jambos *or* Jambeiro. Among the fruit trees of *Malabar*, that which the inhabitants call *Jambos*, and the *Portuguese Jambeiro*, must not be pass'd by in silence. The *Malabars* and *Canarins* call the fruit *Jambali*, the *Arabians Tufa Indi*, the *Turks Alma*, and the *Persians Tufat*. It is the common opinion, that this was first of all for the pleasantness of its blossom, and excellency of its fruit, transplanted from *Malacca* (where it is found in great plenty) into all the other parts of the *Indies*. There are two kinds, resembling one another in most respects, except in their fruit, which is somewhat different. Both are not unlike, as well in shape as bigness to our *European* apple-trees, and will grow without much cultivating in any ground, and bear fruit within 5 years; they take root very deep, a thing seldom observ'd among the *Indian* trees. These trees are of a pleasant aspect, spreading their branches to the height of a good plumb-tree. The bark, as well of the tree as of the branches, is of an ash-colour and smooth; the wood brittle; the leaves also resemble those of the plumb-tree, but are somewhat more pointed at the end, being a palm in length, and not unlike the iron point of a long pike or lance. The upper side is dark, and the undermost pale green, with a strait vein in the middle, which sends out divers others on both sides. The blossoms are both for scent and colour like our roses, but inclining more to a purple colour; the first is of the bigness of a large pear, or of a goose egg, or rather bigger. They are of two sorts; one of which is a dark red, inclining to black, generally without stones, excelling the other in taste; the other is pale red, has a longish white stone of the bigness of a peach-stone, cover'd with a white rough skin; this, tho' inferior to the former, yet is of a most pleasing taste. Sometimes the first is absolutely red, and these are of a purple colour, and smell like a rose; the fruit is cover'd with so thin a peel, that no knife can separate it from the pulp, which is accounted cold and moist; and so are the blossoms, notwithstanding which they are very well scented, and for that reason in high esteem among the inhabitants. The fruit is commonly eaten before dinner, or at the beginning of a meal; neither are they useless in physick, both the fruit and flowers preserved, being prescribed in violent burning fevers; having besides their cooling quality, a certain virtue of comforting the spirits. This tree may well be accounted among the number of those, which by the excellency of their fruit, and the agreeableness of their flowers, surprizes the beholders; for, whilst you see one side of the tree bare of leaves and blossoms, the other is stor'd with fruit, which last, till the other side begins to renew its leaves; so that in one and the same tree you see a continual spring and autumn at once. Thus you never can cast your eye upon this tree but you meet there either with blossom or fruit; and as the blossom drops underneath on the ground (which is frequently cover'd with those purple colour'd flowers) others come forth in their stead; and whilst some of the fruit are ripening, others are to be gathered. The best way to gather their fruit is to shake the tree, then they fall with ease; but if you endeavour to pull them off, the tacks are apt to break. Karkapuli.

The fruit *Karkapuli*, call'd *Kerkapoli* by the *Canarins*, is in shape and bigness like an orange; they are green at first, afterwards

1662. terwards turn yellow, and when ripe, white, of ſweet taſte, but a little tartiſh. In the centre of the pulp lies the ſeeds, flat and long, of the bigneſs of a joint of a finger, and are of a dark brown colour.

Koddam Pulli. The tree which bears this fruit is very tall, call'd *Koddam Pulli* by the *Malabars*, ſometimes *Otta Pulli*, and by the *Brahmans Danubos*, by the inhabitants of the iſle of *Ceylon Choroka*; the fruit is eaten, and uſed in phyſick among the *Indians*, being accounted an excellent remedy againſt looſeneſs, eſpecially if occaſioned by too much venery. Beſides which, the fruit before it is quite ripe, or the juice of it mix'd with butter-milk, or the fruit dried and powder'd mix'd with butter-milk and boil'd rice, is excellent good to acuate the appetite of the ſtomach. This juice alſo, as well as the dry fruit powder'd, is accounted a good remedy againſt the dimneſs, cataracts, and other infirmities of the eyes; they apply the juice, mix'd with ſome other herbs, to the nail of the great toe, on that ſide where the defect of the eye is. The midwives give it to women lately brought to bed, to expel the after-birth, and produce plenty of milk for ſuck. This fruit, when dried, is tranſported to foreign countries. There is another kind of this tree, bearing a round fruit and ſweet, of the bigneſs of a cherry, call'd *Karkapuli* by Mr. *Dinſhoten*; this tree is call'd *Karue Choraka* by thoſe of *Ceylon*, i. e. *ſweet Choraka*; out of the bark of both of theſe trees, if ſlit with a knife, iſſues a gum call'd *Gutta*, but that which comes from the *Kanka Choraka* is the beſt.

The uſe of aloe leaves among the Malabars. The uſe of aloe leaves is very frequent among the *Malabars*, a purge they boldly give not only to children, but alſo to women with child. They take of the aloe leaves 3 ounces cut very ſmall, theſe they boil with two drachms of black ſalt over an eaſy fire, and after they have ſtrain'd it, add to it an ounce of ſugar, and ſo let it ſtand the whole night in the air. The next morning about ſix a clock they give the patient this decoction cold, ordering him to abſtain from ſleep, and to walk about to promote its operation; three hours after he hath taken it, they give him a little chicken broth, with a few grains of maſtich in it, and an hour after that allow him to eat, and to take a little wine of the ſmalleſt ſort. They either increaſe or diminiſh the doſe of the decoction, according to the conſtitution of the patient.

There grows in *Malabar* a certain fruit of the bigneſs of a hazle nut, but is not quite ſo round and white; it grows on the tacks of a certain ſhrub which they ſow; it has no peculiar uſe in phyſick, tho' *Serapio* aſcribes to it a virtue of augmenting the ſeed, and promoting the birth in women; the ſame the *Malabars* do to this day, who call the fruit *Chevique lenga*, and in ſome places *Kurkas*, and thoſe of *Cambaiak Karpata*. If *Garcias* may be credited, this is the ſame fruit deſcribed by *Serapio* by the broken name of *Habel-culcul*, whereas it ſhould have been *Hab-alcul*, which ſignifies as much as the ſeed of *Culcul*. 1662. Chevique Lenga.

The tree call'd *Kumbulu* by the *Malabars*, and *Bon-Varo* by the *Brahmans*, grows very tall, with a trunk of that thickneſs, that a man can ſcarce graſp it. The leaves are a ſpan, and two or three inches long, and two palms broad, woolly at the end of the ſtalks, which are round, long and thick; at the extremities of the tacks, which ſprout forth out of the branches, grow certain yellow flowers in cluſters on ſhort ſtalks, conſiſting of five round and thick leaves. After theſe comes a fruit that's like a pear, full of juice, the pulp being of a yellowiſh colour, and a ſweetiſh taſte, but the juice when preſs'd out is deep yellow. They are green at firſt, next of a pale yellow, and turn reddiſh at laſt; in the centre of the fruit is a white ſmooth ſtone, ſhap'd like a pear, with a ſmall kernel in it. The decoction of the root, mix'd with a little rice, is a good remedy againſt the ague, which often follows the gout or rheumatiſm. Taken in butter-milk, or mix'd with the oil of *Sirchelem*, it expels the wind, and eaſes the pain; and the juice of the leaves taken with butter-milk, is good againſt the cholick.

The tree call'd *Ganſchi* by the *Malabars*, and *Schivanni* by the *Brahmans*, grows in ſandy grounds a great height and thickneſs, ſo that a man can ſcarce graſp the trunk, which as well as the branches has a bark of an aſh-colour without, but green within. The leaves hang on long, round and green ſtalks, being above a ſpan in length, and two palms broad, of an oblong figure. The bloſſoms faſtened to ſtalks which are pale green, ſweet, round and thin, each flower conſiſting of no more than three, and ſeldom of four leaves. After theſe comes the fruit, which is of a triangular figure, flattiſh, and of a green colour, hanging on long and green ſtalks, the ſeed being triangular, and the pulp very ſubſtantial; the decoction of the root is uſed againſt the gout, and apply'd to the affected part. *The tree* Ganſchi.

Of the tree *Palega* there are two kinds; one is call'd *Palega-Pajaneli* by the *Malabars*, and the other barely *Pajanel*. The *Palega-Pajaneli*, called *Davandiku* by the *Brahmans*, is very tall, with a trunk enough for a man to graſp, having an aſh-coloured bark, as well as the branches, which grow ſtrait upright, of a conſiderable thickneſs. *The tree* Palega-Pajameli.

1662. The leaves hang on ſtalks, which ſhoot forth both out of the ſtem and branches of the tree. On the extremities of the branches grow certain cluſters of flowers ſhap'd like bells, conſiſting of ſix thick leaves; whitiſh or pale yellow within, and ſtreak'd with red on the out-ſide, the ſcent of which is offenſive to the noſtrils. The fruit which follows the flowers is about three ſpans long, of the breadth of a hand, and an inch thick, with a dark green peel. The pulp juicy and tender at firſt, but grows hard at laſt; the ſeed is very flat. The bark of the tree powder'd and mix'd with wine, applied to a wound, or broken bones, heals them. The decoction of the root is good againſt the dropſy; and the leaves, whilſt yet very young, mix'd with *Malabar* ſaffron, cures all ſorts of ulcers, if apply'd to them outwardly.

The ſecond kind of Pajaneli. The ſecond kind of the *Pajaneli*, called *Davandiku* by the *Brahmans*, is likewiſe a very tall tree, whoſe branches ſhoot forth upright to a great height; it delights in ſandy grounds: The root ſpreads at a great diſtance, having a thick aſh-coloured rind. The trunk is of that thickneſs, that a man can ſcarce graſp it, of a brittle wood, with a dark aſh-coloured bark: The flowers are like the former, ſhap'd like bells, but have no more than five leaves. The fruit is the ſame: Of the juice of the leaves, and that of the fruit *Kareka*, or *Mirobolans* mix'd together, the *Malabars* make a black dye to dye their mourning cloaths with. The decoction of the rind of the root diſpels hard tumours if they be fomented with it.

Of the tree *Pala*, called *Santeru* by the *Brahmans*, there are four kinds; 1. *Pala*; 2. *Kuruta Pala*; 3. *Kadaga Pala*; 4. *Kaikotten Pala*: The firſt kind, called only *Pala*, is a high tree growing in ſandy places, and ſpreading its branches into a great circumference: The root, which has a dark yellow rind, reaches very deep into the ground, and contains a milky juice: The trunk is two or three fathoms thick, the bark of an aſh-colour, as is likewiſe the bark of the branches. The leaves grow four or five together, on ſtalks of an oblong figure, and towards the ſtalks full of a milky ſubſtance; the flowers grow in cluſters, having five whitiſh leaves of a ſtrong ſcent, but offenſive to the brains. The fruit which comes immediately after the bloſſom, do likewiſe hang in cluſters on ſmall tacks, being green huſks of about two ſpans length, but ſmall and flat, full of a milky juice or ſubſtance, as is the tree itſelf, which produces fruit but once a year, *viz.* in *January*.

The ſecond kind of *Pala* is by the *Malabars* called *Kurutu Pala*, by the *Brahmans* *Kudo*, being a tree from ſix to twelve foot high, the trunk about the thickneſs of a foot, with an aſh-coloured bark, as well as the branches. The leaves come forth out of the branches with their ſtalks, being of an oblong figure, and pointed at the end. The flowers grow on the extremities of the ſmall tacks, are white, and bigger than thoſe of the firſt kind, and have five long leaves. The fruit grows likewiſe in cluſters, being of an oblong figure, dark green at firſt, and as they ripen turn yellow. The huſk contains five, ſix or ſeven ſeeds. The tree bears fruit all the year round, but moſt in the rainy ſeaſon. The bark of the tree beaten to powder, and taken in warm water, is good againſt the looſe piles, but if taken in milk ſtops the bloody flux. 1662.

The third kind of *Pala*, called *Kadaga-Pala* by the *Malabars*, and *Alego-Kugo* by the *Brahmans*, is no higher than the *Kurutu-Pala*, and delights in ſandy grounds. The root does not go ſo deep underground as that of the *Pala*, the bark is of a dark brown colour; the trunk is of a foot circumference like the ſecond kind, but the leaves and bloſſom being alſo like the ſame. It bears long huſks like the *Pala*, but are ſomewhat thicker, of a green colour, a ſpan long, and full of a milky liquor. The bark of the trunk beaten to powder, and taken in butter-milk, ſtops the looſeneſs; and the rind of the root, taken in the ſame manner, cures the bloody flux. The decoction of the ſeeds is given in burning fevers, and kills the worms. The fourth kind, called *Kaikotten-Kala*, is very near the ſame with the third. Kaikotten-Kala.

There are two kinds of the tree called *Parva* by the *Malabars*; the firſt they call *Tindaparva*, and the ſecond *Anaparva*, and the *Brahmans Bendarli*. The *Tindaparva* grows to a great height in ſandy grounds, having a thick whitiſh root with a ſoft rind: The trunk is ſo thick that a man can ſcarce graſp it with his arms, having an aſh-coloured bark as well as the branches, which underneath the bark are of a dark brown colour. The leaves which are long, and pointed at the end, hang on ſhort ſtalks, as do likewiſe the flowers, conſiſting of four pale green and pointed leaves. The fruits are a kind of round berries, with a very thin peel, green at firſt, afterwards inclining to white, and turn red as they ripen. In the peel is encloſed a round kernel. The root beaten to powder and taken inwardly, is a ſovereign remedy againſt epileptick fits; and the decoction of the leaves diſperſes all pain, if the affected parts be well fomented with it.

The tree *Kavalkan*, as the *Malabars* call it, and *Bankar* by the *Brahmans*, grows in ſtony

1662. stony and sandy grounds; its root, which is very thick, and covered with an ash-coloured but softish rind, stretching very deep underground. The trunk is so thick that a man can scarce grasp it with both his arms, covered with a thick bark, of an ash-colour without, and pale green within. The wood is also white, and may be drawn into thread. The leaves are of an oblong figure, a span and 2 or 3 inches long, pointed at the ends, hanging on long round and green stalks: The flowers consisting of five small leaves sprout out in clusters, with green and hairy stalks. The fruit comes forth in bunches, three, four, or five together, being of the shape of an egg, with a thick and hard rind, containing nine or ten beans of the length of a finger each, but round and smooth, with a double peel: These beans, when roasted are good food. This tree bears blossom but once a year, *viz.* in *May*, and is not used in physick among the *Malabars*.

The tree Ambalam. Of the tree *Ambalam* there are two kinds in *Malabar*; one is simply called *Ambalam*, or *Koduko Ambado*, (i. e. *Sweet Ambado*) by the *Brahmans*; the other, *Kat Ambalam*, or *Pee Ambalam*. The tree *Ambalam* grows to a great height in sandy grounds, with its branches not spreading, but upright. The root which is very large, stretching with many twigs under ground. The trunk is of a great circumference, covered with a very thick bark; the wood being very soft: The leaves hang on small green stalks or sprouts, in bunches of five together; they are generally as long again as they are broad, smooth and soft, and of a light green on both sides. Those leaves which are nearest to the small twigs, are not so large as the rest, of an agreeable scent, and tartish, not unlike the rind of the *Indian Mangoes*. The blossom or flower do likewise come forth out of small and green sprouts, are of a whitish colour, shaped like stars, having five or six leaves. The buds of these flowers are round, and green at first, but turn white before they open; which when it happens, the leaves fall from the tree, which continues bare as long as it stands in blossom, but as the fruit grows, new leaves come forth by degrees. The fruit grows in clusters, being of an oval figure, and pretty hard, not unlike to the *Indian Mangoes*: Before they come to maturity their rind is dark brown, and full of sour juice, but when they begin to ripen turn light green, and at last yellow, of an agreeable tartish taste, and are eaten by the inhabitants. In the midst of the fruit is a very large stone. This tree bears twice every year, *viz.* in *January* and *May*. The root of it thrust into the matrix stops the superfluous monthly times. The bark powder'd and taken in butter-milk is good against the looseness, and so is the juice mix'd with ice. The decoction of the wood is a good remedy against the involuntary emission of the seed, and the juice of the leaves mix'd with that of the fruit instill'd into the ears, eases the pain in those parts. 1662.

The second kind of the *Ambalam*, *Kat Ambulam*, or *Pee Ambalam*, as the *Malabars* call it, and *Kaduko Ambado* by the *Brahmans*, resembles the first in a great many respects, except that its leaves are less, and so are the fruit, being somewhat rounder, and the taste a mixture of sour and bitter, which is the reason they are never eaten. *Kat Ambalam*, or *Pee Ambalam*, signifies in the *Malabar* tongue as much as *Wild Ambalam*, and *Kaduko Ambado* among the *Brahmans*, as much as the *Bitter Ambado* from its taste. *The tree* Katambalam.

The tree called *Agaty* by the *Malabars*, and *Agasto* by the *Brahmans*, runs up to the height of ten or twelve yards, the branches growing strait upright: The trunk is so big in circumference that a man can scarce grasp it, having a very soft wood, and the pith much tender. If an incision be made into the bark, a certain watery substance distils thence, which turns to gum afterward. The leaves come forth out of small and green sprouts or buds, being near a span and a half long, and growing two and two on long green stalks. The flowers consist of five small leaves, and grow in clusters on stalks of a pale green colour. After the blossom come thin, strait and green husks, of about a span in length, and an inch in breadth, having a thick peel, in which are enclosed certain beans, not unlike in taste to, but somewhat smaller than, our *French* beans, being white at first, but turn pale green by degrees, and are very good food. This tree bears fruit twice or thrice in the rainy season, and indeed the whole year round, but not so frequently in the summer. The juice of the bark of this tree, either by itself, or mix'd with honey, is an excellent remedy against all the inflammations of the throat and mouth. The juice of the leaves taken into the nostrils like a liquid snuff, cures the quartan ague. *The tree* Agaty.

The tree call'd *Appel* or *Nalla-Appella*, by the *Malabars*, and *Karo-Nervoloe* by the *Brahmans*, has a very thick and hairy root, the rind of which is of a saffron colour. The circumference of the stem is of five or six palms; the branches growing directly upright: Its wood is white, but the peel dark red. The leaves sprout forth out of the branches in small green and square buds, the stalks being round, very short, and of a pale green colour, commonly two and two together. The *The tree* Appel.

1662. leaves are of an oval figure, round near the ſtalk, and pointed toward the end. The flowers grow in cluſters, conſiſting of four round white and ſmall leaves each. The fruit are round berries, having a round ſtone in the middle; are pale green at firſt, but when ripe turn black. The tree bears but once a year. The root of this tree powdered and taken in water, ſtops the looſeneſs, and boiled in ſea-water and applied outwardly, appeaſes the pain of the gout. The decoction of the leaves is a good remedy againſt the pain of the belly and ſtomach, occaſioned by wind; the ſame effect has the oil drawn out of the root, if anointed on the painful part; this oil is yellow and tranſparent, of an agreeable ſcent, and a picquant bitteriſh taſte.

Schageri-Kottam. The tree call'd *Schageri Kottam* by the *Malabars*, and *Sahali* by the *Brahmans*, ſeldom exceeds the heighth of ſix foot, and delights in ſandy grounds: Its ſtem is of the thickneſs of a man's arm, the root red within, and black on the out-ſide. The leaves ſprout forth out of the twigs and hang on round, and green ſtalks; they are very large, and pretty long, broad towards the ſtalk, and pointed at the ends; the upper-ſide dark green, and the undermoſt ſide of a pale green colour. At the very extremities of the ſmall twigs grow the flowers in cluſters on ſmall ſtalks, conſiſting of four or five great leaves, of a white and pale yellow colour. The fruit is in ſhape like an *European* pear, dark green at firſt, and when ripe, turns black; it is of a ſweetiſh taſte, and eaten by the *Malabars*. The juice of the leaves boil'd with ſugar, and taken inwardly, ſtrengthens the liver, and ſtops the looſeneſs.

Kolinil. The tree call'd *Kolinil* by the *Malabars*, and *Scheara Punka* by the *Brahmans*, does not grow above two or three foot high, its ſtem being not above three or four inches thick, the branches ſpreading round about it. The wood of the ſtem is very hard, and the green bark which covers it of a picquant bitteriſh taſte. The leaves come forth out of ſmall and green ſprouts, hanging on very ſmall ſtalks; they are of an oval figure, round at the ends, and ſomewhat pointed towards the ſtalks, of a ſharp and bitter taſte: The bloſſom is like our bean bloſſom, having each four leaves: The fruit is a kind of a ſmall, ſmooth, and long huſk, yet not above two or three inches in length, are green in the beginning, and dark red at laſt, having within them certain beans, which are green at firſt, and black at laſt. This tree produces fruit twice a year, once in the winter, and once in the ſummer. The root powdered and boiled in milk, or the juice of the coco-tree, is a good remedy againſt the falling-ſickneſs. 1662.

Alu, or Fig-tree. There are four kinds of fig-trees in *Malabar*, call'd by one general name *Alu*; the firſt they call *Atty-Alu*, the ſecond *Itty-Alu*, the third *Arêalu*, and the fourth *Peralu*.

Atty-Alu. The fig-tree *Atty-Alu*, call'd *Roembadoe* by the *Brahmans*, grows to a great height, ſpreading its branches at a good diſtance. The trunk is of that thickneſs, that a man cannot well graſp it; the fruit is round, but flat, and leſſer towards the ſtalk, and ſomewhat hairy and rough, not unlike our figs. Before they are ripe, they are green and full of a milky juice, but turn red when ripe, and are not ſo juicy. Within the pulp, you ſee ſmall kernels like thoſe in our figs, and as ſoon as they are ripe, the piſmires get into them. Theſe figs are the only ones that are eaten by the *Malabars*, and eaten raw when ripe are accounted good againſt the looſeneſs. If the inhabitants may be believed, theſe trees are produced out of the ſeed of the fruit, after it is eaten by the ravens, and diſcharged again with their dung.

Itty-Alu. The ſecond ſort call'd *Itty-Alu*, and *Areka Goli* by the *Brahmans*, is the ſmalleſt of all the four kinds, its trunk being to be graſpt by any ordinary man. It bears a ſmall and round fruit, which is green, whilſt not come to maturity, and full of a milky juice, but when ripe turns yellow. It has alſo abundance of kernels, like the firſt kind.

Arealu. The tree of the third kind, call'd *Arealu*, and *Bipaloe* by the *Brahmans*, is as tall as the former, ſpreading its branches very loftily, at a good diſtance: The trunk is of ſuch a thickneſs, that two men can ſcarce graſp it: The fruit is like that of the *Itty-Alu*, ſmall and round, and not forced, as that of the *Atty-Alu*. Theſe *Pagans* have dedicated this tree to their idol *Viſtnu*, who they ſay was born under this tree, and took of its bloſſoms: For this reaſon it is, that they ſurround it with a ſtone wall, and worſhip it. The chriſtians call it the *Devil's-tree*.

Peralu. The fourth ſort call'd *Peralu*, and *Vadhoe* by the *Brahmans*, exceeds all the others in height; for which reaſon the *Brahmans* have given it the name of *Vadhoe*, *i. e.* large. The fruit is much the ſame with that of the *Atty-Alu*, but very round, and of a very high red colour, being covered with a kind of a *Lanugo* or woolly ſubſtance when they are ripe.

Of the tree call'd *Paniti* by the *Malabars*, are likewiſe four different kinds, *viz.* *Pariti*, *Bupariti*, *Kadupariti* and *Schem-Pariti*. The tree *Bupariti*, call'd *Valli-Kari-Kapoeſi* by the *Brahmans*, is a very high tree, with very lofty branches, growing in the

1662. the ſhape of a crown round the tree, which is never infeſted with any inſects. The leaves reſemble in ſhape a man's heart, of the bigneſs of the palm of a man's hand, ſomewhat pointed at the end, of a lovely green on the upper-ſide, and a pale green on the other. The flowers are of the ſhape of bells conſiſting of ſeveral white leaves; after theſe comes a certain round ſpongeous fruit, which emits a gummous liquor, if an inciſion be made with a knife. For the reſt, the tree produces flowers all the year round.

The tree Bupariti.

Pariti. *Pariti*, or the tree of the ſecond kind, call *Karikapreſs* by the *Brahmans*, grows to the height of 18 foot, the trunk being however within the compaſs of a man's graſping. The flowers are like thoſe of the *Bupariti*, only ſomewhat leſſer; and after theſe come certain oval ſponges, covered with a *Lanugo* or hairy ſubſtance. The bloſſom bruiſed and mix'd with womens milk, and infuſed into the ears, cures the head-ach.

Kudupariti. The tree *Kudupariti* of the third ſort, called *Kapuſſi* by the *Brahmans*, runs to the height of 12 foot, tho' its ſtem is not above two palms thick. The flowers are likewiſe like bells, of the ſame ſhape and colour as the precedent, only that they are a little leſſer, and inclining to green. The ſpongeous fruit are three corner'd, pointed at the top, and within diſtinguiſh'd by three ſkins in as many different concavities, each of which contains three or four ſeeds encloſed in a thick white *Lanugo* or woolly ſubſtance: This tree is never without bloſſom throughout the whole year. The leaves bruiſed and mixed with cow's milk, and apply'd outwardly to the head, procures ſleep, and conſequently cures the head-ach. The fruit bruiſed and taken inwardly in water ſtops the bloody flux. The fourth ſort is very near the ſame with the third.

Chavanna Mandaru. Of the tree *Mandaru* are likewiſe four different ſorts, *viz. Chavanna Mandaru*, of which two bear the ſame name; *Velutta Mandaru*, and *Kanſchenapou*. The firſt call'd *Chavanna Mandaru* by the *Malabars*, and *Tambido Mandaru* by the *Brahmans*, grows up to the height of 24 foot, ſpreading its branches far round about. The trunk is not above a foot thick. The leaves hang on very ſhort ſtalks, being even in two at the upper-end, like goats feet, whence the *Portugueſe* have given them the name of *Pee de Capra*. The flowers have five leaves of an oval figure, among which the largeſt and broadeſt is rounder than the reſt, white on the outſide, and of a purple colour within; the other four are more oval, of a pale red colour without, but high red within; two of thoſe four, *viz.* thoſe next to the biggeſt leaf are on the inſide whitiſh towards the bottom, but the other two all over of a roſe-colour within; from which roſe-colour the *Malabars* have given the name of *Chavanna Mandaru* to this tree. In ſome of thoſe leaves you ſee ſtreaks as red as blood, which they ſay are the remnants of the blood of St. *Thomas*, who preach'd the goſpel on the coaſt of *Malabar*, and in the iſle of *Ceylon*. After theſe come certain flat, long and ſmooth huſks, of the length of ſeven or eight inches, in which are encloſed flat and long beans, which at firſt are ripe, but afterwards turn dark red. This tree produces flowers all the year round, but in the rainy ſeaſon in greater plenty. The flowers preſerved with ſugar, are uſed with good ſucceſs for a laxative, as we do with our roſe-ſugar. The ſecond ſort of the *Chavanna Mandaru* is a very tall tree like the firſt, with ſuch like branches, a trunk of the ſame thickneſs, and the ſame leaves, only ſomewhat larger. The flowers have five oval leaves of a purple colour, both in and outſide with white ſtreaks. The huſks of this tree are the largeſt of all the four kinds, being two ſpans long, an inch thick, flat and ſmooth; the beans are the ſame both in ſhape and colour as the firſt; and this tree bloſſoms at the ſame time, and in the ſame manner. The flowers of this tree eaten raw are laxative; the bark, flowers and fruit bruiſed together and mix'd with the liquor of the decoction of rice, is a ſovereign remedy to bring to maturity, and to open all ſorts of tumors. The bark chew'd cures the tooth and head-ach. 1662.

The third ſort, call'd *Velutta Mandaru* by the *Malabars* and *Dove Mandaru* by the *Brahmans*, is not above ſix foot high, and an arm thick; the leaves are cloven like thoſe of the firſt, but the flowers white without the leaſt ſcent, having five round leaves. The huſks are not ſo big as thoſe of the others, *viz.* not above four or five inches long, and an inch thick, for the reſt flattiſh and ſmooth. The beans are long and round, of a yellowiſh colour, neither ſo big nor ſo red as thoſe of the *Chavanna Mandaru*. This tree bloſſoms two or three times every year, but chiefly in the rainy ſeaſon. The flowers bruiſed and mix'd with ſome pepper, and applied outwardly to the head cures the head-ach; and if you waſh yourſelf with the decoction of the root, it lays all ſorts of itching of the ſkin. Velutta Mandaru.

The fourth ſort called *Kanſchenapou* by the *Malabars*, and *Kantſanu* by the *Brachmans*, is a tree which runs up to the height of 12 foot or more, with lofty branches, but the ſtem is not above half a foot thick. Kanſchenapou.

1662. The leaves are cloven like the reſt, but not ſo big, very ſtrong ſcented if rubb'd betwixt your fingers, eſpecially in the night-time: The flowers conſiſt alſo of five leaves, of a pale yellow colour, without the leaſt ſcent. The huſks are the ſame with thoſe of the *Chavanna Mandaru*, very ſmooth on the outſide, but ſomewhat hairy whilſt very young. The beans are ſmall, in ſhape and colour reſembling thoſe of the *Velutta Mandaru*. The tree bears flowers twice or thrice a year, but moſt plentifully in the rainy ſeaſon. The decoction of the root taken inwardly, is a good remedy againſt the worms and inflammations of the liver, and the piles. The bark powder'd diſperſes tumors, cleanſes the wounds, and is an excellent narcotick.

The tree Nilikamaram. The tree call'd *Nilikamaram* by the *Malabars*, and *Anvali* by the *Brahmans*, grows up to the height of 24 foot, tho' its trunk be no bigger than a man's arm, which as well as the branches, are covered with a black bark. The leaves ſprout forth out of thin and round twigs, with very ſhort ſtalks; they grow two and two together, of an oval figure, and very ſmall, being dark green on the upper ſide, and light green on the other ſide. Every night the leaves cloſe up like tulips; the flowers grow on ſmall twigs in cluſters, conſiſting of ſix very ſmall leaves. It bears a round, but flattiſh fruit, of a pale green colour when ripe, and ſomewhat tranſparent; the pulp being likewiſe green and very juicy, of an agreeable aſtringent taſte: In the midſt is a ſtone, diſtinguiſh'd into ſix different concavities, each of which contains a ſmall triangular ſeed or ſmall kernel. The fruit is much uſed by the *Malabars*: The water diſtill'd from this fruit cools the liver, and dry'd and power'd, and mix'd with ſour coagulated milk, ſtops the bloody-flux.

Odollam. The tree call'd *Odollam* by the *Malabars*, and *Uro* by the *Brahmans*, grows to the height of 18 foot, its trunk being ſo thick as ſcarce to be encompaſs'd by a man with both his arms, with crooked branches. The wood of the ſtem is very ſoft, and the pith red, the bark of an aſh colour, bitter and very hot upon the tongue. The leaves grow ſcattering upon the twigs and long ſtalks, are of the ſhape of a tongue, thick, ſmooth, dark brown on the upper-ſide, bitter and biting upon the tongue. The flowers grow in cluſters like cornets, on long, thick, and green ſtalks, having five very white and pointed leaves. It bears a kind of ground-apple, with a green and ſmooth rind, under which is a white pulp of a wateriſh taſte. The ſtone which is in the midſt, is ſhap'd like the heart of a man, of a pretty large ſize, with two kernels within it. Some will have this tree to be the ſame which the *Indians* call *Mongas*. 1662.

The tree call'd *Nurotti* by the *Malabars*, and *Kaitu* by the *Brahmans*, riſes up Nurotti. to a great height, its branches ſpreading very lofty round about it: The trunk is ſo big as ſcarce to be graſped by a man; the wood white, with a thick bark, which is green without and red within. The leaves are ſcattered here and there on the twigs with ſhort, round and green ſtalks, of the length of a ſpan, and the breadth of four or five inches, of an oval figure, pointed at the ends, not unlike the laurel leaves. The flowers ſprout forth ſix or ſeven together out of the extremities of the ſmall twigs, conſiſting of three rows of ſmall leaves. The firſt row makes up a ſtar of five ſmall pointed and dark brown hairy leaves. The ſecond row contains five round and ſmall leaves of a roſe-colour, and the third or outermoſt row, five pointed green leaves. The fruit grows on ſhort and thick ſtalks, being of an oval figure, having a roſe colour'd rough peel, and within a large yellowiſh ſtone, containing 10 or 12 kernels of an oleaginous ſubſtance. This tree produces both flowers and fruit in great plenty all the year round: From the kernels or ſeeds an oil is drawn, which has an anodyne quality, and applied outwardly, cures all ſorts of ſcurfs and itchings: The ſame oil, mixed with a certain fruit, the *Malabars* call *Palego*, kills the corns in the feet, if applied to the affected part.

Of the tree call'd *Kaniram* there are four Kaniram. ſeveral kinds: One is call'd *Kaniram* only; the ſecond *Karakaniram*, and the third and fourth *Vallikaniram*, The tree call'd *Kaniram*, and by the *Brahmans*, *Karo*, grows up to a great height, with lofty and far ſpreading branches. The root is very thick, exceeding bitter, and covered with a yellow rind. The trunk is of that thickneſs as ſcarce to be graſped by two men, having a dark aſh colour'd bark. The leaves, which are of an oval figure, are very broad in the middle, and pointed towards the ends, of a bitteriſh taſte and an odd ſcent, growing two and two over againſt the other: The flowers ſprout forth in cluſters, having each five or ſix pale green and pointed leaves. No ſooner begins the bloſſom to bud, but the tree loſes all its leaves, inſtead of which new ones come ſoon after. It bears a kind of round and ſmooth apple, which is green at firſt and turns yellow afterwards, two, three, four or more hanging together on ſhort ſtalks. The pulp, before they are ripe, is white and inſipid, but when ripe, bitter with a thick rough peel. It bloſſoms in the

1662. summer, and brings forth fruit in the winter. In the pulp are round but flattish seeds, which are also very bitter. The juice of the leaves taken in the decoction of the same leaves cures the head-ach, but if used in too great a quantity is mortal, the only antidote against which is man's dung taken inwardly. Two or three of those seeds taken every day for two years successively, is a preservative against the biting of the serpent, called *Cobra de Capelo* by the *Portuguese*.

Manjapumeram. The tree called *Manjapumeram* by the *Malabars*, and *Pariataku* by the *Brahmans*, rises up to the height of 18 or 24 foot, with very thick and lofty branches spreading round about it, but the stem is not above the thickness of an arm, having an ash-coloured bark: The leaves hang crosswise over one another, being pointed at the ends, the uppermost side of a dark green, and the other of a light green colour, of an astringent and bitterish taste; the flowers grow on stalks which stand upright five in a cluster, are very agreeable and sweet scented, having six, seven, and sometimes eight leaves each, of a whitish colour both in and outside. The fruit is of an oval figure, but flat, of a green colour, containing two round and flattish seeds. This tree is of no use among the *Malabar* physicians.

Champakam. This tree *Champakam*, as the *Malabars* call it, and the *Brahmans Champo*, is a very tall tree, with many lofty branches spreading at a good distance: The trunk is of that thickness as scarce to be grasp'd by a man, with a thick bark of an ash-colour without, and soft within, of a bitter astringent taste. The wood is white: The leaves are of an oval figure pointed a good way towards the ends, of the length of a span, and the breadth of four or five inches; the uppermost side dark green and shining, the other side light green, bitter and biting upon the tongue. At the extremities of the small twigs sprout forth pale green flowers, of a quick odoriferous scent, having oval leaves placed in three rows within one another. In the first root are about eight leaves, being as broad again as those of the second row, round but pointed at the ends; but those in the second row are more pointed still, and those in the third more than the second, and pale yellow. The fruit grows in bunches of an oval figure, with a thick rind. Whilst not come to maturity it is green, but turns pale yellow when ripe, being sharp of taste, and of no agreeable scent: Within are three or four seeds, round on one, and flat on the other side; within those seeds, when they are come to their full perfection, is a thin milky substance enclosed in a skin of a purple colour, and within it a black stone. The tree, if not too old, blossoms twice a year; out of these flowers they distil a good cordial water.

Elengi. The tree call'd *Elengi* by the *Malabars*, and *Vavalli* by the *Brahmans*, grows up very high, with many far-spreading branches: The trunk is of that thickness, that two men can scarce well grasp it, with a dark brown and rough bark, containing a milky liquor within. The wood is full of the same juice, and will keep a great while under water, but not very long in the air. The leaves grow on small round and green stalks, being of an oval figure, but pointed at the ends. The flowers have pale green stalks, growing five or six in a cluster, of a white colour, consisting of 16 leaves of an odoriferous scent. The *Malabars* make nosegays of them. The fruit is shap'd live an olive, green at first, but turns yellow and red by degrees: The pulp is yellow and meally. The *Malabars* eat this fruit, which has two oval but flat and dark brown stones within. This tree bears flowers twice a year, out of which the *Malabars* distil a well-scented water, which is look'd upon as a great cordial, and revives the spirits. The fruit bruised and taken inwardly in warm water, promotes the birth.

Besides these there also grows here *Cassia Fistula*, called *Konna* by the *Malabars*, and *Bajo* by the *Brahmans*; and *Tamarinds* call'd *Balam-Pulli*, or *Maderam-Pulli* by the *Malabars*, and *Sinza* by the *Brachmans*. The coast of *Malabar* produces likewise *Cardamom*, *Berbery* ginger, and some aloes; as also bezoar-stones, salt-petre, honey, lacca, and cotton; to be short, this countrey abounds in all sorts of *Indian* trees and fruits.

Living creatures of Malabar. The woods afford vast plenty of birds of all kinds, and among the rest most excellent peacocks, the flesh of which is very white and well tasted. No place in the world abounds more in all sorts of water-fowl, and there are a great many birds here so tame, and so plentiful, that you may kill them with a stick, the reason of which is, that as the *Pagans* adhere to the opinion of *Pythagoras*, concerning the transmigration of the soul; so they won't kill any living creature, which makes all sorts of wild creatures multiply here, almost *in infinitum*. The flesh of their hogs (of which they likewise have great plenty) is also excellent good; but above all, tame fowl is *Plenty of fowl.* so prodigious cheap here, that you may buy a very good pullet for two-pence, and thirty eggs for the same price. I remember I had once bought up 300 pullets against the arrival of our ships, which being put in the old church of *St. Thomas*, we

1662. we found all dead one morning; we could not guess at the cause of this disaster, till a certain *Malabar* told us, that it could not be otherwise, but that a *Cobre Kapel* (a very venomous serpent) must be hidden in the place; whereupon strict search being made we found the serpent under a heap of old wood, which was no sooner removed, but the serpent set herself upright upon the tail, spitting fire and flame, so that no body durst approach her, till one of our soldiers kill'd her with his sword. Of venison there is also great plenty. 1662.

Bats. They have likewise bats of divers kinds; and among the rest a certain sort of that bigness, that their wings when extended are

as long as man can stretch with both his arms together. They have red heads and necks, black bodies, and are shaped like a fox. They are extremely nimble, and having very sharp teeth do a great deal of damage to the fruit. Their wings are bare, like those of our bats, unto which are fastned their legs and tails, so that they can neither walk nor stand; to recompence which defect they have a kind of a hook, of the thickness of a finger on each wing, wherewith they fasten to the branches of the trees: You see here vast multitudes of them in the woods, so that it is no difficult thing to kill them; but whatever you kill, remains hanging among the trees: They are naturally so fierce that they are not to tamed; for if taken alive, they will bite their own wings and flesh as far as they can reach; I once had the curiosity to set two of these creatures a fighting, which they did with such fierceness, that they both remained dead upon the spot. They will drink of the liquor of the coco-tree till they are drunk; they commonly bring forth two young ones at a time, and that generally in the hollow of trees; the *Malabars* eat the flesh, which has no agreeable taste.

Jackall. Here you meet also with *Jackalls*, as our people call them, being not unlike a large fox, of the bigness of an ordinary peasant's dog, of a red grey colour, but thinly covered with hair. They assemble in the night in whole troops, and approaching (especially about the new-moons) to the villages or plantations, make a hideous noise, like the outcries of women or men; they are very greedy after mens flesh, and will scratch the dead carcasses out of the graves, unless they be well covered with stones: They are scarce ever to be tamed. The *Malabars* eat the flesh of these *Jackalls*. And thus much of the coast of *Malabar*.

The author pursues his voyage. After, as I told you, we had set sail the 12th of *March* from *Koulang*, the wind turn'd against us the same evening, but about eleven

1662. ven a clock at night we ſet ſail again with the land wind. The 13th we kept along the ſhore with a gentle breeze and very fair weather; but the wind turning ſoon after to the E. S. E. we were forced to chuſe the main ſea, but made to the ſhore again towards evening, and took the benefit of the land-wind. The 14th there being but little wind we advanced no farther than 12 leagues from *Koulang*; and the 15th finding ourſelves off of the city of *Tengepatnam*, we gave the ſignal by a cannon ſhot for the reſident Mr. *Koek* to come aboard us, which he did accordingly; and after I had diſcourſed with him of what I had in commiſſion to tell him, we continued our voyage, but being towards evening overtaken by a tempeſt, were forced to come to an anchor. The 16th early in the morning the winds being ſomewhat laid we ſet ſail again, but by reaſon of the contrary winds were forced to return towards *Pulon*, near the cape of *Comorin*, where the *Portugueſe* have a ſmall church dedicated to St. *Martin*. The 17th we made this cape, but the winds continuing ſtill againſt us, it was not till the 18th that we could reach *Toutekoriin*, the chief among the ſeaports of the coaſt of *Madure*. Here I tarried for ſome time to obſerve the intereſt of the company, both in reſpect of their traffick hither, and in the government of the inhabitants, who live under their juriſdiction along the ſea-coaſt, in ſeven large villages, the chief of which is *Toutekoriin*, the other ſix are *Manapara*, *Alendale*, *Wiranypatnam*, *Pommekiel*, *Baypaer* or *Vaypaer*, and *Bempaer*. After a ſtay of ſix months here, I received orders from Mr. *Van Goens* to return to *Koulang*, and to take once more upon me the government of this city, being very well known to the queen there; accordingly having ſurrendred my accounts to Mr. *Lawrentz Piil*, in the preſence of captain *Van Reede*, I left this place the 19th of *May* 1665, and went by land to *Koulang*. The number of the inhabitants of the before-mentioned ſeven villages amounted in 1664 to above 20000 ſouls, *viz.* in *Toutekoriin* about 3000, in *Mannapara* 4000, in *Alendale* 800, in *Wiranpatnam* 900, in *Pommekiel* or *Punikael* 2800, in *Baypaer* 700, and in *Bempaer* 800; beſides thoſe inhabiting on the coaſt of *Comorin*, which amounted to a conſiderable number: All theſe villages are adorn'd with ſtately churches, built by the *Portugueſe*, eſpecially thoſe of *Mannapara* and *Bempaer*, but are now in a decaying condition, ſince the *Portugueſe* have been chaſed thence. Some of the *Romiſh* prieſts now and then come to ſay maſs in the neighbouring villages, whither the people flock in great numbers; tho' to ſpeak truth, they are more heathens than chriſtians. *Toutekoriin* conſumes yearly abundance of foreign commodities, by reaſon of the great numbers of inhabitants living along this coaſt, who muſt be provided from abroad with moſt things they ſtand in need of; *Toutekoriin*, otherwiſe *Tutukuriin*, or rather *Tutukury*, or *Tutukuriin*, or *Totokury*, is now, as we told you, the chief of all thoſe ſeaports, being an open place; but beautified with ſtately ſtone buildings. It has three large churches built by the *Portugueſe*, which are to be ſeen at a great diſtance at ſea, the countrey round about being flat and low. In one of theſe the reformed exerciſe their religious worſhip: Beſides which the convent of the *Franciſcans* is lately fitted up for the ſame uſe. 1662.

Come over againſt Tengepatnam. *Come to* Toutekoriin. *The ſeven ſeaports of* Madure. *Their inhabitants.* *The village of* Toutekoriin.

The *Dutch Eaſt-India* company have a factory here, managed by a merchant as chief governor; by a factor as his deputy; two or three aſſiſtants, and a military officer, under whoſe command are ſome ſoldiers, but the *Nayk* of *Madure* will not allow them to erect any fortifications: During my ſtay here, I begun to erect a brick-wall round the garden, but finding the *Jentives* to look with a jealous eye upon it, I deſiſted; yet I took care to repair the houſe of the company, and ſet their flag on the top of it, which might be ſeen a good way at ſea.

This place was taken by the *Dutch* from the *Portugueſe* 1658, without much reſiſtence. In the road of *Toutekoriin*, is good anchorage at five fathom water in a ſandy bottom.

The village Punikael.

Three ſmall leagues from *Toutekoriin* near the rocks of *Remanekor*, not far from the kingdom of *Narſinga* lies the village of *Punikael*, where the *Portugueſe* formerly had a fort, and a garriſon of 40 men. Two leagues from thence there was a *Pagan* temple of the *Brahmans* call'd *Trichanduri*, againſt which and the prieſts thereof the *Portugueſe* would frequently utter very injurious words, which ſo exaſperated the inhabitants, that they entred into a league with their neighbours, *viz.* the *Badagas* of *Narſinga*, in order to drive the chriſtians thence: Accordingly, having with a great deal of ſecreſy got together a body of 6000 men, and received certain intelligence that the *Portugueſe* in the fort were but ill provided with gunpowder (the chief terror of theſe *Barbarians*) they march'd directly to *Punikael*; the *Portugueſe* being not a little ſurprized at ſo unexpected a ſight, were put to the greateſt nonplus that could be, being in want of ammunition, and no great account being to be made upon the *Parvas* (the chriſtian inhabitants) as being not trained up to military affairs, but living upon

War betwixt the inhabitants and the Portugueſe.

1662. upon fishing and swimming: These being sensible of their inability to resist the enemy, no sooner heard of his approach, but they began to betake themselves with their moveables to their boats which lay near the shore, which the *Badagas* endeavouring to prevent, some retired to unpassable places, others to the sea-side, whilst others were exposed to the mercy of the enemy, and with most dreadful outcries implored the assistance of the *Portuguese* in the fort.

Bravery of Anthony Kriminalis.

About that time a certain priest, named *Anthony Kriminalis*, who was come some days before thither to take care of the christians there, seeing this miserable spectacle, applied himself to *John Ferdinando Korrea*, governor of the fort, remonstrating to him, that since they were not in a condition to oppose the enemy, to endeavour to bring things to an accommodation; but the governor answer'd, that it was against the glory of his king to submit in the least respect to those *Barbarians*; *Kriminalis* made what haste he could to return to his flock, which he met in the church where he had preached the same morning, and led them to the sea-shore, endeavouring as much as he could to see them embark in their boats, whilst he refused to enter himself, being resolved to stay ashore, and to expect the utmost fury of the *Barbarians*, who were advancing apace, and with their arrows had already kill'd several of the *Portuguese* and others, among whom was the interpreter of *Kriminalis*, who was shot by his side, notwithstanding which he remained immoveable in his resolution, and wringing his hands up to heaven, fell upon his knees; the first troop of the *Bagadas* pass'd by without doing him the least harm, except that they took his hat, and so did the second, but one of the third troops (consisting of *Mahometans*) run a lance into his left side, whilst others let fly their arrows at him, and thinking he had been kill'd came to take his cloaths, which he, being yet alive, gave to them, and so retreated into the church, with an intention to spend the small remainder of his life at the foot of the altar; and being follow'd by the *Bagadas*, he there received a second thrust, and soon after a third, which put a period to his life: They afterwards cut off his head, which together with his bloody cloaths they carried in triumph to their temple of *Trichanduri*; the trunk of the body was afterwards buried by the christians.

Is killed.

Not far from *Punikael* or *Pommekiel*, lieth a great village call'd *Putanam*, and so further up the coast *Bembar* or *Bempaer*, *Kalekure*, *Beadal*, *Nianankor*, or rather *Romanakoris* and *Kanhameira*; next you see *Negapatnam*, the first frontier of the coast of *Coromandel*, but one of the chiefest towns of this coast is *Periapatan*, situate near the rocks of *Romanankoris* being the capital city of the *Maravas*, who inhabit the mountains, a barbarous generation, living only upon robbing; the jesuites that formerly belonged to the church of *Periapatan*, did endeavour to reclaim them in some measure from their barbarity, but most of them soon return'd to their old way of living. There is another village seated on the other side of the rocks of *Romanankoris*, directly opposite to *Negapatnam*, the inhabitants of which are all christians. All along the sea-coast are about 30 villages, among which, besides the before-mention'd, are the chiefest, *Trichandar* or *Trekandar*, *Kallegrande* and *Cherakalle*. 10[illegible]6.

Manners and customs of the inhabitants.

The inhabitants of those places are very black and strong; they are deceitful and cunning, make but little account of their wives, but generally keep two or three harlots, by whom they have sometimes 16 or 18 children. The men wear nothing but a single piece of callicoe wrap'd about their middle, and another piece about their head, which they call *Romare*. The ordinary women commonly wear painted callicoe, those of fashion are adorn'd with gold rings and bracelets when they are abroad, but are very nasty at home. They tie their hair up in a truss behind, like those of *Malabar*, for the rest they have very good features. They live upon meat and rice, but drink nothing but water, which they are fain to fetch half a league from the sea-shore; they live by pearl fishing and catching of fish, by weaving and shipping, there being some who drive a considerable trade with the painted callicoes to *Kalpentien*, *Kolomba* and the *Malabar* coast. They have abundance of callicoe and linnen weavers here, and great numbers of people are employed in painting of callicoes, which they do very artificially. This trade was in great request whilst I was here, because I used to give all imaginable encouragement to them; the inhabitants are govern'd by judges of their own, who are chosen every year by the chief director of the *Dutch* company there, whom they stile the *Captain of the seven Seaports*. Each village has the privilege to propose four, out of which the *Captain* chuses two, who swear fealty to the company; all civil causes are transacted in their respective villages, but criminal matters are decided at *Toutekoriin* in the council of nine, whereof the *Captain* is president. The remaining *Portuguese* pay no taxes to the *Dutch* company, but to the *Nayk* of *Madure*; however, this tax is paid with the approbation of the chief director, who allots

Their clothing.

Way of living.

Government.

1662. lots every one his ſhare according to his ſubſtance; thoſe who are backward in their payment, muſt expect ſpeedy execution, which is done by the ſoldiers of the *Nayk*, and cauſes frequent quarrels betwixt the inhabitants and the ſoldiers, as it happened in my time; when the *Nayk* peremptorily demanded the tax from the *Parvas*, which they were not able to pay, I ſent to him a ſerjeant with ſome ſoldiers, to deſire that he would ſend a commiſſioner with whom they might treat, and obtain ſome time for the payment thereof; upon which the *Nayk* having ſent one of his great officers with a body of horſe, I remonſtrated to him the impoſſibility of the matter, telling him that the ſeven ſeaports were willing to make a preſent of two ſilver diſhes fill'd with ducats to his maſter, which was well accounted of, and the *Nayk*, as a token of his ſatisfaction, ſent me a ſcarf richly embroidered with gold. Theſe ſeven ſeaports were formerly (before the *Portugueſe* fleets appear'd in theſe parts) under the government of the king of *Marten*, a vaſſal of the queen of *Tengauſy*, unto whom they were forc'd to pay many taxes; at which time the *Parvas* lived deeper in the countrey, and uſed to ſerve in the wars to ſuch princes as would pay them beſt.

Wars betwixt the Parvas *and* Moors.

One time a certain *Parvas* happening to fall out with ſome *Moors*, theſe cut off his noſe and ears, which ſo exaſperated the *Parvas*, that they reſolved to take up arms, and to revenge the quarrel of their countreyman. To begin the fray, they took one of the *Mooriſh* merchants priſoners, whoſe noſe and ears they likewiſe cut off, and ſo ſent him home. Hereupon the *Moors* having aſſembled a body of 30000 men, they march'd to, and pitch'd their tents near *Toutekoriin*; on the other hand, the *Parvas* were not above 5000 men, and well arm'd, and truſting more to their bravery than number, fell upon the *Moors* ſo couragiouſly, that they made them quit the field, with the ſlaughter of 7000 of their men; a great number of them being forc'd to the ſea-ſhore, ſaved themſelves in boats, but were ſcarce got to ſea, when by a ſtrong tempeſt from the S. W. they were ſo diſpers'd, that no news was ever heard of them ſince. After this victory the *Parvas* having made themſelves maſters of theſe ſeaports, came to a compoſition with the queen, promiſing to pay her the ſame taxes as the *Moors* had done, which being impoſſible for them to perform, this proved the occaſion of unſpeakable miſeries; ſome of them being impriſoned for want of payment, others ſold for ſlaves to that degree, that at laſt they reſolved to ſhake of the yoke, coſt it what it would: The *Portugueſe* who 1490 appear'd firſt thereabouts with their ſhips from *Cochin*, having at that time traded there for 40 years before, and conſequently their ſtrength at ſea, being not unknown to the *Parvas*, they ſent their deputies to *Cochin* to implore their protection, and to promiſe their obedience, and that they were ready to embrace the chriſtian faith. The *Portugueſe*, willing to improve this opportunity, came with their fleet 1533 on that coaſt, and having made themſelves maſters of the ſeaport towns, the *Parvas* received baptiſm all on one day. However they met with great oppoſition afterwards from thoſe on the coaſts of *Coromandel* and *Malabar*, encouraged underhand by the *Parvas*, till at laſt matters were adjuſted thus, that the *Portugueſe* ſhould remain maſters of the coaſt, that the *Parvas* ſhould pay them a certain annual tribute, according to their ability, and that all the chief men of that coaſt ſhould have their ſhare in the pearl fiſhing, which was to be perform'd on a certain day. After all, the *Nayk* of *Madure* having found means to get into the poſſeſſion of this countrey, left the *Portugueſe* in the full poſſeſſion of their juriſdiction over the *Parvas*, and of the free exerciſe of their religion, in which ſtate it continued till the year 1630, when the king of *Portugal* having ſent thither a governor, to clip the wings of the *Romiſh* clergy, who were grown two powerful there, this occaſion'd new troubles; for the *Parvas* being a zealous kind of people, and for the moſt part at the devotion of the prieſts, they were divided into two factions, during which inteſtine commotions the clergy did not forget to improve their authority, and to enrich themſelves at the expence of their flock, but the *Jentyves* or *Pagans* alſo began to encreaſe to ſuch a degree, that being become formidable to the *Parvas*, they often forc'd them to ſhelter themſelves againſt their forces in the neighbouring iſlands. Since that time the *Parvas* acknowledged the juriſdiction of the *Portugueſe* governor; each village has two judges, who are changed every year, they keep courts twice a week, and in conjunction with the *Petangiins* (who are hereditary officers) decide all controverſies of leſs moment; they raiſe the taxes, and are accountable once a year to the people for all their tranſactions; whilſt the *Portugueſe* were maſters here, the *Jentyves* or *Pagans* durſt not exact more taxes from the *Parvas* than was agreed for, unleſs they would ſee them go with wife and children to the neighbouring iſlands, from whence they did not return till they had obtain'd ſome conſiderable

1662. derable abatement; but of late years the *Parvas* having left off that custom, the *Jentyves* improve it to their advantage, and force them to pay three times as much as they used to do formerly.

The kingdom of the Nayk of Madure.

The kingdom of the *Nayk* of *Madure*, under whose jurisdiction the seven before-mention'd sea-ports are, borders to the west upon the kingdom of *Travankor* to the east upon the sea, and to the north-west upon the countrey of the *Nayk* of *Tanjaor* or *Tanjauwer*, betwixt the coast of *Malabar* near the cape *Comorin* and *Coromandel*; its whole extent being along the whole eastern gulph or coast opposite to *Ceylon* from the cape *Comorin* (where the coast of *Malabar* ends) to the town of *Bempaer* or the river *Ulton*, a tract of 75 leagues in length, and 30 in breadth. The sea-shore, commonly call'd the *Pearl-Coast*, from the many pearl-banks that are hereabouts, extends from south to north in length, and in some places about half a league deep into the countrey. The capital city and ordinary residence of the *Nayk* is *Madure*, five days journey to the north of *Koulang*; being adorn'd with many most magnificent *Pagodes*, or pagan temples, which have very high turrets gilt on the top. Along the coast of *Madure* neither grass or herb, or plant is to be seen, except thistles and house-leek; it having been found by experience, that the coco-trees would not thrive here no more than several other *Indian* trees; notwithstanding which they are sufficiently provided with all manner of necessaries from the circumjacent countrey, as well as from abroad, by the way of *Toutekoriin*; besides that, the sea-shore abounds in hares and partridges, the first of which resemble our rabbits, their flesh being tough, yet in taste like our hares. The flesh of the partridges, which have red legs and round bills here, is of an agreeable taste.

They have here mice as big as cats, which dare not approach them, for if they be pursued, they will settle upon a chair or chest, and sitting upright, fight and bite like dogs: They are in colour and shape like the *European* mice, except that they are without hair, and have a rough skin like an elephant. They will dig underneath the doors, and do considerable mischief to the merchandizes in the warehouses.

There is also here another sort of mice, red and much lesser than the first, but so fierce, that they will make the cats run before them.

This countrey also produces serpents, and divers other sorts of venomous creatures. One morning, as I was rising, I found the skin of a serpent sticking to one of the posts of my bedstead, which she had cast there the night before, without being perceived by me or any body else. In 1662. *October*, *November* and *December*, the western winds blow with such violence, the sand from the adjacent mountains to the shore, that you are not able to open your eyes. Much rain falls deeper in the countrey, and near the cape *Comorin*, but never at *Toutekoriin*, instead of which a thaw falls every night, which is very cold, and consequently, by the sudden alteration of the weather, very unwholesome; the winds being sometimes so excessive hot here, as if they did blow out of a fiery furnace; as long as these winds last, the inhabitants dare not go abroad into the fields for fear of being overwhelm'd by the sand.

The *Nayk* of the kingdom of *Madure* is master of several considerable countries, each of which are govern'd by a peculiar governor; besides which, there is one governor-general, who has the chief management of the whole kingdom, who ruled all our time the countrey, which was called *Boomalapelles*; besides the governors, each village has two judges, who are much respected by the inhabitants. The *Nayk* to secure himself of the fidelity of his governors, detains always their wives and children in a certain castle call'd *Zwela Baddy*, about seven leagues from *Madure*, under the guard of 300 eunuchs; neither are the husbands permitted to see them without peculiar licence from the *Nayk*, and are oblig'd to depart again in two or three days; some to avoid this inconveniency, content themselves with harlots. Most of the inhabitants of the countrey of *Madure* are *Jentyves* or pagans, (by some they are call'd *Badagas*) tho' some of them have been converted to the *Romish* faith by the *Portuguese*. The *Jentyves* are accounted good soldiers, yet much inferior to the *Malabars*, witness the wars the *Nayk* of *Tanigos*, tho' much inferior in power, wages against them.

There are three *Nayks* in this part of the *Indies*, *viz.* the *Nayk* of *Madure*, the *Nayk* of *Tanjaor*, by the *Dutch* call'd the *Tanjower* and *Tanjouwer*, and sometimes *Teaver*, and the *Nayk* of *Gingi*, otherwise called *Cingie*, or *Chengier*. The word *Nayk*, *Neyk*, or *Najeka*, signifies as much as a governor, vassal or viceroy, their predecessors having in ancient times been only governors of those countries they are now possessed of under the jurisdiction of the kings of *Vidia Najar* or *Bisnagar*, or *Narsinga*; but having revolted against their liege lord, each of them assumed the royal power and title. The *Nayk* of *Madure* had been for a considerable time in war with the *Nayk* of *Tanjaor*, and taken many

5 places

1662. places from him: At my time the war was renewed with more vigour than ever; and the Nayk of *Tanjaor* having gathered a great army, attack'd the *Nayk* of *Madure* so briskly, that he took from him in a few days all the places he had conquered from him before. The army of the *Nayk* of *Madure* being much disheartened by the victories of their enemies, the *Madure* sent to me, to *Koulang*, his chief governor, desiring assistance from the company; but as it was not our interest to engage on any side, I excused it as handsomely as I could.

The Pearl-Banks. Betwixt the coast of *Madure*, where the seven villages are, and the isle of *Ceylon*, are divers famous pearl banks by the sea, for which reason this tract is called the *Pearl-Fishery.* These pearl-banks are properly rocks of white coral stone, which sometimes are covered with sand; on these rocks, the oyster-shells, containing the pearls, are fastened, but in what manner no body knows. Some of those banks are about 12 or 13 fathoms, and others at 15 fathoms distance from the shore, so that they can scarce be seen from thence: Some of those banks are five, six or seven fathom under water. The oysters live six years, after which time the shells open and the pearls are lost; of which I have seen several that were shown me by the divers. These pearl-banks are search'd every year to see whether the shells are come to their full maturity: This is commonly done in *October*, when the weater is calm, and the sea clear hereabouts. After they are convinced that the said oysters are come to their full perfection, the time of pearl-fishing is appointed and proclaimed throughout the countrey, so that the merchants resort thither from the other part of the *Indies*, nay, from *Arabia* and *Turkey* it self, who set up their tents near the sea-side, to buy the pearls.

Pearl-fishing how perform'd. They fish for pearls, or rather the oyster-shells containing the pearls, in certain boats called *Toniis*, being about 28 foot long, (of these you shall see 3 or 400 at time,) each of which has 7 or 8 stones, which serve instead of anchors, and 5, 6 or 7, nay sometimes 8 divers, who are to dive one after another. These divers are quite naked, being covered only with a kind of thin wastecoat; they have each a net hanging down from the neck, and gloves on their hands, wherewith they are to pick the oysters from the rocks; each of them has also a stone of about a foot in length, and 50 pound weight, to make him dive the swifter: This stone has a hole on the top, wherewith it is fasten'd to a rope; when they are going to dive, they set their foot into a kind of a stirrup, laying hold with their left-hand of the rope, the other end of which is held by one in the boat, stopping their nose with the right-hand to hold in their breath, and so go to the bottom; where they are no sooner come, but they give a signal, by pulling the rope, for those in the boat to pull up the stone. This done, to work they go, and scraping the shells from the rocks, fill their nets, and then pull again the rope, when those in the boat draw up the nets first, and soon after the divers, who are succeeded continually by fresh ones. These divers can hold their breath four times as long as other people; they are obliged to dive from 3 fathoms to 15, being not able to hold their breath any longer. These boats commonly go to sea every morning by break of day, with the land-winds, and return in the afternoon with the sea-winds. Those who equip those boats, hire both the divers and the rest of the boat's crew at a certain price *per diem*, like as we do our day-labourers. All the oyster-shells are brought ashore, and there laid up in a great heap, till the pearl fishery is over, which begins immediately after *October*, and continues all the *November* and *December*, which makes the oysters smell very strong, and sometimes occasions distempers. The pearl-fishing being over, a wooden house is erected for the company and the *Nayk*, where each receives his share, the boats being obliged to fish one day for the *Nayk*, and another for the company; and these take care that they be not disturbed in their fishing, the governor and two judges being every day near the sea-shore, to decide such differences as arise betwixt them. At last the oyster-shells are opened in the before-mention'd house, in the presence of certain commissioners; every oyster-shell does not contain pearls, nay, the most are either without any, or have at least very small ones: On the other hand, some shells contain five, six, seven, nay eight pearls apiece. Some of these pearls are found in the liquor, some in the flesh of the oysters, others, but few, are fasten'd to the shells, of which last I keep several by me. The pearls being all taken out of the shells, are put into sifts of different holes, and according to their different sizes are sold to the fairest bidder: The pearl-dust is bought and sold by the *Dutch*. They stew and eat the flesh of these oysters, but it is somewhat rank and hardy, not comparable in taste to our *English* oysters. They give the pearls a glance by rubbing them with salt and powder'd rice. Out of the shells they make a very fine mortar. *Pearl-dust.*

They have two sorts of pearl-dust, the old and the new: The new pearl dust is

1662. search'd after daily by the women among the dirt and rubbish of the oysters: The old pearl-dust is dug out upon the very brink of the sea-shore, dirt, sand and all, sometimes six, seven or eight foot deep; this they let dry altogether in the sun, and by degrees the dust being blown away by the wind, the black pearl-dust remains behind, which they bring to those in small parcels, who have given them some money beforehand. This pearl-dust being the worst of the two, and of no great value, these poor wretches can scarce get a half-penny a day for their labour, a wretched gain indeed, but sufficient to keep them from starving in this countrey.

The horns of Siankos.

Besides the pearl-oyster, they also catch on this coast certain horns call'd *Siankos* by the inhabitants, being in shape long, round and thick, and very white; out of these they make bracelets and thumb-rings, which they make use of in drawing their bows, being valued much beyond Ivory. This product of the sea is found at 8 or 12 fathom depth, in a tract of the sea of about 10 leagues in length, from the coast of *Vyraamdes Laam* to *Ilha Doce*. They begin to fish for it in the middle of *December* till the middle of *May*, when the sea hereabouts beginning to be unclear, the divers cannot without great danger go to the bottom. Among these sea-horns they now and then, (tho' scarce once in 100 years) meet with one they call the *King's-Horn*, being not to be distinguish'd from the rest, except by the opening, which is on the contrary side, being red within and green without; they are said to swim before the rest, which follow them like their king; for which reason it is, that the kings of *Golconda*, and several other *Indian* kings are accounted out of one of these horns, which makes them to be in great esteem here, especially among the *Jentyves*, who will sometimes give 800 reals for such a horn. Whilst I was hereabouts, a certain fisherman dream'd that he had taken a king's-horn, which he telling to one of his comrades, they agreed, that they would go immediately to try, and divide the booty; accordingly they did, and he who had dreamed the night before, catch'd a king's-horn, but refusing to give to his comrade his share, they went before the judges, who were obliged to decide in favour of the dreamer, the other having no witnesses to prove his bargain. I bought the same horn afterwards for 170 reals, and was offered 20 reals gain immediately after, by one of the judges. These *Siankos* are sold at a dear rate at *Bengal*, where they have a way of polishing them, that they shine with a most lovely white, much beyond any ivory: They make bracelets and other ornaments of them. 1662.

As the fishing of those horns is one of the main subsistence of the inhabitants on this coast, so they must be carefully look'd after, that under pretence of fishing for them, they don't dive for oysters, for which reason certain people are maintained to watch them. I remember they once brought up a moorish boat belonging to *Kalitpatnam*, which under pretence of fishing for *Siankos*, had been found among the pearl-banks; when they came before me, I found upon a strict examination, that extreme poverty had inforced them thereunto, and so dismissed them for that time. Some are of opinion, that the pearl-dust dug on the sea-shore, has lain there ever since the isle of *Ceylon* and the *Maldive* islands, were torn from the continent, when the pearl-shells were cast up by the floods here, and opening themselves, were consumed by degrees, leaving the pearls under ground. The pearl-dust is gather'd by the men during those intervals, when they can't go a fishing, but when they are abroad at sea their wives and children do it in their stead. Abundance of divers are devoured by the sharks, against which they pretend to defend themselves by certain incantations, notwithstanding they are christians.

The author retires to Koulang.

After I had settled my accounts at *Toutekoriin*, I prepared for my journey to *Koulang* cross the mountains of *Balligate*; and accordingly as I told you, set out the 19th of *May* 1665, under a guard of some soldiers, and with an attendance of some porters to carry my baggage and provisions, there being no inns by the way, and in many places not the least thing to be got for money. We had scarce travell'd a day but were met by a troop of *Malabar* robbers, arm'd with bows and arrows ready to let fly at us: They had already laid hold of two slaves, who were carrying some *Persian* wine, but seeing the soldiers ready to discharge their firelocks among them, they thought it their best way to retire, and finding us continually upon our guard, quite to leave us at last. We pass'd that dreadful ridge of mountains call'd *Balligate*, extending 120 leagues in length, and is cover'd with a very fine red sand, which being as light as dust, is in *October*, *November* and *December* blown by the continual strong west winds as far as the isle of *Ceylon*, a tract of at least 50 leagues; whence it is probable, that these mountains are not so high now as they were in former ages. When the sun casts its rays upon this red land, the reflection thereof appears most dreadful to the eyes in the sky, which seems to be all on fire. This high ridge of mountains

The mountains of Balligate.

1662. mountains does likewise occasion most surprizing alterations in the season; so that whilst on the north side of the cape *Comorin*, it is winter during the months of *May*, *June*, *July*, *August*, and *September*; it is summer at the same time on the south-side of that cape; on one side you meet with continual tempests, thunder and lightning, whilst the other enjoys an agreeable and lovely season. About that time black clouds are gathering upon these mountains by the winds, which break out into very hard and sudden rains, occasioning great water floods, by the overflowing of the rivers, which are oftentimes thereby choak'd up with sand to that degree, that they are rendered unnavigable for a considerable time after.

Comes to Koulang. Having at last passed the mountains I arrived the 25th of *May* at *Koulang*, whereabouts I found all the fields under water. Pursuant to the orders I had received, to draw the city of *Koulang* into a narrower compass, and to fortify it on the land-side with one wall and two demibastions, I ordered all the houses, churches, trees, and what else stood in our way to be cut or pull'd down; and 30000 stones, each of two foot long and one broad, to be cut out of the quarries; so that the first foundation of these fortifications being laid the 1st of *July*, the same was continued with all imaginable diligence. In the mean while *Goes to* Cochin. I went in an inland bark to *Cochin*, by the way of *Kalkolang*, to confer with the governor *Kolster* how to regulate the factories of *Koulang*, *Kalkolang* and *Karnopoly*, to the best advantage of the company.

After a stay of three days at *Cochin*, in my return to *Koulang*, we were surprized by so violent a tempest, that we were forced to leave the bark and to get ashore, but the next day the violence of the wind being much abated, we prosecuted our journey to *Koulang*, where I arrived the 4th day after I left *Cochin*.

The war among some of the *Indian* kings continuing as yet, it was generally reported, that the king of *Travankoor* (who was then at *Mansassi*, tho' the queen resided at the same time at *Koulang*) was marching with a considerable force to attack the fort of *Kalkolang*, whereupon I sent our factor with letters from our chief director Mr. *Kolster* to the king, to know the reason of this enterprize: But he was forced to return without any other answer from his courtiers, than that the king being employed in his devotions, no body could be admitted into his presence till that time was expired, which was likely to hold for some time; however the army did remain all the time in its former camp, without committing any hostilities: In the mean while I had taken effectual care to provide for the security of *Koulang*, the walls advancing apace, and being in such forwardness, that we hoped in a little time to bring them to perfection; this being the only thing that stay'd me at *Koulang*; for as the time of my contract with the company began to come near a period, I began to make preparations for my return into *Holland*. But Mr. *Jacob Hustart* being gone to *Batavia*, and Mr. *Goens* put in his place, I happened to have some difference with him concerning the government of *Toutekoriin*, which rose to that height, that he ordered me immediately from *Koulang* to the city of *Kolombo* in the isle of *Ceylon*, leaving captain *Van Reede* governor of *Koulang*. *The author is sent to* Kolombo.

The season for sea-voyages (which must be exactly observed in these parts) being then expired, I was forced to travel for above 60 leagues along the sea-shore, with no small difficulty, there being no such thing as an inn to be met with hereabouts, or any other convenient lodgings, unless you meet with some charitable popish priest or other, who will receive you into his house, most of the inhabitants along this shore being *Roman Catholicks*, who have here and there a small church. However, after some troublesome days journey I came safely to *Toutekoriin*, where I found the *Mary* yacht ready to transport me to *Kolombo*, where I arrived the next day, *viz.* the 18th of *Sept.* 1666, I stay'd here above a whole year; when I resolv'd to go aboard the *Brederoo* yacht bound for *Batavia*, where I landed the 20th of *August* 1667, without meeting with any thing remarkable at sea. I continued for three whole years at *Batavia*, without being engaged in the companies service, and in 1670 return'd thence into *Holland*. During those three years, I had sufficient opportunity to take a full view of the city, both within and without, in which I was so curious, as not only to make draughts of all its publick structures, but also of such plants and trees as grow in and about that city; tho' to confess the truth, the same could oftentimes not be undertaken without great hazard, as well from the wild beasts, as form the barbarous *Javanese*, so that I durst not venture far out of the town without a good guard; but before I proceed to give you a description of the living creatures, trees, fruits and plants, and of the city of *Batavia* itself, in the isle of *Java*, it will be requisite I should give you an account before-hand of the situation of this great island. *Comes to* Kolombo.

The isle of Great Java. The isle known generally by the name of *Great Java*, to distinguish it from the *Lesser Java*, otherwise call'd *Bati*, lies six degrees

1662. degrees to the south of the line, directly opposite to the south-point of the isle of *Sumatra*, from which it is separated only from the streights of *Sunda*, where the same is not above four or five leagues over. To the north lies the isle of *Borneo*, betwixt which and this isle there is a convenient passage for small vessels; to the east it has the isle of *Bati*, or the *Lesser Java*, from which it is divided by the channel of *Balambuam*, and to the south by the main ocean. Its length from the streights of *Sunda* to the channel of *Balambuam*, *viz.* from E. to W. inclining however a little to the S. and N. is about 130 or 140 leagues; its breadth is very different, but the whole circumference is computed at 300 leagues; The north coast of *Java* has abundance of very commodious creeks, bays, harbours, and goodly towns, with many little islands near the shore. In former times the isle of *Java* had as many petty kings as there were cities, but now adays it is divided into two kingdoms only, the one of which is under the jurisdiction of the emperor of *Mataram*, the other under the king of *Bantam*. The first is in the possession of the eastern and greatest part of the isle, the other of the western and lesser part; for since the emperor of *Mataram* (call'd also the emperor of *Great Java* by the *Dutch*) had once found means to subdue his petty neighbours, he soon extended his conquests all over the eastern parts of this isle: The emperor who reign'd all the time of my being there, was a young prince named *Sousouhounan Ingelaga*, the son of *Sulthan Mahomet*.

Java has two kingdoms.

Unto one or other of these two potent princes all the rest are obliged to pay homage, tho' there be also as yet remaining some petty sovereignties along the sea-coasts, besides what belongs to the city of *Batavia*.

Cities of Java.

In the eastern parts of *Batavia* are the cities *Balambuam*, *Panarukan*, *Passarvan*, *Joartan*, *Surabaaya*, *Brandaon*, *Sydayo*, *Tubaon*, *Kajaon*, *Japare*, *Pati*, *Dauma*, *Samarang* and *Mataram*, the residence of the emperor of *Java*. To the west, near the sea are *Taggel*, *Charabaon*, *Dermayaon*, *Manukaon*, *Karavaon* and *Batavia*; of the coast of which we intend to give you a short but exact account. About 10 or 12 leagues from *Batavia* is the famous city of *Bantam*, where the *English* have a factory, and a considerable traffick.

Manners and customs of the Javanese.

The *Javanese* are a barbarous, proud, and fierce nation, of a brown colour, with flat faces, and thin, short, coal black hair, large eye-brows, and large cheeks. They boast themselves to be descended from the ancient *Chinese*, unto whom they resemble in some respects, having very small eyes with large eye-lids. The men are very robust and strong limb'd, and wel fitted for the war; the women are but smal. The men wear a piece of callicoe wrap'd two or three times round their bodies; people of fashion have them with gold flowers or streaks. The women wear it from under their arm-pits down to their knees, all the rest bare. They marry sometimes two or three wives, and perhaps keep divers concubines besides, according to their ability. Lying and cheating is a daily practice with them. Those living near the sea-side are for the most part *Mahometans*, which was introduced there about 150 years ago. In the inland countries they are generally *Pagans*, abstaining from feeding upon any living creatures. When they are to consult about matters of moment it is done in the night time. 1662.

Their clothing.

Religion.

Its fertility.

The isle of *Java* is very fertile, tho' a great part thereof be not known hitherto; it has very high mountains, reaching to the very clouds, witness the pepper mountain on the south-side of the island; it has likewise impassable forests and wildernesses; but to the north, betwixt *Batavia* and *Bantam*, is a very populous countrey, full of rice fields, and all sorts of tame and wild creatures; hereabouts also is salt and pepper to be found, but not so good as that at *Malabar*, besides most other sorts of *Indian* fruits, which are sold in great plenty at *Batavia*. They abound also in fish, are well stor'd with hogs, oxen, sheep and other tame beasts, the flesh whereof is of a very good taste; fowl both wild tame they have in great plenty; but the woods have also large tigers, rhinoceros's and divers other wild beasts; in the rivers you see also often *Crocodiles*, call'd *Kaymans* by the *Indians*.

The air and seasons.

The air or climate of *Batavia* is in my opinion as temperate and healthy as any place whatever in the *Indies*; the east and west winds blowing all the year long along the shore, besides the ordinary land and sea winds. The seasons of the year run here in the same manner as in *Europe*, except that the sun passes twice a year directly over their heads; the most agreeable season begins in *May*, which continues with continual breezes from the east, and a very serene sky till *November*; when the winter season approaching it rains sometimes continually for three or four days without intermission, which sets all the low grounds under water, which however has this convenience, that it kills and washes away all insects, which else would prove very noxious to the fruits. This season ends about *May*, when the dark clouds beginning to

1662. to disperse, the sky assumes its former serenity; in *December* the west winds blow so violently, that there is no going by sea here; in *February* it is changeable weather, intermix'd with sudden storms of thunder and lightning; in *March* they begin to sow, and this month produces some fruit; in *June* is the most agreeable time of the year. In *July* the sugar and rice begins to ripen; in *September* it is the best time, and the *October* affords them plenty of all sorts of fruits.

The happy temperature of the climate produces such plenty of all sorts of necessaries, that there are very few countries that can compare with this island; the pleasant river rising in the mountains divides itself into many branches, and waters the circumjacent countrey, and afterwards recollecting its channels, passes thro' the midst of *Batavia*, (which it divides in two parts) and there exonerates into the sea. 1662.

Batavia. The city of *Batavia*, which got its name many years ago from the *Dutch* after their first establishment in those parts, was first, and is now by the *Javanese* and *Chinese* call'd *Kalakka*; from the fruit of a palm or cocotree, which grows very plentiful hereabouts; the fruit of which the *Javanese* call *Kalakka*. The *Indians* call it *Jacata*, derived likewise from a certain fruit call'd *Jaccas* by the *Indians*, and *Schrookzak* by the *Dutch*. Not long before the *Mahometans* settled in the *Indies*, *Batavia* was no more than an open village, inhabited by *Pagans*; at first it was surrounded only with a row of palladoes of bamboo canes, but as it became more populous, the inhabitants began to wage war against the king of *Bantam*, and some other neighbouring princes, and that with very good success. The city of *Batavia* lies at 5 deg. 50 min. off southern latitude, at the north-side of the isle of *Java*, in a large but fenny plain before it to the south; it is surrounded with abundance of small islands, and to the north or landside with woods and high mountains. It is divided into two parts by a river, is of a quadrangular figure, fortified with a wall of stone, and 22 bastions; the names whereof are *Amsteldam*, *Middelburgh*, *Delft*, *Rotterdam*, *Hoorn*, *Enkahuissen*, *Vienna*, *Gelderland*, *Katzenelbogden*, *Orange*, the *New-gate*, *Hollandia*, *Diest*, *Nassaw*, *Zealand*, *Utrecht*, *Friesland*, *Overysel*, *Groningen*, *Zewburgh*, *Kuilenburgh*, and the *Middlepoint*. The ditch underneath the wall was in the year 1670, surrounded with a quick-set hedge of thorns; it has four great gates, two whereof are very stately and artificially built by the famous *John Listing*, on the south-side; the first 1630, and the other 1657. The third gate

1662. gate is on the east-side call'd *Rotterdam*, and the fourth call'd *Utrecht* on the west-side. The city of *Batavia* is situate in a bay, extending to the east as far as the cape of *Karovant*, and to the west as far as the cape call'd the *Rough Point*, towards *Bantam*, which lies on the same shore, about twelve leagues from *Batavia*. 1662

The harbour. Both within and without this bay lie about 17 or 18 islands, upon which the violence of the winds and waves being broken and check'd, this renders the road of *Batavia* one of the safest harbours of the whole world, being able to contain above 1000 vessels at once; small vessels and barks lie commonly close under the banks of the river, where they may lie without anchors in a muddy bottom; the river is lined with stones on both sides as far as the boom, which is shut up every night at nine a clock, and guarded by a good number of soldiers. besides which, there is cut a channel out of the main river, for the reception of smaller vessels; no vessel passes the boom without paying a certain custom, every vessel that fetches salt pays a real, and those that carry stones two reals. The ditch without the wall is very broad and deep, and sometimes rises so high, that some of the lowermost streets without the city are laid under water; all the buildings of this city are well contriv'd, most even of the private houses having handsome gardens, well planted with fruit trees and plants and flowers, adorn'd with pearls, springs, pumps, &c.

Its streets. All the streets of this city run in a streight line, most of them being 30 foot broad; and on both sides near the houses paved with bricks; there are eight streets, which are all well built and inhabited, among which the *Princes-Street* is the chiefest, beginning at the middle point of the castle, and running in a strait line to the town-house, having on each side a cross street. Next to this is the *Lords-street*, beginning on the north-side over-against the castle, reaching in a direct line to the new gate. The first cross street on the east-side has got the name of *John Tirment*, who built abundance of houses in this street. The second is call'd the *Market-Street*, opposite to which lies the third call'd the *Petawins-Street*: The fourth is call'd the *Street of the Hospital.* As you come out of the castle at the first entrance into the *Princes-Street* is the *Princes-Lane* on the left-hand. These are on the east-side of the river; we will now pass over to the western side; the bank of which is planted with pleasant trees, and adorn'd with houses all in a straight line as far as the *Diest-Gate*. The first street on this side is

1662. call'd the *Gentlemans-Street*, being divided into two streets by a gracht that comes cross it: The second street comes crosswise thro' this part of the city, beginning at the *Utrecht Bastion*, from whence it has got the name of the *Utrecht-Street*. But now we must look back and take a view of the *Burghwalls* or *Grachts* (being streets with water channels in them) of these there are no less than 15 among which the *Tygers Gracht* is the most stately and most pleasant, both for the goodliness of its buildings, and the ornament of its streets, which afford a very agreeable shadow to those that pass along the street; the channel is edged and lined with stones from the bottom, over which are four stone bridges, sustain'd by as many high stone arches, twelve foot broad each; beside which, there is a wooden bridge at one end. The inward *Gracht* behind the *Carpenters-wharf* (where is also the founding-house) has three bridges; next to this is the *Kaymans Gracht* with four bridges. The first *Gracht* which runs crosswise, is the *city's Inward Burghwall*, having only one bridge: Next to this the *Herb Gracht*, without any bridge at all. The *Sesons Gracht* extending from the *Middle Point* directly to the *Rotterdam-Gate*, with six bridges, and the *Inward Gracht* with one bridge only. These are all the *Burghwalls* and *Grachts* on the east-side; now we must come to those on the west-side. The first is the *Gentlemans Gracht*, with three bridges; the second is call'd the *Rhinoceroses Gracht*, having likewise three bridges; the third is the *City's Inward Gracht*, with three bridges. The first *Gracht* running crosswise to the north, is the *City's Inward Gracht*; the second faces the *Carpenters Wharf*, and is called the *Javanese Gracht*; and the third is call'd the *Chinese Gracht*, having only one bridge. The fourth *Gracht* which runs crosswise, begins at the bastion call'd *Friesland*, and ends at the new bridge near the *Fish-Market*, having three bridges; last of all, the *City's Inward Gracht* with one bridge. These are all the *Grachts* and *Burghwalls* within the city, over which are laid 56 bridges, most of which are sustain'd by large stone arches, not to mention here the wooden draw-bridges which are over the *Gracht* without the walls. At my first coming to *Batavia* I lodg'd upon the *Tygers Gracht*, so that having sufficient opportunity to take a draught of it, I thought fit to insert it here.

The publick buildings of the city.

Among the publick buildings of this city, the church call'd the *Cross-Church* claims the precedency, being built in 1640, of solid stone: In the midst of the church stands the steeple, being exceedingly beautify'd with iron-work. It has but one bell, which is only rung before church-time; the stone edgings in the front of the church are artificially carved, and adorned on the top with *Cherubims*. But time which defaces all things, and the air, which is much sharper here than in *Europe*, has in a few years wrought a considerable change in this magnificent structure. The pulpit and seats of the chief men here are very finely wrought and adorned with iron-work and ebony-wood. The vestry is of the same workmanship. This structure is very lightsome and lofty, within being adorned with five clear branches of brass brought thither from *Holland*. In the other part of the city, the foundation of the new church was laid during my stay there, and before my departure the brick-work was almost finished. In the year 1644, there was also a church built in the castle, of an octagonal figure, being very light within, and flat on the top; the floor covered with well polish'd white and blue stones neatly done: The glass of the lanthorn on the top was of the best kind, and the pews of the church carv'd very artificially and made of the best kind of wood the *Indies* afford. 1662. *The cross church.*

The Town House.

The *Town-House* stands very near in the centre of the city, in a spacious place, being built of brick in 1652. It is two stories high, and you ascend into the second by a pair of winding stairs. The great gate is exactly in the middle of the structure, artificially wrought, of the *Corinthian* order, over which is a balcony or gallery of stone, unto which you enter out of the upper-hall. When criminals are to be try'd, a scaffold is erected before the *Town-House*. The windows of this building are in proportion very high and lofty, finely glazed, and on the out-side guarded with iron-work. In this house the courts of justice are kept; here is the meeting of the *Shepen* or senators, as also of the masters of the hospitals, and of the overseers of other places; as also of the court for the direction of military affairs within the city. The inward court is enclosed with a high wall, and a double row of stone-pillars; here the officers of justice have their habitations, and the prison-keeper with his attendants on the west-end of it. It extends from the *Tygers Gracht* to the *Lords-Street*.

The hospital for the sick.

The hospital for the sick stands upon the bank of the great river, which runs through the city, betwixt the *New-Gate* and the *Diest-Gate*. Here such as are sick, and have not wherewithal to provide for themselves, are entertained and cured, there being sometimes 200 or 300 to be seen here at a time, who are all provided with neat lodgings, beddings and other conveniencies. In

the

The Hospital for the Sick.

1662. the out-houſes are the apartments for the overſeers and their ſervants, for the doctor, apothecary, ſurgeon, miniſter, caſh-keeper, treaſurer and others, who are to keep the houſe clean and look after the ſick; all theſe are plentifully maintain'd by the company. Beſides thoſe before-mention'd, three perſons of note belonging to the company are conſtituted overſeers, who take their turns every week, and ſee that every thing be done as it ought to be, and eſpecially whether any of them are recovered ſo far as to be fit for ſervice. Behind it is a ſquare encloſed with a high wall, and planted with trees, which ſerves for a walking place for thoſe who are upon their recovery; and a door with a wooden bridge reaching a good way into the river, is alſo made for the taking of the freſh air of the river. The miniſter, who is appointed to viſit the ſick, ſays prayers every morning and evening, when a bell is rung; every ſunday there is a ſermon, where all thoſe that are able are obliged to be preſent.

The Spin-Houſe. For the encouraging of virtue, and ſuppreſſing of debauchery in lewd women, a ſpin-houſe has been erected here, having no windows or proſpect but only on the eaſt-ſide towards the *Burghwall*, where certain iron-rails are made in the gate, with wooded ſhutters within, which are ſhut and bolted as often as the overſeer pleaſes. 1662. Here the women are reclaim'd from their lewdneſs by keeping them continually at work, under the tuition of a governeſs whoſe buſineſs is to look after the Houſe, and to ſet them their taſk, which if they miſs to perform, they are ſure to be ſcourged. For the reſt, there two members of the ſenate conſtituted on purpoſe for the government of this houſe, whoſe buſineſs is to be preſent there every ſunday at the ſermon that is held there, for the reclaiming thoſe lewd creatures from their ill courſe of life. If they commit any miſdemeanor which cannot be corrected by ſcourge, they are puniſh'd by the ordinary court of juſtice.

Upon the very brink of the river are built two ſlaughter-houſes or fleſh-halls, *Slaughter-houſes or fleſh-halls.* ſuſtain'd by wooden piles, by which means they may with conveniency throw the excrements of the kill'd beaſts into the river. They kill twice a week, each butcher having his peculiar ſtall, where he ſells his meat at ſuch a price as the magiſtrates ſhall think fit to ſet, tho' moſt of them find means to ſell it as dear as they can. Whilſt I was there beef was ſold at the rate of four pence *per* pound, and pork at the ſame rate; but mutton being moſt eſteem'd was ſold dearer. All the beaſts that are to be kill'd

muſt

1662. must be taxed by the farmer of the excise upon cattle; according to which the butcher is obliged to pay the tenth-penny excise: But if the farmer should be extravagant in his taxation, the butcher who thinks himself injur'd, may appeal to the general judgment of all the butchers, who if they do not agree to the price set by the farmer, he is obliged to tax it himself at his own set rate.

The hall for the sale of stuffs. On the west-side of that spacious place which faces the *Town-House*, is a certain structure, in which are sold all sorts of cloaths ready made, as also stuffs and callicoes, white and painted, besides divers other commodities exposed to sail there, by the *Chinese*. These have here their peculiar shops, for each of which they pay 3 crowns *per* month. The whole building is of wood, being divided into 5 walks or galleries, having shops on each side; and as many doors from without, which are kept open day and night, because the shop-keepers don't put up their commodities till very late at night, and lay them out again early in the morning, with a great deal of curiosity, to invite the buyers to give them a good price, at which the *Chinese* are very dextrous and quick, so that unless you be upon guard, you are over-reach'd before you are aware of it; however, these little shops have this conveniency, that you may furnish your self here at an easier rate, and that all at once, with abundance of small things, which you can't buy so conveniently at the great shops where they will not be satisfied with a small gain. 1662.

The city stables. On the east-side of the *Town-House* is a goodly structure, fitted up for stables for horses, being all of brick-work without, and provided with racks, mangers, and partitions, and paved with stones, so that the horse-dung may be removed and wash'd away with all imaginable conveniency. The place where they manage their horses is very airy and well situated, having two doors, one whereof leads to the city's *Binne Gracht*, for the conveniency of watering and washing the horses. In this stable are kept, besides the coach and cart-horses, above 100 saddle-horses, that are managed daily by certain persons kept for that purpose. Their best horses are the *Arabian* and *Persian* horses, which they buy here at a high rate, 200 crowns being a common price for an indifferent *Persian* horse, the best being not to be got for money. It is worth observation, that the *Persians* train up and manage their horses without blows, whereas our managers are used to make use of whips and spurs, which makes them unfit for the due management of those horses. Abundance of horses are also brought to *Batavia*

1662. *via* from *Japara* in the iſle of *Java*; but theſe are not comparable to the *Perſian* horſes: Some of theſe however are very tractable, if well handled from the beginning, but many of them are broken mouthed before they come to *Batavia:* The natives being uſed to ride their horſes with a light hunting-bridle, they are apt to toſs up their heads, when they are rid afterwards with a curb-bridle, to prevent which, our managers faſten a leather ſtring to the girt under their belly, the other end of which being buckled to the bridle, makes them keep their heads ſteady. 1662.

The Chineſe hoſpital for ſick and aged perſons.

On the *Rhinoceroſes Gracht*, near the ſpin-houſe, is the *Chineſe* hoſpital for ſick and aged perſons, built of brick, and divided into convenient apartments, and a pleaſant court to walk in: It was built in the year 1640. In this houſe ſuch as are ſick and ſuperannuated, and have not wherewithal to ſubſiſt, are received and maintain'd. For the maintenance of which a certain duty is laid upon marriages and burials; as alſo upon actors of plays, farces, and ſuch like ſhews. And as, beſides this, many of the rich *Chineſe*, either by voluntary contributions or legacies, give great encouragement to this houſe; it is provided with a conſiderable revenue. The whole management of this houſe is committed to two *Hollanders*, and as many *Chineſe*, who have a ſecretary to keep their accounts.

The hoſpital for children.

At the extremity of the weſt-end of the *Rhinoceroſes Gracht*, you ſee the hoſpital wherein poor orphans are maintain'd and educated, being of brick, with convenient lodgings for the ſervants of the houſe: It has hitherto no ſettled revenue, being maintain'd by the voluntary contributions of well-diſpoſed people.

The houſe of the artiſans.

In the eaſt-corner is the houſe wherein are lodged all the artiſans belonging to the company, as carpenters, bricklayers, gun-founders, ſtone-cutters, glaſs-makers, turners, ingineers, ſeal-cutters, pewterers, painters, &c. all which are diſpoſed into their proper quarters, under the direction of three *Hollanders* appointed by the company. Beſides the ſlaves belonging to the houſe, there is alſo a chirurgeon and a ſchoolmaſter; the laſt of which is obliged to ſay prayers every night; at which all are obliged to be preſent under a certain forfeiture. In this houſe the ſurveyor-general has his lodgings, which are very handſome, and keeps two clerks under him. He overſees the workmen. In this houſe alſo are maintained ſuch criminals as have been condemned to the chains, who are kept here.

1662. here to hard labour, and well guarded. Every night at nine a clock, the doors of the houſe are ſhut up, and a guard of ſlaves is placed to prevent any diſorders which might happen among ſo great a number of people of different callings. I had for ſome time my lodgings in this houſe; and here it was that I firſt made the draught, and afterwards made the deſcription of *Batavia.* The wharf belonging to this houſe is only fitted for the building of ſmall yachts and boats, ſuch as are uſed only in the road for the loading or unloading of ſhips: But ſhips of bulk are built at the iſle of *Ormus*, about a league to the weſt of *Batavia*, where are conſiderable magazines for ropes, and other implements belonging to ſhips, which are defended by certain fortifications. 1662.

The Rope-Alley. The *Rope-Alley*, where they are employed in twiſting ropes, is likewiſe in one corner of the city, oppoſite to the carpenter's wharf, being planted with large nut-trees, which afford an agreeable ſhade to the rope-makers. A little beyond it to the weſt you ſee the pack-houſes of the company; wherein are laid up pepper, cinnamon, nutmegs, cloves, mace, &c. The overſeer has a goodly habitation for his own uſe.

The LODGINGS of the ARTISANS belonging to the COMPANY.

The magazine of rice. Not far from thence, *viz.* near the baſtion call'd *Amſterdam*, ſtands the company's magazine of rice, a large ſtructure, having a door looking to the water-ſide, where ſhips may be laden and unladen. It was built in my time 1670, of brick-work. There is a ſquare encloſed with a wall at the inward wharf, where the receivers and other ſervants of the company have their habitations.

The *Prawenhouſe*, ſo call'd from the word *Praw*, which in the *Malayan* tongue ſignifies a *boat or ſmall veſſel*, ſtands upon the brink of the river, for conveniency of ſuch ſmall boats as are built or refitted there; here ſeveral ſhipwrights, and a good number of ſeamen have their quarters, the laſt being obliged to be ready upon call, wherever they are ordered to row by the deputy governor, under whoſe tuition they are. On the eaſt-ſide of the little wharf, the overſeer has a ſmall houſe. Having thus given you an account of the publick ſtructures of this city, with ſuch draughts thereof as time and opportunity would permit us to take, we will now proceed to the four great markets of *Batavia*, and begin with the fiſh-market.

The fiſh market. The fiſh-market is on the weſtern-ſide of the great river, being ſuſtained by ſtrong wooden

1662. wooden piles, and covered on top with pan-tiles. Oppofite to it is the dwelling place of the *Aflager* (or *Outroper)* where the fifher boats are oblig'd to ftop, and their cargo is fold immediately by publick fale, to the faireft bidder; the fifhmongers are generally *Chinefe*, each of which has his own ftall, for which he pays two reals *per* month. The *Outroper* pays ready money to the fifhermen for what they fell to thefe *Chinefe*, who allow him twopence in the crown, and are obliged to repay it at a fet time. Here you may furnifh yourfelf with fea, river, or fhell-fifh, according to your own pleafure, from 10 a clock in the morning till four in the afternoon; when the fifhmongers leave their ftalls here, and fell the remnants near the river-fide behind the flefh-hall.

The rice or corn market. The rice or corn market is adjoining to the former, or rather oppofite to it at the north-end; being built after the fame manner, except that it has no ftalls or banks; here you meet with grains of all forts which are fold here, according to the market price, by a certain fmall meafure called *Ganting*, containing about 13 or 14 pounds of rice, which is commonly fold for fixpence. He that has the overfight of the market and meafures, has a houfe at one end; his bufinefs among other things is to fet the mark upon the meafures and weights, which is done twice a year; *viz.* in *January* and *July*, at the town-houfe, in the prefence of two *fhepemen* or aldermen. They pay two-pence for each mark. 1662.

The fowl-market. Near the new bridge, as you pafs along the river-fide to the *Crofs-Church*, is the fowl-market, where the *Mardiikers* and *Topaffen* (a kind of negroes) fell all forts of fowl in great plenty, fo that you may buy an ordinary pullet for three-pence, but the

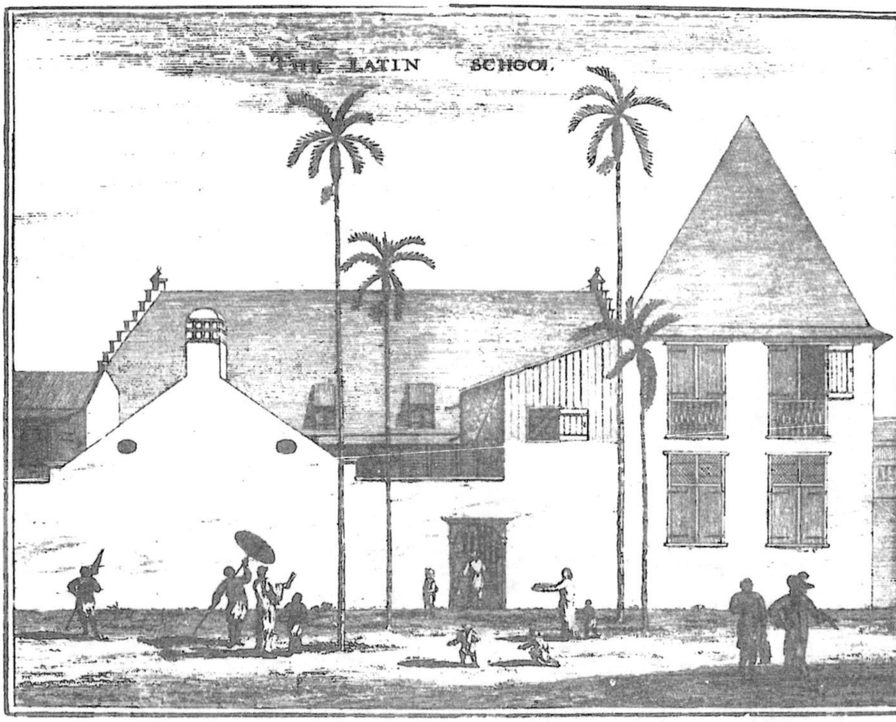

beft fort are dearer. In this market you fee many huts, in which they fell dried fifh, eggs and courfe earthen ware.

The fruit market. The fruit-market begins at the new-bridge, extending by the river-fide to the *Middlepoint*. Here you meet with all forts of fruits and herbs, fold by the *Chinefe* and *Negroes*, who pay the 10th penny excife. From four a clock in the afternoon till night, this market is fo crowded with people, that there is fcarce any paffing in it.

The Latin and Greek fchools. On the *Tyger's-Gracht* is the *Latin* and *Greek* fchool, the back-fide of it reaching to the *Kaymans-Gracht*, with a lofty ftone-gate. It has a very pleafant court, where the fchoolboys may divert themfelves at

7 certain

1662. certain times. The rector or head ſchoolmaſter has a very handſome houſe. Beſides this ſchool, there are divers other ſchools at *Batavia* for the inſtruction of young people in reading and writing; in which ſome of the natives, and eſpecially the *Topaſſes* are ſo ingenious, that they don't give way in that point to any other nation. What books are uſed here are brought out of *Holland*; but in the year 1667, a printing houſe was erected, and ſeveral books have been printed here with good ſucceſs.

The caſtle. The caſtle is a quadrangle, ſituate in a level ground, two baſtions of which, *viz.* the *Diamond* and the *Rabbet* front the city, one facing the *Tyger*'s-*Gracht*, and the other in a ſtrait line thro' the *Lord-ſtreet* to the *Middlepoint* of the new-gate.

On the weſt-ſide the river waſhes the very walls, being encloſed by part of the city, which lies open on that ſide; the two other baſtions call'd the *Pearl* and the *Sapphire* face the ſea; the low grounds toward the weſt are well planted with gardens and orchards; the baſtions, as well as the *Courtins* of the caſtle, are faced with white ſtone 1662. from the bottom to the top, and provided with watch-houſes at convenient diſtances; the ditch is very broad and deep, being incloſed 1669, within a quick-ſet hedge, ſerving not only for an ornament, but alſo as an additional ſtrength to the place, from whence they fire with advantage upon an approaching enemy.

In this caſtle the *Dutch* governor general of the *Indies*, and all the members of the council of the *Indies*, reſiding at *Batavia*, have their places of reſidence; as likewiſe the head factors who keep the accounts, and of what is paid to the ſervants of the company; and the general bookkeeper, the ſecretary of the great council, the captain of the armory, the phyſician, chirurgeon, and commander of the ſoldiery; all theſe I ſay, beſides ſeveral others, have their fix'd habitations here. But the houſe or rather palace of the governor-general ſurpaſſes all the reſt in magnificence.

It is built of brick, two ſtories high, yet ſo lofty, that the top of the roof ſurpaſſes in height all the other buildings, and may be ſeen a great way at ſea; eſpecially the lanthorn or turret, which ſtands in the midſt of it, having inſtead of a weather-cock a ſhip of iron, very artificially wrought. The door is juſt in the middle, unto which you aſcend ſeveral broad ſtone ſteps; in this palace is the council-chamber for the great council to meet in, and near it the ſecretaries office and chamber of accompts. The great hall is hung about with bright and well poliſh'd armour, enſigns, ſtandards

1662. and flags, which have been taken by the *Dutch* in several sea and land engagements; in this hall prayers are said every night, and here it is that the governor at certain times gives audience to all such as have occasion to represent their grievances to him. Behind it are pleasant walks planted with trees, among which a *Tamarind* tree of an excessive height, and standing in the center of the garden, affords a most agreeable sight. Out of this garden you pass thro' a little gate of the *Courtin*, by a small bridge to a summer-house, built upon piles in the midst of the water, from whence you have a very pleasing prospect, not only of the fortifications of the castle, but also of the rivers mouth, and the road where the great ships ride at anchor. At the eastern corner of this summer-house is a door leading thro' a gallery, to the before-mentioned chamber of accompts, which has a flat roof, convenient offices, and pleasant walks belonging to it; the floor is covered with a kind of grey-stone neatly done. In this apartment most of the bookkeepers and clerks are boarded at a certain rate by the treasurer.

The houses of the members of the great council are on the south-side of the castle, the land-gate being in the midst of them.

The armoury is built much after the same manner as the chamber of accompts; it extends along the east-side of the *Courtin*, having separate apartments for sword cutlers, gunsmiths, and other artificers of that kind.

The governor of the sea affairs has his house on the north-side just opposite to it, and on the same side dwell the factors, physician, chirurgeon and apothecary. Hereabouts stand also the magazines of flesh, bacon, wine, *Brunswick* mum, *Holland* butter, oil, vinegar, and divers other provisions; and under ground are made certain vaults for gunpowder and artificial fireworks. The castle has four avenues, and as many gates. The first and largest is call'd the *Landgate*, built 1636, where you see a stone-bridge, supported by 14 arches over the ditch, being 26 rods long, and 10 foot broad, paved with *Dutch* bricks set on edge. The *Watergate* faces the north, where is a large watch-house for the garrison, and some apartments on both sides for the overseers of the magazines and storehouses.

This was built 1630, according to the inscription. Besides these, two lesser gates are in the *Courtins* to the E. and W. which are scarce ever made use of, unless that some vessels laden with ammunition, and such like things, are generally unladen here. There is a small plain before the *Rabbet* bastion, where the new listed soldiers are exercised and taught the use of arms, by an officer appointed for that purpose. Not many years ago a wooden drawbridge was built near the bastion call'd the *Sapphire*, by which means you may walk all round the city to the boom, where you must be ferried over. 1662.

Before my departure, a project was on foot of building a tower and steeple upon the *Rabbet* bastion, making some additions to the *Rotterdam* and *Utrecht* gates, and to enlarge the cit to the E. and N. as far as to the turning of the great river, so that the north-side of the castle should front the bastion call'd the *Middlepoint*. Thus far of the city of *Batavia* itself, we will now take a view of its outside.

It is easy to be guess'd at, what moved the regents of this city to surround it with forts at such a distance, *viz.* to the E. as far as the river *Antjol*, and to the W. as far as the river *Anke*, along the bay of *Batavia*, and on the landside to the S. by the forts *Northwiik*, *Riswick* and *Jacatra*; these serving the inhabitants of the flat countrey, as a defence against the incursions of the neighbouring barbarians, so that they may quietly enjoy the fruits of their labour; the countrey all about this city being well cultivated and stored with rice and sugar-reed fields, gardens and orchards, countrey-houses, brick and tile wharfs and sugar-mills, which are of great consequence to the city. To give all possible encouragement for the manuring of the ground, the main channel of the great river was ordered to be stop'd up 1659, instead of which two branches being made, one leading to *Riswick*, the other to *Jacatra*, these serve to lay the ground thereabouts under water upon occasion. One of these branches is to the W. brought into another channel, leading directly to the middle of the city, and being stop'd near the second bridge of the new gate by a dike and sluice. Here you see seven mills, one whereof is a corn-mill, four gunpowder-mills, one saw-mill for wood, and one paper-mill, which are driven by the force of the water; near it the millers have their habitations.

Before the dike, just at the entrance of the city is the place where they refine the brimstone; near this place 1658, a very strong sluice was built for the conveniency of bringing countrey commodities into the cities with less charge, but the same was ruin'd in a little time after by the force of the water.

Not many years ago, a certain contagious distemper began to rage at *Batavia*, which proving mortal to many, it was resolved, (to stop the infection) to build a

The PEST HOUSE.

1662. kind of hoſpital or peſt-houſe, where ſuch as were ſeiz'd with this evil, might be provided with lodgings, diet, and ſuitable remedies. This houſe, which has with it the *Deiſt-Gate* near the road to *Arke*, is under the government of ſeveral of the richeſt citizens of *Batavia*.

By the eaſt-ſide of the dike where the mills are, a houſe was built in 1609, for the waſhing and whitening of linen apparel, the latter being carried thither by bamboo canes faſtened together. Without the city

Their out-works. are beſides theſe many other houſes erected partly by the company, and partly by the liberality of ſome of the inhabitants, which I will paſs by in ſilence here, and ſay a word or two more of their out-works or forts: All theſe lie in a flat even countrey, made of earth, ſurrounded with ditches and quickſet-hedges, except the quinquangular fort call'd the *Riſwick*, and the fort *Ansjol*, both which are faced with brick-work. They are all well provided with great artillery, and proviſions for nine months, or perhaps for a whole year, as well as the garriſon of the city of *Batavia* it ſelf. There is a certain officer appointed to keep the cannon and other arms neat and clean, the which being under the over-ſight of a captain of the artillery, who commands alſo the fire-workers, and has his habitation upon the baſtion call'd the *Diamond*. The garriſon conſiſts chiefly in foot, there being only a troop of horſe, which ſerves as a guard to the governor-general, who are obliged to be upon the guard in their turns. Theſe enjoy great privileges, are commanded by one of the beſt officers, and are obliged to appear every *Sunday* in their armour well poliſh'd, and with their piſtols, carabines, and broad ſwords. 1662.

The inhabitants. The inhabitants of *Batavia* conſiſt either of the citizens, or ſuch as are ſervants to the company, being of divers nations; among whom the *Dutch* exceed the reſt both in riches and dignity, moſt places of honour and profit being in their hands.

Chineſe. The *Chineſe* drive here a conſiderable traffick, being more induſtrious than any of the other *Indians*; they deal much in fiſh, and cultivate moſt of the rice, reed and corn-fields; ſome alſo maintain themſelves by fiſhing, but the chiefeſt upon merchandizing; they farm the exciſes and cuſtoms; but of late years ſome of the other nations have found ways to imitate them in their thriftineſs and cozenings, at which they are great artiſts, which I know by my own experience. They live here according to the laws and cuſtoms of their own countrey, under the tuition of a *Chineſe* governor, who manages all their af-

fairs

1662. fairs with the company. They are dreſs'd after their own faſhion, in a coat with wide ſleeves, either callicoe or ſilk, according to their abilities. They don't ſhave their heads here according to the *Tartarian* faſhion, as they do now in *China*, but wear their hair long and neatly twiſted. Their habitations are ſettled thro' the whole city, but live for the moſt part on the weſt-ſide, near the great river, and many of them on the eaſt-ſide; their houſes are low, with the roof cover'd over the firſt floor.

The Malayans. The *Malayans* as they are not ſo much addicted to trading as the *Chineſe*, live for the moſt part upon fiſhing; their boats are made after the *Indian* faſhion, with large ſails. They have alſo a governor of their own, who lives in the *Rhinoceroſes Gracht*, whereabouts moſt of them have their dwelling-places. They wear light callicoes or ſilks, tho' ſome of their women of faſhion uſe flower'd and ſtrip'd ſilk; their hair, which is very black, they tie behind in a knot, but the men wear a piece of cloath about their heads. Thoſe few merchants that are among them, are next to the *Chineſe*, accounted the cunningeſt traders; the houſes of the *Malayans* are but very indifferently built there, being covered with leaves, and planted round with coco-trees. They have a cuſtom of chewing the *Bethel* leaves continually, and take tobacco through ſugar-canes lackered over with ſtone ball. 1662.

The Moors. The *Moors* or *Mahometans* here maintain themſelves almoſt in the ſame manner, and live near the *Malayans*; ſome however drive a kind of pedling-trade, and ſell coral and glaſs beads in the ſtreets, ſome have ſmall ſtalls in market-towns. A few of them merchandiſe, eſpecially in free-ſtone, which they fetch in their veſſels from the adjacent iſlands. They are clad after the *Mahometan* faſhion.

Amboyneſe. The *Amboyneſe* inhabit a particular part of the ſuburbs, on the left-hand, as you come from *Jacatra* to the city, near the burying place of the *Chineſe*; near it their governor (who has done great ſervice to the company) has built himſelf a ſtately houſe, after the manner of the *Amboyneſe*. They live for the moſt part upon carpenters work, being extremely dextrous in building of houſes of bamboo-canes, and have a peculiar way of ſplitting and twiſting of canes in divers figures for windows, which afford a free paſſage to the air. The *Amboyneſe* are a courageous nation, of a dreadful aſpect, with long black hair, and much inclined to mutiny; their chief weapons are cymeters, and ſhields of an oval figure, where with they know how to ward

A Melayā Captain.

Betwixt pag. 276. 277.

The habit of a Malayan and his Wife at Batavia.

A Souldier of Amboina

29

Betwixt pag. 276, 277.

A Negro Pedler with his Wife.

1662. a blow, and to intercept their enemies arrows: The men wear a piece of callicoe wrapt ſeveral times about their heads, both ends hanging down, and adorned with flowers and ſome other ornaments. The women have only a piece of callicoe wrapt about them, and another piece round their ſhoulders, their arms being left bare; their houſes are made of wooden planks, carved with leaves, indifferently high built: Their dreſs is like that of the *Moors*.

Javaneſe. The *Javaneſe* inhabit in houſes of bamboo-canes, on the other ſide of the burying-place of the *Chineſe*, ſome of which are neatly built and cover'd with the twigs of coco-trees. Some maintain themſelves with huſbandry, and eſpecially with planting of rice, others with building of boats, uſed by the inhabitants for the carrying of their commodities to the city; they alſo go abroad a fiſhing, their boats which are turn'd like horns in the figure of a half-moon, being ſo nimble, that they call them the *Flying-Boats*. The *Javaneſe* men go for the moſt part naked, being only covered from the middle to the knees; ſome wear a kind of a ſcarf, whereon they faſten their ſwords; on the head they wear a cap, but go bare-footed. Their houſes excel in neatneſs thoſe of the reſt of the *Indians*.

The *Mardiikers* or *Topaſſers* are a mixture of divers *Indian* nations, call'd *Topaſſers*, i. e. *Accommodators*, becauſe they will accommodate themſelves eaſily to the manners, cuſtoms and religion of ſuch as they live among; tho' ſome will have them derive their name from a precious ſtone call'd a *Topaz*. They live both within and without the city, the chiefeſt of which being merchants, who traffick in their own veſſels with the adjacent iſles, live in very ſtately houſes. The reſt live upon huſbandry, graſing and gardening, and have ſome artiſans among them; they have their own captains, who ſit in the council of war, and ſchool-maſters who teach their children to read and to write. Their dreſs approaches near to the *Dutch* faſhion, but their breeches reach down to their ankles, and wear a kind of caps on their heads. Their women are clad like other *Indian* women. Their houſes are better built than thoſe of the other *Indians*, generally of ſtone, and cover'd with tiles, ſtately built and arch'd. Before their houſes they plant coco-trees, and all ſorts of *Indian* fruits and flowers, but the backſide they reſerve for the keeping of pigs, pidgeons, fowl and other ſorts of poultry, which they bring to ſale in the market. 1662. Mardikers *or* Topaſſers.

1662.

The soldiers of Makassar. The chief arms of the soldiers of *Makassar* are certain poison'd arrows of a foot long, pointed at one end with fish teeth, and on the other with a kind of hard wood; when they are to go into the wars, they provide a good number of these arrows dipt a good while before in a poisonous liquor which they let dry upon them. This poison is the juice issuing out of the bark of a certain tree growing in the isle of *Makassar*, and two or three adjacent isles of the *Bougisses*; it is of the height of a clove tree; its leaves resembling also those of that tree; the juice of which, while yet fresh, is mortal, and not to be cured by antidotes. These poison'd arrows the soldiers of *Makassar* don't shoot out of their bows, but thro' trunks, as we let fly at the birds in *Europe* with small earthen balls; with these they will hit any mark within four rods distance. This poison is so pernicious, and penetrates with that swiftness thro' the whole mass of the blood, and seizes upon the spirits, that the *Makassars* themselves know no remedy against it. The most approved remedy against it is man's dung, which taken immediately after the wound is given, causes a vomiting, and hinders the operation of the poison: I have known several of our soldiers cured by this remedy, tho' some others I have seen die not long after they had been wounded, notwithstanding the use of it, and others after two or three days. In the isle of *Makassar* grows a certain root, of a bitterish taste, which is look'd upon as a great antidote against this poison, and is often used as such by the *Dutch*; they chew the root, and lay it about the orifice of the wound.

Timorese *soldiers.* The *Timorese* soldiers or inhabitants of the isle of *Timoor*, use swords of sandel wood, wherewith they can cut a man through the middle at one stroke: For in this isle, and the *Molucca-Islands*, and all along to the S. S. E. beyond the *Lesser-Java*, to the 10th deg. of southern latitude, grow whole woods of white and yellow sandel wood, call'd *Chandava* by the inhabitants. The *Timorese* are very barbarous, but warlike; formerly they were all pagans, but of late years most are turn'd mahometans, and some *Roman* catholicks.

Bougisses. The *Bokjes* or *Bougisses*, who formerly inhabited divers isles near that of *Makassar*, are a warlike people, arm'd with cymeters, arrows, and shields, which they handle with great dexterity. They go for the greatest part naked, having only a piece of stuff about the middle down to the knees. The women are clad like the other *Indians*. After the *Dutch* became engaged in a war with the king of *Makassar*, these *Bougisses* fixt their habitations in and about *Batavia*, till the event of the war; their king having his residence near the out-guard, betwixt the forts of *Riswick* and *Northwick*, the queen being permitted to reside within the city; but after the *Makassars* were conquered by the *Dutch*, under the conduct of *Cornelius Spellman*, and a firm peace was settled with the neighbouring nations, both the king and queen had a house assign'd them in the *Lords-Street*. This house or palace extends to the brink of the river, with very pleasant walks, flower-gardens, and a most delightful vineyard, which in my time, 1676, bore vast branches of grapes. The gate facing the street is very neatly built, of the *Ionick* order, with a gallery on the top of it, and the apartments so spacious and well-contrived, that most of the *Indian* kings and their retinue might live here. 1662.

Number of foreigners at Batavia. Among the foreign nations residing here, there may, according to computation, be raised 6720 fighting men, *viz.* 400 *Topassars* or *Mardiiken* under two captains, within the city, besides 710 without the city, under three captains, making in all 1110; of *Regantiins* 70; *Amboynese* 600; *Malayans* 201; *Chinese* 1200; *Moors* 200; of the *Javanese* in their quarter within the *New-Gate* 750; near the burying-place of the *Chinese* 1500; in their quarter beyond the *New-Fort* 800; and of *Brasilians* beyond the fort 300. That this island is sufficiently fruitful, and able to maintain its inhabitants, is evident from the exportations that are made yearly thence to *Amboyna* and other places: It is true no wheat grows here, but supposing the supplies that are brought of that grain from *Suratte* and *Japan* should be stopt, the defect thereof may very well be supplied with rice. The chief artisans here are *Dutch*, most of which live very well, and the *Chinese* have many carpenters and bricklayers among themselves, who will work as journeymen. Their cabinet-makers have a way of joining the wood of their cabinets, so that the jointures are not to be seen. Others get a livelyhood by selling of sugar-beer, cookery, and the sale of *Sury* or coco-liquor, and *Arack* or *Indian* strong-waters, of which they make punch, (as the *English* call it) a liquor that opens both the hearts and purses of the inhabitants. But the chief inns and taverns are kept by the *Dutch*, who pay, as well as all the other nations, two reals *per* month for their license, besides 70 reals excise of every pipe of *Spanish* wine they sell. The distillers of *Arack* are most *Chinese*, who pay 50 reals excise for every chaudron or gosper *per* month.

The

Betwixt pag. 270. 277.

A Marchant of Java.

A Javanese Man and Wooman.

32

A Makaſser with his Wife as they are habited at Batavia

Tymorian Souldiers.

34.

35.

A Bougis of Bokjes.

Makassar Souldiers who blow poison'd darts out of Trunks. 36

Betwixt pag. 278. 279.

A Topas or Mardick with his Wife 37

1662. The government of the city of *Batavia* is settled upon the same basis as in the *United Provinces*, being administer'd by six peculiar colleges or councils.

The first and chief is composed of the members of the council of the *Indies*, in which the governor-general of the *Indies* presides, whose name was Mr. *Maetzuiper* at that time. In this council all affairs of state are transacted: Their chamber is in the palace of the governor, where audience is given every day to redress the grievances of the people.

The second college or council consists of nine persons, besides the president, who commonly is one of the members of the great council, and is the keeper of the great seal, representing a woman placed in a tower, with a balance in one, and a sword in the other hand, with this inscription; *The seal of the council of justice of the castle of* Batavia; this college being generally called the *Council of Justice*. Here are debated and decided all matters relating to the publick revenue and treasury. They also take cognizance of differences arising about customs. The president in conjunction with the council has a voice in the determination of civil causes, and has a third part of all the fines; but if they exceed 100 reals, he has only a sixth part. His chief business is to take care that no incroachments be made upon the prerogatives of the sovereignty of the *United Provinces*. The secretary is to keep an exact register of all things transacted in this assembly, without any other reward but his salary: He also has in his custody the money which comes from the fines, of which he must give an account. The door-keeper is to attend whilst they are sitting, and to summon such persons as are to appear before them: He wears a stick and a silver-shield on the left-side, with the seal of the council. The goal-keeper keeps three tables for the prisoners; who are to pay half a real for turning the key. This council assembles in the council-chamber of the town-house, twice, and sometimes thrice a week.

The third college or council consists of the aldermen or senators, chosen out of the best citizens. They assemble three times a week, *viz. Mondays*, *Wednesdays* and *Thursdays*, from 7 till 11 in the forenoon. At their election they are presented with 50 rixdollars, and with 100 more every 6 months. In this council are determin'd all the causes betwixt the citizens, (from whom however lies an appeal to the council of justice;) if any difference arises betwixt a servant of the company and a citizen, the last must be summoned before this court; and no citizen is obliged to appear before the council of justice, but must be summon'd before this assembly first, and there answer for himself. This council issue their orders in relation to the publick structures, bridges and streets, yet not without the approbation of the great council. The president has the custody of the seal, and calls the assembly together when he thinks fit: He may peruse the register, and proposes all matters to the council: He has a double voice, and is commonly one of the members of the great council. The *Landrost* or chief judge, has in this assembly a decisive sentence in criminal causes, and is allowed a third part of all the fines. This council consists of nine persons, among whom are two *Chinese*. They have also a door-keeper, who is called the city messenger, having a shield with the city's arms in it. 1662. *The government of Batavia.*

The fourth council consists of the overseers of the hospital of the orphans, being chosen out of the best citizens, except the president, who is generally a member of the great council. It consists of five members only, three whereof are citizens, the other two servants of the company: Their business is to provide for the poor-orphans, and to enquire into their condition, and what is left by their parents.

The fifth is the council appointed for the determination of matters of less moment; the president whereof is a member of the council of justice. They are to give licences for marriages, and not to permit men before they are twenty one, and maids before eighteen years of age, to marry; nor mahometans or pagans to marry with christians, nor any *Hollanders* with the natives that don't understand *Dutch*. They sit twice a week in the town-house, where causes of little moment are pleaded and soon decided.

The sixth council of *Batavia* is the council of war, in which the chief officer of the militia of the city is president. Here are determined all matters relating to the militia of less moment, which are brought before them by the city major; but matters of consequence are referr'd to the determination of the judge and court of the senators. They also meet in the town-house once a week.

All these courts have each their own secretary, clerks and waiters.

The ecclesiastical government of *Batavia* is administred by the ministers, church-wardens and overseers of the poor, who assemble in the vestry of the church upon the summons of their president, who is chosen every month. The ministers being chosen in, and sent hither out of *Holland*, are *The ecclesiastical government.*

1662. are confirm'd here, and live in great esteem among the citizens.

The original and rise of Batavia.

Batavia, the capital city of all the *Indies* under the *Dutch* jurisdiction, has been frequently attempted by the natives or *Javanese*; for no sooner had the *Hollanders* in 1618. (after the taking of *Jacatra*, unto which they gave the name of *Batavia*) erected a fortress here, but the natives being encouraged by the *English* of *Bantam*, endeavour'd to drive them from thence. To effect which, the *English* persuaded them to erect a redoubt or great battery, upon which they planted their great guns, from whence they play'd so furiously upon the new bastion of the *Dutch* fort, that they were not able to bring it to perfection. *John Peterson Koen*, the *Dutch* governor, having thereupon call'd together a council of war, it was resolved, that to hinder the further progress of the enemy, they should make a salley the next morning by break of day, in order to attack the redoubt, and the quarters of the *Chinese* and *English* at the same time. Accordingly our men were divided into three troops, commanded by *Peter Van Broek*, (afterwards governor-general of the *Dutch-Indies*) *Peter Van Dirks*, and *Peter Van Rey*, with these they attack'd the before-mentioned posts at once. The *Javanese* fought bravely at first; but seeing the *Hollanders* persisted in the attack, resolved either to die or overcome, they retreated, leaving their strong hold to the enemy, who destroy'd all their work in a few hours. But being sorely gall'd by the fire of the city, they had not the same success at the new redoubt erected by the enemy near the river-side; so, that having endeavoured, but in vain, to make a breach there, they were forced to retire with the loss of 15 men killed and 10 wounded. Besides this redoubt, the *Javanese* had another battery raised in the midst of the city, which being mounted with heavy cannon taken out of the *English* ships, did also considerable mischief to the besieged, who were day and night at work in raising batteries, and putting their fortifications in a state of defence; whereas the enemy being much superior in number, had had time enough to provide themselves with all things for this enterprise. In the mean while the *Hollanders* made a second attempt upon the redoubt near the river-side, but were repulsed with the loss of 7 or 8 of their men, and a lieutenant, whose head the *Javanese* carried in triumph on the top of a launce. The *English* then living at *Bantam*, would fain have revenged themselves upon the *Dutch* inhabitants there, for the damages their countreymen had received at *Batavia*, had they not been prevented therein by the *Pangerang*. Whilst the *Dutch*, who were not above 240 fighting men strong in the fortress, were thus defending themselves against some thousands of the *Javanese*, (besides the *English*) an *English* squadron of 11 ships appeared in the road of *Batavia*, coming from *Bantam*; whereupon the governor of the fort, having recommended the defence thereof to *Peter Van Broek* the deputy governor, he went on board a man of war, with an intention to engage the *English*, but finding himself two weak, left what ammunition he could spare, in the castle, and so set sail for the *Molucca* islands, being pursued for some days by the *English*, but to no purpose; who after their return, came again to an anchor in the road of *Batavia*. Thus the *Dutch* were attack'd both by sea and land, yet did not lose their courage, but defended themselves with so much bravery, that the enemy thought fit to offer a truce, to settle, as they pretended, the preliminaries of a peace. 1662.

Hostages being exchang'd on both sides, the *Dommagon* or prime minister, the king of *Jacatra*'s brother demanded the sum of 4000 crowns from the *Hollanders*, which he said they had forfeited according to agreement, for having attack'd the *English* without the king's leave, and 4000 more for the letting them finish the new bastion, which he said was not comprehended in the said contract; after many debates and contests, certain articles were at last agreed on, which the *Dutch* (who wanted ammunition) were willing to sign; but the *English* finding those conditions against their interest (the *Dutch* being thereby permitted to remain in the possession of their fortress and habitations at *Bantam*) found out the following trick to break off the treaty; they so far prevail'd, first with *Peter vander Broek* the deputy-governor of the fortress, that he came out to meet the king of *Jacatra* at an appointed place, but no sooner appear'd there but he was taken prisoner, with those few that attended him, and laid in irons; being threatned with present death, unless he would prevail with those in the fortress to surrender it immediately; but finding the garrison resolved to defend the place, the *English* brought more of their heavy cannon ashore, in order to batter it with the utmost fury; at the same time they drag'd the deputy-governor, loaden with irons and a rope about his neck, to the walls of the castle, threatning him once more with immediate death upon the spot, unless the garrison would prevent it by an immediate surrender; the deputy-governor was so far from being overcome by the fear of present death,

Bravery of the Dutch *governor of* Batavia.

1662. that on the contrary, like a brave and faithful commander, he exhorted them to defend the place to the last drop of blood, which so exasperated some of the *Javanese* and *English* that stood near him, that they threw him backwards by the rope, and so drag'd him back to the council, all which he took patiently, and with so undaunted courage, that some of the *English* being asham'd of so barbarous an action, afterwards beg'd his pardon. By this time the *Dutch* having spent all their ammunition, and quite tir'd out with continual labour and watching, without any hopes of present relief, saw themselves under an indispensable necessity to surrender the place under condition, that the garrison and castle with all the artillery should be deliver'd to the *English*, and the merchandizes, money and jewels to the *Javanese*; it was sign'd the first of *February* 1619, by *Wydurk Bama*, king of *Jacatra*, and the *English* chief commander on one side, and by those in the fortress on the other side.

The *Hollanders* being now upon the point of delivering themselves and the fortress up to their enemies, a sudden accident robb'd the *Javanese* and the *English* of all their hopes; for the *Pangerang* of *Bantam* had no sooner notice of this capitulation, in which he had no share, but he order'd his *Dommagon* or chief minister to march with a body of 4000 men to secure the *Dutch* deputy-governor, and the castle with all that was found in it for his use. Accordingly he march'd with all secrecy to *Jacatra*, and meeting with the king in his apartment, put his dagger to his breast with these words: *King, surrender yourself prisoner, or expect no quarter*, which so terrify'd the king, that he comply'd not only with his demands, but soon after retir'd with the queen into the mountains, without ever being heard of since. The *Dommagon* of *Bantam* having taken the deputy-governor into his custody, summon'd the fortress to surrender, which those refus'd to do, except upon the before-mention'd conditions, which the *Bantamese* refusing to agree to, and the *English* in the mean while (seeing they were like to be disappointed in aim) beginning to reimbark their cannon, thro' contrivance of the besieged, these finding their enemies at variance about the booty, began to take fresh courage, and having in several attacks bravely repulsed the *Javanese*, were now so confident of maintaining the fort, that they gave it the name of *Batavia*; thus matters stood, when on the 25th of *March* 1619, their so long look'd for relief, consisting of 17 men of war, under the command of *John Peterson Koen*, came from the *Moluque* islands in the road of *Batavia*: Within a few days after they landed 1100 men, divided into 12 several bodies, and edged on with revenge, attack'd the city of *Jacatra* with incredible fury, the *Javanese* defended themselves with great obstinacy for some time, but no longer able to endure our fire, they left their entrenchments, and look'd for their safety in an open flight, being closely pursued by the *Dutch*, who gave no quarter; this happened the 30th of *March* 1619, which day is yearly celebrated here in memory of this great action. This done, Mr. *Koen* sail'd with the fleet to *Bantam*, demanding the immediate restitution of all the prisoners; the *Pangerang* being at first unwilling to grant his demand, he began to thunder with his cannon into the city, which soon terrify'd him into a compliance. The *English* seeing themselves now quite out of all hopes of accomplishing their design, by the coming of the *Dutch* fleet, made the best of their way thro' the streight of *Sunda*, and those of *Bantam*, finding themselves forsaken by their confederates, thought it most convenient to give over their project. 1662.

The *Hollanders* having now their hands free, and seeing the situation of their new fortress in so fertile a countrey, near a very advantageous bay, capable of containing 1000 ships with safety, resolved and gave immediate orders for the building of the city, under the cannon of the fortress, the adjacent islands furnishing them with sufficient stone and mortar, and what else was requisite for this undertaking, being purchased from the neighbouring confederates. But the *Javanese* not being able to brook the rise and encrease of this new city, the *Mataran* (or *Javanese* emperor) 1629, laid close siege to it with 12000 men, under the conduct of the prince of *Madure*; and being advanc'd with their works within musket shot of the walls, they made several furious attacks in the night-time, but were as often repulsed by the fire of the besieged, who besides this made frequent sallies, and ruin'd their works, without giving them leisure to repair them. The *Javanese* being resolv'd to try all means to reduce the place, stop'd the current of the great river with piles ram'd into the bottom, behind which they threw all the dead carcasses of men and beasts, which not only infected the water, but also the air, which occasion'd distempers among the besieg'd, who were forced to drink salt water for a considerable time, till at last by continual digging having found some springs of tolerable good water, they began to refresh themselves with less danger and more ease. The *Javanese* finding also this design

1662. ſign to prove unſucceſsful, had recourſe again to force, and the 2d of *October* 1629, made a general aſſault on the ſouth-ſide of the city, relieving their troops continually with freſh men, but were repulſed bravely without any conſiderable loſs of the *Dutch*. At the ſame time they aſſaulted a ſmall outwork or tower call'd *Maaſland-Waerberg*, defended only by 15 men, who defended themſelves courageouſly, as that they were attack'd. At laſt, having ſpent all their powder and ball, they went to work with the tiles and bricks of the caſtle within; the *Javaneſe* being ſenſible of their want, advanced to the very foot of the walls, and having found means to bring a great rope round the building, were endeavouring to pull down the tower; but the beſieged ſeeing themſelves in extremity, made a furious ſally upon the *Javeneſe*, who thought not fit to ſtand the ſhock, but ſoon retreated to their entrenchments, except a few that were ſlain upon the ſpot. The firſt of *November* 1629, about ſix hours after ſunſet, the *Javaneſe* ſet fire to their camp in three ſeveral places, and march'd off with all imaginable ſecrecy, after a ſiege of three months and three days. No booty worth mentioning was found there, but 800 men miſerably murthered all on a ſpot; a miſerable ſpectacle! occaſion'd as we learn'd afterwards by the haughty courage of the prince of *Madure*, which happened thus: During the firſt ſiege of the caſtle of *Batavia*, the emperor of *Mataran* having ſent a body of troops under the command of one of his beſt officers to the king of *Jacatra*, and the ſame returning unſucceſsful, the prince of *Madure* ſpoke ſlightly of the matter, telling openly at court, *That if he had been ſent with ſuch troops, he would have carried the caſtle or died in the attempt*. The *Materan* being inform'd thereof, and reſolv'd to try his fortune againſt *Batavia*, gave the ſupreme command of his army to the ſaid prince, who proving unſucceſsful, juſt as he was ready to march off with his troops, was order'd to be ſlain with all his followers, *to verify his own words* (as he ſaid) *that he would either carry the caſtle or periſh in the attempt*.

Batavia *beſieged by the* Javaneſe.

The *Javaneſe* loſt above 30000 men in this unfortunate ſiege, notwithſtanding which, thoſe of *Bantam* in the year 1655, had a mind to try their fortune againſt the *Dutch*; who meeting them in the open field, this occaſioned many ſkirmiſhes, in which the *Javaneſe* commonly had the worſt, ſo that being pretty well tired with the war, and hearing of the approaching ſuccours from the *Molucca* iſlands, under the command of *Arnold Ulaming*, they thought it their beſt way to come to a compoſition with them, ſince which time they have not thought fit to come to any rupture, but maintain a good correſpondence with thoſe they know are able to cope with them; eſpecially ſince they have ſtrengthned their city with divers conſiderable outworks and forts. 1662.

The fort *Anſjol* on the ſea-ſide, the fort *Aake* to the weſt-ſide, and on the *Quinquangular* fort, the *Riſwick*, *Noothwick* and *Jacatra* on the land-ſide. The fort *Aake* is built 1200 rods from *Batavia* to the eaſt, near the ſea-ſide juſt by the lime-kills, and faced with ſtone. The fort *Aake* lies about 500 rods from the city, more towards the land-ſide, being alſo a free quadrangular figure; hereabouts live abundance of farmers along the river, the grounds being very fertile here. Near it is the *Peſt-houſe*. The fort *Jacatra* ſtands upon the bank of the river, not above 500 paces to the north-eaſt of the city; from whence there is a ſtrait and pleaſant walk thither, planted on both ſides with gardens and orchards. The *Chineſe*, *Amboyneſe*, and ſome other foreigners have their habitations hereabouts. The fort of *Northwick* lies to the north of the city near the river, betwixt that of *Jacatra* and *Riſwick*.

The outworks of Batavia.

Without the city many of the citizens have very pleaſant gardens and houſes. Upon the great river without *Batavia* you ſee a houſe belonging to captain *Burghs*, built flat on the top after the *Indian* faſhion, being ſurrounded with all ſorts of *Indian* trees. Upon the brink of the river is a pleaſant ſummer-houſe. Without the city, near the great river, ſtands another houſe belonging to a rich citizen call'd *Strantwich*, belonging formerly to Mr. *John Maetzuicker*, governor-general of the *Dutch Indies*: It is very airy and pleaſantly built, with a very fine front, the gardens being well ſtored with trees and flowers of moſt ſorts.

Without the new gate, in a grove of pleaſant trees, you ſee the tomb of a *Chineſe* governor, named *Sequa*; being no more than a heap of earth raiſed above the ſurface of the ground, and encloſed with brickwork, plaiſtered white all over: In the midſt you ſee a table, and upon it a cup, into which the *Chineſe* put ſometimes money, ſometimes victuals, to appeaſe the manes of the deceaſed.

A Chineſe *tomb*.

The grounds about *Batavia*, and indeed of the whole iſle of *Java*, are extremely fertile in all ſorts of fruits the *Indies* afford; but what is moſt ſurprizing is, that divers plants, which in *Europe* grow on ſmall and tender ſtalks, riſe up here very thick, and with hard ſtalks; whereas

Trees, plants and flowers of Java.

on

1662. on the other hand, divers sorts of beans and flowers grow in *Java* upon trees. The soil about *Batavia* is so rich, that the seeds brought hither out of *Holland*, *Persia*, and from *Suratte*, thrive extremely, and yield plentiful fruits.

Fruits of the earth. *Holland* cabbages, if sown in due time, and well look'd after, come here to a good perfection, but if neglected they will not cabbage. Provident nature seems to have been careful in abundance of astringent plants for this climate, where the bloody flux and other distempers occasioned by the gall, are so frequent. Of trefoil or clover they have great store here; and in their gardens purslain, asparagus, endive, lettice, bekabung, water-cresses, parsley, radishes, red and white beetes, and such like: The radishes grow longer and better tasted here than in *Europe*, and there is a certain kind of them shorter but thicker than the rest, which are boil'd like our turnips. The *Chinese* pickle radishes, and use them to create an appetite to their victuals. Here also is found a certain kind of *Mandragora*, called *Bella Donna* by the *Italians*, in great request among the *Indians* in burning fevers; they pickle it in vinegar, and eat the fruit roasted in the ashes as a disert.

Vines. Vines are very plenty and good here if well cultivated; whether or by whom the vines have been translated hither is uncertain, there being no mention made of it in the journals of the voyages made into those parts since the year 1595. They grow very lusciously upon the walls of the houses of *Batavia*, which bear fruit in a manner all the year round, provided they be pruned in due time; for 14 days after they are pruned the buds come out, which in 14 days more stand in full blossom, and in two months longer produce ripe grapes; so that every vine brings forth ripe grapes every three months, and consequently four times in the year. But they don't thrive so well without the city; whether the lands be too low, or not sufficiently purged from the salt-petre, I will leave to the enquiry of others; since it is certain, that vineyards would be of prodigious consequence to the inhabitants, there being vines here which bear grapes, each bunch weighing 16 or more ounces; and there are some grapes as big as the *Spanish Muscadine* grape.

Blue beans. All along the roads about *Batavia* grow a certain plant among the woods, with small branches not unlike the hops, which spread very plentifully upon the ground, or will rise up to a good height on stalks like our *French* beans, having leaves like our rose-trees. The flower comes forth out of a bud as large as our ordinary roses, pointed at the end; they are of a lovely sky blue colour, and yellow in the middle, but the fruit being rank is not regarded. 1662.

Indian garden-herbs. The *Indian* beets grow in the gardens of *Batavia*, their leaves being not unlike our sorrel leaves, with a pale vein thro' the middle: They bring forth pursley flowers on green stalks; some are white, others a mixture of purple and green. The leaves and stalks when boil'd, are in taste like the *Indian Bajan:* All sorts of garden-herbs are in great request among the *Indians* here, because most of the *Indian* foreigners that come from *Suratte*, and the coast of *Coromandel*, feed for the most part upon fruits of the earth; for believing the transmigration of the soul, they will not eat the flesh of any living creature; for which reason also they abstain from red beans, or herbs of a red colour, as having a resemblance to blood; and for the same reason it is, that the *Indians*, tho' otherwise very ignorant, yet are very well versed in the knowledge of plants and trees. The *Malayans* call all pot-herbs or other eatable herbs *Seir*, but medicinal and poisonous herbs *Oubat*. About *Batavia* are to be found divers sorts of pot and other garden herbs; as red and white beets, parsley, divers sorts of lettices, dill, fennel, asparagus, &c. And of fruits of the earth water-melons, pompions, cucumbers, citruls, &c. And of pulse, all sorts of beans and peas, which grow up to a great height on stalks or trees.

Fokky-Fokky. The fruit call'd *Fokky-Fokky* by the *Indians* is shaped like a pear, sometimes near a yard long, and of the thinness of a man's arm: It contains abundance of small seeds, the rind being thin, but so smooth and bright, that you may see your face in them like as in a looking-glass: The leaves are green but rough, and as it were covered with a hairy substance: They grow up to a good height. This fruit is one of the best and most esteem'd of all the *Indies*, being of a delicious taste, and when boil'd with wine and pepper, not unlike our artichoak bottoms. They are frequently eaten both by the *Dutch* and *Indians*, instead of the *European* turnips, being look'd upon as very nourishing and easy to be digested; besides, that by their diuretick quality they are good against the gravel and stone. There is another wild kind of *Fokky-Fokky*, the fruits wereof are round, and when ripe turn yellow, but these are only food for the hogs.

Jamboes. In the plains of *Java* grows a tree, the fruit whereof the *Malayans* call *Jamboes*, and the *Dutch* sloes or small plumbs: This tree resembling in all respects our sloe or wild plumb-tree; the fruits being also of an astringent but not disagreeable taste: The fruit when ripe is yellow, and the juice

1662. juice thereof mix'd with *Champana* and rose water, is used against the inflammation of the throat. The juice taken inwardly is good against the bloody flux, and other bileous distempers. Thus this juice of the *Indian* fruit *Jangomas* is equivalent in its virtue to the *Acacia* of the antients, or to our *European* sloes.

Cubebes or Kumuk. In the isle of *Java* only, *viz.* in the woods near the shore of the streight of *Sunda*, grows wild a certain fruit called *Cubebes* and *Quabeb* by the *Arabians*, *Kumuk* by the *Javenese*, and by the rest of the *Indians*, except the *Malayans*, *Kubab Sini*, i. e. *Chinese Kubebe*, not because it grows in *China*, but because it is transported thither in great quantities. The tree which bears this fruit is both in leaves and branches not unlike to our apple-tree, but somewhat lesser. The fruit is round, smaller than pepper, of a dark brown colour, and if pinch'd with the nails, will emit a certain liquor like unto the cloves. This fruit is in so high an esteem among the *Javanese*, that they will not permit them to be transported, unless they are boil'd before-hand, to prevent their being transplanted into another place. They gather some of them before they are ripe; these are light, with a rough rind, within which is a small soft and whitish kernel. When they are ripe the rind is smooth, have a bigger kernel, and are much heavier than the others. Before they are quite ripe, they have an aromatick, biting, and bitterish taste, and when chew'd offend the brain: But the ripe ones are neither so sharp nor so bitter, and don't send so much of their offensive vapours up to the head; they are reckoned hot and dry in the third degree; are good to attenuate slime in the stomach and breast, expel wind, and correct the cold symptoms of the womb. Chew'd with mastick, they draw the phlegmatick humours from the head, and strengthen the brains. They are in great request among the *Javanese* and other *Indians*, who steep them in wine, and take them to raise their appetite to venery, and to warm the stomach. Three or four chew'd, disperse the vapours which occasion giddiness in the head, but care must be taken to spit out both the phelgm and *Cubebes*, and to keep the nostrils close while you are a chewing, that so the smell and scent of them may penetrate with the more efficacy, and affect more immediately the head.

Assafetida. The *Javanese*, *Malayans*, and other *Indians*, use very frequently for the relishing of their sauces, a certain drug called *Hin*, by the *Arabians Altit*, and by the *Europeans Assafetida*, by reason of its ill scent. This shrub, out of the root of which this juice is express'd, grows in *Persia*, betwixt *Gamron* and *Lara*. It is of two sorts; 1662.
the first is not unlike our *Osier*, out of the leaves and sprigs of which is squeezed the *Hin* by a press, and the juice afterward coagulated in the sun: The second sort is much stronger and worse scented, being the juice express'd out of the root of this shrub. This juice, and that of *Amfion* or *Opium*, are two of the chiefest commodities of the *Dutch* trade in the *Indies*. Our *East-India* ships bound to *Java* and other *Indian* ports, do always carry a considerable quantity of this juice from *Persia*, which they exchange with the *Javanese* for such of their countrey commodities as they have occasion for.

Both great and small *Cardamome*, (as the *Arabians* call it) called *Malignetus* by the *Indians*, grows likewise in the isle of *Java*. Cardamome.
The small *Cardamome* grows on a stalk with small joints like reeds, (the leaves being also like theirs, and grow in clusters like them;) but the *Cardamome* seldom grows above two or three foot high, and the leaves rub'd betwixt your fingers, emit a very odoriferous scent. From the root first sprout forth in ears like the *Spicknard*, the flowers being of a pale colour, not unlike the orange-flowers. After these come certain husks, which contains these well-scented seeds, which are green, but in time turn of a dark vermillion colour. The *Cardamome* is a most excellent spice of extraordinary virtues, having an agreeable heat consonant to our nature, without leaving any heat behind it, which is the reason that it is chew'd without any addition. It promotes urine, and the monthly terms of the women; opens the obstructions of the spleen and liver, and procures a sweet breath. The great *Cardamome* grows plentifully in the woods of *Java*; the flowers grow on the stalk like the hyacinth; it differs from the small *Cardamome* in divers respects: It grows to the height of six foot, the leaves are larger, and the stalks not knotty like the reeds. The small *Cardamome* sends forth an ear from the root, and the husks are sometimes a finger long. However, the leaves and flowers are of the same scent in both, but the leaves of the great *Cardamome* are not only much larger, but also covered with a *Lanugo* on the under side. This shrub is very pleasant to behold, of a light green colour, with white flowers tip'd with purple red at the extremities.

The plant called by the *Malayans Moulit Bebek*, i. e. the *Ducks-Beak*, from its shape, grows in the gardens of *Batavia* on a somewhat longer stalk than the *Cardamome*, being a sempervirent herb; the leaves also differ from those of the *Cardamome*, being carved or edged in the circumference. Moulit. Bebek.

1662. The inhabitants use the juice of this herb against pustules and other exulcerations of a bileous nature; and steep'd in vinegar, it is a good remedy against the St. *Anthony*'s *Fire*; the *Malayan* women lay it upon the heads of their children to corroborate the brains.

Indian *Sorrel.* In the isle of *Java*, and adjacent islands, grows an odd kind of sorrel, having no resemblance to the *European* sorrel, growing up to the height of six foot, with a strong, hard, and three corner'd stalk not unlike the hemp; the leaves being also not unlike those of the hemp, beset with sharp small prickles. The flower has but one single leaf of a pale yellow colour, but of a purple colour below. The leaves chew'd have the same taste as our sorrel, but are more oily: The seed is thorny like that of *Carduus*, and of a cooling and drying quality. The *Malayans* eat this herb among their sallads; they also take the leaves, and after they have mix'd them well with the sawdust of sandel-wood upon a marble-stone, and a little coco oil and vinegar, make a cataplasm of it, which they apply to the head to cure the tooth-ach, proceeding from a hot cause.

Benzoin *tree.* In the isle of *Java* grows likewise the tree, out of the bark of which, after an incision made, flows that well scented gum called *Benzoin* or *Benjuin*, being a shrub or tree spread into many branches, of the thickness of a man's arm.

Nardus. About *Batavia* grows a plant in great plenty call'd *Nardus*, most in request among the *Javanese*, who used it in their fish and boil'd meat sauces, to give them a relish. They steep the *Nardus* in vinegar, and make a syrup of it with sugar, which is esteem'd a good remedy against the coldness of the bowels, and opens the obstructions of the spleen and liver. This vinegar and syrup cures also the stings of the serpents and scorpions, if applied outwardly and taken inwardly at the same time.

Amsion, *or* Opium. *Amsioen* or *Amsion*, as it is called by the *Indians*, and *Opium* by the *Europeans*, is nothing else but the juice of poppies, much used by the *Javanese* and other *Indians*, especially when they are upon the point of engaging their enemies. The *Amsion* is a very useful drug to the *Indians*, without which they would be at a stand how to cure many distempers in this hot climate, as the bloody flux, burning fevers, and such like distempers proceeding from the gall. The poorer sort of the *Indians* boil the leaves and sprouts of the *Amsion*, out of which they make a slighter sort of *Opium*, by coagulating the decoction called *Poust*.

Pyzang. The fruit called *Pyzang* or *Indian* figs, as also *Bachovees* from the *Portuguese* word *Bakovia*, are called *Pyzang* or *Banana*'s by the *Malayans*, *Gedars* by the *Javanese*, *Thio* by the *Chinese*, by the rest of the *Indians* *Oucelli*, by the inhabitants of the isle of *St. Thomas Oucella*; and by the *Arabians* *Maus* and *Muza*. The stem or trunk of this tree grows up in long oval scollops to the height of 20 or 30 foot in six months time; its circumference being of four foot, but so soft, that you may cut it with a knife like a cabbage stalk. It spreads its branches very loftily, and bears leaves, some of which are a foot and a half broad, and five, six, or seven foot long; green on the uppermost side, but dark on the other side, with a thick vein through the middle. The fruit has an ear, the stalk a yellowish brown, is very pleasing to the sight, and shap'd like a cucumber, turning at the extremities towards one another as they hang on the tree: Before they are ripe they are of a parrot green colour, but when come to full perfection, yellow both in and outside. When the fruit is fit to be gathered the stem is cut down to the ground, and the fruit, which is green as yet, taken and hung up in the house, where it ripens and turns pale yellow in a few days. The rind is so thin, that it may be taken off without a knife. Neither the tree nor fruit produces any seed, but a very handsome flower of the bigness of an ostriches egg, which sprouts forth on the top out of large buds, and opens its leaves by degrees. Whilst the stem has fruit enough to nourish, the leaves fall off one after another: Out of the before-mentioned knot or flower comes forth a branch, on which grows the fruit in a cluster, sometimes 1 or 200 together, so that sometimes one branch is as much as a man can carry, and each stem or trunk brings forth no more than one cluster. There are divers sorts of these figs, distinguish'd by the inhabitants by different names, shapes and tastes; and they put them to various uses; some have a way of drying them in the sun, when they taste as pleasantly as the *Portuguese* figs: Of this kind I tasted at *St. Anthony*, one of the salt islands.

The *Dutch* fry them with butter and eggs, or with butter alone, and eat it for a dainty; thus dress'd they are accounted cooling, nourishing and opening. The fruit raw is very astringent, and consequently not to be eaten thus, because they are windy, and will create a nauseousness in the stomach; and sometimes will produce the bloody flux. However, they being of so agreeable a scent and taste, they are sometimes eaten raw, provided they are cut off the trees a good while before they come to full maturity; when the rind will remain green

1662. green, and the pulp by degrees acquires a very agreeable taste, not unlike our sugar pears: If you cut the fruit thro' the middle, you will see th figure of a cross within: The leaves of this tree are used like as we do our mats, to pack up goods with: And I remember, that in 1660, when I travell'd with Mr. *James Hustart* to the isle of *Buro*, the inhabitants served up their victuals in those leaves instead of dishes, and covered their meats with the same: They also used them instead of napkins to wipe their hands on: When one of our servants offered them a glass with liquor, they refused to take it; but instead thereof brought forth a leaf of a certain tree, which being accommodated for that purpose, they drunk out of it, telling us, that their cup needed no washing: The *Javanese* being of opinion, that the leaves of these fig-trees have a great virtue to extinguish the fire, they plant them near their houses, to make use of them in case of necessity. So soon as the stem or trunk is cut to the root, after the fruit is come to maturity, the root sends forth new ones, round about the old one, which coming to their full growth in a little time, and producing new fruits, the same may be had fresh all the year long. This tree grows without much trouble and in such plenty, that for a penny you may buy a whole bunch; they grow best in a fat and mellow soil. Some will have this fruit the same, which by the spies of *Israel* were brought out of the *Land of Promise* into the camp of the *Israelites*: Others are of opinion, that these were the leaves wherewith *Adam* and *Eve* covered their nakedness: Others again maintain, that *Adam* eat of this fruit, which occasioned his fall, whence they call them *Paradise Apples*.

The Bamboe.

The *Bamboe* grows all over *Batavia*, being strait reeds clove in two at the upper-end, having no root fastened in the ground, but grows without the least portion of earth from the surface of the water, having on the bottom a thick knob, from whence sprout forth small twigs like threads, which being nourished by the air and thaw, bring forth leaves and flowers. Its flowers are very white, having five long leaves somewhat crumpled, not unlike the white lillies; they have also a very odoriferous scent, and a yellow seed within. The leaves sprout forth at the extremity of the twigs bending downwards, which bear long and narrow leaves. It is very surprizing both for its natural growth, and its most agreeable scent.

Button *flower*.

The flower called by the *Malayans*, *Borago Soesan*, by the *Javanese*, *Bunbang Ungo*, and *Licuboa* by the *Chinese*; the *Portuguese* call *Fule de Botano*, i. e. the *Button Flower*, from its resemblance to a button. It grows in great plenty in the gardens, by reason of its pleasing purple colour, (which remains even after it is dried) but has no scent. It grows like our clover, except that the leaves grow closer to one another on thin brown stalks; The flower comes forth with green buds betwixt two leaves. 1662.

The white sweet-briar.

The white sweet briar, called *Boenga Dadu* by the *Javanese* and *Malayans*, and *Tyntsou* by the *Chinese*, bears leaves and flowers like our rose-tree, except that the flowers, which are very white, are not altogether so large, and have pointed leaves; they scent like our roses, but not altogether so strong. They say, that this tree was first transplanted from *Persia* near *Batavia* by the *Dutch*, when they first settled here: Out of the leaves of the flowers they distil rose-water, used in the same manner as our rose-water, for which reason they are very industrious to propagate this tree.

Jakkas.

The tree which bears the fruit called *Jakka*, or *Jakkas* by the *Portuguese*, and *Nanka* by the *Javanese*, is one of the largest fruit-trees of the *Indies*, which delights in high and dry grounds, where it will grow up to the height of an oak-tree. The leaves are blue on the underside, but green on the other side, round and less than the leaves of our cherry-trees. It bears no flowers, the fruit growing out of stem and branches, of such a bigness, that one of them weighs sometimes nine or ten pounds, being commonly eight inches thick, and a foot and a half long: They are very pleasing to look upon, not unlike the pompions or large melons, but on the outside like the *Ananas* or pine-apples. The fruit is green at first, but after it is gathered and ripened, yellow: It has a thick rind, covered with a kind of three cornered thorny *Lanugo*, but don't prick. Within this rind you have certain divisions like as in a honey comb, which contain certain kernels or chesnuts larger than dates, enclosed in a yellow pulp, which is eaten. The kernel is generally of the bigness of a joint of a man's thumb, and two of them be sometimes found in one of these fruits if it be of the largest size; some are yellow, others white within; the harder the sweeter they are. The fruit is of an agreeable scent, yet of a rough taste, and if eaten raw create winds, but if roasted like chesnuts are well tasted, and a provocative to venery, for which reason they are frequently eaten by the common people. If you eat too much of this fruit it inflames the blood, produces loosenesses, exulcerations in the bowels and bloody fluxes. In short, this fruit is very unwholesome by reason of its lusciousness,

1662. and is commonly evacuated by stool just as it is eaten; the pulp about the kernels being so tough, that it is scarce to be manag'd with the teeth; the kernels are eaten boil'd by the inhabitants with a little salt instead of rice. Of this fruit there are two sorts; one is call'd *Barka*, and is the best, the other *Papa* or *Girasol*, which is softer than the other; as you may perceive by pressing it with your fingers. They grow all over the *Indies*, but those of the isle of *Ceylon*, and the coast of *Malabar* are the best; I remember that the queen of *Signati* presented me with one, which was of so delicious a taste, that I could meet with none afterwards like it.

The flower Siampin. This flower is called by some the flower of *Camboja*, because it was transplanted from thence to *Batavia*, tho' others look for its original as far as *China*, whence it is call'd *Pakjaboa*. It grows all about *Batavia* in the gardens, on knotty trees, which grow sometimes twelve foot high. It bears no seed, but thick oily leaves, white on the extremities, but a pale yellow towards the stalk; some have red spots on the upper side. The flower sprouts far at the ends of the twigs in a broad knot, which produces several flowers, the scent whereof is like our *May* flowers, but stronger and not so agreeable. The leaves of the stem are long, pointed at the end, green and full of veins; the wood is grey, and near the top where the flower buds out, surrounded with many young sprigs.

The flower Katsiepiri. The flower call'd *Katsiepiri* by the *Malayans*, *Korban* by the *Javaneses*, and *Micuhoa* by the *Chinese*, grows in the gardens of *Batavia*, the tree being not unlike a palm-tree, but somewhat higher, and with larger leaves. The flowers sprout out of pale green buds, are well scented with thick, oily and snow white leaves, with yellow seeds in the middle. This flower is in great request for its pleasing scent, being sold sometimes for two-pence a piece.

Ar z or ri[illegible] flower. The rice-flower is called by the *Portuguese Fulo di Arroz*, by the *Malayans Boingo rutsia Pria*, and by the *Javanese Pella Sidanga*, all in the same sense from its scent, which is like rice when it comes boiling hot out of the pot. It grows on a kind of vine which spreads its branches like our vines, with very fair broad leaves, like those of the quince pear-tree, and are as green as a leek. The branches grow so thick that the sun cannot penetrate them, being supported by bamboo sticks. The flower has single white leaves, streaked with white within, and in the middle a pointed sprout surrounded with small buds.

Jamboa. The apples called *Pompions* by the *Dutch*, *Jamboa* by the *Portuguese*, and *Yboe* by the *Chinese*, grow scarce any where else in the *Indies* but in the isle of *Great-Java*, especially in the gardens of *Batavia*. This tree is produced by no other ways than either by laying off of the branches, like as we do our vines, or from the seed of the fruit; the first bears fruit the second year, but the tree which comes from the kernel or seed does not bear till the third or fourth year. The apples are of a gold colour without, and some of them red within; their taste being not unlike our cherries. Some are white and somewhat sweeter; they are very like oranges, both in and out side, except that they are five times as big, some weighing 10 or 12 pounds, and being 10 or 12 inches in circumference, so that one apple is sufficient for two or three at a time. They grow in clusters four or five together, on thin twigs supported by bamboo-canes, without which they would either break or hang down to the ground. The tree also grows like the orange-tree, except that the branches are somewhat thicker and closer, and the leaves broader. The blossoms have white leaves, with a yellow seed within, being of the bigness of our apple blossoms: The fruit continues almost all the year round, and after it is gathered will keep four or five months. It delights in a fat soil, and the ground must be kept clear of weeds near the stem.

Most and the best of the *Indian* fruits continue throughout the whole year, except few, among which that call'd *Mangas* by the *Javanese*, and *Pao Ampelan* by the *Malayans* is one; the trees which bear this fruit are sometimes as tall, thick and well spread as the largest oak trees in *Europe*. The flowers which are white, sprout forth of certain small twigs growing on the branches, which produce such vast plenty of fruit, that when they begin to ripen, they are forced to support them with sticks. Their time of gathering is chiefly in *September* and *October*; tho' less or more they continue throughout the year. And most of the trees bear fruit but every other year. The fruit is something larger than a plumb; green at first, but when ripe of an orange colour; some are spotted, and being of the same colour on the inside are very pleasing to the eye, but somewhat crabbed in taste. The inhabitants make divers relishing pickles of them; they boil them in a certain pickle, and make them as good in taste as the best *Portuguese* olives; others are pickled with vinegar and green pepper, and are used with roasted meats like our pickled cucumbers. They are also preserved with sugar for the use of the women; they have another way of taking off the rind and the kernel, the space of which they Mangaes *or* Manges.

1662. they fill up with sugar, butter and eggs, and so make a delicious dish of them, very pleasing both to the palate and stomach. The fruit, if eaten in any great quantity after it is ripe, is very unwholsome, but moderately used, is good against the bloody-flux. The tree is produced out of the kernel, and does not bear till some years after, neither does it bear fruits for several years before it dies.

Mangostan.

The fruit call'd *Mangostan* by the *Malayans* and *Manges Tanges* by the *Javanese*, carries the bell before all the other *Indian* fruits, for its agreeable taste. It grows chiefly about *Bantam*, and in some places of *Malacca*. The tree which bears this apple, grows no higher than a plumb or mulberry-tree, having a streight stem of the bigness of a man's calf of his leg; with a rough bark, its branches growing up like those of the clove tree; both the leaves and branches affording a very agreeable sight. The apples hang at the extremities of the small twigs, each being cover'd with two leaves, of two palms in length, having abundance of veins; they are somewhat of a pale green on the outside, but light green on the inside. This agreeable fruit comes forth from a pale green bud, which opening produces the blossom, and these the fruit. On the top of the apple is a kind of a coronet, which opens as soon as it begins to ripen. The several points of this coronet has so many marks to direct you how many kernels are contained in the apple; which are sometimes six, sometimes eight; but those which have the most kernels, are generally the best. The fruit has a very thick rind, not unlike our granate apples, of a purple colour without and whitish on the inside; Its taste is somewhat crab-like, not unlike the rind of the granate apple, and somewhat inclining to bitter; the pulp which is round the inward kernels, is sometimes white, sometimes inclining to red, being exceeding pleasing to the palate, and not unwholsome for the stomach, notwithstanding its cooling quality, it being scarce ever known, that any body surfeited himself by the eating of this fruit, a thing otherwise very common to the cooling fruits of the *Indies*. These are accounted very proper even in agues, and have towards the bottom, about the stalks, three or four different rinds or shells. These are brought in such vast quantities from *Bantam* to *Batavia*, that you may buy many of them for six-pence, and I have seen several of them in the gardens about *Batavia*, one whereof bore fruit very plentifully, which makes me believe they would thrive very well hereabouts.

Indian *Almond-tree*.

As far as I remember, there is scarce any kind of fruit tree in the *Indies* which casts its leaves so as to remain bare except this tree, which as well as the fruit is call'd *Katopper*. The tree grows up very tall, with thick branches and leaves, which afford a very plentiful shade; it is in all respects like an elm-tree, except that its leaves are above a palm in length and very narrow, with yellow veins. The stem of this tree is very strait, out of which come forth the branches one above the other in due order. The fruit grows in clusters on the extremities of the twigs with the blossoms, which are small white flowers with a yellow seed, and many green buds not open'd yet near them: The fruit is enclosed in a hairy substance, which turns yellow, and shrinks as it ripens; within which is a hard shell, which contains commonly one, and sometimes two kernels. These are as sweet as almonds, being not unlike them in shape, and are eaten and used otherwise like almonds; the shell is so hard that you can scarce crack them with your teeth. There are divers sorts of them; some having a pale red shell, which are bigger, others a yellow one.

The Javanese Rottangs.

The *Javanese Rottangs* grow in those countries wild, and are different in their kind; some would have them to be a kind of reed, because they grow sometimes with knots or joints; whereas otherwise they have no resemblance either in the stem or leaves to the cane or reed kind. This grows so fast, and twists its self sometimes so closely up to the very tops of the highest trees, that they die for want of air. They are much used in the *Indies*; however the best walking canes are brought from *Japan* and *Siam*. They bear also a kind of fruit of a brown colour like our earth-nuts, with a very thin rind, containing two kernels, which are white, but of an unpleasant taste, and therefore scarce ever eaten, except a small portion thereof next to the rinds which is well tasted. The *Chinese* make divers sorts of pickles of this fruit, in the nature of the pickled olives, and draw an oil from them, which is very good to heal wounds.

The tree and fruit Anrae.

The tree and fruit call'd by the *Portuguese* and *Dutch Anrae*, is call'd *Sarborosia* by the *Malayans*. It grows in divers places of the *Indies*, to the height of an ordinary apple-tree, with rough leaves, which are green at first, but turn brown as the fruit begins to ripen, and grow directly opposite to one another, like those of the tree *Gojovas*, but are not so broad. It bears no blossom, the fruit coming forth of buds like the *Portuguese* figs, which has a rough rind, with pale green knots, not unlike the pine-apple; it comes to full maturity in three months time, when it is gathered, and

1662. kept till it grows soft, that it may be broken with ones hands; within it resembles a rotten medlar, being full of seeds, and the pulp of so agreeable a taste, that one can scarce be satisfied with it. The inhabitants make many incisions in the bark, to make the tree bear the better, as we say of our walnut-trees, when the twigs are well beaten whilst they are gathering the fruit. There is another sort of these figs called *Atanoane* by the inhabitants, which are lesser, as is likewise the tree, which resembles a shrub, with narrow leaves, but above a palm in length. The fruit is of the bigness of a *China* apple, yellow and shadowed with an orange colour, but white within, with brown seeds; they are much more luscious, and when cut open emit a scent like rose-water, being accounted very comfortable to the brains, and therefore held in great esteem. This fruit likewise sprouts forth out of long green buds, which opening, contain another round nut or bud, which produces the fruit.

Date-tree. The date trees grow in great plenty in *Persia* near *Gamron*, and delight much in sandy grounds. Some of these trees have of late years been transplanted to *Batavia*, of which I saw a young one in Mr. *Peter Moleth*'s garden, the draught of which I have inserted, but whether it will bear fruit time will shew. The date trees continue in their full vigour for many years; they have, like the coco-trees, very small roots, and the trunk is thicker near the top, than towards the root. The pith of the three is accounted excellent good to encrease sperm and an appetite to venery, and the *Persians* about *Gamron* are so fond of this fruit, that they eat it at their meals as we do bread, or the *Indian* rice. The dates hang in yellow shells on the trees, being of a delicious taste, especially if eaten green. There is a male and female date-tree, the last of which bears fruit only; they differ also in this, that the female has a thicker and longer stem, but the blossom is the same in both, and shoots forth in a great bunch or cluster on the top of the tree, of the thickness of an arm, which opening after some time produces the flowers, and those the fruit. The *Persians* cut off this knot from the male tree before it opens, which they cut into divers pieces, one of which they put into the knot or cluster of the female tree, (which they have a way to open) pretending thereby to make the tree bear greater plenty of fruit.

They have many stories of the male and female trees, tho' not worth the inserting here.

Water-melons or Patekas. The water-melons, call'd *Batiek* by the *Indians*, as also *Patekas* or *Pateko*, grow almost in all the countries betwixt the two tropicks of *Cancer* and *Capricorn*, yet the nearer to the *Equinoctial* line, the better they are, and continue in vigour all the year round, except in the heighth of the rainy season. Some are white without, as at *Batavia*, but the red ones are the best; they have a thin green rind, which is soft and tender within. The pulp is bright, and so tender as to melt in ones mouth like sugar. The seeds are black, not unlike our pompion seeds: The plant creeps with its stalks and leaves along the ground like the pompions, and at their opening resemble our cucumbers. The fruit is sufficient for four persons to feed upon, and is, among all other fruits that are eaten raw, the most pleasant and harmless, tho' you eat ever so much of it. However, moderately eaten they are best, when they are very refreshing and acuate the stomach; whereas in too great a quantity they are obnoxious, and may occasion the bloody flux: They grow best in sandy grounds. I have seen some of them in the gardens of *Holland*, but the fruit has a watery taste.

Ananas. The fruit called *Ananas*, by the *Portuguese* and *Dutch*, is called *Nuna* by the *Malayans* and *Javanese*, and *Unglay* by the *Chinese*. The plant which produces this fruit delights to grow in shady places and a fat soil: First shoots forth a stalk of an inch thick and a foot long, on which near to the ground grows the fruit, not unlike a melon, with a well colour'd rind, being of a pale red colour mixed with orange colour'd streaks, which towards the extremities are green. The fruit looks yellow within. They are sometimes five inches in circumference, and nine long, weighing perhaps five or six pounds. Below and round about the stalk come forth certain sprouts like house-leek or aloes, with 15 or 16 carved leaves of the same colour as the fruit, green in the middle, and of an orange colour about the edges. The *Ananas*, after it is come to its full perfection, is one of the most delicious fruits of all the *Indies*; but before they are well ripe, they contain a corroding poisonous quality, of which the ripe ones even have some remnants, and therefore ought not to be eaten in too great a quantity, unless you cut them into small slices, and by pouring some *Spanish* wine upon them draw out the sharp humour. Some use water instead of wine, notwithstanding which they often create a heat in the throat; but as they are diuretick, so they are accounted good against the gravel: But without being steep'd in wine or water, they would exulcerate the palate of the mouth and the tongue, and cause a mortal bloody-flux. They have a way of preserving them with

1662. ſugar, and are thus tranſported frequently from the *Weſt-Indies* into *Europe.* This fruit has ſo fragrant a ſmell, that when it is cut it fills the room with a ſmell like roſe-water: In taſte they approach next to our large ſtrawberries, which being very inviting to the pallate, makes one eat too much, and inflames the bowels, or occaſions burning fevers, for which reaſon they ought to be eaten with caution. Thoſe of the iſle of *Ceylon* exceed the reſt in taſte; thoſe growing near *Batavia,* and in other parts of *Java,* are not ſo fine. The fruits ripen in ſix months; when they are cut from the ſtalks, which remain thus; or elſe 1662.
they take the ſprouts, and having cut them from the main ſtalk, put them thus without any root in the ground, which afterwards produce new plants. The fruit *Ananas* grows in moſt parts of both the *Indies,* and ſome are of opinion that the firſt plants thereof have been tranſplanted many years ago from *Braſil* unto the *Eaſt-Indies.*

Among other *Indian* plants, which are beneficial to human kind, is that called *Betel* or *Betele* by the *Indians,* and *Siry* by Betel.
the *Malayans, Sury* by the *Javaneſe,* and *Lauheu* by the *Chineſe,* which is one of the

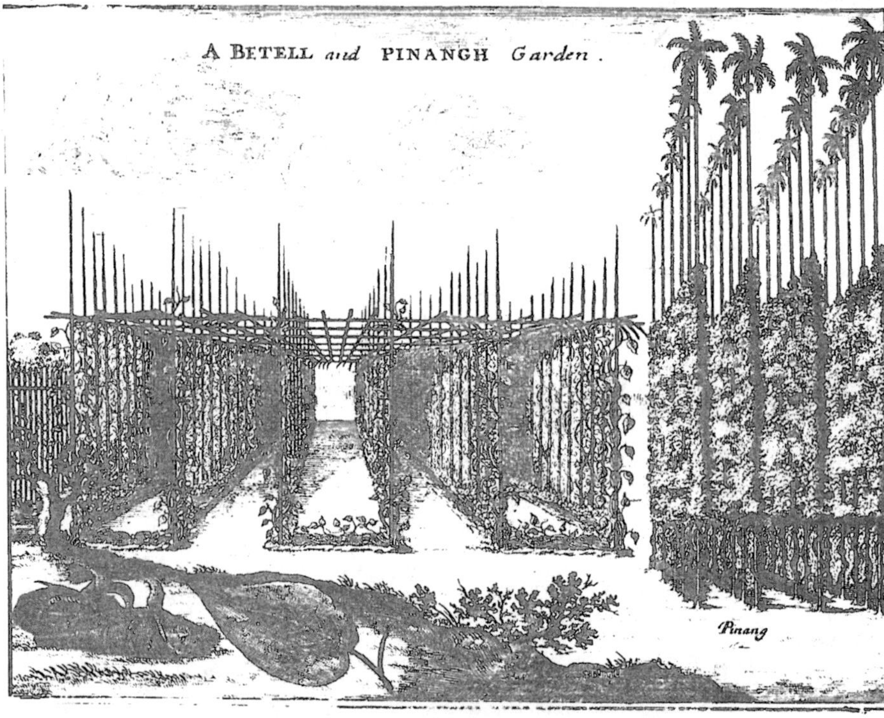

moſt inconſiderable ones. It reſembles at a diſtance the black pepper, and runs up with its branches round trees, ſtalks, poſts, or any other thing it meets with, like our hops, to a good height, delighting eſpecially in a well dung'd ſoil, and ſhady places; and growing but ſlowly in the open air: It requires alſo a conſiderable heat, which is the reaſon that it is planted near the ſeaſide, and after all muſt be defended and covered againſt the cold night blaſts, being ſo tender, that it can't bear the leaſt cold. Both the branches and leaves are in all reſpects like thoſe of the pepper; the leaves being ſometimes ſix inches broad, and as many long, of a dark green colour, having ſeveral veins thro' the length, and 5 or 6 croſſwiſe; the ſtalks are an inch broad. The leaves have a ſpicy taſte, very penetrant and ſomewhat aſtringent. They are ſo generally uſed in the *Indies,* as if the inhabitants could not live without them. They take a ſingle leaf, and a ſmall quantity of lime made of burnt oyſter ſhells, then folding the leaf together, they put into it the lime, and a fourth part of the nut *Areka,* (or *Pinang*) which augments the aſtringent quality of the *Betel,* and draws the ſpittle: After they have chew'd it thus a while, the firſt ſpittle is red, like ſtagnated blood, which being paſs'd, they ſwallow the reſt. The firſt ſpittle taints

1662. the lips with a pleasing red, as soon as it affects the brains, which is chiefly attributed to the *Areka*; and I have seen some, who, tho' used to chew this mixture, were seized with swooning fits: It never fails to create a giddiness in the head to such as are not used to it, which is soon cured by rubbing their gums with a little salt. The juice thereof, which is swallowed down, has an astringent and corroborating quality of the stomach, after the first spittle which contains the lime, is spitted out: It closes the upper orifice of the stomach, disperses the vapours arising from drunkenness, and revives the spirits. It corrects a stinking breath, cures the tooth-ach and scurvy, fastens the teeth and strengthens the gums, but makes the teeth as black as jet, an ornament much affected by the *Indians*; and if you chew too much of this mixture, it will loosen and corrode the teeth. *Betel* chew'd without lime, produces a green spittle, but with lime, makes it red; persons of quality mix some musk, ambergreece or camphire with it: The use of it is so frequent here, that no body pays a visit to another, but a small dish of *Betel* is brought immediately. Nice people spit in pots.

Pynang *tree.* The ancient herbalists have placed the *Pynang* tree among the palm-trees, perhaps because its stem, leaves and branches, are not unlike the coco-tree. It owes its original to the kernel of the nut like the coco-tree, and grows all over the *Indies*, especially in the isle of *Ceylon*, where they drive a great traffick with these nuts, and transport them in prodigious quantities to the coast of *Madura* and other places. In a few years after it is planted it bears nuts. From underneath the leaves sprout forth certain twigs, which grow close together, and are full of small of small white leaves, emitting a most fragrant scent at a considerable distance, especially mornings and evenings. After these flowers come the nuts, called *Fausel* by the *Arabians*, *Areka* by the *Indians*, and *Pynang* by the *Malayans*: They grow very thick together on both sides of very strong stalks, being green at first, but turning yellow by degrees; some are of an orange colour. Some of these nuts grow not so close on tender twigs; others, which are of an orange colour, grow out of certain green husks, in bunches like grapes; they are covered on the out-side with a hairy substance. This tree equals in heighth the coco-tree, but the stem seldom exceeds six or seven inches in thickness, neither has it so long and many branches as the coco-tree, and the leaves are shorter and broader. These trees look very odly at a distance, being so thin of stem and almost without branches, so that they are beat by the wind on all sides, yet never break. The stem is spongy within, but the bark very hard, of which they make laths for the coverings of their houses, for which they are very useful by reason of their straightness. The fruit resembles an acorn, but is four bigger; however, when cleansed from the hairy threads, the nut scarce exceeds the bigness of a nutmeg, and looks like it within. The kernels are astingent, and good for the stomach. They make no other use of them but for chewing with the *Betel* leaves and lime, as we told you before. They cleanse the nuts from the hairy strings with a pair of scissors, and cut the nut if large in four, or else in two pieces; and this put into a leaf of *Betel*, and mix'd with a little lime, they chew so long as it will draw the spittle, and spit out what remains; but the old *Pynang* nuts with the *Betel* leaf will dissolve insensibly in the mouth. Such as are not used to the chewing of *Pynang*, especially if used before it is come to its full maturity, will certainly be seiz'd with giddiness in the head, and will fall down without sense or motion.

Suryboa is a certain plant which runs up close round the *Pynang* tree to a great heighth, and being planted in rows, afford shady and agreeable walks. The leaves and branches are like those of the *Betel* or of pepper: The fruit is not unlike in shape to the *Bengal* pepper, growing on small and green stalks of two fingers length: It is green and chequer'd, of the length of a palm, but scarce an inch thick, containing a white kernel with small seeds. These kernels are used with the *Areka* instead of *Bethel*, being a pleasant chew. They cut them throught the middle, and taking one half of the *Pinang* kernel likewise cut in the middle, they tie both together wirh a cotton thread, and with the addition of a small quantity of lime made of oyster-shells, use it like as they do the *Bethel*; it has the same effects, and being not so common as the *Betel*, is more esteem'd among persons of quality. Suryboa.

Dap-Daf or *Dap-Dap*, is a very agreeable fruit both raw and dress'd, having a very plesant taste, of a mixture of sweet and sour, and of a cooling quality. It grows out of the bottom of a stem of a tree, having very fine leaves, the flowers or blossom consisting of small red leaves. The fruit is inclining to red, mix'd with black spots of an oval figure, and ragged, bent a little at the end like a cucumber. It contains a white kernel of a delicious taste, being enclosed in a whitish rind. These trees bear fruit all the year long, Dap-Daf *or* Dap-Dap.

long, and grow properly in the *Molucca* iſlands, from whence they have been tranſplanted into the gardens of *Batavia*, but do not thrive ſo well there as in their native ſoil, being much peſter'd with aunts or piſmires, which do incredible miſchiefs to the fruits there. The tree whereof I took the draught at *Batavia*, was ſurrounded with rails, within which the ground was paved with ſtone, and a ſmall ciſtern in it with water, notwithſtanding which the fruit was ſo covered with piſmires as ſcarce to be diſcerned.

Takkatak. The fruit call'd *Takkatak*, or *Boa Burun* by the *Malayans*, and *Kannekoeni* by the *Javaneſe*, are by the *Dutch* called *Red-Currants*, from their reſemblance to our currants, tho' in their qualifications they are very different. Theſe berries grow on high trees with large leaves, not unlike the cheſnut trees, and ſprout forth in large buds in cluſters, on the twigs of the trees, being of the ſame bigneſs as ours, but are of a ſour taſte; notwithſtanding which they are much coveted, and ſold and uſed in great quantities at *Batavia*, in the ſame manner as we do our red-currants. They grow in the gardens about *Batavia*, and bear fruit every three months, but moſt in *September*.

Moringo. The tree call'd *Moringo* by the *Portugueſe* and *Dutch*, *Ramongy* by the *Malayans*, and *Kelor* by the *Chineſe*, is found not only in all the gardens, but alſo before the houſes: It has a white bloſſom, which ſprouts forth from white buds, having a yellow ſeed within. The fruits grow ſeveral together, being encloſed in hard huſks, not unlike our *French* beans, except that the huſks are round and longer. So ſoon as they are ripe, they are gathered, and the twigs on the top being cut off, others ſprout forth in their ſtead, which bear new fruit. The leaves are very ſmooth and thick, in taſte not unlike the coco leaves in *Holland*, but not ſo biting and penetrant. They ſtew theſe leaves with meat, or eat them alone, as we do our ſpinage, being well taſted and cooling; the ſame they do with the huſks, whilſt they are young, but when old are tough; ſo that both the uſefulneſs and pleaſantneſs of this tree is a ſufficient encouragement to the people to afford it a place in their gardens, eſpecially ſince it wants no great induſtry to plant it, as growing out of a ſprig of the tree planted only in the ground without any root, which in a few months begins to bloſſom and to bear fruit.

Torre. The tree called *Torre* by the *Malabars*, *Tary* by the *Portugueſe*, *Rombang Juri* by the *Javaneſe*, and *Huſk-Tree* by the *Dutch*, does not riſe above the heighth of an ordinary apple-tree: It brings forth certain huſks hanging ſtrait down on thin ſtalks of about a quarter of a yard in length, and the thickneſs of a little finger. The huſks contain 8 or o ſmall peaſe, which are eaten as well as the leaves, which are round and ſmall, growing on ſmall twigs, and the flowers, which are ſurpriſing at firſt ſight. They ſprout forth out of green buds in the ſhape of a half-moon, with purple-coloured points, and ſtreaks of the ſame colour within: From the innermoſt leaf come forth certain long and thin ſprouts like fillets, with yellow hairy points; the ſtalk is green, but the beginning of the leaves of the flower are white, interſpers'd with veins to the extremities, with a parrot-green colour intermix'd with ſome red, which affords a moſt agreeable ſpectacle to the eye: The inhabitants alſo make uſe of the leaves as a ſovereign remedy againſt the ſtings of the ſerpents, in which caſe they ſqueeze them betwixt two ſtones, and mixing a little ſalt with them, apply them to the tumor, which give immediate relief.

The *Portugueſe* have given it the name of *Folio di Inverno*, or *Devil's-Leaf*, or *Helliſh-Leaf*, becauſe it will over-run all places wherever it lights; the *Malayans* call it *Garrak*, and the *Javaneſe Klatte*: It has ſeveral phyſical virtues againſt divers diſtempers. Devil's-Plant. There are two ſorts, diſtinguiſh'd by their different colours, one having green leaves, and growing very faſt, the other being brown and red, like the leaves of our red-cabbages, and growing up to the heighth of 12 or 14 foot, with carved leaves hanging on very long ſtalks. On the top ſprouts out a bunch of green buds, which opening by degrees, produce yellowiſh flowers; after which comes the fruit, not unlike a cheſnut, containing a bean or kernel, which is very good food.

The broad Nomerado. The plant or herb called the *Broad-Numerado* by the *Portugueſe*, and *Bajan Dierdia* by the *Malayans*. The ſhape of the leaf which grows on the ſtalk of this plant chequered with various colours like a tulip, is altogether like our beetes, and uſed in the ſame manner, but is preſerved for the beauty of its leaves, which are on the top, as an ornament of the gardens. There is another ſort reſembling in colour our red cabbages, and is frequently planted by the *Chineſe*, who ſell it in great quantities in the market of *Batavia*; it is of an agreeable taſte, either boil'd with meat or ſtew'd by it ſelf.

Kappok. The tree which produces the *Javaneſe* cotton, is call'd *Kappok* by the *Malayans*, *Jerondo* by the *Javaneſe*, and *My* by the *Chineſe*, grows up to the heighth of a great maſt, ſpreading its branches directly ſtraight-

1662. straightways on all sides. The bark of this tree is white, as far as the lowermost branches, but from thence to the top green; the flowers which are white come forth out of certain buds growing out of the branches; then come the fruits of the bigness of a hen's egg, pointed at the end, being green at first, but turn brown like a dried oak-leaf. These fruits hang on the middle and end of the branches, two and two together, seldom one alone. They open at last near the stalks, and produce the cotton-wool, which covers the seed, and extends its self when exposed to the air. The seeds are black, not unlike the brown pepper, but somewhat smoother. The cotton-wool is gathered in the *Indies* in *October* and *November*, wherewith they drive a considerable traffick all over the *Indies*, where they are used instead of feathers, to stuff their cushions, bolsters and quilts withal, feather-beds being unknown here, but is not long enough for combing, or for weaving: Great care is to be taken that no fire come near it, for if it takes fire it burns with such violence, that scarce any water can quench it. This tree grows whereever it is planted.

Jamboes. The tree *Jamboes*, as the *Indians* and *Javanese* call it, the *Portuguese Rosado*, the *Malayans Jamboe Ramus*, and the *Chinese Ileapont*, affords a very agreeable entertainment to the eye, while it stands in full blossom. It grows up very regularly, in the shape of a pyramid, the branches growing in good order, neither entangled within one another, neither above one another. It rises to the heighth of a large pear-tree in *Europe*, and takes deep root. The leaves are long and green, at the extremities of the small twigs sprout out green buds, which produce flowers with leaves as red as blood, containing certain red fillets within: The fruits are of an oval figure, resembling in bigness and shape our sugar-pears, which grow in clusters 23, 24 or 25 together: Some are red, others white, but both of the same taste, tho' the white ones are reckoned the best. They smell very sweet, but are somewhat mellow: The stone which lies in the middle has a large but bitter kernel, which is never eaten. Abundance of these flowers which produce no fruit, fall from the tree upon the ground, which cover the ground underneath, and afford a pleasant sight. The stalks of the flowers are red, not unlike the sea-lion's, but not so long. These flowers have so pleasing and savory a taste, that they are used and eaten as a delicious sallad. The fruit has a sweet, yet relishing rest, and allays the excessive heat of the stomach; if stew'd with sugar, and a little wine, they eat like stew'd pears. The best I ever met with were in the isle of *Ceylon*, where they grow in great plenty. These trees are produced from the seed, and bear fruit in the 4th year, and three times in a year, so that they never are in want of this fruit throughout all the seasons: 'Tis generally believed that this tree, for his sweet scented flowers and well tasted fruit's sake, was transplanted from *Malacca* into other distant countries. There is yet another sort of *Jamboes*, which grow in the isle of *Amboyna*, on trees no bigger than our cherry-trees, but they are not so well tasted; so that this tree is cultivated there rather for its blossom, which is red also, than the goodness of the fruit.

Among many other fruits, which if eaten raw, are crabbed and sour upon the tongue, we must not pass by in silence what the *Portuguese* call *Nelyka*, the *Malayans* and *Javanese Boa Malakka*, the *Chinese Soaly*, and the *Dutch Wild-Plumbs*: They grow in vast numbers on thin twigs, and are greenish of colour; the twigs have small green leaves growing close together. The fruit has a sourish taste, and is very cooling, for which reason it is in request by some, tho' generally no great account is made of it. They are in their prime in *August*, and are then to be sold in the market in *Batavia*. Boa Malakka.

Canary tree. The tree called *Canary* by the *Malayans*, *Javanese* and *Chinese*, is an *Indian* oak-tree, which grows very high with lofty branches and very smooth leaves, interwoven with divers veins. The stem grows thick, and extends it self into several protuberances near the root. The rangers of the forests keep a watchful eye over these trees at convenient distances, when the acorns begin to fall, because the wild-boars appearing in great numbers, they shoot them; so that during that season, the wild-boars flesh is sold at a cheap rate in the market of *Batavia*. The fruit is nothing else but an acorn or nut, produced out of a yellow blossom growing on small twigs. The nut or acorn is enclosed in a green shell, and next to that another, which is so hard, that you must break it with a hammer, if you will come at the kernel, which is as white as an almond, and of as good a taste, being covered by a thin skin.

In and near the city of *Batavia*, grows in the gardens a certain flower, both in scent and figure not unlike our camomile-flower, but whether it obtains the same virtue, is unknown hitherto. The *Topasses* call it after the *Portuguese*, *Fulo di Madre*, i. e. *Mother-Flower*, because its leaves and the flower are somewhat like the *Matricaria*, and perhaps of the same kind. It Camomil tree or Fulo di Madre.

1662. grows about a foot high, with large carved leaves: The flower which is white, sprouts forth out of green buds, with double leaves carv'd at the ends.

The flower call'd *Four-Lights* comes forth out of small buds, being not unlike a single gilliflower, but of a bright red colour. It consists of four carved leaves, which have certain pleasant curls at the ends. The leaves are dark green on the inside, and pale green without, checquered with streaks which run all along to the point of the leaf, which has the shape of an heart. This flower is kept only for ornaments sake, but is soon faded.

Alli *or water-flower.* There is scarce a lake or pool in this countrey, but what produces some flower or other; but the flower called *Alli* is found in great plenty all along the ditch or *Gracht* betwixt *Ansjol* and *Jacatra*. It is a pretty sort of a flower, which may be kept a pretty while in water: It comes forth out of long and large buds, is pale green without, and white within with yellow seeds. After it is opened, it is not unlike a tulip or lilly, except that the leaves are green on the out-side. Its virtues are unknown as yet, but is kept for ornament's sake.

White violet or Jarron. The leaves of this flower growing close within one another like our violets, it has got the name of a white violet, scarce differing from it in any thing but the scent. It grows wild on certain shrubs without *Batavia*; when they are planted in the gardens, the stalks thereof are cut down close to the ground, when new stalks sprout forth, which bring flowers in great plenty. The inhabitants who call this flower *Jarron*, say it was brought hither from the isle of *Baly*. The *Malayans* call it *Benja Susun*, the *Javanese Malati Rompah*, and the *Chinese Beleboa*. It much resembles the *Katsiopiri*, but is not so strong of scent, tho' it has no scent at all, except in the morning, before the sun-beams have dry'd up the dew from its leaves. The leaves are pale green, in shape not unlike peach leaves, but something broader: The flower issues out of a pale green turned bud, of the bigness of a double daffadil, and is snow white.

Cotton of Bengale. There is a certain sort of cotton which is transplanted from *Bengal* to *Batavia*, called by the *Chinese Algocdan*, but by the *Malayans* and *Javanese Kapas* or *Kappas*; the tree bears flowers and fruit throughout the whole year. So soon as the flowers are gone, there buds out a knot, containing the cotton or wool: The leaves are carved in three places, being not unlike a certain herb the *Dutch* call *Ducksfoot*. The flower is brown red, having within certain pointed fillets. This cotton is fit for weaving. 1662.

The fruit called *Batsjan* by the *Javanese* *Malayans* and *Chinese*, is a kind of wild *Mangas* of so strong a scent, that you may smell it before all other herbs in the market. The tree which bears this fruit, is very delightful to the eye, and not unlike the *Mangas* tree, but the leaves are somewhat bigger than those of the almond-tree, of a dark green colour. The blossom is also like that of the *Mangas* tree, and yellow. The fruit is green, of the bigness and shape of a limon, within which grow certain almonds, which are much more taking to the eye than toothsom, tho' the smell is much more disagreeable than the taste, which is bitterish, and somewhat nauseous, and not comparable to the true *Mangas*, which is the reason they are not much planted near *Batavia*, but abundance of them are brought to market there from *Bantam*, in *October* and *November*. *Wild Mangas.*

About *Batavia* and all over the isle of *Java* grows a certain tree called *Marokko* or *Morukko* by the *Portuguese*, *Dap-Dap* or *Dadap* by the *Javanese*, *Darradap* by the *Malayans*, and *Oysensio* by the *Chinese*. Its leaves are like those of the poplar-tree, but as big again, smell very well, and grow on yellow stalks. These leaves being interspersed with many yellow veins, appear at a distance as if the tree were cover'd with flowers. The inhabitants lay these leaves over their pots, in which they have their boiled rice, the steam of which draws out from thence a very agreeable scent; but have no other use that I know of. Marokko.

The plant call'd *Ratsiobonk* by the *Malayans* and *Javanese*, *Bantoboa* by the *Chinese*, *Datura* by the *Turks* and *Persians*, *Duroa* by the *Indians*, and in a broken dialect *Dutter* by the *Dutch*, grows wild in the woods, almost all over the *Indies*; it seldom rises above the heighth or thickness of our red cabbages, the stalk being very like the same, but the leaves brown, pale, green and carved. It bears divers flowers, which open every morning, and close up again about noon; they are white within, and pale yellow without, some being near a palm in length, and of the figure of a bell, others carved at the extremities; after these comes the fruit, which has a pale green rind, cover'd with thorny prickles; they seldom exceed the bigness of our yellow palms, and contain yellowish seeds. Whether this plant has the virtue of intoxicating to a degree of madness for a certain time, as some would have it, I am not able to determine; but this I am certain of, that the *Topasses* and other negroes, who keep it in their gardens near *Batavia* *The plant* Dutter.

1662. *Batavia*, look upon it as a fable. It is properly a kind of nightshade or henbane.

Kananga. The trees call'd *Kananga* by the *Malayans*, *Javanese* and *Chinese*, bear leaves of a parrot green colour, above which comes forth the blossom; they are planted near the *Betel*, which winds about them; and growing to a great heighth, their lofty tops are conspicuous above most of the other fruitful trees in the gardens; as far as I know, they have no other use. Besides that, these trees are easily to be discerned from the rest by their crooked hanging boughs, they commonly set a little wind-mill in the tops to frighten the birds out of the garden, especially the great bats here, which keep their rendezvouses in these trees, and are seen hanging with their claws to the branches thereof with their heads downwards, and that in such numbers, that you see sometimes more batts than leaves on a tree.

Indian oak. The *Indian* oak-tree produces no eatable fruit, yet does its wood make a sufficient amends for this defect, being the most lasting of all, and as good as our *European* oak. This tree grows up to a great heighth, as may be seen by the long pieces of timber in many of the churches, and other lofty buildings of *Batavia*. This tree is sufficiently known by its large branches and broad leaves, which sprout forth out of the boughs and branches, being intermix'd with green veins of a pale brown colour, and somewhat rough, something resembling the fig-leaves, but are not carv'd; at the extremities of the boughs sprout forth certain flowers not unlike the hops, which produce acorns, the seeds from whence this large tree takes its root; the inhabitants use the leaves in the pleurisy: They take a certain quantity of the liquor contain'd in the coco-nuts, in which they boil some of these leaves, to the consumption of half the liquor, and this decoction they give the patient to take inwardly, which appeases the pain. I have seen pieces of this oak-timber as streight as an arrow, no less than forty foot long, and of 2½ foot diameter to the very top in thickness; and nothing more common than to meet with boards of this wood of three and more foot broad. The *Malayans* call this tree *Kyati*, from whence they call this oak-wood, *Kiaten-wood*; which is exceeding hard, and has the same veins as our oak, being very lasting, and not subject to be worm-eaten, being proof, especially against the mice, which sometimes will eat whole pieces of the timber within, tho' the out side appear very sound.

Water-pompions. The fruit call'd water-pompions by the *Dutch* from their shape, are call'd *Katolas* by the *Malayans* and *Javanese*, and with a broken name *Katilas* by the *Portuguese*. It is neither a tree, shrub, herb nor plant, 1662. but sprouts forth in the nature of small branches, from a small seed, and spreads to that degree, that it runs over the tops of the houses with its leaves and flowers. The *Indians* frequently lead them over their cisterns in which they bathe, being sustain'd by bamboo-canes to keep off the heat of the sun-beams. They bring fruits the whole years round, but especially in *April* and *August*. The flowers are like those of our pompions, and fade without producing any fruit. The fruit is of two sorts, one grows to the bigness of our ordinary pompions, but the other which is the best, scarce exceeds in bulk our cucumbers or melons. They are used in the same manner for salad. There is another sort of the length of a man's arm. but no thicker than a good walking-cane, the rind being full of spots; that of which I took the draught was 13 inches long and 3½ diameter, weighing 3¼ pounds. When the gardners have a mind to make this grow longer than their ordinary size, they fasten a weight with wire-thread to the extremities of it, which stretches it downwards to a prodigious length. The leaves and branches are like those of the pompions; the fruit green inclining to yellow on the rind without, but white within; as are also the seed.

If we should enter upon giving you an account of all the flowers that grow in the isle of *Java*, it would require an entire volume; among the chiefest and best is that flower call'd *Champakka* of *Siampakka* by the *Malayans* and *Indians*, and *Vinhoa* by the *Chinese*. The tree which produces these flowers, grows up to the heighth of our moderate pear-trees or peach-trees, with large wrinkled leaves, intermix'd with many veins. The branches or boughs grow all in a strait line from the tree, and afterward turn upwards; they are generally so weak that no body can climb up to the tree, so that the flowers which grow on the top, must be taken down with bamboo-canes or reeds. These flowers are in great request among the *Indians*, for their odoriferous scent, and used in garlands: The scent is betwixt a rose and a violet, and so strong, that it may be smell'd in the houses, as the flowers are carried by in the streets; they are of two colours, *viz.* of an orange colour and green, not unlike the blossom of a *Spanish* orange-tree, but resemble in figure the *English* saffron. This flower is one ingredient of that famous ointment made by the *Indian* women call'd *Borbory*; they also adorn their hair among the rest with this flower. This tree also bears fruit, which grows out of the sprigs like bunches of grapes, Champakka.

1662.

grapes, and are of the same colour and bigness, but fit for nothing.

The great creeping-beans. The branches which produce the beans, call'd by the *Dutch* the *Large Creeping-Beans*, are call'd *Katsjang Parang* by the *Malayans* and *Javanese*, and run up in many small branches to such a heighth, that their curl'd sprigs on the top grow beyond the pinacles of the highest buildings. At the bottom they are of the thickness of a man's arm, and change their leaves and fruits, without any alteration to themselves; they bear fine green and thick leaves, intermix'd with small veins; the blossoms are of a purple colour, and before they open pointed at the end: The husks which contain the beans, are green like ours, having a purple colour'd string all round the husk. They are of divers sorts, among which these following are most in request.

Fabas de Moro. The *Moors-Bean* call'd *Fabas de Moro* by the inhabitants, are very large, and run up to a great heighth; they commonly plant them near the *Pynang* trees, which serve them for supporters. The husks are about a foot in length, and an inch in breadth; they are chiefly used by the *Chinese* and *Javanese*, but neglected by the *Dutch*, by reason of their unsavoury taste.

Gondola. The bean call'd *Gondola* runs up likewise to good heighth, affording a very agreeable shade; the leaves boil'd or stew'd are very cooling; the ranks don't hold above one year, tho' the beans will keep green three or four years; I did plant some of the large creeping-beans at *Koulang* about a summer-house, four or five of which yielded me near six bushels of beans.

Kadjang. *Kadjang* as the *Javanese* and *Malayans* call it, and the *Chinese Petau*, is a kind of pease known by all the inhabitants of *Batavia*, which grow in vast plenty in the fields about *Batavia*. When they are ripe, they are gather'd and dry'd in the air. These pease are of the bigness of our vetches, which grow among the winter-corn, and grow with green shells at first, but turn black afterwards. Betwixt each two leaves sprouts forth a bud, which produces a flower, and this the pea. These peas are of great advantage to the ships in their return home, and when boil'd with bacon and well butter'd, are very good for the stomach. If you plant them in a pot, with earth and keep them well water'd, they will come in twice 24 hours, and make a good sallad aboard a ship.

Makandou. The tree, the fruit whereof the *Javanese* call *Makandou*, has very broad, thick and fine leaves, the blossom is long and white, after which comes the fruit *Makandou*, in all respects like a pine-apple, except that it is not pointed at the end, neither so hard, but soft. Before it is ripe, it is green, but afterwards yellow, and almost insipid. The *Malayans* roast it in the ashes, and take it inwardly against the bloody-flux, asthma and pleurisy. In the isle of *Java* grows a certain tree with leaves like those of the ash-tree, and a knotty stem or trunk. It bears a fruit like unto our hazle-nuts, the kernels whereof, after they are taken nut of the shells, are of no ill taste, yet a little astringent. The leaves apply'd to wounds and ulcers, cleanse them and render them fit for healing; a spoonful of the juice of the leaves is a good remedy against the worms. Out of the stem grows a twig, but to no great heighth, which brings forth yellow flowers, like those of the nightshade; after these come the fruits, which before they are ripe are green, but afterwards red, and of a circular figure; if you squeeze them betwixt your hands, they send forth such an ill scent, that no *Assa Fœtida* or *Segapenum* is comparable to it; for which reason the *Indian* women apply to the nostrils of such persons as are afflicted with fits of the mother: The *Indians* look upon them as not fit to be eaten.

1662.

In the woods of *Java* grows a certain shrub, call'd *Daulontas*, to the heighth of six foot, spreading its branches at a good distance, like our water-willow in *Holland*; and that in such vast quantities, that the *Chinese* are forced to root them out with fire and steel: The leaves are not unlike those of the *Balsamina*, and cover'd likewise at the ends. It bears clusters of flowers like coronets, not unlike those of the elder-der-tree; after which come certain berries that are very better, both the leaves and flowers smell like the camomile-flowers, and contain the same virtues: its decoction is excellent good against the cough, and nothing provokes the monthly terms of the women beyond this remedy. Daulontas.

The fruit *Mangam* is look'd upon by the *Javanese* as the greatest antidone in the world, even beyond *Bezoar*, *Malaive* nuts, &c. The tree which bears this fruit grows upon the graves of their kings, and the fruit is of the bigness of a coco-nut. Whenever the king of *Bantam* intends to give a mark of his particular favour to any of his particular favour to any of his great men, or some foreign minister, he first puts his drinking-cup upoe this fruit, and then drinks to the person he intends to honour. Mangam.

In the isle of *Java*, on the banks of rivers, but especially about *Bantam* grows a certain plant, the leave, whereof resemble altogether the horn of *Alce*, from whence the

1662. the *Javanese* have given it the name of *Simbar Mangiram*, and the *Malayans* that of *Tanda rousa*; it has no root, but instead thereof a veiny knot or lump, which lies not under ground, but either upon stones, or in hollow trees, sending forth its leaves on all sides. This plant is sempervirent and full of juice, and if some of the leaves happen to rot by the rains, the next sunshine produces others in their stead. The *Javanese* use these leaves like as we do the roots and leaves of the white-lillies, *viz.* to make poultices of to apply to tumors; but they are not proficuous in the St. *Anthony*'s fire, which shews that this plant is very hot, which its bitterish and biting taste seems also intimate. Taken inwardly it purges by stool, and applied to the navel kills the worms.

Simbar mangiram.

Water-flower. The flower called *Tratty*, or *Tongjong Tratty* by the *Malayans* and *Javanese*, *Tienboa* by the *Chinese*, and *Fulo de Tranke*, i. e. *The Flower of the Lake*, by the *Portuguese*, is very large and fair, and grows most commonly in pools and standing waters. The stalk grows to the heighth of a fathom above the surface of the water, and the flower resembling our tulips, except that it has broader leaves, and is at least as big again. Some are of a purple colour near the points of the leaves, which by degrees turns pale yellow or white towards the stalk. Some are quite white, but of the same shape as the former. At the first opening of the buds, these flowers emit a most fragrant scent, and discover to us their beauty, which by reason of its pleasant colour attracts the sight of all that pass by. They sprout forth out of a green bud, which bursts open like those of the peony-flowers: Some of the leaves grow upwards like the flowers, being of the breadth of a brim of a hat, and bright green; some lie flat and close to the surface of the water, being round, out of the midst of which comes forth a stalk with the flower. After the leaves are fallen off come forth round husks or buds of the bigness of a man's hand, of a green colour, containing a pale yellow seed, and many small and yellowish beans, which lying bare in part, resemble the *Faba Ægyptiaca* of *Dioscorides*, *viz.* this husk being flat on one side, is as if it were cut asunder in the middle with a knife, and discovers about 30 beans placed in a circle. As these beans grow to their full bigness, they are enclosed in a peculiar husk, and when ripe, resemble the green husk of a hazel-nut without the shell, and are not unlike it in taste, being very sweet, but somewhat phlegmatick; they are sold daily in the market of *Batavia*: It seems to me to be a kind of water-lilly, having broad and red leaves, and being the same both in the stalk and root, tho' it differs from our *Dutch* water-lillies, which are white or yellow, but are of a purple colour in the *Indies*: It also differs from ours in the fruit and husk. The leaves of this plant are steemed cold in the third degree, like our *European* water-lillies; wherefore also the *Dutch* here, after the example of the *Malayans*, give the decoction thereof in burning fevers, frensies, bloody-fluxes and other hot diseases. There is also another sort, with pale purpled flowers; and a third also worth seeing. There grows also in the rivers and pools abundance of what is commonly called ducks-meat, being a food the ducks are mighty fond of, whereof the *Chinese* keep here great numbers. In the standing pools and rivers grows also the *Potamo Geyton*, or fountain-herb, and water-plantine, which if chew'd causes great burning in the throat and upon the tongue. 1662.

Nothing is more frequent in the *Indies* than to see the trees bear fruit all the year round; but the fruit called *Langzap* by the *Malayans*, *Kakasan* by the *Javanese*, and in a broken dialect *Lansen* by the *Portuguese* and *Dutch*, is gathered but once a year, *viz.* in *February*. The trees which bear these fruits, hanging in bunches like grapes, in vast quantities, spread in a large circumference, with lofty branches, and pale green leaves like the lawrel leave, or those of the chesnut-tree, but are not carved. The fruits have a soft and yellow rind like our peaches, containing a white and sharpish liquor. They resemble most our yellow plumbs, but are inclining to red and white within, the pulp being divided by certain partitions, is of a somewhat astringent taste like our red currants, and so luscious, that one can scarce be satisfied with them; they are in great request here, being accounted very good to allay the heat of burning fevers: Each has commonly two or three kernels, from which you must suck the pulp, the kernels and skin being both bitter. The fruit sprouts out of small yellowish buds or knots, after the blossom. They grow in vast plenty in the isle of *Amboyna*, and especially ar *Gilolo*, where I have seen prodigious quantities of them brought to market. The isle of *Java* produces another sort of this fruit, called *Boa Rampi* by the *Malayans*, and *Kapandung* by the *Javanese*, differing from the former only in the outside, being for the rest the same in taste and virtue; for which reason they might well be call'd the *Javanese Lansen*: These are ripe in *October*, and are brought out of the countrey to *Batavia*. Langzap.

These purple plumbs are so called by the *Dutch* from their colour, but by the *Purple plumbs.*

1662. *Javaneſe Gapak*, and by the *Malayans Boka Gobok*: They grow in great plenty on trees of a moderate ſize; they re of purple colour without, but white within, with red ſtones. They have a ſouriſh taſte.

Jambu-lang.

The fruit *Jambulang* is the ſame with our black-cherries, which is the reaſon the *Dutch* call it by that name here, but the *Javaneſe Duat*, and the *Malayans Kriango*; tho' they are of an oval figure, and not of ſo agreeable taſte, approaching to our great ſloes; they ripen in *Autumn*. The tree which bears theſe fruits is alſo much taller than the black-cherry trees, and ſpread their branches at a great diſtance. The leaves are dark green, taper towards the ſtalk, and broader at the ends, being intermix'd with many ſtrings or veins. The flowers have red leaves with ſmall filets within: The fruit is brought to market at *Batavia* by whole large baſkets full in the months of *September* and *October*. It is look'd upon among the inhabitants as a very good remedy againſt the bloody-flux.

Fulo de Sapato, *a ſingle and douple ſhoe-flower.*

The ſingle ſhoe-flower is call'd by the *Portugueſe Fulo de Sapato*, i. e. *Shoe-flower*, becauſe the flower chew'd affords a juice, which is excellently good for blacking and beautifying of ſhoes. There are two ſorts of it, which may be diſtinguiſh'd as male and female, like our peony-flowers. Out of the flower, which is darken'd, and not unlike our common roſes, ſprouts forth on the top a yellow ſtalk, at the end of which bud out leaves like a coronet, covered with a yellow wool: The leaves are green, and carved at the extremities like our nettles. Theſe produce large buds containing the flower. They are aſtringent of taſte, and conſequently cooling: The water diſtill'd thereof is good in burning-fevers, and applied outwardly to the forehead procures ſleep. There is alſo another kind of theſe flowers, with ſingle leaves, of an iſabella colour, which grow upon ſmall trees like our ſweet-briars: They ſpread their branches at ſuch a diſtance, that they are frequently uſed for arbours; they alſo make baſkets of the twigs. The inhabitants waſh their heads with the decoction of theſe leaves, and when ſteept in vinegar, uſe it againſt the looſeneſs; they alſo apply it to bruiſes. Theſe buſhes or ſmall trees require an exceſſive heat for their growth, which is the reaſon they commonly plant them againſt the eaſt-walls here, as we do in *Europe* againſt the ſouth-walls, for the exerciſe of heat. There is likewiſe a ſhoe-flower with double leaves not differing from the former, except in its leaves, and the coronet in the middle, which are both of a bright red colour like a ruby.

The flower Dukol.

The flower called *Dukol* by the *Javaneſe*, *Bale Adap* by the *Malayans*, and *Fulo di Poco*, i. e. *Flower of the Buſh*, by the *Portugueſe*, grows every were in the hedges, to the heighth of 12 or 13 foot; it produces at the top a white leaf growing ſtraight upwards, near unto which the flowers, which are of an orange colour, grow in cluſters. The other leaves are dark green, with white veins running through the middle. 1662.

Crab or wild-plumbs.

The fruit called *Boenga Tanjong* by the *Malayans*, *Kombang* by the *Javaneſe*, *Kauky* by the *Chineſes*, and *Crab-Plumbs* by the *Dutch*, grows on very high trees with wrinkled leaves. The flowers, which are very ſmall and of an iſabella colour, open every morning, and ſend forth a moſt fragrant ſcent, but cloſe up again againſt ſun-ſet. The fruit is of the bigneſs and ſhape of a hazel-nut, green at firſt, but turns yellow afterwards, and of an orange colour at laſt: The pulp which is of the ſame colour, grows about a brown ſtone, but being of a ſour taſte, this tree is admired and planted chiefly for its flowers ſake.

Karem-bolas.

The fruit called *Karembolas*, and likewiſe *Kamozia*, *Karabelli*, *Chamarah* and *Bolunbach* by the *Indians*, grows in many places of the *Indies* on a tree, with a ſlender ſtem, twig and leaves, which is produced from the ſeed, and growing to the heighth of an ordinary cherry-tree, bears a flower of a pale blue colour, after which comes the fruit, which is green at firſt, but turns yellow, reſembling in ſhape our pompions. Some of theſe trees (which is very ſtrange) produce a fruit of ſo delicious a taſte, that nothing can be beyond it; whilſt others of the ſame kind bear a fruit ſo aſtringent and ſour as can ſcarce be imagined; when they are cut in the middle, they repreſent in the inſide a ſtar. The leaves of the tree are green, not unlike the roſe-tree leaves, but not carved and full of ſmall veins.

Boca Bidara, *or* Maſſam.

The tree which produces the fruit called *Boca Bidara* by the *Malayans* and *Javaneſe*, and *Maſſam* by the *Chineſe* and *Portugueſe*, and by the *Dutch Prick-Plumbs* from their thorney prickles, grows up to the heighth of our cherry-trees, with aſh coloured leaves, with a triple vein. Its twigs are covered all over with almoſt inviſible thorns or prickles: It produces fruit all the year round, in ſuch plenty, that the twigs bend to the very ground. The fruit is of the bigneſs of a hazel-nut, of a dark green colour without, but white within, containing a ſtone of an iſabella colour: The flowers are yellow, having no more than five leaves, with as many ſmall ſtalks betwixt them. This fruit being of an agreeable taſte, tho' ſomewhat aſtringent, is eaten raw, and very cooling. The tree

1662. grows wild at some distance from *Batavia*, but has been of late years cultivated in their gardens.

Javanese Turnips. The root called *Gadang* by the *Javanese* and *Malayans*, has got the name of a *Javanese* turnip among the *Dutch*, because it grows like our potatoes in the earth, and is of the bigness of our turnips, tho' it differs much from them both in its substance and taste. It bears dark green leaves, with white streaks or veins, betwixt which sprouts forth a twig with flowers of a purple colour. They are accounted very nourishing and wholesome, if not used in too great a quantity.

Mushrooms. Here grow divers sorts of mushrooms or toadstools, called *Kulet* by the *Malayans*, and *Jamor* by the *Javanese*. Some are of a red, others of a pale green colour; they grow without any seed out of the moisture of the earth. Some of them are used here like as in *Europe*, and are eaten with wine and sugar.

Indian Saffron, or Borbori. The plant, the root whereof is called *Borbori* by the *Javanese*, *Saffran di Terra*, i. e. *Saffron under Ground* by the *Portuguese*, *Kurkum* by the *Arabians*, and by the *Latins* *Radix Curcume* or *Curcumy-root*, has its leaves not unlike those of the white-hellebore, *viz.* thick, long, and broad, smooth and interspersed with many veins. The stalk is thick, and grows up to a considerable heighth: The flower is of a purple colour, and the root resembles the gentian-root. After the flower comes the fruit, like a chesnut, containing a round seed not unlike our peas. The root contains a saffron yellow tincture, whence it has got the name of *Indian* saffron. The *Malayans* boil and eat them both with fish and flesh, and look upon them as the most sovereign remedy in the world, against all the obstructions of the liver, lungs and spleen; again the gravel and stone, the stoppage of the monthly flowers, and other diseases of the womb, but most especially against the yellow jaundice: This root is one of the main ingredients in that oinment, called *Borbori* by the *Javanese*, wherewith they anoint the whole body.

The Indian *tree housleek.* The *Indian* tree housleek, grows in the isle of *Java*, on the *Mango* trees, and a certain *Indian* oak called *Kyati* by the *Malayans*. The shrub has long leaves, in taste not unlike our sorrel, but are more juicy, and much thicker, like our common houseleek. It has long round roots, out of which sprout forth certain threads, which fasten to the trees and stones, and grow thus till they come to their full perfection. It has a small white flower of an aromatick, smell approaching to the smell of citrons, for which reason the *Malayans* look upon it as a great strengthener of the sinews and brains. The leaves and flowers made up into a conserve, are good against the cramp, and very cordial, like our borage-flowers. After the flower comes the fruit, of the length of a finger, and an insipid taste, containing seeds as big as our barley. This plant has a certain quality of resisting all putrefactions and poisons; for which reason the *Malayan* physicians prescribe it as an infallable remedy against poison'd wounds occasion'd by the poison'd darts and other weapons of the *Javanese*, which they poison with the blood of a certain serpent called *Gekko* by the *Dutch*. 1662.

The fields and woods of *Java* produce a certain herb called *Veronica* by the *Europeans*, with a white flower; the *Malayans* and *Javanese* call it *Oribat Matta*, i. e. *a Remedy for the eyes*, because its juice allays the inflammations and defluxions in the eye. The same juice or the decoction of the herb, they also use against old coughs and consumptions: By reason of its diuretick quality, they also prescribe it for the gravel and stone, and the *Gonorvirulenta*. The leaves bruised are also apply'd outwardly to ulcers, as having a singular drying quality. Indian Veronica.

The plant call'd *Kolkas* by the *Arabians* and *Moors*, has a very thick root, large broad leaves, and bears a red fruit growing in clusters, not unlike the *Arum*. It contains a slimy poisonous substance, for which reason the *Javanese* cut them in slices, and steep them three or four days in river water; after which they squeeze the remaining juice out by a press, and having laid the roots to dry, make a kind of meal or flour of it, of which they make cakes instead of rice. The *Malayans* and *Chinese* prepare them in the same manner. The bread made of these roots, which the *Javanese* of *Materan* were forced to eat 1629, at the siege of *Batavia*, for want of rice (their magazine of *Tengel* being destroy'd by the *Dutch*) occasioned a pestiferous bloody-flux in their camp; the *Chinese* and *Malayans* also boil these roots, but throw away the the first decoction, and putting on fresh water, boil them again, and afterwards eat them with vinegar, oil of coco and pepper, as we do the red beat-root. Kolkas.

The *Indian Betony* tree has speckled leaves like our *Pulmonaria*. The flowers sprout forth like ears, sometimes a thousand in one ear, of a pale blue colour, like our rosemary-flowers. The decoction of this plant they account a good remedy against spiting of blood, the consumption and coughs, call'd *Sabit Haty*, i. e. *the disease of the heart*, by the *Malayans*, who comprehend the liver, lungs, and even the spleen, under, *The Indian Betony tree.*

1662. der the general name of the heart. The *Indian* women uſe the juice thereof as an antidote againſt the ſting of ſerpents, ſcorpions, and ſuch like venomous creatures.

Indian *graſs.*

Java produces all ſorts of graſs, and among the reſt, a peculiar kind, which has four ears croſſwiſe on the top of the ſtalk, the leaves being for the reſt like thoſe of common graſs. There alſo grows here another ſort of graſs, of the ſame kind with ſix or eight ears, which contain ſmall ſeeds. The *Malayan* phyſicians preſcribe the root and the graſs it ſelf for the bloody-flux, ſtoppage of urine, exulcerations and pains of the kidneys, and to promote the monthly times in women. *Java* produces likewiſe another kind of graſs differing from the reſt in the roots, which are three or four ſmall knots, which when chew'd have a flavour like cloves, but are not ſo hot in the mouth.

The Indian *primeprint.*

The *Indian* primeprint has got its name from its reſemblance to ours, in its leaves as well as flowers; tho' the leaves thereof have a more odoriferous ſcent than our primeprint, and the flowers, tho' the ſame in ſhape, yet differ in their colour from ours, thoſe of the *Indian* primeprint being inclinable to a blue, whereas ours are as white as ſnow, but the berries of both are black. Like unto this is a certain ſhrub called *Alkanna* and *Henne* by the *Arabians*, and *Chinnets* by the *Perſians*, except that its leaves are ſomewhat leſs. The leaves of *Alkanna* are in great requeſt throughout the *Indies*, to give their teeth, lips, but eſpecially their nails, a red tincture, a thing much eſteemed among the *Moors.* They prepare the tincture, by ſteeping the leaves after they have been rubb'd ſmall upon a marble ſtone, in fair water mixt with a ſmall quantity of lime; with this the *Turks* and *Perſians* alſo die their horſes tails. The leaves chew'd leave a piquant taſte upon the tongue, yet without any ſharpneſs. Both theſe ſhrubs are in high eſteem among the *Indian* women, who uſe the decoction of the leaves in all diſeaſes of the womb, and have an opinion that it keeps them young; and to confeſs the truth, they have a peculiar virtue (if boil'd in water) to cure the *Indian* gout or barenneſs, called *Beribery*; it grows all over the *Indies*, and the *Malayans* call it *Sagondi.*

The Indian *ſage-tree.*

The *Indian* ſage-tree grows twelve foot high, whole woods of them being to be ſeen about *Batavia*; and if planted in the gardens, ſpreads its roots to that degree, as not to be eaſily rooted out again. The flowers are white, the leaves very long and of an agreeable ſcent. They cultivate the trees in the gardens by pruning and cuting the roots and ſhoots at certain times, and by this means make it as good and as wholeſome as our garden ſage. The *Malayan* women uſe it againſt the diſtempers of the womb, mixt with the *Sagandi* and the *Daulontas*, wherewith they bathe themſelves. The flowers are preſcribed by the phyſicians to correct the cold humours of the brain and ſinews, and by reaſon of their diuretick quality are very proper in the dropſy. Our garden ſage as well as roſemary, are a kind of rarity here, the exceſſive heat of this climate being as unnatural to them, as the cold is with us in winter. 1662.

The Indian *Verbena.*

The *Indian Verbena* grows alſo in *Java*, being altogether like ours, except that the ears are ſomewhat longer and harder. They apply the flowers bruiſed to exulcerated legs, by reaſon of their drying quality, requiſite in the healing of wounds eſpecially at *Batavia*, where the moiſt and hot climate renders the cure thereof very difficult. A ſpoonful of the juice of the leaves taken inwardly, cures the cholick and bloody-flux; and the *Indian* women attribute to this plant a ſecret virtue againſt witchcraft.

The Indian *Eſula.*

In the woods of *Java* grows a certain kind of *Eſula*, which ſhoots up to a great heighth, with a three corner'd ſtalk, ſometimes of the thickneſs of a man's leg; it has abundance of thorny knobs, which being however not very hard, don't prick: The leaves grow at ſome diſtance from one another, being not unlike thoſe of our houſleek; out of the ſtalk, (after an inciſion made) iſſues a milky yellow juice, of a ſharp taſte. This juice reduced to the conſiſtency of an extract is adminiſtred in the dropſy, lameneſs and other diſtempers proceeding from cold; it purges both by ſtool and urine. This plant differs not either in ſhape or the manner of growing from that, which affords that yellow juice, call'd corruptly by the apothecaries *Gutta Gemou*, and by the *Indians Lonan Cambodia*, becauſe it is of the product of the kingdom of *Kambodia.*

Mitium Solis.

In *Java* alſo grows a certain kind of *Mitium Solis*, reſembling ours in its flowers, leaves and the ſtalk; but the fruit is much larger, and as hard as a ſtone, containing a mealy pulp. The *Portugueſe* have given it the name of *Yerva da Roſarios*, the roſary herb, becauſe the *Malayan* women uſe to make their roſaries of the fruit, and wear it about their neck inſtead of necklaces. Both the berb and fruit is proficuous in the diſtempers of the kidnies and bladder.

Boa Kamba *or* Indian *Pears.*

The fruit called *Boa Kamba* or *Kaman* by the *Javaneſe*, *Boa Binſel* by the *Malay-*

1662. *ans*, and *Letsise* by the *Chinese*, is by the *Dutch* called the *Indian* pear, by reason of its bigness and resemblance to our pears. When ripe they are of a pale yellow with black spots, hollow within, with blue seeds, the pulp adhering close to the peel. They are scarce ever cultivated in the gardens of *Batavia*, by reason of their crabbed taste, tho' very agreeable to the eye; they are brought in great quantities into the market there, especially in *February*. The tree grows up to a great heighth, having a brittle and coarse wood and leaves.

Rambustan *or* Rampostan.

Rambustan or *Rampostan* as the *Malayans* call it, is one of those fruits, which are produced without flowers, for this comes forth only out of a green bud. They grow in clusters on very small twigs of a tree, of the heighth of our cherry-trees, are of a purple colour, and resemble at a distance our chesnuts, whilst they are hanging on the trees. Within is a slender quantity of a pulp, of an acid agreeable taste, and in this a stone. They come to maturity in *February*. There is another kind of *Rambustan* growing on shorter twigs than the former, and being covered with a hairy substance; but tho' these two fruits are very different in outward appearance, their taste is much the same.

Romani *or* Satarra.

The fruit called *Satarra* by the *Malayans*, *Gandaria* by the *Javanese*, and *Romani* by the *Portuguese*, resemble our yellow plumbs, but are somewhat bigger. The inside is not unlike the *Mangas*, and in taste like the *Batsian*, yet not altogether so four. They are green at first, but turn yellow mixt with an orange colour; the pulp is likewise yellow. The inhabitants pickle and use them like as we do olives; they are of no disagreeable taste, but something more hairy than the *Mangas*.

The Javanese *flower.*

The *Javanese* flower called *Fule de Japan* (in the same sense) by the *Portuguese*, *Benga Japan* by the *Malayans*, and *Quiboa* by the *Chinese*, delights in shady places; the stalk is not above a foot high, some of which produce white flowers, others of an isabella and purple colour, sprouting forth with small knobs between the leaves; and no sooner do the leaves of the lowermost flowers fall off, but others come forth on the top in their stead. The stalk, after the leaves have been cast, produces a bud, containing a black seed, as small as tobacco seed, tho' this plant will grow without it, if you put only a twig of it in the ground. These flowers have no other use but to divert the eye.

The tree Patty.

The tree called *Patty* by the *Malayans* and *Javanese*, grows in many gardens about *Batavia*, being cherish'd by the inhabitants, by reason of its spacious branches and fine leaves, which afford an agreeable shade; it rises up to the heighth of an apple-tree, with thin branches, on which you see the fruit hanging on the stalks, three and three together, of a crabbed taste, and therefore not regarded; they resemble the pine-apple on the one side, and have a seed within. The leaves are of a lively green colour, and grow very close together. 1662.

Marygolds.

The flowers called marygolds by our people, have got their name rather from their colour, than any other resemblance to ours. The leaves are dark green, like those of the apple-tree, but somewhat less: On the tops of the twigs sprout forth certain orange colour'd buds, which opening produce the orange colour'd flowers with four leaves, they have no other use than to please the eye-sight.

The huntsman's tree.

The huntsman's tree is a kind of wild palm-tree, the stem whereof is covered with a grey rind or bark, twisted about as it were with circles. The leaves which are bright green, grow on long yellowish stalks, the lowermost of which turn yellow by degrees, and hang downwards; being for the rest very agreeable to the eye. The fruit is not near so big as the least coco-nuts, and has no other use, except that the inhabitants draw from it a certain syrup and sugar, which they sell to the neighbouring countries. The wood of the stem is very durable, provided it be kept from the air, and so hard, that they can neither saw nor cut it, but are forced to split it by pieces of wood in it; some of the *Indians* make their bows of the twigs of this tree; and the *Chinese* at *Batavia* make of the leaves and tender sprouts, fans to cool themselves with. The *Malabars* make use of the leaves instead paper, which they know how to order with a great deal of dexterity; for the leaves being about three inches broad, and above a yard long, they make holes at one end of them, and so tie as many of them together with a string, as they have occasion for at a time. They write with an iron pencil, wherewith they know how to imprint and cut their characters on the uppermost surface of these leaves, as that they remain indelible. This they perform for the most part without keeping their eyes so close and earnestly upon them, as we do. These leaves are also very durable and will not easily putrefy, even in water; I have several letters writ to me upon these *Olen* or leaves by persons of great quality among the *Malabars*. This tree also yields a juice like the coco-tree, which if boil'd, tastes very sweet, and is apt to inebriate, but if not boil'd, turns four immediately. But the chief use they make

1662. of it is, to boil it into ſugar. This huntſman's tree is none of the loweſt rank among the many kinds of palm-trees of the *Indies*, being much eſteem'd and cultivated for its uſefulneſs, eſpecially in the iſle of *Ceylon* and in *Javapatnam*, where you ſee whole woods of this tree.

The tree and fruit Billingbing *or* Blingbing.

About *Batavia* grows a tree of a moſt delightful aſpect, with moſt pleaſant leaves hanging downwards. The ſtem, which is very thick, and branches ſend forth ſmall ſprouts full of green buds or knobs, which produce red flowers, not unlike a ſmall lilly; after which comes the fruit, growing in cluſters, reſembling both in bigneſs and ſhape our ſmall cucumbers, about the thickneſs of an inch, and a fingers length. They have a green rind, and within it a ſeed, not unlike that of the cucumbers, but ſomewhat more round. The *Malayans* and *Javaneſe* call this fruit *Billingbing* and *Blinbing*. This tree is among the trees what the ſheep are among the beaſts, for they not only rob it of its flowers and fruit, but alſo of its leaves and rind, ſometimes to the very root, as having their peculiar uſe in phyſick; ſo that this tree would make but a very ſlender appearance for the moſt part, were it not that provident nature did almoſt cover its ſtem and branches with odoriferous flowers and well-taſted fruits. The fruit is very juicy and cooling, but ſomewhat aſtringent, for which reaſon it is ſeldom uſed alone, but in ſauces, to give a good reliſh: The fruit is alſo preſerved with ſugar. Our phyſicians there prepare a ſyrup out of the juice, and preſcribe it in the exceſſive heat of the liver and blood; and this ſyrup is alſo mixed with the decoction of the rice, before it is peel'd, called *Pady*, and given in fevers. This juice alſo quenches the thirſt, and has one peculiar quality, that notwithſtanding its aſtringency, it takes away that ſour taſte of divers other fruits which ſets the teeth on edge.

The Indian *dog's-tongue.*

The herb call'd hound's or dog's-tongue, from its reſemblance to ours, which bears the ſame name, is by the *Javaneſe* called *Suroe*, by the *Malayans Sudu-Sudu*, and by the *Chineſe Kautſu*. The ſtalk is thick below, but grows thin towards the top. As you pull off the leaves, you ſee a milky juice drop out of it; of which two or three drops dropt into the ear, cures the earach; as its uſe is only in phyſick, it generally grows wild.

Bitter-green.

The plant called bitter-green by our people, has got its name from its bitter taſte: It grows in the gardens of *Batavia*, and creeps up to the next tree or ſtalk, almoſt like the branches of the cucumbers, but that it leaves are deeper carved, and more pointed. The fruit is alſo not unlike a cucumber, yellow with green ſtreaks and a thick rind, yellow within, with a red kernel. When it comes to its full perfection, it is marbled with an orange colour. The *Dutch* make no account of this fruit, by reaſon of its bitter taſte; but the inhabitants uſe it in their ſawce call'd *Karry*, and put the root and leaves in their ordinary drink, which preſerves it for two or three days, whereas otherwiſe it would turn immediately. They cure the bitterneſs with ſugar. 1662.

Durions.

Among all the garden fruits, there is ſcarce any that exceed the *Durions*; 'tis true the ſcent of it is not unlike that of rotten figs, and conſequently not very inviting to ſearch after the kernel, which makes amends for the ſmell, being of a luſcious taſte. The tree which produces this fruit, grows crooked, with abundance of branches, and very harſh leaves pointed at the ends, of a palms length, ſometimes grey on the outſide, but bright green on the other ſide. They are not inferior in heighth to the talleſt trees of *Europe*. The fruit *Durions* grows in cluſters on the thicke ſtends of the twigs, and ſprouts forth out of a green bud, which growing bigger and bigger by degrees, opens at laſt into an iſabella colour'd flower, ſurrounded on the out-ſide with hard leaves, like a rind: This flower produces a thorny fruit of the bigneſs of a melon, covered with a thorny rind, not unlike the fruit *Jaka*; it is green at firſt, but turns yellow. It has four partitions within, in each of which you ſee a ſtone like a peach-ſtone, of the bigneſs of a cheſnut, containing a delicious ſweet and white kernel. Before they take out the kernels they ſtamp the fruit under foot, to avoid being wounded by the thorney prickles. The *Durions* are always eaten raw, being reckon'd one of the wholeſomeſt fruits in the *Indies*, if uſed moderately, but if in exceſs, inflame the blood, and raiſe pimples in the face. They ſeem to have an antipathy againſt the *Bethel*, becauſe they will not grow near it, but die. They come to maturity in three months time, and chiefly in *October* and *November*, tho' I have ſeen them alſo in the market of *Batavia* in *Auguſt*, for they are to be had all the year round, but not in ſuch plenty. They grow much about *Bantam*, whence they are brought to *Batavia*. The firſt that I ſaw was in the grounds of *Chriſtian Chandellour*, near the great river of *Batavia*; and ſince that I have met with them in divers other places thereabouts; ſo that this fruit thrives as well here as at *Bantam*, but no where better than near *Malacca*, where the *Durions* are of an exceſſive bigneſs.

1662. The pepper, called *Lada* or *Laden* by the *Malayans*, and *Maritsia* by the *Javanese*, grows on tender branches, with abundance of knots, and creeps up along stalks or trees like our hops. Sometimes they will climb beyond the pinnacle of the highest trees, and afterwards hang downwards. On the stalks or twigs of these branches the pepper grows in such thick clusters, that they are scarce to be discern'd from the leaves. These sprout forth out of the buds of the branches, being green and interspersed with veins, not unlike those of the cinnamon-tree, pecked at the extremity, sometimes of the breath of a hand, and long in proportion, of a bitterish taste, and hot upon the tongue: After the leaves come forth certain twigs or stalks not unlike those of the hazel-nut trees, on which hang the berries, like our red-currants, but in larger clusters; these berries turn black as they ripen. The pepper is one of the chiefest commodities in the spice-trade; the best grows along the coast of *Malabar*, near *Koulang*, where I used to buy great quantities for the company's use. The pepper must be planted in a rich soil, and bears fruit within the year. In *Malabar* it ripens chiefly in *January*, but in other places sooner or later, according to the difference of the climate. In the isle of *Java* it ripens in *October*, and is gathered in *November* and *December*, and is then green, but turns black as it is a drying in the sun; after which it is made up into balls of 80 or 90 pounds. The best pepper is white, close and biting within: There is also a sort of long pepper. The *Indians* also make a pickle of green pepper. Of the *Sagon* tree, represented in the next print, we have treated before.

Wild onions. The *Portuguese* have given the name of a wild onion, or *Sabollos de Matte*, to a certain flower, because its root resembles that of an onion, tho' for the rest it has not least congruity with it. The *Javanese* and *Malayans* call it *Hakung*, and the *Chinese* *Taukio*. This flower grows in a bunch on the top of a thin stalk, but near three foot high. They come forth out of red buds, are of a high red colour, with purple colour'd streaks of a palm in length; are very delightful to the eye, and of no disagreeable smell, especially in the morning before the dew is dry'd up by the sun-beams, for which reason they are much cherish'd in the gardens of *Batavia*. The leaves of this plant are above three foot long, and spread all round about, being pointed towards the extremities.

Potatoes. The Roots of potatoes, called *Patattes* by the *Portuguese*, after the *Brasilians*, are called *Ubi Tora* by the *Malayans*, *Ubi* by the *Javanese*, and *Hantsoa* by the *Chinese*. These 1662. roots grow in the ground on branches, with leaves not unlike the cucumber leaf; some of these branches bearing white, others blue flowers, shaped like bells. The *Chinese* cultivate these roots in the fields near *Batavia*, which must be well dung'd beforehand: They cut the ranks near the extremity, which they put into the ground, and let them grow for some time. Then they cover these ranks with rich earth, at a foot distance perhaps, into which the ranks send forth their roots, which come to maturity in a short time, and sometimes grow to the thickness of a man's arm, and a foot long. Some are red on the outside, and these are in greatest esteem at *Batavia*, but don't approach in goodness to those of *Brasil*, especially near *Rio St. Francisco*, where these roots are red both within and without. This root is frequently boil'd by the *Dutch* both with fish and flesh, excelling in taste and sweetness much our parsnip-roots or artichokes; they are also eaten raw with salt, oil and vinegar, like a salad, but are not so easy a digestion then: The best way is to roast them in the ashes, which makes them taste like chesnuts, and are good to stop the looseness, a symptom very frequent to those that inhabit near the line; for which reason this root is in great request here, and cultivated with a great deal of care, which makes them very cheap here; for you may buy as much for a half-penny as will suffice for a whole meal. In the isle of *St. Thomas* they use them instead of bread. They also make a kind of drink of them. They boil a considerable quantity of these roots in a kettle well cover'd, till they are soft or tender; then they stamp them well, and put them in a vessel with water, where they begin to ferment in twice 24 hours, when the vessel must be stopp'd up; which done, it turns clear, and as strong as good beer.

Besides the potatoes, there grows another root about *Batavia* called *Injames* by the *Portuguese*, after the *Brasilians*, by the *Javanese* and *Malayans* *Byra*, and *Siatsini* by the *Chinese*. It has a very fine green leaf, and interspersed with veins: The root has commonly five or six inches diameter, and is one foot and a half long, having a brown rind, but is white within. The flower is of a greenish colour. These roots are sold in the market of *Batavia* by the piece, weighing each 15 *Katty*, or thereabouts, a *Katty* being a pound and a quarter, according to our weight, so that 30 persons may dine upon one root. Its taste is however not near to good as the potatoes, and being of a hard digestion and very dry, they are not much look'd after by the *Injames or Byra.*

1662. the *Dutch*, but the natives are very fond of them.

Blue plumbs. The tree which bears a kind of blue plumbs, spreads its branches very loftily, not unlike the mulberry-tree, except that its leaves are of a different shape. You see this tree frequently at one and the same time laden with flowers and fruit, both ripe and unripe: The wood is very tough, so that you may venture to climb up by the smallest branches. The flowers are of an agreeable scent, especially in the morning before the dew is gone. This fruit is not regarded at *Batavia*, because the markets are over-stock'd with them by the country people, who bring them in vast quantities thither out of the mountains; tho' for the rest it is of an agreeble taste, somewhat like the dates. They are rarely to be met with here in the gardens. This plumb comes forth out of certain buds, consisting of five white leaves each, and grows on the twigs like our oval plumbs. It is green at first, but turns to a dark red, but the pulp is white, within which are three stones. The *Malayans* and *Javanese* call these plumbs *Boa Soa*, or *Sau*, the *Chinese Theely*, and the *Portuguese Fruite de Manilha*, i. e. *Fruit of Manilha*. At *Batavia* I never saw but one tree, bearing at the same time flowers and ripe plumbs.

Oranges. *Java* produces divers sorts of oranges, among which threee are prefer'd before the rest, *viz.* the common ones, and those of *Japan* and *China*. The trees are much of the same heighth, but different in their leaves; those of *Japan* have broader leaves than the ordinary ones, and these again broader than those of *China*. They all are of a different taste, yet very agreeable. The *Javanese* oranges are the biggest and most juicy, but somewhat inclining to a sour taste; among the ordinary ones, some are exceeding sweet, others quite crab-like. The *China* oranges have a pleasant taste, betwixt sweet and sour, being prefer'd here before the rest, having a very thin rind: They are preserved with sugar, like the *Portuguese* figs, and thus transported all over the *Indies*.

Wild Jamboes. Tho' this fruit called the wild *Jamboe* by our people, and *Jamboe* by the *Malayans* and *Javanese*, has not the least resemblance to the *Jamboe* we have given a description of before, in outward appearance, because that grows upon high trees, with a most delightful blossom; whereas this grows upon a low tree not unlike our mulberries, without any blossom, but is produced out of certain green buds, not unlike the figs; yet are they the same in taste, and divers other qualities. Some of them are extremely well tasted, and quench the thirst. Some are dark red, others white, mix'd with red, and that on the same tree, where they grow in clusters in such prodigious quantities, that they cover the very leaves and twigs, as if they had been spread over with a scarlet cloth. They are of the bigness of a sugar-pear. In *Amboyna* they grow in such plenty, that you may see the ground under the trees covered with them, every one being free to gather them; one reason whereof is, that they being used there as we do our acorns, for the fattening of hogs, which the *Moors* and *Mahometans* abominate, they are not much regarded. 1662.

The weed call'd *Tobako* by the *Malayans* and *Javanese*, after the *Portuguese*, grows in all parts of the *Indies*; the *Chinese* call it *Hun*. Tobacco being frequently used by the inhabitants, is consequently in great request, and carefully look'd after: that of *Ternate* being esteem'd the best, is most generally made use of at *Batavia*. They have a way of tying several leaves, weighing about two pounds together, with small twisted canes, each parcel of the best being commonly sold for six-pence; but you may buy also very good tobacco at *Batavia*, for two pence. In *Amboyna* each family commonly plants as much tobacco in their garden as they have occasion for, not troubling themselves with any other plantations. About *Batavia* the plantations of tobacco are chiefly managed by the *Chinese* and *Javanese*, and this weed grows here and thrives extremely well, provided it be planted in a rich soil, when it will grow up to the heighth of eight foot, with leaves of 18 inches long and eight broad. The *Indians* don't take tobacco through pipes, but have a way of rowling one or more leaves (according as they are big) together, and lighting the same at one end, suck in the smoke as we do with our pipes. The women commonly take of the worst sort, and rowl up their leaves in a piece of dry'd *Pysang*. *Tobacco.*

Among all the flowers of the *Indies*, that call'd *Fula Mogori* or *Mugri*, i. e. *the Flower Mogori*, by the *Portuguese*, *Kombans Malati* by the *Javanese*, and *Badiboa* by the *Chinese*, is more esteemed by the inhabitants, which they plant with singular care upon long and well dunged beds, with little walks betwixt them: The stalk on which this flower grows, seldom exceeds two foot in heighth, and grows like briars: The leaves are smooth like the quince-pear tree leaves, the flowers exceeding white, consisting of four leaves, which seldom open, and imitate in their odoriferous scent our white-lillies, but are no bigger than the blossom of an apple-tree. The *Javanese* of both sexes wear these flowers upon strings on their *Fula Mogori.*

1662. their festival days. I remember that at a certain turnament on horseback at *Japara*, I saw the *Javanese* thus adorn'd with these flowers, some of which had these strings tied several times round above their ears, with the two ends hanging down before upon their breasts. They also distil a water out of these flowers, which they esteem a great cordial in fainting-fits especially, much beyond our rose-water, it being reckoned equal with orange-flower water. They prescribe it in burning-fevers, and head-achs, proceeding from a hot cause. The *Javanese* also wash their faces with this water, to make them smooth. The leaves bruised are a good remedy against the rheum or defluxions of the eyes: These flowers grow in vast plenty all the year round, and are sold in the streets by the slaves.

The tree called the melancholy-tree, has got its denomination from its opening its flowers not till after sun-set, which continues no longer than the night time. Hence the *Portuguese* have given it the name of *Arvore da Noyte*, i. e. *the Night-tree*; at *Goa* they call it *Pareavtako*, at *Malacca Singadi*, in the kingdom of *Dekan Pul*, the *Arabians Guart*, the *Persians* and *Turks Gul*, and the *Malabars Mogli*, i. e. *trees*, for its excellency's sake; for which reason the same *Malabars* call the water distill'd from the flowers *Mogli-water*: There is another kind of this tree, which begins to blossom in the morning, and is bereaved of its leaves by night: These trees grow for the most part about *Cochin* and *Malacca*.

Arvore da Noyte *or the melancholy-tree.*

Boenga Mera.

The plant called *Boenga Mera* by the *Malayans*, *Kombang Merak* by the *Javanese*, and *Konkusiou* by the *Chinese*, has very fine green leaves, growing on small stalks, close together. The flowers, which are not unlike our gilliflowers, are high red, but yellowish at the extremities; they no sooner open, but drop of, leaving small husks behind them, which contain a kind of pease, but are not eatable.

Katsian.

Among several other sorts of beans which grow and are eaten at *Batavia*, those called *Katsian Goedi* by the *Malayans*, and *Katsian* only by the *Javanese*, but by the *Chinese Lak Goetuin*, exceed the rest. They grow in the fields all about *Batavia*, especially in those belonging to the *Chinese*: The stalks and husks of these beans are pale green, and somewhat woolly, but the leaves are smooth, and resemble those of our *French* beans, being interspersed with many veins. The blossoms are white, and sprout forth out of green knobs or buds. These beans grow almost all the year round, and consequently are no small advantage to the inhabitants of *Batavia*, affording very good food to the labouring men; as likewise for our ships, because they will keep a great while at sea. 1662.

Turkey wheat or Maiz.

The *Turkey* wheat, called *Maiz* by a general name among the *Indians*, and *Jangon* by the *Malayans*, *Javanese* and *Chinese*, grows in many places in the *Indies*, and in good plenty about *Batavia*; for they take the corn fresh out of the ears, and put it into the ground, which produces fresh corn in three months time. It is boiled and roasted with the chaff, and look'd upon as a great dainty; some of this corn is white, some red. The *Indies* produce also rice, ginger, cotton, and sugar in many places, figs, quince-pears, apples, lemons, besides many other fruits.

Thus much concerning the trees, fruits and plants of the *Indies*, and of *Java* and *Batavia* in particular; we will now proceed to give some account of the living creatures of the *Indies*, and begin with the fishes.

The sea-porpoise or hog-fish, sea-hog.

The sea-porpoise or hog-fish is about 15 or 16 inches long, and and about seven in breadth. It has a very thick skin, and such close and hard scales, that scarce any instrument will pierce them, but when boil'd the scales come off with ease, and the skin is very soft. Their flesh is very white resembling the breast of a boiled capon; the mouth is but small in proportion of the rest of the body, but is armed with two rows of white glistering teeth, one above, the other below. Upon the back, which is brown, you see a sharp fin of half a finger's length, which the fish can erect at pleasure, and such another is below near the navel; the other fins are not so strong, of a pale blue colour. The belly is white, and glistering like silver, but the sides are mix'd with yellow, which by degrees, towards the back, turns into an ash colour. It has large brown shining eyes, and when boil'd is of a very pleasant taste.

Amboynese *fish.*

The *Amboynese* fish has got its name because it is found chiefly in the rivers of *Amboyna*, but being very scarce, and of a very good taste, is look'd upon as a dainty here. It is about a span in length, something like our perch both in shape and taste. Its colour is inclining to brown, with blue streaks under the head, the fins below the mouth are likewise blue, but those on the sides are green and speckled. It is both a very wholesome and toothsome fish, especially with good sauce.

The stone-bream.

The stone-bream is a most excellent fish, some of which are four foot long; they resemble our breams, (which has begot them their name) but are much bigger.

1662. ger. Their eyes are very large, with a large red mouth, as are also the fins and extremity of the tail. They are catched at sea with a hook, being not easily to be taken with the net, and are eaten either broil'd or boil'd. There is another kind, but not so good as the former, the flesh of which shrinks when they are cut, from whence some call them shrinkers.

The baldpate. The fish called baldpate has got its name from its head and neck, being without scales, whereas the rest of the body is covered with them. It is of a greyish colour, its mouth, which is very wide, being spotted with red. The eyes are large, yellow and starting out of the head: It is one of the best sorts of fish that can be eaten, of a very agreeable taste: It is taken both in the sea and rivers.

Among the great variety of fish found in the *Indies*, most of which turn immediately after they are catch'd; there are however a few that will take salt like our herrings; such is the sea-bleak, a fish much of the bigness of a herring, but not so long and something broader: It is green on the back, but white on the belly, with a forked tail: The head is of a very odd shape, with a wide mouth and large eyes. They are catch'd in prodigious quantities, because they swim in vast shoals like the herrings, especially on the coast of *Malabar*, where they dung their rice-fields with them. They are of a tolerable good taste, but not so good as our herrings.

The sea-bleak.

The thurd fish. This fish is called thurd fish, because it delights in nasty places, tho' otherwise it is of no ill taste, but is not regarded. It is very flat, about a span in length, and near of the same breadth. The belly is blue, and the body is full of brown spots.

The yellow-tail. The fish called yellow-tail is in shape and bigness like a bream, with very sharp prominent teeth in the fore part of the mouth. The back all along to the tail is inclining to a yellow, and the tail very yellow, whence it has got its name. The belly is blue, inclining to a brown towards the forepart. It has red fins, and is catch'd with hooks at sea near the rocks: It is both a wholsome and toothsome fish.

The Kaelt *fish.* The *Kaelt* fish, as our people call it, is a kind of pike with a large piked mouth full of teeth, and large bright eyes. The belly and tail is of a purple colour, but the back brown: It is very thick and plump, about a foot and a half long, swims very swiftly, and of a good taste, but somewhat hard.

Ravens fish. The raven fish, has got its name from its mouth, like a bill under the head. It is about a span in length, red on the back and tail, but inclining to yellow on the belly, and has two yellow streaks on each side, which vanish by degrees. It is a very firm fish, and very wholesome to eat, and is taken in salt waters. 1662.

The king's fish. The king's-fish has obtain'd his title from its excellent taste, being one of the best and most wholesome fishes of the *Indies*. Some are five foot long, and have long forked tails. The back and sides are full of brown spots, but the belly is white. They can open their mouths very wide, and are very greedy after carrion.

Eels. The rivers and standing pools afford also abundance of eels; they are generally black on the back, which turns pale towards the belly, and are full of blackish spots. It is the general opinion here, that they are a kind of water-serpents. There is another sort of a ruddy colour with yellow streaks, having a sharp head with very small eyes; some of them are a foot and a half long. They are eaten by none but the natives.

The sea-eel. There is another kind of sea-eels, or rather water-serpents in the *Indies*, of about three foot long, of a brown colour, chequered with black spots like the skin of a serpent. The forepart of the body is slender, but is as thick again towards the tail. It has a long head and mouth with sharp teeth, but so small as scarce to be discerned. It delights in rocky places, and serves the natives for a dainty. This fish has one peculiar quality, *viz.* That those who kill or exenterate it, are commonly seized with a trembling, and sometimes with fainting, which however continues not long, which seems to intimate that this creature contains something of poison, which exerts its vigour at the time of its expiration.

The sea-cock. The sea-cock is a fish of a very odd shape, more like a sea-monster than a fish. Some are about two foot long, very broad and thick; a great part whereof is nothing but head. On the back it has two long fins, but one longer than the other, and below three other very long fins; a forked tail of a brown colour, but is yellow on the belly. The skin is glistering like silver, and the fins on both sides are red: It is catch'd in salt-water.

The white fish. The white-fish has a thick short head, a brown back, and blue belly inclining to yellow; it is of a tolerable good taste, and catch'd in prodigious quantities in the sea near the shoar with nets, but is generally not much regarded.

The grunting fish. The grunting fish has got its name from a certain grumbing noise it makes when it is taken; cross the back run along both sides two brown and one yellow streak; it is very plump, with little scales, not above

1662. bove a ſpan in length; the head not unlike a pope. It is of an agreeable taſte, and eaten like as we do our popes or ſmall perches.

The ſea-hog. The ſea-hog or ſea-porpoiſe called *Pixoporkas*, in the ſame ſenſe by the *Portugueſe*, is of a different kind from the former, this being not above a ſpan in length, inclining to a green with blackiſh ſcales, the fins and tail of the ſame colour, but the eyes are yellow: It is a freſh-water fiſh, very plump and fat and well taſted.

Another kind of grunting fiſh. There is alſo another kind of grunting-fiſh, ſo call'd for the ſame reaſon with the former; it is almoſt round, with a ſmooth ſkin, but full of knobs and ſpots; it is of a browniſh colour ſtreaked with black. The head is very thick, ſhort, and full of knobs, with a large mouth and red eyes. The tail is alſo very round and ſhort; on each ſide of the body is a red fin, and the fiſh is of a tolerable good taſte.

The ſea-louſe. The ſea-louſe is a ſtrange kind of ſhell-fiſh, of above a foot in length. It appears like a round lump, with a large tail, with many legs on both ſides. Its colour is gray inclining to green. It is catched near *Batavia*, but is ſeldom eaten, unleſs it be by the *Javaneſe* and *Chineſe*.

The lamprey. The *Lamprey* is a kind of an eelpoute, above a foot long, with a ſmooth ſkin, and fat like an eel, but of a different ſhape. It is brown on the belly, with yellow ſpots on the back, and has purple coloured fins under the belly. The head is not unlike that of a ſnail, with horns, and its fins are venomous. It is catch'd in ponds and pools, and eats beſt ſtew'd.

Kabos. *Kabos* is a kind of an eelpoute, but bigger than the laſt; theſe being above two foot long and very fat. The ſkin is likewiſe ſmooth, without ſcales, of a browniſh colour, but the belly is ſomewhat paler, with black ſpots. The head is thick and ſhort, with the eyes in the forehead; they are well taſted.

The pen fiſh. The pen fiſh is alſo a kind of eelpoute, with a ſmooth ſkin without ſcales; of the length of a foot, the back brown, and the belly of a pale blue colour. The fins are brown, very ſharp and venomous, ſo that if the leaſt part of it remains in a wound, it will ſcarce heal; the fiſh is of a good taſte, but unwholeſome if eaten in any quantity. It is likewiſe a freſh-water fiſh, and taken in pools and ponds.

The elephant's-noſe. The fiſh called the elephant's-noſe is of an odd ſhape, its undermoſt jaw being as ſharp as a pin. The body is prettily ſpotted, with a broad ſtreak running croſs the middle. It is a very thick fiſh, which is taken in the ſea, and in bigneſs and taſte is not unlike our large ſmelts.

Jacob Evertſon. The fiſh called *Jacob Evertſon*, is above ten foot long, weighing ſometimes 400 pound. It is blue on the belly, and brown on the body, with many dark red ſpots near the head and tail. It has a large white mouth, with a ſhort brown tail, and many fins turning up towards the back.

The crooked-back. The fiſh crooked-back has got its name from its ſhape: It has a ſmooth ſkin without ſcales, a white belly, and yellow tail and fins. It is in great requeſt all over the *Indies*, by reaſon of its agreeable taſte; ſome are four foot long.

The horn fiſh. The horn fiſh is about a ſpan in length or ſomething more, with a large head, but a little mouth; half of the body being taken up with the head. The ſkin is very bright, the back bluiſh, the belly white, but the fins and tail yellow. The body repreſents it ſelf in various colours, according to its ſeveral turnings.

Kneſſen. The fiſh called *Kneſſen*, is a baſtard carp, about a ſpan long, and pretty broad with thick ſcales. It is a well taſted freſh-water fiſh.

The flounder. Their flounders are in ſhape and bigneſs like ours, except that they have teeth, wherewith they take hold of all they light on; they alſo are as well taſted as the *Dutch* flounders; they have here alſo turbuts and ſoals, little different from ours both in ſhape and taſte.

The Klip *fiſh.* The *Klip* fiſh is a kind of fiſh with a ſmooth ſkin without ſcales, flat, broad, and of the bigneſs of our plaiſe: It is brown on the back, ſpotted with white, but very white towards the belly, with many ſtreaks of various colours. The mouth and eyes are like thoſe of the bream, and it is a well taſted fiſh.

The cod fiſh. The cod fiſh here is of the ſame ſize and colour with ours, except that it has very ſharp fins on the back and the under part of the mouth jets out beyond the uppermoſt.

The horn fiſh. The horn fiſh has got its name from the horn upon his head, and two more underneath, which being very brittle are alſo very poiſonous, and if part thereof remain in a wound, will ſcarce admit of a cure; and if you happen only to be wounded by it, it will exulcerate immediately.

The flat fiſh. The flat fiſh is about a foot long, with a ſmooth ſkin without ſcales, and a white mouth: It gliſters all over like ſilver; on the back it has a ſmall fin, and one more on each ſide. Underneath the belly, it has only one fin which is inſtead of the tail. It is a freſh-water fiſh, of a very good taſte, but full of ſmall bones, and therefore not much regarded.

1662.

The red fish. The red-fish is a kind of a bream, of a dark red colour, as are likewise the fins; however the belly is blue, and has two yellow fins; it is very thick of body, and the head is sharp at the end, with a large mouth and yellow eyes, some are four foot long.

The bitter fish. The bitter fish is of the shape and bigness of a carp, with large scales and red fins, and two black streaks round the tail. It is a fine well tasted fish, but being full of small bones, is not much in request.

The parrot fish. The parrot fish has got its name from its mouth, which turns like the bill of a parrot. It is a foot long, and sometimes bigger. It is of a greenish colour, marbled or checquered towards the head with yellow. Both the fins and eyes are of a blue colour; the last very large and sprightly, and surrounded with a yellow circle. It has very large scales, and two rows of very hard teeth, wherewith they often bite off the hooks. This fish is very greedy after muscles and oysters, which it cracks to pieces to come at the fish. It is a very firm fish, and of a good taste.

Short nose. The short nose is a fish like our haddock, having a round body; it is yellow on the belly, and the fins are of the same colour. The mouth is just under the nose, which is very short; it is a well tasted fish.

The bone fish. The bone fish is of the bigness and shape of our carps, but flatter, and has another head: It has large scales, and a forked tail; its taste is very good, but being full of small bones, is not much regarded.

The sand smelt. The sand smelt resembles in colour and bigness a small whiting, and is round of body, and inclining to a yellow on the belly: It is a sea fish, and of an excellent taste.

The pock fish. The pock fish is generally above a foot long, with a smooth skin, without scales; but being very bright, it varies in colour according to the various position of its body, appearing sometimes blue, then green, and soon after of a purple, or some other colour. It is a long fish, but not broad, not unlike a great smelt, with a forked tail, and teeth in its mouth. Tho' it is a well tasted fish, yet being full of small bones, is not eaten, except by the natives.

The Chinese fish. The *Chinese* fish is round, and about a span long; the head is like an eel, with small eyes, and a long tail. It is green on the back, but white on the belly. It is a fresh water fish, and well tasted, but those catch'd in ponds are accounted unwholesome.

The pit fish. The pit fish is no bigger than a large smelt, with a round body, full of green and yellow spots, and without scales. The eyes, which they can draw in or out, are starting out of the head. On the back they have sharp pointed fins; they delight in muddy places, notwithstanding which they are well tasted; they are very nimble, and will leap a great way. 1662.

The mullet. The mullet is a very fine fish, which being catch'd in particular places only, is dry'd in the sun, and transported all over the *Indies*. It is white of colour, chequered with blue and purple; it swims with great swiftness, and is so nimble, that it will not only leap over the net, but even over the fisher-boat. These fishes are of a dainty taste whilst in season, but at certain times they are pestered with worms, at which time they are neither toothsome nor wholesome.

The sea snipe. Nothing more common than to give names to fishes in foreign countries from what they most resemble; whence it is, that the sea snipe has got its name from tis mouth, which is like the bill of a snipe. Some of them are five foot long, with a head like that of a hog, and large bright eyes: On the back are large and sharp fins, reaching from the head to the tail, and full of spots.

The korets. Some korets are six or seven foot long, have large yellowish eyes, and a forked yellow and greyish tail, with yellow fins; under the belly, which is blue, inclining to green, and under the tail, are divers fins. They are very bright, and shine like silver, when they are catch'd at sea with hooks: They are very well tasted and not unwholesome, being sometimes a great refreshment to those ships that come to these parts.

The sea devil. This kind of fish has deservedly got the name of sea devil, by reason of its ugly shape; having the eyes on one side, and the mouth in the concavity below the head. Its tail is like that of a roach, with two teats on each side, pointed towards the end. The skin on the head is full of brown spots; some are near seven or eight foot long, but afford very course food.

The stip fish. The stip fish has a skin full of spots, is well tasted, and taken generally with hooks near the isle of St. *Vincent*.

The sea pidgeon. The sea pidgeon has got its name from the resemblance of its head to that of a pidgeon; and of its breasts protuberating like those creatures. This fish is without scales, but not without divers spots. It is but rarely catch'd, and none of the best tasted.

The sea hedge-hog. The sea hedge-hog is justly so called from its sharp fins about the head and mouth, which is round, and has very large eyes. They can't swim very swiftly, and consequently would soon fall a prey to other fish, were it not that nature has arm'd them with these pointed fins against any attempt.

1662.

The ſuckers. The ſuckers are repreſented at length in the cut, tho' there are ſome much bigger. They are blue, with bright yellow eyes, a ſmooth ſkin without ſcales: They have no teeth, but broad lips, wherewith they will ſuck, and adhere ſo cloſe to other fiſh, that they will rather be kill'd than let go their hold. They will ſtick ſo cloſe to the ſhark, that they are often catch'd with them. They are eaten ſometimes for want of better food, but are but of an indifferent taſte.

The ſhark. Some ſharks are eight, ten, or fourteen foot long: Their ſkin is rough and ſharp, and they have a double row of teeth, and ſome three or four rows, which are covered with the gums. Their eyes lie forward near the mouth. It is a very pernicious fiſh, which oftentimes bites off an arm or a leg of thoſe that divert themſelves with ſwimming. The ſharks bring forth their young ones alive, which follow the ſhe-ſhark wherever ſhe goes, and in bad weather creep into her belly, and come out again after the ſtorm is over. It is obſervable that certain fiſhes of a foot long always ſwim after the ſhark, which are plainly to be ſeen in ſtill weather.

The ſea cat. The ſea cat, (the draught whereof you ſee in the cut) is a very odd creature, both for its colour and ſhape. The eyes are exceeding large in proportion to the body, the back is of a purple colour, and the belly blue, with divers purple ſpots. The tail is in compariſon of the reſt of the body, vaſtly large, and pale red, wherewith it ſwims, it being deſtitute of fins. However, juſt on the front of the head, it has ſeven fins, which ſtand out ſtrait forward like thoſe of the ſhrimps. It affords very good food, eſpecially if dry'd in the ſun.

Souldier-fiſh. The klip-fiſh, or ſoldier-fiſh, is a kind of bream, but ſometimes grows not above to the length of a ſpan: It is flat and of a pale colour: On the back it has ſharp fins like a perch; a ſharp tail, and yellow eyes. It is one of the beſt fiſh in the *Indies*, of a very delicious taſte.

The ſea eagle. The ſea eagle is an odd kind of fiſh: It has a tail like a roach, with large fins like wings, a thick head, and taſtes like a roach.

The ſea cat. The ſea cat is a round fiſh of a ſpan in length, of a very odd ſhape; the hindermoſt part of the body being an oval lump, on which hangs the head. It has long and large eyes, a ſmooth ſkin, inclining to blue, but brown upon the belly. The entrails of this fiſh contain a certain gum, out of which the *Chineſe* make their ink. They dry this fiſh in the ſun, as the *Dutch* do the plaiſe; and they are in great requeſt among the *Indians*, tho' they are of no eaſy digeſtion.

1662.

The leaping fiſh. The leaping fiſh is ſo called, becauſe they leap and play continually upon the ſurface of the water. They are of the bigneſs of a herring, and are without fins on the back, from the head to the tail. They have a knotty head, and the body of a greyiſh colour, with black ſpots; but toward the belly they begin to be white. They look very fiercely before they begin to leap. They are ſea fiſhes, and of a very good taſte, eſpecially broiled.

Pampus. The fiſh *Pampus* is above a foot long, and about a ſpan in breadth; for the reſt in colour and ſhape, not unlike our plaiſe, with a ſmooth ſkin: The eyes ſtand on both ſides, and the mouth ſtrait forward. It is a well taſted fiſh, eſpecially if dry'd and eaten as the *Dutch* do their plaiſe.

Peyxe Kok. *Peyxe Kok*, i. e. the *Fiſh Kok*, ſo called by the *Portugueſe*, becauſe when taken it makes a noiſe or ſound like *Kok*. It is taken near the iſle of *St. Vincent*, and is but an indifferent fiſh.

The blower. The blowers are huge fiſhes which appear now and then in the open ſea. They have got this name from their drawing in of the water, and ſpouting it out again with great force into the air.

The white fiſh. The white fiſh is about the bigneſs of a whiting, with a round hanging belly, a ſtrait back, and turn'd up mouth: Its tail is forked, it has one large fin upon the back, and abundance of ſmall ones betwixt the belly and the tail. It is full of ſtreaks all over the body, and on the mouth it has two long teats: It is of a very good taſte.

Five-finger-fiſh. The five-finger-fiſh has got its name from five black ſpots on each ſide, reſembling the prints of fingers. Its length is about a foot and a half, with a ſmall head, large mouth, and brown pointed fins towards the tail. It is of a ſhining blue colour mix'd with purple, without ſcales. It is of a pretty good taſte, and taken in the ſea all over the *Indies*.

Karappa, or round fiſh. Karappa, or round-fiſh, is not unlike a whiting, of a very good taſte: It has but a ſmall head and tail, but a pretty bulky belly. Below it has ſome ſome fins not unlike thoſe of an eel.

Flying-fiſh. Some of the flying-fiſh are near as big as corette, of a blueiſh colour on the back, but inclining to a brown towards the tail. They have large eyes, and large yellowiſh fins, and reſemble in ſhape our ſmelts: They are of an agreeable taſte, but not eaſy to be catch'd, except when they fly againſt the ſails, which they frequently do, and ſo fall upon the ſhips deck.

The fork-tail. The fork-tail is a long and round fiſh, with a very long forked tail, whence it has got its name. Its head is not unlike that

1662. that of a herring, with a long teat on the top of it, and two more below near the mouth, like those of the shrimps, but larger; they keep them close to the body when they are swimming. They are of the bigness of a mackrel, but of no extraordinary good taste.

Soals. Some soals here are a foot long, of the same colour as ours, and as well-tasted; but their heads are strangely shaped, the mouth turning quite to one side, as well as their eyes.

Bonites. The bonites are not unlike the corettes, but with lesser fins and blue streaks, which vanish by degrees towards the tail. The back is of a dark brown, and the belly white, the eyes blue, surrounded with a yellow circle. Some are a foot and a half long, and very bright when first taken, which is done without much difficulty, because they follow the ships, and are very greedy after a bait. They eat best if they are salted a little before they are broil'd.

The sword-fish. The sword-fish has a very odd head, not unlike that of an owl, with a very wide mouth: The skin is hard, the back grey, the belly white without any scales. On each side of the sword, which is above five foot long, are 27 teeth: Their whole length, including the sword, is generally 25 foot long, and so thick, that scarce two men can grasp them. Near the eyes they have two nostrils, through which they draw the water in and out.

Siap Siap. The fish called *Siap Siap* by the *Javanese*, is a river fish in great request among the *Javanese*, and is taken in considerable quantity near *Batavia*.

The pyed-fish. The pyed-fish has got its name from its colour; its tail and fins being brown, spotted with pale blue spots: It is about a foot long, and pretty thick, without scales. The eyes, which are yellow, are surrounded by a blue circle; underneath the throat hangs a crop extending it self to the tail: It has a little mouth, and on each side a yellow fin. It is in great esteem among the inhabitants, and well tasted, but contains a certain venomous matter, which must be carefully taken out when it is gutted.

Five-eyes. The five-eyes have got their name from five black eyes, enclosed in yellow circles, which are in the fins near the tail. They are smooth and yellow without scales, pretty thick with a small head and sharp nose, which turns over the mouth, near which they have two red fins; they are catch'd in the rivers and are well-tasted.

Sea-bats. The sea-bat has got its name from its resemblance to a bat: It has two yellowish wings streak'd with three blue streaks; a long tail, thick head and large mouth. By its taste it seems to be a kind of thornback.

The gudgeons of *Java* are of the length of a finger, but scarce an inch thick. They are speckled with pale blue, and other colours without scales; they have small forked tails, are catch'd in the rivers and are exceeding well tasted. There is another kind of them taken in the sea, in such prodigious quantities, that they sell a whole canoe full for eight or ten pence, and fatten their ducks and geese with them. 1662. *The gudgeon.*

The *Indian* carps are taken in the rivers, being not in the least different from ours either in shape or taste. *Carps.*

The sea-monster is an odd kind of fish, having a knobby star of eight tacks upon the head, and upon that a certain excrescence resembling a bishop's mitre: From the sides of the head issue two fins of the same length with the body of the monster. It has a very dreadful wide mouth, and very broad tail, wherewith it guides it self in swimming. *The sea-monster*

They have divers sorts of shrimps and creafishes in the *Indies*; and of the latter sort, a certain kind which have teeth like a saw on the back; some of them are of that bigness as to weigh six pounds, of a delicious taste, and very wholsome, being accounted good for such as are troubled with the asthma, or spit-blood. The sea-shrimps are a salt-water fish, the biggest of which are near a span in length, and have shells like ours, of a fallow colour with a red fork'd tail. Out of the head come forth divers fins, on which hang two small thin horns. They are very well tasted, and five or six are sufficient for one man's meal. The river-shrimps are about the bigness of our sea-shrimps, of a blue colour, with a small head and thick body. Out of the head come two long fins, as fine as a thread. Their shell is not so hard as the former, neither are they so well-tasted. The rivers here afford also abundance of creafishes, which are taken in holes among the oysters. They are better tasted than our lobsters. *Shrimps and creafishes.*

The sea-star is an odd shaped fish with five branches or tacks like a star: They are of a pale red colour, an inch thick, covered with a knobby skin, underneath which are many small bones: They have a hole in the middle, through which they draw their sustenance: They are never to be seen at sea, except in calm weather, and are taken and kept rather for curiosity's sake than any other use. *The sea-star.*

The sea-crabs are of about the bigness of a span, of a most curious colour, the shell being specked with yellow spots; besides which they have three purple spots enclosed within white rings. Their claws are yellowish towards the body, afterwards white, *Sea-crabs or lobsters.*

1662. white, and at the extremities of a high purple colour; their eyes are fixt upon certain small tacks an inch breadth without the head. There is also a kind of blue-crabs, some of which are a foot and a half long: They are of a purple colour spotted with white; the claws are blue, and of a purple colour towards the body; their eyes are fixt upon small tacks like the former, and stand a fingers length without the head. They are a salt-water fish, and very well-tasted.

Lobsters. There is another kind of lobsters not quite so big as the former, which run very swiftly: Their eyes stand likewise about two inches breadth without the head, especially whilst they are running, but otherwise can draw them back, and lay them close under two fins. Their bodies are marbled with divers colours, the claws of a purple colour; behind they have two small round and blue shells edged with yellow. Some are of a considerable bigness, and of a very good taste. There is another sort of sea-crabs, of the same bigness as the blue-lobsters, but easily to be distinguished from them by their colour, which is inclining to green, with red claws, and by their taste, which is exceeding delicious, these being the best sort throughout the *Indies*. Their eyes stand likewise an inch's breadth without the head. Some sea-crabs here are of a prodigious bigness, and are, as well as all other shell-fish, best in the encrease of the moon. Some crabs here cast their shells, and during a certain season of the year abide under ground till they grow again. The *Indian* oysters are prefer'd before those of *Europe*.

Muscles and oysters. The muscles of the *Indies* are like ours, but somewhat bigger; the shell is brown both in and outside. There is another sort of muscles called tail muscles by our people; these are of a greenish colour; they have on that end where they open, two sharp horns, and on the other end, a pale yellow tail, wherewith they can fasten themselves in the mud. They are of the same taste, and used like ours, as well as those we commonly call St. *James*'s muscles. Of oysters they have also several sorts, the biggest adhere to the rocks, some to the roots and tacks of the trees; they are all of a very good taste; and are either stew'd with spices, or eaten raw with lemon-juice and pepper.

Purple-snails. Abundance of purple-snails are found in the islands over against *Batavia*: The scallop or shell is of a yellow colour, of the bigness of a good citron, with curious windings at one end. Within this shell is the *snail*, which is round, plump and yellow, streak'd with black. They are boil'd and eaten by the *Chinese*, who have a way of polishing the shells, and pick out of the middle of the snail a certain purple colour'd substance, which they use in colouring and making of red ink. There is also another kind with green shells, streak'd with black, white within, and of the bigness of a child's head: The snail is of the same colour, and is not ill tasted. Another sort has a shell pale-red, marbled with white, and curiously twisted, of the bigness of an orange: The snail is of the same colour, and is eaten as we do our perewinkles, but is of a hard digestion. 1662.

Quallen. The *Quallen* are a certain product of the sea, of a mucilaginous substance, without head or tail, or entrails; they commonly are of the bigness of a trencher, and sometimes less. They have purple edges all round them, wherewith they swim. In the midst is a certain white spot, (which is sometimes blueish) wherein perhaps their victuals are contained. If they are forced ashore, they are dissolved. The *Chinese* have a way of distilling a certain *Arack* or strong-water out of them, which is excessive hot, sharp and unwholesome, causing exulcerations in the body. For if this substance happen to adhere to the bare skin of a man in swimming or otherwise, it burns with violence, and raises blisters immediately.

The Dorades. The *Dorades*, by some called sea-breams, are a kind of dolphins. They have long and sharp fins on the back, and a very long tail; underneath the belly they have three fins, the last of which extends as far as the tail. Some are 4 or 5 foot long, and rather broad than thick. They eat tolerably well, if salted before they are dress'd, but are of a hard digestion: They are sometimes taken with the hook, being not easily catched with the harpiron, by reason of their nimbleness, which is such, that they will leap sometimes five or six foot high above the water, after the flying-fish.

Scates or thornbacks. The *Indies* afford excessive large thornbacks, some of which are as big in circumference as a moderate table, and will suffice to dine forty people. They have vast long tails, but are of the same colour with ours, and of the same taste, but are hard of digestion, but the young ones are much better. Their fins, which are very large, are of a purple colour. All fish with scales cast their spawn; but those without scales bring forth their young ones alive.

Indian *and* Javanese *birds and four leg'd beasts.*

The bird Emeu. In the isles of *Sumatra*, *Banda*, and the other adjacent *Molucca* islands, is to be found

1662. found a certain bird, called *Emeu* or *Eme* by the inhabitants, and *Casuaris* by the *Dutch*. He walks constantly with his head straight upright, when he is above five foot high, and about three in length from the breast to the tail. The head is in proportion of the body, but small, very smooth, and of a dark blue colour. Before, on the neck, hang two red teats or bags. The eyes are large and fierce, behind which are the ear-holes, and almost at the extremities of the bill two nostrils; and from the midst of the bill to the crown of the head, grows a hard yellow substance, like a cockle-shell, especially in the males. They have very long and gross legs, covered with a yellowish rind, their feet are thick, knobby, and without spurs, instead of which, they have on the forepart three long horny claws, in which they differ from the ostriches, whose feet are cloven both before and behind. They are covered all over with feathers, or rather with plumes of a dark red mix'd with black. Those upon the breast and thighs, grow two and two together, but those on the tail are much longer and stronger. Underneath the feathers, which grow on both sides, are hidden certain pens, which serve them in running, for these birds are scarce able to raise themselves from the ground. They are exceeding greedy, devouring every thing 1662.

they meet with, even to iron and burning coals, all which they evacuate backwards without any alteration; nay, they sometimes throw out what they have eat, not till a year after, without the least sign of any digestion: For the rest they live upon herbage. Their strength consists in their legs and feet; and run so fast that no man can overtake them, and when exasperated, kick with their feet backwards and sideways like a horse. They lay greenish eggs upon the ground among the shrubs, scarce so big as our hen-eggs, speckled with dark green spots; the yolks thereof are eaten by the inhabitants. They have neither tongue nor tail.

Among the several sorts of flitter-mice or bats, that which by some is called a flying-cat, may well challenge a place; its head, tail, nay the whole body and bulk resembing to a cat. It differs from the bats in this, that whereas they hang on certain tacks, this hangs on its claws, and hides its self within its wings: The hair brown red, except on the back, where it is black. Betwixt the fore and hindermost legs grows two skins, a little hairy on the outside, which serves them for wings. There is also a sort of flying-apes, these have very sharp teeth and claws, and very lively eyes. *Flying-cat.*

In

1662. *The hunter's bird.* In some parts of the *Indies* you meet with a certain bird call'd the hunter's-bird. The breast and whole body is black, but the tail grayish; the head is dark yellow, but without feathers; below the neck hangs a bag, not unlike those of our turkeys: The bill is distinguish'd by certain twisted rings, by which they discern their age, every year producing one like our oxes horns. On the top of the bill grows a horny substance; they are look'd upon as a rarity, and sold at a dear rate.

Dronte *or* Dodaers. In the isle of *Mauritius* you meet with a certain bird call'd *Dronte* by the inhabitants, and *Dodaers* by the *Dutch*. In bigness it is betwixt an ostrich and a large turkey, and has also some resemblance to them in his feathers and tail. His head is very large, not unlike that of a cuckow, but covered all over with a skin. The eyes are large and black, the neck crooked and very thick: The bill is very long, thick and pale blue, except towards the extremities, the uppermost whereof is blackish, and the undermost yellowish, but both sharp and bent. He is very thick and round of body, covered with soft grey feathers, like those of the ostrich; the belly and hindermost part are so thick as to touch almost the ground, which is the reason he is easily catch'd. On both sides he has certain pens instead of wings, of a pale yellow colour, and instead of the tail five curl'd plumes of the same colour: His legs are short and thick, with four large claws. The meat, especially that of the breast, is fat and toothsome enough, and three or four of these creatures afford a meal for 100 persons. In his stomach is sometimes found a certain porous hard stone.

Parraquets. The parraquets are of a green colour, of the bigness of a sterling; their bills are yellow, the neck red mix'd with green, and the wings yellow at the extremities: They are found in vast numbers in the woods, and are easily tamed and taught to speak. There are divers sorts of them of different colours.

The martin. The martins here are as big as our magpies, of a black colour with a yellow bill, and a yellow tuft upon the head. The midst of the wings is white, the feet yellow, with large crooked claws. The *Javanese* are great admirers of this bird, and teach him to whistle and speak, which he does as distinctly as a man, but with somewhat a rough voice. There is another sort of them not so big as these; they are found all

1662. all over the *Indies*, and feed upon rice and other fruits of the earth.

Crows. The *Indian* crows are pale blue, in ſhape betwixt a heron and ſtork. The head and neck is ſomewhat of a darker colour, with a curl'd tail and ſharp bill. They live moſt in wilderneſſes, and fly (as they ſay) ſometimes as far as *Europe*, under a certain leader, who flies ſometimes before and ſometimes behind.

The bird Rubus. The bird *Rubus* is of the bigneſs of a ſtarling, with a blue bill and legs, the back and tail red, and white and black wings. The head is green, and in his tail he has two large feathers, like the *Paradiſe* bird.

Bats. In divers parts of the *Indies* are very large *bats*, exceeding in bigneſs our cats. In the iſle of *Java* are ſome of the ordinary ſort, no bigger than a pidgeon; they live in the woods, and are accounted a dainty by the *Javaneſe*. In the night-time they will get ſometimes into the chambers, if the windows be left open, and draw blood from ſuch as are aſleep there.

Gwira. There are two ſorts of the bird called *Gwira*, they are both white, mix'd with ſome brown feathers. One ſort has a red belly, and the other a blue tail, with one very long feather in it.

Poreo. The *Poero* is a long, but ſlender bird, of a ſpan in length, including the bill and tail. The bill is ſomewhat crooked, and the tail like that of the bird *Gwira*. His feathers are blueiſh, mixt with yellow, and his feet very ſmall. He feeds upon piſmires.

Cormorants. In *Java* you meet often with cormorants, not unlike our geeſe, except that they are much bigger; underneath the bill hangs a large bag, which they can extend and draw together at pleaſure, and in it keep ſuch fiſh as they have ſwallow'd. Their feet are like thoſe of the ſwan, and their bills are crooked towards the extremities. They are ſo greedy after prey, that they ruſh out from among the flags with ſuch violence, that they are eaſily taken by that means. They ſwallow oyſters with the ſhells, and keep them in their bags till they open, when they ſpew them out again and pick out the oyſter. They are frequently found in the iſle of *Din Ding*, and ſoon diſcovered by their noiſe.

Ducks. All over the *Indies* you meet with ducks in great numbers, reſembling ours both in bigneſs and taſte. They are generally dark yellow, with a black bill and legs, large bellies, and tufts on their heads. But whereas the *Weſt-India* ducks have hanging bellies, theſe carry them more upright. By reaſon of the exceſſive heat they are not eaſily brought to ſit upon their eggs, which are generally laid under hens, or fomented in horſedung or ovens. Their meat is very wholeſome, provided they are well fed. 1662.

Wide-bill. The wide-bill has got his name from his bill, which reaches up on both ſides to the eyes: He is ſcarce of the bigneſs of a pidgeon, of a pale black colour, with black wings, and underneath the eyes and bill white. They are brought to market in great quantities at *Batavia*, their meat being well taſted.

The ſtrand bird or ox-eye. The ſtrand bird is a kind of ſnipe of the bigneſs of our wood-cocks. Their feathers are green mixed with black, they are ſold in great numbers at *Batavia*, and in taſte are not unlike our wood-ſnipes.

Turtles. The *Indian* turtles are not altogether ſo big as ours, and of a yellowiſh colour mix'd with grey: They have a black feather in each wing, and the tail is black and white; under the neck they are ſomewhat brighter, and the breaſt almoſt red. They are taken in great quantities in the rice-fields, and are fat and well-taſted.

Geeſe. The *Indian* geeſe are much finer and larger than the *European* geeſe, reſembling rather our ſwans, their necks being exceſſive long, of a yellowiſh colour, but their bills black. Along the back, upon the wings and tail they have dark grey feathers mix'd with ſome light ones, but on the belly they are white. They have not ſo ſhrill a voice as our geeſe, but differ not in the leaſt from them either in ſhape or taſte, their feet being likewiſe red. They have both wild and tame ones.

Birds of prey. In divers places of the *Indies* are great quantities of birds of prey, as eagles, hawks, kites, and ſuch like, which do prodigious miſchief both among the wild and tame fowl, and are of ſuch ſtrength, that they carry ſometimes a young pig away and devour it in the woods or among the rocks. There is a certain bird of prey here, which you ſee moving in the air without moving its wings; and another called *Jin* by the *Chineſe*, exceeding all the reſt in nimbleneſs: It is greeniſh on the back, but white on the belly. The eyes are quick and red, and the bill yellow, bent like a hook at the end. Their feet are likewiſe yellow, arm'd with long and very ſharp claws.

Kokoy. The *Kokoy* is a kind of a heron, but much exceeding ours in beauty, being yellow before and green in the hindermoſt part. On the head he has a delicious plume, ſpreading all over the neck. The young ones eat tolerably well, but the old ones are tough and taſte much after fiſh.

Kolibry. *Kolibry* is the leaſt of all the birds, being no bigger than a horſe-fly; it has a very ſharp bill, wherewith it ſucks its ſuſtenance out of the flowers, though ſome are

1662. of opinion it feeds upon the dew. It has all the colours of the rain-bow, and its wings are not unlike those of the pidgeons or ducks: It builds a nest to the south under the branches of orange, limon, or cotton-trees, to defend itself against the injuries of the north winds: Its eggs are no bigger than peas. There is another which sings exceeding fine, but is not so well colour'd; it weighs not above 24 grains, and is catch'd by throwing hot any thing else upon it.

Birds like quails or throstles. In the woods of *Java* you see vast numbers of birds not unlike our quails or throstles, but of the bigness of our wild pidgeons; their bills are however somewhat longer than those of our quails, and their noise is very different. They are of so cold a constitution, that if exposed on the cold ground, they are in danger of perishing by cold; for which reason they hide themselves, cover'd with their wings in the hollowness of trees, immediately after sun-set, and at sun-rising come forth again and begin to chirp with a great deal of chearfulness.

Quails. The *Indian* quails resemble those of *Europe*, are brown on the back and blue on the belly: they have a yellow bill and four claws, *viz.* three before, and one behind; they don't make any noise, but are very good meat.

Rice-birds. The rice-bird is of the bigness of one of our pullets, but something longer leg'd, with brown feathers on the body, a red head, and very large claws; they live among the rice, whence they have got their name, and eat very deliciously roasted.

Pheasants. In many parts of the *Indies* are also pheasants with long and pointed tails; some are white on the breast and about the eyes.

Butterflies. They have prodigious numbers of butterflies of various colours; they have long bills, which they can stretch out when they suck the juice of the flowers, or draw back at pleasure. Some are of a most delicious colour, intermix'd with blue, white and red, beyond what can be express'd. They are generally of the bigness of the palm of the hand, when their wings are spread; some have larger wings than others, and have two small feathers on their heads.

Wood-pidgeons. The *Indian* wood-pidgeons are of the bigness of our tame pidgeons, with brown spots on their backs; a white belly, purple colour'd breast, and red feet; they resemble entirely our turtle-doves, or common pidgeons; live generally in the woods or in the rice-fields, and are a most delicious food; when they are tamed they will breed in our houses.

The Lory. The *Lory* bird is a bird as big as a parrot, but of a much finer colour, with a lofty round breast, cover'd with yellow feathers. The wings are green, the head black and shining, with a yellow bill. The *Indians* give sometimes 30 crowns for such a bird, because they will learn and speak several languages, and are very tame: There is another with large and long tails, sometimes three quarters of a yard long, these are blue on the back, and yellow under the belly, and commonly call'd *Kakkataws* or *Indian* ravens. Another kind there is, which is white all over, except a yellow tuft on the head, which they set upright, when they are vexed. They have also some resemblance both in shape and bigness to our magpies or blackbirds; these imitate a man's voice much more distinctly than the parrots: They are of a blueish colour, mix'd with dark blue spots and streaks, they have a yellow tuft on the head, which is black, and as smooth as velvet.

The Yelamber. The *Yelambers* are as big as our larks, with a thick bill and red feet; their feathers are yellow, chequered with grey, they are catch'd in prodigious numbers, and sold in the markets of *Batavia*, being look'd upon as a dainty.

Rice-sparrows. The rice-sparrows are no bigger than our ordinary sparrows, and of the same colour, except that their bills are somewhat thick, with a few black feathers near the tail, and some white ones underneath on the belly; their feet are blue. They are found in such prodigious quantities, that the inhabitants are scarce able to preserve the rice from being devour'd by them.

Parrokets. These birds properly called parrokets, are no bigger than our larks, but have a very fine green head and wings; the back underneath the wings is of a high red colour, the breast light green, and the tail of a most agreeable colour: They are found in the woods in great numbers, feed upon rice and fruits, but will not speak, being kept only for their feather's sake.

Pullets. The *Indian* pullets are generally white, with long red tails, and their feet almost cover'd with feathers, and a bright red comb on the head. They are not much bigger than our largest tame pidgeons, but very well tasted. They were first transported to *Batavia* from *Siam*. They have also a kind of tame fowl with black feathers, legs and flesh, which however is not ill tasted, and accounted very wholsome: Another kind there is that have hair instead of feathers, others have their feathers turn'd towards the head, in lieu of declining backwards.

Herons. About *Batavia* and many other parts of the *Indies* abundance of herons are to be seen in the low grounds; they are in bigness

1662. ness the same with our herons, with long gray feathers and black wings; they are generally seen near the water-side, where they are looking for their prey, but build their nests in trees; the meat is tough, and tastes much after fish.

The jumpers. The jumpers have got their name from their continual motion from branch to branch: They are of the same bigness with our blackbirds, and will whistle like them; they have a black head, wings and tail, but are white on the breast and belly; I have seen them kept at *Batavia* with a chain to one leg for diversion sake, and they feed them with boil'd rice. They are easy to be tamed.

Stock doves. The stock-doves are in shape and bigness like our pidgeons, but of a much finer colour; the neck and breast is green, the rest of the body purple colour'd, and the tail and wings blue with a white edge. They are catch'd in great numbers in the woods near *Batavia*, and eat very well roasted.

The goldfinch or linnet. The goldfinches here are very agreeable for their fine colour'd feathers, being for the rest no longer than our linnets or goldfinches; their bill is pale red, the head white, the back and wings blue, the belly red, and the tail dark blue. They are taken in prodigious quantities near *Batavia*, and sometimes kept in cages: They feed upon rice.

Scorpions. At *Batavia* you see often large scorpions of a quarter of a yard long; but those of a lesser size are so frequent, that you can scarce move a stool, bench, chest, lookinglass or picture, without being in danger of being stung by them, unless you be very careful to avoid them. The small ones are about a fingers length, composed of many joints, of the thickness of a goose-quill. They are yellow, speckled with brown streaks; before they have two claws, with two sharp pinchers; their tail is long, and lies turn'd upon the back, at the end of which is the sting, wherewith they poison such as they touch. They have eight long legs, not unlike those of a creafish. The sting of a scorpion is accounted mortal, unless prevented in a little time; tho' some are of opinion that the scorpions in the *Indies* are not so venomous as those of *Italy* and *Spain*. A scorpion bruised to death, or stifled in oil, and apply'd to the wound, draws out the poison. They say that a radish sliced and laid upon a scorpion, kills him in a minute: They have also another story, *viz.* that the scorpion is sometimes so pester'd with the pismires, that he stings himself to death in the head with his tail, and so becomes a prey to the pismires.

The thousand-legs are about five or six inches long, of the thickness of a man's finger, of a ruddy colour, and composed of many joints and bones. They have two claws or pinchers, wherewith they wound as dangerously as the scorpions; occasioning such violent pain, as is almost unspeakable: The cure is perform'd by stifling them in oils like as with the scorpions, and they are generally found like them, in holes, and behind old chests or benches. 1662. *Thousand-legs.*

Both the *East* and *West-Indies* produce snakes of divers sizes and colours: Among others they have a certain sort in the isle of *Java*, not exceeding a foot in length, which are frequently met with in the fields among the grass: They have others with large shining scales on the back, and their eyes so bright, that in a sun-shiny day you see them at a great distance; others are so full of spots, that they are terrible to behold. Besides these, they have another kind of snakes much lesser than the field snakes; these dwell in houses, and feed upon flies, ants and other insects. They will stick so close to a wall or roof, as if they were immoveable, but no sooner perceive their prey, but they shoot down all on a sudden to catch it. The tail of a snake separated from the body, will grow to it again. These snakes are not in the least pernicious, and will pass over the bare faces of persons sleeping in their chambers, without doing the least harm.

In the woods of *Java*, as likewise in the fens and pools is found a certain sort of snakes, or rather a kind of crocodile call'd *Legoaen* by the *Indians*; it resembles altogether a crocodile, except that it is less, being not above five or six foot long, whereas the crocodiles are from 15 to 20 foot: The *Javanese* however affirm, that those in the mountains are much larger. They have a knobby green skin, but the meat is white, like that of our rabbets, and very well tasted. They have a long head, wide mouth, and a tail as long as the whole body; each leg has four paws arm'd with sharp and long claws. *Snakes.*

In the woods of *Java* are certain flying-snakes, or rather drakes, they have four legs, a long tail, and their skin speckled with many spots; their wings are not unlike those of the bat, which they move in flying, but otherwise keep them almost unperceived close to the body. They fly nimbly, but can't hold it long, so that they fly from tree to tree at about 20 or 30 paces distance. On the outside of the throat are two bladders, which being extended when they fly, serve them instead of a sail; they feed upon flies and other insects: The *Javanese* don't in the least ac- *The flying-snake or drake.*

1662. count them poisonous, but handle them just like the common snakes, without the least danger.

Frogs. The frogs here are about the same bigness with ours; of a dark yellow colour, with brown spots: They are sold daily in the markets of *Batavia*, the *Chinese* accounting them a dainty, but eat only the hindermost parts. There is another sort of frogs in *Java* near as big as a rabbet, but are not eaten. They make a noise like the bellowing of an ox.

Fireflies. The fire-flies have got their name, because they appear in the dark shining like a light, and are catch'd by means of a fire or candle, through which they will fly till they are taken. They are about an inch broad and long, and sometimes bigger: The head, which is brown, has two small horns; the neck is red, but their hard wings brown, underneath which they have two softer wings, which they make use of in flying, and then it is you discover that shining substance, which is contained in a black bladder on their backs, which they hide with their wings whilst they are not a flying. In the rainy season they dwell in prodigious numbers among the trees, and draw their chief sustenance from the blossom. There are divers sorts of them.

Horse-flies. The horse-flies here are a most pernicious insect, which sting most furiously. They are about two inches broad and long, of a brown colour, with a yellow streak along the body. They build their nests very curiously on the roof or rafters, as the wasps do on the sprigs of trees: In these they lay their eggs and hatch their young ones. They feed upon fruits, and emit a most nauseous scent after they are kill'd.

Kakkerlakken, *or* Kakalakkas. The *Kakkerlakken* are so called by a corrupted name from the *Portuguese* word *Kakalakkas*, because their eggs are both in colour and smoothness like to the *Lacca*. They are much of the same bigness with the horse-flies, of a brown colour, with two long horns on the head. They both run and fly very nimbly, and are very pernicious, there being no chest or trunk so strong, but they will gnaw through it. They are also to be found in ships, tho' newly built, in their way from *Europe*, especially at the time of their passing under the line; when the lice die, these begin to appear; and in their return, as soon as they are pass'd the line again, and the lice appear, these begin to vanish by degrees. They are very pernicious to paper, linen, and woollen cloaths.

Jakalat. The *Jakalat* is a mischievous insect, but only in the lower parts of the houses, its delight being in moist grounds.

Locusts. About *Batavia* you find a kind of locusts of a finger's length, but no thicker than a pen or goose-quill, distinguish'd by divers joints. They walk upon six feet, and have two small horns. The locusts here are however of divers kinds; some are yellow on the belly, with brown wings, and two horns on the head; they can leap a great way, and fly together in great numbers. There is another sort of the same shape, but green, and of a finger's length. These come sometimes in such prodigious swarms, that they darken the sky as they pass by, and devour all in those parts where they settle, so that the inhabitants are often obliged to change their habitations for want of sustenance, as it has happened frequently in *China* and the isle of *Tajowak*.

A kind of Spanish *flies.* The blister-drawers are so called, because when they sting they raise blisters. They are of divers sorts, different both in colour and bigness, but commonly of the length and breadth of a finger. They have very large eyes, and delight in marshy places. They are most frequent at *Batavia* in *October* and *November*.

Hornets. There is here a kind of hornets that have a certain claw like a pincher on the head, wherewith they pinch to that degree, that they will not let go their hold unless you cut off their heads. They are of divers sorts, bigness and shape, some being above five inches long, of a dark brown colour; they have double wings, the uppermost are hard, the undermost soft; the last they make use of in flying, the others being only for the defence of the undermost ones. They feed upon herbs, and the fruits of certain trees, which they know how to choose among all the rest.

Ants or pismires. Of ants or pismires there are in *Java* and throughout all the *Indies* prodigious quantities of divers sorts; some of them are above a finger in length, of a ruddy colour, inclining to black, some with, others without wings. They are very pernicious to the fruits of the earth; and even in the houses scarce any thing can be preserved against them without a great deal of care. It is observable, that an ant meeting another with something in her mouth, will give way to her, if she be not loaden her self.

Catterpillars. The gardens about *Batavia* are extremely pestered with catterpillars; they are about 5 Inches long, with long brown horns standing upright on their heads. The head and whole body is yellowish, but the wings inclining to a green spotted with yellow. They feed upon herbs and leaves like the locusts.

Schrankels *or Knobs.* This insect has got its name from the knotty composition of its body, which, as well as

1662. as the feet is of a pale-green colour. It has two fore legs covered with a hard ſhell like a crab or creafiſh. It ſeems to be a kind of locuſt, and feeds upon greens, but can neither fly nor run very faſt. There is another kind with a monſtrous head and neck, and a thick body, on the hindermoſt part of which are two ſmall pins like thorns. The two fore-feet are encloſed in a hard ſhell and of a very odd ſhape; it has two wings, but can ſcarce fly, by reaſon of the weight of its body. 1662.

Spiders. There are many ſorts of ſpiders in the *Indies*, and of a very different bigneſs; ſome are above four inches long, and have very thick legs; others have eight feet, a thick ſpeckled body, and round head with brown eyes. Theſe have two teeth bent like hooks, wherewith they bite fiercely. I have ſeen toothpicks made of theſe teeth.

The lynx. The lynx is a fierce creature, of the bigneſs of a large dog, and in ſhape ſeems to participate both of that and a cat. He is of a brown colour chequer'd with red, with black ſtreaks; his tail is very ſhort, and the ears very black; he lives upon prey, and is extremely nimble.

Sucotyro *or* Sucotario. The *Sukotyro*, as the *Chineſe* call it, is a very odd ſhaped beaſt; it is of the bigneſs of a large ox, with a ſnout like a hog, two long rough ears, and a thick buſhy tail. The eyes are placed upright in the head, quite different from other beaſts: On the ſide of the head, next to the eyes ſtand two long horns, or rather teeth, not quite ſo thick as thoſe of the elephant: It feeds upon herbage, and is but ſeldom taken. Of the jackal we have given a deſcription before.

Oxen with bunches. On the *Cape of Good-Hope*, but eſpecially in the iſle of *Madagaſcar*, are certain oxen with bunches upon their necks and ſhoulders, which being nothing but fat, is melted and uſed by the inhabitants like butter; but theſe oxen have not ſo great a quantity of ſuet about their kidneys as ours. The cows of this kind frequently bear two or three calves at a time.

The Macaſſar-fox. The macaſſar-fox has got his name from the iſle of *Macaſſar*, where he is moſt found. He has an exceſſive long buſhy tail, which ſtands upright, flat feet, long claws, and ſhort ears, juſt as he is repreſented in the cut.

Apes and monkeys. There are divers ſorts of apes and monkeys diſtinguiſh'd by peculiar names. Some are very ſmall, others middle ſized, and others as big as a boy of eight years of age; ſuch a one I ſaw my ſelf once at *Batavia*. In many parts of the *Indies*, where the inhabitants think it a crime to kill any living creature, they multiply to a prodigious degree, and are very tame: They

1662. They live for the moſt part in woods, and feed upon fruits. Some are green with a long beard and large eye-brow, like an ancient man: Some, call'd *Cicatic* by the *Indians*, have long buſhy tails, for which reaſon they are reckon'd by ſome among the fox kind. There is another ſort call'd *Saragoſe*, with long tails, which they carry ſtraight upright. Another ſort are called death's heads by the *Dutch*, from their pale faces. The *Suri* monkeys are in bigneſs and ſhape not unlike a ſquirrel, but of a yellow colour; they have ſhort and round ears, large eyes, and a large buſhy tail, wherewith they can cover the whole body: They can leap at a great diſtance from tree to tree, and guide themſelves with the tail ſo exactly, that they ſeem to fly. There is a certain ſort of monkeys or apes that are not in the leaſt miſchievous; they are no bigger than a rat, but have a long tail, which they carry upright. They have a green, ſoft and woolly hair, ſomewhat inclining to a grey about the eyes, and a little white on the feet. They have ſhort ears, a ſharp mouth and brown noſe, the feet being like thoſe of an ape; but theſe are very ſcarce. Thoſe call'd *Sangwyns* are likewiſe of the bigneſs of a rat, and very nimble; their face, hands and ears are black, and the reſt of the body of a cheſnut colour, except that they have ſome dark yellow hair along the back; they have very long tails, feed upon fruits, and are very diverting. 1662.

The piſmire-eater or ants-bear.

The piſmire-eater or ants-bear, is ſo call'd, becauſe he feeds chiefly upon ants: There are three ſeveral ſorts of them; the firſt is of the bigneſs of a young hog, the ſecond ſomewhat leſſer, and the third like a cat, but longer. They are all of a ruddy colour like a fox, with a long ſharp mouth, ſmall ears, and a head like that of a pig.

Stags.

Abundance of deer or ſtags are found in the foreſts of the *Indies*, they are eaſily to be tamed here, ſo that they will feed among the cattle. They are generally red, ſpeckled with white, and much of the ſame bigneſs as ours. They have large ears, long legs, and are white underneath the belly. The horns of the male are wrought towards the head, and brown and very hard towards the extremities. Their fleſh is very well taſted. With the deer-ſkins a great traffick uſed to be carried on in the iſle of *Tayowan*, whilſt the *Dutch* were maſters of it; for they uſed to take many thouſands of them only for the ſkin's ſake, which were ſold to the *Japoneſe*; and ſcarce to preſerve any part of their

1662. their flesh, except the tongue, which is accounted a dainty here.

The iron-pig or porcupine. About *Batavia*, and in the woods of *Java* are abundance of iron-pigs or porcupines. They grunt like hogs, and are covered with certain painted pens or pegs like iron, whence they got their name: They are of different sizes, some of the bigness of a good large dog, but somewhat longer, and more short leg'd. They are generally brown, with a grey tuft on the head, and a mouth like a hare, with two great teeth both below and above, like a horse, the two fore-feet like those of a deer, and the hindmost like a bear. The pens or pegs are very sharp, a foot long, and checquered with black and white. When they are at rest, they lay them close to the body, but if they are vexed, they can, by contracting themselves, cast them forth with such strength, that they kill man or beast: Thus some years ago, a dead lion was found at the *Cape of Good-Hope* with a porcupine's pen sticking in his body, wherewith he had doubtless been killed. In the winter they retire into holes, where they remain without either eating or drinking. They feed upon herbs and roots, and cast their pens as other creatures do their hair. In the stomachs of some of these animals grows a certain stone, which by reason of its sudorifick quality is accounted very good in pestilential fevers; just as the stone found in the *Vesica Bilearis* or gall-bladder of the wild boars, is reputed the most sovereign remedy in that distemper called *Morderi* by the *Javanese*, and as much dreaded among them as the plague in *Europe*, because it commonly kills in a few hours time.

Tame and wild boars. There are several sorts of hogs in the *Indies*, some with, but the most without any hair; hogs flesh is accounted wholsomer and better than beef or mutton, and is by the *Chinese* prescribed even for sick persons. The wild boars feed upon what roots or fruits they can meet with; and I remember that I saw a considerable number of them swim cross the water in the isle of *Dingding* near *Malacca*, to look after provisions. In the gall-bladder of the *Indian* wild boars, grows a certain porous stone, called thence *Piedra da Puerco*, i. e. hog's stone by the *Portuguese*; it is sudorifick, and expedient in malignant distempers; they steep it in wine for twelve hours, and give the infusion to the patients; or they give the quantity of 25 grains poudered in wine. Women with child must be cautious of it, because it makes them miscarry, it being a general opinion among the *Malayan* women, that they can procure their monthly times, with only holding this stone in their hands. 1662.

Sheep. The *Javanese* sheep are much of the same bigness as ours, some being white, others pyed white and red, with short legs and little or no wool. Their meat is not so good as the *European* mutton, pork being much prefer'd before it here. The sheep have sometimes teats hanging below their throats like some of our hogs, others have such long ears that you may tie them together underneath the throat. Others have tails of 20, 30 or 40 pounds, being one lump of fat, which eats best boil'd. Some have a plain hair like our goats, others a curled wool like our sheep, and are milked like cows.

He and she goats. The goats here are not near so big as the sheep, nor is their flesh so well tasted, tho' the kids in some parts of the *Indies* afford excellent good meat. Some are white, some pyed, and have generally long hair. Others have very long ears, and horns standing upright on the head. In some places they bear three or four young ones at a time: They make cheese of their milk.

Bouffles. The Bouffles are bulkier and stronger than an ordinary ox; they have no hair, their flesh is very good, but not so juicy nor so digestible as beef, for which reason it is most used among the slaves, and other labouring people. Their horns lie close to the head; some of them are black, and, when polish'd, are very useful for several things to be made out of them. The tame bouffles are used in the sugar-mills, plough and cart: They guide them by means of a chain drawn through their nostrils: Their milk is accounted very wholsome. The wild bouffles that live in the forests are very fierce, and not easy to be taken.

Oxen and cows. Many places of the *Indies* afford oxen and cows, the flesh whereof, as well as the milk and butter, are very good; some are red, others white, others pyed, and of several other colours. Some have horns standing upright on the head, others crooked horns like ours; and others long ears hanging downwards: However, the beef is much better in some places than in others. It is generally eaten fresh, because it will scarce take salt well in this hot climate, and is not to be kept above three or four days. They bring a certain kind of oxen from *Suratte* to *Batavia*, not much bigger than a large dog; they look very fierce, notwithstanding which they are used in small carts to draw children, or any other odd thing.

Horses. The horses here are of different sorts and colours, some black, others of a chesnut

1662. nut colour, and others white and grey. The *Javanese* horses are not very tall, but thick and well-set, like the *Norwegian* or *Westphalian* horses, very strong and hardy, but are not near so high-spirited as the *Persian* horses that are transported from *Suratte* to *Batavia*, and excel all the rest in swiftness, courage and beauty. The *Indians* carry on their wars for the most 1662.
part with foot soldiers, and preserve their horses for the draught and travelling.

Thus much of the isle of *Java* and the city of *Batavia:* We will now proceed to give an account of our return into *Holland.*

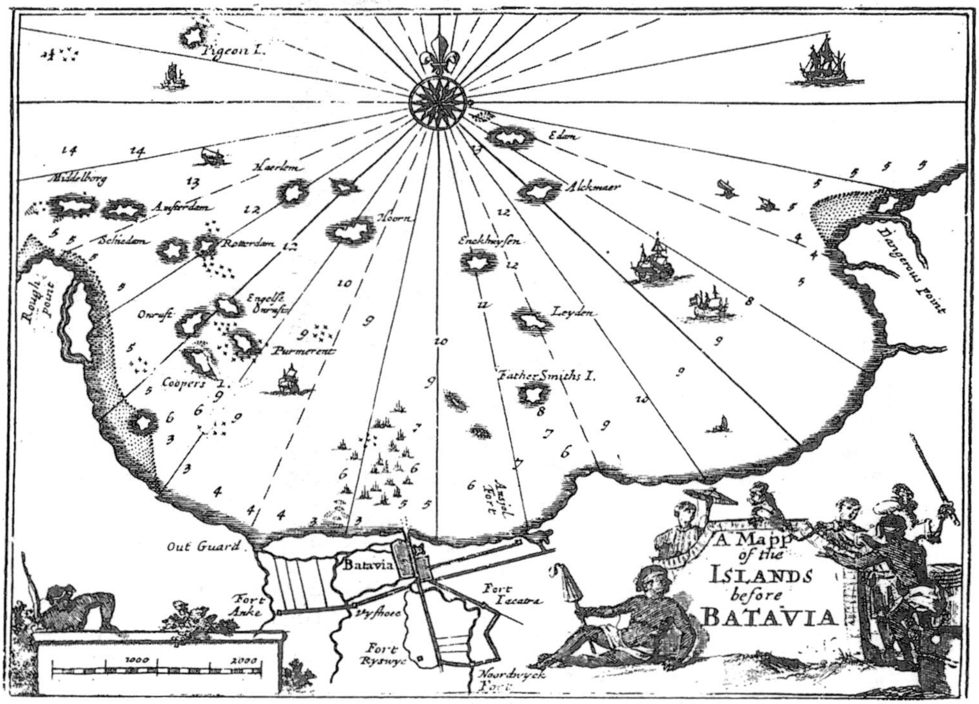

The author's return into Holland.

Every thing being got ready for our voyage, we weigh'd anchor in the road of *Batavia*, the 17th of *December* 1670, and with the land-wind, pass'd betwixt the isles to the south of *Batavia*, situate betwixt the *Ruigenhoeck* or *Rough-Point*, and *Karowan*, most of which have borrow'd their names from some places or other in the *United Provinces*; as the *Coopers-Isle*, the *Schiedam*, *Amsterdam*, *Middleburgh*, *Purmerent*, *Rotterdam*, the *Pigeon-Island*, the *Harlem*, *Hoorn*, *Enckhuysen*, *Edam*, *Alcmar*, &c. we came the same evening to an anchor near the isle call'd the *Men-eaters Island*, near which the ship called the *South-Pole* struck upon the sands, but got off again. Here a general review being taken of all the persons on board the ships, such as were found to be indebted to the company, were sent back to continue in the service 'till they had discharged their debts.

Then we set sail again, and had the 19th the point of *Bantam* to the west of us, and *Pulo Paly* to the north; but being becalm'd were forced to come to an anchor at 15 fathom water. The 20th, having received some refreshments by the *Golden-Lion* from *Bantam*, we set sail again, but the calm obliged us to come to an anchor again at 15 fathom. The 21st we continued our voyage, and had the 23d the point of *Java*, called *Krakketou* to the east-south-east, at 23 fathom water. The commodore having, by the usual signal of the white flag, summon'd all the commanders of ships aboard him, to know whether they were provided with what was necessary for so long a voyage; the *Golden-Lion* was sent back, and we had the north point of the *Princes Isle*, west to the north; and the 25th the south-point about four leagues from us.

1662. About noon the commodore went aboard and took a view of all the ships under his command, and in the afternoon set sail again: We met with several fierce but short travadoes or storms, at 7 deg. and 41 min. southern latitude. The 31st we had another most violent travado at 9 deg. 54 min. but continued not long.

Isle of Mony. The first of *January* one of our ships crew died, and we got sight of land to the south-east, which we found to be the isle of *Mony*, and that we were 64 leagues to the south-south-west of the *Princes Isle*, being forced thus far to the east by the tide; we were at the latitude of 10 deg. 29 min. The 2d we had the said isle to the south-east, and found its situation to be 52 min. more to the north than it is placed in the maps. The 3d, we were within four leagues of the said island, at 11 deg. 15 min. Hereabouts one of our ships crew was found dead in his cabin. The 6th we were at 13 deg. 40 min. and the 9th at 14 deg. 17 min. The same day Mr. *Dirk Indiik* died of a long and lingering distemper: As he had been factor and fiscal at *Suratte*, and was accounted very rich, his goods were all sealed up in the presence of the commodore and the other commanders. The next following day we made 32 leagues, and so continued our voyage with a prosperous gale till the 19th, when we found our selves at 20 deg. 54 min. of latitude, and at 105 deg. 14 min. longitude. The 26th the commodore having by the usual signal summon'd the chief officers aboard him, to adjust the difference in the compasses, and the same being found only 1 degree 33 minutes, no alteration was made therein.

The 2d of *February* we were at the heighth of 29 deg. overtaken by a most furious tempest, with thunder and lightening from the west, and had frequent travadoes till the 4th, and for many days after had very changeable weather, sometimes good, sometimes bad. The 26th with break of day we found 112 fathom depth, but saw no land: About noon we found our selves at 35 deg. 17 min. steering our course westward, the weather being very fair, we saw divers whale-fish sporting in the water, and some sea-birds, which together with the colour of the water, was a sufficient sign that we were not very far from land. The next day we found seven fathom water without seeing the land.

They discover land. The 28th very early in the morning we discovered land to the north-north-west of us, at 45 fathom depth, and the next day after sun-rising at 38, being then within three leagues of the shore, which appeared hilly and white. About noon we were at 34 deg. 36 min. the weather cold and fair. The first of *March* we found our selves at 35 deg. and steering our course to the south-east in sight of the land, which was very hilly to the north-east, found 65 fathom depth at night, in sight of a mountainous shore. The 4th we still saw land at 48 fathom water, and in the evening at 20. 1662.

The 6th before sun-set, we saw the famous point of the *Table-Bay* of the *Cape of Good-Hope*, where we cast anchor before the fort, at eight fathom water. Here we met with three ships, *viz.* the *Crown'd-Peace*, the *Damiata*, and a yacht bound for the *Indies*; and heard the good news that the commodore *Ysbrand Gotske* did come to the cape, the last 2d of *February*, and thence continued his voyage with three ships the 24th for *Holland*. Our commodore being then sick, he sent one to the commander in chief of the cape, named Mr. *Hakkius*, to notify his arrival, and the next day went ashore himself. *Arrive at the Cape of Good-Hope.*

The 8th the *Mary Yacht* arrived at the cape from the isle of *Madagascar*, having on board the marquis *de Mondeverguin*, a *French* governor of *Madagascar*, and the other adjacent places under the *French* jurisdiction. He was a person of 70 years of age, and of a goodly aspect. He sent word to Mr. *Hakkius*, commander in chief of the cape, that he should be glad to come ashore, provided he might be sure of a reception suitable to his quality: However, he set sail again on a sudden, without coming ashore, perhaps by reason of the rumour that was then already spread abroad of a war betwixt *France* and the *Dutch*. *The marquis de Mondeverguin arrives at the Cape.*

The same evening the ship called the *Spanbroeck* came into that road from *Ceylon*, with advice, that the *Cingalese* had taken up arms under their king *Radya*, and we were in the mean while not idle to provide our selves with what necessaries we could get for the prosecution of our voyage, till the 17th of *March*, when the commodore summoning all the officers aboard him, told them, that he intended to set sail the next sunday, *viz.* the 22d of *March*, without staying for the two ships we left behind, and a war betwixt us and the *French* being then much talk'd of, he ordered every body to be upon his guard, and to prepare for a vigorous defence in case of an atrack.

The 20th was spent in letting the seamen go ashore in their turn.

The 21st the goods of the before-mention'd Mr. *Indyck*, deceased were exposed to publick sale, and 13 diamonds, besides four more of an extraordinary bigness, with

1662. with some bezoar-stones, being found concealed in a private pocket in his breeches, the same were sealed up, seized by the commodore as contraband goods, for the use of the company.

They leave the Cape of Good Hope.

The 22[d] after dinner, the commodore having given the signal to sail, to the five ships, the *Peace*, the *Arms of Veer*, the *Count of Breda*, *South-Pole* and *Spanbroeck*, they weighed their anchors, and after sunset were about two leagues and an half from the *Table-Bay*.

The 23[d], a consultation being held aboard the commodore about regulating the compass, and the same being fix'd to 3 deg. to the west we found our selves that evening at 33 deg. and about 18 leagues to the south-east of the *Table-Mountain*.

Sail to St. Helens *isle*.

From hence we steer'd our course to the isle of St. *Helens*, of which we got sight the 12th of *April*, at 16 deg. 44 min. without any remarkable accident.

The 13th with sun-rising we were within five or six leagues of the said isle, when the commodore summoned again all the officers aboard him, in order to consult what course they should take towards the *Ascension* island.

The 24th we were at 4 deg. 32 min. and the 27th at 16 min. of southern latitude, steering our course north-west to the west with an easterly wind and brisk gale.

They pass the line.

The next following day we were at 15 min. of northern latitude; and the 29th at 2 deg. 38 min. having been much pestered with sudden storms and travadoes.

The 14th of *May* the *Breda* gave a signal as if they had seen land, but it proved only a refraction of the sun-beams through the clouds. The sea hereabouts seem'd in the night-time all on fire, a thing usual in hot weather.

See the Brasil *voyage*.

The 24th, at 25 deg. 29 min. we found our selves in the *Kroos* or *Cross-Sea*, (so called from a kind of water-cresses or ducksmeat that floats in prodigious quantity upon the surface of the water) and the 25th finding these sort of herbage encrease, we judged our selves to be more eastward than we intended.

The 30th at 26 deg. 15 min. our constable *Mans Timmer* died, and we were still much pestered with these *Cresses*, which continued the 1st and 2[d] of *June*.

We continued the same course till the 13th, when it being agreed to fix the compass 4 deg. more to the west, we took our course north to the east, towards the *Dutch* coast.

The 15th being a foggy day, we discharged every hour a musquet, as a signal to the ships to prevent their being separated from one another.

About midnight the commodore sent for me, and in the presence of the master of the ship, *Henry Span*, the first chirurgeon, and the minister, told me, that finding himself very ill, he was resolved to make his last will, which he did accordingly, recommending his affairs, and what he had of the companies in his hands, to our care.

About six in the morning he sent for me again, with an intention to make some alterations in his testament, but before the clerk could finish it, he expired, without signing of it. We took care to summon immediately the council of war, where every thing being settled for the prosecution of our voyage, we discovered land the 29th to the north-east at 115 fathom water.

The commodore dies.

The 30th we found our selves over against the isle of *Fulo*, and understood by one of their fisher-boats, that the peace continued betwixt *France*, *England* and *Holland*, and that 14 days before, 11 stout ships pass'd that way.

The isle of Fulo.

Having provided our selves with some cods, which we bought or exchanged at the rate of two pence a piece, we gave the signal by a cannon shot, to our convoy, which we expected to meet us hereabouts.

The first of *July* meeting a boat betwixt *Fulo* and *Hitland*, we charged the master thereof with the body of our deceased commodore, in order to his burial in *Hitland*: He had six crowns given him for his pains and charges, with a promise of six more, after we had received certain advice, that he had well discharged his trust. About noon our two convoys, the *Middleburgh* and *Leyden* came up with us, and after the usual salute, brought us fresh orders from the company.

The 2[d] and 3[d] of *July*, several of our seamen, and among the rest, the quarter-master died of the dropsy, an usual distemper to those that return from the *East-Indies*, and many more falling sick daily for want of provisions; the rest were hardly put to it, especially in our ship, which being leaky, four men were continually employed at the pump.

The 5th we advanced bravely with a very cold wind and air.

The 6th it was fair weather, and we had 18 fathom water.

The 7th it proved cold and rainy, at 16 fathom: The same evening the ship called the *Arms Vanter Veer* left us, and soon got out of sight.

The 8th of *July* we got sight of the *Dutch* coast, and the ship *Spanbroeck* having taken its course towards the *Spaniards-Gate*, we were forced to lie by till four in the

1662. *They arrive in the* Texel.

the afternoon, when with turning of the tide, we made the *Texel*, where we came to an anchor the same night.

The 9th Mr. *Silvius*, Mr. *Bekker*, and Mr. *Schagen* came aboard us, three directors of the company; who having given the necessary orders for the unloading of our vessels, and taken the diamonds belonging to the company into their custody, discharged the ships crew from their service; and I embark'd in a boat for *Enkhuysen*, and arrived at *Amsterdam* the 11th. Count *Maurice* of *Nassau* happening to pass at the same time through *Amsterdam* in his way over *Zealand* to *Cleves*, he sent for me; and I having shew'd him my observations and draughts of *Brasil* and the *East-Indies*, he engaged me to meet him the next day again at dinner, at the house of Dr. *William Piso*, where I took my leave of the said earl, he being just upon his departure. 1662.

Nieuhoff *gives an account to the company.*

Some days after I appeared in the assembly of the directors of the company, unto whom having given a satisfactory account of all my transactions, they return'd me thanks; and as a mark of their satisfaction, bestow'd upon me another factor's place; so that accordingly I undertook my third voyage to the *East-Indies*, in the ship called the *Arrow*, before the expiration of the year.

The third sea and land voyage of Mr. JOHN NIEUHOFF *aboard the* Arrow *to the isles of* Majotte, *upon the* African *coast of* Mosambique, *extracted from his own journals, and brought over and deliver'd by capt.* Reiner Klacson *to his brother* Henry Nieuhoff.

MR. *John Nieuhoff* having embarked aboard the *Arrow*, they pass'd by the *French* coast the 18th of *December*, and the 1st of *Jan.* 1672, at 29 deg. by the *Canary* isles, about three leagues off of *Teneriff*, where they met with the *Lion* bound for the *East-Indies*. They continued their voyage with a prosperous gale, without any remarkable accident, and passing the 4th of *Feb.* the line, and the 16th the high islands of *John Christian de Akonga* at 36 deg. 36 min. southern lat. arriv'd the 8th of *April* within sight of the *Cape of Good-Hope*, at 33 deg. 30 min. lat. and cast anchor in the *Table-Bay* the same night. Here they met with seventeen vessels, thirteen of which were bound from the *East-Indies* for *Holland*, and accordingly set sail the twenty forth. The ship the *Arrow* had aboard her a large chaloop or boat, which being taken to pieces before they left *Amsterdam*, was now set together again, for its more convenient passage along the shore of *Sofala*, *Mosambique* and the island of *Majotte*.

They come to the Cape of Good-Hope.

They leave the Cape *of* Good-Hope.

In this chaloop (unto which they gave the name of the *Bow*) they embark'd, and in company of the *Arrow* and another small vessel called the *Goldfinch*, bound for the isle of *St. Maurice*, having aboard Mr. *Huigens*, governor of that isle, set sail the 30th of *April*. The 6th of *June* being at 36 deg. 3 min. latitude, the *Goldfinch* steer'd her course towards *St. Maurice*, leaving the *Bow* and *Arrow* to prosecute their voyage towards the isle of *Madagascar*, which they got first sight of the 20th. They kept along the coast which was high and rocky, and near a large point of land found 20 fathom water at a league distance from the shore, and near it a long sand-bank. They were then at 24 deg. and being, by reason of the land wind, obliged to advance sometimes nearer the shore, sometimes to keep off at sea; they at last cast anchor at 30 fathom, whereas three leagues from the shore, they could find no bottom. The *Bow* afterwards follow'd the *Arrow*, but kept closer to the shore.

The twenty second they discover'd a small isle not above half a league from the shore, where the *Arrow* cast her anchor at 17 fathom; they went a fishing, and brought back along with them two canoes belonging to the inhabitants, loaden with coco-nuts and water-limons. The *Bow* being sailed before, and come to an anchor in the bay of *St. Austin* near a small isle, the *Arrow* followed her thither, and found at the mouth of the river two white points of land jetting out into the sea.

1672. The inhabitants brought some fruits aboard us, and Mr. *Hugo* and Mr. *Nieuhoff* went ashore the next day, to see whether they could traffick with them, but could only exchange a few slaves with them; however Mr. *Nieuhoff* catch'd abundance of fish at the mouth of the river.

They land at Madagascar.

The second of *July* the *Bow* sail'd within the mouth of the river to refit, having received some damage; they endeavour'd to catch some *Tortoises* but could not take any: About noon the captain of the *Madagascarians* came aboard us to exchange some slaves; and the seventh the *Bow* in which was Mr. *Nieuhoff*, and the *Arrow* separated, the first some leagues to the north, but were to meet again at the island of *Majotte*.

The 14th the *Bow* after 17 leagues sail was at 16 deg. 56 min. latitude within sight of the continent of *Mosambique*, and at 3 leagues distance from the shore; found 100 fathom water near a sand-bank: The next day they came within 1½ league off of the isle of *Paimibris*.

The 18th at 16 deg. 15 min. they saw white downs, and in the evening cast anchor near a sand-bank at 18 fathom, whereas at the stern of the ship there were at least 60 fathoms. The 20th they passed by a large bay, cover'd with a great sand-bank, which at low water has six fathom water. The 22d they pass'd betwixt the southern islands of *Mosambique*, named *St. James* and *St. Joris*, where coming to an anchor at nine fathom, they met here with a stout *Portuguese* ship at anchor behind the fort, having aboard the governor of *Goa* lately come from *Portugal* with three lesser vessels. The *Arrow* coming likewise afterwards to an anchor here, divers *Portuguese* officers came aboard us, to buy certain commodities, and about the same time three other *Portuguese* ships, one of which had the governor of *Mosambique* aboard her, arrived here from *Sofala*. It prov'd a very tempestuous day.

The first of *August* the *Bow* and *Arrow* set sail again, steering their course eastward to the isles of *Madagascar* and *Masyeleyn*. The 10th they got sight of the shore of *Madagascar* at 15 deg. 53 min. and about half a league from a round mountain cast anchor at ten fathom water. The *Bow* entred the river, and discovered two boats with masts, and divers canoes, but could not come up with them. As the wind hereabout turns every 24 hours thro' all the points of the compass, so it is easy sailing along this coast. The 12th Mr. *Nieuhoff* in the *Bow* sail'd towards the isles of *Makandari* and *Magelagie*, taking a *Madagascarian* slave along with him.

The 15th the *Bow* and *Arrow* met again, but had not been able to traffick much: They saw nine boats with four square sails pass in sight of them, and in a small river met with another boat, that furnish'd them with eight pullets, and told them, that farther to the north they might meet with fresh provisions enough. So they set sail again, and after five days came to a large bay, where they cast anchor at seven fathom. Here they were told, that it was a plentiful coast, and that *Magelagie* and the islands of *Makandari* were farther to the east. The 22d they came within a league of an Island, where they cast anchor at 11 fathom. The 24th Mr. *Nieuhoff* sail'd in the *Bow* up the river *Magelagie* and returning the 26th reported, that this was the river upon which *Magelagie* stood, a populous and plentiful place; that he had seen there an *English* ship, that had bought slaves there to be carried to *Barbadoes*, besides several other *Moorish* vessels trading in slaves. Hereupon Mr. *Hugo* and Mr. *Nieuhoff* went thither, and return'd the 30th. About two leagues into the country you see a high ridge of land. The 31st Mr. *Nieuhoff* carried certain commodities ashore, but could not agree about the exchange, the inhabitants offering very little, and holding their slaves at sixteen crowns a piece: however the second of *September* Mr. *Hugo* and Mr. *Nieuhoff* went ashore with some cloves, for which the king had offered some money before, but return'd unsuccessful; and the *Madagascarians* (a very malicious generation) having besides this spoil'd the ponds where we used to fetch our fresh water; they set sail again for the river *Marigando*; where they cast anchor the ninth on the east-side of the cape, and met with good fresh water on the west-side of the bay. Mr. *Hugo* and Mr. *Nieuhoff* had the good fortune to exchange some of their commodities with the king of the place, and brought back 22 slaves, 13 cows, some sheep and other provisions, of which they stood in great want. The 22d it being resolved to sail 36 or 40 leagues farther to the *North*; Mr. *Nieuhoff* sail'd before with the *Bow* to discover the lands and rocks, and came into the *Young Man's Bay*, where there is 10, 12 and 15 fathom water. Hence continuing their voyage, they came the 27th about noon to the point or cape of *Parmira* near one of the five islands at 13 deg. 13 min. The 29th they were near the cape of *Konquiso*, where they saw some fisher boats. The middlemost of these islands is a high, steep and unaccessible rock, which may be discovered a great way at sea. Some of the fishermen having shew'd them where their king kept his court, Mr. *Nieuhoff* set sail thither in the *Bow*, leaving the 1672.

1672. *Arrow* in the bay, and in company with the ships mate, and some few seamen went ashore, in hopes to exchange some of his commodities; but on the 7th the *Arrow* was much surprized to see the *Bow* making towards them, and with two cannon shot to give the signal of distress. They sent out their boat to meet them, which returning with the master of the *Bow*, gave an account, that Mr. *Nieuhoff* being gone ashore with some of the company in the bay of *Antegoa*, or *Ant Osy Sambo*, by some styled the *Murtherers Bay*, to traffick, was not returned, and that therefore the *Bow*, after a stay of three whole days, had weighed her anchors, and set sail again without them. It was concluded on all hands, that the *Bow* ought to return thither, but Mr. *Hugo* alledging that having at first no more than six months provisions, they would be in great danger of being starved, if they tarried any longer here, he insisted upon returning to the cape first, which they did accordingly, and set sail the same afternoon at 25 and 30, and again at 20 and 25 fathom water. In the evening they pass'd near a great sand-bank south to the west, and north to the east, of the biggest of the three islands near the cape of *Koaquiso*, about three leagues from the said isle, and the northern point and the great isle of *Naushy*.

This was the end of Mr. *John Nieuhoff*, who had spent so many years in viewing the *West* and *East-Indies*, and consequently deserved a better fortune. What *Hugo* alledged, concerning their scarcity of provisions, was indeed true enough; but on the other hand, it is unquestionable, they needed not to have bestow'd much time in looking after him. The *Bow* and *Arrow* prosecuted their voyage, and on the 8th found themselves at 12 deg. 40 min. latitude, having the west cape of *St. Sebastian* six leagues to the north-east. The next 1672.
following day they came in sight of a small isle full of trees, about three leagues from the cape of *St. Sebastian*, near which place being toss'd to and fro by tempests and contrary winds, they were reduced to that extremity, that they were forced to live upon a spoonful of rice 24 hours: So that after having endured a great deal of misery, and lost many of their men, both the *Bow* and *Arrow* return'd to the *Cape of Good-Hope* the 17th of *December*, where Mr. *Hugo* met but with an indifferent reception, and the master of the *Bow* was cashier'd for having not tarried longer near the place where Mr. *Nieuhoff* went ashore. The first of *Jan.* 1673, the *Bow* and *Arrow* being provided with sufficient provisions, set sail again, the first for the bay where they had left Mr. *Nieuhoff*, the second for the isle of *St. Maurice*, whither she was to carry Mr. *Hugo*. After their parting at sea, no news was heard of the *Bow* for a long time after, till at last it was discovered that the ships crew mutinied and sold the vessel to the *French* at *Mosambique*; so that it remains uncertain, whether any of them had any intelligence concerning Mr. *Nieuhoff*. At the request of his brother, Mr. *Henry Nieuhoff*, the directors of the chamber of *Amsterdam* dispatch'd, the 2d of *May* 1676, the yacht called the *Voerhout* from the *Cape of Good-Hope* to the place where Mr. *Nieuhoff* went ashore; which returning to the said cape the 20th of *September* with 250 slaves, brought no farther account than that they had seen the king of the place, and that he had declared to them, that he knew nothing of the matter; so that it is very probable that Mr. *Nieuhoff* and his company were at their first landing massacred by the barbarous inhabitants.

THE TRUE

TRAVELS, ADVENTURES AND OBSERVATIONS

OF

Captain *JOHN SMITH,*

INTO

EUROPE, ASIA, AFRICA and *AMERICA,*

From *Anno Dom.* 1593, to 1629.

To the Right Honourable

WILLIAM Earl of *PEMBROKE*,

Lord Steward of his Majeſty's moſt Honourable Houſhold;

ROBERT Earl of *LINDSEY*,

Great Chamberlain of England;

HENRY Lord *HUNSDON*,

Viſcount Rochford, Earl of Dover;

AND

All your Honourable Friends and Well-willers.

My Lords,

SIR *Robert Cotton*, that moſt learned treaſurer of antiquity, having by peruſal of my general hiſtory, and others, found that I had likewiſe undergone divers other as hard hazards in the other parts of the world, requeſted me to fix the whole courſe of my paſſages in a book by it ſelf; whoſe noble deſire I could not but in part ſatisfy; the rather, becauſe they have acted my fatal tragedies upon the ſtage, and rack'd my relations at their pleaſure. To prevent therefore all future miſpriſions, I have compiled this true diſcourſe. Envy hath taxed me to have writ too much, and done too little; but that ſuch ſhould know how little I eſteem them, I have writ this, more for the ſatisfaction of my friends, and all generous and well diſpoſed readers. To ſpeak only of my ſelf were intolerable ingratitude; becauſe, having had ſo many co-partners with me, I cannot make a monument for my ſelf, and leave them unburied in the fields, whoſe lives begot me the title of a ſoldier; for as they were companions with me in my dangers, ſo ſhall they be partakers with me in this tomb.

For my *Sea-Grammar* (cauſed to be printed by my worthy friend Sir *Samuel Saltonſtall*) hath found ſuch good entertainment abroad, that I have been importuned by many noble perſons, to let this alſo paſs the preſs. Many of the moſt eminent warriours, and others, what their ſwords did, their pens writ: Though I be never ſo much their inferior, yet I hold it no great error to follow good examples; nor repine at them will do the like.

And now, *My moſt Honourable good Lords*, I know not to whom I may better preſent it, than to your lordſhips, whoſe friendſhips, as I conceive, are as much to each others, as my duty is to you all; and becauſe you are acquainted both with my endeavours and writings, I doubt not, but your honours will as well accept of this, as of the reſt, and patronize it under the ſhadow of your moſt noble virtues, which I am ever bound in all duty to reverence, and under which I hope to have ſhelter againſt all ſtorms that dare threaten.

5

Your Honours to be commanded,

John Smith.

THE TRUE TRAVELS, ADVENTURES AND OBSERVATIONS OF Captain *JOHN SMITH*.

CHAP. I.

His Birth; Apprenticeſhip; going into France; *his beginning with ten ſhillings and three pence; his ſervice in the* Netherlands; *his bad paſſage into* Scotland; *his return to* Willoughby, *and how he lived in the woods.*

HE was born in *Willoughby* in *Lincolnſhire*, and a ſcholar in the two free-ſchools of *Alford* and *Louth*. His father anciently deſcended from the ancient *Smiths* of *Crudley* in *Lancaſhire*; his mother from the *Rickands* at *Great-Heck* in *Yorkſhire*. His parents dying when he was about thirteen years of age, left him a competent means, which he not being capable to manage, little regarded, his mind being even then ſet upon brave adventures, ſold his ſatchel, books, and all he had, intending ſecretly to get to ſea, but that his father's death ſtay'd him. But now the guardians of his eſtate more regarding it than him, he had liberty enough, though no means, to get beyond the ſea. About the age of fifteen years, he was bound an apprentice to Mr. *Thomas Sendall* of *Lyn*, the greateſt merchant of all thoſe parts; but becauſe he would not preſently ſend him to ſea, he never ſaw his maſter in eight years after. At laſt he found means to attend Mr. *Peregrine Berty* into *France*, ſecond ſon to the right honourable *Peregrine*, that generous lord *Willoughby*, and famous ſoldier; where coming to his brother *Robert*, then at *Orleans*, now Earl of *Lindſey*, and lord great chamberlain of *England*, being then but little youths under tutorage: His ſervice being needleſs, within a month or ſix weeks they ſent him back again to his friends, who when he came from *London*, they liberally gave him (but out of his own eſtate) ten ſhillings to be rid of him; ſuch oft is the ſhare of fatherleſs children: But thoſe two honourable brethren gave him ſufficient to return for *England*. But it was the leaſt thought of his determination, for now being freely at liberty in *Paris*, growing acquainted with one Mr. *David Hume*, who making ſome uſe of his purſe, gave him letters to his friends in *Scotland* to prefer him to king *James*. Arriving at *Roan*, he better bethinks himſelf, ſeeing his money near ſpent, down the river he went to *Haver de Grace*, where he firſt began to learn the life of a ſoldier. Peace being concluded in *France*, he went with captain *Joſeph Duxbury* into the *Low-Countries*, under whoſe colours having ſerved three or four years, he took his journey for *Scotland*, to deliver his letters. At *Ancuſan* he imbark'd himſelf for *Lethe*, but as much danger, as ſhipwreck and ſickneſs could endure, he had

had at the holy isle in *Northumberland* near *Berwick*. Being recovered, into *Scotland* he went to deliver his letters. After much kind usage among those honest *Scots* at *Ripweth* and *Broxmoth*, but neither money nor means to make him a courtier, he returned to *Willoughby* in *Lincolnshire*; where within a short time, being glutted with too much company, wherein he took small delight, he retired himself into a little woody pasture, a good way from any town, invironed with many hundred acres of other woods: Here by a fair brook he built a pavillion of boughs, where only in his clothes he lay. His study was *Machiavil's Art of War*, and *Marcus Aurelius*; his exercise a good horse, with his lance and ring; his food was thought to be more of venison than any thing else; what he wanted his man brought him. The country wondering at such an hermit, his friends persuaded one *Seignior Theodora Polaloga*, rider to *Henry* Earl of *Lincoln*, an excellent horseman, and a noble *Italian* gentleman, to insinuate into his woodish acquaintance, whose language and good discourse, and exercise of riding drew him to stay with him at *Tattersall*. Long these pleasures could not content him, but he returned again to the *Low-Countries*.

CHAP. II.

The notable villany of four French *gallants, and his revenge*; Smith *thrown overboard*; *Captain* La Roche *of* St. Malo *relieves him*.

A notable villany of four French gallants.

THus when *France* and the *Netherlands* had taught him to ride a horse, and use his arms, with such rudiments of war, as his tender years in those martial schools could attain unto; he was desirous to see more of the world, and try his fortune against the *Turks*, both repenting and lamenting to have seen so many christians slaughter one another. Opportunity casting him into the company of four *French* gallants well attended, faining to him the one to be a great lord, the rest his gentlemen, and that they were all devoted that way; over-persuaded him to go with them into *France*, to the duchess of *Merceur*, from whom they should not only have means, but also letters of favour to her noble duke, then general for the emperor *Rodulphus* in *Hungary*; which he did, with such ill weather as winter affordeth; in the dark night they arrived in the broad shallow inlet of *St. Valleries sur Soame* in *Picardy*: His *French* lord knowing he had good apparel, and better furnished with money than themselves, so plotted with the master of the ship, to set his and their own trunks ashore, leaving *Smith* aboard till the boat could return, which was the next day after, towards evening: The reason he alledged was, the sea went so high he could come no sooner, and that his lord was gone to *Amiens*, where they would stay his coming; which treacherous villany, when divers other soldiers and passengers understood, they had like to have slain the master, and had they known how, would have run away with the ship.

A carralue is in value a penny.

Coming on shore he had but one carralue, was forced to sell his cloak to pay for his passage. One of the soldiers, called *Curzianvere*, compassionating his injury, assured him that this great lord *Dupreau* was only the son of a lawyer of *Mortagne* in base *Britany*, and his attendants *Cursell*, *La Nelie* and *Monferrat*, three young citizens, as arrant cheats as himself; but if he would accompany him, he would bring him to their friends, but in the interim supplied his wants: Thus travelling by *Diepe*, *Codebeck*, *Humphla*, *Pount-demer* in *Normandy*, they came to *Caen* in base *Normandy*; where both this noble *Curzianvere*, and the great prior of the great abby of *St. Stephen* (where is the ruinous tomb of *William the Conqueror*) and many other of his friends kindly welcomed him, and brought him to *Mortagne*, where he found *Dupreau* and the rest, but to small purpose; for Mr. *Curzianvere* was a banished man, and durst not be seen but to his friends; yet the bruit of their cozenage occasioned the lady *Collumber*, the baron *Larshan*, the lord *Shasghe*, and divers other honourable persons, to supply his wants, and with them to recreate himself so long as he would: But such pleasant pleasures suited little with his poor estate, and his restless spirit, that could never find content to receive such noble favours, as he could neither deserve nor requite: But wandering from port to port to find some man of war, spent that he had, and in a forest, near dead with grief and cold, a rich farmer found him by a fair fountain under a tree: This kind peasant relieved him again to his content, to follow his intent. Not long after, as he passed thorow a great grove of trees, between *Pounterson* and *Dina* in *Britany*, it was his chance to meet *Cursell*, more miserable than himself: His piercing injuries had so small patience,

Here he incountred one of the thieves.

I as

as without any word they both drew, and in a ſhort time *Curſell* fell to the ground, where, from an old ruinated tower, the inhabitants ſeeing them, were ſatisfied, when they heard *Curſell* confeſs what had formerly paſſed; and that how, in the dividing that they had ſtolen from him, they fell by the ears amongſt themſelves, that were actors in it; but for his part, he excuſed himſelf to be innocent as well of the one, as of the other. In regard of his hurt, *Smith* was glad to be ſo rid of him, directing his courſe to an honourable lord, the earl of *Ployer*, who during the war in *France*, with his two brethren, viſcount *Poomory*, and Baron *de Mercy*, who had been brought up in *England*; by him he was better refurniſhed than ever. When they had ſhewed him *St. Malo* mount, *St. Michael*, *Lambal*, *Simbreack*, *Lanion*, and their own fair caſtle of *Tuncadeck*, *Gingan*, and divers other places in *Britany* (and their *Britiſh Cornwaile*) taking his leave, he took his way to *Raynes*, the *Britains* chief city, and ſo to *Nants*, *Poyters*, *Rochel* and *Bourdeaux*. The rumour of the ſtrength of *Bayon* in *Biſky*, cauſed him to ſee it; and from thence took his way from *Leſkar* in *Bicarne* and *Paw* in the kingdom of *Navarre* to *Tolouza* in *Gaſcoigne*, *Bezers* and *Carcaſſone*, *Narbone*, *Montpelier*, *Nimes* in *Languedock*, and thorow the countrey of *Avignion*, by *Arles* to *Marſeilles* in *Provence*, there imbarking himſelf for *Italy*; the ſhip was inforced to *Tolonne*, and putting again to ſea, ill weather ſo grew upon them, that they anchored cloſe about the ſhore, under the little iſle of *St. Mary*, againſt *Nice* in *Savoy*. Here the inhuman provincials, with a rabble of pilgrims of divers nations going to *Rome*, hourly curſed him, not only for a hugonot, but his nation they ſwore were all pirates, and ſo vilely railed on his dread ſoveraign queen *Elizabeth*, and that they never ſhould have fair weather ſo long as he was aboard them; their diſputations grew to that paſſion, that they threw him over-board, yet God brought him to that little iſle, where was no inhabitants, but a few kine and goats. The next morning he eſpied two ſhips more riding by them, put in by the ſtorm, that fetched him aboard, well refreſhed him, and ſo kindly uſed him, that he was well contented to try the reſt of his fortune with them. After he had related unto them his former diſcourſe, what for pity, and the love of the honourable earl of *Ployer*, this noble *Britain* his neighbour, captain *La Roche* of *St. Malo*, regarded and entertained him for his well reſpected friend. With the next fair wind, there ſailed along by the coaſt of *Corſica* and *Sardinia*; and croſſing the *Gulf of Tunis*, paſſed by cape *Bona* to the iſle of *Lampadoſa*, leaving the coaſt of *Barbary* till they came at cape *Roſuta*, and ſo along the *African* ſhore for *Alexandria* in *Ægypt*. There delivering their fraught, they went to *Scandaroone*, rather to view what ſhips were in the road, than any thing elſe; keeping their coarſe by *Cypres* and the coaſt of *Aſia*, ſailing by *Rhodes*, the *Archipelagus*, *Candia* and the coaſt of *Græcia*, and the iſle of *Zefolonia*. They lay to and again a few days, betwixt the iſle of *Corfu*, and the cape of *Otranto*, in the kingdom of *Naples*, in the entrance of the *Adriatick* ſea.

The nobleneſs of the earl of Ployer.

An inhuman act of the provincials in caſting him over-board.

Capt. La Roche *relieves him.*

CHAP. III.

A deſperate ſea-fight in the Streights; *his paſſage to* Rome, Naples, *and the view of* Italy.

A deſperate ſea-fight.

BEtwixt the two capes they met with an *Argoſie* of *Venice*; it ſeemed the captain deſired to ſpeak with them, whoſe untoward anſwer was ſuch, as ſlew them a man; whereupon the *Britaine* preſently gave them the broad-ſide, then his ſtern, and his other broad-ſide alſo, and continued the chaſe, with his chaſe-pieces, till he gave them ſo many broad-ſides one after another, that the *Argoſies* ſails and tackling was ſo torn, ſhe ſtood to her defence, and made ſhot for ſhot; twice in one hour and a half the *Britaine* boarded her, yet they cleared themſelves; but clapping her aboard again, the *Argoſie* fired him, which with much danger to them both was preſently quenched. This rather augmented the *Britaine*'s rage, than abated his courage; for having reaccommodated himſelf again, ſhot her ſo oft betwixt wind and water, ſhe was ready to ſink, then they yielded; the *Britaine* loſt fifteen men, ſhe twenty, beſides divers were hurt, the reſt went to work on all hands; ſome to ſtop the leaks, others to guard the priſoners that were chained, the reſt to rifle her. The ſilks, velvets, cloth of gold and tiſſue, piaſters, chiequeens and ſultanies, which is gold and ſilver, they unloaded in four and twenty hours, was wonderful, whereof having ſufficient, and tired with toil, they caſt her off with her company, with as much

much good merchandize as would have freighted ſuch another *Britaine*, that was but two hundred tuns, ſhe four or five hundred.

To repair his defects he ſtood for the coaſt of *Calabria*; but hearing there was ſix or ſeven galleys at *Meſſina*, he departed thence for *Malta*; but the wind coming fair, he kept his courſe along the coaſt of the Kingdom of *Sicilia*, by *Sardinia* and *Corſica*, till he came to the road of *Antibo* in *Peamon*, where the ſet *Smith* on ſhore with five hundred chicqueens, and a little box God ſent him, worth near as much more. Here he left this noble *Britaine*, and embarked himſelf for *Leghorn*, being glad to have ſuch opportunity and means to better his experience by the view of *Italy*; and having paſſed *Tuſkany* and the countrey of *Siena*, where he found his dear Friends, the two honourable brethren, the lord *Willoughby* and his brother cruelly wounded in a deſperate fray, yet to their exceeding great honour. Then to *Viterbo* and many other cities he came to *Rome*, where it was his chance to ſee pope *Clement* VIII. with many cardinals, creep up the holy-ſtairs, which they ſay, are thoſe our ſaviour Chriſt went up to *Pontius Pilate*, where blood falling from his head, being prick'd with his crown of Thorns, the drops are marked with nails of ſteel, upon them none dare go but in that manner, ſaying ſo many *Ave-Maries* and *Pater-Noſters*, as is their devotion, and to kiſs the nails of ſteel: But on each ſide is a pair of ſuch like ſtairs, upon which you may go, ſtand, or kneel, but divided from the holy-ſtairs by two walls: Right againſt them is a chapel, where hangs a great ſilver lamp, which burneth continually, yet they ſay the oil neither increaſeth nor diminiſheth. A little diſtant is the ancient church of *St. John de Lateran*, where he ſaw him ſay maſs, which commonly he doth upon ſome *Friday* once a month. Having ſaluted father *Parſons*, that famous *Engliſh* jeſuit, and ſatisfied himſelf with the rarities of *Rome*, he went down the river *Tiber* to *Civita Vecchia*, where he embark'd himſelf, to ſatisfy his eye with the fair city of *Naples*, and her kingdom's nobility; returning by *Capua*, *Rome*, and *Siena*, he paſſed by that admired city of *Florence*, the cities and countreys of *Bolonia*, *Ferrara*, *Mantua*, *Padua* and *Venice*, whoſe gulf he paſſed from *Malamoco* and the *Adriatick-Sea* for *Ragouza*, ſpending ſome time to ſee that barren, broken coaſt of *Albania* and *Dalmatia*, to *Capo de Iſtria*, travelling the main of poor *Sclavonia* by *Lubbiano*, 'till he came to *Grates* in *Styria*, the ſeat of *Ferdinando*, archduke of *Auſtria*, now Emperor of *Almania*, where he met an *Engliſhman* and an *Iriſh* jeſuit, who acquainted him with many brave gentlemen of good quality, eſpecially with the lord *Eberſbaught*, with whom, trying ſuch concluſions, as he projected to undertake, preferred him to baron *Kiſell*, general of the artillery, and he to a worthy colonol, the earl of *Meldrich*, with whom, going to *Vienna* in *Auſtria*, under whoſe regiment, in what ſervice, and how he ſpent his time, this enſuing diſcourſe will declare.

The popes holy-ſtairs, brought from Jeruſalem, *whereon (they ſay) Chriſt went up to* Pontius Pilate.

CHAP. IV.

The ſiege of Olumpagh; *an excellent ſtratagem by* Smith; *another not much worſe.*

The ſiege of Olumpagh.

AFter the loſs of *Caniza*, the *Turks* with twenty thouſand beſieged the ſtrong town of *Olumpagh* ſo ſtraitly, as they were cut off from all intelligence and hope of ſuccour, till *John Smith*, this *Engliſh* gentleman, acquainted baron *Kiſell*, generall of the archdukes artillery, he had taught the governor, his worthy friend, ſuch a rule, that he would undertake to make him know any thing he intended, and have his anſwer, would they bring him but to ſome place where he might make the flame of a torch ſeen to the town; *Kiſell* inflamed with this ſtrange invention, *Smith* made it ſo plain, that forthwith he gave him guides, who in the dark night brought him to a mountain, where he ſhewed three torches equidiſtant from the other, which plainly appearing to the town, the governor preſently apprehended, and anſwered again with three other fires in like manner; each knowing the others being and intent; *Smith*, though diſtant ſeven miles, ſignified to him theſe Words: *On* Thurſday *at night I will charge on the eaſt, at the alarm ſalley you*; *Eberſbaught* anſwered, *he would*, and thus it was done: Firſt he writ his meſſage as brief, you ſee, as could be, then divided the alphabet into two parts thus,

A. b. c. d. e. f. g. h. i. k. l.
1. 1. 1. 1. 1. 1. 1. 1. 1. 1. 1.

m. n. o. p. q. r. ſ. t. v. w. x. y. z.
2. 2. 2. 2. 2. 2. 2. 2. 2. 2. 2. 2. 2.

The

An excellent stratagem. The first part from *A.* to *l* is signified by shewing and hiding one link, so oft as there is letters from *A* to that letter you mean; the other part from *m* to *z*, is mentioned by two lights in like manner. The end of a word is signified by shewing of three lights, ever staying your light at that letter you mean, till the other may write it in a paper, and answer by his signal, which is one light, it is done, beginning to count the letters by the lights, every time from *A* to *m*; by this means also the other returned his answer, whereby each did understand other. The guides all this time having well viewed the camp, returned to *Kisell*; who doubting of his power, being but ten thousand, was animated by the guides, how the *Turks* were so divided by the river in two parts, they could not easily second each other. To which *Smith* added this conclusion; that two or three thousand pieces of match fastened to divers small lines of an hundred fathom in length, being armed with powder, might all be fired and stretch'd at an instant before the alarum, upon the plain of *Hysnaburg*, supported by two staves, at each lines end, in that manner would seem like so many musketeers; which was put in practice, and being discovered by the *Turks*, they prepared to encounter these false fires, thinking there had been some great army; whilst *Kisell* with his ten thousand being enter'd the *Turks* quarters, who ran up and down as men amazed, it was not long ere *Ebersbaught* was pell-mell with them in their trenches; in which distracted confusion, a third part of the *Turks* that besieged that side towards *Knousbruck*, were slain, many of the rest drowned, but all fled. The other part of the army was so busied to resist the false fires that *Kisell* before the morning put two thousand good soldiers in the town, and with small loss was retired; the garrison was well relieved with what they found in the *Turks* quarters, which caused the *Turks* to raise their siege and return to *Caniza*; and *Kisell* with much honour was received at *Kerment*, and occasioned the author a good reward and preferment, to be captain of two hundred and fifty horsemen, under the conduct of colonel *Voldo* earl of *Meldritch*.

Another stratagem.

CHAP. V.

The siege of Stoll-weissenburg; *the effects of* Smith's *fire-work*; *a worthy exploit of earl* Rosworme; *earl* Meldritch *takes the bashaw prisoner.*

A General rumour of a general peace, now spread it self over all the face of those tormented countries; but the *Turk* intended no such matter, but levied soldiers from all parts he could. The emperor also, by the assistance of the christian princes, provided three armies, the one led by the archduke *Matthias*, the emperor's brother, and his lieutenant duke *Merceur* to defend *Low-Hungary*; the second by *Ferdinando* the archduke of *Styria*, and the duke of *Mantua* his lieutenant to regain *Caniza*; the third by *Gonzago*, governor of *High-Hungary*, to join with *Georgio Busca* to make an absolute conquest of *Transilvania*.

The siege of Alba-Regalis. Duke *Merceur* with an army of thirty thousand, whereof near ten thousand were *French*, besieged *Stoll-weissenburg*, otherwise called *Alba Regalis*, a place so strong by art and nature, that it was thought impregnable. At his first coming, the *Turks* sallied upon the *German* quarter, slew near five hundred, and returned before they were thought on. The next night in like manner they did near as much to the *Bemers* and *Hungarians*; of which fortune still presuming, thinking to have found the *French* quarter as careless, eight or nine hundred of them were cut in pieces and taken prisoners. In this encounter monsieur *Grandvile*, a brave *French* colonel, received seven or eight cruel wounds, yet followed the enemy to the ports, he came off alive, but within three or four days died.

Earl *Meldritch*, by the information of three or four christians (escaped out of the town) upon every alarm, where there were greatest assemblies and throng of people, caused captain *Smith* to put in practice his fiery dragons he had demonstrated unto him, and the earl *Van Sulch* at *Comora*, which he thus performed: Having prepared forty or fifty round-bellied earthen pots, and filled them with hand gun-powder, then covered them with pitch, mingled with brimstone and turpentine, and quartering as many musket-bullets, that hung together, but only at the center of the division, stuck them round in the mixture about the pots, and covered them again with the same mixture; over that a strong searcloth, then over all, a good thickness of towze-match, well tempered with oil of linseed, camphire and powder of brimstone: These he fitly placed in slings, graduated so near as *The effect of good fire-works.*

they could to the places of these assemblies. At mid-night upon the alarm, it was a fearful sight to see the short flaming course of their flight in the air, but presently after their fall, the lamentable noise of the miserable slaughtered *Turks* was most wonderful to hear: Besides, they had fired that suburb at the port of *Buda* in two or three places, which so troubled the *Turks* to quench, that had there been any means to have assaulted them, they could hardly have resisted the fire and their enemies. The earl *Rosworme*, contrary to the opinion of all men, would needs undertake to find means to surprize the segeth and suburb of the city, strongly defended by a muddy lake, which was thought unpassable.

A worthy exploit of earl Rosworme.

The duke having planted his ordnance, battered the other side, whilst *Rosworme* in the dark night, with every man a bundle of sedge and bavins still thrown before them, so laded up the lake, as they surprised that unregarded suburb before they were discovered: Upon which unexpected alarm, the *Turks* fled into the city; and the other suburb not knowing the matter, got into the city also, leaving their suburb for the duke, who, with no great resistance took it, with many pieces of ordnance; the city being of no such strength as the suburbs, with their own ordnance was so battered, that it was taken by force, with such a merciless execution, as was most pitiful to behold. The *Bashaw* notwithstanding, drew together a party of five hundred before his own palace, where he intended to die; but seeing most of his men slain before him, by the valiant captain, earl *Meldritch*, who took him prisoner with his own hands; and with the hazard of himself saved him from the fury of other troops, that did pull down his palace, and would have rent him in pieces, had he not been thus preserved. The duke thought his victory much honoured with such a prisoner; took order he should be used like a prince, and with all expedition gave charge presently to repair the breaches, and the ruins of this famous city, that had been in the possession of the *Turks* near threescore years.

Earl Meldritch *takes the Bashaw prisoner.*

CHAP. VI.

A brave encounter of the Turks *army with the christians; duke* Merceur *overthroweth* Assan Bashaw; *he divides the christian army; his nobleness and death.*

MAhomet the great *Turk*, during the siege, had raised an army of sixty thousand men to have relieved it; but hearing it was lost, he sent *Assan* bashaw, general of his army, the bashaw of *Buda*, bashaw *Amaroz*, to see if it were possible to regain it: The duke understanding there could be no great experience in such a new levied army as *Assan* had, having put a strong garrison into it, and with the brave colonel *Rosworme*, *Culnits*, *Meldritch*, the *Rhine-Grave*, *Vahan* and many others, with twenty thousand good soldiers, set forward to meet the *Turk* in the plains of *Girk*. Those two armies encountred as they marched, where began a hot and bloody skirmish betwixt them, regiment against regiment, as they came in order, till the night parted them: Here earl *Meldritch* was so invironed among those half circular regiments of *Turks*, they supposed him their prisoner, and his regiment lost; but his two most couragious friends, *Vahan* and *Culnits*, made such a passage amongst them, that it was a terror to see how horse and man lay sprawling and tumbling, some one way, some another on the ground. The earl there at that time made his valour shine more bright than his armour, which seemed then painted with *Turkish* blood; he slew the brave *Zanzack Bugola*, and made his passage to his friends, but near half his regiment was slain. Captain *Smith* had his horse slain under him, and himself sore wounded; but he was not long unmounted, for there was choice enough of horses that wanted masters. The *Turk* thinking the victory sure against the duke, whose army, by the siege and the garrison he had left behind him, was much weaken'd, would not be content with one, but he would have all; and lest the duke should return to *Alba Regalis*, he sent that night twenty thousand to besiege the city, assuring them, he would keep the duke or any other from relieving them. Two or three days they lay each by other, entrenching themselves; the *Turks* daring the duke daily to a set battle, who at length drew out his army, led by the *Rhine-Grave*, *Culnits* and *Meldritch*, who upon their first encounter, charged with that resolute and valiant courage, as disordered not only the foremost squadrons of the *Turks*, but enforced all the whole army to retire to the camp, with the loss of five or six thousand, with the bashaw of *Buda*, and four or five zanzacks, with divers other great commanders, two hundred prisoners, and nine pieces of

A brave encounter of the Turks *army with the christians.*

Duke Merceur *overthroweth* Assan *Bass.*

of ordnance. At that instant appeared, as it were another army coming out of a valley over a plain hill, that caused the duke at that time to be contented, and to retire to his trenches, which gave time to *Assan*, to reorder his disordered squadrons: Here they lay nine or ten days, and more supplies repaired to them, expecting to try the event in a set battle; but the soldiers on both parties, by reason of their great wants, and approach of winter, grew so discontented, that they were ready of themselves to break up the leager; the bashaw retiring himself to *Buda*, had some of the rear troops cut off. *Amaroz* bashaw hearing of this, found such bad welcome at *Alba Regalis*, and the town so strongly repaired with so brave a garrison, raised his siege, and retired to *Zigetum*.

The duke understanding that the archduke *Ferdinando* had so resolutely besieged *Caniza*, as what by the loss of *Alba Regalis*, and the *Turks* retreat to *Buda*, being void of hope of any relief, doubted not, but it would become again the christians. To the furtherance whereof, the duke divided his army into three parts. The earl of *Rosworme* went with seven thousand to *Caniza*; the earl of *Meldritch* with six thousand he sent to assist *Georgio Busca* against the *Transilvanians*, the rest went with himself to the garrisons of *Strigonium* and *Komara*; having thus worthily behaved himself, he arrived at *Vienna*, where the archdukes and the nobility with as much honour received him, as if he had conquered all *Hungaria*; his very picture they esteemed would make them fortunate, which thousands kept as curiously as a precious relique. To requite this honour, preparing himself to return into *France*, to raise new forces against the next year, with the two archdukes, *Matthias* and *Maximilian*, and divers others of the nobility, was with great magnificence conducted to *Nurenburg*, there by them royally feasted, (how it chanced is not known,) but the next morning he was found dead, and his brother-in-law died two days after; whose hearts, after this great triumph, with much sorrow were carried into *France*.

Duke Merceur *divideth his army.*

Duke Merceur *and his Brother in-law die suddenly.*

CHAP. VII.

The unhappy siege of Caniza; *earl* Meldritch *serveth prince* Sigismundus; *prince* Moyses *besiegeth* Regall; Smith'*s three single combats; his patent from* Sigismundus, *and reward.*

The unhappy siege of Caniza.

THE worthy lord *Rosworme* had not a worse journey to the miserable siege of *Caniza*, (where by the extremity of an extraordinary continuing tempest of hail, wind, frost and snow, the christians were forced to leave their tents and artillery, and what they had, it being so cold, that three or four hundred of them were frozen to death in a night, and two or three thousand lost in that miserable flight in the snowy tempest, though they did know no enemy at all to follow them,) than the noble earl of *Meldritch* had to *Transilvania*, where hearing of the death of *Michael*, and the brave duke *Merceur*, and knowing the policy of *Busca*, and the prince his royalty, being now beyond all belief of men, in possession of the best part of *Transilvania*, persuaded his troops, in so honest a cause, to assist the prince against the *Turk*, rather than *Busca* against the prince.

Earl Meldritch *serveth prince* Sigismundus.

The soldiers being worn out with those hard pays and travels, upon hope to have free liberty to make booty upon what they could get possession of from the *Turks*, were easily persuaded to follow him whithersoever. Now this noble earl was a *Transilvanian* born, and his fathers countrey yet inhabited by the *Turks*; for *Transilvania* was yet in three divisions, though the prince had the hearts both of country and people; yet the frontiers had a garrison amongst the unpassable mountains, some for the emperor, some for the prince, and some for the *Turk*: To regain which small estate, he desired leave of the prince to try his fortunes, and to make use of that experience, the time of twenty years had taught him in the emperor's service, promising to spend the rest of his days, for his countrey's defence in his excellency's service. The prince glad of so brave a commander, and so many expert and ancient soldiers made him camp-master of his army, gave him all necessary relief for his troops, and what freedom they desired to plunder the *Turks*.

Earl Meldritch *maketh incursions to discover* Regall.

The earl having made many incursions into the land of *Zarkam*, among those rocky mountains, where were some *Turks*, some *Tartars*, but most bandittoes, rennegadoes, and such like, which sometimes he forced into the plains of *Regall*, where is a city, not only of men and fortifications, strong of it self, but so environed with mountains, that made the passages so difficult,

cult, that in all theſe wars no attempt had been made upon it to any purpoſe: Having ſatisfied himſelf with the ſituation, and the moſt convenient paſſages to bring his army unto it. The earth no ſooner put on her green habit, than the earl overſpread her with his armed troops. To poſſeſs himſelf firſt of the moſt convenient paſſage, which was a narrow valley betwixt two high mountains; he ſent colonel *Veltus* with his regiment, diſperſed in companies to lie in *Ambuſcado*, as he had directed them, and in the morning to drive all the cattle they could find before a fort in that paſſage, whom he ſuppoſed would ſally, ſeeing but ſome ſmall party to recover their prey; which took ſuch good ſucceſs, that the garriſon was cut off by the ambuſcado, and *Veltus* ſeized on the ſkonces, which were abandoned. *Meldritch* glad of ſo fortunate a beginning, it was ſix days ere he could with ſix thouſand pioneers make paſſage for his ordnance. The *Turks* having ſuch warning, ſtrengthened the town ſo with men and proviſion, that they made a ſcorn of ſo ſmall a number as *Meldritch* brought with him before the city, which was but eight thouſand. Before they had pitched their tents, the *Turks* ſallied in ſuch abundance, as for an hour they had rather a bloody battle than a ſkirmiſh, but with the loſs of near fifteen hundred on both ſides. The *Turks* were chaſed till the cities ordnance cauſed the earl to retire. The next day *Zachel Moyſes*, general of the army, pitched alſo his tents with nine thouſand foot and horſe, and ſix and twenty pieces of ordnance; but in regard of the ſituation of this ſtrong fortreſs, they did neither fear them nor hurt them, being upon the point of a fair promontory, environed on the one ſide within half a mile with an unuſeful mountain, and on the other ſide with a fair plain, where the chriſtians encamped, but ſo commanded by their ordnance, they ſpent near a month in entrenching themſelves, and raiſing their mounts to plant their batteries; which ſlow proceedings the *Turks* oft derided, that their ordnance were at pawn, and how they grew fat for want of exerciſe, and fearing leſt they ſhould depart ere they could aſſault their city, ſent this challenge to any captain in the army.

Moyſes *beſiegeth* Regal.

That to delight the ladies, who did long to ſee ſome court-like paſtime, the lord *Turbaſhaw* did defy any captain, that had the command of a company, who durſt combate with him for his head: The matter being diſcuſſed, it was accepted, but ſo many queſtions grew for the undertaking, it was decided by lots, which fell upon captain *Smith*, before ſpoken of.

Three ſingle combates.

Truce being made for that time, the rampires all beſet with fair dames and men in arms, the chriſtians in batalia; *Turbaſhaw* with a noiſe of hautboys entered the field well mounted and armed; on his ſhoulders were fixed a pair of great wings, compacted of eagle's feathers, within a ridge of ſilver, richly garniſh'd with gold and precious ſtones, a *Janizary* before him, bearing his lance, on each ſide another leading his horſe; where long he ſtay'd not, 'ere *Smith*, with a noiſe of trumpets, only a page bearing his lance, paſſing by him with a courteous ſalute, took his ground with ſuch good ſucceſs, that at the ſound of the charge, he paſſed the *Turk* thorow the ſight of his beaver, face, head and all, that he fell dead to the ground, where alighting and unbracing his helmet, cut off his head and the *Turks* took his body; and ſo returned without any hurt at all. The head he preſented to the lord *Moyſes*, the general, who kindly acceped it, and with joy to the whole army he was generally welcomed.

The death of this captain ſo ſwelled in the heart of one *Grualgo*, his vowed friend, as rather inraged with madneſs than choler, he directed a particular challenge to the conqueror, to regain his friend's head, or loſe his own, with his horſe and armour for advantage, which according to his deſire, was the next day undertaken: As before upon the ſound of the trumpets, their lances flew in pieces upon a clear paſſage, but the *Turk* was near unhorſed. Their piſtols was the next, which marked *Smith* upon the placard; but the next ſhot the *Turk* was ſo wounded in the left arm, that being not able to rule his horſe, and defend himſelf, he was thrown to the ground, and ſo bruiſed with the fall, that he loſt his head, as his friend before him, with his horſe and armour; but his body and his rich apparel were ſent back to the town.

Every day the *Turks* made ſome ſallies, but few ſkirmiſhes would they endure to any purpoſe. Our works and approaches being not yet advanced to that heighth and effect, which was of neceſſity to be performed; to delude time, *Smith* with ſo many incontradictible preſuading reaſons, obtained leave, that the ladies might know he was not ſo much enamoured of their ſervants heads, but if any *Turk* of their rank would come to the place of combat to redeem them, ſhould have his alſo upon the like conditions, if he could win it.

The challenge preſently was accepted by *Bonny Mulgro*. The next day both the champions entring the field as before, each diſcharging their piſtol, having no lances, but ſuch martial weapons as the defendant appoint-

I

appointed, no hurt was done; their battle-axes were the next, whoſe pierceing bills made ſometime the one, ſometime the other to have ſcarce ſenſe to keep their ſaddles; ſpecially the chriſtian received ſuch a blow, that he loſt his battle-axe, and failed not much to have fallen after it, whereat the ſuppoſed conquering *Turk*, had a great ſhout from the rampires. The *Turk* proſecuted his advantage to the uttermoſt of his power; yet the other, what by the readineſs of his horſe, and his judgment and dexterity in ſuch a buſineſs, beyond all men's expectation, by god's aſſiſtance, not only avoided the *Turks* violence, but having drawn his faulſchion, pierced the *Turk* ſo under the culets, thorow back and body, that altho' he alighted from his horſe, he ſtood not long ere he loſt his head, as the reſt had done.

CHAP. VIII.

Georgio Buſca *an* Albane, *his ingratitude to prince* Sigiſmundus; *prince* Moyſes *his lieutenant, is overthrown by* Buſca, *general for the emperor* Rodulphus; Sigiſmundus *yieldeth his country to* Rodulphus; Buſca *aſſiſteth prince* Rodol *in* Wallachia.

THIS good ſucceſs gave ſuch great encouragement to the whole army, that with a guard of ſix thouſand, three ſpare horſes, before each a *Turk*'s head upon a lance, he was conducted to the general's pavilion with his preſents. *Moyſes* received both him and them with as much reſpect as the occaſion deſerved, embracing him in his arms, gave him a fair horſe, richly furniſhed, a ſchimitar and belt worth three hundred ducats; and *Meldritch* made him ſergeant major of his regiment. But now to the ſiege, having mounted ſix and twenty pieces of ordnance, fifty or ſixty foot above the plain, made them ſo plainly tell his meaning, that within fifteen days two breaches were made, which the *Turks* as valiantly defended as men could; that day was made a darkſome night, but by the light that proceeded from the murdering muſkets, and peace-making cannon, whilſt their ſlothful governor lay in a caſtle on the top of a high mountain, and like a valiant prince aſketh what's the matter, when horror and death ſtood amazed each at other, to ſee who ſhould prevail to make him victorious: *Moyſes* commanding a general aſſault upon the ſloping front of the high promontory, where the barons of *Budendorfe* and *Oberwin*, loſt near half their regiments by logs, bags of powder, and ſuch like, tumbling down the hill, they were to mount ere they could come to the breach; notwithſtanding with an incredible courage, they advanced to the puſh of the pike with the defendants, that with the like courage repulſed, till the earl *Meldritch*, *Becklefield* and *Zarvana*, with their freſh regiments ſeconded them with that fury, that the *Turks* retired and fled into the caſtle, from whence by a flag of truce they deſired compoſition. The earl remembering his father's death, battered it with all the ordnance in the town, and the next day took it; all he found could bear arms, he put to the ſword, and ſet their heads upon ſtakes round about the walls, in the ſame manner they had uſed the chriſtians, when they took it. *Moyſes* having repaired the rampires, and thrown down the work in his camp, he put in it a ſtrong garriſon, though the pillage he had gotten in the town was much, having been for a long time an impregnable den of thieves; yet the loſs of the army ſo intermingled the ſowre with the ſweet, as forced *Moyſes* to ſeek a further revenge, that he ſacked *Veratio*, *Salmos* and *Kupronka*, and with two thouſand priſoners, moſt women and children, came to *Eſenberg*, not far from the prince's palace, where he there encamped.

Regal *aſſaulted and taken.*

Sigiſmundus coming to view his army, was preſented with the priſoners, and ſix and thirty enſigns; where celebrating thanks to Almighty God in triumph of thoſe victories, he was made acquainted with the ſervice *Smith* had done at *Olumpagh*, *Stoll-Weiſſenburgh* and *Regal*; for which, with great honour, he gave him three *Turks* heads in a ſhield for his arms, by patent, under his hand and ſeal, with an oath ever to wear them in his colours, his picture in gold, and three hundred ducats yearly for a penſion.

The patent.

SIGISMUNDUS BATHORI *Dei gratia, dux* Transilvaniæ, Wallachiæ, *&* Vandalorum; *comes* Anchard, Salford, Growenda; *cunctis his literis significamus qui eas lecturi aut audituri sunt, concessam licentiam aut facultatem* Johanni Smith, *natione* Anglo *generoso*, 250. *militum capitaneo sub illustrissimo & gravissimo* Henrico Volda, *comite de* Meldri, Salmariæ, *&* Peldoiæ *primario, ex* 1000 *equitibus &* 1500. *peditibus bello* Ungarico *conductione in provincias supra scriptas sub authoritate nostra: Cui servituti omni laude, perpetuaque memoria dignum præbuit se seerga nos, ut virum strenuum pugnantem pro aris & focis decet. Quare e favore nostro militario ipsum ordine condonavimus, & in sigillum illius tria* Turcica *capita designare & deprimere concessimus, quæ ipse gladio suo ad urbem* Regalem *in singulari prælio vicit, mactavit, atque decollavit in* Transilvaniæ *provincia: Sed fortuna cum variabilis ancepsque sit, idem forte fortuito in* Wallachiæ *provincia, Anno Domini* 1602, *die mensis* Novembris 18, *cum multis aliis etiam nobilibus & aliis quibusdam militibus captus est à domino* Bascha *electo ex* Cambia *regionis* Tartariæ, *cujus severitate adductus salutem quantam potuit quæsivit, tantumque effecit Deo omnipotente adjuvante, ut deliberaverit se, & ad suos commilitones reverterit; ex quibus ipsum liberavimus, & hæc nobis testimonia habuit ut majori licentia frueretur qua dignus esset, jam tendet in patriam suam dulcissimam: Rogamus ergo omnes nostros charissimos, confinitimos, duces, principes, comites, Barones, gubernatores urbium & navium in eadem regione & cæterarum provinciarum in quibus ille residere conatus fuerit, ut idem permittatur capitaneus libere sine obstaculo omni versari. Hæc facientes pergratum nobis feceritis. Signatum* Lespriziæ *in* Misnia *die mensis* Decembris 9, *Anno Domini* 1603.

Cum privilegio propriæ majestatis.

Sigismundus Bathori.

UNIVERSIS *& singulis, cujuscunque joci, status, gradus, ordinis, ac conditionis aa quos hoc præsens scriptum pervenerit,* Gulielmus Segar, *eques auratus aliàs dictus garterus principalis rex armorum* Anglicorum, *salutem.* Sciatis, *quod ego prædictus garterus, notum, testatumque facio, quod patentem suprascriptum, cum manu propria prædicti ducis* Transilvaniæ *subsignatum, & sigillo suo affixum, vidi: Et copiam veram ejusdem (in perpetuam rei memoriam) transcripsi, & recordavi in archivis, & registris officii armorum. Datum* Londini 19 *die* Augusti, *Anno Domini* 1625. *Annoque regni domini nostri* CAROLI *Dei gratia* Magnæ-Britanniæ, Franciæ *&* Hiberniæ *regis, fidei defensoris, &c. primo.*

Gulielmus Segar, Garterus,

The same in English.

SIGISMUNDUS BATHORI, by the grace of God duke of *Transilvania*, *Wallachia* and *Moldavia*, earl of *Anchard*, *Salford* and *Growenda*; to whom this writing may come or appear. Know that we have given leave and licence to *John Smith* an *English* Gentleman, captain of 250 soldiers, under the most generous and honourable *Henry Volda*, earl of *Meldritch*, *Salmaria* and *Peldoia*, colonel of a thousand horse, and fifteen hundred foot, in the wars of *Hungary*, and in the provinces aforesaid under our authority; whose service doth deserve all praise, and perpetual memory towards us, as a man that did for God and his countrey overcome his enemies. Wherefore out of our love and favour, according to the law of arms, we have ordained, and given him in his shield of arms, the figure and description of three *Turks* heads, which with his sword before the town of *Regal*, in single combat he did over-come kill, and cut off, in the province of *Transilvania*. But fortune, as she is very variable, so it chanced and happened to him in the province of *Wallachia*, in the year of our lord 1602, the 18th day of *November*, with many others, as well noble men as also divers other soldiers, were taken prisoners by the lord bashaw of *Cambia*, a country of *Tartaria*, whose cruelty brought him such good fortune, by the help and power of Almighty God, that he delivered himself, and returned again to his company and fellow soldiers, of whom we do discharge him, and this he hath in witness thereof, being much more worthy of a better reward; and now intends to return to his own sweet countrey. We desire therefore all our loving and kind kinsmen, dukes, princes, earls, Barons, governors of towns, cities or ships, in this kingdom, or any other provinces he shall come in, that you freely let pass this the aforesaid captain, without any hindrance or molestation, and this doing, with all kindness, we are always ready to do the like for you. *Sealed at* Lipswick *in* Misenland, *the ninth of* December, *in the year of our Lord* 1603.

With the proper privilege of his majesty.

SIGISMUNDUS BATHORI.

TO all and singular, in what place, state, degree, order or condition whatsoever, to whom this present writing shall come; I *William Segar*, Kt. otherwise garter and principal king of arms of *England*, wish health. Know, that I the aforesaid garter, do witness and approve, that this aforesaid patent, I have seen, signed and sealed, under the proper hand and seal manuel of the said duke of *Transilvania*, and a true copy of the same, as a thing for perpetual memory, I have subscribed and recorded in the register and office of the heralds of arms. Dated at *London*, the nineteenth day of *August*, in the year of our Lord 1625, and in the first year of our soveraign lord *Charles*, by the grace of God, king of *Great-Britain*, *France* and *Ireland*, defender of the faith, &c.

WILLIAM SEGAR.

CHAP. IX.

Sigismundus *sends ambassadors unto the emperor; the conditions re-assured; he yieldeth up all to* Busca, *and returneth to* Prague.

BUsca having all this time been raising new forces, was commanded from the emperor again to invade *Transilvania*, which being one of the fruitfullest and strongest countries in those parts, was now rather a desart, or the very spectacle of desolation; their fruits and fields overgrown with weeds, their churches and battered palaces, and best buildings, as for fear, hid with moss and ivy; being the very bulwark and rampire of a great part of *Europe*, most fit by all christians to have been supplied and maintained, was thus brought to ruin by them it most concerned to support it. But alas, what is it, when the power of majesty pampered in all delights of pleasant vanity, neither knows, nor considers the labour of the ploughman, the hazard of the merchant, the oppression of statesmen, nor feels the piercing torments of broken limbs and inveterate wounds, the toilsome marches, the bad lodging, the hungry diet, and the extreme misery that soldiers endure to secure all those estates; and yet by the spight of malicious detraction, starve for want of their reward and re-

 compences,

compences; whilst the politique courtier, commonly aims more at his own honours and ends, than his countries good, or his prince's glory, honour or security, as this worthy prince too well could testify. But the emperor being certified how weak and desperate his estate was, sent *Busca* again with a great army, to try his fortune once more in *Transilvania*. The prince considering how his country and subjects were consumed, the small means he had any longer to defend his estate, both against the cruelty of the *Turk*, and the power of the emperor, and the small care the *Polanders* had in supplying him, as they had promised, sent to *Busca* to have truce, till messengers might be sent to the emperor for some better agreement, wherewith *Busca* was contented. The ambassadors so prevailed, that the emperor re-assured unto them the conditions he had promised the prince at their confederacy for the lands in *Silesia*, with 60000 ducats presently in hand, and 50000 ducats yearly as a pension. When this conclusion was known to *Moyses*, his lieutenant, then in the field with the army, that would do any think, rather than come in subjection to the *Germans*, he encouraged his soldiers, and without any more ado, marched to encounter *Busca*, whom he found much better provided than he expected; so that betwixt them, in six or seven hours, more than five or six thousand, on both sides, lay dead in the field. *Moyses* thus overthrown, fled to the *Turks* at *Tameswⱥare*, and his scattered troops, some one way, some another.

Busca *in* Transilvania *overthroweth* Moyses.

The prince understanding of this so sudden and unexpected accident, only accompanied with an hundred of his gentry and nobility, went into the camp to *Busca*, to let him know how ignorant he was of his lieutenant's error, that he had done it without his direction or knowledge, freely offering to perform what was concluded by his ambassadors with the emperor; and so causing all his garrisons to come out of their strong holds, he delivered all to *Busca* for the emperor, and so went to *Prague*, where he was hourably received, and established in his possessions, as his imperial majesty had promised. *Busca* assembling all the nobility, took their oaths of allegiance and fidelity, and thus their prince being gone *Transilvania* became again subject to the emperor.

Sigismundus *yieldeth his countrey to* Busca.

Busca *assisteth* Rodol *in* Wallachia.

Now after the death of *Michael*, vavoid of *Wallachia*, the *Turk* sent one *Jeremy* to be their vavoid or prince, whose insulting tyranny caused the people to take arms against him, so that he was forced to flie into the confines of *Moldavia*; and *Busca* in the behalf of the emperor, proclaimed the lord *Rodol* in his stead. But *Jeremy* having assembled an army of forty thousand *Turks*, *Tartars* and *Moldavians*, returned into *Wallachia*. *Rodol* not yet able to raise such a power, fled into *Transilvania* to *Busca*, his ancient friend; who considering well of the matter, and how good it would be for his own security, to have *Wallachia* subject to the emperor, or at least such an employment for the remainders of the old regiments of *Sigismundus*, (of whose greatness and true affection he was very suspicious) sent them with *Rodol* to recover *Wallachia*, conducted by the valiant captains the earl *Meldritch*, earl *Veltus*, earl *Nederspolt*, earl *Zarvana*, the lord *Becklefield*, the lord *Budendorfe*, with their regiments, and divers others of great rank and quality, the greatest friends and alliances the prince had; who with thirty thousand, marched along by the river *Altus*, to the streights of *Rebrinck*, where they entred *Wallachia*, encamping at *Raza*; *Jeremy* lying at *Argish*, drew his army into his old camp, in the plains of *Peteske*, and with his best diligence fortified it, intending to defend himself, till more power came to him from the *Crim-Tartar*. Many small parties that came to his camp, *Rodol* cut off, and in the nights would cause their heads to be thrown up and down before the trenches. Seven of their porters were taken, whom *Jeremy* commanded to be flayed quick, and after hung their skins upon poles, and their carcases and heads on stakes by them.

CHAP. X.

The battle of Rottenton; *a pretty stratagem of fire-works by* Smith.

RODOL not knowing how to draw the enemy to battle, raised his army, burning and spoiling all where he came, and returned again towards *Rebrink* in the night, as if he had fled upon the general rumour of the *Crim-Tartars* coming, which so inflamed the *Turks* of a happy victory, they urged *Jeremy* against his will to follow them. *Rodol* seeing his plot fell out as he desired, so ordered the matter, that having regained the streights, he put his army in order, that had been near two days pursued with continual skirmishes in his rear, which now making head against the

enemy,

A battle betwixt Rodol *and* Jeremy.

enemy, that followed with their whole army in the best manner they could, was furiously charged with six thousand *Heydukes*, *Wallachians* and *Moldavians*, led by three colonels, *Oversall*, *Dubras* and *Calab*, to entertain the time till the rest came up; *Veltus* and *Nederspolt* with their regiments, entertained them with the like courage, till the zanzacke *Hamesbeg*, with six thousand more, came with a fresh charge, which *Meldritch* and *Budendorfe*, rather like enraged lions, than men, so bravely encounter'd, as if in them only had consisted the victory; *Meldritch*'s horse being slain under him, the *Turks* pressed what they could to have taken him prisoner; but being remounted, it was thought with his own hand he slew the valiant zanzacke; whereupon his troops retiring, the two proud bashaws *Aladin* and *Zizimmus*, brought up the front of the body of their battle. *Veltus* and *Nederspolt* having breathed, and joining their troops with *Becklefield* and *Zarvana*, with such an incredible courage, charged the left flank of *Zizimmus*, as put them all in disorder, where *Zizimmus* the bashaw was taken prisoner, but died presently upon his wounds. *Jeremy* seeing now the main battle of *Rodol* advance, being thus constrained, like a valiant prince in his front of the vantgard, by his example so bravely encouraged his soldiers, that *Rodol* found no great assurance of the victory. Thus being joyned in this bloody massacre, there was scarce ground to stand upon, but upon the dead carcasses, which in less than an hour were so mingled, as if each regiment had singled out other. The admired *Aladin* that day did leave behind him a glorious name for his valour, whose death many of his enemies did lament after the victory, which at that instant fell to *Rodol*. It was reported *Jeremy* was also slain; but it was not so, but fled with the remainder of his army to *Moldavia*, leaving five and twenty thousand dead in the field, of both armies. And thus *Rodol* was seated again in his soveraignty, and *Wallachia* became subject to the emperor.

Wallachia *subjected to the emperor.*

But long he rested not to settle his new estate, but there came news, that certain regiments of stragling *Tartars*, were foraging those parts towards *Moldavia*. *Meldritch* with thirteen thousand men was sent against them, but when they heard it was the *Crim-Tartar*, and his two sons, with an army of thirty thousand; and *Jeremy*, that had escaped with fourteen or fifteen thousand, lay in ambush for them about *Langanaw*, he retired towards *Rottenton*, a strong garrison for *Rodol*; but they were so invironed with these hellish numbers, they could make no great hast for skirmishing with their scouts, foragers and small parties that still encountred them. But one night amongst the rest, having made a passage through a wood, with an incredible expedition, cutting trees thwart each other to hinder their passage in a thick fog; early in the morning, unexpectedly they met two thousand loaded with pillage, and two or three hundred horse and cattle; the most of them were slain and taken prisoners, who told them where *Jeremy* lay in the passage, expecting the *Crim-Tartar* that was not far from him. *Meldritch* intending to make his passage by force, was advised of a pretty stratagem by the *English Smith*, which presently he thus accomplished; for having accommodated two or three hundred trunks with wild-fire, upon the heads of lances, and charging the enemy in the night, gave fire to the trunks, which blazed forth such flames and sparkles, that it so amazed, not only their horses, but their foot also; that by the means of this flaming encounter, their own horses turned tails with such fury, as by their violence overthew *Jeremy* and his army, without any loss at all to speak of to *Meldritch*. But of this victory long they triumphed not; for being within three leagues of *Rottenton*, the *Tartar*, with near forty thousand so beset them, that they must either fight, or be cut in pieces flying. Here *Busca* and the emperor had their desire; for the sun no sooner displayed his beams, than the *Tartar* his colours; where at mid-day he stayed a while to see the passage of a tyrannical and treacherous imposture, till the earth did blush with the blood of honesty, that the sun for shame did hide himself from so monstrous sight of a cowardly calamity. It was a most brave sight to see the banners and ensigns streaming in the air, the glittering of armour, the variety of colours, the motion of plumes, the forests of lances, and the thickness of shorter weapons, till the silent expedition of the bloody blast from the murdering ordnance, whose roaring voice is not so soon heard as felt by the aimed at object, made among them a most lamentable slaughter.

CHAP. XI.

The names of the English *that were slain in the battle of* Rottenton; *and how captain* Smith *was taken prisoner, and sold for a slave.*

IN the valley of *Veristhorne*, betwixt the river of *Altus* and the mountain of *Rottenton*, was this bloody encounter, where the most of the dearest friends of the noble prince *Sigismundus* perished. *Meldritch* having ordered his eleven thousand in the best manner he could, at the foot of the mountain upon his flanks, and before his front, he had pitched sharp stakes, their heads hardened in the fire, and bent against the enemy, as three battalion of pikes, amongst the which also, there was digged many small holes. Amongst those stakes were ranged his footmen, that upon the charge were to retire, as there was occasion. The *Tartar* having ordered his 40000 for his best advantage, appointed *Mustapha* bashaw to begin the battle, with a general shout, all their ensigns displaying, drums beating, trumpets and hautboys sounding. *Nederspolt* and *Movazo* with their regiments of horse most valiantly encountred, and forced them to retire; the *Tartar Begolgi* with his squadrons, darkening the skies with their flights of numberless arrows, who was as bravely encounter'd by *Veltus* and *Oberwin*, which bloody slaughter continued more than an hour, till the matchless multitude of the *Tartars* so increased, that they retired within their squadrons of stakes, as was directed. The bloody *Tartar*, as scorning he should stay so long for the victory, with his massie troops prosecuted the charge: But it was a wonder to see how horse and man came to the ground among the stakes, whose disordered troops were there so mangled, that the christians with a loud shout cried *Victoria*; and with five or six field pieces, planted upon the rising of the mountain, did much hurt to the enemy that still continued the battle with that fury, that *Meldritch* seeing there was no possibility long to prevail, joined his small troops in one body, resolved directly to make his passage, or die in the conclusion; and thus in gross gave a general charge, and for more than half an hour, made his way plain before him, till the main battle of the *Crim-Tartar*, with two regiments of *Turks* and *Janizaries* so overmatched them, that they were overthrown. The night approaching, the earl with some thirteen or fourteen hundred horse, swam the river, some were drowned, all the rest slain or taken prisoners: And thus in this bloody field, near 30000 lay, some headless, armless and legless, all cut and mangled; where breathing their last, they gave this knowledge to the world, that for the lives of so few, the *Crim-Tartar* never paid dearer. But now the countries of *Transilvania* and *Wallachia* (subjected to the emperor) and *Sigismundus*, that brave prince, his subject and pensioner, the most of his nobility, brave captains and soldiers, became a prey to the cruel devouring *Turk*; where, had the emperor been as ready to have assisted him, and those three armies led by three such worthy captains, as *Michael*, *Busca* and himself, and had those three armies joined together against the *Turk*, let all men judge, how happy it might have been for all christendom, and have either regained *Bulgaria*, or at least have beat him out of *Hungaria*, where he hath taken much more from the emperor, than hath the emperor from *Transilvania*.

The battle of Rottenton.

Extracted out of a book intituled, the wars of Hungaria, Wallachia *and* Moldavia, *written by* Francisco Ferneza, *a learned* Italian, *the prince's secretary, and translated by Mr.* Purchas.

In this dismal battle, where *Nederspolt*, *Veltus*, *Zarvana*, *Mavazo*, *Bavel*, and many other earls, barons, colonels, captains, brave gentlemen, and soldiers were slain, give me leave to remember the names of our own countreymen, with him in those exploits, that as resolutely as the best in the defence of Christ and his gospel, ended their days, as *Baskerfield*, *Hardwick*, *Thomas Milemer*, *Robert Mollineux*, *Thomas Bishop*, *Francis Compton*, *George Davison*, *Nicholas Williams*, and one *John a Scot*, did what men could do; and when they could do no more, left there their bodies in testimony of their minds; only ensign *Charlton* and sergeant *Robinson* escaped: But *Smith* among the slaughtered dead bodies, and many a gasping soul, with toil and wounds lay groaning among the rest, till being found by the pillagers, he was able to live, and perceiving by his armour and habit, his ransome might be better to them than his death, they led him prisoner with many others; well they used him till his wounds were cured, and at *Axopolis* they were all sold for slaves, like beasts in a market-place, where every merchant, viewing their limbs and wounds, caused other slaves to struggle with them, to try their strength. He fell to the share of bashaw *Bogal*, who sent him forthwith to *Adrianopolis*, so for *Constantinople* to his fair mistress for a slave. By twenty and twenty chained by the necks, they marched in file to this great city where they were delivered to their several Masters, and he to the young *Charatza Tragabigzanda*.

The Englishmen *in this battle.*

CHAP. XII.

How Captain Smith *was ſent priſoner thorow the* Black *and* Diſſabacca-Sea *in* Tartaria; *the deſcription of thoſe ſeas, and his uſage.*

THIS noble gentlewoman took ſometime occaſion to ſhew him to ſome friends, or rather to ſpeak with him, becauſe ſhe could ſpeak *Italian*; would feign herſelf ſick when ſhe ſhould go to the *Bannians*, or weep over the graves, to know how *Bogal* took him priſoner; and if he were, as the baſhaw writ to her, a *Bohemian* lord conquered by his hand, as he had many others, which ere long he would preſent her, whoſe ranſomes ſhould adorn her with the glory of his conqueſts.

But when ſhe heard him proteſt he knew no ſuch matter, nor ever ſaw *Bogal*, till he bought him at *Axopolis*, and that he was an *Engliſhman*, only by his adventures made a captain in thoſe countries; to try the truth, ſhe found means to find out many who could ſpeak *Engliſh*, *French*, *Dutch* and *Italian*, to whom relating moſt part of theſe former paſſages ſhe thought neceſſary, which they ſo honeſtly reported to her, ſhe took (as it ſeem'd) much compaſſion on him; but having no uſe for him, leſt her mother ſhould ſell him, ſhe ſent him to her brothat the *Tymor Baſhaw* of *Nalbrits*, in the county of *Cambia*, a province in *Tartaria*.

How he was ſent into Tartaria.

Here now let us remember his paſſing in, this ſpeculative courſe from *Conſtantinople* by *Sander*, *Screw*, *Panaſſa*, *Muſa*, *Laſtilla* to *Verna*, an ancient city upon the *Black-Sea*. In all which journey, having little more liberty, than his eyes judgment, ſince his captivity, he might ſee the towns with their ſhort towers, and a moſt plain, fertile and delicate countrey, eſpecially that moſt admired place of *Greece*, now called *Romania*, but from *Varna*, nothing but the *Black-Sea* water, till he came to the two capes of *Taur* and *Pergilos*, where he paſſed the ſtreight of *Niger*, which (as he conjectured) is ſome ten leagues long, and three broad, betwixt two low lands, the channel is deep, but at the entrance of the ſea *Diſſabecca*, there are many great oſie ſhaulds, and many great black rocks, which the *Turks* ſaid were trees, weeds and mud thrown from the in-land countries, by the inundations and violence of the current, and caſt there by the eddy. They ſailed by many low iſles, and ſaw many more of thoſe muddy rocks, and nothing elſe but ſalt-water, till they came betwixt *Suſax* and *Curuſke*, only two white towns at the entrance of the river *Bruapo* appeared: In ſix or ſeven days ſail, he ſaw four or five ſeeming ſtrong caſtles of ſtone, with flat tops and battlements about them, but arriving at *Cambia*, he was (according to their cuſtom) well uſed. The river was there more than half a mile broad. The caſtle was of a large circumference, fourteen or fifteen foot thick, in the foundation ſome ſix foot from the wall is a palliſado, and then a ditch of about forty foot broad, full of water. On the weſt-ſide of it, is a town all of low flat houſes, which as he conceived, could be of no great ſtrength, yet it keeps all them barbarous countreys about it in admiration and ſubjection. After he had ſtayed there three days; it was two days more before his guides brought him to *Nalbrits*, where the *Tymor* was then reſident, in a great vaſt ſtone caſtle, with many great courts about it, invironed with high ſtone walls, where were quartered their arms, when they firſt ſubjected thoſe countries, which only live to labour for thoſe tyrannical *Turks*.

The Deſcription of the Diſſabecca-Sea.

Smith's uſage in Tartaria.

To her unkind brother, this kind lady writ ſo much for his good uſage, that he half ſuſpected as much as ſhe intended; for ſhe told him, he ſhould there but ſojourn to learn the language, and what it was to be a *Turk*, till time made her maſter of her ſelf. But the *Tymor*, her brother, diverted all this to the worſt of cruelty; for within an hour after his arrival, he cauſed his *Drubman* to ſtrip him naked, and ſhave his head and beard ſo bare as his hand, a great ring of iron, with a long ſtalk bowed like a ſickle, riveted about his neck, and a coat made of ulgries hair, guarded about with a piece of an undreſt ſkin. There were many more chriſtian ſlaves, and near an hundred *Forſados* of *Turks* and *Moors*, and he being the laſt, was ſlave of ſlaves to them all. Among theſe ſlaviſh fortunes there was no great choice, for the beſt was ſo bad, a dog could hardly have lived to endure, and yet for all their pains and labours, no more regarded than a beaſt.

CHAP.

CHAP. XIII.

The Turks *diet; the slaves diet; the attire of the* Tartars; *and manner of wars and religion,* &c.

The Tymor's *diet of* Cambia *is as the* Turks.

THE *Tymor* and his friends fed upon pillaw, which is boiled rice and garnances, with little bits of mutton or buckones, which is roasted pieces of horse, bull, ulgrie or any beasts. *Samboyses* and *Muselbit* are great dainties, and yet but round pies, full of all sorts of flesh, they can get chopped with variety of herbs. Their best drink is coffee, of a grain they called *Coava*, boiled with water; and sherbeck, which is only honey and water; mares milk, or the milk of any beast, they hold restorative; but all the commonalty drink pure water. Their bread is made of this *Coava*, which is a kind of black wheat, and *Cuskus* a small white seed, like *Millia* in *Biskay*: But our common victuals, the entrails of horse and ulgries; of this cut in small pieces, they will fill a great cauldron, and being boiled with *Cuskus*, and put in great bowls in the form of chaffing-dishes, they sit round about it on the ground; after they have raked it thorow, so oft as they please with their foul fists, the remainder was for the christian slaves. Some of this broth they would temper with *Cuskus* pounded, and putting the fire off from the hearth, pour there a bowl full, then cover it with coals till it be baked, which stewed with the remainder of the broth, and some small pieces of flesh, was an extraordinary dainty.

The slaves diet.

The attire of those Tartars.

The better sort are attired like *Turks*, but the plain *Tartar* hath a black sheeps-skin over his back, and two of the legs tied about his neck; the other two about his middle, with another over his belly, and the legs tied in like manner behind him: Then two more, made like a pair of bases, serveth him for breeches; with a little close cap to his skull of black felt, and they use exceeding much of this felt for carpets, for bedding, for coats and idols. Their houses are much worse than your *Irish*, but the in-land countries have none but carts and tents, which they ever remove from countrey to countrey, as they see occasion, driving with them infinite troops of black sheep, cattle and ulgries, eating all up before them as they go.

The Tartars *of* Nagi *and their manners.*

For the *Tartars* of *Nagi*, they have neither town, nor house, corn nor drink, but flesh and milk. The milk they keep in great skins like burrachoes, which though it be never so sower, it agreeth well with their strong stomachs. They live all in *Hordias*, as do the *Crim-Tartars*, three or four hundred in a company, in great carts fifteen or sixteen foot broad, which are covered with small rods, wattled together in the form of a bird's nest, turned upwards, and with the ashes of bones, temper'd with oil, camels hair, and a clay they have; they loam them so well, that no weather can pierce them, and yet very light. Each *Hordia* hath a *Murse*, which they obey as their king. Their gods are infinite. One or two thousand of those glittering white carts drawn with camels, deer, bulls and ulgries, they bring round in a ring, where they pitch their camp; and the *Murse*, with his chief alliances, are placed in the midst. They do much hurt, when they can get any *Stroggs*, which are great boats used upon the river *Volga*, (which they call *Edle*) to them that dwell in the countrey of *Perolog*, and would do much more, were it not for the *Muscovite* garrisons that there inhabit.

CHAP. XIV.

The Description of the Crim-Tartars; *their houses and carts, their idolatry in their lodgings.*

The description of the Crim-Tartar's *Court.*

NOW you are to understand, *Tartary* and *Scythia* are all one, but so large and spacious, few or none could ever perfectly describe it, nor all the several kinds of those most barbarous people that inhabit it. Those we call the *Crim-Tartars* border upon *Moldavia*, *Podolia*, *Lithuania*, and *Russia*, are much more regular than the interior parts of *Scythia*. The great *Tartarian* prince, that hath so troubled all his neighbours, they always call *Chan*, which signifieth emperor; but we the *Crim-Tartar*. He liveth for the most part in the best champion plains of many provinces; and his removing court is like a great city of houses and tents drawn on carts, all so so orderly placed east and west, on the right and left hand of the prince's house, which is always in the midst towards the south, before which none may pitch their houses, every one knowing their order and quarter, as in an army. The prince's houses are very artificially wrought, both the foundation, sides and roof of wickers, ascending round to the top like a dove-coat; this they cover with white salt, or white earth, tempered with the powder of bones, that it may shine the whiter; sometimes with black felt, curiously painted with vines, trees, birds and beasts; the breadth of the carts are eighteen or twenty foot, but the house stretcheth four or five foot over each side, and is drawn with ten or twelve, or for more state twenty camels and oxen. They have also great baskets, made of smaller wickers, like great chests, with a covering of the same, all covered over with black felt, rubbed over with tallow and sheeps milk, to keep out the rain, prettily bedecked with painting or feathers; in those they put their houshold stuff and treasure, drawn upon other carts for that purpose. When they take down their houses, they set the door always towards the south, and their carts thirty or forty foot distant on each side, east and west, as if they were two walls: The women also have most curious carts; every one of his wives hath a great one for herself, and so many other for her attendants, that there seem as many courts as he hath wives. One great *Tartar* or nobleman, will have for his particular, more than an hundred of those houses and carts, for his several offices and uses, but set so far from each other, they will seem like a great village. Having taken their houses from the carts, they place the master always towards the north; over whose head is always an image like a puppet, made of felt, which they call his brother; the women on his left-hand, and over the chief mistress's head such another brother, and between them a little one, which is the keeper of the house; at the good wife's bed's-feet is a kid's-skin stuffed with wool, and near it a puppet looking towards the maids; next the door another, with a dried cow's udder, for the women that milk the kine, because only the men milk mares: Every morning those images in their orders, they besprinkle with that they drink, be it *Cossmos*, or whatsoever, but all the white mares milk is reserved for the prince. Then without the door, thrice to the south, every one bowing his knee in honour of the fire; then the like to the east, in honour of the air; then to the west, in honour of the water; and lastly to the north, in behalf of the dead. After the servant hath done this duty to the four quarters of the world, he returns into the house, where his fellows stand waiting, ready with two cups and two basons, to give their master, and his wife that lay with him that night, to wash and drink, who must keep him company all the day following, and all his other wives come thither to drink, where he keeps his house that day; and all the gifts presented him till night, are laid up in her chests; and at the door a bench full of cups, and drink for any of them to make merry.

His houses and carts. *Baskets.* *Their idolatry in their lodgings.* *Cossmos is mares milk.*

CHAP. XV.

Their feasts, common diet, princes estate, buildings, tributes, laws, slaves, entertainment of ambassadors.

Their feasts.

FOR their feasts they have all sorts of beasts, birds, fish, fruits and herbs they can get, but the more variety of wild ones is the best; to which they have excellent drink made of rice, millet and honey, like wine; they have also wine, but in summer they drink most *Cossmos*, that standeth ready always at the entrance of the door, and by it a fidler; when the master of the house beginneth to drink, they all cry ha, ha, and the fidler plays, then they all clap their hands and dance, the men before their masters, the women before their mistresses; and ever when he drinks, they cry as before; then the fidler stayeth till they drink all round; sometimes they will drink for the victory; and to provoke one to drink, they will pull him by the ears, and lug and draw him, to stretch and heat him, clapping their hands, stamping with their feet, and dancing before the champions, offering them cups, then draw them back again to increase their appetite; and thus continue till they be drunk, or their drink done, which they hold an honour and no infirmity.

Their common diet.

Though the ground be fertile, they sow little corn, yet the gentlemen have bread and hony-wine; grapes they have plenty, and wine privately, and good flesh and fish; but the common sort stamped millet, mingled with milk and water. They call *Cassa*

Caſſa for meat, and drink any thing; alſo any beaſt unprofitable for ſervice they kill, when they are like to die, or however they die, they will eat them, guts, liver and all; but the moſt fleſhy parts they cut in thin ſlices, and hang it up in the ſun and wind without ſalting, where it will dry ſo hard, it will not putrefy in a long time. A ram they eſteem a great feaſt among forty or fifty, which they cut in pieces boiled or roaſted, and put it in a great bowl with ſalt and water; for other ſawce they have none; the maſter of the feaſt giveth every one a piece, which he eateth by himſelf, or carrieth away with him. Thus their hard fare makes them ſo infinite in cattle, and their great number of captivated women to breed upon, makes them ſo populous. But near the chriſtian frontiers, the baſer ſort make little cottages of wood, call'd *Uluſi*, daubed over with dirt, and beaſts dung covered with ſedge; yet in ſummer they leave them, beginning their progreſs in *April*, with their wives, children and ſlaves, in their carted houſes, ſcarce convenient for four or five perſons; driving their flocks towards *Precopia*, and ſometimes into *Taurica* or *Oſow*, a town upon the river *Tanais*, which is great and ſwift, where the *Turk* hath a grrriſon; and in *October* return again to their cottages. Their clothes are the ſkins of dogs, goats and ſheep, lined with cotton cloth, made of their fineſt wooll; for of their worſt they make their felt, which they uſe in abundance, as well for ſhoes and caps, as houſes, beds and idols; alſo of the coarſe wool mingled with horſe hair, they make all their cordage. Notwithſtanding this wandering life, their princes ſit in great ſtate upon beds or carpets, and with great reverence are attended both by men and women, and richly ſerved in plate, and great ſilver cups, delivered upon the knee, attired in rich furs, lined with pluſh, or taffity, or robes of tiſſue. Theſe *Tartars* poſſeſs many large and goodly plains, wherin feed innumerable herds of horſe and cattle, as well wild as tame; which are elkes, biſons, horſes, deer, ſheep, goats, ſwine, bears and divers others.

How they become populous.

Their princes ſtate.

Ancient buildings.

In thoſe countries are the ruins of many fair monaſteries, caſtles and cities, as *Bacaſaray*, *Salutium*, *Almaſſary*, *Precopia*, *Cremum*, *Sedacom*, *Capha*, and divers others by the ſea, but all kept with ſtrong garriſons for the great *Turk*, who yearly by trade or traffick, receiveth the chief commodities thoſe fertile countries afford, as bezoar, rice, furs, hides, butter, ſalt, cattle and ſlaves, yet by the ſpoils they get from the ſecure and idle chriſtians, they maintain themſelves in this pomp. Alſo their wives, of whom they have as many as they will, very coſtly, yet in a conſtant cuſtom with decency.

Commodities for tribute to the Turk.

Good laws, yet no lawyers.

They are mahometans, as are the *Turks*, from whom alſo they have their laws, but no lawyers nor attornies, only judges, and juſtices in every village or hordia; but capital criminals, or matters of moment, are try'd before the *Chan* himſelf, or privy-councils, of whom they are always heard, and ſpeedily diſcharged; for any may have acceſs at any time to them, before whom they appear with great reverence, adoring their princes as gods, and their ſpiritual judges as ſaints; for juſtice is with ſuch integrity and expedition executed, without covetouſneſs, bribery, partiality and brawling, that in ſix months they have ſometimes ſcarce ſix cauſes to hear. About the prince's court, none but his guard wear any weapon, but abroad they go very ſtrong, becauſe there are many bandittoes and thieves.

Their ſlaves.

They uſe the *Hungarians*, *Ruſſians*, *Wallachians* and *Moldavian* ſlaves (whereof they have plenty) as beaſt to every work; and thoſe *Tartars* that ſerve the *Chan* or noblemen, have only victuals and apparel, the reſt are generally naſty and idle, naturally miſerable, and in their wars better thieves than ſoldiers.

His entertainment of ambaſſadors.

This *Chan* hath yearly a donative from the king of *Poland*, the dukes of *Lithuania*, *Moldavia*, and *Nagayon Tartars*; their meſſengers commonly he uſeth bountifully and very nobly, but ſometimes moſt cruelly: when any of them do bring their preſents, by his houſhold officers, they are entertained in a plain field, with a moderate proportion of fleſh, bread and wine, for once; but when they come before him, the *Sultans*, *Tuians*, *Ulans*, *Marhies*, his chief officers and councellors attend; one man only bringeth the ambaſſador to the court gate, but to the *Chan* he is led between two councellors; where ſaluting him upon their bended knees, declaring their meſſage, are admitted to eat with him, and preſented with a great ſilver cup full of mead from his own hand, but they drink it upon their knees. When they are diſpatched, he invites them again; the feaſt ended, they go back a little from the palace door, and are rewarded with ſilk veſtures, wrought with gold down to their anckles, with an horſe or two, and ſometimes a ſlave of their own nation; in thoſe robes preſently they come to him again, to give him thanks, take their leave, and ſo depart.

CHAP.

CHAP. XVI.

How he levieth an army; their arms and provision; how he divideth the ſpoil, and his ſervice to the great Turk.

How he levieth an army. WHEN he intends any wars, he muſt firſt have leave of the great *Turk*, whom he is bound to aſſiſt when he commandeth, receiving daily for himſelf and chief of his nobility, penſions from the *Turk*, that holds all kings but ſlaves, that pay tribute, or are ſubject to any: ſignifying his intent to all his ſubjects, within a month commonly he raiſeth his army, and every man is to furniſh himſelf for three months with victuals, which is parch'd millet, or ground to meal, which they ordinarily mingle with water (as is ſaid,) hard cheeſe or curds dried and beaten to powder; a little will make much water like milk, and dried fleſh, this they put alſo up in ſacks: The *Chan* and his nobles have ſome bread and *Aquavitæ*, and quick cattle to kill when they pleaſe, wherewith very ſparingly they are contented. Being provided with expert guides, and got into the countrey he intends to invade, he ſends forth his ſcouts to bring in what priſoners they can, from whom he will wreſt the utmoſt of their knowledge fit for his purpoſe: Having adviſed with his council, what is moſt fit to be done, the nobility, according to their antiquity, doth march; then moves he with his whole army: If he find there is no enemy to oppoſe him, he adviſeth how far they ſhall invade, commanding every man (upon pain of his life) to kill all the obvious ruſticks, but not to hurt any women or children.

The manner of his wars. Ten or fifteen thouſand, he commonly placeth, where he findeth moſt convenient for his ſtanding camp; the reſt of his army he divides in ſeveral troops, bearing ten or twelve miles ſquare before them, and ever within three or four days return to their camp, putting all to fire and ſword, but that they carry with them back to their camp; and in this ſcattering manner he will invade a countrey, and be gone with his prey, with an incredible expedition. But if he underſtand of an enemy, he will either fight in ambuſcado or flie; for he will never fight any battle if he can chuſe, but upon treble advantage; yet by his innumerable flights of arrows, I have ſeen fly rrom his flying troops, we could not well judge, whether his fighting or flying was moſt dangerous, ſo good is his horſe, and ſo expert his bowmen; but if they be ſo intangled they muſt fight, there is none can be more hardy or reſolute in their defences.

Regaining his own borders, he takes the tenth of the principal captives, man, woman, child or beaſt (but his captains that take them, will accept of ſome particular perſon they beſt like for themſelves;) the reſt are divided amongſt the whole army, according to every man's deſert and quality; that they keep them, or ſell them to who will give moſt; but they will not forget to uſe all the means they can, to know their eſtates, friends and quality, and the better they find you, the worſe they will uſe you, till you do agree to pay ſuch a ranſome as they will impoſe upon you; therefore many great perſons have endured much miſery to conceal themſelves, becauſe their ranſoms are ſo intolerable; their beſt hope is of ſome chriſtian agent, that many times cometh to redeem ſlaves, either with money or man for man; thoſe agents knowing ſo well the extreme covetouſneſs of the *Tartars*, do uſe to bribe ſome jew or merchant, that feigning they will ſell them again to ſome other nation, are oft redeemed for a very ſmall ranſom. *How he divides the ſpoil.*

But to this *Tartarian* army, when the *Turk* commands, he goeth with ſome ſmall artillery; and the *Nagayans*, *Precopeans*, *Crims*, *Oſovens* and *Circaſſians* are his tributaries; but the *Petigorves*, *Oczaconians*, *Bialogordens* and *Dobrucen Tartars*, the *Turk* by covenant commands to follow him, ſo that from all thoſe *Tartars* he hath had an army of an hundred and twenty thouſand excellent, ſwift, ſtomachful *Tartarian* horſe, for foot they have none. Now the *Chan*, his ſultans and nobility, uſe *Turkiſh*, *Caramanian*, *Arabian*, *Parthian* and other ſtrange *Tartarian* horſes; the ſwifteſt they eſteem the beſt; ſeldom they feed any more at home, than they have preſent uſe for; but upon their plains is a ſhort wood-like heath, in ſome countries like gail, full of berries, much better than any graſs. *How the* Chan *doth ſerve the great* Turk.

Their arms. Their arms are ſuch, as they have ſurpriſed or got from the chriſtians or *Perſians*, both breſt-plates, ſwords, ſcimiters, and helmets; bows and arrows they make moſt themſelves; alſo their bridles and ſaddles are indifferent, but the nobility are very handſome, and well armed like the *Turks*, in whom conſiſteth their greateſt glory; the ordinary ſort have little armour, ſome a plain young pole unſhaven, headed with a piece of iron for a lance; ſome an old chriſtian pike, or a *Turk*'s cavarinel; yet thoſe tattertimallions will have two or three

three horſes, ſome four or five, as well for ſervice, as for to eat; which makes their armies ſeem thrice ſo many as there are ſoldiers. The *Chan* himſelf hath about his perſon, 10000 choſen *Tartars* and *Janizaries*, ſome ſmall ordnance; and a white mare's tail, with a piece of green taffity on a great pike, is carried before him for a ſtandard; becauſe they hold no beaſt ſo precious as a white mare, whoſe milk is only for the king and nobility, and to ſacrifice to their idols, but the reſt have enſigns of divers colours.

For all this miſerable knowledge, furniture, and equipage, the miſchief they do in *Chriſtendom* is wonderful, by reaſon of their hardneſs of life and conſtitution, obedience, agility, and their emperor's bounty, honours, grace, and dignities he ever beſtoweth upon thoſe, that have done him any memorable ſervice in the face of his enemies.

A deſcription of the Caſpian *ſea.*

The *Caſpian* ſea, moſt men agree that have paſſed it, to be in length about 200 leagues, and in breadth 150, environed to the eaſt, with the great deſarts of the *Tartars* of *Turkomania*; to the weſt by the *Circaſſes* and the mountain *Caucaſus*; to the north, by the river *Volga*, and the land of *Nagay*; and to the ſouth, by *Media* and *Perſia*: This ſea is freſh water in many places, in others as ſalt as the great ocean; it hath many great rivers which fall into it, as the mighty river of *Volga*, which is like a ſea, running near 2000 miles, thro' many great and large countries, that ſend into it many other great rivers; alſo out of *Saberia*, *Yaick*, and *Yem*, out of the great mountain *Caucaſus*, the river *Sirus*, *Araſh*, and divers others, yet no ſea nearer it than the black ſea, which is at leaſt 100 leagues diſtant: In which countrey live the *Georgians*, now part *Armenians*, part *Neſtorians*; it is neither found to increaſe or diminiſh, or empty itſelf any ways except it be under ground, and in ſome places they can find no ground at 200 fathom.

Many other moſt ſtrange and wonderful things are in the land of *Cathay*, towards the north-eaſt, and *China* towards the ſouth-eaſt, where are many of the moſt famous kingdoms in the world, where moſt arts, plenty, and curioſities are in ſuch abundance, as might ſeem incredible, which hereafter I will relate, as I have briefly gathered from ſuch authors as have lived there.

CHAP. XVII.

How captain Smith *eſcaped his captivity; ſlew the* Baſhaw *of* Nalbrits *in* Cambia; *his paſſage to* Ruſſia, Tranſilvania, *and the midſt of* Europe *to* Africa.

*How*Smith *eſcaped his captivity.*

ALL the hope he had ever to be delivered from this thraldom, was only the love of *Tragabigzanda*, who ſurely was ignorant of his bad uſage; for altho' he had often debated the matter with ſome chriſtians, that had been there a long time ſlaves, they could not find how to make an eſcape, by any reaſon or poſſibility; but God beyond man's expectation or imagination helpeth his ſervants, when they leaſt think of help, as it hapned to him. So long he lived in this miſerable eſtate, as he became a threſher at a grange in a great field, more than a league from the *Tymor*'s houſe; the *Baſhaw*, as he oft uſed to viſit his granges, viſited him, and took occaſion ſo to beat, ſpurn, and revile him, that forgetting all reaſon, he beat out the *Tymor*'s brains with his threſhing bat, for they have no flails; and ſeeing his eſtate could be no worſe than it was, clothed himſelf in his clothes, hid his body under the ſtraw, filled his knapſack with corn, ſhut the doors, mounted his horſe, and ran into the deſart at all adventures; two or three days, thus fearfully wandring he knew not whither, and well it was, he met not any to aſk the way; being even as taking leave of this miſerable world, God did direct him to the great way or caſtragan, as they call it, which doth croſs theſe large territories, and generally known among them by theſe marks.

Their guides in thoſe countries.

In every croſſing of this great way is planted a poſt, and in it ſo many bobs with broad ends, as there be ways, and every bob the figure painted on it, that demonſtrateth to whrt part that way leadeth; as that which pointeth towards the *Crim*'s countrey, is marked with a half moon; if towards the *Georgians* and *Perſians*, a black man, full of white ſpots; if towards *China*, the picture of the ſun; if towards *Muſcovia*, the ſign of a croſs; if towards the habitation of any other prince, the figure whereby his ſtandard is known. To his dying ſpirits thus God added ſome comfort in this melancholly journey, wherein if he had met any of that vile generation, they had made him their ſlave, or knowing the figure engraven in the iron about his neck, (as all ſlaves have) he had been ſent back again

again to his master; sixteen days he travelled in this fear and torment, after the cross, till he arrived at *Æcopolis*, upon the river *Don*, a garrison of the *Muscovites*. The governor after due examination of those his hard events, took off his irons, and so kindly used him, he thought himself new risen from the dead, and the good lady *Calamata*, largely supplied all his wants.

The description of Cambia, *and his passage to* Russia.

This is as much as he could learn of those wild countries, that the countrey of *Cambia* is two days journey from the head of the great river *Bruapo*, which springeth from many places of rhe mountains of *Innagachi*, that join themselves together in the pool *Kerkas*; which they account for the head, and falleth into the sea *Dissabacca*, called by some the lake *Mœotis*, which receiveth also the river *Tanais*, and all the rivers that fall from the great countries of the *Circassi*, the *Cartaches*, and many from the *Tauricaes*, *Precopes*, *Cummani*, *Cossunka*, and the *Crim*; thro' which sea he sailed, and up the river *Bruapo* to *Nalbrits*, and thence thro' the desarts of *Circassi* to *Æcopolis*, as is related; where he stayed with the governor, till the convoy went to *Caragnaw*; then with his certificate how he found him, and had examined with his friendly letters, sent him by *Zumalack* to *Caragnaw*, whose governor in like manner so kindly used him, that by this means he went with a safe conduct to *Letch* and *Donko* in *Cologoske*, and thence to *Berniske*, and *Newgrod* in *Siberia*, by *Rezechica*, upon the river *Nieper*, in the confines of *Lithuania*; from whence with as much kindness, he was convoyed in like manner by *Coroski*, *Duberesko*, *Duzihell*, *Drohobus*, and *Ostroge* in *Volonia*; *Saslaw*, and *Lasco* in *Podolia*; *Halico* and *Colonia* in *Polonia*; and so to *Hermonstat* in *Transilvania*. In all this his life, he seldom met with more respect, mirth, content and entertainment; and not any governor where he came, but gave him somewhat as a present, besides his charges; seeing themselves as subject to the like calamity. Through those poor continually forraged countries, there is no passage, but with the caravans or convoys; for they are countries rather to be pitied than envied; and it is a wonder any should make wars for them. The villages are only here and there, a few houses of streight fir trees, laid heads and points above one another, made fast by notches at the ends, more than a man's heighth, and with broad split boards, pinned together with wooden pins, as thatched for covertura. In ten villages you shall scarce find ten iron nails, except it be in some extraordinary man's house. For their towns *Æcopolis*, *Letch* and *Donko*, have rampires made of that wooden walled fashion, double, and betwixt them earth and stones, but so latched with cross timber, they are very strong against any thing but fire; and about them a deep ditch, and a palizado of young fir trees; but most of the rest have only a great ditch cast about them, and the ditches earth, is all their rampire; but round well invironed with palizadoes. Some have some few small pieces of small ordnance and slings, calievers and muskets, but their generallest weapons are the *Russe* bows and arrows; you shall find pavements over bogs, only of young fir-trees laid cross one over another, for two or three hours journey, or as the passage requires, and yet in two days travel, you shall scarce see six habitations. Notwithstanding to see how their lords, governors and captains are civilized, well attired and accoutred with jewels, sables and horses, and after their manner with curious furniture, it is wonderful; but they are all lords or slaves, which makes them so subject to every invasion.

His observations in his journey to Transilvania, *through the midst of* Europe.

In *Transilvania* he found so many good friends, that but to see, and rejoyce himself (after all those encounters) in his native countrey, he would ever hardly have left them, though the mirrour of virtue their prince was absent. Being thus glutted with content, and near drowned with joy, he passed *High-Hungaria* by *Fileck*, *Tocka*, *Cassovia* and *Vnderoroway* by *Ulmicht* in *Moravia*, to *Prague* in *Bohemia*; at last he found the most gracious prince *Sigismundus*, with his colonel at *Lipswick* in *Misenland*, who gave him his pass, intimating the service he had done, and the honours he had received, with fifteen hundred ducats of gold to repair his losses: With this he spent some time to visit the fair cities and countries of *Dresden* in *Saxony*, *Magdeburgh* and *Brunswick*, *Cassel* in *Hessen*; *Wittenberg*, *Vilum*, and *Minekin* in *Bavaria*; *Augsburg* and her universities; *Hama*, *Frankford*, *Mentz*, the *Palatinate*; *Worms*, *Spires* and *Strasburg*; passing *Nancie* in *Lorain*, and *France* by *Paris* to *Orleans*, he went down the rivir of *Loyer* to *Angiers*, and imbarked himself at *Nantz* in *Britain*, for *Bilboa* in *Biskay*, to see *Burgos-Valladolid*, the admired monastery of the *Escurial*, *Madrid*, *Toledo*, *Corduba*, *Cuedyrial*, *Sevil*, *Cheries*, *Cales* and *St. Lucas* in *Spain*.

CHAP. XVIII.

The observations of captain Smith; *Mr.* Henry Archer, *and others in* Barbary.

BEing thus ſatisfied with *Europe* and *Aſia*, underſtanding of the wars in *Barbary*, he went from *Gibraltar* to *Ceuta* and *Tangier*, thence to *Saffee*, where growing into acquaintance with a *French* man of war, the captain and ſome twelve more went to *Morocco*, to ſee the ancient monuments of that large renowned city: It was once the principal city in *Barbary*, ſituated in a goodly plain countrey, 14 miles from the great mount *Atlas*, and ſixty miles from the *Atlantick-Sea*, but now little remaining but the king's palace, which is like a city of it ſelf, and the chriſtian church, on whoſe flat ſquare ſteeple is a great broach of iron, whereon is placed the three golden balls of *Africa*: The firſt is near three ells in circumference, the next above it ſomewhat leſs, the uppermoſt the leaſt over them, as it were an half ball, and over all a pretty gilded *Pyramid*. Againſt thoſe golden balls hath been ſhot many a ſhot, their weight is recorded 700 weight of pure gold, hollow within, yet no ſhot did ever hit them, nor could ever any conſpirator attain that honour as to get them down. They report, the prince of *Morocco* betrothed himſelf to the king's danghter of *Æthiopia*, he dying before their marriage, ſhe cauſed thoſe three golden balls to be ſet up for his monument, and vowed virginity all her life. The *Alfantica* is alſo a place of note, becauſe it is inviſoned with a great wall, wherein lie the goods of all the merchants ſecurely guarded. The *Inderea* is alſo (as it were) a city of it ſelf, where dwell the *Jews*: The reſt for the moſt part is defaced; but by the many pinnacles and towers, with balls on their tops, hath much appearance of much ſumptuouſneſs and curioſity. There have been many famous univerſities, which are now but ſtables for fowls and beaſts, and the houſes in moſt parts lie tumbled one above another: the walls of earth are with the great freſh floods waſhed to the ground; nor is there any village in it, but tents for ſtrangers, *Larbes* and *Moors*. Strange tales they will tell of a great garden, wherein were all ſorts of birds, fiſhes, beaſts, fruits and fountains, which for beauty, art and pleaſure, exceeded any place known in the world, though now nothing but dung-hills, pigeon-houſes, ſhrubs and buſhes. There are yet many excellent fountains, adorned with marble, and many arches, pillars, towers, ports, and temples; but moſt only reliques of lamentable ruins and ſad deſolation.

The three golden balls of Africa.

The deſcription of Morocco.

When *Muly Hamet* reigned in *Barbary*, he had three ſons, *Muly Sheck*, *Muly Sidan* and *Muly Bufferres*, he a moſt good and noble king, that governed well with peace and plenty, till his empreſs, more cruel than any beaſt in *Africa*, poiſoned him, her own daughter, *Muly Sheck*, his eldeſt ſon, born of a *Portugal* lady, and his daughter, to bring *Muly Sidan*, to the crown, now reigning, which was the cauſe of all thoſe brawls and wars that followed betwixt thoſe brothers, their children, and a ſaint that ſtarted up, but he played the devil.

A bloody empreſs.

King *Huly Hamet* was not black, as many ſuppoſe, but *Molata* or tawny, as are the moſt of his ſubjects; every way noble, kind and friendly, very rich and pompous in ſtate and majeſty, though he ſitteth not upon a throne nor chair of ſtate, but croſs leg'd upon a rich carpet, as doth the *Turk*, whoſe religion of *Mahomet*, with an incredible miſerable curioſity they obſerve. His ordinary guard is at leaſt 5000, but in progreſs, he goeth not with leſs than 20000 horſemen, himſelf as rich in all his equipage, as any prince in chriſtendom, and yet a contributor to the *Turk*. In all his kingdom were ſo few good artificers, that he entertained from *England*, goldſmiths, plummers, carvers and poliſhers of ſtone, and watch-makers, ſo much he delighted in the reformation of workmanſhip, he allowed each of them ten ſhillings a day ſtanding fee, linen, woollen, ſilks, and what they would for diet and apparel, and cuſtom free to tranſport or import what they would; for there were ſcarce any of thoſe qualities in his kingdom, but thoſe, of which there are divers of them, living at this preſent in *London*. Amongſt the reſt, one Mr. *Henry Archer*, a watch-maker, walking in *Morocco*, from the *Alfantica* to the *Juderea*, the way being very foul, met a great prieſt, or a *Sante* (as they call all great clergymen) who would have thruſt him into the dirt for the way, but *Archer* not knowing what he was, gave him a box on the ear; preſently he was apprehended, and condemned to have his tongue cut out, and his hand cut off: But no ſooner it was known at the king's court but 300 of his guard came and broke open the priſon, and delivered him although the fact was next degree to treaſon.

King Muly Hamet, *or the great* Zeriff *of* Barbary.

His great love to Engliſhmen.

2

Concern-

The strange love of a lion.

Concerning this *Archer*, there is one thing more worth noting: Not far from mount *Atlas*, a great lioness in the heat of the day, did use to bathe her self, and teach her young puppies to swim in the river *Cauzef*, of a good breadth; yet she would carry them one after another over the river; which some *Moors* perceiving, watched their opportunity, and when the river was between her and them, stole four of her whelps, which she perceiving, with all the speed she could passed the river, and coming near them, they let fall a whelp (and fled with the rest) which she took in her mouth, and so returned to the rest: A male and a female of those they gave Mr. *Archer*, who kept them in the king's garden, till the male killed the female, then he brought it up as puppy-dog lying upon his bed, till it grew so great as a mastiff, and no dog more tame or gentle to them he knew: But being to return to *England*, at *Saffee* he gave him to a merchant of *Marseilles*, that presented him to the *French* king, who sent him to king *James*, where it was kept in the tower seven years: After one Mr. *John Bull*, then servant to Mr. *Archer*, with divers of his friends, went to see the lions, not knowing any thing at all of him; yet this rare beast smelled him before he saw him, whining, groaning and tumbling, with such an expression of acquaintance, that being informed by the keepers how he came thither, Mr. *Bull* so prevail'd, the keeper opened the grate, and *Bull* went it: But no dog could fawn more on his master, than the lion on him, licking his feet, hands and face, skipping and tumbling to and fro, to the wonder of all the beholders; being satisfied with his acquaintance, he made shift to get out of the grate: But when the lion saw his friend gone, no beast by bellowing, roaring, scratching and howling, could express more rage and sorrow; nor in four days after would he either eat or drink.

Another kind lion in Morocco.

In *Morocco* the king's lions are altogether in a court invironed with a great high wall; to those they put a young puppy-dog: The greatest lion had a sore upon his neck, which this dog so licked, that he was healed: The lion defended him from the fury of all the rest, nor durst they eat till the dog and he had fed; this dog grew great, and lived amongst them many years after.

The description of Fez.

Fez also is a most large and plentiful countrey, the chief city is called *Fez*, divided into two parts; old *Fez*, containing about 80 thousand housholds, the other 4000 pleasantly situated upon a river in the heart of *Barbary*, part upon hills, part upon plains, full of people and all sorts of merchandize. The great temple is called *Carucen*, in breadth seventeen arches, in length 120, born up with 2500 white marble pillars; Under the chief arch, where the tribunal is kept, hangeth a most huge lamp, compassed with 110 lesser, under the other also hang great lamps, and about some are burning 1500 lights: They say they were all made of the bells the *Arabians* brought from *Spain*. It hath three gates of notable heighth, priests and officers so many, that the circuit of the church, the yard, and other houses, is little less than a mile and half in compass; there are in this city 200 schools, 200 inns, 400 water-mills, 600 water-conduits, 700 temples and oratories; but 50 of them most stately and richly furnished. Their *Alcazer* or *Burse* is walled about, it hath twelve gates, and fifteen walks covered with tents, to keep the sun from the merchants, and them that come there. The king's palace, both for strength and beauty is excellent, and the citizens have many great privileges. Those two countries of *Fez* and *Morocco*, are the best part of all *Barbary*, abounding with people, cattle, and all good necessaries for man's use. For the rest, as the *Larbs* or mountainers, the kingdoms of *Cocow*, *Algier*, *Tripoli*, *Tunis* and *Ægypt*; there are many large histories of them in divers languages, especially that writ by that most excellent statesman, *John de Leo*, who afterwards turned christian.

A brief description of the most unknown parts of Africa.

The unknown countries of *Guine* and *Binn*, these 26 years have been frequented with a few *English* ships only to trade, especially the river of *Senega*, by captain *Brimstead*, captain *Brocket*, Mr. *Crump*, and divers others. Also the great river of *Gambria*, by captain *Jobson*, who is returned in thither again, in the year 1626, with Mr. *William Grent*, and thirteen or fourteen others, to stay in the countrey, to discover some way to those rich mines of *Gago* or *Tumbatu*, from whence it is supposed the *Moors* of *Barbary* have their gold, and the certainty of those supposed descriptions and relations of those interior parts, which daily the more they are sought into, the more they are corrected: For surely those interior parts of *Africa*, are little known to either *English*, *French* or *Dutch*, though they use much the coast; therefore we will make little bold with the observations of the *Portugals*.

CHAP.

CHAP. XIX.

The strange discoveries and observations of the Portugals *in* Africa.

How the Portugals *coasted to the* East-Indies.

THE *Portugals* on those parts have the glory, who first coasting along this western shore of *Africa*, to find passage to the *East-Indies*, within this 150 years, even from the *Streights of Gibralter*, about the cape of *Bonne Esperance* to the *Persian Gulf*, and thence all along the *Asian* coast to the *Moluccas*, have subjected many great kingdoms, erected many commonwealths, built many great and strong cities; and where is it they have not been by trade or force? No not so much as *Cape de Verd* and *Sermleone*; but most bays or rivers, where there is any trade to be had, especially gold, or conveniency for refreshment, but they are scattered; living so amongst those blacks, by time and cunning, they seem to be naturalized amongst them. As for the isles of the *Canaries*, they have fair towns, many villages, and many thousands of people rich in commodities.

Or Edward.

Ordoardo Lopez, a noble *Portugue*, *Anno Dom.* 1578, imbarking himself for *Congo*, to trade, where he found such entertainment, finding the king much oppressed with enemies, he found means to bring in the *Portuguese* to assist him, whereby he planted there christian religion, and spent most of his life to bring those countries to the crown of *Portugal*, which he describeth in this manner.

The kingdom of Congo.

The kingdom of *Congo* is about 600 miles diameter any way, the chief city, called *St. Savadore*, seated upon an exceeding high mountain, 150 miles from the sea, very fertile, and inhabited with more than 100000 persons, where is an excellent prospect over all the plain countries about it well water'd, lying (as it were) in the center of this kingdom, over all which the *Portuguese* now command, though but an handful in comparison of the negroes. They have flesh and fruits very plentiful of divers sorts.

Wild elephants.

This kingdom is divided into five provinces, *viz.* *Bamba*, *Sundi*, *Pango*, *Batta* and *Pembo*; but *Bamba* is the principal, and can afford 400000 men of war. Elephants are bred over all those provinces, and of wonderful greatness; though some report, they cannot kneel nor lie down, they can do both, and have their joints as other creatures for use: With their fore-feet they will leap upon trees to pull down the boughs, and are of that strength, they will shake a great *Coco* tree for the nuts, and pull down a good tree with their tusks, to get the leaves to eat, as well as sedge and long grass, *Coco* nuts and berries, *&c.* which with their trunk they put in their mouth, and chew it with their smaller teeth; in most of those provinces, are many rich mines, but the negroes opposed the *Portuguese* for working in them.

The kingdom of Angola.

The kingdom of *Angola* is wonderful populous, and rich in mines of silver, copper, and most other metals; fruitful in all manner of food, and sundry sorts of cattle, but dogs flesh they love better than any other meat; they use few clothes, and no armour; bows, arrows and clubs are their weapons. But the *Portuguese* are well armed against those engines, and do buy yearly of those blacks more than five thousand slaves, and many are people exceeding well proportioned.

The kingdom of Anchios.

The *Anchios* are a most valiant nation, but most strange to all about them. Their arms are bows, short and small, wrapped about with serpents skins of divers colours, but so smooth, you would think them all one with the wood, and it makes them very strong; their strings little twigs, but exceeding tough and flexible; their arrows short, which they shoot with an incredible quickness. They have short axes of brass and copper for swords; wonderful, loyal and faithful, and exceeding simple, yet so active, they skip amongst the rocks like goats. They trade with them of *Nubea* and *Congo* for *Lamach*, which is a small kind of shell-fish, of an excellent azure colour,' male and female, but the female they hold most pure; they value them at divers prices, because they are of divers sorts, and those they use for coin, to buy and sell, as we do gold and silver; nor will they have any other money in all those countries, for which they give elephants teeth; and slaves for salt, silk, linen cloth, glass-beads, and such like *Portugal* commodities.

A strange money.

Shambles of men's flesh.

They circumcise themselves, and mark their faces with sundry slashes from their infancy. They keep shambles of mens flesh, as if it were beef or other victuals; for when they cannot have a good market for their slaves, or their enemies they take, they kill, and sell them in this manner; some are so resolute, in shewing how much they scorn death, they will offer themselves and slaves, to this butchery to their prince and friends; and though there be many nations will eat their enemies in *America* and *Asia*, yet none but those are known to be so mad, as to eat their slaves and friends also.

Religions and idols they have as many as nations and humours; but the devil hath the greatest part of their devotions, whom all those blacks do say is white; for there are no saints but blacks.

Divers nations yet unknown, and the wonders of Africa.

But besides those great kingdoms of *Congo*, *Angola* and *Azichi*, in those unfrequented parts are the kingdoms of *Lango*, *Matania*, *Battua*, *Sofola*, *Mozambeche*, *Quivola*, the *Isle of St. Lawrence*, *Mombaza*, *Melinda*, the empires of *Monomotapa*, *Monemugi* and *Presbyter John*, with whom they have a kind of trade, and their rites, customs, climates, temperatures and commodities by relation: Also great lakes, that deserve the names of seas, and huge mountains of divers sorts, as some scorched with heat, some covered with snow; the mountains of the sun, also of the moon, some of chrystal, some of iron, some of silver, and mountains of gold, with the original of *Nilus*; likewise sundry sorts of cattle, fishes, fowls, strange beasts and monstrous serpents; for *Africa* was always noted to be a fruitful mother of such terrible creatures, who meeting at their watering places, which are but ponds in desart places, in regard of the heat of the countrey, and their extremities of nature, make strange copulations, and so ingender those extraordinary monsters. Of all these you may read in the history of this *Edward Lopez*, translated into *English* by *Abraham Hartwel*, and dedicated to *John* lord archbishop of *Canterbury*, 1597. But because the particulars are most concerning the conversion of those pagans, by a good poor priest, that first converted a noble man, to convert the king, and the rest of the nobility; sent for so many priests and ornaments into *Portugal*, to solemnize their baptisms with such magnificence, which was performed with such strange curiosities, that those poor negroes adored them as gods, till the priests grew to that wealth, a bishop was sent to rule over them, which they would not endure, which endangered to spoil all before they could be reconciled. But not to trouble you too long with those rarities of uncertainties; let us return again to *Barbary*, where the wars being ended, and *Befferres* possessed of *Morocco*, and his father's treasure, a new bruit arose amongst them, that *Muly Sidan* was raising an army against him, who after took his brother *Befferres* prisoner; but by reason of the uncertainty, and the perfidious, treacherous, bloody murthers rather than war, amongst those perfidious, barbarous *Moors*, *Smith* returned with *Merham*, and the rest to *Saffee*, and so aboard his ship, to try some other conclusions at sea.

CHAP. XX.

A brave sea-fight betwixt two Spanish *men of war, and captain* Merham, *with* Smith.

MErham, a captain of a man of war then in the road, invited captain *Smith* and two or three more of them aboard with him, where he spared not any thing he had to express his kindness, to bid them welcome, till it was too late to go on shore, so that necessity constrained them to stay aboard; a fairer evening could not be; yet ere midnight, such a storm did arise, they were forced to let slip cable and anchor, and put to sea; spooning before the wind, till they were driven to the *Canaries*; in the calms they accommodated themselves, hoping this strange accident might yet produce some good event; not long it was before they took a small bark coming from *Tenerif*, loaded with wine; three or four more they chased, two they took, but found little in them, save a few passengers, that told them of five *Dutch* men of war, about the isles; so that they stood for *Boiadora*, upon the *African* shore, betwixt which and cape *Noa*, they descry'd two sail. *Merham* intending to know what they were, hailed them; very civilly they danced their topsails, and desired the man of war to come aboard them, and take what he would, for they were but two poor distressed *Biskayners*. But *Merham*, the old fox, seeing himself in the lion's paws, sprung his louf, the other tacked after him, and came close up to his nether quarter, gave his broad-side, and so loufed up to windward; the vice-admiral did the like, and at the next bout, the admiral with a noise of trumpets, and all his ordnance, murtherers and muskets, boarded him on his broad-side; the other in like manner on his ley quarter, that it was so dark, there was little light, but fire and smoak; long he stayed not, before he fell off, leaving 4 or 5 of his men sprawling over the grating; after they had battered *Merham* about an hour, they boarded him again as before, and threw four ked-gars or grapnels in iron chains, then ſhearing off, they thought ſo to have torn down the grating; but the admiral's yard was ſo intangled in the ſhrouds, *Merham* had time to diſcharge two croſs-bar ſhot amongſt them, and divers bolts of iron made for that purpoſe, againſt his bow, that made ſuch a breach, he feared they both ſhould have ſunk for company; ſo that the *Spaniards* was as yare in ſlipping his chained grapnels, as *Merham* was in cutting the tackling, kept faſt their yards in his ſhrouds; the vice-admiral preſently cleared himſelf, but ſpared neither his ordnance nor muſkets to keep *Merham* from getting away, till the admiral had repaired his leak; from twelve at noon, till ſix at night, they thus interchanged one volly for another; then the vice-admiral fell on ſtern, ſtaying for the admiral that came up again to him, and all that night ſtood after *Merham*, that ſhaped his courſe for *Mamora*; but ſuch ſmall way they made, the next morning they were not three leagues off from cape *Noa*. The two *Spaniſh* men of war, for ſo they were, and well appointed, taking it in ſcorn as it ſeemed, with their chaſe, broad-ſide and ſtern, the one after the other, within muſket ſhot, plying their ordnance; and after an hours work, commanded *Merham* amain for the king of *Spain* upon fair quarter; *Merham* drank to them, and ſo diſcharged his quarter-pieces: Which pride the *Spaniard* to revenge, boarded him again, and many of them were got to the top to unſling the main-ſail, which the maſter and ſome others from the round-houſe, cauſed to their coſt to come tumbling down; about the round-houſe the *Spaniards* were ſo peſter'd, that they were forced to the great caben and blew it up; the ſmoak and fire was ſo vehement, as they thought the ſhip on fire; they in the fore-caſtle were no leſs aſſaulted, that they blew up a piece of the grating, with a great many of *Spaniards* more; then they cleared themſelves with all ſpeed, and *Merham* with as much expedition to quench the fire with wet cloaths and water, which began to grow too faſt. The *Spaniard* ſtill playing upon him with all the ſhot they could; the open places preſently they covered with old ſails, and prepared themſelves to fight to the laſt man. The angry *Spaniard* ſeeing the fire quench'd, hung out a flag of truce to have but a parley; but that deſperate *Merham* knew there was but one way with him, and would have none, but the report of his ordnance, which he did know well how to uſe for his beſt advantage. Thus they ſpent the next afternoon, and half the night, when the *Spaniards* either loſt them or left them. Seven and twenty men *Merham* had ſlain, and ſixteen wounded, and could find they had received 140 great ſhot. A wounded *Spaniard* they kept alive confeſſed they had loſt 100 men in the admiral, which they did fear would ſink ere ſhe could recover a port. Thus reaccommodating their ſails, they ſailed for *Sancta Cruſe*, cape *Goa* and *Magadore*, till they came again to *Saffee*, and then he returned into *England*.

CHAP. XXI.

The continuation of the general hiſtory of Virginia, *the* Summer-Iſles *and* New-England; *with their preſent eſtate from* 1624 *to this preſent* 1629.

Concerning theſe countries, I would be ſorry to trouble you with repeating one thing twice, as with their maps, commodities, people, government and religion yet known; the beginning of theſe plantations, their numbers and names, with the names of the adventurers, the yearly proceedings of every governor both here and there. As for the miſpriſions, neglect, grievances, and the cauſes of all thoſe rumours, loſſes and croſſes that have happened; I refer you to the general hiſtory, where you ſhall find all this at large, eſpecially to thoſe pages where you may read my letter of advice to the council and company, what of neceſſity muſt be done, or loſe all and leave the countrey, page 70, what commodities I ſent home, page 163, my opinion and offer to the company, to feed and defend the colonies, page 150, my account to them here of my actions there, page 163, my ſeven anſwers to his majeſty's commiſſioners: Seven queſtions what hath hindered *Virginia*, and the remedy, page 165. How thoſe noble gentlemen ſpent near two years in peruſing all letters came from thence; and the differences betwixt many factions, both here and there, with their complaints; eſpecially about the ſallery which ſhould have been a new office in *London*, for the well ordering the ſale of tobacco, that 2500 pounds ſhould yearly have been raiſed out of it, to pay four or five hundred pounds yearly to the gover-

nor

nor of that company, two or three hundred to his deputy; the rest into stipends of forty or fifty pounds yearly for their clerks and other officers which were never there, page 153; but not one hundred pounds for all them in *Virginia*, nor any thing for the most part of the adventurers in *England*, except the undertakers for the lotteries, fetters out of ships, adventurers of commodities, also their factors and many other officers, there imploy'd only by friendship to raise their fortunes out of the labours of the true industrious planters by the title of their office, who under the colour of sincerity, did pillage and deceive all the rest most cunningly: For more than 150000 pounds have been spent out of the common stock, besides many thousands have been there consumed, and near 7000 people that there died, only for want of good order and government, otherwise long ere this there would have been more than 20000 people, where after twenty years spent only in complement and trying new conclusions, was remaining scarce 1500, with some few cattle.

Then the company dissolved, but no account of any thing; so that his majesty appointed commissioners to oversee and give order for their proceedings. Being thus in a manner left to themselves, since then within these four years, you shall see how wonderfully they have increased beyond expectation; but so exactly as I desired, I cannot relate unto you: For altho' I have tired my self in seeking and discoursing with those returned thence, more than would a voyage to *Virginia*; few can tell me any thing, but of that place or places they have inhabited, and he is a great traveller that hath gone up and down the river of *James-Town*, been at *Pamaunke*, *Smith*'s-*Isles*, or *Accomack*; wherein for the most part, they keep one tune of their now particular abundance, and their former wants having been there, some sixteen years, some twelve, some six, some near twenty, &c. But of their general estate, or any thing of worth, the most of them do know very little to any purpose.

Their estate 1627. Now the most I could understand in general, was from the relation of Mr. *Nathaniel Cawsey*, that lived there with me, and returned *Anno Dom.* 1627; and some others affirm, Sir *George Yerely* was governor, captain *Francis West*, Dr. *John Pott*, captain *Roger Smith*, captain *Matthews*, captain *Tucker*, Mr. *Clabourn* and Mr. *Farrer*, of the council: Their habitations many. The governor, with two or three of the council, are for most part at *James-Town*, the rest repair thither as there is occasion; but every three months they have a general meeting, to consider of their publick affairs.

Their numbers. Their numbers then were about 1500, some say rather 2000, divided into seventeen or eighteen several plantations; the greatest part thereof, towards the falls, are so inclosed with pallisadoes they regard not the *Salvages*; and amongst those plantations above *James-Town*, they have now found means to take plenty of fish, as well with lines as nets, and where the waters are the largest, having means they need not want.

Their condition with the salvages. Upon this river they seldom see any *Salvages*, but in the woods many times their fires: Yet some few there are, that upon their opportunity, have slain some few straglers, which have been revenged with the death of so many of themselves; but no other attempt hath been made upon them this two or three years.

Their increase of cattle and poultry. Their cattle, namely, oxen, kine, bulls, they imagine to be about 2000; goats great store and great increase; the wild hogs, which are infinite, are destroy'd and eaten by the *Salvages*; but no family is so poor that hath not tame swine sufficient; and for poultrey, he is a very bad husband, that breedeth not an hundred in a year, and the richer sort doth daily feed on them.

Plenty of corn. For bread they have plenty, and so good, that those that make it well, better cannot be: Divers have much *English* corn, especially Mr. *Abraham Perce*, which prepared this year to sow two hundred acres of *English* wheat, and as much with barley, feeding daily about the number of sixty persons at his own charges.

Their drink. For drink, some malt the *Indian* corn, others barley, of which they make good ale, both strong and small, and such plenty thereof, few of the upper planters drink any water: But the better sort are well furnish'd with sack, *Aquavitæ* and good *English* beer.

Their servants diet. The servants commonly feed upon milk homily, which is bruised *Indian* corn pounded and boil'd thick, and milk for the sawce; but boil'd with milk, the best of all will feed oft on it, and leave their flesh; with milk, butter and cheese; with fish, bulls-flesh, for they seldom kill any other, &c. And every one is so applied to his labour about tobacco and corn, which doth yield them such profit, they never regarded any food from the *Salvages*, nor have they any trade or conference with them them, but upon meer accidents and defiances: And now the merchants have left it, there having gone so many voluntary ships within these two years, as have furnished them with apparel, sack, *Aquavitæ*, and all necessaries, much better than any before.

Their arms and exercise. For arms, there is scarce any man but he is furnish'd with a piece, a jack, a coat of of male, a ſword or rapier; and every holyday, every plantation doth exerciſe their men in arms, by which means hunting and fowling, the moſt part of them are moſt excellent markſmen.

Their health and diſcoveries.

For diſcoveries they have made none, nor any other commodity than tobacco do they apply themſelves unto, tho' never any was planted at firſt. And whereas the countrey was heretofore held moſt intemperate and contagions by many, now they have houſes, lodgings, victuals, and the ſun hath power to exhale up the moiſt vapours of the earth, where they have cut down the wood, which before it could not, being covered with ſpreading tops of high trees; they find it much more healthful than before; and for their numbers few countries are leſs troubled with death, ſickneſs or any other diſeaſe, or have their overgrown women become more fruitful.

The preſent eſtate of Virginia 1629.

Since this, Sir *George Yerely* died 1628, captain *Weſt* ſucceeded him, but about a year after, returned for *England:* Now Dr. *Poot* is governor, and the reſt of the council as before: *James-Town* is yet their chief ſeat, moſt of the wood deſtroy'd, little corn there planted, but all converted into paſture and gardens, wherein doth grow all manner of herbs and roots we have in *England*, in abundance, and as good graſs as can be. Here moſt of their cattle do feed, their owners being moſt ſome one way, ſome another, about their plantations, and return again when they pleaſe, or any ſhipping comes in to trade. Here in the winter they have hay for their cattle, but in other places they browze upon wood, and the great huſks of their corn, with ſome corn in them, doth keep them well.

Mr. Hutchins. *Five thouſand people. Five thouſand cattle. Goats hogs and poultry infinite.*

Mr. *Hutchins* ſaith, they have 2000 cattle, and about 5000 people; but Maſter *Floud*, *John Daves*, *William Emerſon*, and divers others ſay about 5000 people, and 5000 kine, calves, oxen and bulls; for goats, hogs and poultry, corn, fiſh, deer, and many ſorts of other wild beaſt, and fowl in their ſeaſon, they have ſo much more than they ſpend, they are able to feed three or four hundred more than they have; and do oft much relieve many ſhips, both there and for their return; and this laſt year was there at leaſt two or three and twenty ſale. They have oft much ſaltfiſh from *New-England*, but freſh fiſh enough, when they will take it; peaches in abundance at *Kekoughtan*; apples, pears, apricocks, vines, figs, and other fruits ſome have planted that proſpered exceedingly, but their diligence about tobacco, left them to be ſpoil'd by the cattle, yet now they begin to revive; Mrs. *Pearce*, an honeſt induſtrious women, hath been there near twenty years, and now returned, ſaith, ſhe hath a garden at *James-Town*, containing three or four acres, where in one year ſhe hath gathered near an hundred buſhels of excellent figs; and that of her own proviſion ſhe can keep a better houſe in *Virginia*, than here in *London* for 3 or 400 pounds a year, yet went thither with little or nothing. They have ſome tame geeſe, ducks and turkies. The maſters now do ſo train up their ſervants and youths in ſhooting deer and fowl, that the youths will kill them as well as their maſters. They have two brew-houſes, but they find the *Indian* corn ſo much better than ours, they begin to leave ſowing it. Their cities and towns are only ſcattered houſes, they call plantations, as our countrey villages, but no ordnance mounted. The forts captrin *Smith* left a building, ſo ruined, there is ſcarce mention where they were; no diſcoveries of any thing more, than the curing of tobacco, by which hitherto, being ſo preſent a commodity of gain, it hath brought them to this abundance; but that they are ſo disjointed, and every one commander of himſelf to plant what he will: They are now ſo well provided, that they are able to ſubſiſt, if they would join together, now to work upon ſoap-aſhes, iron, rape-oil, mader, pitch and tar, flax and hemp; as for their tobacco, there comes from many places ſuch abundance, and the charge ſo great, it is not worth the bringing home.

Good hoſpitality.

Commodities worth making, black wallnut, aſh for pikes, oak for planks, knees for ſhips, cypreſs for cheſts, &c.

There is gone, and now a going, divers ſhips, as captain *Perſe*, captain *Prine*, with Sir *John Harvey* to be their governor, with two or three hundred people; there is alſo ſome from *Briſtol* and other parts of the weſt-countrey a preparing, which I heartily pray to God to bleſs, and ſend them a happy and proſperous voyage.

Nathaniel Cauſie, maſter *Hutchins*, maſter *Floud*, *John Davis*, *William Emerſon*, maſter *William Barnet*, maſter *Cooper*, and others.

CHAP.

CHAP. XXII.

The proceedings and present estate of the Summer Isles, *from* Anno Dom. 1624, *to this present* 1629.

FROM the *Summer Isles*, Mr. *Ireland*, and divers others report, their forts, ordnance and proceedings, are much as they were in the Year 1622. as you may read in the general history, pag. 199. Captain *Woodhouse* governour. There are few sorts of any fruits in the *West Indies*, but they grow there in abundance; yet the fertility of the soil in many places decayeth, being planted every year; for their plantains, which is a most delicate fruit, they have lately found a way by pickling or drying them, to bring them over into *England*, there being no such fruit in *Europe*, and wonderful for increase. For fish, flesh, figs, wine, and all sorts of most excellent herbs, fruits and roots they have in abundance. In this governour's time, a kind of whale, or rather a *Jubarta*, was driven on shore in *Southampton* tribe from the west, over an infinite number of rocks so bruised, that the water in the bay where she lay, was all oily, and the rocks about it all bedasht with parmacitty, congealed like ice, a good quantity we gathered, with which we commonly cured any boil, hurt or bruise; some burnt it in their lamps, which blowing out, the very snuff will burn so long as there is any of the oil remaining, for two or three days together.

The present estate of the Summer Isles, 1629. The next governour was captain *Philip Bell*, whose time being expired, captain *Roger Wood* possess'd his place, a worthy gentleman of good desert, and hath lived a long time in the countrey; their numbers are about 2 or 3000 Men, Women and Children, who increase there exceedingly; their greatest complaint is want of apparel, and too much custom, and too many officers; the pity is, there are no more men than women, yet no great mischief, because there is so much less pride: the cattle they have increase exceedingly; their forts are well maintained by the merchants here, and planters there; to be brief, this isle is an excellent bit to rule a great horse.

All the cohow birds and egbirds are gone; seldom any wild cats seen; no rats to speak off; but the worms are yet very troublesome; the people very healthful, and the ravens gone; fish enough, but not so near the shore as it used, by the much beating it; it is an isle that hath such a rampire and a ditch, and for the quantity so manned, victualled, and fortified, as few in the world do exceed it, or is like it.

The 22d of *March*, two ships came from thence; the *Peter-Bonaventure*, near 200 Tons, and sixteen Pieces of ordnance; the captain, *Thomas Sherwin*; the master, Mr. *Edward Some*, like him in condition, a goodly, lusty, proper, valiant man: The *Lydia*, wherein was Mr. *Anthony Thorne*, a smaller ship, were chased by eleven ships of *Dunkirk*; being thus over-match'd, captain *Sherwin* was taken by them in *Torbay*, only his valiant master was slain; the ship with about seventy *English* men they carried betwixt *Dover* and *Calais* to *Dunkirk*; but the *Lydia* safely recovered *Dartmouth*. *An evil mischance.*

These noble adventurers for all those losses patiently do bear them; but they hope the king and state will understand it is worth keeping, tho' it afford nothing but tobacco, and that now worth little or nothing, custom and fraught pay'd, yet it is worth keeping, and not supplanting; tho' great Men feel not those losses, yet gardiners, carpenters and smiths, do pay for it.

From the Relation of *Robert Chestevan* and others.

CHAP. XXIII.

The proceedings and present estate of New England, *since* 1624, *to this present* 1629.

Considerations about the loss of time. WHEN I went first to the north part of *Virginia*, where the westerly colony had been planted, it had dissolved it self within a year, and there was not one christian in all the land. I was set forth at the sole charge of four merchants of *London*; the countrey being then reputed by your westerlings, a most rocky, barren, desolate desart; but a good return I brought from thence, with the maps and relations I made of the countrey, which I made so manifest, some of them did believe me, and they were well embraced both by the *Londoners* and the *Westerlings*, for whom I had promised to undertake it, I thinking to have joined them all together; but that might well have

have been a work of *Hercules*. Betwixt them long there was much contention; the *Londoners* indeed went bravely forward; but in three or four years, I and my friends consumed many hundred pounds amongst the *Plimothians*, who only fed me with delays, promises and excuses, but no performance of any thing to any purpose. In the interim, many particular ships went thither, and finding my relations true, and that I had not taken that I brought home from the *Frenchmen*, as had been reported; yet farther, for my pains to discredit me, and my calling it *New-England*, they obscured, and shadowed it, with the title of *Canada*, till at my humble suit, it pleased our most royal king *Charles*, whom God long keep, bless and preserve, then prince of *Wales*, to confirm it with my map and book, by the title of *New-England*; the gain thence returning, did make the fame thereof so increase, that thirty, forty, or fifty sail went yearly only to trade and fish; but nothing would be done for a plantation, till about some hundred of your brownists of *England*, *Amsterdam* and *Leyden*, went to *New Plimouth*, whose humorous ignorances, caused them for more than a year to endure a wonderful deal of misery, with an infinite patience; saying my books and maps were much better cheap to teach them than myself; many other have used the like good husbandry, that have pay'd soundly in trying their self-will'd conclusions; but those in time doing well, divers others have in small handfuls undertaken to go there, to be several lords and kings of themselves, but most vanished to nothing. Notwithstanding the fishing ships, made such good returns, at last it was ingrossed by twenty patentees, that divided my map into twenty parts, and cast lots for their shares; but money not coming in as they expected, procured a proclamation, none should go thither without their licences to fish; but for every thirty tuns of shipping, to pay them five pounds; besides, upon great penalties, neither to trade with the natives, cut down wood for the stages, without giving satisfaction, tho' all the countrey is nothing but wood, and none to make use of it, with many such other pretences, for to make this countrey plant itself, by its own wealth: Hereupon most men grew so discontented, that few or none would go; so that the patentees, who never a one of them had been there, seeing those projects would not prevail, have since not hindred any to go that would, that within these few last years, more have gone thither than ever.

The effect of negardliness.

A new plantation, 1629.

Now this year 1629, a great company of people of good rank, zeal, means and quality, have made a great stock, and with six good ships in the months of *April* and *May*, they set sail from *Thames*, for the bay of the *Massachusets*, otherwise called *Charles*'s river, *viz.* the *George Bonaventure*, of twenty pieces of ordnance, the *Talbot* nineteen, the *Lions-wheip* eight, the *May-flower* fourteen, the *Four Sisters* fourteen, the *Pilgrim* four, with three hundred and fifty men, women and children; also an hundred and fifteen head of cattle, as horse, mares, and neat beast; one and forty goats, some conies, with all provision for houshold and apparel; six pieces of great ordnance for a fort, with muskets, pikes, corselets, drums, colours, with all provision necessary for a plantation, for the good of man; other particulars I understand of no more, than is writ in the general history of those countries.

But you are to understand, that the noble lord chief justice *Popham*, judge *Doderege*, the right honourable earls of *Pembroke*, *Southampton*, *Salisbury*, and the rest, as I take it, they did all think, as I and they that went with me, did; that, had those two countries been planted, as it was intended, no other nation should complant betwixt us. If ever the king of *Spain* and we should fall foul, those countries being so capable of all materials for shipping, by this might have been owners of a good fleet of ships, and have relieved a whole navy from *England* upon occasion; yea, and have furnished *England* with the most easternly commodities; and now since, seeing how conveniently the *Summer Isles* fell to our shares, so near the *West-Indies*, we might with much more facility than the *Dutchmen* have invaded the *West-Indies*, that doth now put in practise, what so long hath been advised on, by many an honest *English* statesman.

Notes of inconveniency.

Those countries, captain *Smith* oft times used to call his children that never had mother; and well he might, for few fathers ever payed dearer for so little content; and for those that would truly understand, how many strange accidents hath befallen them and him; how oft up, how oft down, sometimes near despair, and ere long flourishing, cannot but conceive God's infinite mercies and favours towards them. Had his designs been to have persuaded men to a mine of gold, though few do conceive either the charge or pains in refining it, nor the power nor care to defend it; or some new invention to pass to the south-sea, or some strange plot to invade some strange monastery, or some portable countrey, or some chargeable fleet to take some rich carocks in the *East-Indies*; or letters of mart to rob some poor merchants, what multitudes

multitudes of both people and money would contend to be first imployed? But in those noble endeavours (now) how few of quality, unless it be to beg some monopoly; and those seldom seek the common good, but the commons goods, as you may read at large in his general history, *pag.* 217, 218, 219, his general observations and reasons for this plantation; for yet those countries are not so forward, but they may become as miserable as ever, if better courses be not taken than are; as this *Smith* will plainly demonstrate to his majesty, or any other noble person of ability, liable generously to undertake it; how within a short time to make *Virginia* able to resist any enemy, that as yet lieth open to all, and yield the king more custom within these few years, in certain staple commodities, than ever it did in tobacco; which now not being worth bringing home, the custom will be as uncertain to the king, as dangerous to the plantations.

CHAP. XXIV.

A brief discourse of divers voyages made unto the goodly countrey of Guinea, *and the great river of the* Amazons; *relating also the present plantation there.*

IT is not unknown how that most industrious and honourable knight, sir *Walter Raleigh*, in the year of our Lord 1595, taking the isle of *Trinidada*, fell with the coast of *Guiana*, northward of the line 10 degrees, and coasted the coast, and searched up the river *Oranoco*; where understanding that twenty several voyages had been made by the *Spaniards*, in discovering this coast and river, to find a passage to the great city of *Mano*, called by them the *Eldorado*, or the golden city: He did his utmost to have found some better satisfaction than relations: But means failing him, he left his trusty servant *Francis Sparrow* to seek it, who wandring up and down those countries, some fourteen or fifteen years, unexpectedly returned. I have heard him say, he was led blinded into this city by *Indians*; but little discourse of any purpose, touching the largeness of the report of it; his body seeming as a man of an uncurable consumption, shortly died here after in *England*. There are above thirty fair rivers that fall into the sea, between the river of the *Amazons* and *Oranoco*, which are some nine degrees asunder. In the year 1605, captain *Ley*, brother to that noble knight, sir *Oliver Ley*, with divers others, planted himself in the river *Weapoco*, wherein I should have been a party; but he died, and there lies buried, and the supply miscarrying, the rest escaped as they could.

Sparrow *left to seek the great city of* Mano.

Captain Charles Ley.

Sir *Thomas Roe*, well known to be a most noble gentleman, before he went lord ambassador to the great *Mogul*, or the great *Turk*, spent a year or two upon this coast, and about the river of the *Amazons*, wherein he most imployed captain *Matthew Morton*, an expert seaman in the discovery of this famous river, a gentleman that was the first shot, and mortally supposed wounded to death, with me in *Virginia*, yet since hath been twice with command in the *East-Indies*; also captain *William White*, and divers other worthy and industrious gentlemen, both before and since, have spent much time and charge to discover it more perfectly, but nothing more effected for a plantation, till it was undertaken by captain *Robert Harcote* 1609.

Sir Thomas Roe.

Captain Morton.

Captain White.

Captain Harcote.

This worthy gentleman, after he had by commission made a discovery to his mind, left his brother *Michael Harcote*, with some fifty or sixty men in the river *Weapoco*, and so presently returned to *England*, where he obtained, by the favour of prince *Henry*, a large patent for all that coast called *Guiana*, together with the famous river of *Amazons*, to him and his heirs: But so many troubles here surprized him, tho' he did his best to supply them, he was not able, only some few he sent over as passengers, with certain *Dutchmen*, but to small purpose. Thus this business lay dead for divers years, till sir *Walter Raleigh*, accompanied with many valiant soldiers and brave gentlemen, went his last voyage to *Guinea*, amongst the which was captain *Roger North*, brother to the right honourable the lord *Dudley North*, who upon this voyage having stayed, and seen divers rivers upon this coast, took such a liking to those countries, having had before this voyage, more perfect and particular information of the excellency of the great river of the *Amazons*, above any of the rest, by certain *Englishmen* returned so rich, from thence in good commodities, they would not go with sir *Walter Raleigh* in search of gold; that after his return for *England*, he endeavoured by his best abilities to interest his countrey and state in those fair regions, which by the way of letters patents unto divers noblemen and gentlemen of quality, was erected into a company and perpetuity for trade and plantation, not knowing of the interest of captain *Harcote*.

Whereupon,

Captain Roger North.

Whereupon, accompanied with 120 gentlemen and others, with a ſhip, a pinnace and two ſhallops, to remain in the countrey, he ſet ſail from *Plimouth* the laſt of *April* 1620, and within ſeven weeks after he arrived well in the *Amazons*, only with the loſs of one old man: Some hundred leagues they ran up the river to ſettle his men, where the ſight of the countrey and people ſo contented them, that never men thought themſelves more happy: Some *Engliſh* and *Iriſh* that had lived there ſome eight years, only ſupplied by the *Dutch*, he reduced to his company and to leave the *Dutch*: Having made a good voyage, to the value of more than the charge, he returned to *England* with divers good commodities beſides tobacco: So that it may well be conceived, that if this action had not been thus croſſed, the generality of *England* had by this time been won and encouraged therein. But the time was not yet come, that God would have this great buſineſs effected, by reaſon of the great power the lord *Gundamore*, ambaſſador for the king of *Spain*, had in *England*, to croſs and ruin thoſe proceedings; and ſo unfortunate captain *North* was in this buſineſs, he was twice committed priſoner to the *Tower*, and the goods detained till they were ſpoiled, who beyond all others, was by the much greateſt adventurer and loſer.

Nota bene.

Notwithſtanding all this, thoſe that he had left in the *Amazons*, would not abandon the countrey. Captain *Thomas Painton*, a worthy gentleman, his lieutenant died. Captain *Charles Parker*, brother to the right honourable the lord *Morley*, lived there ſix years after; Mr. *John Chriſtmas* five years, ſo well, they would not return, altho' they might, with divers other gentlemen of quality and others: All thus deſtitute of any ſupplies from *England*. But all authority being diſſolved, want of government did more wrong their proceedings, than all other croſſes whatſoever. Some relief they had ſometime from the *Dutch*, who knowing their eſtates, gave what they pleaſed, and took what they liſt. Two brothers, gentlemen, *Thomas* and *William Hixon*, who ſtayed three years there, are now gone to ſtay in the *Amazons*, in the ſhips lately ſent thither.

The buſineſs thus remaining in this ſort, three private men left of that company, named Mr. *Thomas Warriner*, *John Rhodes*, and *Robert Bims*, having lived there about two years, came for *England*, and to be free from the diſorders that did grow in the *Amazons*, for want of government amongſt their countreymen, and to be quiet amongſt themſelves, made means to ſet themſelves out for St. *Chriſtophers*; their whole number being but fifteen perſons that paid for their paſſage in a ſhip going for *Virginia*, where they remained a year before they were ſupplied, and then that was but four or five men. Thus this iſle, by this ſmall beginning, having no interruption by their own countrey, hath not got the ſtart of the continent and main land of *Guinea*, which hath been laid apart, and let alone until that captain *North*, ever watching his beſt opportunity and advantage of time in the ſtate, hath now again purſued, and ſet on foot his former deſign: Captain *Harcote* being now willing to ſurrender his grant, and to join with captain *North*, in paſſing a new patent, and to erect a company for trade and plantation in the *Amazons*, and all the coaſt and countrey of *Guinea* for ever. Whereupon, they have ſent this preſent year in *January*, and ſince 1628, four ſhips, with near 200 perſons; the firſt ſhip with 112 men, not one miſcarried; the reſt went ſince, not yet heard of; and they are preparing another with their beſt expedition; and ſince *January* are gone from *Holland*, 100 *Engliſh* and *Iriſh*, conducted by the old planters.

This great river lieth under the line; the two chief head lands north and ſouth, are about three degrees aſunder, the mouth of it is ſo full of many great and ſmall iſles, it is an eaſy matter for an unexperienced pilot to loſe his way. It is held one of the greateſt rivers in *America*, and as moſt men think in the world; and cometh down with ſuch a freſh, it maketh the ſea freſh, more than thirty miles from the ſhore. Captain *North* having ſeated his men about 100 leagues in the main, ſent captain *William White*, with thirty gentlemen and others, in a pinnace of thirty tun, to dicover farther, which they did ſome 200 leagues, where they found the river to divide itſelf into two parts, till then all full of iſlands, and a countrey moſt healthful, pleaſant and fruitful; for they found food enough, and all returned ſafe and in good health: In this diſcovery, they ſaw many towns well inhabited, ſome with three hundred people, ſome with five, ſix, or ſeven hundred; and of ſome they underſtood to be of ſo many thouſands, moſt differing very much, eſpecially in their languages: Whereof they ſuppoſe by thoſe *Indians*, they underſtand are many hundreds more, unfrequented till then by any chriſtians, moſt of them ſtark naked, both men, women and children, but they ſaw not any ſuch giant-like women as the rivers name importeth. But for thoſe where captain *North* hath ſeated his company, it is not known where *Indians* were ever ſo kind to any nation, not ſparing any pains, danger or labour, to feed

2 and

and maintain them. The *English* following their buildings, fortifications and sugar works; for which they have sent most expert men, and with them all things necessary for that purpose; to effect which, they want not the help of those kind *Indians* to produce; and many other good commodities, which (God willing) will ere long make plain and apparent to this kingdom, and all the adventurers and well-willers to this plantation, to be well worthy the cherishing and following with all alacrity.

CHAP. XXV.

The beginning and proceedings of the new plantation of St. Christopher *by Captain* Warner.

MAster *Ralph Marifield* and others, having furnished this worthy industrious gentleman, he arrived at St. *Christophers*, as is said, with fifteen men, the 28th
1623. of *January* 1623, viz. *William Tested*, *John Rhodes*, *Robert Bims*, Mr. *Benifield*, Sergeant *Jones*, Mr. *Ware*, *William Ryle*, *Rowland Grascock*, Mr. *Bond*, Mr. *Langley*, Mr. *Weaver*, *Edward Warner*, their captain's son, and now deputy governor, till his father's return, sergeant *Aplon*, one sailor and a cook: At their arrival, they found three *Frenchmen*, who sought to oppose captain *Warner*, and to set the *Indians* upon us; but at last we all became friends, and lived with the *Indians* a month, then we built a fort, and a house; and planting fruits, by *September* we made a crop of *Tobacco*; but up-
A hurricano. on the 19th of *September* came a hurricano and blew it away. All this while we lived upon cassado bread, potatoes, plantanes, pines, turtles, guanes, and fish plenty; for drink we had *Nicknobby*.

1624. The 18th of *March* 1624, arrived captain *Jefferson*, with three men passengers in the *Hopewell* of *London*, with some trade for the *Indians*, and then we had another crop of tobacco, in the mean time the *French* had planted themselves in the other end of the isle; with this crop captain *Warner* returned for *England* in *September* 1625.

In his absence came in a *French* pinnace, under the command of *Monsieur de Nombe*, that told us, the *Indians* had slain some *Frenchmen* in other of the *Caribbee* isles, and that there were six peryagoes, which are huge great trees, formed as your canoos, but so laid out on the sides with boards,
Their fight with the Indians. they will seem like a little galley: Six of those, with about four or five hundred strange *Indians* came unto us, we bad them be gone, but they would not; whereupon we and the *French* joined together, and upon the 5th of *November* set upon them, and put them to flight: Upon new-years even they came again, found three *English* going about the isle, whom they slew.

1626. Until the 4th of *August*, we stood upon our guard, living upon the spoil, and did nothing. But now captain *Warner* arriving again with near an hundred people, then we fell to work and planting as before; but upon the 4th of *September*, came such a hurricano, as blew down all our *A hurricano.*
houses, tobacco, and two drums into the air we know not whither, drove two ships on shore that were both split; all our provision thus lost, we were very miserable, living only on what we could get in the wild woods, we made a small party of *French* and *English* to go aboard for provision, but *Eight* French *slain.*
in their returning home, eight *French* men were slain in the harbour.

Thus we continued till near *June* that the *Tortles* came in 1627, but the *French* 1627.
being like to starve, sought to surprize us, and all the cassado, potatoes, and tobacco we had planted, but we did prevent them. The 26th of *October*, came in captain *William Smith*, in the *Hopewell*, with some ordnance, shot and powder, from the earl of *Carlisle*, with captain *Pelham* and thirty men; about that time also came the *Plow*, also a small ship of *Bristow*, with captain *Warner*'s wife, and six or seven women more.

Upon the 25th of *November*, the *Indians* set upon the *French*, for some injury about *Three* Indians *slain*
their women, and slew six and twenty *French* men, five *English*, and three *Indians*. Their weapons are bows and arrows, their bows are never bent, but the string lies flat to the bow; their arrows a small reed, four or five foot long, headed some with the poisoned sting of the tail of a stingray, some with iron, some with wood, but all so poisoned, that if they draw but blood, the hurt is incurable.

The next day came in captain *Charles Saltonstall*, a young gentleman, son to sir *Samuel Saltonstall*, who brought with him good *The arrival of many* English *ships.*
store of all commodities to relieve the plantation; but by reason some *Hollanders*, and others had been there lately before him, who carried away with them all the tobacco, he was forced to put away all his commodities upon trust till the next crop; in the mean time he resolved there to stay, and imploy himself and his company in planting

ing tobacco, hoping thereby to make a voyage, but before he could be ready to return for *England* a hurricano happening, his ſhip was ſpiit, to his great loſs, being ſole merchant and owner himſelf, notwithſtanding forced to pay to the governor the fifth part of his tobacco, and for fraught to *England*, three pence a pound, and nine pence a pound cuſtom, which amounts together to more than threeſcore pound in the hundred pound, to the great diſcouragement of him and many others, that intended well to thoſe plantations. Nevertheleſs he is gone again this preſent year 1629, with a ſhip of about three hundred tons, and very near two hundred people, with Sir *William Tuffton* governor for the *Barbadoes*, and divers gentlemen, and all manner of commodities fit for a plantation.

Captain *Prinn*, captain *Stone*, and divers others came in about *Chriſtmas*; ſo that this laſt year, there hath been about thirty ſail of *Engliſh*, *French* and *Dutch* ſhips, and all the *Indians* forced out of the iſle, for they had done much miſchief amongſt the *French*, in cutting their throats, burning their houſes, and ſpoiling their tobacco; amongſt the reſt *Tegramund*, a little child, the king's ſon, his parents being ſlain or fled, was by great chance ſaved, and carefully brought to *England*, by maſter *Meriſield*, who brought him from thence, and bringeth him up as his own children.

The deſcription of the iſle.

It lieth ſeventeen degrees Northward of the line, about an hundred and twenty leagues from the *Cape de tres Puntas*, the neareſt main land in *America*; it is about eight leagues in length, and four in breadth; an iſland amongſt 100 iſles in the *Weſt-Indies*, called the *Caribbees*, where ordinarily all them that frequent the *Weſt-Indies* refreſh themſelves; thoſe, moſt of them are rocky, little and mountainous, yet frequented with the canibals; many of them inhabited, as *St. Domingo*, *St. Mattalin*, *St. Lucia*, *St. Vincent*, *Granada* and *Margarita*, to the ſouthward; northward, none but St. *Chriſtophers*, and that but lately; yet they will be ranging *Marigalanta*, *Guardalupo*, *Deceado*, *Mountſerat*, *Antegua*, *Mevis*, *Bernardo*, *St. Martin* and *St. Bartholomew*, but the worſt of the four iſles poſſeſſed by the *Spaniard*, as *Portorico* or *Jamaica*, is better than them all; as for *Hiſpaniola* and *Cuba*, they are worthy the title of two rich kingdoms, the reſt not reſpected by the *Spaniards*, for want of harbours, and their better choice of good land, and profit in the main. But captain *Warner* having been very familiar with captain *Painton*, in the *Amazon*, hearing his information of this *St. Chriſtophers*; and having made a years tryal, as it is ſaid, returned for *England*, and joining with maſter *Meriſield* and his friends, got letters patents from king *James* to plant and poſſeſs it. Since then, the right honourable the earl of *Carliſle* hath got letters patents alſo, not only of that, but all the *Caribee Iſles* about it, who is now chief lord of them, and the *Engliſh* his tenants that do poſſeſs them; over whom he appointeth ſuch governors and officers as their affairs require; and although there be a great cuſtom impoſed upon them, conſidering their other charges, both to feed and maintain themſelves; yet there is there, and now a going, near upon the number of three thouſand people; where by reaſon of the rockineſs and thickneſs of the woods in the iſle, it is difficult to paſs, and ſuch a ſurff of the ſea goeth on the ſhore, ten may better defend, than fifty aſſault. In this iſle are many ſprings, but yet water is ſcarce again in many places; the valleys and ſides of the hills very fertile, but the mountains harſh, and of a ſulphurous compoſition; all over-grown with *Palmetas*, cotton trees, *Lignum Vitæ*, and divers other ſorts, but none like any in chriſtendom, except thoſe carried thither; the air very pleaſant and healthful, but exceeding hot, yet ſo tempered with cool breaths, it ſeems very temperate to them, that are little uſed to it; the trees being always green, the days and nights always very near equal in length, always ſummer; only they have in their ſeaſons great guſts and rains, and ſometimes a hurricano, which is an over-grown, and a moſt violent ſtorm.

The ſprings, temper and ſeaſons.

In ſome of thoſe iſles, are cattle, goats and hogs, but here none but what they muſt carry; *Guanes* they have, which is a little harmleſs beaſt, like a crocodile or aligator, very fat and good meat; ſhe lays eggs in the ſand, as doth the land crabs, which live here in abundance, like conies in boroughs, unleſs about *May*, when they come down to the ſea-ſide to lay in the ſand, as the other; and all their eggs are hatched by the heat of the ſun.

A ſtrange hatching of eggs for beaſts.

From *May* to *September*, they have good ſtore of *Tortoiſes* that come out of the ſea to lay their eggs in the ſand, and are hatched as the other; they will lay half a peck at a time, and near a buſhel ere they have done, and are round like tennis-balls: This fiſh is like veal in taſte, the fat of a browniſh colour, very good and wholeſome. We ſeek them in the nights, where we find them on ſhore, we turn them upon their backs, till the next day we fetch them home, for they can never return themſelves, being ſo hard, a cart may go over them; and

Fiſh.

and ſo big, one will ſuffice forty or fifty men to dinner. Divers ſorts of other fiſh they have in abundance, and prawnes moſt great and excellent, but none will keep ſweet ſcarce twelve hours.

Birds. The beſt and greateſt is a *Paſſer Flaminga*, which walking at her length, is as tall as a man; pigeons and turtle-doves in abundance; ſome parrots, wild hawks, but divers other ſorts of good ſea-fowl, whoſe names we know not.

Roots. *Caſſado* is a root planted in the ground, of a wonderful increaſe, and will make very good white bread, but the juce rank poiſon, yet boiled, better than wine; potatoes, cabbages and radiſhes plenty.

Fruits. Maize, like the *Virginia* wheat; we have pine-apple, near ſo big as an artichoke, but the moſt daintieſt taſte of any fruit; *Plantnais*, an excellent and moſt increaſing fruit; apples, prickle-pears and peaſe, but differing all from ours. There is pepper that groweth in a little red huſk, as big as a walnut, about four inches in length, but the long cods are ſmall, and much ſtronger and better for uſe, than that from the *Eaſt-Indies*. There is two ſorts of cotton; the ſilk-cotton, as in the *Eaſt-Indies*, groweth upon a ſmall ſtalk, as good for beds as down; the other upon a ſhrub, and beareth a cod bigger than a walnut, full of cotton-wool: *Anotto* alſo groweth upon a ſhrub, with a cod like the other, and nine or ten on a bunch, full of *Anotto*, very good for dyers, tho' wild; ſugar-canes, not tame, four or five foot high; alſo maſtick and locuſt-trees; great and hard timber, gourds, muſk-melons, water-melons, lettice, parſly; all places naturally bear purſlain of it ſelf; ſope-berries like a muſquet bullet, that waſheth as white as ſope; in the middle of the root is a thing like a ſedge, a very good fruit. we call pengromes; a pappaw is as great as an apple, coloured like an orange, and good to eat; a ſmall hard nut, like a hazel-nut, grows cloſe to the ground, and like this grows on the palmetas, which we call a mucca-nut; muſtard-ſeed will grow to a great tree, but bears no ſeed, yet the leaves will make good muſtard; the mancinel tree, the fruit is poiſon; good figs in abundance; but the palmeta ſerveth to build forts and houſes, the leaves to cover them, and many other uſes; the juice we draw from them, till we ſuck them to death, it is held reſtorative, and the top for meat doth ſerve us as cabbage; but oft we want powder'd beef and bacon, and many other needful neceſſaries.

By *Thomas Simons*, *Rowland Graſcocke*, *Nicholas Burgh*, and others.

CHAP. XXVI.

The firſt planting of the Barbadoes.

THE *Barbadoes* lies ſouth-weſt and by ſouth, an hundred leagues from *St. Chriſtophers*, threeſcore leagues weſt and ſouth from *Trinidada*, and ſome fourſcore leagues from *Cape de Salinos*, the next part of the main. The firſt planters brought thither by captain *Henry Powel*, were forty *Engliſh*, with ſeven or eight negroes; then he went to *Diſacuba* in the main, where he got thirty *Indians*, men, women and children of the *Arawacos*, enemies both to the *Caribbees* and the *Spaniards*. *A deſcription of the iſle.* The iſle is moſt like a triangle each ſide forty or fifty miles ſquare, ſome exceeding great rocks, but the moſt part exceeding good ground, abounding with an infinite number of ſwine, ſome turtles, and many ſorts of excellent fiſh; many great ponds wherein is duck and mallard; excellent clay for pots, wood and ſtone for building, and a ſpring, near the midſt of the iſle, of *Bitume*, which is a liquid mixture like tar, that by the great rains falls from the tops of the mountains; it floats upon the water in ſuch abundance, that drying up, it remains like great rocks of pitch, and as good as pitch for any uſe.

The mancinel apple, is of a moſt pleaſant ſweet ſmell, of the bigneſs of a crab, *Fruits and trees.* but rank poiſon, yet the ſwine and birds have wit to ſhun it; great ſtore of exceeding great locuſt-trees, two or three fathom about, of a great heighth, that beareth a cod full of meal, will make bread in time of neceſſity. A tree like a pine beareth a fruit ſo great as a muſk-melon, which hath always ripe fruit, flowers or green fruit, which will refreſh two or three men, and very comfortable; plum-trees many, the fruit great and yellow, which but ſtrained into water in four and twenty hours, will be very good drink; wild fig-trees there are many; all thoſe fruits do fat the hogs, yet at ſometimes of the year they are ſo lean as carrion; guane trees bear a fruit ſo big as a pear, good and wholſome; palmetaes of three ſeveral ſorts; pappaws, prickle-pears, good to eat or make drink; cedar trees very tall and great; fuſtick trees

trees are very great, and the wood yellow, good for dying; ſoap-berries, the kernel ſo big as a ſloe, and good to eat; pompions in abundance; goads ſo great as will make good great bottles, and cut in two pieces, good diſhes and platters; many ſmall brooks of very good water; *Guiney* wheat, caſſavo, pines and plantains; all things we there plant, do grow, exceedingly, ſo well as tobacco; the corn, peaſe, and beans, cut but away the ſtalk, young ſprigs will grow, and ſo bear fruit for many years together, without any more planting; the iſle is overgrown with wood or great reeds, thoſe woods which are ſoft are exceeding light and full of pitch, and thoſe that are hard and great, they are as hard to cut as ſtone.

Their numbers. Mr. *John Powel* came thither the 4th of *Auguſt* 1627, with forty five men, where we ſtayed three weeks, and then returning, left behind us about an hundred people, and his ſon *John Powel* for his deputy, as governor; but there have been ſo many factions amonſt them, I cannot from ſo many variable relations, give you any certainty for their orderly government: For all thoſe plenties, much miſery they have endured, in regard of their weakneſs at their landing, and long ſtay without ſupplies; therefore thoſe that go thither, it were good they carry good proviſion with them; but the iſle is moſt healthful, and all things planted do increaſe abundantly; and by this time there is, and now a going, about the number of fifteen or ſixteen hundred people.

Sir *William Curtine*, and captain *John Powel*, were the firſt and chief adventurers to the planting this fortunate iſle; which had been oft frequented by men of war to refreſh themſelves, and ſet up their ſhallopes; being ſo far remote from the reſt of the iſles, they never were troubled with any of the *Indies*. Harbours they have none, but exceeding good roads, which with a ſmall charge, might be very well fortified; it doth ebb and flow four or five foot, and they cannot perceive that there hath ever been any hurricano in that iſle.

From the relations of captain *John White*, and captain *Wolverſtone*.

CHAP. XXVII.

The firſt plantations of the iſle of Mevis.

The deſcription of the iſle. BEcauſe I have ranged and lived amongſt thoſe iſlands, what my authors cannot tell me, I thing it no great error in helping them to tell it my ſelf. In this little iſle of *Mevis*, more than twenty years ago, I have remained a great time together, to wood and water, and refreſh my men; it is all woody, but by the ſeaſide ſouthward, there are ſands like downs, where a thouſand men may quarter themſelves conveniently; but in moſt places the wood groweth cloſe to the water-ſide, at a high-water mark, and in ſome places ſo thick of a ſoft ſpungy wood like a wild fig-tree, you cannot get through it, but by making your way with hatchets or fauchions: Whether it was the dew of thoſe trees, or of ſome others, I am not certain, but many of our men became ſo tormented with a burning ſwelling all over their bodies, they ſeemed like ſcalded men, and near mad with pain; here we found a great pool, wherein bathing themſelves they found much eaſe; and finding it fed with a pleaſant ſmall ſtream that came out *The bath.* of the woods, we found the head half a mile within the land, diſtilling from many rocks, by which they were well cured in two or three days. Such factions here we had, as commonly attend ſuch voyages, that a pair of gallows were made, but captain *Smith* for whom they were intended, could not be perſuaded to uſe them; but not any one of the inventers, but their lives by juſtice fell into his power to determine of at his pleaſure, whom with much mercy he favoured, that moſt baſely and unjuſtly have betray'd him.

The laſt year 1628, Mr. *Littleton* with ſome others, got a patent of the earl of *Carliſle* to plant the iſle called the *Barbadoes*, thirty leagues northward of *St. Chriſtophers*; which by report of their informers and undertakers, for the excellency of the pleaſantneſs thereof, they called *Dulcina*, but when they came there, they found it ſuch a barren rock they left it; altho' they were told as much before, they would not believe it; perſuading themſelves thoſe contradicters would get it for themſelves, they were thus by their cunning opinion, the deceivers of themſelves; for ſeeing it lie conveniently for their purpoſe in a map, they had not patience to know the goodneſs or badneſs, the inconvenience or probability of the quantity or quality; which error doth predominate in moſt of our home bred adventurers, that will have all things as they *A great miſpriſon.*

they conceit and would have it; and the more they are contradicted, the more hot they are; but you may see by many examples in the general history, how difficult a matter it is, to gather the truth from amongst so many foreign and several relations, except you have exceeding good experience, both of the countries, people and their conditions; and those ignorant undertakings, have been the greatest hindrance of all those plantations.

Their numbers.

At last, because they would be absolute, they came to *Mevis*, a little isle by *St. Christophers*; where they seated themselves, well furnish'd with all necessaries, being about the number of an hundred, and since increased to an hundred and fifty persons, whereof many were old planters of *St. Christophers*, especially Mr. *Anthony Hinton*, and Mr. *Edward Thompson*. But because all those isles for the most part are so capable to produce, and in nature like each other, let this discourse serve for the description of them all. Thus much concerning those plantations, which now after all this time, loss and charge, should they be abandon'd, suppressed and dissolved, were most lamentable; and surely seeing they all strive so much about this tobacco, and that the fraught thereof, and other charges are so great, and so open to any enemy by that commodity, they cannot long subsist.

And it is a wonder to me to see such miracles and mischiefs in men; how greedily they pursue to dispossess the planters of the name of Christ Jesus, yet say they are christians, when so much of the world is unpossessed; yea, and better land than they so much strive for, murthering so many christians, burning and spoiling so many cities, villages and countries, and subverting so many kingdoms, when so much lieth wast, or only possessed by a few poor savages, that more serve the devil for fear, than God for love; whose ignorance we pretend to reform, but covetousness, humours, ambition, faction and pride hath so many instruments, we perform very little to any purpose; nor is there either honour or profit to be got by any that are so vile, to undertake the subversion, or hindrance of any honest intended christian plantation.

Certain exploits of captain Smith.

Now to conclude the travels and adventures of captain *Smith*; how first he planted *Virginia*, and was set ashore with about an hundred men in the wild woods; how he was taken prisoner by the savages, by the king of *Pamaunke* tied to a tree to be shot to dath; led up and down their countrey to be shewed for a wonder; fatted, as he thought, for a sacrifice for their idol, before whom they conjured him three days, with strange dances and invocations, then brought him before their emperor *Powhatan*, that commanded him to be slain; how his daughter *Pocahontas* saves his life, return'd him to *James-Town*, relieved him and his famished company, which was but eight and thirty to possess those large dominions; how he discover'd all the several nations upon the rivers falling into the bay of *Chisapeacke*; stung near to death with a most poisoned tail of a fish called stingray; how *Powhatan* out of countrey took the kings of *Pamaunke* and *Paspahegh* prisoners; forced thirty nine of those kings to pay him contribution; subjected all the savages; how *Smith* was blown up with gun-powder, and returned for *England* to be cured.

Also how he brought our *New-England* to the subjection of the kingdom of *Great-Britain*; his fights with the pirates, left alone amongst a many *French* men of war, and his ship ran from him; his sea-fights for the *French* against the *Spaniards*; their bad usage of him; how in *France* in a little boat he escaped them; was adrift all such a stormy night at sea by himself, when thirteen *French* ships were split or driven on shore by the isle of *Ree*, the general and most of his men drowned, when God, to whom be all honour and praise, brought him safe on shore to all their admirations that escaped; you may read at large in his general history of *Virginia*, the *Summer-Isles* and *New-England*.

CHAP. XXVIII.

The bad life, qualities and conditions of pirates; and how they taught the Turks *and* Moors, *to become men of war.*

As in all lands where there are many people, there are some thieves, so in all seas much frequented, there are some pirates; the most ancient within the memory of threescore years, was one *Callis*, who most refreshed himself upon the coast of *Wales*; *Clinton* and *Purser* his companions, who grew famous till queen *Elizabeth* of blessed memory hanged them at *Wapping*: *Flemming* was as expert and as much sought for as they, yet such a friend to his countrey, that discovering the *Spanish Armada*, he voluntarily came to *Plimouth*, yielded himself freely to my lord admiral, and gave him notice of the *Spaniards* coming; which good warning came so happily and unexpectedly; that he had his pardon, and a good reward; some few pirates there then remained; notwithstanding it is incredible how many great and rich prizes the little barques of the west country daily

daily brought home, in regard of their ſmall charge; for there are ſo many difficulties in a great navy, by wind and weather, victual, ſickneſs, loſing and finding one another, they ſeldom defray half the charge: But for the grace, ſtate and defence of the coaſt and narrow ſeas, a great navy is moſt neceſſary, but not to attempt any far voyage, except there be ſuch a competent ſtock, they want not wherewith to furniſh and ſupply all things with expedition. But to the purpoſe.

The difficulties of a great navy.

What occaſioneth pirates.

After the death of our moſt gracious queen *Elizabeth*, of bleſſed memory, our royal king *James*, who from his infancy had reigned in peace with all nations; had no imployment for thoſe men of war, ſo that thoſe that were rich reſted with that they had; thoſe that were poor, and had nothing but from hand to mouth, turned pirates; ſome, becauſe they became ſlighted of thoſe for whom they had got much wealth; ſome for that they could not get their due; ſome that had lived bravely, would not abaſe themſelves to poverty; ſome vainly, only to get a name; others for revenge, covetouſneſs, or as ill; and as they found themſelves more and more oppreſſed, their paſſions increaſing with diſcontent, made them turn pirates.

Their chief rendezvouz.

Now becauſe they grew hateful to all chriſtian princes, they retired to *Barbary*, where altho' there be not many good harbours, but *Tunis*, *Algier*, *Sally*, *Mamora*, and *Tituane*, there are many convenient roads, or the open ſea, which is their chief lordſhip: For their beſt harbours *Maſſalquebar*, the towns of *Oran*, *Mellila*, *Tangier*, and *Ceuta*, within the ſtreights, are poſſeſſed by the *Spaniards*; without the ſtreights they have alſo *Arzella* and *Mazagan*; *Mamora* they have likewiſe lately taken and fortified. *Ward*, a poor *Engliſh* ſailer, and *Danſker* a *Dutchman*, made firſt here their marts, when the *Moors* knew ſcarce how to ſail a ſhip; *Biſhop* was ancient and did little hurt; but *Eaſton* got ſo much as made himſelf a marqueſs in *Savoy*; and *Ward* lived like a baſhaw in *Barbary*; thoſe were the firſt that taught the *Moors* to be men of war. *Gennings*, *Harris*, *Tompſon*, and divers others, were taken in *Ireland*, a coaſt they much frequented, and died at *Wapping*. *Haws*, *Bough*, *Smith*, *Walſingham*, *Ellis*, *Collins*, *Sawkwel*, *Wollingſtone*, *Barrow*, *Wilſon*, *Sayres*, and divers others, all theſe were captains amongſt the pirates, whom king *James* mercifully pardon'd; and was it not ſtrange, a few of thoſe ſhould command the ſeas? Notwithſtanding the *Malteſes*, the pope, *Florentines*, *Genoeſes*, *French*, *Dutch* and *Engliſh* gallies and men of war, they would rob before their faces, and even at their own ports, yet ſeldom more than three four, five or ſix in a fleet; many times they had very good ſhips, and well mann'd, but commonly in ſuch factions amongſt themſelves, and ſo riotous, quarrellous, treacherous, blaſphemous and villanous, it is more than a wonder they could ſo long continue, to do ſo much miſchief; and all they got, they baſely conſumed it amongſt *Jews*, *Turks Moors* and whores.

Their conditions.

The beſt was, they would ſeldom go to ſea, ſo long as they could poſſibly live on ſhore, being compiled of *Engliſh*, *French*, *Dutch* and *Moors*, (but very few *Spaniards* or *Italians*) commonly running one from another, 'till they became ſo disjointed, diſordered, debauched and miſerable, that the *Turks* and *Moors* began to command hem as ſlaves, and force them to inſtruct hem in their beſt ſkill, which many an accurſed renegado or chriſtian turned *Turk* did, till they have made thoſe *Sallymen* or *Moors* of *Barbary* ſo powerful as they be, to the terror of all the *Streights*, and many times they take purchaſe in the main ocean, yea ſometimes in the narrow ſeas in *England*, and thoſe are the moſt cruel villains in *Turkey* or *Barbary*, whoſe natures are very noble and of good natures, in compariſon of them.

Renegadoes.

Advertiſement for wild beaſts.

To conclude, the miſery of a pirate, (altho' many are ſufficient ſeamen as any) yet in regard of its ſuperfluity, you ſhall find it ſuch, that any wiſe man would rather live amongſt wild beaſts, than them; therefore let all unadviſed perſons take heed how they entertain that quality; and I could wiſh merchants, gentlemen, and all ſetters forth of ſhips, not to be ſparing of a competent pay, nor true payment; for neither ſoldiers nor ſeamen can live without means, but neceſſity will force them to ſteal; and when they are once entred into that trade, they are hardly reclaimed. Thoſe titles of ſeamen and ſoldiers, have been moſt worthily honoured and eſteemed, but now regarded for the moſt part, but as the ſcum of the world; regain therefore your wanted reputations, and endeavour rather to adventure to thoſe fair plantations of our *Engliſh* nation; which however in the beginning were ſcorned, contemned, yet now you ſee how many rich and gallant people come from thence, who went thither as poor as any ſoldier or ſailor, and gets more in one year, than you by piracy in ſeven. I intreat you therefore to conſider how many thouſands yearly go thither; alſo how many ſhips and ſailors are imployed to tranſport them, and what cuſtom they yearly pay to our moſt royal king *Charles*, whoſe proſperity and his kingdom's good, I humbly beſeech the immortal God to preſerve and increaſe.

TWO

TWO

JOURNALS:

THE FIRST

Kept by ſeven SAILERS

IN THE

Isle of St. Maurice in *GREENLAND*,

In the years 1633, 1634;

Who paſs'd the winter, and all died in the ſaid ISLAND.

THE SECOND

Kept by ſeven other *SAILERS*, who in the years 1633 and 1634, wintered at *SPITSBERGEN*;

WITH

An account of their Adventures and Sufferings from the Bears and Whales, inſupportable cold and ſtorms, *&c*.

Done out of LOW-DUTCH.

TO THE

READER.

IT *having pleased God, the Creator and Preserver of the Universe, by whose uncontroulable will, the counsels of men are governed, to influence the committee of the* Greenland *company, to take a resolution of making the most exact enquiry that could be, concerning the true condition of the countrey of* Greenland, *during the winter: Concerning the nights there, and other curious observations (disputed among the astronomers) it was resolved to select seven of the boldest and ablest seamen, out of the fleet, who for that purpose should tarry there all the winter, which resolution being published, the following seven offered themselves for that service, and were accepted of accordingly:* Outgert Jacobson *of* Grootenbrook, *their commander*; Adrian Martin Carman *of* Schiedam, *Clerk*; Thaunifs Thauniffen *of* Shermerhem, *as cook*; Dick Peterson *of* Veenhuyse; Peter Peterson *of* Harlem; Sebastian Gyse *of* Delfts-Haven, *and* Gerard Beautin *of* Bruges. *These seven being left* 1633, *by their own choice, in the isle of St.* Maurice *in* Greenland, *the* Dutch *fleet set sail from thence the* 26th *of* August, *and the seamen left us the following account.*

TWO

TWO

JOURNALS:

THE FIRST,

Kept by Seven SAILERS in *GREENLAND*:

THE SECOND,

Kept by Seven other SAILERS at *SPITZBERGEN*, in the Years 1633 and 1634.

THE 26th of *August* our fleet set sail for *Holland* with a strong N. E. wind and a hollow sea, which continued all that night. The 27th, the wind still at N. E. we went four or five times up to an adjacent hill, but did not observe the least darkness all that night. The 28th the wind the same, it began to snow very hard; we then shar'd half a pound of tobacco betwixt us, which was to be our allowance for a week; towards evening we went about together, to see whether we could discover any thing worth our observation, but met with nothing. The 29th proving a sun-shiny and clear day, we ascended together in the afternoon the before mentioned hill, when, (and at several other times when it was clear weather) we could distinctly see the *Bears Mountain*. The 30th the wind turn'd to the N. W. with some snow in the afternoon, the night cloudy, the wind at N. E. The 31st, being a clear and sun-shiny day, we had a perfect sight of the *Bears Mountain*, with a fresh gale from the N. E. a fair star-light night.

The 1st of *September* prov'd a fair day, the wind at N. W. with some snow in the evening, and a windy night from the N. E. We went three or four times by the hill, but saw nothing. The 2d, the same wind continued, with some snow and cloudy night. The 3d, was a fair day, with some snow; the wind as the day before, which continued the 4th and 5th, with some snow; the night fair and star-light. The 6th, was a fair forenoon, but the night rainy, the wind the same. The 7th, the wind continued as before all the day, with fair weather, but turning to the S. E. by S. at night produced a great deal of rain. On the 8th 'twas a rainy morning, the wind at S. E. but in the afternoon fair, and the night star-light; at the beginning whereof we were frightned by a noise, as if something had fallen very heavy upon the ground, but saw nothing, the wind at S. E. still. The 9th, the wind the same; it prov'd a sun-shiny day, and so warm that we pull'd off our shirts and sported in the sun on the side of the hill; we had also a sight of the *Bears Mountain*; the night was rainy, the wind at S. E. The 10th was very stormy, the night rainy and the wind the same. The 11th was a foggy and rainy day, the wind at S. E. by S. but turn'd to the S. W. in the afternoon, and to the N. E. in the night, the weather cloudy; we made a shift to get some salleting, being fond of a change of diet. The 12th it blew hard from the N. E. the weather clear, but the night snowy, the wind as before. The 13th was a fair sun-shiny day, the wind at S. E. but the wind turning to the N. E. by N. it began to snow, the night was still and close, the wind at N. W. The 14th it was fair weather, the wind in the west, with some snow; we went up the hill, but saw nothing worth our observation, except that at night we observed the setting of the sun; the wind at N. W. by W. a clear night, and the wind at S. W. The 15th it blew very hard, so that the sea foam'd; we observ'd the sun from the S. to the S. W. when it clouded in, but the night prov'd star-light, the wind at W. The 16th it was a fair sun-shiny day, the wind at S. W. which made us go about to gather some herbs for salletting; it being a very star-light moon-shining night, we saw abundance of ſea-gulls. The 17th it blew very hard out of the S. W. which made the ſea foam, yet the day was clear and the night calm, the wind as before. The 18th it was a rainy day, the wind at S. W. by S. This was the firſt time we took each of us our allotment of brandy, being a certain meaſure which was to ſerve us for eleven days. The 19th it was a clear day, the wind at W. the night ſtar-light, the wind at S. E. The 20th it was ſun-ſhine, the wind at S. E. by S. we then diſcharged our great guns, having no more to fear from the *Biſcay* privateers for this ſeaſon; the night was ſtar-light, the wind at S. W. The 21[ſt], day and night miſty and rainy; the wind at S. W. The 22[d], it blew and rain'd very hard, the wind at S. W. The 23[d], being a cloudy day, the wind at E. we diſcover'd a whale near the ſhore, which made us ſet out our ſloop in order to catch him; but he got clear of us, it turning a dark ſky, with rain and miſt on a ſudden, and in the night it rain'd very hard; the wind at S. E. The 24th, the wind was at S. E. by S. with rainy weather in the forenoon, but the afternoon being fair, we went to the *Red-Hill* for ſome ſalletting, but found none; at night the wind was at S. E. The 25th proved very rainy in the morning, the wind at S. E. by E. but the afternoon and night it was very ſtormy weather. The 26th it was cold froſty weather, with an eaſterly wind. The 27th being a fair day, the wind at N. E. we went towards the ſouth-ſide of the iſle for ſome ſalletting, but found none, being ſpoiled by the cold rains; in the night the wind turn'd to the W. with very foul weather. The 28th a violent ſtorm aroſe from the north, with ſome ſnow and running clouds, but the night prov'd fair, the wind at S. E. The 29th it blew very hard from the S. E. with ſome ſnow, we obſerved the height of the ſun ſomething above the mountains; the night was fair, and the wind S. The 30th it was a cloudy rainy day, the wind at S. W. by W. the night proved very wet, mix'd with ſnow, and very ſtormy.

THE 1[ſt] of *October* it was fair in the morning, the wind at N. E, but in the afternoon ſtormy, and a cloudy night, the wind as before; it being froſty weather, we reſolved to go to the ſouth-ſide of the iſle. The 2[d] it froze ſo hard, that the ice would bear even on the ſouth part of the iſland, the wind the ſame as the day before: We found there a fine ſpring of freſh water, and the night was very clear, the wind at eaſt. The 3[d] the wind was the ſame in the forenoon, but turn'd to the weſt afterwards, with froſt and ſnow, but the night was very fair. The 4th prov'd a froſty day, the wind ſouth; in the morning we ſaw the *Bears Mountain*; the afternoon was very warm, and the night foggy and rainy, the wind very ſharp from the S. W. The 5th, the wind continued the ſame, with rain from morning till night, which made us keep our tents all that day; at night the wind turn'd to the ſouth. The 6th, the wind was the ſame, with froſty weather, we obſerved the ſun in the ſouth, from our huts, about half a pace above the hill; we alſo could ſee the *Bears Mountain:* In the night it blew very hard from the S. W. by S. with a hollow ſea and very dark ſky. The 7th it was very ſtormy, the wind at S. W. by W. we went upon the hill, but met with nothing there, the night proved very wet. The 8th the wind continued the ſame, in the morning with ſnow, but turn'd to the S. W. by S. in the afternoon; towards night it grew very tempeſtuous, which ſhook our huts to that degree, that we were not able to reſt, the ſtorm increaſing with ſnow and froſt till late in the night; the wind at N. E. and afterwards to the N. with a very hollow ſea. The 9th, the tempeſt continued with ſuch violence, that no ſhip could have rid ſafely at anchor, with froſt and ſnow, the waves riſing by the northerly wind above the fort. It being exceſſive cold, we began the firſt time to make a fire; we had ſtill very ſtrong winds from the N. E. by N. all that night, which continuing the ſame the 10th; the exceſſiveneſs of the cold forced us to keep at home near the fire ſide; we found a conſiderable alteration in our bodies, being troubled with a ſudden giddineſs in our heads, the wind the ſame as before. The 11th it was very cold and ſnowy weather, the wind at N. E. we had hung ſome of our linen in the air to whiten, but were glad to bring them near the fire, they being in a moment frozen as hard as a board; we went along the ſea-ſhore to the ſouthern rocks, but found nor ſaw any thing there. The 12th it froze, ſnow'd, and blew ſo very hard; that our barrel of beer, (tho' laid within a fathom from the fire) was frozen, the wind at N. E. we went upon the hill that day but ſaw nothing. The 13th the cold weather continued, we took a view about us on the hill as uſual, but diſcovered nothing, except that we ſee the ſun ſet between S. and W. very clear, the wind at the north; the beginning of the night was ſtar-light, but towards the morning it was ſtormy with ſnow. The 14th the wind and weather the ſame, and we obſerved the ſun to ſet at S. W. by W. part of the night was ſtar-light. The 15th in the morning, finding two whales caſt a-ſhore near the old furnace of *Amsterdam*, we went to work with our harp-irons, launces and hangers, but notwithstanding all our endeavours, they got clear of us by the advantage of the tide; the weather proved indifferently well that day, the wind as the day before; we went upon the hill but without seeing any thing. The 16th the weather continued very cold with snow, the wind the same, which occasioned no small alteration in our bodies; we took a view round about us on the hill, but observed nothing. The 17th it was still frosty weather, and cloudy, and blew very hard from the north; the evening was star-light; we went in the day upon the hill, but saw nothing. The 18th the frost continued, the wind N. we observed the sun to set at S. W. by N. or almost S. W. it was a very moon-light night. The 19th the wind kept in the N. we saw from the hill the *Bears Mountain*, and some ice we saw about a mile to the north of the shore; it was a sun shiny day, but the sun did not rise high enough to reach over the hill, into our huts in the bay; it was a bright moon-light night. The 20th being a fair day, the wind at N. E. we had sight of a bear, the first we saw here, but could not catch him; we saw great shoals of ice, a good way at sea, from the shore, and the night proved very cold, with an east wind. The 21st. it blow'd and snow'd very hard, with a N. E. wind, which continued all night, with very thick snow. The 22d it snow'd all day, and the night continued cloudy, the wind the same. The 23d was cloudy, the wind at N. E. we took a view again round about us from the hill, but saw nothing; the night was very fair. The 24th the wind and weather the same, with some frost, we went upon the red hill, where we saw nothing except the tracks of some beasts, whence we concluded that they began to come down towards the sea-side. The night was clear and frosty. The 25th we had an excessive cold, yet sun-shiny day, the wind at S. W. but the sun could not send its beams over the hills to our huts; it being a star-light night, a bear came in sight of our huts, but we could not take him; the wind was the same as the day before. The 26th the wind continuing the same corner, we went upon the hill, where we saw nothing but ice, the night was very clear, the wind at the W. The 27th it was fair weather, the wind the same, the night very clear and star-light. The 28th, the wind blew from the same corner all day and night, with clear frosty weather; we went up the hill but saw nothing. The 29th being an excessive cold day, the wind in the N. not only the bay, but also the sea, as far we could see, was full of ice; in the night it snowed very hard, the wind as before. The 30th it continued freezing very hard, with the same wind, and the sea was so full of ice, that we could see no water; the night proved very tempestuous. The 31st the north-wind produced such an excessive frost and snow, that not the least drop of water was to be seen, wherever you turn'd yourself, and some of our vessels were frozen to pieces, tho' we sav'd our beer and other strong liquors, by putting them in the buttery cellar.

The 1st of *November*, a N. E. wind vehemently encreased the cold, so that when we came upon the hill, we could see nothing but ice on the north-side; yet we had still ten hours day, tho' we seldom got sight of the sun-beams, the same not appearing except on the south-side, whither we could not come by reason of the snow and ice. Towards evening we got sight of a bear, but he no sooner saw us making up towards him, but he saved himself upon the ice at sea, these creatures being excessive shy here; the cold grew so fierce by this time, that to preserve our beer, and other liquors, we were forced to kindle a fire in the buttery cellar. Towards night, the bears appeared in such numbers about our hutts, that we scarce durst venture abroad; the wind continued as before. The 2d, it being a very hard frost, we discovered five or six bears upon the ice in the bay, whereof we kill'd one, but the rest saved themselves upon the ice. The 3d, it was tolerable good weather, the wind at N. E. we saw four bears, one whereof being kill'd by a gun, he got upon the ice in the bay, but was pull'd ashore by the help of some ropes we had by us. The night was star-light, and the wind as before. The 4th, the wind being at N. E. it froze very hard, tho' it was very cloudy; we saw three bears, but we could shoot none of them, they betaking themselves immediately to the ice at sea; the wind was W. The 5th a south wind produced so violent a snow, that we durst not venture out of our huts; we had of late not seen any sea gulls; all that night the wind continued in the south, as well as the 6th, with some tempestuous weather, the wind turned east in the night. The 7th it was still, the wind at N. E. we went up the hill, but discovered nothing; the wind turning to the north in the night, fill'd the bay with great shoals of ice. The 8th the wind continued at the north, with excessive cold weather; for want of water we were forced to make use of melted snow. The 9th, the north-wind holding still, we made shift to get to the southern shore, where we saw no ice, but plainly discovered the sun, this being the first time we had sight of of it in 21 or 22 days laſt paſt, being then above half an hour above the horizon; the wind continued in the north, all that night as well as the next day, being the 10th when we got ſight of a great number of bears. The 11th the north wind encreaſed, with thick clouds; at night the wind turned N. E. which continued the 12th, with very thick fogs, we went upon the hill, but could ſee nothing but ice, and ſome ſea-gulls; the night proved very light by reaſon of the moon; the wind at eaſt. The ſame wind continuing the 13th, it froze moſt ſeverely; and the 14th the wind turned to the weſt; the cold weather held on and brought vaſt quantities of ice into the bay; it was a bright moon-ſhiny night, but we ſaw no bears that day, tho' the next being the 15th we ſaw three or four, but had only the pleaſure of ſeeing them, they not coming within the reach of our guns. The 16th the wind continued in the ſame corner all that day and night; we let fire at a bear that came in ſight of us, but miſſing him he betook himſelf to the ice in the bay. The 17th the wind turned to the north, with dark ſnowy weather, yet the cold was not ſo exceſſive as before. The 18th the froſt encreaſed again with a N. E. wind, which however prov'd very tolerable to us hitherto; we ſpending moſt of our time in rehearſing to one another, the adventures that had befaln us both by ſea and land; it prov'd a very fair and ſtar-light night. The 19th the wind turning to the north again, we paſs'd the hill to the ſouth-ſide, yet not without a great deal of difficulty, being often knee deep in the ſnow; we then had a full ſight of the *Bears-Mountain*, and ſaw the ſun juſt above the ſurface of the ſea, having yet ſo much daylight left, that we could write and read in the open air, but not within our huts, which made us very melancholy; the wind continued the ſame as it did the 20th, with dark ſnowy weather; in the night the wind turning to the weſt, continued there the 21ſt, when going up the hill we looked to the north-ſide, but could ſee nothing but ice. The 22d, the wind held weſterly, with very cold weather. The 23d the wind ſhifted to the N. W. by W. and being a fair day, we paſſed the hill to the *Red-hill*, but could ſee nothing but ice wherever we turned our faces; two or three bears came within ſight of us, but not within the reach of our guns: The beginning of the night proving very clear and calm, we diſcover'd a bear, at whom we diſcharged our guns immediately (they being always ready charged) and wounded him ſorely, as we found by the tracks of blood near the ſea-ſhore; yet he eſcaped to the ice, nothing being more frequent than to be ſhot quite thro' the body, without receiving much harm. The 24th proving a cloudy dark day, a S. E wind forced moſt of the ice out of the bay into the ſea, but yet not quite out of ſight; at night the wind turning to the weſt, the bay was filled again with ice; the weather being very froſty; we ſaw a vaſt quantity of ſea-gulls, but they kept cloſe among the mountains; the wind as before. The 25th the wind being in the W. with froſty weather, we ſaw a vaſt number of ſea-gulls, but they returned to the mountains before night; the wind was as before. The 26th the wind turning to the ſouth, it prov'd a tolerable mild day, and moſt of the ice was carried out of the bay into the ſea; the wind as before. The 27th it was fair weather, the wind at S. W. but turned to the eaſt in the night. The 28th the wind was at S. E. with fair weather; we got ſight of a bear again, whom we purſued over the hill, but he proving too nimble for us, eſcaped our hands. The weather was (to our great ſurpriſe) ſo mild for theſe five or ſix days laſt paſt, that we believed the cold to be no more intenſe here than it was in *Holland*; at the ſame time the wind as before. The 29th, the wind continuing the ſame, we went over the hill again to the ſouth-ſide of the iſle, where we found all covered with ice; tho' at the ſame time there was ſcarce any ice to be ſeen within half a mile of the northern ſhore; it was a ſtar-light night. The 30th the wind blew from the ſame corner, and ſeeing ſome bears, we made what haſte we could after them, but in vain, not being able to overtake them; the wind continued as before, with violent rains.

The 1ſt of *Dec.* a ſouthern wind produced ſome rain, but turned to the S. E. at night. The 2d the wind continued the ſame, with rainy weather, which carried the ice from the ſhore to the N. at ſea: It continued thawing all that night, the weather mild. The 3d the wind at S. with rainy weather and ſtrong winds at night. The 4th the wind continuing day and night the ſame, with cloudy weather, we heard ſome bears near our huts, and purſued two or three of them, but could take none. The 5th the wind ſtill ſouth, with mild calm weather, ſo that to the beſt of our judgment, it could ſcarce be better in *Holland* at that time of the year: We ſhot one bear as we perceived by the track of blood; but he had ſtrength enough to get upon the ice, out of our reach. The 6th the wind blew from the S. E. cloudy ſky, but mild weather, with a ſtar-light night; the wind as before. The 7th the wind continued the ſame with foggy weather; but the wind turning to the ſouth, at night it began to ſnow, and the froſt return'd. The 8th a N. E. wind produced a dark a dark and frosty day, but at night it turn'd to the west: Which continued thus the 9th, with very clear and cold weather, there being nothing but ice to be seen as far as our eyes could reach. It was a frosty star-light night. The 10th was a bright day, the wind still at west; we found our selves surrounded on all sides with nothing but ice, it being a moon-shiny night, we discovered three or four bears, one of which we wounded in two places, yet he escaped our hands upon the ice: We went upon the hill, from whence we could discern nothing but ice; the wind continued at west all night, and the 11th with fair weather, but could discover no bears that day; those that had once heard or felt the effects of our guns, beginning to be very shy; it was a very frosty night. The 12th in the morning, we had the good fortune to shoot a bear on the head, who dropt immediately; we roasted a leg of him immediately, which happened to be a young one, it relish'd exceedingly well with us, having fed upon nothing but salt meat for a considerable time. The wind held still in the west, with very cold weather, and a calm moon-light night. The 13th was a cloudy dark day, the wind at S. W. we went cross the hill to the *Red-Hill*, but saw nothing but vast heaps of ice in the sea, to the north-side; at night the wind turned to the S. E. with snow. The 14th proved a clear frosty day, the wind at the south, and a bright moon-light night; we found the ice removed from the shore, a great way into the sea. The 15th the wind being the same, it proved a dark day, and the ice was forced back into the bay: In the night (which was exceeding dark) the wind changed to the S. W. The 16th, the wind continuing as before, we went up the hill, but observed nothing; it was a moon-light night. The 17th prov'd a very cloudy dark day, the wind still at south. We went again up the hill, but saw nothing; it snowed and thawed very hard at night, with the same south wind, which brought us abundance of sea-gulls (as it frequently does) to the sea-side; these make the same noise, here, as they do at *Holland* in *May*, but retire every night among the mountains, their ordinary receptacle. The 18th was a rainy dark day; the wind still at south, which changed to the E. the 19th with a hard frost, and a calm and cloudy night; the wind as before, which continued the 20th with calm weather, and a dark night. The 21st, the wind kept still in the same corner, with dark snowy weather, the snow lying so high upon the ground, that we could not stir out without boots; it froze and snow'd severely, the wind at north. The 22d in the morning, we found the bay fill'd with ice again, but the cold was so severe, that this was the coldest day we had met with as yet; we had still four hours day-light; the night was star-light and calm. The 23d an easterly wind produced a bright frosty day and stormy night, with so much snow, that we durst scarce venture out of our huts, but could see the ice turn'd back into the bay; the wind still at east, which continued the 24th, with a foggy air; yet the latter part of the night was star-light, with a hard frost and storm from the N. E. The 25th, a south wind produced a fair day, but at night the wind turned to the north. The 26th it was a clear frosty day, the wind at E. but turn'd to the N. W. at night. The 27th, the wind and weather as before, but the night proved dark and calm, with an easterly wind, which continued thus the 28th, with very dark snowy weather: In the night it blew hard out of the west, with so violent a snow, that we could not stir out of our huts; weather and wind as before. The 29th the wind veering about to the west, produced a clear and excessive cold day, the fore-part of the night prov'd star-light and calm, but the wind turning afterwards to the S. E. it snowed very hard; we found the bay clear of ice in the morning. The 30th it blew hard from the S. W. it was a cloudy but calm day; we saw neither bears nor fish. The 31st proved an indifferent good calm day. a S. W. wind produced a great deal of snow in the night, but the cold was very tolerable.

In the year 1634, the 1st of *January*, having wished one another a happy new year, and good success in our enterprise, we went to prayers to disburthen our hearts before God; the weather was dark, cold and frosty, and the wind as before; two bears came near our huts, but being a dark day and a very deep snow, it was impossible to take them. The 2d of *January* a N. E. wind produced a clear day; and the ice was forced out of the bay to sea, yet remained within sight; the fore-part of the night was star-light, but afterwards an east wind brought a cloudy sky along with it. The 3d it rained a little, the wind at S. E. which encreased at night, the wind blowing hard from the S. W. The 4th we had a fierce westerly wind and cold weather; the bay was so filled with ice again, that we could see no water. The night was pretty mild, with an easterly wind; which continued the 5th with a thick fog and frost; the night was star-light, the wind at W. The 6th was a clear frosty day, the wind at N. which increased all night with some snow. The 7th the wind and weather continued

tinued as before, but with abundance of ſnow, more than we obſerved before, ſince our coming hither; beſides which, it froze hard all the day and night, that we durſt not venture to ſtir abroad, for fear of being ſwallow'd up in ſome pit or other fill'd with ſnow. The 8th the wind blew from the N. E. with very froſty weather, but turned cloudy afterwards; the night was exceſſive cold and ſtormy; whereof we now began to feel the effects in our bodies. The 9th the wind and weather continued as before, and the bay was fill'd with ſuch vaſt ice-ſhoals, that at a diſtance they appear'd from the tops of our huts, (where we uſed often to make our ſpeculations) like white hills or land-ſkies; it was a clear moon-light night, tho' we never got ſight of the moon, before ſhe was ſeven or eight days old, by reaſon of the high hills betwixt her and us; the wind and weather continued as before. The 10th, a N. E. wind produced a bright, calm and pleaſant day, but exceſſive cold, whereof we found the effects. The bay continued full of ice; the greateſt part of the night was ſtar-light, but very cold, which ſeem'd likely to hold. The 11th the forenoon proved clear and calm, but the wind turning to the ſouth in the afternoon, it was cloudy, but nevertheleſs cold, which not a little annoy'd us, eſpecially after the wind brought with it a vaſt quantity of ſnow from the S. E. The 12th, the ſame wind and ſnow continued, ſo that we could not ſtir out, tho' the cold was not altogether ſo exceſſive as for ſome days before; in the night the wind and the weather continued as before; and in the morning the ice was forced out to ſea, quite out of ſight. The 13th a S. E. wind brought abundance of ſnow, and ſeeing a bear near our huts, we kill'd him with a fuſee upon the ſpot, and ſo drawing him with roaps into our tent, flay'd him, the weather being ſo cold, and ſnow ſo high, that we could not do it without doors; the night was very clear. The 14th it being a tolerable clear day, the wind at eaſt, we went croſs the hill to the *Red-hill*, but ſaw nothing; it was a moon-light night, and the ſtars appeared ſometimes; the wind as before. The 15th it was a ſtrong eaſterly wind with ſnow, we ſaw the ice about a mile from the ſhore; the night was moon-light, the wind at N. E. The 16th a ſouth wind produced good tolerable weather; for we made this obſervation during our ſtay here, that with a ſouth wind the weather was not ſo cold as otherwiſe; in the night the wind turned to the eaſt; it was a dark but froſty night. The 17th the wind continued as before, with cold foggy weather; at night the wind turning to the north, it froze ſo fiercely that the whole bay was cover'd with ice, there being not the leaſt water to be ſeen in the morning. The 18th was a cold foggy day; in the afternoon the wind turned to the weſt, and in the night it began to ſnow, the wind as before, which continued thus the 19th, with abundance of ſnow, ſo that we were not able to ſtir abroad. The 20th the ſnow continued with a weſterly wind, which lay ſo high, that we ſcarce peept out of our tent or hut; tho' for the reſt, it was not quite ſo cold, as ſome days before; and in the Night an eaſterly wind brought us more ſnow. The 21ſt the ſame wind continued very ſtrong, with a violent ſnow; in the night the wind turn'd to the weſt. The 22d the ſnow and weſterly wind continued with great vehemency, which was follow'd by a very hard froſt at night. The 23d it was a clear froſty morning, which made us get a little way out of our huts, (tho' not without a great deal of difficulty) to the ſouth ſide of the iſle, to obſerve the heighth of the ſun; but growing cloudy ſoon after, could not make an exact obſervation; however, we ſaw in the bay thereabouts, the ice and ſnow at leaſt 6 foot high; the wind was eaſt all night, ſometimes we could ſee the ſtars; the weather as before. The 24th a weſt wind had blown the ice a great way into the ſea; it was firſt clear weather, then ſnowy and ſtar-light in the beginning of the night; but in the morning a ſouth wind produced a cloudy ſky. The 25th the ſtrong ſouth wind and clouds continued, with a very cold night. The 26th it ſnow'd hard, the wind at weſt: At night we ſaw the ice again all over the bay; at night (which was cloudy) the wind turn'd to the ſouth. The 27th the wind being weſt, it proved a mild cloudy day, and more ice was forced into the bay; the night was dark and ſnowy, with an eaſt wind. The 28th the wind was at weſt at firſt, but veering about to the S. E. it began to ſnow; the ſame night the ice was carried a good way into the ſea again. The 29th the wind turn'd to the S. W. and to the W. at night, with dark rainy weather: In the morning the bay was full of ice again; the wind and weather as before. The 30th proving a calm, clear and froſty day, we went (tho' not without a great deal of difficulty) upon the hill; and looking to the ſouth, obſerved (according to gueſs) the ſun about an hour and half high. In the night the wind turn'd to the eaſt, with fair weather; the ſtars appeared ſometimes; the wind and weather as before. The 31ſt a weſterly wind brought us abundance of ſnow, in the night the wind turn'd to the north, with ſtar-light froſty weather.

The

The 1ſt of *Feb.* the wind continuing as before; it was clear and calm weather, which made us go upon the hill, where we ſaw the body of the ſun very clear; and on the north-ſide of the iſle nothing but ice as far as we could ſee; the night was very calm and ſtar-light. The 2^{d}, a N. E. wind produced clear but very cold weather, with a bright moon-light night, to our no ſmall ſatisfaction; we found the bears to grow very ſhy of us, for we ſeldom ſaw any; the wind and weather as before. The 3^{d} the wind was eaſterly, the weather the ſame, but the night was ſomewhat cloudy, with a S. E. wind; it was not ſo cold as before. The 4th the wind continued as the day before, in the forenoon, when the ice was carried out of the bay into the ſea; in the afternoon the wind turn'd to the ſouth, with ſnowy weather, but was not ſo cold as before; it was a ſtar-light night. The 5th it was a ſullen day, the wind at S. E. and at the eaſt in the night, with ſome ſnow; but the cold was ſomewhat abated. The 6th the wind continued as before; the weather calm and cloudy; the wind turning to the S. W. it proved a very clear and moon-ſhiny night. The 7th it blew ſtrong from the E. the weather cloudy. The 8th was a very calm day, the wind at ſouth; the ice was carried away quite from the ſhore, beyond the reach of our eye-ſight; it was a clear moon-light night. The 9th the wind being northerly, it ſnowed ſo violently, that we could not ſtir abroad, it continued thus all night; the wind at ſouth. The 10th proved a pretty mild day, tho' the wind was at the N. but turn'd to the S. W. at night, which was very dark and ſtormy. The 11th was a cloudy day, the wind at the ſouth, but turned to the eaſt at night, but tolerable good weather. The 12th the wind continued the ſame, with ſome ſnow; it was a dark night, but not exceſſive cold, conſidering the climate and ſeaſon. The 13th the wind ſtood ſtill in the ſame corner, with ſnowy but calm weather; and it was a moon-light night. The 14th we had the ſame wind, and a clear day; but in the night it thawed and grew very ſtormy. The 15th the wind blew as yet from the eaſt, and the ſnow was ſo high, that we ſunk to the waſte in it, ſo ſoon as we ſtir'd out of our huts. The ſame wind continued the 16th, the weather pretty mild, but cloudy: This day we got ſight of two wild-fowls, which in reſpect of their bigneſs, did appear to us not unlike geeſe, but were ſo ſhy, that they would not come within reach of our guns, we alſo eſpied a faulcon, but could likewiſe not come near enough to hit him. The 17th the wind blew ſtill from the eaſt, and had a great deal of ſnow: In the night the ſtars appeared ſometimes. The 18th the wind continued the ſame, with cloudy but mild weather. The 19th it was eaſterly wind ſtill; and being a fair day, we made ſhift to get over the hill to the *Red-Hill*, but ſaw nothing worth taking notice of, not ſo much as any ice; the weather as before. The 20th the weather and wind continued with very little alteration, and was tolerably mild. The 21ſt the wind turned to the N. E. with very bright weather, which made us again get up the hill (tho' not without a great deal of trouble) but could ſee nothing worth mentioning. The night proved fair and calm, but afterwards froſty with ſome ſnow. The 22^{d} the wind continued N. E. with much ſnow; the night was dark and froſty. The 23^{d} the wind blew out of the ſame corner; the weather was very cold, which brought abundance of ice into the bay, but the main ſea was clear of it as far as we could ſee; the night was dark and froſty. The 24th an eaſterly wind produced a moſt violent froſt; the day cloudy, but the night clear, with a north wind, which held the 25th, with a cloudy ſky; in the afternoon it clearing up in the weſt, we ſaw the ſun again the firſt time from our huts, and found it to ſet at S. W. by W. the night was very dark. The 27th it was very calm and mild weather, but at night a ſouth wind brought us a thaw. The 28th the ſouth wind and open weather continued, the ice being forced out of the bay into the main ſea, yet not quite out of ſight, the night was very dark, the wind at S. W.

The 1ſt of *March* the wind and weather continued as before, with ſome ſunſhine in the forenoon, but afterwards it changed and proved rainy: We ſaw the ſun-beams on the S. W. of our hut; the night was very dark, with a S. W. wind. The 2^{d} it blew hard from the W. the weather clear and cold; the night was dark and froſty, and the wind very high from the N. E. The 3^{d} the wind and weather continued with little alteration; a violent north wind forced the ice into the bay, but in ſmall pieces. The 4th the wind turned to the N. E. with cloudy, but calm weather; the cold very tolerable. The 5th was cloudy, the wind at N. E. the night the ſame. The 6th the wind and weather continued as the day before; the night proved very calm and pleaſant, yet by reaſon of the ſnow we could not as yet ſtir from our huts. The 7th it was cloudy but calm, and the night ſtormy from the N. E. The 8th the wind continued as before, with dark and cloudy weather, but a ſtar-light night. The 9th the wind blew ſtill from the

the same corner; both the day and night were cloudy with a sharp frost. The 10th it froze very hard, the wind at N. E. with excessive cold weather; the night was very clear and frosty. The 11th the weather changed on a sudden, being a calm pleasant sun-shiny day; the south wind in the night brought us such pleasant weather, that we extremely rejoyced at it. The 12th the same wind continued, and the ice was carried out of the bay into the main sea, beyond the reach of our eye-sight; the night proved dark, but not very cold; the wind at S. E. The 13th was a cloudy day; in the night the wind and weather as before, very dark, but only moderately cold, the wind at N. E. The 14th it blew all day and all night, being very cold from the N. E. The 15th the wind turning to the south, produced milder weather; and perceiving a bear near our huts (a thing we had not seen many days before) we let fly at him so successfully, that he dropt down dead upon the spot; being glad to find our selves some imployment, and to feed upon fresh meat (having lived upon powdered beef for a considerable time) we soon flay'd him, and having hung his skin up in the air to dry, we feasted upon part of the flesh, and sprinkled the rest with a little salt only, by reason we were exceedingly afflicted with the scurvy; the night proved dark, the wind at S. W. The 16th the wind continued the same, but the weather was very cold; we fix'd some traps to catch foxes, and in the night the wind turn'd to the N. which held thus the 17th, with cloudy weather, and fill'd the bay with ice from the sea; at night the wind was as before, which continued thus the 18th, being a cloudy, but frosty day, but a star-light night. The 20th proving a calm sun-shiny day, we went upon the hill, but could discover nothing, (as far as we could see) but ice; the night was cloudy, the wind in the south, which held thus the 21st, with dark rainy weather, the ice was all caried out to sea again; the night was cloudy, the wind still in the south. The 22d the wind turn'd to the S. E. with thick clouds; for want of refreshments we began to be very heartless, being afflicted with the scurvy to that degree, that our legs were scarce able to bear us; the night was cloudy, and the wind as before. The 24th proved a pretty pleasant sun-shiny day; in the afternoon the wind shifted to the S. E. with some snow clouds; the night was exceeding dark. The 25th was a sun-shiny and calm day, from morning till night; towards evening a southerly wind produced some clouds, but the night proved clear again and calm. The 26th the sea had forced the ice into the bay again; the day was very bright, the wind at S. E. and S. the night was very clear. The 27th the same wind continued with fair and clear weather both day and night. The 28th proved a cloudy day, the wind at S. E. The ice was carried so far into the sea, out of the bay, that we could scarce see it. The same day we saw a whale, a huge beast, in the bay, but could not come at him: This day going also over the hill to the *Red-Hill*, we spied from thence five whales near the shore, and towards evening four more in the bay, being ten in all we had seen that day; had we had hands enough, and been provided with instruments for such a purpose, we might have taken as many of these fish, as would have freighted a good fleet immediately, without being obliged to stay for the taking of them after their arrival, as they generally do: The wind and weather was in the night as before. The 29th a southerly wind produced a cloudy, but very mild day: Innumerable whales appeared near the shore that day, so that had we not wanted men and tools, we might have made a considerable advantage, which we now durst not so much as attempt, being but seven in all, and disabled by the scurvy: In the night the wind and weather as before, which continued the 30th, when we saw abundance of fishes, as we did almost every day after; the night was very dark, the wind as before. The 31st it blew a brisk gale from the N. E. with some snow; we got sight of four or five whales again, which came so near the shore, that they were likely to have been cast upon the sands; but if they had, we had not strength enough to have catch'd them: We saw likewise a she bear with three young ones, about the bigness of a small sheep: We did what we could to kill them, but our first shot failing, they all got of, to our grief, tho' it was no unpleasant sight to see the young ones follow the old: In the night the wind and weather as before.

The first of *April* was a cloudy day, the wind at E. We saw four or five whales again at the entrance of the bay, but had only the pleasure of looking at them; the night was star-light, the wind in the south. The 2d proved a snowy day, the wind at S. E. but not very cold; the night was dark, the wind as before. The 3d the wind turning to the W. produced a cloudy day; there being at this time no more than two of us in health, (the rest being very ill and crippled by the scurvy) we killed the only two pullets we had left, at their request, and they fed pretty heartily upon them, in hopes it might prove a means to recover part of their strength, which was much decayed

cayed and which we heartily wished, being sorry we had not a dozen more for their sake: In the night the weather and wind was much the same as before, which continued thus all day and all night. The 4th a westerly wind produced a sun-shiny day. The 5th we saw two very large whales in the bay; the night was dark, the wind at S. E. The 6th it was clear weather, but the night dark, the wind N. E. we saw four or five whales more in the bay; at night the wind and the weather as before, which continued the 8th, with cold sun-shiny weather; we saw innumerable whales both at sea and in the bay: In the night the wind and the weather continued as before, and so it did the 9th, when we saw abundance of whales again; the night was cold and frosty, the wind at north. The 10th, the wind continued the same, with very clear weather; the bay was full of ice, and we saw some whales, in the night the wind and weather as before. The 11th we saw neither fishes nor bears, having not seen any of the last these several days; it continued to be very cold weather; in the night the wind as before. The 12th the wind turning to the N. E. it proved a very clear frosty day; at night the wind and weather as before, which continued the 13th; the bay was full of ice, the night very cold and dark. The 14th the wind held still in the same corner, with sun-shine; at night the wind turning to the south, the ice was carried out of the bay, a great way from the shore. The 15th proved a calm mild day, we saw four whales in the bay, tho' we don't now stir out so often as formerly, our clerk being very ill; the greatest part of the night the wind was at west. The 16th being *Easter-day*, our clerk died, the Lord have mercy upon his soul, and upon us all, we being all very sick; the wind was at W. with a clear day and dark night. The 17th the wind continued as the day before, but was very cloudy, the bay was full of ice again; the greatest part of the night weather and wind as before. The 19th both wind and weather proved as the day before; and now having not the least refreshment left, we grew worse and worse every day, and that without any hopes of recovery, partly for want of necessaries, partly by reason of the excessiveness of the cold; for being scarce able, whilst in health, to keep ourselves tolerably warm, by exercising our bodies, we were but in little hopes of doing it now we were sick, and not able to stir out of our cabins, all our dependence being on God's mercy; the wind and weather as before. The 20th proved a cloudy day, the wind at S. we saw the ice forced a great way to the N. at sea, the night was snowy, with an easterly wind. The 21st was a bright calm and sun-shiny day, but we could make but slender observations, being not able to stir from our huts, by reason of the scurvy, which encreases upon us every day; the night was cloudy, the wind at N. E. which continued thus the 22d; the ice was forced so near the shore, that we could scarce see any water; at night a south wind carried the ice quite out of sight again. The 23d the wind blew from the same corner with small rain; we were by this time reduced to a very deplorable state, there being none of them all, except myself, that were able to help themselves, much less one another; so that the whole burthen lay upon my shoulders, and I perform my duty as well as I am able, as long as God pleases to give me strength: I am just now a going to help our commander out of his cabin, at his request, because he imagined by this change to ease his pain, he then struggling with death; the night was dark, and the wind as before. The 24th was a cloudy day and night, the wind at S. which continued the 25th with some sun-shine: The ice kept about half a mile from the shore to the north-side, but on the south-side of the same bay, no ice was to be seen. We had sight of many whales again; the night was dark, with a strong N. W. wind; the ice was forced nearer to the shore, tho' there remained a good interval of water betwixt both; the wind and weather as before. The 26th it was a calm, but cloudy day, the night fair, the wind at W. The 27th it was thawing weather: That day we kill'd our dog for want of other refreshment; the night was cloudy, yet without rain, the wind at E. which continued thus the 28th, with cloudy weather: The ice was this day carried to sea, quite out of sight; the night was cloudy with a strong N. wind. The 29th the wind and weather as before, but turn'd to blow hard from the N. E. at night. The 31st was a clear sun-shiny day, with the same wind: [*Die*] *Memorandum.* This word *DIE*, was the last, questionless he writ, intending probably to set down afterwards his observation concerning the night, according to his usual way. This person being one, who (according to the report of others) had learned to write of the other six, he writ as long as he was able, *viz.* to the last day of *April*; when perhaps, being seized by a fainting fit, he was forced to retire to his cabin, where he delivered up his soul to his creator, as will appear more fully by the following additions.

 Among

AMong all the ſhips that were ſent the next year from *Holland* to *Greenland*, thoſe of *Zealand* being the firſt that came in ſight of the iſle of *St. Maurice*, ſome of the ſeamen being eager to know what was become of their comrades, went aſhore in a boat, ſtriving who ſhould be the firſt to come to their huts, tho' by their not appearing upon the ſea-ſide, they did not preſage any good to themſelves. They were no ſooner entred the hut, but they found they were not deceived in their gueſs, every one of the poor wretches, left there laſt year, lying dead in their cabins, the news whereof they brought to their commander.

The firſt of theſe ſeven unfortunate fellows, died the 16th of *April* 1634, whom they had put in a coffin, and depoſited in one of the huts. The other ſix died in the beginning of *May*, as we believe by the concluſion of the journal at the end of *April*.

The before-mention'd ſhips of *Zealand* came to an anchor in the bay of *St. Maurice*'s iſle the 4th of *June* 1634, where they found the dead carcaſſes of theſe unfortunate wretches, each in his own hut; near one of them ſtood ſome bread and cheeſe, upon which probably he had fed not long before his death; another had a box with ointment by his cabin-ſide, wherewith he had rubb'd his teeth and joints, his arm being ſtill extended to his mouth; there alſo lay a prayer-book near him, wherein he had been reading; the reſt being found each in his cabin.

If we ſeriouſly reflect upon the condition of theſe wretches, it muſt needs have been very miſerable, eſpecially after all were fallen ſick, ſo as not to be able to aſſiſt one another; eſpecially in reſpect of him that out-lived the reſt, being the ſame, who according to his own teſtimony, attended them to the laſt; and had learn'd to write from the others, as did appear by his hand-writing, till the concluſion of the journal, who, as we gueſs, lived ſome days after he left off writing; it being very probable, that ſome might grow ſooner ſtiff, by the exceſſive cold, than others, in proportion of the quantity of natural heat they had left; tho' it is beyond all queſtion, that the ſource of their diſtemper was the ſcurvy, occaſioned by their ſalt food without any manner of refreſhment, which having put the cramp into their limbs, and rendred them incapable of exerciſe, they ſoon grew quite ſtiff, and were quite overcome by the cold; it being certain, that without the ſcurvy they needed not have dreaded the cold, which was not ſo exceſſive, but that once within three or four days they could ſtir abroad, after the ſnow was a little ſettled.

Our commodore had no ſooner received the diſmal news from the ſeamen that had been aſhore, but he order'd the ſix dead carcaſſes to be put in coffins, and to be buried with the ſeventh under the ſnow, till the ground ſhould become more pliable; which being done, they were afterwards, *viz.* on St. *John*'s day, honourably interr'd (according to the circumſtances of time and place) under a general diſcharge of the cannon of the whole fleet.

It is furthermore left to the conſideration of the courteous reader, that he was appointed clerk for this deſign, having never been in that ſtation before, his want of ability ought to plead ſtrongly for the ſimplicity of theſe obſervations; which having (at the requeſt of ſome friends) been put to the preſs, were publiſhed, and made as intelligible as the nature of the matter would allow of, without impoſing upon the publick, which has been done with the utmoſt ſincerity, after the true original, which ſtill remains in my cuſtody, in oppoſition to divers fabulous relations, which have been publiſhed upon the ſame ſubject.

A SHORT

A SHORT JOURNAL OF Seven other SEAMEN, who being left in 1634, AT SPITZBERGEN, To pass the Winter, died there in 1635.

IN the year 1633, seven persons being left much at the same time as well at *Spitzbergen*, as in the isle of *St. Maurice*; the ships that were sent thither in 1634, had orders from the *Greenland* company, to release those that had stay'd there, and to leave in their room seven others, who should offer their service for that purpose. Accordingly the following seven were (with their consent) appointed to remain the next following winter at *Spitzbergen*; *Andrew Johnson* of *Middleburgh*, *Cornelius Thysse* of *Rotterdam*, *Jerome Carcoen* of *Delfts-Haven*, *Tiebke Jellis* of *Friseland*, *Nicholas Florison* of *Hoorn*, *Adrian Johnson* of *Delft*, *Fettje Otters* of *Friseland*.

These being provided with all manner of necessaries, as meat, drink, physical preparations, herbs, &c. were left ashore to continue all the winter there; during which time, they kept a journal of all remarkable occurrences; the chief heads whereof I thought only fit to insert here, leaving out the more unnecessary observations, such as of the wind and weather, &c. to avoid prolixity. The 11th of *September* 1634, the ships being sail'd thence for *Holland*, they got sight of abundance of whales, at whom they discharged their guns, but could not take any; they went also in search for green herbs, foxes and bears, but met with none. The 20th or 21st of *October*, they had no more sight of the sun. The 24th of *November* the scurvy beginning to appear among them, they search'd very earnestly after green herbs, bears and foxes, but to their great grief could find neither of them; so they comforted one another with hopes that God would provide for them something or other for their refreshment. The 2[d] of *December* *Nicholas Florison* took a dose of a scorbutic potion, and they set some traps to catch foxes. The 11th, *Jerome Carcoen*, took such another potion; and they resolved for the future, every one to eat separately from the other, some being not so much afflicted with the scurvy as the rest. They went often in quest after some refreshments, but meeting with none, they recommended themselves to God's providence. The 12th *Cornelius Thysse* did likewise take a medicinal potion against the scurvy. The 23[d], as the cook was throwing out some water, he saw a bear just by the hut, but he run away at the noise, before they could come at their guns. The 24th they discovered another bear; three of them advancing towards him, he rose upon his hindermost legs, and being shot through the body by one of our guns, he began to bleed and to roar, and to bite one of our halberts with a great deal of fierceness; but finding us too hard for him, he betook to his legs; being excessive eager after some fresh meat, (of which we stood in great need for the recovery of our health) we pursued him with lanthorns and candles a great way, but to our sorrow could not overtake him; which made us say to one another, that in case we were not supply'd by God's peculiar providence, with some refreshments speedily, the pain we endured must needs kill us before the return of our ships; but God's will be done. The 25th *Cornelius Thysse* took another potion against the scurvy, being in a deplorable condition. The 14th of *Jan.* *Adrian Johnson* of *Delft* died, being the first of the seven, tho' the other six were full of pain, and very ill. The 15th *Fettje Otters* died likewise; and on the 17th *Cornelius Thysse*, being the man of all the rest, in whom they had

had put their most hopes next to God. The remaining four were very weak, and had scarce strength left to stand upon their legs, yet they made shift to make coffins for these three, and put their bodies into them. The 28th they saw the first fox, but could not take him. The 7th of *February* they had the good fortune to take a fox, to their no small satisfaction, tho' in effect they were too far gone to receive any benefit thereby.

They saw many bears, three or four, nay sometimes six or ten together, but had not strength enough to manage their guns; or if they had had, they could not have pursued them, being not in a condition to set one foot before another, nay not even to bite their biscuits, for they were seized with most cruel pains, especially in their loins and belly, which encreased generally with the cold; one did spit blood, and another was afflicted with the bloody-flux, *Jerome Carcoen* was still something better than the rest, being still able to fetch them some fewel for firing. The 23d they began to be so weak, that they kept close in their cabins, recommending themselves to God's mercy. The 24th they saw the sun again, which they had not seen since *October* 20 or 21 in the preceeding year. The 26th, being the last day (as we guess) they were able to write, and lived not long after; they left this following memorial behind them: Four of us that are still alive, lie flat upon the ground in our huts; we believe we could still feed, were there but one among us that could stir out of his hut to get us some fewel, but no body is able to stir for pain; we spend our time in constant prayers, to implore God's mercy to deliver us out of this misery, being ready whenever he pleases to call us; we are certainly not in a condition to live thus long without food or fire, and cannot assist one another in our mutual afflictions, but must every one bear our own burthen.

When the ships from *Holland* arrived there in 1635, they found them all dead, shut up close in their tent, to secure their dead bodies against the bears and other ravenous creatures. This being the tent of *Middleburgh*, a baker who got a shore first, happened to come to the back door, which he broke open, and running up stairs, found there upon the floor, part of a dead dog that was laid there to dry; but making the best of his way down again, he trod upon the carcass of another dead dog (for they had two) at the stair foot in the buttry. From hence passing thro' another door, towards the fore-door, in order to open it, he stumbled in the dark over the dead bodies of the men, whom they saw, (after the door was opened) altogether in the same place, *viz.* three in coffins, *Nicholas Florison* and another, each in a in a cabin, the other two upon some sails spread upon the floor, with their knees drawn up to their chins. Coffins being ordered to be made for the four that had none; they were buried with the other three under the snow, till the ground becoming more penetrable, they were buried one by another, and certain stones laid upon their graves, to hinder the ravenous beasts from digging up their carcasses: These were the last that pretended to pass the winter at *Spitzbergen*.

A TRUE

A TRUE and SHORT

ACCOUNT

OF

FORTY TWO PERSONS

Who perished by shipwreck near

SPITZBERGEN,

In the year 1646.

JOHN CORNELIUS of *Muniken*, being ordered to *Spitzbergen*, to catch whales, he set sail from the *Texel* in a galliot, the 6th of *May* 1646, and arrived the 3d of *June* following near *Spitzbergen*, with an intention to anchor in the bay, but was by the vast floats of ice-shoals forced to keep out at sea. After having in vain cruized up and down among the ice-shoals, they got into the bay, but perceiving two whales farther at sea, they sent out their sloop in pursuit of the whales.

Whilst they were rowing up and down to watch the motion of these creatures, they discovered at a distance a great ice-shoal, with something white upon it, which at first sight they imagined to be bears, (they being generally white here;) but one *Ellert Johnson*, (who was in the sloop to manage the harpcock or iron wherewith they strike the whale) judging by the motion that it was something else, persuaded them to row that way, which being done accordingly, they not long after perceived the same to be a piece of a rope belonging to the sails of a ship, which was held up by a man as a signal of their utmost distress; so they rowed up to it with all the oars they had, and coming near them, found (to their great surprize) four living men, and one dead one, (all *Englishmen*) upon the ice-shoal, who upon their bended knees express'd their joy and thankfulness for so unexpected a deliverance from the jaws of death. They were taken into the sloop, and carried into the bay aboard the ship.

They had cut a great hole, in the nature of a subterraneous cave, into the ice, and round the entrance thereof had placed the pieces of ice that were cut out of the concavity, to defend themselves against the violence of the winds and waves. In this hole they had spent fourteen days, (it being so long since they had lost their ship.)

At first there were in all forty two of them, and they had saved some victuals and tools with their sloop. The commander perceiving, after a little while, that it was impossible for them to hold out long upon the ice-shoal, resolved to go ashore in the sloop, with seventeen of his men, if he could, and to send them word afterwards, how matters stood there. This was done accordingly, but it blowing very hard, and they having not heard the least tidings of them since, they were afraid that they were drowned before they reached the shore.

There were then twenty four left upon the ice-shoal, but the want of provisions encreasing daily among them; and they being reduced to a starving condition, and expecting nothing but present death, resolved to divide themselves, and to get upon several other ice-shoals, in hopes by some chance or other, to come near to the shore; but whether some of them got ashore, or whether they were taken up by some ship or other, or whether they were swallowed up by the merciless waves, they were not able to tell.

Certain it is, that we found four of them (the miſerable remnants of forty two) ſitting together upon this ice ſhoal, overwhelmed with affliction, without any hopes of being ſaved, from the laſt extremity they were reduced to by froſt and hunger, before we came in full ſight of them with our ſloop, having had nothing to feed upon for ſome time, but a leather-belt, (belonging to one them) which they had divided and eat, ſhare and ſhare alike, till all was conſumed.

After they were brought to our ſhip, our ſurgeon took all imaginable care for their recovery; notwithſtanding which, three of them died in a few days after; ſo that of forty two wherewith their ſhip was manned, no more than one eſcaped with life, who arriving in *September* 1646, in the galliot the *Delft* upon the *Meuſe*, from thence return'd to his native country in *England*.

A N.

AN ACCOUNT OF ISELAND, SENT TO Monsieur *de la MOTHE de VAYER.*

S I R,

PUrsuant to your request, I am going to give you the best account I am able of what I could learn concerning the condition of *Iseland* and *Greenland*, during our stay in the north. As nothing is more agreeable to my sentiments than to serve you to the utmost of my power, so I will treat of both one after another.

Iseland is a large isle, and *Greenland* of a vast extent: I will begin with the first, and give you an account of all the most material passages I have met with concerning it, in their best authors, especially in *Angrim Jonas*, (erroneously call'd *Arngrim* by some) and by conversing with several persons of note and learning in *Denmark*; upon which score I am particularly obliged to *Olaus Wormius*, a doctor of physick of *Copenhagen*, a person very curious in all the affairs of the north. I will also not pass by in silence, what I have read in *Blefkenius*, a *Dane* by birth, and who has been in *Iseland* himself, at least as far as relates to those things he has been an eye-witness of; for which I have the same regard, as for what *Herodotus* assures us to have seen with his own eyes; it appearing very improbable to me, that men of honour and learning should be so careless of their reputation, as to impose things upon the world, never seen by them, under a false notion of their own experience. To be short, I will follow the footsteps of *Salust*, and rehearse to you what I have either read in *Blefkenius* or *Angrim Jonas*, or heard from Dr. *Wormius* and others, upon whose authority we are obliged to rely in this point.

The isle of *Iseland* lies in the *Deucalidonian* ocean, at 13 deg. 30 min. longitude, and 65 deg. 44 min. latitude, according to the elevation taken in the bishoprick of *Hole*, the most northern part of the isle, as *Angrim Jonas* tells us in his *Crimogea*; adding, that he had the same of *Gundebrand de Thorlac*, bishop of *Hole*, his familiar friend, and once a disciple of the famous astronomer *Tycho Brahe*.

Iseland is to the east washed by the *Hyperborean* sea, and on the south side by the *Deucalidonian* sea; to the west it lies opposite to *Greenland*, towards the cape *Farewell*, and on the north side is inclosed by the frozen sea of *Greenland*. Its length from east to west, is computed to be twenty days journey; and its breadth, where it is broadest, at four days journey, from the south to the north. But *Angrim Jonas*, who has given us this account, does not mention whether these days journeys are to be perform'd on foot or on horseback.

It is generally believed to be twice as big as the isle of *Sicily*; and by its elevation and the globe, you will soon be convinced of the truth of what I am going to tell you, *viz.* That about the summer solstice, whilst the sun is in the *Twins* and *Cancer*, the sun does never go entirely below the horizon for two months, in the north of *Iseland*; but some part of it remains above it, and one half of it whilst the longest days last, from ten at night till two in the morning, when it rises quite above the horizon; whence it appears, that about the winter solstice, whilst the sun is in the signs of *Sagittary* and *Capricorn*, the whole body of the sun does for two months successively not rise above the horizon; and in the shortest days not above

half

half of it, from ten a clock in the morning till two in the afternoon, the ordinary time of ſun-ſet here at that ſeaſon.

This iſle has got its name from the whiteneſs of its ice, *Quaſi Iceland*; it was formerly reputed fertile in wheat, and well ſtored with wood, fit for the building of large ſhips; the roots whereof being of a vaſt bulk, are to this day found underground where theſe foreſts ſtood, and are as black as ebony-wood. But now-a-days *Iſeland* produces no wheat, nay not ſo much as a tree, except ſome few ſhrubs. And were it not that they are furniſhed with grain from the neighbouring countries, and ſupplied with ſufficient quantities of wood, both for fuel, and their buildings, (which are like thoſe of other parts in the north) by the ice, which in the month of *May* is, together with the wood, forced from the more northern parts on this ſhore, they muſt periſh with hunger and cold. In their building they alſo make uſe of the bones of whales and other great fiſhes; and for firing, of two ſorts of turfs, (or *Ceſpes Bituminoſus*, called *Gleba Foſſilis* by *Angrim Jonas*) which they dig and dry in the ſun. Theſe ſhoals of ice, which come from the north thither, bring along with them ſuch vaſt trunks of trees, that according to the *Iſeland* chronicles, a tree was carried thither of ſixty three cubits long, and ſeven in compaſs.

For no ſooner come the ice ſhoals from the north to the *Iſeland* coaſt, but the inhabitants go in queſt of theſe trees, and of ſeveral beaſts, which are carried along with it thither; ſuch as white and red foxes, ſtags, wolves, white and black bears and unicorns. For that fine and large horn preſerved in the king of *Denmark*'s palace at *Frederickſburgh*, (the *Fontainbleau* of that kingdom) belonged to a fiſh taken upon the ice near *Iſeland*; it is much larger than that of St. *Denys* in *France*. Count *Ulefeld*, great marſhal of *Denmark*, ſhew'd me another of theſe unicorns, which was entire, but not above two foot long, likewiſe taken upon the ice near *Iſeland*; he told me, that when he firſt had it, there was to be ſeen ſtill part of the fleſh and ſkin.

Iſeland is a ſtrong and mountainous countrey: their paſtures are of ſuch goodneſs, that they are fain to remove the cattle for fear they ſhould burſt themſelves; the graſs having ſo agreeable a ſcent here, that foreigners tranſport and dry it, to lay it among their linen. However, their beef is not reckoned of the beſt ſort, and their mutton is rank; which the *Iſelanders* don't much regard, becauſe they dry their meat in the ſun and wind, which preſerves it better than ſalt, and takes away much of its rankneſs. Butter they make in abundance, and keep it in tubs, or for want of ſuch, only pile it up in the houſe. Their ordinary drink is milk or whey, ſometimes with water, ſometimes without. They don't want good horſes; theſe feed during the winter upon dry'd fiſh, as well as their oxen and ſheep, when hay begins to fall ſhort: Of theſe dry'd fiſh they alſo make flour and bread, when by the rigour of the winter ſeaſon, they can't ſometimes be ſupplied with grain from abroad.

Iſeland is full of clear and fine ſprings, the water whereof is not only very wholeſome to drink, but ſome of them have alſo a nouriſhing quality like beer: they are alſo not deſtitute of hot ſprings for bathing; of ponds and lakes, they have great abundance, which furniſh them with great quantities of fiſh; as alſo great numbers of brooks and navigable rivers, the names whereof, as well as of their bays and capes, I will not inſert here, they being to be found in other authors.

Blefkenius tells us of a certain lake in the weſtern part of the iſle, which always ſmoaks, and yet is ſo cold, that it petrifies every thing that is put into it; for, ſays he, if you put a ſtick into the ground near it, the ſtick changes into iron as far as it is under ground; as far as it lies under water it turns into ſtone, and that part above the water remains wood as before. *Blefkenius* ſays, he ſaw this try'd twice, and that part which ſeem'd to be iron, being put into the fire, it burnt like charcoal. He alſo tells us of another lake in the middle of the ſame iſle, the exhalations whereof are ſo malignant, that they kill the birds in an inſtant that fly over it. This lake ſeems to be of the ſame ſtamp with the *Avernus* of the *Greeks* mentioned by *Virgil*, *lib.* 6. *Æneid.*

Quam ſuper haud ullum poterant impune volantes
Tendere iter pennis: tali ſeſe halitus atris
Faucibus effundens, ſupera ad convexa ferebat:
Unde locum Graji dixerunt nomine Aornum.

Blefkenius adds, (beſides what *Angrim Jonas* relates of the hot ſprings of *Iſeland*) that certain ſprings are ſo hot here, that the water thereof burns the ſkin; and after it is ſet to cool, it leaves a ſulphur upon its ſurface, as the ſea water leaves a ſaline ſubſtance in the ſalt pits. Upon the ſurface of the water of theſe ſprings, ſwims alſo a certain red ſubſtance, which plunges under water as ſoon as you come near it, but no ſooner do you turn your back, but it appears again above water. The ſame author aſſures us, that in a certain place of

this

this isle, named *Turleskhaven*, there are two fountains or springs, one very cold, the other excessive hot; the waters whereof being conveyed by two different pipes or channels, and mix'd together in one trunk or basin, make a convenient and most excellent bath. Near it (says he) is another spring, the water whereof having the taste of wheat, is a good remedy against the venereal distemper, which, according to *Blefkenius*, is very common here.

Iseland affords not any mines of metal or minerals; except brimstone, whereof there is abundance in most parts of the isle, but especially in the mount *Hecla* in the east of the isle, extending towards the south, and which sometimes appears all in flames like mount *Vesuvius*. *Blefkenius* says, that mount *Hecla* not only sends forth flames, but also whole torrents of sulphureous liquor, which burns like spirit of wine: sometimes these eruptions are followed by vast quantities of black ashes and stones. These eruptions cease commonly with a west wind; which makes the inhabitants living thereabouts, who know the avenues of the mountains, to chuse that time to go to the top of it, and throw great stones into the hole, through which the flames break forth: it being otherwise very dangerous to approach so near it, there being divers instances that men have been swallow'd up by the earth that has given way as they were going up the mountain.

It is a received opinion among the *Iselanders*, that this mountain is the place where the souls of wicked persons are tormented with fire; for they will tell you, that they see sometimes whole troops of infernal spirits carrying the damn'd souls into the abyss of this mount, and returning back again to fetch more. *Blefkenius* says, this is generally observed after some bloody battle has been fought in some place or other. Thus the *Iselanders* believe, that the noise which arises from the many sea shoals forced against the shore, are the groans and lamentations of the damn'd souls, by reason of the excessive cold they endure; it being their opinion, that some souls are condemn'd to suffer eternal cold, as well as everlasting fire.

The same *Blefkenius* tells us, that whilst he was in *Iseland*, there arose so prodigious a fire about midnight in *November*, on the sea near the mount *Hecla*, that it was seen all over the isle, to the no small astonishment of the inhabitants; the most sensible among whom were however of opinion, that the same proceeded from mount *Hecla* itself. Within an hour after they perceived an earthquake all over the isle, which was followed soon after by so dreadful a noise, (like a thunderclap) that every one expected the day of judgment to be at hand. Some few days after, the sea was found dry near the place where the fire had appear'd, and was retreated at least two leagues within its old bounds from the shore.

As the use of corn is unknown among the *Iselanders*, so they neither buy nor sell; but what commodities are brought to them, such as flour, beer, wine, strong-waters, iron, woollen and linen cloths, *&c.* they exchange for the products of their countrey; such as dry'd fishes, butter, tallow, course woollen cloths, brimstone, foxes, bears, stag and wolves skins. *Blefkenius* says, that the *Germans* who traffick thither, set up their tents upon the shore, where they expose their commodities, as cloaks, shoes, looking-glasses, knives, and such like toys, which they exchange for what the *Iselanders* bring to them. He further adds, that the young women of *Iseland* (who are handsome enough, but miserably clad) come to these strangers to prostitute themselves for some bread, biscuit, or some other trifle; nay, their fathers often carry them to these foreigners, and look upon it as a lucky chance, if they happen to be with child by them; they being afterwards in greater esteem among, and sooner married by the *Iselanders* than others.

So soon as an *Iselander* has bought (or rather exchanged) some wine or beer from these strangers, he invites his kindred, relations, and friends, to make merry with him; when they seldom part as long as any strong liquor is left. During the merriment, they sing the atchievements of their ancient warriours, but without any art, order, or rule. It is accounted a singular piece of ill breeding among them, to go away from the table to piss, whilst they are drinking. The young wenches (who as I told you are not ugly) commonly creep under the benches, to reach them the chamber-pots.

Angrim Jonas is very angry with *Blefkenius* upon this account, and accuses him of falshood, in reflecting upon the reputation of his countrey-women, and accusing them of barbarity; as also, in regard of what he says concerning their washing their mouths and teeth every morning with their own urine, tho' the same has been observed in the *Celtiberians* by *Catullus*:

Nunc Celtiber in Celtiberia Terra,
Quod quisque minxit, hoc sibi soleat mane
Dentem, & russam defricare Gingivam.

To tell you my opinion upon this matter; it's possible the *Iselanders* are not now so barbarous as formerly, tho' it may rationally

nally be ſuppoſed, that a nation living ſo near the north pole, may not be ſo refined and poliſhed as ſome others, eſpecially among the vulgar ſort, for people of faſhion ought to be exempted of this rule (leſs or more) in moſt places.

Blefkenius aſſures us, that the *Iſelanders* have familiar ſpirits, who attend them like ſervants, and give them notice from time to time when they ſhall be ſucceſsful in hunting or fiſhing. *Ortelius* adds, that they call theſe dæmons or ſpirits *drolla's*; which ſeems to have ſome reference to the *Daniſh* word *troll*, which ſignifies a *devil*. *Blefkenius* further tells us, that the *Iſelanders* ſell what wind they pleaſe to ſtrangers. *Angrim Jonas* ridicules this ſtory called *Ging*, that the *Iſeland* ſeamen being very expert in diſcerning in the evening, by the diſpoſition of the air, what wind is likely to blow the next day; which if they find ſuitable to the wiſh of ſuch ſtrangers as lie ready to ſail near the ſhore, they pretend to ſell them ſuch a wind, which (to cover the deceit) they do thus: They aſk the ſtranger to give them his handkerchief; which done, they pretend to mutter certain words into it, and immediately after tie it into knots, for fear the words ſhould evaporate into the air. Afterwards he returns him his handkerchief thus knotted, with a ſtrict charge to keep it thus with extraordinary care, till he arrives in the deſired port: ſometimes it happens, that the wind proves according to wiſh, but much oftner it proves quite otherwiſe. So ſoon as the poor ſtranger is got out to ſea, if he be overtaken by a tempeſt, he is put to no ſmall nonplus what to do, imagining that he carries the devil in his pocket, and conſequently thinking it a point of conſcience to keep it, yet is unwilling to part with it. If, ſays *Angrim*, once in a great many times the wind proves according to what the *Iſelander* has foretold the ſtranger, this is a ſufficient precedent in oppoſition to many other experiments made to the contrary; the perſon who fancies to have bought his favourable wind, not failing to tell it where-ever he comes, that with the aſſiſtance of the wind he purchaſed in *Iſeland*, he was happily carried to the deſired port.

Tho' ſuch like ſtories are not likely to make any impreſſion upon men of judgment, they may ſerve for variety's ſake, there being ſome pleaſure in underſtanding what is ſaid and believed by other people. *Blefkenius* tells us alſo, that there are ſorcerers in *Iſeland*, who can ſtop a ſhip under full ſail; againſt which (ſays he) they make uſe of certain ill-ſcented ſuffumigations, (deſcribed by him) as counter charms, by virtue of which they force the dæmon that retains them, to let the ſhip purſue its former courſe. But it's time to return to more ſerious matters relating to the hiſtory of *Iſeland*.

Iſeland was in ancient times divided into four provinces, according to the four corners of the world; each whereof was ſubdivided into three bailliages, called *repes* by the *Iſelanders*, except the northern province, which being the largeſt and moſt conſiderable of all, had four bailliages; each of which was again ſubdivided into ſix, ſeven, eight, or ten diſtricts or judicatures, in proportion to their extent. Every year there was an aſſembly held of the bailliages in each province, who were convened by certain ſmall croſſes of wood, ſent by the governour of the province to his reſpective bailiffs, who were to diſtribute them among the judges, and theſe among ſuch of the heads of families, as had a right to appear at this aſſembly. Beſides which, the lord chief juſtice, or preſident of the whole iſle, who being the interpreter or conſervator of the laws of the land, who was alſo conſidered as the ſovereign of the four provinces, uſed at certain times to call together the general eſtates of the whole iſle; which was done by four wooden hatches, ſent to the four governours of the provinces.

Each bailliage had three principal *pagodes*, or pagan temples, for the adminiſtration of juſtice, and their devotion; whence the office of *bailiff* was honoured with the ſurname of *godorp*, i. e. *divine*. The principal care of theſe bailiffs was to provide for the poor, whereof there were great numbers in ſo deſolate a countrey; to take care that the poor of one *repe* did not go thence to another; and to refrain the licentiouſneſs of ſturdy beggars, againſt whom the laws were very ſevere; for they had liberty to kill, or to emaſculate them, to prevent their multiplication. They had alſo a law, forbidding (under pain of baniſhment) not only a poor fellow to marry a poor woman, but alſo any man, who had but juſt enough for his own ſuſtenance, to marry a woman without ſomething to maintain herſelf.

This ariſtocratical form of government, and manner of adminiſtring juſtice, continued in this iſle till the year of *Chriſt* 1263. when the kings of *Norway* conquered the ſaid iſle, and forced them to pay them an annual tribute; being invited thereunto by the inteſtine broils ariſen among the great ones, about the adminiſtration of the government. The kings of *Denmark*, after having made themſelves maſters of *Norwegen*, did ſend into *Iſeland* their governours or or viceroy* ; from which time on, they had nothing but the ſhadow left of their antient liberty. Theſe governours have their reſidence in a certain caſtle, called *Beſeſtat*, ſeated in the weſtern part of the iſle. They are however not obliged to reſide there conſtantly, unleſs in caſe of neceſſity, and when they gather the yearly tribute, which is paid in the ſame commodities I had occaſion to mention before, and which they exchange with ſtrangers; which ſerve in ſome meaſure the king of *Denmark* to provide his navy with proviſions, and clothing for the ſeamen.

The laſt viceroy, or governour of *Iſeland* (ſince our coming into the north) was Mr. *Proſmoel*, admiral of the *Daniſh* fleet, lately defeated by the *Swedes* in the *Baltick* ſea. The admiral fought with incredible courage, and died upon the deck of his ſhip with ſword in hand, having refuſed to accept his life from the hands of his enemies.

Angrim Jonas dates chriſtianiſm in *Iſeland*, from the thouſandth year after the birth of Chriſt; not but that there were chriſtians there a conſiderable time before; but that paganiſm was not abſolutely aboliſhed till that time. The *Iſelanders*, whilſt pagans, did, beſides other gods, adore *Thor* and *Odin*. The firſt was to them inſtead of *Jupiter*, and *Odin* in lieu of the *Mercury* of the antient *Greeks* and *Romans*. Hence they call to this day their Thurſday *Thorſday*, and their Wedneſday *Odin's Daguir*. The altars conſecrated to their gods were covered with iron plates, upon which they kept an everlaſting fire. Upon the altar ſtood a certain veſſel of tin, containing the blood of the ſacrifice, wherewith they beſprinkled the ſpectators. On one ſide of this veſſel lay a ſilver ring, of about twenty ounces weight, which they uſed to beſmear with the blood of the ſacrifice, and lay their fingers upon it when they were to take a ſolemn oath. The chronicles of *Iſeland* tell us, that they uſed to offer ſacrifices of men to their idols. Theſe they threw down from the rocks, or into deep pits made for that purpoſe near the gates of their temples. The pagan *Iſelanders* had their two principal temples, one in the north, the other in the ſouth part of the iſle. In lieu whereof the *Iſeland* chriſtians have erected two, and the only two biſhopricks in theſe parts of the iſle, *viz.* that of *Hole* in the north, and that of *Scalhold* in the ſouth. They at preſent profeſs the *Lutheran* religion, as well as in *Denmark*.

The antient *Iſelanders* were tall, and well made, robuſt, nimble, and active, famous gladiators, and much addicted to pyracies. *Monomachies*, or ſingle duels, were publickly allowed among them; nay, even their law-differences were decided by duels, the vanquiſhed loſing their pretenſions, as did likewiſe he who refuſed to accept the challenge, and was uſed in the ſame manner as if he had been vanquiſhed. This was the chief method of acquiring poſſeſſions among them; for, if two gladiators entred upon a ſingle combat, the conqueror became by his victory maſter of the whole eſtate of his conquered enemy, againſt which his heirs had but one remedy, which was to bring a large bull or ox to the conqueror, which he was to kill with one ſtroke, which if he fail'd to do, he loſt his whole pretenſion upon the eſtate of his conquer'd adverſary.

Beſides that the *Iſelanders* were very ſtrong and couragious, they had alſo a ſufficient ſhare of wit, and were ſo curious in their annals, that they not only carefully preſerved their own hiſtory from oblivion; but alſo embelliſhed the ſame with the moſt memorable tranſactions that happened in the neigbouring kingdoms. Hence it is, that *Angrim Jonas*, in his *Specimen Iſelandicum*, ſpeaking of his countrymen, calls them *ad totius Europæ res hiſtoricas lynciæ*, i. e. quickſighted in the whole hiſtory of *Europe*. Certain it is, that *Saxo Grammaticus*, in his preface to his *Daniſh* hiſtory, confeſſes to have made uſe with good ſucceſs of the *memoirs* taken out of the *Annals of* Iſeland, called *Tylenſes*. Dr. *Wormius*, I remember, told me concerning theſe Annals, that they were curiouſly written, and contained many exquiſite matters (not to be found elſewhere) relating to the iſles of *Orcades*, the *Hebrides*, *Scotland*, and *England*, nay, even in the dukedom of *Normandy*: The reaſon whereof might probably be, that theſe *Iſelanders* were very powerful in the *Deucalidonean* or *Scots* ſea, and perhaps carried from thence their commerce as far as *Normandy*.

The moſt antient hiſtories of *Iſeland*, and ſuch as are moſt in eſteem among them, were written in verſe; it being obſervable upon this head, that the antient kings and heroes of the north uſed conſtantly to carry ſome poets along with them to the wars, who uſed to celebrate their hiſtories in verſe. Theſe were ſung by the ſoldiers in their armies, and conſequently divulged in the adjacent countries. The *Iſelanders* were ſo famous for their poetry among the neighbouring nations, that it was generally believed that there was a certain kind of magick hidden in their verſes, whereby they could ſummon the dæmons from the infernal regions, and change the influence of the planets. Their poets are born, and not made ſuch; for the moſt ingenious perſon among them cannot write a verſe, without his natural genius prompts him to it, the rules of their

their poetry being moſt ſtrict and ſevere; whereas ſuch as are endowed with this qualification by nature, write them with ſuch facility, that they can ſpeak ſcarce any thing but in metre. They are commonly ſeized with this poetical frenzy in the new moon, when their faces appear dreadful, with a pale countenance, and hollow eyes; not unlike as the ſybil of *Cumæ* is deſcribed by *Virgil*. At that time it is very dangerous to converſe with theſe furious fellows, the wound given by a mad dog being ſcarce more dangerous than their venomous ſatires.

I cannot forbear to tell you what Dr. *Wormius* related to me upon this head: Some years before, when he was *rector magnificus*, (or vice-chancellor of the univerſity of *Copenhagen*) a certain young ſtudent, a native of *Iſeland*, made his complaint to him againſt one of his countrymen, who, as he ſaid, had moſt highly affronted him in one of his ſatires. *Wormius* having ſent for the poet, he did not diſown the poem, but denied that it was intended againſt his countryman; and in effect, the vice-chancellor, according to the knowledge he had of the *Iſeland* tongue (being a dialect of the antient *Runic* language) could not find out any great reaſon of complaint in the ſaid poem. The plaintiff, finding the vice-chancellor inclinable to his adverſary's ſide, burſt out into tears; telling him, with a mournful countenance, that if he did not aſſiſt him, he was loſt for ever. Then rehearſing to him the fables, figures, and other malicious deſigns, under which the malignity of this ſatire was couched; he further told him, that he muſt be looked upon as an infamous perſon in his country, if this poem ſhould ever come thither; that all his welfare lay at ſtake; nay, that the malicious deſign of it reached even his life, and that the charms contained therein would purſue him, and have their effects upon him wherever he went. Dr. *Wormius*, not a little moved in compaſſion, when he ſaw him in this agony, took the poet aſide, repreſenting to him the duty and charity of a chiſtian, and likewiſe the ſeverity of the *Daniſh* laws againſt ſorcerers; with ſevere threats to deliver him into the hands of juſtice, if the other ſhould happen to fall ſick, tho' only out of fear: Which made ſuch impreſſion upon the poet, that at laſt he confeſſed the malicious deſign of his ſatire, tore it to pieces, and promiſing never to write it, or ſpeak of it again, embraced the young ſtudent, who was raviſhed with joy, becauſe he had made his peace with the poet.

The *Iſeland* poets have a certain mythology or explanation of their fables, called *Edda*. Among other matters, they ſuppoſe a certain giant, named *Immer*, the firſt principle of things. They ſay, that the chaos produced dwarfs, who getting upon the giant, took him to pieces. Out of his ſkull they made the heavens, out of his right eye the ſun, out of his left the moon, out of his ſhoulders the mountains, the rocks of his bones, the ſea of his bladder, and the rivers of his urine; and ſo with the other parts of his body: Whence it is, that theſe poets call the heavens *Immer's* ſkull, the ſun his right eye, the moon his left eye, the rocks his bones, the mountains his ſhoulders, the ſea his bladder, the rivers his urine, and ſo forth. Dr. *Wormius* did ſhew me a very antient copy of this *Edda*, written in the *Iſeland* tongue by an *Iſelander*, and interpreted it to me, whence I have taken what I have related to you now.

The Edda.

If we may believe the *Iſelanders* annals, they uſed in former ages to be ſo formidable at ſea, that both the kings of *Denmark* and *Norway* were jealous of their naval ſtrength; whereas now they have not wood enough to build a fiſher-boat. They formerly traffick'd into all the circumjacent countries, whereas now they ſcarce ever leave the iſle, unleſs ſome few of them who come to *Copenhagen* to ſtudy, and are generally ſo eager to return to their native countrey, that there is not ſo much as one inſtance to be given of their ſtaying in *Denmark* afterwards, tho' good livings have been offered them there, there being ſome among them who have applied themſelves to their ſtudies with very good ſucceſs. They are ſo bigotted to their miſery, that whatever you tell them concerning the advantage of the *Daniſh* climate beyond theirs, has not the leaſt effect upon them. There were at that time about fourteen or fifteen ſtudents at the univerſity of *Copenhagen*, who were generally ſpeaking of a low ſtature, and ſlender; tho' I remember, *Blefkemius* ſays in one place, that he ſaw an *Iſelander* in *Iſeland* of ſuch a prodigious ſtrength, that he could lift a *Hamborough* barrel of beer (holding forty-eight gallons) to his mouth.

The *Iſelanders* retain to this day ſome relicks or rather a ſhadow of their antient government; their laws being now ſo interwoven with thoſe of *Norway* and *Denmark*, that whilſt they are fond, not quite to part with their own, and at the ſame time are obliged to obey the others, they entangle themſelves into no ſmall difficulties concerning the concordance betwixt their and the *Daniſh* laws; which has made *Angrim Jonas* ſay, that there are as many *Pantinomies* in the laws of *Iſeland*, as there are *Antinomies* in the *Roman* law.

The *Iſelanders* retain to this day their antient

tient custom of building their houses at a considerable distance from one another, without any order or rule, for fear of fire, being all of wood: They have no other windows but a hole on the top; their houses being very low, and sometimes half under ground, by reason of the high winds that often blow here. They are commonly covered (like those in *Sweden*) with the bark of beech-tree covered with turfs, much after the same manner as *Virgil* describes the hut of *Tityrus* in his *Bucolics*:

Pauperis & Tuguri congestum cespite culmen.

These are their dwelling-houses, wherein they live to a hundred years of age, and more, without making use of any physick or physicians.

The whole isle of *Iseland* has no more than two villages, which are the seats of their two bishops, *viz. Hole* and *Schalholt*; the first whereof, being the biggest, has only a few houses; and as they have neither towns nor villages, so they have no highways; which obliges those that travel here from one province to another, to make use of the needle and compass (as they do at sea) for their guide; and near those pits or holes, which by reason of their being filled with snow, might prove dangerous to travellers, they set up marks to forewarn them of the danger. The *Iselanders* seldom inhabit but near the sea shore, or near a river, for the conveniency of fishing and pasture, so that the inland country is in a manner a desart. At *Hole* there is a college or school for boys, till they come into rhetorick, when they are sent to *Copenhagen* to study philosophy and divinity. Here is also a printing-press, where they did sometime ago print the Old Testament, translated into the *Iseland* tongue. The New Testament is still in the press for want of paper, which is a dear commodity in that country.

There have been divers bishops of note in *Iseland*, especially in the see of *Hole*, a catalogue of whom you may see in the *Crimogee* of *Angrim Jonas*. *Gundebrand Torlac* was bishop of this see, a person of great probity and learning. *Angrim Jonas* being his coadjutor, had the survivance of this bishoprick granted him by the king of *Denmark*; but after the death of *Gundebrand*, refused to accept of the same, having for some time before devoted most of his time to his private studies. He is still living; and, as Dr. *Wormius* told me, above ninety years of age, notwithstanding which he married a very young woman about four years ago. He is both a man of learning and probity, and much consider'd for his knowledge in the affairs of the north, as his writings sufficiently testify.

I had almost forgot to mention one thing, worth our observation among the *Iselanders*, *viz.* that they are great chess-players, there being not a peasant in the country, but what has a set of it, which they make themselves out of fish-bones. The whole difference betwixt theirs and ours, being only that our fools stand for their bishops; because, say they, the clergymen ought to be near the king's person. Their rooks represent little captains, whence the *Ieland* scholars call them *Centuriones*. They are represented with swords on their sides, with bloated cheeks, as if they were blowing the horn they hold in both their hands. I shall have occasion to speak more concerning the horns used by the northern generals in the wars, which are not unlike that of our *Rowland*, or the horn, or rather trumpet of *Misenus*, whom *Virgil* styles *Hectoris magni comes*, or, *Hector*'s companion; it being certain, that in *Germany*, as well as the northern parts, trumpeters are not considered as servants, but officers of the troop; but of this more another time. We return to our chess-game.

Chess-play much used in the north.

This game is not only of antient standing, and generally used, in *Iseland*, but all over the north. The *Norwegian* chronicle tells us, that *Drosen* the giant, foster-father of *Herald* surnamed the *Hairy*, (as *Chiron* was of *Achilles*) having understood the great actions of his pupil, then king of *Norway*, sent him, among other presents (mention'd in that chronicle) a very fine and rich chess-table. This *Herald* reign'd about the year of Christ 870. And if *Encolpius* in *Petronius* could brag that he had seen *Trimalcion* play at draughts upon tables made of turpentine wood and chrystals, with men of gold and silver; I may boast to have play'd at chess with the countess *Eleonore*, natural daughter to the king of *Denmark*, married to count *Ulefeld*, great marshal, and chief minister to the king of *Denmark*. The tables were inlaid with a white and yellow amber; the pieces of gold, curiously wrought, and enamell'd with the same colours as the tables. The kings and queens were dressed in their royal robes, seated upon a throne, with a crown on the head. The bishops had their mitres and habits, richly adorned; and the knights were mounted on horses, with fine trappings. The rooks were represented by elephants with towers on their backs. The men were little musqueteers, presenting their guns close to their cheeks, as if they were expecting the word, to fire.

Iseland a dialect of the Runick.

I told you before, that the *Iseland* tongue was founded upon the antient *Runic* language; and Dr. *Wormius*, who is well ver-sed fed in the *Runic*, and has writ a whole treatise of it, has assured me, that the *Iseland* tongue is the purest dialect of the *Runick* that is to be found now. For a farther proof whereof it is to be observed, that the alphabet given us by *Blefkenius* are *Runick* characters; adding, that some of them being designed for hieroglyphicks, express entire words. *Angrim Jonas* has also a whole chapter of it in his *Crimogea*. And since this book is very scarce to be had here, and consequently much more in *France*, you will I hope not take it amiss, if I entertain you with some things I have observed there, it being certain, that by explaining to you the antiquity of the *Iseland* tongue, I shall at once give you a considerable insight into the antient state of the north.

Angrim Jonas tells us, that the *Iseland* chronicles, speaking of the first inhabitants of the northern part of the world, deduce their origin from a certain *Asiatick* prince, named *Odin* or *Ottin*, who being forced out of the *lesser Phrygia* by the victorious arms of *Pompey the great*, retired with the remainder of his *Phrygian* forces into the north. *Angrim* is forced to confess, that the *Iseland* chronicles don't begin but with *Odin*, though at the same time some other northern countries trace their origin much further, *viz.* of a certain prince, named *Norus*, who first erected *Norway* into a kingdom, and provided them with wholesome laws. This *Norus* was son to *Therre* king of *Gothland* and *Finland*, the most potent, brave, and most virtuous prince of that age; for which reason he was by his subjects reverenced like a God; and the *Norwegians* to this day call the month of *January Therre*, after his name. King *Therre* had a most beautiful daughter, named *Goa*, who being ravished by a foreign prince, her brother *Norus* went in pursuit of the ravisher; and the name of *Goa* was given to the month of *February*, to her memory, the same being retained to this day among the *Iselanders*. *Angrim* has given us the genealogy of all the anceſtors of *Norus*, who were reckon'd among the number of the gods by the northern nations; one whereof represented the god of the sea, another of the winds, another of snow, another of the winter. Among the rest they worshipped one under the name of the god of fire, whose statue was extremely fine and handsome; whence they gave him the name of *Halogie*, i. e. *a fierce and glorious flame*. This genealogy reaches to *Giloe*, a nephew of *Norus*, in whose reign (as the chronicle tells us) the great *Odin* came out of *Asia* into the north.

Angrim Jonas finding such a diversity in the chronicles, saw himself obliged to look farther backwards, beyond the first kings of *Norway*, for the first original of the northern nations, which he deduces from the antient giants that were forced out of the land of promise by *Joshua*, and afterwards settled their habitations in the northern parts, from whom the *Goths* derive their race, the word *Got* signifying as much as a giant; wherefore I think it not amiss to say something as well in reference to these giants as of *Odin* the *Asiatick* prince.

This famous *Odin* was worshipped as a God all over the north, under the name of *Mercury*, by reason of his excellent wit. It is he who laid the first foundation of the northern poesy, and of their *magi*, so much celebrated in other parts of the world. Of the first I have said something already, and upon the *magi* I could say much more, were it not that it both deserves and requires a most particular account, which I intend to reserve for another opportunity. I can't however forbear to put you in mind upon this occasion, of the negligent temper of many of our modern authors, who, without making any serious reflection upon the circumstances of things imposed upon the world (without the least sense or reason) by antiquity, are not only taken by them for granted, but also improved by them, in order to make them pass current in the world. I would desire any body to consider how little coherence there is betwixt the fabulous relations of *Odin* their *Asiatick* prince, and the time of *Pompey*, so much celebrated in history?

Is it not a most surprizing thing, to see most of the antients, represent the founders of nations, or other great men, like giants? Thus they make *Hercules* three times bigger than other men. And *Virgil* represents his *Æneas* and *Turnus* like mountains, *quantus Athos, aut quantus Erix*; and compares *Sandarus* and *Bitias* to two tall oaks. Thus all the pictures and statues of *Charles the great* (in the *German* churches) are much beyond the size of an ordinary man. I remember that I saw the statue of a *Rowland* in the market-place of *Bremen*, of the heighth of a pike. *Saxo Grammaticus* makes his *Danes* to be descended from giants. *Job.* and *Olaus Magnus*, two brothers, and both *Swedish* historians, do the same with their countrymen, as *Angrim Jonas* describes his first *Iselanders* as giants, the word *Got*, as he says, signifying a giant, and that the antient *Goths* were actually such. And because the giants of *Canaan*, who were drove thence by *Joshua*, were the first giants mentioned in the holy scripture after the deluge, these must be brought into the north; because *Palestine* was too hot for them to abide in.

The

The two before-mentioned *Swedish* historians (who being brothers, succeeded one another in the archbishoprick of *Upsal*) outdo even *Angrim Jonas* himself in deducing the origin of the *Swedes* from the children of *Japhet*; and take a great deal of pains to persuade the world, that the city of *Upsal* was built in the time of *Abraham*. I wonder how *Angrim Jonas* happened not to follow their footsteps, in deducing the origin of his *Iselanders* from the race of *Japhet*; seeing it is said of the children of *Japhet*, in the tenth chapter of *Genesis*, *Ab his divisæ sunt insulæ gentium in regionibus suis, unusquisque secundum linguam suam, & familias suas in nationibus suis*; *By these were the isles of the Gentiles divided in their lands, every one after his tongue, after their families in their nations.* For it being a general and orthodox opinion, that the children of *Noah* did repeople the world after the deluge, and that those of *Japhet* in particular, settled in the isles: *Angrim* might with much better pretence affirm, that of the first inhabitants of his isle, than *Olaus Magnus* had told us of the *Swedes* being descended from the race of *Japhet*; for besides that *Angrim* has the history of *Genesis* on his side (which the *Swedes* have not) it saves the trouble of tracing the original of the *Iselanders* from the giants of *Canaan* coming into the northern parts.

To tell you my real opinion concerning those gentlemen, who have taken so much pains in making so nice a scrutiny into the first inhabitants of the world, after the deluge, they have taken a great deal of pains in vain; it being certain, that since we are destitute of true histories concerning these most antient times, all their relations are founded only upon conjectures, or some fabulous chronicle or account ill digested and worse explained. I don't apply this only to Mr. *Angrim Jonas*, for whom I have a singular respect: The error is general, he having not been the first who traced the original of the northern nations from the giants of *Canaan*; besides that, he has no insignificant plea for his assertion, because he found some *Iseland* words to have no small congruity with the *Hebrew*, which was called the language of *Canaan*, after the *Jews* had made themselves masters of the *land of promise*, by chacing the giants thence. Our author had unhappily forgot, that these giants did not speak *Hebrew*, which being foreign to them, they could not possibly introduce it in the north, if we would take it for granted, that they actally inhabited there.

Many errors of this nature are to be met with in the writings of most of the best authors, who have run upon the same mistake in looking for the true origin of nations among the interpretation or etymology of certain *German* or *Hebrew* words, which to them seem'd to have a near relation to the language of those nations they were treating of. Thus Mr. *Grotius*, in his treatise of the origin of the *Americans*, deduces their race from the *Germans*, because, says he, many of their words terminate in *Lan*, *Land* being a *German* word. Mr. *Sact* says, that there is a certain nation in *America*, called *Alavardes*, who have got their name from one *Alvarado*, a *Spanish* commander, who conquered them. But *Grotius* traces the origin of the *Alavardes* from the *Lombards*, by a corruption of the word; as to this day the *French* call *Hallbards*, certain arms of the *Lombards*, called *Lombards* by the antient *French*.

Mr. *Bechard*, a person not inferiour in learning to *Grotius*, takes the same road in his treatise called *Phaleg*, of the partition and inhabitants of the earth after the deluge, his reasons being founded upon conjectures of the same nature; tho' I must confess I could not but be surprised at his stupendous knowledge in the eastern languages, in finding out the interpretation of the *Carthaginian* verse in *Plautus* his comedy, called the *Carthaginian*, out of the *Hebrew*. I told you just now, that his invention is full of ingenuity; but can't however agree with him, that the *Carthaginian* tongue had any relation to the *Hebrew*; for *Dido*, (who founded *Carthage*) being a native of *Phœnicia*, (which language was very different from the *Hebrew*) the *Carthaginians* questionless were so far from speaking *Hebrew* in the days of *Plautus*, that it is most likely they retained the same language that *Dido* had introduced there, *viz.* the *Phœnician*. Mr. *Samuel Petit*, a learned man and great critick, having before Mr. *Bechard* found out quite another interpretation of the same words in *Plautus*, I am apt to imagine, that if a third person (as well skill'd as they in the *Hebrew*) should undertake the same task, he would find out another interpretation of the same *Carthaginian* verses in *Plautus*, by virtue of the transposition of the letters and points, which these two gentlemen have made use of to attain their end, according to the liberty allowed to the criticks in the *Hebrew*; by which rule they are able to give almost what sense they please to a sentence, just as we can make our chimes sound a tune at pleasure.

I hope, Sir, you will pardon this digression, which I thought not altogether foreign to our present purpose, when I observed Mr. *Angrim Jonas* to be misguided by the same error, as many others have been

been beſides him, in looking for the origin of the *Iſelanders* among the *Hebrew*, it being certain, that nothing can be more fallacious than conjectures founded upon ſuch like etymologies.

I am apt to believe, that *Angrim Jonas* would have acknowledged the ſame giants, who, according to his opinion, firſt peopled the north, for the firſt founders of the *Iſelanders*, were it not that he believes that iſle not to have been inhabited till for a conſiderable time after; wherefore it will not be amiſs to relate the chief heads of his relation upon that account. He ſays, that *Iſeland* was firſt of all diſcovered by one *Naddocus*, who, as he was going to the iſles of *Faro*, was caſt by a tempeſt on the eaſtern part of *Iſeland*, unto which he gave the name of *Sneeland*, i. e. *Snowland*, from the vaſt heaps of ſnow he ſaw there, which made *Naddocus* not to ſtay there long. The next who went in queſt after this iſle, was a certain *Swede*, named *Garderus*, who hearing *Naddocus* ſpeak of this iſle, found it, and landed there in the year 864; and having paſs'd the whole winter there, called it *Garderſholm*, i. e. *Garders iſle*. The third perſon who came into this iſle, was a famous *Norwegian* pirate named *Flocco*, who having underſtood ſomething of the ſituation of this iſle, made uſe of a peculiar invention for his direction, the compaſs being then a thing as yet unknown in the world. As he was going from *Hittland*, (one of the *Orcades* or *Orkney* iſlands) he ventured boldly into the main ſea, and having taken three ravens along with him, he let one of them fly as ſoon as he thought himſelf at a good diſtance from the ſhore; but finding the raven returning towards *Hittland*, from whence he was come, he kept on his courſe farther at ſea; and then letting go the ſecond raven, he ſoon found by her return to the ſhip, that ſhe could diſcover no land; ſo ſteering his former courſe for ſome time, he ſent forth the third raven, which diſcovering the *Iſeland* ſhore, *Flocco* followed her with all the ſails he could make; and thus with a favourable wind landed in the eaſtern part of *Iſeland*, then call'd *Garderſholm*, where he paſs'd the winter, and finding himſelf againſt the ſpring ſurrounded with whole mountains of ice, (called the *Greenland* ice by the inhabitants) he gave it the name of *Iſeland*, i. e. *Iceland*, which name it has retained ever ſince; *Flocco* paſs'd another winter in the ſouth part of the iſle; but being as little pleaſed with that part as with the other, he return'd to *Norway*, where they gave him the name of *Refnafloke*, i. e. *Flocco the Raven*, becauſe he had made uſe of that creature in the diſcovery of *Iſeland*.

The true founder of the *Iſelanders*, was a certain baron of *Norway*, named *Ingulph*, who having with his brother-in-law *Hiorleifus*, killed two of the greateſt men of that countrey in a duel, were baniſh'd for that fact. And it being the cuſtom of this countrey for exiles to take along with them the doors or gates of their houſes, *Ingulph* having caſt anchor near the *Iſeland* ſhore, threw his gates over-board, in order to facilitate his landing upon them. But being forced to another part of the iſle, *viz.* in the ſouthern part, he landed there; but finding his gates caſt aſhore three years after, he thought fit to fix his habitation thereabouts. *Ingulph* and his brother-in-law firſt landed in this iſle in the year 870, but did not ſettle there till four years after, *viz.* 874, whence the *Iſeland* chronicles take their epocha; this being the time of the firſt peopling of this iſle, which the ſame chronicle ſays, *Ingulph* found deſart and uncultivated. However, it is ſaid, that ſome *Engliſh* and *Iriſh* miners were before that time caſt aſhore here, the ſame having been diſcovered by ſome bells, croſſes, and other pieces made in *England* and *Ireland*, and ſome books they had left behind them. It is agreed on all hands, that the *Iriſh* had been aſhore in this iſle ſeveral times before the time of *Ingulph*; for their chronicles ſay, that the ancient *Iſelanders* called theſe *Iriſh*, *Papa's*, and the weſtern part of the iſle, *Paper*, from the *Iriſh* who uſed to land there.

Becauſe the *Iſeland* chronicle calls *Iſeland*, *A wilderneſs and uncultivated*, at the time of the arrival of *Ingulph*, *Angrim Jonas* aſſures us boldly, that it was not inhabited before that time; nay, is angry with thoſe who diſagree with him in this point, as *Pontanus*, and others, who would have *Iſeland* be the *Thule* of the ancients mentioned by *Virgil*, who ſpeaking of *Auguſtus*, ſays,

—— *Tibi ſerviat ultima Thule.*

For (ſays he) in his *Specimen Iſelandicum*, if *Iſeland* is ſuppoſed to have been the *Thule* of the ancients, it muſt have been inhabited in *Auguſtus*'s time; which is contrary to our *Iſeland* chronicles, which tell us, that it was not inhabited till *Auguſtus* his time.

But I would have this gentleman to call to mind, what he himſelf has alledged in another place, *viz.* That the *Iriſh* uſed to come aſhore in *Iſeland* before the time of *Ingulph*, and that theſe *Iriſh* were called *Papa*'s by the ancient *Iſelanders*. I would fain know of him, who were theſe ancient *Iſelanders*. I agree with *Angrim*, that *Iſeland* was not converted to the chriſtian religion till ſome years after *Ingulph* landed there; but on the other hand, he will, I hope, easily allow me, that there were a considerable number of christians at that time in the northern countries: 'tis certain that the *Irish* were such, the marks they had left behind them, and found by *Ingulph*, sufficiently testify the same. *Angrim* mentions in his *Crimogea*, that *Ingulph*'s brother-in-law, who came along with him into *Iseland*, had many sentiments which inclined to christianity, if he was not an absolute christian. And it is certain, that the christian religion was at that time spread all over the northern countries, and among the rest in *Iseland*, as I shall have occasion to shew anon. This being granted, what time is it that *Angrim* pretends to allow to the pagan *Iselanders*, who were, as he says, so zealous in their idolatry, and especially in their adoration of *Odin*, by whom they used to swear, and call him the grand protector of *Asia*. It is beyond all dispute, that among all the heathenish superstitions, the sacrifices of men are of the most ancient date, which, that they were practised among the ancient *Iselanders*, I have sufficiently demonstrated before. Their own chronicle tells us, that in the western part of the isle there was a certain cirque, in the center whereof stands a high rock, from whence they tumbled down the miserable wretches design'd for the sacrifice, the blood whereof was afterwards offered to their Gods. The same chronicle mentions, that after the said custom was abolished here, as well as in other places, the rock retained still a red tincture, the remnants of the blood spill'd there before. I must, I say, upon this account, once more ask *Angrim*, where he will fix these many ages mentioned in his annals? And from whence he dates the introduction or invention of their mythology call'd *Edda*, which are of such antiquity, and so peculiar to the *Iselanders*, that the other nations have but very little knowledge of it, and all the other *Europeans* none at all.

Add to this, *Sir*, that the *Iseland* chronicles, when they speak of the voyages of *Naddocus*, of *Garderus*, and *Flocco* (all which happened before the time of *Ingulph*) don't make the least mention of the isle of *Iseland* having been a desert at that time: certain it is, that *Flocco* lived there for two whole years, and in all probability, not without such provisions as are the products of a countrey not destitute of inhabitants. Besides this, how will *Angrim Jonas* come off of what he had said of the *Iselanders*, that they were very exact and curious, in recording the histories of all other nations of *Europe*; *ad totius Europæ res historicas Lyncæi*, says he: *Herodotus* and *Plato* mention the same of the ancient *Egyptians*: For (says he) they preserve in their libraries, the most ancient monuments of the history of foreign nations, looking upon it as the best argument they can alledge for the antiquity of their own nation. To add as much weight as I can unto what *Angrim Jonas* says upon this head concerning his *Iselanders*, I must tell you, that Dr. *Wormius* shew'd me a copy of a chronicle of the western part of *Iseland*, wherein (by his interpretation) I found many remarkable passages in the history of *Norway*, *Denmark*, *England*, the *Orcades*, *Hebrides*, and among the rest, of the invasion of that part of *France* by the *Normans*, unto which they gave that name after their conquest. The arrival of *Ingulph* being not mentioned till afterwards, it seems very probable, that there were certain people that took care of the records of *Iseland*, and that consequently that isle was inhabited before that time. I am of opinion, that the *Iseland* chronicles (which speak of *Ingulph*) cited by *Angrim Jonas*, are authentick, and that the said *Ingulph* did not come into *Iseland* till about the year 874. But it is possible, that the southern parts, where he landed, were at that time dispeopled either by mortality, or the ravages of certain pirates; yet does it not follow from thence, that the whole isle was destitute of inhabitants. It is not likely, that *Ingulph* could settle a sufficient colony there to people the whole isle; besides, that the *Iseland* chronicles tell us, that divers neighbouring nations did settle in divers parts thereof. *Angrim Jonas* himself, makes mention of a certain inhabitant of the *Hebrides*, named *Kalman*; who, he says, was the first who made a settlement in the western part of *Iseland*, where it is worth our observation, that *Angrim Jonas* does not tell us the time when this *Kalman* came thither, no more than when the *Irish*, *Scotch*, those of the *Orkney* isles, and others, who inhabited there, fix'd their first habitations in *Iseland*. 'Tis for this reason, that I imagine, that a considerable difference ought to be made betwixt the isle of *Iseland*, whilst inhabited by pagans, and betwixt that since christianity was established there: the chronicles of the christian *Iseland* don't trace their origin beyond the time of *Ingulph*; which, according to the christian *Æra* of this countrey, begins with the year 874. whereas the chronicles of the pagan *Iseland* have no certain beginning.

Taking this for granted, (as it easily may be) nothing is more easy than to reconcile the chronicles in reference to the pagan and christian *Iseland*; and consequently to make *Angrim Jonas* to agree with himself; and to allow what *Pontanus* says, *viz.* that the

the modern *Iseland* is the *Thule* of the ancients, which he proves from the authority of divers *Greek* and *Latin* authors, from the history of *Adam* of *Bremen*, who writ in the year 1067. of *Saxo Grammaticus*, who lived soon after, and of *Andreas Vellejus*, who has translated *Saxo* into the *Danish* tongue, and in his translation always takes the *Tyleasses* for the modern *Iselanders*. *Angrim Jonas*, as I remember, alledges, that *Adam* of *Bremen* has inserted many fabulous relations in his history, and among the rest, that in his time it was received as an ancient tradition, that the ice in *Iseland* was sometimes found so old and dry, that if thrown into the fire, it would burn as fierce as a certain kind of coal, called *Hoville* by the *Flemings*. But to answer this objection, it is not so much the question here, whether the ancients were not guilty of certain follies; but rather, whether the more ancient the history is, the more it savours of folly; which seems to be an argument for the antiquity of *Iseland*, and its being known in other parts. Perhaps *Angrim Jonas* will tell us, that if the ancient authors did take the modern *Iseland* for the same they called *Thule*, they are much out in its true situation; but to this I answer, that the same authors have committed many errors of this nature in reference to other places; the question being not at this time, whether the said authors have given us an exact description of *Iseland*, either as it was then, or as it is now; but, whether the isle they described to us was the same with our *Iseland*.

What confirms me in this opinion is, that *Casaubon* declares for it; for in his commentaries upon *Strabo*, he tells us expresly, that the *Thule* mentioned in this great geographer, is our modern *Iseland*: and, to confess the truth, the thing argues in its own behalf; the modern *Iseland* being now as well as in former ages, placed by the joint consent of all the geographers, at the extremity of the *Deucalidonian* sea, or that of *Scotland*, or the *British* sea; and the ancient *Thule* has always been accounted the furthermost of the *Britannick* isles. 'Tis a thing beyond all dispute, that the *Scots* sea has been formerly called the *Caledonian* sea, from that vast *Caledonian* forest, whereof there is not so much as a single tree to be seen at this time in *Scotland*. *Selden* says, that the *Scots* inhabiting the northern parts of that kingdom, were called *Deucalidonians*, which in their language signifies as much as *Black and Swarthy*, as the ocean which washes the northern shore of *Scotland*, and the adjacent isles, has been called the *Deucalidonian* sea, from the dark and cloudy air which is generally observed thereabouts. *Pliny* calls it for the same reason, *mare pigrum*, or the *Lazy Sea*; and *Adam* of *Bremen*, *Mare Jecoreum* and *Pulmoneum*, because it has a heavy motion like those troubled with an asthma, in the same sense as *Plautus* speaks of asthmatick legs; *pedibus pulmoneis mihi advenisti*.

Angrim Jonas, as it seems, would not be so averse, to allow that *Iseland* is the same with the ancient *Thule*, provided he could be convinced, that that isle was inhabited before the time of *Ingulph*; wherefore, though I have said enough upon this head for the satisfaction of unbyass'd persons; yet will I not think it beyond the purpose, to alledge some undeniable reasons for the proof thereof, *viz*. that *Iseland* was inhabited before that time. I have by me two chronicles of *Greenland* written in *Danish*, one in verse, the other in prose. That written in verse, begins with the year 770. when it says, *Greenland* was first discovered. The other assures us, that the person that went first from *Norway* into *Greenland*, pass'd through *Iseland*, and tells us expresly, that *Iseland* was inhabited at that time; whence it is evident, that *Iseland* was not first of all inhabited in the year 874.

Angrim Jonas will perhaps object, that my *Danish* chronicles don't agree with that of *Iseland*, which says, that *Greenland* was not discovered till the year 982, nor inhabited till 986. But I must tell him, that my *Danish* chronicles are founded upon the authority of *Ansgarius* a great prelate, a native of *France*, who has been acknowledged the first apostle of the northern world. He was made archbishop of *Hamburgh* by *Lewis the Mild*, his jurisdiction extending from the river *Elbe*, all over the north, as far as the frozen sea; the emperor's patents, constituting the said *Ansgarius* the first archbishop of *Hamburgh*, are dated in the year 834, and were confirmed by pope *Gregory* IV's bull in 835. The true copy, both of the patent and of the bull, may be seen in the 4th book of *Pontanus* his *Danish* history of the year 834. where it is expresly said in the patent, that *the gates of the Gospel are set open, and that* Jesus Christ *had been revealed both in* Iseland *and* Greenland; for which the emperor gives his most humble thanks to God.

Two inferences are to be made from thence: first, that *Iseland* was inhabited by christians in the year 834; and consequently forty years before the arrival of *Ingulph* there: secondly, that *Greenland* was inhabited by christians in the same year 834, which agrees with my *Danish* chronicle, where

where the first discovery of *Greenland* is fix'd to the year 770. *Angrim Jonas* being put to a nonplus, tells us, that he questions the authority of the bull of *Gregory* IV. alledged by *Pontanus*, which he would fain make us believe is suppositious; but to be plain with him, I think he has taken a notion of maintaining the credit of his native countrey, by adhering too strictly to the authority of its chronicles; whereas it would have been more for his reputation, not to have insisted so much upon that authority, than to rob this isle of the glory of its antiquity; who is so ignorant as not to know, that the age wherein *Ingulph* lived was very barbarous? The *Goths* having carried the same together with their arms throughout all *Europe*; whoever should go about to persuade me into a belief of all what is inserted in the ancient chronicles of these barbarous ages, might as soon make me believe the romances of *Oger* the *Dane*, or the four sons of *Aymon*, of the archbishop of *Turpin*, and other such like nonsensical stories relating to the same time.

I could wish, *Sir*, you had the opportunity of reading the writings of *Angrim Jonas*, which I had scarce time to peruse. Perhaps you might discover some reasons for the antiquity of *Iseland*, which I have either not discovered or neglected. His *Specimen Iselandicum*, was printed at *Amsterdam* 1643. Perhaps his *Crimogea* is not so easy to be had; that which I saw was printed at *Hamburgh* in 1609. As I don't question but you will take abundance of pleasure in reading of them, so I will refer myself to them for a more ample account, of what I have related to you now by way of an epitome; it being all I was able to learn, and thought worthy your knowledge concerning *Iseland*. If I find this to have met with a favourable reception at your hands, I will send you a farther account of *Greenland*, though at the same time I am ready to acknowledge, that considering your merits and reputation you have acquired, by those excellent treatises you have obliged the world with of late, I ought for the future not to offer any thing but what is more polite than this; the defect thereof you will, I hope, attribute in a great measure to the want of time, and my readiness to obey your commands, which must at this juncture serve as a plea to you to excuse its errors; in hopes of which I beg you to be persuaded that I am,

SIR,

Your most humble, and

most obedient servant,

Copenhagen,
Dec. 18. 1644.

LA PEYRERE.

AN

AN ACCOUNT OF GREENLAND.

ADVERTISEMENT

Concerning the

MAP of *GREENLAND.*

AS I dare assure my self, that monsieur Chaplain *is the true author of this map; having judg'd the same absolutely necessary for the understanding this historical account; so I thought I could not do amiss, in following the advice of a person so highly and so universally esteemed.*

I have compiled this map answerable to four elevations, particularly known to me, viz. that of cape Farewell, *of* Iseland, *of* Spitzbergen, *and of that part of the* Christian's-Sea, *where captain* Monk *being stopt by the ice, gave it the name of* Monk's Winter-haven.

I have computed the longitude of all those places, from the meridian of the Iron *island of the* Canaries, *by the advice of* Mr. Roberval, *a famous mathematician; and of* Mr. Sanson, *an excellent geographer, whose steps I have follow'd in that map.*

A great lunar eclipse. *The longitude of* Monk's Winter-Haven, *was more exactly discover'd to me beyond the rest, by an eclipse of the moon, mention'd in the journal of that captain, who declares to have seen it in that harbour, about eight a clock at night, the 20th of* December *in the year* 1619. *This eclipse must have been seen at* Paris, *(according to the tables of the celestial motions) about three in the morning, the 21st day of that month. But in regard, that eclipse continued above three hours, and that captain* Monk *did not see it, either in its beginning, middle or end, I have consulted* Mr. Gassendus, *concerning this doubt; whose abilities and learning being sufficiently known to all, who make profession of these sciences, I thought I might with probability enough, suppose this eclipse discovered at* Monk's-Haven. *between its beginning and end; that is to say, about the middle of its duration, or about the hour that it must have been seen at* Paris; *whence it is evident, that when it was three a clock in the morning at* Paris, *it was no more than eight a clock of the preceding evening at* Monk's-Harbour; *and that consequently there are seven hours difference between the one place and the other. Now supposing* 15 *degrees for every hour, (according to the rules of astronomy) the meridian of* Monk's-Harbour *must be distant from the meridian of* Paris 105 *degrees, and* Paris *being at the* 23 *degree and a half of longitude,* Monk's-Haven *ought to be placed in the* 178 *degree and a half; that is to say, in the* 81 *degree and half beyond the meridian of the* Canaries: *And consequently allowing twelve ordinary leagues of* France *for every degree of this parallel, the degrees (whereof are one less than the degree of the great circle's moity) this haven must be distant from* Paris *about* 1260 *leagues. I have divided the southern part of* Greenland, *taken at cape* Farewell, *into two islands, in the manner they are represented here. This I have done, not from the* Danish *accounts I made use of to compose this history (for they don't mention it) but from a map communicated to me out of the library of my lord cardinal* Mazarin, *by monsieur* Naude, *(the ornament of that excellent collection of books, and other raritias that make up that renowned library.) These are the words in* Latin, *written at the bottom of the said map:* This delineation was made by *Martin*, the son of *Arnold*, born at the *Briel*, a city of *Holland*; who twice, *viz.* 1624, and 1625, went as commodore to the isle, known by the name of *Old-Greenland. This* Martin, *the son of* Arnold, *calls* Greenland *an island; tho' it is not certainly known, whether it be an island or part of the continent, or made up of several isles. He declares it to be the map of* Old-Greenland; *tho' he might rather have call'd it both the old and new, for none else has been discovered; and that which we know, ought rather to be called the new* Greenland, *than the old. Because, tho' the old* Greenland *must undoubtedly be fix'd hereabouts near the west of* Iseland; *nevertheless, this certain place is not known to this day, even not to the inhabitants of* Norway, *tho' their fore-fathers were the first discoverers of it, and dwelt in it some entire ages, as will more fully appear out of the following relation.*

The old new and Greenland.

The nearness of their situation between cape Farewell, *and the streights called* Christian's-Streights, *with the sea of that name, and* Monk's Winter-Haven, *has been represented according to the map captain* Monk *caused to be made of his voyage, and was annexed to his journal. I was the rather inclined to follow his foot-steps, for as much as it agrees with that of captain* Hudson, *who first discovered these streights and this sea; which map* Mr. Chaplain *was pleased to communicate to me, in order to compare it with that of captain* Monk.

I dare not affirm, that all the coast of the Christian's-Sea, *and so westerly from thence, between the Gulph of* Davis, *and* Monk's Winter-haven, *belongs to* Greenland, *because perhaps some great river or streight unknown, may separate* Greenland *from* America. *What makes me more doubtful upon this, is, that I never heard in* Denmark, *that all this coast did belong to* Greenland, *as I have heard it declared of all the coast on the N. E. between cape* Farewell *and* Spitzbergen. *I refer the solution of this question to those who have got a better insight into this matter, from the* English *and* Dutch *relations; my only design being to give an account of what I understand of this country out of the* Danish *books, and from the conversation I have had in* Denmark.

The Ambassador, mentioned in this relation, was *Monsieur de la THUILLERIE*, who was so instrumental in concluding that famous peace between the two northern crowns.

A N

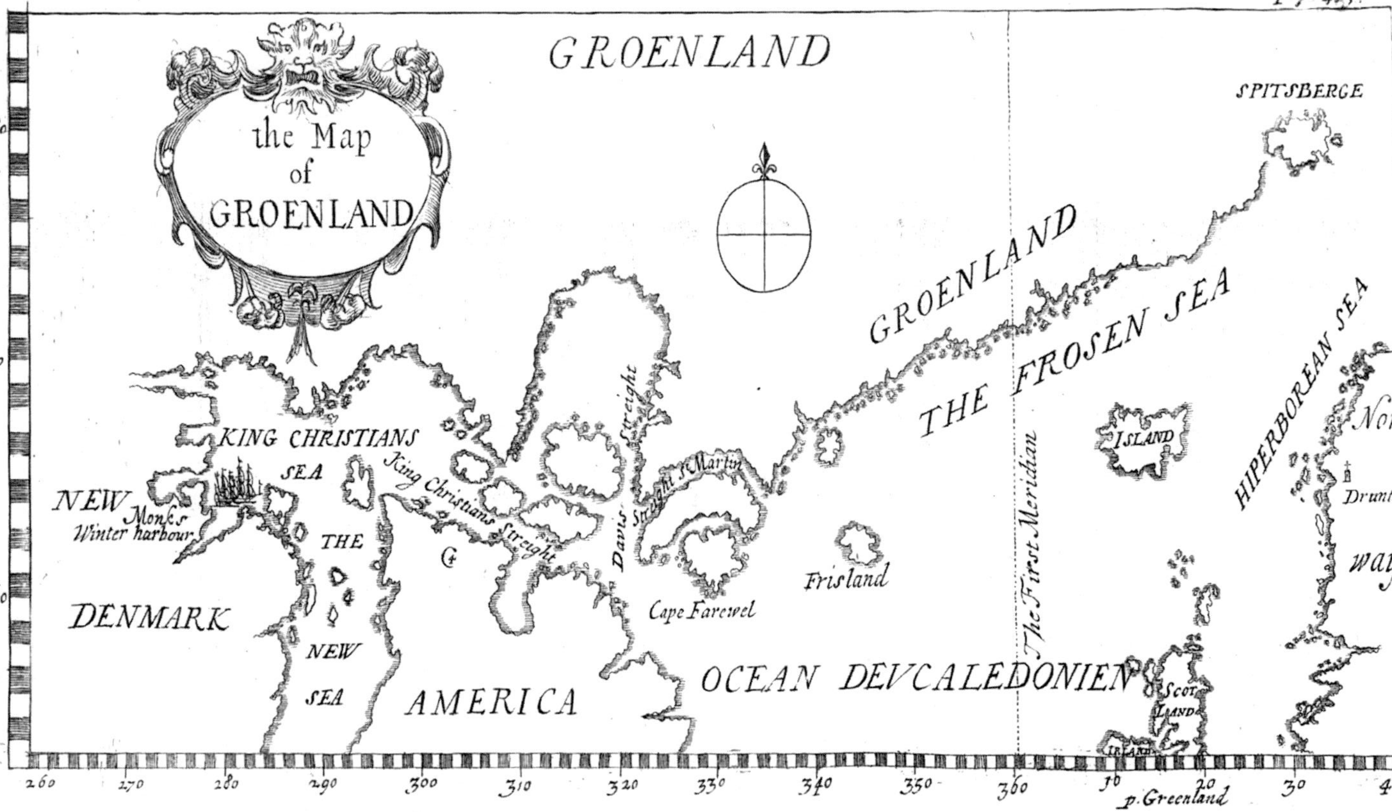
the Map
of
GROENLAND
GROENLAND
SPITSBERGE
GROENLAND
THE FROSEN SEA
HIPERBOREAN SEA
Nor
way
Drunthen
ISLAND
KING CHRISTIANS
SEA
King Christians Streight
NEW
Monks
Winter harbour
THE
NEW
SEA
DENMARK
AMERICA
Davis Streight
Streight S. Martin
Cape Farewel
Frisland
The First Meridian
OCEAN DEVCALEDONIEN
SCOT LAND
p. Greenland
80
70
60
260
270
280
290
300
310
320
330
340
350
360
10
20
30
40
41.

AN ACCOUNT OF GREENLAND, TO Monsieur *de la MOTHE le VAYER.*

SIR,

I Perceive that I have not satisfied your curiosity, in writing to you a long letter concerning *Iseland:* 'Tis but just therefore, that I should perform my promise, to send you a relation of *Greenland.* Don't wonder at the time that I have taken to pass between these two islands. If you weigh the difficulties and the dangers that attend such a voyage, you will be satisfied that I ought to inform my self with leisure of the true condition of this northern country, which deserves rather the name of *Incognita, unknown,* than the southern part of the world. Nevertheless, it has been inhabited by the *Norwegians,* during the space of five or six hundred years, who traffick'd and settled their colonies there. But that I may not confound matters, I will tell you what I have understood of this country, (which is almost inaccessible,) with all imaginable exactness, from whatever I could learn either by conversation, or from the most confused writings, I will not say that ever I read, because they were explained to me out of a tongue I understood not, as were the *Danish* books, and which Mr. *Rets,* a *Danish* gentleman, was so kind to read and to interpret to me, whom you will see speedily at *Paris*; the king of *Denmark* having named him, in consideration of his merits, his resident in *France.*

Of Greenland.

Greenland is that northern tract of land which extends from the south to the east, and thence to the north from cape *Farewell,* to the *Deucaledonian* ocean, all along the coasts of the frozen sea towards *Spitzbergen* and *Nova Zembla.* Some are of opinion, that it joins to the *Great-Tartary*; but this is uncertain, as you shall see anon.

On the east it hath the *Frozen-Sea,* on the south the *Deucaledonian* ocean, on the west the streights of *Hudson* or *Christian,* and the *Christian* or *Hudson*'s-*Sea,* that divides it from *America.* Its extent towards the north is unknown hitherto. The *Danish* chronicle informs us, that it is the farthest part of the world towards the north, and that beyond it, there is no land on that side. Some believe, that *Greenland* is join'd to *America,* because the *English,* who have attempted to pass the *Streights of Davis,* to seek a passage that way to the east, have found, by experience, that what *Davis* fansied to be the streights, is nothing but a gulf; tho' according to the account of a certain *Danish* captain, named *John Monk,* who ventured to find a passage to the east, by the north-west of the *Gulf of Davis,* there is great likelyhood, that this country is altogether separated from *America,* as will appear in its proper place, when we shall discourse of this voyage. The elevation of *Greenland* taken at cape *Farewell,* (the most southern part of it) according to the computation of captain *Monk,* a most expert seaman, is sixty degrees and thirty minutes: The other part extending much nearer to the pole. The elevation of *Spitzbergen,* which the *Danes* judge to belong to *Greenland,* is according to their computation 78 degrees or thereabouts. I don't say any thing concerning the longitude of that country, because my accounts being silent here, I have learn'd nothing more than what our maps inform upon this head. It will be sufficient for me to take notice in this place, that cape *Farewell* is beyond the *Canaries,* and our first meridian: As to the history of *Greenland,* I have chiefly made use of two chronicles, one

Its latitude.

one of *Iseland*, the other of *Denmark*; the first being very ancient and in prose, the other of a later date in verse, but both in the *Danish* language. However the original of that of *Iseland* was written in the *Iseland* tongue, by one *Snorro Storlefonius* an *Iselander*, who was *Nomophylax*, as *Angrim Jonas* call him; that is, chief justice of that island, in the year 1215. the same who compil'd the *Edda*, or the *Iseland* fables in verse I have formerly mentioned to you. The *Danish* chronicle was written in *Danish* verse, by a *Danish* priest, named *Claudie Christopherson*; within these 15 years, or thereabouts. This *Danish* chronicle says, that some *Armenians* being long toss'd at sea by a furious tempest were forced into the northern sea, at last got ashore in *Greenland*, from whence they pass'd over into *Norway*, where they inhabited the rocks of the *Hyperborean-Sea*: But this relation is founded only upon ancient fables and customs, to deduce the original of remote places and nations: But thus much is certain, that the *Norwegians* did first discover and inhabit *Greenland*.

Snorro Storlefonius, *author of the* Edda.

Torwald *and his son* Erick.

A certain gentleman of *Norway*, named *Torwald*, and his son *Erick*, surnamed the *Red-hair'd*, having committed a murder in his country, fled over into *Iseland*, where *Torwald* died. His son *Erick* being a cholerick person, kill'd soon after another man in *Iseland*; so that to escape the severity of the law, he resolved to seek for shelter in a country which one *Gundebuirne* had told him he had seen to the west of *Iseland*; *Erick* landed by his direction, in a certain harbour, made by two capes or points of land, *viz.* one at the end of an island, opposite to the continent of *Greenland*, the other on the continent. The cape of the isle was named *Huidserken*, that of the continent *Huarfs*; having between both a very good harbour call'd *Sanstaffin*, where ships may ride safely at anchor, even in the greatest storm.

Huidserken is a prodigious high mountain, without comparison much bigger than *Huarf*. *Erick* called it *Mukla-jokel*, i. e. the *Ice-mountain*; but it has been since named *Bloserken*, i. e. the *Blue-Shirt*; and a third time *Huidserken*, i. e. the *White-Shirt*. The reason of these two last alterations, seems to be founded upon the change of its colour; for the ice that melts and freezes at the same time, appears in colour at first not unlike the moss or grass or little trees growing upon these rocks. But when by a long continued snow, vast heaps are gathered, the ice becomes extraordinary thick and returns to its former colour and natural whiteness. This I can affirm by my own experience in *Swedeland*, where we have seen rocks, some whereof appeared to us of a bluish, and others of a white colour for the same reason. I will assure you, and my lord embassador can testify, that in our return the same winter from *Swedeland* to *Denmark*, as we pass'd in a coach over the sea, betwixt *Elsenore* and *Copenhagen*, we met vast shoals of ice piled upon one another; some whereof appeared to our sight very white; others of the finest azure, which being not able to give a sufficient reason for this difference, as being produced by the same water; and situate in respect of our eyes, at no such distance as to cause so remarkable a difference: This put me in mind of what *Virgil* says concerning the frozen *Zones*.

Ice of several colours.

Cærulea glacie concretæ atque imbribus atris.

Tho' I am apt to believe that the words *Cærulea glacie* ought to be interpred in this passage, the *Black Ice*, as *Virgil* fancies to be in these dark and black countries; in the same sence he says in another place,

Olli cæruleus supra caput adstitit imber.

And in another place,

——— *Stant manibus aræ,*
Cæruleis mæstæ vittis atraq; cupresso.

In both which passages the word *Cæruleus* signifies *black*, without all dispute.

But to return to our purpose, *Erick* before he would venture on the continent, thought it adviseable to land in the isle unto which he gave the name of *Ericksand*, i. e. *Erick's Isle*, and continued there all the winter. In the spring he passed over to the continent, which he called *Greenland*, i. e. the *Green-Country* from the verdure of its pastures and trees. Unto the place where he landed, he gave the name of *Ericksfiorden*, i. e. *Erick's-Haven*, at a small distance from whence he built certain habitations, called *Ostraburg*, i. e. the *East-borough* or plantation. Next *Autumn* he went to the western-side, where he erected another plantation called *Vestreburg*, i. e. the *Western-Borough*. But whether the continent seem'd to him colder and sharper than that of *Iseland*; or whether he found it less secure, he returned the next winter to *Ericksand*; yet returned from thence next summer to the continent, taking his course towards the north, to the foot of a great rock which he named *Sneefiel*, i. e. the *Snow-Rock*, and thence to a certain harbour, upon which he bestowed the name of *Ravensfiorden*, i. e. *Rookeshaven*, from a great number of crows or ravens he found there. *Ravensfiorden* lies directly opposite to the north-sine of the *Ericksfiorden*, which is seated on the south-

I side

ſide, being divided only by a branch or arm of the ſea. About the end of autumn, *Erick* returned to his iſland, where he paſs'd the third winter. In the ſpring he reſolved to go in perſon to *Iſeland* to engage the inhabitants of that iſle (with whom he had good correſpondence) to follow him into *Greenland*; he was not backward in telling them wonders of this new diſcovered country, of its plenty of great and ſmall cattle, of excellent paſtures, of fiſhes and all ſorts of game. His rhetorick proved ſo prevailing, that a good number of them croſſed the ſea with him into *Greenland*.

Olaus Trugger *King of* Norway, a *chriſtian.*

Erick had a ſon named *Leiffe*, accompanied his father into *Iſeland*, and from thence croſſed over to *Norway*; where, as my chronicle of *Iſeland* tells us, he gave a favourable account to king *Olaus Trugger* of the country diſcover'd by his father. The king of *Norway* having then but lately embraced the chriſtian religion, cauſed *Leiffe* to be inſtructed in the ſame, and to be baptiz'd, who continued at his court all the winter. The next ſummer he ſent him back to his father into *Greenland*, in company of a certain prieſt, to inſtruct *Erick* and his people in the chriſtian faith. *Leiffe* being returned to his father in *Greenland*, had the name of *Leiffdenhepne*, i. e. *Leiffe the fortunate* beſtow'd upon him, becauſe he had eſcaped great dangers in his voyage: On the other hand, he met with but an indifferent reception from his father, becauſe he had brought along with him certain ſtrange ſeamen, who being ſhipwrecked during the ſame tempeſt he ſo narrowly eſcaped, he found upon the keel of their ſhip, caſt upon the ice-rocks, and receiv'd them into his ſhip, and carried them into *Greenland*. *Erick* was diſpleaſed becauſe *Leiffe* had, as he alledged, ſhew'd to the ſtrangers the way to a country he deſired not to diſcover to all the world: But the generous *Leiffe* knew ſo well how to manage his father's ſavage temper, by repreſenting to him the true duty of humanity, and of charity the chief ornament of chriſtians, that he began to reliſh his and the prieſt's advice, ſent to him by the king of *Norway*, with ſuch ſucceſs, that he was perſuaded to ſuffer himſelf to be baptized, as did all the inhabitants under his juriſdiction. This is all I could learn concerning *Erick*, his ſon *Leiffe*, and thoſe firſt *Norwegians* that inhabited *Greenland*. The *Iſeland* chronicle mentions the departure of *Torwald* and of *Erick* his ſon from the harbour of *Jedrem* in *Norway* to have happened under the reign of *Hakon Jarle*, ſurnamed the *Wealthy*, where this chronicle begins under the reign of *Olaus Trugger* king of *Norway*, who reign'd about the year of our lord 982. But the *Daniſh* chronicle put it about the year 770. I have proved to you in my relation of *Iſeland*, that this computation is more probable than the firſt, by a bull of pope *Gregory* IV. granted about the year of our Lord 835, to biſhop *Anſgarius*, to encourage the propagation of the chriſtian religion in the northern countries, and particularly in *Iſeland* and *Greenland*. I will not pretend in this place to weigh all the arguments alledged on this head, but will content my ſelf to mention two particulars only, in relation to this opinion. The firſt is, that the ſame *Daniſh* chronicle ſays, that the kings of *Denmark* being continued chriſtians, during the reign of the emperor *Lewis the Mild*, *Greenland* was much talk'd of in thoſe days. The ſecond is, that Mr. *Gunter*, ſecretary to the king of *Denmark*, a perſon of more than ordinary learning and ingenuity, and my intimate friend, has aſſured me, that he himſelf ſaw among the records of the archbiſhoprick of *Bremen*, an ancient MS. chronicle containing a copy of a bull, by vertue whereof the archbiſhop of *Bremen* was conſtituted metropolitan of all the north, and particularly of *Norway*, and of the iſlands thereunto belonging, *viz.* thoſe of *Iſeland* and *Greenland*. He had indeed forgot the date of the bull, but remembred very well that it was granted before the year of our lord 900.

Green-land *firſt receives chriſtianity.*

Archbiſhop of Bremen *metropolitan of the north.*

The *Daniſh* chronicle ſays, that as the ſucceſſors of *Erick* increaſed in number in *Greenland*, they ventured deeper into the countrey, and met with a fruitful ſoil, meadows and rivers in the valleys between the mountains. They divided *Greenland* into eaſt and weſt *Greenland*, according to the different ſituation of the two boroughs. *Oſtreburg* and *Veſtreburg* built by *Erick*. In the eaſt they laid the foundation of a town named *Garde*, whither (as the chronicle tells us) the *Norwegians* tranſported every year, divers merchandizes, and ſold them to the inhabitants.

Garde *a town in* Greenland.

Their poſterity went farther in, and built a city, unto which they gave the name of *Albe*. And as their zeal increaſed, they built a monaſtery upon the ſea-ſhore, dedicated to St. *Thomas*. The city of *Garde* was the reſidence of their biſhops, and the church of *St. Nicholas* (the patron of ſeamen) built in the ſame town, the cathedral church of *Greenland*. A catalogue, together, with the ſucceſſion of thoſe biſhops, is to be ſeen in that part of the *Specimen Iſeandicum* of *Angrim Jonas* which treats of *Greenland* from the time of their ſettlement there, 'till the year 1389. And *Pontan* obſerves in his hiſtory of *Denmark*, that in

St. Nicholas *Church.*

in the ſame year 1389, one named *Henry* biſhop of *Garde* was preſent at the aſſembly of the ſtates of *Denmark* held at *Nieuburg* in the iſle of *Funen*, at the entrance of that part of the *Baltick* ſea, commonly call'd the *great Balt*. As *Greenland* was under the juriſdiction of the kings of *Norway* in temporal matters, ſo their biſhops acknowledg'd the ſuperiority of the biſhops of *Drunthen* in *Norway*, in eccleſiaſtical matters; and the biſhops of *Greenland* uſed frequently to croſs the ſea into *Norway* to adviſe with the biſhops of *Drunthen* about ſuch difficulties as ſometimes intervened in points of religion. *Greenland* was then governed by the laws of *Iſeland*, under certain governours, appointed by the kings of *Norway*. The names of whom, with the actions performed by ſome *Iſeland* heroes in *Greenland*, you may read in the *Specimen Iſelandicum*, where good *Angrim* their affectionate countryman has remembred them to the beſt advantage.

Magnus *K. of* Norway, *and* Erick *of* Denmark *conquers* Greenland.

The *Daniſh* chronicle tells us, that in the year 1256, *Greenland* revolted and refuſed to pay their tribute to king *Magnus* of *Norway*; which induced king *Erick* of *Denmark* (at the requeſt of king *Magnus* who had married his neice) to equip a fleet againſt them; but they no ſooner ſaw the *Daniſh* flags diſplay'd on the coaſt of *Greenland*, but they were ſeized with ſuch fear, that they ſued for pardon, and deſired peace. The king of *Denmark* (in reſpect of the love he bore to his niece, and her children) would not take any advantage of the weakneſs of the king of *Norway*, but left him in full poſſeſſion of *Greenland*: This peace was concluded in the year 1261. *Angrim Jonas* further mentions the names of the three principal inhabitants of *Greenland*, who were inſtrumental in concluding the treaty of peace in *Norway*. By virtue thereof thoſe of *Greenland* were for the time to come to ſwear fealty, and to pay tribute to the kings of *Norway*.

The chronicle of *Iſeland* being only a collection of other ſtories; has among the reſt a chapter entituled a deſcription of *Greenland*, which as it ſeems to relate to its moſt flouriſhing ſtate during the ſettlement of the *Norwegians* there; ſo I will tranſcribe to you *verbatim* the whole chapter, as it was interpreted to me from the *Daniſh* tongue into *French*. But don't require from me either time or method in this relation, for I can warrant neither.

Skagefiord.

In the moſt eaſtern part of *Greenland* lies the city of *Skagefiord*, ſeated near an inacceſſible rock; and further at ſea, a ſandbank hinders ſhips from entring the road, except at high water, when if the wind blows hard, many whales and other fiſh come into the bay, and are taken in great abundance. A little higher towards the eaſt, there is another harbour called *Funchebuder*, having borrow'd its name from a certain page of St. *Olaus* king of *Norway*, who was with ſeveral others ſhipwrecked there. A little higher nearer the *Ice-mountains*, there is an iſland called *Roanſon*, well ſtor'd with all ſorts of wild beaſts, and particularly with white bears, but beyond it nothing is to be ſeen but ice, both on the ſea and land ſide. On the weſtern coaſt lies the bay of *Kindelfiord*, inhabited all along the ſhore. On the right hand of this bay ſtands a church called *Korskirk*, i. e. the *Craſs-Church*; the land whereof reaches to *Petreſuik* near *Vandaleburg*; and beyond it monaſtery of monks, dedicated to St. *Olaus* and St. *Auſtin*. The juriſdiction of a monaſtery extends to *Bolton*. Next to *Kindelfiord* is *Rumpeſinfiord*, where is a nunnery, and near it ſeveral little iſlands, having divers hot ſprings of ſuch an exceſſive heat in the winter, that no body can endure it, tho' in the ſummer they are pretty cool and temperate; theſe waters are very wholeſome, and proper for the cure of divers diſeaſes. A little beyond them is *Eynetsfiord*: Between *Eynetsfiord* and *Rumpeſinfiord*, ſtands a royal palace call'd *Fos*; and a great church dedicated to St. *Nicholas*. Near the bay of *Lunesfiord* is the cape of *Klining*, and beyond it another bay called *Grantevig*, and beyond that a houſe named *Daller*, that belongs to the cathedral of *Greenland*. To this cathedral appertains all the country about *Lunesfiord*, and particularly the great iſland beyond *Eynetsfiord* called *Reyatſen*, becauſe of the many *Renes* (a kind of ſtags frequent in the north) found there. This iſland produces a certain ſtone called *Talgueſtein*, of ſuch ſolidity as not to be corrupted by fire, and ſo eaſy to be cut, that drinking veſſels, kettles, and vats containing ten or twelve ton, are made of it. More towards the weſt is an iſland called *Langen*, where are eight farms. This iſland belongs to the cathedral. Near to the church of *Eynetſfiord* is a royal palace named *Halleſtad*. Not far from it is the bay of *Ericksfiord*; at the entrance whereof lies an iſland called *Herrieven*, i.e. the *Lord's-iſland*, one half whereof belongs to the cathedral, the other half to the church called *Diurnes*, the firſt church you meet with in *Greenland*, as you enter on *Ericksfiorden*. To the church of *Diurnes* belongs all the country as far as *Midfiord*, and the whole track of land from *Ericksfiord* to the north eaſt. Near it is *Bondefiord* to the north, where are many iſlands and good harbours. The country is not inhabited, but altogether deſart between *Oſtreburg* and *Veſtreburg*. Near to this deſart is a church named

Old Greenland *deſcrib'd.*

A hard ſtone.

named *Strosnes*, formerly the cathedral, and residence of the bishop of *Greenland*. The *Skreklinguers* or *Skreklingres* inhabit all the country about *Vestrebug*. These desarts produce horses, goats, oxen, sheep, and all manner of wild beasts, tho' not inhabited either by christians or pagans. The author of this account was one *Iver Ben*, who was a long time steward of the bishop of *Greenland*, and an eye-witness of what he says, having been with others employed by the judge of *Greenland* to suppress the *Skreglingres*. At their arrival they found no living men, but abundance of cattle, of which they took as much as their ship could carry. Beyond *Vestrebug* is a great rock call'd *Himmelradsfield*; beyond this rock there is no safe passage for ships, by reason of the many whirlpools on that coast.

Of the Skreglingres.

These are the contents of the whole chapter which I have set down here with as much exactness as I was able; and as I had neither map, nor any other history of *Greenland*, to justify or contradict this account, I have given it you in the same manner as I had it. What puzzles me most is, what is said of the church of *Strosnes*, between *Ostreburg* and *Vestreburg*, to have been ever since *Greenland* began to be inhabited, the cathedral and the bishop's residence; there being not the least doubt but that the city of *Garde* has always had that prerogative. The *Danish* chronicle lamenting the loss of this countrey, assures us, that if the city of *Garde*, the residence of the bishop, were yet in being, and the passage thither could be recovered, we might from thence be supply'd with sufficient memoirs for the comprizing of a good history of *Greenland*. *Angrim Jonas*, a native of *Iseland*, speaking of this residence, says expresly, *Fundata in Bordum* (we must read *Garden*) *episcopali residentia in sinu Eynetsfiord Greenlandiæ Orientalis*; An episcopal see was settled in the city of *Garden* in the bay of *Eynetsfiord*, on the eastern coast of *Greenland*. The author of that relation may perhaps have been a good steward, but has proved himself but an indifferent historian, having not given us the least account who were these *Skreglingres*, against whom he was sent. I will therefore tell you what Mr. *Wormius*, the most curious person that ever I met with in the affairs of the north, has communicated to me by word of mouth, and in writing. They were savages, the original natives of *Greenland*, unto whom 'tis probable, the *Norwegians* gave that name, but for what reason I know not. 'Tis likely they inhabited the west side of the bay of *Kindelfiord* in *Greenland*; the other being inhabited by the *Norwegians*. What this author says concerning the *Skreglingres* being in possession of *Vestreburg* must be understood of the west side; the east part being possessed by the *Norwegians*. 'Tis very probable that some few of the *Norwegian* adventurers having passed the other side of the bay of *Kindelfiord*, were worsted by those *Skreklingres*. The viceroy or governour of *Greenland*, called the judge of *Greenland* (according to the *Iseland* idiom) being resolved to revenge this affront, sent against them a ship well equipp'd, and mann'd with land-forces, which those savages no sooner saw approach their shore, but according to their usual custom (when they find they are too weak to resist) they fled into the woods and rocks. The *Norwegians* finding no living body upon the coast, plunder'd the country, and carried the booty aboard their ship. This did induce our author to tell us, that amongst the *Skreklingres* were horses, goats, oxen, sheep, *&c.* but neither christians nor pagans.

Mr. *Wormius* is of opinion, that those *Skreglingres* were not far distant from the gulph of *Davis*, and perhaps were *Americans*, or the native inhabitants of *New Greenland*, discover'd by the *Danes* in the reign of *Christiern* IV. their king; of which I shall have occasion to speak more hereafter: That they lived near the *Old Greenand*, inhabited by the *Norwegians*, and that they peopled part of *Vestrebug*, before ever *Erick* possessed himself of the other part.

To tell you my opinion, I see no reason why we should transplant the *Americans* hither; Mr. *Wormius*'s opinion is more reasonable; unto which I shall add only, that by the same reason that *Vestreburg* was inhabited by the natives of that country, when the *Norwegians* came thither, *Ostreburg* had likewise its inhabitants. And as the eastern shore was nearer to the *Frozen Sea*, it was less fruitful, and by consequence more desart than the western coast. The *Norwegians* finding less resistance on that side than on the other, took possession of *Ostreburg* with less resistance than *Vestreburg*; and according to all the relations that I have seen, they were not so resolute in attempting a passage on the western coast, but to the north where they travell'd eight days together, without discovering any thing but snow and ice in the valleys. From whence you may infer, that the track of land inhabited by the *Norwegians* in *Greenland* was enclosed between the southern and eastern seas; to the north by inaccessible ice-mountains, and to the west by the *Skreglingres*, who stopp'd their farther progress on the side of *Vestreburg*. It is also observable, that the *Iseland* chronicle affirms it for a certain truth, that the *Norwegians* were possessed of so small a track

track of land in *Greenland*, as would not amount to above a third part of a biſhoprick in *Denmark*, notwithſtanding their biſhopricks are no larger than thoſe of *France*. The *Daniſh* chronicle declares the ſame, tho' in different words, *viz.* that the *Norwegians* did not inhabit the hundredth part of *Greenland*; that it was inhabited by divers nations, governed by their peculiar lords, moſt of whom were never known to the *Norwegians*.

Greenland *barren.* The *Iſeland* chronicle ſpeaks variouſly concerning the fruitfulneſs of *Greenland*, according to the different relations that compoſe it. It ſays in one place, that there grows the beſt wheat in the world, and high and lofty oaks, which bear acorns as big as apples. In another place he tells us, that nothing grows in *Greenland*, becauſe of the cold, and that its inhabitants know not what bread is. This agrees with the *Daniſh* chronicle, which affirms, that when *Erick* firſt came into this country, his people were forced to live altogether upon fiſh, by reaſon of the ſterility of the land. Neverthelefs the ſame *Daniſh* chronicle relates, that *Erick's* ſucceſſors, who went farther into the countrey, found between certain mountains, fruitful lands, meadows, and rivers, not diſcover'd by *Erick*. The contradictions in the *Iſeland* chronicle are not to be regarded, when it declares that nothing grows in *Greenland*, becauſe of the cold, the reaſon itſelf alledged to back this aſſertion, rendring it very dubious; it being moſt certain, that that part of *Greenland*, inhabited by the *Norwegians*, was ſituate under the ſame degree of elevation with *Upland*, the moſt fruitful province of *Swedeland*, which produces very good and fine wheat. Add to this what the ſame chronicle obſerves in another place, *viz.* that the cold is not ſo violent in *Greenland* as in *Norway*. Now 'tis moſt certain, that *Norway* produces very good wheat; and what I am going to tell you upon this head, would perhaps ſeem ſtrange to you, if the ſame was not founded upon the authority of creditable perſons, who have informed me that there are certain places in *Norway*, where they have two crops within the ſpace of three months. This muſt be underſtood of the plains betwixt the rocks, which being continually enliven'd by the reverberated ſunbeams againſt theſe rocks, in the months of *June*, *July*, and *Auguſt*, become ſo fertile, that in ſix weeks time they ſow and reap good corn. The ſoil being ſo fat and moiſt there by reaſon of the great quantity of ſnow melted and carried into the plains from the mountains, that immediately after they ſow again, and at the end of another ſix weeks, never fail of a ſecond harveſt as good as the former. Norway *wonderfully fruitful.*

'Tis very likely, that in *Greenland*, as well as other countries, are ſome good and ſome bad grounds; ſome plains, ſome mountains. 'Tis certain it has many rocks; the *Iſeland* chronicle tells us expreſly that it produces marble of all colours. And it is agreed on all hands, that their paſture grounds are excellent, and maintain abundance of great and ſmall cattle, many horſes, hares, ſtags, renes and other deer, ordinary wolves, and ſtag-wolves, foxes, bears white and black; and if credit may be given to the *Iſelandian* chronicle, they have taken caſtors and martins alſo, the furs whereof were not inferior to the martin ſable of *Muſcovy*. *Greenland* abounds more in falcons (white and grey) than any other place in the world. Formerly theſe birds uſed to be ſent to the kings of *Denmark* as rarities, becauſe of their extraordinary goodneſs; and the kings of *Denmark* preſented them frequently to other kings and princes, becauſe falcons and hawks are not uſed in *Denmark*, nor in any of the northern countries. Greenland *beaſts.*

The ſea produces great plenty of fiſhes all along the coaſts of *Greenland*; as likewiſe ſea-wolves, ſea-dogs, and ſea-calves, and an incredible number of whales. I know not whether I ought to reckon the white bears of *Greenland* amongſt the terreſtrial or marine creatures; for, as the black bears never forſake the land, and live altogether upon fleſh; ſo white bears never leave the ſea, and live upon what fiſh they catch. They are much larger and wilder than the black. They hunt after the ſea-wolves and dogs, who ſave their young ones upon the ice for fear of the whales. They are greedy after the young whales, their fleſh being a greater dainty to them than that of any other fiſh. They never of their own accord venture into the main ſea when the ice is melted. 'Tis not but that they can ſwim, and live in the water as well as the fiſh, but they much dread the whales purſuing them by the ſcent, out of a natural antipathy, and becauſe they devour their young ones. It happens ſometimes that vaſt ice ſhoals are from the north part of *Greenland* driven towards the ſouth, ſo that the bears not daring to venture from the ice are carried along with it, either into *Iſeland* or *Norway*, and being enraged with hunger, *Its fiſhery.* *White bears.*

(Heu male cum ſolis Norwegum erratur in oris.)

deſtroy all they meet in their way, whereof they tell you ſtrange ſtories in theſe countries.

Greenland has ever yielded plenty of horned beaſts, *Unicorns.*

beasts, called unicorns. In *Denmark* we have frequent opportunity to see many of them entire, and some pieces of these horns. If you enquire what sort of animals bear these horns, I must tell you, Sir, that they are horned creatures, improperly named unicorns, having nothing common with that so much celebrated horn of the creature which bears that name, of what nature soever it be. And as this name is ambiguous, some do yet question whether the creatures that have them are flesh or fish. You may observe, that the horns of the unicorns which I saw in *Denmark*, (whether whole or in pieces) are of the same substance, fashion, and virtue, as those seen in *France* and elsewhere. That beautiful entire horn I have sometimes spoken of to you, in the king of *Denmark*'s palace at *Fridericksbourg*, is without dispute bigger than that at St. *Denys*. I confess, 'tis not so streight, and bends within two or three foot of the point; but for the rest, 'tis of the same colour, shape, and weight as that of St. *Denys*; for the pieces of those horns I have seen in divers places at *Copenhagen*, are esteemed great preservatives against poison, as those in *Paris*, and elsewhere are. Now taking it for granted, that all those horns in *Denmark* are altogether the same with those of *France*, and that these of *Denmark* are brought thither from *Greenland*, the main question is, What sort of animals bear these horns in *Greenland?* Mr. *Wormius* being the first who informed me that they are fishes. This occasioned a smart dispute betwixt us at *Christianople*, this opinion being contradictory to the sentiments of all the naturalists, who have discoursed of it; who represent the unicorn as a terrestrial four-legg'd creature, which agrees with divers passages of holy Scripture, which cannot be understood but of four-legg'd unicorns. A curious and learned person having had the goodness to give me a farther account thereof in his letter from *Copenhagen*, I will insert the copy thereof here.

" SOME years ago being at Mr. *Frise* " the lord chancellor of *Denmark*'s " house (the predecessor of Mr. *Thomasson*, the present lord chancellor) I took an " occasion to complain to that great man, " of the negligence and want of curiosity " of our merchants and seamen that frequented *Greenland*, in not enquiring into the nature of those animals, the horns " whereof they brought in such plenty " to us, without giving themselves the " trouble of bringing along with them " some part of their flesh or skin, for the " better discovery of the whole. The " lord chancellor answer'd, they are more " curious than you imagine, and instantly " sent for a great piece of a dry'd skull, " with part of that kind of horn on it, " of about four foot long. Being extremely rejoyced to see me hold in my " hands so great a rarity, and could " scarce sufficiently feast my eyes with " the sight of it, as not understanding " at first what it was, I entreated my lord " to give me leave to carry it home to " my house, to look upon it there at my " own leisure, which he readily granted. " I found this *cranium* or skull much like " that of the head of a whale, having two " holes on the top, and which penetrate " to the palate or throat; these two holes, " being doubtless the two passages thro' " which this fish spouts up the water it " drinks: I took also notice, that what " they called the horn, proceeded out of " the left-side of its jaw. I invited the " most curious and ingenious of my auditors, to be eye witnesses of so extraordinary a sight in my closet, and among " the rest sent for a painter, who in the " presence of all the company drew the " picture of that skull, with the horn, " as it really was in figure, and answerable to its bigness, according to the original.

" My curiosity stopt not here; but understanding that such another creature " had been taken near, and carried into " *Iseland*; I writ to the bishop of *Hole*, " whose name was *Thorlac Schalonius*, and " who had been formerly my disciple at *Copenhagen*, to send me the draught of that " animal, which he did accordingly; and " sent me word at the same time, that the " *Iselanders* call it *Narhual*, that is, a whale " that feeds upon dead carcasses; for *Hual* " signifies a whale, and *Nara* a dead carcass. 'Twas really the picture of a true " fish, like a whale; I promise to shew " it to you in your return from *Christianople*, with that of the skull I had from " my lord chancellor *Frise*.

Narhual; *a great Fish.*

Mr. *Wormius* fail'd not at our return to fulfill his promise and even beyond it; for not satisfied to shew me the draughts of those fishes, he led me into his closet, where I saw upon a table the skull it self of that animal, which my lord chancellor had formerly delivered to him. He had got it, (at his request) from a *Danish* gentleman, a kinsman of monsieur *Frise*, who being one of his co-heirs, had got it for his share, and valued it at 8000 rixdollars, and had brought it 20 leagues to *Copenhagen*, to shew it to my lord embassador. I must confess, that I could not sufficiently admire

admire so exquisite a piece of curiosity. After he had carried it to my lord embassador, he was desirous to look upon it in the same closet. His excellency viewed it with more than ordinary satisfaction, and intreated Mr. *Wormius* to lend it him, in order to have a draught made of it, which he intended to carry with him to *Paris*. This great man, who has a great veneration for all vertuosoes, will be glad to shew this draught among his other curiosities he brings along with him from the north. As he has a particular affection for you, and for all those gentlemen of the famous and ingenious society of the library of monsieur *Bourdelot*: So I am certain that his closet (which he designs to furnish and accomplish, if God grants him life) will after his return into *France*, be free for you, and for all those gentlemen.

Unicorns. There is no doubt, but that the name of unicorn is equivocal, and belongs to several animals, as to the onyx and *Indian* ass, mentioned by *Aristotle*, and to that wild beast, described by *Pliny* to have the head of a stag, the body of a horse, and the feet solid, all of a piece, like the elephant; and besides this, of a wonderful swiftness and strength, being the same unicorn, mention'd in several places of the holy scripture. As to its its swiftness, the same is represented as so marvellous that God will cause *Syrion* (a mountain of *Libanus*,) to skip as the foal of an unicorn, and its strength so exalted that the power of God is compared to it. The strength of God, (saith *Moses*, the leader of the children of *Israel*,) is like that of the unicorn. Whence it appears that our unicorns of the north, which we know to be fish, must be of a different kind from the unicorns believed to be in the south or eastern parts of the world, and are without doubt terrestrial animals, when the prophet *Isaiah* foretells the *Jews* that God would drive them and their kings (whom he names unicorns) from *Jerusalem*. The unicorns, saith he, shall descend with them: This cannot be understood but of a terrestrial creature; if the prophet had supposed those unicorns to be fishes, 'tis likely he would have said, they shall swim, instead of, they shall descend. I will therefore call them a kind of sea-unicorns, as others have done with sea-dogs, sea-calves and sea-wolves. This name is not new, seeing *Bartholine* a *Danish* author hath inserted a peculiar chapter of sea-unicorns, in his treatise of unicorns. Notwithstanding which, there remains still another difficulty, *viz.* whether these sea-unicorns (of which we are now speaking) be really unicorns, and whether that we call their horns, be truly horns, or rather their teeth. The resolution of the first doubt depends upon the second; for if they be teeth, those fishes cannot properly be called unicorns, because they have no horns; and if they be horns, they are doubtless unicorns, because they have but one horn. Mr. *Wormius* affirms, that they are teeth and not horns. And I find that *Angrim Jonas* calls them *Dentes* in that place of his *Specimen Iselandicum*, where he speaks of a bishop of *Greenland* named, *Arnoldus*, being shipwrack'd as he was sailing to *Norway*; the ship being shatter'd to pieces by a storm in the *Isthmus* to the west of *Iseland*. This shipwreck happened in the year 1126: He mentions the several things taken up out of this shipwreck; *Reperti sunt*, saith this old man, *Dentes Balenarum*, &c. There were cast ashore by the tide, precious and rare teeth of whales, *Runick* letters done upon them, with a red gum, not to be blotted out, that every one of the seamen at the end of their voyage might know their own. And 'tis certain, that this *Angrim Jonas* understands by these precious teeth of whales, the same which in *Denmark* they call, and ought to be understood of, those horns we attribute to unicorns, and of which we now treat; what makes me suppose them to be teeth and not horns is, that *Aristotle* lays it down as an undoubted truth, that all unicorns carry their horns in the middle of their foreheads; but these fish have that which we name horns, at the end of their snout or under-jaw or gum, in the same place where teeth are fixed: That the horns are growing in the forehead *per symphysim*, *i. e.* by an adjunction or natural union with the bone, but the teeth are sunk into the gums *per Gomphosim* *i. e.* as a wedge or nail that enters the substance. This was plainly to be seen in that skull monsieur *Wormius* shew'd us, which was sunk into the jaw near a foot deep, and stretch'd out in length like a lance, laid flat in the same manner as the fish named *Pristis* carries its sythe, and the *Xiphias* or sword-fish wears its sword. *Lasting Runick letters.*

I have taken notice of a very good reason, or rather observation in *Aristotle*, concerning the horn of these unicorns. He says, that all the animals that have two horns, are cloven-footed; but all unicorns have but one solid claw: That nature had made the same union, and the same conjunction of claws in the feet, as of the horns in the head of the unicorns, as it has made the same division of claws and horns in the feet and hands of other animals. From whence it follows, that the

the only distinction of the unicorns from the other animals, consists in the unity and solidity of their claws and horns; and by the same reason that the unicorns have their claws in their feet, as the other animals, they bear their horns in the same place of the head, namely in the forehead: And as the other beasts that have two horns, carry them on both sides of their front, they that have but one, have it in the middle of the fore-head. But as the fish we are speaking of, that have neither claws nor feet, cannot have any horns in their head, we may from hence conclude, that what some suppose their horns, being fixed deep into their jaws, and not fastned to their front, cannot properly be said to be horns, and therefore are to be reckon'd as teeth.

At first I my self was not of this opinion, but as I was disputing about it with monsieur *Wormius*, the great marshal of *Denmark*, (of whose high birth, eminent vertues and dignities he possesses next to the king, my letters have informed you before.) This great person, who has honoured me with his particular favour, and taken a singular satisfaction to satisfy my curiosity in every thing I could desire, told me in relation to this matter something that confirm'd me in my first opinion, that they were horns and not teeth. He acquainted me, that the king of *Denmark*, his master, designing to make a present of a piece of this sort of horns, that should be extraordinary beautiful and handsome, he order'd him to cause an entire horn to be sawed near the root, where 'tis biggest and most beautiful. As soon as he had sawed a little of the horn, (which he fansied to be solid) he found it hollow within, and what surprised him most, in the same concavity, another less horn, of the same figure and substance as the great one. He order'd the great horn to be sawed round, without touching the little one, and found it to be grown in the inside of the great one, about a foot long within the concavity, the remainder of the great one being solid. This made me imagine that the animals which bear those horns, cast them as the stags do theirs, that their great horns fall off, and others come in their stead; and that it was doubtless for this reason, that so many horns separated from their heads, were carried by the ice-shoals unto the coast of *Greenland* over *Iseland*: But I was soon convinced to the contrary, when I saw the skull before mentioned, and observed that long root that was fixed in its jaw-bone, and that the very same thing that the said minister told me he had caused to be sawed, was a tooth and no horn. That also 'tis possible that the teeth fall, and others grow in their steads, in these fishes, as well as they fall and grow again in children, and some persons of a more advanced age. 'Tis very frequent that such teeth as fall are put out and forced away by other new teeth that begin to appear before the old ones fall away. The like never happens to the stags, whose heads, after having cast their horns, remain as bare as if they never had any, until such time as their new horns grow again.

The horn of St. Denys.

But for fear so long a discourse of horns should seem tedious, I will conclude it with saying something of the pretended unicorn's horn of *St. Denys*. I have told you that it is altogether, and every where like that of *Denmark*. I will add to this, that the *Danes* are of opinion, (as most certainly it is) that all those kind of horns found in *Muscovy*, *Germany*, *Italy* and *France*, came originally out of *Denmark*, where this sort of merchandize was very frequent, whilst there was a passage between *Norway* and old *Greenland*, and that they constantly cross the seas from one coast to the other. The *Danes*, who brought them to sale in foreign countries, had no reason to declare them to be fishes teeth; but sold them for unicorn's horns, to sell them at the higher rate; this they have not only practised formerly, but also continue to do it this day. 'Tis not long since, that the company of *New-Greenland* at *Copenhagen*, sent one of their agents into *Muscovy*, with several great pieces of these kind of horns, and amongst the rest, one end of a considerable bigness, to sell it to the great duke of *Muscovy*. The great duke being extremely taken with the beauty thereof, he shew'd it his physician, who understanding the matter, told the great duke, 'twas nothing but the tooth of a fish; so that this agent returned to *Copenhagen* without selling his commodity. After his return, giving an account of the success of his journey, he exclaimed against the physician, who had spoiled his market by disgracing his commodities: Thou art a half-headed fellow, replied one of the directors of the company, (as he told me since) why didst thou not offer two or three hundred ducats to the physician, to persuade him that they were the horns of unicorns? You need not doubt, sir, but that the horn of *St. Denys*, did come originally from the same place, and was sold in the same manner. I can't exactly tell you the time since I saw it; but if the remembrance of the idea that remains in me, deceives me not, 'tis a tooth like those

Fishes teeth sold for horns of an unicorn.

those they show in *Denmark*; for it has the same root as the rest, hollow and worm-eaten at the end like a rotten tooth; this being granted, as it is really true, I will positively affirm it to be a tooth fallen out of the jaw-bone of the same fish known in *Iseland*, by the name of *Narhual*, and that consequently it is no horn.

But it is time to return into *Greenland*: The chronicle of *Iseland* tells us, that the air of *Greenland* is milder and more temperate than in *Norway*: That there is not so much, nor such frequent snow, neither the cold so excessive; not but that it freezes very hard, and sometimes they have grievous tempests; but those violent frosts and great storms happen not often, nor do they continue for any considerable time. The *Danish* chronicle mentions it as a very strange thing, that in the year 1308, they were afflicted with such dreadful thunders and lightening in *Greenland*, that a church named *Skalholt*, was burnt to the ground: That this thunder and lightening was followed by such a prodigious tempest, that it overthrew the tops of several rocks, which cast out such abundance of ashes that they fansied it rain'd ashes. This tempest was succeeded by an excessive cold winter, the like whereof had never been known in *Greenland*; the ice continuing a whole year without melting. One time as I was relating this stupendous rain of ashes to my lord embassador, he informed me, that being at *Rochel*, a sea captain lately come from the *Canaries*, assured him, that lying at anchor about six leagues from those islands, there happen'd to fall just such a shower of ashes, which lay as thick upon the deck of his ship, as if it had snowed very hard. The cause of this sudden accident was attributed to a violent earthquake, which having shaken the fiery mountains in the *Canaries*, the ashes were by the wind carried six leagues into the sea. 'Tis very probable, that the ashes cast out from the *Greenland* rocks proceeded from the same cause, and that there are in that countrey sulphurous mountains and subterraneous places, which burn like these of the *Canaries* and elsewhere. This may be verified by the neighbourhood of mount *Hecla* in *Iseland*, which lies much more northerly than this part of *Greenland*, as also by several instances of other fiery mountains in *Lapland*, much farther than the *Arctick* circle: Besides, what questionless you may have taken notice of before, in the old description of that country, *viz.* That there are baths there of such an excessive heat, that they are useful only in winter.

Air of Greenland.

A violent storm.

A strange shower of ashes.

The summer in *Greenland* is always pleasant both night and day, if that continual twilight, that in summer abides all the night in the air, may be called night. As the days in winter are very short, the nights are consequently very long. Besides that, nature produces there a wonder which I should scarce relate upon my own credit, did not the *Iseland* chronicle record the same as a miracle, and had I not an entire confidence in monsieur *Rets*, who did read and interpret it to me.

In *Greenland* with the beginning of the night, a certain light arises either with the new-moon, or just before it, which gives light to all the country, in the same degree and manner, as if it were full moon; and the darker the nights are, the more conspicuous the light appears. It takes its course towards the north, whence it is called the *Northern-Light*. It appears like a flying fiery meteor, streaming along in the air, as a high and long palisado. As it moves from one place to another, it leaves behind it a smoak in those places, through which it had passed; its swiftness being such, that none but such as have seen it are able to imagine it. It lasts all the night, and vanishes with sun rising. The enquiry into the true cause of this meteor, I will leave to those who are better versed in natural philosophy than my self, whether certain vapours arising out of the earth, enflamed by a continual motion, are not the most probable cause thereof, as we see with the same swiftness those long fuzees or fiery tongues to kindle, which fall from, or pass thro' the sky, or in the same manner as the flaming meteors fly about the church-yards. I have been told for certain, that this northern light is plainly seen as far as *Iseland* and *Norway*, when the air is clear, and the nights not clouded with any mists: It gives light, not only to the people of this northern climate; but also discovers itself in our parts. Doubtless this light is the same which I have heard mention'd by the most learned and judicious philosopher monsieur *Gassendi*, to have been frequently seen by him, and named *Aurora Borealis* or the *Northern Twilight*. The most remarkable that he ever saw, was that seen all over *France*, *silente Luna*, or about the new-moon, (for it was but one day old) in the night betwixt the 12th and 13th of *September*, *Anno* 1621. He has mentioned it only *en passant* in the life of monsieur *Perest*, but described it at large, more compleat in his learned observations, and at the end of his exercitations against Dr. *Flud*, whither I refer you, to avoid prolixity; and to return to my former relation.

A strange light.

The

The *Danish* chronicle says, that in the year 1271, a violent wind from the north east forced such a vast quantity of ice shoals loaden with bears and wood to the coast of *Iseland*, that from thence they conjectured, that what was discovered in the west of *Greenland*, was only a small part thereof; and that it extended a great way farther to the north-east. This persuaded some seamen of *Iseland* to venture upon this discovery, but could meet with nothing but ice shoals; some kings of *Norway* and *Denmark* having a long time before the same thought and design in their heads, they had sent thither several ships, nay some of them went thither in person, but with no better success than the seamen of *Iseland*: What had induced them to attempt this voyage, was either the fame, or the general received opinion grounded upon certain reports that this countrey abounded in veins of gold and silver, and precious stones. Or perhaps that passage in *Job* had made some impression upon their mind, *Gold comes from the north*. Upon which account I can't forbear to tell you what the same *Danish* chronicle says upon that subject, *viz.* that in former times certain merchants return'd from thence with great riches. It says also, that in the reign of St. *Olaus* king of *Norway*, some mariners of *Frizeland* undertook that voyage for the same purpose; but being by violent tempests forced among the rocks of this coast, they were forced to shelter themselves in some creek. He further tells us, that when they adventured ashoar, they found not far from the sea shoar some ill built huts or cabins half under ground; and about those cabins a great many mineral stones, glittering like gold and silver ore, which made them resolve to take a good quantity along with them. *Riches in the north.* In effect every one of them having taken as much as they could well carry away, as they were marching off to their ships, they saw coming out of these under-ground huts, a good number of ill shap'd and ill look'd fellows, resembling more the devils than men, with their bows and slings, and great dogs at their heels. This oblig'd these mariners to hasten their pace, to preserve both themselves and their treasure; but one of them loitering behind, had the misfortune to fall into the hands of those salvages, who tore him immediately in pieces, in the sight of his companions. This *Danish* author adds, that this countrey is full of riches, and therefore 'tis commonly said, that Saturn has hid here his treasures, and planted a set of devils here to guard them.

In the *Iseland* chronicle he has a peculiar chapter intituled, *The course and navigation from* Norway *to* Greenland. The course into *Greenland*, according to the account given by the most skilful pilots, born either in *Greenland*, or returned from thence lately, is as followeth. From *Nordstadensundmur* in *Norway*, you direct your course towards the west, till ye come to *Horensunt*, on the eastern side of *Iseland*, is seven days sail. *The strait course to Greenland.* From *Suofuels Jokel*, a sulphureous mountain of *Iseland*, to *Greenland*, the shortest way is to sail towards the west. Half way between *Iseland* and *Greenland*, lies *Gundebuirne skeer*. This was the old passage before the ice from the north rendred this navigation very dangerous. 'Tis also recorded (but in a separate paragraph) from *Langueries* to *Iseland*, (which is the most northerly part towards the pole) are eighteen leagues to *Ostreborn*, which signifies the *eastern born*. From *Ostreborn* to *Hualsbredde*, is twice twenty four hours sail. I would not have any body to undertake a voyage into *Greenland*, according to this direction; the same having always been, as far as I was able to learn, very difficult and dangerous; you may perhaps have taken notice of this from what I have said before, of the return of *Leiffe* into *Greenland*, to his father *Erick*, surnamed the *red hair'd*, from the foremention'd shipwreck of bishop *Arnold*, and the disasters that befel the mariners of *Friseland*. The same *Iseland* chronicle has another chapter, entituled, *A copy taken out of an old book, call'd,* Speculum Regale, *or,* the Royal Looking-glass. Concerning the affairs of *Greenland*, the contents whereof are plainer than the former; it says, that in former days three large sea-monsters of a strange shape, were seen in the sea of *Greenland*. *Three strange monsters.* The first was by the *Norwegians* call'd *Haffstramb*, which appear'd from the girdle upwards above water; its neck, head, face, nose and mouth, were altogether like those of a man, only the head was extraordinary high, and pointed towards the crown. It had very large shoulders, and at the extremities thereof two stumps like arms, but without hands. The body was but slender towards the middle, and keeping constantly under water, below the girdle, none ever saw the whole shape of this monster. Its countenance appear'd like ice, and as often as it was seen above water, it prov'd the forerunner of violent storms.

The second monster. The second monster was call'd *Marguguer*; in shape (as far as the girdle) not unlike a woman with large breasts, its hair hanging down behind, large hands, at the extremities of its stumps of arms with long fingers join'd together, with a skin like the feet of geese. Sometimes this monster has been seen holding a fish in its hands upon which it fed. It always portended an approaching

proaching violent ſtorm; if it dived under water with the face towards the mariners, 'twas a ſign they ſhould not be ſhipwrack'd; but if it turn'd its back to them, 'twas an ill omen, foretelling that they ſhould be caſt away.

The third monſter. The third monſter was call'd *Hafgierdinguer*; being no monſter to ſpeak properly, but three mountains of water raiſed by violent ſtorms, which occaſioned a whirlpool, that ſwallowed up all the ſhips that had the misfortune to light within this triangular whirlpool, made by the poſition of theſe watery mountains, out of which ſeldom any eſcaped without ſhipwracking. This pretended monſter or whirlpool, was occaſioned by the currents of the ſea, which meeting with turbulent winds contrary to the current, uſed to ſurprize and ſwallow up the ſhips.

This ſame book declares, that in this ſea are great heaps of ice raiſed upon one another, appearing at a diſtance like huge ſtatues of ſtrange ſhapes: it adviſes thoſe that go into *Greenland*, to bend their courſe towards the ſouth weſt, before they come near the ſhoar of that countrey, by reaſon of the great quantity of ice that ſwims on theſe ſeas, at a great diſtance from the ſhoar, even in the ſummer. It adviſes thoſe that happen to be entangled among the great ice ſhoals, to put in practice what others have done in ſuch like emergencies, *viz.* to put their long boat upon the thickeſt part of theſe ice ſhoals, with all the proviſion they have, and to ſtay there till this ice carries them to ſome land or other, or elſe it diſſolves, when they may ſave themſelves in their long-boat. *How to eſcape from the ice ſhoals.*

Here ends the hiſtory of old *Greenland*; but the hiſtory of *Denmark* tells us preciſely, that in the year 1348, a furious plague, call'd the *black peſtilence*, carried away the greateſt part of the inhabitants of the north, and among the reſt, the ſeamen and merchants of *Norway* and of *Denmark*, that were members of the *Greenland* company in both kingdoms. And it is obſervable, that from this time on, the voyages and traffick into *Greenland* were diſcontinued, and began to be loſt. Monſieur *Wormius*, as I remember, told me nevertheleſs, to have read in an old *Daniſh* manuſcript, that about the year 1484, in the reign of king *John*, there were in the city of *Bergen* in *Norway*, above forty ſeamen living that ſailed every year into *Greenland*, and brought from thence ſeveral commodities of great value: but having refuſed to ſell them to certain *German* merchants, come on purpoſe to *Bergen* to buy them, theſe *Germans* (without diſcovering their deſign) invited thoſe mariners to a ſupper, and deſtroyed them all in one night. This ſtory as 'tis related carries but little probability along with it; there being at that time no ſuch free and frequent paſſage betwixt *Norway* and *Greenland*; the narrative I am entring upon being moſt certain that the trade and traffick which *Norway* and *Denmark* formerly had with *Greenland*, was then either quite decayed, or totally ruined.

You muſt underſtand, Sir, that the tributes and cuſtoms of *Greenland* were anciently deſigned and employed to defray the charges of the table of the kings of *Norway*; and that not a mariner durſt ſail into *Greenland* without leave, upon pain of death. It happened in the year 1389, that *Henry* biſhop of *Garde*, went over into *Denmark*, to be preſent, as I told you before, at the aſſembly of the ſtates of this kingdom, then aſſembled in *Funen*, in the reign of queen *Margaret*, who united the two crowns of *Norway* and *Denmark*. It happened about the ſame time, that certain merchants of *Norway*, who had croſs'd the ſeas to *Greenland* without leave, were accuſed of having embezzled the tributes and cuſtoms belonging to the queen's table. The queen treated thoſe merchants ſeverely enough, for they had been infallibly hang'd, if they had not taken a ſtrict oath upon the holy Bible, that they had been carried over into *Greeenland*, not deſignedly, but by a ſtorm; and that what merchandiſes they had brought from thence were purchaſed with ready money, without meddling in the leaſt with the queen's revenues; they were diſcharged upon this oath. However the ſevere prohibitions made upon this occaſion, together with the danger of the ſeas, produced this fatal effect, that ſince that time, neither merchant nor mariner durſt venture on this voyage. The queen, ſome time after, ſent thither ſome ſhips, which were never heard of ſince, ſuppoſed to be caſt away, tho' it was never known either how or where, or in what manner they were loſt. This put ſuch a conſternation among the old mariners of *Norway*, that none of them could be prevailed upon to venture again upon thoſe ſeas. The queen being at that time engaged in a war with *Sweden*, and conſequently meeting no great account of *Greenland*, was not very forward to force them to theſe voyages.

Of the tributes of Greenland.

The danger of adventurers into Greenland.

The cauſe of the interruption of the commerce with Greenland.

The *Daniſh* chronicle, unto which I ſtand indebted for this hiſtory, ſays, that about the ſame time, *viz.* in the year of our Lord 1406, *Eſkild* biſhop of *Drunthem* in *Norway*, willing to take the ſame care of *Greenland* as his predeceſſors had done before; ſent thither a certain perſon named *Andrew*, to ſucceed in the place of *Henry* biſhop

2

bishop of *Garde*, in case he was dead, or to send him word if he was alive. But since this *Andrew* took shipping for *Greenland*, not the least news could be heard of him; and notwithstanding all the inquiry that could be made, it was impossible to hear the least tidings, either of him or of bishop *Henry*. This was the last bishop that was sent from *Norway* into *Greenland*.

Queen Margaret *of* Norway.

The same *Danish* chronicle gives us a catalogue of the names of all the kings of *Denmark*, since queen *Margaret*, to the reign of *Christian* IV. the present king, with an exact account of what happen'd in reference to the recovery of *Greenland*, in their respective reigns. It is absolutely requisite, Sir, you should not be ignorant of this succession, and of the fatalities or misfortunes which have made us lose even the knowledge of this renowned countrey, which in former days was so well known, inhabited, and frequented by the people of our world.

The kings of Denmark.

Erick of *Pomerania* succeeded to queen *Margaret*, but as he was a foreigner newly come into *Denmark*, he never took the pains as much as to enquire, whether there was such a countrey in the world as *Greenland*.

Christopher of *Bavaria* was crown'd next after *Erick*, but being all the time of his reign imployed in a war against the *Vandals*, then inhabiting *Pomerania*, had but little leisure to look after *Greenland*.

The family of *Oldenbourg*, that now sways the *Danish* scepter, began to reign in the year of our lord 1448. But king *Christian*, the first of that name, and of that race, instead of bending his thoughts towards the north, employed them in the south: for going in pilgrimage to *Rome*, he got from the pope the propriety of the countrey of *Dithmarsen*, to be annexed to the crown of *Denmark*, and leave to establish an university at *Copenhagen*.

Christian II. succeeded *Christian* I. and solemnly promised at his coronation, to use his utmost endeavours for the recovery of *Greenland*: but instead of recovering a countrey lost by his predecessors, he was forced to forsake his own kingdoms. His cruelties having caused him to be driven out of *Sweden*, which queen *Margaret* had united with the two kingdoms of *Norway* and *Denmark*, and establish'd in these three kingdoms but one government. He departed into *Denmark*, with the same furious spirit that had possessed him in *Sweden*, so that the *Danes*, not able to suffer him any more than the *Swedes*, deposed him. Whence it is, that he is represented amongst the kings of *Denmark*, with a broken scepter in his hand. His lord chancellor *Erick Valkanor*, a *Danish* gentleman, remarkable for his virtue, wisdom and wit, being made archbishop of *Drunthem* after his master's disgrace, retired to his archbishoprick, where he employed his mind and skill in the recovery of *Greenland*. He perused all the books that mention'd it: he examin'd all the merchants and mariners of *Norway* that could in the least be supposed to have any knowledge of it, and caused a map to be made of the passage leading to it. But just as he was upon the point of putting in execution so laudable a design in the year 1524, a great lord of *Norway* pick'd a quarrel with him, and forc'd him to abandon both his archbishoprick and the kingdom, whence he departed to *Rome*, where he died.

Frederick I. uncle to king *Christian*, had took possession of the kingdoms of *Denmark* and *Norway*; and because the faction of *Christian* was not altogether extinct, *Frederick* fearing the interest of *Valkanor*, caus'd him to be driven out of *Norway*, and annull'd the charters given to the respective companies erected for the discovery and recovery of *Greenland*.

Christian III. succeeded *Frederick*, who caused the passage into *Greenland* to be attempted, but those he sent return'd without being able to find it out. This oblig'd this king to repeal all the severe prohibitions and orders publish'd by the king's predecessors, *viz.* that none should sail into *Greenland* without peculiar licence. Instead whereof he granted full liberty to every one that had a mind to go thither without his leave. But the *Norwegians* being in those days so weak in shipping, and so miserably poor, were not in a condition to provide ships for so difficult and dangerous a voyage.

King Frederick II. *of* Denmark, *his endeavours to recover* Greenland.

King *Frederick* II. inherited with the kingdom his father *Christian* III's design. He sent a certain person named *Magnus Heigningson* to discover *Greenland*. If we we may rely upon the author's credit in reference to this voyage, there is a secret and hidden cause unknown to all the world, that visibly stops and hinders the designs of recovering this countrey. For after *Magnus Heigningson* had wandered and passed through many difficulties; he discovered *Greenland* at a distance, but could not come near it, for as soon as he had made the coast, his ship stopt immediately, at which he was astonish'd (and not without reason) for it was in the main sea, in a great depth of water, without any ice; besides, the wind blew fresh and fair, and the ship was under full sail. Thus being unable to go forward, he was forced to return to *Denmark*, where he gave an account

of

of what had happen'd to the king; whom he told by way of excuse, that in the bottom of those seas there are rocks of loadstone, which had stopp'd his ship. If he had but known the story of the *Remora*, perhaps he might have alledg'd that as a pretence, more probable than that of the loadstone. This expedition happen'd in the year 1588, or thereabouts, when king *Frederick* II. reigned. Our *Danish* chronicle tracing exactly the sequel of the time, hath inserted between the reigns of king *Christian* and king *Frederick*, a long narrative of the voyage of captain *Martin Forbisher*, an *English* captain, who undertook the discovery of *Greenland* in the year 1577. As this narrative gives us a much clearer insight into the affairs of *Greenland* and of its inhabitants than any other now extant, as far as ever I saw till this time; so I thought it not amiss to send you a translation of the matters contain'd therein.

The Voyage of Martin Forbisher *into* Greenland.

Martin Forbisher set sail out of *England* for *Greenland*, in the said year 1577; he discover'd it, but could not land nor come near it that year, by reason of the night, the ice and the winter, which came very suddenly upon him in that voyage. After his return into *England*, he acquainted queen *Elizabeth* with what he had seen. The queen upon his relation thought to have recovered this unknown countrey. She with the first beginning of the spring, gave him three ships. With these *Forbisher* set sail, and having got sight of the land, came to an anchor on the east side of it. The inhabitants of the countrey where he landed, fled away at the approach of the *English*, leaving their houses to hide themselves up and down; nay, some of them for fear climb'd up to the top of the sharpest and highest rocks, from whence they cast themselves down into the sea. The *English*, who could never so far prevail upon, or engage these savages to come near them, enter'd into their forsaken dwellings, being properly speaking no more than tents made with skins of sea-calves or whales, spread upon four great poles, sowed together very artificially with dry'd nerves. They took notice that all those tents had two entrances, the one on the western side, the other towards the south, whereby they sheltred themselves from the winds that most troubled them from the east and north. In all those dwellings, they found nothing but an old woman of a frightful look, and a young woman big with child, whom they took away with them, with a little infant that she held by the hand. As they took them away by force from the old woman, she howl'd and cried most vehemently. From whence they sailed along the coast towards the east, and saw a monster upon the water as big as an ox, with a horn at the end of its snout of a * yard and a half long, which they fancy'd to be an unicorn. Thence they steer'd their course to the north east, and discovering land, they cast anchor there, the countrey thereabouts appearing very pleasant to them. And though this place was within the continent of *Greenland*, they named it *Anavavick*, that they might keep it under another name. They found this countrey much subject to earthquakes, which overthrew great massy rocks, and rowled them into the plains, and that there was no abiding there without manifest danger. However they stay'd there a while, and because they met with a sand, glittering as if it were intermix'd with gold oar; they loaded three hundred tuns of it in their vessels. They did what they could to draw the salvages of this countrey to a conversation with them, which they seem'd not to be unwilling to; for they answered by signs, to the signs the *English* made to them, giving them to understand, that if they would go higher, they would find what they sought for. *Forbisher* answered he would, and for that purpose took his long boat with some soldiers, giving order to his three ships to follow. He passed along the coast higher up, and saw a great number of those salvages upon the rocks, which made him apprehensive of a surprize. The salvages who conducted him along the coast and were ashoar, perceiving his jealousy, (that they might not fright him by their numbers) caused three men only to appear from behind an intrenchment, much handsomer and better habited than the rest. These desired the *English* by signs and demonstrations of love to come ashoar. *Forbisher* seeing no more than three near the shoar, the rest appearing on the rocks at a distance, row'd towards the shoar without the least fear, but some that were conceal'd in a ditch being impatient (when they saw *Forbisher* rowing towards them) of delay, ran in a croud to meet the *English*; this made him keep off at a distance. However these salvages being not in the least discouraged for that reason, endeavoured still to draw to them the *English*, by casting a great deal of raw flesh upon the coast, as if they had dogs to deal withal. But finding the *English* to be afraid to approach them, these salvages contrived another artifice. They carried a pretended cripple to the sea shoar, and there leaving him they departed, and never appeared for some time, as if they were gone a great way off, or for good and all. They supposed that the *English*, according to the custom

The houses of Greenland. (margin)

* *Of the* Danish *measure.*

Of gold sand.

The salvages of Greenland.

custom of strangers, would come and carry away that weak and infirm man, (who could not easily escape their hands) to make use of him as an interpreter. But the *English* smelling the rat, discharged a musquet at the cripple, which rous'd him to that degree, that he was glad to run away as fast as he could set his feet to the ground. Then the salvages flock'd in vast numbers to the shoar, and sending whole showers of stones and arrows out of their slings and bows, the *English* only laugh'd at it, but in lieu thereof gave them a volley of shot and cannon ball that dispers'd them all in a moment.

The salvages temper. According to this relation, those salvages are treacherous, wild, and so barbarous, as not to be civilized by flattery. They are gross of body, and of an olive colour; though some are of opinion, that there are amongst them negroes as well as in *Ethiopia*. *Their cloathing, &c.* Their cloathing is of skins of sea dogs sewed together, with dry nerves. Their women walk with their hair loose, they cast it behind their ears to shew their faces, painted with blue and yellow: they wear no petticoats as our women do, but many drawers made of fish skins, which they put one over another; each pair of drawers has its pockets, where they keep their knives, thread, needles, and small looking-glasses, and other trifles brought to them by strangers, or cast ashoar by the tide of the sea after shipwrecks, which often happen here. The shifts of men and women are made of the bowels of great fish sewed together with very small nerves. Both sexes wear a kind of loose garments which they girt with straps of the skins of fish. They stink most nauseously, are nasty and filthy: their tongues serve them instead of a napkin or handkerchief, neither are they ashamed of what other men conceal and cover. Amongst them those are reckoned the richest who have most bows, slings, boats, and oars; their bows are but short, and their arrows slender, pointed with bone or sharp horns. They are very dexterous in handling their bows and slings, and in darting at the fish in the water with their javelins. Their boats are covered all over with skins of sea-dogs which hold no more than one man at a time. Their great boats are made of wood fastened together with strong wooden pegs and ribs, and covered with whales skins sewed together with very strong nerves; these boats carry at most but twenty men at one time; their sails are of the same substance as their shifts, *viz.* of the bowels of fish sowed together with small nerves; and though there be no iron in those ships, they are so artificially and strongly join'd together, that they dare adventure in them a great way into the main sea, without dreading the most violent storms or tempests. This countrey produces no venomous creatures except spiders. They have also abundance of gnats, which with their stings raise large pustules and swellings in the face. They have no fresh water but what they procure from the dissolved snow.

The author of this chronicle is of opinion, that the violent frosts bind and stop the veins of the earth to such a degree, as to hinder the passage of all fresh water springs. Their dogs are of an extraordinary size, so that they couple them together, and use them to draw their carriages in the same manner as other people do with their horses.

Here ends this relation, which whether this *Danish* author has taken out of the *English* travels of *Martin Forbisher*, or whether he has written by hear-say, in imitation of those ancient *Danes*, who made up and compos'd the history of their times according to the tales that were spread abroad in the world, I am not able to determine. But it is time to return to the kings of *Denmark*.

Christian V. son of *Frederick* II. undertook once more the business of *Greenland*, resolving to leave no stone unturn'd for the discovery thereof, notwithstanding the ill success his father and grandfather had met with in this attempt: in order to this design, he sent for a captain and skilful pilot from *England*, both well acquainted with those seas, and the course they were to take in this voyage. The captain and pilot being arrived in *Denmark*, three stout ships were equipp'd, and committed to the conduct of *Gotske Lindenau*, a *Danish* gentleman, as commodore, who set sail from the *Sound* in the beginning of the warm season in the year 1605. These three ships kept together for some time, till the *English* captain being come to the elevation he long'd for, he steer'd his course towards the south west for fear of the ice, that he might with the more safety and convenience approach the coast of *Greenland*. The course he took seem'd suitable to the ancient passage from *Iseland* mention'd before. The relation whereof gives the same directions. The *Danish* commodore judging the *English* captain to have taken the wrong course to the south west, steer'd his course to the north east, and arrived alone with his ship in *Greenland*. As soon as he cast anchor, divers salvages that had discover'd him from the high shoar, (where they inhabited) leap'd into their little boats, and came on board him. He receiv'd them with a great deal of civility, and welcomed them

Christian V. *of* Denmark.

His endeavours to recover Greenland.

Gotske Lindenau *sailing to* Greenland.

Two courses into Greenland.

them with several bumpers of excellent wine; but these savages fancying it to be bitter, made very ugly faces at it; but seeing some whale oil, they desired something of that; accordingly great pots being fill'd with it, they did drink them off very greedily. These salvages brought skins and furs, of foxes, bears, sea-calves, and a great many horns, (which the author calls precious) or at least some pieces, ends and stumps of them, which they exchanged for needles, knives, looking-glasses, buckles, and other such like trifles, which the *Danes* shewed them: They making not the least account of the gold and coined silver that was offer'd them, but express'd an earnest desire for all steel works, a thing most in request among them, above all other commodities. To purchase which they were ready to part with what they esteem'd most precious, *viz.* their bows, arrows, boats, and oars, and when they had nothing else to give, they stripped themselves of their shirts. *Gotske Lindenau* continued three days in this road, but the chronicle does not say that he landed here. Doubtless he was afraid to venture ashoar, and to hazard his small number of men amongst such multitudes of salvages of this countrey. He weighed anchor and departed the fourth day, but before he set sail, detain'd on board his vessel two of those salvages that were come to traffick with him, who made such violent efforts to get out of the hands of the *Danes*, that they attempted to leap over-board into the sea, so that they were forced to bind them. Those that remained a shoar, seeing their companions chained and carried away, made a most dreadful noise, and sent whole showers of arrows and stones after the *Danes*; but these firing a great gun at them, they were soon dispersed. The commodore return'd alone with his ship into *Denmark*.

Davis's gulph.

The *English* captain with his and the other *Danish* ship arrived in *Greenland* (as the chronicle tells us) at the furthermost end of the land to the west, which could be no other place but *Cape Farewel*: For 'tis most certain that he enter'd *Davis*'s gulph, and sailed along the eastern coast of that gulph. He discovered a great many good harbours, a beautiful countrey, and large verdent plains. The salvages of this part of the countrey barter'd with them, as the salvages of the other part of *Greenland* had done with *Gotske Lindenau*. These indeed seem'd to be much more wary, timorous and mistrustful than the others, for as soon as they had made any exchange of goods with the *Danes*, they would run and leap into their boats as if they had stollen them, or as if they had been pursued by an enemy. The *Danes* being very desirous to land in one of these harbours, went ashoar well provided with all sorts of weapons. The countrey where they set foot ashoar, appear'd to them pleasant and pretty good, but sandy and stony like the grounds in *Norway*. By the exhalations and vapours that issued out of the earth, they concluded that there were divers sulphureous mines here, especially since they found a great many stones supposed to belong to the silver mines which they had carried over into *Denmark*; where out of one hundred weight of these stones, they extracted twenty six ounces of silver. This *English* captain finding so many fine harbours along this coast, gave them *Danish* names, and caused a map to be drawn of them before his departure thence. He also seized four of those salvages, the most comely they could meet with, one of which was so enraged at his captivity, that the *Danes* finding they could not drag him along with them, they beat out his brains with the but end of their musquets, which so frighted the other three, that they followed them without any farther opposition. At the same time a body of salvages got together, either to revenge the death of him that was kill'd, or to relieve those that were leading away into captivity. To effect this, they got betwixt the sea and the *Danes*, with an intention to engage them before they could reach the harbour, and prevent their getting on board. But the *Danes* having sent a volley of their small shot, seconded by their cannon, among them, the salvages frighted both with the noise and the fire, fled in great confusion, suffering the *Danes* to embark without any farther disturbance; who were no sooner got on board, but they weighed anchor and returned into *Denmark* with the three salvages, whom they presented to the king their master, who declared that he thought them much better shaped, and less barbarous, than those two *Gotske Lindenau* brought along with him, being also very different from them in their habit, language and manners.

Silver stones.

The king's second adventure into Greenland.

The king of *Denmark*, well satisfied with this first voyage, resolved on a second. Accordingly the next year 1606, he sent the same gentleman *Gotske Lindenau*, with five good ships into *Greenland*: He set sail from the *Sound* the 8th day of *May*, carrying along with him the three salvages, the *English* captain had taken in *Davis*'s gulph, for to make use of them as his interpreters. Those poor harmless creatures express'd an unspeakable joy when they understood that they were returning back into their own countrey. One of them fell sick at sea, died, and

Savages of Groenland
A Savage fishing in his boate
A little Groenland boate
The fish the Islanders call Narwall, which has the horn, or tooth call'd the Unicorns horn
The head of the fish Narwall, with a piece of the tooth or horn, four foot long

was cast over-board. *Gotske Lindenau* steering his course directly towards *America* (as the *English* captain had done before) came to the south-west point of the gulph of *Davis* by cape *Farewel*. One of his five ships lost her company in a mist, but the other four arrived in *Greenland* the 3[d] of *August*. In the first road where the *Danes* cast anchor, the salvages appear'd in great numbers near the shore, but would not traffick with them, so that as they seem'd to be afraid of the *Danes*, those likewise would not trust them. This obliged them to hoist their sails, and go up higher to another place, where they met with an harbour much more commodious than the first; but the inhabitants were as ill-humour'd as the former; for, being jealous of the *Danes*, they threatned to fight them if they offer'd to set foot on shore. The *Danes*, not willing to trust these any more than the others, or venture upon a landing, sailed farther; and as they coasted along the shore, these salvages rowed along in their small boats, and following them at some distance; the *Danes* found a means to surprize, at several times, six of these salvages, whom they carried aboard in their boats belonging to their ships. It happen'd that when the *Danes* had cast anchor at the third road, a servant of *Gotske Lindenau*, a bold fellow, earnestly entreated his master to suffer him to go alone on shore, in order to try the temper of those salvages, alledging, that he hoped either to intice them by the commodities he would carry along with him, or to save himself by flight if they had any mischievous design against him. The admiral yielded at last to the importunity of his servant, but no sooner had he set his foot on the shore, but he was taken, kill'd and torn in pieces by these salvages, who after this tragedy withdrew from the shore, sheltring themselves behind the hills, beyond the reach of the *Danish* cannon. The knives and swords of these salvages are made of the horns or teeth of fishes, commonly call'd unicorns, sharpen'd with stones, and are as keen as if they were of iron or steel. *Gotske Lindenau* being convinced that he was not likely to get much advantage by staying in this countrey, set sail for *Denmark*, but one of his *Greenland* prisoners was so much afflicted at his removal from his native countrey, that in despair he cast himself over-board into the sea, and was drown'd.

The salvages jealous of the Danes refuse to traffick with them.

A bold adventure to the destruction of the adventurer.

The *Danes* in their return home met with the first ship that was separated from them in this voyage, but did not keep together above five days, when by a most violent storm they were again separated and scatter'd from one another in such a manner, that they did not meet again till a month after the storm ceas'd. After much labour, hazard, and a thousand difficulties, they return'd to *Copenhagen* the 1st day of *October* following.

The third adventure.

The king of *Denmark* having taken a resolution, undertook the third and last voyage into *Greenland*; he sent two great ships under the command of a certain captain, a native of *Holstein*, named *Karsten Richkardtsen*, who took into his service some of the best mariners of *Norway* and *Iseland*, who being well versed in those seas, were to serve him as guides in the dangerous enterprize. The chronicle says, this captain set sail from the *Sound* the 13th day of *May*, without mentioning the year, which I could never learn. The 8th day of *June* following, he discovered the tops of the mountains of *Greenland*, but he could not come near the shore, by reason of the vast ice shoals that were settled near to the shore, and extended a great way into the sea. The ice being heap'd upon one another, appear'd at a distance like mountains or high rocks. Upon this occasion the author observes, that some years the ice of *Greenland* never melts all the summer. Thus the captain of *Holstein*, finding no means to approach the shore; and being besides this separated by a storm from the other ship, before he came to these vast ice mountains, was obliged to return without being able to encompass his design. However, the king of *Denmark* was pleased to admit of his excuses, and the difficulties he alledg'd in his behalf. Perhaps you will be curious to know what became of the four first salvages, and of the five last, the remnants of all they had taken in the two first voyages into *Greenland*: I will give you, sir, a brief account of them.

Is prevented to approach the shore by the ice.

An account of some salvages carried from Greenland into Denmark.

The king of *Denmark* appointed certain persons to take particular care of their food, and to look after them, with this proviso, however, that they should be at liberty to walk where they pleased. Their food was milk, butter, cheese, raw flesh, and fishes, after the same manner as they used to feed in their own countrey. It being found impracticable to accustom them to our bread, or roasted or boil'd meat, much less to our wines; but they swallow'd nothing more greedily than great draughts of oil, or of whales grease. They often turn'd their heads towards the north, and by their sighs express'd the desire and affection they bore to their native countrey; that after their keepers were removed, some of them who could get to their little boats and oars, put off to sea, with an intent questionless to cross the seas; but being surprized by a storm about ten or twelve leagues from the *Sound*, were forced upon the shore of *Schonen*, where being taken by the peasants, they were brought back to *Copenhagen*, where they

they were more ſtrictly guarded by their keepers afterwards, which put them into ſuch a melancholly humour, that they pined themſelves to death.

However there being five of theſe ſalvages alive, a *Spaniſh* ambaſſador came into *Denmark*, the king being willing to give the ſaid miniſter the divertiſement of ſeeing theſe ſalvages to row in their little canoo's or boats, they perform'd the ſame with extraordinary dexterity.

But to give you the beſt idea I can of the ſhape of theſe boats, I would have you fancy the weaver's ſhuttle, of ten or twelve foot long, compos'd of large whale bones, of the thickneſs of an inch, or thereabouts, cover'd both within and without, (not unlike the ſticks of an umbrello) with the ſkins of ſea-dogs, and ſea-calves, ſtitched together, with the nerves of the ſame creature.

Their boats and manner of uſing them.

We muſt alſo ſuppoſe this engine or boat to have a round hole on the top, in the middle about the compaſs of both the thighs of a man; and that it grows narrower and narrower by degrees, at both ends proportionably to its bigneſs, (like our watermen's boats upon the *Thames*.) The chief ſtrength and ingenuity of the whole engine, conſiſting chiefly in the junctures at both ends, where theſe whale bones are join'd and faſtened together; and in the opening, hole, or circle above, in the circumference whereof all the whale bones from the lowermoſt parts meet; the demi-circle underneath being faſtened to the uppermoſt circle, or round hole like a rundlet, where it opens towards its paniers: It is farther to be obſerved, that all the whale-bones underneath and of the ſides of the boat either paſs thro' or end in this demi-circle; and that every thing is ſo well join'd together, that what with its light weight, and the good management of the rower, it will bear againſt the moſt violent ſtorms at ſea.

The ſalvages, when they are to make uſe of theſe boats, get into them by the hole or open, at the top, and ſtretching their legs towards one or other of theſe two ends, ſtop the overtures left with their waſtcoats, made of dog or ſea-calves ſkins; theſe they faſten cloſe to their middle, and the hole wherein they ſit, and cover their heads with certain bladders or caps tied to the upper part of their waſtcoats, that let the weather be never ſo bad, and the ſea never ſo boiſterous; nay tho' they are dip'd ſometimes over head and ears, (which often happens) they are never the worſe for it, no water entring either thro' their cloaths, or into their boat. Thus they always ſwim on the ſurface of the water, and are in leſs danger in tempeſtuous weather than a large ſhip.

They uſe only one oar, not above five or ſix foot long, and half a foot broad at both ends, which they manage with both hands, graſping it in the middle where it is round.

I did not tell you without very good reaſon, that the ſhape of theſe boats reſembles a weaver's ſhuttle, it being certain that the ſhuttle manag'd by the moſt dexterous workmen, does not go forward with the ſame ſwiftneſs as theſe boats do upon the water, by the dexterity of theſe ſalvages: The *Spaniſh* ambaſſador was extreamly delighted to ſee five of them perform their taſk with ſuch incredible ſwiftneſs, and to croſs and paſs by one another with ſo violent a motion, without touching their oars or boats.

The king of *Denmark* being curious to try the uttermoſt of their ſtrength, order'd a ſloop to be mann'd with eight pair of oars, to row againſt them, but they were ſo nimble, that the ſloop could ſcarce overtake them. The ambaſſador was ſo generous as to give a preſent of money to every one of theſe ſalvages, which they beſtow'd in cloaths after the *Daniſh* faſhion: Now ſome of them bought themſelves boots and ſpurs, and feathers in their hats, offering to ſerve the king on horſeback.

They attempt to return into Greenland.

But they were ſoon after ſeiz'd with their former ſplenetick fits; all their thoughts being bent upon their native countrey. Two of theſe mention'd before, who got out at ſea, and were caſt upon the ſhore of *Schonen*, being not ſo ſtrictly guarded as the reſt, becauſe no body believed they would run the ſame hazard again, (after their firſt deliverance) did once more attempt to row in their boats croſs the ſeas, ſteering their courſe towards the north; they were purſued as far the entrance of the *Sound*, but could not be overtaken; ſo that 'tis probable they were loſt, it being not likely they could reach *Greenland* in their ſmall boats.

It was generally obſerved, that theſe ſalvages would burſt out into tears, as often as they ſaw a child on his mother's or a nurſe's breaſt; queſtionleſs becauſe they were married and could not forget their wives and children, they had been forced to leave behind them.

Thoſe that remained at *Copenhagen* had a ſtrict guard put upon them, which ſerved only to encreaſe their deſire to return to their native countrey, becauſe they now deſpaired of ever ſeeing it again.

This had ſuch a powerful influence upon their minds, that they all died with vexation, except two who outliv'd their companions about ten or twelve years. The *Danes* did what they could to render their capti-

captivity easy, representing to them, that they were, and always should be treated among them like friends and countreymen; which seem'd to have some influence upon them.

The next thing they did, was to endeavour to instruct them in the christian faith; but as they could never be brought to learn the *Danish* tongue, and that faith comes by hearing, it was impossible to make them truly sensible of the mysteries of the christian religion.

Some people who had taken particular notice of their actions, did observe them frequently lifting up their eyes towards heaven, and to worship the rising-sun. One of them died at *Colding* in *Jutland*, being employed in fishing of pearls in the water.

For it is observable, sir, that the mussels in *Denmark* are so full of seed pearls, (as they call them) that scarce any are without them; of these mussels, vast quantities are taken in the river of *Colding*; and some among the rest, which contain very good and round ones: The *Greenland* salvage having often mention'd, that they had pearls in his countrey, and that he used to be employed in fishing for them, the governor of *Colding* took him along with him to his government, where he gave him sufficient employment in the river; the salvage being an excellent diver, brought up abundance of the best mussels, and for the most part some of that kind, which contained very good pearls; the governor was so pleased at this success, that imagining no otherwise, but that in a little time he should be able to sell his pearls by the bushel, he made this poor salvage dive continually for pearls (notwithstanding the rigour of the winter season) to such a degree, that at the last the cold kill'd him.

His companion, now become inconsolable by his death, made shift to get into one of their little boats, and taking the opportunity of the next fair day, cross'd the seas to the opposite shore of the *Sound*, before any body had the least suspicion of his flight; however he was pursued and overtaken, but not before he was got betwixt 30 and 40 leagues at sea. Being given to understand by certain signs, that he must have been infallibly swallow'd up by the waves of the sea, before he could reach the *Greenland* shore; he answered by signs, that his intention was to keep along the coast of *Norway*, to a certain light, from whence he would have cross'd over to *Greenland*, by the direction of the stars. After his return to *Copenhagen*, he died for grief. This was the end of the unhappy *Greenlanders*.

They were much the same, as I formerly described to you the *Laplanders*, of a low stature and broad shoulder'd, *forti pectore & armis*, strong limb'd, flat nosed, with large thick lips. The remnants of their boats, oars, bows, arrows, slings and garments, are to be seen to this day in *Denmark*. I had the opportunity of seeing two of their boats with their oars at *Copenhagen*, one at Mr. *Wormius*'s, and the other at the landlord's of our ambassador. The said Mr. *Wormius* has also some of their garments made of dogs and sea-calves skin,, some of their shirts made of the guts of fishes, one of their vests made of the skin of a bird, with the feathers on it of various colours; as also their bows, arrows, slings, knives, hangers, and their javelins or darts, which they use in fishing, pointed at the extremities (as well as their arrows) with horns, or teeth sharpened at the points. I also saw here a *Greenland* almanack, compos'd of 25 or 30 small canes or reeds, fastened to a piece of a sheep-skin, but the use thereof was known to nobody but the *Greenlanders* themselves.

The kings of *Denmark* being quite discouraged by so many disappointments in these voyages, some merchants of *Copenhagen* entred into a society with some persons of quality (known to this day by the name of the *Greenland* company) in order to prosecute the same design. This company sent in 1636, two ships to the gulph of *Davis*, where they came to an anchor near the shore, which surrounds that bay. They had not been there long, before they saw eight salvages of the countrey coming towards them in their small canoos or boats; coming aboard, the *Danes* laid out their knives, looking-glasses, needles and such like trifles, and the salvages their fur and dog skins, and sea-calves skins; besides a considerable quantity of what they call the unicorns horns.

The Danish Greenland *company*.

Whilst they were busy in exchanging these commodities, a cannon aboard one of these ships happened to be discharged at the drinking of a health; the sudden noise whereof put these poor wretches into such a consternation, that they run over-board into their boats, and so put to sea, with such swiftness, that they could scarce well perceive them, till about 200 or 300 paces from the ship. The *Danes*, surprized at their unaccountable fear, gave a signal to these salvages to return, which they did, as soon as they saw the fire and smoke quite gone. Their manner of traffick is thus: Having chosen what commodities they like best, they put them together in one bundle; this done, they put in another bundle what commodities they are willing to exchange for them;

them; and thus adding or diminishing till both parties are satisfied, the bargain is struck at last.

Much about the same time that the *Danes* were busy in exchanging their commodities with those of the salvages, they saw one of these marine unicorns lying upon the shore, where being cast by the tides, it was left wallowing upon the sands. As it is generally reported of these sea-calves, that they love to feed upon grass; so it is likely that these fishes (which may well be call'd sea-oxen) take delight to come now and then ashore.

The salvages had no sooner discovered the prey, but they attack'd and kill'd the fish, and after they had beaten his horn or teeth into several pieces, carried them aboard immediately and sold them to the *Danes*. This fish which appears so defenceless ashore, is very fierce at sea, being the same thing at sea to the whale, that the rhinoceros is to the elephant among the terrestrial beasts; for he will engage the whale, and run his tooth into his sides. Some affirm, that they are of such strength as to be able to split a vessel at sea, if they run their teeth against it, and that several ships have been sunk by them.

However this traffick was not the main reason that had induced the *Danes* to bestow such vast charges upon those voyages: The pilot it seems, who was the chief conductor of these ships, had formerly taken notice of a certain tract near the sea-shore on that coast, the sand whereof had both the colour and full weight of gold oar; he thought it best to improve this opportunity, he gather'd as much of it, as the ship aboard of which he was could well carry, and so set sail for *Denmark*, telling the ships crew, that they were all rich enough, if they could come safely thither.

The great marshal of *Denmark*, who was governor and the first establisher of this company, being surpriz'd at their sudden return, the pilot told him, that his ship being loaden with gold, they had done their business beyond expectation. But the great marshal being a person not easily to be impos'd upon, he sent some of this sand to the goldsmiths of *Copenhagen*, who not being able to bring as much as one single grain of gold out of it, the grand marshal was so enraged at the folly of the pilot, that, to give all possible demonstrations that could be to the rest of the company, that he had not the least hand in so gross a miscarriage, he commanded the pilot immediately to weigh anchor, and to throw the whole charge of this pretended gold oar into the *Baltick* sea: The pilot was forced to obey, but finding himself at once despoiled of all his hopes, died soon after, as it is supposed, for grief.

However, the great marshal had sufficient occasion afterwards to repent of this rash resolution; for (as he told me himself) not long after, such another gold dust or sand being found in the mines of *Norway*, an assay-master, who was lately settled at *Copenhagen*, found means to separate a considerable quantity of gold, in proportion of the oar, so that the *Danes* in all probability, lost a great treasure by the ignorance of the other goldsmiths (in whose skill they confided) who perhaps would not have drawn any gold ever out of the oar of *Peru*.

This was the last voyage undertaken by the *Danes* for the discovery of *Greenland*; in this voyage they brought along with them that great piece of an unicorn's horn, which, as we told you before, the great duke of *Muscovy*'s physician discover'd to be the tooth of a fish; which the master of the house, where the ambassador lodged, and who belong'd to the *Greenland* company, shew'd us, being valued at 6000 rixdollars.

The *Danish* ship, at the time of their departure from the *Greenland* coast, seized two of the salvages of that countrey aboard them, in order to carry them to *Denmark*: After they were come into the main sea, they loosened these poor wretches of their bonds, who guided by a violent desire after their native countrey, laid hold of the first opportunity, and throwing themselves overboard, did endeavour to reach that shore by swimming, tho' questionless they were devoured by the waves, they being too great a distance from it.

I have hitherto given you an account of what I was able to learn, as well of the *Old* as the *New Greenland*, the first inhabited by the *Norwegians*, the second discover'd by the *Norwegians*, *Danes* and *English*, whilst they were endeavouring to recover the passage in the first. 'Tis very probable that the passage between the *Old Greenland* and *Iseland*, has been stop'd up by the vast ice shoals forced thither during the extremity of the winter season; and by the strong north-east winds from the *Frozen-Sea*, and gathered into vast ice mountains in these streights; whereby the free passage for ships being quite interrupted, those mariners who were sent in quest after the recovery of *Old Greenland*, were forced to steer their course towards the cape *Farewel*, and the gulph of *Davis*, lying to the east, being that part of the countrey now known by the name of *New Greenland*; it being certain by so many reiterated trials and experiments, that the

the paſſage betwixt *Iſeland* and the *Old Greenland*, has been quite loſt, which muſt be attributed to its being ſtopped up by the ice mountains.

The *Iſeland* chronicle, in that chapter which treats of the old paſſage, mentions ſomething which ſeems much to confirm the truth of this aſſertion, *viz.* That half ways betwixt *Iſeland* and *Old Greenland*; there were a conſiderable number of ſmall rocky iſles, frequented only by bears; betwixt which, it is likely, theſe ice ſhoals might be forced in betwixt thoſe rocks, with ſuch violence, and in ſuch vaſt heaps, that the ſun being not ſtrong enough to melt them in the ſummer ſeaſon, they became in proceſs of time to be petrified, and conſequently ſtop'd up the whole paſſage into the *Old Greenland*; ſo that ever ſince there has not been the leaſt news heard of the poſterity of thoſe *Norwegians* that ſettled there.

'Tis not unlikely, that the ſame plague which raged in 1348, all over the north, being tranſplanted out of *Norway* into *Greenland*, did ſweep away moſt of their inhabitants, as it happened in divers other countries of the north. I am apt to perſuade myſelf, that *Gotſke Lindenau*, who, as I told you, ſteer'd his courſe to the north-eaſt, in his voyage, did either actually come to the ſhore of the *Old Greenland*, or at leaſt very near it; and that the two ſalvages he took in thoſe parts, were actually of the poſterity of the antient *Norwegians*, that ſettled in *Old Greenland*.

On the other hand, I have heard it affirm'd by very conſiderable perſons, who ſaw and converſed with them at *Copenhagen*, that neither theſe, nor the other ſalvages, brought from the gulph of *Davis* (tho' much different both in their manners and language) had any thing either in their language or manners, that had the leaſt relation either with *Denmark* or *Norway*; nay, that the language of thoſe ſalvages was ſo far from having any congruity with that of the *Danes* and *Norwegians*, that even they could not as much as underſtand one word they ſaid.

The *Daniſh* chronicle takes particular notice, that the three ſalvages brought from the gulph of *Davis* by the *Engliſh* pilot, ſpoke ſo faſt and thick, that one could not hear them ſpeak diſtinctly, except theſe words, *Oxa indecha*; the ſignification of which words, no body has been able to underſtand hitherto. 'Tis beyond all diſpute, that that part of *Greenland*, known by the name of the *Old Greenland*, is only a ſlender part of that vaſt tract of northern land, ſo often mentioned in this treatiſe; and, that the ſhore is oppoſite and neareſt to *Iſeland*, as alſo that the *Norwegians*, who ſettled there, did not advance very far into the countrey, no more than thoſe, who ſince that time have diſcover'd the *New Greenland*, did ever advance farther than to the ports, and upon the ſhore; the moſt of them (as we told you before) not daring as much as to venture to ſet foot aſhore.

I had it from the lord great marſhal of *Denmark*'s own mouth, that in the laſt voyage made thither by the *Danes* in 1636, they by certain ſigns enquired of the *Greenlanders*, who came to traffick with them, whether there lived another people like themſelves, beyond the mountains they ſaw, about ten or twelve leagues diſtant from the ſea ſide; whereupon the ſalvages did give them to underſtand by certain ſigns, that there actually lived other men, having no hair upon their heads, on the other ſide of thoſe mountains; that they were of a gigantick ſtature, with vaſt bows and arrows, killing all ſtrangers that came into their countrey. But no real certainty can be given of theſe people, no more than of the countrey they inhabit; both the ancient and modern hiſtories being ſilent in this point; the only thing we are certain of is, that *Greenland* is without compariſon of a much larger extent, than has been hitherto diſcovered by the *Norwegians*, *Danes* and *Engliſh*.

I was willing to enlarge my ſelf the more upon this ſubject, in order to the repreſenting to you two other things: (1.) That it is not very certain, whether *Greenland* is coherent with the continent of *Aſia*, near the *Grand-Tartary*: (2.) No more, than whether it be contiguous to *America*. Concerning the firſt, I can tell you, that the vaſt ice mountains near *Nova-Zembla*, have hitherto ſo infeſted the paſſage thereabouts, that no body has been able to determine, whether there be a paſſage that way into the ſea of the eaſt; for tho' the moſt ſkilful pilots and mariners have been employed in finding it out, they could never come beyond the cape of *Spitzbergen*, accounted by the *Danes* a part of *Greenland*, whereabouts they catch moſt of the whales tranſported afterwards into *Europe*: The *Dutch* here have their huts for the management of their trade, and with other nations ſend thither ſhips every year.

I can't upon this occaſion forbear to give you an account of what I had the honour to learn from the grand-marſhal of *Denmark*'s own mouth, concerning this part of *Greeland*, and the adjacent ſea; nay, ſuch was his generoſity, that not ſatisfied to have told it me by way of mouth, he would give himſelf the trouble of writing it in a letter to me, which I carefully preſerve as a glorious proof of his generoſity and

and favour towards me, in hopes of meeting before long, with a favourable opportunity of showing the same to you. But what do I say of showing you his letter, when there is so great a prospect, that you may suddenly see his excellency in person; it being at present reported here at the *Hague*, as a thing unquestionable, that this great person, with the countess *Eleonor* his spouse, the daughter of the king of *Denmark*, are gone lately from *Copenhagen* to *France*, where this great personage is to reside with the character of ambassador extraordinary from his majesty of *Denmark*: This is the same great person, of whose most excellent qualifications, I have sent such ample praises to our dear friend Mr. *Burdelot*, when I gave him an account of that famous interview betwixt the two plenipotentiaries of *Sweden* and *Denmark* at the bridge of *Brensbroe*, on account of a negotiation of peace, betwixt the two northern crowns; which was at last happily concluded by the intercession and indefatigable care of my lord ambassador from our most illustrious king: This interview was one of the most glorious that had been seen for a long time, where the two greatest men of the two northern crowns, *viz.* the grand marshal of *Denmark*, and the lord chancellor of *Sweden*, did meet one another with an inexpressible veneration, and all the marks of a most generous courage; and our ambassador had there the honour to establish a most intimate friendship between those two great personages.

Of the lord chancellor of *Sweden*, I shall have occasion to speak upon another occasion, and it is beyond my present purpose to enter upon a panegyrick of the grand marshal of *Denmark*; so I will only assure you, that whenever you shall have the opportunity of seeing this great minister, you will be satisfied both in respect of his extraordinary courage and refined wit, and by his noble presence, that he not only deserves the honour of managing all the affairs of moment in the north, but also of a far greater empire.

Add to these his historical virtues, that he is a compleat philosopher who disdains all pomp and vanities, but in lieu hereof is endowed with the most generous inclinations in the world, which renders his conversation the most agreeable in the universe. This great person had in his service, among many others, a certain *Spanish* gentleman named *Leonin*, who being a great naturalist, he sent him to *Spitzbergen*, in order to give him an account of what observations he could make there; whereof I will give a brief account.

This countrey is situate under the 78 degree of elevation, and not improperly call'd *Spitzbergen*, i. e. *peaked Mountains*, from those peaked mountains wherewith it is covered. These mountains are a mixture of sand, or rather gravel, and small flat stones joined pretty close together, not unlike that which we commonly call the grey *Ardoise* stone. The mountains increase in bulk every year, so as to be plainly discovered by those who sail that way; *Leonin* went ashore, as deep into the countrey as he durst venture, and found the whole countrey, as far as his eyesight could carry, all covered with these peaked hills; and met with no living creature except some few foxes; he was not a little surprized to discover upon one of these hills, about a league from the seaside, a small mast of a ship, with one of its pulleys still fastened to it; this made him ask the seamen how that mast came there, who told him they were not able to tell, but were sure they had seen it as long as they had used that coast. Perhaps formerly the sea might either cover or come near this mountain, where some ship or other being stranded, this mast is some remnant of that wreck.

A description of Spitzbergen.

They have some grass, but so short, that it is scarce to be seen above ground, or beyond the stones; for to speak properly, here is scarce any earth, but only small stones or gravel, betwixt which comes forth a sort of moss, like that which grows upon the barks of trees, in other parts of the northern climate, which serves for food for the reendeer, and is so nourishing to them, that they become absolutely fat by it; and I remember, that the grand marshal had once one of these creatures kill'd, which had at least four inches of fat.

This countrey is a desart, and not habitable, by reason of the excessive cold; for though the sun does not set here for four whole months in the year; and that for six weeks more, it does not go below the horizon above three ells: To speak after the *Danes*, who seem to have taken their mensuration of the heaven from *Virgil*; meaning that at midnight (if you may so call it) the sun does approach only within eleven degrees and half of the horizon in this countrey for the space of six weeks: As the cold is very fierce here, so the sunbeams are very bright and piercing, and consequently this subtilty of the air, encreases the effects of the cold.

There is no living near these mountains, which scarce having any solidity, they constantly send forth certain exhalations, which pierce the whole body in a very little time; to prevent which, the best remedy is to expose yourself to the sunbeams

beams in a place where they may ſurround you on all ſides without any obſtacle.

They have great quantities of bears in that countrey; they are all white, ſome living in the water, others upon the ſhore. They are commonly ſeen ſwimming a good way out at ſea, or elſe upon the great ice ſhoals. The grand Marſhal had cauſed ſeveral of theſe creatures to be taken alive, which he kept at *Copenhagen*; and when he had a mind to ſhew ſome ſport to his acquaintance, they uſed to take a walk along the ſea-ſhore, and in ſome ſandy but deep place where the water was very clear, cauſe theſe bears to be thrown into the water, where they could ſee them dive quite to the bottom; he told me, that it was one of the beſt diverſions in the world, to ſee thoſe creatures plunge themſelves down to the bottom of the ſea, and to ſport there for two or three hours ſucceſſively; nay, he believed they would have continued there for a whole day, had they not been drawn out by the ropes and chains that were faſtened round their bodies.

Whales of Spitzbergen. The ſea of *Spitzbergen* produces abundance of whales of ſuch a bigneſs, that ſome taken hereabouts have been found to be no leſs than two hundred foot long, and of a proportionable bigneſs in the circumference of their bodies. But they frequently take thoſe of a hundred and thirty and a hundred and ſixty foot long. Theſe vaſt creatures have no teeth, and within theſe vaſt bodies they ſeldom find any thing except ten or twelve handsful of a kind of ſmall black ſpiders, progenerated by the corrupted air of the ſea, and ſome ſmall quantity of green herds tore up from the bottom of the ſea; it is moſt probable that theſe whales don't live upon theſe ſpiders, neither upon theſe herbs, but upon the ſea, which produces both; the ſea hereabouts being ſo covered with theſe inſects, that it appears quite black, an infallible ſign to thoſe who go about catching of whales, that they are likely to make a good booty; the whales generally delight in that part of the ſea which produces theſe inſects.

Sometimes they take of theſe whales in ſo vaſt numbers, and of ſo prodigious bigneſs, that the ſhips are not ſufficient to carry all the lard, but are forced to leave part of it behind them, in order to carry it away the next year.

It is obſervable that never any thing corrupts or putrifies in this countrey; even the dead carcaſſes buried thirty years before, appear as entire and as well coloured as they did at the ſame moment they gave up the ghoſt.

Here are certain huts erected a long time ago for the convenience of boiling the whale oil or greaſe; theſe appear the ſelfſame, without the leaſt alteration, now, as they did from the beginning, when they were built, the wood being as firm and as freſh, as it was the day it was cut from the tree. To ſpeak the truth of theſe northern parts, the dead fare better here than the living; for if the firſt don't corrupt, the living don't keep long in health; witneſs poor *Leonin* (before mentioned) who returned from this voyage ſo cramp'd with cold, that he lived not long after.

All the birds you meet with here, are water-birds, there being not one kind of them living upon land. They have ducks in great abundance, beſides divers other ſorts of water-fowl not known to ſtrangers. The grand marſhal of *Denmark* has ſeveral of them by him ſtuffed out, it being impoſſible to bring them to *Copenhagen* alive. Their feathers and beaks are not unlike thoſe of the *Paroquets*, and their feet are like thoſe of the ducks. Thoſe that have taken them, aſſure us, that they ſing very deliciouſly, eſpecially when many of them ſing together, they make a moſt harmonious noiſe.

Thoſe that failed to *Spitzbergen* to catch whales, arrive there in the month of *July*, and return from thence in *Auguſt*. If they come before *July*, they can't approach the ſhore, by reaſon of the vaſt ice-ſhoals, and for the ſame reaſon they muſt not venture to ſtay longer than about the middle of *Auguſt* at fartheſt; for nothing is more frequent than to ſee vaſt ice-ſhoals in theſe ſeas, ſometimes 60, 70 or 80 fathoms thick.

——Quæ tantum vertice ad auras
Æthereas tantum radice ad Tartara tendunt.

For in certain places near this ſhore, the ice-ſhoals are ſo thick, that they reach the bottom of the ſea, and theſe encreaſing by degrees, by the occaſion of new ice-ſhoals, ariſe as high above the ſurface of the water, as they are deep below it. Theſe Ice-ſhoals are as bright and tranſparent as glaſs: What renders the navigation hereabouts moſt dangerous is, the uncertainty of the currents, occaſioned, as I ſuppoſe, by the ſudden melting of the ice, which ſometimes congeals and melts in different places, at no great diſtance, at the ſame time.

Uncertainty about Greenland *whether a continent or iſle.* It ought therefore not to ſeem ſtrange to you, if I am not able to reſolve abſolutely the firſt propoſition, *viz.* whether *Greenland* is coherent to the continent of *Aſia*, and the *Grand-Tartary* or not, by reaſon of the vaſt diſtance there is between us and the *Frozen-Sea*; the uncertainty of the

 melting

melting of the ice, the violence of the tempests that reign frequently near these coasts, the uncertainty of the true course to be taken, the desarts you meet with there, and what is worst, the want of all manner of subsistence and conveniencies in these desarts: All these taken together, are such insurmountable obstacles, as render this discovery past all hopes of success. The second proposition being involved in no less difficulties than the first; we can with no more certainty affirm of this, than of the former, whether *Greenland* joins with the continent of *America* or not.

Of this I can give you not a more convincing proof, than what I intended to oblige you with, *viz.* The account of a voyage made by a *Danish* captain named *John Munek* (which I promised you long ago) who attempted the discovery of the *eastern passage*, towards the north-west, betwixt *Greenland* and *America*; the same being not in the least foreign to my present purpose; for besides that it contains no small varieties, it has a particular relation to *Greenland* and the adjacent isles.

Munek's voyage to discover a passage between Greenland *and* America.

The king of *Denmark* (that now reigns) being prevailed upon to encourage by his authority, the discovery of a passage to the *East Indies*, thro' a supposed streight betwixt *Greenland* and *America*, engaged one captain *Munek* to undertake this voyage. A certain *English* captain named *Hudson*, had some time before attempted the discovery of this sea and streights with the same design, but was lost in the voyage, tho' no body knows how; it is likely that his boldness having some relation to the presumption of *Icarus*, his wings were render'd useless by the cold, as the others were by the heat of the sun, and so met with the same fate of perishing in the sea; which like that of *Icarus*, got from him the name of *Hudson's streights*, and *Hudson's bay*.

Captain *Munek* set sail from the *Sound* the 16th of *May* 1619, with two vessels, equipped at the charge of the king of *Denmark*, one mann'd with forty eight, and the other with sixteen men. He arrived the 28th of *January* on the cape *Farvel* (as the *Danes* call it) i. e. *Farewell*; having got its name questionless from the opinion the *Danes* have conceived, that such as go beyond it, are passing into another world, and take a long farewel from this part of it. This cape *Farewell*, as I told you before, lies under 60 degrees and a half of elevation, in a mountainous country, covered always with snow and ice; and as these vary frequently in colour, and with their whiteness and transparency dazzle the eye, the true shape of this cape has not been discovered hitherto.

Comes to Hudson's *streights.*

From this cape captain *Munek* steering his coast to the west by north, entered *Hudson's streights*, where meeting with abundance of ice, he avoided the danger thereof, by keeping out at sea. Hence it is that he advises those that will attempt this passage, not to go too far to the west, by reason of the many ice shoals, and impetuous currents that are near the *American* coast. He tells us, that the eighth of *July* there arose so thick and strong a frost in these seas, that all his ship tackling were covered with ice-tags, so that they were scarce able to manage them; but that the next day from three a clock in the afternoon till sun-set, it was so excessive hot, that they were forced to pull off their clothes.

A sudden change of weather.

Coming into *Hudson's streights*, he gave it the name of *Christian's streights*, after the king of *Denmark* his master; and landed some of his men the 17th of *July* in an isle upon the coast of *Greenland*. Those that were sent to view this isle, assured the captain, that they had discovered some footsteps of men, but no inhabitants. However the next day they saw a whole troop of them near the sea-shore, who being amazed and frightned at the sight of the *Danes*, did run away as fast as they could, but had no sooner hid their arms, they carried along with them, behind an adjacent huge mass of stones, but they advanced towards the *Danes*, and in an obliging manner returned the salute given by them, with this caution however, to keep betwixt the *Danes* and the place, where they had concealed their arms. But the *Danes* found means by several turnings and windings to amuse them so long, till coming near to the stone heap, they seized upon their bows, quivers, and arrows.

The inhabitants.

The poor salvages, quite dismay'd at their loss, did in most submissive posture, and with all the engaging signs in the world, beg the *Danes* to restore them their weapons, giving them to understand, that as they lived upon hunting, and must perish for want of them, they would give them their clothes in exchange for them. The *Danes*, moved with compassion, restored them their arms, which they joyfully received upon their bended knees. The *Danes* to engage them the more, produced their toys, and made some trifling presents to the salvages, who were infinitely delighted with them, and in lieu thereof gave to the *Danes* divers sorts of birds, and some fat of fishes. One of these salvages casting his eyes upon a little looking-glass, in which he saw his face, was so taken with it, that he put it in his bosom, and run away as fast as as his legs would carry him, the *Danes* having the diversion of laughing at his simplicity, as they had occasion to do soon after at the rest of the salvages, who seeing one of their ship's crew, with black hair and flat-faced, not unlike themselves, mistook him for one of their countrymen, and caress'd him as if they had been very old acquaintance.

Captain *Muneck* left this isle the next day, being the 19th of *July*, with an intention to pursue his voyage, but by reason of the vast ice shoals, was forced to return to his old station, but could not get sight of any of the salvages again, tho' they did all they could to entice them to the sea shore, by hanging little knives, looking-glasses, and other toys on small ropes. Whether it was out of fear of the *Danes*, or that they were forbidden to keep any farther correspondence with them by the chief judge or governour, is uncertain.

Captain *Muneck* meeting with no men, went often a hunting, and having taken abundance of reen-deer in this isle, he gave it the name of *Reinsundt*, i. e. *the gulph of Renes*, and the road where they lay at anchor, *Muneckens*, after his own name. This isle lies at 61 deg. 20 min. elevation; where after having set up the arms of the king of *Denmark* his master, he departed a second time, the 22d of *July*; but was soon after surprized by such violent tempests, and vast ice shoals, that with much ado he made shift to save himself the 28th of *July* betwixt two isles, where he cast all his anchors, and for his better security, was forc'd to fasten his vessels with long ropes on the shore.

Muneck *comes to an anchor betwixt two isles.*

It was no sooner low water, but the *Danes* found themselves all upon dry land, and the water beginning to rise again, carried along with it such a prodigious quantity of ice shoals, that had they not been day and night upon their guard, they would have been in greater danger here than in the open sea.

Betwixt these two isles, there was a huge ice shoal, about twenty two fathom high; which being loosen'd from the shore, and broken in two pieces, did sink to the bottom of the sea with so violent a motion, that the waves did arise like mountains, as if it had been a violent tempest, and put our ship in great danger of being swallow'd up by them.

They did not see any inhabitants here, but discovered several foot-steps, and other marks which sufficiently convinced them, that they were either at that time, or had been formerly inhabited by men. They found here divers minerals, and among the rest, great store of *Talc*, of which they carried off several tons into ships. They saw several other isles thereabouts, which in all probability were inhabited as well as these; but the shore being so rocky and full of ice, that there was scarce ever any thing seen like it, the *Danes* durst not venture too near them. These isles are situated at 62 deg. 20 min. about fifty leagues within the *Christian*'s *streights*. Captain *Muneck* gave that part where he lay at anchor, the name of *Haresound*, i. e. *the bay or road or hares*, from the vast number of hares they saw in this isle, and set up *Christian* IV. there, which the *Danes* generally express by this character *C*4.

He left these isles the 9th of *August*, steering his course to the W. S. W. with a N. W. wind, and the 10th came on the southern shore of *Christian*'s *streights*, being the *American* coast itself. Pursuing his course, he discovered a large isle to the N. W. unto which he gave the name of *Sneoeuland*, i. e. *the Snow-isle*.

Breadth of Hudson's *or* Christian's *streights.*

The 20th of *August* he steer'd his course from the W. to the N. *and then* (as the journal says) *I took the right course at the elevation of* 62 *deg.* 20 *min.* But it being a very thick fog, they could discover no land; tho' as the same journal says, *The streights of* Christian *is thereabouts not above sixteen leagues broad.* From whence 'tis reasonable to conclude, that it is broader in other places.

Hudson's *or* Christians *sea.*

Out of the streight he sailed into *Hudson*'s sea, the name whereof he changed likewise, as he had done that of the streights, giving it two names instead of one; for that part which washes the shore of *America*, he called the *New-sea*, and the other part towards the side of *Greenland* (if it may be supposed to belong to that countrey) *Christian's sea*.

He steer'd his course as much as possible he could to the W. N. W. till finding themselves at 63 deg. 20 min. elevation; they were so entangled amongst the ice, that they were forced to seek for shelter on the *Greenland* coast, and to pass the winter there; whence it is that they gave the name of *Muneckens vinter haven*, i. e. *Muneck's winter haven*, to that road; and to the track of land along the coast, the name of *New Denmark*.

The author of this journal has pass'd by in silence several places they saw in their passage thither, because having inserted their names in a peculiar map, he directs his readers thither for farther instructions. He speaks only of two isles in the *Christian's sea*, call'd by him the *two sister isles*, and of one more much larger than the former,

towards

towards the *New-sea*, unto which he has given the name of *Dikes Oeuland*. He advises those that intend to pass the *Christian's streights*, to keep in the middle of the streights as much as possibly they can, by reason of the rapidity of the contrary currents, occasion'd by the flux and reflux of the seas on both coasts, which carrying along with them vast ice shoals, put the vessels in frequent danger of being lost. He adds, that the tides in the *Christian's sea*, keep their certain times, from five to five hours, and that these tides are regulated according to the course of the moon.

Muneck's Haven.

Captain *Muneck* came to an anchor the 7th of *September* at *Munecken's vinter haven*, where after having somewhat refresh'd his men, he order'd his ships to be drawn into a little creek near the harbour, in order to have them refitted, and to preserve them against the force of the ice. The next thing they had to do, was to erect some huts, to defend themselves against the extremity of the cold of the approaching winter season, which would not permit them to return homewards at that time. *Muneck's haven* is situate at the entrance of a river, which was not frozen in *October*, tho' the sea was already full of ice near the shore.

The countrey near it.

Captain *Muneck* says, that the 7th of *October* he went up the river in a sloop, to view the situation of the adjacent countrey, but could not go farther than a league and a half, being stop'd by the rocks that are cross the river. Finding the passage by the river thus closed up, he took along with him some soldiers and seamen, and marched along with them about three or four leagues deep into the countrey, in hopes of meeting with some of the inhabitants, but found nothing like it that way. However, in his return thro' another part of the country, he found a pretty broad and high stone, and upon it the figure of a devil, with his horns and claws very distinctly painted. Near it was a place inclosed with small stones about eight foot square: On one side of this square place he saw a little hill composed of small stones, intermix'd with the moss of trees. On the opposite side of the same square, stood another square stone, not unlike an altar, resting upon two other stones, and upon the altar, he saw three pieces of charcoal laid crossways upon one another.

One of their altars.

Their sacrifices.

Captain *Muneck* saw several such like altars in his return, with charcoal upon them, just like the former; and tho' he could not as much as get sight of one single person of the natives, yet was it observable, that near every one of these altars they saw, they observed the foot-steeps of men; whence they conjectured, that the natives of the countrey used to assemble near these altars, to perform their sacrifices, which in all likelihood they celebrated either with fire, or to the fire. They farther took notice, that near those places, where they discovered these foot-steps of men, they found abundance of bones gnawed, which as they supposed, were the remnants of the sacrificed beasts, eaten by the salvages at the sacrifice, after their fashon, or rather torn or gnaw'd to pieces with their hands and teeth, as our dogs do with a bone.

Inhabitants.

In the woods, thro' which they pass'd, they found abundance of trees, sawed or cut in pieces by iron instruments; as also abundance of dogs muzzled with small twigs of trees. But what confirm'd them most of all in their opinion, *viz.* That this was not destitute of inhabitants was, that they had discovered the marks where tents or huts had been erected in divers places, and many pieces of bears and wolf-skins, as also of stags, sea-calves and dogs-skins, which had questionless served to cover these tents withal; it being more than probable, from what has been said upon this head, that these inhabitants lead a vagabond life, like the *Scytes*, or encamp in troops like the *Laplanders*.

Living creatures of this countrey.

The *Danes* having fix'd their huts, which were to serve them all the winter, began to provide wood to keep themselves warm, and venison for their food. Captain *Muneck* was the first who shot a white bear with his own gun, which they eat with a good appetite, and say, did relish and digest very well. They also kill'd abundance of hares, partridges, and other birds; which tho' not express'd by their peculiar names, he says are very frequent in *Denmark*. He adds, that they catch'd also four black foxes, and some sables, a name the northern nations generally give to the sable martins.

What most surprized the *Danes* was, that they discovered in the sky divers phenomena they never observed in *Denmark*. Thus, (as the journal assures us) there appeared the 27th of *November*, three distinct suns in the firmament, tho' it was a very thick and gross air. The 24th of *January* next following, two suns appeared very dictinctly; and the 10th of *December*, or the 20th of the old stile, they observed an eclipse of the moon about eight a clock at night; and the same night, they saw for two hours together, the moon surrounded by a very bright circle, with a cross in it, dividing the whole body of the moon into four

four parts. This meteor ſeem'd to be the fore-runner of the enſuing miſeries, and almoſt total deſtruction of the *Danes*, as you will ſee out of the following account.

Extremity of cold. The extremity of the cold began by this time to increaſe to ſuch a degree, that there lay ice-ſhoals near the ſhore of 300 and 360 foot thick; and their beer and wines, nay, even the moſt ſpirituous *Spaniſh* wines and ſtrong brandies, froze from top to bottom in the veſſels that contained them, which breaking aſunder, and the liquors being congealed into entire pieces of ice, they were forced to cut out pieces of them with their hatchets, which being melted, before the fire, they afterwards uſed to drink; nay, ſuch was the exceſs of the cold, that if they happened to forget a ſmall quantity of water in any of their tin or leather veſſels, they found them certainly crack'd the next morning, in that very place where the water had begun to freeze.

Thus the merciless cold, which even did not ſpare the metals encreaſed its rigour with ſuch violence, upon the bodies of the miſerable *Danes*, that they fell all ſick, one after another, their ſickneſs encreaſing according to the rigour of the ſeaſon; for being ſeized with a violent looſeneſs, they were emaciated to the laſt degree, till they dropt one after another, there being about the middle of *March* not enough left to keep the guard; ſo that captain *Muneck* himſelf was forced to ſtand centinel at his own hut. *Miſery of the* Danes.

The worſt was, that this diſtemper inſtead of abating did augment with the approach of the ſpring, when their teeth began to looſen in their gums, and their mouths were ſo full of ulcers within, that they could eat no bread, except what was ſteep'd in water. Towards *May*, the miſerable remnants of the *Danes* were attack'd by the bloody flux, and ſuch exceſſive pains in the nervous parts, as if they had been pricked without intermiſſion, with the points of knives. Their bodies did decay viſibly day by day, turned livid and black at laſt, no otherwiſe than if they had been beaten with ſticks, and ſome of them loſt their arms and legs by the violence of the cold. This is properly nothing elſe than the higheſt degree of ſcurvy, a diſtemper very common, and ſufficiently known in the northern parts of the world. Such as died were forced to be kept above ground, the reſt wanting ſtrength to bury them.

By this time the want of bread encreaſing, they were conſtrained to dig under the ſnow, where by good chance they found a certain ſort of berries, which they did feed upon for ſome time; but the worſt was, that they would not keep in the leaſt, wherefore they were obliged to boil and eat them immediately. The journal mentions the 12th of *April* as a very remarkable day, because it then rained the firſt time, after ſeven months, there having not fallen a drop of rain in all that time. *No rain in ſeven months.*

Birds of Greenland. The ſpring rejoyced them with the ſight of many ſorts of birds, none of which had appeared all the winter long, but their weakneſs would not permit them to catch or ſhoot any of them. About the middle of *May* they ſaw abundance of wild geeſe, ſwans, ducks, an infinite number of ſmall birds, patridges, ravens, faulcons, and ſome eagles. Not long after, captain *Muneck* happened to fall ill among the reſt, and on the 4th of *June* was ſo miſerably afflicted with tormenting pains in his limbs, that for four days together he could nor ſtir out of his hut: Not imagining otherwiſe than that his laſt hour was near at hand, he made his laſt will, in which he prayed the next that came to that ſhore, to bury his body, and to be careful of his journal, in order to deliver it to the king of *Denmark*. But about four days after, finding his ſtrength ſomewhat recovered, he made ſhift to peep out of his hut to ſee whether any of his crew were living or not; and out of ſixty four that came along with him, found only two alive. Theſe poor wretches raviſh'd with joy to ſee their captain, revived as it were from the dead, run to him with open arms, and carried him ſtreightways to a fire, wherewith rubbing his joints, they brought him pretty well to himſelf. They then encouraged one another, reſolving to live if poſſible they could, but how was the difficulty; they were forced to look for food under the ſnow, where now and then they found ſome herbs and roots, which had that happy effect upon them, that they began to recover more and more every day. It being then the 10th of *June*, the ice began to melt, which gave them opportunity to catch ſome trouts, ſalmons and other fiſhes: Thus what they catch'd by fiſhing and hunting, furniſhed them with ſufficient food; by which means having now recovered their full ſtrength, they reſolved notwithſtanding all the difficulties and dangers they were to ſurmount, to endeavour to get back to *Denmark*; what haſtened their reſolution was, that about that time the ſummer ſeaſon and rainy weather brought aſhore ſuch vaſt quantities of gnats, that they were not able to abide there. *Captain* Muneck *makes his laſt will.* *Recovers.*

According to this reſolution, they left their greateſt ſhip behind them, and embark'd bark'd aboard the small frigate, the 16th of *July*, and set sail from the same port, where I told you they had laid up their ships, and was by the captain named *Jans Muneckes Bay*, i. e. *John Muneck's Bay* or port, after his own name. Coming into the *Christian-Sea*, they met with abundance of floating ice-shoals, where they lost their sloop, and with much ado got their vessel clear; for having lost their rudder, they were forced to fasten their ship to a vast ice-rock till it could be refitted. The ice beginning to melt they found their sloop again, about ten days after; but this lasted not long, for the sea freezing and thawing again by turns, they got, not without a great deal of trouble, thro' the *Christian Streight*, and thence by cape *Farewel* into the ocean, where they were surprised the 3d of *September*, by so violent a tempest, that they were in great danger of being lost; the two seamen being so tired out by the long continuance of the tempest, that being forced to commit themselves to the mercy of the wind and waves, their mast was brought by the board, and with much ado they got the sails out of the sea into the ship.

Muneck *reimbarks with two seamen only.*

Arrive in Norway.

The fury of the tempest being somewhat allay'd for some days, gave them leisure and opportunity to get the 21st of *September*, into a part of *Norway*, where they came to an anchor with one anchor, the only one they had left.

But when they thought themselves freed from all danger, they were assaulted by another tempest, which put them in more danger than ever they had seen before; however they had the good fortune once more to escape this danger, having found means to run their ship among the rocks, they made shift to get ashore, 'till the fury of the tempest being past, they refitted their vessel, and in some days after got safe into *Denmark*, where captain *Muneck* gave an account of the success of his voyage, to the king, who received him no otherwise, than if had been returned from the dead.

One might reasonably suppose, that this voyage would put a period to captain *Muneck*'s misfortunes; but his ill fate not tired yet of pursuing so brave a man, the odness of the accident that befel him hereafter ought not to be pass'd by in silence.

Muneck *prepares for a second voyage into* Greenland.

After some stay in *Denmark*, (during which time he mused upon his last miscarriage, for want of knowledge of the country) he began to be persuaded within himself that there was still a possibility of finding out a passage to the east that way, and therefore resolved to attempt the same a second time. But this being a thing of such a nature, as to require the assistance of other people, he engaged divers gentlemen of quality, and rich citizens of *Denmark* in the same design, who entring into a society, they equip'd two vessels, which they committed to the care of captain *Muneck*.

Having taken effectual care to provide his ships with all necessaries, and to remedy all the inconveniencies he had been made sensible of in his former voyage; when being just ready to depart, the king of *Denmark* demanded the captain (as he was taking his leave of him) the day fix'd for his departure; and thus entring upon the discourse of his late voyage into *Greenland*, the king began to upbraid his conduct, as if his ships had been lost by the captain's ill management. His reply happening to be somewhat rougher than the king expected, he pushed him with his cane against the breast, which the captain taking to heart, went home to bed, and what with grief and want of food (which he refused to take) died in ten days after.

Dies of grief.

But it is time to return to the subject, that did lead us into this long digression; from what has been said, it seems to be evident, that there is a long and broad canal, if not an entire sea, betwixt *Greenland* and *America*; notwithstanding which, as we know but very little of that coast, it remains doubtful, whether *Greenland* is upon the same continent with *America* or not; tho' it seems most probable it is not, as I told you before. And captain *Muneck* was questionless of the same opinion, without which he would never have taken so much pains to engage a whole society of gentlemen to attempt the finding out of this passage to the east.

This leads me to a discovery of the mistake of the author, who has published his dissertations concerning the origin of the *Americans*, which he deduces from the *Greenlanders*; the first inhabitants of which he would make us believe were *Norwegians*, and consequently that the first inhabitants of *America*, were originally of *Norway*. He pretends to justify his opinion by a certain imaginary affinity betwixt some *American* words that terminate in *Lan* and the termination of *Land*, so frequent in the *German*, *Lombard* and *Norwegian* languages, and the resemblance of the manner of living; that is, as he tells you, betwixt the *Americans* and *Norwegians*, who are, if you will believe him, the *Allemanni* of *Tacitus*: But I don't question to convince you of his mistake, by the following reasons: (1.) because the *Norwegians* were not the first inhabitants

The Norwegians *were not the first inhabitants of* Greenland.

habitants of *Greenland*, as is apparent from what has been ſaid upon the head before; and Mr. *Wormius*, that learned and famous antiquary of the north, is ſo far from tracing the original of the firſt inhabitants of *America* out of *Greenland*, that on the contrary, he believes the *Skreglingers* or original natives of *Greenland*, about *Weſternburgh*, to have been deſcended from the *Americans*. (2.) He is grievouſly miſtaken in his gueſs, there being little or no likelihood that *Greenland* is joined to the continent of *America*, neither is that paſſage ſo well known, nor ſo eaſy as he would have us imagine. (3.) He is no leſs in an error, in what he ſays concerning the affinity of the languages and manner of living, betwixt the *Norwegians* and *Americans*; the contrary being made ſufficiently evident by the preceeding relation: But ſuppoſing the *Norwegian* language to have been introduced in *America*; he muſt find out another paſſage for theſe northern people into *America*, than by the way of *Greenland*.

I will not trouble you with the other miſtakes this author has been guilty of in ſeveral paſſages of his diſſertations, knowing that you are conſtantly employed in matters of much more moment, wherewith you have obliged the learned world; and as I muſt look upon it as an eternal obligation, that you would throw away part of your precious time, in reading ſo unpoliſhed a work, that has ſo little reſemblance to the nicety of your own excellent pieces, I don't queſtion, but that you are as well pleaſed to have done with reading of this letter, as I am ſatisfied to have finiſhed it, and to declare to you, that I ſhall always be

SIR,

From the *Hague*
Jan. 18, 1646.

Your moſt humble and

moſt affectionate Servant.

Captain

Captain *THOMAS JAMES*'s

STRANGE and DANGEROUS

VOYAGE

In his intended DISCOVERY of the

North-Weſt PASSAGE

INTO THE

SOUTH SEA,

In the years 1631 and 1632.

Wherein the MISERIES indured, both

GOING, WINTERING, RETURNING,

And the RARITIES obſerved, both

PHILOSOPHICAL and *MATHEMATICAL*,

Are RELATED at Large.

Publiſhed by His Majeſty's Command.

To which are added

A PLAT or CARD for the ſailing in thoſe Seas.

ALSO

Divers little TABLES of the AUTHOR's, of the VARIATION of the COMPASS, &c.

WITH

An *APPENDIX* concerning LONGITUDE,

By Mr. HENRY GELLIBRAND, Aſtronomy Reader of *Greſham-College, London.*

AND

An ADVICE concerning the PHILOSOPHY of theſe late DISCOVERIES.

By *W. W.*

THE PREPARATIONS TO THE VOYAGE.

HAVING been for many years importuned, by my honourable and worſhipful friends, to undertake the diſcovery of that part of the world, which is commonly called, *The North-Weſt Paſſage into the South-Sea*, and ſo to proceed to *Japan*, and ſo round the world to the weſtward; being preſt forward withal, by ſignifying to me the earneſt deſire the King's Moſt Excellent Majeſty had, to be ſatisfied therein: I acquainted my much honoured friends, the merchants of *Briſtol*, therewith; who, as ever they have been benefactors and advancers of them that purſue the ways of honour (together with the enlargement and benefit of his Majeſty's kingdoms) did freely offer to be at the charge of furniſhing forth ſhipping for this purpoſe. And now being thus enabled, I addreſſed my ſelf to the honourable Sir *Thomas Roe*, Kt. (as to a learned, and furtheſt employed traveller by ſea and land, this day in *England*) who joyfully preſented theirs and mine own voluntary willingneſs, to do His Majeſty ſervice in this kind; who moſt graciouſly accepted of the offer; and encouraged me by many favours, in my weak undertakings. Wherefore with all ſpeed, I contrived in my mind, the beſt model I could, whereby I might effect my deſign. The adventurers moneys were inſtantly ready, and put into a treaſurer's hand, that there might be no want of preſent pay, for any thing I thought neceſſary for the voyage.

I was ever of the opinion, that this particular action might be better effected by one ſhip, than by two conſorted; becauſe in thoſe icy ſeas, ſo much ſubject to fogs, that they might be eaſily ſeparated; I forbear to ſpeak of ſtorms and other accidents; as that of a rendezvous in diſcoveries, cannot ſurely, or without much hindrance be appointed; and that ſpeedy perſeverance is the life of ſuch a buſineſs: Wherefore I reſolved to have but one ſhip, the ſhip-boat, and a ſhallop.

A great ſhip (as by former experience I had found) was unfit to be forced thorow the ice, wherefore I made choice of a well-conditioned ſtrong ſhip, of the burthen of 70 ton; and in GOD, and that only ſhip, to put the hope of my future fortunes.

The ſhip reſolved upon, and that in leſs time than eighteen months our voyage could not be effected. I next conſidered how our ſhip of ſeventy tons in bulk and weight might now be proportioned, in victuals, namely, and other neceſſaries; this was all done, as contractedly as we could; and the number of men it would ſerve, at ordinary allowance for the forementioned time, was found to be twenty two, a ſmall number to perform ſuch a buſineſs, yet double ſufficient to ſail the ſhip with provident carefulneſs.

The baker, brewer, butcher, and others, undertake their offices upon their credits, knowing it to be a general buſineſs, and their utter undoing if they failed in performance; but truly they proved themſelves maſters in their arts, and have my praiſe for their honeſt care; in them conſiſting a great part of the performance of the voyage.

The carpenters go in hand with the ſhip, to make her as ſtrong and ſerviceable as poſſible in their underſtandings they could.

Every thing being duly proportioned, and my ſmall number of men known, I began to think of the quality and ability they ſhould be of.

Voluntary loyterers I at firſt diſclaimed, and publiſhed I would have all unmarried, approved, able and healthy ſeamen: In a few days an abundant number preſented themſelves, furniſhed with general ſufficiency in *Marine* occaſions. I firſt made choice of a *Boatſwain*, and ſome to work with him, for fitting the rigging of the ſhip; and as things went forward, ſhipped the *ſubordinate Crew*. And all things being perfectly ready, I ſhip'd the *Maſter's Mates*; and laſt of all, the *Maſter* of my ſhip, and my *Lieutenant*. The whole company were ſtrangers to me, and to each other, (as by way of familiarity) but yet privately recommended by worthy merchants, for their ability and faithfulneſs. I was ſought to by divers, that had been in places of the chiefeſt command in this action formerly, and others alſo that had uſed the *northerly Icy-Seas*; but I utterly refuſed them all, and would by no means have any with me that had been in the like voyage or adventures, for ſome private reaſons unneceſſary here to be related. Keeping thus the power in my own hands, I had all the men to acknowledge immediate dependance upon my ſelf alone, both for direction and diſpoſing of all, as well of the navigation, as all other things whatſoever.

In the mean time, the better to ſtrengthen my former ſtudies in this buſineſs, I ſeek after *Journals*, *Plots*, *Diſcourſes*, or whatever elſe might help my underſtanding.

I ſet ſkillful workmen to make me *Quadrants*, *Staves*, *Semicircles*, &c. as much, namely, as concern the fabrick of them, not truſting to their mechanick hands to divide them, but had them divided by an ingenious practitioner in the *Mathematicks*. I likewiſe had *Compaſs-Needles*, made after the reaſonableſt and trueſt ways that could be thought on: And by the firſt of *April*, every thing was ready to be put together into our hopeful ſhip.

In the mean ſpace I made a journey up to *London*, to know his Majeſty's further pleaſure, and to make known to him my readineſs; who calling for the before mentioned honourable knight, I ſpeedily after received his Majeſty's royal letters, with directions for proceeding in my voyage, and my diſcharge; whereupon I had forth the ſhip into the road, expecting a fair wind to begin the voyage.

A VOYAGE

A VOYAGE For the DISCOVERY of a North-West Passage INTO THE SOUTH SEA.

THE 2d of *May* 1631, I took my leave of the worshipful merchant-adventurers in this action, in the city of *Bristol*; and being accompanied with a reverend divine, one Mr. *Thomas Palmer*, and divers of the merchants, with others of my kindred and native countreymen, I repaired on board. Here Mr. *Palmer* made a sermon, exhorting us to continue brotherly love amongst us, and to be bold to profess the true christian religion, wherever we should happen in this our peregrination. After they had received such entertainment as my estate could afford them, they departed for *Bristol*. This afternoon I made a review of all things, as well of clothes, and other necessaries, as of victuals; and where there was found any want, we were presently furnished.

The 3d of *May* (after prayer for a prosperous success to our endeavours) about three a clock in the afternoon, we came to sail, and stood down the channel of *Severne*, with little wind, but slowly got forward to the westward of *Lundy*; and then the wind opposed itself so strongly against us, that we were driven to bear up and come to an anchor in *Lundy* road the 5th in the evening, where we remained until the 8th in the morning. Now hoping the wind would favour us, we came to sail, but we were forced to put into *Milford*, where we came to an anchor about midnight. Here we remained till the 17th in the morning; when with the first favouring wind, we proceeded and doubled about cape *Cleere* of *Ireland*.

The 22d we were in the latitude 51. 26. and the *Blaskes* did bear of us north east, about twelve leagues off; which *Blaskes* is in latitude 52. 4. Here I ordered the course that should be kept, which was generally west north west, as the wind would give leave, which in this course and distance is very variable and unconstant.

The 4th of *June* we made the land of *Greenland*, standing in with it to have knowledge of the trending of it; it proved very thick foul weather.

The 5th, by two a clock in the morning, we found ourselves encompassed about with ice; and endeavouring to clear ourselves of it, (by reason we could not see far about us) we were the more engaged, and struck many fearful blows against it: at length we made fast to a great piece, (it blowing a very storm) and with poles wrought day and night to keep off the ice; in which labour we broke all our poles.

The 6th, about two a clock in the morning, we were beset with many extraordinary great pieces of ice that came upon us, as it were with wilful violence; and doubtless had crushed us to pieces, if we had not let fall some sail, which the ship presently felt. In escaping that danger we ran against another great piece, that we doubted whether our ship had not been stav'd to pieces; but pumping, we found she made no water. The former pieces of ice had crushed our shallop all to pieces; wherefore I caused our long boat speedily to be had up from betwixt the decks, and put over-board; by help whereof we again recovered our broken shallop, and had her up up on the decks, intending to new build her. All this day we did beat, and were beaten fearfully amongst the ice, it blowing a very storm. In the evening, we were inclosed amongst great pieces, as high as our poop; and some of the sharp blue corners of them did reach quite under us. All these great pieces (by reason it was the outside of the ice) did heave and set, and so beat us, that it was wonderful how the ship could endure one blow of it; but it was God's only preservation of us, to whom be all honour and glory. In this extremity, I made the men to let fall, and make what sail they could, and the ship forced herself thorough it, tho' so tossed and beaten, as I think never ship was. When we were clear, we sayed the pumps, and found her stanch; upon which we went instantly to prayer, and to praise God for his merciful delivery of us.

The 7th and 8th days, we endeavoured to double about cape *Farewel*, being still pestered with much ice.

The 9th. we were in latitude 59.00. and we made account the cape *Farewel* bare of us due east, and some ten leagues off. The *Blaskes* in *Ireland*, is in lat. 52. 4. and cape *Farewel* in lat. 59.00. The course is west north west, and the distance about 410 leagues. I know very well these latitudes, courses, and distance, do not exactly agree with mathematical conclusions; but thus we found it by practice. The variation of the compass in lat. 52. 30. and thirty leagues to the westward of *Ireland*, is about 3.00. to the eastward; in lat. 57.00. about 310 leagues west north-west from the *Blaskes*, the compass doth vary 9.00. to the westward: In lat. 59.15. some forty leagues to the eastward of cape *Farewel*, the variation is about 14.45. In this course I have been observant, whether there were any current that did set to the N. E. as some have written there did, and that as well in calm weather, as otherwise; but I could not perceive any. The winds here are variable, and the sea of an unsearchable depth. We have not seen from *Ireland* hitherto any whales or other fish; the weather for the most part was foggy and misty, that wets as bad as rain.

The 10th, all the morning, was very foul weather, and a high-grown sea, although we had ice not far off about us, and some pieces as high as our top-mast-head. Our long boat, which we were fain to tow at stern, (by reason we were building our shallop on our decks) broke away, and put us to some trouble to recover her again. This we did, and made means to have her into the ship, though very much bruised; and that I had two men sore hurt, and like to be lost in the heaving of her in. By eight of the clock this evening, we were shot up as high as cape *Desolation*; for finding here the land to trend away north and by east, we certainly knew it to be the cape. It stands in lat. 60. 00. and the land from cape *Farewel* to it, trends N. W. the distance about forty leagues. The distance from cape *Desolation*, to the south end of the island of *Resolution*, is about 140 leagues; the course west, half a point north. The lat. of the south end of the island, being 61. 20. some twelve leagues to the westward of cape *Desolation*, the variation is 16. 00. In this course we were much tormented, pestered and beaten with the ice, many pieces being higher than our top-mast-head. In our way we saw many grampusses amongst the ice, and it seemeth the sea is full of them: The weather for the most part a stinking fog, and the sea very black; which I conceive to be occasioned by reason of the fog.

The 17th at night we heard the rut of the shore, as we thought; but it proved to be the rut against a bank of ice that lay on the shore. It made a hollow and hideous noise, like an overfall of water, which made us to reason amongst ourselves concerning it; for we were not able to see about us, it being dark night and foggy. We stood off from it till break of day, then in again; and about four a clock in the morning we saw the land above the fog; which we knew to be the island of *Resolution*. This last night was so cold, that all our rigging and sails were frozen. We endeavoured to compass about the southern point of the island; for that we were so much pestered with the ice, and blinded with a very thick fog. Here runs a quick tide into the straight, but the ebb is as strong as the flood: The fog was of such a piercing nature, that it spoiled all our compasses, and made them flag, and so heavy withal, that they would not traverse. Wherefore I would advise any that shall sail this way hereafter, to provide compasses of *Muscovy* glass, or some other matter that will endure the moisture of the weather. As the fog cleared up, we could see the entrance of the straight to be all full of ice close thronged together. Endeavouring to go forward, we were fast inclosed amongst it; and so drove to and again with it, finding no ground at 230 fathom, four leagues from the shore.

The 20th in the morning, we had got about the southern point of the island; and the wind came up at west, and drove both us and the ice upon the shore. When we were driven within two leagues of the shore, we came amongst the most strange whirlings

whirlings of the sea that possibly can be conceived: there were divers great pieces of ice aground in 40 fathom water, and the ebb coming out of the broken grounds of the island, amongst these isles of ice, made such a distraction, that we were carried round, sometimes close by the rocks, sometimes close by those high pieces, that we were afraid they would fall upon us. We were so beaten likewise with the encountring of the ice, that we were in a most desperate estate. We made fast two great pieces of ice to our sides with our kedger and grapnels that drew nine or ten fathom, that so they might be a-ground before us, if so be we were driven on the shore. But that design failed us; and now from the top seeing in amongst the rocks, I sent the boat (for now we had finished her) to see if she could find some place of security; but she was no sooner parted, but she was inclosed, and driven to hale up on the ice, or else she had been crushed to pieces. They ran her over the ice from piece to piece; and in the mean space, with the whirling and incountring of the ice, the two pieces brake away from our sides, and carried away our kedger and grapnels: then we made signs to the boat, to make all the haste she could to us, which she perceiving did; the men being with much difficulty inforced to hale her over many pieces of ice. In the mean space we made some sail, and got to that piece of ice that had our grapnel on it, which we again recovered. By this time was our boat come, and we put a fresh crew into her, and sent her to fetch our kedger, which she endeavoured with much danger of boat and men. By this time the ship was driven so near the shore, that we could see the rocks under us and about us; and we should be carried with the whirlings of the waters, close by the points of rocks, and then round about back again; and all this notwithstanding the sail we had abroad; that we expected continually when she would be beaten to pieces. In this extremity I made them to open more sail, and to force her in amongst the rocks and broken grounds, and where there was many great pieces of ice a-ground. We went over rocks, that had but twelve or thirteen foot water on them; and so let fall an anchor. This anchor had never been able to wind up the ship, but that (by good fortune) the ship ran against a great piece of ice that was a-ground. This rush brake the main knee of her beak-head, and a corner of it tore away four of our main shrouds, and an anchor that we had at the bow, fastened into it, and so stopt her way, that she did wind up to her anchor. We saw the sharp rocks under us, and about us; and had but fifteen foot water; being also in the sides way, where all the ice would drive upon us: Our boat we could not see, which made us doubt she had been crushed to pieces. In her was the third part of our company; but by and by we saw her come about a point amongst the rocks. She had recovered our kedger, which made us something joyful; with all speed we laid out hawsers to the rocks, and every one did work to the best of his strength, to warp her out of this dangerous place to the rock's side, where we had three fathom water, and were under the shelter of a great piece of ice that was aground, which should keep off the ice, that otherwise would have driven upon us. Here we lay very well all the ebb; but when the flood came, we were assaulted with pieces of ice, that every half hour put us into despairable distress. We did work continually and extreamly, to keep off the ice. At full sea our great piece of ice (which was our buckler) was afloat; and do what we could got away from us, and left us in a most eminent danger, by reason of the ice that drove in upon us. But the ebb being once made, this great piece of ice came again a-ground very favourable to us, and sheltered us all the rest of the ebb. All night we wrought hard, to shift our cables and hawsers; and to make them fast aloft on the rocks, that the ice might the better pass under them. All day and all night it snowed hard, and blew a very storm at west, which drove in all the ice out of the sea upon us. In working against the violence of the ice, the flooke of our kedger was broken, two arms of our grapnels, and two hawsers, our shallop being again very much bruised; whereupon to work we go on all hands to repair it.

This tide the harbour was choaked full of ice, so that it did seem firm and unmoveable; but when the ebb was made, it did move. Some great pieces came aground, which did alter the course of the other ice, and put us on the rocks. Here, notwithstanding all our uttermost endeavours, she settled upon a sharp rock, about a yard above the main mast; and as the water ebbed away, she hung after the head, and heel'd to the offing. We made cables and hawsers aloft to her masts, and so to the rocks, straining them tough with our tackles; but she as the water ebbed away, sunk still; that at length she was so turned over, that we could not stand in her. Having now done all to the best of our understandings, (but to little purpose) we went all upon a piece of ice, and fell to prayer, beseeching God to be merciful unto us. It wanted yet an hour to low

2 water,

water, and the tide did want a foot and a half to ebb, to what it had ebbed the last tide. We were careful observers of the low waters, and had marks by stones and other things which we had set up, so that we could not be deceived. The ship was so turn'd over, that the portless of the forecastle was in the water; and we did look every minute when she would overset. Indeed at one time the cables gave way, and she sunk down half a foot at that slip; but unexpectedly it began to flow, and sensibly we perceived the water to rise apace, and the ship withal. Then was our sorrow turned to joy, and we all fell on our knees, praising God for his mercy, in so miraculous a deliverance.

As soon as she was freed from this rock, we wrought hard to get her further off. All the flood we were pretty quiet from the ice, but when the ebb was made, the ice came all driving again upon us, which put us to a great extremity. We got as many pieces betwixt us and the rocks as we could, to fence us from the rocks. There came a great piece upon our quarter, which was above 300 of my paces about, but it came a-ground. Thus did divers great pieces besides, which was the occasion that this tide the harbour was quite choakt up; so that a man might go any way over it from side to side. When it was three quarters ebb, these great pieces that came a-ground, began to break with a most terrible thundering noise; which put us in a great fear, that those about us would break us all to pieces. But God preserved us.

The 22d in the morning, the water veer'd to a lower ebb than the last tide had done by two foot, whereby we saw God's mercies apparent in our late extremity. That flood we had some respite from our labours; but after full sea our hopes ebb too. The great piece that was by us, so stopt the channel, that the ice came all driving upon us; so that now undoubtedly we thought we should have lost our ship. To work thereupon we go with axes, bars of iron, and any thing proper for such a purpose; to break the corners of the ice, and to make way for it to drive away from us. It pleased God to give good success to our labours; and we made way for some, and fended off the rest; and got so much of the softer sort of the ice betwixt us and the rocks, that we were in pretty security. But at low water, those pieces that were a-ground, breaking, kept a most thundering noise about us. This day I went ashore, and built a great beacon with stones upon the highest place of the island, and put a cross upon it, and named this harbour, *The harbour of God's providence.* In the evening, the harbour was fuller of the ice than ever it had been since we came hither; and the greater pieces grounded and stopt the rest, that none went out the ebb, but the ship lay as if she had lain in a bed of ice.

The 23d in the morning, with the flood, the ice drove up amongst the broken grounds; and with the ebb, drove all out (it being then very calm) except one extraordinary great piece; which coming aground not far from us, settled itself in such a manner, that we much fear'd him. But there came no more great ice after him; otherwise we must have expected as great danger as at any time heretofore. I took the boat, and went ashore upon the eastern side, to see if I could find any place freer from danger than this unfortunate place, where amongst the rocks I descried a likely place. From the top of the hill where I was, I could see the ship. It was now almost low water; at which instant the forementioned piece of ice brake with a terrible noise into four pieces, which made me doubtful if it had not spoiled the ship, it being full half mast high. I made what haste I could to the boat, and so to the ship, to be satisfied; where I found all well, God be thanked, for that the ice had broken from the ship-ward. I instantly sent away the boat, to sound the way to a cove that I had found; which was a very dangerous passage for the boat. At her return we unmoor'd the ship, and with what speed possible warpt away from amongst this terrible ice. We were not a mile from them, but they brake all to pieces; and would surely have made us bear them company, but that God was more merciful unto us. We got about the rocks, and so into this little cove which I had so newly discovered. Here we made fast to the rocks, and thought ourselves in indifferent safety; which being done, I went ashore again, to wander up and down, to see what I could discover. I found it all broken rocky grounds, and not so much as a tree, herb, or grass upon it: Some ponds of water there were in it, which were not yet thawed, and therefore not ready for the fowl: We found not in the snow any footing of deer, or bears, but foxes we saw one or two.

We found where the salvages had been, but it was long since. They had made five hearths, and we found a few firebrands about them; and some heads and bones of foxes, with some whale-bones: I could not conceive to what purpose they should come thither; for we could find none or very little wood on the shore side, and no fish at all; though we did daily endeavour to take some. But it may be the season was not yet come. I named this cove by the master's name of my ship, *Price's Cove*. The latitude of it is 61. 24. the variation. The firebrands and chips which I spake of, had been cut with some hatchet or instrument of iron. From the top of the hills, we could see the islands that are on the south shore, and commonly called Sir *Thomas Button*'s isles: They did bear south and by east, half a point easterly; some 14 or 15 leagues distant upon the change day, it flows here seven a clock and a half, and the tide highest at most three fathoms. The flood comes from the eastward, and thither it returns. I have been observant from the top of the hills, whence I might descry the great pieces of ice two or three leagues from the shore, drive to and again with the flood and ebb indifferently. Hence I collected, that assuredly there is no current sets in here, but that it is a meer tide. Near the shore, the eddies whirl into twenty manners, when the ebb is made; which is, because it comes out of the broken ground amongst the ice that is aground near the shore: Besides which reason, there be divers rocks lying under water, on which you shall have now 30, then 12, and anon but 8, and then 20 fathom; and these uncertainties occasion such distractions. I would therefore advise none to come too near those dangerous shores, for fear he lose his ship, and so by consequence all: The last night we took better rest than we had done in ten nights before.

And this morning, being the 24th, there sprung up a fare gale of wind at east; and after prayer we unfastened our ship, and came to sail, steering betwixt great pieces of ice, that were aground in 40 fathom, and twice as high as our topmast head.

We went forth of this cove, upon the flood, and had none of those whirlings of the waters, as we had at our going into it. We endeavoured to gain the north shore, and kept ourselves within a league of the shore of the island of *Resolution*, where we had some clear water to sail thorough. In the offing, it was all thick throng'd together, as might be possible. By twelve a clock we were fast inclosed, and notwithstanding it blew very hard at east, yet we could make no way through it; but the hard corners of the ice did grate us with that violence, as I verily thought it would have grated the planks from the ships sides. Thus we continued in torment till the 26th day, driving to and again in the ice, not being able to see an acre of sea from topmast head.

The 26th was calm sun-shine weather, and we took the latitude and variation. The latitude is , the variation we sounded, and had ground at 140 fathom, small white sand. I caused the men to lay out some fishing lines, but to no purpose; for I could not perceive that the bait had been so much as touched. The nights are very cold, so that our rigging freezes, and the fresh ponds of water stand upon the ice above half an inch thick.

The 27th, there sprung up a little gale at south-east, and the ice did something open. Hereupon we let fall our foresail, and forced the ship thorough the throng of ice. In the evening, the wind came contrary, at W. N. W. and blew hard, which caused us to fasten to a great piece, to which we remained moor'd till the 29th.

The 29th I resolved, that here is no current, and that by many experiments which I have made: namely, by taking marks on the land, and noting our drift to and again with the ebb and flood for many days together, as well in calm weather as otherwise. By all these experiments, I found exactly, that the tide was no stronger there than that betwixt *England* and *France*.

The 29th in the morning, there sprung up a fine gale at east, and the ice did open something, so that we did force the ship thorough it with her foresail. By twelve a clock, we were gotten into some open water, with a fine gale of wind at east, and so clear weather, that we could see the island of *Resolution*. The north-end did bear of us E. N. E. some twelve leagues off.

From the 29th till the 5th of *July*, we sailed continually thorough the ice, with variable winds and fogs, and sometimes calm. At noon we had a good observation, and were in latitude 63. 15. and then we saw *Salisbury* island, bearing W. by N. some seven leagues off, with much ice betwixt it and us; to weather which we were driven to stand to the northward. Soon after we saw *Prince Charles*'s cape and *Mill* island; and to the N. N. W. (and indeed, round about us) the sea most infinitely pestered with ice. This did grieve me very much; for whereas I had determined to prosecute the discovery to the north-westward, I saw it was not possible this year. We were moreover driven back again with contrary winds, still closed and pestered with ice, and with all the perils and dangers incident to such adventures, so that we thought a thousand times that the ship had been beaten to pieces.

By the 15th of *July* we were got betwixt *Digge*'s island and *Nottingham*'s island, not being able to get more northward. There for an hour or two we had some open water.

2 But

But before I proceed farther, it were not amiss in some manner to describe the streight, which begins at the island of *Resolution*, and ends here at *Digges*'s island. If you go down into the bay, the streight is about 120 leagues long; and trends W. N. W. and E. S. E. generally. In the entrance it is about 15 leagues broad; and then on the southward side is a great bay. About the middest it is likewise about 15 leagues broad, and then the land opens something wider; so that betwixt *Digge*'s island and cape *Charles*, it is about 20 leagues broad: Betwixt which two stands *Salisbury* island and *Nottingham* island. If it be clear weather, you may see both the south and the north shores; ordinarily, the depth in the middle of the streight is 120 fathoms, white sand: A certain tide runs in it, and no current: The north shore is the straitest, and the clearest from ice too. Along the north shore you have many low small islands, which cannot be seen far off from the land; and in many places, the land makes as if it had small sounds in it. The main land on both sides is indifferent high land. And so much for discourse may suffice, referring you to the plot for the particulars.

The 16th, being now resolved of the impossibility to do any thing to the north westward, for the reasons aforesaid, I gave order to the master of my ship to steer away, W. S. W. to have a sight of *Mansfield*'s island, which the next day by three a clock in the afternoon we had; having had so much dangerous foul weather amongst the ice, that we struck more fearful blows against it than we had ever yet done. This was the first day that we went to half allowance of bread flesh days, and I ordered things as sparingly as I could. Two of our men complained likewise of sickness, but soon afterward recovered. In the evening we came to an anchor, and I sent the boat ashore to try the tides. They brought me word, that whilst the boat was ashore, it flowed about some three foot; and as we found by the ship, and by the ice, the water at that time came from the W. S. W. and that at the highest tides (so far as they could perceive) it had not highed above two fathom: They found that the savages had been upon it, by certain fires which they found, and heaps of stones, tracks of other beasts, but foxes they could not find. The wind was so contrary, and the weather so foggy, that we were fain to spend some powder to recover our boat again.

Next morning, being the 17th, the wind came something favourable, and we weighed. The shore being something clear of ice, (though very thick all to the offing) we stood along it S. and S. by W. some ten leagues. In the afternoon, the wind came contrary, and we came again to an anchor, within a mile of the shore; for to sea-board was all thick ice and unpassable. I went ashore myself, to be resolved of the tide, and found whilst I was ashore, that it did flow two foot; and at that time the flood came from the S. W. by W. I doubted it was an half tide, which afterwards I found to be true. I found where the savages had been upon the island, but could see little or no drift wood on the shore, no beasts on the island, nor fishes in the sea. It flows on the change day about a eleven a clock. We saw some fowl on it, of which we killed one, and returned on board. This island is very low land, little higher than a dry sand-bank. It hath ponds upon it of fresh water, but no grass; and is utterly barren of all goodness.

The 18th in the morning, the wind came something favourable, and we weighed and came to sail; for the ice was all come about us. We endeavoured to proceed to the westward, intending to fall with the western-land about the latitude 63. 00. By twelve a clock (having been much pestered) we were come to a firm range of ice; but it pleased God that the wind larged, and we stowed away S. S. W. at noon in latitude 62. 00. By four in the evening (having escaped dangerous blows) we were come as we thought) into an open sea, and joyfully steered away W. and W. by N. although that joy was soon quailed. By ten at night we heard the rut of the ice, and it grew a thick fog, and very dark with it: nevertheless we proceeded, and the nearer we came to it, the more hideous noise it made.

The 19th, by three in the morning, we were come to it, and as it did clear a little, we could see the ice; which were as thick rands of ice, as any we had yet seen. These being unpassable, and moreover the wind at N. W. we stowed alongst it, hoping to weather it to the southward; but at last, we became so blinded with fog, and so incompassed with ice, that we could go no farther.

The 20th in the morning (notwithstanding the fog) we endeavoured to get to the westward, our ship beating and knocking all this while most fearfully.

It this wilfulness we continued till the 21st. when being fast amongst the ice, I observed we were in latitude 60. 33. and then looking what damage our ship might have received, we could perceive that below the plate of iron, which was before her cut-water, she was all bruised and broken; the two knees she had before to strengthen her, spoiled and torn; and many other defects, which we could not by any means come

come to mend. Notwithstanding all this, and the extraordinary thick fog, (that we could not see a pistol shot about us) we proceeded with the hazard of all.

Till the 27th, which was the first time we had clear weather to look about us: The wind withal came up at south, and the ice did open something; so that we made some way thorough it to the westward. In the evening we were fast again, and could go no farther; the wind veering from the south to the east, and blowing a fresh gale. This occasioned our griefs the more, that with a good wind we could not go forward; putting therefore a hawser upon a piece of great ice, to keep the ship close to it, we patiently expected for better fortune. Since we came from *Mansfield*'s island, our depth was commonly 110 and 100 fathom oozie ground. Now the water begins to shoal; for this present 27th, driving fast to and again in the ice, we have but 80 fathom ground as before.

The 28th and 29th, we were so fast inclosed in the ice, that notwithstanding we put abroad all the sail that was at our yards, and that it blew a very hard gale of wind, the ship stirred no more than if she had been in a dry dock. Hereupon we went all boldly out upon the ice, to sport and recreate ourselves, letting her stand still, under all her sails. It was flat, extraordinary large ice, the worst to deal withal that we had yet found. I measured some pieces, which I found to be 1000 of my paces long. This was the first day that our men began to murmur, thinking it impossible to get either forwards or backwards. Some were of the opinion, that it was all such ice betwixt us and the shore. Others, that the bay was all covered over; and that it was a doubt whether we could get any way, or to any land to winter in. The nights were long, and every night it did so freeze, that we could not sail amongst the ice by night, nor in thick foggy weather. I comforted and encouraged them the best I could; and to put away these cogitations, we drank a health to his majesty on the ice; not one man in the ship, and she still under all her sails. I most ingeniously confess, that all their murmuring was not without reason: Wherefore doubting that we should be frozen up in the sea, I ordered that fire should be made but once a day; and that with a certain number of shides, that the steward should deliver to the cook by tail, the better to prolong our fuel, whatsoever should happen.

The 30th we made some way thro' the ice; we heaving the ship with our shoulders, and with mawls and croes of iron breaking the corners of the ice, to make way. As we got forwards, the water shoal'd apace; so that I believe it to be some island. At noon we observed thro' the fog, with the quadrant, upon a piece of ice, and were in latitude 58. 54. our depth 30 fathom. We put out hooks, to try to catch some fish, but to no purpose, for there is not any in this bay.

The 31st we laboured as aforesaid, and got something forward. At noon we were in lat. 58. 40. our depth 23 fathom. It was very thick hazy weather, or else I think we should have seen the land.

The first of *August* the wind came up at west, which drove us to the eastward, where our depth increased to 35 fathom. At noon (by observation with the quadrant, on the ice) we were in latitude 58. 45. At six a-clock this evening we might perceive the ice to heave and set a little; which was occasioned by a swelling sea that came out of the south-west. This did comfort us very much, hoping shortly we should get out of the ice.

The 2d it did blow hard at S. W. and yet we could not feel the forementioned swelling sea; which did again quench the hopes we had formerly conceived.

The 3d we did see a little open water to the Norwestward, and did feel a swelling sea from the west; which doth assure us, that there is an open sea to the westward.

The 5th we saw the sea clear; but could by no means work ourselves to it with our sails; wherefore about six in the evening we let fall an anchor in 50 fathom water, and stood all with poles and oars to fend off the ice, and let it pass to leeward. We continued this labour all night.

The 6th in the morning the wind came up at N. W. and we weighed with much joy, as hoping now to get into an open sea to the southward. This by noon we had done, and were in lat. 58. 28. very free of ice. The wind did large upon us, so that we stood away N. W. to get up as high to the northward as we could, and so to come coasting to the southward. We went to prayer, and to give God thanks for our delivery out of the ice.

The 9th (being in lat. 59. 40.) we came again to the ice, which lay very thick to the north. Since we came out of the ice, our depth increased to 110 fathom, and now decreaseth again: So that I think we approached towards the shore.

The tenth proved very thick foggy weather; the wind contrary, and the water shoaling apace, we came to an anchor in 22 fathom.

The 11th in the morning we weighed, and made in for the shore, and about noon saw the land, our depth being 16 fathom, in in lat. 59. 40. The land to the N. of us did trend N. by E. and so made a point to the southward, and trended away W. by S. which we followed, making it for that place which was formerly called *Hubbert's* hope. And so it proved indeed, but it is now hopeless.

Two or three words now concerning the bay that we have passed over. It is from *Digge's* island to the western land (in latitude aforesaid) about 160 leagues, the course W. S. W. the variation.

The tides do set in the middle of the bay, east and west, as we have often try'd by our lead a ground. But nearer the shores, as they are forced by the land, I am of the opinion, that in the ocean, or in large bays, the tides do naturally set E. and W. and that this doth give little hope of a passage. The greatest depth we had in the bay was 110 fathom, and so shoaling as you approach to land, we coasted round about this forementioned little bay, which is some 18 leagues deep in 8 and 6 fathoms, and in the bottom of it we were in 2 fathom and a half water, and saw the firm land almost round about us. Then we proceeded to the southward six and seven fathom water, within sight of the breach of the shore, keeping the lead continually going, and in the night we would come to an anchor. This night, here being little wind, we came to an anchor with our kedger; but in weighing of him, we lost him, having no more aboard us.

The twelfth we were in lat. 58. 46. some two leagues from the shore, The variation is about 17 deg.

The 13th in the afternoon (it being something hazy) we saw some breaches a-head us; our depth was 9 and 10 fathom; and luffing to clear ourselves of them, we suddenly struck upon the rocks; the ship then being under our two topsails, foresail, and spritsail, with a fresh gale of wind. In this fearful accident, we struck all our sails amain; and it did please God to send two or three good swelling seas, which did heave us over the rocks into three fathom, and presently into three fathom and a half, where we chopt to an anchor, and assayed the pumps; but we found she made no water, although she had three such terrible blows, that we thought her mast would have shiver'd to pieces, and that she had been assuredly bulged. We hoisted the boat overboard, and doubly mann'd her, to go seek and sound a way out of this perilous place. She was no sooner gone, but there rose a fog; so that we were fain to spend some powder, that she might hear whereabouts we were. The wind dull'd something, otherwise it had been doubtful whether she could ever have recovered to us again. After she had been absent about two hours, she brought us word, that it was all rocks and breaches round about us, and that withal, she had found a way, where there was not less than two fathom and a half, and that afterwards the water did deepen. We did presently weigh, and follow the boat, and past over two ledges of rocks, on which there was scarce fourteen foot water: Then it did deepen to three, four, and so to fourteen fathom; then it shoal'd again to nine. It being now night, we came to an anchor; where we rid indifferent well all the night. In the morning the wind came contrary, so that we could not go that way we intended to clear our selves, and therefore we went to work, to fit our holds, to splice our cables, and make ready two shot, and so placed them in the hold, that they might upon all occasions run clear; the ends of them being fasten'd to the main-mast. We likewise look'd to our anchors, and fitted our spare ones. We got out our long boat from betwixt the decks; which was very much broken and bruised. The carpenter went to work to fit her, (for I intended to tow the shallop at stern) and so to have the boats ready at an instant, either to lay out anchors, or be serviceable to what God should be pleased to try our faith and patience withal; for in him was our only trust, and our hope upon his favour in our honest endeavours. At noon, in lat. 57. 45. we could see the land from the N. W. to S. E. by E. with rocks and breaches; and the rocks that we came over, dry above water; whereby I knew it flows here two fathoms at least. At noon I sent the boat off to sound to the eastward, because the water shoaled when we came to an anchor. She brought us word, the shoalest water she had been in was seven fathom. We intending thereupon to weigh, the wind came easterly, so that we could not budge; but lay here the 14th all night with a stiff gale of wind.

The 15th in the evening our cable galded off; by reason of which perilous and sudden accident, in which we had not time to put a buoy to it, we lost our anchor, and were driven into four fathom water, before we could set our sails. This when we had done, we stowed S. S. E. the wind being at east, but the water shoaled to three fathom. Then we stowed N. N. E. and it did deepen by degrees to ten fathom; and because it grew dark, we came to an anchor, and rid a good stress all night.

The 16th in the morning the wind came up at N. a fresh gale; and we weighed and came to sail. By nine a clock it grew to be be a very storm; and we turned to and again in ten fathom water. In the evening the wind dull'd; and we stood S. W. to have a sight of port *Nelson*; which course we stood all night, by the stars, being in lat. 57. 25. the variation about 17 degrees.

The 17th in the morning we stood south; and our depth decreased by degrees to eight fathoms. At noon we had good observation, being in lat. 57. 15. and we make account that we are some six or seven leagues off the southern side of port *Nelson*. Here the colour of the water changed, and was of a puddleish and sandy red colour. We stood into six fathoms, and could not see the land from top-mast-head? so night coming on, and it beginning to blow hard at east by south, we stood off again into ten and twelve fathoms, where the water was again of the colour of the sea.

The 18th, as the wind and weather favoured us, and the storm was broken up, we stood in again south, and came again into thick puddleish water, into eight, seven, and six fathom, and then off again, for that it grew thick foggy weather, keeping our lead continually going, night and day.

The 19th, being fine clear sun-shine weather, we stood in again into the thick puddlish water, into eight fathom, where we came to an anchor to try the tides; for that from top-mast-head we could not now see the land. We were at noon (by good observation) in lat. 57. 20. and the tide did set N. W. by W. and S. E. by E. It did run two knots and a half in two glasses. I resolved that this was nothing but shoals to the land. In the afternoon it began to snuffle and blow, so that we had much ado to get up our anchor. This being done, we stood E. S. E. but the water shoaled apace. Then we stood E. and it deepen'd a little. In the evening the wind came up at W. and then we stood E. S. E. into ten and eight, and afterwards S. E. as our depth did guide us by our lead and the colour of the water, into seven and six fathoms.

The 20th at six in the morning we saw the land, it being a very low flat land. We stood into five fathoms, to make it the better, and so stood along it. At noon we were in lat. 57. 00. We named it *the new principality of south Wales*, and drank a health in the best liquor we had to prince *Charles* his highness, whom God preserve. We stood along it, and came to a point where it trends to the southward; near to which point there are two small islands. In the evening it was calm, and we came to an anchor. The tide set as aforesaid. There we rid all that night, and the next day, by reason the wind was contrary. There went a chopping short sea; and the ship did labour at it exceedingly leaping in spreetsail-yard, fore-castle, and all; for as yet we had not trimm'd her well, to ride. About nine at night it was very dark, and it did blow hard. We did perceive by the lead the ship did drive; wherefore bringing the cable to capstan, to heave in our cable (for we did think we had lost our anchor) the anchor hitch'd again, and upon the chopping of a sea, threw the men from the capstan. A small rope in the dark had gotten foul about the cable, and about the master's leg too; but with the help of God he did clear himself, tho' not without sore bruising. The two mates were hurt; the one in the head, the other in the arm. One of our lustiest men was stricken on the breast with a bar, that he lay sprawling for life; another had his head betwixt the cable, and hardly escaped. The rest were flung where they were sore bruised; but our gunner (an honest and a diligent man) had his leg taken betwixt the cable and the capstan, which wrung off his foot, and tore all the flesh off his leg, crush'd the bone to pieces, and sorely withal bruised all his whole body; in which miserable manner he remained crying till we had recovered ourselves, our memory, and strengths to clear him. Whilst we were putting him and the rest down to the chirurgeon; the ship drove into shoally water, which put us all fear; we being so sorely weaken'd by this blow, which had hurt eight of our men. It pleased God, that the anchor held again; and she rid it out all night. By midnight the chirurgeon had taken off the gunner's leg at the gartering place, and dress'd the others that were hurt and bruised; after which we comforted each other as well as we could.

The 22d we weighed, and stood a little off into deeper water, expecting a better wind; which in the afternoon favoured us. We stood in again for the shore, and along it we proceeded. It is very shoal about four leagues off, and full of breaches.

The 23d at noon we were in lat. 56. 28. In the evening, the wind came contrary; and we were fain to turn to and again. All this month the wind hath been very variable, and continued not long upon one point; yet it happened so, that we could get but little forward.

The 26th there sprung up a fine gale at west, but very thick weather; nevertheless we stood into seven and six fathom, the water very thick and puddleish. At noon it cleared; and we could see that we were imbayed in a little bay, the land being almost round about us.

We stood out of it, and so along it, in sight, till the 27th in the morning; when

2 we

we came to higher land than any we had yet ſeen ſince we came from *Nottingham* iſland. We ſtood into it, and came to an anchor in five fathom. I ſent off the boat, well mann'd and arm'd, with order in writing what they were to do, and a charge to return again before ſun-ſet. The evening came, and no news of our boat; we ſhot and made falſe fires, but had no anſwer, which did much perplex us, doubting that there had been ſome diſaſter befaln her, thro' careleſſneſs, and in her we ſhould loſe all. We aboard, at preſent, were not able to weigh our anchor, nor ſail the ſhip. At laſt we ſaw a fire upon the ſhore, which made us the more doubtful, becauſe they did not anſwer our ſhot, nor falſe fires with the like. We thought withal, that it had been the ſalvages, who did now triumph in their conqueſt. At length they came, all ſafe and well; and excuſed themſelves, in that upon their coming aſhore, it did ebb ſo ſuddenly, that a bank of ſand was ſo preſently dry without them, as they could not come away, till that was covered again; and with that they pacified me. They reported, that there was great ſtore of drift-wood on the ſhore; and a good quantity growing on the land. That they ſaw the tracks of deer and bears, good ſtore of fowl (of which they had killed ſome) but no ſign of people: That they paſs'd over two little rivers, and came to a third, which they could not paſs: That it did flow very near three fathoms ſometimes, as appeared by the ſhore. That it was low water at four a clock; that the flood came from the N. W. and that it flow'd half tide, which both they and we had perceived by the ſhip. At low water we had but three fathom, where we did ride. The wind began to blow hard at E. whereupon we weighed and ſtood to the northward till midnight, then in again; and in the morning we ſaw the land, and then it began to blow hard, and as we ſtood off, it encreaſed to a very ſtorm; ſo that at length we could not maintain a pair of courſes, but tried under our main courſe, all day and all night; ſome time turning her head to the landward, ſome time to the offing.

The 29th in the morning we made account we had droven back again ſome 16 or 18 leagues; and in the morning (as it cleared) we ſaw a ſhip to leeward of us ſome three or four leagues; ſo we made ſail, and bore up with her. She was then at an anchor in 13 fathom. It was his majeſty's ſhip, and captain *Fox* commanded in her.

I ſaluted him according to the manner of the ſea, and received the like of him. So I ſtood in to ſee the land, and thought to tack about, and keep weather of him, and to ſend my boat on board of him; but the wind ſhifted, ſo that for that time I could not. In the evening, I came to weather of him, and ſent my boat on board of him, who preſently weighed, and ſtood off with me till midnight, and then we ſtood in again.

In the morning, captain *Fox* and his friends came on board me; where I entertained them in the beſt manner I could, and with ſuch freſh meat as I had gotten from the ſhore: I told him, how I had named the land, *The ſouth principality of* Wales. I ſhewed him how far I had been to the eaſtward, where I had landed; and in brief, I made known to him all the dangers of this coaſt, as far as I had been. He told me, how he himſelf had been in port *Nelſon*, and had made but a curſory diſcovery hitherto; and that he had not been aland, nor had not many times ſeen the land. In the evening, after I had given his men ſome neceſſaries, with tobacco and other things which they wanted, he departed on board his ſhip; and the next morning ſtood away S. S. W. ſince which time I never ſaw him. The wind ſomething favouring me, I ſtood in for the ſhore, and ſo proceeded along it in ſight.

This month of *Auguſt* ended with ſnow and hail; the weather being as cold as at any time I have felt in *England*.

The firſt of *September* we coaſted along the ſhore in ten fathoms, and when it cleared, in ſight of land. At length the water ſhoaled to ſix and five fathom, and as it cleared, we ſaw it all breaches to leeward, ſo we hull'd off, N. N. E. but ſtill raiſed land. By night we had much ado to get ſafely out of this dangerous bay. At midnight the wind came up at S. and ſo we took in our ſails, and let the ſhip drive to the northward into deeper water. This day was the firſt time the chirurgeon told me, that there were divers of the men tainted with ſickneſs. At noon we were in lat. 55.12.

The ſecond we ſtood in again for the ſhore, but as we came into ſhoal water it began to blow, the weather being winterly and foul, threatning a ſtorm; wherein we were not deceived, for that in ſtanding off we had a violent one.

By midnight it broke up, and the third in the morning we ſtood in again, and by eleven we ſaw it. Here we found the land to trend S. S. E. and S. ſo that we knew we were at a cape land; and named it *cape Henrietta Maria*, by her majeſty's name, who had before named our ſhip. At noon we were in lat. 55. 05. and that is the height of the cape.

From port *Nelſon* to this cape, the land trends (generally) E. S. E. but makes with points and bays; which in the particulars doth

doth alter it a point, two or three. The distance is about 130 leagues, the variation at this cape taken by amplitude, is about 16 deg. a most shoald and perilous coast, in which there is not one harbour to be found.

The 3d day in the afternoon, we had a tearing storm at N. which continued till midnight in extreme violence.

The 4th in the morning (the storm being broke up) we stood in again S. W. The weather was very thick, and we sounded continually; but by noon it cleared, and we saw the land. Here it did trend S. by E. and the tides did set along it, with a quick motion. In the evening there came a great rolling sea out of the N. N. E. and by eight a clock it blew very hard at S. E. and by reason of the incounter of the wind and this great sea, the sea was all in a breach; and to make up a perfect tempest, it did so lighten, snow, rain and blow all the night long, that I was never in the like: We shipt many seas, but one most dangerous, which rack'd us fore and aft, that I verily thought it had sunk the ship, it strook her with such a violence. The ship did labour most terribly in this distraction of wind and waves, and we had much ado to keep all things fast in the hold and betwixt decks.

The 5th in the morning, the wind shifted to S. W. but changed not his condition, but continued in his old anger and fury. In the afternoon it shifted again to the N. W. and there showed his uttermost malice; and in that tearing violence, that nor I, nor any that were then with me, ever saw the sea in such a breach. Our ship was so tormented and did so labour, with taking it in on both sides, and at both ends, that we were in a most miserable distress in this so unknown a place. At eight a clock in the evening the storm brake up, and we had some quietness in the night following, not one having slept one wink in 30 hours before. If this storm had continued easterly, as it was at first, without God's goodness we had all perished.

The 6th, the wind was at S. W. so that we could do no good to the westward. We spent the time therefore in trimming of our ship; we brought all our coals (which for the most part was great coal) aft; as we also did some other things, and all to lighten her afore. Others did pick our bread, whereof there was much wet; for do what we could, we ship'd abundance of water betwixt decks, which ran into the hold, and into our bread-room; for the sea indeed, so continually over-rackt us, that we were like *Jonas* in the whales belly. We over-looked our tacks and shoots, with other riggings of stress, because that hence forward we were to look for no other but winter weather. This evening our boatswain (a painful man, and one that had labour'd extremely these two or three days) was very sick, swooning away three or four times; insomuch that we thought verily he would presently have died.

The 7th in the morning the wind came up at S. E. and we stood away S. W. under all the sail we could make. In this course we saw an island, and came close aboard it, and had 20 fathom water, which was some comfort to us; for hitherto we could not come within four or five leagues of the shore, at that depth. This island stands in latitude 54. 10. In the afternoon we stood away S. W. and in the evening had the shoaling of the western shore, in ten, eight and seven fathom, but it was so thick, that we could not see the land. It is about 14 leagues betwixt this island and the main.

The 8th was thick, foggy and calm; which so continued till the 9th, about six in the morning; the wind then coming up at S. S. W. (though very foggy) we stood to the eastward, keeping our lead going continually. In the evening the water shoaled to ten and nine fathom, wherefore we stood off and on all night.

The 10th we made it, finding it an island of about eight or nine leagues long. It stands in latitude 53. 5. and about 15 leagues from the western shore. The part of it that we coasted, trends W. N. W. I named it my lord *Weston's Island*. We stood still away to the eastward, it being broken foggy weather. In the afternoon, we descry'd land to the eastward of us, which made like three hills or hummocks: Towards them we sail, keeping our lead still going, and very circumspect. At length we also saw land to the southward of us; whereupon we loof up, and now make for that, by course, as we had set it in the thick dark fog. We came in amongst such low broken grounds, breaches and rocks, that we knew not which way to turn us; but God be thanked it was but little wind, and so we came to an anchor. Soon after it cleared, at which time we could see nothing but sands, rocks and breaches round about us; that way only excepted which we came in. I sent presently the boat to sound amongst the shoals and rocks, that if we should be put to extremity, we might have some knowledge which way to go. This night proved calm and fair weather, and we rid quietly.

The 11th in the morning, I went in the boat ashore my self; and whilst I was a land, I sent the boat about amongst the broken

broken grounds to sound. I found this island utterly barren of all goodness, yea, of that which I thought easily to have found; which was scurvy-grass, sorrel, or some herb or other, to have refreshed our sick people. I could not perceive that the tide did flow here (ordinarily) above two foot. There was much drift wood on the shore, and some of it drove up very high, on the north-side of the island; whereby I judged, that the storms were very great at north in the winter. Thus I returned aboard; and sent many of our sick men to another part of island, to see if they themselves could fortunately find any relief for their griefs. At noon, by good observation, we were in latitude 52. 45. In the evening our men returned comfortless; and then we weigh'd and stood to the westward, coming to an anchor under another island, in 20 fathoms.

The 12th in the morning it began to blow hard at S. E. which was partly off the shore, and the ship began to drive, it being soft oozy ground. We heaved in our anchor thereupon, and came to sail under two courses. Whilst the most were busy in heaving out of top-sails; some that should have had special care of the ship, ran her ashore upon the rocks, out of meer carelesness, in looking out and about, or heaving of the lead after they had seen the land all night long, and might even then have seen it, if they had not been blinded with self-conceit, and been enviously opposite in opinions. The first blow struck me out of a deep sleep; and I running out of my cabin, thought no other at first, but I had been wakened (when I saw our danger) to provide my self for another world.

After I had controul'd a little passion in my self, and had checkt some bad counsel that was given me, to revenge my self upon those that had committed this error; I ordered what should be done to get off these rocks and stones: First, we halled all our sails a-back-stays, but that did no good, but make her beat the harder: Whereupon we struck all our sails amain; and furled them up close, tearing down our stern to bring the cable through the cabin to the capstan, and so laid out an anchor to heave her astern. I made all the water in hold to be stav'd, and set some to the pumps to pump it out, and did intend to do the like with our beer: Others I put to throw out all our coals, which was soon and readily done. We quoiled out our cables into our long boat; all this while the ship beating so fearfully that we saw some of the sheathing swim by us. Then stood we, as many as we could, to the capstan; and heaved with such a good will, that the cable brake, and we lost our anchor. Out with all speed therefore, we put another. We could not now perceive whether she did leak or no; and that by reason we were imployed in pumping out the water, which we had bulged in hold; though we much doubted, that she had received her death's wound; wherefore we put into the boat the carpenter's tools, a barrel of bread, a barrel of powder, six muskets, with some match, and a tinder-box, fish-hooks and lines, pitch and okum; and to be brief, whatever could be thought on in such an extremity. All this we sent ashore, to prolong a miserable life for a few days. We were five hours thus beating, in which time she struck 100 blows, insomuch that we thought every stroke had been the last that it was possible she could have endured. The water we could not perceive in all this time to flow any thing at all: At length it pleased God, she beat over all the rocks, though yet we knew not whether she were stanch. Whereupon to pumping we go on all hands, 'till we made the pumps suck; and then we saw how much water she did make in a glass. We found her to be very leaky; but we went to prayer and gave God thanks it was no worse; and so fitted all things again, and got farther off and came to an anchor. In the evening it began to blow very hard at W. S. W. which if it had done whilst we were on the rocks, we had lost our ship without any redemption. With much ado we weighed our anchor, and let her drive to the eastward amongst the broken grounds and rocks, the boat going before, sounding. At length we came amongst breaches, and the boat made signs to us that there was no going farther. Amongst the rocks therefore we again came to an anchor, where we did ride all night, and where our men, which were tired out with extreme labour, were indifferently well refreshed. Here I first noted, that when the wind was at S. it flowed very little or no water at all, so that we could not bring our ship aground to look to her, for we did pump almost continually.

The 13th at noon we weighed and stood to the westward; but in that course it was all broken grounds, shoals and sunken rocks, so that we wondered with our selves, how we came in amongst them in a thick fog. Then we shaped our course to the northward, and after some consultation with my associates, I resolved to get about this land, and so to go down into the bottom of *Hudson*'s *Bay*, and see if I could

could discover a way into the river of *Canada*; and if I failed of that, then to winter on the main land, where there is more comfort to be expected, than among rocks or islands. We stood along the shore, in sight of many beaches: When it was night we stood under our fore-sail, the lead still going. At last the water shoaled upon us to ten fathom, and it began to blow hard: We tackt about, and it did deepen to 12 and 14 fathom, but by and by it shoaled again to eight fathom. Then we tackt about again, and suddenly it shoalded to six and five fathom, so we struck our sail amain, and chopt to an anchor, resolving to ride it out for life and death. We rid all night a great stress, so that our bits did rise, and we thought they would have been torn to pieces.

At break of day the 14th, we were joyful men; and when we could look about, we descried an island some two leagues off, at W. by N. and this was the shoal that lay about it. Here did run a distracted, but yet a very quick tide, of which we taking the opportunity, got up our anchor, and stood N. W. to clear our selves of this shoal. In the afternoon the wind came up at N. E. and we stood along the eastern shore in sight of a multitude of breaches. In the evening it began to blow a storm not sail-worthy, and the sea went very high, and was all in a breach. Our shalop, which we did now tow at stern, being moor'd with two hawsers was sunk, and did spin by her moorings, with her keel up, twenty times in an hour. This made our ship to hull very broad, so that the sea did continually over-rake us, yet we endured it and thought to recover her. All night the storm continued with violence, and with some rain in the morning, it then being very thick weather. The water shoalded apace, with such an over-grown sea withal, that her sail was not to be endured, and what was as ill, there was no trusting to an anchor. Now therefore began we to prepare ourselves, how to make a good end of a miserable tormented life. About noon as it cleared up, we saw two islands under our lee; whereupon we bare up to them, and seeing an opening betwixt them, we endeavoured to get into it before night, for that there was no hope of us, if we continued out at sea that night; therefore come life, come death, we must run this hazard. We found it to be a good sound, where we rid all night safely, and recovered our strengths again, which were much impaired with continual labour. But before we could get into this good place, our shallop broke away, (being moor'd with two hawsers) and we lost her to our great grief. Thus now had we but the ship-boat, and she was all torn and bruised too. This island was the same that we had formerly coasted the western side of, and had named my lord *Weston*'s island. Here we remained till the 19th, in which time it did nothing but snow and blow extremely, insomuch that we durst not put our boat over-board.

The 19th, the wind shifted N. N. E. and we weigh'd and stood to the southward; but by noon the wind came up at S. and so we came to an anchor under another island, on which I went ashore, and named it *The earl of Bristol's island.* The carpenter wrought hard in repairing our boat; whilst I wandered up and down on this desart island, I could not perceive that ever there had been any salvages on it; and in brief, we could find neither fish, fowl nor herb upon it, so that I returned comfortless on board again. The tides do high about some six foot, now that the wind is northerly: The flood comes from the north, and it doth flow half-tide. The full sea this day was at one a clock. Here seeing the winds continue so northerly, that we could not about to go into *Hudson*'s bay, we considered again what was best to do, to look out for a wintering-place. Some advised me to go for port *Nelson*, because we were certain that there was a cove, where we might bring in our ship. I liked not that counsel, for that it is a most perilous place, and that it might be so long ere we could get thither, that we might be debar'd by the ice. Moreover, seeing it was so cold here, as that every night our rigging did freeze, and that sometimes in the morning we did shovel away the snow half a foot thick off our decks, and in that latitude too; I thought it far worse in the other place. I resolved thereupon to stand again to the southward, there to look for some little creek or cove for our ship.

The 21st, the wind came up at N. and we weighed, although it was a very thick fog, and stood away S. W. to clear our selves of the shoals that were on the point of this island. This island is in lat. 53. 10. When we were clear, we steer'd away S. At noon the fog turned into rain, but very thick weather, and it did thunder all the afternoon, which made us doubt a storm; for all which we adventured to proceed. In the evening the wind increased, and blew hard; wherefore we took in all our sails, and let her drive to the southward, heaving the lead every glass. Our depth, when we took in our sails, was thirty fathom, and it did increase to 45, which was a great comfort to us in the dark: At midnight, our depth began suddenly to decrease; and as fast as the lead could be heaved,

heaved, it shoaled to twenty fathom, wherefore we chopt to an anchor, and trimmed our ship aft, to mount on the sea, and fitted all things to ride it out. There was no need to bid our men watch, not one of them putting his eyes together all the night long. We rid it out well all the night, although the sea went very lofty, and that it did blow very hard.

The 22d in the morning, when we could look about us, we saw an island under our lee some leagues off, all being shoals and breaches betwixt us and it. At noon (with the help of the windward tide) we attempted to heave up our anchor, although the sea still went very lofty. Joining all our strengths therefore, with our best skills, God be thanked, we had it up; but before we could set our sails we were driven into nine fathom. Endeavouring thereupon to double a point, to get under the lee of this island, the water shoaled to seven, six, and five fathom, but when we were about, it did deepen again, and we came to an anchor in a very good place; and it was very good for us that we did, for the wind increased to a very storm. Here we rid well all the night, took good rest, and recovered our spent strengths again. The last night and this morning it did snow and hail, and was very cold: Nevertheless, I took the boat and went ashore, to look for some creek or cove to have in our ship, for she was very leaky, and the company become sickly and weak, with much pumping and extreme labour. This island, when we came to the shore, was nothing but ledges of rocks, and banks of sand, and there went a very great surf on them. Nevertheless I made them row thorough it, and ashore I got with two more, and made them row off without the breaches, and there to come to an anchor and to stay for me: I made what speed I could to the top of a hill, to discover about, but could not see what we looked for: Thus because it began to blow hard, I made haste towards the boat again. I found that it had ebbed so low, that the boat could not by any means come near the shore for me; so that we were fain to wade thro' the surf and breaches to her; in which some took such a cold, that they did complain of it to their dying day. But now it began to blow hard, so that we could not get but little to windward toward our ship, for the wind was shifted since we went ashore; and return to the shore we could not, by reason of the surf. Well, we row for life; they in the ship let out a buoy by a long warp, and by God's assistance we got to it, and so haled up to the ship, where we were well welcomed, and we all rejoyced together. This was a premonition to us, to be careful how we sent off the boat, for that it was winter weather already. I named this island, *Sir* Thomas Roe's *island:* It is full of small wood, but in other benefits not very rich, and stands in lat. 52.10. At noon we weighed, seeing an island that bare S. S. E. of us, some four leagues off, which was the highest land we had yet seen in this bay; but as we came near it, it suddenly shoaled to six, five, and four fathom, wherefore we struck our sails amain, and chopt to an anchor; but it was very foul ground, and when the ship was winded up, we had but three fathom at her stern. As it cleared, we could see the breaches all along under our lee; holding it safe therefore to stay long here, we settled every thing in order, for the ship to fall the right way. We had up our anchor, got into deep water, and stood over again for Sir *Thomas Roe*'s island, which by night we brought in the wind of us, some two leagues off, which did well shelter us. The tides run very quick here amongst these shoals; and their times of running ebb or flood, be very uncertain: Their currents are likewise so distracted, that in the night there is no sailing by the compass; wherefore we were fain to seek every night some new place of security to come to an anchor.

The 24th in the morning it did lower, and threaten a storm, which made us with the windward tide weigh to get nearer under the island. It was very thick foggy weather, and as we stood to the north eastward, we came to very uncertain depths; at one cast twenty fathom, the next seven, then ten, five, eight, and three, and coming to the other tack, we were worse than we were before, the currents making a fool of our best judgments in the thick fog, when we could see no land marks. It pleased God that we got clear of them, and endeavoured to get under the lee of the island. This being not able to do, we were fain to come to an anchor in 35 fathom, some two leagues off the shore. All this afternoon (and indeed all night too) it did snow and hail, and was very cold.

The 25th we weighed, and thought to get to the eastward; but as we tack'd to and again, the wind shifted so in our teeths, that it put us within a quarter of a mile of the very shore; where we chopt to an anchor, and rid it out for life and death. Such miseries as these we endured amongst these shoals and broken grounds, or rather more desperate than I have related (very unpleasant perchance to be read) with snow, hail, and stormy weather, and colder than ever I felt it in *England* in my life. Our shoot-anchor was down twice or thrice a day, and

and extreme pains made a great part of the company sickly.

All this lasted with us until the 30th of this month of *September*, which we thought would have put an end to our miseries; for now we were driven amongst rocks, shoals, over-falls, and breaches round about us, that which way to turn we knew not; but there rid amongst them in extremity of distress. All these perils made a most hideous and terrible noise in the night season; and I hope it will not be accounted ridiculous, if I relate with what meditations I was affected, now and then, amongst my ordinary prayers; which I here afford the reader, as I there conceived them in these few ragged and torn rhimes.

Oh my poor soul, why dost thou grieve to see,
So many deaths muster to murder me?
Look to thyself, regard not me; for I
Must do (for what I came) perform or die.
So thou mayst free thyself from being in
A dunghil dungeon, a mere sink of sin;
And happily be freed, if thou believe,
Truly in God through Christ, and ever live.
Be therefore glad: yet e'er thou go from hence,
For our joint sins, let's do some penitence,
Unseignedly together. When we part,
I'll wish the angels joy, with all my heart.
We have with confidence relied upon
A rusty wire, touch'd with a little stone,
Incompass'd round with paper, and alass,
To house it harmless, nothing but a glass,
And thought to shun a thousand dangers, by
The blind direction of this senseless flie;
When the fierce winds shatter'd black nights asunder,
Whose pitchy clouds, spitting forth fire and thunder,
Hath shook the earth, and made the ocean roar;
And run to hide it in the broken shore:
Now thou must steer by faith; *a better guide,*
'Twill bring thee safe to heaven against the tide
Of Satan's malice. Now let quiet gales
Of saving Grace inspire thy zealous sails.

The first of *October* was indifferent fair weather, and with a windward tide, out went our boat to sound a channel to help us out of this perilous place. The boat within two hours returned, and told us how she had been a way where there was no less than 12 fathom. We presently thereupon weigh'd, but found it otherwise, and came amongst many strange races and over-falls, upon which there went a very great and breaking sea. As we proceeded, the water shoal'd to six fathom. Well! there was no remedy, we must go forward, happy be lucky, seeing there neither was any riding, and as little hope to turn any way with a sail, but that there appear'd present death in it. It pleased God so to direct us, that we got thro' it, having no less than five several, and all very uncertain depths. The water sometimes deepen'd to twenty fathom, then upon a sudden, it shoal'd to seven, six, and five fathoms; so we struck all our sails amain, and chopp'd to an anchor, where we rid till midnight, for life and death, it blowing a merciless gale of wind, and the sea going very lofty, and all in a breach. The ground was foul ground too, insomuch that we doubted our cable every minute.

The second in the morning was little wind; wherefore taking the opportunity of the tide, the boat went forth to sound; which returning again in two hours, told us how they had sounded about that shoal, and had found a place of some safety to ride in, and had been in no less water than five fathom. We weighed, and found our cable galled in two places; which had soon failed us, if the foul weather had continued. We stood the same way that the boat did direct us; but it proved so calm, that we came to an anchor in eighteen fathom. I took the boat, and went ashore on an island that was to the southward of us, which I named, *The earl of* Danby's *island*. From the highest place in it, I could see it all broken grounds and shoals to the southward; and rather worse than any thing better than that which we had been in. I found that the salvages had been upon it, and that it was full of wood. I made haste to the boat to sound the bay for fear of shoals and sunken rocks, but found it indifferent good. Toward the evening it began to blow hard; wherefore we made towards the ship. She put forth a buoy and a warp; and we rowing for life to recover her, were put to the leeward of her; but by getting hold of the warp, we hall'd up to her. The boat we left half full of water, ourselves being as wet as drown'd rats; and it made us the more rejoice, that we had escap'd this great danger. All this night we had a very hard rodesteed, it blowing a most violent gale of wind, with snow and hail.

The third about noon the wind dull'd, and we had up our anchor, standing in farther into the bay into four fathom and a half water. Here we came again to an anchor, with our second anchor; for many of our men are now sick, and the rest so weaken'd, that we can hardly weigh our shoot-anchor. I took the boat, and went presently ashore to see what comfort I could find. This was the first time that I put foot on this island, which was the same that we did after winter upon. I found the tracks of deer, and saw some fowl; but that that did rejoice

rejoice me moſt, was, that I did ſee an opening into the land, as if it had been a river. To it we make with all ſpeed, but found it to be barr'd, and not two foot water at full ſea on the bar; and yet within a moſt excellent fine harbour, having four fathom water. In the evening I returned aboard, bringing little comfort for our ſick men more than hopes.

The fourth it did ſnow and blow very hard, yet I got aſhore, and appointed the boat to go to another place (which made like a river) and to ſound it. In the mean time I went with four more, ſome four or five miles up into the country, but could find no relief all that way for our ſick, but a few berries only. After we had well wearied ourſelves in the troubleſome woods, we returned to the place I had appointed the boat to tarry for me; where at my coming I ſtill found her, ſhe having not been where I had order'd her, for it had blown ſuch a fierce gale of wind, that ſhe could not row to windward. Thus we returned aboard with no good news. It continued foul weather, with ſnow and hail, and extreme cold, till the ſixth, when with a favouring wind, we ſtood in nearer to the ſhore, and here moor'd the ſhip.

The ſeventh it ſnow'd all day, ſo that we were fain to clear it off the decks with ſhovels, and it blew a very ſtorm withal. It continued ſnowing and very cold weather, and it did ſo freeze, that all the bows of the ſhip, with her beak-head, was all ice; about the cable alſo was ice as big as a man's middle. The bows of the boat were likewiſe frozen half a foot thick, ſo that we were fain to hew and beat it off. The ſun did ſhine very clear, and we tore the topſails out of the tops, which were hard frozen in them, into a lump; ſo that there they hung a ſunning all day, in a very lump; the ſun not having power to thaw one drop of them. After the boat was fitted, we rowed towards the ſhore, but could not come near the place where we were uſed to land, for that it was all thicken'd water with the ſnow that had fallen upon the ſands, that are dry at low water. This made it ſo difficult to row, that we could not ſet through it with four oars, yet ſomething higher to the weſtward, we got aſhore. Seeing now the winter to come thus extremely on upon us, and that we had very little wood aboard, I made them fill the boat, and went aboard; and ſent the carpenter and others to cut wood, others to carry it to the water-ſide, whilſt the boat brought it aboard; for I doubted that we were likely to be debar'd the ſhore, and that we ſhould not go to and again with the boat. It was miſerable and cold already aboard the ſhip; every thing did freeze in the hold, and by the fire-ſide. Seeing therefore that we could no longer make uſe of our ſails (which be the wings of a ſhip) it raiſed many doubts in our minds that here we muſt ſtay and winter. After we had brought ſo much wood aboard as we could conveniently ſtow, and enough as I thought would have laſted two or three months, the ſick men deſired that ſome little houſe or hovel might be built aſhore, whereby they might be the better ſheltered, and recover their healths. I took the carpenter (and others whom I thought fit for ſuch a purpoſe) and chuſing out a place, they went immediately to work upon it. In the mean ſpace, I myſelf, accompanied with ſome others, wandered up and down in the woods, to ſee if we could diſcover any ſigns of ſavages, that ſo we might the better provide for our ſafeties againſt them. We found no appearance that there were any on this iſland, nor near unto it. The ſnow by this time was half-leg high; and ſtalking thro' it, we return'd comfortleſs to our companions, who had all this time wrought well upon our houſe. They aboard the ſhip took down our top-ſails in the mean while, and made a great fire upon the hearth in the hatch-way; ſo that having well thaw'd them, they folded them up, and put them betwixt decks, that if we had any weather, they might bring them again to yard. Thus in the evening we returned aboard.

The twelfth we took our main-ſail from the yard, which was hard frozen to it, and carried it aſhore to cover our houſe withal, being firſt fain to thaw it by a great fire. By night they had covered it, and had almoſt hedged it about; and the ſix builders did deſire to lie in it aſhore that night, which I condeſcended unto, having firſt fitted them with muskets and other furniture, and a charge to keep good watch all night. Moreover, they had aſhore two greyhounds, (a dog and a bitch) which I had brought out of *England*, to kill us ſome deer, if happily we could find any.

By the 13th at night our houſe was ready; and our ſix builders deſired they might travel up into the country to ſee what they could diſcover.

The 14th, betimes in the morning, being fitted with munition, and their order to keep together (but eſpecially to ſeek out ſome creek or cove for our ſhip) they departed. We aboard took down our own top-maſts and their rigging, making account if we did remove, to make uſe of of our foreſail and mizen.

The 15th in the evening our hunters returned very weary, and brought with them a ſmall lean deer, in four quarters, which

 rejoiced

rejoiced us all, hoping we should have had more of them to refresh our sick men withal. They reported, that they had wander'd above twenty miles, and had brought this deer above twelve miles, and that they had seen nine or ten more. The last night they had a very cold lodging in the woods; and so it appeared, for they look'd all almost starved, nor could they recover themselves in three or four days after. They saw no sign of salvages, nor of any ravening wild beasts, nor yet any hope of harbour.

The 17th my lieutenant, and five more, desired they might try their fortunes in travelling about the island. But they had far worse luck than the others, although they endured out all night, and had wandered very far in the snow (which was now very deep) and returned comfortless, and miserably disabled with the coldness. But what was worse than all this, they had lost one of their company, *John Barton*, namely, our gunner's mate; who being very weary, merely to save the going about, had attempted to go over a pond, that was a quarter of a mile over; where when he was in the very midst, the ice brake and closed upon him, and we never saw him more. Considering these disasters, I resolved to fish no more with a golden hook, for fear I weaken'd myself more with one hunting, than twenty such deers could do me good. Being now assured, that there were no savages upon the island, nor yet about us on the other islands; no, nor on the main neither, as far as we could discover (which we farther proved by making of fires) and that the cold season was now in that extremity, that they could not come to us, if there were any; we comforted and refreshed our selves, by sleeping the more securely. We chang'd our island garrison every week, and for other refreshing we were like to have none till the spring.

From this 10th to the 29th it did (by *interims*) snow and blow so hard, that the boat could hardly adventure ashore, and but seldom land, unless the men did wade in the thick congealed water, carrying one another. We did sensibly perceive withal, how we did daily sink into more miseries. The land was all deep cover'd with snow, the cold did multiply, and the thick snow-water did increase; and what would become of us, our most merciful God and preserver knew only.

The 29th I observed an eclipse of the moon, with what care possibly I could, both in the tryal of the exactness of our instruments, as also in the observation. I refer you to the observation in the latter end of this relation, where it is at large describ'd. This month of *October* ended with snow and bitter cold weather.

The first of *November* I cast up my accounts with the steward concerning our victuals, the third part of our time being this day out. I found him an honest man; for he gave me an account every week what was spent, and what was still in the hold remaining under his hand. I would take no excuse of leekage or other waste, unless he did daily shew it me. Every month I made a new survey; and every six months put what we had spared by itself; which now was at least a month's provision of bread, and a fortnight's of peas, and fish, *&c.*

The third the boat endeavoured to get ashore, but could not set thro' the thick congealed water.

The fourth they found a place to get ashore, and so once in two or three days, till the ninth, bringing beer to our men ashore in a barrel, which would freeze firmly in the house in one night. Other provision they had store. The ice beer being thaw'd in a kettle, was not good; and they did break the ice of the ponds of water, to come by water to drink. This pond-water had a most loathsom smell with it; so that doubting lest it might be infectious, I caus'd a well to be sunk near the house. There we had very good water, which did taste (as we flatter'd our selves with it) even like milk.

The tenth (having store of boards for such a purpose) I put the carpenter to work, to make us a little boat, which we might carry (if occasion were) over the ice, and make use of her, where there was water. At noon I took the latitude of this island by two quadrants, which I found to be 52.00. I urged the men to make traps to catch foxes, for we did daily see many. Some of them were pied, black and white; whereby I gathered that there were some black foxes, whose skins, I told them, were of a great value; and I promised, that whosoever could take one of them, should have the skin for his reward. Hereupon they made divers traps, and waded in the snow (which was very deep) to place them in the woods.

The twelfth our house took fire, but we soon quenched it. We were fain to keep an extraordinary fire night and day; and this accident made me order a watch to look to it continually; seeing, that if our house and clothing should be burnt, that all we were but in a woful condition. I lay ashore till the 17th, all which time our miseries did increase. It did snow and freeze most extremely. At which time we looking from the shore towards the ship, she did look like a piece of ice in the fashion of a ship, or a ship resembling a piece of ice. The snow was

was all frozen about her, and all her fore-part firm ice, and ſo was ſhe on both ſides alſo. Our cables froze in the hawſe, wonderful to behold. I got me aboard, where the long nights I ſpent, with tormenting cogitations; and in the day time, I could not ſee any hope of ſaving the ſhip. This I was aſſured of, that it was moſt impoſſible to endure theſe extremities long. Every day the men muſt beat the ice off the cables; while ſome within board, with the carpenters long calking iron, did dig the ice out of the hawſes; in which work, the water would freeze on their clothes and hands, and would ſo benumb them, that they could hardly get into the ſhip, without being heav'd in with a rope.

The 19th, our gunner (who as you may remember, had his leg cut off) did languiſh irrecoverably, and now grew very weak; deſiring, that for the little time he had to live, he might drink ſack altogether, which I ordered he ſhould do.

The 22d in the morning he died. An honeſt and a ſtrong-hearted man. He had a cloſe boarded cabin in the gunroom, which was very cloſe indeed; and as many clothes on him as was convenient, (for we wanted no clothes) and a pan with coals, and a fire continually in his cabin: For all which warmth, his plaiſter would freeze at his wound, and his bottle of ſack at his head. We committed him at a good diſtance from the ſhip unto the ſea.

The 23d, the ice did increaſe extraordinarily, and the ſnow lay on the water in flakes, as it did fall; much ice withal drove by us, yet nothing hard all this while. In the evening, after the watch was ſet, a great piece came athwart our hawſe, and four more following after him, the leaſt of them a quarter of a mile broad; which in the dark did very much aſtoniſh us, thinking it would have carried us out of the harbour, upon the ſhoal's eaſtern-point, which was full of rocks. It was newly congealed, a matter of two inches thick, and we broke thorough it, the cable and anchor induring an incredible ſtreſs, ſometimes ſtopping the whole ice. We ſhot off three muſkets, ſignifying to our men aſhore, that we were in diſtreſs; who anſwered us again, but could not help us. By ten a clock it was all paſt; nevertheleſs, we watched carefully, and the weather was warmer than we had felt it any time this month. In the morning, at break of day, I ſent for our men aboard, who made up the houſe, and arrived by ten, being driven by the way, to wade thorough the congealed water, ſo that they recovered to the boat with difficulty. There drove by the ſhip many pieces of ice, though not ſo large as the former, yet much thicker: One piece came foul of the cable, and made the ſhip drive.

As ſoon as we were clear of it, we joined our ſtrengths together, and had up our eaſtermoſt anchor; and now I reſolved to bring the ſhip aground, for no cables nor anchors could hold her: But I will here ſhow you the reaſons why I brought her no ſooner aground. Firſt, it was all ſtony-ground, ſome ſtones lying dry, three or four foot above water; ſo that it was to be ſuſpected, that it was the like all about us. Secondly, it did ordinarily flow but two foot and a half here; and if ſhe ſhould bed deep in the ſands, we could not ever come to dig her out again; for that ſhe would not be dry, by four or five foot. Thirdly, it was a looſe ſand, which might riſe with the ſurf, or ſo mount about her, that all our weak powers could not heave it away in the next ſpring time. Fourthly, we doubted the tides would not high ſo much in the ſummer as they did now. Fifthly, We could not bring her out of the tides way, which doth run ſomething quick here; and the ice, beſides, might drive and mount up upon her, and ſo overſet her, or tear her, and carry away her planks, iron works and all; ſo that we ſhould have nothing left to finiſh our pinnace with. Sixthly, If it did blow a ſtorm at N. W. or thereabouts, the water would flow ten foot and upwards; and that wind being off the ſhore, it would blow away all the ice, and there would come in an extraordinary great ſurf about the ſhoaled eaſtern-point, which was occaſioned by a deep overfall. Moreover, ſhe would beat extremely; and if ſhe were put up by the ſea, or that ſurf, it was very doubtful that we ſhould never have her off again. For theſe reaſons we endured all the extremity, ſtill hoping upon ſome good and fortunate accident. But now all our provident deſigns we ſaw to become fooliſhneſs; and that a great deal of miſerable labour had been ſpent in vain by us. With the flood we weighed our weſtermoſt anchor, perceiving God's aſſiſtance manifeſtly, becauſe it happened to be fine warm weather; otherwiſe we had not been able to work. The wind was now ſouth, which blew in upon the ſhore, and made the loweſt tides. We brought the ſhip into twelve foot water, and laid out one anchor in the offing, and another in ſhoaled water, to draw her a land at command. Our hope alſo was, that ſome ſtones that were to the weſtward of us, would fend off ſome of the ice. We then being about a mile from the ſhore, about ten a clock in the dark night, the ice came driving upon us, and our anchors came home. She drove ſome two cables length; and the wind blowing

blowing on the fhore, by two a clock fhe came aground, and ftopt much ice; yet fhe lay well all night, and we took fome reft.

The 25th the wind fhifted eafterly, and put abundance of ice on us. When the flood was made, we encouraged one another, and to work we go, drawing home our anchors by main force, under great pieces of ice, our endeavour being to put the fhip to the fhore. But to our great difcomforts, when the half tide was made, (which was two hours before high water) the fhip drove amongft the ice to the eaftward, (do what we could) and fo would have on the fhoaled rocks. As I have formerly faid, thefe two days, and this day, was very warm weather, and it did rain, which it had not yet but once done, fince we came hither; otherwife, it had been impoffible we could have wrought. Withal, the wind fhifted alfo to the fouth, and at the very inftant, blew a hard puff, which fo continued for half an hour. I caufed our two topfails to be had up from betwixt decks, and we hoifted them up with ropes in all hafte, and we forced the fhip afhore, when fhe had not half a cable's length to drive on the rocky fhoals. In the evening we broke way thorough the ice, and put an anchor to fhoreward in five foot water, to keep her to the fhore if poffible it might be. Here fir *Hugh Willoughby* came into my mind, who without doubt was driven out of his harbour in this manner, and fo ftarved at fea. But God was more merciful to us. About nine a clock at night, the wind came up at N. W. and blew a very ftorm. This wind was off the fhore, which blew away all the ice from about us, long before we were afloat. There came in a great rowling fea withal about the point, accompanied with a great furf on the fhore. And now were we left to the mercy of the fea on the ground. By ten, fhe began to rowl in her dock; and foon after, began to beat againft the ground. We ftood at the capftang as many as could, others at the pumps; for we thought that every fifth or fixth blow would have ftaved her to pieces. We heaved to the uttermoft of our ftrengths to keep her as near the ground as we could. By reafon of this wind, it flowed very much water, and we drew her up fo high, that it was doubtful if ever we fhould get her off again. She continued thus beating, till two a clock the next morning, and then fhe again fettled. Whereupon we went to fleep to reftore nature; feeing the next tide we expected to be again tormented.

The 26th, in the morning tide, our fhip did not float, whereby we had fome quietnefs. After prayers, I called a confultation of the mafter, my lieutenant, the mates, carpenter, and boatfwain; to whom I propofed, that now we were put to our laft fhifts, and therefore they fhould tell me what they thought of it: Namely, whether it were not beft, to carry all our provifion afhore; and that when the wind fhould come northerly, it were not fafeft to draw her farther off, and fink her. After many reafonings they allowed of my purpofe, and fo I communicated it to the company, who all willingly agreed to it. And fo we fell to getting up of our provifions; firft our bread, of which we landed this day two dry-fats with a hogfhead of beef; having much ado to fet the boat thorough the thick congealed water. In the evening, the wind came up at N. E. and E. and fill'd the bay choakful of ice.

The 27th, the bay continued full of ice, which I hoped would fo continue and freeze, that we fhould not be put to fink our fhip. This day we could land nothing.

The 28th, at break of day, three of our men went afhore over the ice, unknown to me; and the wind coming up at W. drove the ice from betwixt us and the fhore, and moft part out of the bay alfo: And yet not fo, that the boat could go afhore for any thing. I made the carpenter fit a place againft all fudden extremities, for that with the firft N. W. or northerly wind, I meant to effect our laft project. In the run of her, on the ftarboard fide, he cut away the fealing and the plank to the fheathing fome four or five inches fquare, fome four foot high from the keel of her, that fo it might be boared out at an inftant. We brought our bread which was remaining in the bread room, up into the great cabbin, and likewife all our powder, fetting much of our light dry things betwixt decks.

The 29th, at five a clock in the morning, the wind came up at W. N. W. and began to blow very hard. It was ordinary for the wind to fhift from the W. by the N. round about. So firft I ordered the cooper to go down in hold, and look to all our cafk; thofe that were full, to mawle in the bungs of them; thofe that were empty, to get up, or if they could not be gotten up, to ftave them. Then to quoil all our cables upon our lower tire; and to lay on our fpare anchors, and any thing that was weighty, to keep it down from rifing. By feven a clock, it blew a ftorm at N. W. our bitter enemy. The fhip was already bedded fome two foot in the fand, and whilft that was a flowing, fhe muft beat. This I before had in my confideration; for I thought fhe was fo far driven up, that we fhould never get her off. Yet we had been fo

2 ferreted

ferreted by her laſt beating, that I reſolved to ſink her right down, rather than run that hazard. By nine a clock, ſhe began to rowl in her dock, with a moſt extraordinary great ſea that was come, which I found to be occaſioned by the forementioned overfall. And this was the fatal hour that put us to our wits end. Wherefore I went down in hold with the carpenter, and took his augur and bored a hole in the ſhip, and let in the water. Thus with all ſpeed, we began to cut out other places to bore thorough, but every place was full of nails. By ten, notwithſtanding, the lower tire was covered with water; for all which, ſhe began ſo to beat in her dock, more and more, that we could not work, nor ſtand to do any thing in her: Nor would ſhe ſink ſo faſt as we would have her, but continued beating double blows; firſt abaft, and then before, that it was wonderful, how ſhe could endure a quarter of an hour with it. By twelve a clock, her lower tire roſe; and that did ſo counterbeat on the inſide, that it beat the bulk heads of the bread-room, powder-room, and forepiece, all to pieces; and when it came betwixt decks, the cheſts fled wildly about, and the water did flaſh and fly wonderfully; ſo that now we expected every minute when the ſhip would open and break to pieces. At one a clock ſhe beat off her rudder, and that was gone we knew not which way. Thus ſhe continued beating till three a clock, and then the ſea came up on the upper deck, and ſoon after, ſhe began to ſettle. In her, we were fain to ſink the moſt part of our bedding and clothes; and the chirurgeons cheſt with the reſt. Our men that were aſhore, ſtood looking upon us, almoſt dead with cold, and ſorrows to ſee our miſery and their own. We look'd upon them again, and both upon each other with woful hearts. Dark night drew on, and I bade the boat to be haled up, and commanded my loving companions to go all into her; who (in ſome refuſing compliments) expreſſed their faithful affections to me, as loth to part from me. I told them, that my meaning was to go aſhore with them. And thus, laſtly, I forſook the ſhip.

We were ſeventeen poor ſouls now in the boat; and we now imagined, that we were leapt out of the frying pan into the fire: The ebb was made, and the water extraordinary thick, congealed with ſnow; ſo that we thought aſſuredly, it would carry us away into the ſea. We thereupon double mann'd four oars, appointing four more to ſit ready with oars; and ſo with the help of God we got to the ſhore, halling up the boat after us. One thing was moſt ſtrange in this thick water: Namely, that there went a great ſwelling ſea. Being arrived upon the land, we greeted our fellows the beſt we could; at which time they could not know us, nor we them by our habits nor voices, ſo frozen all over we were, faces, hair, and apparel. And here I mean to take breath awhile, after all this long and unpleaſant relation of our miſerable endeavours, craving leave firſt of all to ſpeak a word or two in general.

The winds, ſince we came hither, have been very variable and unconſtant; and till within this fortnight, the ſoutherly wind was the coldeſt. The reaſon I conceive to be, for that it did blow from the main land, which was all covered with ſnow; and for that the north winds came out of the great bay which hitherto was open. Add to that, we were now under a ſouth bank which did ſhelter us, ſo that we were not ſo ſenſible of it.

A N. W. a N. W. by N. and a N. W. wind (if it blew a ſtorm) would raiſe the tides extraordinarily: And indeed, from the W. N. W. to the N. N. E. would raiſe the tides in proportion, as they did blow from the middle point: The wind being on the oppoſite points (if it blew) it would flow very little at all. The harder it blew, the leſs water it would flow. If it were little wind or calm, it would flow indifferently. The tides do high ordinarily (without being forced) about three foot; but being forced with the forementioned winds, upwards of ten foot. I could perceive no difference betwixt neap and ſpring tides: It flows half tide; that is, the flood comes from the northward, and thither returns again, two hours before it be high water; and it is commonly ſo ſeen in moſt bays or inlets.

OUR

OUR
WINTERING.

AFTER we had haled up the boat, we went along the breach side in the dark, towards our house, where we made a good fire; and with it and bread and water, we thawed and comforted ourselves, beginning after that to reason one with another, concerning our ship. I requir'd that every one should speak his mind freely. The carpenter (especially) was of the opinion, that she was founder'd, and would never be serviceable again. He alledged, that she had so beaten, that it was not possible, but that all her joints were loose, and seams open; and that by reason it flowed so little water, and no creek nor cove being near, wherein to bring her aground, he could not devise how he might come to mend it. Moreover, her rudder was lost, and he had no iron work to hang on another. Some alledged, that we had heaved her up so high upon the sands, that they thought we should never have her off again, and that they were assured she was already dock'd three foot. Others, that she lay in the tides way, and that the ice might tear her to pieces off the ground; besides which, two of our anchors we could not now get from under the ice; which when the ice brake (which would be of a great thickness by the spring) would break our anchors to pieces, and then we should have no anchors to bring us home withal, supposing we got off the ship, and that she proved sound also. I comforted them the best I could with such like words; My masters and faithful companions, be not dismay'd for any of these disasters, but let us put our whole trust in God; it is he that giveth and he that taketh away; he throws down with one hand, and raiseth up with another: His will be done. If it be our fortunes to end our days here, we are as near heaven as in *England*; and we are much bound to God Almighty for giving us so large a time of repentance, who as it were daily calls upon us, to prepare ourselves for a better life in heaven. I make no doubt, but he will be merciful to us both here on earth, and in his blessed kingdom; he doth not in the mean time deny, but that we may use all honest means to save and prolong our natural lives withal; and in my judgment, we are not yet so far past hope of returning into our native countries, but that I see a fair way by which we may effect it. Admit the ship be foundered, (which God forbid, I hope the best) yet have those of our own nation, and others, when they have been put to these extremities, even out of the wreck of their lost ship, built then a pinnace, and recovered to their friends again. If it be objected, that they have happened into better climates, both for temperateness of the air, and for pacifick and open seas; and provided withal, of abundance of fresh victuals; yet there is nothing too hard for couragious minds, which hitherto you have shown, and I doubt not will still do, to the uttermost.

They all protested to work to the uttermost of their strength, and that they would refuse nothing that I should order them to do, to the uttermost hazard of their lives. I thank'd them all, and to the carpenter for his cheerful undertaking, I promised to give him so much plate presently, as should be worth ten pound sterling; and if so be I went to *England* in the pinnace, I would give her him freely, and fifty pounds in money over and above; and would moreover gratify all them, that I should see painful and industrious. Thus we then resolved, to build us a new pinnace with the timber we should get upon the island; that in the spring, if we found not the ship serviceable, we might tear her up, and plank her with the ships planks. And so for this night we settled ourselves close about the fire, and took some rest till day-light.

The 30th betimes in the morning, I caused the chirurgeon to cut the hair of my head short, and to shave away all the hair of my face, for that it was become intolerable, and that it would be frozen so great with isicles: The like did all the rest.

The first of *November* we fitted our selves to work. The first thing we were to do, was to get our clothes and provisions ashore, and therefore I divided the company. The master and a convenient company with him, were to go aboard, and get things out of the hold. The cock-swain with his gang, were to go in the boat, to bring and carry things ashore. Myself, with the rest, to carry it half a mile thro' the snow, unto the place

place where we intended to build a store-house: As for the heavier things, we purposed to lay them upon the beach. In the afternoon the wind was at south south west, and the water veer'd to so low an ebb, that we thought we might get something out of our hold. We launched our boat therefore, and with oars set thro' the thick congealed water: It did freeze extream hard, and I did stand on the shore with a troubled mind, thinking verily that with the ebb the boat would be carried into the sea, and that then we were all lost men. But by God's assistance, they got safely to the ship, and made a fire there, to signify their arrival aboard. They fell presently to work, and got something out of the hold, upon the decks; but night coming on, they durst not adventure to come ashore, but lay on the bed in the great cabbin, being almost starved.

The first of *December* was so cold, that I went the same way over the ice to the ship, where the boat had gone yesterday. This day we carried upon our backs in bundles, 500 of our Fish, and much of our bedding and clothes, which we were fain to dig out of the Ice.

The 2d was mild Weather; and some of the men going over the ice, fell in, and were very hardly recovered; so that this day we could land nothing, neither by boat nor back: I put them therefore to make us a store-house ashore. In the evening, the wind came up at west; and the ice did break and drive out of the bay: It was very deep and large ice, that we much doubted it would have spoiled the ship.

The 3d day, there were divers great pieces of ice that came athwart the ship, and she stopt them, yet not so, that we could go over them. We found a way for the boat; but when she was loaden, she drew four foot water, and could not come within a flight-shot of the shore. The men therefore must wade through the thick congealed water, and carry all things out of the ship upon their backs. Every time they waded in the ice, it so gathered about them, that they did seem like a walking piece of ice, most lamentable to behold. In this extream cold evening they cut away as much ice from about the boat as they could, and pickt it with hand-spikes out of her, and endeavouring to hoise her into the ship: There being small hope that she could go to and again any more. But use what means they could, she was so heavy, that they could not hoise her in, but were fain there to leave her in the tackles by the ship's side.

The 4th, being sunday we rested; and performed the sabbath-duties of a christian.

The 5th and 6th were extream cold; and we made bags of our store-shirts, and in them carried our loose bread over the ice ashoar upon our backs. We also digged our clothes and new-sails with hand-spikes of iron, out of the ice, and carried them ashoar, which we dried by a great fire.

The 7th day was so extreamly cold, that our noses, cheeks, and hands, did freeze as white as paper.

The 8th and 9th it was extream cold, and it did snow much, yet we continued our labour, in carrying and rowling things ashoar. In the evening the water raised the ice very high, and it did break two thoughts of our boat, and break in the side of her; but for that time we could not help it.

The 10th, our carpenter found timber to make a keel, and a stern, for our pinnace; the rest wrought about our provisions until the 13th day; and that we spent in digging our boat out of the ice, which we were fain to do to the very keel; and dig the ice out her, and then we got her up on the ice; in which doing, many had their noses, cheeks, and fingers, frozen as white as paper. The cold now encreased most extreamly. By the 19th, we could get no more things out of our hold; but were fain to leave five barrels of beef and pork, all our beer, and divers other things which were all firm frozen in her.

The 21st was so cold, that we could not go out of the house.

The 23d we went to heave our boat ashore, running her over our oars, but by ten a clock there came such a thick fog, that it was as dark as night. I made them give over, and make what haste we could to the shore; which we had much ado to find, for the time, losing one another. At the last, we met all at the house, the miserablest frozen that can be conceived. Upon divers, the cold had raised blisters as big as wall-nuts. This we imagined to come, by reason that they came too hastily to the fire. Our well was now frozen up; so that dig as deep as we could, we can come by no water. Melted snow water is very unwholesome, either to drink or to dress our victuals. It made us so short-breathed, that we were scarce able to speak. All our sack, vinegar, oil, and every thing else that was liquid, was now frozen as hard as a piece of wood, and we must cut it with a hatchet. Our house was all frozen on the inside, and it froze hard within a yard of the fire-side. When I landed first upon this island, I found a spring under a hill-side; which I then observing, had caused some trees to be cut for marks to know the place again by. It was about three quarters of a mile from our house. I sent three of our men which had been formerly with me, thither upon the

24th: These wading thorow the snow, at last found the place, and shoveling away the snow, they made way to the very head of it. They found it spring very strongly, and brought me a can of it, for which I was right joyful. This spring continued all the year, and did not freeze, but that we could break the ice and come to it. We labour'd very hard these three or four days, to get wood to the house, which we found to be very troublesome, through the deep snow.

We then settled our bedding and provisions, providing to keep *Christmas-day* holy, which we solemnized in the joyfullest manner we could; so likewise did we St. *John*'s day; upon which we named the wood we did winter in, in memory of that honourable knight, sir *John Winter*, *Winter*'s *Forest*, And now instead of a *Christmas* tale, I will here describe the house that we did live in, with those adjoining.

When I first resolved to build a house, I chose the warmest and convenientest place, and the nearest the ship withal. It was amongst a tuft of thick trees under a south-bank, about a flight-shot from the sea's side. True it is, that at that time we could not dig into the ground, to make us a hole or cave in the earth, (which had been the best way) because we found water within two foot digging, and therefore that project fail'd. It was a white light sand, so that we could by no means make up a mud-wall. As for stones, there were none near us, which moreover were all now covered with the snow. We had no boards for such a purpose, and therefore we must do the best we could, with such materials as we had about us.

The house was square, about twenty foot every way, as much namely, as our main-course could well cover: First we drove strong stakes into the earth, round about, which we watteled with boughs, as thick as might be, beating them down very close. This our first work was six foot high on both sides, but at the ends almost up to the very top, there we left two holes for the light to come in at, and the same way the smoak did vent out also. Moreover I caused at both ends, three rows of thick bush-trees, to be stuck up, as close together as might be possible. Then at a distance from the house, we cut down trees, proportioning them into lengths of six foot, with which we made a pile on both sides, six foot thick, and six foot high, but at both ends ten foot high, and six foot thick: We left a little low door to creep into, and a portal before that, made with piles of wood, that the wind might not blow into it. We next of all fastened a rough-tree aloft over all, upon which we laid our rafters, and our main-course over those again; which lying thwart-ways over all, did reach down to the very ground on either side. And this was the fabrick of the outside of it. On the inside we made fast our bonnet-sails round about. Then we drove in stakes and made us bedstead frames, about three sides of the house, which bedsteads were double one under another, the lowermost being a foot from the ground. These we first fill'd with boughs, then we laid some spare sails on that, and then our bedding and cloaths. We made a hearth or causie in the middle of the house, and on it made our fire; some boards we laid round about our hearth to stand upon, that the cold damp should not strike up into us. With our wast-clothes we made us canopies and curtains, others did the like with our small sails.

Our second house was not past twenty foot distant from this, and made for the watteling much after the same manner, but it was less, and covered with our fore-course: It had no piles on the south-side, but in lieu of that we piled up all our chests on the inside; and indeed the reflex of the heat of the fire against them, did make it warmer than the mansion-house. In this house we drest our victuals, and the subordinate crue did refresh themselves all day in it.

A third house (which was our store-house) we likewise made some twenty paces off from this, for fear of firing. This house was only a rough-tree fastened aloft, with rafters laid from it to the ground, and covered with our new suit of sails. On the inside we had laid small trees, and covered them over with boughs, and so stor'd up our bread and fish in it, about two foot from the ground, the better to preserve them. Other things lay more carelesly.

Long before *Christmas* our mansion-house was covered thick over with snow, almost to the very roof of it: And so likewise was our second house; but our store-house all over, by reason we made no fire in it. Thus we seemed to live in a heap and wilderness of snow; forth a-doors we could not go, but upon the snow, in which we made us paths middle-deep in some places, and in one special place, the length of ten steps. To do this we must shovel away the snow first; and then by treading make it something hard under foot: The snow in this path was a full yard thick under us; and this was our best gallery for the sick men, and for mine own ordinary walking. And both houses and walks we

 did

did daily accommodate more and more, and make fitter for our uses.

The 27th we got our boat ashore, and fetcht up some of our provisions from the beach-side into the store-house; and so by degrees did we with the rest of our provisions, with extremity of cold and labour, making way with shovels thorow the deep snow, even from the sea-side unto our store-house. And thus concluded we the old year 1631.

January 1632.

The first of *January* (and for the most part of all the month) was extreme cold.

The 6th, I observed the latitude with what exactness I could, (it being very clear sun-shine weather) which I found to be 51. 52. This difference is, by reason that here is a great refraction.

The 21st I observed the sun to rise like an oval, along the horizon: I call'd three or four to see it, the better to confirm my judgment; and we all agreed that it was twice as long as it was broad. We plainly perceived withal, that by degrees as it gate up higher, it also recovered its roundness.

The 26th I observed, when the eastern-edge of the moon did touch the planet *Mars*, the *Lion's-Heart* was then in the east-quarter 21. 45. above the horizon; but all this was not done with that exactness that I have done other observations.

The 30th and 31st there appeared in the beginning of the night, more stars in the firmament than ever I had before seen by two thirds. I could see the cloud in *Cancer* full of small stars, and all the *Via Lactea* nothing but small stars, and amongst the *Pleiades* a great many small stars. About ten a clock the moon did rise, and then a quarter of them was not to be seen. The wind for the most part of this month hath been northerly and very cold; the warmest of which time we imployed our selves in fetching wood, working upon our pinnace, and other things that happened. In the beginning of this month the sea was all firmly frozen over, so that we could see no water any way. I hope it will not seem tedious to the readers, if I here deliver mine own opinion, how this abundance of ice comes to be ingendered.

The land that encircles this great bay, (which lies in a broken irregular form, making many little shoald bays and guts, being moreover full of islands and dry sands) is for the most part low and flat, and hath flat shoalds adjoining to it, half a mile or a mile, that are dry at low water. Now you must know that it flows half tide (as I have often experienced) that is, from whence the flood cometh, the water thither returneth, two hours before it be high-water or full sea. It seldom rains after the middle of *September*, but snows, and that snow will not melt on the land nor sands: At low water when it snows (which it doth very often) the sands are all covered over with it, which the half-tide carries officiously (twice in 24 hours) into the great bay, which is the common rendezvous of it. Every low water are the sands left clear, to gather more to the increase of it. Thus doth it daily gather together in this manner, till the latter end of *October*, and by that time hath it brought the sea to that coldness, that as it snows the snow will lie upon the water in flakes, without changing its colour, but with the wind is wrought together, and as the winter goes forward, it begins to freeze on the surface of it, two or three inches or more in one night; which being carried with the half-tide, meets with some obstacle, (as it soon doth) and then it crumples, and so runs upon itself, that in a few hours it will be five or six foot thick. The half-tide still flowing, carries it so fast away, that by *December* it is grown to an infinite multiplication of ice. And thus by this storing of it up, the cold gets the predomination in the sea, (which also furnisheth the springs and water in the low flat lands) that it cools it like itself. This may appear by our experience, though in all this I freely submit myself unto the better learned. Our men found it more mortifying cold to wade thorow the water in the beginning of *June*, when the sea was all full of ice, than in *December* when it was increasing. Our well, moreover, out of which we had water in *December*, we had none in *July*.

The ground at ten foot deep was frozen: The quantity of the ice, may very easily be made appear, by mathematical demonstration; and yet I am not of the opinion, that the bay doth freeze all over. For the 21st the wind blowing a storm at north, we could perceive the ice to rise something in the bay.

February 1632.

The cold was as extreme this month as at any time we had felt it this year; and many of our men complained of infirmities, some of sore mouths, all the teeth in their heads being loose, their gums swoln, with black rotten flesh, which must every day be cut away. The pain was so sore on them, that they could not eat their ordinary

dinary meat. Others complained of pain in their heads and their breasts, some of weakness in their backs, others of aches in their thighs and knees, and others of swellings in their legs. Thus were two thirds of the company under the chirurgeon's hand; and yet nevertheless they must work daily, and go abroad to fetch wood and timber, notwithstanding the most of them had no shoes to put on. Their shoes upon their coming to the fire, out of the snow, were burnt and scorcht upon their feet, and our store-shoes were all sunk in the ship. In this necessity they would make this shift, to bind clouts about their feet, and endeavoured by that poor help, the best they could to perform their duties. Our carpenter likewise is by this time faln sick to our great discomforts. I practised some observations by the rising and setting of the sun, calculating the time of his rising and setting, by very true running-glasses: As for our clock and watch, notwithstanding we still kept them by the fires-side, in a chest wrapt in clothes, yet were they so frozen, that they could not go. My observations by these glasses, I compared with the stars coming to the meridian. By this means we found the sun to rise 20 minutes before it should; and in the evening to remain above the horizon 20 minutes (or thereabouts) longer than it should do; and all this by reason of the refraction.

Since now I have spoken so much of the cold, I hope it will not be too coldly taken, if I in a few words make it some way to appear unto our readers.

We made three differences of the cold, all according to the places. In our house; in the woods; and in the open air, upon the ice, in our going to the ship.

For the last, it would be sometimes so extreme, that it was not indurable, no cloaths were proof against it, no motion could resist it. It would, moreover so freeze the hair on our eye-lids, that we could not see; and I verily believe that it would have stifled a man in a very few hours. We did daily find by experience, that the cold in the woods would freeze our faces, or any part of our flesh that was bare, but it was yet not so mortifying as the other. Our house on the out-side was covered two third parts with snow, and on the inside frozen and hang'd with ice-sickles. The cloathes on our beds would be covered with hoar-frost, which in this little habitacle, was not far from the fire. But let us come a little nearer to it. The cook's tubs, wherein he did water his meat, standing about a yard from the fire, and which he did all day ply with melted snow-water; yet in the night-season, whilst he slept but one watch, would they be firm frozen to the very bottom. And therefore was he fain to water his meat in a brass-kettle close adjoining to the fire; and I have many times both seen and felt by putting my hand into it, that side which was next the fire was very warm, and the other side an inch frozen: I leave the rest to our cook, who will almost speak miracles of the cold. The surgeon, who had hung his bottles of syrups and other liquid things, as conveniently as he could to preserve them, had them all frozen: Our vinegar, oil and sack, which we had in small cask in the house, was all firm frozen. It may farther in general be conceived, that in the beginning of *June* the sea was not broken up, and the ground was yet frozen; and thus much we found by experience in the burying of our men, in setting up the king's standard towards the latter end of *June*, and by our well our coming away in the beginning of *July*, at which time upon the land, for some other reasons, it was very weather.

March 1632.

The first of this month being St. *David*'s day, we kept holiday, and solemnized it in the manner of the antient *Britains*, praying for his highness's happiness *Charles* prince of *Wales*.

The 15th, one of our men thought he had seen a deer; whereupon he with two or three more desired that they might go to see if they could take it: I gave them leave; but in the evening they returned so disabled with cold, which did rise up in blisters under the soles of their feet, and upon their legs, to the bigness of walnuts, that they could not recover their former estate (which was not very well) in a fortnight after.

The 26th three more desired that they also might go out to try their fortunes, but they returned worse disabled, and even almost stifled with the cold.

This evening the *Moon* rose in a very long oval along the horizon.

By the last of this month, the carpenter had set up 17 ground timbers and 34 staddles, and (poor man) he proceedeth the best he can, though he be fain to be led unto his labour.

In brief, all this month hath been very cold. The wind about the N. W. the snow as deep as it hath been all this winter: but to answer an objection, that may be made; you were in a wood (may some men say unto us) and therefore you might

might make fire enough to keep you from the cold. It is true, we were in a wood, and under a south-bank too, or otherwise we had all starved. But I must tell you withal, how difficult it was to have wood in a wood: And first, I will make a muster of the tools we had. The carpenter in his chest had two axes indeed, but one of them was spoiled in cutting down wood to pile about our house before *Christmas.* When we came first a-land, we had but two whole hatchets, which in a few days broke two inches below the sockets. I called for three of the cooper's hatchets: The carpenter's axe and the cooper's best hatchet I caused to be lockt up; the other two hatchets to be new helv'd, and the blades of the two broken hatchets to be put into a cleft piece of wood, and then to be bound about with rope-yarn, as fast as might be, which must be repaired every day; and these were all the cutting-tools we had: Moreover, the 6th of *Feb.* the carpenter had out his best axe about something, and one of the company in his absence, by his undiscreet handling of it, brake that too, two inches below the socket; we must henceforth order these pieces of tools the best we could; wherefore I gave order that the carpenter should have one of the cooper's hatchets; they that lookt for timber in the woods the other; and they that cut down wood to burn, were to have the two pieces: And this was before *Christmas.*

The three that were appointed to look crooked timber, must stalk and wade (sometimes on all four) thorow the snow; and where they saw a tree likely to fit the mould, they must first heave away the snow, and then see if it would fit the mould, if not, they must seek farther; if it did fit the mould, then they must make a fire to it, to thaw it, otherwise it could not be cut; then cut it down and fit it to the length of the mould, and then with other help get it home, a mile thorow the snow.

Now for our firing. We could not burn green wood; it would so smoke, that it was not indurable; yea, the men had rather starve without in the cold, than sit by it. As for the dry wood, that also was bad enough in that kind, for it was full of turpentine, and would send forth such a thick smoke, that would make abundance of soot, which made us all look as if we had been free of the company of chimney-sweepers. Our clothes were quite burnt in pieces about us, and for the most part we were all without shoes: but to our fuellers again. They must first (as the former) go up and down in the snow, till they saw a standing dry tree; for that the snow covered any that were fallen. Then they must hack it down with their pieces of hatchets, and then others must carry it home thorow the snow. The boys with cutlasses must cut boughs for the carpenter; for every piece of timber that he did work, must first be thaw'd in the fire, and he must have a fire by him, or he could not work. And this was our continual labour throughout the forementioned cold, besides our tending of the sick and other necessary imployments.

April 1632.

The first of this month being *Easter-day*, we solemnized as religiously as God did give us grace. Both this day, and the two following holy-days were extreme cold: And now sitting all about the fire, we reasoned and considered together upon our estate. We had five men (whereof the carpenter was one) not able to do any thing. The boatswain and many more were very infirm; and of all the rest we had but five that could eat of their ordinary allowance. The time and season of the year came forwards apace, and the cold did very little mitigate. Our pinnace was in an indifferent forwardness, but the carpenter grew worse and worse. The ship (as we then thought) lay all full of solid ice, which was weight enough to open the seams of any new and sound vessel, especially of one that had lain so long upon the ground as she had done. In brief, after my disputations, and laying open of our miserable and hopeless estates, I resolved upon this course: That notwithstanding it was more labour, and tho' we declined weaker still and weaker; yet that with the first warm weather, we would begin to clear the ship, that so we might have the time before us, to think of some other course. This being ordered, we lookt to those tools we had, to dig the ice out of her; we had but two iron-bars ashore, the rest were sunk in the ship, and one of them was broken too: Well, we fell to fitting of those bars, and of four broken shovels that we had, with which we intended (as after we did) to dig the ice out of her, and to lay that ice on a heap, upon the larboard-bow, and to sink down that ice to the ground so fast, that it should be a barricado to us, when the ice brake up, which we feared would tear us all to pieces.

The 6th was the deepest snow we had all this year, which filled up all our paths and ways, by which we were used to go unto the wood; this snow was something moist-er er and greater than any we had all this year; for formerly it was as dry as dust, and as small as sand, and would drive like dust with the wind.

The weather continued with this extremity until the 15th; at which time our spring was harder frozen, than it had been all the year before. I had often observed the difference betwixt clear weather and misty refractious weather, in this manner. From a little hill which was near adjoining to our house, in the clearest weather, when the sun shone with all the purity of air that I could conceive, we could not see a little island which bare off us S. S. E. some four leagues off; but if the weather were misty (as aforesaid) then we should often see it from the lowest place. This little island I had seen the last year, when I was on *Danby* island.

The 13th, I took the height of it instrumentally, standing near the sea-side, which I found to be 34 minutes, the sun being 28 degrees high. This shows how great a refraction here is. Yet may this be noted by the way, that I have seen the land elevated, by reason of the refractious air, and nevertheless the sun hath risen perfect round.

The 16th was the most comfortable sunshine day that came this year; and I put some to clear off the snow from the upper decks of the ship, and to clear and dry the great-cabin, by making fire in it. Others I put to dig down thorow the ice, to come by our anchor, that was in shoal water, which the 17th in the afternoon we got up and carried aboard.

The 18th I put them to dig down thorow the ice, near the place where we thought our rudder might be. They digged down and came to water, but no hope of finding of it: We had many doubts that it might be sanded, or that the ice might have carried it away already the last year; or if we could not recover it by digging before the ice brake up and drove, there was little hope of it.

The 19th we continued our mineing work aboard the ship, and returned in the evening to supper ashore. This day the master and two others desired that they might lie aboard, which I condescended to; for indeed they had lain very discommodiously all the winter, and with sick bed-fellows, as I my self had done, every one in that kind taking their fortunes. By lying aboard they avoided the hearing of the miserable groanings, and lamenting of the sick men all night long, enduring (poor souls) intolerable torments.

By the 21st we had laboured so hard, that we came to see a cask, and could likewise perceive that there was some water in the hold. This we knew could not be thawed water, because it did still freeze night and day very hard aboard the ship, and on the land also.

By the 23d in the evening, we came to pierce the forementioned cask, and found it was full of very good beer, which did much rejoyce us all, especially the sickmen, notwithstanding that it did taste a little of bulge-water. By this we at that time thought that the holes we had cut to sink the ship were frozen, and that this water had stood in the ship all the winter.

The 24th we went betimes in the morning to work, but found that the water was risen above the ice, where we had left work, about two foot; for that the wind had blown very hard at north the night before. In the morning the wind came about south, and blew hard, and although we had little reason for it, we yet expected a lower veer of the water. I thereupon put them to work on the out-side of the ship, that we might come to the lower hole, which we had cut in the stern-shootes. With much labour by night, we digged down thorow the ice to it, and found it unfrozen, (as it had been all the winter) and to our great comforts, we found that on the inside, the water was ebb'd even with the hole; and that on the outside it was ebbed a foot lower. Hereupon I made a shot-board to be nail'd on it, and to be made as tight as might be, to try if the water came in any other way. As to the other two holes, we had digged on the inside, we found them frozen. Now I did this betimes, that if we found the ship foundered, we might resolve of some course to save or prolong our lives, by getting to the main before the ice were broken up; for as for our boat it was too little, and bulged; besides that, our carpenter was by this time past hope, and therefore little hope had we of our pinnace: But which was worst of all, we had not four men able to travel through the snow over the ice, and in this miserable estate were we at this present.

The 25th we satisfied our longing; for the wind now coming about northerly, the water rose by the ship's-side (where we had digged down) a foot and more above the hold, and yet did not rise within board. This did so incourage us, that we fell very lustily to digging, and to heave out the ice out of the ship. I put the cook and some others to thaw the pumps, who by continual pouring of hot water into them, by the 27th in the morning they had cleared one of them, which we assaying, found that it did deliver water very sufficiently. Thus we fell to pumping; and having cleared

cleared two foot water, we then left to have a second trial. Continuing our work thus in digging the ice, by the 28th we had cleared our other pump, which we also found to deliver water very well: We found likewise that the water did not rise any thing in hold.

The 29th it rained all day long a sure sign to us, that winter was broken up.

The 30th we were betimes aboard at work, which day and the 31st were very cold with snow and hail, which did pinch our sick men more than any time this year. This evening being *May* even, we returned late from our work to our house, and made a good fire, and chose ladies, and did ceremoniously wear their names in our caps, endeavouring to revive ourselves by any means. And because you hear us in this merry humour, I will make known to you what good cheer we kept at *Christmas* and *Easter*; and how we had dieted our selves all the winter.

At our coming forth of *England*, we were stored with all sort of sea provisions; as beef, pork, fish, *&c.* but now that we had little hope of refreshing, our cook did order it in this manner.

The beef which was to serve on *Sunday* night to supper, he did boil on *Saturday* night, in a kettle full of water, with a quart of oat-meal, about an hour. Then taking the beef out, he boiled the rest till it came to half the quantity; and this we called porridge, which with bread we did eat, as hot as we could; and after this we had our ordinary of fish. *Sunday* dinner we had pork and peas, and at night the former boiled beef made more porridge. In this manner our *Tuesday*'s beef was boiled on the *Monday* nights, and the *Thursday*'s upon the *Wednesday*. And thus all the week (except *Friday* night) we had some warm thing in our bellies every supper. And (surely) this did us a great deal of good. But soon after *Christmas* many of us fell sick, and had sore mouths, and could neither eat beef, pork, fish, nor porridge. Their diet was only this. They would pound bread or oatmeal in a mortar to meal; then fry it in a frying-pan with a little oil, and so eat it. Some would boil peas to a soft paste, and feed as well as they could upon that. For the most part of the winter, water was our drink. In the whole winter we took not above a dozen foxes; many of which would be dead in the traps two or three days oftentimes; and then when the blood was settled, they would be unwholesome. But if we took one alive, that had not been long in the trap, him we boiled, and made broth for the weakest sick men of him; the flesh of it being soft boiled, they did eat also.

Some white partridges we kill'd; but not worth the mentioning towards any refreshing.

We had three sorts of sick men: Those that could not move nor turn themselves in their beds, who must be tended like an infant. Others that were as it were crippled with scurvy-aches. And others, lastly, that were something better. Most of all had sore mouths. You may now ask me, how these infirm men could work? I will tell you: Our surgeon (who was diligent, and a sweet-condition'd man as ever I saw) would be up betimes in the mornings; and whilst he did pick their teeth, and cut away the dead flesh from their gums, they would bathe their own thighs, knees, and legs. The manner whereof was this: There were no trees, buds, nor herb, but we made trial of it; and this being first boiled in a kettle, and then put in a small tub and bason, they put it under them, and covered themselves with clothes upon it. This would so mollify the grieved parts, that although when they did rise out of their beds they would be so crippled, that they could scarce stand; yet after this done half an hour, they would be able to go (and must go) to wood through the snow, to the ship, and about their other business. By night they would be as bad again; and then they must be bathed, anointed, and their mouths again drest, before they went to bed. And with this diet, and in this manner, did we go through our miseries.

I ever doubted that we should be weakest in the spring; and therefore had I reserv'd a ton of *Alicant* wine unto this time. Of this, by putting seven parts of water to one of wine, we made some weak beverage; which (by reason that the wine, by being frozen, had lost his virtue) was little better than water. The sicker sort had a pint of *Alicant* a day, by itself; and of such poor *aqua vitæ* too, as we had, they had a little dram allowed them next their hearts every morning; and thus we made the best use of what we had, according to the seasons.

May, 1632.

The first of this month we went aboard betimes to heave out the ice.

The second it did snow and blow, and was so cold, that we were fain to keep house all day. This unexpected cold at this time of the year did so vex our sick men, that they grew worse and worse; we cannot now take them out of their beds, but they would swoon, and we had much ado to fetch life in them.

The third, those that were able went aboard betimes to heave out the ice. The snow

ſnow was now melted in many places upon the land, and ſtood in plaſhes; and now there came ſome cranes and geeſe to it.

The fourth, while the reſt wrought aboard, I and the ſurgeon went with a couple of pieces, to ſee if we could kill any of theſe fowl for our ſick men, but never did I ſee ſuch wild-fowl, they would not indure to ſee any thing move. Wherefore we returned within two hours, not being able to indure any longer ſtalking thro' the ſnow, and the wet plaſhes. I verily thought that my feet and legs would have fallen off, they did ſo torment me with aching.

The ſixth, *John Warden*, the maſter of my ſhip's chief mate, died; whom we buried in the evening (in the moſt chriſtian-like manner we could) upon the top of a bare hill of ſand, which we called *Brandon-Hill*.

The weather continued very cold; freezing ſo hard in a night, that it would bear a man.

By the ninth we were come to, and got up our five barrels of beef and pork, and had found four buts of beer, and one of cyder, which God had preſerved for us. It had lain under water all the winter; yet we could not perceive that it was any thing the worſe. God make us ever thankful for the comfort it gave us.

The tenth it did ſnow and blow ſo cold, that we could not ſtir out of the houſe; yet nevertheleſs by day the ſnow vaniſheth away apace on the land.

The eleventh we were aboard betimes, to heave out ice.

The twelfth at night we had cleared out all the ice out of the hold, and found likewiſe our ſtore-ſhoes, which had lain ſoak'd in the water all the winter; but we dried them by the fire, and fitted our ſelves with them. We ſtruck again our cables into the hold. There ſtow'd we a butt of wine alſo, which had been all the winter on the upper-deck, and continued as yet all firm frozen. We fitted the ſhip alſo, making her ready to ſink her again, when the ice brake up. We could hitherto find no defect in her, and therefore well hop'd that ſhe was ſtanch. The carpenter, nevertheleſs, did earneſtly argue to the contrary; alledging, that now ſhe lay on the ground, in her dock; and that the ice had fill'd her defects; and that the ice was the thing that kept out the water; but when ſhe ſhould come to labour in the ſea, then doubtleſs ſhe would open. And indeed we could now ſee quite through her ſeams betwixt wind and water. But that which did trouble us as ill as all this, was the loſs of her rudder; and that ſhe now lay in the very ſtrength of the tide, which, whenever the ice drove, might tear her to pieces. But we ſtill hoped the beſt.

The thirteenth, being the ſabbath-day, we ſolemniz'd, giving God thanks for thoſe hopes and comforts we daily had; the weather by day-time was pretty warm, but it did freeze by night; yet now we could ſee ſome bare patches of land.

The fourteenth we began a new ſort of work. The boatſwain and a convenient number ſought aſhore the reſt of our rigging, which was much ſpoiled by pecking of it out of the ice; and this they now fell to fitting, and to ſerving of it. I ſet the cooper to fit our cask, although (poor man) he was very infirm; my intent being to paſs ſome cables under the ſhip, and ſo to buoy her up with theſe caſks, if otherwiſe we could not get her off. Some others I ordered to go ſee if they could kill ſome wild-fowl for our ſick men, who grew worſe and worſe. And this is to be remember'd, that we had no ſhot but what we did make of the aprons of our guns, and ſome old pewter that I had; for the carpenter's ſheet-lead we durſt not uſe.

The fifteenth I manured a little patch of ground, that was bare of ſnow, and ſowed it with peaſon, hoping to have ſome of the herbs of them ſhortly to eat; for as yet we can find no green thing to comfort us.

The eighteenth our carpenter, *William Cole* died, a man generally bemoaned of us all, as much for his innate goodneſs, as for the preſent neceſſity we had of a man of his quality. He had endured a long ſickneſs with much patience, and made a godly end. In the evening we buried him by Mr. *Warden*, accompanied with as many as could go; for three more of our principal men lay then expecting a good hour. And now were we in the moſt miſerable eſtate that we were in all the voyage. Before his extreme weakneſs he had brought the pinnace to that paſs, that ſhe was ready to be boulted and trennel'd, and to be joined together to receive the plank; ſo that we were not ſo diſcouraged by his death, but that we did hope of our ſelves to finiſh her, if the ſhip proved unſerviceable.

This our pinnace was 27 foot by the keel, 10 foot by the beam, and 5 foot in hold. She had 17 ground timbers, 34 principal ſtaddles, and eight ſhort ſtaddles. He had contrived her with a round ſtern, to ſave labour; and indeed ſhe was a well proportioned veſſel. Her burthen was twelve or fourteen ton.

In the evening the maſter of our ſhip, after burial, returning aboard ſhip, and looking about her, diſcover'd ſome part of our gunner, under the gun-room ports. This man

man we had committed to the sea at a good distance from the ship, and in deep water, near six months before.

The nineteenth in the morning I sent men to dig him out. He was fast in the ice, his head downward, and his heel upward, for he had but one leg, and the plaister was yet at his wound. In the afternoon they had digged him clear out; after all which time he was as free from noisomness as when we first committed him to the sea. This alteration had the ice and water, and time only wrought on him, that his flesh would slip up and down upon his bones, like a glove on a man's hand. In the evening we buried him by the others. This day one *George Ugganes* (who could handle a tool best of us all) had indifferent well repaired our boat; and so we ended this mournful week. The snow was by this time prettily well wasted in the woods; and we having a high tree, on the highest place of the island, which we called our watch-tree, from the top of it we might see into the sea, but found no appearace of breaking up yet.

The twentieth, being *Whit-sunday*, we sadly solemnized, and had some taste of the wild-fowl, but not worth the writing.

The 21st was the warmest sun-shine day that came this year. I sent two a fowling; and my self taking the master, the surgeon, and one more, with our pieces and our dogs, we went into the woods to see what comfort we could find. We wandered from the house eight miles, and search'd with all diligence; but returned comfortless, not an herb nor leaf eatable, that we could find. Our fowlers had as bad success. In the woods we found the snow partly wasted away, so that it was passable. The ponds were almost unthaw'd; but the sea from any place we could see all firm frozen.

The snow doth not melt away here with the sun or rain, and so make any land-floods, as in *England*; but it is exhaled up by the sun, and suck'd full of holes, like honey-combs, so that the sand whereon it lies will not be at all wetted. The like observation we also had; that let it rain ever so much, you shall see no land-floods after it.

The 22d we went aboard the ship, and found that she had made so much water, that it was now risen above the ballast, which made us doubt again of her soundness. We fell to pumping, and pump'd her quite dry. And now by day sometimes we have such hot glooms, that we cannot endure in the sun, and yet in the night it would freeze very hard. This unnaturalness of the season did torment our men, that they now grew worse and worse daily.

The 23d our boatswain (a painful man) having been long sick, (which he had heartily resisted) was taken with such a painful ach in one of his thighs, that we verily thought he would have presently died. He kept his bed all day in great extremity; and it was a maxim amongst us, that if any one kept his bed two days, he could rise no more. This made every man to strive to keep up for life.

The 24th was very warm sun-shine, and the ice did consume by the shore's side, and crack'd all over the bay, with a fearful noise. About three in the afternoon, we could perceive the ice with the ebb to drive by the ship; whereupon I sent two with all speed unto the master to beat out the hole, and to sink the ship; as likewise to look for the rudder betwixt the ice. This he presently performed; and a happy fellow, one *David Hammon*, pecking betwixt the ice, struck upon it, and it came up with his lance; who crying that he had found it, the rest came and got it up on the ice, and so into the ship. In the mean space, with the little drift that the ice had, it began to rise and mount into high heaps against the shoal shores and rocks; and likewise against the heap of ice, which we had put for a barricado to our ship, but with little harm to us. Yet we were fain to cut away 20 fathom of cable, which was frozen in the ice. After an hour, the ice settled again, as not having any vent outwards. Oh! this was a joyful day to us all; and we gave God thanks for the hopes we had of it.

The 25th was a fine warm day, and with the ebb the ice did drive against the ship, and shake her shrewdly.

The 26th I took the surgeon with me, and went again to wander the woods; and went to that bay, where last year we had lost our man *John Barton*. But we could find no sign of him, nor of other relief.

By the 28th it was pretty clear betwixt the ship and the shore, and I hoped the ice would no more dangerously oppress us; wherefore I caused the lower hole to be firmly stopp'd, the water then remaining three foot above the ballast.

The 29th, being prince *Charles*'s birth-day, we kept holy-day, and display'd his majesty's colours both a-land and a-board, and named our habitation, *Charles-town*, by contraction *Charlton*; and the island, *Charlton-island*.

The 30th we launched our boat, and had intercourse sometimes betwixt the ship and the shore by boat, which was news to us.

The last of this month we found on the beach some vetches to appear out of the ground, which I made the men to pick up, and to boil for our sick men.

This

This day we made an end of fitting all our rigging and sails; and it being a very hot day, we did dry and new make our fish in the sun, and aired all our other provisions. There was not a man of us at present able to eat of our salt provisions, but myself and the master of my ship. It may be here remember'd, that all this winter we had not been troubled with any rheums, nor flegmatical diseases. All this month the wind hath been variable, but for the most part northerly.

June, 1632.

The four first days it did snow, hail, and blow very hard; and was so cold, that the ponds of water did freeze over; and the water in our cans did freeze in the very house; our clothes also that had been washed, and hung out to dry, did not thaw all day.

The fifth it continued blowing very hard in the broad-side of the ship, which did make her swag and wallow in the dock for all she was sunken, which did much shake her. The ice withal did drive against her, and gave her many fearful blows. I resolved to endeavour to hang the rudder; and when God sent us water (notwithstanding the abundance of ice that was yet about us) to have her farther off. In the afternoon we under-run our small cable to our anchor, which lay a-stern in deep water, and so with some difficulty gate up our anchor. This cable had lain slack under foot, and under the ice, all the winter, and we could never have a clear slatch from ice, to have it up before now; we found it not a jot the worse. I put some to make colrakes, that they might go into the water, and rake a hole in the sands to let down our rudder.

The sixth we went about to hang it. And our young lustiest men took turns to go into the water, and to rake away the sand; but they were not able to endure the cold of it half a quarter of an hour it was so mortifying; yea, use what comforts we could, it would make them swoon and die away. We brought it to the stern-post, but were then fain to give it over, being able to work at it no longer. Then we plugg'd up the upper holes within board, and fell to pumping the water again out of her.

The seventh we wrought something about our rudder, but were again forced to give over, and to put out our cables over-board, with messengers unto them; the anchors lying to that pass, that we might keep her right in her dock, when we should have brought her light.

By the eighth at night we had pump'd all the water out of her; and she at a high water would fleet in her dock, though she were still dock'd in the sands almost four foot. This made us to consider what was to be done. I resolved to heave out all the ballast, for that the bottom of her being so soak'd all the winter, I hoped was so heavy, that it would bear her. If we could not get her off that way, I then thought to cut her down to the lower deck, and take out her masts; and so with our cask to buoy her off.

The ninth betimes in the morning we fell to work. We hoisted out our beer and cyder, and made a raft of it, fastening it to our shore-anchor. The beer and cyder sunk presently to the grouud, which was nothing strange to us; for that any wood or pipe-staves that had lain under the ice all the winter, would also sink down, so soon as ever it was heav'd over-board. This day we heav'd out ten tun of ballast. And here I am to remember God's goodness towards us in sending those forementioned green vetches; for now our feeble sick men, that could not for their lives stir these two or three months, can indure the air and walk about the house; our other sick men gather strength also, and it is wonderful to see how soon they were recovered. We used them in this manner: Twice a day we went to gather the herb or leaf of these vetches, as they first appeared out of the ground; then did we wash and boil them, and so with oil and vinegar that had been frozen, we did eat them. It was an excellent sustenance and refreshing; the most part of us eat nothing else. We would likewise bruise them, and take the juice of them, and mix that with our drink. We would eat them raw also with our bread.

The eleventh was very warm weather, and we did hang our rudder. The tides did now very much deceive us; for a northerly wind would very little raise the water. This made us doubt of getting off our ship.

The thirteenth I resolved of the latitude of this place; so that having examined the instruments, and practised about it this fortnight, I now found it to be in 52 deg. and 3 min.

The fourteenth we had heaved out all the ballast, and carried all our yards, and every thing else of weight ashore, so that we now had the ship as light as possible it could be.

The fifteenth we did little but exercise ourselves; seeing that by this time our men that were most feeble, are now grown strong, and can run about. The flesh of their gums became settled again, and their teeth fasten'd; so that they can eat beef with their vetches.

This day I went to our watch-tree; but the sea (for any thing I could perceive to the contrary) was still firm frozen; and the bay we were in, all full of ice, having no way to vent it.

The sixteenth was wondrous hot, with some thunder and lightning, so that our men did go into the ponds ashore to swim and cool themselves; yet was the water very cold still. Here had lately appeared divers sorts of flies; as butter-flies, butchers-flies, horse-flies, and such an infinite abundance of blood-thirsty muscatoes, that we were more tormented with them than ever we were with the cold weather. These (I think) lie dead in the old rotten wood all the winter, and in the summer they revive again. Here be likewise infinite company of ants, and frogs in the ponds upon the land; but we durst not eat of them, they look'd so speckled like toads. By this time were neither bears, foxes, nor fowl to be seen; they are all gone.

The seventeenth the wind came northerly, and we expecting a high tide in the morning betimes, put out our small cable astern out at the gun-room-port; but the morning tide we had not water by a foot. In the evening I had laid marks, by stones, *&c.* and methoughts the water did flow apace. Making signs therefore for the boat to come ashore, I took all that were able to do any thing with me aboard; and at high-water (altho' she wanted something to rise clear out of her dock) yet we heav'd with such a good-will, that we heav'd her thro' the sand into a foot and a half deeper water. Further then so, we durst not yet bring her, for that the ice was all thick about us. After we had moor'd her, we went all to prayers; and gave God thanks that had given us our ship again.

The eighteenth we were up betimes; the cooper, and some with him, to fill fresh water; myself with some others to gather stones at low water; which we piling up in a heap, at high water the cockswain and his gang fetch'd them aboard; where the master with the rest stowed them. The ship at low water had a great lust to the offing; by which means we could the better come and stop the two upper holes firmly; after which we fitted other convenient places, to make others to sink here, if occasion were.

The nineteenth we were all up betimes to work, as afore specified. These two days our ship did not fleet, and it was a happy hour when we got her off, for that we never had such a high tide all the time we were here. In the evening I went up to our watch-tree; and this was the first time I could see any open water any way, except that little by the shore-side, where we were. This put us in some comfort, that the sea would shortly break up, which we knew must be to the northward, seeing that way we were certain, there was above two hundred leagues of sea.

The twentieth we laboured as aforesaid. The wind at N. N. W. The tide rose so high, that our ship fleeted, and we drew her further off, into a foot and a half deep water. Thus we did it by little and little, for that the ice was still wonderful thick about us.

The 22d there drove much ice about us, and within us; and brought home our stern anchor. At high water (notwithstanding all the ice) we heav'd our ship farther off; that so she might lie a-float at low water.

The next low water we sounded all about the ship, and found it very foul ground; we discovered stones three foot high above the ground, and two of them within a ship's breadth of the ship, whereby did more manifestly appear God's mercies to us; for if when we forced her ashore, she had strucken one blow against those stones, it had bulged her. Many such dangers were there in this bay, which we now first perceived, by the ice's grounding and rising against them. In the evening we tow'd off the ship unto the place where she rid the last year, and there moor'd her, sheering the ship night and day, flood and ebb, amongst the dispers'd ice that came athwart of us.

The 23d we laboured in fetching our provisions aboard; which to do we were fain to wade to carry it to the boat a full flight shot, and all by reason the wind was southerly. This morning, I took an observation of the moon's coming to the south, by a meridian-line of one hundred and twenty yards long, which I had rectified many weeks before-hand.

The 24th I took another observation of the moon's coming to the meridian; for which I refer you to the observations in the latter end of this journal.

Whereas I had formerly cut down a very high tree, and made a cross of it, to it I now fastened (uppermost) the king's and queen's majesties pictures drawn to the life, and doubly wrapt in lead, and so close, that no weather could hurt them. Betwixt both these I affixed his majesty's royal titles; *viz.* Charles *the first, king of* England, Scotland, France, *and* Ireland; *as also of* Newfoundland, *and of these territories; and to the westward as far as* Nova Albion; *and to the northward, to the latitude of* 80 *degrees*, &c.

On the out-side of the lead, I fasten'd a shilling and a six-pence of his majesty's coin; under that we fasten'd the king's arms fairly cut in lead, and under that the arms of the city of *Bristol*. And this being *Mid-summer-Day*, *summer-day*, we raised it on the top of the bare hill, where we had buried our dead fellows; formally by this ceremony taking possession of these territories to his majesty's use.

The wind continuing southerly, and blowing hard, put all the ice upon us; so that the ship now rid amongst it, in such apparent danger, that I thought verily we should have lost her. We labour'd, flood and ebb, both with poles and oars, to heave away and part the ice from her. But it was God that did protect and preserve us; for it was past any man's understanding, how the ship could endure it, or we by our labour save her. In the night the wind shifted to the westward, and blew the ice from us, whereby we had some rest.

The 25th in the morning, the boatswain, with a convenient crew with him, began to rig the ship, the rest fetching our provisions aboard. About ten a-clock, when it was something dark, I took a lance in my hand, and one with me with a musket and some fire, and went to our *watch-tree*, to make a fire on the eminentest place of the island, to see if it would be answer'd. Such fires I had formerly made, to have knowledge if there were any savages on the main or the islands about us. Had there been any, my purpose was to have gone to them, to get some intelligence of some christians, or some ocean sea thereabouts. When I was come to the tree, I laid down my lance, and so did my consort his musket; and whilst my self climbed up to the top of the tree, I ordered him to put fire unto some low tree thereabouts. He (unadvisedly) put fire to some trees that were to windward; so that they (and all the rest too, by reason it had been very hot weather) being sear and dry, took fire like flax or hemp; and the wind blowing the fire towards me, I made haste down the tree. But before I was half way down, the fire took in the bottom of it, and blazed so fiercely upwards, that I was fain to leap off the tree, and down a steep hill, and in brief, with much ado, escap'd burning. The moss on the ground was as dry as flax; and it would run most strangely, and like a train along the earth. The musket and the lance were both burnt. My consort at last came to me, and was joyful to see me; for he thought verily I had been burned. And thus we went homeward together, leaving the fire increasing, and still burning most furiously. We could see no answer of it. I slept but little all night after; and at break of day I made all our powder and beef to be carried aboard. This day I went to the hills to look to the fire; where I saw how it did still burn most furiously, both to the westward and northward: leaving one upon the hills to watch it, I came home immediately, and made them take down our new suit of sails, and carry them to the seaside. ready to be cast in, if occasion were, and to make haste to take down our houses. About noon the wind shifted northerly; and our centinel came running home, bringing us word, that the fire did follow him hard at his heels, like a train of powder. It was no need to bid us take down and carry all away to the sea-side. The fire came towards us with a most terrible rattling noise, bearing a full mile in breadth; and by that time we had uncovered our houses, and laid hand on, to carry away our last things, the fire was come to our town, and seized on it, and (in a trice) burnt it down to the ground. We lost nothing of any value in it; for we had brought it all away into a place of security. Our dogs in this combustion would sit down on their tails, and howl, and then run into the sea, on the shoals, and there stay. The wind *shifted easterly*; and the fire ranged to the westward, seeking what it might devour. This night we lay all together aboard the ship, and gave God thanks that he had shipt us in her again.

The 27th, 28th, and 29th, we wrought hard in fetching our things aboard, as likewise our water, which we must tow off with the ebb, and bring it to the ship with the flood. Moreover, we must go about the easter-point for drift-wood; for our tools were all so spent, that we could cut none. Wherefore, about some three days agone I had caused our pinnace to be sawed to pieces, and with that we stowed our cask, intending to burn it at low waters, and such other times as we could not work in carrying things aboard. I employed the men in fetching stones; and we did build three tombs over our three dead fellows, filling them up with sand in a decent and handsome fashion. The least tomb had two tons of stones about it.

The 30th we most earnestly continued our labour, and brought our sails to yard; and by eleven a-clock at night had made a priddy ship; meaning to have finished our business with the week and the month, that so we might the better solemnize the sabbath ashore to morrow, and so take leave of our wintering island.

The wind hath been variable a great while, and the bays are now so clear of ice, that we cannot see a piece of it, for it was all gone to the northward. Hoping therefore that it give content to some readers, I will relate the manner of the breaking of it up. It is first to be noted, that it doth not freeze (naturally) above six foot, the rest is by accident. Such is that

that ice that you may see here, six fathom thick. This we had manifest proof of, by digging the ice out of the ship, and by digging to our anchors before the ice broke up.

In *May*, when the heat increaseth, it thaws first on the shoal by the shore side; which when it hath done round about, then the courses of the tides (as well by the ebb and flood, as by their rising and falling) do so shake the main ice, that it cracks and breaks it. Thus, when it hath gotten room for motion, then runs one piece of it upon another; and so bruises and grinds it self against the shoals and rocks, that it becomes abbreviated, insomuch that a ship may have well passage through it. Besides this, much of it is thrust upon the shoals, where it is much consumed by the heat of the sun. The season here in this climate is most unnatural; for in the day-time it will be extreme hot, yea, not indurable in the sun, which is, by reason that it is a sandy countrey. In the night again it will freeze an inch thick in the ponds, and in the tub about and in our house; and all this towards the latter end of *June*.

The muscatoes, upon our coming away, were most intolerable. We tore an old ancient in pieces, and made us bags of it to put our heads in; but it was no fortification against them. They would find ways and means to sting us, that our faces were swoln hard out in pimples, which would so itch and smart, that we must needs rub and tear them. And these flies, indeed, were more tormenting to us than all the cold we had heretofore endured.

July, 1632.

The first of this month, being *Sunday*, we were up betimes. And I caused our ship to be adorned the best we could; our antient on the poop, and the king's colours in the main-top. I had provided a short brief of all the passages of our voyage to this day: I likewise wrote in what state we were at present, and how I did intend to prosecute the discovery, both to the westward, and to the southward, about this island. This brief discourse I had concluded, with a request to any noble minded traveller, that should take it down, or come to the notice of it; that if we should perish in the action, then to make our endeavours known to our sovereign lord the king. And thus with our arms, drum and colours, cook and kettle, we went ashore, and first we marched up to our eminent cross, adjoining to which we had buried our dead fellows. There we read morning prayer, and then walked up and down till dinner-time. After dinner we walked to the highest hills, to see which way the fire had wasted. We descried that it had consumed to the westward sixteen miles at least, and the whole breadth of the island. Near about our cross and dead it could not come, by reason it was a bare sandy hill. After evening prayer I happened to walk along the beach-side; where I found an herb resembling scurvy-grass. I made some to be gathered, which we boiled with our meat to supper. It was most excellent good, and far better than our vetches. After supper we went all to seek and gather more of it; which we did to the quantity of two bushels, which did afterwards much refresh us. And now the sun was set, and the boat come ashore for us; whereupon we assembled our selves together, and went up to take the last view of our dead, and to look unto their tombs, and other things. Here leaning upon mine arm, on one of their tombs, I uttered these lines, which though perchance they may procure laughter in the wiser sort (which I shall be glad of) they yet moved my young and tender-hearted companions at that time with some compassion. And these they were:

I were unkind, unless that I did shed,
Before I part, some tears upon our dead;
And when my eyes be dry, I will not cease
In heart to pray, their bones may rest in peace:
Their better parts (good souls) I know were given,
With an intent they should return to heaven.
Their lives they spent, to the last drop of blood,
Seeking God's glory, and their countrey's good;
And as a valiant soldier, rather dies,
Than yields his courage to his enemies;
And stops their way, with his hew'd flesh, when death
Hath quite depriv'd him of his strength and breath:
So have they spent themselves, and here they lie
A famous mark of our discovery.
We that survive, perchance may end our days
In some employment meriting no praise:
And in a dunghil rot; when no man names
The memory of us, but to our shames,
They have out-liv'd this fear, and their brave ends,
Will ever be an honour to their friends.
Why drop you so, mine eyes? Nay rather pour
My sad departure in a solemn shower.

The winter's cold, that lately froze our blood,
Now were it so extreme, might do this good,
As make these tears, bright pearls: which I would lay,
Tomb'd safely with you, till doom's fatal day.
That in this solitary place, where none
Will ever come to breathe a sigh or groan,
Some remnant might be extant, of the true
And faithful love I ever tender'd you.
Oh, rest in peace, dear friends, and let it be
No pride to say the sometime part of me.
What pain and anguish doth afflict the head,
The heart and stomach, when the limbs are dead;
So griev'd, I kiss your graves; and vow to die
A foster-father to your memory.

FAREWEL.

So fastening my brief to the cross, which was securely wrapt up in lead, we presently took boat and departed, and never put foot more on that island.

This island and all the rest (as likewise the main) is a light white sand, covered over with a white moss, and full of shrubs and low bushes; excepting some bare hills, and other patches. In these bare places the sand will drive with the wind like dust. It is very full of trees, as spruce and juniper; but the biggest tree I saw was but a foot and a half over. At our first coming hither, we saw some deer, and kill'd one, but never any since. Foxes all the winter we saw many, and kill'd some dozen of them; but they went all away in *May.* Bears we saw but few, but kill'd none. We saw some other little beasts. In *May* there came some fowl, as ducks and geese; of which we kill'd very few. White partridges we saw, but in small quantities; nor had we any shot to shoot at them. Fish we could never see any in the sea; nor no bones of fish on the shore side, excepting a few cockle-shels, and yet nothing in them neither. Other things remarkable I have before mentioned.

OUR

OUR DISCOVERY AND Coming Home.

July 1632.

MONDAY being the 2d of *July*, we were up betimes, about ſtowing and fitting our ſhip and weighing of our anchors, which when the laſt was a-trip, we went to prayer, beſeeching God to continue his mercies to us, and rendering him thanks for having thus reſtored us. Our ſhip we found no defect in; we had abundance of ſuch proviſions as we brought out of *England*, and we were in indifferent health, and did gather ſtrength daily. This being done, we weighed and came chearfully to ſail: The wind at N.W. bad to get away; wherefore we ſtood over to *Danby* iſland, to take in more wood, and there to be ready to take the opportunity of a fair wind. I went aſhore my ſelf with the boat; for that ſome of the company had told me, that they had ſeen ſtakes the laſt year droven into the ground. When we came aſhore, whilſt ſome gather'd wood, I went to the place, where I found two ſtakes droven into the ground about a foot and a half, and firebrands, where a fire had been made by them. I pull'd up the ſtakes, which were about the bigneſs of my arm; and they had been cut ſharp at the ends with a hatchet, or ſome other good iron tool, and driven in as it were with the head of it. They were diſtant about a ſtone's throw from the water-ſide. I could not conceive to what purpoſe they ſhould be there ſet, unleſs it were for ſome mark for boats. This did augment my deſire to ſpeak with the ſalvages; for without doubt they could have given notice of ſome chriſtians, with whom they had ſome commerce. About four in the evening I returned aboard with a boat's lading of wood, and the wind ſomething favouring we weighed, with our lead ſeeking out a channel amongſt theſe perilous ſhoalds. In the evening the wind oppoſing it ſelf, we came to anchor betwixt *Charleton* iſland, and that iſland we named the laſt year, (in memory of that honourable gentleman, Mr. *Thomas Carie*, one of the bed-chamber to the king) *Carie*'s iſland, where we rid all night.

The 3d at break of day, we weighed with a bare wind, and ſounding up and down for a channel, we were many times in five and four fathom water. The wind larging upon us, we ſtood away weſt: By noon we ſaw all ice to the northward of us; endeavouring therefore to compaſs about the weſtern point of *Charleton* iſland, and ſo to ſeek to the ſouthward, we found it all ſhoalds, rocks and breaches. By four in the afternoon we ſaw the weſtern land, but all full of ice; whereupon as the wind favoured us, we ſtood along it in ſight to the northward.

The 4th was calm, but ſo very thick fog with all, that we could not ſee a piſtol-ſhot about us: Wherefore we came to an anchor, and there rid all this day and the next night.

The 5th at three in the morning we weighed; but ice being all about us, we knew not which way to turn us: Now to avoid telling the ſame thing twenty times, we were continually, 'till the 22d, ſo peſtered and tormented with ice, that it would ſeem incredible to relate it: ſome-we were ſo blinded with fog, that we could not ſee about us; and being now become wilful in our endeavours, we ſhould ſo ſtrike againſt the ice, that the fore-part of the ſhip would crack again, and make our cook and others to run up all amazed, and think the ſhip had been beaten all to pieces. Indeed we did hourly ſtrike ſuch unavoidable blows, that we did leave the hatches open, and twenty times in a day the men would run down into the hold, to ſee if ſhe were bulged.

Sometimes when we had made her faſt in the night, to a great piece of ice, we ſhould have ſuch violent ſtorms, that our faſtning would break, and then the ſtorm would beat us from piece to piece moſt fearfully; otherwhile we ſhould be faſt incloſed among great ice as high as our poop. This was made (as I have formerly ſaid) by one piece running upon another, which made it draw eight or ten fathom water.

 Beſt

Besides which, the lowermost would rise from underneath, and strike us under the bulge, with pieces of five, six, yea of eight tun; that many times we have pump'd clear water for an hour together; before we could make the pump suck. Amongst these several and hourly dangers, I overheard the men murmur and say, that they were happy that I had buried; and that if they had a thousand pounds they would give it, so they lay fairly by them; for we (say they) are destined to starve upon a piece of ice. I was fain to indure all this with patience, and to comfort them up again, when I had them in a better humour.

The 22d having been vext with a storm all last night, and this morning with a thick fog, we drove in thirteen fathom water. About noon it cleared, and we saw land, and at the instant had a good observation, whereby we knew it to be cape *Henrietta Maria*. I made the master stand in with it, and in the mean time we fitted a cross, and fastened the king's arms and the arms of the city of *Bristol* to it; we came to an anchor within a mile of the shore, in six fathom water; so we hoisted out the boat, and took our arms and our dogs, and went ashore. Upon the most eminent place we erected the cross, and then seeking about, we soon saw some deer, and by and by more and more: We stole to them with the best skill we had, and then put our dogs on them, but the deer ran clear away from them at their pleasure. We tired the dogs and wearied ourselves, but to no purpose, neither could we come to shoot at them. I saw in all about a dozen (old and young) very goodly beasts. We took half a dozen young geese on the pools, by wading in to them; and so returned to our boat vext, that now we had found a place where there was refreshing, and we could get none of it: Whereas therefore we had kept our dogs with a great deal of inconvenience aboard the ship all the winter, and had pardoned them many misdemeanors, (for they would steal our meat out of the steeping tubs) in hope they might hereafter do us some service; and seeing they now did not, and that there was no hope they could hereafter, I caused them to be left ashore. They were a dog and a bitch; buck-dogs of a very good race. The dog had a collar about his neck, which it may be hereafter may come to light. I did see no sign at all of any salvages, nor could we find any herbs or other refreshing here.

In the evening, (being returned aboard) and the wind blowing fair at south, I caused the master to weigh and come to sail, and to lose no time, for we did hope for an open sea to the N. W. This cape hath a very shoald point that lies off it, which we endeavoured to compass about.

Sailing therefore amongst shattered ice, we came to very shoald water, (four and five fathom deep) and could not avoid it. At length standing N. the water deepened, but we came amongst great pieces of ice; which by reason of some open water, there went a pretty sea. These hard pieces of ice made a most fearful noise. It proved a fair moon-shine night, otherwise it had gone ill with us. We turned amongst this ice, staying the ship sometimes within her length of great pieces, as bad as rocks; but by reason we were often forced to bear up, we did sag upon the main rand of ice, and that we thought would be worse for us, we let fall an anchor, and stood all on the decks to watch the ice's sheering of the ship (to and again) to avoid it. Thus having poles and oars to fend it, we could not keep our selves so clear, but many pieces came foul of us. We brake two of our great poles with it, which were made to be handled by four men, besides some other damages. At break of day we weighed, and sought all ways to clear ourselves of ice, but it was impossible. I conceive it impertinent to relate every particular days passages, which was much alike to us. Our endeavours were sometimes with our sails, giving and receiving 500 fearful blows in a day. Sometimes we would stop at an anchor, when we could get a little open water, and so suffer the ice to drive to leeward; other whiles we should be enclosed amongst it, and then it would so break and rise, and leap up under us, that we expected to be beaten every hour to pieces.

Moreover, we should have such storms in the dark nights, that would break the mooring we had made fast to some piece of ice for security in the night season; and then we should beat most dangerously from piece to piece till day-light, that we could see to make her fast again. I forbear to speak of thick fogs which we had daily, which did freeze our rigging day and night; besides all which, we should come into most uncertain depths, sometimes twenty fathom, next cast ten, next fifteen, then nine, rocky foul ground. The great deep ice withal, driving on these uncertain depths, did so distract the tides, and deceive us so much in our accounts, that by the 30th we were driven back so far to the eastward, and to the southward of the cape, that at five a clock in the evening it bare N. W. of us some three leagues off, contrary to our expectations. With all these mischiefs our ship is now become very leaky, that we must pump every half watch. Here I called a consultation; and after consideration of all our experience, we were all of the same opinion, that it was impossible to get to the northward, or to the eastward, by reason of the ice; wherefore I resolved upon this course; when the wind blew south, it would blow the ice off the south shore, then we would seek to get to the westward, betwixt it and the shore. I must confess, that this was a desperate resolution, for all the coast we knew to be shoald and foul ground, all rocks and stones; so that if the wind should shift to the northward, there would be (without God's mercies) little hope of us. But here we must not stay; the nights grew long, the cold so increased, that betwixt the pieces of ice, the sea would be frozen. I caused the ship to be fitted, and places convenient again prepared to sink her the second time, if so be we were put to extremities. We presently put our project in execution (the wind being at south) and got about the shoals of the cape, standing then into the shoreward, to get betwixt it and the ice, we came into four fathom water (very foul rocky ground) thinking to come to an anchor all night, and let the ice drive to leeward. But still there was so much ice betwixt us and the shore, that we were fain to bear up amongst it into deeper water, and to let the ship drive amongst it. The wind increasing, we endured a most dangerous dark night of it. In the morning we fell to work to get the ship again out of the ice into some clear water, which we saw W. by S. of us. Some of our company went out upon the ice, to heave her with their shoulders, whilst others stood aboard with poles; the rest stood to spill and fill the sail. By nine in the morning we had gotten into some clear water, and stood west and by south, and into four fathom water foul grouud. But being not able to weather some rands of ice which did drive, we were fain to stand off again, and (when the evening grew dark) to come to an anchor.

About midnight there came a great piece of ice (which we could not avoid) athwart of our cable, and made the ship drive and drag her anchor. This drove her into shoald water, it being very rocky and foul ground. We brought the cable to capstan, and heav'd with such a courage, that we heaved home our anchor from under it. Thus we did endeavour (the best we could) to keep our selves in eight and ten fathom water. It then pleased God that the wind blew along the shore, otherwise it had gone far worse with us.

August 1632.

The first of this month at break of day, when we could see a little about us, we fell to struggle and strive again with the ice, and to get in nearer to the shore. There by reason the wind was opposite to come to an anchor, we let the ice drive to leeward, hoping that there was a clear sea to the westward. The ice drove very thick upon us, and one piece came foul of us, which did touch our spritsail-yard, and made the ship drive, but we soon clear'd ourselves of it. Then we weigh'd and stood in nearer to the shore, but the water shoalded, and there were so many great rands of ice betwixt us and the shore, that there was no coming to an anchor: So we turned betwixt the ice, many pieces of it being a-ground in shoald water, and few pieces distant one from the other a cables length. This day we saw two sea-morses on the ice.

The 2d in the morning we were glad of the break of day, having most dangerously turned amongst the ice all night, and endured many a heavy blow. We stood in again to the shoreward, to see if we could get some clear water; for to the northward it was all impassable ice. We stood into five and four fathom, but still all incompast with ice; so we stood off again into deeper water, and in the evening we were inclosed amongst extraordinary great pieces; it was a very thick fog withal, so that we made fast the ship to a great flat piece, and went to sleep and refresh ourselves after our extreme pains-taking.

The 3d, 4th and 5th we were inclosed amongst very great ice, and it blew such a storm of wind, that we sometimes endeavouring to get forward to the westward, did strike such heavy blows, that made all the forepart of the ship crack again: Then we would give over working, and let her alone amongst it; but then the ice would break and rise under us, that would endanger us as bad as the former. Our ship doth make above a ton of water every watch, which we must pump out, beside our other labour. God think on us, and be merciful to us amongst all these dangers.

The 5th at noon we were in latitude 55. 30. the cape bearing off us S. E. by E. some twelve leagues off; and this is all we have gotten since the 22d of *July*. All night it blew a violent gale of wind at W. N. W. and about midnight our hawser (which we had made fast to a piece of ice) broke, and we lost fourteen fathom of it. We beat all night most fearfully, being tost from piece to piece, because that in the dark we durst not venture our men to go forth on the ice for fear of losing them.

All the 6th the storm indured and drove us again with the ice, almost to the cape.

 The

The 7th was the moſt comfortable day we had ſince we came out of our wintering-place; the wind came up fair at eaſt, and we got (although with our former inconveniencies and dangers) nearer to the ſhore, and into ſome open water, making good way to the weſtward. Moreover, our leak now ſtopt of its own accord, ſo that now we pumpt but little. We ſailed all night, keeping good watch on the forecaſtle, bearing up for one, and looffing for another.

Thus did we the 8th alſo, but then the wind ſhifting to the N. W. it drove the ice on the ſhore, and we came to an anchor in eight fathom water. The main ice we had ſome two mile to windward of us, but the ſet of the tide kept it off from us. At noon we were in latitude *55. 34.* In the evening a rang of ice drove upon us, which made us weigh and ſtand in nearer the ſhore, into ſix fathom, and there to come to an anchor. The wind increaſing about midnight, the ſhip did drive, and was quickly in five fathom water; wherefore we let fall our ſhoot-anchor, and both held her. But that that troubled us was, that we expected every minute, when the main ice would come upon us, and then there would be no hope but to be put aſhore.

The 9th in the morning we weighed our ſecond anchor, the ice being within leſs than a mile of us. About eight in the morning a point of it came foul of us, which we prevented by weighing, and came to an anchor in three fathom and a half water. The wind continued N. N. W. which was in on the ſhore. This morning I cauſed all our empty caſk to be filled with water, and the ſhip to be left unpumpt, and the places lookt to that we had prepared to ſink her; for we were at preſent in as apparent danger as any time this voyage, and (to our great griefs) it was all foul rocky ground: The danger of this was, if we made faſt to a piece of ice that drew deep water, then as ſoon as it came to ground on theſe rocks, it would break all to pieces, and betray us to our deſtruction. About noon there came foul of us the point of a range of ice, which we reſolved to endure the extremity of with an anchor, thinking to ride and break through it, we now perceiving ſome open water beyond it; thruſting therefore and fending with our poles, at laſt a great piece came thwart our hawſer, and there went a pretty ſea amongſt it. The ſhip did now fall upon it ſo violently, that I expected every blow ſhe would beat out her bows. At length ſhe did drive with it, ſo that I thought the cable had been broken. We brought it to capſtan to heave it in, but found that our ſhoot-anchor was broken in the middle of the ſhank. We preſently ſet our ſails thereupon, endeavouring that way to edge in amongſt the ice off of this perilous ſhore. It pleaſed God to favour our labour ſo, that by eight in the evening we got off into ſeven fathom; and a dark night coming on, we made faſt to the biggeſt piece we could find. It blew fairly all night, but about midnight the wind came up at north, which was more on the ſhore than before.

By break of day on the 10th we were driven into four fathom, very foul ground, ſo that the lead did fall off the rocks three or four foot; we ſet our ſails, and uſed our uttermoſt endeavours to edge off. Some of us went upon the ice to hale her; others ſtood with poles to thruſt by night. At night we had gotten off into eight fathom, and made faſt to the biggeſt piece we could find. If any man ſhould aſk why we now kept ſo near to the ſhore, in this continual danger? I anſwer, Becauſe that in the offing the ice was ſo extraordinary thick, that we could make no way, any way through it. Moreover, when we were in that great thick ice, and that the wind came up fair at S. or S. E. or E. we could not get out of it. Wherefore we choſe to run this adventure, and ſo prevent and overcome all dangers with God's aſſiſtance and our extreme labour.

The 11th in the morning was a thick fog, yet there ſprung up a gale of wind at eaſt, and we made in for the ſhore.

From the 11th till the 14th the wind continued fair, and we made all the ſail we could (night and day) as the ice would ſuffer us. We had the ſhore in ſight by day on one ſide, and the ice within two miles on the other, and we ſail'd amongſt diſperſt pieces, luffing for one, and bearing up for another.

The 14th at noon we were in latitude *57. 55.* In the evening we were imbayed in ice, and ſtood S. W. to clear ourſelves of it, but could not. But ſeeing from topmaſt-head clear water over it, we put into it; but there roſe a very thick fog, and night came on withal, that we were fain to faſten to a piece of ice, expecting day and better weather.

The 15th in the morning (although the fog was very thick) we endeavoured to get out of the ice, and ſtood away weſt; but within two hours the water ſhoalded from forty fathom to twenty five, whereby we knew that we had the ſhoalding of the weſtern ſhore. Then we ſhaped our courſe to the northward, the fog continued ſo thick, that we could not ſee a piſtol-ſhot about us. We had not ſtood this way two hours, but we heard the rut of the

the ice a-head of us, which made the most hideous noise of any we had heard this voyage. We halled our tacks aboard, and stood to the westward in this day, hearing of it sometimes, and sometimes seeing of it, which was very large, deep and high ice above the water. We weathered it all, except some few pieces, and got into open water. About sunset there came a sudden gust N. N. W. and before we could handle our sails, it was with us, and put us to some tronble. It dallied with us by gusts till nine a clock, and then it fell into a most violent storm. We considered where we might have the clearest drift, and so took in all and let her drive her head to the shoreward. Before midnight the water shoalded on us to fifteen fathom. Then we turned her head to the eastward, and set our main-course low set, but as much as she could indure. The water deepen'd but little, and we knew that we were on those rocky shoalds which we struck on the last year; God be merciful to us. Here was the first great breaking sea that we had this year.

The 16th in the morning we were driven to a great rand of ice; to avoid which we set our fore course to, and stood to the shoreward in 13 fathom water, and then about again: We stood in a mile into the ice; but there went such a great swelling sea in it, that it was indurable, so we stood out again. About three a clock in the afternoon the storm broke up, and blew fair at N. W. which proved good for us, for we had not drift for four hours; besides, it was but two leagues betwixt the shoalds and the ice. We set all our sails and endeavoured to weather the ice, but in the evening we were still pester'd with it. By midnight we knew not which way to turn, nor what to do; so we took in all our sails, and let her drive amongst it. The ice beat us on every side, for there went amongst it a very great full sea.

The 17th in the morning, when we could see about us, we were in the midst of the ice; but with the last storm it was all broken into mammocks, as big as a boat of three or four tons, which did give us many a heavy blow in the dark night. If this storm had taken us amongst it, it had beaten us all to pieces, without God's miraculous preservation. We made sail and endeavoured to clear ourselves of it to the northward, which by eight in the morning we had done.

We then went to prayer, and gave God thanks that had delivered us out of it. For we were hourly, for the space of six weeks, as it were in the jaws of death; yea, never any (that I have heard of) have been so long in such long nights upon a foul shoald shore, tormented with ice, as we have now been. At noon we were in latitude 58. 20.

Now as touching the dissolution or ruin of the ice, we found that this storm had torn and shattered this rand of ice, which was on the outside, although it must have a long time to work into the main body of it. I have in *July*, and in the beginning of *August*, taken some of the ice into the ship, and cut it square two foot, and put it into the boat, where the sun did shine on it with a very strong reflex about it: And notwithstanding the warmth of the ship (for we kept a good fire) and all our breathings and motions, it would not melt in eight or ten days.

It was our practice, when we should be two days together fast to a piece of ice, to set marks on it, to see how it did consume, but it yielded us small hope of dissolving. We could not in that time perceive any diminution by the sinking of it or otherwise. Nevertheless, I think that it is ruined with storms, or consumed with heat some years, or else the bay would be filled choke-full; but I confess that these secrets of nature are past my apprehension.

Being out of it, (but no otherways than that we yet saw it from off the decks, all to the eastward) I ordered the master to steer away north and by east, keeping the shoalding of the western shore.

The 18th at noon we were in latitude 59. 30.

The 19th we continued our course betwixt N. N. E. and the N. by E. and at noon were in latitude 61. 7. some 12 leagues off the shore. I ordered the master to shape his course north east, to look to that place betwixt *Carie*'s *Swans-nest* and *Ne ultra*.

The 20th we were in latitude 61. 45. This day we saw some few seols about the ship.

The 21st the water shoalded so that we made account we did approach the land; but about noon the wind came up at N. E. our direct opposite. We looft as near it as we could, and as it larg'd we came to stand E. and E. and by N.

The 22d we fell with the land to the westward of *Carie's Swan's-Nest*, where we had forty fathom three leagues off. We stood in within a league of the shore, into thirteen fathom; and seeing the land to the southward of us, we compast about it, it being *Carie*'s *Swan's-Nest*, which is in latitude 52. 00.

All the 23d we sailed N. E. and for the most part in sight of land.

The

The 24th at noon, (by judgment) we were in latitude 63. 30. having sail'd a N. E. course. All this day was a very thick fog, which about one a clock clear'd a little, so that I expected to see the land. Some of our men being better sighted, spied it out about some two leagues off from us. I knew it could be no other than *Nottingham* island, though it were something contrary to the expectation of our best mariners. We stood into it to make it. It was the north end of it, and it bare off us due east; I was soon assured of it, and I ordered the master to shape his course N. W. and by N. Both he and others were unwilling, but without much ado submitted themselves, (how loth soever) for that it was so very foul thick weather. The reasons of my resolution were these; the time of the year was far spent, and the discommodities of winter came upon us, and therefore would I make the shortest way, betwixt the lands already discovered. If I found an open sea, I had my desire, and did then intend to proceed to the utmost of our power; if we met with the land, I should then finish the discovery, it being not passing fifteen leagues from land to land, and not passing ten leagues from *Nottingham* island to the main of the north shore. We made what sail we could, it blowing a very stiff gale of wind until eight in the evening; then it began to blow fiercely, and we took in our top-sails, and stood under our two courses and bonnets. At nine it blew a violent storm at S. S. E. so that we took in our foresail, and let her drive N. W. All the night it continued an extraordinary storm; so that we heaved the lead every half watch; but the ship did drive so fast, that she would be past the lead before there was twenty fathom of line out, all the night being exceeding cold withal.

The 25th the storm continued in his utmost malice, and did so perplex us, that there were but few that did sleep or eat a bit these 24 hours. About six a clock in the afternoon the storm began to slacken, yet blew there a fierce gale of wind betwixt the S. and S. W. We stood W. N. W. and made a N. W. way, when suddenly the sea became very smooth. We reasoned thereupon amongst ourselves, what might be the cause of it. We all thought it to be the leeward tide, nothing doubting what afterwards we encountered. The ship had very quick way in this smooth water.

The 26th by two a clock in the morning, we were suddenly come in amongst the ice; and it pleased God that the moon at the instant gave us so much light, that we could see a little about us. We would have staid the ship, but it was so thick to windward, and so near us, that we durst not. We then bore up in this unexpected accident; and (I verily believe) did not escape striking the length of a foot against the ice as hard as rocks, two or three times; the ship now having way, after twelve leagues a watch. Then we stood close by a wind to the eastward, expecting day, that we might see about us: We could from topmast-head see the ice to N. N. W. the N. W. and so round about by the S. to the E. and some there was to leeward of us. It was all flat sound ice, in main rands, and the sea as smooth as a well amongst it. This struck us all into a dump, whereupon I called a consultation of my associates; namely, *Arthur Price* master, *William Clemens* lieutenant, *John Whittered* master's mate, *Nathaniel Bilson* chirurgeon, and *John Palmer* boatswain, requiring them to advise and counsel me, how to prosecute our business to effect. These all went together, and reasoned amongst themselves, and then brought me their opinions in writing under their hands, *viz.* Our advice is, That you repair homeward from this present 26th, and that for these reasons:

First, For that the nights are long and so extreme cold withal, that we can hardly handle our sails and riggings. Secondly, The times are now subject to stormy and gusty weather, as witnesseth the present season, it having continued a storm ever since the 24th, and doth yet continue no weather to discover in. Thirdly, we doubt whether *Hudson's Streights* be so clear of ice, that it may be passable in convenient time, (winter coming now on apace) before we be frozen up, seeing the ice lies here all over the seas in rands and ranges. Fourthly, We must have a set of fair weather to pass the straight, which we may stay a long time for, if we neglect the first opportunity. Fifthly, For that our ship is very leaky, so that in foul weather we are fain to pump every glass, which is great labour. Moreover we know her to be so sorely bruised with rocks and blows of the ice, that she is no more to be adventured amongst it, but in saving of our lives homewards. Besides all this, our men grow very weak and sickly, with extreme labour. Sixthly, the season of the year is so far spent, that we can expect no other weather than we have had, both lately and at present; that is to say, snow and fog freezing our rigging, and making every thing so slippery, that a man can scarce stand; and all this with the wind southerly, which if it should come to the northward,

ward, then we are to expect far worse. Seventhly and lastly, that the ice lies all in thick rands and ranges, in the very way we should go, as you and all men here may see. And therefore we conclude as aforesaid, that there is no possibility of proceeding farther; wherefore we here counsel you to return homeward, hoping that God will give us a favourable passage, and return us home safe into our native countries, if we take time, and not tempt him too far by our wilfulness.

Indeed most of these reasons were in view, and I could not tell what to say to oppose them; nor any reason could I give, how we might proceed farther; wherefore (with a sorrowful heart, God knows) I consented that the helm should be born up, and a course shap'd for *England*, well hoping that his majesty would graciously censure of my endeavours, and pardon my return. And although we have not discovered populous kingdoms, and taken special notice of their magnificence, power and policies, brought samples home of their riches and commodities, pried into the mysteries of their trades and traffick, nor made any great fight against the enemies of God and our nation; yet I wish our willingness in these desart parts may be acceptable to our readers. When we bore up helm, we were in latitude 65. 30. at least N. W. and by N. from *Nottingham* island. Some were of an opinion, that we were farther to the northward; but by reason it was by judgment, I chose to set down the lesser distance.

The 27th the wind came up at N. W. with which wind we could not have gone on in our design: That wind made no great swelling sea. By noon we were athwart of cape *Charles*, so that we went in betwixt that cape and *Mill* Islands. The last night it did snow very much, and was very cold, so that all our rigging and sails were frozen, and all the land covered over with snow. And here (sithence I have formerly spoken that it snows very much) it will not be amiss to consider of the reasons of it. When I was upon *Charleton* island, (our wintering place) and in *June*, when the snow was clearliest gone off the ground, I have in the nights, (and some of them following the hottest days) observed, whether there fell any dew or no; but I could never perceive any, and (under correction of the learned) from moss and sand, little (methoughts) was to be expected. Now of what was exhal'd from the snowy ice, and cold sea; what could there probably be returned but the like again? Generally we continued on our course, blinded with foggy and dirty weather; and that, intermixt with snow and frost, amongst disperst pieces of ice, many of them higher than our topmast-head.

With great variety of winds, we were also driven within three leagues of both shores; so that the last of this month, we were in the narrow of the straight, which is about fifteen leagues over; the south shore was much pestred with ice.

September 1632.

The 1st and 2d we continued our endeavour to get on our way.

The 3d in the evening, as the weather cleared up, we did see the south end of the *Island of Resolution*.

These three days and nights had been extreme cold with fog and frost, insomuch that our men in the evening could hardly take in our topsails and spreetsail. We have sailed thorow much mountainous ice, far higher than our topmast-head; but this day we sailed by the highest that I ever yet saw, which was incredible indeed to be related. Now as the wind comes easterly we feel another sea out of the ocean, and the ship labours with another motion, than she hath done with any that ever we observed to come out of the westward.

From the 3d to the 8th we had variety of winds, and were gotten clear out of the streights, but were now come into such a tumbling sea, (the weather dirty and gusty, and by interims calm again) that the ship did so labour and rowl, that we thought verily she would have rowled her masts by the board. This made her so leaky, that we were fain to pump every glass; yea, her seams did so open aloft, we lay all wet in her.

This was the last day that we saw any ice. The wind now favouring us, we made all the haste we could homeward. By the way, (having endeavoured, observed and experimented some things in my unfortunate voyage) I perfected up my said observations, which being after commanded to publish, I here most submissively offer unto the judicious readers, and raine our private opinion withal, concerning the feiseableness of the action intended, which was to find a *Passage into the South-Sea*.

What hath been long ago fabled by some *Portuguese*, that should have come this way out of the *South-Sea*, the meer shadows of whose mistaken relations have come to us, I leave to be confuted by their own vanity. These hopes have stirred up from time to time, the more active spirits of this our kingdom, to research that merely imaginary passage. For my own part, I give no credit to them at all; and as little to the vicious and abusive wits of later

later *Portuguese* and *Spaniards*, who never ſpeak of any difficulties, as ſhoald water, ice, nor ſight of land, but as if they had been brought home in a dream or engine. And indeed their diſcourſes are found abſurd, and the *Plots* (by which ſome of them have practiſed to deceive the world) meer falſities, making ſea where there is known to be main-land, and land where is nothing but ſea.

Moſt certain it is, that by the only induſtry of our own nation, thoſe northern parts of *America* have been diſcovered to the latitude of 80 degrees and upwards. And it hath been ſo curiouſly done, (the labours of ſeveral men being joined together) that the main land hath been both ſeen and ſearcht, and they have brought this ſuppoſed paſſage to this paſs, that it muſt be to the north of 66 degrees of latitude. A cold clime peſtered with ice and other diſcommodities, and where the *Spaniards* diſpoſitions and their weak ſpeeke ſhips can hardly long endure it. And withal it is thus known, that the entrance of *Hudſon's Streights* is but fifteen leagues broad, in the middle not ſo much; and betwixt *Saliſbury* iſland and the main, that it is but eight leagues. Then proceeding to the northwards, towards the forementioned latitude, it is but fifteen leagues from main to main. This in length is but about 140 leagues, as may more plainly appear by the map. Moſt infinitely peſtered withal it is with the ice until *Auguſt*, and ſome years not paſſable then; yea I believe the ſtreight is never clear of ice thorowly.

Now moſt probable it is, that there is no paſſage, and that for theſe reaſons following.

Firſt, that there is a conſtant tide flood and ebb ſetting into *Hudſon's Streights*, the flood ſtill coming from the eaſtward, which as it proceeds (correſpondent to the diſtance) it alters his time of full ſea. This alſo entering into bays, and broken ground, it becomes diſtracted, and reverſes with half tides.

Secondly, here is no ſmall fiſh, as cod, *&c.* and very few great ones, which are rarely to be ſeen; nor are there any bones of whales, ſea-horſes, or other great fiſh to be found on the ſhore, nor any drift-wood.

Thirdly, That we found the ice in the latitude of 65. 30. to be lying all over the ſea in rands; and I am moſt certain that the ſhoalds and ſhoald-bays are the mother of it. Had there now been any ocean beyond it, it would have been broke all to pieces; for ſo we found it coming thorow the ſtreight into the ſea to the eaſtward.

Fourthly, the ice ſeeks his way to the eaſtward, and ſo drives out at *Hudſon's Streights*, which I have often obſerved, being a land upon the iſland of *Reſolution*, and driving amongſt the ice in the ſtreight.

Now admit there were a paſſage, yet is it known, that it is partly narrow, for 140 leagues, and to be infinitely peſtered with ice withal, as every one have found, who have gone that way. Comparing therefore ſome obſervations taken at *Bantam*, *Gulolo*, and at *Firando* in *Japan*, and the diſtance betwixt *Japan* and the weſtern part of *Califurnia*, with the obſervations taken at *Charleton* iſland, (referring all to the meridian of *London*) and then the diſtance betwixt the meridians of cape *Charles* and the weſtern part of *Califurnia*, will be found to be about 500 leagues in the latitude of 66. 00. where yet the meridians incline very much together.

To this may be added, that near about cape *Charles*, the variation is 29 degrees to the weſt, which is a probable argument, that there is much land to the weſtward; and that this ſtreight muſt be very long, and that you have no time to paſs it but in *Auguſt* and *September*, when the nights are ſo long, and the weather ſo cold, that it will not be indurable.

Add to this, that neither can any great ſhips, which are fit for carrying of merchandize, indure the ice, and other diſcommodities, without extraordinary danger.

Moreover, a thouſand leagues is ſooner ſailed to the ſouthward, and about the cape *de Bona Speranza*, (where the winds are conſtant) and that with ſafety, than a hundred in theſe ſeas, where you muſt daily run the hazard of loſing ſhip and lives: Put hereunto that comfort for the ſick, or refreſhing for your men, here is none to be had in theſe quarters.

Towards the latter end of *Auguſt* and in *September*, the weather grows tempeſtuous, and the winds incline to be weſterly, that there will be but ſmall hope of performing your voyage this way.

But let us (by way of imagination only) inlarge this ſtreight, in this latitude, and free it of ice; yet what advantage, in ſpeedy performance, will be gotten by this paſſage, if the winds be withal conſidered? To *Japan*, *China*, and the northern parts of *Aſia*, it may be the nearer cut; but in navigation, the fartheſt way about is well known, in fewer days to be performed, yea with leſſer pains, and more ſafety of ſhip and goods.

Again: To the *East-Indies* and other parts, where we have the greatest commerce and employment of shipping, the other way is as near. What benefit of trade might have been obtained in those northern parts of *Asia*, I will not presume to speak of; holding that there is a great difference betwixt those parts and the northern parts of *America*; whereas I am sure that there is none in any place where I have been all this voyage.

The 22d of *October* we arrived in the road of *Bristol*, having been hindered and crost with much contrary tempestuous winds and weather. The ship being brought into harbour, and hal'd dry a ground to look to her, it was there found, that all her cut-water and stern were torn and beaten away, together with fourteen foot of her keel; much of her sheathing cut away, her bows broken and bruised, and many timbers crackt within board; and under the starboard bulge a sharp rock had cut thorow the sheathing, the plank, and an inch and a half into a timber that it met withal. Many other defects there were besides, so that it was miraculous how this vessel could bring us home again. Being all here arrived, we went all to church and gave God thanks for his preservation of us amidst so many dangers. I very well know that what I have here hastily written, will never discourage any noble spirit, that is minded to bring this so long tried action to absolute effect; and it is likely withal, that there be some, who have a better understanding, and a surer way of prosecuting of it, than myself have: To whose designs I wish a happy success. And if they do but make a review of what hath been done, and give more certain celestial observations, hydrographical descriptions, or exacter practice in navigation, it will be a most commendable labour. For although I have spent some years of my ripest age, in procuring vain intelligence from foreign nations, and have travelled unto divers honourable and learned personages of this kingdom, for their instructions; have bought up whatever I could in print or manuscript, and what plot or paper soever conducing to this business, that possibly I could procure; and have served voluntarily besides, and spent some time in rendering a relation, (since my coming home) and expended withal of my own monies, in my aforesaid endeavours, and in furnishing of extraordinary necessaries above 200 *l.* in ready money; yet I repent not myself, but take a great deal of comfort and joy, in that I am able to give an account (in some reasonable way) of those parts of the world, which heretofore I was not so well satisfied in.

THE

THE
COPY of the LETTER
Which I left at
CHARLETON,
Fastened to the Cross, *July* 1, 1632.

BE it known to any that shall haply arrive here, on this island of *Charleton*, that whereas our sovereign lord, *Charles* I. king of *England*, *Scotland*, *France*, and *Ireland*, Defender of the Faith, *&c.* having a desire to be certified, whether there were any passage or not, by the north-west or north-westward, thorough these territories into the south sea: Some of the better minded merchants, of the worshipful company of merchant-adventurers of the city of *Bristol*, to satisfy his majesty therein, did voluntarily offer to set forth a convenient ship for that purpose, well mann'd, victualled, and furnished with all other necessaries. This free offer of theirs was not only commended, but graciously accepted of by his majesty. Whereupon, they fitted and furnished forth a ship, called the *Henrietta Maria*, of the burthen of 70 tuns, victualled for 18 months. A number thought convenient to manage such a business was 22 men, whereof 19 were choice able men, two younkers, and my unworthy self their commander. All which, the *Bristol* merchants did most judiciously and bountifully accommodate, and had in a readiness, the first of *May*, 1631.

The 3d of *May* we began our voyage out of the road of *Bristol*, commonly called *King's Road*, passing about the cape *Cleere* of *Ireland*, upon many courses, but reduced to a west north-west, we sailed along, and upon the 4th of *June*, we made the land of *Greenland* to the northward of cape *Farewell*, where for the space of two days, we were dangerously ingaged amongst the ice. Being clear of it, we doubled cape *Farewell* to the southward, and so continued our course to the westward, continually sailing and thrusting the ship thorough much ice.

The 19th of *June* we made the island of *Resolution*, and endeavouring to compass about it to the southward, we were taken with a strong westerly wind, which drove the ice and it us, upon the shore. In that distress, (seeing it was broken grounds and main inlets into it) I sent the shallop to seek and sound a place for our refuge; but when she was departed, she was in as great danger as we, and could not return to us by reason of the ice. We being now driven very near the rocks, were fain to set our sails, and force the ship into an opening, adventuring her amongst unknown dangers to avoid apparent, before we could moor her in a place (as we thought) safe from danger.

The 22d of *June*, (this inlet being full of ice) that ice upon the ebb, so jamb'd one piece into another, that it altered the ordinary course of it, and it came upon the ship, and put her against the rocks, notwithstanding our utmost resistance. As the water ebb'd away, the ship hung by the keel upon a rock, and heel'd to the offing. As soon as we perceiv'd this, we made fast some hawsers to her masts, and to the rocks, to hold her upright; but all in vain; she sunk still, as the water ebb'd away; so that she was so turned over, that we could not stand in her. Hereupon, we got all upon a piece of ice, looking upon her, and praying God to be merciful to us. The rock that she hung upon, was a little abaft the mainmast, which made her hang after the head, and she sunk over so much, that the portlass of the forecastle was in the water. At length, it pleased God the flood came, before it had ebb'd so low as the tide before and after, by a foot; and the ship rose, and was safe and sound: And thus were we miraculously delivered. With the

the first wind, we proceeded to the westward, continually being pestred with so much ice, that it was about the middle of *July* before we could attain to Sir *Dudley Digg*'s island. And here I was put to my consideration; for whereas by my directions, I was to search especially two places; one from *Digg*'s island to the northward, and failing there, to go to the *Checks* and *Hubbart*'s hope, and so to search it to the southward; I now finding the sea much pestered with ice in the latitude of 64. 00. and as far as we could see to the northward; and that the time was so far spent, as that before I could do any thing that way, it would be *August*, and then as much trouble to return again to *Digg*'s island; and that by that time, the year would be so far spent, the nights so long and cold, that I fear'd I should be forced with shame to return into *England* again that year. Wherefore I took my way to the westward, by *Mansfield*'s island; on which I landed twice, still hindred and incumbred with ice. Thence I proceeded westward, hoping for an open sea in the bay. We were there more troubled with ice, than in any place before; so that it was the 11th of *August*, before we had sight of the western land, which we made in latitude 59. 30. something to the southward of the *Checks*. We were not able to attain thither, by reason of the contrary winds and ice, but were observant of the current of the tides; which after, by experience, we found to come from the northward. We coasted along the shore, in sight of land, and in ten fathom water to the southward; and entred that inlet, which heretofore was called *Hubbart*'s hope; which was the very place where the passage should be, as it was thought by the understandingest and learnedest intelligencer of this business in *England*. We sailed to the very bottom of it, into three fathom water, and found it to be a bay of some eighteen or nineteen leagues deep. From thence we proceeded to the southward, in sight of land for the most part; and although I was as careful to keep the lead always going (it blowing a fresh gale of wind, and a pretty big sea) our depth eight, nine, and ten fathom; yet before the lead was up, the ship struck upon a flat rock; (she then being under foresail, foretopsail, maintopsail, and spritsail) and gave three sore knocks, and got over it. Being past this danger, we proceeded, and pass'd by port *Nelson*. Finding the land trend to the eastward, we began our discovery of it more carefully; because that no man (that ever I could hear or read of) did ever see this land before. We stood into six and five fathom; for it is very low land, and trends for the most part E. S. E. and E. by S.

The 27th of *August* I entred upon it, and in the name of the merchants-adventurers of *Bristol*, took possession of it to his majesty's use, naming it, *The New South-West Principality of Wales*. I brought from the land some small trees and herbs, and killed divers sorts of fowl, in sign of seizure, which I brought aboard. Not long after, (being put back to the westward with contrary winds) we spake with captain *Fox*, in a ship of his majesty's, set forth for the same purpose that we were: I invited him aboard, and entertained him with such fare as we had taken in this new discovered land; and made him a relation of all our endeavours: The like did he to us, and withal told us, that he had been in port *Nelson*, where he had put up a shallop, and found there many things which Sir *Thomas Button* had left there. The next day he departed from us, and stood to the westward, and we never saw him since. His ship, he, and all his company were very well. We continued our discovery to the eastward, and came to the eastern-point, which is in latitude 55. 06. which we named cape *Henrietta Maria*. There the land trends to the southward, and we followed it in sight, but were put off with foul weather; which being over-blown, we stood in again for the western shore, (that we might leave no part unseen) and followed it again to latitude 54. 40. The second time we also put off, with like foul weather, which made us stand to the eastward. In this way we past by some islands, and happened amongst broken grounds and rocks, in latitude 53. 30. where we came to an anchor, and sheltred ourselves some few days, shifting roads. Now the winter began to come on, and the nights to be long and cold; that amongst these dangerous places, we were fain to spend the day to look for security for the night. Here, by misfortune, our ship came aground; and that amongst great stones, as big as a man's head, where she did beat for the space of five hours most fearfully. In this time, we lightned her, and carried some of our things ashore; so that by the great favour of God, we got her off again; whereupon we named this island, *The island of God's Favour*. After that again, amongst those rocks, we were put to many extremities. At length, (having a gentle southerly wind) we stood along the eastern shore to the northward, now looking for a convenient place to winter in. And here again, were we assaulted with a violent storm, in which we lost our shallop, and were driven amongst divers dangers; and

and ſeeing an opening betwixt two iſlands, we ventured to go in, in very foul weather. We found it to be a very good ſound, and there we came to an anchor. We landed on one of them, which we named, *The Lord Weſton's Iſland*; and mann'd out our old ſhip boat upon it. The other iſland, we named my *Lord of Briſtol's Iſland*. Parting from hence, we ſtood to the ſouthward, to look for a wintering place, becauſe the time of diſcovery was paſt for this year. Many were our troubles amongſt theſe iſlands, ſhoals and broken grounds, which made us ſtrain our ground tackle for life many a time.

The 6th of *October* we arrived in this bay, it ſeeming a very likely place to find a harbour in; but ſearching the likelieſt places, we found it all ſo ſhoaled flats and rocks, and ſtony by the ſhoreſide, that we could by no means bring our ſhip near the ſhore, but were forced to ride a league off, in three fathom and a half water.

The winter came on apace, the weather proved tempeſtuous, and the cold ſo multiplied, that our ſails froze in lumps to the yards unmanuable. Neither could our only boat go from the ſhip, by reaſon of the weather. About the middle of *October*, I cauſed a houſe to be made aſhore, where our ſick men might the better recover; but always with an intent to take it down, if we found otherwhere a place for our ſhip. I ſent likewiſe men afoot, (ſeeing the boat could not go) to diſcover the iſland, and to ſee if they could find ſome creek or cove, but all in vain; we ſpent the time with hope of fairer weather, till now the cables began to freeze in the houſe, and the ſhip to be frozen over with the ſprew of the ſea; ſo that we were fain to ſhovel the ſnow off our decks. Moreover, the water began ſo to congeal by the ſhore ſide, that the boat could hardly get aſhore. Yet for all that, if the wind blew N. W. there went a very great ſurf on the ſhore, and ſuch a great ſea in the bay, that there was no bringing of our ſhip aground. Beſides this, ſhe would have then lain open to the E. and S. E. and S. and indeed the neareſt land, all about that way, was two leagues off. Hereupon, we continued out the extremity at an anchor.

The 29th of *November*, the ice came about us on all ſides, and put us from our ground tackle, and would have driven us out of the bay upon rocks and ſhoals, (where undoubtedly we had periſhed) but that by God's great goodneſs, it proved ſo warm a day, (the wind at S.) that ſuddenly we brought up ſome ſail, and hoiſt it up with ropes, and ſo forced her aſhore; where ſhe beat all that night very ſorely. The ſhip being now grounded and quiet, we conſidered what was beſt to do with her, and reſolved to ſink her; but the next tide, before we had any of our proviſions aſhore, the wind came N. W. ſo that the ſhip beat moſt fearfully. We got all our dry proviſions up to the upper deck, and made a hole to ſink her; but before ſhe was ſunk, ſhe beat ſo extraordinarily, that we all thought ſhe had been foundered. Being ſunk down ſo low, that the water came on the upper deck, we took our boat and went all aſhore, in ſuch pitiful cold weather, that we were all ſo white frozen, that ſome ſick men that were aſhore before, did not know us one from another.

The next day we fell to land our proviſions: Firſt our bread, fiſh, and dry things, the men driven to wade in the water up to the middles, moſt lamentable to behold. Within two days, what with great flat pieces that ſtuck about us, and that which froze, it was become firm ice, betwixt the ſhip and the ſhore; ſo that then we were fain to carry all things on our backs a mile from the ſhip to the houſe. Within few days, the hold became ſo frozen, that we could not get all our things out of it, but were fain there to leave it frozen till the next year. Then we made us two other houſes: Our firſt houſe was our manſion houſe, wherein we did all lie together; our other was to dreſs our victuals; and the third for a ſtore-houſe; which we built a pretty diſtance off, for fear of fire. And now we conſidered of the eſtate we were in, we all doubted that the ſhip was foundered, eſpecially our carpenter. But ſuppoſe ſhe were ſound, yet was it a queſtion, whether we could get her off in the ſummer, when the tides are low. Moreover, ſhe might be ſpoiled, lying in the tides way, when the ice brake up; and then we ſhould be deſtitute of any veſſel to bring us home. The carpenter undertook to build a pinnace, of the burthen of twelve or fourteen tun, that ſhould be ready by the ſpring; that if we found the ſhip unſerviceable, we might tear her up, and plank her with the ſhips plank. Upon this we reſolved, and by *May* brought it to that paſs, that ſhe was ready to be joined together to receive the plank. But God mercifully provided otherwiſe for us: We indured a bitter cold winter, in which it pleaſed God to viſit us with ſickneſs; ſo that in the beginning of *May* 1632, there was but myſelf, and the maſter and ſurgeon, perfectly ſound, and he began to find ſome defect alſo. About the beginning of *April*, we began to dig the ice out of our ſhip, which by the middle of *May*, we had effected.

The

The 24th of *May* the ice began to break up betwixt the ſhip and the ſhore; and about the middle of *June* we had off our ſhip, and found her to be ſtanch and ſound, contrary to all our expectations. Before this time, about the middle of *May*, our carpenter died; and with him the hope of our pinnace: Maſter *Wardon* died the 6th of *May*; our gunner, *Richard Edwards*, had his leg broken (which was cut off) at the capſtang in *Auguſt* 1631, and languiſhed till the 22d of *November*, on which day he died. Theſe three men lie buried here under theſe tombs of ſtones. We loſt another man, one *John Barton* our quarter-maſter, who miſcarried in the little bay that is due weſt from this croſs three miles; the ice breaking under him, ſo that he ſunk down, and we never ſaw him more. The two pictures which are wrapt in lead, and faſtened uppermoſt on this croſs, are the lively pictures of our ſovereign lord and lady, *Charles* I. and queen *Mary* his wife, king and queen of *England*, *Scotland*, *France* and *Ireland*, &c. The next under that is his majeſty's royal arms; the lowermoſt is the arms of the city of *Briſtol*.

And now we are in a readineſs to depart this day, and I intend to proſecute our diſcovery to the weſtward, in this latitude of 52. 03. and to the ſouthward alſo, although with little hope. Failing there, I mean to haſte to *Digg*'s iſland, and endeavour to diſcover to the northward. Thus having had ſome experience of the dangers of the ice, ſhoals, and rocks of unknown places, I thought it neceſſary to leave this teſtimony of us and our endeavours, if God ſhould take us into his heavenly kingdom, and fruſtrate our return into our native countrey. Wherefore I deſire any noble minded traveller, that ſhall take this down, or come to the knowledge of it, that he will make relation of it to our ſovereign Lord the king's majeſty, and to certify his grace, that we cannot as yet find any hope of a paſſage this way; and that I do faithfully perſevere in my ſervice; accounting it but my duty to ſpend my life to give his majeſty contentment, whom I beſeech God to bleſs with all happineſs. And that they would likewiſe advertiſe our worſhipful adventurers of all our fortunes; and that if as aforeſaid, we periſh, it was not by any want or defect in ſhip or victual, or other neceſſaries; all which we have in abundance for four months and above; which if occaſion be, we can prolong to ſix months. Thus being at preſent unable to expreſs a grateful mind otherwiſe but in my prayers to God, I heartily beſeech him to pour out his bountiful bleſſing upon all their honeſt endeavours, and to continue their noble diſpoſitions in actions of this kind. And I faithfully promiſe, that if I ſhall come where the like letters and tokens ſhall be left, to make a true relation of it, as it ſhall be deſired. So deſiring the happineſs of all mankind, in our general Saviour *Chriſt Jeſus*, I end,

Charleton, July 2. 1632. *Thomas James.*

The NAMES *of the several* INSTRUMENTS, *I provided and bought for this Voyage.*

A *Quadrant* of old seasoned pear-tree wood, artificially made; and with all care possible divided with *diagonals*, even to minutes. It was of four foot (at least) *semidiameter*.

An *equilateral triangle* of like wood, whose *radius* was five foot at least, and divided out of *Petiscus*'s table of *tangents*.

A *quadrant* of two foot *semidiameter* of like wood; and with like care projected.

The *sights*, *centers*, and every other part of them look'd to, and tried with convenient *compasses*, to see if they had been wrong'd or alter'd. And this continually, before they were made use of.

Staves *for taking* altitudes *and* distances *in the heavens.*

A *staff* of seven foot long, whose *transome* was four foot, divided into equal parts by way of *diagonals*, that all the *figures* in a *radius* of ten thousand, might be taken out, actually.

Another of six foot, near as convenient, and in that manner to be used.

Mr. *Gunter*'s *cross-staff*.

Three *Jacob's staves*, projected after a new manner, and truly divided out of the table of *tangents*.

Two of Mr. *Davis*'s *back-staves*, with like care made and divided.

Of Horizontal Instruments.

Two *semicircles*, two foot *semidiameter*, of seasoned pear-tree wood, and divided with *diagonals*, to all possible exactness.

Six *meridian compasses*, ingeniously made; besides some dozens of others, more common.

Four *needles* in square boxes, of six inches *diameter*, and other six of three inches *diameter*.

Moreover, four special *needles* (which my good friends Mr. *Allen* and Mr. *Marre* gave me) of six inches *diameter*, and touch'd curiously, with the best *load-stone* in *England*.

A *load-stone* to refresh any of these, if occasion were, whose *poles* were marked for fear of mistaking.

A *watch-clock* of six inches *diameter*, and another lesser *watch*.

A *table* every day *calculated*, correspondent to the *latitude*, according to Mr. *Gunter*'s directions in his book, the better to keep our *time* and our *compass*, to judge of our *course*.

A *chest* full of the best and choicest *mathematical books*, that could be got for money in *England*; as likewise Mr. *Hackluite*, and Mr. *Purchas*; and other books of *journals* and *histories*.

Study instruments, of all sorts.

I caused many small *glasses* to be made, whose part of time, I knew to a most insensible thing, and so divided and appropriated the *log-line* to them; making use of *Wilbrordus Snellius* his numbers of feet answering to a *degree*, and approved of by Mr. *Gunter*.

I made a *meridian-line* of 120 yards long, with six *plumb-lines* hanging in it; some of them being above 30 foot high, and the weights hung in a hole in the ground, to avoid wind. And this to take the *sun*'s or *moon*'s coming to the *meridian*. This line we verified, by setting it by the *pole* itself, and by many other ways.

Two pair of curious *globes*, made purposely; the workman being earnestly affected to this voyage.

This was the manner that we took the variation of the Compass, *and that as often as conveniently we could, but divers of the tables, by negligence of my boy are lost; but these (I hope) may suffice to give satisfaction of our care in navigation.*

July 13, 1631. These 13 *Azimuths*, with the *Altitu. Dec.* were taken upon a great piece of ice, with three *Needles* together; then the *Declination* was not equated, the last three set forth by themselves, proves the rest; *viz.* the *Azimuth* of W. with his *Variation*, the *Azimuth* at due W. and the *Variation* by the *Altitude* and *Azimuth* at due W.

These were taken 20 leagues to the eastward of *Salisbury* island; and two *Quad.* one of four, another of two foot, *Semid. Semicircle* of two foot *Semid.*

Latitud.		*Declin.*		*Al. Sun.*		*AZM.*		*F.*	*T. AZ.*		*F.*	*Variat.*	
63	01	20	14	39	42	77	50	S.	50	11	S	27	39
63	01	20	14	35	33	90	00		62	12	S	27	48
63	01	20	14	34	24	76	30	*N*	65	07	S	27	23
63	01	20	14	31	24	80	18	*N*	72	12	S	27	30
63	01	20	14	30	57	78	53	*N*	73	21	S	27	46
63	01	20	14	29	00	74	50	*N*	77	28	S	27	42
63	01	20	14	27	10	71	00	*N*	98	42	*N*	27	42
63	01	20	14	25	52	68	28	*N*	96	02	*N*	27	34
63	01	20	14	25	00	66	40	*N*	94	16	*N*	27	36
63	01	20	14	24	00	64	50	*N*	92	16	*N*	27	26
63	01	20	14	23	30	64	00	*N*	91	18	*N*	27	44
63	01	20	14	22	30	27	55	*N*	89	58	*N*	27	33
63	01	20	14	22	20	61	34	*N*	89	18	*N*	27	44

The mean variation is 27 36 00

The variation of the altitude and azimuth of West. 27 33 00
The variation of the azimuth of West.——— 27 48 00
The variation by azimuth a due West.——— 27 35 00

The mean of these three, is, 27 38 00

July 22, 1631. These three *Azimuths* and *Altitudes* were taken upon a piece of ice, the *Magnetical Azimuths* by the sun's shade in the water, the air thick of fog, that the sun gave no perfect shade otherways, ten leagues west from *Mansfield*'s island.

Latitud.		*Declin.*		*Al. Sun.*		*AZM.*		*F.*	*T. AZ.*		*F.*	*Variat.*	
60	33	18	25	34	06	90	00	S	64	34	S	25	26
60	33	18	25	31	34	84	48	N	70	08	S	25	04
60	33	18	25	18	25	71	35	N	82	54	N	25	21

The mean is 25 17 00

July 24, 1631. These 11 *Azimuths* were taken upon a piece of ice about the middle of the great bay; some of them by the shade, and some by the sight of the sun in the water, the weather being thick of fog.

Latitud.		*Declin.*		*Al. Sun.*		*AZM.*		*F.*	*T. AZ.*		*F.*	*Variat.*	
59	20	17	40	36	44	82	50	S	59	04	S	22	46
59	20	17	40	35	44	83	40	S	61	18	S	22	22
59	20	17	40	33	02	90	00		67	14	S	22	46
59	20	17	40	29	49	84	25	N	73	40	S	21	55
59	20	17	40	27	25	79	50	N	75	10	S	22	00
59	20	17	40	26	27	78	10	N	87	14	S	22	14
59	20	17	40	23	48	72	35	N	84	38	S	22	47
59	20	17	40	21	16	68	47	N	88	38	S	22	35
59	20	17	40	20	40	67	30	N	90	00		22	30
59	20	17	40	20	10	67	00	N	89	00	N	22	12
59	20	17	40	19	34	66	00	N	88	10	N	22	10

The mean is 22 23 21

 July 31,

July 31, 1631. These several *Azimuths* were taken upon a piece of ice, 50 leagues off the western shore.

Alt. Sun		*AZ. M.*		*F.*	*T. AZ.*		*F.*	*Variat.*		
24	00	76	26	N	99	20	N	22	54	
23	35	76	00	N	98	38	N	22	38	Latitude
22	50	75	00	N	97	18	N	22	18	58 43 43
22	05	73	40	N	96	04	N	22	24	
20	32	71	20	N	93	32	N	22	12	Declinat.
18	40	67	55	N	90	24	N	22	29	15 43 43
18	30	67	30	N	90	02	N	22	32	

The mean is 22 29 34

August 1, 1631. These several *Azimuths* were taken upon a piece of ice about forty leagues off the western shore.

Alt. Sun		*AZ. M.*		*F.*	*T. AZ.*		*F.*	*Variat.*		
26	36	83	05	N	104	36	N	21	31	
25	24	81	25	N	103	06	N	21	41	Latitude
24	26	78	38	N	100	42	N	22	04	58 45 00
22	30	75	16	N	97	22	N	22	06	
21	31	73	50	N	95	42	N	21	52	Declinat.
20	10	71	27	N	93	24	N	21	57	15 25 00
18	42	68	40	N	90	58	N	22	18	
18	07	67	25	N	89	56	N	22	31	

The mean is 22 00 00

August 5, 1631. These *Azimuths* were taken upon a piece of ice, and calculated by all the figures of the canon, about forty leagues off the western shore.

Alt. Sun		*AZ. M.*		*F.*	*T. AZ.*		*F.*	*Variat.*		
23	14	79	12	N	101	02	N	21	50	
22	11	76	40	N	99	12	N	22	32	Latitude
21	11	75	11	N	97	28	N	22	17	58 37 00
20	00	73	02	N	95	48	N	22	46	
18	59	71	24	N	93	47	N	22	23	Declinat.
17	15	68	35	N	90	53	N	22	18	14 12 00
16	42	67	28	N	90	00		22	32	
15	39	65	32	N	88	18	N	22	46	

The mean is 22 25 30

These observations were taken the 10th of *November*, 1631. the latitude 52. 03. the difference may be conceived, to grow by reason of the sun's low altitude and refraction. The others about the summer solstice, where difference of Meridians is avoided, and are more exact.

Alt. Sun		*AZ. M.*		*T. AZ.*		*Var. West.*	
G.	*M.*	*G.*	*M.*	*G.*	*M.*	*G.*	*M.*
14	25	42	25	26	11	16	14
14	00	45	25	27	30	17	55
13	15	47	25	29	54	17	31
12	18	48	10	32	33	15	37
12	03	49	20	33	16	16	04
11	41	51	07	34	15	16	52
10	57	53	25	36	04	17	21
9	42	55	25	38	58	16	27
9	15	57	45	40	00	17	14
8	50	58	37	40	52	17	45

The mean is 16 57 00 West.

An Appendix *touching Longitude.*

Latitude and longitude are two primary affections of the earth; by the help of these two, doth the geographer strive to represent the parts of the earth that they may keep symmetry and harmony with the whole. Latitude then is an arch of the Meridian, comprehended between the æquator and a parallel; but longitude is an arch of the æquator, intercepted between the prime meridian and the meridian of a place, the difference of longitudes being the difference of two meridians. The measure of the former is the meridian, the æquator of this latter. For the exact settling of latitudes we have many and absolute helps, so that the error, if any happen, ought to be imputed to the imperfect handling of the artist. But the longitude of a meridian is that which hath, and still wearieth, the greatest masters of geography. Nevertheless hath not the wise creator left man unfurnished of many excellent helps to attain his desire: For besides eclipses, especially of the moon, (whose leisure we must often wait, and perhaps go without, if the heavens be not propitious to us) we have the concourse of quick pac'd inferior planets, with superior slow ones, or their appulses with some fixed star of known place, or else some other artifice derived from their motions and positions. As for the magnetical needle to argue a longitude from its variation, is altogether without ground. And though well furnish'd seamen are able by their dead reckonings (as they term them) to determine the difference of meridians somewhat near, yet by reason of the unknown quantity of a degree in a given measure, (which is the rule of the ships way) varieties of adverse winds, different sets of tides, and other involved incumbrances, they come often wide of the mark they aim at. The best way yet known to the world, is that which is deduced from the cælestial apperences, which being performed by judicious artists, may in short time rectify our geographical and hydrographical charts hitherto in most places foully distorted. It is my intent here, to give an instance from two several observations drawn from the cœlestial bodies, by the author of this discourse, in his discovery for the N. W. at the bottom of the bay, being his wintering place, and called by the name of *Charlton*, which for judgment, circumspection, and exactness, may compare with most: The first, from the eclipse of the moon; the second, from the moons mediation of heaven, or her coming to the plan of his meridian of *Charlton*.

The captain then mindful of the lunar eclipse, which was to happen *October* 29, *Anno* 1631, was waiting on the moon with his instruments, but by reason of the interposition of the clouds, could make no observation on the beginning of her obscuration, but at her emersion or total recovery of light, the heavens being more serene, he took the altitude of the superior limb of the moon 29 deg. 11 min. the latitude of *Charlton* being 52 deg. 3 min.

At that very time, myself, with some friends, found the exact time of the moons emersion at *London* in *Gresham* college, (by a quadrant of six foot *Radius*, actually cut to each minute of the quadrant) to be *October* 29. 13 h. 7 min. 28 sec. or *October* 30 day, at one of the clock, 7 min. and about a half in the morning.

Now because the tables of the cœlestial motions, lately published by the most learned and industrious *Lansberg*, do much amuse the world, with that lofty title of perpetuity, it shall not be amiss to enquire after the time of the captain's observation from them, that so by comparing the one with the other, we may obtain the difference of meridians, which is the matter now sought after.

The middle motions of the luminaries answerable to the equal time of the emersion of the moon, are these which follow.

		Sex.	Deg.	M.	Sec.
The middle motion of the	Sun	3	47	39	26
	Center of the sun	3	15	49	58
	Apogæum of the sun	1	35	45	44
The middle motion of the	Longitude of the moon	2	59	29	1
	Anomaly of the moon	0	5	11	39
	Latitude of the moon	4	32	8	15
The Prosthaphæresis of the æquinox		0	0	12	30

Being thus furnished with these middle motions, we are next to enquire for the true places of the luminaries and their concomitants, as their right ascensions, the declination, latitude, semidiameter, parallax, and refraction of the moon, that so the true altitude of of the moons center, and consequently the time of the emersion may be had at *Charlton.*

For the sun's true place.	Sex.	Deg.	M.	Sec.
The middle motion of the sun's center	3	15	49	58
The Prosthaphæresis of the center add	0	1	37	0
The proportional scruples				
The middle motion of the sun's apogæum	1	35	45	44
The true motion of the apogæum subtr.	1	37	22	24
The middle motion of the sun is	3	47	39	26
The anomaly of the sun's orb	2	10	16	42
The prosthaphæresis of the sun's orb	0	1	32	43
The excess to be added	0	0	0	20
The absolute prosthaphæresis of the sun's orb subtr.	0	1	33	3
The middle motion of the sun from the true equinoctial	3	47	51	56
The true motion of the sun from the true æquinoctial	3	46	18	53
Therefore the sun's true place was in *Virgo*	0	16	18	53
And his right ascension		223	49	53
For the moon's true place.				
The anomaly of the moon's center	5	59	18	2
The prosthaphæresis of the moon's center	0	0	5	36
The proportional scruples	0			
The anomaly of the moon's orb	0	5	11	30
The æquated anomaly of the moon's orb	0	5	5	54
The prosthaphæresis of the moon's orb subtr.	0	0	24	4
The middle motion of the moon's longitude from the sun	2	59	39	1
The true motion of the moon's longitude from the sun	2	59	14	57
The middle motion of the sun from the true æquinoctial	3	47	51	56
The true motion of the moon from the true æquinoctial	0	47	6	53
Therefore the moon's true place was in *Taurus*	0	17	6	53
For the moon's latitude.				
The middle motion of the moon's latitude	4	32	8	15
The moon's absolute prosthaphæresis of her orb subtr.	0	0	24	4
The moon's true motion of latitude	0	31	44	11
The moon's northern latitude was	0	0	9	5
And her reductive scruples subtr.	0	0	0	26
But the moon's true motion in her proper orb was	0	17	6	53
Therefore the moon's true place reduced to the eclipt. *Taurus*	0	17	6	27
And because the north latitude of the moon was	0	0	9	5
Therefore will her right ascension be	0	44	35	10
And her declination	0	17	7	49
And because we have the distance of the moon, from the earth in semidiameters of the earth	0	64	15	0
Therefore shall the moon's apparent semidiam. be	0	0	15	0
And her parallax of altitude	0	0	47	0
Now because the altitude of the limb of the moon was found by observation to be	0	29	11	0
If we shall substract her semidiameter	0	0	15	0
And the refraction	0	0	2	0
We have the apparent altitude of the moon's center	0	28	54	0
To this if we add the parallax of altitude	0	0	47	0
We shall have the true altitude of the moon's center	0	29	41	0
Having thus the latitude of the place, the moon's true altitude with her declination, by the resolution of a sphærical triangle, according to the 11 *Prob. Lib.* 2. *Part.* 2. of our *British* Trigonometry, we have the distance of the moon from the merid.	0	63	26	0

And by comparing this arch with the difference of the ascensions of the luminaries, the time of the moon's total recovery of her light at *Charlton*, will be 7 h. 49 min. 28 sec. which subtr. from the time of the emersion at *London*, 13 h. 7 min. 28 sec. The difference of meridians, in respect of time, will be 5 h. 18 min. so that *Charlton* is removed from *London* westwards, 79 deg. 30 min.

This may likewise be confirmed by a second different observation made at the instant of the moon's culmination or mediation of heaven, at which time the altitude of the brightest star in the asterism of the northern crown, (being of the second magnitude) was found to be 33 deg. 27 min. easterly, *Anno* 1632, *June* 23.

It

It may be problematically delivered after this manner.

Having the latitude of a place, with the altitude of a known fixed star at the moment of the moon's culmination, to find the longitude.

This fixed star is of known longitude and latitude, therefore was his declination 27. 59. and right ascension 229. 46. Now by the resolution of a sphærical triangle of three known sides, we have the distance of this star from the meridian, and by consequence the right ascension of the moon, whence we conclude her culmination to be with the 28 deg. 10 min. of *Aquarius*; but the moon's true place was much less. Here note, that the scrupulosity of time is unknown, and therefore we cannot argue the moon's true place from thence, (though I grant it might be evinced) for that were to beg the question, and to know that first, which we look after.

In the next place we are to enquire with what point of the ecliptick the moon did culminate with us here at *London*, that so from the difference of her places of the like affection, we may deduce the difference of meridians.

Observation on the moon's culmination here at *London* we made none; therefore must we have recourse to the aforesaid tables of *Lansberg*, and from thence calculate the same. Now because the moon was not far removed from the sun's opposite point, it will not be amiss to enquire first the moon's place at midnight.

	Sex.	Deg.	M.	Sec.
The sun's opposite place at midnight in *Aquarius*	0	11	18	15
The moon's true place at midnight reduced to the eclip. was in *Aquarius*	0	23	33	18
The south latitude of the moon was	0	4	56	38
Therefore the difference of ascensions will be	0	14	6	0
The diurnal motion of the moon	0	14	24	0
Therefore the moon's proper motion answerable to the difference of ascensions is	0	0	33	59
Which added to the moon's true place at midnight	0	23	33	18
Gives us the moon's true place reduced to				
The ecliptick at her culmination at *London*	0	24	7	8

Now because the moon's southern latitude was 4 deg. 56 min. 38 sec. the arch therefore of the ecliptick comprehended between the moon's true place and the culminating point of the ecliptick, will trigonometrically be found to be 54 min. 38 sec. which added to the moon's true place before found, gives us the culminating point of the ecliptick, 25 d. 1 min. 46 sec. which is less than that found at *Charleton*, the difference being 3 d. 8 min. 24 sec. therefore is the place of observation westerly of *London*. Having therefore the moon's diurnal motion, and the difference of the culminating points, we conclude the meridian of *Charlton* to be distant from this of *London* 5 h. 14 min. of time, of 78 deg. 30 min. of the equator.

The difference between that of the eclipse, and this latter observation, is only 4 min. of time, or one deg. a difference easily pardoned, especially if we shall compare the same with some other places, yea even such as border nearly on each other. To give an instance on two eminent places which lie in the heart of *Europe*, *Rome* and *Norenberg*: Their difference of longitude, *Regiomotnanus* makes 36, *Werner* 32, *Appian* 34, *Mæstlin* and *Origan* 33, *Stofler* 18, *Maginus* 26, *Schoner* 12, *Mercator* and *Hondius* as much, *Stadius* 13, *Jansonius* 10, *Longomontanus* 16, *Lansberg* 10, *Kepler* by two observations on two lunar eclipses, but 4 min. of time.

This variety among these great artists, will I hope, pardon us this difference of 4 min. and be a means to encourage our *English* seamen, and others, to make such or the like observations in foreign parts as the heavens shall be offered unto them.

H. GELLIBRAND.

To the Venerable Artists and younger Students in Divinity, in the famous University of Cambridge.

YOU nobly-witted and ingenuously studied *academians*, whose excellency in all kinds of learning, all foreign universities do admire, and none attain unto; I here present you a voyage to *Cholcos*, though not the golden fleece with it; the search, I mean, but not the finding, of that so much talk'd of, so often sought for, north-west passage, and nearer way into the *South-Sea*. That, wherein so much time and treasure have been expended, so many brave spirits employed, and yet none discovered. Perchance, there is no such passage to be found, and that the *Spaniards*, by the gullery of their false sea-charts, and the fable of an old *Greek* pilot, have but diverted our *English* and *Dutch* seamen, from their golden *Indies*. This plot of theirs hath taken, for these many years, and it appears to be but a plot, for that themselves never make use of this passage. For mine own part, I suppose that the philosopher's stone is in the north-west passage. My argument for it, is, for that there's so much philosophy in the way to it.

So much, and such variety; such variety, and that so various (I think) from what is received in the schools; that it were well worth the disquisition of an university, (and I wish you the first honour of it) either to find out, how these observations may be reduced to *Aristotle*'s philosophy; or whether they need any other enquiry, and ought to be examined by some other rules, than *Aristotle* hath yet light upon. This is my purpose of inscribing it unto you. Of this one thing am I confident: that you are all so rational and ingenious, as to prefer truth before authority: *Amicus Plato, amicus Aristoteles*, but *magis amica veritas*. Your sciences, then, being liberal; your studies, I know, have so far passed into your manners, that your minds are so too, and that such as have already profited beyond the credulity required in a young learner, and are themselves promoted to be masters of the arts; though they still reverence their old *Greek* tutor, yet they will not suffer that of *Pythagoras*'s school, so to domineer in *Aristotle*'s, as to let an *ipse dixit*, go away with it: much less allow it the authority of a mayor's hammer, with one knock to silence all arguments.

Upon this confidence, I with all due respects here prefer two *propositions* unto your discussing.

The first this, *Whether those rules of* Aristotle'*s philosophy be to be allowed so universal, that they hold all the world over.*

The second this, *Whether they ought to be so magisterial, as to prescribe against all other examinations.*

The first of these I shall but *problematically* propound unto you: but in the second, I hope a man of my cloathing may be allowed the freedom of being something more earnest.

But that I may not come with prejudice to the making of these motions, or be thought upon some *ignorance* or *ambition*, to speak against the *incomparable Aristotle*; I shall desire all my fellow *academians* to allow me so much discretion, as to know, that he that shall in your hearings oppose your *Aristotle*, does like the ship here spoken of, run against a rock, endanger his own bulge, and the staving of his vessel. No, I so far honour the old *Aristotle*, that I will allow him to be *master* and *moderator of the schools*; and that there is the same respect due to him in the *schools*, which, by *reason* and *long custom*, is due to one of the *king's ships* in the *narrow seas*; *That in acknowledgment of a sovereignty, every other name ought to strike sail to him. Aristotle* (it must be confess'd) hath made all learning beholden to him: no man hath learned to confute him, but by him; and unless he hath plow'd with his heifer. He had the most incomparable wit, and was the most logical and demonstrative deliverer of himself, of all the sons of nature: One who best of all deserved to be called, *her principal secretary*; one who not only *adorns* a *library*, but *makes it*: *Qui habet Aristotelem, habet bibliothecam*, is truer of him, than of the *great comparer*. This is my opinion of him; and I wish him more studied.

'Tis not therefore the name or the authority of the great *Aristotle*, that my propositions meddle withal; but whether his observations gathered out of this part of the world alone, could, like a *royal pass* or *commission*, carry a man all the world over?

It must be confest, that in respect of the *equinoctial*, and the *latitude* that *Aristotle* lived in, he was but a *northern man*; and 'twas his own rule, that *nihil agit extra sphæram activitatis suæ*. So then it would be put to voices, to consider whether he that knew but these northern parts, and the *Mediterranean* sea, could possibly make such collections, by what was here to be learned, as should be unfailable in the *southern hemisphere*

sphere and the two *Indies?* Plainly, those that are conversant in *navigations* and *books of voyages* into those parts, have found so many contrarieties to observe, that it were rather *tedious* than difficult, to fill up a *note-book* with them.

The antients, we know (as if they had measured the world by the yard-wand) restrained the *limits* of *temperature* and *habitation*, by the five *zones*, without consideration of any interloping or concurring causes, which experience hath now found out, to have quite altered their observation. I add, that a good leisure and diligence might observe, how in the contrary part of the world there be found clean contrary *causes* and effects, unto those in this part of the world. The *south* wind there brings *cold* and *winter*, and the *north* is the rainy wind. How will the *thunder* and the *wind* be made agree with *Aristotle*'s definition of a *meteor?* In some places of the mountains *Andes* by *Peru*, it thunders ever. The *East Indies* have their *Monsons* and their steady winds, constant for six months together; and who shall assign their causes? Then the *doctrine* of the *tides*, nothing so uncertain; which *ebb* and *flow* in some places *different*, and in others *contrary* to the *moon* and her *motions*. This (as I remember) is *Aristotle*'s definition of a
Aristoteles, 1. *meteor* 1. *meteor*, that it is *an imperfect mix'd body, generated out of an infirm and inconstant concretion of the elements, which therefore cannot be durable.* Now the *Monson* is both constant in his continuance this year, and in his return next year; most constantly keeping his seasons half year one way, and half year another way for all ages, nothing more constantly or durably, and therefore nothing like *Aristotle*'s *meteor*. And so for the *thunder* upon the *Andes*: It is first, perpetual; secondly, not caused by a *dry exhalation* (as *Aristotle* wills) but hanging over such hills as are covered with snow, and a perpetual winter. Witness the *thunder* on the *Alps* also; yea, and that in the middle of the sea, five hundred leagues from the shore, or any thing that is dry. Yea, it frequently both *snows* and *thunders* upon the *Andes*, at one instant; and in *dry* places that are hard by, scarce ever *thundering*.

But not to pass the *line* for it; you see in this little book how *Charleton* island, which is no more northerly than your *Cambridge*, is yet so unsufferably cold, that it is not habitable; and that there encounter so many different (at least so seeming) occurrences of nature, as were well worth the disquisition of a *philosopher*. I could (in my small reading) instance in many other particulars, which I had rather should be found out by some industrious searchers after *nature*, in the *modern relations* of our *discoverers*, than in this my short *proposition*. 'Tis not to be doubted, but that the careful reading of of our *books of voyages*, would more elucidate the *history of nature*, and more conduce to the improvement of *philosophy* than any thing that hath been lately thought upon. These *navigations* have in part fulfill'd that of the prophet, *many shall pass to and fro, and knowledge shall be encreased.* Dan. 12. 4. This, I suppose, might be observed from this study, that the great and infinite *creator* hath so disposed and varied every thing, that it is impossible for man's reason and observation to conclude him; and therefore, tho' vulgar and received *philosophy* may give a man a *general* hint, all the world over; yet no *universal* and unfailing certainty.

This brings me to my *second proposition*, That seeing God will not have his works, (no more than his kingdom) to come by Luk. 17. 20. observation; *Whether then ought any human dictates to be so magisterial, as to prescribe against all other examination?*

No human study more conduces to the setting forth of God's glory, than the contemplation of his great works in *philosophy*: For tho' a smattering knowledge in *second causes* warps the mind towards *atheism*; yet a higher speculation of them, brings it about again to religion. No man, I believe, will think it fit for us to have a *pope in philosophy*; one that no body shall presume to censure of, but all be bound to advance his *decretals* above the *holy scriptures*. This is the scandal that myself and divers good men take at the undue authority in some heats pinn'd upon the *Stagyrite*.

I am sorry that the *Israelites* dotage upon *Solomon*'s *philosophy*, should have caused the *Suidas*, & *Rabbini*. zealous *Hezekiah* to call in and to suppress those unvaluable *physicks*; for fear, I suppose, lest their credit should have as much derogated from the authority of the *holy Scriptures*; as the *brazen serpent* (which he destroy'd about the same time) had done from *religion*. None will believe, that *Solomon*'s *philosophy* was contrary to the *scriptures*, seeing the *scripture* commends *Solomon* for them. 'Twas not *Hezekiah*'s fear, therefore (or not only) lest there might have been a competition between them, but a neglect of one of them: He was jealous lest the *scripture* might have any writing set up *by* it, tho' not against it.

Can *divines* then be blamed for speaking, when they hear *Aristotle*'s *philosophy* to be solely magnified, and the study of the *scripture philosophy*, disrespected? Or that when 'tis confessed, that such a thing is true in *divinity*, and yet in the *moderating* of the point, *determine* for *philosophy?* Nay, to hear it call'd *absurd* and *ridiculous*, to have scripture urged at all in point of *philosophy?* No doubt

doubt there is; *But whatsoever is false in divinity, is also false in nature*, how much shew of truth soever it passes with in *philosophy*. *Philosophy* hath taken its turn in the *schools*; and the *holy texts* by the *schoolmen*, have even been submitted unto *Aristotle*'s: Yea, to the great corruption of *theology*, as the complaint is, hath this man been so far advanc'd, that *contra est philosophus, & contra est apostolus*, have familiarly passed up and down for equal *oppositions*; so that it hath been a *measuring cast* oftentimes betwixt the *prophet* and the *peripatetick*, and by foul play hath the measure been made to stand the harder at the *peripatetick*, for that the *prophet* hath been enforced to comply with him, by a *wrested interpretation*. Thus had St. *Paul* need give his caveat unto *theology* as well as unto *theologues*, *Beware lest any man spoil you through philosophy*.

All this were to no purpose, unless the *text of God* were excellent in this kind, and embellished here and there with most admirable *philosophy*. What incomparably rare foot-steps of it have we in the books of *Genesis*, *Job*, and the *Psalms*? How noble a study then were it, and how worthy the leisure of some excellently learned to bestow some time upon it? *Valesius* the *physician*, hath in his *Sacra philosophia* done something in this kind; who yet might have done better here and there, for the honour of the scriptures. I am not so sottish to believe, that every particular is to be drawn out of *scripture*; 'tis none of my dotage, that: Or, that *God* in *scripture* did intend, every where, the accurateness of *philosophy*; or stand to be so curious in *definitions* and *decisions*. Nor so foolish would I be thought, as to have all *philosophy* taken in pieces, and new moulded by the *scriptures*: Nor, that nothing should be determined on, till a *text* confirm'd it. But this perchance might profitably be thought upon, that where the *scriptures* have any thing in this kind, it should more reverently be esteemed; collections out of scatter'd places (as is done out of *Aristotle*, made; these compared, and their *resultances* observ'd. This surely would amount to more than is yet thought of; and, a-God's name, let scholars be so bold with *Aristotle*, as to examine him upon good assurance, by what is *truth's touchstone*. Received *philosophy* is a most necessary handmaid to the *scriptures*; but let her not be set above her lady, nor no competition be maintained betwixt them.

Something else remains to be thought of: That seeing the same *God*, who gave *Aristotle* these good parts, hath, in like manner, raised up many excellent spirits moe, whether it were not injurious unto what is done, and a discouragement to what might be done; to have the inventions or observations of those excellent wits and great industries, so abash'd with *Aristotle*'s authority, that they can have no credit in the world, for that his *dictates* have pre-occupated all good opinion? Let it not then be thought unequal to examine the *first cogitations* of the *old philosophy*, by the *second thoughts* of our more modern *artists*: For that the same improvement may by this means accrue unto our *physicks*, that hath advanced our *geography*, our *mathematicks*, and our *mechanicks*. And let it not be thought so insolent, to refuse *Aristotle*'s authority singly, where his reason is not so concluding; seeing other men have taken the boldness to do that before us in several kinds. Some have perfected, and others controul'd his *ethicks* by the *scriptures*; as *Scultetus*, *Wallæus*, and some others. *Justin Martyr*, surnamed the *philosopher*, hath purposely written *contra dogmata Aristotelis*. *Basson* and *Gassendus* (two brave men) have newly written point-blank against him: nor have they taken away all liberty from those that are to follow them.

And thus, with renewing my former protestation for mine own respects to *Aristotle*, I conclude my two *propositions*; which I desire may receive a favourable construction from all ingenuous, incapricious *scholars*. I meant them out of good-will to promote learning; to encourage and countenance future undertakings: and in such a case, a little too much saying, may be thought not to have exceeded an *honest rhetorician*; for I would not be thought too earnest in it. The hint for all this I took from this book; which in mine own and some better judgments, is (to say no more) as well done, and enriched with as sure and useful observations, as any in this kind. I was desired by the able author, and some other friends, to overlook the written copy of it, and to amend the *English* here and there; in which I did not despair of doing something, for that, in my younger time I had a little acquainted myself with the *language of the sea*. That which put me in the head to inscribe it unto your names (most excellently learned *Academians*) was, for that the place of this *wintering*, was within a *minute* or two of the *heighth* of our *Cambridge*; which my prayer to *God* is, that your studies may make famous.

Yours, X. Z.

AN

ACCOUNT

OF TWO

VOYAGES;

The FIRST of

Feodor *ISKOWITZ BACKHOFF*,

The MUSCOVITE Envoy,

INTO

CHINA.

The SECOND of

Mr. *ZACHARY WAGENER*,

A Native of DRESDEN in MISNIA,

Thro' a great part of the WORLD,

As alſo into CHINA.

Tranſlated from the High-Dutch *original printed at* Berlin.

Adverti∫ement

TO THE

READER.

A*MONG tho∫e many voyages which lately have been u∫hered into the World, the following* Mu∫covite *emba∫∫y may ju∫tly challenge a place, e∫pecially for its u∫efulne∫s in geography, which I here pre∫ent to the reader, without the lea∫t alteration, according to the copy thereof, ∫ent to me by* Johannes Scultetus, *councellor of ∫tate of his electoral highne∫s of* Brandenburgh. *And as the voyages of Mr.* Zacharias Wagener, *are very famous in* Holland, *and the following ab∫tract thereof being communicated to me by his brother-in-law Mr.* Chri∫tian Bothe, *a con∫iderable merchant in* Dre∫den, *I thought it not un∫ea∫onable to ∫ubjoin the ∫ame, for the benefit of the courteous reader.*

THE

THE TRAVELS OF Feodor *Iskowitz Backhoff* FROM *MUSCOW* into *CHINA*.

(1.) *The road from* Muſcow *to* Siberia.

MOST generally they take their way over *Uſtingha*, ſeated upon the river *Dwina*, from whence we continu'd our journey to *Tobolſko*, the capital city of *Siberia*, being three thouſand verſts, or ſix hundred *German* leagues from the city of *Muſcow*. Before you have travell'd the third part of your way, you come to a great ridge of mountains, called *Camiani Rojas*, i. e. *the ſtone girdle*, by the *Muſcovites*; it being their opinion, that they extend round the terreſtrial globe. I ſuppoſe them to be the ſame the antients called *montes Siberei*. This mountain being fifty leagues over, and interwoven with deep valleys, which are generally, but eſpecially in *Autumn*, overflown with water, is impaſſable in the ſummer; but theſe being well frozen in the winter, afford a ſwift and convenient paſſage for ſleds, ſo that in twenty four hours you may travel eighteen or twenty leagues, and conſequently perform the whole journey from *Muſcow* to *Tobolſko* in ſix or ſeven weeks. The firſt city you come to in *Siberia* is called *Worchaturia* from the river *Tura*, upon which it lies.

(2.) *Of the cities, rivers, and fertility of* Siberia.

Siberia has twenty three cities, the capital of which *Tobolſko*, ſituate upon a hill near the river ſide, is a place of no great traffick; the inhabitants being for the moſt part *Bouchar* and *Calmuck Tartars*, who are very poor; the chiefeſt place of trading being *Jeneſſay*, lying a great way beyond *Tobolſko*, which conſiſts in ſables, martins, and ſuch like furs. *Dauri* is the utmoſt frontier place of *Siberia*, on the *Calmuck* ſide. *Siberia* is watered by many rivers, among which the river *Oby* is the chiefeſt. It contains many iſlands well ſtor'd with trees. This river is in ſome places a *German* league, in other places about half a league broad, and falls into the *Tartarian ſea*. It produces abundance of fiſh, and among the reſt *Beluja's* or *white fiſh*. The cities of *Siberia* are, *Worchaturia*, *Japonſoi*, *Tumen*, *Tobolſko*, *Damianſky*, *Samara*, *Sergouz*, *Berofott*, *Narin*, *Tomoko*, *Koſneotz*, *Kraſnozar*, *Ket*, *Jeneſſay*, *Nallen*, *Dauri*, *Takow*, *Magaſcy*. Theſe as well as all the other cities of *Siberia*, are not very populous. There are very good corn-fields here, the ſoil whereof is ſo good, that it bears very well without dung. It has no ſea-ports, the *Tartarian ſea* being cover'd with ice ſummer and winter; however fiſher-boats venture as far as the iſle of *Malgamſay*, over-againſt the mouth of the river *Oby*.

(3.) *Of the inhabitants of* Siberia.

THE antient inhabitants were *Tartars*, governed by their own princes or kings; one of the family of their last prince living not long ago, with the *Czar*'s permission, in *Siberia*, till his house was plunder'd, and he forced to fly the country, by the *Russians* that trade that way in salt, with the *Calmuck Tartars*, which they bring thence in great barges. This prince having afterwards married among the *Calmuck Tartars*, makes sometimes an inroad into *Siberia*, and takes a severe revenge of the *Muscovites* there. The natives being not very forward to oppose him, as living still in hopes, that one time or other he may be instrumental in delivering them from the *Muscovite* yoke. The *Calmuck* and *Mogul Tartars* border upon *Siberia*, (besides divers other *Tartarian* nations) their country extending from thence to the frontiers of *China*. There are also divers other hords, living on the frontiers of *Siberia*; as the *Tingoskoy*, the *Watzkoy*, *Tyrgyskoy* and *Barrabanskoy*, which have each their particular captains or leaders. The natives of *Siberia* are much addicted to sorcery. There are not many *Russians* living among them, by reason of the great distance of this country from *Muscow*.

(4.) *How* Siberia *was brought under the obedience of the* Muscovites.

ABove a hundred years ago, under the reign of the *Czar Joan Bazilowitz*, a certain *Cosaen* named *Jormac Timorsof*, leader of a certain gang of robbers, having taken some vessels loaden with ammunition belonging to the *Czar*; he issued his strict orders to seize the said *Jormac*, cost it what it wou'd; so that *Jormac* dreading the *Czar*'s revenge, got with his gang into the river *Cama*, and so to *Czotrava*, an isle about five or six hundred *Versts* above *Casan*, which at that time belong'd to a vast rich *Russian* merchant named *Daniel Stroginot*, living in a city built by him, and called *Stroginot* after his name. Having represented to this merchant the easy conquest of *Siberia*, he obtained some arms and ammunition of him to accomplish his design; accordingly he went up the river *Tagit*, till he came to the river *Toura*, where is a considerable island, inhabited by *Tartars*; these he soon chased thence, and continuing his march to the city of *Tumen*, he soon made himself master of it, the same he did afterwards with *Tobolsko* the residence of their king. However he march'd forward fifty leagues to the river *Irtish*, in pursuit of the enemy, who retreated before him. Having refreshed his people hereabouts for six weeks, he sent three hundred of them to pursue the flying *Tartars*, which they did with so much eagerness, that being surrounded by the enemy, they were almost all kill'd, few escaping their hands. *Jormac* having no more than two hundred men left, intrench'd himself in an isle, but being attack'd in the night-time by the *Tartars*, he was killed with all his followers, except forty, who made a shift to get into *Muscovy*; and having represented unto the *Czar* all the circumstances of the matter, he sent six hundred chosen men under the command of one of these *Cosacks* (who had been *Jormac*'s lieutenant) who retook the city of *Tobolsko*; where having fortify'd himself, and being recruited with fresh troops, he made such frequent excursions into the neighbouring *Tartarian* countries; that they at last grew weary of the war, and submitted to the *Czar* of *Muscovy*. The same fortune attended the *Czar* in his conquest of the kingdom and city of *Astracan*, which he made himself master of in one campaign, but he paid pretty dear for *Casan*, having been forced to raise the siege of that city, the first time, but took it in the second siege.

(5.) *The revenues of the kingdom of* Siberia.

THE *Czar*'s revenues in this kingdom arise from the tribute of the sables, martins, red and white foxes skins, and other furs, out of which he has the fifth for his share; certain officers being appointed by the *Czar* for that purpose. Mr. *Fletcher*, who was *English* envoy in *Muscovy* in 1588, affirms, that in one year there were brought into the *Czar*'s treasury out of *Siberia*, no less than 466 *Zimmer* of sable (40 sables to each *Zimmer*) and 180 *Siberian* fox skins. The ordinary revenue of *Siberia* amounts now to 200000 *Roubles*. They have different ways of catching the sables; either by wooden

wooden traps, not unlike our mice-traps, or by ſnares, which being laid under the trees where they feed, the trees are cut down, and they entangled in the ſnares. They alſo go a ſable hunting in ſleds drawn by dogs, and kill them with their bows and arrows.

The Journals of Feodor Iskowitz Backhoff *from* Tobolsko, *the capital city of* Siberia, *into* China, *called* Kattay *by the* Ruſſians.

* *Underſtand from the beginning of the world according to the* Ruſſians *computation,* viz. *in the year of Chriſt* 1644.

IN the year 7162 *, in the month of *May*, I left *Tobolſko*, purſuant to his *Czariſh* majeſty's orders, and travell'd to the city *Tax* upon the river *Irtiſh*, where I arriv'd the 27th of *July*, having ſpent a month and three days in this journey. From *Tax* I went up the river the firſt of *Auguſt*, and for want of horſes ſpent four weeks of my journey to the *white lake*, where being furniſhed with forty camels and fifty horſes from *Snablai Tniſcha*, or prince of the *Bouchar Tartars*, we left the ſaid lake the 16th of *October*, and continued our journey in three weeks time to *Kabalgakuna*, inhabited by the *Calmuck Tartars*, who live in brick houſes, built after the *Ruſſian* manner. From *Kabalgakuna* to the *ſeven elms* is two days travelling; and from thence to the rivulet of *Jelkuſa*, which ariſes from among the mountains, and falls into the *Irtiſh*, another day's journey. From the river of *Jelkuſa*, along the right ſide of the *Irtiſh*, to the reſidence of that *Calmuck prince* (who is a prieſt) reſiding on the left ſide of the ſaid river, is three days journey. Their fields, which produce wheat, barley, and peas, are plowed by ſome of the *Bouchar Tartars*. From hence, all along the right ſide of the river *Irtiſh* to *Ablawich* (near the *Bouchar* cornfields) is fourteen days journey, thro' high mountains, full of birch-trees.

We arrived at *Ablawich* the 22d of *November*, where they live in plaiſter'd houſes; their fruits are wheat, barley, and peas; and they abound in fiſh. Their prince named *Albai Tonſcha* did invite me to his houſe, where after he had demanded the *Czar's* preſents (which I gave him) he entertained me very handſomly. The 30th of *November* I continued my journey thro' the *Bouchar Tartars*, who are for the moſt part huſbandmen, among whom I tarried four months and ten days.

The third of *April* 7163, I went from thence to the brook of *Botka*, twelve days journey from the *Bouchar* cornfields; near this brook the before-mentioned prince *Ablai Tonſcha* was building for himſelf two houſes of ſtone, by *Chineſe* workmen. Here I ſtayed five weeks and five days.

The 30th of *June*, 7163, having receiv'd my paſſport from *Ablai Tonſcha*, I continu'd my journey from the brook *Botka* to *Conjaja Toucha*, or *Koltaſching's children* in fourteen days, and in five days more to the ſmall city of *Rontaſhina*, inhabited by *Calmuck* prieſts. From this place to the lake, through which paſſes the river *Irtiſh*, is fourteen days journey.

From hence to *Miſganſko Teſcha* is two days journey, and from thence through the mountains ſeven days more. Hereabouts live the princes of the *Mogul Tartars*, who ſpeak both the *Mogul* and *Calmuck* languages; there is three days journey from hence to the reſidence of the prince named *Dobruna*, whoſe territories extend fifteen days journey to the frontiers of *China*. However many petty princes have their territories interſperſed here, who are alſo of the race of the *Moguls*.

From the uttermoſt frontiers of *China* to *Cokatana*, their firſt city, is a journey of three months. The mountains along the river *Irtiſh* and the *white lake* to the frontiers of *China*, are inhabited by the *Moguls* and *Calmuck Tartars*; the firſt live very poorly, and I was often obliged to ſtay among them to furniſh my ſelf with water and proviſions. After I had ſtayed nine days at *Cokatana* in expectation of two guides, we continued our journey thence the twelfth day of *January* 7164 to *Koſki*, a journey of twelve days. Hereabouts alſo live divers petty princes of *Mogul Tartars*, who call themſelves *Tiobetzanſky*, but are under the *Chineſe* juriſdiction. *Kanki* is ſituate among the rocks; here I ſaw the famous *Chineſe* wall, being three fathoms high, and one and a half thick, fill'd up in the inſide with ſmall ſtones; the ſtone towers ſtand not in the ſame line cloſe to the wall, but at ten fathoms diſtance, and are a hundred fathoms diſtance from one another, reaching as long as the wall to the ſea-ſide. The 20th of *February*, having received orders from the king of *China* for the continuation of my journey, we ſet out the 21ſt from *Capki*, ſeven days journey from *Cambalu*, (or *Pekin*) having twenty eight cities lying between them, ſurrounded with ſtone walls, upon which we ſaw ſome canon, but of a ſmall ſize. The ſoldiers that keep the guard at the gates were armed with a kind of carabines, not above half a yard long, with threefold muzzles, but without firelocks. They have generally ſtone-bridges built over their canals or rivulets, but have not

not many rivers of note; the governours of the places are generally carried in *Palanka's* or litters, upon mens shoulders, attended by a guard on both sides.

We came to *Cambalu* the third of *March* 7164; about an *English* mile out of town, we were met by two deputies, one whereof was the chancellor of the *Pricas*, or secretary's office of the foreign affairs, the other of that of the *Chinese* affairs. They received us in a spacious structure of stone, inhabited by some priests, and built as we were told, for the reception of the *Dalac Lama*, or the *Tartarian* high-priest, who is reverenced among them like a god. At the entrance of this house they desired me to alight from my horse, and to pay my respects to their king upon my knees: Unto which I replied, that it was not our custom to salute even our *Czar* upon our knees, but only with a very low bow, and bare-headed; unto which they gave no other answer, but that the *Dutch* never refused it, and therefore I ought not. They then presented me with some *Thee*, made with cow's milk and butter, in the king's name; it being *Lent*, I refused to drink it. They told me, that I being sent from one great *Czar* to another mighty prince, I ought at least to accept it, which I did, and so returned back. As we were making our entry, I saw in the gate standing three brass cannon, and so we marched forward for three *Versts*, thro' most markets, before we came to the court prepared for our reception, which had two houses of stone, hung with tapestry. Our daily allowance of provisions was one sheep and a small cask of *Spanish* brandy, two fishes, a middle-sized *Jasy*, a certain quantity of wheaten flour, *Sichay*, and rice, and two cups of brandy. The 4th of *March* certain persons sent by the *Chinese* king came to my lodgings to demand the presents I had brought along with me from the *Czar*; I told them, that it was not customary at our *Czar*'s court to deliver the presents till we had been admitted to the audience of the king, and delivered our credentials. Unto which they replied, *One king ought not to prescribe laws to another; our customs are different from yours. Our* Bogday (king) *has sent us to demand the presents, but if you come to sell them, let us know your price.* I replied, That I was not sent by the *Czar* to merchandize, but to establish a friendly concurrence betwixt the two kings, and to offer him some presents. They then told me, That since I own'd I was sent with presents to their king, they would take by force what our *Czar* had sent; and as for my credentials, care should be taken of them hereafter; and thus actually took the presents by force.

The 6th of *March* word was sent me to bring my credentials to the secretary's office; which I refused to comply with, telling the messenger that I was sent with these credentials to the king, and not to his ministers.

August 21, they sent again upon the same errand; but I refusing the same, they told me, That since I had disobey'd their king's command, they had orders to punish me; I gave them no other answer, but, if they cut me limb by limb, I would not part with them till I had been admitted to the king's presence.

The 31st of *August* all the presents were brought back by certain officers, who told me that it was done by special command from their king, because I had refused to deliver my credentials into the *Prica*'s or secretary's office; and one among them told me, *No foreign minister, come he from what country he will, is admitted into the presence of our king, but only of his great ministers, call'd* Inoanol Boyarde. I can give you no true account of the bigness of the city of *Cambalu*, because we had no liberty to take a view of it; but if we may credit the *Moguls* and *Chinese*, they told us it was sixty *Versts* (twelve *German* leagues) in compass. Vast quantities of silk stuffs are made and sold here, but their pearls and precious stones they have from *Karatscho*, two months journey with camels from *Cambalu*, and then in the possession of a son of the late king. The king's palace fronts a spacious market-place, whither all sorts of people come to salute the king, at least three times a month. Every new moon they put out flags as a signal to the people to come to make their submission; and the the same is done every 22d and 29th day of the month, when they appear in rich brocado'd clothes, upon their bended knees, and among the rest twenty six elephants trained up for that purpose. The *Bogday* then regent, was a *Mogul Tartar*; but the late *Chinese* emperor, after these *Tartars* had made themselves masters of the *Chinese* empire (about thirty years before) kill'd himself, securing only a young son, named *Young Sie*, behind two of the *Chinese* lords carried to *Karatscho* in old *China*. The *Chinese's* are much stronger in the city of *Cambalu* than the *Moguls*. In the year 7164, the 7th of *July*, 25 *Hollanders* [a], the

(a) *Nieuhoff* p. 181. We understand by the said father *Adam*, that there was there a *Muscovite* embassy, with an attendance of 100 persons (among whom were some *Moors*) to treat about certain points relating to traffick; but were not as yet admitted to audience, because the emperor resided at that time sometimes in the city, sometimes at some distance thence.

remainders

remainders of the three ſhips (who had each of them 100 men aboard, two whereof were loſt) arrived at *Cambalu*, but for want of an interpreter could not converſe with them; they gave me two letters for *Muſcow*. Having obtained my paſſport in 7164 in *September*, I left *Cambalu*, and returned thro' the ſame way I came to *Muſcow*, having had but ill ſucceſs in my negotiation, becauſe I would not reverence their idols ([b]).

And here it is to be obſerved that *Cambalu* is the capital city of *China*, otherwiſe it is called *Peking*, the firſt being the name given them by the *Tartars*, whence ſome geographers have been miſlead, who have placed *Cambalu* in their maps, in the great *Tartary*. *Tamerlane* a *Tartar* by birth, having conquered *China*, is the reaſon that frequent mention has been made of *Cambalu* in his hiſtory, which has introduced this error of placing *Cambalu* in *Tartary*; add to this, that our ancient hiſtorians of *China* have call'd it *Kattay*, the ſame name that is given to it by the *Ruſſians* to this day; *Kattay* being a *Tartarian* word, ſignifying as much as an incloſed or wall'd place, (ſuch as *China* is) given by them to *China*, whilſt they were in poſſeſſion of it. And becauſe *China* was known or firſt deſcribed by the ancient hiſtorians at the ſame time the *Tartars* were maſters of it, they were eaſily led into that miſtake, by taking the *Grand Tartary* for *China*, and ſo put it down accordingly in their maps, placing *Cambalu* in *Tartary*, whereas it is the ſame with *Peking* the capital city of the *Chineſe* empire. For the ſame reaſon it is, that they have deſcribed *Tartary* as a rich plentiful countrey, whereas it is very mean, and above one half of it not fit for tillage. *Kattay* is indeed a *Tartarian* word, but not a name of their own countrey, but given by them to *China*.

([b]) *Introcetta* p. 313. Speaking of this embaſſy: *In quos* (ſc. ritus) *quoniam Muſcoviæ ante biennium legatione functi conſentire nollent, eum dedecore muneribus, quæ attulerunt, redditis rejecti ſunt.* And *Nieuhoff* p. 187, the 14th of *September* our envoys underſtood that the *Muſcovite* Ambaſſador was upon his departure, without being admitted to audience, becauſe he refuſed to bend his knees before the imperial ſeat, as looking upon it as a degrading to his maſter's honour. About noon, juſt as our enjoys were at dinner, one of the ſaid ambaſſador's domeſticks came to take leave of us, deſiring in behalf of all the reſt, that we would be pleaſed to give them a certificate to teſtify that they had met with us here, which was readily granted. Afterwards we heard, that the ſaid ambaſſador was ſtopped in the countrey, becauſe he was not provided with a ſufficient paſſport.

A SHORT

A SHORT ACCOUNT OF THE VOYAGES OF Mr. *ZACHARY WAGENER*,

Perform'd in thirty five Years,

Through *Europe*, *Asia*, *Africa* and *America*;

Taken out of his own JOURNAL.

ANNO 1633, the 3d of *June*, I left *Dresden* (my native city) with consent of parents and embarked in a small vessel upon the river *Elbe* in company of Mr. *Frederick Lebzelter*, one of the grooms of the chamber to his electoral highness of *Saxony*, for *Hamburgh*, where we arrived safely some time after; but not meeting with any opportunity of preferment there, I embarked for *Amsterdam*, where I was entertained for a whole year by Mr. *William Johnson Blawe*, one of the most noted booksellers of that city; and after that, being resolved upon travelling farther, engaged my self in the service of the *West-India* company, in the quality of a private centinel, and in 1634, the 18th of *July*, embarked aboard a stout two deck'd ship, bound for *Brasil*, where we arrived after a most troublesome voyage of sixteen weeks, and came to an anchor before the *Receif*. Not long after our arrival, I was advanced to a muster-master's place in major *Bajart*'s company then in garrison in the fort *Ernestus*, and sometime after was made clerk of the kitchin of his excellency count *John Maurice* of *Muscow*, general of *Brasil*.

Anno 1638, the 20th of *April*, the beforementioned earl embark'd with 8000 *European* soldiers, and 3000 *Brasilians* aboard 47 ships, steering their course from the *Receif* to the *Bay of all Saints*, in order to besiege the city of *St. Salvador*; I went along with his excellency in that expedition, which proved unsuccessful; for the city being impossible to be begirt on all sides, we returned after two months to the *Receif*. *Anno* 1630, I went along with the said earl to *Anthony Vaez*, by the way of the cape of *St. Austin* and *Sexinhain*, and so farther by land to *Porto Calvo*: In our return we pass'd thro' the middle of the *Dutch-Brasil*, by the way of *Bosiovegid*, to the city of *Paraiba*, and as we passed along took a view of all the garisons and fortresses, so that this progress took up above, three months. After I had spent this seven years in *Brazil*, *viz.* three years in the service, and four in his excellency's family, I desired leave to return home, which being granted, and a passport given me, I embark'd in 1641, in *April*, aboard a vessel called the *Tiger*, bound with two other vessels freighted with sugar, tobacco and *Brasil* wood, Mr. *William Honton* commodore for *Holland*. We arrived the 17th of *January* in the *Texel*, when a man of war being then just ready to sail for *Enkhuisen*, I when aboard her, and lodged that night in the said city. The 18th, early in the morning I went by land over *Horn* to *Burmerent*, and from thence thro' the *Beemstes* by water to *Amsterdam*. The 20th early in in the morning, I went in the *Trackshuit* over *Harlem* to *Leyden*, and from thence to the *Hague* and *Delft*, where I delivered the letters and presents wherewith I was intrusted by his excellency the earl of *Nassaw*.

But having a longing desire to see my native countrey, I set out from *Amsterdam*, *Anno* 1641, the 14th day of *August*, and taking my way over *Harlem*, thro' *Friseland*, arrived safely at *Hamburgh* the 23d, but the roads being then much infested by straggling parties, I went up the river *Elbe* as far as *Magdeburg*, where taking coach for *Leipzick*, I continued my journey afterwards from thence to *Dresden*, the place of my nativity, where I arrived the 12th of *October*, and to our mutual joy, found my parents in good health. I stayed with them about fourteen months, but not being able to comply with their manner of living, so different from what I had been used to of late years, I took a resolution (with their consent) to return into *Holland*, and to take a voyage thence into the *East-Indies*.

Accordingly in 1642, the 10th of *February*, I took shipping upon the river *Elbe*, in company of the young Mr. *Dillichius*, and the son of the count marshal, Mr. *Henry Van Tauben*, and passing down the river *Elbe*, where my fellow travellers left me, intending to continue their journey thro' *Holland* for *France*; and the river beginning to be full of ice by this time, our vessel could not get farther than *Tangermunden*, where we were forced to stay till the 2d of *March* and then went forward (tho' not without great danger of the ice) for *Hamburgh*, where I arrived the 6th, and soon after agreed with a *Dutch* master of a vessel to carry me to *Amsterdam*. The 11th we set sail, and passing by *Gluckstadt*, came to an anchor near *Zell*, where going ashore, I diverted my self for a short time with one of my relations, and so went aboard again, and continued our voyage towards the *Dutch* coast. Our Master it seems was born in a certain village on the *Friseland* coast, called *Maccon*, and being seiz'd with a curiosity to see his birth-place, took this opportunity to come to an anchor near it, which proved so unprosperous, that in a few days after being surprised by a storm with a violent frost, I was obliged to spend thirteen days at the house of a rugged *Friseland* countrey fellow, whose language I did not understand. All the comfort I had was to take this opportuny to go to *Franeker*, an university in those parts; and after my return the tempest being laid, we set sail again the 26th, and arrived the 28th at *Enkhuisen*, where changing my vessel for another, I came the 29th early in the morning to *Amsterdam*; here I received the unwelcome news that the ships wherewith I intended to have sailed to the *East-Indies*, were already gone some days before, and that the next were not to sail till *August*; being afraid that my money would scarce hold out till that time, I was forced to take a journey into *North-Holland*, to expect the coming of their *East-India* ships, wherewith I returned afterwards. *Anno* 1642, the 10th of *May* we came to an anchor with nine ships before the *Texel*, where in two months after, we saw ten ships richly freighted, Mr. *Francis Caron* commodore, and came along with them in *August* into *Holland*.

Having in vain endeavoured, by the interest of Mr. *Beirmthellen* to get an assistants place in the chamber of *Amsterdam*, I was forced to take up with a *Cadee*'s place, at the rate of ten *guilders per* month; and being furnished with recommendatory letters to the regency of *Batavia*, I sail'd out of the *Texel* the 29th of *September*, in a new vessel call'd the *Swan*, in company of two others; and having refreshed ourselves at the *Isle of Wight*, (belonging to *England*) and in the isle of *St. Vincent*, we came in 1643, the 17th of *April*, safely to an anchor in the road of *Batavia*, having outstrip'd the two others, that were no such sailers as ours. After I had stay'd here for some time, the then governor-general *Anthony Van Diemen* removed me from the military service to an assistant's place worth 20 *guilders per* month. *Anno* 1647, the 20th of *May*, Mr. *Cornelius Vander Lyn*, his successor, bestow'd upon me one of the head clerks places worth 28 *guilders per* month, besides six *Reals* board wages: *Anno* 1648, I being then in the 35th year of my age, married at *Batavia* a certain widow born in the city of *Wesel*, named *Mary*, the relict of Mr. *Aux Brebis*, who then lived with the head factor, Mr. *James Schwern*. *Anno* 1649, the 29th of *September*, the said governor-general Mr. *Van Lyn*, was pleased to bestow upon me the employment of a factor (besides my clerks place) for five years, with a monthly salary of 56 *guilders per* month, and 13 *reals* board wages.

In what quality I first went to the East-Indies.

Anno 1650, I was sent in an open chaloop from *Batavia* to the *Streights of Sunda*, *Thys Crab* commander, to fetch certain instructions, which Mr. *Maximilian le Maire* (who was lately arrived there with the ship the *Walfisch* from *Holland*) had brought along with him; but before we reach'd the said vessel, we met the ship the *Nassaw*, coming from the western coast of *Sumatra*, loaden with pepper, and being willing to speak with them, by the carelessness of our master the chaloop run so violently against the poop of the ſhip, that it was ready to ſink; I did endeavour to lay hold of the lion's head of the great ſhip, but miſſing my aim, fell into the water, where I narrowly eſcaped being drowned; for the ſhip being under ſail, I got under her, and with much ado got upon the other ſide (yet not without being ſorely cut by the muſſel-ſhells that ſtuck to the bottom) from whence, with much ado they dragged me up with a rope into the ſhip. Afterwards it being reſolved to ſend me along with Mr. *William Verſtegen*, extraordinary councellor of the *Indies*, and commiſſary of the northern quarter, from *Tonquin* to *Taiwan*, my ſalary was raiſed to 66 *guilders per* month.

Anno 1651, the 20th of *April*, we embark'd aboard the *Delfthaven* yacht at *Batavia*, in order to proſecute this intended voyage, which having been accompliſh'd with good ſucceſs, we ſtop'd in our return near the kingdom of *Quinam*, and after having ſettled a firm peace with that king, and obtained the releaſement of our priſoners, we came to an anchor again in the road of *Batavia*, the laſt day of *December*, where in a few days after my arrival, I was conſtituted a member of the council of juſtice by Mr. *Reimerſon*, then governor-general in the abſence of Mr. *Lyn*.

Anno 1653, the 14th of *July*, the time of my former contract being expired, I engaged myſelf again in the companies ſervice for three years longer, at the rate of 85 *guilders per* month; I was ſoon after as commiſſary or envoy of the company ſent with two yachts the *Shellfiſh* and the *Brownfiſh* to *Kanton* in *China* ([a]) to endeavour the eſtabliſhment of a free commerce for our company there, with the *Tartarian* viceroy; but the *Tartarian* commanders aiming at nothing but our money, and little to be relied upon, I left theſe covetous wretches, and made the beſt of my way with my two yachts towards *Tonquin*, where having left the *Brownfiſh* to refit, I returned, notwithſtanding I was very dangerouſly ill, with the *Shellfiſh* alone the 29th of *December* to *Batavia*. Having immediately after my recovery, given an account of my negotiation, I had ſoon after a place aſſign'd me in the council of juſtice.

Anno 1656, the 12th of *July*, I was ſent in the quality of director in the ſhip call'd the *Calf* to *Japan*, ([b]) to relieve according to cuſtom, Mr. *John Brichlinus*, his year being expired; where I arrived the 18th of *Auguſt*, and immediately delivered the preſents ſent by the company to the emperor; but had ſcarce been here three days when on the north-ſide of the capital city of *Jedo*, a ſudden fire broke out, which being increaſed by a violent wind, laid not only the whole city (which might for its bigneſs be compared to a whole province) in aſhes in 48 hours, but alſo conſumed the royal palace and near 160000 ſouls; however we had the fortune to eſcape the fury of the flames thro' God's mercy, tho' not without a great deal of danger.

Anno 1657, the 27th of *October*, I returned out of *Japan* ([c]) in the ſhip the *Flower-Valley*, in company of the head factor, Mr. *John Betgens*, who had received orders to go and reſide at *Tajoan* in the quality of deputy-governor to Mr. *Coyets*; we were put to no ſmall trouble to get into the road of that place, where having ſtay'd ſix days, I ſet ſail again thence, in company of the *Hercules* and the *Watchman*, and came ſafely before *Batavia* the 18th of *December*, where we found ſeveral *Dutch* ſhips (which on the 31ſt returned for *Holland*, under the command of Mr. *John Canæus*) riding at anchor.

Anno 1658, being ready to go a ſecond

([a]) Of this voyage *Nieuhoff p.* 29. Hereupon it was reſolved to ſend as commiſſioners Mr. *Schedal* and Mr. *Wagener*, the firſt in the *Brownfiſh*, the other in a veſſel call'd the *Shellfiſh*. They ſet ſail together from *Batavia*, and after a voyage of four weeks, came to the weſtern point of *Haitamon*. From whence they went up the river *Kanton*, as far as *Wangſoe*, three leagues diſtance from *Kanton*, where having ſtaid for ſome time, but in vain, in expectation of the *Mandarins* to conduct them to *Kanton*; Mr. *Schedel*, without leave from the regency of *Kanton*, and againſt the advice of the interpreters, went to ſee his old friend *Haitau*, in whom he much confided; being directed by him to go to ſee *Tautans*, he did accordingly, but finding neither him nor his ſecretary at home, was forced to come aboard again immediately, as not knowing where to lodge all that night.

The ſame *Nieuhoff p.* 32. Mr. *Wagener* finding all his courtſhips to the *Mandarins* of no effect, he returned with both the yachts to *Batavia*, he having not with all his cunning, been able to ſettle a commerce there for his countreymen: What vexed him moſt was, that theſe avaricious wretches had the impudence to demand ſo vaſt a ſum of money, only to procure the reception of his letters, by the viceroy, without the leaſt promiſe of entring afterwards into a conference upon the propoſed commerce.

([b]) Concerning this commiſſion, *Arnold Montan* ſays, *p.* 356. Next to this the embaſſy performed by Mr. *Zachary* of *Miſnia*, is no leſs remarkable; and *p.* 369. ſpeaking of this conflagration: Mr. *Wagener* returning early in the morning into the city, found the whole ſouthern part of it in a flame; About noon the fire got into the imperial palace, with ſuch violence, that in an inſtant the ſtrong towers and ſtone watch-houſes were ſeen tumbling into the ditch, where the fire ſtop'd on that ſide; but continuing on the other hand, the emperor's lodgings were conſumed before the night, he having ſcarce time given him to retire with his chief councellors to their ſummer-houſes, built on the north-ſide at ſome diſtance from the palace; in ſhort, in two days time above 100000 houſes were laid in aſhes, inhabited before the fire by 1000000 of ſouls, together with a vaſt number of moſt ſtately palaces, and pagodes or pagan temples.

([c]) The ſame *Montan*, *p.* 377. In the mean while Mr. *Wagener* taking a ſhort voyage to *Batavia*, ſoon returned to prepare for his ſecond intended embaſſy to *Japan*. *Anno* 1659, he had made all the neceſſary preparations for it.

time

time as director to *Japan*, to take care of the company's intereſt there, Mr. *John Maetzucker*, who ſucceeded Mr. *Reymers* as governor-general, was pleaſed to appoint me 100 *guilders per* month, without any limited time; I embark'd immediately after aboard the ſhip call'd the *Venenburgh* at *Batavia*, and ſet forward with a proſperous gale till *Auguſt*, when being among the *Maccauſche* iſlands upon the *Chineſe* coaſt, we were overtaken by ſo violent a tempeſt, that we expected every moment to be daſhed againſt the rocks, but thro' God's mercy this ſtorm laſted not above twelve hours; after which the wind proving pretty favourable, we continued our voyage, and the 17th of *September* arrived ſafely in the bay of *Nangaſacka*. Our commerce in *Japan* being eſtabliſh'd upon a good foot, and all other matters ſettled to our ſatisfaction, I began to prepare for my return to *Batavia*; and in 1659, ſet ſail in the ſhip called the *Haverſen*, from the bay of *Nangaſacki*; but the maſter of our veſſel being not well acquainted in thoſe ſeas, we got one night among the rocks *de Paraelles* (a branch of the ſea, formerly part of the continent, but ſwallow'd up by the waves) I was no ſooner awake the next morning, but ſeeing ourſelves among theſe rocks, and that we had miſſed the entrance of the *Streight of Banca*, I gave myſelf over for loſt, and certainly had been ſo, if by the indefatigable labour of the ſeamen, and a favourable gale, we had not made ſhift to get the 20th of *December* into the harbour call'd *Pauloſingen*, where we were forced to ſtay four days before we could get out to make the ſaid ſtreight, from whence we ſailed without any ſiniſter accident to *Batavia*.

Anno 1660, the 22d of *Auguſt*, Mr. *Jacob Carack*, and I were ſent as commiſſioners to *Macaſſar* in the *Poſtilion* yacht, to treat with the king concerning a peace, purſuant to the inſtructions given us for that-purpoſe.

The 12th of *November* I returned alone in the ſame veſſel, in order to give an account of my negotiation there, Mr. *Carack* being obliged to ſtay behind about ſome buſineſs of moment in our fortreſs of *Pannebolla*.

In the beginning of the year 1661, being without employment, I thought fit to accept of the ſurveyorſhip over the buildings, vacant by the death of Mr. *John Liſtingen*, whereby I a third time obtained a place in the council of juſtice; but finding this office too burthenſome for my gouty carcaſs, which was not able to endure ſuch continual going from place to place, I quitted that employment, and in lieu thereof was ordered to relieve the commander in chief on the *Cape of Good-Hope*, Mr. *John Van Riebeck*, who was to have been ſucceeded by Mr. *Gent Van Hoom*, but he dying in his voyage thither, I was pitch'd upon to ſupply his place. Accordingly I left *Batavia Anno* 1662, the 30th of *January*, with all my family, and with two ſhips in ſixteen days time, with a proſperous gale, came in ſight of the cape or utmoſt point of *Africa*. As I was entring the bay, we heard the unwelcome news, that of the ſeven ſhips we ſaw at anchor before *Batavia*, and parted thence about a month before us, four were loſt in a ſtorm near the iſland of St. *Maurice*.

Anno 1663, in *February* I received letters out of *Holland* from the governors of the company, wherein they not only confirm'd me in my governors place here, but alſo appointed me the ſame allowance my predeceſſor had enjoy'd.

Anno 1664, being advertiſed by ſeveral letters ſent to me over land from the bay of *St. Helens*, by captain *Henry Van Wallen*, intimating that a conſpiracy had been diſcovered in the ſhip call'd the *Arms of Horn*, and that he had been obliged to take into cuſtody the maſter of the ſhip and another officer; I embark'd the next day with three horſes, aboard the ſhip called the *Watercock*, but not being able to go beyond the cape of *Satannia*, I landed there, with two ſervants on horſe-back, continued my journey thither by land; but were no ſooner arrived there, when being inform'd by the *Hottentots* (inhabitants of the cape) that the ſaid ſhip was ſailed thence the day before towards the cape; we were forced to make the beſt of our way back to the bay of *Satanbia*, where we arrived the 3d day, but to our great regret, found that the captain had again quitted his firſt ſtation there, and was gone up two leagues farther into the bay; ſo that we ſaw ourſelves under an abſolute neceſſity to take up our reſting place all that night upon the ground near the ſea-ſhore but were not a little ſurpriſed, when the next morning we diſcovered in the land the foot-ſteps of a great lion that had paſſed but a few paces from us, without doing us any harm.

After my return to the cape, *viz. Anno* 1666, my wife, after a month's ſickneſs, departed this life, after I had lived with her in marriage 18 years and four months, but had no children by her; I ordered a ſmall chapel to be built on the cape, wherein ſhe was interred. Not many months after, *viz.* the 16th of *September* Mr. *Cornelius Van Qualbergen*, who was ſent in the ſhip the *Dordrecht* to ſucceed me in my command,

mand, arrived at last on the cape, after a most tedious and troublesome voyage of eight months, in which they had lost 190 men by the scurvy and other distempers. Having pursuant to the orders sent me by the council of seventeen, given the said Mr. *Qualbergen*, all the necessary instructions, and surrendered the government into his hands, I embark'd with all my moveables the 1st of *October*, in the beforementioned ship the *Dordrecht*, together with my daughter-in-law, whose name was *Mary Bucqui*, the relict of *Cornelius Vorburgh*, one of the head factors of the company, and with a very moderate and prosperous wind, arrived safely at *Batavia*, where being lodged at Mr. *John Bolan*'s house, she and I shared the inheritance of her mother, according to the determination of two arbitrators chosen for that purpose.

Anno 1667, the 1st of *September* I embark'd at *Batavia* in the ship called the *Erasmus*, being sent as an envoy of the companies to the emperor of great *Java* or of *Materan*, with two very fine *Persian* horses, besides other presents to renew the ancient friendship, and good neighbourly correspondency betwixt them; we came to an anchor near the river *Samaran*, where leaving our ship, we travell'd in six or seven days to the capital city *Materan*, where having discharged my commission, I return'd from thence by land, with a numerous attendance to *Samaran*, and from thence set sail towards *Japan*, where having stayed a few days to dispatch some business of moment, we embarked, and arrived the last day of *November*, with the same yacht, we came in from *Batavia* in that road, where I gave an ample account of my transactions to the great council of the *Indies*.

Having by this time spent twenty five years in the *East-India* company's service, I took a full resolution to return to my native countrey, for which reason having desired my discharge from the just now mentioned council, the governor-general, Mr. *Maetzucker*, would fain have prevailed upon me to continue there for some time longer, offering me his garden-house without the gate of *Batavia* for my habitation.

But being resolved to return to my native countrey, I was forced to refuse his kind offer, and having obtained my passport, I left *Batavia* in 1667, the 8th of *December*, with a squadron of six ships, whereof *John Vander Lahn* was admiral, and my self carrying the vice-admiral's flag aboard the ship call'd the *Arms*, bound for *Middleburg* on account of the chamber of *Zealand*. Having happily pass'd the *Streights of Sunda*, we arrived *Anno* 1668, the 22d of *February*, with fair wind and weather, in the *Table-Bay* of the *cape of Good-Hope*, where to our great satisfaction we received the news of the late concluded peace betwixt his *Britannick* majesty and the states-general at *Breda*.

Whilst we lay at anchor here, four more ships that were left behind at *Batavia* to take in their cargo, arrived likewise in the said bay the 10th of *March*; as also not long after, the ship called *Thuys de Telsen*, being sent from the chamber of *Amsterdam*, having aboard fourteen conspirators, (for the most part northern country men) who had laid a plot to kill the captain and the other officers of their ship, whilst they were at dinner, and afterwards to seize the vessel; five of the ringleaders of them were sentenced to be hanged on a gibbet near the fort; seven others to be whip'd and burn'd with a red hot iron, and the rest to be kept in irons for their life-time, and to work in such places as should be appointed by the company, which was put in execution accordingly. *Anno* 1668, the 26th of *March* we set sail from the *Table-Bay* with the whole fleet, consisting of ten ships richly laden, *viz.* the *Holland Hayn*, the *Arms of Middleburgh*, the *Dordrecht*, *Liberty*, *Amerongen*, *Cattenburgh*, the *Sprecaw*, *Outshorn*, the *Tiger* and the *Young Prince*; and taking our course betwixt the continent and the *Red-Island*, passed the *Green-Sea*, and so with a prosperous gale continued our voyage till the month of *July*, when we arrived happily in *Holland*.

N. B. *Mr.* Zachary Wagener, *being in the month of* July *arrived with ten ships as vice-admiral in* Zealand, *found himself so much indisposed, that after some stay at* Middleburgh, *he thought fit to go to* Amsterdam, *to take the advice of the physicians of that city; and having accordingly taken up his quarters at the sign of the city of* Prague, *in the* Warmer-street, *nothing was left unattempted to remove the indisposition of his body; which notwithstanding all the endeavours of the best physicians not availing, he died the 1st of* October 1668, *and was inter'd the 6th following, in the* Old Church *of* Amsterdam. *He was then 54 years old and four months, the greatest part of which he had spent in travelling by sea and land; having spent seven years in* Brasil, *and served the* Dutch East-India *company no less than 25 years.*

THE

THE

HISTORY

OF THE

Life and Actions

OF

Adm. *CHRISTOPHER COLUMBUS*,

AND OF HIS

DISCOVERY

OF THE

WEST-INDIES,

CALL'D

The NEW WORLD,

Now in Possession of his Catholick Majesty.

Written by his own Son D. Ferdinand Columbus.

THE

Author's Preface.

I Being the son of the admiral Christopher Columbus, *a person worthy of eternal memory, who discovered the* West-Indies; *and having myself sail'd with him some time, it seem'd to me but reasonable, that among other things I have writ, one and the chiefest should be his life, and wonderful discovery of the* West-Indies, *or* New-World; *because his great and continual sufferings, and the distempers he laboured under, did not allow him time to form his notes and observations into a method fit for history; yet knowing there were many others who had attempted this work, I forebore, till reading their books I found in them, that which is usual among historians,* viz. *that they magnify some things, lessen others, and sometimes pass that over in silence, which they ought to give a very particular account of. For this reason I resolved to undergo the labour of this task, thinking it better I should lie under the censure my skill and presumption shall be subject to, than to suffer the truth of what relates to so noble a person to lie buried in oblivion. For it is my comfort, that if any fault be found in this my undertaking, it will not be that, which most historians are liable to,* viz. *that they know not the truth of what they write; for I promise to compose the history of his life of such matter only as I find in his own papers and letters, and of those passages of which I myself was an eye-witness. And whosoever shall imagine, that I add any thing of my own, may be assured I am satisfied, I can reap no benefit thereby in the life to come; and that the reader alone will have the benefit of it, if it be capable of yielding any.*

The author having given this account of himself, I have not much to add, but to inform the reader before he enters upon the work, that in it he will find all the reasons which induced the admiral to such an undertaking; he will see how far he proceeded in person upon the discovery in four several voyages he made; how great and honourable the articles were, upon which he entered upon the discovery, and which were afterwards confirm'd to him by those two famous princes, king Ferdinand *and queen* Isabel *or* Elizabeth; *how basely they were all violated; and he, after such unparalleled services, most inhumanly treated; how far he settled the affairs of the island* Hispaniola, *the first place the* Spaniards *planted in; what care he took that the* Indians *should not be oppress'd, but rather by good usage and example, prevail'd upon to embrace the* Catholick *faith; also the customs and manners of the* Indians; *their opinions and practice as to religious worship; and in a word, all that can be expected in a work of this nature, the foundation whereof was laid by so great a man as was the admiral, and finished by his own son, who had all the education that could contribute to make him capable of writing so notable a life.*

THE

THE DISCOVERY OF THE *WEST-INDIES*, BY *CHRISTOPHER COLUMBUS*,

Together with his

LIFE and ACTIONS, *&c.*

CHAP. I.

Of the country, original, and name of admiral Christopher Columbus.

Columbus's *original.*

IT being a very material point in the history of any man of note, to make known his countrey and original, because they are best look'd upon, who are born in noble cities and of illustrious parents; therefore some would have had me spent my time in shewing that the admiral was honourably descended, tho' his parents, thro' the peevishness of fortune, were fallen into great poverty and want; and that I should have proved they were the offspring of that *Junius Colon*, of whom *Tacitus* in his 12th book says, That he brought king *Mithridates* prisoner to *Rome*; for which service the people assign'd him the consular dignity, the eagle or standard and consular court. And they would have me give a large account of those two illustrious *Coloni*, his predecessors, who, *Sabellicus* tells us, gained a mighty victory over the *Venetians*, as shall be mention'd in the 5th chapter: But I refused to undertake that task, believing he was particularly chosen by Almighty God for so great an affair as that was he performed; and because he was to be so truly his apostle as in effect he proved it was his will he should in this part be like the others, who were called to make known his name from the sea and rivers, and not from courts and palaces, and to imitate himself, whose progenitors being of the blood royal of *Jerusalem*, yet it pleased him that his parents should not be much known. Therefore, as God gave him all the personal qualities for such an undertaking, so he would have his countrey and original more hid and obscure. So it is that some, who would cast a cloud upon his fame, say he was of *Nervi*, others of *Cugureo*, and others of *Bugiesco*, all small towns near the city of *Genoa*, and upon its coast. Others, who were for exalting of him say, he was a native of *Savona*, others of *Genoa*; others more vain, make him of *Piacenza*, in which city there are some honourable persons of his family, and tombs with the arms and inscriptions of the family of *Columbus*; this being then the usual surname of his predecessors; tho' he complying with the

His Name.

the countrey whither he went to live, and begin a new state of life, modelled the word, that it might be like the ancient, and distinguished the direct from the colateral line, calling himself *Colon.* This made me apt to believe, that as most of his affairs were guarded by some special providence, so this very particular, concerning his name and surname, was not without some mystery. We may instance many names which were given by secret impulse, to denote the effects those persons were to produce, as in his is foretold and expressed the wonder he performed. For if we look upon the common surname of his ancestors, we may say he was true *Columbus* or *Columba*, for as much as he convey'd the grace of the Holy Ghost into that new world which he discovered, shewing those people who knew him not, which was God's beloved son, as the Holy Ghost did in the figure of a dove at St. *John*'s baptism; and because he also carried the olive branch and oil of baptism over the waters of the ocean, like *Noah*'s dove, to denote the peace and union of those people with the church, after they had been shut up in the ark of darkness and confusion. And the surname of *Colon* which he reviv'd, was proper to him, which in *Greek* signifies a member, that his proper name being *Christopher*, it might be known he was a member of Christ, by whom salvation was to be convey'd to those people. Moreover, if we would bring his name to the *Latin* pronunciation, that is *Christophorus Colonus*; we may say, that as St. *Christopher* is reported to have bore that name, because he carried Christ over the deep waters, with great danger to himself, whence came the denomination of *Christopher*; and as he convey'd over the people whom no other could have been able to carry; so the admiral, *Christophorus Colonus*, imploring the assistance of Christ in that dangerous passage, went over safe himself and his company, that those *Indian* nations might become citizens and inhabitants of the church triumphant in heaven; for it is to be believ'd, that many souls, which the devil expected to make a prey of, had they not pass'd through the water of baptism, were by him made inhabitants and dwellers in the eternal glory of heaven.

CHAP. II.

Of the admiral's father and mother, and their quality, and of the false account one Justiniani *gives of his employ, before he had the title of admiral*

No certainty of Columbus's *parentage.*

NOT to go upon the etymology, derivation and meaning of the word admiral; but to return to the quality and persons of his progenitors; I say, that how considerable soever they were, being reduced to poverty and want by the wars and factions in *Lombardy*; I do not find after what manner they lived, tho' the admiral himself in a letter says, that his ancestors and he always traded by sea. For my farther information in this particular, as I passed thro' *Cugureo*, I endeavoured to receive some information from two brothers of the *Columbi*, who were the richest in those parts, and reported to be somewhat a kin to him; but the youngest of them being above 100 years old, they could give me no account of this affair. Nor do I think that this is any dishonour to us who descend from him, because I think it better that all the honour be deriv'd to us from his person, than to go about to enquire whether his father was a merchant or a man of quality, that kept his hawks and hounds; whereas it is certain there have been a thousand such in all parts, whose memory was utterly lost in a very short time among their neighbours and kindred, so as it is not known whether there ever were any such men. But I am of opinion that their nobility can add less lustre to me, than the honour I receive from such a father. And since his own honourable exploits made him not stand in need of the wealth of his predecessors, (who notwithstanding their poverty, were not destitute of virtue, but only of fortune) he ought at least by his name and worth, to have been raised by authors above the rank of mechanicks and handicrafts. Which yet, if any will affirm, grounding his assertion on what one *Augustin Justiniani* writes in his chronicle; I say, that I will not set my self to deny it, begging time or means to prove the contrary by testimonials; for as much as *Justiniani*'s writing it does not make that to be look'd upon as an article of faith, which is no longer in the memory of man; so neither will it be thought undeniable, should I say I received the contrary from a thousand persons. Nor will I show his falsehood by the histories others have

Falshood of Justiniani's *history.*

have writ of *Christopher Columbus*, but by this same author's testimony, and writing, in whom is verified the proverb; *that lyers ought to have good memories*, because otherwise they contradict themselves, as *Justiniani* did in this case; saying in his comparison of the four languages, upon that expression of the psalm, *in omnem terram exivit sonus eorum*, these very words. This *Christopher Columbus* having in his tender years attain'd some elements of learning, when he came to manly years, applied himself to the art of navigation, and went to *Lisbon* in *Portugal*, where he learn'd cosmography, taught him by a brother of his who there made sea charts; with which improvement, and discoursing with those that sail'd to *S. George de la Mira* in *Africk*, and his own reading in cosmography, he entertain'd thoughts of sailing to those countries he discover'd. By which words it appears, that he follow'd no mechanick employment, or handicraft; since, he says, he employed his childhood in learning; his youth in navigation and cosmography, and his riper years in discoveries. Thus *Justiniani* convinces himself of falshood, and proves himself an inconsiderate, rash, and malitious countryman; for when he speaks of a renowned person who did so much honour to his country, whose historiographer *Justiniani* made himself, tho' the admiral's parents had been very mean, it had been more decent, to speak of his origin, as other authors in the like case do; saying he was of low parentage, or come of very poor friends, than to use injurious words, as he did in his psalter; and afterwards in his chronicle, falsly calling him a mechanick. And supposing he had not contradicted himself, reason it self made it appear, that a man, who had been employed in art manual or handicraft, must be born and grow old in it to become a perfect master; and that he would not from his youth have travelled so many countries, as also that he would not have attained so much learning and knowledge, as his actions demonstrate he had, especially in those four principal sciences required, to perform what he did, which are, astrology, cosmography, geometry and navigation. But it is no wonder that *Justiniani* should dare to deliver an untruth in this particular, which is hidden, since in affairs well known concerning his discovery and navigation, he has inserted above a dozen falshoods in half a sheet of paper in his psalter, which I shall briefly hint at without staying to give him an answer, to avoid interrupting the series of the history, since by the very course of it, and what others have writ on that subject, the falshood of his writing will be made out. The first therefore was, that the admiral went to *Lisbon* to learn cosmography of a brother of his own that was there; which is quite contrary, because he liv'd in that city before, and taught his brother what he knew. The second falshood is, that at his first coming into *Castile*, their catholick majesties *Ferdinand*, and *Isabel*, or *Elizabeth* accepted of his proposal, after it had been seven years bandy'd about and rejected by all men. The third, that he set out to discover with two ships, which is not true, for he had three caravals. The fourth, that his first discovery was *Hispaniola*, and it was *Guarabani*, which the admiral called *S. Salvador*, or *S. Saviour*. The fifth, that the said island *Hispaniola* was inhabited by *Canibals*, that eat men's flesh; and the truth is, the inhabitants of it were the best people, and most civiliz'd of any in those parts. The sixth, that he took by force of arms, the canoo, or *Indian* boat he saw, whereas it appears that he had no war that first voyage with any *Indian*, and continued in peace and amity with them till the day of his departure from *Hispaniola*. The seventh, that he return'd by way of the *Canary* islands, which is not the proper way for those vessels to return. The eighth, that from the said island he dispatch'd a messenger to their majesties aforesaid, whereas it is certain, that he was not first at that island, as was observ'd, and he himself was the messenger. The ninth, that the second voyage he return'd with twelve ships, and it is manifest he had seventeen. The tenth, that he arrived at *Hispaniola* in twenty days, which is a very short time to reach the nearest islands, and he perform'd it not in two months, and went to others much farther distant. The eleventh, that he presently made from *Hispaniola* with two ships; and it is known there were three he took to go from *Hispaniola* to *Cuba*. *Justiniani's* twelfth falshood is, That *Hispaniola* is four hours distant from *Spain*, and the admiral reckons it above five. And farther, to add a thirteenth to the dozen, he says, the western point of *Cuba*, is six hours distant from *Hispaniola*, making it further from *Hispaniola* to *Cuba*, than from *Spain* to *Hispaniola*. So that by his negligence and heedlessness, in being well inform'd and writing the truth of these particulars, which are so plain, we may plainly discern what inquiry he made into that which was so obscure, wherein he contradicts himself, as has been made appear. But laying aside this controversy, wherewith I believe I have by this time tired the reader, we will only add, that

that considering the many mistakes and falshoods found in the said *Justiniani*'s history, and psalter, the senate of *Genoa* has laid a penalty upon any person that shall read or keep it; and has caus'd it to be carefully sought out in all places it has been sent to, that it may by publick decree be destroy'd and utterly extinguish'd. I will return to our main design, concluding with this assertion, that the admiral was a man of learning and great experience; that he did not employ his time in handicraft or mechanick exercises, but in such as became the grandeur and renown of his wonderful exploits, and will conclude this chapter with some words taken out of a letter he writ himself to prince *John* of *Castile*'s nurse, which are these.

I am not the first admiral of my family, let them give me what name they please; for when all is done, David, *that most prudent King, was first a shepherd, and afterwards chosen king of* Jerusalem, *and I am servant to that same Lord, who rais'd him to such dignity.*

CHAP. III.

Of the admiral's person, and what sciences he learn'd.

The admiral describ'd.

THE admiral was well shap'd, and of a more than middling stature, long visag'd, his cheeks somewhat full, yet neither fat nor lean; he had a hawk nose, his eyes white, his complexion white, with a lovely red: In his youth his hair was fair, but when he came to thirty years of age, it all turn'd grey. He was always modest and sparing in his eating, drinking, and his dress. Among strangers he was affable, and pleasant among his domesticks, yet with modesty and an easy gravity. He was so strict in religious matters, that for fasting and saying all the divine office, he might be thought profest in some religious order. So great was his aversion to swearing and cursing, that I protest I never heard him swear any other oath, but by *S. Ferdinand*; and when in the greatest passion with any body, he would vent his spleen by saying, *God take you for doing or saying so.* When he was to write, his way of trying his pen was by writing these words, *Jesus cum Maria sit nobis in via*, and that in such a character, as might very well serve to get his bread. But passing by other particulars of his actions and manners, which may be mention'd at their proper time in the course of this history; let us proceed to give an account to what science he most addicted himself. In his tender years he apply'd himself so much to study at *Pavia*, as was sufficient to understand cosmography; to which sort of reading he was much addicted, for which reason he also apply'd himself to astrology and geometry, because these sciences are so link'd together, that the one cannot subsist without the other: And because *Ptolemy* in the beginning of his cosmography, says, that no man can be a good cosmographer unless he be a painter too; therefore he learn'd to draw, in order to describe lands, and set down cosmographical bodies, plains or rounds.

CHAP. IV.

How the admiral employ'd himself before he came into Spain.

Testimonies out of Columbus's *own writings.*

THE admiral having gain'd some insight in sciences, began to apply himself to the sea, and made some voyages to the east and west; of which and many other things of those his first days, I have no perfect knowledge, because he died at such time as I being confin'd by filial duty, had not the boldness to ask him to give an account of things; or to speak the truth, being but young, I was at that time far from being troubled with such thoughts. But in a letter writ by him in the year 1501, to their catholick majesties, to whom he durst not have writ any thing but the truth; he has these following words.

Most serene princes, "I went to sea very "young, and have continued it to this day; "and this art inclines those that follow it, to "be desirous to discover the secrets of this "world; it is now forty years that I have "been sailing to all those parts, at present "frequented; and I have dealt and conversed with wise people, as well clergy "as laity, *Latins*, *Greeks*, *Indians* and "*Moors*, and many others of other sects; "and our Lord has been favourable to this

" my inclination, and I have received of " him the ſpirit of underſtanding: He has " made me very ſkilfull in navigation, " knowing enough in aſtrology, and ſo " in geometry and arithmetick. God hath " given me a genius and hands apt to " draw this globe, and on it the cities, ri- " vers, iſlands and ports, all in their pro- " per places. During this time I have ſeen, " and endeavoured to ſee, all books of coſ- " mography, hiſtory and philoſophy, and " of other ſciences; ſo that our Lord has " ſenſibly opened my underſtanding, to the " end I may ſail from hence to the *Indies*, " and made me moſt willing to put this in " execution. Fill'd with this deſire, I came " to your highneſſes. All that heard of my " undertaking, rejected it with contempt " and ſcorn. In your highneſſes alone, " faith and conſtancy had their ſeat". In another letter written from *Hiſpaniola*, in *January* 1495, to their catholick majeſties, telling them the errors and miſtakes commonly made in voyages and piloting; he ſays thus, " It happened to me that king " *Renee*, whom God has taken to himſelf, " ſent to me to *Tunis* to take the galeaſſe " call'd *Fernandina*; and being near to the " iſland of *St. Peter* by *Sardinia*, I was told " there were two ſhips and a barack with " the ſaid galeaſſe, which diſcompos'd " my men, and they reſolved to go no far- " ther, but to return to *Marſeilles* for ano- " ther ſhip and more men; and I perceiv- " ing there was no going againſt their wills, " without ſome contrivance, yielded to their " deſires, and changing the point of the " needle, ſet ſail when it was late, and next " morning at break of day, we found our " ſelves near cape *Cartegna*, all aboard " thinking we had certainly been ſailing for " *Marſeilles*." In the ſame manner in a *Memorandum*, or obſervation he made to ſhow, that all the five zones are habitable, and proving it by experience in navigation, he ſays, " In *February* 1467, I ſail'd my ſelf " an hundred leagues beyond *Thule*, *Iſeland*, " whoſe northern part is 73 degrees diſtant " from the equinoctial, and not 63 degrees " as ſome will have it to be; nor does it lie " upon the line where *Ptolemy*'s weſt begins, " but much more to the weſtward; and to " this iſland which is as big as *England*, the " *Engliſh* trade, eſpecially from *Briſtol*. At " the time when I was there, the ſea was " not frozen, but the tides were ſo great, " that in ſome places it ſwell'd 26 fathoms, " and fell as much." The truth is, That the *Thule Ptolemy* ſpeaks of, lies where he ſays, and this by the moderns is call'd *Frizeland*. And then to prove that the equinoctial or land under it is habitable, he ſays, " I was in the fort of St. *George de la Mira* " belonging to the king of *Portugal*, which " lies under the equinoctial, and I am a wit- " neſs that 'tis not uninhabitable, as ſome " would have it." And in his book of his firſt voyage, he ſays, " He ſaw ſome mer- " maids on the coaſt of *Menegueta*, but that " they are not ſo like ladies, as they are " painted." And in another place he ſays, " I obſerved ſeveral times in ſailing " from *Liſbon* to *Guinea*, that a degree on " the earth, anſwers to 56 miles and two " thirds." And farther he adds, " That " in *Scio*, an iſland of the *Archipelago*, he " ſaw maſtick drawn from ſome trees." In another place he ſays, " I was upon the ſea " 23 years, without being off it any time " worth the ſpeaking of; and I ſaw all the " eaſt and all the weſt, and may ſay towards " the north, or *England*, and have been at " *Guinea*; yet I never ſaw harbours for " goodneſs, like thoſe of the *Weſt-Indies*." And a little farther he ſays, " That he took " to the ſea at 14 years of age, and ever " after follow'd it." And in the book of the ſecond voyage, he ſays, " I had got " two ſhips, and left one of them at *Porto* " *Santo*, for a certain reaſon that occurr'd " to me, where ſhe continued one day, " and the next day after I join'd it at " *Liſbon*, becauſe I light of a ſtorm and " contrary winds at ſouth-weſt, and ſhe had " but little wind at north-eaſt, which was " contrary." So that from theſe inſtances we may gather, how much experience he had in ſea affairs, and how many countries and places he travell'd before he undertook his diſcovery.

CHAP.

CHAP. V.

The admiral's coming into Spain, *and how he made himself known in* Portugal, *which was the cause of his discovering the* West-Indies.

Another Columbus.

AS concerning the cause of the admiral's coming into *Spain*, and his being addicted to sea-affairs, the occasion of it was a famous man, of his name and family, call'd *Columbus*, renown'd upon the sea, on account of the fleet he commanded against infidels, and even in his own country, insomuch that they made use of his name to frighten the children in the cradle; whose person and fleet, it is likely were very considerable, because he at once took four *Venetian* galleys, whose bigness and strength I should not have believ'd, had I not seen them fitted out. This man was call'd *Columbus the Young*, to distinguish him from another, who was a great seaman before him. Of which *Columbus the Younger*, *Marc Antony Sabellicus*, the *Livy* of our age, says in the eighth book of his tenth decade, That he lived near the time when *Maximilian*, son to the emperor *Frederick* the 3d, was chosen king of the *Romans*: *Jerome Donato* was sent embassador from *Venice* into *Portugal*, to return thanks in the name of the republick to king *John* the 2d, because he had cloathed and relieved all the crew belonging to the aforesaid great galleys, which were coming from *Flanders*, relieving them in such a manner, as they were enabled to return to *Venice*, they having been overcome by the famous Corsair *Columbus the Younger*, near *Lisbon*, who had strip'd and turn'd them ashoar. Which authority of so grave an author as *Sabellicus*, may make us sensible of the afore-mention'd *Justiniani*'s malice, since in his history he made no mention of this particular, to the end it might not appear, that the family of *Columbus* was less obscure than he would make it. And if he did it thro' ignorance, he is nevertheless to blame; for undertaking to write the history of his country, and omitting so remarkable a victory, of which its enemies themselves make mention. For the historian, our adversary, makes so great account of his victory, that he says, ambassadors were sent on that account to the king of *Portugal*. Which same author in the afore-mentioned eighth book, somewhat further, as one less obliged to inquire into the admiral's discovery, makes mention of it, without adding those twelve lyes which *Justiniani* inserted. But to return to the matter in hand, I say, That whilst the admiral sail'd with the aforesaid *Columbus the Younger*, which was a long time; it fell out that understanding the before-mentioned four great *Venetian* galleys were coming from *Flanders*, they went out to seek, and found them beyond *Lisbon*, about Cape *St. Vincent*, which is in *Portugal*, where falling to blows, they fought furiously, and grappled, beating one another from vessel to vessel with the utmost rage, making use, not only of their weapons, but artificial fire-works; so that after they had fought from morning till evening, and abundance were kill'd on both sides; the admiral's ship took fire, as did a great *Venetian* galley, which being fast grappled together with iron hooks and chains, used to this purpose by sea-faring men, could neither of them be relieved, because of the confusion there was among them, and the fright of the fire, which in a short time was so increased, that there was no other remedy, but for all that could, to leap into the water, so to die sooner, rather than bear the torture of the fire. But the admiral being an excellent swimmer, and seeing himself two leagues or a little further from land, laying hold of an oar, which good fortune offered him, and sometimes resting upon it, sometimes swimming, it pleased God, who had preserved him for greater ends, to give him strength to get to shore; but so tired and spent with the water, that he had much ado to recover himself. And because it was not far from *Lisbon*, where he knew there were many *Genoeses* his countrymen, he went away thither as fast as he could, where being known by them he was so courteously received and entertain'd, that he set up house and marry'd a wife in that city. And forasmuch as he behav'd himself honourably, and was a man of a comely presence, and did nothing but what was just; it happened that a lady whose name was *Donna Felipa Moniz*, of a good family and pensioner in the monastery of all saints, whither the admiral used to go to mass, was so taken with him, that she became his wife. His father-in-law *Peter Moniz Perestrello*, being dead, they went to live with the mother-in-law, where being together, and she seeing him so much addicted to cosmography, told him that her husband *Perestrello* had been a a great sea-faring man, and that he with two other captains having obtained the king of *Portugal*'s leave, went to make discoveries

The admiral serves under him.

Comes to Lisbon *and marries.*

coveries, upon condition, that dividing what they found into three parts they were to cast lots who should chuse first. Being thus agreed, they sail'd away to the south-west, and arriv'd at the island of *Madera* and *Porto Santo*, places never before discovered. And because the island of *Madera* was biggest; they divided it into two parts; the island of *Porto Santo*, being the 3d which fell to the lot of the said *Perestrello*, *Columbus*'s father-in-law, who had the government of it till he died.

The admiral bring much delighted to hear such voyages and relations, his mother-in-law gave him the journals and sea charts left her by her husband, which still more inflam'd the admiral; and he enquired into the other voyages the *Portugueses* then made to *St. George de la Mira*, and along the coast of *Guinea*, being much pleased to discourse with those that had failed thither. To say the truth, I can not certainly tell whether whilst this wife lived, the admiral went to *Mira* or *Guinea*, as I said above, the reason seems to require it. However it was, as one thing leads to another, and one consideration to another, so whilst he was in *Portugal*, he began to reflect, that as the *Portugueses* travel so far southward, it were no less proper to sail away westward, and land might in reason be found that way. That he might be the more certain and confident in this particular, he began to look over all the cosmographers again, whom he had read before, and to observe what astrological reasons would corroborate this project; and therefore he took notice of what any persons whatsoever spoke to that purpose, and of sailors particularly, which might any way be a help to him. Of all which things he made such good use, that he concluded for certain, that there were many lands west of the *Canary* islands, and *Cabo Verde*; and that it was possible to sail to, and discover them. But that it may appear from what mean arguments he came to deduce, or make out so vast an undertaking, and to satisfy many who are desirous to know particularly, what motives induced him to discover these countries, and expose himself in so dangerous an undertaking, I will here set down what I have found in his papers relating to this affair.

CHAP. VI.

The principal motives that inclin'd the admiral to believe he might discover the West-Indies.

Three reasons for the discovery.

BEING about to deliver the motives that inclin'd the admiral to undertake the discovery of the *West-Indies*, I say they were three, *viz.* natural reasons, authority of writers, and the testimony of sailers. As to the first, which is natural reason, I say, he concluded that all the sea and land compos'd a sphere or globe; which might be gone about from east to west, travelling round it, till men came to stand feet to feet one against another in any opposite parts whatsoever. Secondly, he gave it for granted, and was satisfied by the authority of approved authors, that a great part of this globe had been already travelled over, and that there then only remained to discover the whole, and make it known, that space which lay between the eastern bounds of *India*, known to *Ptolemy* and *Marinus*, round about eastward, till they came thro' our western parts to the islands *Azores*, and of *Cabo Verde* the most western parts yet discovered. Thirdly, He considered, that this space lying between the eastern limits known to *Marinus*, and the aforesaid island of *Cabo Verde*, could not be above a third part of the great circumference of the globe, since the said *Marinus* was already gone 15 hours, or 24 parts into which the world is divided towards the east; and therefore to return to the said isles of *Cabo Verde*, there wanted about eight parts; for the said *Marinus* is said to have begun his discovery towards the west. Fourthly he reckoned, that since *Marinus* had in his said cosmography, given an account of 15 hours, or parts of the globe towards the east, and yet was not come to the end of the eastern land, it followed of course, that the said end must be much beyond that; and consequently, the farther it extended eastward, the nearer it came to the islands *Cabo Verde*, towards our western parts; and that if such space were sea, it might easily be sail'd in a few days, and if land, it would be sooner discovered by the west, because it would be nearer to the said islands. To which reason

Arguments from reason.

ſon may be added, that given by *Strabo* in the 15th book of his coſmography, that no man with an army ever went ſo far as the eaſtern bounds of *India*, which *Cteſias* writes is as big as all the reſt of *Aſia*; *Oneſicritus* affirms, it is the third part of the globe; and *Nearchus*, that it is four months journey in a ſtrait line; beſides that, *Pliny* in the 17th chapter of his 6th book, ſays, That *India* is the third part of the earth: Whence he argu'd, that being ſo large, it muſt be nearer *Spain* by way of weſt. The 5th argument that induced him to believe, that the diſtance that way was ſmall, he took from the opinion of *Alfragranus* and his followers, who make the circumference of the globe, much leſs than all other writers and coſmographers, allowing but 56 miles and two thirds to a degree. Whence he would infer, that the whole globe being ſmall, that extent of the third part muſt of neceſſity be ſmall, which *Marinus* left as unknown; therefore that part might be ſail'd in leſs time than he aſſign'd; for ſince the eaſtern bounds of *India* were not yet diſcover'd, thoſe bounds muſt lie near to us weſtward, and therefore the lands he ſhould diſcover, might properly be call'd *Indies*. By this it plainly appears, how much, one Mr. *Roderick*, arch-deacon of *Seville*, was in the wrong as well as his followers, who blame the admiral; ſaying, He ought not to have call'd thoſe parts *Indies*, becauſe they are not ſo, whereas the admiral did not call them *Indies*, becauſe they had been ſeen or diſcover'd by any other perſon, but as being the eaſtern part of *India* beyond *Ganges*, to which no coſmographer ever aſſign'd bounds, or made it border on any other country eaſtward, but only upon the ocean; and becauſe theſe were the eaſtern unknown lands of *India*, and have no particular name of their own; therefore he gave them the name of the neareſt country, calling them *Weſt-Indies*, and the more becauſe he knew all men were ſenſible of the riches and wealth of *India*; and therefore by that name he thought to tempt their catholick majeſties, who were doubtful of his undertaking, telling them he went to diſcover the *Indies* by way of the weſt. And this mov'd him rather to deſire to be employed by the king of *Caſtile*, than by any other prince.

Why call'd Indies.

CHAP. VII.

The ſecond motive inducing the admiral to diſcover the Weſt-Indies.

A ſecond motive from authors.

THE ſecond motive that encouraged the admiral to undertake the aforeſaid enterpriſe, and which might reaſonably give occaſion to call the countries he ſhould ſo diſcover *Indies*, was the great authority of learned men, who ſaid that it was poſſible to ſail from the weſtern coaſt of *Africk* and *Spain*, weſtward to the eaſtern bounds of *India*, and that it was no great ſea that lay between them, as *Ariſtotle* affirms, at the end of his 2d book of heaven and the world; where he ſays, That they may ſail from *India* to *Cadiz* in a few days. Which ſome think *Averroes* proves, writing upon that place. And *Seneca* in his firſt book of nature, looking upon the knowledge of this world, as nothing in reſpect of what is attain'd in the next life; ſays, a ſhip may ſail in a few days with a fair wind from the coaſt of *Spain*, to that of *India*. And if as ſome would have it, this ſame *Seneca* writ the tragedies; we may conclude it was to the ſame purpoſe, that in the chorus of his *Medea*, he ſpeaks thus;

Venient annis
Sæcula ſeris, quibus Oceanus
Vincula rerum laxet, & ingens
Pateat tellus, Typhyſque novos
Detegat orbes, nec ſit terris
Ultima Thule.

That is, There will come an age in later years, when the ocean will looſe the bonds of things, and a great country be diſcovered, and another like *Typhys* ſhall diſcover a new world, and *Thule* ſhall no longer be the laſt part of the earth. Which now moſt certainly has been fulfill'd in the perſon of the admiral. And *Strabo* in the firſt book of his coſmography, ſays, the ocean encompaſſes all the earth; that in the eaſt, it waſhes the coaſt of *India*, and in the weſt, thoſe of *Mauritania* and *Spain*, and that if the vaſtneſs of the atlantick did not hinder, but they might ſoon ſail from the one to the other upon the ſame parallel. The ſame he repeats in the ſecond book. *Pliny* in the ſecond book of his natural hiſtory, *Chap.* III. adds, That the ocean ſurrounds

surrounds all the earth, and that the extent of it from east to west, is from *India* to *Cadiz*. The same author, book the 6th. *chap*. 31, and *Solinus*, *chap*. 68, of the remarkable things in the world, say, that from the islands *Gorgones*, supposed to be those of *Cabo Verde*, was forty days sail on the *Atlantick* ocean, to the islands *Hesperides*, which the admiral concluded were those of the *West-Indies*. *Marcus Paulus Venetus*, and *John Mandiville* in their travels say, they went much farther eastward than *Ptolemy* and *Marinus* mention, who perhaps do not speak of the eastern sea; yet by the account they give of the east, it may be argued, that the said *India* is not far distant from *Africk* and *Spain*. *Peter Aliacus* in his Treatise, *De imagine mundi*, chap. 8. *De quantitate terræ habitabilis, & Julius Capitolinus, de locis habitabilibus*; and in several other treatises, say, that *Spain* and *India* are neighbours westward. And in the 19th chapter of his cosmography, he has these words; according to the philosophers and *Pliny*, the ocean that stretches between the western borders of *Spain* and *Africk*, and from the beginning of *India* eastward, is of no great extent, and there is no doubt but it may be sail'd over in a few days, with a fair wind, and therefore the beginning of *India* eastward, can not be far distant from the end of *Africk* westward. These and the like authorities of such writers, inclined the admiral to believe that the opinion he had conceived was right, and one Mr. *Paul* physician to Mr. *Dominick* of *Florence*, contemporary with the admiral, much encouraged him to undertake the said voyage. For this Mr. *Paul* being a friend to one *Ferdinand Martinez*, a canon of *Lisbon*, and they writing to one another concerning the voyages made in the time of king *Alphonso* of *Portugal* to *Guinea*, and concerning what might be made westward; the admiral who was most curious in these affairs, got knowledge of it, and soon by the means of *Laurence Girardi*, *a Florentine* residing at *Lisbon*, writ upon this subject to the said Mr. *Paul*, sending him a small sphere, and acquainting him with his design. Mr. *Paul* sent his answer in *Latin*, which in *English* is thus.

CHAP. VIII.

A Letter from Paul, *a physician of* Florence, *to the admiral, concerning the discovery of the* Indies.

To *Christopher Columbus*, *Paul* the physician wishes health.

I Perceive your noble and earnest desire to sail to those parts where the spice is produced; and therefore in answer to a letter of yours, I send you another letter, which some days since I writ to a friend of mine, and servant to the king of Portugal, *before the wars of* Castile, *in answer to another he writ to me by his highnesses order, upon this same account, and I send you another sea chart like that I sent him, which will satisfy your demands. The copy of that letter is this.*

To *Ferdinand Martinez* canon of *Lisbon*, *Paul* the physician wishes health.

A letter concerning the discovery westward.

I Am very glad to hear of the familiarity you have with your most serene and magnificent king, and though I have very often discoursed concerning the short way there is from hence to the Indies, *where the spice is produced, by sea, which I look upon to be shorter than that you take by the coast of* Guinea; *yet you now tell me, that his highness would have me make out and demonstrate it, so as it may be understood and put in practise. Therefore, tho' I could better show it him with a globe in my hand, and make him sensible of the figure of the world; yet I have resolved to render it more easy and intelligible, to show this way upon a chart, such as are used in navigation; and therefore I send one to his majesty, made and drawn with my own hand, wherein is set down the utmost bounds of the west from* Ireland, *in the north, to the farthest part of* Guinea, *with all the islands that lie in the way: opposite to which western coast is described the beginning of the* Indies, *with the islands and places whither you may go, and how far you may bend from the north pole towards the equinoctial, and for how long a time; that is, how many leagues you may sail before you come to those places most fruitful in all sorts of spice, jewels, and precious stones. Do not wonder if I term that country where the spice grows west, that product being generally ascrib'd to the east, because those who shall sail westward, will always find those places in the west; and they that travel by land eastward, will ever find those places in the east. The strait lines that lie lengthways in the chart, show the distance there*

there is from west to east, the other cross them, show the distance from north to south. I have also mark'd down in the said chart, several places in India, *where ships might put in upon any storm or contrary winds, or any other accident unforeseen. And moreover, to give you full information of all those places, which you are very desirous to know; you must understand, that none but traders live or reside in all those islands, and that there is there as great a number of ships and seafaring people with merchandize, as in any other part of the world, particularly in a most noble part call'd* Zacton, *where there are every year an hundred large ships of pepper loaded and unloaded, besides many other ships that take in other spice. This country is mighty populous, and there are many provinces and kingdoms, and innumerable cities under the dominion of a prince call'd the* great cham, *which name signifies king of kings, who for the most part resides in the province of* cathay. *His predecessors were very desirous to have commerce, and be in amity with christians; and 200 years since, sent embassadors to the pope, desiring him to send them many learned men and doctors to teach them our faith; but by reason of some obstacles the embassadors met with, they returned back without coming to* Rome. *Besides there came an embassador to pope* Eugenius *IV. who told him the great friendship there was between those princes, their people and christians. I discours'd with him a long while upon the several matters of the grandeur of their royal structures, and of the greatness, length and breadth of their rivers, and he told me many wonderful things of the multitude of towns and cities founded along the banks of the rivers, and that there were 200 cities upon one only river, with marble bridges over it of a great length and breadth, and adorn'd with abundance of pillars. This country deserves as well as any other, to be discover'd; and there may not only be great profit made there, and many things of value found, but also gold, silver, all sorts of precious stones, and spices in abundance, which are not brought into our parts. And it is certain that many wise men, philosophers, astrologers, and other persons skill'd in all arts, and very ingenious, govern that mighty province, and command their armies. From* Lisbon *directly westward, there are in the chart 26 spaces, each of which contains 250 miles, to the most noble and vast city of* Quisay, *which is 100 miles in compass, that is 35 leagues; in it there are 10 marble bridges: the name signifies a heavenly city, of which wonderful things are reported, as to the ingenuity of the people, the buildings and revenues. This space above mentioned, is almost the third part of the globe. This city is in the province of* Mango, *bordering on that of* Cathay, *where the king for the most part resides. From the island* Antilia, *which you call the seven cities, and whereof you have some knowledge, to the most noble island of* Cipango, *are ten spaces, which make 2500 miles, or 225 leagues, which island abounds in gold, pearls, and precious stones: and you must understand, they cover their temples and palaces with plates of pure gold. So that for want of knowing the way, all these things are hidden and conceal'd, and yet may be gone to with safety. Much more might be said, but having told you what is most material, and you being wise and judicious, I am satisfied there is nothing of it, but what you understand, and therefore I will not be more prolix. Thus much may serve to satisfy your curiosity, it being as much as the shortness of time and my business would permit me to say. So I remain most ready to satisfy and serve his highness to the utmost, in all the commands he shall lay upon me.*

Florence, June 25.
1474.

After this letter, he again writ to the admiral as follows.

To *Christopher Columbus*, Paul the physician wishes health.

Another letter to the admiral.

I *Received your letters with the things you sent me, which I take as a great favour, and commend your noble and ardent desire of sailing from east to west, as it is markt out in the chart I sent you, which would demonstrate it self better in the form of a globe. I am glad it is well understood, and that the voyage laid down is not only possible, but true, certain, honourable, very advantageous, and most glorious among all christians. You cannot be perfect in the knowledge of it, but by experience and practice, as I have had in great measure, and by the solid and true information of worthy and wise men, who are come from those parts to this court of* Rome, *and from merchants who have traded long in those parts, and are persons of good reputation. So that when the said voyage is perform'd, it will be to powerful kingdoms, and to most noble cities and provinces, rich, and abounding in all things we stand in need of, particularly in all sorts of spice in great quantities, and store of jewels. This will moreover be grateful to those kings and princes, who are very desirous to converse and trade with christians of these our countries, whether it be for some of them to become christians, or else to have communication with the wise and ingenious men of these parts, as well in point of religion, as in in all ſciences; becauſe of the extraordinary account they have of the kingdoms and government of thoſe parts. For which reaſons and many more that might be alledged, I do not at all admire, that you who have a great heart, and all the* Portugueſe *nation, which has ever had notable men in all undertakings, be eagerly bent upon performing this voyage.*

This letter, as was ſaid before, encouraged the admiral much to go upon his diſcovery, tho' what the doctor there writ was falſe, as believing that the firſt land they ſhould meet with, would be *Cathay*, and the empire of the *Great Cham*, with the reſt he there relates; ſince as experience has made appear, the diſtance from our *Indies* to that, is greater than from hence to our *Indies*.

CHAP. IX.

The third motive and inducement, which in ſome meaſure excited the admiral to diſcover the Weſt-Indies.

A third motive from the hope of finding ſome land, before unheard of.

THE third and laſt motive the admiral had to undertake the diſcovery of the *Weſt-Indies*, was the hopes of finding, before he came to *India*, ſome very beneficial iſland or continent, from whence he might the better purſue his main deſign. This his hope was grounded upon the authority of many wiſe men and philoſophers, who look'd upon it as moſt certain, that the greateſt part of this terraqueous globe was land, or that there was more earth than ſea; which if ſo, he argued, that between the coaſt of *Spain* and the bounds of *India* then known, there muſt be many iſlands, and much continent, as experience has ſince demonſtrated, which he the more readily believed, being impoſed upon by many fables and ſtories which he heard told by ſeveral perſons and ſailers, who traded to the iſlands and weſtern ſea, and to *Madera*; which teſtimonies making ſomewhat to his purpoſe, they were ſure to gain a place in his memory. Therefore I will not forbear relating them, to ſatisfy thoſe that take delight in ſuch curioſities. It is therefore requiſite to be underſtood, that a pilot of the king of *Portugal*, whoſe name was *Martin Vicente*, told him, that he being once 450 leagues weſtward of cape *St. Vincent*, found and took up in the ſea, a piece of wood ingeniouſly wrought, but not with iron; by which, and the winds having been weſt for many days, he gueſſed that piece of wood came from ſome iſland that way. Next one *Peter Correa*, who had married the admiral's wife's ſiſter, told him, that in the iſland of *Porto Santo* he had ſeen another piece of wood brought by the ſame winds, well wrought, as that above mentioned; and that there had been canes found ſo thick, that every joint would hold above four quarts of wine; which he ſaid he affirmed to the king of *Portugal* himſelf diſcourſing with him about theſe affairs, and that they were ſhown him; and there being no place in our parts, where ſuch canes grow, he look'd upon it as certain, that the wind had brought them from ſome neighbouring iſlands, or elſe from *India*. For *Ptolemy* in the firſt book of his coſmography, chap. 17, ſays, there are ſuch canes in the eaſtern parts of *India*: And ſome of the iſlanders, particularly the *Azores* told him, that when the weſt wind blew long together, the ſea drove ſome pines upon thoſe iſlands, particularly upon *Gratioſa* and *Fayal*, there being no ſuch in all thoſe parts. And that the ſea caſt upon this iſland of *Flores*, another of the *Azores*, two dead bodies of men, very broad faced, and differing in aſpect from the chriſtians. At cape *Verga* and thereabouts, they ſay, they once ſaw ſome cover'd *Almadies* or boats, which it is believed were drove that way by ſtreſs of weather, as they were going over from one iſland to another. Nor were theſe only the motives he then had, which yet ſeemed reaſonable; but there were thoſe that told him they had ſeen ſome iſlands, among whom was *Anthony Leme*, married in the iſland of *Madera*, who told him, that having made a conſiderable run in a caraval of his own weſtward, he had ſeen three iſlands. Theſe he did not give credit to, becauſe he found by their own words and diſcourſe, that they had not ſailed 100 leagues to the weſtward, and that they had been deceived by ſome rocks, taking them for iſlands; or elſe perhaps they were ſome of thoſe floating iſlands that are carried about by the water, call'd by the ſailers *Aguadas*, whereof *Pliny* makes mention the firſt book, chap. 97, of his natural hiſtory; where he ſays, that in the northern parts the ſea diſcover'd ſome ſpots of land, on which there are trees of deep roots, which parcels of land are carried about

Floating-iſlands.

about like floats or islands upon the water. *Seneca* undertaking to give a natural reason why there are such sorts of islands, says in his third book, that it is the nature of certain spungy and light rocks, so that the islands made of them in *India*, swim upon the water. So that were it never so true, that the said *Anthony Leme* had seen some island, the admiral was of opinion, it could be no other than one of them, such as those called *St. Brandam* are supposed to be, where many wonders are reported to have been seen. There is also an account of others that lie much northward, and always burn. *Juventius Fortunatus* relates, that there is an account of two islands towards the west, and more southward than those of *Cabo Verde*, which swim along upon the water. These and the like grounds might move several people of the islands of *Ferro* and *la Gomera*, as also of the *Azores*, to affirm that they saw islands towards the west every year, which they look'd upon as most certain, and many persons of reputation swore it was true. He says moreover, that in the year 1484, there came into *Portugal*, one from the island of *Madera* to beg a caraval of the king, to go to discover a countrey, which he swore he saw every year, and always after the self-same manner, agreeing with others, who said they had seen it from the islands *Azores*. On which grounds in the charts and maps formerly made, they placed some islands thereabouts; and particularly because *Aristotle* in his book of wonderful natural things, affirms, it was reported that some *Carthaginian* merchants had sail'd through the *Atlantick* sea, to a most fruitful island, as we shall declare more at large hereafter, which island some *Portuguese* inserted in their maps, calling it *Antilla*; tho' they did not agree in the situation with *Aristotle*, yet none placed it above 200 leagues due west from the *Canaries* and *Azores*, which they conclude to be certainly the island of the seven cities, peopled by the *Portuguese* at the time that *Spain* was conquered by the *Moors* in the year 714. At which time they say, seven bishops with their people embark'd and sailed to this island, where each of them built a city; and to the end none of their people might think of returning to *Spain*, they burnt the ships, tackle and all things necessary for sailing. Some *Portuguese* discoursing about this island, there were those that affirmed several *Portuguese* had gone to it, who could not find the way to it again. Particularly they say, that in the time of *Henry* infant of *Portugal*, a *Portuguese* ship was drove by stress of weather to this island *Antilla*, where the men went ashore, and were led by the islanders to their church, to see whether they were christians, and observed the *Roman* ceremonies, and perceiving they did, they desired them not to depart till their lord came, who was then absent, and would make very much of them, and give them many presents, and to whom they would presently send advice; but the master and seamen were afraid of being detained, suspecting those people had not a mind to be discovered, and might therefore burn their ship, and for that reason they sail'd back to *Portugal*, hoping to be rewarded for what they had done by the *Infante*. He reproved them severely, and bid them return quickly; but the master for fear run away from *Portugal* with the ship and men; and it is reported, that whilst the seamen were at church in the said island, the boys of the ship gathered sand for the cookroom, the third part whereof they found to be pure gold. Among others that set out to discover this island, was one *James de Fiene*, whose pilot *Peter Velasquer*, of the town of *Palos de Moguer*, told the admiral in the monastery of *St. Mary de la Rabida*, that they set out from *Fayal*, and sailed above 150 leagues south-west, and in their return discovered the island *Flores*, being led to it by abundance of birds they saw fly that way, because those being land and not sea-fowls, they judged they could not rest but upon land: After which they sailed so far north-east, till they came to cape *Clare*, in the west of *Ireland*, where they met with stiff westerly winds, and yet a smooth sea, which they imagined was caused by some land that shelter'd it towards the west. But it being then the month of *August*, they would not turn towards the island for fear of winter. This was above forty years before our *Indies* were discovered. This account was confirm'd by the relation a mariner at port *St. Mary* made, telling him that once making a voyage into *Ireland*, he saw the said land, which he then thought to be part of *Tartary*, falling off towards the west, which it is like was the land we now call *Bacallaos*, and that they could not make up to it by reason of the bad weather. This he said agreed with what one *Peter de Valasco* of *Galicia* affirm'd to him, in the city of *Murcia* in *Spain*, which was, that sailing for *Ireland*, they went away so far to north-west, that they discovered land west of *Ireland*, which land he believes to be the same, that one *Femaldolmos* attempted to discover after the manner as I shall here faithfully set down, as I found it in my father's writings; that it may appear how some men lay the foundation of great matters

ters upon slight grounds. *Gonzalo de Oviedo*, in his history of the *Indies*, writes, That the admiral had a letter, wherein he found the *Indies* describ'd, by one that had before discovered them, which was not so, but thus: *Vincent Dear, a Portuguese of Tavira*, returning from *Guinea* to the *Tercera* islands, and having pass'd the island of *Madera*, which he left east of him, saw, or imagin'd he saw, an island which he certainly concluded to be land. Being come to the *Tercera* island, he told it to one *Luke de Cazzana*, a *Genoese* merchant, who was very rich, and his friend, persuading him to fit out some vessel to conquer that place; which he was very willing to do, and obtain'd licence for it of the king of *Portugal*. He writ therefore to his brother *Francis de Cazzana*, who resided at *Sevil*, to fit out a ship with all speed for the said pilot. But the said *Francis* making a jest of such an undertaking, *Luke de Cazzana* set out a vessel in the *Tercera* island, and the pilot went out three or four times to seek the said island, sailing from 120 to 130 leagues, but all in vain, for he found no land. Yet for all this, neither he nor his partner gave over the enterprize till death, always hoping to find it. And the brother aforesaid, told me and affirm'd it, that he knew two sons of the captain that discovered the *Tercera* island, their names *Michael* and *Jasper Cotereal*, who went several times to discover that land, and at last in the year 1502, perish'd in the attempt, one after another, without ever being heard of; and that this was well known to many.

CHAP. X.

Proving it to be false, that the Spaniards *had formerly the dominion of the* Indies, *as* Gonzalo de Oviedo *endeavours to make out in his history.*

IF all we have said above, concerning so many imaginary islands and countries, appears to be a mere fable and folly, how much more reason have we to look upon that as a falshood, which *Gonzalo Fernandez de Oviedo* conceits in his natural history of the *Indies*, looking upon his own imagination as a certain truth, and saying he has fully made out, that there was another discoverer of this navigation of the ocean, and that the *Spaniards* had the dominion of those lands; alledging to make out his assertion, what *Aristotle* writes of the island *Atlantis*, and *Sebosus* of the *Hesperides*. This he affirms upon the judgment of some persons, whose writings we have duly weigh'd and examin'd, and I would have omitted to talk on this subject, to avoid condemning some, and tiring the reader, had I not consider'd, that some persons, to lessen the admiral's honour and reputation, make great account of such notions. Besides I thought I did not perform my duty fully, by setting down with all sincerity the motives and inducements that inclin'd the admiral to undertake his unparallel'd enterprize, if I should suffer such a falshood, which I know to be so, to pass uncensur'd. Therefore, the better to discover his mistake, I will in the first place, set down what *Aristotle*, as related by one *F. Theophilus de Ferrariis*, says as to this point; which *F. Theophilus* among *Aristotle*'s problems collected by him, brings in a book call'd, *De admirandis in natura auditis*, a chapter with these following words: Beyond *Hercules*'s pillars, it is reported there was formerly found an island in the atlantick sea, by certain *Carthaginian* merchants, which had never before been inhabited by any but brute beasts. It was all wooded and covered with trees, had a great many navigable rivers, and abounded in all things nature usually produces, though removed not many days sail from the continent. It happened that some *Carthaginian* merchants coming to it, and finding it a good country, as well for the richness of the soil, as temperature of the air, they began to people it. But the senate of *Carthage* being offended at it, soon made a publick decree, That for the future, no person upon pain of death, should go to that island, and they that went first were put to death; to the end that other nations should not hear of it, and some more powerful people take possession of it; by which means it might become an enemy to their liberty. Now I have faithfully quoted this authority, I will give the reasons that induce me to say, That *Oviedo* has no just cause to affirm that this island was *Hispaniola* or *Cuba*, as he asserts. In the first place, because *Gonzalo de Oviedo* not understanding

A mistaken account of a Spanish author disproved.

underſtanding *Latin*, he of neceſſity took ſuch interpretation of this place, as ſome body made him; who, by what we ſee did not well know how to tranſlate out of one language into another, ſince he alter'd and chang'd the *Latin* text in ſeveral particulars, which perhaps deceiv'd *Oviedo*, and inclin'd him to believe that this quotation ſpoke of ſome iſland in the *Indies*; becauſe

Atlantis *neither* Hiſpaniola *nor* Cuba.

we do not read in the *Latin* text, that theſe people went out of the ſtreights of *Gibraltar*, as *Oviedo* writes; nor much leſs, that the iſland was large, nor its trees great, but that it was an iſland much wooded. Nor is it found there, that the rivers were wonderful; nor does it ſpeak of its fatneſs, or ſay it was more remote from *Africk* than *Europe*, but in plain terms, ſays, it was remote from the continent: Nor does it ſay any towns were built there, for traders who happened upon it could build but little: Nor is it ſaid to be famous, but that they were afraid its fame would ſpread abroad into other nations. So that the expoſitor who interpreted this place to him, being ſo ignorant, it cauſed *Oviedo* to imagine it to be another thing than really it was: and if he ſhould ſay, that it is otherwiſe in *Ariſtotle*'s text, and that what the friar writes, is as it were a compendium of what *Ariſtotle* writ; I muſt aſk him who gave him authority to beſtow ſo many kingdoms on whom he pleaſes, and to rob one of his honour, who has gain'd it ſo fairly; and tell him he ought not to have been ſatisfied with reading that authority as it lies in the friar's pamphlet, but ſhould have ſeen it in the original, that is, in *Ariſtotle*'s works. Beſides that he was miſinform'd in this caſe, for tho' *Theophilus* in all his other books following *Ariſtotle*, delivered the ſubſtance and ſumm of what he ſays; yet he did not ſo in his book *De admirandis*, he himſelf owning in the beginning, that he does not in that his book abridge *Ariſtotle*, as he has done in the others; but that he there inſerts all the text word for word; and therefore it cannot be ſaid there was either more or leſs in *Ariſtotle*, than what he ſet down. Add to this, That *Anthony Beccaria of Verona*, who tranſlated this book out of *Greek* into *Latin*; of which tranſlation *Theophilus* made uſe, did not render it ſo faithfully, but that he inſerted ſeveral matters differing from the *Greek* original, as will appear to any man that ſhall obſerve it.

In the ſecond place I ſay, that tho' *Ariſtotle* had writ ſo, as *Theophilus* delivers it, yet *Ariſtotle* himſelf quotes no author, but ſpeaking as of a thing, for which there is no good authority, ſays, *Fertur*, which implies that what he delivers concerning this iſland, he writes as doubtful and ill grounded. Beſides, He writes of a thing not then new but which had happened long before; ſaying, It is reported, that formerly an iſland was found, and therefore it may well be ſaid according to the proverb, *That in great travells there are great lyes*: Which proverb is now verify'd; for in that narration there are circumſtances no way agreeable to reaſon, for as much as it ſays, That this iſland abounded in all things, but had never been inhabited, which is not conſonant, nor likely, for as much as fruitfulneſs in land proceeds from its being cultivated by the inhabitants; and where there are no inhabitants, the land is ſo far from producing any thing of it ſelf, that even thoſe things which art produces, grow wild and uſeleſs. Nor is it more likely, that the *Carthaginians* ſhould be diſpleaſed, becauſe their people had found ſuch an iſland, and ſhould put to death the diſcoverers; for if it was ſo remote from *Carthage* as the *Indies* are, it was a folly to fear that thoſe who ſhould come to inhabit there would conquer *Carthage*, unleſs, that as *Oviedo* affirms, the *Spaniards* poſſeſs'd thoſe iſlands before. He would farther aſſert, That the *Carthaginians* were prophets, and that now their jealouſie and propheſie were fulfill'd, the emperor taking *Tunis* or *Carthage*, with the money brought from the *Indies*, which I am ſatiſfied he would have ſaid, to gain more favour by telling ſuch news, than he did, but that his book was publiſh'd before. So that any judicious perſon may conceive it is a folly to ſay, that iſland was never more heard of, becauſe the *Carthaginians* quitted the dominion of it, for fear any other nation ſhould take it from them, and come afterwards to deſtroy their liberty; for they ought to have fear'd this much more from *Sicily* or *Sardinia*, that lay but two days ſail from their city, than from *Hiſpaniola*, between which and them, there lay one third of the world. And if it ſhould be objected that they apprehended the wealth of that country, might impower their enemies to do them harm; I anſwer, they had more cauſe to hope, that being themſelves maſters of thoſe riches, they might oppoſe and ſubdue whom they pleaſed, and that if they left that iſland unpeopled, they left it in the power of another to diſcover it; whence the ſame miſchief might follow, which they feared. And therefore they ought rather to fortify it and ſecure their trade to it, as we know they did another time upon the like occaſion; for having found the iſlands which they then call'd *Caſſiterides*, and now we call the *Azores*, they kept that voyage very private, becauſe of the tin they brought from thence; as *Strabo* tells us at the latter end of the third book of his *cosmography*. Wherefore, granting it were true, what *Aristotle* had writ in this fable, it might be said he meant it of the voyage to the islands *Azores*, which either for want of better understanding, and the great antiquity of the testimony, or through affection, which blinds men, *Oviedo* argues, should be understood of the *Indies* we now possess, and not of the said islands *Azores*, or any of them. If it should be replied, that this cannot be, because *Strabo* does not say they were the *Carthaginians* who were possessed of the islands *Azores*, but the *Phœnicians* : I answer, that the *Carthaginians* being come from *Phœnicia* with their queen *Dido*, therefore she and they were called *Phœnicians* at that time, as the christians born in the islands are now called *Spaniards*. And should it be again urged, that the place of *Aristotle* which speaks of this island, says, it had many navigable rivers, which are not to be found in the islands *Azores*, but in *Cuba* and *Hispaniola*. I answer, that if we will take notice of this particular, they add, that there were abundance of beasts in them, which there are not in *Cuba* or *Hispaniola*; and it may well be, that in a thing of such antiquity, there might be some mistake in relating that particular, as often happens in many of these uncertain and so far distant antiquities. Observe that neither *Cuba* nor *Hispaniola* have any deep navigable rivers, as the place quoted intimates; and that any ships may enter the mouths of the biggest rivers of those islands, but not conveniently sail up them. Besides that, as has been said, how great soever *Aristotle*'s authority may be, the word might possibly be corrupted, and it might be writ *navigandum*, instead of *potandum*; which better agreed with what he treated of, commending it for plenty of drinking water, as well as fruitfulness in producing things to eat. This might well be verify'd of any one of the *Azores*, and with more reason, because neither *Cuba* nor *Hispaniola* lie so, as that the *Carthaginians* could be carried to them either by reason of their nearness, or by any mischance; for if those who went purposely with the admiral to discover, thought the way so long, that they would have turned back, how much longer must it seem to them who designed no such tedious voyage, and who, as soon as the time would permit, had turned back towards their countrey! Nor does any storm last so long, as to carry a ship from *Cadiz* to *Hispaniola*; nor is it likely, that because they were merchants, they should have any mind to run farther from *Spain* or *Carthage*, than the wind obliged them, especially at a time when navigation was not come to that perfection as now it is. For which reason very inconsiderable voyages were then look'd upon as great, as appears by what we read of *Jason*'s voyage to *Colchos*, and that of *Ulysses*, thro' the *Mediterranean*, in which so many years were spent; and therefore they were so famous, that the most excellent poets have given an account of them, because of the little knowledge they had then of sea-affairs, whereas it has been so approved of late in our age, that there have been those who had the boldness to sail round the world, which has contradicted the proverb that said, *He that goes to cape* Nam, *will either return or not*; which cape is in *Africk*, not very much distant from the *Canaries*. Besides, it is a notorious mistake, to think the island, whither those merchants were carried, could be either *Cuba* or *Hispaniola*; for it is well known, that with all the knowledge we have at this present, 'tis almost impossible to come at them, without meeting with any other islands that encompass them all round. But if we would say that land or island was none of the *Azores*, as has been said above, one lye ought to be grafted upon another, by alledging that it was the same island of which *Seneca* in his fourth book, makes mention, where he tells us, that *Thucydides* speaks of an island called *Atlantica*, which in the time of the *Peloponnesian* war was all, or mostly drowned. Whereof *Plato* also makes mention in his *Timæus*. But because we have discoursed too long concerning these fables, I will proceed to the next point, where it is said, that the *Spaniards* had entirely the dominion of the said islands; which opinion is grounded on what *Statius* and *Sebosus* say, that certain islands called *Hesperides*, lay forty days sail west of the islands *Gorgones*. And hence it is argued, that since those must of necessity be *Indies*, and are called *Hesperides*; that name came from *Hesperus*, who was king of *Spain*, who of consequence, and the *Spaniards* were lords of that countrey. So that rightly considering his words, he endeavours from uncertain premises to deduce three infallible consequences, contrary to *Seneca*'s rule, who in his sixth book of Nature, speaking of of such like things, says it is hard to affirm any thing as sure and certain upon grounds that are no other than conjectures, as here *Oviedo* does; forasmuch as only *Sebosus* is said to have made mention of those islands *Hesperides*, declaring towards what part they lie, but not mentioning that they were the *Indies*, or of whom they took the name, or by whom conquered. And if *Oviedo* out of *Berosus*, affirms that *Hesperus* was King of *Spain*; I grant it to be true, but not that he gave the name to *Spain*, or

Hesperides *none of the* Indies.

Italy. But he, like a true historian, owning that *Berosus* fails him in this particular, took up with *Hyginus*, yet cautiously without mentioning in what book or chapter; and thus he conceals his authority; for in short, no place is to be found where *Hyginus* speaks of any such matter; but on the contrary, in one only book of his that is extant, entitul'd, *De poetica astronomia*, he has not only no such words; but in three several places where he speaks of these *Hesperides*, he says thus; *Hercules* is painted as killing the dragon that guarded the *Hesperides*. And somewhat farther he says, that *Hercules* being sent by *Euristheus* for the golden apples to the *Hesperides*, and not knowing the way thither, he went to *Prometheus* on mount *Caucasus*, and entreated him to shew him the way, whence follow'd the death of the dragon. Now according to this we shall have other *Hesperides* in the east, to whom also *Oviedo* may say, *Hesperus* king of *Spain* gave his name. *Hyginus* says farther, in the chapter of planets, that it appears by several histories, that the planet *Venus* is called *Hesperus*, because it sets soon after the sun. From all which we may infer, that if we ought to make use of any testimonies or quotations from persons used to relate poetical fables, as *Hyginus* does, that very same which *Hyginus* says, rather makes against *Oviedo* than for him; and we may suppose and affirm, they were called *Hesperides* from a certain star. And as the *Greeks* for the same reason call'd *Itar Hesperia*, as many write; so we may say, *Sebosus* called these islands *Hesperides*, and made use of the same conjectures, and some reasons to shew whereabouts they lay, which we said above, moved the admiral to believe for certain, that there were such islands westward.

Thus we may conclude, that *Oviedo* did not only presume to counterfeit authorities for what he said, but that either through inadvertency, or to please him who told him these things (for it is certain he did not understand them himself) he maintain'd two contradictions, the disagreement between which were sufficient to discover his error. For if the *Carthaginians*, who, as he says, arrived at *Cuba* or *Hispaniola*, found that countrey inhabited by none but brute beasts, how could it be true, that the *Spaniards* had been possessed of it long before, and that their king *Hesperus* gave it his name? Unless perhaps he will say, that some deluge unpeopled it; and that afterwards some other *Noah* restored it to that condition it was discovered in by the admiral. But because I am quite tired with this dispute, and methinks the reader is cloy'd with it, I will not dilate any more upon this point, but follow on our history.

CHAP. XI.

How the admiral was disgusted by the king of Portugal *on account of the discovery he proposed to him.*

Proposals made to the king of Portugal.

THE admiral now concluding that his opinion was excellently well grounded, he resolved to put it in practice, and to sail the western ocean in quest of those countries. But being sensible that such an undertaking was only fit for a prince, who could go through with and maintain it; he resolved to propose it to the king of *Portugal*, because he liv'd under him. And though king *John* then reigning, gave ear to the admiral's proposals, yet he seemed backward in embracing them, because the great trouble and expence he was at upon account of the discovery and conquest of the western coast of *Africk*, call'd *Guinea*, without any considerable success as yet, or being as yet able to weather the cape of *Good Hope*, which name some say was given it instead of *Agesingue*, its proper denomination, because that was the farthest they hoped to extend their discoveries and conquests, or as others will have it, because this cape gave them hopes of better countries and navigation. Be it as it will, the aforesaid king had but little inclination to lay out more money upon discoveries; and if he gave any ear to the admiral, it was because of the excellent reasons he gave to prove his opinion, which so far prevailed upon him, that there remained only to grant the admiral those terms he demanded. For the admiral being a man of a noble and generous spirit, would capitulate to his great benefit and honour, that he might leave behind him such a reputation, and so considerable a family, as became his great actions and merits. For this reason the king by the advice of one doctor *Calzadilla*, of whom he made great account, resolved to send a caraval privately, to attempt that which the admiral had proposed to him; because in case those countries were so discovered, cover'd, he thought himself not oblig'd to bestow any great reward, which might be demanded on account of the discovery. Having thus speedily equipp'd a caraval, and going out, it was to carry supplies to the islands of *Cabo Verde*, he sent it that way the admiral had proposed to go. But those he sent wanted the knowledge, constancy, and spirit of the admiral. After wandring many days upon the sea, they turned back to the islands of *Cabo Verde*, laughing at the undertaking, and saying, it was impossible there should be any land in those seas. This being come to the admiral's ear, and his wife dead, he took such an aversion to that city and nation, that he resolved to go to *Castile*, with a little son he had left him by his wife, call'd *D. James Columbus*, who inherited his father's estate. But fearing lest if the king of *Castile* should not consent to his undertaking, he might be forced to propose it to some other prince, which would take up much time, he sent a brother he had with him, called *Bartholomew Columbus*, into *England*, who tho' he was no *Latin* scholar, was a skilful and judicious man in sea affairs, and could make sea charts, globes, and other instruments fit for that profession, having been taught by the admiral his brother. *Bartholomew Columbus* being on his way for *England*, it was his fortune to fall into the hands of pyrates, who stripp'd him and the rest of his company. For this reason, and being sick and poor in that countrey, it was a long time before he could deliver his message, till having got some supply by making sea-charts, he began to make some proposals to King *Henry* the VIIth, then reigning, to whom he presented a map of the world, on which were these verses, which I found among his papers, and shall be here inserted, rather for their antiquity than elegancy.

King Henry VII. *of* England.

Terrarum quicunque cupis fœliciter oras
Noscere, cuncta decens docte pictura docebit,
Quæ Strabo, affirmat, Ptolemæus, Plinius, atque
Isidorus; non una tamen sententia cuique.
Pingitur hic etiam nuper sulcata carinis
Hispanis Zona illa, prius incognita genti,
Torrida, quæ tandem nunc est notissima multis.

Pro auctore, sive pictore.

And a little lower.

Genoa cui patria est, nomen cui Bartholomæus
Columbus de terra rubra, opus edidit istud,
Londiniis Ann. Dom. 1480. *atque insuper anno.*
Octava Decimaque die cum tertia mensis
Febr. Laudes Christo cantentur abunde.

The sense of the first lines is to this effect. Whosoever thou art that desirest to know the coasts of countries, must be taught by this draught, what *Strabo*, *Ptolemy*, *Pliny*, and *Isidorus* assert, tho' not agreeing in all points. Here is also set down, the formerly unknown torrid zone, now known to many. For the author or painter. The second verses implied, That his name was *Bartholomew Columbus* of the red earth, a *Genoese*, published this work at *London*, *Anno* 1480, the 21st of *February*. Praise to God.

And because it may be observed, that he says, *Columbus of the red earth*; I must acquaint the reader, that I have seen some subscriptions of the admiral's, before he had that title, where he writ *Columbus de terra rubra*. But to return to the king of *England*; I say, that he having seen the map, and what the admiral offer'd him, readily accepted of it, and ordered him to be sent for. But God having reserved it for *Castile*, the admiral had at that time gone his voyage, and was returned with success, as shall be shewn in its place.

CHAP. XII.

The admiral's departure from Portugal, *and the conferences that he had with their catholick majesties, king* Ferdinand, *and queen* Isabel *or* Elizabeth.

The admiral goes into Spain.

I Will now forbear relating how *Bartholomew Columbus* proceeded in *England*, and will return to the admiral, who about the end of the year 1484, stole away privately out of *Portugal*, with his son *James*, for fear of being stopped by the king; for he being sensible how faulty they were, whom he had sent with the caraval, had a mind to restore the admiral to his favour, and desired he should renew the discourse of his enterprize; but not being so diligent to put this in execution, as the admiral was in getting away; he lost that good opportunity, and the admiral got into *Castile* to try his fortune, which was there to favour him. Therefore leaving his son in a monastery at *Palos*,

Palos, called *la Rabida*, he presently went away to the catholick king's court, which was then at *Cordova*; where being affable, and of pleasant conversation, he contracted friendship with such persons as he found most inclinable to his undertaking, and fittest to persuade the king to embrace it; among whom was *Lewis de Santangel* an *Arragonian* gentleman, clerk of the allowances in the king's houshold, a man of great prudence and reputation. But because the matter required to be handled with learning, rather than empty words and favour, their highnesses committed it to the prior of *Prado*, afterwards archbishop of *Granada*, ordering him together with some cosmographers to take full information in this affair, and report their opinions therein. But there being few cosmographers at that time, those that were called together were not so skilful as they ought to be; nor would the admiral so far explain himself as that he might be served as he had been in *Portugal*, and be deprived of his reward. For this reason, the answer they gave their highnesses was as various as were their judgments and opinions. For some said, that since in so many thousand years as had pass'd since the creation, so many skilful sailers had got no knowledge of such countries; it was not likely that the admiral should know more than all that were then, or had been before. Others, who inclin'd more to cosmographical reason, said the world was so prodigious great, that it was incredible three years sail would bring him to the end of the east, whither he design'd his voyage; and to corroborate their opinion, they brought the authority of *Seneca*, who in one of his works, by way of argument, said, that many wise men among them disagreed about this question, whether the ocean were infinite, and doubted whether it could be sail'd, and tho' it were navigable, whether habitable lands would be found on the other side, and whether they could be gone to. They added, that of this lower globe of earth and water, only a small compass was inhabited, which had remained in our hemisphere above water, and that all the rest was sea, and not navigable, but only near the coasts and rivers. And that wise men granted it was possible to sail from the coast of *Spain* to the farthest part of the west. Others of them argued almost after the same manner as the *Portuguese* had done about sailing to *Guinea*, saying, That if any man should sail streight away westward, as the admiral proposed, he would not be able to return into *Spain*, because of the roundness of the globe, looking upon it as most certain, that whosoever should go out of the hemisphere known to *Ptolemy*, would go down, and then it would be impossible to return, affirming it would be like climbing a hill, which ships could not do with the stiffest gale. Tho' the admiral sufficiently solv'd all these objections; yet the more powerful his reasons were, the less they understood him thro' their ignorance; for when a man grows old upon ill principles in mathematicks, he cannot conceive the true, because of the false notions at first imprinted in his mind. In short, all of them holding to the *Spanish* Proverb, which, tho' it be contrary to reason, commonly says, *dubitat Augustinus*, St. *Augustin* questions it, because the said saint in his 21st book, and 9th chapter *Of the city of God*, denies and looks upon it as impossible that there should be *Antipodes*, or any going out of one hemisphere into the other; and further urging against the admiral those fables that are current about the five zones, and other untruths, which they looked upon as most certainly true, they resolved to give judgment against the enterprize, as vain and impracticable; and that it became not the state and dignity of such great princes, to be moved upon such weak information. Therefore after much time spent upon this subject, their highnesses answered the admiral, that they were then taken up with many other wars and conquests, and particularly the conquest of *Granada*, which they had then in hand, and therefore could not conveniently attend that new undertaking, but that in time there would be more conveniency to examine and execute that which he proposed. And to conclude, their majesties would not give ear to the great proposals the admiral made.

Reasons against his undertaking.

CHAP.

CHAP. XIII.

How the admiral not agreeing with the king of Castile, *resolved to go elsewhere to offer his service.*

The admiral meets with more disappointments.

WHilst this was in agitation, their catholick Majesties had not been always settled in one place, because of the war they made in *Granada*, for which reason it was a long time before they came to a resolution and gave their answer. The admiral therefore went to *Sevil*, and finding their highnesses no way resolved more than at first; he concluded to give the Duke of *Medina Sidonia* an account of his project. But after many conferences, seeing there was no likelyhood of coming to such conclusion as he wish'd for in *Spain*, and that the execution of his design was too much delay'd; he resolved to apply himself to the King of *France*, to whom he had already writ concerning this affair, designing, if he were not admitted there, to go into *England*, next to seek out his brother, of whom he had as yet no manner of news. Being so resolved to set out for the Monastery of *Rabida*, to send his son *James*, whom he had left there, to *Cordova*, and then proceed on his journey. But to the end what God had decreed, should not be disappointed, he put it into the heart of *F. John Perez*, guardian of that house, to contract such friendship with the admiral, and be so taken with his project, that he was concern'd at his resolution, and for the loss *Spain* would sustain by his departure. Therefore he intreated him by no means to put his design in execution, for that he would go to the queen, of whom he hoped, that he being her father confessor, she would give gredit to what he should say to her. Tho' the admiral was quite out of hopes and disgusted to see so little resolution and judgment in their highnesses councellors, yet, being on the other side very desirous that *Spain* should reap the benefit of his undertakings, he complied with the father's desires and request, because he now look'd upon himself as a natural born *Spaniard*, because he had so long resided there: whilst he was following his project, and because he had got children there which was the cause he rejected the offers made him by other princes, as he declares in a letter he writ to their highnesses in these words, *that I might serve your highnesses, I have refused to take up with* France, England *and* Portugal, *the letters from which princes your highnesses may see in the hands of doctor* Villalan.

CHAP. XIV.

How the admiral returned to the camp before Granada, *and took his leave of their catholick majesties, having concluded nothing with them.*

THE admiral departing from the monastery of *Rabida* near *Palos*, together with *F. John Perez*, to the camp of S. *Faith*, where their catholick majesties then were to carry on the siege of *Granada*; the said father further inform'd the queen, and press'd the business so home, that her majesty was pleased the conferences about the discovery should be renewed. But the opinions of the prior of *Prado* and others of his followers varying, and on the other side, *Columbus* demanding to be made admiral and vice-roy, besides other matters of great consequence; it was thought too much to grant him, because if what he propos'd succeeded, they judg'd his demand too considerable, and in case it did not, they thought it a folly to give such titles, which made the business come to nothing. I cannot forbear declaring that I make great account of the admiral's wisdom, resolution and foresight, for he being so unfortunate in this affair, having so earnest a desire, as I have said before, to remain in this kingdom, and being reduced to such a condition, that he ought to take up with any thing; it was a greatness of spirit in him not to accept of any but great titles and honours, demanding such things as if he had foreseen and been most certainly assured of the success of his project, he could not have articled better, or more honourably than he did, so that at last they were forced to grant, that he should be admiral on the ocean, and enjoy all the allowances, privileges and prerogatives, that the admirals of *Castile* and *Leon* had in their several seas, and that all civil employments

The admiral's demands.

ments, as well of government as administration of justice, in all the islands and continent should be wholly at his disposal, and that all government should be given to one or three persons he should name; and that he should appoint judges in all parts of *Spain* trading to the *Indies*, who should decide all matters relating to those parts. As for profit and revenue, he demanded, over and above the salary and perquisites of the aforesaid employments of admiral, vice-roy and governour, the tenth of all that was bought, bartered, found, or got within the bounds of his admiralship, abating only the charge of the conquest; so that had there been 1000 ducats in an island, one hundred were to be his. And because his adversaries said he ventured nothing in that undertaking, but had the command of a fleet as long as it lasted, he demanded the eighth part of what he should bring home in his fleet, and he would be at the eighth part of the expence. These being matters of such great consequence and their highnesses refusing to grant them; the admiral took leave of his friends and went away towards *Cordova*, to take order for his journey into *France*, for he was resolved not to return to *Portugal*, tho' the king had writ to him, as shall be said.

CHAP. XV.

How their catholick majesties sent after the admiral, and granted him all he demanded.

Reasons that prevail'd with the queen.

IT was now the month of *January*, in the year 1492, when the admiral departed from the camp of St. *Faith*, and that same day *Lewis de Santangel* before mentioned, who did not approve of his going away, but was very desirous to prevent it; went to the queen, and using such words as his inclination suggested to persuade and reprove her at once, said, he wondered to see that her highness, who had always a great soul for all matters of moment and consequence, should now want the heart to venture upon an undertaking, where so little was ventured, and which might redound so much to the glory of god and propagation of the faith, not without great benefit and honour to her kingdoms and dominions; and such in short, that if any other prince should undertake it, as the admiral offered, the damage that would accrew to her crown was very visible, and that then she would with just cause be much blam'd by her friends and servants, and reproached by her enemies, and all people would say, she had well deserv'd that misfortune; and tho' she herself should never have cause to repent it, yet her successors would certainly feel the smart of it. Therefore, since the matter seemed to be grounded upon reason, and the admiral who proposed it was a man of sense and wisdom, and demanded no other reward but what he shou'd find, being willing to bear part of the charge, besides venturing his own person; her highness ought not to look upon it as such an impossibility as those scholars made it, and that what they said that it would be a reflexion on her if the enterprise did not succeed, as the admiral proposed, was a folly, and he was of a quite contrary opinion, rather believing they would be look'd upon as generous and magnanimous princes, for attempting to discover the secrets and wonders of the world, as other monarchs had done, and it had redounded to their honour. But tho' the event were never so uncertain, yet a considerable sum of money would be well employ'd in clearing such a doubt. Besides that, the admiral only demanded 2500 crowns to fit the fleet, and therefore she ought not to despise that undertaking, that it might not be said it was the fear of spending so small a sum that kept her back. The queen knowing the sincerity of *Santangel*'s words, answered, thanking him for his good advice, and saying, she was willing to admit of the proposals, upon condition the execution were respited, till she had a little breathing after the war. And yet if he were of another opinion, she was content that as much money as was requisite for fitting out the fleet should be borrowed upon her jewels. But *Santangel* seeing the queen had upon his advice condescended to what she had refused to all other persons, replyed, there was no need of pawning her jewels, for he would do her highness that small service as to lend his money. Upon this resolution the queen immediately sent an officer post, to bring the admiral back, who found him upon the bridge of *Pinos*, two leagues from *Granada*; and tho' the admiral was much concerned at the difficulties and delays he had met with in his enterprise, yet understanding the queen's will and resolution, he returned to the camp of St. *Faith*, where he was well entertained by their catholick

The admiral's demands granted.

lick majesties, and his dispatch and articles committed to the secretary *John Coloma*, who by their highnesses command and under their hand and seal, granted him all the articles and clauses we said above, he had demanded, without altering or diminishing any thing in them.

CHAP. XVI.

How the admiral fitted out three caravals to go upon his discovery.

The admiral sets out. THE aforesaid articles being granted by their catholick majesties, he set out from *Granada* on the 12th of *May*, this year 1492, for *Palos*, the port where he was to fit out his ships, that town being oblig'd to serve their highnesses three months with two caravals, which they ordered should be given to the admiral. These and another ship be fitted out with all care and diligence. The ship he went in was call'd the *St. Mary*, another was *La Pinta*, whereof *Martin Alonzo Pinzon* was captain, and *Vincent Yanez Pinzon*, brother to *Alonzo*, both of the town of *Palos*, of the 3d which was call'd *La Nina*, and had square sails. They being furnished with all necessaries, and 90 men, set sail directly towards the *Canaries* on the 3d of *August*, and from that time forwards, the admiral was very careful to keep an exact journal of all that happened to him during the voyage, specifying what wind blew, how far he sail'd with every wind; what currents he found, and what he saw by the way, whether birds, or fishes, or other things; which he always did in four voyages he made from *Spain* to the *Indies*. I will not write all those particulars; for tho' to give an account of his voyage, and to shew what impressions and effects answered the course and aspects of the stars, and to relate what difference there is between that and our sea and our countries, would be now very beneficial; yet I do not think all those particulars would now be pleasing to the reader, whom such long and superfluous relations must tire. Therefore I shall only discourse of those things I shall think necessary and convenient.

CHAP. XVII.

The admiral arriv'd at the Canary *islands, and there furnish'd himself compleatly with all he wanted.*

The rudder of a caraval gives way. THE next day after the admiral's departure for the *Canary* islands, being *Saturday* the 4th of *August*, the rudder of one of the caravals, call'd *La Pinta*, broke loose, and being therefore forced to lie by, the admiral soon came by her side, but the weather blowing hard, could give no assistance; yet commanders at sea are oblig'd so to do, to encourage those that are in distress. This he did the more readily, as misdoubting this had happened by the contrivance of the master, to avoid going the voyage, as he attempted to do before they set out. *Pinzon* the captain being an able seaman, soon repaired that fault with the help of some ropes, so that they were able to continue their voyage, till on *Tuesday* following, the weather being rough, the ropes broke, and they were forced again to lie by to mend what had given way. From which misfortune of breaking of the rudder twice, any body that had been superstitious, might have foreboded its future disobedience to the admiral, when thro' the malice of *Pinzon*, it twice got away from him, as shall be mentioned hereafter.

To return to what we have in hand, they apply the best remedy they could for the present, that they might at least reach the *Canary* islands, which all three ships discovered on *Thursday* the 9th of *August* about break of day, but the wind being contrary, they could not come to an anchor at *Gran Canaria*, tho' very near it, that day nor the two following. Here the admiral left *Pinzon*, that going ashore he might endeavour to get another ship; and he to the same purpose went away to the island *Gomera*, with the caraval call'd *La Mina*, that if they fail'd of a vessel in one island, they might find it in the other. *The admiral at Gomera.* Thus he came to *Gomera* on the *Sunday* following, being the 12th of *August*, and sent his boat ashore, which return'd in the morning, with the news that there was never a vessel in the island at that time, but that they hourly expected the lady *Beatrix de Bobadilla*, proprietress of that same island, who was then at *Gran Canaria*, an and had hired a vessel of 40 tun, belonging to one *Gradenna* of *Sevile*, which being fit for the voyage he design'd, he might have taken. Therefore the admiral resolved to expect him in that port, believing that if *Pinzon* had not been able to repair his own vessel, he might himself have got another at *Gomera*. Having stay'd there the two following days, and the vessel above mentioned not appearing, he sent a man aboard a bark that was bound from *Gomera* to *Gran Canaria*, to acquaint *Pinzon* where he lay, and assist him in fixing his rudder, writing to him that he did not go himself to assist him, because that vessel could not sail. But it being long after the departure of that bark, before the admiral received any answer; he resolved on the 23d of *August* to return with his two vessels to *Gran Canaria*, and sailing the next day, met in the way the aforementioned bark, which was not yet arriv'd at *Gran Canaria*, by reason of the contrary winds. Having taken out the man he had sent aboard the bark, that night he sail'd close by *Tenerife*, where they saw flames gush out of the high rock commonly call'd the *Peake*, or rather *El Pico*, which his men admiring at, he told them the occasion of that fire, proving what he said by the example of mount *Etna* in *Sicily*, and of many others like it. Leaving that island they arrived at *Gran Canaria* upon *Saturday* the 25th, whither *Pinzon* with much difficulty was got in but the day before. By him he was inform'd that the lady *Beatrix* was sail'd the *Monday* before, with that vessel he took such pains to get, and the others being much troubled at it, he made the best of whatever happen'd; affirming, that since it did not please God he should meet with that vessel, it was perhaps because in finding it, he would at the same time have met with some obstacle or opposition in pressing of it, and have lost time in shipping and unshipping the goods, which would be a hindrance to his voyage: for this reason, fearing if he returned to seek it at *Gomera*, he might miss of it by the way; he resolved to repair his caraval the best he could at *Gran Canaria*, making a new rudder, she having lost hers, and to change the sails of the other caraval call'd *La Nina*, which were square, to round, that she might follow the other ships with less danger and agitation.

At Gran Canaria.

CHAP. XVIII.

How the admiral set sail from the island of Grand Canaria *upon his discovery and what happened to him on the ocean.*

WHEN the ships were refitted and in order to sail on *Friday*, (this by what follows ought to be *Saturday*) the first of *September*; in the afternoon the admiral weighed anchor, and departed from *Gran Canaria*, arriving the next day at *Gormra*, where four days more were spent in laying in provisions, wood and water; so that next *Thursday* in the morning which was on the 6th of *September* 1482, which may be accounted the first setting out upon the voyage on the ocean, the admiral departed from *Gomera*, and stood away to the westward, but made but little way by reason of the calm. On *Sunday* about day, he found himself nine leagues west of the island *Ferro*, where they lost sight of land, and many fearing it would be long before they should see it again, sigh'd and wept, but the admiral after comforting them all with great promises of lands, and wealth to raise their hopes, and lessen the fear they had conceiv'd of the length of the way, tho' they sail'd 18 leagues that day, he pretended by his computation it was but 15, resolving all the voyage to keep short in his reckoning, that his men might not think themselves so far from *Spain* as they were, if he should truly set down the way he made, which yet he privately mark'd down. Continuing thus his voyage, on *Wednesday* the 12th of *September*, about sun-setting, being about 150 leagues west of the island *Ferro*, he discovered a large body of the mast of a tree of 120 tun, which seem'd to have been a long time upon the water. There and somewhat further the current set strong towards the north east, but when he had run 50 leagues farther westward, on the 13th of *September*, he found that at night fall, the needle vary'd half a point towards the north-east, and at break of day, half a point more, by which he understood that the needle did not point at the north star, but at some other fix'd and visible point. This variation no man had observ'd before, and therefore he had occasion to be surpriz'd at it, but he was more amaz'd the 3d day after, when he was almost 100 leagues further; for at night the needles vary'd about a point to the north east, and in the morning they pointed upon the star. On *Saturday*

The admiral sails westward.

day the 15th of *September*, being almost 300 leagues west of *Ferro*; at night they saw a wonderful flash of light fall from the sky, into the sea, about four or five leagues distance from the ships towards the south-west, tho' the weather was then fair, like *April*, the wind favourable at north east, the sea still, and the current setting north-east. The men aboard the caraval call'd *la Ninna*, told the admiral, they had the *Friday* before seen a heron and another sort of bird, which the *Spaniards* call *Rabo de Junco*, which they were amaz'd at, those being the first birds they had seen; but they were more surprised the next day, which was *Sunday*, at the great abundance of weeds between green and yellow, that appeared upon the water, which seem'd to be newly wash'd away from some island or rock. They saw enough of these weeds the next day, which made many affirm they were already near land, especially because they saw a small lobster alive among those weeds, which they said somewhat resembled the herb *Star-wort*, but that the stalk and branches were long, and it was all full of small seeds. Afterwards they observed that the sea-water was but half as salt as before: besides, that night abundance of *Tunny* fishes follow'd them, running along, and sticking so close to them, that those aboard the caraval *Ninna*, kill'd one with a bearded iron. Being now 360 leagues west of *Ferro*, they saw another of those birds the *Spaniards* call *Rabo de Junco*, because of a long feather their tail consists of, and in *Spanish*, *Rabo* signifies a tail, as *Junco* is a rush, so that *Rabo de Junco* imports rush tail. On *Tuesday* following, being the 18th of *September*, *Martin Alonzo Pinzon*, who was gone a-head with the caraval call'd *Pinta*, which was an excellent sailor, lay by for the admiral, and told him he had seen a great number of birds fly away westward, for which reason he hop'd to find land that night, and he thought he saw the land to the northward, 15 leagues distant; that day about sun-setting, looking very dark and cloudy. But the admiral knowing for certain it was no land, he would not lose time to discover it, as all his men would have had him; forasmuch as he was not yet come to the place where he expected by his computation to find land, therefore they took in their top-sails at night, because the wind freshned, having for eleven days never abated one handful of sail, going still before the wind westward.

He sees birds and sea-weeds.

CHAP. XIX.

How all the men carefully observed what signs they discovered, being eager to discover land.

ALL the men aboard the ships being unacquainted with that voyage, and fearfull of the danger, because far from any relief, there were some that began to mutter, and seeing nothing but sky and water, carefully observed every thing that appear'd, at greater distance from land, than any had been before. For which reason I will relate all they made any account of, and this only in the first voyage; for I shall not mention lesser tokens generally seen upon such occasions. On the 19th of *September*, in the morning, a fowl call'd *Alcatraz*, which is a sort of sea gull, flew over the admiral's ship, and others in the afternoon, which made him conceive hope of land, he imagining they would not fly very far from it. Upon these hopes, as soon as the wind abated, they sounded with 200 fathom of line; and tho' they found no bottom, they perceived the current now set south-west. On *Thursday* the 22d, two hours before noon, two *Alcatrazes* came to the ship, and another some time after; besides, they took a bird like a heron, but that it was black, and had a white tuft on the head, the feet like a duck, as commonly water-fowls have; they also caught a little fish, and saw abundance of weeds; and about evening there came aboard three land-fowls singing, but at break of day they flew away, which was some comfort to them, considering that the other fowls being large, and used to the water, might better go far from land, but that these little ones could not come from any far distant countrey. Three hours after they saw another *Alcatraz*, that came from the W. N. W. and the next day after noon, they saw another *Rabo de Junco* and an *Alcatraz*, and there appear'd more weeds than before, towards the north, as far as they could see; which things sometimes were a comfort to them, believing they might come from some near land, and sometimes they caused dread, because they were so thick, that in some measure they staid the ships, and fear making things worse than they are, they apprehended that might befal them, which is fabulously reported of St. *Amaro* in the frozen sea, who is said not to suffer ships to stir backwards or forwards, and therefore they steer-ed

More birds and other tokens.

ed away from those shoals of weeds, as much as they could. But to return to the tokens. The next day they saw a whale, and on *Saturday* following, being the 22d of *September*, some small birds; and the wind those days blew at south-west, sometimes more and sometimes less west, which tho' contrary to their voyage, the admiral said he look'd upon as very good, and a help to them, because the men continually muttering, among other things that increased their fear, said this was one, That since the wind was always right a stern, they should never in those seas have a gale to carry them back; and tho' sometimes they found the contrary, they alledg'd that it was no settled wind, and that not being strong enough to swell the sea, it would never carry them back so far as they had to sail. Whatsoever the admiral could say, telling them that the reason was, the lands being now near, which did not suffer the waves to rise, and using the best argument he could, yet he affirms he stood in need of God's particular assistance, as *Moses* did when he led the *Israelites* out of *Egypt*, who forbore laying violent hands upon him, because of the prodigies God wrought by his means. So said the admiral, it happened to him in that voyage; for upon *Sunday* following, the wind started up at W. N. W. with a rowling sea, as the men wish'd, and three hours before noon, they saw a turtle fly over the ship, and about evening an *Alcatraz*, a river fowl, and other white birds, and some crabs among the weeds; and the next day they spy'd another *Alcatraz*, and several small birds that came from the west, and small fishes, whereof the men of the other vessels stuck some with harping irons, because they would not bite at the hook.

Muttering among the seamen.

CHAP. XX.

How the men mutiny'd to turn back, and seeing other signs and tokens of land, went on well enough satisfied.

The men mutiny.

THE more the aforesaid tokens were found vain, the more they took occasion to apprehend and mutter; caballing together, and saying, the admiral out of a foolish fancy of his own, had designed to make himself a great lord at the expence of their lives and danger; and since they had done their duty in trying their fortune, and had gone farther from land and any succour than any others had done, they ought not to destroy themselves, nor proceed in that voyage, since if they did, they should have cause to repent; for provisions would fall short, and the ships fail, which they knew were already so faulty, that it would be hard to get back so far as they were gone, and that none would condemn them for so doing, but they would rather be look'd upon as very brave men, for going upon such a design, and venturing so far; and that the admiral being a foreigner, and having no favour at court, and so many wise and learned men having condemn'd his opinion, there would be no body now to favour and defend him, and they should sooner find credit if they accused him of ignorance and mismanagement, than he whatsoever he could say for himself. Nor did there want some who said, that to end all dispute, in case he would not acquiesce to them, they might make short, and throw him overboard, and give out, that as he was making his observations he dropped into the sea, and no man would go about to enquire into the truth of it, which was the readiest way for them to return home and secure themselves. Thus they went on from day to day, muttering, complaining and consulting together: nor was the admiral without apprehensions of their inconstancy, and ill intentions towards him. Therefore sometimes with good words, and sometimes with a full resolution to expose his life; putting them in mind of the punishment due to them if they obstructed the voyage, he in some measure quell'd their apprehensions, and suppress'd their ill designs. To confirm the hope he gave them, he put them in mind of the aforesaid signs and tokens, assuring them they would soon find land; which signs they were so attentive to, that they thought every hour a year till they saw land. On *Tuesday* the 25th of *September*, about sun-setting, as the admiral was discoursing with *Pinzon*, whose ship was very near, the said *Pinzon* on a sudden cry'd out, land, land, sir! Let not my good news miscarry: And shew'd him towards the south-west, a bulk which look'd very like an island, about 25 leagues from the ships. This was so pleasing to the men, that they returned thanks to God; and the admiral who had given no credit to these words, to please the men and that they should not obstruct his voyage, stood that way a great part of the night. Next morning they perceived that what they had seen were only clouds, which often look like land, for which reason, to the great dissatisfaction of most of the sailers, they turn'd the sterns of their ships westward, as they had always done, except when the wind hindred. Continuing ſtill attentive to the ſigns; they ſaw an *Alcatraz*, a *Rabo de Junco*, and other birds like thoſe above mentioned. On *Thurſday* the 27th of *September* in the morning, they ſaw another *Alcatraz* coming from the weſt, and ſailing eaſtward, and abundance of fiſhes with gilt backs appeared, whereof they ſtruck one with a harping-iron. A *Rabo de Junco* flew by them, and they founds that the currents, for thoſe laſt days, were not ſo regularly fixt, as they uſed to be before, but turned with the tide, and there were not ſo many weeds as before. On *Friday* following, all the ſhips took ſome fiſhes with gilt backs, and on *Saturday* they ſaw a *Rabo de Junco*, which tho' it be a ſea-fowl does not reſt on it, but flies always in the air, purſuing the *Alcatrazes*, till it makes them drop their excrement for fear, which it catches in the air for its nouriſhment, and thus it maintains its ſelf on the ſea, and it is reported there are many of them about the Iſlands of *Cabo Verde*. Soon after they ſaw two other *Alcatrazes*, and abundance of flying fiſhes, which are about a ſpan long, and have two little wings like a bat; they fly about a pike high from the water, and a muſket-ſhot in length, more or leſs, and ſometimes they drop upon the ſhips. Afternoon they ſaw abundance of weeds lying in length north and ſouth, as they had done before, beſides three *Alcatrazes* and a *Rabo de Junco* that purſued them.

On *Sunday* morning four *Rabo de Juncoes* came to the ſhip, by reaſon of whoſe coming ſo together, it was thought the land was nearer, eſpecially becauſe ſoon after there flew by four *Alcatrazes*, and abundance of weeds were ſeen in a line lying W. N. W. and E. S. E. and alſo a great number of thoſe fiſhes they call *Emperadores*, which have a very hard ſkin, and are not fit to eat. How much ſoever the admiral regarded theſe tokens, yet he never forgot thoſe in the heaven, and the courſe of the ſtars. He therefore obſerved in this place, to his great admiration, that the *Charles Wain* at night appeared in the weſt point, and in the morning they were directly N. E. by which he gathered, that their whole nights courſe was but three lines or nine hours, that is, ſo many parts of twenty four, and this he made out every night. He alſo perceived, that at night fall the compaſs varied a whole point to the north-weſt, and at break of day it came right with the ſtar. Theſe things confounded the pilots, till he told them the cauſe of it was the compaſs the ſtar took about the pole, which was ſome ſatisfaction to them; for this variation made them apprehend ſome danger in ſuch an unknown diſtance from home, and ſuch ſtrange regions.

CHAP. XXI.

How they ſaw not only the aforementioned ſigns and tokens, but others better than they, which were ſome comfort to the men.

They diſagree in their computations.

ON *Monday* the 1ſt of *October*, after ſun-riſing, an *Alcatraz*, came to the ſhip, and two more about ten in the morning, and long ſtreams of weeds lay from eaſt to weſt. That day in the morning the pilot of the admiral's ſhip ſaid, they were 578 leagues weſt of the iſland *Ferro*, the admiral ſaid by his account, they were 584 leagues, but in private he concluded it was 707, which is 129 leagues more than the pilot reckon'd. The other two ſhips differed very much in their computation, for the pilot of the caraval *Ninna* on *Wedneſday* following afternoon ſaid, they had ſail'd 540 leagues, and the other of the caraval *Pinta* ſaid 634. Adding all they had ſail'd during thoſe three days, they were ſtill much ſhort of truth, for they went always before the wind, and had run much more. But the admiral, as has been ſaid, wink'd at this groſs miſtake, that the men might not be quite dejected, being ſo far from home. The next day, being the 2d of October, they ſaw abundance of fiſh, catch'd a ſmall tunny, and ſaw a white bird, and many other ſmall ones, and the weeds they ſaw were withered and almoſt fallen to powder. The next day after, ſeeing no birds, but ſome fiſh, they miſtruſted they had left ſome iſlands on both hands, and were ſlip'd between without diſcovering them; gueſſing that thoſe many birds they had ſeen were paſſing from one iſland to another. They were very earneſt to ſteer either one way or the other, to ſeek out thoſe lands they imagined; but the admiral would not conſent, being unwilling to loſe the fair wind that carry'd him away to weſtward, which he accounted his ſureſt courſe; and beſides, becauſe he thought it was a leſſening the reputation of his undertaking, to run from one place to another, ſeeking that which he always affirmed he well knew where to find. For this reaſon the men were ready to mutiny, continuing to mutter and conſpire againſt him; but it pleaſed God, as

was

was said above, to assist him by the means of fresh tokens; for on *Thursday* the 4th of *October*, afternoon, above forty sparrows together and two *Alcatrazes* flew so near the ships, that a seaman killed one of them with a stone; and before this they had seen another bird like a *Rabo de Junso*, and another like a swallow, and a great many flying fishes fell into the ships. Next day there came a *Rabo de Junco*, and an *Alcatraz*, from the westward, and abundance of sparrows were seen. On *Sunday* the 7th of *October*, about sun-rising, some signs of land appeared westward, but being imperfect, no man would speak of it, not so much for the shame that would follow of asserting what was not, as for fear of losing 30 crowns a year, their catholick majesties had promised for life, to him that should first discover land; and to prevent their crying land, land at every turn, as they might do without cause at every turn, out of covetousness of that allowance, it was ordered, that whosoever said he saw land, if it were not made out in three days after, should lose the reward, though afterwards he should prove the first discoverer. All aboard the admiral being thus forewarned, none of them durst cry out land; but those in the caraval *Ninna*, which was a better sailer, and kept a head, believing it to be certainly land, fired a gun, and put out their colours in token of land. But the farther they sailed, the more their joys vanished, till that appearance quite vanished, tho' it pleased God soon after to give them some manner of comfort, for they saw great flights of great fowl, and others of small land birds, flying from the west towards the south-west. Therefore the admiral being now so far from *Spain*, and sure that such small birds would not go far from land; he alter'd his course, which till then was west, and stood to the south-west, saying, that if he changed his road, it was, because he deviated but little from his first design, and because he would follow the example of the *Portuguese*, who had discovered most of their islands by means of such birds, and the more because those they saw followed almost the same way; he had always proposed to himself to find land, according to the place they were then in; since as they well knew he had often told them, he never expected to find land till he was 750 leagues to the westward of the *Canaries*; within which distance he had farther said, he should discover *Hispaniola*, which he then call'd *Cipango*, and there is no doubt but he had found it, had not he known it was reported to lie in length from north to south: For which reason he had not inclined more to the south to run upon it, and therefore that and others of the *Caribbea* islands lay now on his larboard-side, south of him, whither those birds were directing their course. Being so near to land was the reason they continually saw such abundance of birds; and on *Monday* the 8th of *October*, there came to the ship twelve singing-birds of several colours, and after flying a turn about the ship, they held on their way. They also saw from the ships, many other birds flying towards the south-west; and that same night abundance of large fowls were seen, and flights of small birds coming from the northward, and flying after the rest. Besides, they saw a good number of tunny fish. In the morning they spy'd a jay, an *Alcatraz*, ducks and small birds, flying the same way the others had done; and they perceived the air to be fresh and odoriferous, as it is at *Sevil* in *April*. But they were now so eager to see land, that they had faith in no signs whatsoever; so that tho' on *Wednesday* the 10th of *October*, they saw abundance of birds pass by both day and night, yet the men did not cease to complain, nor the admiral to blame their want of courage; declaring to them, that right or wrong they must go on in discovering the *Indies*, their catholick majesties had sent them to.

The admiral alters his course.

CHAP. XXII.

How the admiral discovered the first land, which was an island called De Los Lucayos.

THE admiral being no longer able to withstand so many as opposed him, it pleased God that on *Thursday* the 11th of *October*, afternoon, the men took heart and rejoyced, having manifest tokens that they were near land, which were that those aboard the admiral, saw a greeen rush swim by the ship, and then a great green fish of that sort, that goes not far from the rocks. Those aboard the caraval *Pinta* saw a cane and a staff, and took up another staff curiously wrought, and a small board, and abundance of weeds fresh wash'd away from the banks. Those in the caraval *Ninna* saw other such like tokens, and a branch of a thorn full of red berries, which seem'd to be newly broke off. By these tokens, and reason it self, the admiral being assured

Other Tokens.

ſured he was near land; at night, after prayers, he made a ſpeech to all the men in general, putting them in mind how great a mercy it was that God had brought them ſo long a voyage, with ſuch fair weather, and comforting them with tokens, which every day were plainer and plainer; therefore he pray'd them to be very watchful that night, ſince they well knew that in the firſt article of the inſtructions he gave each ſhip at the *Canary* iſlands, he ordain'd that when they had ſail'd 700 leagues to the weſtward, without diſcovering land, they ſhould lie by from midnight till day. Therefore, ſince they had not yet obtained their deſires in diſcovering land, they ſhould at leaſt expreſs their zeal in being watchful. And forasmuch, as he had moſt aſſured hopes of finding land that night, every one ſhould watch in his place; for beſides the gratuity their highneſſes had promiſed of 30 crowns a year for life, to him that firſt ſaw land, he would give him a velvet doublet. After this, about ten at night, as the admiral was in the great cabin, he ſaw a light aſhore, but ſaid it was ſo blind, he could not affirm it to be land; tho' he called one *Peter Gutierres*, and bid him obſerve whether he ſaw the ſaid light, who ſaid he did; but preſently they called one *Roderick Sanchez* of *Segovia*, to look that way, but he could not ſee it, becauſe he came not up time enough where it might be ſeen; nor did they ſee it afterwards above once or twice, which made them judge it might be a candle or torch belonging to ſome fiſherman or traveller, who lifted it up, and let it fall down; or perhaps that they were people going from one houſe to another; becauſe it vaniſh'd and ſuddenly appeared again, ſo that few would gueſs but that they were near land. Being now very much upon their guard, they ſtill held on their courſe, till about two in the morning the caraval *Pinta*, which being an excellent ſailer, was far a-head, gave the ſignal of land, which was firſt diſcovered by a ſailer, whoſe name was *Roderick de Triana*, being two leagues from ſhore. But the thirty crowns a year was not granted by their catholick majeſties to him, but to the admiral; who had ſeen the light in the midſt of darkneſs, ſignifying the ſpiritual light he was then ſpreading in thoſe dark regions. Being now near land, all the ſhips lay by, thinking it a long time till morning, that they might ſee what they had ſo long deſired.

Land diſcover'd.

CHAP. XXIII.

How the admiral went aſhore, and took poſſeſſion for their catholick Majeſties.

St. Salvador *the firſt iſland diſcovered.*

DAY appearing, they perceived it was an iſland fifteen leagues in length; plain, without hills and full of green trees, and delicious waters, with a great lake in the middle, inhabited by abundance of people, who ran down to the ſhore, aſtoniſhed and admiring at the ſight of the ſhips, believing them to be ſome living creatures, and were impatient to know certainly what they were. Nor were the chriſtians leſs haſty to know them, whoſe curioſity was ſoon ſatisfied, for they ſoon came to an anchor; the admiral went aſhore with his boat well armed, and the royal ſtandard diſplay'd, as did the captains of the other two ſhips in their boats, with their particular colours of this enterprize, which were a green croſs with an F on the one ſide, and on the other the names of *Ferdinand* and *Iſabel* or *Elizabeth* crown'd. Having given thanks to God, kneeling on the ſhore, and kiſs'd the ground with tears of joy, for the great mercy received, the admiral ſtood up, and called that iſland *St. Salvador*. After that he took poſſeſſion for their catholick majeſties, in the uſual words, and with the ſolemnity proper in thoſe caſes; abundance of the natives that were come out, being preſent, and conſequently the chriſtians admitted him as admiral and viceroy, and ſwore to obey him as repreſenting their highneſſes perſons, and with ſuch expreſſions of joy, as became their mighty ſucceſs, all of them begging his pardon for all the affronts they had done him thro' their fear and irreſolution. Abundance of the *Indians* being come down to this rejoycing, and the admiral perceiving they were peaceable, quiet and very ſimple people, he gave them ſome red caps, and ſtrings of glaſs beads, which they hung about their necks, and other things of ſmall value, which they valued as if they had been ſtone of high price.

CHAP. XXIV.

The manners and customs of those people, and what the admiral saw in that island.

Descripti-on of the Islanders.

THE admiral being gone off to his boats, the *Indians* follow'd him to them and to the ships swimming, and others in their canoes, carrying parrots, bottoms of spun cotton, javelins, and other such trifles to barter for glass-beads, bells, and other things of small value. Like people in their original simplicity, they went naked as they were born, and a woman that was among them had no other cloathing. Most of them were young, not above thirty years of age; of a good stature, their hair lank, thick, very black and short, being cut above their ears, except some few who had let it grow down to their shoulders, and had ty'd it with a strong thread about their head like womens tresses. Their countenances were pleasant, and their features good, but their too high foreheads made them look somewhat wild. They were of a middle stature, well shaped, plump, but of an olive colour, like the people of the *Canaries* or peasants that are sun-burn'd. Some were painted with black, some with white and others with red; some only the faces, others the whole body, and others nothing but the eyes and nose. They had no weapons like our men, nor knowledge of them; for when the christians shew'd them a naked sword, they took it simply by the edge. Nor had they any knowledge of iron, and therefore they made their javelins we mentioned, of wands, with the points hardened at the fire, arming them with a fish bone instead of iron. Some of them having scars of wounds about them, and being ask'd by signs how they came by them, they answered by signs, that people came from other islands to take them away, and they received those wounds in their own defence. They seem'd ingenious and of a voluble tongue, for they easily repeated the words they once heard. There were no sort of creatures there but parrots, which they carried to barter among the other things we have spoke of, and in this trade they continued till night. Next day being the 13th of *October* in the morning, many of them came down to the shore, and went aboard in their boats called canoes, which were made of one piece, being the body of a tree hollow'd like a tray. The biggest of them were so large, they contained 40 or 45 men, and so less and less, till some would hold but one. They row'd with a paddle like a baker's peal, or those they use in dressing hemp; true it is, that the oars are not fixed on the side with pins to turn as ours are, but they dip them in the water, and pull back as if they were digging. These canoes are so light and so artificially built, that if they overset they soon turn them right again swimming, and empty the water by throwing the vessel from side to side like a weaver's shuttle; and when it is above half out, they lade out what remains with dry'd calabashes cut in two, which they carry for that purpose. That day they brought such things to barter for as they had the day before, giving all they had for any small things they could get. Jewels or any sort of metal were not seen among them, except some small plates of gold which hung at their nostrils, and being asked whence they had that gold, they answered by signs, towards the south, where there was a king who had abundance of pieces and vessels of gold, expressing that towards the south and south-west, there were many other islands and large countries. Being very covetous of any thing of ours, and being themselves but poor, and having nothing to give in exchange, as soon as they came aboard, if they could lay their hands on any thing, tho' it were but a piece of a broken earthen glazed dish or porringer, they leaped into the sea, and swam ashore; and if they brought any thing aboard, they would give it for any trifling thing of ours, or bit of broken glass, so that some of them gave 16 bottoms of cotton for three small pieces of *Portuguese* brass coin not worth a farthing; these bottoms weighed 25 pounds, and the cotton was very well spun. Thus they spent the day, and at night they all went ashore. It is to be observed, that their liberality in dealing did not proceed from the great value they put upon those things themselves, which they had of our men, but because they valued them as being ours, looking upon it as most certain that our men were come down from heaven, and therefore they earnestly desired to have something left them as a memorial.

Canoes.

CHAP.

CHAP. XXV.

How the admiral departed from that island, and went to discover others.

NEXT *Sunday*, being the 15th of *October*, the admiral run along the coast of the island, towards the north-west, in his boats, to discover something about it; and that way he went, he found a large bay or harbour, capable of containing all the ships in christendom. The people seeing him scour along, ran after, along the shoar, crying out, and promising to give him provisions, calling others to come to see the people drop'd from heaven upon earth, and lifted up their hands to heaven, as it were giving thanks for their coming. Many of them swimming, or in their canoes, as best they could, came to the boats, asking by signs, whether they were come down from heaven, and praying them to land and rest themselves. The admiral gave them all glass beads, pins, and other trifles, rejoycing at their great simplicity, till he came to a *Peninsula*, which made a good port, and where a good fort might be made. There he saw six houses of the *Indians* with gardens about them, as pleasant as they are in *Castile* in *May*. But his men being weary of rowing, and he plainly perceiving that was none of the land he looked for, nor so beneficial, as that he should make any longer stay there, he took seven of those *Indians* to serve him as interpreters; and returning to his ships, sailed for other islands that could be discovered from the *Peninsula*, and appeared to be plain, green and very populous, as the *Indians* themselves affirm'd. The next day being *Monday*, the 16th of *October*, he came to one that was seven leagues from the other, and called it St. *Mary of the Conception*. That side of this island next St. *Salvador* extended north-west five leagues in length, but the admiral went to that side which lies east and west, and is above 10 leagues in length; and being come to an anchor towards the west, landed to do as he had done in the other. Here the people of the island ran together to see the christians, admiring as the others had done. The admiral perceiving this was the same thing as the last: The next day being *Tuesday*, sail'd westward to another island considerably bigger, and anchored upon the coast of it, which runs north-west and south-east, above 28 leagues. This was like the others, plain, had a fine strand, and was called *Fernandina*. Before they came to this island, and that of the *Conception*, they found a man in a small canoe, who had a piece of their bread, and a calabash of water, and a little earth like vermillion, wherewith those people paint their bodies, as was said above; and some dry leaves which they value, as being of a sweet scent and wholesome; and in a little basket he had a string of beads of green glass, and two small pieces of *Portuguese* money, by which it was guessed that he was coming from St. *Salvador*, that he had passed by the *Conception*, and was going to *Fernandina* to carry news of the christians: But because the way was far, and he weary, he came to the ships, was taken up with his canoe, and courteously treated by the admiral, designing as soon as he came to land to send him ashore, which he did, that he might spread the news. The good account he gave, caused the people of *Fernandina* to come aboard in their canoes, to exchange the same sort of things the others had done before, for these people were like the rest; and when the boat went ashore for water, the *Indians* very readily show'd where it was, and carry'd a small cask full on their shoulders to fill the hogsheads in the boat. They seemed to be a wiser and discreeter people than the first, and as such bargain'd harder for what they exchanged, had cotton cloath in their houses, and bed-cloaths; and the women covered their privities with short hanging cotton-cloaths, and others with a sort of swathe. Among other notable things they saw in that island, were some trees which seemed to be grafted, because they had leaves and branches of four or five several sorts, and yet were natural. They also saw fishes of several shapes and fine colours, but no sort of land creatures but lizards and snakes. The better to discover the island, they sailed away north-west, and came to an anchor at the mouth of a beautiful harbour; at the entrance whereof was a small island, and therefore they could not get in, there being but little water; nor did they much care, because they would not be far from a town that appeared at a distance: For in the biggest island they had yet seen they had not found above 12 or 15 houses together, built like tents, in which they saw no other ornaments or moveables, but what they carry'd to the ships to exchange. Their beds were like a net, drawn together in the nature of a sling tied to two posts in their houses, in which they lie. Here they saw some dogs like mastiffs, and others like beagles, but none of them bark'd.

Marginal notes: Conception *Island*. — *Island* Fernandina.

CHAP.

CHAP. XXVI.

How the admiral sailed by other islands that were in sight where he was.

Island Isabella.

FInding nothing of value in this island, *Fernandina*, on *Friday* the 19th of *October*, they sailed away to another, called *Saomotto*, to which he gave the name of *Isabella*, to proceed regularly in his names; for the first which the *Indians* call'd *Guanabani*, he call'd St. *Salvador*, or St. *Saviour* in honour of god, who had show'd it and delivered him from many dangers. The second for his particular devotion, to the conception of the virgin *Mary*; and because she is the great patroness of christians, he called St. *Mary of the Conception*; the third he called *Fernandina*, in honour of the catholick king, and the fourth *Isabella*, in memory of the catholick queen; and the next after it which was *Cuba*, he stiled *Joanna*, in respect to prince *John*, heir of *Castile*, having in these names regard both to spirituals and temporals. True it is, that as to goodness, extent, and beauty, he said this *Fernandina* far exceeded the others; for besides that it abounded in delicious waters, pleasant meadows and trees, among which were many of *Aloes*; there were in it some hills, which the others wanted, being very plain. The admiral enamoured with its beauty, and to perform the ceremony of taking possession, landed upon some meadows as pleasant and delightful as they are in *Spain* in *April*; and there was heard the singing of nightingales and other birds, so sweet, that he could scarce depart. Nor were they only about the trees, but flew thro' the air in such swarms, that they darkened the sun, and most of them differed much from our birds. There being abundance of waters and lakes; near to one of them they saw a sort of alligator seven foot long, and above a foot wide in the belly, which being disturbed by our men, threw its self into the lake. But it not being deep, they killed it with their spears, not without dread and admiration, because of its fierce and frightful look. Time afterwards made them look upon this as a dainty, it being the best food the *Indians* had; forasmuch as when that horrid skin, and the scales that cover it are taken of, the flesh is very white and very delicious, the *Indians* call them *Yvanas*. Being very desirous Yvanas. to know more of that countrey, and it being then late, they left that creature for the next day, when they killed another, as they had done the first; and travelling up the land found a town, the people whereof fled, carrying away as much of their goods as they could. The admiral would not suffer any thing of what they had left to be taken away, lest they should look upon the christians as thieves. Therefore their fear being soon over, they came of their own accord to the ships to barter, as the others had done.

CHAP. XXVII.

How the admiral discovered the island of Cuba *and what he found there.*

Island of Cuba,

THE admiral having learned the secrets of the island *Isabella*, its product, and the manners of the people, would lose no more time among those islands, because they were many and like one another, as the *Indians* said. He therefore set sail with a fair wind for a very large countrey, much applauded by them all, called *Cuba*, which lay towards the south, and on *Sunday* the 28th of *October*, he came up with the coast of it, on the north side. This island at first sight appeared to be better and richer than those before named, as well by reason of the beauty of its hills and mountains, as for the variety of trees, the large plains, and the greatness and extent of its coasts and rivers. Therefore to get some knowledge of its people, he came to an anchor in a large river, where the trees were very thick and tall, adorned with fruit and blossoms, differing from ours, and where there were abundance of birds, the place most delicious, for the grass was high, and nothing like ours; and tho' there were several sorts of herbs known to us, yet the great variety made our men not know them. Going to two houses that were not far off, they found the people were fled for fear, and had left their nets, and all other fishing tackle, and a dog that did not bark. As the admiral had ordered, nothing was touched, for it was enough for him at present to see what their food and necessaries were. Returning to their ships they held on their course westward, and came to another river, which the admiral called *de Mares*, or of seas. This much exceeded the other, because a ship could turn it up, and the banks were much inhabited; but the people seeing the ships, fled towards the mountains, which appear'd, and were high, round, and covered with trees and pleasant plants, whither the *Indians* convey'd all they could carry away. The admiral being disappointed, by the peoples fear, of learning any thing of the nature of the island, and considering if he landed with many men, it would increase their terrour, he resolved to send two christians, with one of the *Indians* he brought from *St. Salvador*, and with one of that country, who ventured to come aboard in his canoo. These he ordered to travel up into the country, making much of the natives they met by the way, and that no time might be lost, whilst they were going, he order'd the ship to be lay'd ashore to careen her, where they observed that all the fire they made was mastick, whereof there was plenty all the country over. This tree is in all respects like our mastick tree, but much bigger.

CHAP. XXVIII.

How the two christians return'd, and the report they made of what they had seen.

A town in Cuba.

THE ship being repaired and ready to sail, the christians returned with two *Indians* on the 5th of *November*, saying, they had travell'd twelve leagues up the land, and came to a town of 50 pretty large houses, all of timber covered with straw, and made after the manner of pavillions, like the others; that they contain'd about 1000 people, because all that were of one family liv'd in a house, that the principal men of the place came out to meet them, and led them by the arms to their town, giving them one of those great houses to lodge in, where they made them sit down upon seats made of one piece, in strange shapes, and almost like some creature that had short legs, and the tail lifted up to lean against, which is as broad as the seat for the conveniency of leaning, with a head before, and the eyes and ears of gold. These seats they call *Duchi*, where the christians being seated, all the *Indians* sate about them on the ground, and then came one by one to kiss their hands and feet, believing they came from heaven; and they gave them some boil'd roots to eat, not unlike chesnuts in taste; earnestly entreating them to stay there among them, or at least to rest themselves 5 or 6 days, because the two *Indians* they took with them, gave those people an excellent character of the christians. Soon after, many women coming in to see them; the men went out, and these with no less respect, kiss'd their feet and hands, offering them what they brought. When their time came to return to the ships, many *Indians* would go along with them, but they would admit only of the king, his son and one servant, whom the admiral did much honour to; and these christians told him, that in their way out, and return, they had found several towns, where they were entertain'd with the same courtesy, but that there were not in them above five houses together: Besides, that by the way they met many people, who always carried a lighted firebrand, to light fire and perfume themselves with certain herbs they carried along with them, and to roast some of those roots they gave them; forasmuch as that was their principal food. They also saw very many sorts of trees and plants, which were not to be seen about the sea-coast; and great variety of birds, far differing from ours, but that among them that were partridges and nightingals. As for four-footed creatures, they had seen none but dumb dogs. That there was a great deal of till'd land, some sow'd with those roots, a sort of beans, and a sort of grain they call *Maiz*, which was well tasted, bak'd, or dry'd and made into flour. They saw vast quantities of cotton well spun, in bottoms, insomuch that in one house only, they saw above 12500 pounds of it. The plants it comes from are not set, but grow naturally about the fields, like roses, and open of themselves, when they are ripe, but not all at the same time; for upon one and the same plant, they had seen a little young bud, another open, and a third coming ripe. Of these plants the *Indians* afterwards carried great quantities aboard the ships, and gave a basket full for a thong of leather; yet none of them make use of it to cloath themselves, but only to make nets for their beds, which they call *Hamacas*, and in weaving aprons for women to cover their nakedness. Being ask'd whether they had gold or pearls, or spice, they made signs that there was great plenty towards the east, in a country they call'd *Bohio*, which is the island of *Hispaniola*, but it is not yet certainly known what place they meant.

CHAP.

CHAP. XXIX.

How the admiral desisted from following the western coast of Cuba, *and turn'd eastward towards* Hispaniola.

THE admiral having this account, and resolving to stay no longer in that river, order'd some natives of that island to be taked, designing to carry some from all parts into *Spain*, to give an account of his country; and accordingly 12 were seiz'd, men, women, and children, and this so peaceably and without any disturbance, that when they were ready to sail with them, the husband of one of the women, and father of two children that had been carry'd aboard, came to the ships in a canoo desiring he might be taken along with them, and not parted from his wife and children, which extreamly pleas'd the admiral, who order'd he should be receiv'd, and they all well us'd and made much of. That same day, being the 13th of *November*, he came about to the eastward, designing for the island they call'd *Bohio*. The wind blowing hard at north, he was forced to come to an anchor again in the same island of *Cuba*, among some high islands, lying near a large port, which he call'd *del Principe*, or the princes port, and the sea, *Our Lady's*. These islands lay so thick and close, there was not above a quarter of a league distance between them at furthest, and but a musquet shot for the most part. The chanels were so deep, and so well adorn'd with trees and greens, that it was very delightful going among them; and among the multitude of other trees, there were abundance of mastick, aloes and palm, the trunk green and smooth, and other plants of sundry sorts. And tho' these islands were not inhabited, yet there appeared the tokens of many fires made by fishermen; for as it afterwards appear'd, the people of *Cuba* went together in great number, in their canoos over to these islands, and abundance more that lie hereabouts uninhabited, and live upon the fish they catch, upon birds, crabs, and other things they find on the earth; forasmuch as generally the *Indians* eat abundance of filthy things, such as great spiders, worms that breed in rotten wood and other corrupt places, and abundance of fish almost raw; for as soon as taken, before they roast it, they digg out the eyes to eat, and many other such things they feed on, which, besides that they are nauseous, would kill any of us, should we eat them. They follow this fishing and birding according to the season, sometimes in one island, sometimes in another, as one that changes his diet, being weary of the last. But to return to the islands of *Our Lady's Sea*, in one of them the christians with their swords, kill'd a beast like a badger, and in the sea found much mother of pearl; and casting their nets, among many other sorts of fish they caught, one was like a swine, all cover'd with a very hard skin, no part whereof was soft but the tail. They also observ'd that in this sea, and the islands, the tide swell'd and fell much lower than in other places, where they had been till then, and their tides were quite contrary to ours; for it was low water when the moon was S. W. and by S.

Conjugal affection in an Indian.

Foood of the Indians.

CHAP. XXX.

How the admiral set sail again eastward for Hispaniola, *and one of the ships forsook him.*

ON *Monday* the 19th of *November*, the admiral departed from the princes port in *Cuba*, and the sea of *Our Lady*, steering eastward for the island of *Bohio* and *Hispaniola*, but the wind being contrary, he was forced to ply two or three days between the island *Isabella*, which the *Indians* call *Somoto*, and the said princes port, which lie almost north and south, about 25 leagues distant, in which sea he still found long traces of these weeds he had seen in the ocean, and he perceived they swam along the current, and never lay athwart it. During this time *Martin Alonzo Pinzon* being inform'd by certain *Indians* he had conceal'd aboard his caraval, that in the island *Bohio*, which we said was *Hispaniola*, there was great plenty of gold; covetously blinding him, on *wednesday* the 21st of *November*, he went away from the admiral without any stress of weather, or any other occasion, for he could have come up to him before the wind, but would not, and so making as much way as possibly he could, his vessel being an excellent sailer, he made forwards all *Thursay*, whereas they had sail'd in sight of one another all the day before, and night coming on, he quite vanish'd. Thus the admiral was left only with two ships, and the weather not being fit

Martin Alonzo *leaves the admiral.*

fit for his vessels to sail over towards *Hispaniola*, he was forced to return to *Cuba*, to another port not far from the princes, which he call'd *St. Catharine's*, there to take in wood and water. In this port he accidentally saw signs of gold on some stones in the river where they were watering, and up the country there were mountains full of such tall pine trees, as would make masts for the biggest ships. Nor was there any want of wood for planks, to build as many ships as they would, and among them oaks, and others like those in *Castile*. But perceiving that all the *Indians* directed him to *Hispaniola*, he run along the coast 10 or 12 leagues farther towards the south-east, meeting all the way excellent harbours, and many large rivers. The admiral says so much of the delightfulness and beauty of that country, that I have thought fit here to set down his own words, speaking of the mouth of the river, which makes a harbour by him called *Puerto Santo*, or holy harbour. Thus he says, when I went with the boats before me to the mouth of the harbour towards the south, I found a river, up whose mouth a gally could easily row, and the way up it was such, that it was not to be discover'd but close by: the beauty of it invited me to go up a boats length, where I found from 5 to 8 fathom water; and proceeding, I went a considerable way up the river in the boats; because, as well the beauty and delightfulness of the river, and the clearness of the water, thro' which I could see the sand at the bottom; as the abundance of palm trees of several sorts, the finest and highest I had yet met with; the other, infinite number of large green trees, the birds, and the verdure of the plain, tempted me to fix there for ever. This country, most serene princes, is so wonderfully fine, as far exceeds all other beauty and delightfulness, as the day in brightness exceeds the night. Therefore I often told my companions, that tho' I should never so much endeavour to give your highnesses a perfect account of it, my tongue and pen would always fall short of the truth. And to say the truth, I was astonished to see so much beauty, and know not how to express it; for I have writ of the other countries, of their trees and fruits, of the plants and ports, and of all that belong'd to them, as largely as I was able, yet not as I ought, since all men affirm'd it was impossible any other country could be more delicious. Now I am silent, wishing this may be seen by others, who will write of it, that they may prove how little credit is to be got more than I have done in writing or speaking of that place considering what it deserves. The admiral going on with his boats, saw a canoo among the trees in the port, drawn upon land under a bower, which canoo was made of the body of one tree, and as big as a twelve oar barge, and in some houses hard by, they found a ball of wax, and a man's skull in two baskets hanging at a post. The same they afterwards found in another house, which made our men judge, they were the sculls of the founders of those houses. No people appeared to receive any information of, for as soon as ever they saw the christians, they fled from their houses to other parts. Afterwards they found another canoo about 70 foot long, that would carry 50 persons, made like the other we spoke of before.

A delicious country.

Two vast canoos.

CHAP. XXXI.

How the admiral sail'd over to Hispaniola, *and what he saw there.*

Hispaniola.

THE admiral having sail'd 106 leagues eastward along the coast of *Cuba*, came to the east point of it, which he call'd *Alpha*, and on *Wednesday* the 5th of *December*, struck off to sail over to *Hispaniola*, distant 16 leagues from *Cuba* eastward, and by reason of some currents, could not reach it till the next day, when he put into port *St. Nicholas*, so call'd by him in memory of that saint, whose festival was that day. The port is large, deep, safe, and encompass'd with many tall trees, but the country is more rocky, and the trees are less, that is, like those of *Castile*, among which there were small oaks, myrtle and other shrubs, and a pleasant river ran along a plain towards the port, all about which, there were large canoos like 15 oar barges. The admiral not being able to meet with any of those people, ran along the coast northward, till he came to a port he call'd the *Conception*, which lies almost due south of a small island about the bigness of *Gran Canaria*, which was afterwards call'd *Tortuga*. Perceiving that this island *Bohio* was very large, and that the land and trees were like those of *Spain*; and that at one draught of a net they had taken several fishes, like those of *Spain*, as soles, salmon, pilchards, crabs, and some others, therefore on *Sunday* the 9th of *December*, they gave it the name of *Espannola*, as call'd in

Tortuga.

in English, Hispaniola. All of them being very desirous to enquire into the nature of this island; whilst the men were fishing on the shoar, three christians travelled along the mountain, and lighted on a company of Indians, as naked as those they had seen before, who seeing the christians draw near them, in a great fright, ran into the thickest of the wood, as having no cloaths to hinder them. The christians to get some information, ran after them, but could only overtake a young woman, who had a plate of gold hanging at her nose. She was carried to the ships, where the admiral gave her several baubles, as bells and glass, and then sent her ashore without the least disgust offer'd her, ordering three Indians of those he brought from the other islands to go with her, and three christians, to the town where she dwelt. The next day he sent 11 men ashoar well arm'd, who having travelled four leagues, found a sort of town or village of above 1000 houses, scattered about a valley, the inhabitants whereof seeing the christians, all fled to the woods. But the Indian guide, whom our men brought from St. Salvador, went after them, and said such things to them of the christians, affirming they were people come from heaven, that he persuaded them to turn back quietly and without any fear. Afterwards full of astonishment, they would lay their hands on our mens heads by way of honour, brought them to eat, and gave them all they desired, without asking any return, praying them to stay that night in their village. The christians would not accept of the invitation, but return'd to their ships carrying the news that the country was very pleasant, abounding in their provisions: that the people were whiter and handsomer, than any they had yet seen in other islands, and that they were tractable and courteous, and told them the country where the gold was found, lay farther eastward. The admiral hearing this account, set sail immediately, tho' the wind was contrary, and on Sunday following, being the 15th of December, as he was plying between Hispaniola and Tortuga, he found one Indian alone in a little canoo, which they all wonder'd was not swallowed by the sea, the wind and the waves were so high. He took him into the ship, carried him to Hispaniola, and set him ashoar with several gifts. He told the Indians how kindly he had been used, and spoke so well of the christians, that abundance of them came presently aboard, but they brought nothing of value, except some small grains of gold hanging at their ears and nostrils, and being ask'd whence they had that gold, they made signs there was a great deal higher up. The next day there came a great canoo from the island Tortuga, which was near the place where the admiral lay at anchor, with 40 men in it, at such time as the Cacique or lord of that port of Hispaniola was upon the shoar, bartering a plate of gold he had brought. When he and his saw the canoo, they all sate themselves down upon the ground, as a sign they would not fight. Immediately almost all those in the canoo landed, again whom the Cacique of Hispaniola got up alone, and with threatning words made them return to their canoo. Then he threw water after them, and taking up stones off the strand, cast them into the sea towards the canoo. But when they were all in submissive manner return'd to their canoo, he took up a stone and delivered it to one of the admiral's officers, to throw at those in the canoo, to express that he took the admiral's part against the Indians, but the officer did not throw, seeing they presently went off in their canoo. After this, discoursing about the affairs of that island, which the admiral had call'd Tortuga, he affirm'd there was more gold in it than in Hispaniola, and that in Bohio there was more than in any other, which was about 15 days journey from the place where they were.

CHAP. XXXII.

How the principal king of the island came aboard, and of the state he came in.

ON Tuesday the 18th of December, the king that came the day before, where the canoo of Tortuga was, and who lived 5 leagues from the place where the ships lay, came in the morning to the town near the sea, some of the Spaniards at the same time being there by the admiral's order to see whether they brought any more gold. These seeing the king come, went to acquaint the admiral, saying he brought above 200 men along with him, and that he came not a foot but was carry'd on a sort of palanquine by four men with great respect, tho' he was very young. This king being at a small distance from the ships having rested a little, drew near with all his men, concerning which, the admiral himself writes thus: There is no doubt but your highnesses had been very much pleas'd to have seen his gravity, and the respect his people pay'd him

Account of the Cacique or Indian king.

him, tho' all naked. When he came aboard, and understood I was under deck, being then at dinner, he surpris'd me, sitting down by me, without giving me time to go out to receive him, or rise from table. When he came down he made signs to all his followers to stay above, which they did with great respect, sitting down upon the deck, except two ancient men that seemed to be his counsellors, that sat down at his feet. They said this man was a *Cacique*. I order'd such meat as I was eating, to be brought him; they just tasted of every thing, and sent the rest to their men, who all eat of it. The same they did as to drinking, for they only kiss'd the cup and gave it about. They were all wonderful grave, and spoke but few words, and those they utter'd, by what I could gather, were very deliberate and staid. The two old men observ'd the king's mouth, and spoke for and to him. After eating, one of his gentlemen with great respect brought him a girdle, not unlike those used in *Castile*, tho' differently wrought, which he took in his hand, and gave me with two pieces of wrought gold very thin. Of which gold I believe there is little here, and I guess'd that place was near to where they took it, which produced very much. I believing he would like a carpet or counterpan that lay on my bed, gave it him, together with some fine amber beads I had about my neck, with a pair of red shoes and a bottle of orange-flower water, with which he was wonderfully pleas'd, and both he and his counsellors express'd much concern because they did not understand me, nor I them, tho' I made out, that if I wanted any thing, all the island was at my command. I presently brought out a letter-case, in which I carry'd a gold medal weighing 4 ducats, on which your highnesses effigies are cut, and showed it him, saying over again, that your highnesses were mighty princes, and possest the best part of the world, and shewed him the royal standard, and the other of the cross, which he made great account of. Therefore turning to his counsellors, he said, your highnesses were certainly mighty princes, since you had sent me so far as from heaven thither, without any fear. Much more pass'd between us, which I did not understand, but perceiv'd they admired at every thing they saw; but it being then late, and he desiring to be gone, I sent him ashore very honourably in my boat, and caused several guns to be fired, and he being ashore got into his palanquine, attended by above 200 men, and a son of his was carried on a man of note's shoulders. He ordered all the *Spaniards* that were ashore, to have meat given them, and to be very courteously used. Afterwards a sailer that met him on the way, told me, that every one of the things I had given him, were carry'd before him by a man of great worth, and that his son went not along with him on the road, but at some distance behind him with as many more attendance as he had, and a brother of his on foot, with near as many more, two great men leading him under the arms, to whom I had given some small matters when he came aboard after his brother.

CHAP. XXXIII.

How the admiral lost his ship upon the flats thro' the carelessness of the sailers, and the assistance he receiv'd from the king of that island.

THE admiral continuing the relation as above, says, That on *Monday* the 24th of *December*, the weather was very calm, without any wind hardly, but so much as carried him from St. *Thomas*'s sea, to *Punta Santa*, or the holy cape, off which he lay by about a league, and about 11 of the clock at night he went to take his rest, for he had not slept in two days and a night; and the weather being calm, the seaman that was at the helm, left it to a grummet, which (says the admiral) I had forbid during the whole voyage, bidding them, whether the wind blew or not, never to leave the helm to a grummet. And to say the truth, I thought my self safe from flats and rocks; for that *Sunday* I sent my boats to the king, they went at least three leagues and a half beyond the said *Punta Santa*; and the seamen had view'd all the coast, and the shoals that lie three leagues E. S. E. of that cape, and observ'd which way to sail, which I had not done during the voyage; and it pleased our lord, that at midnight, seeing me gone to bed, and we being in a dead calm and the sea as still as the water in a dish, all the men went to rest, leaving the helm to a grummet. Thus it came to pass, that the current easily carried away the ship upon one of those shoals, which tho' it was night, made such a roaring noise, that they might be heard and discover'd a league off. Then the fellow who felt the rudder strike and heard the noise, began to cry out, and I hearing it, got up immediately; for none

The admiral's ship lost.

had yet perceived that we were a ground. Presently the master, whose watch it was, came out, and I order'd him and other sailers to take the boat, and carry out an anchor a stern; whereupon he and others leap'd into the boat, and I believing they would have done as I ordered, they row'd away, flying with the boat to the other caraval, which was half a league off. I then perceiving they ran away with the boat, that the water ebb'd, and the ship was in danger, caused the masts to be cut down, and lightned her as much as I could to see to get her off; but the water still ebbing, the caraval could not budge, but turning athwart the streams, the seams open'd, and all below deck was full of water. Mean while the boat returned from the caraval to relieve me; for the men aboard perceiving the boat fled, would not receive it, which oblig'd it to return to the ship. No hopes of saving the ship appearing, I went away to the caraval to save the men, and because the wind blew from the land, and great part of the night was spent, and yet we knew not which way to get from among those flats; I lay by with the caraval till day appeared, and then I drew towards land within the shoals, having first sent *James de Arana* the provost, and *Peter Gutierres* your highnesses secretary, to acquaint the king with what had happened, telling him, That as I was going to visit him in his own port, as he had desired the last *Saturday*, I had lost my ship opposite to his town, and a league and a half from it upon a flat. The king understanding it, with tears in his eyes, expressed much grief for our loss, and immediately sent aboard all the people in the place, with many large canoes. So they and we began to unload, and in a short time carried off all that was upon deck. The assistance this king gave was great; and afterwards he himself, with his brothers and kindred, took all possible care both aboard and ashore, that all things might be done orderly; and from time to time he sent some of his kindred weeping, to beg of me not to be dejected, for he would give me all he had. I do assure your highnesses, better order could not have been taken in any part of *Castile*, to secure our things; for we lost not the value of a pin, for he caused all our cloaths to be laid together near his palace, where he kept them till the houses were voided, which he had appointed for us. He placed armed men to keep them, who stood there all day and all night, and all the people lamented, as if our loss had concern'd them much; so loving, tractable and free from covetousness they are, that I swear to your highnesses, there are no better people, nor a better countrey in the world. They love their neighbour as themselves, and their conversation is the sweetest in the universe, being pleasant and always smiling. True it is, both men and women go as naked as they were born; yet, your highnesses may believe me, they have very commendable customs, and the king is serv'd with great state; and he is so staid, that it is a great satisfaction to see him, as it is to think what good memories these people have, and how desirous they are to know every thing, which moves 'em to ask many questions, and to enquire into the cause and effects of every thing.

Great kindness of the Indians *to the* Spaniards.

CHAP. XXXIV.

How the admiral resolved to plant a colony where the king resided, and call'd it the nativity.

ON *Wednesday* the 26th of *December*, the chief king of that countrey came aboard the admiral's caraval, and expressing much grief and sorrow, comforted him, offered all he would have, and saying he had already given the christians three houses to lay up all they got out of the ship, and that he had given them many more, had they stood in need of them. In the mean while a canoe came with some *Indians* from another island, bringing some plates of gold to exchange for bells, which they valued above any thing. Besides the seamen came from shore, saying abundance of *Indians* resorted from other places to the town, who brought several things in gold and gave them for points, and other things of small value, offering to bring much more if the christians would. Which the great *Cacique* perceiving was pleasing to the admiral; he told him he would cause a great quantity to be brought from *Cibao*, a place that yielded much gold. Being ashore, he invited the admiral to eat *Axis* and *Cazabi*, which is their principal diet, and gave him some vizor masks, with the eyes, nose and ears of gold, and other pretty things which they hung about their necks. Then complaining of the *Caribbes*, who carried away his men to make slaves and eat them, he was much comforted, when the admiral comforting him, show'd him our weapons, saying, he would defend him with them. He was much astonish'd

The admiral builds a fort and leaves men in the island.

ſtoniſh'd at our canon, which ſo terrified them, that they fell down as if they were dead, when they heard the report. The admiral therefore finding ſo much kindneſs among thoſe people, and ſuch ſigns of gold, almoſt forgot the grief conceiv'd for the loſs of his ſhip; thinking God had permitted it that he might fix a colony there, and leave chriſtians to trade, and get farther knowledge of the people and countrey, learning the language, and converſing with the natives, that when he returned from *Spain* with ſuccours, he might have ſome body to direct him in his affairs, for peopling and ſubduing that countrey. To this he was the more inclined, becauſe many voluntarily offered themſelves to ſtay and inhabit there. For this reaſon he reſolved to build a tower with the timber of the ſhip that was wrecked, whereof he loſt no part, but made uſe of it all. To forward his deſign, the next day being *Thurſday*, the 27th of *December*, news was brought, that the caraval *Pinta*, was in a river towards the eaſt point of the iſland. To be aſſured of it, the *Cacique*, whoſe name was *Guacanagari*, ſent a canoe with ſome *Indians*, who carried a chriſtian thither: he having gone 20 leagues along the coaſt, returned without any news of it, which was the reaſon that no credit was given to another *Indian*, who ſaid he had ſeen her ſome days before. Nevertheleſs the admiral did not alter his reſolution of leaving ſome chriſtians in that place, who were all ſtill more ſenſible of the goodneſs and wealth of the countrey, the *Indians* bringing maſks and other things of gold to give them, and telling them of ſeveral provinces in the iſland where it was found. The admiral now being ready to depart, and diſcourſing with the king concerning the *Caribbes*, or *Canibals*, of whom they complained and were in great dread, therefore to pleaſe him with leaving ſome chriſtians there, and at the ſame time make him afraid of our arms, he cauſed a gun to be fired againſt the ſide of the ſhip, which ſhot quite thro' it, and the bullet fell into the water, which not a little terrified the *Cacique*. Beſides, he ſhowed him all our other weapons, and how they offended with them, and defended themſelves, telling him, that ſince ſuch weapons were left to defend him, he needed not to fear the *Caribbes*, for the chriſtians would deſtroy them all, and he would leave them for his guard, and return himſelf to *Caſtile* for jewels and other things to give him. Then he particularly recommended to him *James de Arana*, ſon to *Roderick de Arana* of *Cordova*, of whom mention has been made above. To him, and *Peter Gutierres* and *Roderick de Eſkovedo*, he left the government of the fort, and command of 36 men, with abundance of commodities, proviſion, arms and cannon, and the boat that belonged to the ſhip, with carpenters, caulkers, and all other neceſſaries for ſettling there, alſo a ſurgeon, gunner, and ſuch like perſons. This done he prepared with all poſſible ſpeed to return directly to *Caſtile*, without making any more diſcoveries, fearing, ſince he had but one ſhip left, leſt ſome other misfortune might beſal him, which might hinder their catholick majeſties from coming to the knowledge of thoſe kingdoms he had newly acquired for them.

CHAP. XXXV.

How the admiral ſet out to return to Spain, *and found the other caraval commanded by* Pinzon.

ON *Friday* the 4th of *January*, at ſun-riſing, the admiral ſet ſail, with the boats a-head, ſtanding north-weſt, to get out of ſhoal water, that was about the port where he left the chriſtians, by him called the port of the *Nativity*. becauſe on *Chriſtmas* day he had landed, eſcaping the danger of the ſea, and begun to build that colony. Thoſe flats reach from cape *Santo* to cape *Serpe*, which is ſix leagues, and run out above three leagues to ſea, and all the coaſt north-weſt and ſouth-eaſt is an open ſtrand, and plain for four leagues up the countrey, where there are then high mountains, and abundance of large villages, in compariſon of what is in the other iſlands. Then he ſailed towards a high mountain, which he called *Monte Chriſto*, and lies 18 leagues E. of cape *Santo*. So that whoſoever would come to the city of the *Nativity*, when he diſcovers *Monte Chriſto*, which is round like a pavillion, and looks almoſt like a rock, muſt keep out at ſea two leagues from it, and ſail weſt till he comes to cape *Santo*, when the city of the *Nativity* will be five leagues from him; and he muſt paſs thro' certain channels among the flats, which lie before it. The admiral thought fit to mention theſe marks, that it might be known where the firſt habitation of chriſtians was in thoſe weſtern parts. Having ſailed eaſt of *Monte Chriſto* with contrary winds, on *Sunday* the 6th of *January*, in the morning, a ſailer from the round

Where the firſt chriſtian colony was.

round top discovered the caraval *Pinta* that was sailing westward, right before the wind. As soon as it came up with the admiral, *Martin Alonzo Pinzon*, the captain, coming aboard the admiral's caraval, began to show some reasons, and give excuses for his leaving of him, saying it had happened against his will. The admiral, tho' he very well knew the contrary, and was satisfied of the man's evil inclination, remembring his bold manner of proceeding before in the voyage, yet connived at him, and bore with all, for fear of ruining his undertaking, which might easily have been done, because most of his crew were *Martin Alonzo*'s countreymen, and several of them his relations. And the truth is, that when he forsook the admiral, which was at *Cuba*, he went away with a design to sail to the island *Bohio*, because the *Indians* aboard his caraval hold him, there was abundance of gold there. When he was there and found nothing of what had been told him, he was returning towards *Hispaniola*, where other *Indians* had told him there was much gold, and thus he had spent 20 days in sailing not above 15 leagues east of the *Nativity*, to a river which the admiral called of *Grace*, and there *Martin Alonzo* had lain 16 days, and had got gold enough, as the admiral had done at the *Nativity*, giving things of small value for it. Of this gold he distributed one half among his crew, to gain and please them, that he as captain might keep the rest, and afterwards he would persuade the admiral that he knew nothing of all this. He now following on his way to come to an anchor at *Monte Christo*; the weather not permitting him to proceed farther, he went in his boat up a river, southwest of the mount, where in the sand he discovered signs of gold dust, and therefore called it the *River of Gold*. This river lies 17 leagues east of the *Nativity*,, and is not much less than the river *Guadalquivar* that runs by *Cordova*.

The other caraval found.

CHAP. XXXVI.

Of the first skirmish between the Christians *and* Indians, *which happened about the gulf of* Samana *in* Hispaniola.

Fierce Indians.

ON *Sunday* the 13th of *January*, being near the cape called *Enamorado*, or the *lovers Cape*, the admiral sent the boat ashoar, where our men found some *Indians* with fierce countenances on the shoar, with bows and arrows, who seemed to be ready to engage, but at the same time were in a consternation. However, having some conference with them, they bought two of their bows and some arrows, and with much difficulty prevailed to have one of them go aboard the admiral. Their speech was suitable to their fierceness, which appeared greater than any people they had yet met with had shown; for their faces were all daubed over with charcoal, it being the custom of all those people to paint themselves, some black, some red and some white, some one way, and some another; their hair was very long, and hung in a bagg made of parrots feathers. One of them standing before the admiral, as naked as he was born, as all the others there till then discovered were, he said in a lofty tone, they all went so in those parts. The admiral thinking this was one of the *Caribbes*, and that the bay parted them from *Hispaniola*, he ask'd of him where the *Caribbes* dwelt who pointed with his finger, in another island eastward, and that there were pieces of *Guanin*, as big as half the stern of the caraval; and that the island *Matinino* was all inhabited by women, with whom the *Caribbes* went and lay at a certain time of the year; and if afterwards they brought forth sons, they gave them to the fathers to carry away. Having answered to all the questions put to them, partly by signs, and partly by that little the *Indians* of St. *Salvador* could understand of their language, the admiral gave them to eat, and some baubles, as glass beads, and green and red cloath, which done, he sent them ashore, that they should cause gold to be brought if the others had any. The boat being ashore, they found on the shore among the trees 55 of them, all naked, with long hair, as the women in *Spain* wear it, and behind on the crown of the head, they had plumes of parrots or other birds feathers, and all of them armed with bows and arrows. When our men landed, the *Indian* that had been aboard made the others lay down their bows and arrows, and a great cudgel they carry instead of a sword, for, as has been said, they have no iron at all: when they came to the boat, the christians stept ashore, and having begun to trade for bows and arrows by order of the admiral, the *Indians* who had already sold two, not only refused to sell any more, but with scorn, made as if they would seize the christians, and run to their bows and arrows where they had left them, taking up with them ropes to bind our men; they being upon their guard seeing them

A fray with the Indians.

them come in that fury, tho' they were but ſeven, fell couragiouſly upon them, and cut one with a ſword on the buttock, and ſhot another with an arrow in the breaſt. The *Indians* aſtoniſhed at the reſolution of our men, and the wounds our weapons made, fled moſt of them leaving their bows and arrows; and many of them had been killed, had not the pilot of the caraval, who commanded the boat, protected them. The admiral was not at all diſpleaſed at this ſkirmiſh, imagining theſe were the *Caribbes* all the other *Indians* ſo much dreaded, or that at leaſt they bordered on them, they being a bold and reſolute people, as appeared by their aſpect, arms and actions, and he hoped that the iſlanders hearing how ſeven chriſtians had behaved themſelves againſt 55 fierce *Indians* of that country, they would the more reſpect and honour our men that were left behind at the *Nativity*, and would not dare to offend them. Afterwards, about evening, they made a ſmoak at land to ſhow their courage; wherefore the boat went again to ſee what they would have, but they could never be brought to venture themſelves, and ſo the boat returned. The bows were of yew, almoſt as big as thoſe in *France* and *England*, the arrows of ſmall twigs growing out of the ends of the canes, which are maſſive and very ſtrait, about the length of a man's arm and a half; the head is made of a ſmall ſtick hardened at the fire, about a quarter of a yard and half long, at the end whereof they fix a fiſh's tooth, or bone, and poiſon it. For this reaſon the admiral gave that gulph the name of *Gulpho de Flechas*, that is, *Gulph of arrows*, whereas the *Indians* called it *Samana*. There appeared a great deal of fine cotton and *Axi*, which is the pepper they uſe, and is very hot, ſome of it long and ſome round. Near land, where there was little water, grew abundance of thoſe weeds our men ſaw in long ſtrings upon the ocean, whence they concluded it all grew near land, and when ripe, broke looſe, and was carried out to ſea by the current.

CHAP. XXXVII.

How the admiral ſet out for Spain, *and the caraval* Pinta *was parted from him in a great ſtorm.*

Diſcoverers return towards Spain.

ON *Wedneſday*, the 16th of *January*, 1493. the admiral ſet forward with a fair wind from the aforeſaid *Gulf of arrows*, now called *Samana*, towards *Spain*, becauſe now both the caravals were very leaky, and they took much pains to keep them up: Cape *Santelmo* being the laſt land they ſaw; 20 leagues north-eaſt of it, there appeared abundance of weeds, and 20 leagues ſtill farther, they found all the ſea covered with ſmall tunny-fiſhes, whereof they ſaw great numbers the two following days, which were the 19th and the 20 of *January*, and after them abundance of ſea-fowls, and all the way the weeds ran with the current in long ropes, lying eaſt and weſt; for they had really found, that the current takes theſe weeds a great way off, and that they keep not on long in the ſame way; for ſometimes they go one way, and ſometimes another; and this they ſaw almoſt every day, till they were almoſt half ſeas over. Holding on their courſe with a fair wind, they made ſo much way, that in the opinion of the pilots, on the 9th of *February*, they were ſouth of the iſlands *Azores*; but the admiral ſaid they were 150 leagues ſhort, and this was the truth, for they ſtill found abundance of weeds, which as they went towards the *Indies*, they did not ſee till they were 263 leagues weſt of the iſland of *Ferro*. As they ſailed on thus with fair weather, the wind began to riſe more and more every day, and the ſea to run ſo high, that they could ſcarce live upon it. For which reaſon, on *Thurſday* the 14th of *February*, they drove which way ſoever the wind would carry them; and the caraval *Pinta*, commanded by *Pinzon*, not being able to lie athwart the ſea, run away due north, before the ſouth wind, the admiral ſteering north-eaſt to draw nearer to *Spain*, which the caraval *Pinta*, could not do, by reaſon of the darkneſs, tho' the admiral had always his light out. Thus when day appeared, they had quite loſt ſight of one another, each looking upon it as moſt certain, that the other was loſt; therefore betaking themſelves to prayers and religious acts; thoſe aboard the admiral caſt lots, which of them ſhould go in pilgrimage for the whole crew to our lady of *Guadalupe*, which fell to the admiral. Afterwards they drew for another to go to *Loretto*, and the lot fell upon one *Peter de Villa*, a ſeaman of *Port St. Mary*. Then they caſt lots for a third, who was to watch a night at St. *Oleve* of *Moguer*, and the ſtorm ſtill increaſing, they all made a vow to go barefoot and in their ſhirts at the firſt land they came to, to ſome church of our lady. Beſides theſe general vows,

A terrible ſtorm.

several others were made by private men, because the tempest was now vehement, and the admiral's vessel could scarce withstand it for want of ballast, which was fallen short, the provisions being spent. To supply which want, they thought convenient to fill all the vessels in the ship with sea-water, which was some help, and made the ship bear more upright, and be in less danger of oversetting. Of this violent storm, the admiral has these words. I had been less concerned for the tempest, had I alone been in danger; for I know I owe my life to the supreme creator, and because I have been other times so near death, that only the least part was wanting to compleat it. But what infinitely grieved and troubled me was the consideration, that as it had pleased our lord to give me faith and assurance to go upon this undertaking, wherein I had now been successful; so now that those who opposed it were to be convinced, and your highnesses served by me with honour and increase of your mighty state, his divine majesty should please to obstruct all this by my death, which had yet been more tolerable, had it not been attended with the loss of all those men I had carried with me, upon promise of happy success. They seeing themselves in that affliction did not only curse their setting out, but the fear and awe my persuasions infused into them, to dissuade their return when outward bound, as they had several times resolved to do. But above all my sorrow was double, when I remembered two sons I had left at school at *Cordova*, destitute of friends, in a strange country, before I had done, or at least could be known to have done any service, which might be believed to incline your highnesses to remember them. And tho' on the one side I comforted my self with the faith, that our lord would not permit a thing which was so much for the exaltation of his church, to be left imperfect, when I had with so much opposition and trouble, almost brought it to perfection: yet on the other side I considered, It was his will, that because of my demerits he would not permit me to obtain such honour in this world, but snatched it from me. Being in this inward confusion, I remembered your highnesses good fortune, which tho' I were dead, and the ship lost, might find some means that a conquest so near atchieved should not be lost, and that it was possible the success of my voyage should by some means or other, come to your knowledge. For this reason as briefly as the time would permit, I writ upon parchment, that I had discovered those lands, I had promised, as also in how many days, and what way I had done it, the goodness of those lands, the nature of the inhabitants, and how your highnesses subjects were left in possession of all I had discovered; which writing folded and sealed, I superscribed to your highnsses, promising in writing upon it a 1000 ducats to him, that should deliver it sealed to you; to the end, that if any foreigners found it, the promised reward might prevail with them, not to give that intelligence to another. Then I caused a great cask to be brought to me, and having wrapped the writing in an oyled cloath and then put it into the cake of wax, I droped it into the cask, and having stopped the bung close, cast it into the sea, all the men fancying, it was some act of devotion. And apprehending that might perhaps never be taken up, and the ship still sailed nearer to *Spain*, I made another pacquet like the first, and placed it at the top of the poop, to the end that when the ship sunk, the cask might take its chance, remaining still above water.

CHAP. XXXVIII.

How the admiral arrived at the islands Azores *and the people of the island of St.* Mary *took away his boat and the men in it.*

They spy land. SAiling on in such mighty danger, and so great a storm, on *Friday* the 15 of *February*, at break of day, one *Ruy Garcia*, from the round top, saw land bear E. N. E. from them. The pilot and seamen judged it was the rock of *Lisbon*, but the admiral concluded it was one of the islands *Azores*, and tho' they were at no great distance from it, yet they could not come to an anchor that day because of the weather. Thus plying about because the wind was east, they lost sight of the island and discovered another, about which they ran struggling against wind and weather, with continual labour and no respite, not being able to get to land. Wherefore the admiral in his journal says, on *Saturday* the 16th of *February*, I arrived at one of those islands at night, and by reason of the bad weather, could not tell which of them it was. That night I took a little rest, because from *Wednesday* till then, I had never slept, and was lame of both my legs, having been continually in the open air and wet, nor was it little that I suffered by provisions. Upon *Monday* morning, being at an anchor, I understood from some of the inhabitants, that it was the island of St. *Mary*, one

one of the *Azores*, and all of them admired I had escap'd, considering the terrible storm, which had held for 15 days without intermission in those parts. These people understanding what the admiral had discovered, seem'd to rejoyce, giving praise to God, and three of them came aboard with some fresh provisions and many complements from the commander of the island, who was far from thence at the town; for about this place, there was nothing to be seen but a hermitage, which as they said, was dedicated to the blessed virgin. Thereupon the admiral and all his crew remembring they had made a vow the *Thursday* before, to go barefoot and in their shirts, the first land they came at, to some church of our lady; they were all of opinion they ought here to perform it, especially it being a place where the people and governour express'd so much affection and tenderness for our men, and belonging to a king, who was so great a friend to him of *Castile*. Therefore the admiral desired those three men to repair to the town, and cause the chaplain to come that had the keys of that hermitage, that he might say mass there. These men consenting, they went into the caraval's boat, with half the ship's crew, that they might begin to perform their vow, and being come back, the rest might go to do their part. Being landed barefooted and in their shirts, as they had vow'd to do, the governour, with abundance of people from the town, who lay in ambush, on a sudden rush'd out upon them and made them prisoners, taking their boat, without which he thought the admiral could never get away from him.

CHAP. XXXIX.

How the admiral weathered another storm, and at last recovered his boat and men.

THE admiral thinking they stay'd too long, who were gone ashoar in the boat; it being then noon, whereas they went off by break of day, he suspected some misfortune had befallen them, either at land or at sea. Therefore not being able from the place where he lay, to discover the hermitage they were gone to, he resolved with his ship to sail about a point, whence the church could be seen. Being come near, he saw abundance of people a horseback, who dismounting, went into the boat to attack the caraval. The admiral therefore mistrusting what might happen, ordered his men to be in a readiness and arm'd, but make no shew of resistance, that the *Portuguese* might come the nearer. When they were near the admiral, the captain of them stood up, demanding to parley, which the admiral granted, thinking he would come aboard, and might be secur'd without breach of faith, since he had seiz'd his men without provocation. But the *Portuguese* durst not come nearer than to be heard, when the admiral told him, he admired at his irregular manner of proceeding, and that none of his men came in the boat since they were gone ashoar upon a safe conduct, and offers of relief, especially since the governour himself had sent to welcome him. He therefore desired him to consider, that besides his doing an action which enemies would not be guilty of, and against the laws of honour, the king of *Portugal* would be highly offended at it, whose subjects were, when they landed, in the dominions of their catholic majesties, or resided there, made much of, and treated with all manner of civility, and were safe without any safe conduct, as if they were in *Lisbon*; besides that their highnesses had given him letters of recommendations to all princes, potentates, and other persons in the world, which he would shew him if he drew near. Therefore since such letters were received with respect in all parts, and he and the king's subjects well treated on their account, much more they ought to be so in *Portugal*, their princes being so near neighbours and allies; especially he being their great admiral of the ocean and vice roy of the *Indies* he had discovered, all which he was ready to show him under their highnesses hands and seals. Accordingly at that distance he show'd his commissions, and told him he might draw near without any apprehension, for as much as in regard to the peace and amity betwixt their catholick majesties and the king of *Portugal*, they had commanded him to pay the utmost civility to such *Portuguese* ships as he met; adding, that though he should obstinately persist in keeping his men, yet that would not prevent his returning to *Spain*, he having still men enough to sail to *Sevil*, and to do him harm, if need were, whereof he himself would be the occasion, and such punishment would be adjudged well deserved of him, besides that his king would punish him, as giving cause for a war between him and their catholick majesties. The captain and his men answered, that they neither knew their catholic majesties, nor their letters, nor did they fear them, and would make him know what

what *Portugal* was. By this answer the admiral suspected, there had some breach happened between the two crowns since his departure and therefore gave him such an answer as his folly deserv'd. At last when they were parting, the captain stood up, and at a great distance said, he might go to the harbour with his caraval, for that all he did was by order of the king his master. The admiral hearing it, call'd all that were aboard to bear witness, and calling to the captain and *Portuguese*, swore he would never go off the caraval, till he had taken an 100 *Portuguese* to carry them into *Castile*, and to destroy all that island. This said, he again came to an anchor in the port, where he was at first, the weather obliging him to it. But the next day the wind still increasing, and the place where he lay being unsafe, he lost his anchors, and was forced to stand out to sea, towards the island of *St. Michael*, where in case he could not come to an anchor, he had resolved to run it out at sea, not without much danger, as well because the sea ran high, as by reason he had but three able seamen left, and some grummets, all the rest being land men, and *Indians* who understood nothing of sea affairs. But supplying the want of the absent in his own person, he passed that night with much labour and danger, till day appearing, perceiving he had lost sight of the island of *St. Michael*, and that the weather was calmer, he resolved to return to the island of *St. Mary*, to endeavour to recover his men, anchors, and boat. He came up with it on *Thursday* the 21st of *January*, after noon, and soon after the boat came off with five men and a notary, who all upon security given them, went aboard and lay there that night, it being late. The next day they said they came from the captain to know for certain whence the ship came, and whether it had the king of *Spain*'s commission, which being made out, they were ready to show them all manner of friendship, which they did because they could not seize the ship nor the admiral, and that they might suffer for what they had done. The admiral suppressing his resentment, said, he thank'd them for their civil offers, and since they proceeded according to the maritime laws and customs, he was ready to satisfy them; and accordingly show'd them the king of *Spain*'s general letter of recommendation, directed to all his subjects and those of other princes, as also his commission for that voyage; which the *Portuguese* having seen, they went ashore satisfied, and soon dismissed the seamen, with their boat, of whom they understood it was reported in the island, that the king had sent orders to all his subjects to secure the person of the admiral by any means whatsoever.

They restore his men.

CHAP. XL.

How the admiral sail'd from the islands of Azores, *and was forced into* Lisbon *by a storm.*

Another terrible storm.

ON *Sunday* the 24th of *February*, the admiral sail'd from the island of *St. Mary* for *Spain*, being in great want of wood and ballast, which he could not take in, because of the bad weather, tho' the wind was fair for his voyage. Being an 100 leagues from the nearest land, a swallow came into the ship, which, as was believ'd, the storm had drove out to sea, which appeared more plainly, because the next day being the 28th of *February*, a great many more swallows and land fowl came aboard, and they saw a whale. On the 3d of *March* the tempest was so great, that after midnight it split their sails; wherefore being in great danger of their lives, they made a vow to send one in pilgrimage to our lady *de Cinta* at *Guelva*, whither he was to go barefoot, and in his shirt. The lot fell again upon the admiral, God showing thereby, that his offerings were more acceptable than those of others; besides which, other private vows were made. Thus running on without a rag of cloath, but bare masts, a mighty sea, high winds and frightful thunder, each of which seem'd enough to destroy the caraval, it pleased God to give them sight of land, about midnight, which offered no less danger than the rest; for to avoid being beaten to pieces, and running into some place where they knew not how to get off, they were forced to make some sail, to bear up against the storm till day, which appearing, they found they were upon the rock of *Lisbon*. The admiral was forced to put in there, to the great astonishment of the people of that country, and their seamen, who ran from all parts to behold, as it were some wonder, a ship that had escap'd so terrible a storm; having receiv'd news of many ships that had perish'd about *Flanders*, and in other countries of late days. He came to an anchor in the river of *Lisbon* upon *Monday* the 4th of *March*, and presently sent away an express to their catholick majesties with the news of his arrival, and another to the king of *Portugal*, asking leave to go up to anchor before the city, the place

The admiral at Lisbon.

place where he was, not being ſafe, againſt any that ſhould deſign to do him harm, upon pretence, it was done by the king's order, as believing by his ruin, they might obſtruct the king of *Spain*'s ſucceſs.

CHAP. XLI.

How the people of Liſbon *came to ſee the admiral, as a prodigy; and he went to viſit the king of* Portugal.

The admiral refuſes to quit his veſſel.

ON *Tueſday* the 5th of *March*, the maſter of a great guard ſhip that lay in the harbour, came with his boat full of arm'd men to the admiral's caraval, requiring him to come along to give an account of himſelf to the king's officers, as was practiſed by all ſhips that came into the harbour. He anſwered, That the king of *Spain*'s admirals, as he was, were not obliged to obey any ſuch ſummons, nor to quit their ſhips, to give any account of themſelves, and he was reſolved to do his duty. The maſter bid him at leaſt to ſend his boatſwain. The admiral reply'd, It was ſtill the ſame thing, whether he ſent a grummet, or went himſelf, and therefore it was in vain to deſire him to ſend any body. The maſter being ſenſible he was in the right, deſired him at leaſt to ſhow him the king of *Spain*'s letter, that he might ſatisfy his captain: This being but reaſonable, the admiral ſhow'd him their catholick majeſties letter, with which he was ſatisfied, and went back to his ſhip to give an account of what had happened, to *Alvaro de Acunna* his captain, who came immediately with trumpets, fifes, drums, and great ſtate, aboard the admiral, expreſſing much kindneſs, and offering his ſervice. The next day it being known at *Liſbon*, that the ſhip came from the *Indies*, ſuch throngs of people went aboard to ſee the *Indians*, and hear news, that the caraval could not contain them, and the water was covered with boats, ſome of them praiſing God for ſo great a happineſs, and others ſtorming that they had loſt that diſcovery, thro' their king's incredulity; ſo that day was ſpent with great concourſe of people. The next day, the king ordered his officers to preſent the admiral with all ſorts of refreſhment, and all things he ſtood in need of either for himſelf, or his men, without aſking any pay. At the ſame time he writ to the admiral, congratulating his happy arrival, and, deſiring, ſince he was in his dominions, he would come to ſee him. The admiral was doubtful what to do in this caſe, but he conſidered the king was in amity with their catholick majeſties, and had treated him courteouſly; and beſides, to take off all ſuſpicion that he came from his conqueſts, he conſented to go to *Valparaiſo*, nine leagues from *Liſbon*, where the king was, whither he came on *Saturday* night, being the 9th of *March*. The king ordered all the nobility of his court to go out to meet him, and being come into his preſence, did him great honour, commanding him to put on his cap, and ſit down, and having with a chearful countenance heard the particulars of his proſperous voyage, offered him all he ſtood in need of, for the ſervice of their catholick majeſties, though he thought, that foraſmuch as he had been a captain in *Portugal*, that conqueſt belong'd to him. To which the admiral anſwered, That he knew of no ſuch agreement, and that he had ſtrictly obſerv'd his orders, which were not to go to the mines of *Portugal*, nor to *Guinea*. The king ſaid, all was well, and he doubted not but juſtice would be done. Having ſpent a long time in this ſort of diſcourſe, the king commanded the prior of *Crato*, the greateſt man then about him, to entertain the admiral, and ſhew him all civility and reſpect, which was done accordingly. Having ſtay'd there all *Sunday* and all *Monday*, till after maſs, the admiral took leave of the king, who expreſs'd great kindneſs, and made him great proffers, ordering *D. Martin de Noronha* to go along with him, and many other gentlemen went for company to honour him, and hear an account of his voyage. As he was thus on his way to *Liſbon*, he paſs'd by a monaſtery, where the queen then was, who ſent earneſtly to intreat him he would not paſs by without ſeeing her. She was much pleaſed to ſee him, and did him all the favour and honour that was due to the greateſt lord. That night a gentleman came from the king, to the admiral, to let him know, that if he pleaſed to go by land into *Spain*, he would attend him, provide lodgings all the way, and furniſh him all neceſſaries, as far as the borders of *Portugal*.

Nobly receiv'd by the king.

CHAP. XLII.

How the admiral left Lisbon *to return to* Castile *by sea.*

The admiral returns to Palos.

ON *Wednesday* the 13th of *March*, two hours after day, the admiral set sail for *Sevil*, and on *Friday* following at noon, arrived at *Saltes*, and came to an anchor in the port of *Palos*, whence he had set out on the 3d of *August* the foregoing year 1492, 7 months and 11 days before his return. He was there received by all the people in procession, giving thanks to God for his prosperous success, which, it was hop'd, would redound so much to the propagation of christianity, and increase of their catholick majesties dominions; all the inhabitants of that place looking upon it as a great matter that the admiral set out from thence, and that most of the men he had with him, belong'd to it, tho' many of them, thro' *Pinzon*'s fault, had been mutinous and disobedient. It happened that when the admiral came to *Palos*, *Pinzon* was arriv'd in *Galicia*, and design'd to go by himself to *Barcelona* to carry the news to their catholick majesties, who sent him orders not to go thither without the admiral, with whom he had been sent to discover, at which he was so concern'd and offended, that he return'd indispos'd, to his native country, where within a few days he died for grief: But before he got to *Palos*, the admiral set out for *Sevil*, designing thence for *Barcelona*, where their catholick majesties were; and he was forced to stay a little by the way, tho' but never so little, to the so great admiration of the people wheresoever he went, that they ran from all the neighbouring towns, down to the roads to see him, the *Indians*, and other things he brought. Thus holding on his way he got to *Barcelona* about the middle of *April*, having before sent their highnesses an account of the happy success of his voyage, which was extraordinary pleasing to them, and they ordered him a most solemn reception, as to a man that had done them such singular service. All the court and city went out to meet him; and their catholick majesties sate in publick with great state, on rich chairs under a canopy of cloth of gold; and when he went to kiss their hands, they stood up to him as to a great lord, made a difficulty to give him their hands, and caused him to sit down. Having given a brief account of his voyage, they gave him leave to retire to his appartment, whither he was attended by all the court; and he was so highly honoured and favoured by their highnesses, that when the king rode about *Barcelona*, the admiral was on one side of him, and the *Infante Fortuna* on the other; whereas before, none went by his majesty but the said *Infante*, who was his near kinsman.

His reception at Barcelona.

CHAP. XLII.

How it was resolved that the admiral should return with a powerful fleet to people the island Hispaniola, *and his holinesses approbation of the conquest was obtain'd.*

The pope's grant.

ORders were given at *Barcelona*, with great care and expedition for the admiral's return to *Hispaniola*, as well to relieve those that were left there, as to enlarge the colony and subdue the island, with the rest that were and should be discovered. To make their title to them the stronger, their catholick majesties, by the advice of the admiral, procured the pope's approbation and consent for the conquest of the said *Indies*, which pope *Alexander* the 6th, who then governed the church, readily granted; not only for what was already, but for all that should be discovered westward, till it should come to the east, where any christian prince was then actually in possession, forbidding all persons in general, to intrude within those bounds. The same his holiness confirm'd the next year, in very significant terms. And their catholick majesties being sensible that the admiral had been the cause of all this favour granted by the pope, and that his discovery had entitled them to the possession of all those parts, they were pleased he should be immediately gratify'd at *Barcelona*, on the 28th of *May*, and therefore granted him a new privilege, or rather an exposition, and explanation of what he had before, confirming to him all they had granted before, and in plain terms declared how far the bounds of his admiralship, and vice-royship extended, being over all that which his holiness had granted them, thus ratifying what they had given him before, which privileges and prerogatives are as follows.

CHAP.

CHAP. XLIV.

Privileges and prerogatives granted by their catholick majesties to the admiral.

The admiral's letters patent.

FErdinand *and* Elizabeth, *by the grace of God king and queen of* Castile, *of* Leon, *of* Aragon, *of* Sicily, *of* Granada, *of* Toledo, *of* Valencia, *of* Galicia, *of* Majorca, *of* Minorca, *of* Sevil, *of* Sardinia, *of* Jaen, *of* Algarve, *of* Algezira, *of* Gibraltar, *of the* Canary Islands, *count and countess of* Barcelona, *lord and lady of* Biscay *and* Molina, *duke and duchess of* Athens *and* Neopatria, *count and countess of* Roussillion *and* Cerdaigne, *marquess and marchioness of* Oristan, *and* Gociano, &c. *Forasmuch as you* Christopher Columbus, *are going by our command with some of our vessels and men to discover and subdue some islands and continent in the ocean, and it is hoped that by God's assistance, some of the said islands and continent in the ocean will be discovered and conquer'd by your means and conduct, therefore it is but just and reasonable, that since you expose your self to such danger to serve us, you should be rewarded for it. And we being willing to honour and favour you for the reasons aforesaid: Our will is, That you,* Christopher Columbus, *after discovering and conquering the said islands and continent in the said ocean, or any of them, shall be our admiral of the said islands and continent you shall so discover and conquer; and that you be our admiral, vice-roy and governor in them, and that for the future you may call and style your self,* D. Christopher Columbus, *and that your sons and successors in the said employment may call themselves dons, admirals, vice-roys and governors of them; and that you may exercise the office of admiral, with the charge of vice-roy and governor of the said islands and continent, which you and your lieutenants shall conquer, and freely decide all causes civil and criminal, appertaining to the said employment of admiral, vice-roy and governor, as you shall think fit in justice, and as the admirals of our kingdoms use to do; and that you have power to punish offenders; and you and your lieutenants exercise the employments of admiral, vice-roy and governor in all things belonging to the said offices, or any of them; and that you enjoy the perquisites and sallaries belonging to the said employments, and to each of them, in the same manner as the high-admiral of our kingdoms does. And by this our letter, or a copy of it sign'd by a publick notary: We command prince* John, *our most dearly beloved son, infantes, dukes, prelates, marquesses, great masters and military orders, priors, commendaries, our counsellors, judges, and other officers of justice whatsoever, belonging to our houshold, courts and chancery, and constables of castles, strong-houses and others; and all corporations, bailiffs, governors, judges, commanders, sea-officers; and the aldermen, common-council, officers and good people of all cities, lands and places in our kingdoms and dominions, and in those you shall conquer and subdue, and the captains, masters, mates and other officers and sailers, our natural subjects now being, or that shall be for the time to come, and any of them, that when you shall have discovered the said islands and continent in the ocean; and you, or any that shall have your commission, shall have taken the usual oath in such cases, that they, for the future, look upon you as long as you live, and after you, your son and heir, and so from one heir to another for ever, as our admiral on our said ocean, and as vice-roy and governor of the said islands and continent, by you* Christopher Columbus *discovered and conquered; and that they treat you and your lieutenants, by you appointed, for executing the employments of admiral, vice-roy and governor, as such in all respects, and give you all the perquisites and other things belonging and appertaining to the said offices; and allow, and cause to be allow'd you, all the honours, graces, concessions, preheminences, prerogatives, immunities and other things, or any of them which are due to you, by vertue of your commands, of admiral, vice-roy and governor, and to be observed compleatly, so that nothing be diminished, and that they make no objection to this, or any part of it, nor suffer it to be made; forasmuch as we from this time forward, by this our letter, bestow on you the employments of admiral, vice-roy and perpetual governor for ever; and we put you into possession of the said offices, and of every of them, and full power to use and exercise them, and to receive the perquisites and sallaries belonging to them, or any of them, as was said above. Concerning all which things, if it be requisite, and you shall desire it, we command our chancellor, notaries and other officers to pass, seal and deliver to you our letter of privilege, in such firm and legal manner, as you shall require or stand in need of. And that none of them presume to do any thing to the contrary, upon pain of our displeasure, and forfeiture of thirty ducats for each offence. And we command him, who shall show them this our letter, that he summon them to appear before us at our court, where we shall then be, within* 15 *days after such summons, under the said penalty. Under which same we also command any publick notary whatsoever, that he give to him that shows it him,*

him, a certificate under his seal, that we may know how our command is obey'd.

Given at *Granada*, on the 30th of *April*, in the year of our *Lord* 1492. I the king, I the queen.

By their majesties command, *John Coloma* secretary to the king and queen.
Entered according to order, *Roderick Doctor*.
Registred, *Sebastian Dolana*, *Francis de Madrid*, chancellors.

The confirmation.

AND now forasmuch as it has pleased our lord, that you have discovered several of the said islands, as we still hope you will by his grace discover and find others and the continent in the said ocean, and those parts of the Indies, *and have desired and requested of us, that we would confirm to you our said grant here set down, and all the contents of it, to the end that you and your children, heirs and successors, one after another, and after your days, may have and enjoy the said employments of admiral, vice-roy and governor of the said ocean, islands and continent, as well of those you have already found and discover'd, as of those you shall for the future find and discover, with all the power, preheminence and prerogative, as the admirals, vice-roys and governors in our kingdoms of* Castile *and* Leon *do enjoy; and that all the perquisites and sallaries appertaining and belonging to the said offices, and granted and allowed to our admirals, vice-roys and governors may be made good to you; or that we make such provision in this case, as in our goodness we shall think fit. And we having regard to the hazard and danger you have exposed your self to in our service, in going to discover and find out the said islands, and that which you now run in attempting to find out the other islands and continent, wherein we have been, and hope to be by you well served: To requite and reward you do by these presents, confirm to you and your children, heirs and successors, one after another, now and for ever the said employments of admiral of the said ocean, and vice-roy and governor of the said islands and continent by you discovered and found out; and of the other islands and continent, that shall be by you or your industry found or discovered for the future in those parts of the* Indies. *And it is our will, that you, and after you your children, heirs and successors, one after another, enjoy the said employment of our admiral of the said ocean, which is ours, and commences at a line, we have caused to be drawn from the islands* Azores, *to those of* Cabo Verde, *and so from pole to pole north and south; so that all beyond the said line westward is ours, and belongs to us. And accordingly we constitute you admiral, and your sons and successors, one after another, of all that part for ever. And we also appoint you our vice-roy and governor, and after you, your sons heirs and successors, one after another, of the said islands and continent discovered, and to be discovered in the said ocean in those parts of the* Indies, *as has been said; and we grant you the possession of all the said employments of admiral, vice-roy and governor for ever, with full commission and authority to use and exercise in the said sea, the office of admiral in all those things, and in the same manner and form, and with the rights and privileges, perquisites and sallaries, as our admirals of* Castile *and* Leon, *have and do use, have enjoy'd or enjoy, as well in the said islands and continent already discover'd, as in those that shall hereafter be discovered in the said ocean and said parts of the* Indies, *that the planters of them all may be the better governed. And we grant you such power and authority, that you may, as our vice-roy and governor, and your lieutenants, judges, commanders and officers by you created, exercise the civil and criminal jurisdiction, the supreme and mean authority, and the absolute and mixt command. And in those places you may remove, turn out, and put in others in their places, as often as you please, and shall think convenient for our service. And that they have power to hear, judge and determine all suits or causes civil or criminal, that shall occur or arise in the said islands or continent; and that they have and receive the fees and salaries usually annex'd, and appertaining to those employments in our kingdoms of* Castile *and* Leon. *And you our said vice-roy and governor may hear and determine all the said causes and any of them, whensoever you shall please, upon the first motion by way of appeal or complaint, and examine, determine and decide them, as our vice-roy and governor; and you and your children may do all that is reasonable in such cases, and all other things appertaining to the office of vice-roy and governor, and that you and your lieutenants and officers appointed to this purpose, may take such cognizance, and use such methods as you shall think proper for our service, and the execution of our justice. All which you and they may do and perform lawfully and effectually, as they might and ought to do, had the said officers been appointed by us. But our will and pleasure is, that such letters patents as you shall grant, be drawn and granted in our name, with these words,* Ferdinand *and* Elizabeth by the grace of God king and queen of *Castile* and *Leon, &c. and be sealed with our seal, which we will cause to be given you for the said islands and continent. And we command all the people, inhabitants and other persons in the said island and continent, to obey you, as our vice-roy and governor of the same; and those that sail on the said seas to obey you as our admiral of the said ocean; and that all of them execute your letters and orders, and take part with you*

you and your officers, for the execution of our justice; and give, and cause to be given you, all the aid and assistance you shall require and stand in need of, upon such penalties as you shall impose on them, which we by these presents do impose on them, and do look upon them as impos'd; and do grant you authority to execute them on their persons and goods. And it is also our will, that if you shall find it for our service, and the execution of justice, That any persons who shall be in the said islands or continent, depart from them, and do not return nor stay in them, and that they come and appear before us, you may in our name command, and make them depart the said islands. All whom by these presents we command, that they presently perform, execute and put in practice all that has been said, without looking farther, or asking advice upon it, nor expecting any other letter or command from us, notwithstanding any appeal or petition they shall make or present against your said order. For all which things, and any other due or belonging to the said offices of our admiral, viceroy, and governour, we give you sufficient authority, with all incidents, dependencies, and emergencies to them annexed or inherent. Concerning all which things, if it shall be your will, we do command our chancellor, notaries, and other officers belonging to our seals, that they give, pass, dispatch, and seal you our letter of privilege, made as effective, firm and strong, as you shall require of them and stand in need of; and that none of them presume to do any thing to the contrary, upon pain of our displeasure, and of thirty ducats to be paid to our treasury by every one that shall be guilty of the contrary. And besides, we command him that shall shew them this our letter to summon them to appear before us at our court, wheresoever we are, within fifteen days upon the said penalty. Under which we command any publick notary, *that shall be called for such purpose, that he give to him that shall shew it him, a certificate sign'd under his hand, that we may know how our commands are obey'd.*

Given in the city of *Barcelona* the 28th of *May*, in the year of our Lord 1493.

I the King, I the Queen.

By their majesties order, *Ferdinand Alvarez de Toledo*, secretary to the king and queen, our lord and lady.

Peter Gutierres, chancellor, without fees for seal or entry.

Deliver'd, *Roderick Doctor.*

Enter'd, *Alonzo Perez.*

CHAP. XLV.

How the admiral went from Barcelona *to* Seville, *and set out thence for* Hispaniola.

The admiral's second voyage.

ALL things necessary for the peopling of those countries being provided, the admiral departed from *Barcelona* for *Seville* in *June*, and being come thither, so diligently sollicited the fitting out of the fleet their catholick majesties had ordered him to provide, that in a short time seventeen ships, between great and small, were made ready, well stored with provisions, and with all things thought necessary for peopling of those countries; as handicrafts of all sorts, labourers, countrymen to till the land; besides, the fame of gold and other rarities in those countries, had drawn together so many gentlemen, and other persons of worth; that it was necessary to lessen the number, and not to allow so many to go aboard, at least till it appeared in some measure how things would succeed in those parts, and till things were a little settled. Yet was it impossible so much to confine the number of people that went aboard, but that it amounted to 1500 of all sorts; among whom some carried horses, asses, and other beasts, which were afterwards of great use and advantage to the planters in those countries. Being thus furnished, the admiral weighed anchor in the road of *Cadiz*, where the fleet had been fitted, upon *Wednesday* the 25th of *September* 1493, an hour before sun-rising, my brother and I being there, and stood south-west for the *Canary* islands, designing there to take in some necessary refreshment. On the 28th of *September*, being 100 leagues from *Spain*, there came aboard the admiral's ship, abundance of land-fowl, turtle-doves, and other sorts of small birds, which seem'd to be passing over to winter in *Africk*, and to come from the islands *Azores*. He holding on his course, on *Wednesday* the 2d of *October* arrived at *Gran Canaria*, and came to an anchor; at midnight sail'd again for *Gomera*, where he arrived on the fifth of *October*, and orders were given for taking up with all speed whatsoever the fleet stood in need of.

He arrives at the Canaries.

CHAP. XLVI.

How the admiral departing from Gomera, *crossed the ocean and discovered the* Caribbee *islands.*

ON *Monday* the 7th of *October* the admiral continued his voyage towards the *Indies*, having first deliver'd a commission shut up and seal'd, to every ship, commanding them not to open it, unless they were separated from him by stress of weather; for he in those letters giving an account of the course they were to steer, to come to the town of the *Nativity* in *Hispaniola*, would not have that course known to any without great need. Thus sailing with a fair gale till *Thursday* the 24th of *October*, when being 400 leagues west of *Gomera*; he yet met with none of the weeds he had seen the first voyage; when he was out but 250 leagues, to the great astonishment of them all. That day and the next a swallow flew about the fleet. On *Saturday* at night the body of St. *Elmo* was seen, with seven lighted candles on the round-top, and there follow'd mighty rains, and frightful thunder. I mean, the lights were seen, which the seamen affirm to be the body of St. *Elmo*, and they sing litanies and prayers to him; looking upon it as most certain, that in those storms where he appears, there can be no danger. Whatsoever this is, I leave to them; for if we will believe *Pliny*, when such lights appeared in those times to the *Roman* sailers in a storm, they said they were *Castor* and *Pollux*, whereof *Seneca* makes mention also, at the beginning of his first book of nature. But to return to our history; on *Saturday* the second of *November*, at night, the admiral perceiving a great alteration in the sky and winds, and taking notice of the mighty rains, he concluded for certain that he was near some land, and for this reason caused most of the sails to be furl'd, and ordered all to be upon the watch; nor without cause; for that same night, as day began to break, they spy'd land seven leagues to the westward, which was a high mountainous island; and he called it *Dominica*, because discovered upon *Sunday* morning. A while after he saw another island north-east of *Dominica*, and then another, and another after that, more northward. For which mercy God had been pleased to bestow on them, all the men assembling in the poop, sung the *Salve regina*, and other prayers and hymns very devoutly, giving thanks to God, for that in twenty days after departing from *Gomera*, they had made that land, judging the distance between them to be between 750 and 800 leagues. And finding no convenient place to come to an anchor on the east side of the island *Dominica*, they stood over to another island which the admiral called *Marigalante*, that being his ship's name. Here landing, he with all necessary solemnity again confirmed the possession he had in his first voyage taken of all the islands and continent of the *West Indies* for their catholick majesties.

Island Dominica *discovered.*

Island Marigalante.

CHAP. XLVII.

How the admiral discovered the island of Guadalupe, *and what he saw there.*

Guadalupe *islands.*

ON *Monday* the fourth of *November*, the admiral sailed from the island *Marigalante* northwards, by another great island, which he called *St. Mary of Guadalupe*, for his own devotion, and at the request of the friars of the house of that name, to whom he had made a promise to call some island by the name of their monastery. Before he came to it, at two leagues distance, they discovered a very high rock, ending in a point, whence gush'd out a stream of water, as thick as a large barrel, which falling made such a noise, that it was heard aboard the ships, tho' many affirmed it was only a white vein in the rock, the water was so white and frothy by reason of its steep fall. Going ashore in the boat to view a sort of town they saw from the shore, they found no body there, the people being fled to the woods, except some children, to whose arms they ty'd some baubles to allure their fathers when they returned. In the houses they found geese like ours, and abundance of parrots with red, green, blue, and white feathers, as big as common cocks. They also found pompions, and a sort of fruit, which look'd like our green pine-apples, but much bigger, and within full of a solid meat, like a melon, and much sweeter both in taste and smell, which grow on long stalks like lillies or aloes, wild about the fields, and are better than those that are brought up by art, as afterwards appeared. They also saw other sorts of fruits and herbs differing from ours. Beds of cotton nets, that is, hammacks, bows, and arrows, and other ſuch things, of which our men took none, that the *Indians* might be the leſs afraid of the chriſtians. But what they moſt admired was, that they found an iron-pan, tho' I believe that the rocks and fire-ſtones in that country being of the colour of bright iron, a perſon of but indifferent judgment that found it, without looking farther, took it for iron, tho' in truth it was not ſo; forasmuch as from that day to this, there was never any thing of iron found among thoſe people, nor did I hear the admiral ſpeak of this. And therefore I am opinion, that he uſing daily to write down whatſoever happened, and was told him, that he might among other things ſet down what was told him concerning this particular, by thoſe that were aſhore. And tho' it were of iron, it was not to be admired, becauſe the *Indians* of the iſland of *Guadalupe*, being *Caribbees*, and making their excurſions to rob as far as *Hiſpaniola*, perhaps they had that pan of the chriſtians, or of the other *Indians* of *Hiſpaniola*; and it is poſſible they might carry the body of the ſhip the admiral loſt, to make uſe of the iron; and tho' it were not the hulk of that ſhip, it muſt be the remainder of ſome other wreck, carried thither by the wind and current from our parts. But be it what it will, they that day took neither the pan nor any thing elſe, but returned to their ſhips. The next day, which was *Tueſday* the fifth of *November*, the admiral again ſent two boats aſhore, to endeavour to take ſome body that might give him an account of the country, and inform him how far off, and which way *Hiſpaniola* lay. Each of the boats brought back a youth, who agreed in ſaying they were not of that iſland, but of another call'd *Borriquen* (now *St. John*) and that the inhabitants of that iſland of *Guadalupe* were *Caribbees* or *Canibals*, and had taken them priſoners from their own iſland. Soon after the boats returning to ſhore, to take up ſome chriſtians they had left there, found ſix women with them, who had fled to them from the *Caribbees*, and came of their own accord aboard the ſhips. The admiral to allure the iſlanders, would not keep them aboard, but gave them ſome glaſs beads and bells, and made them be ſet aſhore againſt their wills. This was not done unadviſedly, for as ſoon as they landed, the *Caribbees* in the ſight of the chriſtians, took away all the admiral had given them. Therefore either thro' the hatred they bore the *Caribbees*, or for the fear they had conceived of thoſe people; awhile after, when the boats returned for wood and water, the ſaid women got into them, begging of the ſeamen to carry them aboard the ſhips, and giving them to underſtand by ſigns, that thoſe people did eat men, and make ſlaves of them, and therefore they would not ſtay with them. So that the men yielding to their intreaties, carried them back to the ſhips, with two children and a young man that had made his eſcape from the *Caribbees*, thinking it ſafer to put themſelves into the hands of people they never ſaw, and ſuch ſtrangers to their nation, than to remain among thoſe they knew to be wicked and cruel, and who had eaten their huſbands and children, and they ſay they do not kill and eat the women, but keep them as ſlaves. One of the women told them, that towards the ſouth there were many iſlands, ſome inhabited, others not, which both ſhe and the other women, ſeverally call'd *Giamachi*, *Cairvaco*, *Huino*, *Buriari*, *Arubeira*, *Sixibei*. *Product of the iſland* Guadalupe. But the continent, which they ſaid was very great, both they and the people of *Hiſpaniola*, called *Zuanta*, becauſe in former times canoes had come from that land to barter with abundance of lads, of whom they ſaid there were two thirds in an iſland not far diſtant; and they alſo ſaid, that a king of that country whither they fled, was gone with ten great canoes, and 300 men, to make incurſions into the neighbouring iſlands, and take people to eat. The ſame women gave information where the iſland *Hiſpaniola* lay; for tho' the admiral had inſerted it in his ſea-chart; yet for his farther information, he would hear what the people of that country ſaid of it. He would immediately have ſailed that way, had he not been told, that one captain *Mark* was gone aſhore with eight men, without his leave, before day, and was not yet returned. He was therefore forced to ſend out to look for him, tho' in vain; for by reaſon of the great thickneſs of the trees, there could be no diſcovering of them. Therefore the admiral, that they might not be loſt, or be obliged to leave a ſhip behind to take them in, which might afterwards miſs her way to *Hiſpaniola*, reſolved to ſtay there till the next day; and becauſe the country, as has been ſaid, was full of great woods, he ordered them to be ſought after again, and that they ſhould carry trumpets and muſkets to bring them to the noiſe. Theſe people having ſtrayed all that day, returned to their ſhips without finding or hearing any news of them. The admiral therefore ſeeing it was now *Thurſday* morning, and no news had been heard of them ſince *Tueſday*, and that they went without leave, reſolved to continue his voyage, or at leaſt make ſhew of ſo doing, that it might be a puniſhment to others, but at the intreaty of ſome of their kindred and friends, he ſtay'd, and ordered the ſhips ſhould in the mean while take in wood and water, and the men waſh

wash their linen; and sent captain *Hojeda*, with forty men, to look for those that were stray'd, and pry into the nature of the country, where he found mastick, aloes, sandal, ginger, frankincense, and some trees in taste and smell like cinamon, abundance of cotton, and many falcons, and saw two of them pursuing the other birds; they also saw kites, herons, daws, turtles, partridges, geese, and nightingals, and affirm'd that in travelling six leagues, they cross'd 26 rivers, several whereof were vast deep, which makes me believe, that the country being uncouth, they often cross'd the same river. Whilst these were admiring at what they saw, and other companies went about the island, seeking the stragglers, they returned to the ships without being met by any that look'd for them, on *Friday* the 8th of *November*, saying the thickness of the woods was the cause they had lost themselves. The admiral to punish their presumption, commanded the captain to be cast into irons, and the rest to suffer by retrenching their allowance of provisions. Then he landed, and went to some houses, where he saw all the things above-mentioned, especially a great deal of cotton spun and unspun, looms to weave, abundance of mens skulls hung up; and baskets full of mens bones. These houses they saw were the best, and more plentifully stored with provisions, and other things necessary for the use of the *Indians*, than any others the admiral saw in the islands at his first voyage.

CHAP. XLVIII.

How the admiral departed from the island Guadalupe, *and of some islands he found in his way.*

Monseratte island. ON *Sunday* the tenth of *November* the admiral weighed anchor, and sailed with the whole fleet along the coast of the island *Guadalupe*, towards the north-west for *Hispaniola*, and came to the island *Monseratte*, calling it by that name, because of its heighth, and understood by the *Indians* he had with him, that the *Caribbees* had unpeopled it, devouring the inhabitants. *Redonda.* Thence he proceeded to St. *Mary Redonda*, so called, because it is so round and upright, that there seems to be no getting into it without ladders, which the *Indians* call'd *Ocamaniro*. Next he came to *St. Maria la Antigua*, which is above 28 leagues in extent. *St. Maria Antigua.* Still holding on his course north-west, there appeared several other islands towards the north, and lying north-west and south-east, all very high and full of woods, in one of which they cast anchor, and call'd it *St. Martin*, *St. Martin.* where they took up pieces of coral, sticking to the anchor flooks, which made them hope they should find other useful things in those countries. Tho' the admiral was very desirous to know every thing, yet he resolved to hold on his course towards *Hispaniola*, to relieve those he had left there, but the weather being bad, he came to an anchor on *Thursday* the thirteenth of *November*, in an island, where he ordered some *Indians* to be taken, to know whereabouts he was. As the boat was returning to the fleet with four women, and three children the men had taken, it met a canoe, in which there were four men and one woman, who perceiving they could not make their escape, stood upon their guard, and hit two of the christians with their arrows, which they let fly with such force and dexterity, that the woman shot a target quite thro'; but the boat furiously boarding, the canoe overset, so that they took them all swimming in the water, and one of them swimming shot several arrows, as if he had been upon dry land. These had their members cut off, for they are taken by the *Caribbees* in other islands, and gelt, as we do to fat capons, that they may be more pleasing to the taste. The admiral departing hence, continued his voyage W. N. W. where he found above fifty islands, which he left to the northward; the biggest of them he called *St. Ursula*, and the others the *Eleven thousand virgins*. *St. Ursula.* Next he came to the island which he call'd St. *John Baptist*, but the *Indians Borriquen*, and the fleet anchored in a bay on the west side of it, *St. John, or Borriquen.* where they took several sorts of fish, as skate, olaves, pilchards, and shads, and saw falcons, and bushes like wild vines. More to the eastward, some christians went to certain houses well built after their fashion, with a square before them, and a broad road down to the sea, with towers made of cane on both sides, and the top of them curiously interwoven with greens, as is seen in the gardens of *Valencia*. At the end of it next the sea, was a rais'd gallery or balcony that could hold ten or twelve people, lofty and well built.

CHAP.

CHAP. XLIX.

How the admiral arrived at Hispaniola, *where he understood the* Spaniards *were dead.*

An Indian *sent ashoar.*

ON *Friday* the twelfth of *November*, the admiral came up with the north side of *Hispaniola*, and presently sent ashore at *Samana*, one of the *Indians* born in that part, whom he brought out of *Spain*, being then converted to our holy faith, who offer'd to reduce all the *Indians* to submit to the christians. The admiral continuing his voyage towards the town of *Natal*, or the *Nativity*, when he came to cape *Angel*, some *Indians* went aboard, to barter their commodities with the christians. Coming to an anchor in the port of *Monte Christo*, a boat that went ashore, found near a river two dead men, one of them seemed to be young, the other old, who had a rope made of a certain sort of broom, or such like furze that grows in *Spain*, called *Esparto*, about his neck, his arms extended, and his hands tied to a piece of wood, in the form of a cross; but they could not discern whether they were christians or *Indians*, but look upon it as an ill omen. The next day being the 26th of *November*, the admiral sent ashoar in several places; the *Indians* came very friendly and boldly to talk with the christians, and touching our men's shirts and doublets, said shirt, doublet in *Spanish*, to shew they knew how those things were called, which delivered the admiral from the jealousy he had conceived, on account of the dead men, judging that if those people had wronged the christians left there, they had not come so boldly aboard the ships. But the next day, when he came to an anchor near the town of *Navidad*, or the nativity, after midnight, a canoe came to the fleet, and asked for the admiral, and being bid to come aboard, for he was there, they would not do it, saying, they were resolved not to go aboard till they saw and knew him. The admiral therefore was forced to come to the ship's side to hear them, and then presently two went up with two masks, which they gave to the admiral, from the *Cacique Guacanagari*, saying, he sent many commendations. They being asked by the admiral concerning the christians left there, answered, that some of them died of distempers, some parted from their company, and some were gone into other countries; but that all of them had four or five wives, tho' it appeared by their way of speaking, that all or most of them were dead; yet the admiral not thinking fit to take any notice at that time, sent back the *Indians*, with a present of some things made of latten, and other baubles, for *Guacanagari*, and themselves, and so they went away that same night, with the gifts for the *Cacique*.

Indians *came boldly aboard.*

CHAP. L.

How the admiral went to the town of Navidad, *or the* Nativity, *found it forsaken and burnt, and had an interview with King* Guacanagari.

ON *Thursday* the 28th of *November*, about evening, the admiral with all his fleet came into the port, before the town of *Navidad* or the *Nativity*, found it all burnt, and that day no body was seen all about there: Next day in the morning, the admiral landed very much concern'd to see the houses and fort burnt, and nothing left belonging to the christians, but only ragged cloaths and such like things, as is usual in a place plunder'd and destroy'd; and seeing no body to enquire of, the admiral went with some boats up a river that was hard by. Whilst he was going up it, he ordered the well he had made in the fort, to be cleansed, thinking to find gold in it; because at his going away, fearing what might happen, he commanded those he left behind, to throw all the gold they could get into that well, but nothing was found in it; and the admiral that way he went up with his boats, could lay hold of no *Indian*, because they all fled from their houses, to the woods. Having therefore found nothing but some of the christians cloaths, he returned to *Navidad*, where he saw eight of the christians, and three others, in the fields near the town, whom they knew to be christians by their cloaths, and they seem'd to have been dead about a month. The christians going about to seek some other tokens, or writings of the dead, a brother of the *Cocique Guacanagari*, came with some *Indians* to talk with the admiral. These could speak some words of *Spanish*, and knew the names all of the christians, that had been left there, and said that those *Spaniards* soon began to fall at variance among themselves, and to take every one what gold and as many women as they could; whereupon *Peter Gutierres* and *Escovedo* kill'd one *James*, and then they and nine others went away with their women to a *Cacique*, whose name was *Caunabo*, who was lord of the mines, and kill'd them all; then many days after came with a great many men to *Navidad*, where there was only *James de Arana*, with ten men, who had remained with him to guard the fort, all the rest being dispersed about the island. The *Cacique Caunabo* coming up by night, fired the houses where the christians liv'd with their women, for fear whereof they fled to the sea, where eight of them were drowned, and three died ashoar, whom they show'd. That *Guacanagari* himself, fighting with *Caunabo* in defence of the christians, was wounded and fled. This account agreed with that given by other christians, sent by the admiral to learn more of the country, who went to a town where *Guacanagari* lay ill of a wound, which he said had hindred him from waiting on the admiral, and giving him an account of what was become of the christians; among whom he said, soon after the admiral returned for *Spain*, there began to be dissension, and every one would barter gold for himself, and take what woman he thought fit; and not satisfied with what *Guacanagari* gave and allowed to be given them, they divided into several parcels, and dispersed some one way and some another, and that some *Biscainers* joyning together, went where they were all kill'd; and this was the truth of what had happened, which they might tell the admiral, desiring him by those same christians, that he would go see him, because he was in such a condition that he could not leave his house. The admiral did so, going the next day to visit him, and he with great signs of sorrow, told him all that had happened, as has been related above, and that he and his men had been all wounded in defence of the christians, as appeared by their wounds, which were not given by christian arms, but with *Aragayas*, or wooden swords, and arrows pointed with fish bones. This discourse being over, he presented the admiral with 8 strings of small beads, made of white, green, and red stones, a string of gold beads, a regal crown of gold, and three little calabashes full of gold sand, all which might be about 4 mark weight in gold, each mark being half a pound. The admiral in return, gave him abundance of our baubles, which might be worth three royals, (or eighteen pence) and were valued by him above a thousand. Tho' he was very ill, he would needs go with the admiral to see the fleet, where he was courteously entertain'd and much pleased to see the horses, of which the christians had before given him an account. And because some of those that were dead, had misinform'd him concerning our holy faith, the admiral was forced to instruct him in it, and afterwards would have him wear an image of the virgin *Mary* about his neck, which at first he had refused to receive.

How the Spaniards left in Hispaniola were destroyed.

CHAP. LI.

How the admiral left the colony of Navidad, *and went to found the city which he call'd* Isabella.

THE admiral reflecting on the disaster of those christians, and his own misfortune at sea, having lost the men and fort ashoar, and his ship upon the water, and that not far off there were better and more commodious places to plant a colony; on *Saturday* the 7th of *December*, he sail'd with the whole fleet eastward, and about evening cast anchor not far from the islands of *Monte Christo*, and the next day at *Monte Christo*, among those seven low little islands, whereof mention has been made already, which, tho' they are without trees, are nevertheless pleasant; for in that winter season, they there found flowers, and nests with eggs, others with young birds, and all other things that are seen in summer. Thence he went to anchor before a town of *Indians*, where resolved to plant a colony, he landed with all the men, provisions and utensils he brought aboard the fleet, in a plain near a rock, on which a fort might conveniently be built, where he built a town and call'd it *Isabella*, in honour of queen *Isabel* or *Elizabeth*. This place was judged very convenient, forasmuch as the port was very large, tho' expos'd to the north-west, and had a most delicate river a bow shot from it, from which canals of water might be drawn to run thro' the middle of the town, and beyond was a mighty open plain, from which the *Indians* said the mines of *Cibao* were not very remote. For these reasons the admiral was so eager upon settling the said colony, that what with the fatigue endured at sea, and what he here went thro', he not only wanted time to write day by day what happened, according to his custom, but it happen'd he fell sick, which interrupted his writing from the

Isabella *the first colony in the* West Indies.

5

the 11th of *December*, till the 12th of *March*, in the year 1494. During which time, having ordered the affairs of the town the best he could, for affairs abroad, he sent one *Alonzo de Hojeda*, with 15 men to seek out the mines of *Cibao*. Afterwards on the 2d of *February*, 12 ships of the fleet returned to *Castile*, under the command of one captain *Anthony de Torres*, brother to prince *John*'s nurse, a man of great judgment and honour, and in whom their catholick majesties and the admiral much confided. He had all in writing at large that had happened, as also the nature of the country, and what it required. Not long after *Hojeda* returned, and giving an account of his journey, said, That the 2d day, after he set out for *Isabella*, he lay at the pass of a mountain, which was very difficult of access, that afterwards, at every league's distance he found *Caciques*, who had been very kind to him; and continuing his journey the 6th day after he set out, he came to the mines of *Cibao*, where the *Indians* immediately before him, took up gold in a small river, as they had done in many others of the same province, were he affirm'd there was great plenty of gold. This news much rejoiced the admiral, who was then recovered of his sickness, and he resolved to go ashoar, to observe the disposition of the country, that he might the better know what was to be done. Accordingly on *Wednesday* the 12th of *March*, 1494, he set out from *Isabella* from *Cibao*, to see the mines, with all the people that were in health, both a foot and a horseback, leaving a good guard in the two ships and three caravals that remained of the fleet, and causing all the ammunition and tackle belonging to the other ships, to be put aboard his own, that none might rebel with them as they had attempted to do whilst he was sick. Because many having gone that voyage, upon the belief, that as soon as they landed they might load themselves with gold, and so return rich home, (which gold, wheresoever it is found, requires time, trouble, and labour to gather it) the thing not falling out as they expected; being therefore dissatisfied and offended, as also because of the building of the new town, and weary of the diseases, the climate and change of diet caused among them, they had privately conspired to revolt from the admiral, and taking the ships that remain'd, by force to return in them to *Spain*. One *Bernard de Pisa*, who had been an officer of justice at court, and went that voyage in the quality of their catholick majesties controller, was the ringleader and head of these mutineers; therefore the admiral, when informed of it, would not punish him any otherwise, than by securing him aboard a ship, with a design to send him afterwards into *Spain*, with his process drawn up, as well for mutinying, as for having writ a false information against the admiral, which he had hid in the ship. Having therefore ordered all these affairs, and having left some persons both at sea and ashoar, together with his Brother *D. James Columbus* to look to, and secure the fleet, he set forwards towards *Cibao*, carrying along with him all the tools and necessaries to build a fort, to keep that province under, and secure the christians left there to gather gold, against any attempts or designs of the *Indians*. And the more to terrify them, and take away all hopes that they might do in the admiral's presence, as they had done in his absence with *Arana*, and the 38 christians left among them; he then carried along with him all the men he could, that they might in their own towns see and be sensible of the power of the christians, and be sensible that whensoever any wrong was done to one single man of ours travelling through the country, there was a force of men to chastize it. And to appear the more formidable, when he set out for *Isabella* and other towns, he made his men march with their arms in rank and file, as is usual in time of war, and with trumpets sounding, and colours flying. In his way he march'd along that river, which lay about a musquet shot from *Isabella*; and a league beyond, he cross'd another less river, and went to lie that night three leagues off in a plain, divided into pleasant fields, reaching to the foot of a craggy hill, and about two bow shots high. This he call'd *Puerto de los Hidalgos*, or the gentleman's port, (the *Spaniards* call passes on mountains, dry ports) because some gentlemen went before to order the road to be made, and this was the first road made in the *Indies*; for the *Indians* make their ways broad enough but for one man to pass at a time. Beyond this pass, he came into a large plain, over which he travelled five leagues the next day, and went to lie near a great river, which the men pass'd upon floats and in canoes. This river which he call'd of *Canes*, fell into the sea at *Monte Christo*. In his journey, he pass'd by many *Indian* towns, the houses whereof were round, thatch'd, and with such a little door, that he who goes in must stoop very low. Here, as soon as some of the *Indians* brought from *Isabella*, went into the houses, they took what they liked best, and yet the owners were not at all displeas'd, as if all things were in common. In the like manner, the people of the country, coming near to any christian, would take from him what they thought fit, thinking our things had been as common as theirs. But

Conspiracy against the admiral.

His journey to the mines.

But they were ſoon undeceiv'd, being told the contrary. In their way they paſs'd over mountains moſt pleaſantly wooded, where there were wild vines, aloes, and cinnamon trees, and another ſort that produces a fruit like a fig, and were vaſtly thick at the foot, but the leaves were like thoſe of the apple tree. Of this ſort of tree, the ſcammony is ſaid to come.

CHAP. LII.

How the admiral came to the province of Cibao, *where he found the gold mines, and built the caſtle of St.* Thomas.

A deſcription of the country.

ON *Friday* the 14th of *March*, the admiral ſet forward from the river of *Canes*, and a league and a half from it, found a great river, which he call'd the river of *Gold*, becauſe in paſſing it, they gathered ſome grains of gold. Having paſſed it with ſome difficulty, he proceeded to a large town, where many of the people fled to the mountains; but moſt of them fortified their houſes, barring their doors with ſome canes, as if that were a great defence, to hinder any body from coming in; for according to their cuſtom, no man dares break in at the door he finds ſo barr'd; foraſmuch as they have no wooden doors, or other means to ſhut themſelves in, and it ſeems theſe bars are ſufficient. Hence the admiral went to another fine river, which he call'd the *Green River*, the banks whereof were covered with bright round ſtones, and there he reſted that night. Holding on his journey the next day, he paſs'd by ſome great towns, where the people had put ſticks croſs their doors, like the others above-mentioned, and the admiral and his men being tired, they ſtayed that night at the foot of a rugged mountain, which he call'd *Port Cibao*; foraſmuch as the province of *Cibao* begins beyond the mountain. From this the firſt mountain they paſs'd was 11 leagues diſtant, all which diſtance is a plain, and the way directly ſouth. Setting out the next day, he travelled along a path, where they were forced with much difficulty, to lead the horſes; and thence he ſent back ſome mules to *Iſabella*, to bring bread and wine, for they began to want proviſions, and the journey was long; and they ſuffered the more, becauſe they were not yet uſed to the *Indian* diet, as they are now who live and travel in thoſe parts, who find the food of that countrey more eaſy of digeſtion, and more agreeable to that countrey, than what is carried from *Europe*, tho' it is not of ſo great nouriſhment. Thoſe that went for proviſions being returned, the admiral paſſing over the mountain on *Sunday* the 16th of *March*, entered the country of *Cibao*, which is rough and ſtony, full of gravel, plentiful of graſs, and watered by ſeveral rivers, in which gold is found. The further they went into this countrey, the more uncouth they found it, and encumbred with mountains, on the tops whereof, there appeared grains of gold ſand; for as the admiral ſaid, the great rains carry it down from the tops of the mountains, to the rivers in ſmall ſand. This province is as big as *Portugal*, and there are in it abundance of mines, and gold in the brooks; but for the moſt part there are very few trees, and thoſe along the banks of rivers, and are moſt of them pines and palms of ſeveral ſorts. Now *Hojeda* having as was ſaid, travell'd that countrey the *Indians* had ſome knowledge of the chriſtians, ſo it happened, that what way ſoever the admiral went, the ſaid *Indians* came out to the road to meet him, with preſents of proviſions, and ſome ſmall quantity of gold duſt they had gathered, after they underſtood they came for it. The admiral perceiving he was now 18 leagues from *Iſabella*, and the countrey he had left behind very craggy, he ordered a fort to be built in a very pleaſant and ſtrong place, which he call'd the caſtle of St. *Thomas*, to command the countrey about the mines, and be a place of ſafety for the chriſtians that went thither. The command of this new fort he gave to *D. Peter Margarite*, a perſon of account, with 56 men, among whom were workmen of all ſorts to build the caſtle, which was built with clay and timber, that being a ſufficient ſtrength to keep out any number of *Indians* that could come againſt it. Here breaking ground to lay the foundation, and cutting a rock to make the ditches, when they were got two fathom below the the ſtone, they found neſts made of hay and ſtraw, and inſtead of eggs, three or four round ſtones, as big as oranges, as artificially made, as if they had been cannon balls; and in the river that runs at the foot of that hill, the caſtle now ſtands upon, they found ſtones of ſeveral colours, ſome of them large, of pure marble, and other of jaſper.

The fort of St. Thomas.

CHAP.

CHAP. LIII.

How the admiral returned to Isabella, *and found that soil was very fruitful.*

THE admiral having given orders for the finishing and fortifying of the castle, set out for *Isabella*, on *Friday* the 21st of *March*, and near the green river met the mules going with provisions, and not being able himself to stay there, because of the great rains, he stay'd there, sending the provisions to the fort. Afterwards endeavouring to find the ford of that river, and of the river *del Oro*, which is bigger than *Ebro*, he stayed some days in those *Indian* towns, eating their bread and garlick, which they gave for a small matter. On *Sunday* the 29th of *March*, he came to *Isabella*, where melons were already grown, fit to eat, tho' it was not above two months since the seed was put into the ground. So cucumbers came up in 20 days, and a wild vine of that countrey being prun'd, had produced grapes, which were good and large. The next day, being the 30th of *March*, a countreyman gathered ears of wheat he had sown at the latter end of *January*. There were also vetches, but much bigger than those they sow'd; and all they sow'd sprung up above ground in three days, and the 25th day they eat of it. The stones of fruit set in the ground, sprouted out in seven days, and the vine branches shot out in the same time, and in 25 days after, they gathered green grapes. The sugar canes budded in seven days, which proceeded from the temperature of the climate, not unlike to that of our countrey, for it was rather cold than hot; besides, that the waters there are very cold, thin, and wholesome. The admiral was well enough pleased with the air, the soil and the people of the countrey. On *Tuesday* the 1st of *April*, there came a messenger from fort St. *Thomas*, who brought news, that the *Indians* of that countrey fled, and that a *Cacique*, whose name was *Caunabo*, was preparing to come and attack the fort. The admiral knowing how inconsiderable the people of that countrey were, made little account of that report, especially confiding in the horses, by whom the *Indians* were afraid to be devoured, and therefore were so much afraid, that they durst not go into any house where a horse stood. However the admiral thought fit to send more men and provisions, considering that since he design'd to go to discover the continent with three caravals he had left him, it was fit all things should remain quiet behind. Therefore on *Wednesday* the 2d of *April*, he sent 70 men with provisions and ammunition to the fort, 25 of which were to keep guard, and the others help to make another road, the first being very troublesome, as were the fords of the rivers. These being gone, whilst the ships were fitted to go upon the new discovery, he attended to order all things necessary for the town he was building, dividing it into streets, with a convenient market place, and endeavouring to bring the river to it along a large cut canal; for which reason he also made a dam that might serve the mills, because the town being almost a cannon shot from the river, the people would have been troubled to fetch water so far, especially then, when most of them were very weak and indisposed, by reason of the sharpness of the air, which did not agree with them; so that some were sick, and had no other *Spanish* provisions but bisket and wine, by reason of the ill management of the captains of the ships, as also because in that countrey nothing keeps so well as in *Spain*. And tho' they had plenty of the countrey provisions, yet not being used to that food, it did not agree with them. Therefore the admiral had resolved to leave but 300 men in the island, and to send the rest into *Spain*, which number, considering the nature of the island, and of the *Indies*, he knew was sufficient to keep that countrey in subjection to their catholick majesties. In the mean while, because the bisket grew towards an end, and they had no flour, but wheat; he resolved to make some mills, tho' there was no fall of water fit for that purpose within a league of the town, at which work, and all others, he was forced to stand over the workmen, they all endeavouring to save themselves from any labour. After that, he resolved to send out all the people that were in health, except handicraft men, and artificers, to the royal plain, that travelling about the countrey, they might pacify it, strike a terror into the *Indians*, and by degrees be us'd to their food, since they daily felt more want of that of *Spain*. *Hojeda* was sent to command these men, till they came to St. *Thomas*, there to deliver them to *D. Peter Margarite*, who was to lead them about the island, and *Hojeda* himself to command in the fort, he having taken the pains, the winter before, to discover that provice of *Cibao*, which in the *Indian* language signifies stony. *Hojeda* set out from *Isabella* on *Wednesday* the 29th of

Great fruitfulness of Hispaniola.

400 men sent about the island. of *April*, towards St. *Thomas*, with all the aforesaid men, being above 400, and having pass'd the river *del Oro*, apprehended the *Cacique* that liv'd there, and a brother a nephew of his, sending them in irons to the admiral, and cut off the ears of one of his subjects, in the great place of his town, because three christians coming from St. *Thomas* to *Isabella*, this *Cacique* gave them five *Indians* to carry their cloaths over the river at the ford, and they being come to the middle of the river, returned to their town with them, and the *Cacique* instead of punishing them, took the cloaths for himself, refusing to restore them. Another *Cacique* who dwelt beyond the river relying on the service he had done the christians, resolved to go with the prisoners to *Isabella*, and intercede with the admiral for them, who entertain'd him courteously, and ordered that the other *Indians*, with their hands bound, would be publickly sentenced to die in the market-place, which the honest *Cacique* seeing, he with many tears obtained their lives, promising they should never be guilty of any other offence. The admiral having discharged them all, a man a horseback came from St. *Thomas's*, and gave an account, that he had found in that same *Cacique*, who had been prisoner in his town, five christians taken by his subjects as they were coming for *Isabella*, and that he frightning the *Indians* with his horse had released them, above 400 men running away from him, of whom he wounded two in the pursuit; and that when he had pass'd the river, he saw they turn'd upon the said christians, whereupon he made as if he would go back against them, but they for fear of his horse, all ran away, least the horse should fly over the river.

CHAP. LIV.

How the admiral settled the affairs of the island, and went to discover Cuba, *supposing it to be the continent.*

A council to govern Hispaniola. THE admiral being resolved to go out to discover the continent, appointed a council to govern the island in his absence, the persons it consisted of, were, *D. James Columbus*, his brother, with the title of president, *F. Boyl*, and *Peter Fernandez Coronell*, Regents, *Alonso Sanchez de Carvajal* Rector of *Bacca*, and *John de Luxan* of *Madrid*, gentlemen to their catholick majesties. And that there might not want meal for support of the people, he hastned the building of the mills, notwithstanding the rain and flood very much obstructed it. From these rains, the admiral says, proceeds the great moisture, and consequently the fruitfulness of the island, which is so wonderful, that they eat fruit of the trees in *November*, when they were blossoming afresh, which shews that they bear twice a year. But herbs and seeds grow at all times, and so they find on the trees, nests with eggs, and young birds. As the fruitfulness of the soil appeared extraordinary, so they daily received fresh advices of the wealth of the countrey; for some of those the admiral had sent out, were always returning with news of new mines discovered, besides the relation of the *Indians* concerning the great plenty of gold found in several parts of the island. The admiral not so satisfied, resolved to go out to discover along the coast of *Cuba*, not knowing whether it was an island or continent. Therefore taking 3 ships along with him, he set sail upon *Thursday* the 24th of *April*, after noon, and came to an anchor that day at *Monte Christo*, west of *Isabella*. On *Friday* he went to *Guacanagari's* port, thinking to find him there, but he seeing the ships, fled for fear, tho' his subjects falsly affirm'd he would soon return. But the admiral not caring to stay without great cause, departed on *Saturday* the 26th of *April*, and went to the island *Tortuga*, which lies 6 leagues to the westward: He lay by it that night, in a calm with his sails abroad, the tide running back against the currents. Next day the north-west winds and currents setting from the west, oblig'd him to go back to an anchor in the river of *Guadalquiver*, which is in the same island, there to wait for a wind that would stem the current, which both then and the year before, he found to run strong there toward the east. On *Tuesday* the 29th of the same month, the wind being fair, he came to cape St. *Nicholas*, and thence cross'd over to the island of *Cuba*, running along the south coast of it, and having sail'd a league beyond *Cabo Fuerte*, *The coast of* Cuba. put into a large bay which he call'd *Puerto Grande*, or great port, the mouth whereof was 150 paces over, and had much water. Here he cast anchor, and took some refreshment of broil'd fish and oisters, whereof the *Indians* had great store. On the 1st of *May* he continued his voyage along the coast, where he found commodious harbours, fine rivers and high mountains. Upon

on the sea, after he left *Tortuga*, he met abundance of the weeds he saw on the ocean, in his voyage to and from *Spain*. He sailing close along the shore, abundance of people came aboard in their canoes from the island, thinking our men were come down from heaven, bring of their bread, water and fish, and giving it all freely, without asking any thing for it; but the admiral to send them home well pleased, ordered they should be paid, giving them beads, bells, and such-like baubles.

CHAP. LV.

The admiral discovers the island of Jamaica.

Coast of Jamaica.

ON *Saturday* the 3d of *May*, the admiral resolved to sail over from *Cuba* to *Jamaica*, that he might not leave it behind, without knowing whether the report of such plenty of gold they had there, was in it, prov'd true, and the wind being fair, and he almost half way over, discovered it on *Sunday*. Upon *Monday* he came to an anchor, and thought it the beautifullest of any he had yet seen in the *Indies*, and such multitudes of people in great and small canoes came aboard, that it was astonishing. The next day he ran along the coast to find out harbours, and the boats going to sound the mouths of them, there came out so many canoes and arm'd men, to defend the countrey, that they were forced to return to the ships, not so much for fear, as to avoid falling to enmity with those people. But afterwards considering, that if they show'd signs of fear the *Indians* would grow proud upon it, they returned together to the port, which the *admiral* call'd *Puerto Bueno*, that is, good harbour. And because the *Indians* came to drive them off, those in boats gave them such a flight of arrows from their cross-bows, that six or seven of them being wounded, they retired. The fight ending in this manner; there came abundance of canoes from the neighbouring places in peaceable manner, to see and barter provisions, and several things they brought, and gave for the least trifle that was offered them. In this port, which is like a horse-shoe, the admiral's ship was repaired, it being leaky, and that done, they set sail on *Friday* the 9th of *May*, keeping so close along the coast westward, that the *Indians* follow'd in their canoes to trade, and get something of ours. The wind being somewhat contrary, the admiral could not make so much way as he wish'd, till on *Tuesday* the 14th of *May*, he resolved to stand over again for *Cuba*, to keep along its coast, designing not to return till he had sail'd 5 or 600 leagues and were satisfied whether it was an island or continent. That same day, as he was going off from *Jamaica*, a very young *Indian* came aboard, saying, he would come into *Spain*, and after him came several of his kindred and other people in their canoes, earnestly intreating him to go back, but they could never alter his resolution; and therefore to avoid seeing his sisters cry and sob, he went where they could not come at him. The admiral admiring his resolution, gave order that he should be used with all civility.

CHAP. LVI.

The admiral from Jamaica *returns to the coast of* Cuba, *still thinking it to be the continent.*

THE admiral leaving *Jamaica* on *Wednesday* the 15th of *May*, came to that point of *Cuba*, which he call'd *Cabo de Santa Cruz*, or cape Holy Cross, and running along the coast, there happened a great storm of thunder and lightning, which together with the flats and currents, put him into no small danger and to very much trouble, being obliged at the same time to struggle against these two evils, which required contrary remedies; for it is a proper remedy against thunder, to strike the sails, and it is requisite to spread them to avoid the flats, and had this calamity lasted for 8 or 10 leagues, it had been insupportable. But the worst of it was, that all over that sea, both north and north-east, the further they went, the more low little islands they met with, and tho' there were trees in some of them, yet others were sandy, and scarce appear'd above the surface of the water, some a league, some more and some less in compass. True it is, that the nearer they sail'd to *Cuba*, the higher and pleasanter the

Infinite small islands.

the little islands appeared, and being a matter of difficulty, and to no purpose, to give every one of them a name, the admiral called them all in general *Jardin de la Reyna*, the queen's garden. But as many islands as he saw that day, he saw many more and bigger the next day, than he had before, and not only to the north-east, but north-west and south-west; insomuch that they counted 160 islands that day, all parted by deep channels, which the ship sail'd through. In some of these islands they saw abundance of cranes, in shape and bigness like those of *Spain*, but that they were as red as scarlet. In others they found abundance of tortoises, and of their eggs, not unlike a hen's, but that the shells are very hard. The tortoises lay these eggs in a hole they make in the sand, and covering them, leave them till the heat of the sun hatches and brings forth the tortoises, which in time grow as big as a buckler, or great target. In these islands they also saw crows and cranes like those of *Spain*, and sea-crows, and infinite numbers of little birds that sung sweetly, and the very air was as sweet, as if they had been among roses and the finest perfumes in the world, yet the danger was very great, there being such abundance of channels, that much time was spent in finding the way out. In one of these channels, they spy'd a canoe of *Indian* fishermen, who very quietly, without the least concern expected the boat which was making towards them, and being come near, made a sign to them in it, till they had done fishing. Their manner of fishing was so strange and new to our men, that they were willing to comply with them; it was thus: they had ty'd some small fishes they call *Reves*, by the tail, which run themselves against other fish, and with a certain roughness they have from the head to the middle of the back, they stick so fast to the next fish they meet, that when the *Indians* perceive it, drawing their line, they draw them both together; and it was a tortoise our men saw so taken by those fishermen, that fish clinging about the neck of it, where they generally fasten, being by that means safe from the other fish biting them, and have seen them fasten upon vast sharks. When the *Indians* in the canoe had taken their tortoise, and two other fishes they had before, they presently came very friendly to the boat, to know what our men would have, and by their directions went along aboard the ships, where the admiral treated them very courteously, and understood by them that there was an infinite multitude of islands in that sea, and they freely gave all they had, tho' the admiral would suffer nothing to be taken of them but the fish, the rest being their nets, hooks, and calabashes full of water to drink. Having given them some small trifles, they went away very well pleased, and he held on his course with a design not to do so long, because he began to want provisions already, whereas, had he been well stored, he thought not to have returned into *Spain*, but cast about, tho' he was very much spent, not only because he fed ill, but also because he had not stript or lain in a bed ever since he sail'd from *Spain*, till the 19th of *May*, when he writ this, except eight nights, when he was much indisposed. And if he had much care upon him at other times it was doubled this voyage, by reason of the innumerable quantity of islands, among which he was sailing, which where so many, that on the 20th of *May*, he discover'd 71, besides many more he saw W. S. W, at sun-setting. Which islands or sands are not only frightful by their multitude, appearing on all sides; but what is yet more terrible, is, that every night there rises off them a great fogg eastward, so dismal to behold, that it seems as if some great shower of hail would fall; the thunder and lightning are so violent, but when the moon rises, it all vanishes, part of it turning to rain and wind, which is so usual and natural in that countrey, that it did not only happen all those nights the admiral was there, but I saw the same in those islands in the year 1503, in my return from the discovery of *Veragua*, and generally here at night the wind is north, coming off the island *Cuba*; and afterwards when the sun is up, it comes about east, and follows the sun till it comes to the west.

Birds and Tortoises in them.

A pretty way of fishing.

CHAP. LVII.

Of the great fatigue the admiral underwent sailing among abundance of islands.

THE admiral still holding on his course westward, among infinite numbers of islands, upon *Thursday* the 22d of *May* came to an island somewhat bigger than the rest, which he call'd St. *Mary*, and landing at a town, there was in it not one *Indian* would stay to talk to the christians, nor did they find any thing in the houses but fish, which is all the food those people live on, and several dogs like mastiffs, who eat fish too

Indians living upon fish.

too. Thus without talking to any body, or seeing any thing remarkable, he sail'd away north-east, among abundance of islands, in which there were many cranes as red as scarlet, parrots, and other sorts of birds, dogs like those before mentioned, and abundance of those weeds he saw on the ocean, when he first discover'd the *Indies*. Thus sailing among so many sands and islands, fatigued him very much; for sometimes he was forced to stand west, sometimes north, and sometimes south, according as the channels would permit; for notwithstanding his care in sounding, and keeping men upon the round-top to look out, yet the ship often touch'd, and there was no avoiding it, there being no end of the flatts on all hands. Sailing on in this manner, he came again to *Cuba*, to take in water, whereof they had much need. And tho' there was no town where they put in, because the place was wooded, yet one of the seamen that went ashoar, going up among the trees with a cross-bow to kill some bird or beast, found 30 people arm'd with such weapons as they use, that is, spears, and staves, which they wear instead of swords, and call *Macanas*. Among them he said he saw one clad with a white coat or a west, down to his knees, and two that carry'd him had them down to their feet, all three of them as white as the *Spaniards*, but that he had no talk with them, because being afraid of such a number, he began to cry out to his companions, and the *Indians* ran away without looking back. Tho' the admiral the next day sent people ashoar to know the truth of it, they could not travel above half a league, because of the thickness of the trees and bushes, and because all that coast is boggy and muddy, for two leagues up the countrey, where there are hills and mountains, so that they only saw footsteps of fishermen on the shoar, and abundance of cranes like those in *Spain*, but bigger. Then sailing about 10 leagues westward, they saw houses on the shoar, from which some canoes came with water, and such things as those people eat, which they brought to the christians, who payed well for 'em; and the admiral caused one of those *Indians* to be stopp'd, telling him, and the rest by his interpreter, that he would let him go freely home, as soon as he had directed him in his voyage, and given some account of that countrey. At which the *Indian* was very much pleased, and assured the admiral that *Cuba* was an island, and that the king or *Cacique* of the western part of it, never spoke to his subjects but by signs by whom all his orders were immediately obeyed, that all that coast was very low, and full of small islands, which was found to be too true, that the next day, being the 11th of *June*, to pass from one channel to another, the admiral was forced to have the ships towed over a flat, where there was not a foot water, and all the breadth of it was not above two ships length. Bearing up closer to *Cuba* they saw tortoises of a vast bigness, and in such numbers, that they covered the sea. At break of day they saw such a cloud of sea crows that they darkened the sun, coming from the seaward to the island, where they all lighted; besides them, abundance of pigeons, and birds of other sorts were seen, and the next day there came such swarms of butterflies, that they darkened the air, and lasted till night, when the great rain carried them away.

An Indian clad.

Infinite tortoises, crows and butterflies.

CHAP. LVIII.

How the admiral returns back towards Hispaniola.

ON *Friday* the 13th of *June*, the admiral perceiving that the coast of *Cuba* ran far west, and that it was a matter of the greatest difficulty to sail that way, by reason of the infinite multitude of islands and sands there were on all sides, and that he already began to want provisions, for which reason he could not continue his voyage as he had intended, he resolved to return to the town he had began to build in *Hispaniola*, and to furnish himself with wood and water, he anchored in the island *Evangelista*, which is 30 leagues in compass, and 700 from *Dominica*. Having provided himself with what he wanted, he directed his course southward, hoping to get out better that way, and sailing thro' the channel, he saw looked clearest, after sailing a few leagues, found it shut up, which did not a little trouble and terrify the men, seeing themselves as it were hemmed in on all sides, and destitute of provisions and all comfort. But the admiral, who was wise and couragious, perceiving their faint-heartedness, said with a chearful countenance, that he thanked God for forcing him back the same way he came; forasmuch as if they had continued their voyage that way they intended to go, it might perhaps have happened they might have run themselves into some place whence it would be hard getting out, and at a time when they had neither ships nor provisions to go back, which at present they could easily

The admiral imbay'd.

easily do. Thus with great satisfaction of all the men, he returned to the island *Evangelista*, where he had watered, and on *Wednesday* the 25 of *June*, sailed thence north-west towards some small islands that appeared 5 leagues off. Going still a little forward he came into a sea so patched with green and white, that it looked like one entire sand, tho' there was two fathom water; along which he sailed 7 leagues, till he met another sea, as white as milk, which he much admired, the water being very thick. This sea dazzled the eyes of all that beheld it, and seemed to be all a shoal without water enough for the ships, yet there were about 3 fathom water. But when he had sailed about 4 leagues upon that sea, he came into another sea, as black as ink, and 5 fathom deep, thro' which he held his course till he came up with *Cuba*. Thence standing to the eastward, with scant winds, thro' narrow channels and shoals. On the 30th of *June* as he was writing his journal of the voyage, his ship run a ground so fast, that neither anchors nor other inventions, being able to get it off; it pleased God it was drawn off a-head, tho' with some damage, because of its beating on the sand. However, with God's assistance they got off at last, and he sailed on as the wind and shoal-water would permit, always thro' a very white sea, and two fathom deep, neither deeper nor shallower, unless he came too close to some of the sands, where there was want of water. Besides which trouble, every day about sun-setting, he was troubled with mighty showers, which rise in the mountains from the morasses near the sea, which were a great fatigue to him, till he came close to *Cuba* towards the east, the way he came at first. Thence, as he had found before, came off a most fragrant scent, as it were of flowers. On the 7th of *July* he landed to hear mass, and there resorted to him an old *Cacique* lord of that province, who was very attentive at mass; when it was ended, by signs, and the best he could express, he said it was very well done to give thanks to God, because the soul which was good, would go to heaven, and the body remain on earth, but that the wicked souls must go to hell. And among other things said, he had been in the island *Hispaniola*, where he knew some of the chief men; that he had been in *Jamaica*, and a great way towards the west of *Cuba*, and that the *Cacique* of that port, was clad like a priest.

Notable words of an Indian.

CHAP. LIX.

The great hunger and other calamities the admiral and his men endured, and how he returned to Jamaica.

THE admiral sailing thence on *Wednesday* the 16th of *July*, still attended by terrible rains and winds, drew near to cape *Cruz* in *Cuba*, where he was on a sudden assaulted by such a violent rain and storm as bore his ship's side under water, but it pleased God they immediately struck all their sails, and drop'd their best anchors; but they took in so much water at the decks, that the men were not able to pump it out, especially in the condition they were, being much spent for want of provisions: For they eat nothing but a pound of rotten biscuit a day, and about half a pint of wine, unless they happened to catch some fish, which yet they could not keep from one day to the next, provisions in those parts being of a very slight nature, and because the weather was always more inclinable to heat than in our countries, and this want being common to all, the admiral in his journal speaks thus concerning it. I my self am at the same allowance, God grant it may be to his honour, and for your highness's service, for I shall never again for my own benefit expose myself to such sufferings and dangers, never a day passing; but I see we are all upon the brink of death. In this danger and distress he arrived at cape *Cruz* the 18th of *July*, where he was friendly entertained by the *Indians*. They brought him abundance of *Cazabi*, so they call their bread made of roots grated, a great deal of fish, store of fruit and such other things as they eat. The wind being contrary to sail for *Hispaniola*, he stood over to *Jamaica* on *Wednesday* the 22d day of *July*, and sail'd along westward close under the shore, the countrey all along most delightful and fruitful, with excellent harbours, at every league distance, and all the coast full of towns, the people whereof followed the ships in their canoes, bringing such provisions as they eat, and much better liked by the christians, than that they found in the other islands. The climate, air, and weather was the same as the rest, for in this western part of *Jamaica* there gathered every evening a storm of rain, which lasted about an hour more or less, which the admiral said, he attributed to the great woods there in those countries, for that he knew this was usual at first in the *Canary* islands, *Madera* and the *Azores*, whereas now the woods are cut down

Great distress.

Great beauty of Jamaica.

down that shaded them, there are not so great and frequent storms and rains, as there were formerly. Thus the admiral sail'd on tho' with contrary winds, which obliged him every night to take the shelter of the land, which appeared green, pleasant, fruitful, abounding in provisions, and so populous, that he thought none excell'd it, especially near a bay which he called *De las Vacas*, because there are nine islands close to the land, which he said was high as any he had seen, and believ'd reached above the region where the storms bred, yet it is all peopled, very fruitful and pleasant. This island he judg'd to be 800 miles in compass, and when fully discovered, computed it to be 50 leagues in length and 20 in breadth. Being much taken with its beauty, he had a great mind to stay there to be fully informed of the nature of it, but the great want of provisions we mention'd, and the leakiness of the vessels would not permit. Therefore as soon as the weather was a little fair, he sail'd away eastward, so that on *Tuesday* the 19th of *Aug.* he lost sight of that island, standing over directly for *Hispaniola*, and call'd the most eastward cape of *Jamaica* on the south coast *Cabo del Farol.*

CHAP. LX.

The admiral discovers the south-side of Hispaniola, *till he returned east about the town of* Isabella.

South coast of Hispaniola *discover'd.*

ON *Wednesday* the 20th of *August*, the admiral had sight of the south-side of *Hispaniola*, and called the first point cape *St. Michael*, which was 30 leagues distant from the easterlyest point of *Jamaica*, yet at present through the ignorance of the sailers it is called cape *Tiburon*. From this cape on *Saturday* the 23d of *August*, there came aboard a *Cacique*, who call'd the admiral by his name, and had some other *Spanish* words, by which he was convinced this was the same land as *Hispaniola*. At the end of *August* he anchor'd in an island, which is called *Alto Velo*, and having lost sight of the other two ships under his command, he caused some men to go ashore in that little island, whence being very high they might see a great way round; but they discovered none of their companions. As they were going aboard they killed eight sea-wolves, that lay asleep on the sand, and took abundance of pidgeons and other birds; for that island not been inhabited, nor those creatures us'd to see men, they stood still to be killed with staves. The same they did the two following days, waiting for the ships which had been astray ever since the *Friday* before, till at the end of six days they came, and all three together went away to the island *Beata* twelve leagues distant from *Alto Velo*. Hence they passed on coasting *Hispaniola*, in sight of a delightful countrey, which was a plain running up a mile from the sea, so populous, that it seem'd to be one continued town for a league in length. In which plain there appear'd a lake five leagues long from east to west. The people therefore of the countrey having some knowledge of the christians, came aboard in their canoes, bringing news that some *Spaniards* from *Isabella* had happened to come among them, and that they were all well, which much pleased the admiral, and to the end they too might hear of his health, and his company's and of his return, being somewhat more towards the east, he sent nine men to cross the island, passing by the forts of *St. Thomas* and the *Magdalen* to *Isabella*, and he with his three ships still keeping along the coast eastward, sent the boats for water to a place, where a great town appeared. The *Indians* came out against them with bows and poison'd arrows, and with ropes in their hands, making signs that they would bind the christians they should take with them. But as soon as the boats came to the shore, the *Indians* laid down their arms, and offered to bring bread and water, and all they had, asking in their lauguage for the admiral. Going hence they saw in the sea a fish as big as a whale, which on its neck had a great shell, like a tortoise, and bore its head, which was as big as a hogshead, above water, had a tail like a tunny fish, very long, and two large fins on the sides. The admiral by this fish and other signs, perceiving there would be some change of weather, he sought for some harbour to secure himself. And on the 15th of *September* it pleased God to show him an island, being near the east part of *Hispaniola*, call'd by the *Indians Adamanai*, and the weather being very stormy drop'd anchor in the channel, between it and *Hispaniola*, close to a small island that lies between both, where that night he saw the eclipse of the moon, which he said varied 5 hours 23 minutes from *Cadiz* to the place where he was. This I suppose made the bad weather last so long, for he was forced to lie close in that very place till the 20th of the month,

A monstrous fish.

not

not without fear for the other ships, which could not get in, but it pleased God to save them. Being afterwards together again, on the 24th of *September* they sail'd to the most easterly point of *Hispaniola*, and thence passed over to a little island lying between *Hispaniola* and *S. John de Borriquen*, called by the *Indians Mona*. From this island the admiral does not continue the journal of his voyage, nor does he say how he returned to *Isabella*, but only that going from *Mona* to *St. John*, the great toil he had gone through, his own weakness and want of provisions cast him into a dangerous disease between a pestilential fever and a lethargy, which presently depriv'd him of all his senses and memory. Whereupon all the men aboard the ships resolved to desist from the design he had in hand of discovering all the islands of the *Caribbees*, and to return to *Isabella*, where they arriv'd in five days, and on the 29th of *September*, and there it pleased God to restore his health, tho' his sickness lasted above five months, which was attributed to the great sufferings he had gone through during that voyage, and to his extraordinary weakness; for sometimes he had not sleep three hours in eight days, which seems almost impossible, were not he himself and his men witnesses of the truth of it.

CHAP. LXI.

How the admiral subdued the island Hispaniola, *and took such order, that they might not revolt again.*

Bartholomew Columbus.

THE admiral returning to *Hispaniola* from the discovery of *Cuba* and *Jamaica*, found there his brother *Bartholomew Columbus*, who, as was said before, had been sent to treat with the king of *England* about the discovery of the *Indies*. He returned to *Spain* with the grant of his demands, understood at *Paris*, by *Charles* king of *France*, that the admiral his brother had discovered the *Indies*, and he supplied him with 100 crowns to proceed on his journey. Upon this news he made all the haste he could to overtake the admiral in *Spain*; yet when he came to *Sevil*, his brother was set out for the *Indies* with seventeen sail. Therefore to fulfil the orders he had left him at the beginning of the year 1494, he went away to their catholick majesties, carrying me and my brother *D. James Columbus*, to serve prince *John* as his pages, as had been appointed by the queen, who was then at *Valladolid*. As soon as we came thither their majesties sent for *D. Bartholomew Columbus*, and sent him to *Hispaniola* with three ships, where he served some years, as appears by a manuscript I found among his papers, in which are these words. "I served as captain from the 14th of "*April* 1494, till the 12th of *March* 1496, "when the admiral set out for *Spain*, and "then I began to act as governor till the "24th of *August* 1498, when the admiral re-"turned from the discovery of *Paria*, when "I again served as captain till the 11th "of *December* 1500, when I returned to "*Spain*." But to return to the admiral, he returning from *Cuba*, made him governor of the *Indies*, tho' afterwards there arose a controversy on this account, because their catholick majesties said they had not granted the admiral power to appoint any such. But to decide this difference their highnesses granted it a-new, and so for the future he was called *Adelantado*, tha is, lieutenant of the *Indies*.

Why the Indians revolted.

The admiral having the assistance and advice of his brother, took some rest, and lived in quiet, tho' on the other side he met with trouble enough, as well from his sickness, as because he found almost all the *Indians* had revolted, through the fault of *D. Peter Margarite*, of whom we spoke above. He tho' obliged to respect and honour him that at his departure for *Cuba*, had left him the command of 360 foot and 14 horse, to travel over the island, and reduce it under the obedience of their catholick majesties and the christians, and particularly the province of *Cibao*, whence the chief profit was expected; yet did all things so much to the contrary, that as soon as the admiral was gone, he went with all his men to the great plain called *Vega Real*, ten leagues from *Isabella*, without stirring to over-run and reduce the island. Hence there ensued discord and factions at *Isabella*; he endeavouring that those of the council instituted by the admiral, should obey his orders, sending them very insolent letters, till perceiving he could not succeed in his design of getting the whole command into his hands, rather than stay the coming of the admiral, who would call him in question for his behaviour, he went aboard the first ships that came from *Spain*, and returned in them, without giving any account of himself, or any ways disposing of the men left under his command. Upon this every one

one went away among the *Indians*, where he thought fit, taking away their goods and their women, and committing such outrages, that the *Indians* resolved to be reveng'd on those they found alone, or straggling; so that the *Cacique* of the *Magdalen*, whose name was *Guatiguana*, had killed ten, and privately ordered a house to be fired, in which there were eleven sick. But he was severely punished, when the admiral returned; for tho' he himself could not be taken, yet some of his subjects were made prisoners and sent into *Spain* in four ships, *Antony de Torres* brought on the 24th of *February* 1495. Six or seven more, who in other parts of the island had done harm to the christians, suffer'd for it. The *Caciques* had certainly killed many, and would have destroy'd more, but that the admiral came in time to curb them all, who found the island in such disorder, that most of the christians committed a thousand insolencies, for which they were mortally hated by the *Indians*, who refused to submit to them. It was no difficult matter for them all to agree to cast off the *Spanish* yoke; because, as has been said, there were four principal kings or *Caciques*, to whom all the others were subject. The names of those four were *Caunabo*, *Guacanagari*, *Behechico* and *Guarionex*; and each of these had under him 70 or 80 others little lords; not that they paid tribute or gave any thing, but were obliged, whensoever called upon, to assist them in their wars, and till the ground; but *Guacanagari*, one of these who was lord of that part of the island where the town of the *Nativity* had been built, continued a friend to the christians. As soon therefore as he heard of the admiral's coming, he went to visit him, saying, he had no way been aiding or advising with the others, which might appear by the great civility the christians had found in his countrey, where 100 men had been always very well used and furnished with all things he could get to please them; for which reason, the other kings were become his enemies, and particularly *Behechico* had killed one of his women, and *Caunabo* had taken another, wherefore he pray'd him to cause her to be restored, and assist him to revenge these wrongs. The admiral resolved to do so, believing what he said was true, because he wept every time he called to mind those that had been killed at the *Nativity*, as if they had been his own children, and he was the more inclineable to it, considering that the discord among them would make it more practicable to conquer the countrey, and punish the revolt of the other *Indians*, and killing of the christians. Therefore on the 24th of *March* 1495, he

One Indian king sides with the Spaniards.

set out from *Isabella* to carry on the war, and the aforesaid *Guacanagari* with him, being very desirous to crush his enemies; tho' the undertaking seem'd very difficult, they having raised above 100000 *Indians*, whereas the admiral had not along with him above 200 christians, 20 horses, and as many dogs. The admiral being acquainted with the nature and qualities of the *Indians*, when he was two days journey from *Isabella*, divided his forces, giving half to his brother the lieutenant, that he might attack that multitude scattered about the plains in two places, believing the terror of hearing the noise in several places would put them to flight sooner than any thing else, as in effect it proved. The batallions of foot on both sides falling upon the multitude of *Indians*, and breaking them with the first discharge of their cross-bows and muskets, the horse and dogs fell in next in most furious manner, that they might not rally, whereupon those faint-hearted creatures fled, some one way, and some another; and our men pursuing and killing a great number, made such havock, that in a short time, through God's assistance they obtained a compleat victory, many of the enemies being slain, and others taken, among whom was *Caunabo*, the chief *Cacique* of them all, together with his wives and children. This *Caunabo* afterwards confessed he had killed 20 of the christians left with *Arana* in the town of the *Nativity*, the first voyage when the *Indies* were discovered, and that afterwards, under colour of friendship, he went in great haste to see the town of *Isabella*, to observe how he might best attack it, and do as he had done at the *Nativity*. Of all which things, the admiral had been fully informed by others; and therefore to punish him for that offence, and this second revolt, and gathering of forces he had now marched against him, and having taken him and his brother, he sent them all prisoners into *Spain*; for he would not without the knowledge of their catholick majesties, execute so considerable a person, being satisfied with punishing some of those that were most in fault. The victory obtain'd, and this man's imprisonment, put the affairs of the christians into such a good posture, that tho' at that time they were but 630, many of them sick, and others women and children; yet in the space of a year, the admiral spent in ranging the island, without being forced to draw sword any more, he reduced it to such obedience, that they all promised to pay tribute to their catholick majesties every three months, that is, all that inhabited the province of *Cibao*, where the gold mines were, from 14 years of

100000 Indians defeated.

of age upward, to pay a large horse-bell full of gold-dust, and all the rest 25 pounds of cotton a head. And that it might be known who had paid this tribute, there was a sort brass and tin coin stamp'd, one of which pieces was to be given to every one that paid, and he to wear it about his neck, that whosoever was found without it might be known not to have paid and punished. And doubtless this order would have proved effectual, had not those troubles we shall speak of afterwards happen'd among the christians; for after the taking of *Caunabo*, the countrey was so peaceable, that for the future one single christian went safely where he pleased; and the *Indians* themselves would carry him about on their shoulders, which the admiral attributed only to God and the good fortune of their catholick majesties, considering it had been otherwise impossible for 200 men, half sick and ill-armed, to overthrow such a multitude, which it pleased his divine majesty not only to bring under his command, but to send such scarcity of provisions, and such violent diseases among them, that they were reduced to one third of what they had been at first, to make it appear the more plain, that such miraculous victories, and the subduing of nations are his gift, and not the effect of our power or conduct, or of their want of courage; for tho' our men had been superiour to them, yet their multitude might make amends for any advantage we had over them.

CHAP. LXII.

Some remarkable things in the island, as the customs, ceremonies and religion of the Indies.

Product of Hispaniola. THE people of the island being brought under, and conversing more freely with our men, many other particulars, and the secrets of their religion were found out, but particularly that there were mines of copper, azure and amber; as also ebony, cedar, frankincense, and other rich gums and spice of several sorts, but wild, which being cultivated, might be brought to perfection; as for instance, cinnamon of good colour, but bitter, ginger, long pepper, abundance of mulberry trees for making of silk, which bear leaves all the year, and many other useful trees and plants not known in our parts. Besides, the *Spaniards* were inform'd of many other things relating to their customs, which to me seem to deserve a place in our history. To begin with their religion, I will here set down the admiral's own words, writ by himself, which are these.

" I could discover neither idolatry nor " any other sect among them, tho' every " one of their kings, who are very many, " as well in *Hispaniola*, as in all the other " islands and continent, has a house apart " from the town, in which there is nothing " at all but some wooden images carved, " by them called *Cemies*; nor is there any " thing done in those houses but what is " for the service of those *Cemies*, they re- " pairing to perform certain ceremonies, " and pray there, as we do to our churches. *Superstitions of* Indians. " In these houses they have a handsome " round table, made like a dish, on which " is some powder, which they lay on the " head of the *Cemies* with a certain cere- " mony; then through a cane that has " two branches clapp'd to their nose, they " snuff up this powder: The words they " say none of our people understand. This " powder puts them besides themselves, as " as if they were drunk. They also give " the image a name, and I believe it is " their fathers or grand-fathers, or both; for " they have more than one, and some above " ten, all in memory of their forefathers, " as I said before. I have heard them " commend one above another, and have " observed them to have more devotion, " and show more respect to one than ano- " ther, as we do in processions in time of " need, and the people and *Caciques* boast " among themselves of having the best " *Cemies*. When they go to these their " *Cemies*, they shun the christians, and " will not let them go into those houses; " and if they suspect they will come, " they take away their *Cemies*, and hide " them in the woods, for fear they should " be taken from them; and what is most " ridiculous, they use to steal one anothers " *Cemies*. It happened once, that the " christians on a sudden rushed into the " house with them, and presently the *Cemi* " cried out, speaking in their language, by " which it appeared to be artificially made; " for it being hollow, they had applied a " trunk to it, which answered to a dark " corner of the house covered with boughs " and leaves, where a man was concealed " who spoke what the *Cacique* ordered " him. The *Spaniards* therefore reflect- " ing on what it might be, kick'd down " the

" the *Cemi*, and found as has been said; " and the *Cacique* seeing they had discovered his practice, earnestly begg'd of " them not to speak of it to his subjects, " or the other *Indians*, because he kept " them in obedience by that policy. This " we may say has some resemblance of idolatry, at least among those who are ignorant of their *Caciques* fraud, since they " believe it is the *Cemi* that speaks, and all " of them in general are imposed upon, " and only the *Cacique* and he that combines with him, abuse their credulity, " by which means he draws what tribute " he pleases from his people. Most of the " *Caciques* have three stones also, to which " they and their people show a great devotion. The one they say helps the corn " and all sorts of grain; the second makes " women be delivered without pain; and " the third procures rain or fair weather, " according as they stand in need of either. " I sent your highness three of these stones " by *Antony de Torres*, and have three more " to carry along with me. When these " *Indians* die, they have several ways of " performing their obsequies, but the manner of burying their *Caciques* is thus. " They open and dry him at the fire, that " he may keep whole. Of others they " take only the head, others they bury " in a grot or den, and lay a calabash of " water and bread on his head; others they " burn in the house where they die, and " when they are at the last gasp, they suffer them not to die, but strangle them, " and this is done to *Caciques*. Others " are turn'd out of the house, and others " put them into a hamack, which is their " bed, laying bread and water by their head, " never returning to see them any more. " Some that are dangerously ill, are carried to the *Cacique*, who tells them whether they are to be strangled or not, and " what he says is done. I have taken pains " to find out what it is they believe, and " whether they know what becomes of them " after they are dead; especially I enquired of *Caunabo*, who was the chiefest king in *Hispaniola*, a man in years, " knowing, and of a most piercing wit. " He and the rest answered, that they go " to a certain vale, which every great *Cacique* supposes to be in his country, where " they affirm they find their parents, and " all their predecessors, and that they eat, " have women, and give themselves up to " pleasures and pastimes, as appears more " at large in the following account, in " which I order'd one *F. Roman*, who understood their language, to set down all " their ceremonies and antiquities, tho' " there are so many fables that nothing " can be made of it, but that they have " all some regard to a future state, and hold " the immortality of the soul.

The MANUSCRIPT of *F. Roman*, concerning the antiquities of the *Indians*, which he, as being skill'd in their tongue, has carefully gather'd by order of the admiral.

I F. Roman, *a poor anchorite of the order of St.* Jerome, *by order of the most illustrious lord admiral, viceroy and governor of the islands and continent of the* Indies, *write what I could hear and learn of the belief, and idolatry of the* Indians, *and how they serve their Gods. Every one observe some particular way and superstition and worshipping idols, which they call* Cemis. *They think there is an immortal being, like heaven, invisible, and that has a mother, but has no beginning, and this being they call* Jocakuvague Maorocon, *and its mother they call* Atabei, Iermaoguacar, Apito *and* Zuimaco, *which are several names. Those I here write of, are the people of the island* Hispaniola, *for I know nothing of the others, having never been in them. They also know whence they came, the original of the sun and moon, how the sea was made, and whither the dead go. And they believe the dead appear to them upon the roads when any of them go alone, for when there are a great many together they do not appear to them. All this their ancestors have made them believe, for they can neither read nor tell beyond ten.*

CHAP I.

Whence the Indians *came, and after what manner.*

Preposterous conceits of the Indians.

THere is a province in *Hispaniola* call'd *Caanan*, in which there is a mountain called *Canta*, where there are two grots or caverns; the one called *Cacibagiagua*, the other *Amaiauva*; most of the people that first inhabited the island came out of *Cacibagiagua*.

gua. These being in those caverns, kept watch by night, and one *Marocael* had the charge of it, who coming one day too late to the door, they say the sun took him away. Seeing therefore that the sun had carried him away for his neglect, they shut the door against him, and so he wus turn'd into a stone near the door. Then they say, that others going a fishing were taken by the sun, and became trees by them call'd *Jobi*, but otherwise *Mirabolans*.

The reason why *Marocael* watch'd and warded, was to observe whether he would send and distribute the people, and it appears he staid to his own harm.

CHAP. II.

How the men parted from the women.

IT happened, that one *Guagugiana*, bid another, whose name was *Giadruvava*, go and gather an herb called *Digo*, wherewith they cleanse their body when they go to wash. He went out before day, the sun took him by the way, and he became a bird that sings in the morning, like the *Nightingale*, and is call'd *Giahuba Bagiaci*. *Guagugiana* perceiving he did not return, whom he had sent to gather *Digo*, resolv'd to go out of the aforesaid grot *Cacibagiagua*.

CHAP. III.

GUagugiana resolv'd to go away in a passion, seeing they did not return whom he had sent to gather *Digo* to wash him, and said to the women, leave your husbands, and let us go into other countries, and we shall get jewels enough. Leave your children, and let us only carry the herbs along with us, and we will come again for them.

CHAP. IV.

GUagugiana set out with all the women, and went to seek another countrey, and came to *Matinino*, where he immediately left the women, and went into another countrey, called *Guanin*, having left the children by a brook. Afterwards, when hunger began to pinch them, they say, they cry'd, and called their mothers, that were gone; and the fathers could not relieve the children, who for hunger, called their mothers, saying, *Ma*, *Ma*, to speak, but in truth to beg of the earth. And they thus crying and begging of the earth, saying, *Too*, *Too*, like one that very earnestly begs a thing, they were transform'd into little creatures like dwarfs, and call'd *Tona*, because of their begging of the earth. And thus all the men were left without women.

CHAP. V.

THAT there went women again to the said island of *Hispaniola*, formerly called *Aiti*, and so the inhabitants of it are called, and the other islands called them *Bouchi*: And forasmuch as they have no letters, nor way of writing, they can give no good account how they understand this story of their ancestors, and therefore they do not agree in what they say, nor is what they relate to be put into any order. When *Guagugiana*, who carry'd away all the women went off, he took with him the wives of his *Caciques*, whose name was *Anacacugia*, deceiving them as he had done the others. Besides, a kinsman of *Guagugiana*, who followed him, went upon the sea, and *Guagugiana* said to his kinsman, when he was in the canoe, look what a fine *Cobo* there is in the water, which *Cobo* is the sea snail, or periwinkle; and he looking down for the *Cobo*, *Guagugiana* his kinsman took him by the feet and threw him into the sea, and so took all the women to himself, and left those at *Matinino*, where it is said there are none but women to this day; and he went away to another island called *Guanin*, and it was so called for what he carried to it when he went thither.

CHAP.

CHAP. VI.

Nonsensical fables.

THAT *Guagugiana* return'd to the same *Canta*, whence he had carried the women: They say that *Guagugiana* being in that countrey whither he went, saw he had left a woman in the sea, at which he was not pleas'd, and look'd about where to wash himself, being full of those blotches we call the *French Pox*. The woman put him into a *Guanara*, that is, a by-place; and being there, he was heal'd of his sores.

Afterwards he ask'd her leave to go his way, and she gave it him. This woman's name was *Guabonito*; and *Guagugiana* chang'd his name, calling himself from that time forwards, *Biberoci Guahagiona*. And the woman *Guabonito*, gave *Biberoci Guahagiona* much *Guanine* and *Cibe*, that he might carry them tied to his arms; for in those countries, the *Colecibi* are of stone, very like marble, and they wear them about their wrists and necks; and the *Guanini*'s wear them at their ears, making holes in them when they are little, and they sound like fine mettle. They say, that *Guabonito*, *Albeborael*, *Guahagiona*, and the father of *Albeborael*, were the first of these *Guanini*'s. *Guahagiona* staid in that countrey with the father, called *Hiauna*, his son from his father took the name *Hia Guaili Guanin*, which signifies son of *Hiauna*, and from thence forward, was called *Guanin*, and is so to this day. And they not knowing how to write, cannot give a good account of these fables, nor can I write them well; wherefore I believe, I mention the last first and the first last. But all I write is related by them, and so I deliver it as I had it from the people of the countrey.

CHAP. VII.

How women came again to the aforesaid island Aiti, *now called* Hispaniola.

THEY say the men went one day to wash themselves, and when they were in the water it rain'd much, and they were very desirous to have women; and that very often, when it rain'd, they had gone to seek out the track of their women, and could find no news of them; but they say, that as they were washing themselves that day, they saw fall down from the trees, as it were sliding down the branches, the shape of people, which were neither men nor women, nor had the secret parts of men or women, which they went to catch, but they fled as swift as if they had been eagles. Therefore by order of their *Cacique*, they call'd 2 or 3 men, since they themselves could not catch them, to watch how many there were of them, and find out for each of them a man that was *Caracaracoli*; for those men had rough hands, and therefore would hold fast. They told the *Cacique* they were four, and so they took four men that were *Caracaracoli*, which is a distemper like the itch, that makes the body very rough. When they had taken those creatures, they held a council about them, how to make them women, since they had neither the privities of man or woman.

CHAP. VIII.

How they found the way to make women.

Women made.

THEY sought out a bird called *Turiri*, formerly *Turire Cahuvail*, that is, a *Woodpecker*, that makes holes in trees, and taking those creatures that had neither the parts of man nor woman, tied them hands and feet, and bound the said bird to their body; the which bird taking them to be trees, began to work as it uses, pecking and boring that part where womens privities should be; and thus say the antientest *Indians*, they came to have women. I writing in haste, and not having paper enough, could not place every thing rightly, but through mistake transpos'd some; but the mistake is not great, for they believe all that is here writ. Let us now return to what we should have said first, that is, their opinion concerning the original and beginning of the sea.

CHAP. IX.

How they say the sea was made.

THere was a man they call *Giaia*, whose right name they know not, his son was call'd *Giaiael*, that is, *Giaia*'s son. This *Giaiael* intending to kill his father, he banish'd him, where he remain'd an outlaw 4 months; after which his father kill'd him, put his bones into a calabash, and hung it to the top of his house, where it continued some time. It happen'd that being desirous to see his son, *Giaia* one day said to his wife, I have a mind to see our son *Giaiael*, and she was content. Taking down the calabash, he turn'd it over to see his son's bones, and there came out of it abundance of great and small fishes. Perceiving that the bones were turn'd into fishes, they resolv'd to eat them. Now they say, that one day, when *Giaia* was gone to his *Conichi*, that is, his lands, he had by inheritance, there came 4 sons of a certain woman called, *Itiba Tahuvava*, all born at one birth; for the said woman dying in labour, they cut her open, and took out the said sons; and the first they cut was *Caracaracol*, that is, *Mangy*; which *Caracaracol* had to name........ the others had no name.

CHAP. X.

HOW the four sons of *Itiba Tahuvava*, who died in labour, went to take down *Giaia*'s calabash; in which was his son *Giaiael* who had been converted into fish, and none of them durst lay hold of it but *Dimivan Caracaracol*, who unhung it; and they all eat their belly full of fish, but whilst they were eating, they perceiv'd *Giaia* was coming from his estate, and going about in that hurry to hang up the calabash; they did not hang it right, so that there ran so much water from it, as overflow'd all the countrey, and with it came out abundance of fish, and hence they believe the sea had its original. Aftewards they went and met with a man whose name was *Cone*, and he was dumb.

CHAP. XI.

What happened to the four brothers, when they fled from Giaia.

AS soon as they came to *Bassamanaco*'s door, and found he brought *Cazzabi*, they said, *Abiacavo Gearocoel*; that is, let us be acquainted with this grandsire of ours. So *Deminan Caracaracol*, seeing his brothers before him, went in to try whether he could get some *Cazzabi*, which is the bread they eat there. *Caracaracol* going into the house of *Aiamavaco*, ask'd some *Cazzabi* of him, which, as has been said, is bread. He clapt his hand on his nose, and threw on him a *Guanguaio*, full of *Cogioba*, which he had made that day, and is a sort of powder they take sometimes to purge them, and for other purposes you shall know hereafter. This they take through a cane half a cubit long, one end whereof they put to their nose, and the other to the powder, and so snuff it up, which purges them very much. So he gave him that *Guanguaio* instead of bread, and leaving what he was about, went away very angry because they ask'd it of him —— After this, *Caracaracol* return'd to his brothers, and told them what had happen'd to him with *Baiamanicoel*, and the stroke he gave him on the shoulder with the *Guanguaio*, and that it pain'd him very much. His brothers look'd upon his shoulder, and perceiv'd it was much swollen, which swelling increas'd so much, that he was like to die. Therefore they endeavoured to cut it open, and could not; but taking an instrument of stone, they opened it, and out came a live female tortoise; so they built their house, and bred up the tortoise. I understood no more of this matter, and what we have writ signifies but little. They say further, that the sun and moon came out of a grotto, that is in the countrey of *Cacique*, whose name is *Maucia-Tiuvel*, and the grotto is called *Giovovava*; and they pay a great veneration to it, and have painted it all after their fashion, without any figure, but leaves, and the like. In the said grotto, there were two little stone *Cemies*, about a quarter of a yard long, their hands bound,

bound, and they look'd as if they ſweated. Theſe *Cemi*'s they honour'd very much; and when they wanted rain, they ſay they uſed to go viſit them, and they preſently had it. One of the *Cemies* is by them called *Boinaiel*, the other *Maroio*.

CHAP. XII.

What their opinion is concerning the wandring of the dead, after what manner they are, and what they do.

Of the dead. THEY hold, there is a place to which the dead go, called *Coaibai*, and lying in a part of the iſland known by the name of *Soraia*. The firſt that was in *Coaibai*, they ſay, was one *Machetaurie Guaiava*, who was lord of the ſaid *Coaibai*, the habitation and dwelling-place of the dead.

CHAP. XIII.

Of the figure they aſſign the dead.

THEY ſay they are ſhut up in the day, and walk abroad in the night; that they feed on a certain fruit, called *Guabazza*, which taſtes like a——, that in the day-time they are——, and at night were converted into fruit, and that they feaſt, and go about with the living; and thus it is they know them: They feel their belly, and if they cannot find their navel, they ſay they are dead; for they ſay the dead have no navel; and therefore they are ſometimes deceiv'd, when they do not obſerve this, and lie with ſome of the women of *Coaibai*, whom when they think they have in their arms, they have none, becauſe they vaniſh on a ſudden. This they ſtill believe as to this affair. Whilſt a man is living, they call the ſoul *Goeiz*, and when dead *Opia*, which *Goeiz* they ſay, often appears to them, as well in the ſhape of a man as of a woman; and they ſay, there have been men that would fight with it, and when they came to cloſe, it vaniſh'd, and the man clapp'd his arms elſewhere about ſome tree, to which he clung faſt. This they believe all in general, great and ſmall, and that it appears to them in the ſhape of their father, mother, brother, kindred, or any other. The fruit they ſay the dead feed on, is about the bigneſs of a quince. The dead do not appear to them in the day-time, but always at night; and therefore if any one ventures to go abroad at night, it is with great fear.

CHAP. XIV.

Whence they have this, and who makes them hold ſuch an opinion.

THere is a ſort of men among them, called *Bohuti*'s, who have many juggling tricks, as we ſhall ſay hereafter, to make them believe, they talk with the dead, that they know all their actions and ſecrets, and when they are ſick, cure them. Thus they impoſe upon them, which I have ſeen with my own eyes, tho' as to other particulars I relate only what I have heard from many of them, eſpecially the principal men, with whom I convers'd more than with others; for theſe believe ſuch fables more firmly than the others; for they have all their ſuperſtitions reduced into old ſongs, and are directed by them, as the *Moors* are by the *Alcoran*. When they ſing theſe ſongs, they play upon an inſtrument, called *Maiohavan*, made of wood, hollow, ſtrong, yet very thin, and as long as a man's arm; that part where they play on it is made like a ſmith's tongs, and the other end like a club, ſo that it looks like a calabaſh with a long neck. This inſtrument they play on, and is ſo loud, that it is heard a league and a half off; and to that muſick they ſing thoſe ſongs they have got by heart. The chief men play on it, who learn it from their infancy, and ſo ſing to it according to their cuſtom. Let us now proceed to ſpeak of many other ceremonies and cuſtoms of theſe *Gentiles*.

CHAP.

CHAP. XV.

Of the observations of the Indian Buhuitihu'*s, how they profess physick, teach the people, and are often deceived in their cures.*

ALL or most of the people of the island of *Hispaniola* have abundance of *Cemies*, of several sorts: some have their father, mother, kindred and predecessors: some figures cut in stone and wood, and many of both sorts, some that speak, others that cause things to grow, some that eat; and others that cause rain, and others that make the wind blow; which things those ignorant people believe the idols perform, or rather those devils. They having no knowledge of our holy faith. When any one is sick, they bring him to *Buhuitihu*, that is, as was said above, the physician. The doctor is obliged to be dieted as the sick man is. and to look like him, which is done thus. He is to purge himself as the sick man does, which is done by snuffing a certain powder, called *Cogioba*, up his nose, which makes him drunk, that he knows not what he does, and so says many extravagant things, which they affirm is talking with the *Cemies*, and that they tell them how the sickness came.

CHAP. XVI.

What these Buhuitihu'*s do.*

Cure of the sick. WHEN they go to visit any sick body, before they set out from their house, they take the soot off a pot, or pounded charcoal, and black all their face, to make the sick man believe what they please concerning his distemper. Then they take some small bones, and a little flesh, and wrapping them all up in something that they may not drop, put them in their mouth, the sick man being before purged with the powder aforesaid. When the physician is come into the sick man's house, he sits down, and all persons are silent; and if there are any children, they put them out, that they may not hinder the *Buhuitihu* in performing his office; nor does there remain in the house any but one or two of the chief persons: Being thus by themselves, they take some of the herb *Gioia* —— broad, and another herb, wrapped up in the web of an onion half a quarter long; one of the *Gioia*'s, and the other they hold, and drawing it in their hands they bruise it into a paste, and then put it in their mouths to vomit what they have eaten, that it may not hurt them; then presently begin their song, and lighting a torch, take the juice. This done, having staid a little, the *Buhuitihu* rises up, and and goes towards the sick man, who sits all alone in the middle of the house, as has been said, and turns him twice about, as he thinks fit; then stands before him, takes him by the legs, and feels his thighs, descending by degrees to his feet; then draws hard, as if he would pull something off; then he goes to the door, shuts it, and says, be gone to the mountain, or to the sea, or whither thou wilt; and giving a blast, as if he blowed something away, turns about, claps his hands together, shuts his mouth, his hands quake as if he were cold, he blows on his hands, and then draws in his blast as if sucking the marrow of a bone, sucks the sick man's neck, stomack, shoulders, jaws, breast, belly and several other parts of his body. This done they begin to cough, and make faces, as if they had eaten some bitter thing, and the doctor pulls out that we said he put into his mouth at home, or by the way, whether stone, flesh or bone, as above. If it is any thing eatable, he says to the sick man, take notice you have eaten something that has caused this distemper; see how I have taken it out of your body; for your *Cemi* had put it into you because you did not pray to him, or build him some temple, or give him some of your goods. If it be a stone, he says, keep it safe. Sometimes they take it for certain, that those stones are good, and help women in labour; wherefore they keep them very carefully, wrapped up in cotton, putting them into little baskets, giving them such as they have themselves to eat, and the same they do to the *Cemies* they have in their houses. Upon any solemn day, when they provide much to eat, whether fish, flesh, or any other thing, they put it all into the house of the *Cemies*, that the idol may feed on it. The next day they carry all home, after the *Cemi* has eaten. And so God help them, as the *Cemi* eats of that, or any other thing, they being inanimate stocks or stones.

CHAP. XVII.

How the aforesaid physicians have been sometimes deceived.

WHEN they have done as has been said, and yet the patient dies, if the dead man has many friends, or was lord of a territory, and can oppose the said *Bubuitibu*, that is, physician, for mean people dare not contend with them; he that would do him harm, does it thus. When they would know whether the patient died through the physician's fault or whether he did not observe what was prescribed; they take an herb, called *Gueia*, whose leaves are like *Basil*, thick and broad, being called by another name *Zachon:* they take the juice of this leaf, pair the dead man's nails, and cut off the hair on his forehead, which they powder between two stones, and mix with the aforesaid juice of the herb, and pour it down the dead man's throat, or nostrils, and so doing, ask him, whether the physician was the occasion of his death? and whether he observed order? this they ask several times, till he speaks as plain, as if he were alive; so that he answers to all they ask of him, saying, the *Bubuitibu* did not observe order, or was the cause of his death; and they say, the physician asks him, whether he is alive, and how he comes to talk so plain; and he answers he is dead. When they have known what they desire of him, they return him to his grave, whence they took him to make this enquiry. They use another method to know what they desire: they take the dead body and make a great fire, like that used for making of charcoal, and when the wood is turned into a live coal, they throw the body into that violent fire, and cover it with earth, as the collier's do the coals, where they let it lie as long as they think fit, and there ask questions, as was said before; who answers, he knows nothing. This they ask ten times, and then he speaks no more. They ask, whether he is dead? but he speaks only those ten times.

CHAP. XVIII.

How the kindred of the party revenge themselves, when they have got an answer by means of the drench.

Physicians punish'd. THE dead man's kindred get together upon a day appointed, wait for the aforesaid *Bubuitibu*, and bastinado him, till they break his legs, arms and head, so that he is all battered, and so they leave him for dead. At night, they say, there come abundance of snakes of several sorts, white, black, green and of several other colours, which lick the said physician's face, and all his body, so left, as has been said, and remains in that manner two or three days. Whilst he is thus, they say the bones of his legs and arms knit together again, he gets up, and walks fair and softly towards his house and they that saw him, ask the question of him, were not you dead? he answers, the *Cemi*'s came to his assistance in the shape of snakes. The dead man's kindred, in a rage, because they thought they had revenged their relations death, seeing him alive, grow desperate, and endeavour to lay hold of him to put him to death; and if they can catch him again, they put out his eyes, and bruise his testicles; for they say none of these physicians can die, tho' never so much bastinadoed, if they do not cut out his testicles.

How they know what they desire of him they burn, and how they take their revenge.

When they uncover the fire, the smoke that comes from it, rises till they lose sight of it, and makes a noise, as it breaks out: Then it turns down again, and goes into the house of the *Bubuitibu* or physician; and that very moment, he that did not observe order, falls sick, is covered with sores, and all the skin of his body flays off; and this they take for a sign, that he did not do his duty, and therefore the patient died; for which reason they endeavour to kill him, as was said in the other case. These are the sorceries they use.

CHAP. XIX.

How they make and keep their wooden and stone Cemies.

The Cemes or idols. THOSE of wood are made thus: when any one is traveling, he says, he sees some tree that shakes its root; the man in a great fright, stops, and asks, who he is? it answers, my name is, *Buhuitibu*, and he will inform you who I am: the man repairing to the said physician, tells him what he has seen. The wizard, or conjurer, runs immediately to see the tree the other has told him of, sits down by it, and makes it *Cogioba*, as was said above in the story of the four brothers. The *Cogioba* being made, he stands up, gives it all its titles, as if it were some great lord; and asks of it, tell me who you are, what you do here, what you will have with me, and why you send for me? tell me whether you will have me cut you, whether you will go along with me, and how you will have me to carry you, and I will build you a house and endow it? immediately, that tree, or *Cemi*, becomes an idol, or devil, answers, telling how he will have him do it. He cuts it into such a shape as he is directed, builds his house, and endows it; and makes *Cogioba* for it several times in the year: which *Cogioba* is to pray to it, to please it, to ask and know of the said *Cemi*, what good or evil is to happen, and to beg wealth of it. When they would know whether they shall be victorious over their enemies, they go into a house, whither none but the chief men are admitted. The lord of them is the first that begins to make the *Cogioba*, and to make a noise; whilst he does it, none of the company speaking till he has done. His prayer being ended, he stands awhile with his head turned about, and his arms on his knees; then he lifts up his head, and looks towards heaven, and speaks. Then they all answer him with a loud voice, and when they have all spoke, giving thanks, he tells the vision he saw, being made drunk with the *Cogioba*, he snuffed up his nose, which flies into his head; and says, he has talked with the *Cemi*, and shall obtain victory, or that his enemies shall fly, or that there shall be a great mortality, or war, or famine, or some such thing, as occurs to him in his drunken fit. Consider, what a condition their brains are in; for they say, the houses seem to them to be turned topsy turvy, and that the men go upon their heads. This *Cogioba* they make for stone and wooden *Cemies*, as well as for the dead bodies, as has been said above. The stone *Cemies* are of several sorts: some there are, which they say, the physicians take out of the body of the sick, and those they look upon as the best to help women in labour. Others there are that speak, which are shaped like a long turnip, with the leaves long, and extended, like the shrub bearing capers. Those leaves for the most part are like those of the elm. Others have three points, and they think they cause the *Giuca* to thrive. Their roots are like a radish. The leaves of *Giuca* have at least six or seven points; nor do I know what to compare them to, for I have seen nothing like it in *Spain*, or elsewhere. The stem of the *Giuca* is as high as a man. Let us now speak of their opinions concerning the idols and *Cemi*'s, and how they are deceived by them.

CHAP. XX.

Of the Cemi, Bugid *and* Aiba.

Barbarous opinions. THEY say, in the time of the wars, he was burnt, and afterwards being wash'd with the juice of *Giuca*, his arms grew out again, his body spread, and he recovered his eyes. The *Giuca* was small, and they wash'd it with the above-mentioned water and juice, to make it grow bigger, and they affirm it made those sick who had made the said *Cemi*, because they had not brought it *Giuca* to eat. This *Cemi* was called *Baidrama*, and when any one fell sick, they called the *Buhuitibu*, and ask'd him, whence the distemper proceeded? He answered *Baidrama* had sent it, because they had not sent him to eat by those that had charge of his house. This the *Buhuitibu* said the *Cemi*, *Baidrama*, had told him.

CHAP.

CHAP. XXI.

Of Guamorete's Cemi.

THEY say, that when they built the house of *Guamorete*, who was a man of note, they put into it a *Cemi*, that was on the top of his other house, which *Cemi* was called *Corocose*; and when they had wars among themselves, *Guamorete*'s enemies burnt the house in which this *Cemi Corocose* was. They say he presently got up, and went a bow-shot from that place, near to a water. They further say, that when he was on the top of the house, he would come down and lie with the women. That afterwards *Camorese* died, and the *Cemi* fell into the hands of another *Cacique*, and still continued to lie with the women; and moreover, that he had two crowns grew on his head; for which reason they said, since such a one has two crowns, he is certainly *Corocose*'s son; and this they look'd upon as most certain. This *Cemi* came afterwards to another *Cacique*, called *Guatabanex*, and his countrey is called *Giacoba*.

CHAP. XXII.

Of another Cemi, *called* Opigielguoviran, *which belonged to a great man, whose name was* Cavavaniova, *who had many subjects.*

THIS *Cemi Opigielguoviran*, they say, has four feet, like a dog's, and is made of wood, and that he would often at night go out of the house into the woods; whither they went to seek him out, and when brought home again, they bound him with cords, yet he would go away to the woods. They say that when the christians came to the island *Hispaniola*, he broke loose, and went into a moras, whither they followed him by the track, but never saw him since, nor know any thing of him. As I receiv'd this, so I deliver it.

CHAP. XXIII.

Of another Cemi, *called* Guabancex.

THIS *Cemi Guabancex* was in the countrey of a great *Cacique*, whose name was *Aumatex*; and they say, it is a woman *Cemi*, and has two others with it; one a crier, the other gatherer, or governor of the waters. When *Guabancex* is angry, they say, it raises the winds and waters, overthrows houses, and shakes the trees. This *Cemi* they say, is a female, and made of stones of that countrey. The other two *Cemi*'s that are with it, are call'd, one of them *Guatauva*, and is a cryer, that by order of *Guabancex*, makes proclamation for all the other *Cemi*'s of that province to help to raise a high wind, and cause much rain: The other is, *Coatrischie*, who they say, gathers the waters in the vallies among the mountains, and then lets them loose to destroy the countrey. This they believe as most certain.

CHAP. XXIV.

Their Belief of another Cemi, *called* Faraguvaol.

THIS *Cemi* belongs to a principal *Cacique* of the island *Hispaniola*, is an idol, has several names, and was found as you shall now hear. They say, that on a certain day in past times, before the island was discovered, they know not how long since, being abroad a hunting, they found a certain creature: they ran back, and that got into a ditch; looking into it, they saw a beam, which look'd like a thing that had life in it. The huntsman seeing it, ran to his lord, who was a *Cacique*, and father to *Guarionel*, telling him what he had seen. They went thither, and found the thing as the huntsman had given information, and taking that log, they built a house to it. They say it went out of that house several times, and return'd to the place whence they brought it, not exactly to the same spot, but near it; for the aforesaid

aforesaid lord, and his son *Guaraionel*, ordering it to be sought out, found it hid; and that another time, they bound and put it in a sack, and yet bound as it was, it went away as before. Those ignorant people look upon this as undoubted truth.

CHAP. XXV.

Of those things they affirm were reported by two principal Caciques *of the island* Hispaniola; *one of them called* Cazziva, *father to the aforesaid* Guaraionel; *the other*, Gamanacoei.

THAT great lord, who, they say, is in heaven, at the beginning of the book, is this *Cazziva*, who kept a sort of abstinence here, which all of them generally perform; for they shut themselves up six or seven days, without taking any sustenance but the juice of herbs, with which they also wash themselves. After this time they begin to eat something that is nourishing. During the time they have been without eating, weakness makes them say, they have seen something they earnestly desir'd, for they all perform that abstinence in honour of the *Cemies*, to know whether they shall obtain victory over their enemies, or to acquire wealth, or any other thing they desire. They say, this *Cacique* affirm'd, he had spoke with *Giocaùvaghama*, who told him, that whosoever surviv'd him, would not long enjoy his power, because they should see a people clad in their countrey, who would rule over, and kill them, and they should die for hunger. They thought at first, these should be the *Canibals*, but afterwards considering, that they only plunder'd and fled; they believ'd it was some other people the *Cemi* spoke of; and now they believe it is the admiral and those that came with him. Now I will give an account of what I saw and knew, when *F. Roman*, a poor anchorite, went to the province *Madalena*, to a fort built by *D. Christopher Columbus*, admiral, viceroy, and governor of the islands and continent of the *Indies*, for their majesties king *Ferdinand* and Queen *Isabel*. I being in that fort, with *Arriaga*, appointed governor of it by the aforesaid viceroy *D. Christopher Columbus*, it pleased God to give the light of his faith to a whole family of ill-principled people of that province of *Madalena*, which province was called *Maroris*, and the lord of it *Guavaouvionel*, that is, son of *Guavaenechin*. In the said house are his servants, and retainers, whose surname is *Giahuvavariu*, and were in all 16 persons, all relations, and among them five brothers. Of these one died, and the other four were baptiz'd; and I believe, they died martyrs, for so it appear'd by the manner of their death and their constancy. The first that receiv'd baptism was an *Indian* called *Guaticava*, afterwards *John*. This was the first christian that suffer'd a cruel death, and to me he seems to have died a martyr; for I have heard from some that were by when he died, that he said, *Dio Aboriðacha, Dio Aboridacha*, that is, I am God's servant. So died his brother *Anthony*, and another with him, saying the same words. All the people of this house attended me, to do whatsoever I pleased. Such as are left alive at this day, are now christians by means of *D. Christipher Columbus*, viceroy and governor of the *Indies*, and by the grace of God they are very numerous at present.

Let us now say what happened in the province of *Madalena*. When I was there, the aforesaid lord admiral came to the assistance of *Arriaga*, and some christians, besieged by the subjects of a principal *Cacique*, called *Caovalto*. The admiral told me, that the language of the province *Madalena Maroris* was different from the rest, and not understood in all parts of the countrey; and therefore bid me go and reside with another principal *Cacique*, called *Guarionex*, lord of many subjects, whose language was understood all over the island. In obedience to his orders, I went to reside with the said *Guarionex*. True it is, I said to *D. Christopher Columbus*, my lord, why will you have me go to live with *Guarionex*, when I know no language but that of *Maroris*? Be pleas'd to give leave that one of those *Nobuirci*'s, (who were afterwards christians, and knew both the languages) may go along with me; which he granted, and bid me carry who I pleas'd; and it pleased God to give me for a companion, the best of the *Indians*, and who was best instructed in the catholick faith; and afterwards took him from me, God be praised who gave and took him away; for indeed, I look'd upon him as a good child and a brother; and it was that *Guaicavanu*, who was afterwards a christian, and called *John*. What happened to us there I shall not relate, and how I and *Guaicavanu* went to *Isabella*, where we waited for the admiral, till he return'd from the relief of *Madalena*. As soon he came, we went where he had ordered, with one *John de Aguada*, who had

had the command of a fort, which *D. Christopher Columbus* had built, half a league from the place where we were to reside. The admiral commanded the said *John de Aguada* to allow us such provisions as there were in the fort, which is called the *Conception*. We continued with that *Cacique*, *Guarionex*, almost two years, instructing him in our faith, and the manners of christians. At first he appear'd well inclin'd, and gave some hopes of complying and becoming a christian, bidding us teach him the lord's prayer, the creed, and all other christian prayers, which many in his house learnt; and he said his prayers every morning, and caus'd all his family to do so twice a day: yet afterwards he fell off from his good purpose, through the fault of some of the principal men of that countrey, who blam'd him for submitting to the law of christ, since the christians were ill men, and drove them out of their countrey by force. Therefore they advised him never to mind any thing that belong'd to the christians; but that he should joyn and conspire with them, for their destruction, because they could not satisfy them, and were resolv'd to submit no longer. Thus he fell off from his good beginning, and we perceiving he neglected what he had learnt, resolv'd to depart thence, and go where we might be more successful in instructing the *Indians* in the faith. We therefore went away to another principal *Cacique*, who show'd a favourable inclination, saying, he would be a christian: his name was *Maviatue*.

Accordingly we set out to go to the said *Maviatue*'s countrey; I *F. Roman Pane*, poor anchorite, and *F. John Borgognon* of the order of St. *Francis*, and *John Mathew* the first that was baptized in *Hispaniola*.

The second day after we set out from the town and habitation of *Guarionex*, to go to the other *Cacique*, called *Maviatue*; we found *Guarionex*'s people building a house near the house of prayer, where we left some pictures for the *Catecumen*'s, to knee, and pray before them. These were the mother, brothers, and kindred, of the aforesaid *John Mathew*, the first christian; afterwards seven more joyn'd them, and at last all the family became christians, and persever'd in the faith; so that all the aforesaid family was left to keep that house of prayer, and some lands I had caused to be till'd. They being so left to keep the house, two days after we were gone towards the aforesaid *Maviatue*, six men went to the aforesaid house of prayer, left in the custody of the seven *Catecumen*'s, and by order of *Guarionex*, told them, they should take those pictures, left by *F. Roman*, and destroy them, since he and his companion were gone, and they knew not what was become of them. These six servants of *Guarionex* found six children keeping the house of prayer, who being so instructed, said, they should not come in; but they went in by force, took the pictures, and carried them away.

CHAP. XXVI.

What became of the pictures, and a miracle God wrought to show his power.

THESE men being gone out of the house, threw the pictures down, cover'd them with earth, and piss'd upon them, saying, now you will yield much fruit. This they said, because they bury'd them in a field that was sown, saying, what grew there would be good, but this they did in scorn. The children that were keeping the house by order of the *Catechumen's*, seeing this, they ran to their friends who were upon their Lands, and told them, that *Guarionex*'s men had abus'd and scorn'd the pictures; which they understanding, left what they were about, and ran crying out to give an account of it to *D. Bartholomew Columbus*, who was then governor, his brother being gone into *Spain*. He as lieutenant to the viceroy, proceeded against the offenders, and having convicted them publickly, burnt them. This did not deter *Guarionex* and his subjects, from their design of murdering all the christians on the day when they were to bring in their tribute; but the conspiracy was discovered, and they apprehended on the same day they were to put it in execution. Still they held on their resolution, and accordingly killed four *Spaniards*, besides *John Matthew* and his brother *Anthony*, who had been baptiz'd; and running where they had hid the pictures, tore them in pieces. Some days after, the owner of that field went to dig up his *Agi*'s, which are certain roots like turnips, and some like radishes; and in the place where the pictures had been buried, two or three *Agi*'s were grown in the shape of a cross, as if they had been stuck one through another; nor could any man find this cross, but only the mother of *Guarionex*, who was the worst woman I knew in those parts, who look'd upon this as a great miracle, and said to the commander of the fort of the *conception*, this miracle has been shown by God, where the images were found: God knows to what end.

Let us now give an account, how they were converted that first became christians, and how much will be requisite to convert them all. To say the truth, that island stands in much need of people to punish the lords, when they will not suffer their people to be instructed in the faith; for they have nothing to say against it, which I can with truth maintain, because it has cost me much labour to know it; as I am satisfied may be gathered by what has been said hitherto; and a word to the wise is enough.

The first christians were those we have beforemention'd in the island of *Hispaniola*, that is, *Gianauvariu*, in whose house there were seventeen persons who all became christians, only giving them to understand, that there is one God, who has made all things, and created heaven and earth, without any further arguments or controversy; for they were easie of belief. With others there must be force and ingenuity used, for all of them are not alike; for as much, as if those had a good beginning and a better end, they were none of those others that begin well, and then fall off from what has been taught them; and therefore there is need of force and punishment.

The first that receiv'd baptism in the island *Hispaniola*, was *John Matthew*, who was baptiz'd on the feast of St. *Matthew* the evangelist, in the year 1496, and after him all his family; where were many christians, and a greater progress had been made, had they been instructed in the faith, and the *Spaniards* been in a condition to keep them under. And if any one should ask, why I make this so easy a matter? I say, it is, because I know it by experience, especially in the person of a principal *Cacique*, called, *Mahuviativire*, who has continued now for three years in his good purpose, saying, he will be a christian, and have but one wife; for they use to have two or three, and the great men twenty five or thirty. This is what I could learn and find out as to the customs and ceremonies of the *Indians* of *Hispaniola*, with all the pains I have taken; wherein I expect no spiritual, nor temporal advantage. May it please our lord, if this turns to his honour and service, to give me his grace to persevere; and if it must fall out otherwise, may he deprive me of my understanding.

The end of the work of the poor anchorite Roman Pane.

CHAP. LXIII.

How the admiral return'd to Spain *to give their majesties an account of the condition he left the island in.*

TO return to the main subject of our history; I say, the admiral having brought the island into a peaceable condition, and built the town of *Isabella*, besides three forts about the countrey, he resolv'd to return into *Spain*, to acquaint their catholick majesties with several matters he thought convenient for their service; but particularly because of many malicious slanderers, who through envy ceased not to give the king a false information of the affairs of the *Indies*, to the great prejudice and dishonour of the admiral and his brothers. For these reasons he went on board on *Thursday* the 10th of *March* 1496, with 225 *Spaniards* and 30 *Indians* sailed from *Isabella* about break of day, and turned it along the coast with two caravals, one call-ed *Santa Cruz*, the other *Nina*, the same he went in to discover the island of *Cuba*. On *Tuesday* the 22d of *March*, he lost sight of the east point of *Hispaniola*, holding on his course eastward as the wind would permit. But the wind for the most part continuing at east, on the 6th of *April*, finding his provisions fell short, and his men were weary and discouraged, he fell off towards the south to the *Caribbee* islands, and came up with them in three days, anchoring at *Marigalante* on *Saturday* the 9th of *April*. The next day, tho' it was not his custom to weigh anchor on a *Sunday*, when in any port, he set sail, because his men mutter'd, saying, when they were to seek their bread, they needed not so strictly observe days. So he anchor'd at the island *Guadalupe*, and sending the boats well-mann'd ashore, before they came to land, abundance of women came out of a wood, with bows and arrows and feathers, as if they would defend their island. For this reason, and because the sea ran somewhat high, those in the boats kept aloof, and sent two *Indian* women, they brought from *Hispaniola*, ashore swimming, of whom those other women particularly enquired concerning

ing the christians; and understanding they only desired provisions in exchange for such things as they had, bid them go with their ships to the north-side, where their husbands were, who would furnish them with what they wanted. The ships sailing close under the shore, saw abundance of people come down to the shore with bows and arrows, who let fly upon our men with great cries, tho' in vain, for their arrows fell short. But perceiving the boats full of men were going ashore, the *Indians* went back into an ambush, and when our men drew near, came out to hinder their landing, till being frighted with the cannon fir'd at them from the ships, they fled to the wood, leaving their houses and goods, where the christians took and destroy'd all they found. Being acquainted with the way of making bread, they fell to work, and made enough to supply their want. Among other things they found in the houses, there were great parrots, honey, wax and iron, whereof they had hatchets to cut, and looms like those for tapistry-work, in which they weave their tents. Their houses were square, and not round, as is usual in the other islands. In one of them was found the arm of a man roasting upon a spit. Whilst the bread was making, the admiral sent forty men up the countrey, to learn something of it; who the next day return'd with ten women and three boys, the rest of the people being fled. Among these women, was the wife of a *Cacique*, whom a *Canaryman*, that was very nimble, had much difficulty to overtake; and she had got from him, but that seeing him alone, she thought to take him, and closing she got him down, and had stifled him, but that others came in to his assistance. These womens legs are swathed with cotton from the ancle to the knee, that they may look thick, which ornament they call *Coiro*, and look upon it as very genteel, and they gird so hard, that if it happens to slip off the leg, that part appears very thin. The same both men and women use in *Jamaica*, who swath their arms up to the arm-pits, that is, about the smallest parts, like the old fashion sleeves used among us. These women are also excessive fat, and there were some thicker than a man could grasp; as soon as children can stand upon their legs and walk, they give them a bow, that they may learn to shoot; and they all wear their hair long, and loose upon their shoulders, nor do they cover any part of the body. That lady they took said, the island was only inhabited by women, and that those who would have hindered the men landing were women, except only four men, who were there accidentally from another island; for at a certain time in the year they come to sport, and lie with them. The same was observed by the women of another island, called *Matrimonio*, of whom she gave the same account we read of the *Amazons*; and the admiral believed it by what he saw among those women, and and because of the courage and strength that appeared in them. They also say, those women seem to be endow'd with clearer understandings than those of the other islands; for in other places they only reckon the day by the sun, and the night by the moon, whereas these women reckoned by other stars, saying, when the *Charles Wain* rises, or such a star is north, then it is time to do so and so.

Women like Amazons.

CHAP. LXIV.

The admiral sails from the island Guadalupe *for* Spain.

WHEN they had made provision of bread for twenty days, besides what they had aboard, the admiral resolved to continue his voyage towards *Spain*; but perceiving that island was an inlet to the others, he thought fit first to satisfy those women with some gifts, in satisfaction for the loss they had sustained, and therefore sent them all ashore, except the chief lady, who chose to go into *Spain* with her daughter, among the other *Indians* of the island *Hispaniola*, one of whom was *Cuonabo*, who it has been said, was the chief man in all the island, and that because he was not a native of it, but of the *Caribbees*, and therefore that lady was content to go into *Spain* with the admiral. He having furnished himself with bread, wood and water, set sail on *Wednesday* the 20th of *April* from *Guadalupe*, with the wind very scant, keeping near the latitude of 22 degrees; for at that time they had not found out the method of running away north to meet the south-west winds.

Having made but little way, and the ships being full of people, on the 20th of *May*, they all begun to be much afflicted for want of provisions, which was so great, that they had but six ounces of bread a day for each, and less than a pint of water, without any thing else. And though there were eight or nine pilots in those two ships, yet none of them knew where they were, but the admiral was confident they were

Great want of Provisions.

7 but

but a little west of the *Azores*, whereof he gives an account in his journal thus.

This morning the *Dutch* compasses varied as they used to do, a point; and those of *Genoa*, that used to agree with them, varied but a very little, but afterwards sailing east vary more, which is a sign we are 100 leagues, or some what more, west of the *Azores*; for when we were just 100, there were but a few scatter'd weeds in the sea; and the *Dutch* needles varied a point, those of *Genoa* cutting the north-point; and when we are somewhat farther E. N. E. they will alter again; which was verified on sunday following being the 22d of *May*; by which, and the exactness of his account, he found he was 100 leagues from the islands *Azores*, which he was surprized at, and assigned this difference to the several sorts of load-stones the needles are made by; for till they come just to that longitude, they all varied a point, and there some held it; and those of *Genoa* exactly cut the north-star. The same was yet farther demonstrated the next day, being the 24th of *May*. Thus continuing their voyage, though all the pilots went like blind men, on *Wednesday* the 8th of *June*, they came in sight of *Odemira*, between *Lisbon* and cape *St. Vincent*, all the pilots for several days having still made for the land, except the admiral, who the night before slack'd his sails for fear of land, saying, he did so because they were near cape *St. Vincent*, which all laugh'd at; some of them affirming they were in the *English* channel, and those that erred least, said, they were on the coast of *Galicia*, and therefore ought not to take in any sail, it being better to die ashore than starve miserably at sea, the scarcity being so great, that there were many, who like the *Canibals*, were for eating the *Indians* they had aboard; and others, to save the little provision there was left, were for throwing them overboard, which they would have done, had not the admiral used all his authority to prevent it, considering they were human creatures, and therefore ought not to be worse used than the rest, and so it pleased God to reward him with the sight of land next morning, as he had promised them all, for which reason he was afterwards looked upon by the seamen as most expert, and almost prophetical in sea affairs.

CHAP. LXV.

How the admiral went to court, and their catholic majesties set him out again for the Indies.

THE admiral being landed in *Spain*, began to prepare for his journey to *Burgos*, where he was favourably received by their catholick majesties, who were there celebrating the nuptials of prince *John* their son, who married *Margaret* of *Austria*, daughter to *Maximilian* the emperor, who was conducted into *Spain*, and received by most of the nobility, and the greatest appearance of persons of quality that had ever been seen together in *Spain*: But tho' I was present as page to prince *John*, I shall not mention the particulars of this solemnity, as well because it does not belong to our history, as because their highnesses historiographers have doubtless taken care to do it. Therefore to return to what concerns the admiral, I say, that being come to *Burgos*, he presented their majesties with several things he brought as samples from the *Indies*, as well birds and beasts, as trees, plants, instruments and other things the *Indians* use for their service and diversion; also several girdles and masks, with eyes and ears of plates of gold, besides much gold sand, gross and small, as nature produced it: Some grains as big as vetches, some as beans, and some as pigeons-eggs. This was not afterwards so much valued, because in progress of time, there were pieces of gold found that weigh'd above thirty pounds. Yet at this time what he brought was much valued, in hopes of what was hoped for, and accordingly their majesties received it in good part. When the admiral had given them an account of all that related to the improving and peopling the *Indies*; he was desirous to return with speed, for fear some disaster should happen in his absence, especially because he had left the people there in great want of all necessaries. Tho' he press'd hard on this account, yet the affairs of that court being subject to delays, he could not be so soon dispatch'd, but that ten or twelve months elapsed before he obtain'd two ships, which were sent before with succours under the command of *Peter Fernandez Coronel*. These set out in *February* 1498. and the admiral stay'd to negotiate the obtaining such a fleet as was requisite for him to return to the *Indies*. But he was forced to stay above a year at *Burgos* and at *Medina del campo*; where in the year 1499. their catholick majesties granted him many favours, and gave the necessary orders for his

Presents to the king and queen.

his affairs, and for the government, and ſettling of the *Indies*. Whereof I here make mention, that it may appear how ready their catholick majeſties were as yet to reward his merits and ſervice, and how much they afterwards alter'd through the falſe informations of malicious and envious perſons, inſomuch as to ſuffer the wrongs to be done him, which we ſhall give an account of hereafter. But to return to his departure from court to *Sevil*, there the fitting out of the fleet was retarded much longer than was convenient, through the negligence and ill-management of the king's officers, and particularly of *D. John de Fonſeca*, arch-deacon of *Sevil*. Whence it proceeded, that the ſaid *D. John*, who was afterwards biſhop of *Burgos*, ever was an utter enemy to the admiral and his affairs, and was chief of thoſe that brought him into diſgrace with their catholick majeſties. And to the end that *D. James* my brother and I, who had ſerved as pages to prince *John*, who was now dead, might not ſuffer by his delays, nor be abſent from court, till the time of his departure; he ſent us on the 2d of *November* 1497, from *Sevil*, to ſerve ſtill as pages to her majeſty queen *Iſabel* or *Elizabeth* of glorious memory.

Delays in the admiral's buſineſs.

CHAP. LXVI.

The admiral ſets out from Spain *to diſcover the continent of* Paria.

THE admiral forwarding his expedition with all poſſible care, on the 30th of *May* 1498, ſet ſail from the bay of *St. Lucar de Berrameda*, with ſix ſhips loaded with proviſions and other neceſſaries for the relief of the planters in *Hiſpaniola*, and peopling of that iſland.

On the 7th of *June* he arrived at the iſland of *Puerto Santo*, where he heard maſs, and ſtaid to take in wood and water, and what elſe he ſtood in need of; yet that ſame night ſailed away towards *Madera*, whither he came on *Sunday* the 9th of *June*, and there at the town of *Fonchal*, was courteouſly received and treated by the governor of that iſland, with whom he ſtaid to provide himſelf farther till *Saturday* in the afternoon, when he ſail'd, and on *Wedneſday* the 19th of *June* arrived at *Gomera*, where there was a *French* ſhip that had taken three *Spaniards*; who ſeeing the admiral's ſquadron, weigh'd and ſtood to ſea with them. The admiral ſuppoſing they had been merchant ſhips, and fled, believing him to be a *Frenchman*, took no care to purſue, till when they were at a great diſtance, he was inform'd what they were, and ſent after them three of his ſhips; for fear of which the *French* left one of the ſhips they had taken, and fled with the other two, ſo that the admiral could not fetch them up. They might have carried the other off too, had they not forſaken it; for when the admiral appeared in the port, in the conſternation they were in, they had not time to man it; ſo that there being but four *Frenchmen* aboard, and ſix *Spaniards* of thoſe that had been taken in it; theſe ſeeing the aſſiſtance coming to them, clapt the *French* under hatches, and return'd to the port, where the ſhip was reſtored to its maſter; and the *French* had ſuffer'd, but that *D. Alvaro de Lugo* the governor, and all the iſland interceded for them, who beg'd them to exchange for ſix of their men the *French* had carried away, which the admiral granted. Still haſtening on his way, he ſailed for the iſland *Ferro* on *Thurſday* the 21ſt of *June*. There he reſolved to ſend away three of his ſix ſhips to *Hiſpaniola*, and to ſail away with the reſt towards the iſlands of *Cabo Verde*; thence to ſail directly over, and diſcover the continent. He therefore appointed a captain over each ſhip, of thoſe he ſent to *Hiſpaniola*, one of which was *Peter de Arana*, couſin to that *Arana* who died in *Hiſpaniola*, the 2d *Alonzo Sancher de Carvagal*, and the third one *John Antony Columbus* his own kinſman, to whom he gave particular inſtruction, that each of them ſhould command a week in his turn. This done, he ſet out for the iſlands of *Cabo Verde*, and thoſe captains for *Hiſpaniola*. But that climate he was then entring upon being unhealthy at that time, he had a terrible fit of the gout in one leg, and four days after he fell into a violent fever; yet notwithſtanding his ſickneſs, he was ſtill himſelf, and diligently obſerved the way the ſhip made, the alterations of the weather that happened, as he had done ſince his firſt voyage.

The admiral recovers a Spaniſh *ſhip.*

Iſlands of Cabo Verde.

On *Wedneſday* the 25th of *June*, he diſcovered the iſland *de Sal*, one of thoſe of *Capo Verde*, paſſing by it, he came to another called *Boa Viſta*, a name remote from the truth, for it ſignifies a good ſight, and the place is dull and wretched. Here he caſt anchor in a channel near a ſmall iſland on the weſt-ſide of it, near to where there are ſix or ſeven houſes of the inhabitants for

Boa Viſta, where lepers are cured, and how.

for persons troubled with the leprosy, who came thither to be cured. And as sailors rejoyce when they discover land, so do these wretches much more, when they see any ships. Therefore they presently ran down to the shore, to speak to those the admiral sent ashore in the boats to take in water and salt, there being also abundance of goats there. Understanding they were *Spaniards*, the *Portuguese*, who had charge of the island for the owner, went aboard to speak to the admiral, and offer him all he demanded; for which the admiral thanked him, ordered him to be well treated, and some provision given him, because by reason of the barrenness of the island, they always live miserably. The admiral being desirous to known what method they used to cure the lepers; that man told him, that the temperature of the air was one main cause of it; and the next was their diet, because there came thither a vast number of tortoises, on which the sick feed, and anoint themselves with their blood, and continuing it a short time they recover; but that those who are born infected with this distemper are longer a curing. That the reason of having so many *Tortoises*, was the shores being all sandy, whither the tortoises, in the months of *June*, *July* and *August*, came over from the shore of *Africk*, most of them as big as an ordinary target, and that every night they came up to sleep and lay their eggs on the sand; that the people went along the shore in the night with lanthorns or other light, seeking the track the tortoise leaves on the sand, which they follow till they find the fish; which being tired with coming so far, sleeps so sound, that it hears not its enemy. He having found and turned his belly up, without doing it any more harm, goes on to seek more; for when turn'd, they cannot stir from the place, or recover their feet. Having got as many as they think fit, they come again in the morning to chuse those they like best; and letting go the least, carry away the others to eat. So wretchedly do the sick live, without any other employment or sustenance, the island being very dry and barren, without trees or springs, so that they drink of certain wells whose water is thick and brackish. Those who had charge of the island, which were only that man and four more, had no other employment but only to kill goats and salt them to send into *Portugal*. He said, there were such multitudes of these goats on the mountains, that some years they killed to the value of three or four thousand ducats, and that they all came from eight goats, carried thither by the proprietor of the island, whose name was *Roderick Alfonso*, the king of *Portugall's* secretary of the customs. That very often the hunters are four or five months without bread, or any other thing to eat, except goats flesh and fish; for which reason he made great account of the provision he had given him. That man and his companions, with some of the admiral's men, went out a goat-hunting; but perceiving it required much time to kill all he had need of, he would stay no longer being in great haste.

Tortoises how caught.

On *Saturday* the 30 of *June*, he sailed for the island of *Santiago*, the chief of *Cabo Verde*, where he arrived the next day in the evening, and anchored near a church, sending ashore to buy some cows and bulls to carry alive to *Hispaniola*: yet observing it was a difficult matter to furnish himself so soon as he desired, and how prejudicial delays were to him, he resolved to stay no longer; and the more for fear his men should sicken, that countrey being unhealthy. He says, that all the while he was at that island, he never saw the sky nor any star; but there was always a thick hot fog, insomuch that three parts of the inhabitans were sick, and they all of them had a base colour.

Santiago island.

CHAP. LXVII.

How the admiral sailed from the islands of Cabo Verde, *to discover the continent; of the violent heat he endured, and great brightness of the* North-Star.

ON *Thursday* the 5th of *July*, the admiral left the island of *Santiago*, sailing south west, with a resolution to hold that course till he was under the equinoctial, and then to steer due-west, that he might find some other land, or cross over to *Hispaniola*. But the currents among those islands setting violently towards the north and north west, he could not sail as he designed; so that he says, on *Saturday* the 7th of *July*, he was still in sight of the island of *Fogo*, which is one of those of *Cabo Verde*; which he says, is very high land on the south-side; and at a distance, looks like a great church, with a steeple at the east end, which is a vast high rock; whence before the east winds blow, there usually breaks out much fire; as is seen at *Tenerif*, *Vesuvius* and mount *Ætna*. From this last countrey of christians he held on his course south west, till he came into only 5 degrees of north latitude, where he was becalmed, having

Fogo island.

having been till then continually attended by the fog we mentioned above. The calm lasted eight days, with such violent heat, that it almost burnt the ships; and there was no man could abide under deck, and had it not rained sometimes, and the sun been clouded, he thought they would have been burnt alive together with the ships; for the first day of the calm, which was fair, the heat was so violent, that nothing could withstand it, had not God miraculously relieved them with the aforesaid rain and fog. Having therefore got off a little to the northward, into seven degrees of latitude, he resolved not to make any more to the south, but sail due-west, at least till he saw how the weather settled; because he had lost many cask with the great heat, the hoops flew, and the corn and all provisions were scorched up. About the middle of *July*, he says, he very carefully took the latitude, and found a wonderful difference between that and the parallel of the *Azores*. For there, when the *Charles's Wain* was on the right, that is, east, then the *North-Star* was lowest, and from that time began to rise; so that when the *Charles's Wain* was over head, the *North-Star* was two degrees and an half higher, and being once passed that, began again to descend, the same five degrees it ascended. This, he says, he observed several times very carefully, the weather being very fit for that purpose. But that where he was at this time in the torrid zone, it happened quite contrary; for when the *Charles's Wain* was in its greatest elevation, he found the *North-Sar* six degrees high, and when the *Charles's Wain* came to the west, in six hours space he found the *North-Star* eleven degrees high; and then in the morning, when the *Charles's Wain* was quite depressed, though it could not be seen because of the inclination of the pole, the *North-Star* was six degrees high, so that the difference was ten degrees, and it made a circle, whose diameter was ten degrees, whereas in the other place it made but five lowering the position; for there it is lowest when the other is west, and here when in its elevation. The reason of it he thought very difficult to comprehend, and not being compleatly master of it, without farther reflexions on it, he says, he is of opinion, that in what relates to the circumference of the stars orb, it may be said, that at the equinoctial the full appears, and the nearer a man goes to the pole it seems the less, because the heaven is more oblique. As for the variation, I believe the star has the quality of all the four quarters, as has the needle, which if touched to the east-side points to the east, and so of the west, north, and south; and therefore he that makes the compass, covers the load-stone with a cloth, all but the north part of it, *viz.* that which has the virtue to make the steel point north.

Maritine observations,

CHAP. LXVIII.

How the admiral discovered the island of the Trinity, *and saw the continent.*

ON *Tuesday* the last day of *July*, 1498, the admiral having sailed many days west, insomuch, that in his judgment, the *Caribbee* islands were north of him, he resolved not to hold that course any longer, but to make for *Hispaniola*, not only because he was in great want of water, but also because all his provisions perished, and he was afraid lest during his absence some mutiny or disorder had happened among the people he left there, as in effect there had, as we shall show hereafter. Therefore altering his course from the west, he stood north, thinking to light on some of of the *Caribbee* islands, there to refresh his men, and take in wood and water, whereof he had great want.

Trinity island discovered.

As he was thus sailing one day about noon, *Alonzo Perez Norando*, a sailor of the town of *Gullva*, going up to the round-top, saw land to the westward at about fifteen leagues distance, and there appeared three mountains all at the same time, but not long after they perceived the same land stretched out towards the north-east, as far as the eye could reach, and that did not seem to be the end. Having given thanks to God, said the *Salve Regina*, and other prayers, the seamen use in time of distress or joy; the admiral called that land the island of the *Trinity*, as well because he had before thoughts of giving that name to the first land that he found, as in return, because it had pleased God to show him three mountains all together, as has been said. He sailed due-west, to make a cape that appeared to the south of him, and making for the south-side of the island, till he came to an anchor, five leagues beyond a point, which he called *de la Galera*, or of the galley, because of a rock that lay near the point, and at a distance look'd like a galley under sail. Having now but one cask of water for all his ships crew, and the other ships being in the same condition, there being no conveniency here to take

take in any, on *Wednesday* following in the morning he continued his course still west, and cast anchor at another point, which he called *de la Plaga*, or, of the strand, where the people landed, and took water, in a delicate brook, without seeing any town or people there, tho' along the coast they left behind they had seen many houses and towns. True it is, they found the tokens of fishermen, who had fled, leaving behind them some of their fishing tackle. They also saw the prints of the feet of beasts, which seem'd to be of goats, and saw the bones of one, but the head being without horns, they thought it might be of some catamountain, or monkey, as they afterwards found it to be, seeing abundance of those cats in *Paria*. This same day, being the first of *August*, sailing between cape *Galera* and that of *la Plaga* southwards, they discovered the continent, about twenty five leagues distance, as they guessed; but they thinking it another island; called it *Isla Santa*, or Holy Island. The land they saw of the *Trinity*, between the two points, was thirty leagues in length east and west, without any harbour, but all the countrey very pleasant with trees down to the sea, and abundance of towns. This space they ran in a very short time, because the current of the sea set so very violent westward, that it looked like a rapid river both day and night, and at all hours, notwithstanding the tide flow'd and ebb'd along the shore above forty paces, as happens at St *Lucar de Barrameda*, when there are floods; for though the water rise and fall never so much, yet it never ceases running towards the sea.

CHAP. LXIX.

How the admiral sailed to the cape, called Puntal del Arenal, *and a canoe came out to talk to him.*

PErceiving they could have no account of the people of the countrey at this cape, and that there was no conveniency of taking water, without excessive labour, and there was no conveniency of careening the ships and getting provisions. the next being the second of *August*, the admiral went on to another point of land, which seemed to be most westerly in that island, and called it *del Arenal*, where he came to an anchor, thinking the easterly winds which reign there would not be so troublesome to the boats in going backwards and forwards. On the way before they came to this point, a canoe began to follow them with twenty five men in it, and stopped at about a cannon-shot distance, calling out and talking very loud. Nothing could be understood, though it was supposed they enquired who our men were, and whence they came, as the other *Indians* used to do at first: there being no possibility of persuading them with any words to come aboard, they began to show them several things, that they might covet to have them, such as little brass basons, looking-glasses, and other things, the rest of the *Indians* used to make great account of. But tho' this drew them a little, yet they soon stopped again, and therefore the more to allure them, the admiral ordered one to get upon the poop with a taber and pipe, and some young fellows to dance. As soon as the *Indians* saw it, they put themselves into a posture of defence, laying hold of their targets, and shooting their arrows at those that danced, who by the admirals command, that those people might not go unpunished, or contemn the christians, leaving their dance began to shoot with their cross bows, so that they were glad to draw off, and made to another caraval, clapping close to its side without any apprehension. The pilot of the ship went over into the canoe and gave them some things they were very well pleased with, and said, if they had been ashore they would have brought him bread from their houses, and so they went towards land, nor would they in the ship stop e'er a one, for fear of displeasing the admiral. The account they gave of them, was, that they were well shaped people, and whiter than those of the other islands, and that they wear their hair long, like women, bound with small strings, and covered their privities with little clouts.

Indians of the Trinity.

CHAP.

CHAP. LXX.

Of the danger the ſhips were in, entering the mouth of the channel, they called Boca del Drago, *or, the* Dragon's Mouth; *and how* Paria *was diſcovered, being the firſt diſcovery on the continent.*

AS ſoon as the ſhips had anchored at *Punta del Arenal*, the admiral ſent the boats aſhore for water, and to get ſome information of the *Indians*, but they could do neither, that countrey being very low, and unpeopled. He therefore ordered them the next day to dig trenches on the iſland, and by good luck they found them ready made and full of excellent water, and it was thought the fiſhermen had made them. Having taken what they wanted, the admiral reſolved to proceed on to another mouth or channel which appeared towards the north-weſt, which he afterwards called *Boca del Drago*, or, the *Dragon's Mouth*, to diſtinguiſh it from that where he was, to which he had given the name of *Boca de la Sierpe*, or, the *Serpent's Mouth*. Theſe two mouths or channels, like the *Dardanels*, were made by the two weſtermoſt points of the *Trinity* iſland, and two others of the continent, and lay almoſt north and ſouth of one another. In the midſt of that, where the admiral anchored, was another rock, which he called *El Gallo*, that is the *Cock*. Through this mouth, he called *Boca de Sierpe*, the water continually ran ſo furiouſly northward, as if it had been the mouth of ſome great river, which was the reaſon of giving it that name, becauſe of the fright it put them into. For as they lay very ſecurely at anchor, there came a ſtronger ſtream of water than uſual, with a hideous noiſe, running through that mouth northward. And another current running out of the gulph now called *Paria*, oppoſite to that before-mentioned, they met with hideous roaring, and cauſed the ſea to ſwell up like a high mountain, or ridge of hills along that channel, which mountain ſoon came towards the ſhips to the great terror of all men fearing they ſhould over-ſet. But it pleaſed God it paſſed under, or rather lifted them up without doing any harm, though it drew the anchor of one of them, carrying the veſſel away, but by the help of their ſails they eſcaped the danger, not without mortal fear of being loſt. That furious current being paſſed, the admiral conſidering the danger he was in there, ſtood for the *Dragon's Mouth*, which was between the north point of the *Trinity* iſland, and the eaſt point of *Paria*; yet went not through it at that time, but ſailed along the ſouth coaſt of *Paria* weſtward, believing it to be an iſland, and hoping to find a way out northwards towards *Hiſpaniola*. And though there were many ports along that coaſt of *Paria*, he would put into none, all the ſea being a harbour locked in with the continent.

The gulph of Paria.

A wonderfulſwelling of water.

CHAP. LXXI.

How there was ſome gold and pearls found in Paria, *and a people of good converſation.*

THE admiral being at an anchor on the *Fifth* of *Auguſt*, and it being his particular devotion never to weigh on a *Sunday*, he ſent the boats aſhore, where they found abundance of fruit of the ſame ſort they had ſeen in the other iſlands; great numbers of trees, and ſigns of people that had fled for fear of the chriſtians. But being unwilling to loſe time, he ſailed down the coaſt fifteen leagues farther without going into any harbour, for fear he ſhould miſs of wind to bring him out. Being at an anchor on the coaſt, at the end of theſe fifteen leagues, there came out a canoe to the caraval called *El Borreo*, with three men in it; and the pilot knowing how much the admiral coveted to receive ſome information from thoſe people, he pretended to talk to them, and let himſelf fall into the canoe, and the *Spaniards* in the boat took thoſe three men, and carried them to the admiral, who made very much of them, and ſent them aſhore with many gifts, where there appeared abundance of *Indians*. Theſe hearing the good account the three gave them, came all in their canoes to barter, for ſuch things as they had, which were much the ſame, as had been ſeen in the iſlands before diſcovered, only that here they had no targets, nor poiſoned arrows, which theſe people do not uſe, but only the *Canibals*. Their drink was a ſort of liquor as white as milk, and another ſomewhat blackiſh, taſting like green wine made of grapes not quite ripe, but they could not learn what fruit it was made of. They wore cottton cloths

Indians *go aboard.*

well wove, of ſeveral colours, about the bigneſs of a handkerchief, ſome bigger and ſome leſs; and what they moſt valued of our things, was braſs, and eſpecially bells. The people ſeem to be more civilized and tractable than thoſe of *Hiſpaniola*. They cover their nakedneſs with one of thoſe cloths above-mentioned, and have another wrapped about their head. The women cover nothing, not even their privities; the ſame they do in the *Trinity* iſland. They ſaw nothing of value here, except ſome little plates of gold they hung about their necks; for which reaſon, and becauſe the admiral could not ſtay to dive into the ſecrets of the countrey, he ordered ſix of thoſe *Indians* to be taken, and continued his voyage weſtward, believing that land of *Paria*, which he called the *Holy Iſland*, was no continent. Soon after another iſland appeared towards the ſouth, and another no leſs than that towards the weſt, all high land, ſowed and well peopled; and the *Indians* had more plates of gold about their necks than the others, and abundance of *Guaninis*, which is very low gold. They ſaid that was produced in other weſtern iſlands inhabited by people that eat men. The women had ſtrings of beads about their arms, and among them very fine large and ſmall pearls ſtrung, ſome whereof were got in exchange to ſend their catholick majeſties as a ſample. Being aſked where they found thoſe things, they made ſigns to ſhow that in the oyſter-ſhels which were taken weſtward of that land of *Paria*, and beyond it towards the north. Upon this, the admiral ſtaid there to know more of that good diſcovery, and ſent the boats aſhore, where all the people of the countrey that had flocked together, appeared ſo tractable and friendly, that they importuned the chriſtians to go along with them to a houſe not far off, where they gave them to eat, and a great deal of that wine of theirs. Then from that houſe, which it is likely was the king's palace, they carried them to another, which was his ſons, and ſhewed them the ſame kindneſs. They were all in general whiter than any they had ſeen in the *Indies*, and of better aſpects and ſhapes, with their hair cut ſhort by their ears, after the *Spaniſh* faſhion. From them they underſtood that land was called *Paria*, and that they would be glad to be in amity with the chriſtians. Thus they departed from them, and returned to the ſhips.

The firſt pearls in the weſt-Indies.

A courteous and obliging people.

CHAP. LXXII.

How the admiral paſſed through Boca del Drago, *and the danger he was in there.*

THE admiral holding on his voyage weſtward, they ſtill found leſs and leſs water, inſomuch that being come through four or five fathom, they found but two and a half at ebb, for the tide differed from that at the *Trinity* iſland; for at the *Trinity*, the water ſwelled three fathom, and here being forty five leagues to the weſtward, it roſe but one; and there always, whether ebb or flood, the current ran weſt; and here upon the ebb they ran eaſt, and upon the flood weſt; there the water was but brackiſh, here it was like river water. The admiral perceiving this difference, and how little water he found, durſt proceed no farther in his ſhip, which required three fathom water, being of a hundred tun, and therefore came to an anchor on that coaſt, which was very ſafe, being a port like a horſeſhoe, locked with that land on all ſides. However, he ſent the little caraval, called *El Boreo*, or the poſt, to diſcover whether there was any paſs weſtward among thoſe iſlands. She having gone but a little way, retur[n]ed the next day, being the eleventh of *Auguſt*, ſaying, that at the weſtermoſt point of that ſea, there was a mouth or opening, two leagues over from north to ſouth, and within it a round bay, with four other little bays, one towards each quarter of heaven, that from each of them flowed a river, whoſe water made that ſea ſo ſweet, which was yet much ſweeter farther in, adding, that all that land which ſeemed to be iſlands, was one and the ſame continent; that they had every where four or five fathom water, and ſuch abundance of thoſe weeds they ſaw in the ocean, that they hindred ther ſailing. The admiral therefore being certain he could not get out weſtward, that ſame day ſtood back to the eaſtward, deſigning to paſs the ſtreights, which he ſaw between the land the *Indians* call *Paria*, and the *Trinity*. In this ſtreight there are four little iſtands eaſt near the point of the *Trinity*, which he called cape *Boca*, becauſe it was blunt, weſt upon the point of the continent, which he called cape *Lapa*, and in the middle. The reaſon why he called this the *Dragon's Mouth*, was, becauſe it is very dangerous, by reaſon of the abundance of freſh water that ſtruggles to get out there into the ſea, and made three boiſterous channels, extending from eaſt to weſt the width of the ſtreight. And becauſe as he was ſailing through, the wind failed

Account of the gulph of Paria.

Boca del Drago.

failed him; and he was in danger of being drove on some sand or rock; therefore he with reason gave it a name answerable to that of the other mouth, where he was in no less danger as was said above. But it pleas'd God, that what they most dreaded should be their greatest safety, the strength of the current carrying them off. Therefore on *Monday* the 17th of *August*, he began to sail westward along the coast of *Paria*, in order to stand over afterwards for *Hispaniola*, giving thanks to God, who deliver'd him from so many troubles and dangers, still showing him new countries full of peaceable people and great wealth, especially that, which he certainly concluded to be the continent, because of the great extent of that gulph of pearls, of the rivers that ran from it, of the sea, which was all sweet water; and by the authority of *Esdras*, in the 8th chapter of the 4th book; where he says, that dividing the globe into seven parts only, one of them is covered with water; for all the *Indians* of the *Caribbee* islands have told him, there was a vast land southward.

CHAP. LXXIII.

How the admiral stood over from the continent to Hispaniola.

THE admiral sailing along westward on the coast of *Paria*, still fell farther off from it towards the north west, the currents in being calm driving him that way; so that on *Wednesday* the 15th of *August*, he left the cape, he called *de las Conchas*, or of shells, south of him, and the island *Margarita* west, which name he gave this island, perhaps by divine inspiration; because close by it lies that of *Cubagua*, where an infinite quantity of pearls has been found; and in *Hispaniola* and *Jamaica* at his return he called some *Mountains of Gold*, where afterwards was found the greatest quantity and largest pieces that ever were carried from thence into *Spain*. But to return to his voyage, he held on his course by six islands, which he called *las Guardas*, or the guards, and three others more to the north, *los Testigos*, or the witnesses. And though they still discover'd much land of *Paria* westward, yet the admiral says, he could not from this time give such an account of it as he would wish, because through overmuch watching, his eyes were inflam'd, and therefore was forced to take most of his observations from the sailors and pilots. He also says, that this same night, being *Thursday* the 16th of *August*, the compasses which till now had not varied, did at this time, at least a point and a half, and some of them two points, wherein there could be no mistake, because several persons had always watch'd to observe it. Admiring at this, and griev'd that he had not the opportunity of following the course of the continent, he held on north-west, till on *Monday* the 20th of *August* he came to an anchor between *Beaca*, and *Hispaniola*; whence he sent a letter by some *Indians* to his brother the *Adelantodo*, acquainting him with his safe arrival and success. He was surpriz'd to find himself so far westward; for though he knew the force of the currents fail'd, yet he did not think it had been so much. Therefore to the end his provisions might not fail him in time of need, he stood to the eastward for *S. Domingo*, into which harbour he sail'd on the 30th of *August*; for here the lieutenant his brother had appointed the city to be built on the east-side of the river, where it stands at present, and was called *Santo Domingo* in memory of his father, whose name was *Dominick*.

Cape Conchas. Margarita *island*.

S. Domingo *in* Hispaniola.

CHAP LXXIV.

The rebellion and troubles the admiral met with in Hispaniola, *raised by the wickedness of one* Francis Roldan, *whom he had left as alcalde mayor, or chief justice.*

THE admiral being come to *S. Domingo*, almost blind with over-watching, he hoped there to rest himself after his voyage, and find peace among his people, but found all quite contrary, for all the people in the island were in disorder and rebellion; for abundance of those he had left were dead, and of those that remain'd, above 160 were sick of the *French* pox, and besides that many were in rebellion with *Roldan*, he found not the three ships, we said he sent before him from the *Canary* islands. Of these things it is requisite we speak orderly, beginning from the time the admiral set out for *Spain*, which as we said, was in *March* 1496, 30 months before his return: the first part of which time the people continued pretty quiet in hopes of his return

return, and of being speedily relieved: But the first year being pass'd, the *Spanish* provisions failing, and sickness and sufferings increasing, they began to be dissatisfied with what was, and to despair of any better; so that the complaints of many discontented persons were heard, who never want some body to stir them up, desiring to be head of a party, as was now done by one *Francis Roldan*, born at *Torre de D. Ximeno*, whom the admiral had left in such power among both *Christians* and *Indians*, by making him chief justice, that he was as much obey'd as himself. For this reason it is to be suppos'd there was not that good understanding between him and the admiral's lieutenant, as ought to have been for the publick good, as time and experience made it appear. For the admiral, neither returning himself, nor sending any supplies, this *Roldan* began to think of possessing himself of the island, designing for this purpose to murther the admirals brothers, as those that could best oppose his rebellion, and waited an opportunity to put this in execution. It happened that the lieutenant of the island, one of the admiral's brothers, went to a province in the west, called *Xaragua*, 80 leagues from *Isabella*, where the said *Roldan* remained in his employ, but subordinate to *D. James*, second brother to the admiral. This *Roldan* was so offended at, that whilst the lieutenant was taking order how the kings of the island should pay tribute to their catholick majesties, as the admiral had rated all the *Indians*, *Orlando* began underhand to draw some of them over to his party. But that it might not prove fatal to rise on a sudden, and without some pretence: that which *Roldan* laid hold of was, that there was a caraval ashore at *Isabella*, built by the lieutenant of the island, to send to *Spain* in case of necessity, and there being no launching of it for want of tackle and other necessaries, *Roldan* feign'd and gave out there was some other reason for it, and that it behov'd the publick, that caraval should be fitted out, that some of them might go to *Spain* in it, to give an account of their sufferings. Thus upon pretence of the publick good, he press'd that it might be launch'd, and *D. James Columbus* not consenting to it for want of tackle, as has been said, *Roldan* began more boldly to treat with some about launching the caraval in despite of him; telling those, he thought to agree with him, that if the lieutenant, and *D. James* were displeas'd at it, the reason was because they would secure to themselves the dominion of the countrey, and keep them in subjection, without any ship that might carry the news of their revolt to their catholick majesties. And since they were satisfied and convinced of the cruelty and ill-nature of the lieutenant, and what a restless life he led them, building towns and forts, and that they had no hopes of the admiral's coming with supplies, it was fit they should take that caraval and procure their liberty, and not suffer themselves under pretence of pay, which they never receiv'd, to be kept under by a foreigner, whereas it was in their power to live at ease and in plenty; for that whatsoever could be had in the island would be equally divided among them, and they would be serv'd by the *Indians* to their own content, without being so much in subjection, that they could not take to wife any *Indian* woman they pleased. That the lieutenant made them keep the three vows of religious men; and besides that, they wanted not for fasts and disciplines, as also imprisonment, and other punishments, which they endured for the least fault. Therefore, since he had the rod of justice and regal authority, which secured them against any thing that might befal them on this account, he advised them to do what he directed, wherein they could not do amiss. With these and the like words, proceeding from the hatred he bore the lieutenant, he drew so many over to his own party, that one day when the lieutenant was come back from *Xaragua* to *Isabella*, some of them resolv'd to stab him, looking upon it as so easie a matter, that they had provided a halter to hang him up after he was dead. What at present the more incens'd them, was the imprisoning of one *Barahona*, a friend to the conspirators, against whom, if God had not put it into the heart of the lieutenant not to proceed to execution of justice at that time, they had then certainly murdered him.

Rebellion among the Spaniards.

CHAP. LXXV.

How Francis Roldan *endeavour'd to make the town of* Conception *mutiny, and plundered* Isabella.

FRancis *Roldan*, perceiving he had miss'd of the murther of the lieutenant, and his conspiracy was discovered, he resolved to possess himself of the town and fort of the *Conception*, thinking from thence he might easily subdue the island. It fell out con-

conveniently for his design, that he was near the said town; for whilst the lieutenant was abroad, he had been sent with 40 men about that province, to reduce the *Indians* that had revolted, with the same design of making themselves masters of that town, and destroying the christians. So that *Roldan*, under pretence of putting a stop to this evil, and punishing the *Indians*, gather'd his men at the residence of one of their *Caciques*, call'd *Marche*, designing to put his project in execution upon the first opportunity. But *Ballester* the commander of the fort, having some jealousie of him, he stood upon his guard, and acquainted the lieutenant of the island with the danger he was in, who with all speed, and what men he could gather, threw himself into the fort. Thither *Roldan* came upon a safe conduct, now his conspiracy was discovered, rather to observe by the lieutenant what might do him harm, than through any desire of coming to an accommodation, and with more boldness and impudence than became him, required the lieutenant to cause the caraval to be launched, or give him leave to launch it, which he and his friends would do. The lieutenant incensed at these words, answered, that neither he nor his friends were seamen, or knew what was proper to be done in that case; and that though they had known how to launch it, yet they could not sail in her for want of rigging, and other necessaries, and therefore it would be only exposing the men and the caraval. And, forasmuch as the lieutenant understood that affair, as a seaman, and they not being such, knew nothing of it, therefore they varied in their judgments. These and other displeasing words having pass'd between them, *Roldan* went away in a passion, refusing to quit his rod of justice, or stand trial, as the lieutenant ordered, saying he would do both, when their majesties, whose the island was, commanded him; knowing he could expect no justice from him, because of the hatred he bore him, but that right or wrong he would find means to put him to death with shame: that in the mean while, not to exceed the bounds of reason, he would go and reside where he should bid him. But he at present appointing him the residence of the *Cacique*, *James Columbus*, he refused it, saying, there were not provisions there for his men, and that he would find a more convenient place. He set out towards *Isabella*, and having gathered 65 men, perceiving he could not launch the caraval, he plunder'd the magazines, he and his followers, taking away what arms, stuffs, and provisions they thought fit, *D. James Columbus*, who was there, not being able to oppose him, but would have been in danger, had he not retired to the fort with some friends and servants. Yet in the process afterwards drawn up on this subject, there were some that depos'd, that *Roldan* promised to submit to him, provided he would take his part against his own brother: which he refusing, and *Roldan* not being able to do him any further harm; as also fearing the succours that were coming from the lieutenant, he went out of town with all the mutineers, and falling on the cattle that graz'd thereabouts, they kill'd such as they lik'd to eat, and took the beasts of burthen to serve them in their journey, resolving to go into the province of *Xaragua*, whence the lieutenant was lately come, designing to settle there, that being the pleasantest and most plentiful part of the island, the people here being more civiliz'd and wiser than the rest of the natives of *Hispaniola*; but above all, because the women were the handsomest, and of the most pleasing conversation of any others, which most invited them to go thither. But that they might not go without making trial of their strength, before the lieutenant could increase his power, and punish them as they deserv'd, they resolved to take the town of the *Conception* in their way, to surprize it, and kill the lieutenant, and in case this did not succeed, to besiege him. The lieutenant having intelligence of their design, stood upon his guard, encouraging his men with good words, and promising them many gifts, and each of them two slaves. And forasmuch as he understood, that most of those that were with him, lik'd the life *Roldan* and his men led so well, that many of them gave ear to his messages; therefore *Roldan* having conceiv'd hopes that they would all go over to him, had the boldness to undertake that enterprize, which did not succeed as he expected. For the lieutenant, having provided as has been said, being himself a man of great resolution, and having the best men on his side, was resolv'd to do that by force of arms, which he could not compass by fair means and arguments. Having therefore gathered his men together, he march'd out of town to attack the rebels on the road.

Farther progress of the rebels.

CHAP. LXXVI.

How Francis Roldan incens'd the Indians against the lieutenant, and went away with his men to Xaragua.

Francis Roldan, perceiving he was so disappointed, and that not one of the lieutenants men came over to him, as he had expected, resolved to retire in time, and go away to *Xaragua* as he design'd at first, not daring to meet him, yet presum'd to talk contemptibly of him, and to stir up the *Indians*, where-ever he went, to rebel against him, telling them, the cause of his forsaking him was his being a man naturally revengeful and morose, as well towards the *Christians*, as *Indians*; and abominably covetous, imposing great burdens and tributes on them; which if they bore with, he would increase every year, tho' against their catholick majesties will; who requir'd nothing of their subjects but obedience, maintaining them in justice, liberty and peace; which, if they fear'd they should not be able to maintain, he with his friends and followers, would assist them to assert, and would declare himself their protector and deliverer. After which, they resolved to forbid paying the tribute, we said had been impos'd on them, by which means it could not be gathered of those that dwelt far from the lieutenant, nor durst he exact it of those near about him for fear of provoking them to join with the rebels. Yet this condescension towards them, had not so good an effect; but that as soon as the lieutenant was gone from the *Conception*, *Guarionex*, who was the principal *Cacique* of that province, with the assistance of *Roldan*, resolv'd to besiege the fort, and destroy the *Christians* that kept it. The better to effect it, he drew together all the *Caciques* of his party, and agreed with them privately, that every one should kill those that were within his precinct, because the territories in *Hispaniola* being too small, for any of them to maintain a great number of people, the *Christians* had been obliged to divide themselves into small parcels of eight or nine in each liberty. This gave the *Indians* hopes, that surprizing them all at the same time, they might have it in their power to suffer none to escape. But they having no other way of fixing a time, or ordering any thing else that requires counting, but only by their fingers, they resolved, that every one should be ready to destroy the *Christians* at the next full moon. *Guarionex* having thus disposed his *Caciques* to put this in execution, the chiefest of them being desirous to gain honour, and looking upon the matter as very easie, and being no good astronomers, to know when the full moon was, fell on before the time appointed, and were forced to fly after many blows. He thinking to find assistance in *Guarionex* found his own ruin; for he put him to death, as he had deserv'd, for having caused the conspiracy to be discovered, and the *Christians* to be upon their guard. The rebels were not a little concern'd at this miscarriage; for as was reported, it had been contriv'd with their consent, and therefore they waited to see, whether *Guarionex* brought affairs to such terms, that joining with him they might destroy the lieutenant: But perceiving this did not succeed, they thought not themselves secure in the province where they were, but went away to *Xaragua*, still proclaiming themselves protectors of the *Indians*, whereas they were thieves in their actions and inclinations, having no regard to God or the world, but following their inordinate appetites; for every one stole what he could, and *Roldan* their leader more than all of them, persuading and commanding every *Cacique* to entertain him that could and would defend the *Indians* and rebels from paying the tribute the lieutenant demanded of them, tho' at the same time he under this pretence took much more from them; for from only one *Cacique*, whose name was *Manicaotex*, he received every three months, a calabash, containing three marks of pure gold, that is, a pound and a half, and to be the more sure of him, kept his son and nephew as hostages. He that reads this, must not wonder that we reduce the marks of gold to the measure of a calabash, which we do to show, that the *Indians* in these cases dealt by measure, because they never had any weights.

Conspiracy of the Indians *to destroy the* Spaniards.

CHAP. LXXVII.

How the ships came from Spain with provisions and supplies.

THE *Christians* being thus divided, as has been said, and no ships yet coming from *Spain* with supplies, neither the lieutenant, nor his brother *D. James*, could keep the people quiet, that had remained with them; for most of them being mean persons,

persons, and desirous to lead that easie life *Roldan* promis'd them, they durst not punish the guilty, for fear of being forsaken; which made them so insolent, that it was impossible to keep them in order, and therefore they were forced to bear with the affronts of the rebels. But it being God's will to afford them some comfort, it pleased him to order that the two ships should arrive, which, as was said before, had been sent a year after the admiral's departure from the *Indies*, not without great application us'd by him at court for fitting them out; for he, considering the nature of the countrey, the dispositions of the people he left behind, and the great danger that might accrue from his long absence, press'd for and obtain'd of their catholick majesties, that those two ships might be sent before, of 18 he had been ordered to fit out. The arrival of these, the supplies they brought of men and provisions, and the assurance that the admiral was safe arrived in *Spain*, encouraged those that were with the lieutenant to serve him more faithfully, and made those that followed *Roldan*, apprehensive of being punish'd. These being desirous to hear news, and furnish themselves with what they wanted, resolved to repair to *S. Domingo*, where the ships had put in, hoping to draw some of the men over to their party. But the lieutenant having intelligence of their march, and being nearer that harbour, he mov'd towards them to hinder their passage; and having left guards on the passes, went to the port to see the ships, and order the affairs of that place. And being desirous the admiral should find the island in a peaceable condition, and all troubles ended, he again made new overtures to *Roldan*, who was six leagues off with his men, sending to him for this purpose the commander of the two ships lately arriv'd, whose name was *Peter Fernandez Coronel*; as well because he was a man of worth and in authority, as because he hop'd his words would prove more effectual, since he as an eye witness, could certifie him of the admiral's arrival in *Spain*, the good reception he had found, and the willingness their majesties express'd to make him still greater. But the chief men among them, fearing the impression this messenger might make upon their followers, would not suffer him to speak in publick; so that they received him with their bows and arrows on the road, and he could only speak some few words to those that were appointed to hear him. Thus having done nothing, he returned to the town, and the rebels to their quarters in *Xaragua*, not without apprehensions, lest *Roldan* and some of the principal men of his gang should write to their friends that were with the lieutenant, desiring them when the admiral came, to intercede for them, since all their complaints were against the lieutenant, and not against the admiral himself, for which reason they desired to be restored to his favour.

The rebels refuse to submit.

CHAP. LXXVIII.

How the three ships the admiral sent from the Canary *islands arrived where the rebels were.*

HAving spoke of the arrival of the two ships the admiral sent from *Spain* to *Hispaniola*, it is fit we give an account of the three that parted from him at the *Canary* islands, which proceeded on their voyage with fair winds till they came to the *Caribbee* islands, which are the first that sailors meet with in their way to the port of *S. Domingo*. The pilots then not being so well acquainted with that voyage, as they have been since, it happened they knew not how to hit that port, and were carried away by the currents so far to westward, that they arrived in the province of *Xaragua*, where the rebels were, who as soon as they understood that those ships were out of their way, and knew nothing of their revolt, some of them went peaceably aboard, pretending they were there by the lieutenant's orders, the better to be supplied with provisions, and keep that countrey under. But it being very easie for a secret, that is among many, to be discovered, *Alonso Sanchez de Carvajal*, who was the skilfullest of the captains of those ships, being aware of the rebellion and discord, began immediately to make overtures of peace to *Francis Roldan*, thinking to bring him to submit to the lieutenant. But the familiar conversation the rebels had before entertain'd aboard the ships, was the cause that his perswasions had not the desired effect; for *Roldan* had privately obtain'd promises from many of those that came fresh out of *Spain*, that they would stay with him, and by that accession he hoped to become still greater. *Carvajal* therefore finding things were not in such a posture, that he might hope for a speedy conclusion of what he had in hand, thought it convenient, with the advice of the other two captains, that the people they brought under pay to work in the mines, and other employ-

Ignorance of pilots carries the ships to the west of Hispaniola.

employments, should go by land to *S. Domingo*, because the winds and currents being set there against that voyage, it was possible they might not perform it in two or three months; so that they would not only consume the provisions, but the men might fall sick, and the time be lost, which ought to have been employed in the service they came for. Having agreed upon this, it fell to *John Anthony Columbus* his lot to march with the men, which were 40, to *Arana* to sail about with the ships, and to *Caravajal* to stay and endeavour to bring the rebels to an accommodation. *John Anthony Columbus* setting forward the 2d day after they landed, those labourers and vagabonds sent over to work, went away to the rebels, leaving their captain with only six or seven men that stuck to him. He seeing their base infidelity, without apprehending any danger, went to *Roldan*, and told him, That since he pretended to promote the service of their catholick majesties, it was not reasonable he should suffer those men, that were come to people and cultivate the countrey, and to follow their callings with wages in hand, to stay there and lose their time, without doing any thing of that they were obliged to; and that if he had turn'd them away, it had been a token that his words and his actions agreed; that his staying there caused the division and disorder with the lieutenant, and not any inclination in him to obstruct the king's service. But that which had happened turning to the account of *Roldan* and his followers, as well for the carrying on their design, as because the crime committed by many is generally soonest conniv'd at; he excus'd himself as to that point, saying, He could not use violence towards them, and that his was a religious order, which refused no man. *John Anthony* knowing it was not the part of a discreet man to expose himself to the danger of pressing farther without hopes of success, resolved to go aboard again with those few that follow'd him; and therefore that they might not be serv'd so by those that were left, they two captains sail'd immediately with their two ships towards *S. Domingo*, with the wind as contrary as they had fear'd; for they spent many days, spoil'd their provisions, and *Caravajal*'s ship was much damaged upon certain sands, where she lost her rudder, and sprung a leak, so that they had much to do to bring her in.

Fresh men desert to the rebels.

CHAP. LXXIX.

How the captains of the ships that came from Xaragua, *found the admiral at* S. Domingo.

THE captains with their ships, arriving at *S. Domingo*, in their return from *Xaragua*, found the admiral there, after his discovery of the continent. He being fully inform'd of the condition of the rebels, and having seen the process his lieutenant had made against them, tho' the crime was plainly made out to deserve severe punishment, yet he thought fit to form a new process, and give their majesties an account of it, resolving at the same time to use all the moderation he could in this matter, and endeavouring to reduce them by fair means. For which reason, and that neither they nor any others, might have cause to complain of him, or say, he kept them there by force, he made proclamation on the 12th of *September*, giving leave to all that would return to *Spain*, and promising them free passage and provisions. And being inform'd on the other hand, That *Roldan* was coming towards *S. Domingo* with some of his men, he ordered *Michael Ballester*, commander of the *Conception*, to secure his own town and fort; and in case *Roldan* came that way, he should tell him from the admiral, that he was much concerned at his sufferings, and all that was past, and would have no more said of it, granting a general pardon to all, and desiring him to come away immediately to the admiral, without fearing any thing, that by his advice things might be ordered, as was for their majesties service; and if he required any safe conduct, he would send it him in such form as he required. *Ballester* return'd answer on the 14th of *February*, That he had received certain information, that *Riquelme* was the day before come to the town of *Bonao*, and that *Adrian* and *Roldan*, who were the ring-leaders, would meet there in seven or eight days, at which time he might there apprehend them, as he did. For having discours'd them according to the instructions given him, he found them obstinate and unmannerly, *Roldan* telling him, They were not come to treat, nor did they desire, or care for peace, for he had the admiral and his authority at his beck, either to support, or suppress it, as he pleased; and that they must not talk to him of any accommodation, till they had sent him all the *Indians* taken at the siege of the *Conception*, since they had met together

The admiral endeavours to reduce the rebels.

together to serve the king, and upon his promise of security. Other things he added, by which it appeared, he would make no agreement, but what was much to his advantage. To this purpose he demanded, that the admiral should send *Caravajal* to him, because he would treat with no other but him, he being a man that would hear reason, and had discretion, as he had found by experience, when the three ships, as has been said, were at *Xaragua*. This answer made the admiral suspect *Caravajal*, and not without much cause.

Caravajal *suspected, yet trusted.*

First, because before *Caravajal* was at *Xaragua*, where these rebels then were, they had often writ and sent messages to their friends that were with the lieutenant, telling them, they would come and deliver themselves up to the admiral as soon as he arrived, and therefore they desired them to intercede for them, and appease him.

Secondly, because, since they did this as soon as they heard there were two ships come to the assistance of the lieutenant, they had much more cause to perform it, knowing the admiral was not come, had not the long conference *Caravajal* had with them prevented it.

Thirdly, because if he would have done his duty, he might have kept *Roldan*, and the chief men of his gang prisoners, aboard his caraval, they having been two days aboard without any security given.

Fourthly, because knowing as he did, that they were in rebellion, he ought not to suffer them to buy aboard the ships, as they did, 56 swords, and 60 cross-bows.

Fifthly, because there being some proofs that the men who were to land with *John Anthony* to go to S. *Domingo*, would join the rebels, he ought not to suffer them to land, or at least when they were gone over to them, he ought to have been more industrious to endeavour to recover them.

Sixthly, because he gave out that he came to the *Indies* as companion to the admiral, that nothing might be done without him, for fear the admiral should commit some offence.

Seventhly, because *Roldan* had writ to the admiral by *Caravajal* himself, acquainting him, that he was drawing near to *S. Domingo* with his men, by the advice of *Caravajal*, to be the nearer to treat of an accommodation, when the admiral arrived in *Hispaniola*; and now he was come, his actions not suiting with his letter, it appeared he had rather invited him to come thither, to the end that if the admiral had been long coming, or had not come at all, he as the admiral's associate, and *Roldan* as chief justice, might govern the island in despite of the lieutenant.

Eighthly, because at the same time that the other captains came with the three caravals to *S. Domingo*, he came by land attended by a guard of the rebels, and one of the chief of them called *Gamir*, who had been two days and two nights with him aboard his ship.

Ninthly, because he writ to the rebels when they came to *Bonao*, and sent them presents and provisions.

Tenthly, and lastly, because, besides that the said rebels would not treat with any body but him, they all unanimously said, if there had been occasion, they would have taken him for their captain.

Yet the admiral on the other side, considering that *Caravajal* was a discreet prudent person, and a gentleman, and that every one of those arguments might be answered, and perhaps what he had been told was not true, and looking upon him, as one that would not do any thing contrary to his duty, having a great desire to put out that fire, he resolv'd to consult with all the chief men he had about him, about *Roldan*'s answer, and resolve upon what was to be done on this occasion. All agreeing upon it, he sent *Caravajal*, with *Ballester*, to treat, who had no other answer from *Roldan*, but that since they had not brought the *Indians* he demanded, they should not without them talk of any accommodation. *Caravajal* discreetly answering to these words, made so taking a discourse, that he mov'd *Roldan* and three or four of the chief men to go wait upon the admiral and agree with him; but the others disliking of it, as *Roldan* and the others were mounting their horses to go with *Caravajal* to the admiral, they fell upon them, saying, they would not allow them to go, and that if any agreement was to be made, it should be drawn up in writing, that they might all know what was doing: So that after some days pass'd upon this resolution, on the 20th of *October*, *Roldan* by the consent of all his men, writ a letter to the admiral, laying the blame of their separation on the lieutenant; and telling the admiral, that since he had not in writing sent them security to come and give an account of themselves, they had resolved to send him their demands in writing, which were the reward of what they had hitherto done, as shall appear hereafter. Though their proposals were extravagant and insolent, yet the commander *Ballester*, the next day writ to the admiral, extolling *Caravajal*'s moving discourse, and

The rebels reject the admiral's offers.

saying, that since it was not of force to remove those people from their wicked design, nothing less than granting them what they demanded would prevail; for he found them so resolute, that he looked upon it as most certain, that most of the people that were with his lordship would go over to the rebels. And tho' he might rely on his servants and men of honour, yet they would not be able to withstand such a number, many daily resorting to them, which the admiral already knew by experience; for when *Roldan* was near *S. Domingo*, he muster'd all that were fit to bear arms, if it were requisite, and observ'd, that some feigning themselves sick, and some lame, he had not found above 70 men, of which there were not 40 that he could confide in. For which reason, the next day, being the 17th of *October* 1498 the aforesaid *Roldan*, and the chief of his followers, who would have gone to the admiral, sent him a letter subscribed by them, telling him, they had withdrawn from the lieutenant to save their lives, he having a design to destroy them; and that they being his lordship's servants, whose coming they had expected, as of one, that would look upon what they had done complying with their duty, as good service, they had hindred their people from doing harm to any that belong'd to his lordship, as they might easily have done. But that since he was come, and was so far from thinking, that he insisted upon taking revenge, and doing them harm, that they might with honour do what they had undertaken, and be at liberty to do it, they took leave of him and his service. Before this letter was delivered to the admiral, he had sent *Roldan* an answer. *Caravajal*, whom he sent to him, telling him what confidence he always repos'd in him, and what a good account he had given his catholick majesty of them, adding, that he did not write to him for fear of some inconveniency, if his letter should be seen by the common sort, which might redound to his disadvantage, and therefore instead of hand and seal, he had sent that person to him, in whom he knew how much he confided, and might regard what he said, as if it were under his seal, which was the commander *Ballester*; and therefore he might consider what was proper to be done, and he should find him most ready to comply. On the 18th of *October*, he ordered five ships to depart for *Spain*, sending their catholick majesties by them, a most particular account of affairs, and saying, he had kept those ships till then, believing that *Roldan* and his men would have gone away in them, as they had given out at first; and that the other three he kept with him, were fitting out for his brother to go in them to pursue the discovery of the continent of *Paria*, and take order about the fishery and trade for pearls, a sample whereof he sent them by *Arogial*.

CHAP. LXXX.

How Francis Roldan *went to treat with the admiral, but came to no agreement with him.*

ROldan having received the admiral's letter, answer'd the third day, seeming to incline to do all he order'd him, but his men not allowing him to go to treat without a safe-conduct, he desir'd him to send one, drawn up according to those heads he sent under his hand, and sign'd by the chief men about him. This safe-conduct was immediately sent him by the admiral on the 26th of *October*, and *Roldan* having received it, soon came, but rather with a design to draw some body over to him, than to conclude any thing, as appeared by his impudent proposals. Thus he return'd without concluding any thing, saying, He would give his company an account of matters, and write word what they resolv'd on. And that there might be some body from the admiral to treat and sign what was agreed on, the admiral's steward went with him, his name was *Salamanca*. After much talk, *Roldan* sent articles of agreement for the admiral to subscribe, telling him, That was all he could obtain of his people, and if his lordship thought fit to grant it, he should send his assent to the *Conception*; for at *Bonao* they had no longer provisions to subsist on, and they would expect his answer till the next monday. The admiral having read their answer and proposals, and considering what dishonourable things they demanded, would not grant them, lest he should bring himself, his brothers, and justice it self into contempt. But that they might have no cause to complain, or say he was too stiff in this affair, he ordered a general pardon to be proclaim'd, and to be 30 days upon the gates of the fort, the purport whereof was as follows.

" THAT for as much as during his " absence in *Spain*, some difference " had happened between the lieutenant, and " the chief justice *Roldan*, and other per- " sons *A general pardon.*

" sons who had fled with him, notwithstanding any thing that had happened, they might all in general, and every one in particular, safely come to serve their catholick majesties, as if no difference had ever been, and that whosoever would go into *Spain* should have his passage, and an order to receive his pay, as was usual with others, provided they presented themselves before the admiral within 30 days, to receive the benefit of this pardon, protesting that in case they did not appear within the time limited, they should be proceeded against according to course of law.

This pardon, subscrib'd by himself, he sent to *Roldan* by *Caravajal*, giving him in writing, the reasons why he neither could nor ought to grant the articles sent by him, and putting him in mind what they ought to do, if they aim'd at their majesties service. *Caravajal* went to the rebels at the *Conception*, where they were very haughty and proud, laughing at the admiral's pardon, and saying, He should soon have occasion to ask one of them. All this happened in the space of three weeks, during which time, under colour of apprehending a man *Roldan* would execute, they kept the commander *Ballester* besieged in the fort, and cut off his water, believing the want of it would oblige him to surrender; but upon *Caravajal*'s arrival, they rais'd the siege, and after many alterations made on both sides, came to the following conclusion.

CHAP. LXXXI.

The agreement made between the admiral, and Roldan *with his rebels.*

THE articles signed and agreed to by *Francis Roldan*, and his company, in order to their return to *Spain*, are as follows.

Articles of agreement.

" I. THAT the lord admiral give him two good ships, and in good order, according to the judgment of able seamen, to be delivered to him at the port of *Xaragua*, because most of his followers were there; and because there is no other port more commodious to provide and prepare victualling and other necessaries, where the said *Roldan* and his company shall embark, and sail for *Spain*, if so God please.

II. " That his lordship shall give an order for the payment of the salaries due to them all till that day, and letters of recommendation to their catholick majesties, that they may cause them to be paid.

III. " That he shall give them slaves for the service they have done in the island, and their sufferings, and certifie the said gift: And because some of them have women big with child, or delivered; if they carry them away, they shall pass instead of such slaves they were to have; and the children shall be free, and they may take them along with them.

IV. " His lordship shall put into the aforesaid ships all the provisions requisite for that voyage, as has been given to others before; and because he could not furnish them with bread, the judge and his company have leave to provide in the countrey, and that they have 30 hundred weight of bisket allowed them, or for want of it 30 sacks of corn; to the end, that if the *Carabi* or *Indian* bread should spoil, as might easily happen, they may subsist upon the aforesaid bisket or corn.

V. " That his lordship shall give a safe-conduct for such persons as shall come to receive the orders for their pay.

VI. " For as much, as some goods belonging to several persons, who are with *Roldan*, have been seiz'd, his lordship shall order restitution to be made.

VII. " That his lordship shall write a letter to their catholick majesties, acquainting them, That the said *Roldan*'s swine remain in the island, for the inhabitants provision, being 120 great ones, and 230 small, praying their highness to allow him the price for them they would have bore in the island; the which swine were taken from him in *February* 1498.

VIII. " That his lordship shall give the said *Roldan* full authority to sell some goods he has, which he must part with to go away, or to do with them as he pleases, or to leave them for his own use with whom he thinks fit to make the best of them.

IX. " That his lordship will order the judges to give speedy judgment concerning the horse.

X. " That if his lordship shall find the demands of *Salamanca* to be just, he shall write to the said judge to cause him to be paid.

XI. " That his lordship shall be discoursed concerning the captain's slaves.

XII. " That forasmuch as the said *Roldan*

“ *Roldan* and his company miſtruſt, that “ his lordſhip, or ſome other perſon by “ his order, may offer them ſome violence “ with the other ſhips that are in the iſland, “ he ſhall therefore grant them a paſs or “ ſafe-conduct, promiſing in their maje- “ ſties name, and upon his own faith, and “ the word of a gentleman, as is uſed in “ *Spain*, that neither his lordſhip, nor any “ other perſon ſhall offend them, or ob- “ ſtruct their voyage.

Having examined this agreement made by *Alonſo Sanchez de Caravajal* and *James de Salamanca*, with *Francis Roldan* and his company, this day being *Wedneſday* the 21ſt of *November* 1498, I am content it be fully obſerved, upon condition that the ſaid *Francis Roldan*, nor any of his followers, in whoſe name he ſubſcribed and ratified the articles by him delivered to the aforeſaid *Alonſo Sanchez de Caravajal* and *James de Salamanca*, ſhall not receive into their company any other chriſtian of the iſland, of any ſtate or condition whatſoever.

I *Francis Roldan*, judge, do promiſe and engage my faith and word for myſelf and all thoſe with me, that the articles above-mentioned ſhall be obſerved and fulfilled, without any fraud, but faithfully as is here ſet down, his lordſhip performing all that has been agreed on between *Alonſo Sanchez de Caravajal* and *James de Salamanca*, and my ſelf, as is in the written articles.

I. “ THat from the day of the date here- “ of, till the anſwer be brought, “ for which ten days ſhall be allowed, I “ will admit no perſon whatſoever of thoſe “ that are with the lord admiral.

II. “ That within fifty days after the “ ſaid anſwer ſhall be delivered to me here “ in the *Conception*, ſigned and ſealed by “ his lordſhip, which ſhall be within the “ ten days before-mentioned, we will em- “ bark and ſet ſail for *Spain*.

III. “ That none of the ſlaves freely grant- “ ed us, ſhall be carried away by force.

IV. “ That whereas the admiral will not “ be at the port where we are to embark, “ the perſon or perſons his lordſhip ſhall “ ſend thither, be honoured and reſpected “ as their majeſties and his lordſhip's officers, “ to whom ſhall be given an account of “ all we put aboard the ſhips, that they “ may enter it, and do as his lordſhip ſhall “ think fit; as alſo to deliver to them ſuch “ things as we have in our hands belong- “ ing to their majeſties. All the afore- “ ſaid articles are to be ſubſcribed and per- “ form'd by his lordſhip, as *Alonſo Sanchez* “ *de Caravajal*, and *James de Salamanca*, “ have them in writing; the anſwer where- “ of I expect here at the *Conception* for “ eight days to come; and if it be not “ then brought, I ſhall not be obliged to “ any thing here mention'd.

In teſtimony whereof, and that I and my company may obſerve and perform what I have ſaid, I have ſubſcribed this writing, given at the *Conception*, on the 16th of *November* 1498.

CHAP. LXXXII.

How after the agreement concluded, the rebels went away to Xaragua, *ſaying, they would embark on the two ſhips ſent them by the admiral.*

THings being adjuſted as above, *Caravajal* and *Salamanca* returned to *St. Domingo* to the admiral, and at their requeſt, on the 21ſt of *November*, he ſubſcribed the aforeſaid articles brought by them, and granted a new ſafe-conduct or leave to all thoſe that would not go to *Spain* with *Roldan*, promiſing them pay, or the liberty of planters, as they liked beſt, and for others to come freely to manage their affairs. Theſe the *Caſtellan Balleſter* delivered to *Roldan* and his company at the *Conception* on the 24th of *November*, and they having received them, went away toward *Xaragua*, to prepare for their departure, as was afterwards known. And tho' the admiral was ſenſible of their villany, and much concerned that the good ſervice his brother might have done in continuing the diſcovery of the continent of *Paria*, and ſettling the pearl fiſhery and trade, was obſtructed by giving them thoſe ſhips, yet he would not give the rebels occaſion to blame him, ſaying, he had refuſed them their paſſage. He began therefore preſently to fit out the ſhips as had been agreed, tho' the equipment was ſomewhat retarded for want of neceſſaries. To ſupply which defect, and that no time might be loſt, he ordered *Caravajal* to go over by land to provide and diſpoſe all things for the departure of the rebels, whilſt the ſhips came about, giving him ample commiſſion for it, reſolving himſelf to go ſoon to *Iſabella*, to ſettle affairs there, leaving his brother *James* at *St. Domingo*, to look to that

Ships fitted to carry away the rebels.

that place. After his departure, about the end of *January*, the two caravals furnish'd with all necessaries for the voyage, set out to take up the rebels, but a great storm rising by the way, they were forced to put into another port till the end of *March*; and because the caraval *Ninna*, one of the two, was in the worst condition, and required most repairs, the admiral sent orders to *Peter de Arana* and *Francis de Garai*, to repair to *Xaragua* with another called *Santa Cruz* or the *Holy Cross*, aboard which *Caravajal* went, and not by land. He was 11 days by the way, and found the other caraval waiting for him.

CHAP. LXXXIII.

How the rebels altered their resolution of going to Spain, *and came to a new agreement with the admiral.*

IN the mean while, the caravals not coming, and most of *Roldan*'s men having no mind to embark, they took that delay for a pretence to stay, blaming the admiral, as if he had not dispatch'd them as soon as he might; whereof he being informed, writ to *Roldan* and *Adrian*, persuading them in a friendly manner to perform the agreement, and not fall into disobedience. Besides, *Caravajal*, who was with them at *Xaragua*, on the 20th of *April*, entered his protestation before a notary, called *Francis de Garai*, afterwards governor of *Panuco* and of *Jamaica*, requiring them, since the admiral had sent the ships, to accept of them, and embark according to articles. And because they would not, on the 25th of *April* he ordered the ships to return to *St. Domingo*, because they were destroyed by the worms, and the men suffered much for want of provisions. The rebels were no way concerned, but rather rejoyced and grew haughty, seeing such account was made of them, and were so far from acknowledging the admiral's civility, that they laid it to his charge in writing, that it was through his fault they staid, saying, he had a mind to be revenged on them, and had therefore delayed the sending of the caravals, which were in such ill case, that it was impossible they should go in them to *Spain*, and that tho' they had been never so good, their provisions were spent expecting them, and they could not get more under a long while, for which reason they had resolved to expect redress from their majesties. *Caravajal* returned with this answer by land to *St. Domingo*, to whom at the time of his departure, *Roldan* said, he would willingly go wait on the admiral, to endeavour for such an accommodation, as might please all parties, provided he would send him his safe-conduct. *Caravajal* sent the admiral word of it from *St. Domingo*, on the 15th of *May*, who answered on the 21st, commending him for the pains he took, and sent the safe-conduct he required, with a short letter to *Roldan*, tho' very pithy, persuading him to peace, submission, and their majesties service; which he afterwards repeated at *S. Domingo*, more at large on the 29th of *June*; and on the 3d of *August*, six or seven of the chief men about the admiral, sent *Roldan* another safe-conduct, that he might come to treat with his lordship. But the distance being great, and the admiral having occasion to visit the countrey, he resolved to go with two caravals to the port of *Azua* in the same island *Hispaniola*, west of *S. Domingo*, to be the nearer the province where the rebels were, many of whom came to the said port; and the admiral arriving there about the end of *August* with his ships, conferr'd with the chief of them, exhorting them to desist from their ill course, and promising them all possible favour and kindness, which they promised to do, provided the admiral granted them four things, *viz.*

The rebels refuse to go to Spain.

I. "THAT he should send fifteen of "them to *Spain* in the first ships "that went.

New articles agreed on.

II. "That to those that remained, he "should give land and houses for their "pay.

III. "That proclamation should be "made, that all what had happened was "caused by false suggestions, and through "the fault of ill men.

IV. "That the admiral shall a-new ap"point *Roldan* perpetual judge.

This being concluded among them, *Roldan* returned ashore from the admiral's caraval, and sent his companions the articles, which were so much to their mind, and so unreasonable, that they concluded, saying, in case the admiral fail'd in any part, it should be lawful for them by force, or any other means, to oblige him to performance. The admiral being eager to conclude this difficult matter, which had lasted above two years; and considering his adversaries continued more obstinate than ever, and that many

many of those, who were with him, had a mind to join companies, and conspire together to go to other parts of the island, as *Roldan* had done; he resolved to sign the articles whatsoever they were, *viz.* To grant *Roldan* a patent for perpetual judge, and the other three above-mentioned particulars, besides all they had sent in writing, a copy whereof was inserted above. On *Tuesday* following, being the 5th of *November*, *Roldan* to exercise his office, and accordingly it being a part of his grant, he constituted *Peter Riquelme* judge of *Bonao*, with power to imprison offenders in criminal cases, but that he should send criminals upon life and death, to be tried by him at the fort of the *Conception*. The substitute being no honester than his master, he presently went about to build a strong house at *Bonao*, had not *Peter de Arana* forbid him, because he plainly perceiv'd it was contrary to the respect due to the admiral.

CHAP. LXXXIV.

How Ojeda *returning from his discovery, excited new troubles in* Hispaniola.

TO return to the course of our history, the admiral having adjusted matters with *Roldan*, appointed a captain with some men to march about the island to pacify it, and reduce the *Indians* to pay the tribute, and be always in a readiness, that upon the least mutiny among the christians, and sign of rebellion among the *Indians*, he might suppress and punish them, which he did with a design to go himself over to *Spain*; and carry with him his brother the lieutenant, because it would be difficult if he were left behind, to forget old grudges. As he was preparing for his voyage, *Alonso de Ojeda*, who had been discovering with four ships, arrived in the island. And forasmuch as this sort of men sailed about to make their fortune; on the 5th of *September* he put into the port the christians called *Brasil*, and the *Indians Yaquimo*, designing to take what he could from the *Indians*, and load with wood and slaves. Whilst he was thus employ'd, he did all the harm he could, and to show he was a limb of the bishop we have mention'd, endeavoured to raise another mutiny, gave out, that queen *Isabel* or *Elizabeth* was ready to die; and as soon as she was dead, there would be no body left to support the admiral, and that he as a faithful servant to the said bishop, might do what he pleased against the admiral, because of the enmity there was between them. Upon these grounds he began to write to some that were not very sound, after the late troubles, and to hold correspondence with them. But *Roldan* being inform'd of his proceedings and designs, by the admiral's order, went against him with 21 men, to prevent him doing the harm he intended: Being come within a league and a half of him on the 29th of *September*, he understood he was with 15 men at a *Caciques*, whose name was *Haniguaaba*, making bread and bisket, and therefore he travelled that night to surprize him. *Ojeda* understanding that *Roldan* was coming upon him, and being too weak to oppose him, to make the best of a bad case, went to meet him, saying, want of provisions had brought him thither, to supply himself in the king his master's dominions, without designing any harm. And giving him an account of his voyage, said, he had been discovering 600 leagues westward along the coast of *Paria*, where he found people that fought the christians even hand, and had wounded 20 of his men, for which reason he could make no advantage of the wealth of the countrey, where he said he had seen deer and rabbets and tygers skins and paws and *Gaaninies*, all which he show'd *Roldan* aboard the caravals, saying, he would soon repair to *S. Domingo* to give the admiral an account of all. He at this time was much troubled, because *Peter de Arana* had signified to him, that *Riquelme*, judge of *Bonao*, for *Roldan*, under colour of building a house for his herds, had made choice of a strong rock, that he might from thence, with a few men, do all the harm he thought fit; that he had forbid him: Whereupon *Riquelme* had drawn up a process, attested by witnesses against him, and sent it to the admiral, complaining that *Arana* used violence towards him, and praying relief, that no disorder might happen among them. Hereupon, tho' the admiral knew that man was not of a quiet disposition, yet he thought fit to conceal his jealousy, yet so as to be upon his guard, being of opinion it was enough to provide against *Ojeda*'s open intrusion, without taking notice of that which might tolerably be connived at. *Ojeda* holding his wicked purpose, and taking leave of *Roldan* in *February* 1500, went away with his ships to *Xaragua*, where a great many of those lived, who had before rebelled with *Roldan*. And because avarice is the most beneficial and ready way to promote any mischief, he began to give out among those people, that their catholick majesties had appointed him

Roldan *goes against* Ojeda.

Ojeda *stirs up the people to rebellion.*

him and *Caravajal* the admiral's councellors, that they might not suffer him to do any thing, which they did not think was for their majesties service; and that among many other things they had ordered him to do; one was, that he should immediately pay in ready money, all those that were in the island in their service; and since the admiral was not so just as to do it, he was ready to go along with them to *S. Domingo*, to oblige him to pay them out of hand; and that done, if they thought fit, to turn him out of the island dead or alive; for they ought not to rely on the agreement made, or the word he had given them, for he would keep it no longer than necessity obliged him to it. Upon these promises many resolved to follow him, and therefore being assisted by them, he one night fell upon others who opposed him, and there were some killed and wounded on both sides. And being satisfied that *Roldan*, who was returned to the admiral's service, would not join with them, they resolved to surprize and make him prisoner; but he being informed of their design, went well attended where *Ojeda* was, to put a stop to his disorders, or punish him, as he should find expedient. *Ojeda* for fear of him, retired to his ships, and *Roldan* continuing ashore, they treated about a conference, each of them fearing to put himself into the power of the other. *Roldan* perceiving that *Ojeda* was unwilling to come ashore, he offered to go treat with him aboard; to which purpose he sent to ask his boat, which he sent him well mann'd, and having taken in *Roldan* with six or seven of his followers, when they least suspected it, *Roldan* and his people on a sudden fell upon *Ojeda*'s men, with their naked swords, and killing some and wounding others, made themselves masters of the boat, returning with it to land, *Ojeda* having only a small skiff left him, in which he resolved to come peaceably to treat with *Roldan*. Having made some excuse for his offences, he agreed to restore some men he had taken by force, that his boat and men might be returned him, alledging, if it were not restored, it would be the ruin of them all and their ships, because he had no other fit to serve them. *Roldan* readily granted it, that he might have no cause to complain, or say, he was lost through his means, yet making him promise and give security that he would depart the island by a time appointed, as he was obliged to do, by the good guard *Roldan* kept ashore. But as it is a hard matter to root out cockle so that it may not sprout up again, so is it no less difficult for people that have got a habit of doing ill to forbear relapsing into their crimes, as happened to some of the rebels a few days after *Ojeda* was gone. For one *D. Ferdinand de Guevara*, being in disgrace with the admiral, as a seditions person, and having taken part with *Ojeda*, in hatred to *Roldan*, because he would not permit him to take to wife the daughter of *Canua*, the principal queen of *Xaragua*, began to gather many conspirators to secure *Roldan*, and succeed him in the ill things he had done. Particularly he gained to his party, one *Adrian de Moxica*, a chief man among the late rebels, and to other wicked men, who about the middle of *July* 1500, had contrived to secure or murder *Roldan*. He having intelligence of the design, stood upon his guard, and ordered his business so well, that he seized the aforesaid *D. Ferdinand*, *Adrian*, and the chief men of their party, and sending the admiral an account of what had happened, asked what his pleasure was he should do with them? The answer was, That since they had endeavoured, without any provocation to disturb the countrey, (and if they were not punished every thing must run to ruin) he should punish them according to their demerits, and as the law directed. The judge did it accordingly, and proceeding legally against them, hanged *Adrian* as chief author of the conspiracy, banished others, and kept *D. Ferdinand* in prison, till on the 13th of *June* he delivered him, with other prisoners, to *Gonsalo Blanco*, to carry them to *la Vega*, that is, *the Plain*, where the admiral then was. This example quieted the countrey, and the *Indians* again submitted themselves to the christians. Such rich gold mines were discovered, that every man left the king's pay, and went away to live upon his own account, applying himself to dig gold at his own expence, allowing the king the third part of all they found. This prospered so well, that a man has gathered five marks, (a mark is eight ounces) of gold in a day, and a grain of pure gold has been taken up worth above 196 ducats; and the *Indians* were submissive, dreading the admiral, and so desirous to please him, that they readily became christians only to oblige him. When any of the chief of them was to appear before him, he endeavoured to be clad; and therefore to settle all things the better, the admiral resolved to take a progress thro' the island, and accordingly he and his brother and lieutenant set out on *Wednesday* the 20th of *Feb.* 1499, and came to *Isabella* on the 19th of *March*. From *Isabella* they set out the 5th of *April* for the *Conception*, and came thither the *Tuesday* following. The lieutenant went thence for *Xaragua* upon *Friday* the 7th of *June*. On *Christmas-day*

Ojeda forced away.

Another rebellion suppress'd.

day following, which was in the year 1499, being forsaken by all the world, the *Indians* and rebel christians fell upon me, and I was reduced to such distress, that to avoid death, leaving all behind me, I put to sea in a little caraval. But our lord presently relieved me, saying, Thou man of little faith, fear not, I am with you, and so he dispersed my enemies, and show'd how he could fulfil my promises: Unhappy sinner that I am, who placed all my hopes on the world. From the *Conception* the admiral designed to go to *S. Domingo* on the 3d of *February*, in order to make ready to return into *Spain* to give their catholick majesties an account of all things.

CHAP. LXXXV.

How their catholick majesties upon false informations, and malicious complaints of some persons, sent a judge to take cognizance of affairs.

WHilst these disorders happened, as has been said, many of the rebels by letters sent from *Hispaniola*, and others that were returned into *Spain*, did not cease to give in false informations to the king and his council, against the admiral and his brothers, saying, they were cruel and unfit for that government, as well because they were strangers and aliens, as because they had not formerly been in a condition to learn by experience how to govern people of condition; affirming, that if their highnesses did not apply some remedy, those countries would be utterly destroy'd; and in case they were not quite ruined by their ill government, the admiral would revolt, and join in league with some prince to support him, he pretending that all was his own, as having been discovered by his industry and labour; and that the better to compass his design, he concealed the wealth of the countrey, and would not have the *Indians* serve the christians, nor be converted to the faith, because by making much of them he hoped they would be of his side, to do what he pleased against their highnesses. They proceeding in these and such like slanders, importuned their catholick majesties, ever talking ill of the admiral, and complaining there were several years pay due to the men, gave occasion to all that were at court to rail. So that when I was at *Granada*, at the time the most serene prince *Michael* happened to die, above 50 of them, like shameless wretches, brought a load of grapes, and sate down in the court of *Albambra*, (a castle and palace) crying out, that their highnesses and the admiral made them live so miserably by not paying them, with many other scandalous expressions. And their impudence was so great, that if the catholick king went abroad, they all got about him, crying, pay, pay. And if it happened that my brother or I, who were pages to her majesty, passed by where they were, they cried out in a hideous manner, making the sign of the cross, and saying, there are the admiral of the *Mosquito*'s sons, he that has found out false and deceitful countries, to be the ruin and burial place of the *Spanish* gentry; adding many more such insolencies which made us cautious of appearing before them. Their complaints running so high, and their constant importunity with the king's favourites, it was resolved to send a judge to *Hispaniola*, to enquire into all these affairs, ordering him in case he found the admiral guilty of what was alledged, to send him to *Spain*, and stay there himself as governor. The person their majesties made choice of for this purpose, was one *Francis de Bovadilla*, a poor knight of the order of *Calatrava*, who on the 21st of *May* 1499, had full and ample commission given him at *Madrid*, and blank letters, subscribed by their majesties, to such persons as he should think fit in *Hispaniola*, commanding them to be aiding and assisting to him. Thus furnished, he arrived at *S. Domingo* at the latter end of *August* 1500, at such time as the admiral was at the *Conception*, settling the affairs of that province, where his brother had been assaulted by the rebels, and where there were more *Indians*, and those more understanding people than in the rest of the island. So that *Bovadilla* at his arrival finding no body to keep him in awe, the first thing he did was to take up his quarters in the admiral's palace, and seize and make use of all he found there, as if it had fallen to him by inheritance; and gathering together all he could find that had been in rebellion, and many others that hated the admiral and his brothers, he presently declared himself governor. And to gain the affections of the people, he caused a general freedom to be proclaimed for 20 years to come; requiring the admiral to repair to him without any delay, because it was convenient for his majesty's service he should do so. And to back his summons on the 7th of *September*, sent him the king's letter by *F. John de la Sera*, which was to this effect.

Complaints against the admiral.

Bovadilla *the judge in* Hispaniola.

To

To *D. Christopher Columbus*, our admiral of the ocean.

W*E have ordered the commendary* Francis de Bovadilla, *the bearer, to acquaint you with some things, from us: There-fore we desire you to give him entire credit, and to obey him.* Given at *Madrid the* 21st of *May* 1499.

I the king,
I the queen.

By command of
their highnesses,
Mich. Perez de Almazan.

CHAP. LXXXVI.

How the admiral was apprehended and sent to Spain *in irons, together with his brothers.*

THE admiral having seen their majesties letter, came away presently to St. *Domingo*, where the aforesaid judge was, who being eager to remain governor there, at the beginning of *October* 1500. without any delay, or legal information, sent him prisoner a board a ship, together with his brother *James*, putting them in irons, and a good guard over them, and ordered upon severe penalties, that none should dare to speak for them. After this, (by *Abington* law) he began to draw up a process against them, admitting the rebels his enemies as witnesses, and publickly favouring all that came to speak ill of them, who in their depositions gave in such villainies and incoherencies, that he must have been blind that had not plainly perceiv'd, they were false and malicious. For which reason, their catholick majesties would not admit of them, and cleared the admiral, repenting that they had sent such a man in that employment; and not without good cause, for this *Bovadilla* ruin'd the island, and squander'd the king's revenues, that all men might be his friends, saying, their majesties would have nothing but the honour of the dominion, and that the profit should be for their subjects. Yet he neglected not his own share, but siding with the richest and most powerful men, gave them *Indians* to serve them, upon condition they should share with him all they got by their means, and sold by auction the possessions and rights the admiral had acquir'd for their majesties, saying, they were no labourers, nor did they desire to make a profit of those lands, but only kept them for the benefit of their subjects. He thus selling all things under this colour, endeavoured on the other side that they should be bought by some of his own companions, for one third of the value. Besides all this, he made no other use of his judicial power but to enrich himself, and gain the affections of the people, being still afraid lest the lieutenant, who was not yet come from *Xaragua*, should put a stop to his proceedings, and endeavour to set the admiral at liberty by force of arms; in which particular, the brothers behav'd themselves very prudently; for the admiral sent them word immediately, that they should come peaceably to him, the king's service so requiring, that the island might not be put into an uproar; for when they were in *Spain*, they should more easily obtain the punishment of such a senseless person, and satisfaction for the wrong done them. Yet this did not divert *Bovadilla* from putting him and his brothers into irons, allowing the baser sort to rail at them publickly, blowing horns about the port where they were shipp'd, besides many scandalous libels set up at corners of streets against them; so that tho' he was inform'd that one *James Ortir*, governor of the hospital, had writ a libel, and read it publickly in the market-place, he was so far from punishing of *him*, that he seem'd to be very well pleas'd, which made every one endeavour to show himself in this sort. And perhaps for fear the admiral should swim back, he took care when they were to sail, to desire *Andrew Martin* the master of the ship, to look to him, and to deliver him in irons as he was, to the bishop *D. John de Fonseca*, by whose advice and direction it was concluded he did all these things; tho' when they were at sea, the master being sensible of *Bovadilla*'s unworthiness, would have knock'd off the admiral's irons, which he would never permit, saying, that since their catholick majesties, by their letter directed him to perform whatsoever *Bovadilla* did in their name command him to do, in virtue of which authority and commission he had put him into irons, he would have none but their highnesses themselves to do their pleasure herein; and he was resolv'd to keep those fetters as relicks, and a memorial of the reward of his many services, as accordingly he did; for I always saw those irons in his room, which he order'd to be buried with his body; notwithstanding, that he having on the 20th of *November* 1500.

The practices of Bovadilla.

The admiral discharg'd. 1500. writ to their majesties, acquainting them with his arrival at *Cadiz*; they understanding the condition he came in, immediately gave orders that he should be releas'd, and sent him very gracious letters, saying, they were very sorry for his sufferings, and the unmannerly behaviour of *Bovadilla* towards him, ordering him to go to court, where care should be taken about his affairs, and he should be shortly dispatch'd with full restitution of his honour. Nevertheless, I cannot but blame their catholick majesties, who chose for that employment a base and ignorant man; for had he been a man who knew the duty of his office, the admiral himself would have been glad of his coming; since he by letter had desired that one might be sent, to take true information of the perverseness of those people, and of the crimes they committed, that they might be punish'd by another hand, he being unwilling to use that severity which an impartial person would have done, because the original of those tumults had been against his brother. And tho' it may be urg'd, that tho' their majesties had such bad accounts of the admiral, yet they ought not to send *Bovadilla* with so many letters, and such power, without limiting the commission they gave him: It may be answer'd in their behalf, that it was no wonder they did so, because the complaints against the admiral were many, as has been said above.

CHAP. LXXXVII.

How the admiral went to court to give their catholick majesties an account of himself.

AS soon as their majesties heard of the admiral's coming, and being in irons, they sent orders on the 12th of *December* for him to be set at liberty, and writ to him to repair to *Granada*, where he was received by their highnesses with a favourable aspect, and kind words, telling him, his imprisonment had not been by their desire or command, and therefore they were much offended at it, and they would take care those that were in fault should be punish'd, and full satisfaction given him. Having spoke these and such like gracious words, they order'd his business should be immediately gone upon, the result whereof was, that a governor should be sent to *Hispaniola*, who was to right the admiral and his brothers, and *Bovadilla* should be obliged to restore all he had taken from them; and that the admiral should be allow'd all that belong'd to him, according to the articles their highnesses had granted him; and that the rebels should be proceeded against and punish'd according to their offences. *Nicolas de Obando*, commendary of laws, was sent with this power; he was a wise and judicious man, but as afterwards appear'd partial, craftily concealing his passions, giving credit to his own surmises, and malicious persons; and therefore acting cruelly and revengefully, as appears by the death of the eighty kings we have spoken of before. But to return to the admiral; as their majesties were pleas'd to send *Obando* to *Hispaniola*, so they thought it proper to send the admiral upon some voyage that might turn to his advantage, and keep him employ'd till the said *Obando* could pacify and reduce the island *Hispaniola*, because they did not like to keep him so long out of his right, without any just occasion, the information sent by *Bovadilla* plainly appearing to be full of malice, and not containing any thing whereby he might forfeit his right. But there being some delay in the execution of this design, it being now the month of *October* 1500. and ill men endeavour'd to prevail that a new information might be expected, the admiral resolved to speak to their majesties, and beg of them that they would defend him against all dangers, which he afterwards repeated by letter. This they promis'd him by letter, when the admiral was ready to set out upon his voyage; the words of it are to this effect:

The admiral well receiv'd at court.

"AND be assured that your imprisonment was very displeasing to us, "which you were sensible of, and all men "plainly saw, because as soon as we heard "of it, we applied the proper remedies. "And you know with how much honour "and respect we have always ordered you "to be treated, which we now direct should "be done, and that you receive all worthy and noble usage, promising that the "privileges and prerogatives by us granted "you shall be preserv'd in ample manner, "according to the tenor of our letters patents, which you and your children shall "enjoy without any contradiction, as is "due in reason: And if it be requisite to "ratify them a-new, we will do it, and "will order that your son be put into possession of all, for we desire to honour "and favour you in greater matters than "these. And be satisfied we will take the "due

" due care of your sons and brothers, which " shall be done when you are departed; " for the employment shall be given to " your son, as has been said. We there- " fore pray you not to delay your departure. *Given at* Valentia de la Torre, *on the* 14th *of* March 1502.

This their majesties writ, because the admiral had resolved not to trouble himself any more with the affairs of the *Indies*, but to ease himself upon my brother, wherein he was in the right; for he said, that if the services he had already done were not sufficient to deserve to have those villainous people punish'd, all he could do for the future would never obtain it, since he had already perform'd the main thing he undertook before he discover'd the *Indies*, which was to show that there was a continent and islands westward, that the way was easy and navigable, the advantage visible, and the people gentle and unarm'd. All which, since he had verified himself in person, there now remained nothing but for their highnesses to pursue what was begun, sending people to discover the secrets of those countries; for now the gate was open'd, any one might follow the coast, as some did already, who improperly call themselves discoverers; not considering they have not discovered any new countrey, but that for the future they pursue the first discovery, the admiral having shown them the islands and province of *Paria*, which was the first land of the continent discover'd. Yet the admiral having always had a great inclination to serve their catholick majesties, and particularly the queen, he was content to return to his ships, and undertake the voyage we shall speak of; for he was convinced there would daily be found out great wealth, as he writ to their highnesses the year 1499. speaking of the discovery in this manner: It is not to be discontinued; for to say the truth, because one time or other something material will be found. As has since appeared by *New Spain* and *Peru*, though at that time, as generally happens to most men, no body gave credit to what he said, and yet he said nothing but what proved true, as their catholick majesties testify in a letter of theirs writ at *Barcelona* on the 5th of *September* 1498.

CHAP. LXXXVIII.

How the admiral went from Granada *to* Seville, *to fit out a fleet for another discovery.*

THE admiral having been well dispatch'd by their catholick majesties, set out from *Granada* for *Seville* in the year 1501. and being there, so earnestly sollicited the fitting out his squadron, that in a small time he had rigg'd and provided four ships, the biggest of 70, the least of 50 tun burthen, and 140 men and boys, of which number I was one.

The admiral's 4th voyage.

We set sail from *Cadiz* on the 9th of *May*, 1502. and sailed to St. *Catherine*'s, whence we parted on *Wednesday* the 11th of the same month, and went to *Arzilla* to relieve the *Portuguese*, who were reported to be in great distress; but when we came thither, the *Moors* had raised the siege. The admiral therefore sent his brother *D. Bartholomew Columbus*, and me, with the captains of the ships ashore, to visit the governor of *Arzilla*, who had been wounded by the *Moors* in an assault. He return'd the admiral thanks for the visit and his offers, and to this purpose sent some gentlemen to him, among whom some were relations to *Donna Philippa Moniz*, the admiral's wife in *Portugal*. The same day we set sail, and arriving at *Gran Canaria*, on the 20th of *May*, cast anchor among the little islands; and on the 24th went over to *Maspalomas* in the same island, there to take in wood and water for our voyage. The next night we set out for the *Indies*, and it pleas'd God the wind was so fair, that without handling the sails, on *Wednesday* the 15th of *June* we arrived at the island *Matinino* with a rough sea and wind. There, according to the custom of those that sail from *Spain* to the *Indies*, the admiral took in fresh wood and water, and made the men wash their linen, staying till *Saturday*, when we stood to the westward, and came to *Dominica*, ten leagues from the other. So running along among the *Caribbee* islands, we came to *Santa Cruz*, and on the 24th of the same month ran along the south-side of the island of St. *John*. Thence we took the way for St. *Domingo*, the admiral having a mind to exchange one of his ships for another, because it was a bad sailor, and besides, could carry no sail, but the side would lie almost under water, which was a hindrance to his voyage, because his design was to have gone directly upon the coast of *Paria*, and keep along that shore, till he came upon the streight, which he certainly concluded was about *Veragua* and *Nombre de Dios*. But seeing the fault of the ship, he was forced to repair to St. *Domingo* to change it for a better.

And

And to the end the commendary *Lores* sent by their majesties to call *Bovadilla* to an account for his male-administration, might not be surpriz'd at our unexpected arrival, upon *Wednesday* the 29th of *June*, being near the port, the admiral sent *Peter de Terreros*, captain of one of the ships to him, to signify what occasion he had to change that ship; for which reason, as also because he apprehended a great storm was coming, he desired to secure himself in that port, advising him not to let the fleet sail out of the port for eight days to come; for if he did it would be in great danger. But the aforesaid governor would not permit the admiral to come into the harbour, nor did he hinder the going out of the fleet that was bound for *Spain*, which consisted of eighteen sail, and was to carry *Bovadilla*, who had imprison'd the admiral and his brothers, *Francis Roldan*, and all the rest, who had been in rebellion against them, and done them so much harm, all whom it pleased God to infatuate, that they might not admit of the admiral's good advice. And I am satisfied it was the hand of God; for had they arrived in *Spain*, they had never been punish'd as their crimes deserv'd; but rather been favour'd and preferr'd, as being the bishop's friends. This was prevented by their setting out of that port for *Spain*; for no sooner were they come to the east point of the island *Hispaniola*, but there arose so terrible a storm, that the admiral of the fleet sunk, in which was *Bovadilla*, with most of the rebels, and made such havock among the rest, that of 18 ships, only three or four were saved. This happen'd upon *Thursday* the last of *June*, when the admiral having foreseen the storm, and being refused admittance into the port, for his security drew up as close to the land as he could, thus sheltering himself, not without much dissatisfaction among his men, who for being with him were denied that reception, which had been allowed to strangers, much more to them that were of the same nation; for they fear'd they might be so serv'd, if any misfortune should befal them for the future. And tho' the admiral was concern'd on the same account, yet it more vex'd him to behold the baseness and ingratitude us'd towards him in that countrey he had given to the honour and benefit of *Spain*, being refused to shelter his life in it. Yet his prudence and judgment secured his ships, till the next day the tempest increasing, and the night coming on very dark, three ships broke from him every one its own way: the men aboard each of them, tho' all of them in great danger, concluded the others were lost; but they that suffer'd most were those aboard the ship called *Santo*, who to save their boat, which had been ashore with the captain *Terreros*, dragg'd it a-stern, where it over-set, and were at last forced to let it go to save themselves. But the caraval *Bermuda* was in much more danger, which running out to sea, was almost cover'd with it, by which it appeared the admiral had reason to endeavour to change it; and all men concluded, that under God the admiral's brother was the saving of her, by his wisdom and resolution; for as has been said above, there was not at that time a more expert sailor than he. So that after they had all suffer'd very much, except the admiral, it pleased God they met again upon *Sunday* following in the port of *Azua*, on the south-side of *Hispaniola*, where every one giving an account of his misfortunes, it appeared that *Bartholomew Columbus* had weather'd so great a storm, by flying from land like an able sailor; and that the admiral was out of danger, by lying close to the shore like a cunning astrologer, who knew whence the danger must come. Well might his enemies blame him therefore, saying, he had rais'd that storm by art magick, to be reveng'd on *Bovadilla*, and the rest of his enemies that were with him, seeing that none of his four ships perish'd; and that of 18 which set out with *Bovadilla*, only one called *la Aguja*, or *The Needle*, the worst of them all held on its course for *Spain*, where it arrived safe, having on board 4000 peso's in gold, worth eight shillings a peso, belonging to the admiral, the other three that escap'd, returning to *S. Domingo* shatter'd, and in a distressed condition.

He foresees a great storm, and is refus'd admittance in Hispaniola.

All his ships escape

Fourteen bound for Spain *cast away.*

CHAP. LXXXIX.

How the admiral departed from Hispaniola, *and discovered the islands of* Guanaia.

THE admiral in the port of *Azua*, gave his men a breathing time after the storm; and it being one of the diversions used at sea, to fish, when there is nothing else to do, I will mention two sorts of fish among the rest, which I remember were taken there; the one of them was pleasant, the other wonderful. The first was a fish call'd *Saavina*, as big as half an ordinary bell, which lying asleep above water, was struck with a harping-iron from the boat of the ship *Bisceina*, and held so fast, that it could

Two strange fishes. could not break loose; but being tied with a long roap to the boat, drew it after it as swift as an arrow; so that those aboard the ship seeing the boat scud about, and not knowing the occasion, were astonished it should do so without the help of the oars, till at last the fish sunk, and being drawn to the ship's side, was there hall'd up with the tackle. The other fish was taken after another manner, the *Indians* call it *Manati*, and there are none of the sort in *Europe*: it is as big as a calf, nothing differing from it in the colour and taste of the flesh, but that perhaps it is better and fatter; wherefore those that affirm there are all sorts of creatures in the sea, will have it, that these fishes are real calves, since within they have nothing like a fish, and feed only on the grass they find along the banks. To return to our history; the admiral having a little refresh'd his men, and repaired his ships, left port *Azua*, and went to that of *Brasil*, which the *Indians* call *Giacchemo*, to shun another storm that was coming. Hence he sailed again on the 14th of *July*, and was so becalm'd, that instead of holding on his course, the current carried him away to certain islands near *Jamaica*, which are very small and sandy, and he called them *Los Poros*, or *The Wells*, because not finding water in them, they dug many pits in the sand, and took up that water for their use. Then sailing southward for the continent, we came to certain islands, where we went ashore upon the biggest only, called *Guanaia*, whence those that make sea charts, took occasion to call all those islands of *Guanaia*, which are almost 12 leagues from the continent, near the province now call'd *Honduras*, tho' then the admiral called it cape *Casinas*. *Great error of some sea charts.* But these men making such charts without having seen the world, they commit vast mistakes; which since it now comes in my way, I will here set down, tho' it interrupts the course of our history. These same islands and continent are by them twice set down in their charts, as if they were different countries; and whereas cape *Gracias a Dios*, and that they call cape .... are but one and the same, they make two of it. The occasion of this mistake was, that after the admiral had discovered these countries, one *John Diaz de Solis*, (from whom the river *de la Plata*, that is, of Silver or Plate, was called *Rio de Solis*, because he was there killed by the *Indians*,) and one *Vincent Yanez*, who commanded a ship the first voyage, when the admiral discover'd the *Indies*, set out together to discover in the year 1508. designing to follow along that coast the admiral had discovered in his voyage from *Veragua* westward; and he following almost the same track, they put into the coast of *Cariari*, and passed by cape *Gracias a Dios*, as far as cape *Casinas*, which they called *Honduras*, and the aforesaid islands they called *Guanaias*, giving the name of the biggest to them all. Thence they proceeded on further, without owning the admiral had been in any of those parts, that the discovery might be attributed to them, and to have it believ'd they had found large countries; notwithstanding that, *Peter de Ledesma*, one of their pilots, who had been before with the admiral in his voyage to *Veragua*, told them, he knew that countrey, and that he had been there with the admiral discovering it, from whom I afterwards had this. But the nature of the charts plainly demonstrates it; for the same thing is twice set down, and the island is in the same shape, and at the same distance, they having at their return brought a true draught of that countrey, only saying, it lay beyond that which the admiral had discover'd. So that the same countrey is twice describ'd in one chart; which, if it please God, time will make appear, when that coast is better known; for they will find but one countrey of that sort, as has been said. But to return to our discovery, being come to the island of *Guanaia*, the admiral order'd his brother *Bartholomew Columbus* to go ashore with two boats, where they found people like those of the other islands, but not of such high foreheads. They also saw abundance of pine-trees and pieces of *Lapis Calaminaris*, us'd to mix with copper, which some seamen taking for gold, kept hid a long time.

The admiral's brother being ashore in that island, very desirous to know something of it, fortune so order'd it, that a canoe as long as a galley, and eight foot wide, all of one tree, and like the others *A cover'd canoe.* in shape, put in there, being loaded with commodities brought from the westward, and bound towards *New Spain*. In the midst of it was a covering like an awning made of palm-tree leaves, not unlike those of the *Venetian Gondola's*, which kept all under it so close, that neither rain nor sea-water could wet the goods. Under this awning were the children, the women, and all the goods, and tho' there were 25 men aboard this canoe, they had not the courage to defend themselves against the boats that pursued them. The canoe being thus taken without any opposition, was carried aboard, where the admiral blessed God, for that it had pleased him at once to give him samples of the commodities of that countrey, without exposing his men to any danger. He therefore order'd such things to be taken, as he judg'd most sightly and valuable

What goods they had.

valuable; such as some quilts, and shirts of cotton, without sleeves, curiously wrought and dy'd of several colours, and some small clouts to cover their privities, of the same sort; and large sheets in which the *Indian* women aboard the canoe wrapp'd themselves, as the *Moorish* women at *Granada* us'd to do; and long wooden swords with a channel on each side, where the edge should be, in which there were sharp edges of flint fix'd with thread, and a bituminous sort of matter, which cut naked men, as if they were of steel, and hatchets to cut wood like those of stone the other *Indians* use, but that these were made of good copper; also bells of the same metal, plates, and crucibles to melt the metal. For their provision they had such roots and grain as they in *Hispaniola* eat, and a sort of liquor made of *Maiz*, like the *English* beer; and abundance of *Cacao* nuts, which in *New Spain* pass for money, which they seemed to value very much; for when they were brought aboard among their other goods, I observ'd that when any of these nuts fell, they all stoop'd to take it up, as if it had been a thing of great consequence: yet at that time they seem'd to be in a manner besides themselves, being brought prisoners out of their canoe aboard the ship, among such strange and fierce people, as we are to them; but so prevalent is avarice in man, that we ought not to wonder that it mould prevail upon the *Indians* above the apprehension of the danger they were in. I must add, that we ought to admire their modesty; for it falling out, that in getting them aboard, some were taken by the clouts they had before their privities, they would immediately clap their hands to cover them; and the women would hide their faces, and wrap themselves up as we said the *Moorish* women do at *Granada*. This mov'd the admiral to use them well, to restore their canoe, and give them some things in exchange for those that had been taken from them. Nor did he keep any one of them, but an old man, whose name was *Giumbe*, that seemed to be the wisest and chief of them, to learn something of him concerning the countrey, and that he might draw others to converse with the christians, which he did very readily and faithfully all the while we sailed where his language was understood. Therefore, as a reward for this his service, when we came where he was not understood, the admiral gave him some things, and sent him home very well pleased, which was before he came to cape *Gracias a Dios*, on the coast of *Orecchia*, whereof mention has been made already.

Modesty of the Indians.

CHAP. XC.

How the admiral would not go to New Spain, *but sail to the eastward to find out the streight in the continent.*

NOtwithstanding the admiral had heard so much from those in the canoe, concerning the great wealth, politeness, and ingenuity of the people westward towards *New Spain*; yet thinking that those countries lying to the leeward, he could sail thither when he thought fit from *Cuba*, he would not go that way at this time, but held on his design of discovering the streight in the continent, to clear a way into the *South Sea*, which was what he aim'd at in order to come at the countries that produce spice, and therefore resolved to sail eastward towards *Veragua* and *Nombre de Dios*, where he imagin'd the said streight to be, as in effect it was; yet was he deceiv'd in the matter; for he did not conceit it to be an *Isthmus*, or narrow neck of land, but a small gulph running from sea to sea. Which mistake might proceed from the likeness of the names; for when they said the streight was at *Veragua* and *Nombre de Dios*, it might be understood either of land or water; and he took it in the most usual sense, and for that he most earnestly desir'd. And yet tho' that streight is land, yet it was and is the way to the dominion of both seas, and by which such immense riches have been discovered and conveyed; for it was God's will, a matter of such vast concern should not be otherwise found out, that canoe having given the first information concerning *New Spain*.

There being nothing therefore in those islands of *Guanaia* worth taking notice of, he without further delay sailed in order to seek out the streight towards the continent, to a point he called *Casinas*, because there were abundance of trees that bear a sort of fruit that is rough, as a spungy bone, and is good to eat, especially boil'd; which fruit the *Indians* of *Hispaniola* call *Casinas*. There appearing nothing worth taking notice of all about that countrey, the admiral would not lose time to go into a great bay, the land makes there, but held on his course eastwards along that coast, which runs along the same way to cape *Gracias a Dios*, and

The admiral sails eastward.

and is very low and open. The people nearest to cape *Casinas*, wear those painted shirts or jerkins before-mentioned, the clouts before their privities, which were like coats of mail made of cotton strong enough to defend them against their weapons, and even to bear off the stroke of some of ours.

But the people higher eastward towards cape *Gracias a Dios*, are almost black, of a fierce aspect, go stark naked, are very savage, and as the *Indian* that was taken, said, eat mens flesh, and raw fish just as it is taken. They have their ears bored with such large holes, that they may put a hens egg into them, which made the admiral call that coast *de las Orejas*, or *of the Ears.* There on *Sunday* the fourteenth of *August* 1502, *Bartholomew Columbus* went ashore in the morning with the colours, the captains, and many of the men, to hear mass; and on *Wednesday* following, when the boats went ashore to take possession of the countrey for their catholick majesties, above a hundred men ran down to the shore, loaded with provisions; who as soon as the boats came ashore came before the lieutenant, and on a sudden retired back without speaking a word. He ordered they should give them horse-bells, beads, and other things; and by means of the aforesaid interpreter, inquired concerning the countrey; tho' he having been but a short time with us, did not understand the christians, by reason of the distance of his countrey from *Hispaniola*, where several persons aboard the ships had learnt the *Indian* language. Nor did he understand those *Indians*; but they being pleased with what had been given them, came the next day to the same place, above two hundred of them loaded with several sorts of provisions, as hens of that countrey, which are better than ours, geese, roasted fish, red and white beans, like kidney beans, and other things like those they have in *Hispaniola.* The countrey was green and beautiful, tho' low, producing abundance of pines, oaks, palm-trees of seven sorts, and *Mirobalans* of those of *Hispaniola* they call *Hobi*, and almost all sorts of provisions that island affords were here to be found. Abundance of leopards, deer, and other sorts of fish there are in the islands and in *Spain.* The people of this countrey are much like those of the islands, but that their foreheads are not so high, nor do they seem to have any religion. There are several languages among them, and for the most part they go naked, but cover their privities; some wear short jumps down to their navel without sleeves, their arms and bodies have figures wrought on them with fire, which make them look oddly; and some have lions, others deer, and others castles with towers, and other things painted on their bodies. Instead of caps, the better sort of them wear red and white cloths of cotton; and some have locks of hair hanging on their foreheads. But when they are to be fine against a festival day, they colour their faces, some black, and some red; others draw streaks of several colours; others paint their nose, and others black their eyes; and thus they adorn themselves to appear beautiful, whereas in truth they look like devils.

CHAP. XCI.

How the admiral left the coast called de las Orejas, *and by cape* Gracias a Dios, *came to* Cariari, *and what he did and saw there.*

THE admiral sailed along the said coast *de las Orejas* eastward to cape *Gracias a Dios*, which was so called, because there being but sixty leagues to it from cape *Casinas*, we laboured seventy days by reason of of the currents and contrary winds upon the tack to gain it, standing out to sea, and then making the shore, sometimes gaining and sometime losing ground, as the wind was scant or large when we came about. And had not the coast afforded such good anchoring we had been much longer upon it; but being clear, and having two fathom water half a league from the shore, and two more at every leagues distance; we had always the conveniency of anchoring at night when there was but little wind, so that the course was navigable by reason of the good anchoring, but with difficulty.

When on the fourteenth of *September* we came up to the cape, perceiving the land turned off to the south, and that we could conveniently continue our voyage with those *Levant* winds that reigned there, and had been so contrary to us, we all in general gave thanks to God, for which reason the admiral called this cape *Gracias a Dios.* *Cape* Gracias a Dios. A little beyond it, we passed by some dangerous sands that ran out to sea, as far as the eye could reach.

It being requisite to take in wood and water; on the sixteenth of *September*, the admiral sent the boats to a river that seemed to be deep, and to have a good entrance, but the coming out proved not so; for winds freshing from sea, and the waves running high against the current of the river, so distressed the boats, that one of them was

was lost with all the men in it, wherefore the admiral called it the river *de la Desgratia*, that is, of the disaster.

In this river and about it, there were canes as thick as a man's leg; and on *Sunday* the twenty fifth of *September*, still running southward, we came to an anchor near a little island called *Quiriviri*, and a town on the continent, the name whereof was *Cariari*, where were the best people, countrey, and situation, we had yet seen; as well because it was high, full of rivers, and abounding in trees, as because the island was thick wooded, and full of forests of palm, mirobalan, and other sorts of trees. For this reason, the admiral called it *Hucite*. It is a small league from the town the *Indians* call *Cariari*, which is near a great river, whither resorted a great multitude of people from the adjacent parts, some with bows and arrows, others with staves of palm-tree, as black as a coal, and hard as a horn, pointed with the bones of fishes, others with clubs; and they came together as if they meant to defend their countrey. The men had their hair braided and wound about their heads; the women short like ours. But perceiving we were peaceable people, they were very desirous to barter their commodities for ours, theirs were arms, cotton-jerkins, and large pieces like sheets, and *Guaninies*, which is pale gold, they wear about their necks, as we do relicks. These things they swam with to the boats, for the christians went not ashore that day nor the next; nor would the admiral allow any thing of theirs to be taken, that we might not be taken for men that value their goods, but gave them some of ours. The less they saw us value the exchange, the more eager they were, making abundance of signs from land. At last, perceiving no body went ashore, they took all the things that had been given them, without reserving any, and tying them together, left them in the same place where the boats first went ashore, and where our men found them on the *Wednesday* following when they landed. The *Indians* about this place, believing, that the *Christians* did not confide in them, they sent an ancient man of an aweful presence with a flag upon a staff, and two girls, the one about eight, the other about fourteen years of age, who putting them into the boat, made signs that the christians might safely land. Upon their request, they went ashore to take in water, the *Indians* taking great care not to do any thing that might fright the christians, and when they saw them return to their ships, they made signs to them to take along with them the young girls with their *Guaninies* about their necks, and at the request of the old man that conducted them, they complied and carried them aboard. Wherein those people showed more friendly than others had done; and in the girls appeared an undauntedness. For tho' the christians were such strangers to them, they express no manner of concern, but always looked pleasant and modest, which made the admiral treat them well, cloathed, fed, and set them ashore again, where the fifty men were, and the old man that had delivered them received them again with much satisfaction. The boats going ashore again that same day, found the same people with the girls, who restored all the christians had given them. The next day the admiral's brother going ashore to learn something of those people, two of the chief men came to the boat, and taking him by the arms between them, made him sit down upon the grass; and he asking some questions of them, ordered the secretary to write down what they answered; but they seeing the pen, ink, and paper, were in such a consternation, that most of them ran away, which, as was believed, they did for fear of being bewitched; for to us they seemed to be sorcerers, or superstitious people, and that not without reason; because, when they came near the christians they scattered some powder about them in the air, and burning some of the same powder endeavoured to make the smoak go towards the christians; besides, their refusing to keep any thing that belonged unto us, shewed a jealousy, for, as they say, *a knave thinks every man like himself*. Having staid here longer than was convenient, considering the haste we were in, after repairing the ships, and provided all we wanted, upon *Sunday* the second of *October*, the admiral ordered his brother to go ashore with some men to view that *Indian* town, and learn something of their manners, and the nature of the countrey. The most remarkable things they saw were, in a great wooden palace covered with canes, several tombs, in one of which there was a dead body dry'd up and embalmed; in another, two bodies, wrapped up in cotton sheets without any ill scent; and over each tomb, was a board with the figures of beasts carved on it; and on some of them, the effigies of the person buried there, adorned with *Guaninies*, beads, and other things they most value. These being the most civilized *Indians* in those parts, the admiral ordered one to be taken, and learn of him the secrets of the countrey; and of seven that were taken, two of the chiefest were picked out, and the rest sent away with some gifts, and civil entertainment, that the countrey might not be left in an uproar, telling them, they were to serve as guides

Indians of Cariari civilized.

guides upon that coast, and then be set at liberty. But they believing they were taken out of covetousness, that they might ransom themselves with their goods and things of value, the next day abundance of them came down to the shore, and sent four aboard the admiral, as their ambassadors, to treat about the ransom, offering some things, and freely giving two hogs of the countrey, which tho' small, are very wild. The admiral therefore observing the policy of this people, was more desirous to be acquainted with them, and would not depart till he had learnt something of them, but would not give ear to their offers. He therefore ordered some trifles to be given to the messengers, that they might not go away dissatisfied, and that they should be paid for their hogs, one of which was hunted after this manner. Among other creatures that countrey produces, there is a kind of cats of a greyish colour, and as big as a small greyhound, but have a longer tail, and so strong, that whatsoever they clap it about is as it were tied with a rope. These run about the trees like the squirrels, leaping from one to another; and when they leap, they do not only hold fast with their claws, but with their tail too, by which they often hang, either to rest them, or sport. It happened that one *Ballester* brought one of these cats out of a wood, having knocked him off a tree, and not daring to meddle with it when down, because of its fierceness, he cut off one of his fore legs, and carrying it so wounded aboard; it frighted a good dog they had; but put one of the hogs they had brought us into a much greater fear; for as soon as the swine saw the cat, it run away, with signs of much dread, which we were surprized at; because before this happened, the hog ran at every body, and would not let the dog rest upon the deck. The admiral therefore ordered it to be put close to the cat, which presently wound her tail about its snout, and with that fore-leg it had left, fastened on its pole to bite it, the hog for fear grunting most violently. By this we perceived that these cats hunt like the wolves or dogs in *Spain*.

Indian *swine, and a fierce wild cat.*

CHAP. XCII.

How the admiral went from Cariari, *to* Caravaro *and* Veragua, *till he came to* Portavelo, *all along a very fruitful coast.*

Bay *of* Caravaro.

UPON *Wednesday* the 5th of *October*, the admiral sailed, and came to the bay of *Caravaro*, which is six leagues in length, and above three in breadth; where there are many small islands, and two or three channels to get in or out at any time. Within these islands the ships sail as it were in streets between islands, the leaves of the trees striking against the shrouds. As soon as we anchored in this bay, the boats went to one of the islands, where there were twenty canoes upon the shore, and the people by, as naked as they were born, and had only a gold plate about their neck, and some an eagle of gold. These, without showing any tokens of fear, the two *Indians* of *Cariari* interpreting, gave a gold plate for three horse-bells; it weighed ten ducats, and they said there was great plenty of that metal up the continent not far from them.

The next day being the seventh of *October*, the boats went ashore upon the continent, where meeting ten canoes full of people, and they refusing to chaffer away their gold plates, two of the chief of them were taken, that the admiral might learn something of them with the assistance of two interpreters. The gold plate one of them wore weigh'd fourteen ducats, and the other's eagle twenty two. These said, that a day or two's journey up the countrey, there was abundance of gold found in some places which they named. In the bay a vast deal of fish was taken, and ashore there were abundance of those creatures above-mentioned at *Cariari*; also great plenty of their food, such as roots, grain, and fruit. The men, who are painted all over face and body of several colours, as red, black and white, go naked, only covering their privities with a narrow cotton cloth.

Product of the countrey.

From this bay of *Caravaro*, we went to another close by it, called *Aburena*, which in some measure is like the other.

Aburena.

On the seventeenth we put out to sea to continue our voyage; and being come to *Guaiga*, a river twelve leagues from *Aburena*, the admiral commanded the boats to go ashore, which as they were doing, they saw above a hundred *Indians* on the strand, who assaulted them furiously, running up to the middle into the water, brandishing their spears, blowing horns, and beating a drum in warlike manner, to defend their countrey, throwing the salt water towards the christians, chewing herbs and spurting it towards them. Our men not stirring endeavoured to appease them, as they did, for at last they drew near to exchange the gold plates

plates they had about their necks, some for two, and some for three horse bells, by which means we got sixteen gold plates, worth a hundred and fifty ducats. The next day being *Friday* the nineteenth of *October*, the boats went to land again to barter; yet before any christian went ashore, they called to some *Indians*, who were under some bowers they had made that night to defend their countrey, fearing the christians would land to do them some wrong. Tho' they called never so much, yet none of them would come, nor would the christians land without knowing first what mind they were in: for, as afterwards appeared, they waited in order to fall on them as soon as they landed. But perceiving they came not out of the boats, they blew their horns, beat the drum, and making a great noise, ran into the water, as they had done the day before, till they came almost to the boats, making signs as if they would cast their javelins if they did not return to their ships. The christians offended at this their proceeding, that they might not be so bold, and despise them, wounded one with an arrow in the arm, and fired a cannon, at which they were so frighted, that all ran away to land. Then four christians landed, and calling them back, they came very peaceably, leaving their arms behind them, and exchanged three gold plates, saying, they had no more, because they came not provided for to trade, but to fight.

All the admiral looked for in this journey, was to get samples of what those parts afforded; and therefore without farther delay, he proceeded to *Catiba*, and cast anchor in the mouth of a great river. The people of the countrey were seen to gather, calling one another with horns and drums; and afterwards sent a canoe with two men in it to the ships, who having talked with the *Indians* that wete taken at *Cariari*, presently came aboard the admiral without any apprehension of fear; and by the advice of those *Indians*, gave the admiral two plates of gold they had about their necks, and he in return gave them some baubles of ours. When these were gone ashore, there came another canoe with three men wearing plates hanging at their necks, who did as the first had done. Amity thus settled, our men went ashore, where they found abundance of people with their king, who differed in nothing from the rest, but that he was covered with one leaf of a tree, because at that time it rained hard; and to give his subjects a good example, he exchanged a plate, and bid them barter for theirs; which in all were nineteeen of pure gold. This was the first place in the *Indies* where they saw any sign of a structure, which was a great mass of wall, or imagery, that to them seemed to be of lime and stone; the admiral ordered a piece of it to be brought away as a memorial of that antiquity.

Catiba.

He went away eastward, and came to *Cobravo*, the people of which place lie near the rivers of that coast; and because none came down to the strand, and the wind blew fresh, he held on his course, and went on to five towns of great trade, among which was *Veragua*, where the *Indians* said the gold was gathered and the plates made.

The next day he came to a town, called *Cubiga*, where the *Indians* of *Cariari* said the trading countrey ended, which began at *Carabora*, and ran as far as *Cubiga*, for fifty leagues along the coast.

The admiral without making any stay, went on till he put into *Porto Bello*, giving it that name, because it is large, beautiful, well-peopled, and encompassed by a well cultivated countrey. He entered this place on the second of *November*, passing between two small islands, within which the ships may lie close to the shore, and turn it out if they have occasion. The countrey about that harbour higher up, is not very rough, but tilled and full of houses, a stone's throw or a bow shot one from the other; and it looks like the finest landskip a man can imagine. During seven days we continued there on account of the rain and ill weather, there came continually canoes from all the countrey about to trade for provisions, and bottoms of fine spun cotton which they gave for some trifles, such as points and pins. Porto Bello.

CHAP. XCIII.

How the admiral came to port Bastimentos, *or* Nombre de Dios, *and continued his voyage till he put into* Retrete.

ON *Wednesday* the 9th of *November*, we sail'd out of *Porto Bello*, eight leagues to the eastward; but the next day were forced back four leagues by stress of weather, and put in among the islands near the continent, where is now the town of *Nombre de Dios*; and because all those small islands were full of grain, he call'd it, *Puerto de Bastimentos*; that is, the port of provisions. Puerto de Bastimentos.

There

There a boat well mann'd, purſuing a canoe, the *Indians* imagining our men would do them ſome harm, and perceiving the boat was within leſs than a ſtone's throw of them, they all threw themſelves into the water to ſwim away, as in effect they did; for tho' the boat row'd hard, it could not in half a league the purſuit laſted, overtake any of them; or if it did happen to overtake one, he would dive like a duck, and come up again a bow-ſhot or two from the place. This chaſe was very pleaſant, ſeeing the boat labour in vain, which at laſt returned empty.

Here we continued till the 23d of *November*, refitting the ſhips, and mending our caſk; and that day we ſailed eaſtward to a place called *Guiga*, there being another of the ſame name between *Veragua* and *Cerago*. The boats going aſhore, found above 300 perſons on it, ready to trade for ſuch proviſions as they have, and ſome ſmall things of gold they wore hanging at their ears and noſes.

But without making any ſtay here, on *Saturday* the 24th of *November*, we put into a ſmall port, which was called *Retrete*, that is, retir'd place, becauſe it could not contain above five or ſix ſhips together, and the mouth of it was not above 15 or 20 paces over, and on both ſides of it rocks appearing above water as ſharp as diamonds; and the channel between them was ſo deep that they found no bottom, tho' if the ſhips inclin'd never ſo little to either ſide, the men might leap aſhore, which was it that ſav'd the ſhips in that narrow place, which was the fault of thoſe who went in the boats to view it, they being covetous to deal with the *Indians*, and perceiving the ſhips would lie there conveniently for it, cloſe to the ſhore. In this place we continued nine days with bad weather; and at firſt the *Indians* came very familiarly to trade for ſuch as they had, but when they ſaw the chriſtians ſteal privately out of their ſhips they retir'd to their houſes, becauſe the ſeamen like covetous, diſſolute men, committed a thouſand inſolencies; inſomuch that they provok'd the *Indians* to break the peace, and ſome ſkirmiſhes hapned between them. They increaſing daily, took courage to come up to the ſhips, which, as we ſaid, lay with their ſides cloſe to the ſhore, thinking to do ſome harm, which deſign of theirs had turn'd to their own detriments, had not the admiral always endeavoured to gain them by patience and civility: but at laſt, perceiving their inſolence, to ſtrike a terror into them, he caus'd ſome pieces of cannon to be fir'd, which they anſwer'd with ſhouts, threſhing the trees with ſtaves, and threatening by ſigns, ſhewing they did not fear the noiſe, for they thought it had been only a thundering to terrify them. Therefore to abate their pride, and make them not contemn the chriſtians, the admiral cauſed a ſhot to be made at a company of them that was got together upon a hillock, and the ball falling in the midſt of them, made them ſenſible there was a thunderbolt as well as thunder; ſo that for the future they durſt not appear, even behind the mountains. The people of this countrey were the propereſt they had yet ſeen among the *Indians*, for they were tall and ſpare, without any great bellies, and well countenanced.

Retrete, *a very ſmall port.*

War with Indians.

The countrey was all plain, bearing little graſs, and a few trees; and in the harbour there were vaſt great *Crocodiles* or *Alligators*, which go out to ſtay and ſleep aſhore, and ſcatter a ſcent as if all the muſk in the world were together; but they are ſo ravenous and cruel, that if they find a man ſleeping, they drag him to the water to devour him, tho' they are fearful and cowardly when attack'd. Theſe *Alligators* are found in many other parts of the continent, and ſome do affirm they are the ſame as the *Crocodiles* of *Nile*.

Alligators.

CHAP. XCIV.

How the admiral being drove by ſtreſs of weather, ſtood again to weſtward, to get intelligence concerning the mines, and enquire concerning Veragua.

ON *Monday* the 5th of *December*, the admiral perceiving the violent eaſt and north-eaſt winds did not ceaſe, and that there was no trading with thoſe people, he reſolved to go back, to be ſatisfied concerning what the *Indians* ſaid of the mines of *Veragua*, and therefore that day he return'd to *Porto Bello*, ten leagues weſtward; and continuing his courſe the next day, was aſſaulted by a weſt wind, which was oppoſite to his new deſign, but favourable to that he had for three months paſt. But he believing this wind would not laſt long, did not alter his courſe, but bore up againſt the wind for ſome days, becauſe the weather was unſettled; and when the weather ſeem'd a little favourable to go to *Veragua*, another wind would ſtart up and drive him towards *Porto Bello*; and when we were moſt in hopes to get into port, we were quite beat off again, and ſometimes with ſuch thunder and lightning, that the men durſt

not

not open their eyes, the ships seem'd to be just sinking, and the sky to come down. Sometimes the thunder was so continued, that it was concluded, some ship fired its cannon to desire assistance. Another time there would fall such storms of rain, that it would last violently for two or three days, insomuch that it look'd like another universal deluge. This perplex'd all the men, and made them almost despair, seeing they could not get half an hour's rest, being continually wet, turning sometimes one way, and sometimes another, struggling against all the elements, and dreading them all; for in such dreadful storms, they dread the fire in flashes of lightning, the air for its fury, the water for the terrible waves, and the earth for the hidden rocks and sands which sometimes a man meets with near the port, where he hop'd for safety, and not knowing them, chuses rather to contend with the other elements in whom he has less share.

Terrible tempests for many days.

Besides all these terrors, there occur'd another no less dangerous and wonderful, which was a spout rising from the sea, on *Tuesday* the 13th of *December*, which if they had not dissolv'd by saying the gospel of St. *John*, it had certainly sunk whatsoever it fell upon; for as has been said, it draws the water up to the clouds like a pillar, and thicker than a butt, twisting it about like a whirlwind. That same night we lost sight of the ship called *Caino*, and had the good fortune to see it again after three dreadful dark days, though it had lost its boat, and been in great danger, being so near land as to cast anchor, which it lost at long run, being forced to cut the cable. Now it appeared that the currents on that coast follow the wind, running westward with the east-wind, and the contrary, the water still going after the prevailing wind. The ships being now almost shattered to pieces with the tempest, and the men quite spent with labour, a day or two's calm gave them some respite, and brought such multitudes of sharks about the ships, that they were dreadful to behold, especially for such as are superstitious; because, as it is reported, that ravens at a great distance smell out dead bodies; so some think these sharks do, which if they lay hold of a man's arm or leg, cut it off like a razor, for they have two rows of teeth in the nature of a saw. Such a multitude of these was killed with the hook and chain, that being able to destroy no more, they lay swimming upon the water, and they are so greedy, that they do not only bite at carrion, but may be taken with a red rag upon the hook. I have seen a tortoise taken out of the belly of one of these sharks, and it afterwards liv'd aboard the ship; but out of another was taken the whole head of one of his own kind, we having cut it off and thrown it into the water, as not good to eat, no more than they are themselves, and that shark had swallowed it; and to us it seem'd contrary to reason, that one creature should swallow the head of another of its own bigness, which is not to be admired, because their mouth reaches almost to their belly, and the head is shaped like an olive. Tho' some look'd upon them to forebode mischief, and others thought them bad fish, yet we all made much of them, by reason of the want we were in, having been now above 8 months at sea, so that we had consum'd all the fish and flesh brought from *Spain*; and what with the heat and moisture of the sea, the bisket was so full of maggots, that, as God shall help me, I saw many that staid till night to eat the pottage or brewice made of it, that they might not see the maggots; and others were so us'd to eat them, that they did not mind to throw them away when they saw them, because they might lose their supper if they were so very curious.

Multitudes of sharks.

Upon *Saturday* the 17th, the admiral put into a port 3 leagues east of *Pennon*, which the *Indians* called *Huiva*. It was like a great bay, where we rested 3 days, and going ashore, saw the inhabitants dwell upon the tops of trees, like birds, laying sticks across from bough to bough, and building huts upon them, rather than houses. Tho' we knew not the reason of this strange custom, yet we guess'd it was done for fear of the griffins there are in that countrey, or of enemies; for all along that coast, the people at every league distance are great enemies to one another.

We sailed from this port on the 20th with fair weather, but not settled; for as soon as we were got out to sea, the tempest began to rage again, and drove us into another port, whence we departed again the third day, the weather seeming somewhat mended, but like an enemy that lies in wait for a man, rush'd out again, and forced us to *Pennon*, where when we hop'd to put in, the wind started up so contrary, that we were drove again towards *Veragua*. Being at an anchor in the river, the weather became again so stormy, that all the favour we had from it, was, that it allowed us to get into that port, where we had been before on *Thursday* the 12th of the same month. Here we continued from the 2d day in *Christmas*, till the 3d of *January* the following year 1503. when having repair'd the ship called *Gallega*, and taken aboard abundance of *Indian* wheat, water, and wood, we turn'd back towards *Veragua* with bad weather, and contrary winds, which chang'd crosly, just as the admiral alter'd his course. And this was so strange and unheard of a thing, that I would not have repeated so many changes, if, besides by being then present, I had not seen the same written by *James Mendez*, who sail'd with the canoes of *Jamaica*, whereof I shall speak hereafter, and writ an account of this voyage; and the letter the admiral sent by him to their catholick majesties, which is printed, will inform the reader how great our sufferings were, and how much fortune persecuted him she ought most to favour. But to return to the changes of weather, and of our course, which put us to so much trouble between *Veragua* and *Porto Bello*, for which reason, that coast was called *Costa de Contrasses*, that is, coast of thwartings.

Wonderful changes of weather.

Upon *Thursday*, being the feast of the *Epiphany*, we cast anchor near a river, which the *Indians* call *Yebra*, and the admiral nam'd *Belem*, or *Bethlem*, because we came to that place upon the feast of the three kings. He caus'd the mouth of that river, and of another westward, to be sounded; the latter the *Indians* call *Veragua*, where he found but shoal water, and in that of *Belem*, 4 fathom at high water. The boats went up this river to the town, where they were inform'd the gold mines of *Veragua* were. At first the *Indians* were so far from conversing, that they assembled with their weapons, to hinder the christians landing. The next day, our boats going to the river of *Veragua*, the *Indians* there did as the others had done, and that not only ashore, but stood upon their guard with their canoes in the water. But an *Indian* of that coast, who understood them a little, going ashore with the christians, and telling them, we were good people, and desir'd nothing but what we paid for, they were somewhat pacified, and truck'd 20 gold plates, some hollow pieces like joints of reeds, and some grains never melted; which to make their value the more, they said were gathered a great way off upon uncouth mountains; and that when they gather'd it, they did not eat, nor carry women along with them, which same thing the people of *Hispaniola* said, when it was first discovered.

Indian policy.

CHAP. XCV.

How the admiral went into the river of Belem, *and resolv'd to build a town there and leave his brother the lieutenant in it.*

On monday the 9th of *January*, the admiral's ship, and that called *Biscaina*, went up the river; and the *Indians* came presently to truck for such things as they had, particularly fish, which at certain times of the year comes out of the sea up these rivers in such quantities as seems incredible to such as do not see it; and they exchang'd some little gold for pins, and those things they most valued, they gave for beads or hawks-bells. Next day the other two ships came in; which they had not done at first, because there being but little water at the mouth of the river, they were forced to stay for the flood; tho' there the sea never rises or falls above half a fathom.

Trade with the Indians.

Veragua being fam'd for mines and extraordinary wealth, the third day after our arrival, the admiral's brother went up the river with the boats to the town of *Quibio*, so the *Indians* call their king, who hearing of the lieutenant's coming, came down the river in his canoes to meet him. They met in very friendly manner, giving one another interchangeably such things as they valu'd most, and having discours'd a long time together, every one went away peaceably. Next day the said *Quibio* came aboard to visit the admiral, and having discours'd together about an hour, the admiral gave him some things, and his men truck'd bells for some gold, and so he return'd without any ceremony the same way he came.

We being thus very easie and secure, on *Wednesday* the 24th of *January*, the river of *Belem* suddenly swell'd so high, that before we could provide against it, or carry a cable ashore, the fury of the water came so impetuously against the admiral's ship, that it broke one of its two anchors, and drove her with such force against the ship *Gallega*, which lay a-stern of it, that it brought the foremast by the board, and were both carried away foul of one another in utmost danger of perishing. Some judg'd the mighty rains to have been the cause of this mighty flood, they having never ceased all the winter in that countrey; but had that been it, the river would have swell'd by degrees, and not all on a sudden, which made it be believed some great shower had fallen on the mountains of *Veragua*, which the admiral called St. *Christophers*, because the highest of them was above the region of the air, where meteors are bred; for no cloud was ever seen above, but all below

A dangerous sudden flood.

below it. To look to, it is like an hermitage, and lies at least 20 leagues up the countrey, in the midst of woody mountains, whence we believed that flood came which was so dangerous, that tho' it brought water enough to carry the ships out to sea, the wind was then so boisterous, that they must have been shatter'd to pieces at the mouth of the river, distant half a mile from whence they broke loose. This tempest lasted so long, that we had time enough to refit and caulk the ships. The waves broke so furiously upon the mouth of the river, that the boats could not go out to discover along the coast, to learn where the mines lay, and chuse a place to build a town; the admiral having resolved to leave his brother there with most of the men, that they might settle and subdue that countrey, whilst he went to *Spain* to send supplies of men and provisions: Upon this prospect, the weather growing calmer, on *Monday* the 6th of *February*, he sent his brother with 68 men by sea to the mouth of *Veragua* river, a league distant from *Belem* westward, and he went a league and a half up the river, to the *Cacique*'s town, where he staid a day enquiring out the way to the mines.

On *Wednesday* they travel'd four leagues and a half and came to lie near a river, which they pass'd 44 times, and the next day advanced a league and a half towards the mines, show'd them by *Indians* sent by *Quibio* to guide them. In two hours time after they came thither, every man gather'd some gold about the roots of the trees, which were there very thick, and of a prodigious height. This sample was much valued, because none of those that went had any tools to dig, or had ever gather'd any. Therefore the design of their journey being only to get information of the mines, they return'd very well pleas'd that same day to *Veragua*, and the next to the ships. True it is, that, as was afterwards known, these mines, were not those of *Veragua*, which lay much nearer, but of *Urira*, a town whose people are enemies to those of *Veragua*, to do whom a displeasure, *Quibio* ordered the christians to be conducted thither, and that they might go away to those and leave his.

Gold Mines of Urira.

CHAP. XCVI.

How the admiral's brother went to see some towns of that province; with an account of the countrey, and customs of those people.

ON *Thursday* the 14th of *February* 1503, the admiral's brother went into the countrey with 40 Men, a boat following with 14. The next day they came to the river of *Urira*, 7 leagues from *Belem* westward. The *Cacique* came out a league from his town to meet him, with 20 Men, and presented him with such things as they feed on, and some gold plates were exchang'd here. Whilst they were here, the *Cacique*, and chief men, never ceased putting a dry herb into their mouths and chewing it, and sometimes they took a sort of powder they carried with that herb, which looks very odd. Having rested here a while, the christians and *Indians* went together to the town, where abundance of people came out to them, and assign'd them a great house to lie in, giving them much to eat. Soon after came the *Cacique* of *Dururi*, which is a neighbouring town, with a great many *Indians*, who brought some gold plates to truck; all these *Indians* said, there were *Caciques* up the countrey, who had plenty of gold, and abundance of men arm'd like ours. Next day, the lieutenant ordered the rest of his men to return by land to the ships, and he with thirty, he kept with him, held on his journey towards *Zobraba*, where the fields for above 6 leagues were all full of *Maiz*, like corn-fields. Thence he went to *Cateba*, another town; at both places he was well entertained, abundance of provisions given him, and some gold plates truck'd, which, as has been said, are like the paten of a chalice, some bigger and some less, weighing 12 ducats more or less; they wear them about their necks, hanging by a string, as we do relicks. The lieutenant being now very far from the ships, without finding any port along that coast, or any river bigger than that of *Belem* to settle his colony, he came back the same way on the 24th of *February*, bringing above —— ducats in gold he had exchanged for. As soon as he return'd, presently order was taken for his stay, and 80 men being appointed to remain with him, they agreed by ten and ten, or more or less in a gang, and began to build houses upon the bank of the aforesaid river of *Belem*, about a cannon shot from the mouth of it, within a trench that lies on the right hand, coming up the river, at the mouth of which there is a little hill. Besides these houses, which were all of timber, and covered with palm-tree leaves, which grew along the shore, another large house

Christians find good reception.

Dururi.

Zobraba.

Cateba.

A colony at Belem.

house was built, to serve as a storehouse and magazine, into which several pieces of cannon, powder, and provisions were put, and other necessaries for the support of the planters. But for wine, bisket, oil, vinegar, cheese, and much grain, which was all they had to eat, these things were left in the safest place, aboard the ship called *Gallega*, that was to be left with the lieutenant, that he might make use of it either at sea, or ashore, having all its cordage, nets, hooks, and other fishing tackle; for as we have said, there is vast plenty of fish in that countrey in every river, several sorts at certain times running along the coast in shoals, on which the people of the countrey feed more than upon flesh; for tho' there be some sorts of beasts they are not enough to maintain them. The customs of these *Indians* are for the most part much like those of *Hispaniola*, and the neighbouring islands; but these people of *Veragua*, and the countrey about it, when they talk to one another, and eat, turn their backs, and are always chewing an herb, which we look upon to be the occasion that their teeth are decay'd and rotten. Their food is fish, which they take with nets and hooks made of tortoise-shell, which they cut with a thread, as if they were sawing; the same they use in the islands. They have another way of catching some very small fishes, which in *Hispaniola* they call *Titi*. These at certain times being drove to the shore by the rains, are so persecuted by the bigger fish, that they are forced up to the surface of the water, where the *Indians* take as many as they will of them in little mats, or small nets, and wrap them up in leaves of trees, as apothecaries do their drugs; and having dried them in an oven, they keep a long time. They also catch pilchards almost in the same manner; for at certain times these fishes fly from the great ones so violently, and in such fear, that they leap out two or three paces upon the dry land, so that there is no more to do, but to take them as they do the others. These pilchards are taken after another manner; for in the middle of their canoes, from stem to stern, they raise a partition of palm-tree leaves two yards high, and plying about the river they make a noise, and beat the shore with their oars, and then the pilchards, to fly from the other fish, leap into the canoe, and hitting against those leaves fall in, by which means they take as many as they please. Several sorts of fish pass along the coast in shoals, whereof wonderful quantities are taken, which they keep roasted a long time. They have also abundance of *Maiz*, which is a sort of grain growing in an ear, or hard head like *millet*, whereof they make white and red wine, as beer is made in *England*, and mix of their spice with it as pleases their palate; it has a pleasant taste like a sharp brisk wine: they also make another sort of wine of certain trees like palms; and I believe they are of that kind, but that they are smooth, and have such prickles on the trunk as the thorn. From the pith of this palm, which is like palmitoes squeez'd, they draw a juice, whereof they make wine, boiling with it water and spice; and this they make great account of. They make another wine of the fruit we said is found in the island *Guadalupe*, which is like a great pine-apple: It is planted in great fields, and the plant is a sprout growing out at the top of the fruit it self, like that which grows out of a cabbage or lattice. One plant lasts three or four years, and bears. They make wine of other sorts of fruit, particularly of one that grows upon very high trees, and is as big as a large limon, and every one has two, three, and some nine stones like nuts, but they are not round, but long, or like a chesnut. The rind of this fruit is like a pomgranate, and when first taken from the tree it resembles it exactly, save only that it wants the prickly circle at the top. The taste of it is like a peach: Of these some are better, some worse, as is usual among other fruit. There are of them in the islands, and the *Indians* call them *Mamei*.

Indians manner of fishing.

Indian wines.

CHAP. XCVII.

How for the greater security of the christian colony, Quibio, *and several of the principal men were made prisoners, and how through the carelesness of his keepers, he made his escape.*

The mouth of the river choak'd up with sand.

ALL things were now settled for the christian colony, and ten or twelve houses built and thatched, and the admiral ready to sail for *Spain*, when he fell into greater danger for want of water, than he had been before by the inundation. For the great rains of *January*, being over, the mouth of the river was so choaked up with sand, that whereas when they came in, there was about ten foot water, which was scant enough, when we would have gone out there were not two foot, so that we were shut up without any help, it being impossible to get the ships over the sand,

sand; and though there had been such an engine, the sea was so boisterous, that the least wave which beats upon the shore was enough to beat the ships in pieces, especially ours, which were at this time like a honey-comb, being all worm-eaten through and through. We had nothing left but to have recourse to God, and beg rain of him, as before we pray'd for fair weather; for the rain we knew would swell the river, and clear the sand from the mouth of it, as is usual in those rivers. It being in the mean while discovered by means of the interpreter, that *Quibio*, the *Cacique* of *Veragua* intended to set fire to the houses and destroy the christians, because all the *Indians* were against their planting upon that river; it was therefore thought fit, as a punishment to him, and a terror and example to others, to make him a prisoner with all his chief men, and send them into *Spain*, and that his town should remain at the disposal of the christians.

To this purpose, the lieutenant on the 30th of *March*, went with 76 men to the town or village of *Veragua*; and because I call it a town or village, it is to be observed that in those parts their houses are not close together, but they live as in *Biscay* at some distance from one another. When *Quibio* understood that the lieutenant was come near, he sent him word not to come up to his house, which stood upon a hill above the river of *Veragua*; and the lieutenant, that he might not fly for fear of him, resolved to go with only five men, ordering those he left behind to come after him, two and two, at some distance from one another; and when they heard a musquet fired, they should beset the house, that none might escape. Being come up to the house, *Quibio* sent another messenger, bidding him not go in, for he would come out to talk to him, tho' he was wounded with an arrow, which they do that their women may not be seen, being wonderful jealous of them. Accordingly he came and sat at the door, bidding only the lieutenant come near him, who did so, ordering the rest to fall on, as soon as he laid hold of his arm. He asked the *Cacique* some questions concerning his indisposition, and the affairs of the countrey by the assistance of an *Indian* he had, whom we had taken not far off, above three months since, and he willingly went along with us. This man was then much afraid, for knowing that *Quibio* design'd to destroy all the christians, and not knowing our strength, he thought that might easily be done by the great multitude of people there was in that province. But the lieutenant minded not his fear, and pretending to look where the *Cacique* was wounded, he took him by the arm, and tho' they were both very strong, yet the lieutenant took such good hold, that he lost it not till the other four came up, which done, one of them fired a musquet, and on a sudden all the christians running out of their ambush, beset the house, in which there were thirty people great and small, most of which were taken, and never a one wounded, for they seeing their king taken, would make no resistance. Among these there were some wives and children of *Quibio*, and other men of note, who offered great wealth, saying, there was a great treasure in the adjoining wood, and they would give it all for their ransom. But the lieutenant not regarding their promises, ordered *Quibio*, with his wives and children, and the principal men, to be carried aboard, before the countrey took the alarm, staying himself there with most of the men, to go after his kindred and subjects who were fled. Then having consulted with the captains and chief men, whom they should intrust to conduct the prisoners to the mouth of the river; he at last delivered them to *John Sanchez de Cadiz*, a pilot, and a man in good reputation, he offering to carry them, the *Cacique* being bound hands and feet; and this pilot being charged to take special care that the *Cacique* should not escape, he answered, he would give them leave to pull of his beard if he got from him. So he took him into his custody, and went down the river of *Veragua*. Being come within half a league of the mouth of it, and *Quibio* complaining that his hands were too hard bound, *John Sanchez* out of compassion, loosed him from the seat of the boat to which he was tied, and held the rope in his hand. A little after, *Quibio* observing he did not mind him, threw himself into the water; and *John Sanchez* not being able to hold fast the rope, let go that he might not draw him after into the water. Night coming on, and those in the boat being all in a confusion, they could not see or hear where he got ashore, so that they heard no more of him than if a stone had fallen into the water: That the like might not happen with the rest of the prisoners, they held on their way to the ships with much shame for their carelessness and oversight. The next day the lieutenant perceiving the countrey was very mountainous and woody, and that there were no regular towns, but one house here, and another at a great distance, and that it would be very difficult to pursue the *Indians* from place to place, he resolved to return to the ships with his men, not one of them being either killed or wounded. He presented

The Cacique apprehended.

Makes his escape.

presented the admiral with the plunder of *Quibio*'s house, worth about 300 ducats in gold plates, little eagles, and small quills which they string and wear about their arms and legs, and in gold twists which they put about their head in the nature of a coronet. All which things, deducting only the 5th part for their catholick majesties, he divided among those that went upon the expedition: And to the lieutenant, in token of victory, was given one of those crowns or coronets above-mention'd.

CHAP. XCVIII.

How after the admiral was gone from Belem *to return to* Spain, Quibio *assaulted the christian colony, in which engagement there were many killed and wounded.*

ALL things being provided for the maintenance of the colony, and the rules and methods for them to be govern'd by, settled by the admiral, it pleased God to send so much rain, as swelled the river and open'd the mouth of it; wherefore the admiral resolved to depart with all speed for *Hispaniola*, to send speedy supplies to this place. Having waited for a calm that the sea might not beat upon the mouth of the river, he went out with three ships, the boats going a-head and towing us. Yet never a one went out so cleverly, but his keel raced upon the sand, and had been in danger notwithstanding the calm but that those are loose moving sands. Then we presently took in all we had unladed to lighten the ships that they might get out. As we lay waiting for a fair wind upon the open coast, a league from the mouth of the river, it pleased God miraculously to give us an occasion of sending the admiral's boat ashore as well for water, as for other necessary affairs, that by the loss of these both those ashore, and those in the ships might be saved, which happened thus. When *Quibio* and the *Indians* saw that the ships were without, and could not relieve them that were left behind, they assaulted the christian colony at the same time that the boat came to the shore. They having not been discover'd by reason of the thickness of the wood, when they came within ten paces of our mens houses, fell on with great shouts, casting javelins at those they spied, and at the very houses, which being covered with palm-tree leaves, were easily struck through and through, and so sometimes they wounded those within. Having thus surprized our men thinking of no such thing, they wounded 4 or 5 before they could put themselves into a posture of defence. But the lieutenant being a man of great resolution, he went out against the enemy with a spear, encouraging his men, and falling furiously on the *Indians*, with 7 or 8 that followed him, so that he made them retire to the wood, which (as we said) was close to the houses. Thence they returned and skirmish'd, casting their javelins and then retiring, as the *Spaniards* use to do in the sport they call *Juego de Cannas*, many of them flying from the christians after they had felt the edge of their swords, and the teeth of a dog, who furiously fell in among them; so that at length they fled, having killed one christian and wounded 7, one of which was the lieutenant, who was hurt with a javelin in the breast; from which danger two christians took care to preserve themselves, which story I will relate to show the comicalness of the one, who was an *Italian* of *Lombardy*, and the gravity of the other who was a *Spaniard*. The *Lombard* running hastily to hide himself in a house, *James Mendez*, of whom mention will be made hereafter, said to him, turn, turn back *Sebastian*, whither are you going? He answered, let me go, you devil, for I am going to secure my person. The *Spaniard* was captain *James Tristan*, whom the admiral sent ashore in the boat, who never went out of it with his men, tho' the fray was just by the river; and being blamed by some for not assisting the christians, he answered, he said he did it that those ashore might not run to the boat and so all perish, because if the boat were lost, the admiral would be in danger at sea, and therefore he would do no more than he had been commanded, which was to take in water, and to see whether there was any need of his assistance. Resolving therefore to take in the water immediately, that he might carry the admiral an account of what had happen'd, he went up the river for it, where the sweet did not mix with the salt, tho' some advised him not to go, for the danger there was of the *Indians* and their canoes; to which he answered, he did not fear that danger, since he was sent for that purpose by the admiral. Accordingly he went up the river, which is very deep within, and shelter'd on both sides with abundance of trees, which come to the edge of the water and so thick that there is scarce any going ashore, except in some places which are the fishermen's paths, and where they hide their canoes. As soon as the *Indians* perceived he was got about a league from the colony up the river, they rushed out from the thickest on both sides the river in their canoes, and making a hideous noise, blowing

The admiral sails.

Indians *attack the new Colony.*

Indians *kill all the* Spaniards *in the boats.*

ing their horns, assaulting him boldly on all sides with great odds on their side, because their canoes being swift, and one man being enough to command and turn them which way they please, especially those that are little and belong to the fishermen, three or four men came in each of them, one of whom row'd, and the rest cast their javelins at those in the boat; I call them javelins because of their bigness, tho' they have no iron-heads, but only points of fish-bones. There being but seven or eight men in our boat who row'd, and the captain with three or four men for fight, they could not cover themselves against the many javelins they threw at them, and therefore they were forced to quit the oars to cake up their targets. But there was such a multitude of *Indians*, who pour'd in on all sides, coming up and retiring in good order, as they thought fit, that they wounded most of the christians, especially the captain, who was hurt in many places; and tho' he stood unmoved incouraging his men, it availed him nothing; for he was beset on all sides, and could not stir, nor make use of his musquets, till at last they struck a javelin into his eye, and he fell down dead; and all the rest came to the like fate, except one *John de Noia* of *Sevil*, who by good luck in the height of the fray fell into the water, and diving got to the shore, and made his way through the thickest of the wood to the colony, to carry the news of what had happened. This so terrified our men, that seeing they were but a few, some of their companions being kill'd and others wounded, and that the admiral was at sea without a boat, and in danger not to return to a place whence he might send them relief, they resolved not to stay there; and accordingly would have gone away immediately without any orders, had not the mouth of the river hindred, the bad weather having shut it up again; for neither could the ship they had left them get out, nor durst any boat attempt it, because the sea beat so violently, so that there was no sending the admiral advice of what had happened. He was in no less danger himself, riding in an open road, having no boat and but few men, so many having been kill-ed: So that we were all in the same trouble and confusion, as they were within, who considering what had happened, and seeing those that had been killed in the boat drive down the river covered with wounds, and followed by the countrey crows, look'd upon these things as ill omens, and dreaded coming to the same end; and the more because they perceived the *Indians* were puff-ed up with their success, insomuch that they gave them not a minute's respite by reason of the ill situation of the colony; and there is no doubt but that they must have all suffer'd, had they not advised to remove to an open strand eastward, where they made a work round them with the casks and other things, and planting the cannon in convenient places defending themselves, the *Indians* not daring to come out of the wood, because of the mischief the bullets did among them.

CHAP. XCIX.

How the Indians *that were kept prisoners aboard made their escape, and the admiral was informed of the success of his men.*

Some Indians *swim ashore, others hang themlelves.*

WHilst these things happen'd, the admiral waited ten days with much trouble, and suspecting what might fall out, till the sea would settle, that he might send another boat to know what it was that detain'd the first; but fortune thwarting him in all things, would not allow us to hear of one another; and to add to our affliction, it happened that the sons and kindred of *Quibio*, whom we kept prisoners aboard the ship *Bermuda*, to carry them to *Spain*, found means to escape thus. At night they were kept under hatches, and the scuttle being so high that they could not reach it, the watch forgot to fasten it with a chain as they used to do, especially because some seamen lay upon it. The prisoners therefore one night gathering the stones that were in the hold under the scuttle, and raising themselves on them, set their shoulders against it, and forced it open, tumbling those that lay on it over and over, and some of the principal men leaping out, cast themselves into the sea. The seamen taking the alarm, many of them could not get out; and the scuttle being fastened with the chain, better care was taken; but those that remained in despair, because they could not get off with their companions, hang'd themselves with the ropes they could come at, and so were found the next morning, their feet and knees dragging upon the bottom of the hold, the place not being high enough for them to hang without touching, so that all the prisoners aboard that ship escaped or died. Tho' this loss was not material to the ships, yet besides that it increased the number of misfortunes, it was fear'd fear'd it might be hurtful to those ashore; because *Quibio* would willingly have made peace with them to get his children, and now there being no hostage left, there was cause to suspect he would make war with the greater fury. Being thus afflicted amidst so many troubles and disasters, having nothing to trust to but our anchors and cables, without knowing any thing from shore, there wanted not those, who said, that since those *Indians* only to obtain their liberty, had ventured to leap into the sea above a league from shore, they to save themselves, and so many more, would be content to swim ashore, provided that boat which remained would carry them as far as where the waves did not break. I say one boat remain'd, which was that of the ship *Bermuda*, for that of the *Biscaina*, we said before, was lost in the fray, so that they had only that one boat at present among the three ships. The admiral hearing these seamens honest proposal, allow'd of it, and so the boat carried them within a musket shot of land, not being able to go nearer without great danger, because of the great waves that broke on it. There one *Peter de Ledesma*, a pilot of *Sevil*, threw himself into the water, and with a good heart got to shore, where he learnt the condition our men were in, and how they all unanimously said, they would not upon any account remain there in that forlorn condition, and therefore desired the admiral not to sail till he had taken them off, for to leave them there was sacrificing of them, and the more because there were already divisions among them, and they obey'd neither the admiral's brother nor the captains, and all their care was upon the first fair weather, to secure a canoe and go aboard, because this could not be conveniently done with only one boat that was left them; and if the admiral would not receive them, they would endeavour to save their lives aboard that ship which was left them, and rather trust fortune than be at the mercy of the *Indians*, who would inhumanly butcher them. With this answer *Peter de Ledesma* returned to the boat which waited for him, and thence to the ships, where he gave the admiral an account how matters stood.

A Spaniard swims ashore.

CHAP. C.

How the admiral brought off the men he had left at Belem, *and struck over to* Jamaica.

The new colony abandon'd.

THE admiral understanding the rout, the confusion and despair those ashore were in, he resolved to stay and bring them off, tho' not without great danger, because his ships lay in an open road, out of all shelter, and without hopes of escaping had the weather grown more boisterous. But it pleased God in eight days he continued there, the weather mended so much, that those ashore with their boat and large canoes fast bound together, that they might not over-set, began to gather their goods, and every one striving to be none of the last, they used such diligence, that in two days nothing was left ashore but the hulk of the ship, which by reason of the worms was unfit for service. Thus rejoycing we were all together again, we sailed up that coast eastward; for tho' all the pilots were of opinion that we might return to *St. Domingo* standing away to the north, yet only the admiral and his brother, knew it was requisite to run a considerable way up that coast, before they struck across that gulph that is between the continent and *Hispaniola*, which our men were much displeased at, thinking the admiral design'd directly for *Spain*, whereas he neither had provisions, nor were his ships fit for that voyage. But he knowing best what was fit to be done, we held on our course till we came to *Porto Bello*, where we were forced to leave the ship *Biscaina*, it was so leaky, being all worm-eaten through and through. And holding along up the coast, we pass'd by the port we called *Retrete*, and a countrey near which there were abundance of small islands, which the admiral called *las Barbas*, but the *Indians* and pilots, call that the territory of the *Cacique Pocorosa*: Hence we held on ten leagues to the last land we saw of the continent, called *Marmora*, and on *Monday* the first of *May* 1503, we stood to the northward, the wind and currents east, which made us lie as near the wind as we could. And tho' all the pilots said, we should be east of the *Caribbee* islands, yet the admiral fear'd he should not make *Hispaniola*, which proved so; for upon *Wednesday* the 10th of the same month of *May*, we were in sight of two very small and low islands, full of tortoises, as was all the sea about, insomuch that they look'd like little rocks, for which reason those islands were called *Tortugas* or *Tortoises*. Sailing on northwards, on *Friday* following about evening, 30 leagues from those islands, we came to those called *Jardin de la Reina*, or *the queen's garden*, which is a great number of islands on the south-side of *Cuba*. Being here at an

Tortugas Islands.

an anchor, ten leagues from *Cuba*, with men and trouble enough, because they had nothing to eat but bisket, with some little oil and vinegar, labouring day and night at the pump, because the ships were so worm-eaten they were ready to sink, a great storm arose in the night, and the ship *Bermuda* not being able to ride it out, ran foul of us, and broke our stem and its own stern, and tho' with much difficulty, because of the roughness of the sea and high wind, it pleas'd God they got loose from one another; and tho' we cast all our anchors none would hold but the sheet-anchor, whose cable when day appeared, we found held but by a thread, which if the night had lasted an hour longer, must have given way, and all that place being full of rocks, we could not miss spliting upon some of those that were a-stern us. But it pleased God to deliver us here, as he had done from many other dangers. And so sailing hence with much toil, we came to an *Indian* town on the coast of *Cuba*, called *Mataia*, where having got some refreshment, we sailed for *Jamaica*; for the east winds and great currents setting westward, would not permit us to stand for *Hispaniola*, especially the ships being so worm-eaten, that as has been said, we never ceased day and night working at three pumps in each of them, and if any one broke, whilst it was mended, we were forced to supply the want of it with kettles. For all this, the night before *Midsummer-Eve*, the water was so high in our ship, that there was no draining of, for it came almost up to the deck; and with much labour we held out in that manner till day appearing we put into a harbour in *Jamaica* called *Puerto Bueno* or *Good Harbour*, which tho' good to take shelter against a storm, had no fresh water, nor any town near it. Having made the best shift we could, on the day after the feast of St. *John*, we set out for another harbour eastward, called *Santa Gloria* or *Holy Glory*, which is enclosed with rocks. Being got in, and no longer able to keep the ships above water, we run them ashore as far in as we could, stranding them close together board and board, and shoaring them up on both sides, fixed them so that they could not budge; and in this posture the water came up almost to the deck, upon which, and the poop and fore-castle, were sheds made for the men to lie in, to secure our selves, that the *Indians* might not hurt us, because the island was not then inhabited or subdued by *Christians*.

The admiral runs his ships aground.

CHAP. CI.

How the admiral sent canoes from Jamaica *to* Hispaniola, *to give advice that he was cast ashore there with his men.*

BEing thus fortified in our ships about a bow shot from land, the *Indians*, who were a peaceable good natured people, came in their canoes to sell provisions, and such things as they had, for our commodities. Therefore, that there might not be some disorder committed among the christians, and that they might not take more in exchange than was fitting, and the others might have their due, the admiral appointed two persons to oversee the buying of such things as they brought, and to divide daily among the men what was exchanged, because there was nothing left aboard to subsist on, as well because most of the provisions were spent, as for that the rest was spoil'd and some lost when the men came away from *Belem*, where the haste and confusion hindred things being brought off as they should. That we might be supplied with sustenance, it pleased God to direct us to that island, which abounds in provisions, and is inhabited by *Indians*, who are willing enough to trade, and therefore they resorted from all parts to barter such commodities as they had. For this reason, and that the christians might not disperse about the island, the admiral chose to fortify himself upon the sea, and not settle a dwelling ashore; because we being naturally disobedient, no command or punishment would have kept the men from running about the countrey, and into the houses of the *Indians*, to take from them what they found, and thus they would have anger'd their wives and children, which would have caused quarrels and made them our enemies, and the taking their provisions by force, would have reduced us to great want and distress. This could not happen now, because the men were aboard, and there was no going ashore without leave, which pleased the *Indians*, who sold two *Huties*, which are little creatures like rabbets, for a bit of tin, and cakes of bread they call *Zabi*, for two or three red or yellow glass beads; and when they brought a quantity of any thing, they had a hawk's-bell, and sometimes we gave a *Cacique* or great man a little looking-glass or red cap, or a pair of scissors to please them. This good order kept the men plentifully supplied with provisions, and the *Indians* were well pleased with our company.

The admiral's care to prevent disorders.

pany. But it being requisite to find some means to return to *Spain*, the admiral sometimes consulted with the captains and principal men about the means of getting out of that confinement, and at least returning to *Hispaniola*; for to stay there in hopes some ships might arrive was a mere folly, and to think to build a vessel was impossible, having neither tools nor workmen fit to do any thing to the purpose, but what would take up a long time, and not produce such a vessel as was fit to sail against the winds and currents that prevail among those islands; and therefore it had been only time lost, and would rather have proved our ruin than relief. Therefor eafter many consultations, the admiral resolved to send to *Hispaniola* to give an account that he was cast ashore on that island, and desired a ship might be sent him with provisions and ammunition. To this purpose he made choice of two persons that might perform it faithfully and couragiously, I say couragiously, because it seemed impossible to go over from one island to the other in canoes, and there was no other way for it: These being boats, as has been said above, made of one single tree hollowed, and so contrived that when they are loaded, they are not a span above water. Besides, they must be indifferently large for that passage, because little ones would be more dangerous, and the biggest by reason of their own weight were not fit for a long voyage, or to perform what was design'd. Two canoes fit for the purpose being chose, the admiral in *July* 1503, ordered *James Mendez de Segura*, his chief secretary, to go in one of them with six christians and ten *Indians* to row, and in the other he sent *Bartholomew Fiesco*, a *Genoese* gentleman, with the like number of men; that as soon as *James Mendez* got over to *Hispaniola*, he might continue his journey to *St. Domingo*, which was 250 leagues from the place where we were, and *Fiesco* might return to bring the news that the other was safe arrived, and we might not be left in fear least some disaster had befallen him, which there was much cause to fear; considering, as has been said, how unfit a canoe is to live upon a rough sea, especially when there were christians in it; for if there were none but *Indians* the danger had not been so great, because they are so dexterous, that tho' a canoe oversets when they are half way over, they turn it up again, swimming, and get into it. But honour and necessity putting men upon bolder attempts than this, the persons abovementioned took their way along the coast of *Jamaica* to the eastermost point of it, that the *Indians* call *Aoamaquique* from a *Cacique* of that province so called, 33 leagues from *Maima*, where we were. There being 30 leagues distance between the two islands, and nothing in the way but one little island or rock eight leagues from *Hispaniola*, it was requisite to expect a calm, in order to cross over so great a sea in such poor vessels, which it pleased God they soon had. Every *Indian* having put aboard his calabash of water and *Carrabi*, or such provisions as they use, and the *Christians* with swords and targets, and the necessary sustenance, they put out to sea; and the admiral's brother, who went to that point of *Jamaica* to see that the *Indians* of the island should no way hinder them, staid there till night coming on, he lost sight of them, and then returned easily towards the ships, in his way perceiving the people of the countrey to converse and be friendly with us.

Canoes sent over to Hispaniola.

CHAP CII.

How the brothers called Porras, *with many of the men, mutiny'd against the admiral, saying, they would go to* Spain.

WHEN the canoes were gone for *Hispaniola*, the men left aboard the ships began to fall sick, as well by reason of the hardships endur'd during the voyage, as the change of diet; for at present they had no *Spanish* provisions, nor wine, nor flesh, except some of those *Huties* we have spoke of, they happened to get in exchange. So that those who were sound, thinking it very hard to be so long confin'd, did not forbear to mutter among themselves in private; saying, the admiral would return into *Spain* no more, because their catholick majesties had turn'd him off, nor much less to *Hispaniola*, where he had been refus'd admittance at his coming from *Spain*, and that he had sent those in the canoes into *Spain* to sollicit his own affairs, and not to bring ships or other succours, and that he design'd, whilst they were solliciting their catholick majesties to stay there to fulfil his banishment; for otherwise *Bartholomew Fiesco* had been come back by this time, as was given out he was to do. Besides, they knew not, whether he and *James Mendez* were drown'd by the way; which, if it had happened, they should never be reliev'd, if they did not take care for it themselves, since the admiral

Mutiny against the admiral.

ral did not seem to look to it for the reasons aforesaid, and because of the gout, which had so seiz'd all his limbs, that he could scarce stir in his bed, much less undergo the fatigue and danger of going over to *Hispaniola* in canoes. For which reasons, they ought with a good heart to fix their resolution, since they were well, before they fell sick, with the rest, that it would not be in the admiral's power to hinder them; and being once in *Hispaniola*, they would be so much the better received, by how much the danger they left him in was greater, because of the hatred and enmity born him by the commendary *Lares*, then governor of that island; and that when they went into *Spain* they might go to the bishop *D. John de Fonseca*, who would favour them, as would the treasurer *Morales*, who kept for his mistress the sister of those *Porras*'s, the ringleaders of the mutineers, and chief fomenters of the sedition, who did not doubt but they should be well received by their catholick majesties, before whom all the fault would be laid upon the admiral, as had been in the affairs of *Hispaniola* with *Roldan*; and their majesties would the rather seize him and take all he had, than be obliged to perform all that was agreed upon between them and him. These and the like arguments they us'd among themselves, and the persuasions and suggestions of the aforesaid brothers, one of whom was captain of the ship *Bermuda*, and the other controller to the squadron, prevail'd with 48 men to join in this conspiracy, taking *Porras* for their captain; and every one provided what he could against the day and hour appointed; and being all ready with their arms, on the 2d of *January* in the morning, the aforesaid captain *Francis de Porras* came upon the quarter-deck of the admiral's ship, and said to him, My lord, what is the meaning that you will not go into *Spain*, and will keep us all here perishing? The admiral hearing these unusual insolent words, and suspecting what the matter might be, very calmly answer'd, He did not see which way they could go, till those that were gone in the canoes sent a ship. That no man was more desirous to be gone than he, as well for his own private interest, as for the good of them all, for whom he was accountable; but that if he had any thing else to propose, he would again call together the captains and principal men to consult, as had been done several times before. *Porras* replied, It was no time to talk, but that he should embark quickly, or stay there by himself; and so turning his back, added in a loud voice, I am going to *Spain* with those that will follow me, at which time all his followers, who were present began to cry out, We will go with you, We will go with you, and running about, possess'd themselves of the forecastle, poop, and round tops, all in confusion; and crying, Let them die; others, For *Spain*, for *Spain*; and others, What shall we do captain? Though the admiral was then in bed so lame of the gout that he could not stand; yet he could not forbear rising and stumbling out at this noise. But two or three worthy persons, his servants, laid hold of, and with labour laid him in his bed, that the mutineers might not murder him. Then they ran to his brother, who was couragiously come out with a half pike in his hand; and wresting it out of his hands, put him in to his brother, desiring captain *Porras* to go about his business, and not do some mischief they might all suffer for, that he might be satisfied they did not oppose his going; but if he should kill the admiral, he could not expect but to be severely punish'd, without hopes of any benefit. The tumult being somewhat appeas'd, the conspirators took ten canoes, that were by the ship's side, and which the admiral had bought all about the island, and went aboard them as joyfully as if they had been in some port of *Spain*. Upon this, many more, who had no hand in the plot, in despair to see themselves as they thought forsaken, taking what they could along with them, went aboard the canoes with them, to the great sorrow and affliction of those few faithful servants, who remain'd with the admiral, and of all the sick, who thought themselves lost for ever, and without hopes of ever getting off. And it is certain, that had the people been well, not 20 men had remain'd with the admiral, who went out to comfort his men with the best words the posture of his affairs would suggest; and the mutineers, with their captain, *Francis de Porras*, in their canoes, went away for the east-point of the island, whence *James Mendez* and *Fiesco* went over for *Hispaniola*; and wheresoever they came, they insulted the *Indians*, taking away their provisions, and what else they pleas'd by force; and telling them, they might go to the admiral and he would pay them, but in case he did not, they might kill him, which was the best thing they could do; because he was not only hated by the *Christians*, but had been the cause of all the mischief had befallen the *Indians* of the other island, and would do the same by them, if they did not prevent it by his death, for that was his design in staying there. Thus travelling to the eastermost point of *Jamaica*, the first calm they set out for *Hispaniola*, carrying some *Indians* in every canoe to row. But the weather not being well settled,

Mutineers go away to the Coast of the Island.

settled, and their canoes overloaded, they resolv'd to return to *Jamaica* before they were four leagues at sea, the wind turning against them, and they being able to make but little way. Besides, they not being skilful at managing the canoes, it happened a little water flash'd in over the sides; to remedy which, they lightened, throwing all they carried over-board; so that nothing remain'd but their arms, and as much provision as would serve them back. The wind still freshing, and they thinking themselves in some danger, it was resolv'd to murder the *Indians*, and throw them into the sea; this they accordingly executed upon some of them; and others, who for fear of death, trusting in their skill in swimming, leap'd over into the water, and being very weary would hang by the canoes to breath a little, had their hands cut off, and were wounded in other parts; so that they butcher'd 18, leaving only a few alive to steer the canoes, because they knew not how to do it. And had not the need they had of them prevented it, they had compleated the greatest act of cruelty imaginable, leaving not one of them alive, after they had by intreaties, and deceitfully drawn them to their assistance in that dangerous voyage. Being come to shore, they differ'd in opinions; for some said it was better to go to *Cuba*, and that from that place where they were, they might take the east winds and currents upon their quarter, and so run over without any trouble in a short time, and so cross over from thence to *Hispaniola*, not knowing they were 17 leagues asunder: Others said it was better to return to the ships, and make their peace with the admiral, or take from him by force what commodities and arms he had left; others were for staying till another calm, to attempt the same passage again. This being thought the best advice, they staid in that town of *Aoamaquique* above a month, waiting for fair weather, and destroying the countrey. When the fair weather came, they imbark'd again twice, but made nothing of it, the wind being contrary. Being thus disappointed of that passage, they set out towards the west from one town to another, with an ill-will, without canoes or any comfort, sometimes eating what they found, and taking it where they could by force, according to their strength, and that of the *Caciques*, through whose territories they pass'd.

Their Barbarities.

CHAP. CIII.

What the admiral did, after the mutineers were gone from him, and the Advantage he made of an eclipse.

TO return to what the admiral did, after the rebels were gone, he took great care that the sick should be furnished with such things as were proper for their recovery, and that the *Indians* should be so civilly treated that they might not forbear bringing provisions to exchange for our commodities; which things were so well manag'd, and with such application by him, that the *Christians* soon recover'd, and the *Indians* continued some days providing all things plentifully. But they being a people that take little pains in sowing; and we eating more in one day than they did in 20; besides having no longer any inclination to our commodities, and making little account of them, they began in some measure to take the advice of the mutineers, since they saw so great a part of our men against us, and therefore brought not such plenty of provisions as we stood in need of. This brought us to great distress; for if we would have taken it by force, the greatest part of us must have gone ashore in warlike manner, and have left the admiral aboard in great danger, he being very ill of the gout; and if we expected they should bring it of their own accord, we must live in misery, and give ten times as much for it as we did at first, they knowing how to make their bargains, as being sensible of the advantage they had over us. But God, who never forsakes those that have recourse to him, as the admiral had, put him in the way how he should be furnish'd with all he wanted, which was thus. He bethought himself, that within three days there would be an eclipse of the moon in the first part of the night; and then sends an *Indian* of *Hispaniola*, who was with us, to call the principal *Indians* of that province, saying, he would talk with them about a matter of concern. Being come that day before the eclipse was, he ordered the interpreter to tell them, That we were *Christians*, and believ'd in God, who dwelt in heaven, and took care of the good, and punish'd the wicked: That he seeing the rebellion of the *Spaniards*, had not permitted them to go over to *Hispaniola*, as *James Mendez* and *Fiesco* had done, but had made them run through all those sufferings and dangers all the

The Indians fail to supply the Spaniards.

the island had heard of: That as for the *Indians*, seeing how negligent they were in bringing provisions for our commodities, he was angry with them, and had decreed to punish them with plague and famine; which because perhaps they would not believe, God had appointed to give them a manifest token of it in the heaven that they might plainly know the punishment was to come from him. Therefore, he bid them that night, observe when the moon appear'd, and they should see her rise angry and of a bloody hue, to denote the mischief God intended should fall on them. Having said this to them, the *Indians* went away, some afraid, and others looking upon it as an idle story: but the eclipse beginning as the moon was rising, and increasing, the higher she was, the *Indians* took notice of it, and were so frighted, that they came running from all parts loaded with provisions, crying and lamenting, and pray'd the admiral by all means to intercede with God for them, that he might not make them feel the effects of his wrath, and promising for the future carefully to bring him all he wanted. The admiral said he would speak with God, and shut himself up whilst the eclipse lasted, they still crying out to him to assist them; and when the admiral saw, the eclipse began to go off, and the moon would soon shine, he came out of his cabin, saying, He had pray'd to his God for them, and promis'd him in their names they would be good for the future, and use the *Christians* well, bringing them provisions and other necessaries; and that therefore God forgave them, and as a token of it they should see the angryness and bloody colour of the moon would go off. This proving so; just as he spoke it, they gave the admiral many thanks, and prais'd God, continuing so till the eclipse was quite pass'd. From that time forwards they always took care to provide all that was necessary, ever praising the God of the *Christians*; for they believ'd the eclipses they had seen at other times, had denoted mischiefs to befal them; and being ignorant of the cause of them, and that they happened at certain times, not believing it possible to know on earth, what was to happen in the heavens, they certainly concluded the God of the *Christians* had reveal'd it to the admiral.

CHAP. CIV.

Of another mutiny among those that remain'd with the admiral, which was quell'd by the coming of a vessel from Hispaniola

Another Mutiny.

EIGHT months being pass'd after *James Mendez* and *Bartholomew Fiesco* went away, and there being no news of them, the admiral's men were very much cast down, suspecting the worst; some saying they were lost at sea; others, that they were kill'd by the *Indians* in *Hispaniola*; and others, that they had died with sickness and hardships; for from the point of that island, which lay next *Jamaica*, there was above 100 leagues to *S. Domingo*, whither they were to go for relief, the way by land being over uncouth mountains, and by sea against the prevailing winds and currents. To confirm their suspicion, some *Indians* assur'd them they had seen a canoe overset and carried on the coast of *Jamaica* by the current, which its likely had been spread abroad by the mutineers to make those that were with the admiral despair of getting off. They therefore concluding for certain that no relief would come to them; one *Bernard*, an apothecary of *Valencia*, with two companions, whose names were *Zamora* and *Villatoro*, and most of those that had remain'd sick, secretly conspir'd together to do the same the others had done before. But almighty God, who knew how dangerous this second sedition must be to the admiral, was pleas'd to put a stop to it by the coming of a vessel sent by the governor of *Hispaniola*. It came to an anchor one evening near the ships that were a ground; and the captain of it, whose name was *James de Escobar*, came in his boat to visit the admiral, saying, The commendary and governor of *Hispaniola* sent him his commendations; and not being able so soon to send a ship fit to carry off all those men, had sent him in his name to visit him, and presenting him a cask of wine and two flitches of bacon, return'd to his caraval, and without taking any letter, sail'd away that very evening. The men, somewhat comforted with his coming, took no notice of what they had conspir'd to do; tho' at the same time they much wondred that the caraval had stole away so privately, and in such haste; and they suspected, that perhaps the governor of *Hispaniola* would not have the admiral go thither. He being aware of it, told them he had so ordered it, because he would not go away without carrying them all off, which that caraval was not big enough to perform; he being willing to prevent any disorders his stay might occasion, from the mutineers. But the

Base Practice of the Governor of Hispaniola.

the governor of *Hispaniola* was afraid that if the admiral return'd to *Spain*, their catholick majesties would restore him to his government, and so he should be forced to quit it; for which reason he would not provide, as he might have done, for the admiral's voyage to *Hispaniola*; and therefore had sent that little caraval to spy and observe the condition the admiral was in; and to know whether he could contrive with safety to have him destroyed, which he knew, by what had happened to *James Mendez*, who sent an account of his voyage in writing, by the caraval, which was as follows.

CHAP. CV.

An account of what happened to James Mendez, *and* Fiesco *in their voyage.*

JAMES *Mendez*, and *Fiesco*, setting out from *Jamaica*, that day they found the weather settled calm, and so held on till night, encouraging and persuading the *Indians* to row with those paddles they use instead of oars; and the weather being violently hot, they would sometimes leap into the water and swim, and then come fresh again to row. Thus holding on their way, at sun-set they lost sight of land, and half the *Christians* and *Indians* taking their watch together at night to row, and take care the *Indians* should not prove treacherous, they advanced all that night without staying, so that when day appeared they were all weary enough. But the commanders encouraging their men, and sometimes rowing to give a good example; after eating to recover their strength, and the fatigue of the night, they fell to their labour again, seeing nothing but sky and water. And tho' this was enough to afflict them sufficiently, yet we may say of them that they were in *Tantalus* his condition; who having water within a span of his mouth, could not quench his thirst; so they were in distress; for through the ill management of the *Indians*, and the great heat of the foregoing day and night, all the water was drank up, without any regard to the future: And all heat and labour being intolerable without drink, the higher the sun ascended the second day after they set out, the more the heat and thirst increased, so that by noon they had no strength left. And as upon such occasions, the head is bound to supply the defect of the hands and feet; so by good fortune, the captains found two casks of water, wherewith now and then relieving the *Indians*, they kept them up till the cool of the evening, encouraging them, and affirming they should be soon near a small island called *Nabazza*, which lay in their way eight leagues distant from *Hispaniola*. This with their extraordinary thirst, and the labour of rowing two days and a night, quite cast them down, believing they had lost their way; for according to their reckoning they had run 20 leagues, and ought now to be in sight of the island. But it was weariness that deceived them, as well because a canoe that rows well cannot in a day and night row above 10 leagues, as by reason the currents are against them that go from *Jamaica* to *Hispaniola*, which they always judge to be more that suffer most by it. Night being come, having thrown one into the sea who died with thirst, and others lying stretch'd out on the bottom of the canoe, they were so afflicted in mind, and so weak and spent, that they hardly made any way. Yet, taking sometimes sea-water to refresh their mouths, which we may say was the comfort given our saviour, when he said, *I thirst*; they gently held on their way till the second night came on without sight of land: But they being of those God intended to save, it pleased him, that in that time of need, when the moon began to rise, *James Mendez* perceiv'd she got up over-land, for a little island cover'd her in the nature of an eclipse. Nor could they have seen it otherwise, because it was small, and at that time of night. Comforting them chearfully, and showing them the land, he so encouraged them, supplying them in their great thirst with a little water out of the barrels, that the next morning they found themselves near the small island, we said was 8 leagues from *Hispaniola*, and called *Nabazza*. They found it to be all round a hard rock, and about half a league in circumference. Landing there the best they could, they all gave God thanks for that mercy; and there being no spring nor tree, they went about taking up rain-water with their calabashes, which lay in holes among the rocks; which it pleas'd God to give them such plenty of, that they fill'd their bellies and vessels; and tho' the wiser sort advis'd the others to use moderation in drinking, yet thirst made some of the *Indians* exceed all measure, whereof some died there, and others got desperate distempers. Having rested that day till evening, diverting themselves, and eating such things as they found along the shore; for *James Mendez* had all utensils to strike fire, rejoycing to be in sight of *Hispaniola*; and fearing some bad weather might start up, they made ready to put an end to their voyage, and accordingly about sun-setting in the cool of the evening, they set out towards cape *St. Michael*, the nearest land of *Hispaniola*, where they arriv'd the next morning

Great Distress for thirst.

Nabazza Island.

morning, being the fourth day after they set out. When they had rested here two days, *Bartholomew Fiesco*, who was a gentleman that stood upon his honour, would have return'd as the admiral had commanded him, but the men who were sailors, and *Indians*; being spent and indispos'd with their past labour, and drinking sea-water, and thought they had been delivered out of the whales belly, their 3 days and nights answering to those *Jonas* lay there, he could not get a man to go with him. *James Mendez*, as being most in haste, was gone up the coast of *Hispaniola* in his canoe, notwithstanding he suffer'd under a quartan ague caus'd by his great sufferings at sea and at land, in that condition, travelling over mountains and bad roads, he came to *Xaragua*, which is a province in the west of *Hispaniola*, where the governor then was, who seem'd to rejoyce at his coming, tho' afterwards he was tedious in dispatching him, for the causes abovemention'd, till after much importunity, it was obtain'd of him, that he should give *James Mendez* leave to go to St. *Domingo*, there to buy and fit out a vessel with the admiral's money; which ship being by him got ready, was sent to *Jamaica* at the latter end of *May* 1504, and sailed for *Spain*, according to the admiral's direction, to give their catholick majesties an account of the success of his voyage.

CHAP. CVI.

How the mutineers set themselves against the admiral, and would hear of no agreement.

NOW to return to the admiral, who with all his company had now receiv'd some comfort and certain hopes of being delivered, by the account of *James Mendez* his arrival, and the coming of the caraval; he therefore thought fit to make it known to the mutineers, that their jealousy ceasing, they might return to their duty. He therefore sent two men of note, who had friends among them, and knowing they would not believe, or at least not seem to believe the coming of the caraval, he sent them part of the bacon, the captain of it had presented him. These two being come where captain *Porras* was, with those he confided most in, he came out to meet them, that they might not move, or persuade the men to repent them of the crime they had committed, imagining, as the truth was, that the admiral sent them a general pardon. Yet it was not in the power of the brothers so to curb their men, but that they heard the news of the coming of the caraval, the health of those that were with the admiral, and the offers he made them. After several consultations among themselves, and the principal men, the result was, that they would not trust to the pardon the admiral sent them, but would go peaceably away to *Hispaniola*, if he would promise to give them a ship to go in, provided two came; and if there came but one, he should assign them half of it; and in the mean while, because they had lost their clothes, and commodities they had to trade upon the sea, he should share what he had with them. To which the messengers answering, that those were no reasonable proposals, they interrupted them saying, that since it was not granted them by fair means, they would have it by force. Thus they dismiss'd the admiral's messengers, misinterpreting his offers, and telling their followers, that he was a cruel revengeful man; and tho' they fear'd nothing for themselves, because the admiral durst not presume to wrong them, because of the favour they had at court, yet they had reason to fear he would be reveng'd on the rest, under colour of just punishment; and that for this reason; *Roldan* and his friends in *Hispaniola* had not trusted him, nor his offers, and it succeeded well with them, they finding so much favour, that they had him sent into *Spain* in irons. And that the coming of the caraval with the news of *James Mendez*, might make no impression on them, they intimated to them, that it was no true caraval, but a phantom made by art magick, the admiral being very skilful in that art, alledging, it was not at all likely, that if it had really been a caraval, the men aboard it would not have had some further discourse with those about the admiral, but would have vanish'd so soon. Nay, it was more probable, that had it been a caraval, the admiral himself would have gone aboard it, with his son and brother. With these and other words to this purpose, they again confirm'd them in their rebellion; and then brought them to resolve to repair to the ships to take what they found by force, and secure the admiral.

The admiral sends and offers pardon to the mutineers.

The rebels obstinate.

CHAP. CVII.

How the mutineers being come to the ships, the admiral's brother went out to fight them, overcame them, and took Porras *their captain.*

THE mutineers continuing obstinate in their wicked resolution, came to a town of the *Indians* within a quarter of a league of the ships, then called *Maima*, where afterwards the *Christians* built the town they called *Sevil*; which the admiral under-

understanding, and being inform'd of their design, he resolved to send his brother against them, to endeavour to reduce them by good words; but so attended, that if they offer'd him any wrong, he might be able to oppose them. To this purpose, the lieutenant drew out 50 men, well arm'd, and ready for any service. These being come to a small hill, a bow-shot from the town where the rebels were, sent those two before, who had gone on the first message, to require them to be peaceable, and that their captain should come peaceably to a conference. But they being nothing inferior in strength or number, and almost all seamen, persuaded themselves, that those who came with the lieutenant were weak men, and would not fight them; therefore they would not permit the messengers to talk to them, but with their naked swords, and the spears, they had all in a body, crying, Kill, kill, fell upon the lieutenant's party; six of the rebels, who were accounted the boldest, having taken an oath, not to part, but go directly against the lieutenant, for if he were kill'd, they made no account of the rest; wherein it pleas'd God they were disappointed; for they were so well received, that 5 or 6 of them drop'd at the first charge, most of them being of those that aim'd at the lieutenant, who fell upon his enemies in such manner, that in a very short time, *John Sanchez de Cadiz*, from whom *Quibio* made his escape, was kill'd, as was *John Barba*; the first I saw draw his sword when they ran into rebellion, and some others fell very much wounded, and *Francis de Porras* their captain was taken. Seeing themselves so roughly handled like base rebellious people, they turn'd their backs and fled as fast as they could. The lieutenant would have pursued, had not some of the chief men about him been against it, saying, it was good to punish, but not so severely, lest when he had killed many of them, the *Indians* should think fit to fall upon the victors, since he saw they were all in arms, waiting the event of the fray, without taking either side. The lieutenant approving of the advice, return'd to the ships, carrying along with him the captain of the rebels and some other prisoners, where he was well receiv'd by the admiral, his brother, and those that had remain'd with him, all of them giving thanks to God for that victory, which they attributed to him, and wherein the guilty had receiv'd their just punishment, and their pride been humbled, none being wounded on our side but the lieutenant in his hand, and one of the anmiral's gentlemen of the chamber, who died of a small wound he receiv'd with a spear in his hip. But to return to the rebels, *Peter de Ledesma*, that pilot we mention'd above, who went with *Vincent Yanez* to *Honduras*, and swam ashore at *Belem*, fell down certain rocks, and lay hid that day and the next, till the evening, no body assisting him, or knowing where he was, except the *Indians*, who with amazement, not knowing how our swords would cut, with little sticks opened his wounds, one of which was in his head, and his brains were seen thro' it, another on his shoulder, so large that his arm hung, as it were, loose, and the calf of one leg almost cut off, so that it hung down to his ankle, and one foot, as if it had a slipper on it, being sliced from the heel to the toes. Notwithstanding all which desperate hurts, when the *Indians* disturb'd him, he would say, Let me alone, for if I get up, *&c.* And they at these words would fly in a great consternation. This being known aboard the ships, he was carried into a thatch'd house hard by, where the dampness and gnats were enough to have kill'd him. Here instead of turpentine, they dress'd his wounds with oil, and he had so many, besides those already mention'd, that the surgeon who dress'd him swore, that for the first 8 days, he still found out new ones; and yet at last he recover'd, the gentleman of the chamber dying, in whom he apprehended no danger. The next day, being the 20th of *May*, all those that had escap'd, sent a petition to the admiral, humbly begging he would be merciful to them, for they repented them of what was past, and were ready to submit themselves to him. The admiral granted their request, and pass'd a general pardon, upon condition the captain should continue a prisoner, as he was, that he might not raise another mutiny. And because they could not be so easy, and conveniently aboard the ships, and there might arise some provoking words among the common sort, which would cause disturbance, and rub up old sores, which might be the cause of fresh tumults, and because it would be a hard matter to quarter, and maintain so many men conveniently, those few there were beginning to suffer want, he resolv'd to send them a commander with commodities to exchange, that he might go with them about the island, and contain them within the bounds of justice, till such time as the ships came, which he daily expected.

The rebels routed.

A wonderful accoun of a wounded man.

The rebels submit, and are pardoned.

CHAP. CVIII.

How the admiral went over to Hispaniola, *and thence into* Spain, *where at* Valladolid *it pleased God to take him to himself.*

THE christians being all again return'd to their duty, and the *Indians* for that same reason being more careful to supply them for their commodities, some days pass'd pass'd which made up a year since we arrived at *Jamaica*. After which, there arrived a ship, which *James Mendez* had bought and fitted out at *St. Domingo* with the admiral's money, aboard which all the men, as well enemies as friends, were shiped, and setting sail on the 28th of *June*, we proceeded on our voyage with much difficulty, the winds and currents, as we have said before, being very contrary to go from *Jamaica* to *St. Domingo*, where we arrived in great need of rest, on the 13th of *August* 1504, and the governor made a great reception for the admiral, lodging him in his own house; tho' this was a treacherous kindness; for on the other side, he set *Porras* who had headed the mutineers at liberty, and attempted to punish those who had a hand in apprehending of him, and to try other causes and offences that belong'd only to their catholick majesties, who had appointed the admiral captain general of their fleet; and yet he fawned upon the admiral, using all demonstrations of kindness in his presence. This lasted till our ship was refitted, and another hired, on which the admiral, his kindred and servants embark'd, most of the rest remaining in *Hispaniola*. We sailed on the 2d of *September*, and being but two leagues at sea, the mast of the ship came by the board; for which reason the admiral caused it to return into the harbour, and we in the other held on our course for *Spain*. Having run about the 3d part of the way, there arose such a terrible storm, that the ship was in great danger. The next day, which was the 19th of *October*, the weather being fair, and we very still, the mast flew into four pieces; but the courage of the lieutenant, and the admiral's ingenuity, tho' he could not rise out of his bed for the gout, found a remedy for this misfortune, making a jury-mast of a yard, and strengthening the middle of it with ropes, and some planks they took from the poop and stern. In another storm we spent our foremast, and yet it pleased God we sailed 700 leagues in that condition, and arrived at the port of *St. Lucar de Barrameda*, and thence to *Sevil*, where the admiral took some rest after the fatigues he had gone through; and in *May* 1505, set out for the catholick king's court; for the glorious queen *Isabel* had the year before exchanged this life for a better, which was no small trouble to the admiral, she having always favoured and supported him, whereas the catholick king had proved unkind and averse to his affairs, which plainly appeared by the reception he gave him; for tho' to appearance he show'd him a favourable aspect, and pretended to restore him to his full power, yet he would have quite stript him of all, had not shame hindred him; which, as has been said, has great power over noble spirits; and the king himself and queen had both ingag'd their faith to him, when he went upon his last voyage. But the *Indies* daily more and more discovering what they were like to be, and the king perceiving how great a share fell to the admiral, by virtue of the articles granted him, he strove to have the absolute dominion in himself, and to dispose of all those employments which belong'd to the admiral, according to his own will and pleasure. Hereupon he began to propose new terms to him, by way of equivalent, which God would not permit to take effect; because just then king *Philip* I. came to reign in *Spain*; and at the time his catholick majesty went from *Valladolid* to meet him, the admiral much oppress'd with the gout, and troubled to see himself put by his right, other distempers coming on him, gave up his soul to God upon *Ascension-Day*, being the 20th of *May* 1506, at the aforesaid city of *Valladolid*, having devoutly received all the sacraments of the church, and said these words last, *Into thy hands, O Lord, I commend my spirit*; which through his infinite mercy we do not question but he received into his glory: To which may he admit us with him.

His body was afterwards convey'd to *Sevil*, and there by the catholick king's order magnificently buried in the cathedral, and an epitaph in *Spanish* cut on his tomb, in memory of his renowed actions, and discovery of the *Indies*. The words are these:

A CASTILIA, YA LEON,
NUEVO MUNDO DIO COLON.

That is,

Columbus *gave* Castile *and* Leon *a new world*,

words well worth observing, because the like cannot be found either among the ancients or moderns.

It will therefore be ever remembred, that he was the discoverer of the *West-Indies*, tho' since then, *Ferdinand Cortez* and *Francis Pizarro* have found out many other provinces and vast kingdoms on the continent; for *Cortez* discovered the province of *Yucatan*, and the city of *Mexico*, called *New Spain*, then possess'd by the great *Montezeuma*, emperor of those parts; and *Francis Pizarro* found out the kingdom of *Peru*, which is of a vast extent, and full of endless wealth, which was under the dominion of the great king *Atabaliba*. From which countries and kingdoms there come every year into *Spain*, many ships laden with gold, silver, brazil, cochineal, sugar, and many other commodities of great value, besides pearls and other jewels, which are the cause that at this time *Spain* and its princes flourish and abound in wealth.

Pyrami-

Pyramidographia:

OR, A

DESCRIPTION

OF THE

PYRAMIDS

IN

ÆGYPT.

By JOHN GREAVES, *Professor of Astronomy in the University of* Oxford.

Romanorum Fabricæ & antiqua opera (cum veniâ id dictum sit) nihil accedunt ad Pyramidum splendorem, & superbiam.
Bellon. lib. II. Observ. cap. 42.

This LETTER *underneath was written by Mr.* Greaves *to the famous* Claudius Hardy, *who published* Euclid's *DATA, and was in great Esteem for his Learning in the Mathematicks, and his skill in the Oriental Languages.*

Clarissimo Doctissimoque Viro D. C. H.

QUatuor anni elapsi sunt (vir clarissimè) ex quo propter longinquam peregrinationem à me in Orientem susceptam, nulla mihi opportunitas data est, affectum, sincerúmque tibi animum testandi. Tandem favente Numine, salvo & incolumi reverso, conceditur nonnihil otii, & de periculis præteritis, & de amicis veteribus, cogitandi. Inter quos si rectè de humanitate, studiisque tuis judico, nemo erit qui de reditu meo, majori, quàm tu, lætitiâ afficiatur. Eáque tantò erit accumulatior, cùm intellexeris iter tam periculosum non alias ob causas initum, nisi ut linguis orientalibus, & studiis astronomicis, peregrè feliciùs incumberem, in quibus utrisque quantum profeceris, eruditis tuis scriptis, literatis omnibus satis comprobasti. Quapropter breviter, strictimque, ubi commoratus sim, quid præstiterim, & quos libros mecum adduxerim, pro veteri amicitiâ tibi indicabo. Primum annum Constantinopoli egi, ut me totum linguæ Arabicæ addicerem, sed spe falsus, idoneis destitutus magistris, ad alias curas animum induxi, eúmque diligenti librorum MSS. disquisitioni applicui. Quo quidem in genere non pœnitendam operam locavi. Nam præter varios codices Arabicos, Persicos, Turcicos, propemodum de universis scientiis scriptos, & præter lexica melioris notæ tribus hisce linguis deservientia, coemi insuper penè omnes antiquos mathematicos Græcos, in idioma Arabicum ante aliquot sæcula traductos, unà cum operibus præcipuè astronomorum recentium, apud Arabes, & Indos, maximè insignium. Inter verò illos antiquos, non leviter gaudeo adhuc superstites reperiri, quatuor libros Apollonii Pergæi geometræ subtilissimi,

في قطع الخطوط علي النسب

quorum Pappus, aliique meminerunt. Constantinopoli cum classe Turcicâ solvi, eo anni tempore, quo solent, multis navigiis simul, pro more gentis, Alexandriam petere. Fretus satis prosperâ navigatione Rhodum appuli, ubi, propter auctoritatem Posidonii, clanculùm in submœnianis Christianorum hortis altitudinem solis sæpe ob-

To the most worthy and most learned D. *C. D.*

*I*T *is now four years, worthy sir, since my long travels into the* East *have deprived me of the opportunity of giving you some testimony of my affection, and sincere inclinations to you. Being at length, by the help of* God, *returned in safety, I have some leisure to think on past dangers, and old friends; among whom, if I be not mistaken in your favour and inclinations, none will more rejoice at my return than you. And your satisfaction will be the greater, when you understand that I undertook so dangerous a journey upon no other account, but to apply my self more successfully in foreign parts, to the study of astronomy, and the oriental languages; in both which, how great a proficient you are, has been sufficiently made appear to the learned world by your writings, full of erudition. I will therefore, in pursuance of our former friendship, briefly inform you in what parts I resided, what I did there, and what books I have brought with me. I spent the first year at* Constantinople, *with a design to apply my self wholly to the* Arabick *tongue; but being deceived in my expectation, and wanting able masters, I bent my mind to other affairs, and applied my self to a diligent search of manscript books. Wherein I have not lost my labour: for besides several* Arabick, Persian, *and* Turkish *books, which treat of almost all sciences, and besides the best lexicons for the understanding of these three languages, I have bought almost all the ancient* Greek *mathematicians, translated some ages since into the* Arabick *tongue, together with the works of the most renowned modern astronomers among the* Arabians *and* Indians. *But among those ancient ones, I do not a little rejoice, that there are still found in being four books of* Apollonius Pergæus, *the most subtle geometrician,*

Conicorum libri quatuor.

of which Pappus, *and others make mention. I sailed from* Constantinople *with the* Turkish *fleet at the same time the great convoy of that nation uses to set out for* Alexandria. *My passage was good, and I arrived at* Rhodes, *where, in respect to* Possidonius's *authority, I often took the sun's altitude privately in the gardens of the Christians without the walls.*

ſervavi: inde poſt ſex dies è portu diſcedens, octo dierum ſpatio, flantibus leniter Eteſiis, Alexandriam perveni; ubi corruptis Judæis, qui vectigalibus ibi præſunt, inſtrumenta mea aſtronomica ſine periculo expoſui. Erant autem diverſa, ex ære ut plurimum fabrefacta, & ab egregio artifice ſummâ cum diligentiâ conſtructa, quorum maximum quadrans erat totus æneus, radium obtinens ſeptem eorum pedum, qui apud Anglos veteri edicto regio uſurpantur. Alexandriæ ſex menſes continuos hæſi, ſoli ſtelliſque intentus, quoties per caligines, aut pluvias, licebat, quas illic, mediâ præcipuè hyeme, contra receptam opinionem, & crebras, & violentas, eſſe ſenſi. Laboribus, & vigiliis defeſſus, relaxandi animi gratiâ bis Memphim petii, ſeu ut rectiùs loquar القاهرة Nam antiquâ Memphi orientalitor eſt hodierna Elkahira ſeptem ad minimum millibus paſſuum: inde ad ſepulcra veterum Ægyptiorum acceſſi, & cryptas illas ſubterraneas ſubii; poſt ad pyramides me contuli, earumque juſtam magnitudinem, idoneis ad eam rem adjutus inſtrumentis, deprehendi, & multa illic, dum omnia curioſiùs perluſtro, nec à priſcis ſcriptoribus, nec à recentioribus, literis mandata, annotavi. Opera ſanè ſtupenda, & ab ipſis antiquis inter orbis miracula meritò judicata, ſed a nemine (quòd ſciam) pro eorum dignitate ſatis deſcripta.

Interiorem cameram, & nonnulla ſecretiora adyta, temporis injuriâ nondum corrupta, nec unquam, ſi rectè judico, corrumpenda, menſuris Anglicis diligenter menſus ſum, adeò exactè, ut è viginti mille partibus, in quas viginti pedes, lineis tranſverſis, ſive potius diagoniis, diviſi, ne unam quidem, vel deeſſe, vel ſupereſſe, exiſtimem. Quod ideò tanto accuratiùs præſtiti, ut ex iſtâ comparatione omnium gentium menſuræ, quæ hodie ſunt, aut olim fuerunt, è duraturo aliquo monumento poſteris ſignari poſſint. Quod quidem ſi à Mathematicis olim præſtitum fuiſſet, ſelectis aliquibus idoneis locis, temporum injuriæ non obnoxiis, minus hodie incerti eſſemus in antiquorum menſuris inveſtigandis. Quid de meo conſilio cenſendum ſit, eruditorum judicio permitto; me certè, neque propoſiti, neque laboris, ſuſcepti pœnitet. Te verò (vir clariſſime) inter alios præcipuè, oro, & obteſtor, ut pondera, & menſuras gallicas, ſummâ diligentia cum archetypis, collatas, & regio ſigillo, ut fieri aſſolet, munitas ad me tranſmittas, & ſi qua numiſmata, vaſa priſca, vel pedes vetuſti, ab hæredibus nobiliſſimi D. viri Pereſcii recuperari poſſint, meo ære compares. Multum ille in hâc palæſtrâ deſudavit, & quantum ex literis

Departing that port after ſix days, a gentle eaſterly gale, in eight days, brought me to Alexandria; *where bribing the* Jews, *who have the collecting the cuſtoms, I landed my aſtronomical inſtruments in ſafety. I had ſeveral of them, moſt of them of braſs, and made by a notable workman, with extraordinary accuracy; the biggeſt whereof was a braſs quadrant, whoſe radius was ſeven ancient ſtatute foot of* England. *I continued ſix whole months at* Alexandria, *obſerving the ſun and ſtars, as often as fogs and rains would permit; which, contrary to the received opinion, I found to be frequent and violent, eſpecially in the depth of winter. Being ſpent with labour and watching, I went twice to divert my ſelf to* Memphis, *or to ſpeak more properly,* Elkahira: *for the preſent* Elkahira (Grand Cairo) *is at leaſt ſeven miles to the eaſtward of the ancient* Memphis. *Thence I repaired to the ſepulchres of the ancient* Egyptians, *and entered thoſe ſubterranean cells, or caverns; thence I went to the pyramids, and having fit inſtruments for that purpoſe, took their exact dimenſions, obſerving there many things, as I curiouſly view'd them, which have not been delivered in writing either by the ancient or modern authors. They are indeed amazing ſtructures, and deſervedly reckoned by the ancients among the wonders of the world, but not yet deſcribed as they ought to be by any one that I know of.*

I carefully took the dimenſions of the inner chamber, and ſome more private places, which time has not yet, nor, if I miſtake not, ever will deſtroy, with Engliſh *meaſures, and that ſo exactly, that I believe there is not one part over or under of* 20000, *into which twenty foot are divided by croſs, or rather diagonal lines. Which I was the more exact in, to the end that the meaſures of all nations that now are, or formerly were, may be tranſmitted to poſterity from ſome laſting monument, by comparing them with theſe. Had this been formerly done by mathematicians, chooſing for the purpoſe ſome proper places not expoſed to the injury of time, we ſhould not at preſent be ſo uncertain in the ſearch after the meaſures of the ancients. I leave it to the learned to determine, what judgment is to be made of this my deſign; for my part I neither repent my attempt nor my labour. I intreat and conjure you (moſt worthy ſir) to ſend me the* French *weights and meaſures, carefully compared with the ſtandards, and ſealed by the king's authority, as is uſual; and if any coins, old veſſels, or ancient feet can be obtained of the heirs of the moſt noble* Pereſcius, *that you will buy them upon my account. He laboured much in this affair, and, as may be conjectured by his letters, had he brought forth what he had ſo long conceived,*

ipsius licet conjicere, si peperisset, quæ tam diu parturivit, omnium industriam, & conatus facilè superasset. Ipse dum peregrè agebam tanquam itineris πάρεργον, Arabum, Persarum, Turcarum, Italorum, Hispanorum, Germanorum, varia, & diversa pondera, & mensuras, meis oculis, manibúsque subjeci, & cum Anglicis sedulò, & fideliter contuli. Idem & de Gallicis in animum induxissem, si per Parisios domum redire contigisset, sed, spe frustratus, istam tibi, tuæque diligentiæ provinciam demando. Tu me interea eâdem benevolentiâ prosequeris, quâ solebas, & si quid, quod mihi adjumento esse possit, repereris, viro doctissimo, meique amantissimo, D. Dorrel in ædibus oratoris Angli, committes. Vale.

Londini 18 Kal. Jun. MDCXLI.

Tibi addictissimus,

JOANNES GRAVIUS.

conceived, he would doubtless have out-done all others. I, during my travels, by the by, view'd and handled the several and sundry weights and measures of the Arabians, Persians, Turks, Italians, Spaniards, *and* Germans, *and carefully compared them with the* English. *I should have done the same by the* French, *had I returned home by the way of* Paris, *but being disappointed of it, I commit this affair to your care. Do you continue your wonted good will to me, and if you happen to find any thing that may be a help to me, deliver it to the most learned gentleman, and my very good friend, Mr.* Dorrel, *at the* English *embassador's. Farewel.*

London, May 14. 1641.

Your most affectionate,

JOHN GREAVES.

THE

THE

PREFACE.

HOW *high an estimation the ancients had of the Ægyptian Pyramids, appears by the several testimonies of* Herodotus, Diodorus, Strabo, *and* Pliny. *For* [a] Herodotus *acknowledges, that though there were a temple at* Ephesus *very renowned, as also at* Samos; *yet the Pyramids were worthier of relation: each of which single, might be compared with many the most sumptuous structures of the the* Grecians. Diodorus Siculus *confirms as much; who, as he prefers the works of the Ægyptians for magnificence before those of other nations, so he prefers the Pyramids before the rest of the Ægyptians*: it is confessed, [b] *saith he*, that these works far excel the rest in *Ægypt*, not only in the massiness of the structures, and in the expences, but also in the skilfulness of the architects. *He farther adds*, The greatness of the work, and art of the workmen, strike an admiration into the spectators. [c] Strabo *also testifies*, That three of them are very memorable, two of these are accounted amongst the seven miracles of the world. *Lastly*, [d] Pliny, *though he judges them* to be an idle and vain ostentation of the wealth of kings, *yet he grants* that three of them have filled the world with their fame. *Which three, by his description, and by such indications as may be collected out of* Diodorus *and* Strabo, *must necessarily be these three, which are now extant, and of which I intend especially to discourse. For* [e] Diodorus *writes*, That they are seated on Libya-side, an CXX stadia (or furlongs) from *Memphis*, and from *Nilus* XLV. *We likewise read in* [f] Strabo, XL stadia from the city *(Memphis,)* there is a certain brow of a hill in which are many Pyramids; *who presently after describing more particularly the three greatest, gives us this character:* These three stand near to one another upon the same plain. *And if this be not sufficient to point them out*, [g] Pliny *delivers many evident marks whereby to discover them:* These three (*as he informs us,*) are very conspicuous to those that sail upon the *Nilus*, they are seated on *Africa* side, upon a rocky and barren hill between the city *Memphis* and that place which we said is called the *Delta*, from the *Nilus* less than IV miles, from *Memphis* VI; there being a village opposite to them, which they name *Busiris*, from whence they use to ascend up to them. *All which characters were, and are applicable to none but only to these three.*

Having thus discovered their true place, or situation, we shall next discourse of the authors who have written of them. Amongst the ancients, there were many who thought it worth their labour to describe them. For Pausanias, *as it were, complaining that the* Grecians *had been very curious in describing these, whilst they had omitted many remarkable structures of their own, writes thus:* [d] That the *Grecians* admired things of stran-

[a] Καίτοι ἀξιόλογός γε καὶ ὁ ἐν Ἐφέσῳ ἐστὶ νηὸς, καὶ ὁ ἐν Σάμῳ, ἦσαν μὲν νῦν αἱ πυραμίδες λόγου μείζονες, καὶ πολλῶν ἑκάστη αὐτέων Ἑλληνικῶν ἔργων καὶ μεγάλων ἀνταξίη. Herod. l. 2.

[b] Ὁμολογεῖται δὲ ταῦτα τὰ ἔργα πολὺ προέχειν τῶν κατ' Αἴγυπτον, οὐ μόνον τῷ βάρει τῶν κατασκευασμάτων καὶ ταῖς δαπάναις, ἀλλὰ καὶ τῇ πολυτεχνίᾳ τῶν ἐργασαμένων. Diod. Sic. Biblioth. l. 1. Τῷ δὲ μεγέθει τῶν ἔργων καὶ τῇ κατὰ τὴν τέχνην χειρουργίᾳ θαυμαστήν τινα κατάπληξιν παρέχονται τοῖς θεωμένοις, Ibid.

[c] Τρεῖς δ' ἀξιόλογοι, τὰς δὲ δύο τούτων καὶ ἐν τοῖς ἑπτὰ θεάμασι καταριθμοῦνται. Strab. l. 17.

[d] *Regum pecuniæ ociosa ac stulta ostentatio.—Tres quæ orbem Terrarum implevêre famâ.* Plin. l. 36. c. 12.

[e] Αὗται δὲ κεῖνται κατὰ τὴν Λιβύην τῆς Μέμφιος ἀπέχουσι σταδίους ἑκατὸν καὶ εἴκοσι, τοῦ δὲ Νείλου πέντε πρὸς τοῖς τετταράκοντα. Diod. Sic. l. 1.

[f] Τετταράκοντα δ' ἀπὸ τῆς πόλεως σταδίους προελθόντι ὀρεινή τις ὀφρύς ἐστιν, ἐφ' ᾗ πολλαὶ μὲν Πυραμίδες εἰσί. Strab. l. 12. Αὗται μὲν οὖν ἐγγὺς ἀλλήλων εἰσὶ τῷ αὐτῷ ἐπιπέδῳ. Idem ibid.

[g] *Reliquæ tres] sanè conspicuæ undique innavigantibus, sitæ sunt in parte Africæ, monte saxeo sterilique inter Memphim oppidum, & quòd appellari diximus Delta, à Nilo minus* IV *millia pass. à Memphi sex, vico apposito, quem vocant Busirin, in quo sunt assueti scandere illas.* Plin. l. 36. c. 12.

[h] Ἕλληνες δ' ἄρα εἰσὶ δεινοὶ τὰ ὑπερόρια ἐν θαύματι τίθεσθαι μείζονι ἢ τὰ οἰκεῖα. ὁπότε ἀνδράσιν ἐπιφανέσιν ἐς συγγραφὴν, πυραμίδας μὲν τὰς παρὰ Αἰγυπτίοις ἐπῆλθεν ἐξηγήσασθαι πρὸς τὸ ἀκριβέστατον, θησαυρὸν δὲ τὸν Μινύου καὶ τὰ τείχη τὰ ἐν Τίρυνθι οὐδ' ἐπὶ βραχὺ ἤγαγον μνήμης, οὐδ' ὄντα ἐλάττονος θαύματος. Pausaniæ Bœotica.

gers more than of their own, seeing that some historians of note had most accurately described the Pyramids of *Ægypt*, whereas the treasury of *Minyas*, and walls of *Tiryns*, *(places in* Bœotia) no less to be admired than these, had been omitted by them. Pliny *gives us a large catalogue of authors that had purposely treated of this argument:* [i] *Those which have writ of them, are,* Herodotus, Euhemerus, Duris Samius, Aristagoras, Dionysius, Artemidorus, Alexander Polyhistor, Butorides, Antisthenes, Demetrius, Demoteles, Apion: *Where we are beholden to him for preserving the names of so many writers, though their works (unless those of* Herodotus) *by the injury and calamity of times, have long since perished. Besides these,* Diodorus Siculus, Strabo, Pomponius Mela, Pliny, Solinus, *and* Ammianus Marcellinus, *(the names of modern authors I purposely omit,) have given us some relations of them. But it may be, if the writings of* Aristides *had not perished, who in his* Λόγ. Αἰγυπτ. *speaks thus of himself,* [k] After that I had enter'd into *Æthiopia*, and four times travelled all over *Ægypt*, and had left nothing unhandled, neither the Pyramids, nor labyrinth, nor temples, nor channels, and partly had procured out of their writings such measures as might be had, and partly with the priests had measured such things as were not obvious, yet could I not preserve them entire for thee, seeing the books which thy servants, by my appointment, transcribed, have perished: *Or, if we had the* sacred commentaries of the *Ægyptians, so often cited by* [l] Diodorus, *we might receive better satisfaction, and be also more content with the loss of those other writings of the* Grecians. *But seeing the vicissitudes and revolutions of times, have deprived us of these, whilst the Pyramids have been too great to be consumed, it will be no superfluous labour to imitate the examples of the ancients, and to supply the loss of them, by giving a distinct narration of the several respective dimensions and proportions of these pyramids: in which I shall tread in as even a path as I can, between truth and the traditions of such of the ancients as are still extant: first, putting down those relations which by them have been transmitted to us; and next, shewing in what manner, upon examination, I found the Pyramids in the years one thousand six hundred thirty eight, and one thousand six hundred thirty nine, or in the thousand forty and eighth year of the* Hegira. *For I went twice to* Grand Cairo *from* Alexandria, *and from thence into the deserts, for the greater certainty to view them; carrying with me a* radius *of ten feet most accurately divided into ten thousand parts, besides some other instruments, for the fuller discovery of the truth. But before I descend to a particular description, I shall make enquiry by whom, at what time, and to what end these monuments were erected.*

[i] *Qui de iis scripserint, sunt Herodotus, Euhemerus, Duris Samius, Aristagoras, Dionysius, Artemidorus, Alexander Polyhistor, Butorides, Antisthenes, Demetrius, Demoteles, Apion.* Plin. Nat. Hist. l. 36. c. 12.

[k] Ἐπειδὴ καὶ τὸ μέχρι τῆς Αἰθιοπικῆς χώρας προελθεῖν καὶ αὐτὴν διερευνησάμενος Αἴγυπτον τετράκις τὸ σύμπαν καὶ παρεὶς οὐδὲν ἀνεξέταστον οὐ πυραμίδας, οὐ λαβύρινθον, οὐχ ἱερὸν, οὐ διώρυχας ἀλλ' ἂν μὲν ἐν ταῖς βίβλοις τὰ μέτρα ὑπῆρχεν ἐκεῖθεν πορισάμενος· ἂν δὲ μὴ ἐξ ἑτοίμου λαβεῖν ἦν ἐκμετρήσας αὐτὸς μετὰ τῶν παρ' ἑκάστοις ἱερέων καὶ προφητῶν· εἶτ' οὐκ ἐδυνήθην αὐτά σοι διασώσασθαι τῶν ὑπομνημάτων διαφθαρέντων ἃ τοῖς σοῖς παισὶ προσέταξα ποιῆσαι, Aristid. Λόγ. Αἰγυπτ.

[l] Ὡς ἐν ταῖς ἱεραῖς ἀναγραφαῖς ὁρᾶν ἐστὶ κατακεχωρισμένον. Diod. Sic. l. 1. Οἱ ἱερεῖς τῶν Αἰγυπτίων ἱστοροῦσιν ἐκ τῶν ἀναγραφῶν τῶν ἐν ταῖς ἱεραῖς βίβλοις. Idem. Ibidem.

Of

Of the Authors or Founders of the PYRAMIDS.

GREAVES

IT is the opinion of ſome [a] modern writers, that the *Ægyptian* Pyramids were erected by the *Iſraelites*, during their heavy preſſure under the tyranny of the *Pharaohs*. And this ſeems to be confirmed by [b] *Joſephus*; who relates, that *when as time had extinguiſhed the memory of the benefits of* Joſeph, *the kingdom of* Ægypt *being tranſplanted into another family, they uſed the* Iſraelites *with much ſeverity, waſting them with ſeveral labours; for they were commanded to cut divers channels for the river* (Nilus) *to raiſe walls, and caſt up banks, whereby to hinder the inundation of the ſtream; they oppreſſed alſo our nation with thoſe fabricks of the Pyramids, compelling them to learn many* (mechanical) *arts, and inured them to the ſupporting of labours.* But the ſacred ſcriptures clearly expreſſing the ſlavery of the *Jews*, to have conſiſted in making and burning of brick, (for the original is לבנים *lebénim*, which the [c] *Septuagint* renders by πλίνθος and πλινθεία,) whereas all theſe Pyramids conſiſt of ſtone, I cannot be induced to ſubſcribe to their aſſertion.

Much leſs can I aſſent to that opinion of [d] *Stephanus*, [e] *Nicetas*, [f] *Nonnus*, and *the author of the Greek* [g] Ἐτυμολογικὸν μέγα, with ſome others, who derive the name of the Pyramids ἀπὸ τοῦ πυρῶ, that is, *from corn*, and not ἀπὸ τοῦ πυρὸς, *from the figure of a flame of fire*, which they reſemble; becauſe, ſay moſt of them, theſe were built by the patriarch *Joſeph*, as σιτοδόχα, *receptacles and granaries* of the ſeven plentiful years. For, beſides that this figure is moſt improper for ſuch a purpoſe, (a Pyramid being the leaſt capacious of any regular mathematical body) the ſtreightneſs and fewneſs of the rooms within, (the reſt of the building being one ſolid and entire fabrick of ſtone) do utterly overthrow this conjecture. Wherefore the relations of *Herodotus*, *Diodorus Siculus*, and of ſome others, but eſpecially of theſe two, both of them having travelled into *Ægypt*, and converſed with the prieſts, (beſides that, the latter made uſe of their *commentaries*, will give us the beſt and cleareſt light in matters of ſo great antiquity.

For *Herodotus* writes thus concerning the firſt of theſe Pyramids, that [h] *until king* Rhampſinitus's *time the* Ægyptians *report the laws to have flouriſhed in* Ægypt: *After whom*, Cheops *ſucceeding in the kingdom, fell into all manner of vice; for, ſhutting up the temples, he forbad the* Ægyptians *to ſacrifice; beſides, he commanded that they ſhould be employed in his works*, (he means this Pyramid of which he diſcourſeth,) *that ſome of them ſhould receive the ſtones dug out of the quarries of the* Arabian *mountain, and that from thence they ſhould carry them to the* Nilus; *theſe being wafted over the river, others were to receive them, and to draw them to the mountain, which is called* Libycus. *There were employed in the work ten* myriads *of men, every three months a* myriad: *the people ſpent ten years in the way in which they drew the ſtones, which ſeems to me no leſs a work than the building of the Pyramid it ſelf.* [i] *Diodorus Siculus* diſcourſing of the ſame argument, gives the erector of this another name, different from that of *Herodotus*, ſtiling him *Chemmis*; but in the time, and perſon, they both agree, each of them affirming him to have ſucceeded *Rhampſinitus*, and to have been the father of *Mycerinus*, and to have reign'd over the *Ægyptians* fifty years. This difference of names between *Herodotus* and *Diodorus*, concerning the ſame king, may probably be thus reconciled, that *Diodorus* expreſſes the genuine denomination in the *Ægyptian* language, and that *Herodotus* renders the ſignification in the *Greek*; a practice not unuſual with him, and with other approved authors. Thus the patriarch *Iſaac* in the ſcriptures, being denominated from צחק, that is, *laughter*, is by *Alexander Polyhiſtor*, as [k] *Euſebius* teſtifies, named Γέλως. Wherefore חם *Cham* in *Hebrew*, (or in the *Greek*

[a] *Henr. Spondanus de cœmeteriis ſacris, lib.* 1. *par.* 1. *cap.* 6. *Brodæus Epigr. Græc.* εἰς ναύς.

[b] Joſeph. lib. 2. Antiq. cap. 5. Ὧν τ' ἤσαν εὖ ὑπὸ Ἰωσήφυ πεκυχηκότες διὰ χρόνυ μῆκος λήθην λαβόντες, καὶ τῆς βασιλείας εἰς ἄλλον οἶκον μετεληλυθυίας δεινῶς ἐνύβριζον τὺς Ἰσραηλίτας, &c.

[c] Exod. cap. v. ſæpè.

[d] Ὀνομάσθησαν δὲ Πυραμίδες ἀπὸ τῶν πυρῶν, ὡς ἐκεῖ συναγαγὼν ὁ βασιλεὺς ἔνδηιαν ἐποίησε σίτυ κατὰ τὴν Αἴγυπτον. Steph. περὶ πόλεων.

[e] Πυραμίδες.] *Id eſt ædificia quædam à Joſeph. ut nonnulli opinantur, ad condenda frumenta ſcitè admodum elaborata,* ἀπὸ τῶ πυρῶ, *id eſt, à frumento nomen conſecuta. Nicetas in* XX *Orat. Nazianzeni.*

[f] *Non à vero, ut inquit Nonnus, abhorret, quin has Pyramides poſt Joſephi tempora, exceſſumque Judæorum ex Ægypto in Regum ſepulchra converterint. Bilius ex Nonno monacho. Ibidem.*

[g] Πυραμίδες δὲ πάλιν λέγον) ὡρεῖα βασίλικα σιτοδόχα ἃ κατεσκεύασε Ἰωσήφ. Ἐτυμόλ. μέγα.

[h] Herod. lib. 2. Μέχρι μὲν νῦν Ῥαμψινίτυ βασιλῆος εἶναι ἐν Αἰγύπτῳ πᾶσαν εὐνομίην ἔλεγον, &c.

[i] Diod. Sic. l. 1.

[k] Euſeb. l. 6. Evangel. præpar. cap. 19.

flection,

GREAVES *flection, Chemmis,*) signifying *adustion*, which anciently might be the same in *Ægyptian*, and χέωψ, or χαίωψ, signifying *swarthy visage* or *adust*; *Herodotus* might call him *Cheops* in *Greek*, whom in the *Ægyptian* language *Diodorus* stiles *Chemmis*. But I go on with *Diodorus*. *This* Chemmis, [l] saith he, *erected the greatest of these three Pyramids, which are reputed among the seven wonderful fabricks of the world*; where he also enlarges the number of the workmen employed by him, to *three hundred and sixty thousand*, which *Herodotus* mentions only to have been *an hundred thousand*; though both of them concur, and [m] *Pliny* with them both, that *twenty years were spent in the building of this Pyramid*.

Concerning the second Pyramid, *Herodotus* and *Diodorus* assign the author of it to have been *Cephren*, brother to the former king. *Diodorus* adds, that by some he is also called *Chabryis*, and was the son of *Chemmis*; a difference which I imagine to have been occasioned out of the diversity of pronunciation of *Chabryis* for *Cephren*; there being an easy transmutation in letters of the same organ, as *grammarians* use to speak. *Cheops*, as [n] *Herodotus* informs us, *being deceased, his brother* Cephren *reigned after him; who imitated him, as in other things, so in the making of a Pyramid, the magnitude of which is less than that of his brother's*. And [o] *Diodorus* relates, *That* Chemmis *being dead, his brother* Cephren *succeeded him in the kingdom, and reigned fifty six years: some say, that not his brother, but his son, which was named* Chabryis, *reigned after him. This is affirmed by the consent of all, that the successor of the former king, in imitation of him, built the second Pyramid like to the first, in respect of the art and workmanship, but far inferior to it in respect of magnitude.*

The third Pyramid was erected by [p] *Mycerinus*, some call him *Mycherinus*, as it is observed by *Diodorus*, who makes him the son of *Chemmis*, as *Herodotus* doth of *Cheops*; the difference between them being, as we noted before, rather nominal than real. The same [q] *Herodotus* also writes, That *some of the* Grecians *make the third Pyramid the work of* Rhodopis *a curtizan; an error in opinion of those who seem not to know who this* Rhodopis *might be of which they speak; for neither could she have undertaken such a Pyramid, on which so many thousand talents were to be spent; neither lived she in this man's time, but in the time of king* Amasis. Now this *Amasis*, as he elsewhere shews, lived long after these Pyramids were in being. The same story is cited both by [r] *Strabo* and *Pliny*, both of them omitting the names of the founders of the former two. *Strabo* gives her a double name; *The third Pyramid is the sepulchre of a curtizan, made by her lovers, whom* Sappho *the poetress calls* Doricha, *mistress to her brother* Charaxus; *others name her* Rhodope. But whether we name her *Doricha*, or *Rhodope*, the relation is altogether improbable, if we consider either her condition or the infinite vastness of the expence. For [s] *Diodorus*, though he rightly acknowledges this Pyramid to be much less than either of the former two, yet in respect of the exquisite workmanship, and richness of the materials, he judges it not inferior to either of them. A structure certainly too great and sumptuous to have been the design and undertaking of a curtizan, which could hardly have been performed by a rich and potent monarch. And yet *Diodorus* hath almost the same relation, only a little altered in the circumstances; [t] *Some say, that this is the sepulchre of the strumpet* Rhodope; *of whom, some of the* Nomarchæ (or prefects of the provinces) *being enamoured, by a common expence to win her favour, they built this monument.* But to pass by this fable, (for it is no better,) and to return to our enquiry. The same author immediately before, ingenuously confesses, that concerning them all three, there is little agreement either amongst the natives or amongst writers: [u] *For they say,* Armæus *made the greatest of these; the second,* Amasis; *the third,* Inaron. And [w] *Pliny* informing us, that *these three were made in seventy eight years and four months*, leaves the founders of them very uncertain: for reciting the names of many authors that had described them, he

[l] Diod. Sic. lib. 1. Χέμμις] κατεσκεύασε δὲ τὴν μεγίστην τῶν τριῶν Πυραμίδων τῶν ἐν τοῖς ἑπτὰ τοῖς ἐπιφανεστάτοις ἔργοις ἐριθμουμένων.

[m] *Pyramis amplissima ex Arabicis lapidicinis constat. Trecenta* LX *hominum millia annis* XX *eam construxisse produntur.* Plin. l. 36. c. 12.

[n] Herod. lib. 3. Τελευτήσαντος δὲ τούτου, ἐκδέξασθαι τὴν βασιληΐην τὸν ἀδελφεὸν αὐτοῦ Χεφρῆνα, &c.

[o] Diodor. lib. 1. Τελευτήσαντος δὲ τοῦ βασιλέως τούτου διεδέξατο τὴν ἀρχὴν ὁ ἀδελφὸς Χεφρὴν, καὶ ἦρξεν ἔτη ἓξ πρὸς τοῖς πεντήκοντα, &c.

[p] Πυραμίδα δὲ καὶ οὗτος ἀπελίπετο πολλὸν ἐλάσσω τοῦ πατρός. Herodot. lib. 2.

[q] Herodot. lib. 2. Τὴν δὴ μετεξέτεροι φασὶ Ἑλλήνων Ῥοδώπιος ἑταίρης γυναικὸς εἶναι, οὐκ ὀρθῶς λέγοντες, &c.

[r] Λέγεται δὲ τῆς ἑταίρας τάφος γεγονὼς ὑπὸ τῶν ἐραστῶν. ἣ Σαπφὼ μὲν ἡ τῶν μελῶν ποιήτρια, καλεῖ Δωρίχαν ἐρωμένην τοῦ ἀδελφοῦ αὐτῆς Χαράξου γεγονυῖαν ἄλλοι δ' ὀνομάζουσι Ῥοδώπην. Strab. lib. 17.

[s] Diod. Sic. lib. 1. [t] Diod. Sic. lib. 1. Ταύτην δ' ἔνιοι λέγουσι Ῥοδώπιδος τάφον εἶναι τῆς ἑταίρας, ἧς φασὶ, τῶν Νομαρχῶν τινὰς ἐραστὰς γενομένους, διὰ φιλοστοργίαν οἰκοδομήσαντας ἐπιτελέσαι κοινῇ τὸ κατασκεύασμα.

[u] Idem. Ibid. Τὴν μεγίστην ποιῆσαι λέγουσιν Ἀρμαῖον τὴν δὲ δευτέραν Ἀμασίν. [γρ. Ἀμμωσίν.] τὴν δὲ τρίτην Ἰνάρωνα. [γρ. Μάρωνα.] [w] *Tres verò factæ annis* LXXVIII. *& mensibus* IV. Plin. lib. 36. cap. 12.

2 concludes,

concludes, [x] *Inter omnes eos non constat à quibus factæ sint, justissimo casu obliteratis tantæ vanitatis authoribus.*

The *Arabians*, whose excellencies I judge to have been in the speculative sciences, and not in the histories and occurrences of ancient times, assign other founders of these three, different from those mentioned by the *Greeks*. The author of the book intitled, *Morat Alzeman*, writes, *They differ concerning him that built the Pyramids: some say* Joseph, *some say* Nimrod, *some* Dalukah *the queen, and some that the* Ægyptians *built them before the flood: for they foresaw that it would be, and they carried thither their treasures, but it profited them nothing.* In another place he tells us, *That the* Coptites *(or* Ægyptians*) report, that these two greater Pyramids, and the lesser, which is coloured, are sepulchres. In the east Pyramid is king* Saurid, *in the west Pyramid his brother* Hougib, *and in the coloured Pyramid* Fazfarinoun *the son of* Hougib: *The* Sabæans *relate, that one of them is the sepulchre of* Shiit, *(that is,* Seth,*) and the second the sepulchre of* Hermes, *and the coloured one the sepulchre of* Sab, *the son of* Hermes, *from whom they are called* Sabæans. *They go in pilgrimage thither, and sacrifice at them a cock, and a black calf, and offer up incense. Ibn Abd Alhokm*, another *Arabian*, discoursing of this argument, confesses, that he could not find amongst the learned men in *Ægypt*, any certain relation concerning them, (wherefore) *what is more reasonable* (saith he) *than that the Pyramids were built before the flood? For if they had been built after, there would have been some memory of them amongst men.* At last he concludes, *The greatest part of chronologers affirm, that he which built the Pyramids, was* Saurid Ibn Salhouk *the king of* Ægypt, *who was before the flood three hundred years.* And this opinion he confirms out of the books of the *Ægyptians:* To which he adds, *The* Coptites *mention in their books, that upon them there is an inscription engraven;* the exposition of it in *Arabick* is this, *I* Saurid *the king, built the Pyramids in such and such a time, and finished them in six years; he that comes after me, and says he is equal to me, let him destroy them in six hundred years; and yet it is known, that it is easier to pluck down than to build; and when I had finished them, I covered them with satin, and let him cover them with mats.* The same relation I find in several others of them, that this *Saurid* was the founder of these three Pyramids, which the admiration of after-times enrolled amongst the miracles of the world. And these are those three, which are still fair and entire, and standing near to one another, formerly not far distant from the great and ancient city *Memphis*, built by [y] *Uchoreus*, of which there is now not so much as the ruins left,) and less distant from the river *Nilus*, as *Diodorus*, *Strabo*, and *Pliny*, rightly describe.

Besides these three, we find mentioned in *Herodotus* and *Diodorus*, the names and authors of some others, not much inferior to these in magnitude, long since ruined and defaced by time. On the contrary, there are many now standing in the *Libyan* desert, whose names and authors, neither *Herodotus* nor *Diodorus*, nor yet any of the ancients, have expressed.

After *Mycerinus*, according to [z] *Herodotus*, (for *Diodorus* is here silent,) *Asychis* succeeded in the kingdom, [a] *who being desirous to excel his predecessors, left for a monument a Pyramid made of bricks, with these words engraven in stone, Compare not me with the Pyramids built of stone, which I as far excel as* Jupiter *doth the other gods. For striking of the bottom of the lake with long poles, and gathering the dirt which stuck to them, they made thence bricks, and formed me in this manner.*

The same author relates, that many ages after this *Asychis*, *Sanacharib* king of the *Arabians* and *Assyrians*, who certainly is the same which is mentioned in the scriptures, having expelled *Sethon* the king of the *Ægyptians*, and the priest of *Vulcan*, [b] *the* Ægyptians *recovering their liberty, made choice of twelve kings,* (which is also confirmed by *Diodorus*,) *dividing* Ægypt *into so many parts; for they could at no time live without a king; these by a common consent, built a labyrinth above the lake of* Mœris: *At the angle where the labyrinth ends, there is a Pyramid of* XL Orgyiæ, (that is, of CCXL feet,) *in which are ingraven huge resemblances of beasts, the passage to it is under ground.* And this is that Pyramid, as may evidently be collected out of [c] *Strabo*, in which *Imandes* lies buried, whom we may probably suppose to have been the builder of it: His words are these, *At the end of this building,* (that is, of this labyrinth,) *which contains a furlong in length, there is a certain* [d] *sepulchre, being a quadrilateral Pyramid,*

[x] Plin. l. 36. c. 12. [y] Οὐχορεὺς ἔκτισε πόλιν Μέμφιν, ἐπιφανεστάτην τῶν κατ' Ἄιγυπτον. Diodor. lib. 1.
[z] Herod. lib. 2. [a] Ὑπερβάλεσθαι δὲ βουλόμενον τοῦτον τὸν βασιλέα τοὺς πρότερον ἑαυτοῦ βασιλέας γενομένους Αἰγύπτου, μνημόσυνον Πυραμίδα λιπέσθαι ἐκ πλίνθων ποιήσαντα, ἐν τῇ γράμματα ἐν λίθῳ ἐγκεκολαμμένα τάδε λέγοντά ἐστι. Μή με κατονοθῇς πρὸς τὰς λιθίνας Πυραμίδας, προέχω γὰρ αὐτέων τοσοῦτον, ὅσον ὁ Ζεὺς τῶν ἄλλων θεῶν· κοντῷ γὰρ ὑποτύπτοντες ἐς λίμνην, ὅτι προσχοῖτο τοῦ πηλοῦ τῷ κοντῷ τοῦτο συλλέγοντες πλίνθους εἴρυσαν, καὶ με τρόπῳ τοιούτῳ ἐξεποίησαν.
[b] Herod. lib. 2. [c] Strab. lib. 17. [d] *Diodorus* relates, that over the sepulchre there was a circle of gold of three hundred and sixty five cubits compass, and a cubit in thickness, in which the days

of

GREAVES *mid, each side of which is* CCCC *feet, and the altitude is the same; the name of him that lies buried there is* Imandes, whom the author of the epitome calls *Maindes*, and *Strabo* himself not long after *Ismandes*; *Diodorus* names him *Osymanduas*. Which of these two, whether *Herodotus* or *Strabo*, hath given the truest measure of it, unless the Pyramid were now extant, cannot be decided by us. Though *Pliny* adheres to the dimensions of *Herodotus*; but whereas *Herodotus* and *Strabo* mention there but one Pyramid, he makes mention of many. And whereas *Strabo* makes this to be quadrilateral, he describes these (if I mistake not his words) to be sexangular. [e] *Superque Nemeses* XV. *ædiculis incluserit Pyramides complures* (that is, above this labyrinth which he places *in Heracleopolite Nomo*,) *quadragenarum ulnarum* VI *radice muros obtinentes.*

Long before these four Pyramids of *Cheops*, *Cephren*, *Mycerinus*, and *Asychis*, who immediately succeeded one another in the kingdom, but after this of *Ismandes*, *Myris* as he is called by *Diodorus*, (but *Herodotus*, *Strabo* and *Pliny*, name him *Mœris*) another *Ægyptian* king, built two admirable Pyramids; the description of which, tho' in *Herodotus*, it immediately follows that of the twelve kings; yet as it may evidently be collected out of him and *Diodorus*, these two of *Mœris* must many ages have preceded. [f] For *Herodotus* tells us, that from *Menes* (the first king of the *Ægyptians*, whom *Diodorus* names *Menas*,) *the priests recited out of their books* CCCXXX *kings, the last of which was* Mœris; long after whom reigned *Sesostris*, who is call'd by *Manethos*, *Sethosis*; and by *Diodorus*, *Sesostris*, and *Sesoosis*; who more particularly than *Herodotus*, expresses *Sesostris* to have been [g] seven ages after *Mœris*, and to have reigned long before these twelve kings. The which *Sesostris*, or *Sethosis*, immediately succeeding *Amænophis*, (according to *Manethos* in *Josephus*, as we shall shew in the ensuing discourse,) must have been before *Cheops*, *Cephren*, *Mycerinus*, and *Asychis*; and therefore consequently, that *Mœris* must long have preceded these twelve kings. This *Mœris* undertook, and finished that most admirable lake denominated after his name, as it is testified by *Herodotus*, *Diodorus*, *Strabo*, and *Pliny*. A work the most useful and wonderful, if it be rightly considered, that I think was ever by any man attempted; in the midst of which, he erected two Pyramids, the one in memory of himself, the other of his wife, each of them being 1ↄc feet in height; the description of both which, and of his lake, we have in *Herodotus*, the latter we find in *Strabo*, but in none so fully as in [h] *Diodorus*, and therefore I shall relate his words. *Ten* schœnes, (that is, 1ↄc furlongs; though *Strabo* and *Artemidorus* before him, observe a difference of *scœnes* in *Ægypt*, *above the city* (Memphis,) Myris *dug a lake of admirable use, the greatness of which work is incredible. For they relate, that the circumference of it contains* CIↄ CIↄ CIↄ 1ↄc *furlongs, the depth of it in many places is fifty fathom*, (that is, two hundred cubits, or three hundred feet,) *who therefore may not deservedly ask, that shall consider the greatness of the work, how many myriads of men, and in how many years they made it? The common benefit of it to those that inhabit* Ægypt, *and the wisdom of the king, no man can sufficiently commend. For since the rising of* Nilus *is not always alike, and the country is the more fruitful by the moderateness of this, he digged a lake to receive the superfluity of the water, that neither by the greatness of the inundation unseasonably drowning the country, it should occasion marshes or lakes; or flowing less than it should do, for want of water, it should corrupt the fruits; he therefore cut a ditch from the river to the lake, eighty furlongs long, and three hundred feet in breadth. By which, sometimes receiving in, and sometimes diverting the river, he exhibited a seasonable quantity of water to the husbandmen, the mouth of it sometimes being opened, and sometimes shut, not without much art, and great expences. For he that would open the bars* (or sluices,) *or shut them, it was necessary that he spent at the least fifty talents. The lake in this manner benefiting the* Ægyptians, *hath continued to our times, and from the author of it at this day, is called the lake of* Myris. *The king that digged it, left a place in the midst, in which he built a sepulchre and two*

of the year were inscribed, and divided into a cubit a piece, with a description according to their nature, of the setting and rising of the stars, and also their operations, after the *Ægyptian* astrologers. They say, this circle was carried away by *Cambyses* and the *Persians*, at what time they conquered *Ægypt*. (*Diod. Sicul. lib.* 1.) He which shall seriously consider this, and several other passages in *Herodotus* and *Diodorus*, of the stupendious works of the *Ægyptians*, must needs aknowledge, that for magnificence, if not for art, they far exceeded the *Grecians* and *Romans*, even when their empires were at the highest, and most flourishing. And therefore, those *admiranda Romæ*, collected by *Lipsius*, are scarce to be admired, if compared with some of these. At this day there is hardly any vast column or obelisk remaining in *Rome*, worthy of note, which hath not anciently been brought thither out of *Ægypt*.

[e] Plin. lib. 36. cap. 13. [f] Herod. lib. 2. Μετὰ δὲ τοῦτον [Μῆνα] κατέλεγον οἱ ἱερέες ἐκ βίβλου ἄλλων βασιλέων τριηκοσίων τε καὶ τριήκοντα οὐνόματα, ἔσχατος αὐτῶν Μοῖρις.

[g] Diod. Sic. lib. 1. [h] Diod. Sic. lib. 1. Ἐπάνω δὲ τῆς πόλεως ἀπὸ δέκα σχοίνων λίμνην ὤρυξε τῇ μὲν εὐχρηστίᾳ θαυμαστήν, τῷ δὲ μεγέθει τοῦ ἔργου ἄπιστον, &c.

GREAVES.

Pyramids, each a furlong in height; the one for himself, the other for his wife, placing upon them two marble-statues, sitting on a throne, imagining by these works he should propagate to posterity an immortal memory of his worth. The revenue of the fish of this lake, he gave to his wife for her unguents, and other ornaments; the fishing being worth to her a talent a day: For they report, there are two and twenty sorts of fishes in it, and that such a multitude is taken, that those who are perpetually imployed in salting them, of which there is a very great mumber, can hardly dispatch the work. Thus far *Diodorus*. Which description, as it is much more full than that of *Herodotus*, so *Herodotus* hath this memorable observation omitted by *Diodorus:* [i] *That this lake was made by hand, and hollowed, it is apparent, because almost in the midst of it, there stands two Pyramids fifty fathoms above the water, and as many fathoms of the building under-water: Upon the top of each of which, there is a* Colossus *of stone sitting upon a throne; so that the Pyramids are an hundred fathoms high. Strabo* I know not by what oversight omits these two Pyramids, whereas he acknowledges the lake of *Mœris* in which they stood, [k] *to be admirable, being like a sea for greatness and for colour.*

Besides these which we have handled, and whose founders are upon record in the writings of the antients, there are many others in the *Libyan* desert where it bounds *Ægypt*, of which there is no particular mention extant, either in the *Greeks, Latins*, or *Arabians*; unless we shall apply these words of [l] *Diodorus* to some of them. *There are three other Pyramids, each side of which contain two hundred feet, the structure of them, excepting the magnitude, is like to the former,* (that is, as he there specifies, to those three Pyramids of *Chemmis, Cephren*, and *Mycerinus*,) *these three kings before-mentioned, are reported to have erected them for their wives.* The bigness of some of these now extant, doth well answer the measure assigned by *Diodorus:* but if these three kings built them for their queens, it may be wondered why they should have placed them so remote from their own sepulchres; or why they should stand at such large and unequal distances of several miles from one another. I find as little satisfaction in [m] *Pliny* where he writes, *Multa circa hoc vanitas illorum hominum fuit, vestigiaque complurium inchoatarum extant, una est in Arsinoite Nomo, duæ in Memphi, non procul labyrintho, de quo & ipsi dicemus.* For not telling us the founders of these, he leaves us still in the same darkness, only we may in general collect out of him, and likewise out of that ode in *Horace:*

> *Exegi monumentum ære perennius;*
> *Regalique situ Pyramidium altius.*
> Horat. ode 30. lib. 3.

That they were the works of *Ægyptian* kings; but of which of them, and at what time, we are altogether uncertain. *Regum pecuniæ*, [n] saith *Pliny, otiosa, ac stulta ostentatio.* Of the same opinion is *Leo Africanus*, in his accurate description of *Africa*, after many years travel in those parts. *Hâc per desertum arenaceum, itur ad Pyramides, nempe ad priscorum Ægypti regum sepulchra, quo in loco Memphin olim extitisse asserunt* [o]. It may be it was the royal prerogative, and that it was prohibited to private men, how wealthy and potent soever to be thus intombed; but without some farther light from the ancients, it would be too great a presumption to determine any thing.

[p] *Lucan*, I know not upon what ground, makes as if the *Ptolemies* had imitated the *Ægyptian* kings in this particular:

> *Cum Ptolemæorum manes seriemque pudendam*
> *Pyramides claudant.*

Surely if they did, these are none of those: For they would have built them at *Alexandria*, which was then the regal seat, and not at *Memphis*, the which as [q] *Diodorus* assures us, began to decay after the building of *Alexandria*, like as the antient *Thebes* (as the [r] *Grecians* stiled it; or *the city of the sun*, as the *Ægyptians*, according to [s] *Diodorus*, called it; or *Diospolis*, as *Diodorus* and [t] *Strabo* also name it,) did after the building of *Memphis*. Those which imagine the monument or sepulchre, mentioned by [v] *Plutarch* at *Alexandria*, into which *Cleopatra* fled for fear of *Augustus*, to have been a Pyramid, are much deceived. For in the life of *Mark Antony*, where he informs us, that there were sepulchres near the temple of *Isis, of exquisite workmanship, and very high*; into which she conveyed the richest of her treasures, he describes one of them, wherein she hid her self, to have

i Herodot. lib. 2. k Θαυμαστὴν δὲ καὶ τὴν λίμνην ἔχει τὴν Μοίριδος καλουμένην πελαγίαν τῷ μεγέθει, καὶ τῇ χρόᾳ θαλαττοειδῆ. Strab. lib. 17.

l Diod. Sic. lib. 1. Εἰσὶ δὲ καὶ ἄλλαι τρεῖς Πυραμίδες, ὧν ἑκάστη μὲν πλευρᾷ δίπλεθρον ὑπάρχει, τὸ δ' ὅλον ἔργον παραπλήσιον τῇ κατασκευῇ ταῖς ἄλλαις, πλὴν τοῦ μεγέθους· ταύτας δὲ φασὶ τοὺς προειρημένους τρεῖς βασιλεῖς ταῖς ἰδίαις κατασκευάσαι γυναιξίν. m Plin. lib. 36. cap. 12. n Ibid. o Leo Afric. lib. 8.

p Lucan. lib. 8. q Diodor. lib. 1. r Plato, & alii. s Diodor. lib. 1. t Strab. lib. 17.

v Plutarch. in Antonio.

GREAVES had a window above the entrance, by which she drew up with cords the body of *Antony*, and by which afterwards *Proculeius* entred, and surprized her. This window is not in any of those Pyramids I have seen; neither can I apprehend, if these were of as solid and massive stones, and of the same shape as those at *Memphis*, and the chambers within as remote from the outward superficies, of what use it could be, either in respect of light or ornament; and therefore I conjecture these monuments of the *Ptolemies* to have been of a different structure from those of the Pyramids.

In all other classical authors, I find no mention of the founders of the rest in the *Libyan* desert; and after such a distance of time, we must be content to be silent with them.

Of the Time in which the PYRAMIDS *were built.*

TO define the precise time in which these Pyramids were erected, as it is an inquiry of much difficulty, so of much importance, in regulating the various and uncertain traditions of the antients concerning the *Ægyptian* chronology. For if we shall peruse those fragments of *Manethos*, an *Ægyptian* priest, preserved by [a] *Josephus*; or those relations of [b] *Herodotus*, of CCCXXX kings to *Mœris*, from *Menes* the first that reigned in *Ægypt*, (who probably is [c] *Mizraim*, the second son of *Cham*, and [d] *father of the* Ægyptians;) or that computation of [e] *Diodorus*, borrowed from their sacred commentaries, that to the CLXXX *Olympiad*, or to the time in which he travelled thither, there had been a succession in the royal throne for XV CIↃ years; or that calculation of [f] *Pomponius Mela*, of CCCXXX *kings to the time of* Amasis, *continued above* XIII CIↃ *years*; or lastly, those *Dynasties* mentioned by *Africanus* and *Eusebius*, but pretermitted by *Herodotus* and *Diodorus*; the first of which [g] *Joseph Scaliger* places in the VII CIↃ and IX year of that *Julian* period, which by him is called *periodus Juliana postulatitia*, and the time *tempus prolepticum*, preceding the creation by CIↃ CCC XXXVI years, we shall find our selves intangled in a labyrinth, and maze of times, out of which we cannot, without much perplexity, unwind our selves. And if we farther consider, that amongst those many names delivered by *Manethos*, and preserved by *Josephus*, *Africanus*, *Eusebius*, and *Syncellus*, how few there are that concur with those of *Herodotus* and *Diodorus*, or with those in *Plato*, *Strabo*, *Pliny*, *Plutarch*, *Censorinus*, and some others: And that which is of greater consequence, how difficult is it to reconcile these names and times to the *Ægyptian* kings recorded in the scriptures, we shall find our selves beset, and as it were invironed on every side with great inextricable doubts. What therefore in inquiries of this nature, is approved as the most solid and rational foundation, that is, to find out some common and received *Epocha*, in which either all or most agree, that shall be our guide in matters of so great antiquity. Now of all the ancient *epocha's* which may conduce to our purpose, that is none that we may safer rely upon than there of *the migration of the* Israelites *out of* Ægypt; which had the same hand faithfully to pen it, that was the most active and miraculous instrument of their departure. And though prophane historians differ much in the manner of this action, either as they were tainted with malice against the *Hebrews*, or misled with the calumnies and false reports of their enemies, the *Ægyptians*; of whom, [h] *Josephus* may seem to have given a true censure, *That all the* Ægyptians *in general are ill affected to the* Jews; yet all agree in this, that *Moses* was the chief author, and conductor of this expedition. If therefore we shall discover the time in which *Moses* flourished, and in which this great enterprize was performed by him, it will follow by way of consequence, that knowing what *Pharaoh*, or king in *Ægypt*, was coetaneous and concurrent with him, we may by *synchronism*, comparing sacred and prophane authors, and following the line of their successions, as it is delivered by good authority, at length fall upon the age in which *Cheops*, and those other kings reigned in *Ægypt*, whom we assigned out of *Herodotus* and *Diodorus*, to have been the founders of these Pyramids.

And here, for our inquiry, what *Ægyptian* king was concurrent with *Moses*, we must have recourse to the relations, not only of the scriptures, but also of other approved authors amongst the *Jews* and *Gentiles*; in which last though we often find more than an *Ægyptian* darkness, yet sometimes through this we may discover some glimmerings of light. By the scriptures alone, it is impossible to infer, what king of

[a] Joseph. lib. 1. contra Apionem. [b] Herodot. lib. 2. [c] Gen. x. 6. [d] Joseph. l. 1. Antiq. cap. 7. [e] Diodor. lib. 1. [f] *Trecentos & triginta Reges ante Amasim, & supra tredecim millium annorum ætates, certis annalibus referunt.* Pomp. Mela, l. 1. c. 9. [g] Scal. in Eusebii chronic.
[h] Φαίνονται γὰρ καὶ ἡ μάλιστα πρὸς ἡμᾶς δυσμενῶς διατεθέντες κοινῇ μὲν ἅπαντες, Αἰγύπτιοι. Jos. lib. 1. contra Apionem.

Ægypt

GREAVES

Ægypt was coetaneous with *Moses*; seeing the name, which is there given him, of *Pharaoh*, is a common denomination applicable to all of them; much like *Cæsar* or *Augustus* with the *Roman* emperors; or some time *Cosroe* with the *Persians*, and no distinctive appellation. Yet in *Herodotus* we find one king, the successor of *Sesostris*, to have been called [i] *Pheron*, which I suppose is *Pharaoh*, and his proper and peculiar name. But who this *Pharaoh* should be, whose heart GOD hardened, and upon whom *Moses* wrought so many wonders, is worth our disquisition. *Josephus* in his first book *contra Apionem*, out of *Manethos* contends, that *Tethmosis* (who is termed also *Amosis* by *Africanus* and *Eusebius*,) reigned then in *Ægypt*. The whole force of his argument lies in this, that *Manethos* mentions the expulsion of the nation of shepherds to have been by *Tethmosis*: but the *Hebrews* were a nation of shepherds: therefore the *Hebrews* were expelled out of *Ægypt*, or in the scripture-phrase, departed out of *Ægypt* under *Tethmosis*; and consequently, that *Moses*, who was their conductor, was coetaneous with him. That the *Hebrews* were a nation of shepherds, and so accounted of themselves, and were esteemed by others, is very perspicuous. [k] *And* Joseph *said unto his brethren, and unto his father's house, I will go up and shew* Pharaoh, *and say unto him, My brethren and my father's house which were in the land of* Canaan, *are come unto me: and the men are shepherds, for their trade hath been to feed cattel, and they have brought their flocks, and their herds, and all that they have. And it shall come to pass, when* Pharaoh *shall call you, and shall say, What is your occupation? that ye shall say, thy servants trade hath been about cattle, from our youth even until now, both we and also our fathers; that ye may dwell in the land of* Goshen. *For every shepherd is an abomination to the* Ægyptians. But before we shall disprove this assertion of *Josephus*, which carries much speciousness with it, and therefore is approved and followed by [l] *Tatianus*, by [m] *Justin Martyr*, and by [n] *Clemens Alexandrinus*, we shall put down the words of *Manethos* himself, as they are reported by [o] *Josephus* in his first book *contra Apionem*. Timanus *by name being our king, under him I know not how* GOD *was displeased, and beyond expectation, out of the eastern countries, men of obscure birth encamped themselves in the country, and easily, and without battle, took it by force, binding the princes, and besides, cruelly burning the cities, and overthrowing the temples of the gods. Last of all, they made one of themselves a king, who was named* Salatis; *he reigning nineteen years, died. After him, another, named* Bæon, *reigned forty four years; next to him* Apachnas; *another, thirty six years, seven months; then* Apophis, *sixty one;* Janias, *fifty, and one month; after all,* Assis, *forty nine years and two months. And these were the first six kings of them always conquering, and desiring to extirpate* Ægypt. *Their nation was called* Hycsos, *that is, kingly shepherds. For* hyc *in the sacred tongue, signifies a king; and* sos *a shepherd, or shepherds in the common dialect, and thence* hycsos *is compounded. But some say, that these were* Arabians. [*In other copies I have found, that by the denomination* hyc, *kings are not signified, but on the contrary, captive shepherds. For* hyc *in the* Ægyptian *language, when it is pronounced with a broad sound, plainly signifies captives; and this seems more probable to me, and better agreeing to the ancient history.*] *Those kings therefore, which we before mentioned, and those which were called* Pastores, *and those which descended of them, ruled* Ægypt *five hundred and eleven years. After this, he mentions that by the kings of* Thebes, *and of the rest of* Ægypt, *there was an invasion made against these shepherds, and a very great and lasting war. The which, he says, were conquered by a king, whose name was* Alisfragmuthosis, *whereby they lost all* Ægypt, *being shut up into a place containing in circuit ten thousand acres. This space* Manethos *says, the shepherds encompassed with a great and strong wall, that they might secure all their substance and their spoils in a defensible place. But* Themosis, *the son of* Alisfragmuthosis *endeavouring to take them with four hundred thousand armed men, beleaguer'd the walls, who despairing to take them by siege, made conditions with them that they should leave* Ægypt, *and go without any damage whither they would: they upon this agreement, no less than two hundred and forty thousand, with all their substance, went out of* Ægypt *by the desart into* Syria, *and fearing the power of the* Assyrians, (*who then ruled* Asia,) *in that country, which is now called* Judæa, *they built a city capable to receive so many myriads of men, naming it* Hierusalem.

[These are the words of *Josephus*, and not of *Manethos*.]

By way of answer to *Josephus*, we say, that though the *Israelites* might properly be called shepherds, yet it cannot hence be inferr'd out of *Manethos*, that these shepherds were *Israelites*. Nay, if we compare this relation of *Manethos*, with that in *Exodus*, which [p] *Josephus* being a *Jew*,

[i] Σεσώστριος δὲ τελευτήσαντος ἐκδέξασθαι ἔλεγον τὴν βασιληΐην τὸν παῖδα αὐτοῦ Φερῶνα. Herodot. l. 2.
[k] Gen. xlvi. 31, 32, &c.
[l] In oratione contra Græcos.
[m] In parænetico ad eosdem.
[n] Lib. 1. Stromatum.
[o] Joseph. lib. 1. contra Apion. Ἐγένετο βασιλεὺς ἡμῖν Τίμαιος ὄνομα, &c.
[p] Exod. i.

GREAVES cannot but approve of, we ſhall find the contrary. For there they live under a heavy ſlavery and perſecution, whereas here they are the perſecutors and afflictors; there they groan under their taſk-maſters the *Ægyptians*, here they make all *Ægypt* to groan under them: *Laſtly*, whereas there they are employed in the loweſt offices, [q] *in mortar and in brick, and in all manner of ſervice in the field:* Here, after the deſtruction of many cities, and men, and infinite outrages committed upon the *Ægyptians*, they make one of themſelves a king, and for ſix deſcents keep themſelves in poſſeſſion of the royal throne, of which, after a long and bloody war, they are deprived. Their building likewiſe of a city in *Judæa*, and naming it *Jeruſalem*, according to *Manethos*, is a ſtrong argument againſt *Joſephus*, that theſe ſhepherds could not have been the *Iſraelites*. For before the entrance of the *Iſraelites* into *Canaan*, we find that *Jeruſalem was a fort of the* Jebuſites *upon mount* Sion, *unconquered by* Joſhua [r]. *As for the* Jebuſites *the inhabitants of* Jeruſalem, *the children of* Iſrael *could not drive them out*. But they were long after ſubdued by *David*. *And* [ſ] David *and all* Iſrael *went to* Jeruſalem, *which is* Jebus, *where the* Jebuſites *were the inhabitants of the land. And the inhabitants of* Jebus *ſaid to* David, *Thou ſhalt not come hither*; *nevertheleſs*, David *took the caſtle of* Zion, *which is the city of* David. Beſides all this, the hiſtory and chronology of thoſe ancient times, if we compare ſacred and prophane authors, will in no ſort admit that theſe ſhepherds muſt have been the *Iſraelites*. For if theſe that departed out of *Ægypt* in the reign of *Tethmoſis*, king of *Thebais*, or of the upper part of *Ægypt*, were the children of *Iſrael*, then muſt *Moſes* their conductor have been as ancient as *Tethmoſis*, or *Amoſis*, that is, as ancient as *Inachus*, the firſt king of the *Argives*. For *Apion*, in his fourth book of the hiſtories of *Ægypt*, ſhews out of *Ptolemæus Mendeſius*, an *Ægyptian* prieſt, that this *Amoſis* lived in the time of *Inachus*, as it is recorded by [t] *Tatianus*, [u] *Juſtin Martyr*, [x] *Clemens Alexandrinus*, and others. *Euſebius*, tho' he doth not approve of it, for he places *Moſes* in the time of [y] *Cecrops*, yet he aſſures us, that it was a received opinion among many learned men, [z] *Moiſen Inachi fuiſſe temporibus eruditiſſimi viri tradiderunt ex noſtris Clemens, & Africanus; ex Judæis, Joſephus, & Juſtus, veteris hiſtoriæ monimenta replicantes.* Now *Inachus* according to [a] *Caſtor* an ancient chronographer, with whom *Euſebius* alſo concurs, began to reign a thouſand and eighty years before the firſt *olympiad*, that is, CIↃ CCLXVIII before the deſtruction of the temple under *Zedekiah*, and before Chriſt's nativity, after the *Dionyſian* or common account, CIↃIↃCCCLVI. That of the *olympiads* is ſo aſſured an *epocha*, and ſo ſtrongly and clearly proved by eclipſes of the ſun and moon, which are the beſt demonſtrations in chronology, theſe being expreſſed by ſome of the ancients to have happen'd in ſuch a year of ſuch an *olympiad*, as by [b] *Ptolemy*; others in ſuch a year of the *epocha* of *Nabonaſſar*, that we cannot err in our calculations an hour, much leſs an intire day. By this therefore we ſhall fix the time of *Zedekiah*, and the deſtruction of the temple: And conſequently, if, by our continuation of the years mentioned in the ſacred ſtory, it ſhall appear, that from the time of *Moſes*, either to the firſt *olympiad*, or to *Zedekiah* and the deſtruction of the temple, there cannot be ſo great a diſtance as theſe ſuppoſe, we may ſafely then conclude, that *Moſes* lived not in the time of this *Tethmoſis*, and is not ſo ancient as *Joſephus* makes him; and that theſe ſhepherds were not the *Iſraelites*, but very probably *Arabians*, as *Manethos* here alſo reports. *Some ſay that theſe were* Arabians; who to this day, for the greateſt part, like the *Nomades*, wander up and down, feeding their cattle, and often make incurſions upon the *Ægyptians* and *Syrians*. Which occaſioned *Seſoſtris* the great (as we find it in [c] *Diodorus*,) *to make a wall on the eaſt-ſide of* Ægypt, *a thouſand and fifty furlongs in length, from* Peluſium *by the deſert to* Heliopolis, *againſt the inrodes of the* Syrians *and* Arabians: As at this day the *Chineſe* have done againſt the irruptions of the *Tartars* on the north and weſt parts of *China*, for many hundred miles, the which appears by a large map of mine of that country, made and printed in *China*. On the contrary, if the ſucceſſion of times from *Moſes*, recorded in the holy writ, better agrees with the age of *Amenophis*, the father of *Rameſſes*, whoſe ſtory [d] *Joſephus* hath preſerved out of *Manethos*, and whoſe time and rank in the *Dynaſties*, *Africanus* and *Euſebius* deliver out of the ſame *Manethos*, we may with more probability affirm, that the migration of the *Iſraelites* and time of *Moſes*, was when *Amenophis* was *Pharaoh*, or king of *Ægygt*, than that it was when *Tethmoſis* reigned, as *Joſephus* and others contend, out of a deſire to make *Moſes* ancienter than in truth he is.

[q] Exod. i. 14. [r] Joſh. xv. 63. [ſ] 2 Chron. xi. 4, 5. [t] In oratione contra Græcos. [u] In parænetico ad Græcos. [x] Lib. 1. Strom. [y] *And ſo doth St.* Auguſtin, eduxit Moſes ex Ægypto populum Dei noviſſimo tempore Cecropis, Athenienſium regis. L. 18. c. 11. de Civ. Dei. [z] Euſeb. Chron. [a] Ibid. [b] Ptolemæus ἐν μεγάλῃ συντάξει. [c] Diod. Sic. lib. 1. [d] Joſeph. lib. 1. contra Apionem.

And

And tho' this argument from the series and successions of time is so demonstrative and conclusive, that nothing can be opposed against it, and therefore might be sufficient to evince our purpose: yet if we considerately examine another relation of *Manethos*, (which is slighted and depressed by *Josephus*, because it made not for his purpose,) it must necessarily be that those shepherds he meant not the *Israelites*, but rather by the *Israelites* the leprous people, which in his computation are three hundred thirty years and six months after the *Dynasty* of the shepherds. And therefore we may oppose the authority of [e] *Manethos* against himself, or rather against *Josephus*. The sum of whose discourse is this, That *Amenophis*, who was a great worshipper of the gods, as *Orus* one of the former kings had been, being desirous to see the gods, *one of the priests of the same name with him, told him he might, if he cleansed the country of leprous and polluted people.* This leprous people chose for their captain one of the priests of *Heliopolis*, named *Osarsiphus*, who changing his name, was called *Moses*; he causing *Amenophis* for fear to fly into *Æthiopia*, was afterwards by him, and by his son *Sethon*, who was also called *Ramesses*, by the name of his father overthrown in battle, and the leprous people were pursued by them unto the confines of *Syria*. Thus far out of *Manethos*. Here, which is very remarkable, we have expresly the name of *Moses*; whereas in the former relation of *Manethos* there is no mention of him, but of six other kings, with their peculiar names. Whereas it is not probable he would have omitted the name of *Moses* if he had lived in that age, being a name so famous and so well known to them; and by [f] *Josephus* acknowledged, *that the* Ægyptians *accounted him to be an admirable and divine man.* The pursuing of them unto the confines of *Syria*, doth very well intimate the following of the *Israelites* by *Pharaoh* and his host. For his terming them a leprous and polluted people, we must consider him to have been an *Ægyptian*, and therefore not unlikely to throw as many aspersions as he could upon the *Israelites*, whom they deadly hated, it may be out of memory of their former plagues. However it were, *Chæremon* hath almost the same history, as [g] *Josephus* confesses. *Chæremon* professing to write the history of *Ægypt*, says, *That under* Amenophis *and his son* Ramesses, *Two hundred and fifty thousand leprous and polluted men were cast out of* Ægypt. *Their leaders were* Moses *the scribe, and* Josephus, *who was also a sacred scribe. The* Ægyptian *name of* Moses *was* Tisithen, *of* Joseph Peteseph. *These coming to* Pelusium, *and finding there three hundred and eighty thousand men left by* Amenophis, *which he would not admit into* Ægypt, *making a league with them, they undertook an expedition against* Ægypt. Upon this *Amenophis* flies into *Æthiopia*, and his son *Messenes* drives out the *Jews* into *Syria*, in number about two hundred thousand, and receives his father *Amenophis* out of *Æthiopia*. I know [h] *Lysimachus* assigns another king, and another time, in which *Moses* led the *Israelites* out of *Ægypt*, and that was *when* Bocchoris *reigned in* Ægypt, *the nation of the* Jews *being infected with leprosies, and scabs, and other diseases, betook themselves to the temple to beg their living, many being tainted with the disease, there happened a death in* Ægypt. Whereupon *Bocchoris* consulting with the oracle of *Ammon*, received answer, *That the leprous people were to be drowned in the sea in sheets of lead, the scabbed were to be carried into the wilderness*; who choosing *Moses* for their leader, conquered that country which is now called *Judæa*. Out of which relation of *Lysimachus*, and some others of like credit, [i] *Tacitus* may have borrowed his in the fifth book of his histories. *Most authors agree, that there arising a contagion in* Ægypt *which defiled their bodies, king* Bocchoris *consulting the oracle of* Hammon *for remedy, was bid to purge his kingdom, and to carry that sort of men, as hated of the gods, into other countries. Thence the vulgar sort being enquired after, and collected together, after they had been left in the desarts, the rest being heavy with tears,* Moses, *one of the banished men, admonished them, not to expect the help either of gods or men, being deserted by both, but that they should trust to him as their captain sent from heaven, to whose assistance by their giving credit at the first, they had overcome*

[e] Manethos apud Joseph. lib. 1. contra Apionem.

[f] Τῦτον δὲ τὸν ἄνδρα θαυμαστὸν μϑ' Αἰγύπτιοι, καὶ θεῖον νομίζουσι. Joseph. lib. 1. contra Apionem.

[g] Lib. 1. contra Apionem. Χαιρήμων] καὶ γὰρ ὗτος Αἰγυπτιακὴν φάσκων ἱστορίαν συγγράφειν καὶ προσθεὶς ταυτὸ ὄνομα τοῦ βασιλέως, ὅπερ ὁ Μανεθὼς, Ἀμένωφιν καὶ τὸν υἱὸν αὐτῦ Ῥαμέσσην, &c.

[h] Lysimachus apud Joseph. lib. 1. contra Apionem. Ἐπὶ Βοκχόρεως τοῦ Αἰγυπτίων βασιλέως τὸν λαὸν τῶν Ἰουδαίων λεπροὺς ὄντας καὶ ψωροὺς, καὶ ἄλλα νοσήματα τινὰ ἔχοντας, εἰς τὰ ἱερὰ καταφεύγοντας μεταιτεῖν τροφὴν, &c.

[i] Tacit. l. 5. Hist. *Plurimi auctores consentiunt, ortâ per Egyptum tabe quæ corpora fædaret: regem Bocchorim, adito Hammonis oracula, remedium petentem, purgare regnum, & id genus hominum ut invisum deis alias in terras avehere jussum. Sic conquisitum collectumque vulgus, postquam vastis locis relictum sit, cæteris per lachrymas torpentibus, Mosen unum exulum monuisse, ne quam deorum hominumvè opem expectarent ab utrisque deserti, sed sibimet ut duci cœlesti crederent, primò cujus auxilio credentes præsentes miserias pepulissent. Assensere atque omnium ignari fortuitum iter incipiunt.*

GREAVES *their present calamities. They assented unto him, and being ignorant of all, they begin their journey as fortune should lead them.* Thus much and more hath *Tacitus* of *Moses* and the *Jews*. But to pass by his and *Lysimachus*'s calumnies, we can no more assent to these testimonies of theirs, that *Moses* lived in the time of *Bocchoris*, than we did to *Josephus* that he was coetaneous with *Tethmosis*. For we find *Bocchoris* to be placed by *Africanus* and [k] *Eusebius*, both following *Manethos* in the twenty fourth *dynasty*, and by [l] *Diodorus* long after *Sesostris* the great, or *Ramesses*; which *Ramesses*, or *Sethosis*, or *Sethon*, (that is, *Sesostris*, and *Sesoosis* in *Diodorus*,) both in *Manethos* and *Chæremon*, is the son of *Amenophis*, who is the last king of the eighteenth *dynasty*, according to *Africanus* and *Eusebius*. I purposely omit the opinion of [m] *Apion*, that *Moses* (whom he makes to be of *Heliopolis*,) *departed with these lepers, and blind, and lame, in the first year of the seventh* olympiad, *in which year*, saith he, *the* Phœnicians *built* Carthage; and that other of [n] *Porphyrius* in his fourth book against the Christians, that *Moses* was before *Semiramis*. Where he places him as much too high, as *Apion* doth too low.

Laying therefore aside these vain and uncertain traditions, we have no more assured way exactly to fix the time of *Moses*, and by *Moses* the time in which the Pyramids were built, than to have recourse to the sacred scriptures, and sometimes to compare such authors of the Gentiles with these, against whom we have no just exceptions. For by those, and these conjointly, we may continue his time to the first olympiad, and thence to the destruction of the temple, by *Nebuchadnezzar* king of *Babylon*: That of the olympiads being a most certain and known epocha with the *Greeks*, as that of the destruction of the temple with the *Jews*. From *Moses* then, or the migration of the *Israelites* out of *Ægypt*, to the building of *Solomon*'s temple, are CCCCLXXX years current, or four hundred seventy nine complete; and so also [o] *Eusebius* computes them. The words of the text plainly conclude this sum: [p] *And it came to pass in the four hundred and fourth-score year, after the children of* Israel *were come out of the land of* Ægypt, *in the fourth year of* Solomon's *reign over* Israel, *in the month* Zif, *which is the second month, that he began to build the house of the* LORD. From the building of the temple to the destruction of it in the reign of *Zedekias*, by the calculation and confession of the best chronologers, are betwixt four hundred and twenty and four hundred and thirty years. Which is thus deduced: After the first foundation of the temple, *Solomon* reigned [q] thirty seven years, [r] *Rehoboam* with [s] *Abia* twenty; in whose time we are to place *Shishak*, or *Sesochosis*, the king of *Ægypt*. [t] *And it came to pass in the fifth year of king* Rehoboam, *that* Shishak *king of* Ægypt, *came up against* Jerusalem; *and he took away the treasures of the house of the Lord, and the treasures of the king's house, he even took away all; and he took away all the shields of gold which* Solomon *had made*. This *Shishak* is named by the *Septuagint* Σουσακίμ, by St *Hierom* *Sesac*, and is the same whom [u] *Josephus* calls Σούσακος, which he imagines to have been *Sesostris* the great, whose victories and conquests are describ'd at large by [w] *Herodotus*. But this *Sesostris*, or [x] *Sesoosis*, as *Diodorus* also terms him, must long have preceded *Rehoboam*'s time, as in the sequel of this discourse it will appear. Therefore the more probable opinion is that of *Scaliger*, that by *Shishak* is meant *Sesochosis*, whom *Manethos* calls Σέσογχις, and the *scoliast* of *Apollonius* Σεσόγχωσις, the time of the twenty second *dynasty*, in which we find him placed by *Africanus* and *Eusebius*, doth well agree with it, and the radical letters in *Shishak*, *Sesac*, and Σέσογχις, being the same, do very much strengthen our assertion. After *Rehoboam* and *Abiah*'s reign, [y] *Asah* and [z] *Jehosaphat* reigned LXVI years, [a] *Joram* and [b] *Ahazia* IX, [c] *Athalia* and [d] *Joas* XLVI, [e] *Amasias* XXIX, [f] *Uzziah* LII, [g] *Jotham* XVI, [h] *Ahaz*

[k] Ex Edit. Jos. Scaligeri. [l] Diod. lib. 1. [m] Apud Jos. lib. 2. contra Apionem.

[n] *Ex Ethnicis verò impius ille Porphyrius in quarto operis sui libro, quòd adversum nos casso labore contexuit, post Moysen Semiramim fuisse affirmat.* Euseb. chron. [o] Ibid. [p] 1 Kings vi. 1.

[q] For 1 *Kings* vi. 1. *In the fourth year of his reign, and in the second month he began to build the house of the Lord.* And in 1 *Kings* xi. 42. *The time that Solomon reigned in Jerusalem over Israel was forty years.* Out of which, if we subduct three complete years that preceded the foundation of the temple, there remains thirty seven years. [r] 1 *Kings* xiv. 21. *He reigned seventeen years in Jerusalem.*

[s] 1 *Kings* xv. 2. *Three years reigned he in Jerusalem.* [t] 1 *Kings* xiv. 25. 26. [u] Joseph Antiq. l. 8. c. 4. [w] Herod. lib. 2. [x] *Diodorus* in the printed copies, always names him *Sesoosis*, but in one of the *MSS.* as *Henr. Stephanus* observes, he is sometimes called *Sesostris*, and sometimes *Sesoosis*. *Vid. edit. Diod. ab Henr. Stephan.* [y] 1 Kings xv. 10. *Forty one years reigned he in Jerusalem.*

[z] 1 Kings xxii. 42. *He reigned twenty five years in Jerusalem.* [a] 2 Kings viii. 17. *He reigned eight years in Jerusalem.* [b] 2 Kings viii. 26. *He reigned one year in Jerusalem.*

[c] 2 Kings xi. 3. *And he was with her hid in the house of the Lord six years; and Athaliah did reign over the land.* [d] 2 Kings xii. 1. *Forty years reigned he in Jerusalem.*

[e] 2 Kings xiv. 2. *He reigned twenty nine years in Jerusalem.* [f] 2 Kings xv. 2. *He reigned fifty two years in Jerusalem.* [g] 2 Kings xv. 33. *He reigned sixteen years in Jerusalem.* [h] 2 Kings xvi. 2. *He reigned sixteen years in Jerusalem.*

XVI, being contemporary with *Hoshea* the last king of *Israel*, in whose time we find *So* to reign in *Ægypt*, (2 *Kings* xvii. 4.) After *Ahaz* succeeded, *Hezekiah* reigning [i] XXIX years.

Now [k] *in the fourteenth year of king* Hezekiah, *did* Sennacharib *king of* Assyria, *come up against all the fenced cities of* Judah, *and took them.* But afterwards, when he came to besiege *Jerusalem* — [l] *It came to pass that night, that the angel of the* LORD *went out and smote in the camp of the* Assyrians *an hundred fourscore and five thousand; and when they arose early in the morning, behold, they were all dead corpses. So* Sennacharib *king of* Assyria *departed, and went, and returned and dwelt at* Nineveh. In the time of this *Sennacharib*, *Sethon* succeeding *Anysis* reigned in *Ægypt*, according to [m] *Herodotus*, who in his *Euterpe* hath plainly the name of *Sanacharib*, stiling him king of the *Arabians* and *Assyrians*, and making him to have received a miraculous defeat, which it may be was that of *Hezekiah*, though he applies it to *Sethon* king of the *Ægyptians*. His story is well worth our observation, which runs thus: [n] *After this* (Anysis) *the priest of* Vulcan, *by name* Sethon, *reigned, who abusing the men of war of the* Ægyptians, *and contemning them as not useful to him, besides other ignominies he deprived them of their lands, which had been given to every company of twelve by the former kings. Whence it happened, that when afterwards* Sanacharib, *the king of the* Arabians *and* assyrians, *invaded* Ægypt, *the* Ægyptian *soldiers refused to assist him. Then the priest destitute of counsel, shut himself up, lamenting before the image how much he was in danger to suffer; in the midst of his mourning falling asleep, a God appeared to him, incouraging him that he should suffer no distress, if he would march against the armies of the* Arabians; *for he would send him succour. He therefore giving credit to this dream, taking with him such volunteers of the* Ægyptians *as followed him, pitched his army at* Pelusium; *for there* Ægypt *is easiest invaded: Neither did any of the soldiers follow him, but trades-men, and artificers, and merchants. Coming thither by night, an infinite number of mice entring upon his enemies, gnawed their quivers and bows, and the leathers of their shields, so that the next day the enemies destitute of arms, fled, many of them being slain. And therefore now this king stands in the temple of* Vulcan, *in a statue of marble, holding in his hand a mouse with this inscription. He that looks upon me let him be religious.* After *Hezekiah*, [o] *Manasses* reigned LV years, [p] *Amon* II, [q] *Josiah* XXXI. [r] *In his days* Pharaoh Nechoh *king of* Ægypt, *went up against the king of* Assyria *to the river* Euphrates, *and king* Josiah *went against him, and he slew him at* Megiddo *when he had seen him.* The same relation we read in *Heredotus*, if we pardon him the mistake of *Magdolo* for *Megiddo*, who writes, that [s] *Necus* (the king of *Ægypt*) *fighting a battle on land with the* Syrians *in* Magdolo, *obtained the victory, and after the fight he took* Cadytus, *a great city in* Syria.

GREAVES

Next to *Josiah* succeeded [t] *Joachaz*, [u] *Jehoiakim*, and [w] *Jechoniah* or *Jehoiakin*, reigning eleven years and six months. And in the eleventh year of [x] *Zedekiah*, the next king after *Jechoniah*, was the temple burnt by *Nebuzaradan*, *in the* [y] *nineteenth year of* Nebuchadnezzar *king of* Babylon, *or the second of* Vaphres *king of* Ægypt, *in the computation of* Clemens Alexandrinus. *This* Zedekiah, *saith* [z] Josephus, *having been a confederate of the* Babylonians *for eight years, broke his faith with them, and joining league with the* Ægyptians, *hoped to overthrow the* Babylonians. This league we find intimated in [a] *Ezekiel*; and we read in [b] *Jeremiah* and [c] *Josephus* of succours

[i] 2 Kings xviii. 2. *He reigned twenty nine years in Jerusalem.* [k] 2 Kings xviii. 13, 16.
[l] 2 Kings xix. 35, 36. [m] Herod. lib. 2. Σαναχάριβος. [n] Herod. lib. 2. Μετὰ δὲ τοῦτον βασιλεῦσαι τὸν ἱρέα τοῦ Ἡφαίστου, τὸ οὔνομα εἶναι Σεθῶν, &c. [o] 2 Kings xxi. 1. *He reigned fifty five years in Jerusalem.* [p] 2 Kings xxii. 19. *He reigned two years in Jerusalem.* [q] 2 Kings xxii. 1. *He reigned thirty one years in Jerusalem.* [r] 2 Kings xxiii. 29. and 2 Chron. xxxv. 20. *Necho* king of *Egypt*, came up to fight against *Carchemish* by *Euphrates*, and *Josiah* went out against him.
[s] Καὶ Σύροισι πεζῇ ὁ Νεκὼς συμβαλὼν ἐν Μαγδόλῳ ἐνίκησε, μετὰ δὲ τὴν μάχην Κάδυτιν πόλιν τῆς Συρίης ἐοῦσαν μεγάλην εἷλε. Herod. lib. 2. [t] 2 Kings xxiii. 31. *He reigned three months in Jerusalem.*
[u] 2 Kings xxiii. 36. *He reigned eleven years in Jerusalem.* [w] 2 Kings xxiv. 8. *He reigned in Jerusalem three months.*
[x] *And the city was besieged unto the eleventh year of king Zedekiah. And on the ninth day of the fourth month the famine prevailed in the city, and there was no bread for the people of the land: and the city was broken up, and all the men of war fled by night.*
[y] *And in the fifth month on the seventh day of the month (which is the nineteenth year of Nebuchadnezzar king of Babylon,) came Nebuzaradan, captain of the guard, a servant of the king of Babylon, unto Jerusalem. And he burnt the house of the Lord, and the king's house, and all the houses of Jerusalem, and every great man's house burnt he with fire,* 2 Kings xxv. 2, 3, 4, 8, 9. The same relation we find in *Jeremiah*, chap. lii. ver. 5, 6, 7, 12, 13. almost word for word, which is remarkable.
[z] Joseph. antiquit. lib. 10. cap. 10. Τὴν συμμαχίαν καὶ τὴν πρὸς τοὺς Βαβυλωνίους ἐπὶ ἔτη ὀκτὼ κατασχὼν, διέλυσε τὰς πρὸς αὐτοὺς πίστεις, καὶ τοῖς Αἰγυπτίοις προσέθετο, καταλύσειν τοὺς Βαβυλωνίους ἐλπίσας.
[a] Ezek. xvii. 15. [b] Jer. xxxvii. 5.
[c] Jos. ant. l. 10. c. 10. Ὁ δὲ Αἰγύπτιος ἀκούσας ἐν οἷς ἐστὶν ὁ σύμμαχος αὐτοῦ Σεδεκίας ἀναλαβὼν πολλὴν δύναμιν ἧκεν εἰς τὴν Ἰουδαίαν, ὡς λύσων τὴν πολιορκίαν.

GREAVES and affiſtance ſent by the king of *Ægypt*, when *Zedekiah* and *Jeruſalem* were firſt diſtreſſed by the *Chaldeans*, or forces of the king of *Babylon*. [d] *Then* Pharaohs' *army was come forth out of* Ægypt, *and when the* Chaldeans *that beſieged* Jeruſalem, *heard tidings of them, they departed from* Jeruſalem. The ſame is reiterated by him: *Behold* Pharaoh's *army which is come forth to help you, ſhall return to* Ægypt *to their own land. And the* Chaldeans *ſhall come again, and fight againſt this city, and take it, and burn it with fire.* All which we ſee was perform'd by *Nebuchadnezzar* in the eleventh year of *Zedekiah*; and a judgment alſo denounced againſt the king of *Ægypt*. [e] *Thus ſaith the* LORD, *Behold, I will give* Pharaoh Hophra *king of* Ægypt, *into the hands of his enemies, and into the hand of them that ſeek his life; as I gave* Zedekiah *king of* Judah, *into the hand of* Nebuchadrezzar *king of* Babylon, *his enemy, and that ſought his life.* The ſame is often threatned by the prophet [f] *Ezekiel*, who lived in the time of *Hezekiah*, as *Jeremiah* did: *I am againſt* Pharaoh *king of Ægypt, and I will ſcatter the* Ægyptians *among the nations, and will diſperſe them throughout the countries: And I will ſtrengthen the arms of the king of* Babylon, *and put my ſword in his hand, but I will break* Pharaoh's *arms.* Which prophecies we may diſcover moſt manifeſtly to have been fulfilled in the reign of *Apries*, as [g] *Herodotus* names him, or *Apries*, as [h] *Diodorus* calls him, or *Vaphres*, as the *Septuagint* and *Euſebius* render the name of that king, which here in *Jeremiah* is called *Pharaoh Hophra*. *Who*, ſaith [i] *Herodotus*, *next to* Pſammiticus *his grandfather, was the moſt fortunate of all the former kings for twenty five years of his reign*; which might occaſion *Zedekiah* to fly to him for ſuccour: But the *Ægyptians* rebelling againſt him, he was overthrown in battle, taken priſoner, and afterward ſtrangled by his own ſervant *Amaſis*, whom they had made their king. The whole ſtory and manner is at large in [k] *Herodotus*, neither did divine vengeance long forbear to purſue the traitor. For *Cambyſes* the king of the *Perſians* and of *Babylon*, coming with an army againſt him, poſſeſſed himſelf of *Ægypt*, as the prophets had foretold. Nor could the *Ægyptians* ever to this day recover the monarchy. For after the *Perſians* ſucceeded the *Macedonians*, after them the *Romans*, then the *Arabians*, next the *Mamalukes* or *Circaſſians*, and laſt of all the *Turks* or *Scythians*. So that we may conclude from the occurrences then happening, (the relations of *Herodotus* exactly agreeing with the threatenings of the prophets,) as alſo from the computation of times, and from the affinity and analogy of names, that *Hophra*, and *Apries*, or *Vaphres*, muſt have been the very ſame *Ægyptian* king coetaneous and concurrent with *Zedekiah*.

To reaſſume then what hath been demonſtrated by us: From the migration of the *Iſraelites* out of *Ægypt*, under the conduct of *Moſes* to the building of *Solomon*'s temple, are four hundred ſeventy nine years complete; and from the building of the temple to the deſtruction of it, are four hundred and thirty years and ſix months. But becauſe it is not probable, that amongſt ſo many kings, all of them ſhould have reigned completely ſo many years as are expreſs'd in the text; it being the uſual ſtile of kings to reckon the years current of their reign as complete, I ſhall limit this uncertainty between CCCCXX and CCCCXXX years, which is a ſufficient latitude. If any one ſhould deſire a more exact calculation, he may compute them by comparing other places of the ſcriptures with theſe, to be but CCCCXXV years current, *according to the opinion of the moſt reverend and judicious primate of* Ireland, to which I willingly ſubſcribe; though either computation be ſufficient for my purpoſe.

This deſtruction of the temple, by our beſt chronographers, is placed *in the firſt year of the forty eight olympiad*, and *in the hundred and ſixtieth of the* epocha *of* Nabonaſſar, *and in the nineteenth* (as the ſcripture often makes mention) *of* Nebuchodonoſor *the ſon of* Nabolaſſar, (as [l] *Beroſus* in *Joſephus* names him,) which *Nabolaſſar* muſt neceſſarily be the ſame with him that is called *Nabopolaſſar* in *Ptolemy*, (the XIV king of the *Babylonians* after *Nabonaſſar*,) whom *Nabocolaſſar* (or [m] *Nabuchodonozor*, or [n] *Nebuchadrezzar*, or [o] *Nebuchadnezzar*, as the ſcripture alſo terms him,) in his *Canon Regnorum* ſucceeds. The nearneſs of the names, and agreement of the times from *Cyrus*, in whom the ſacred ſcriptures and prophane authors equally concur, do ſtrongly prove them to be the ſame. Wherefore we may conclude, that from the time of *Moſes*, or the migration of the *Iſraelites* out of *Ægypt*, or from the end of the *Amenophis*, (coetaneous with *Moſes*,) the laſt king of the eighteenth *Dynaſty*, (as *Euſebius* out of *Manethos* ranks him,) to the

[d] Jer. xxxvii. 6, 8. [e] Jer. xliv. 30. [f] Ezek. xxx. 22, 23. [g] Herod. l. 2.
[h] Diodor. lib. 1. [i] Ὃς μετὰ Ψαμμιτιχὸν τὸν ἑαυτοῦ προπατορὰ ἐγένετο εὐδαιμονέστατος τῶν πρότερον βασιλέων ἐπ' ἔτεα πέντε καὶ εἴκοσι ἄρξας. Herod. l. 2. [k] Herodot. lib. 2.
[l] Ναβουχοδονόσορος] ὁ πατὴρ αὐτοῦ Ναβολάσσαρος. Beroſ. apud Joſeph. l. 1. contra Apionem.
[m] So *Joſephus*, and the *Vetus vulgata*, always name him. [n] Jer. lii. 12, 28, 29.
[o] 2 Kings xxv. 8. Ezra i. 7. ii. 1.

reign

reign of *Apries*, or *Vaphres*, or *Hophra*, the eighth king of the twenty sixth *Dynasty*, (according to the same *Eusebius* following *Manethos*,) being coetaneous with *Zedekiah* king of *Judah*, and *Nebuchadnezzar* king of *Babylon*, are IↃCCCCIV years, and from *Moses* to the first olympiad IↃCCXV and not CIↃLXXX as they who make *Moses* as ancient as *Inachus* affirm. In which space we may with much certainty, if we give credit to *Herodotus* and *Diodorus*, place the kings the founders of the three greatest and fairest Pyramids; which is the principal intention of this discourse. For [p] both of them describe these to have reigned many ages before *Apries*, and long after *Sesostris* the great. Which *Sesostris*, or *Sesoosis*, as *Diodorus* also stiles him, must have been the same king whom *Manethos* in *Josephus* calls *Sethosis*, and *Ramesses*, and [q] *Ægyptus*, son to *Amenophis* before-mentioned, and brother to *Armais*, or *Danaus*; and *Eusebius* of *Scaliger*'s edition in *Greek* names *Sethos*, the *Latin* translations of St. *Hierom*, both *MSS*. and printed copies *Sethus*, and by all of them is the first king of the XIX *Dynasty*. The great acts and conquests assigned by *Herodotus* to *Sesostris*, and as great attributed by *Manethos* to *Sethosis*, or *Ramesses*, which cannot well be applied to any other precedent or subsequent kings; together with the relation of them both, that while he was in pursuit of his victories abroad, his brother, whom *Manethos* names *Armais*, and [r] *Danaus* (in *Herodotus* his name is omitted,) rebelled against him at home, and the nearness of the time, which may be collected out of both, do very much confirm the probability of this assertion. *Sesostris* then, and *Sethosis*, being one and the same, is by *Manethos* in *Josephus* ranked immediately after *Amenophis*, (coetaneous with *Moses*, as we have prov'd,) and is the same *Manethos* in the tradition of *Eusebius* after *Menophis* that is *Amenophis*, both in the *Greek* and *Latin* copies. Wherefore the founders of these Pyramids having lived after *Sesostris*, must likewise have been after *Amenophis*. If we will come to a greater preciseness yet of time, (for this latitude of nine hundred and four years, which we assigned from *Moses* to the destruction of the first temple, in the time of *Zedekiah* king of *Judah*, and *Apries* king of *Ægypt*, is so great that we may lose our selves in it,) we have no other possible means left, after the revolution of so many ages, and the loss of so many of the commentaries and monuments of the *Ægyptians*, but by having recourse to those *Dynasties* of *Manethos*, as they are preserved by *Africanus* and *Eusebius*. And yet in neither of these shall we find the names of *Cheops* or *Chemmis*, or *Cephren* or *Chabryis*; or of *Mycerinus*, the authors of the greater Pyramids, mentioned by *Herodotus* and *Diodorus*; or of *Asychis*, the builder of a fourth, according to *Herodotus*. Wherefore what their writings have not supplied us with, that reason must. For since these *Ægyptian* kings, as we have proved, lived between *Amenophis* and *Apries*, and by [s] *Eusebius* out of *Africanus*, *Amenophis* is the last of the XVIII *Dynasty*, and *Apries* or *Vaphres*, the VIII of the XXVI *Dinasty*, we must necessarily place them in one of the intermediate *Dynasties*. But seeing all the intermediate *Dynasties* have their peculiar kings, unless it be the XX, we have no reason to exclude them, and to bring these in their places as usurpers: But rather with great probability, (for I must say here with [t] *Livy*, *Quis rem tam veterem pro certo affirmet?*) we may assign to them the XX *Dynasty*. In which we find not the name of any one king, but yet the space left vacant of CLXXVIII years, according to *Eusebius*.

GREAVES

Here therefore we shall place,

First, *Cheops* or *Chemmis*, the founder of the first Pyramid, who began his reign in the CIↃ CIↃ CIↃ CCCC XLVIII year of the *Julian* period, that is CCCCLXXX years before the first olympiad, and IↃ CLXXVII before the first destruction of the temple, and CIↃ CCLXVI before the beginning of the years of our LORD. He reigned fifty years, saith *Herodotus*, and built this Pyramid, as *Diodorus* observes, a thousand years before his time, or the CLXXX olympiad, whereas he might have said a thousand two hundred and seven.

[p] Herodot. lib. 2. Diodor. Sic. lib. 1.

[q] Λέγει γὰρ ὅτι ὁ μὲν Σέθωσις ἐκαλεῖτο Αἴγυπτος, Ἄρμαϊς δὲ ὁ ἀδελφὸς αὐτοῦ Δαναός. Manethos apud Jos. l. 1. contra Apionem. Where in the same place *Manethos* calls this Σέθωσις, also Ῥαμέσσης, and son of *Amenophis*: and therefore *Scaliger* rightly observes, that *Ramesses* with *Manethos* is *Trinominis*. *Scal. in Euseb. Chron.*

[r] This *Danaus* (for his rebellion, being expelled by his brother out of *Ægypt*,) sailed into *Greece*, and possessed himself of *Argos*, as it is testified by *Josephus*, (*lib. 1. contra Apionem*,) by *Africanus* and *Eusebius*, (*vid. Euseb. chron.*) by *Pausanias*, and several others. From whom descended the *Danaidæ*, one of the races of the kings at *Argos*; of all which there is frequent mention in the *Greek* historians and chronographers: Wherefore we cannot be ignorant either of *Danaus* or of his brother's time. I shall only add, for farther illustration, what I find in *Africanus*, Ἄρμαϊς ὁ καὶ Δαναὸς φεύγων τὸν ἀδελφὸν Ῥαμεσσῆν τὸν καὶ Αἴγυπτον ἐκπίπτει τῆς κατ' Αἴγυπτον βασιλείας αὐτοῦ, εἰς Ἑλλάδα τε ἀφικνεῖται. Ῥαμεσσῆς δὲ ὁ ἀδελφὸς αὐτοῦ ὁ Αἴγυπτος καλούμενος ἐβασίλευσεν Αἰγύπτου ἔτη ξη. Μετωνόμασεν τὴν χώραν Αἴγυπτον τῷ ἰδίῳ ὀνόματι, ἥ τις πρότερον Μεστραία παρ' Ἕλλησι δὲ Ἀερία ἐλέγετο. Δαναὸς δὲ ὁ καὶ Ἄρμαϊς κρατήσας τοῦ Ἄργους, καὶ ἐκβαλὼν Σθένελον τὸν Κροτωποῦ Ἀργείων ἐβασίλευσεν, καὶ οἱ ἀπόγονοι αὐτοῦ μετ' αὐτὸν Δαναΐδαι καλούμενοι, ἐπ' Εὐρυσθέα τὸν Σθενέλου τοῦ Περσέως, μεθ' οὓς οἱ Πελοπίδαι. Afr. apud Euseb. chron.

[s] Euseb. chron.

[t] Liv. l. 1.

Secondly,

GREAVES

Secondly, *Cephren* or *Chabryis*, the builder of the second, who reigned fifty [u] six years.

Thirdly, *Mycerinus*, the erector of the third, seven years.

Fourthly, *Asychis* the author of the fourth.

Fifthly, *Anysis* the blind.

How long these two reigned is no where expressed.

Sixthly, *Sabachus* the *Ethiopian*. He conquered *Ægypt*, and reigned [x] fifty years.

The sum is CLXIII years, this being subducted out of CLXXVIII years, (the whole time allowed by *Eusebius* to this *Dynasty*,) the remainder is XV years; which space we may without any inconvenience, divide between *Asychis* and *Anysis*.

If any shall question why the names of these kings are omitted by *Manethos*, an *Ægyptian* priest, in the XX *Dynasty*, I can give no other reason than what we read in *Herodotus*: [y] *These kings* (speaking of *Cheops* and *Cephren*,) *the* Ægyptians *out of hatred will not so much as name, but they call them the Pyramids of* Philition *a shepherd, who in those times, at that place, fed his cattel.* The which hatred, occasioned by their oppressions, as [z] *Diodorus* also mentions, might cause him to omit the rest, especially *Sabachus*, an *Æthiopian*, and an usurper.

Following this computation of *Eusebius* of CLXXVIII years for the XX *Dynasty*, and not that of *Africanus*, who assigns only an CXXV, of whom [a] *Joseph Scaliger* hath this censure, *In istis Dynastis, aliquid turbasse videtur Africanus, ut consuleret rationibus suis*; it will follow by way of consequence, as the *most reverend and learned primate of* Ireland, in his *Chronologiâ Sacrâ* hath singularly well observed.

First, That the XVIII *Dynasty* ends with the migration of the *Israelites* out of *Ægypt*, and with the death of *Amenophis*; which is clearly signified by *Manethos*, and the times of *Belus* and *Danaus*, noted by the *Greek* chronographers, do evidently confirm it. I mean the Ægyptian *Belus* or *Amenophis*, the father of *Ægyptus*, or *Sethosis* and *Danaus*, not the *Babylonian Belus* the father of *Ninus*, whom *Mythologists* confound with this, feigning him to have transported colonies out of *Ægypt* to *Babylon*. The time allotted by [b] *Thallus*, an antient chronographer, to *Belus* of CCCXX years before the *Trojan* war, doth exactly agree with this Ægyptian *Belus* or *Amenophis*.

Secondly, That the XX *Dynasty* will receive those six kings, which out of *Herodotus* we have placed there; the number of whose years exceed the time limited by *Africanus*.

Thirdly, That the XXII *Dynasty* will fall upon the latter time of king *Solomon*, whereby *Sesonchis* the first king of it, may be the same with *Sesac*, or *Shishac*, who in the [c] fifth year of *Rehoboam*, the son of *Solomon*, invaded *Judæa*; which was the only reason that moved [d] *Scaliger* to suspect, that something had been altered by *Africanus* in these *Dynasties*.

By the same series and deduction of times, we may conclude, that the *labyrinth* adjoining to the Pyramid of *Osymanduas*, raised by a common expence of the XII kings, who [e] succeeded *Sethon* to have been CIↃ CIↃ CCCXXIV years since, IↃ CLXXX before Christ. For *Sethon* living in the time of *Sennacharib*, and these immediately following *Sethon* in the government of the kingdom, they must have reigned either in the same age the scripture assigns to *Sennacharib*, or not long after.

Those other Pyramids, the one of *Osymanduas* in [f] *Diodorus*, or *Ismandes*, in [g] *Strabo*, and those two of *Mæris*, or *Myris*, in [h] *Herodotus*, and [i] *Diodorus*, it is evident they preceded *Sesostris* the great, and must therefore have been above three thousand years since, but by how many kings or how many ages, is hard to be defined.

[u] Herod. lib. 2. Diodor. lib. 1. [x] Ibid. [y] Τούτους ὑπὸ μίσεος ἐ καρτα θέλουσι Αἰγύπτιοι ὀνομάζειν, ἀλλὰ ϗ τὰς πυραμίδας καλέουσι ποιμένος Φιλιτίωνος, ὃς τοῦτον τ̓ χρόνον ἔνεμε κτήνεα κατὰ ταῦτα χωρία. Herodot. lib. 2. [z] Diodor. lib. 1. [a] Scalig. in Euseb. chron: [b] Thallus apud Euseb. [c] 1 Kings xiv. 25, 26. [d] Scalig. in Euseb. chron. [e] Herodot. lib. 2. [f] Diodor. lib. 1. [g] Strabo, lib. 17. [h] Herodot. lib. 2. [i] Diodor. lib. 1.

Of the end or intention of the PYRAMIDS, *that they were for ſepulchres; where, by the way is expreſſed, the manner of imbalming uſed by the* ÆGYPTIANS.

Greaves

THAT theſe Pyramids were intended for ſepulchres and monuments of the dead is the conſtant opinion of moſt authors, which have writ of this argument. [a] *Diodorus* expreſly tells us, that *Chemmis* and *Cephren, although they deſigned* (theſe two greater) *for their ſepulchres, yet it happened that neither of them were buried in them.* [b] *Strabo* judges all thoſe near *Memphis* to have been the ſepulchres of kings. *Forty ſtadia from the city* (Memphis,) *there is a certain brow of an hill in which are many Pyramids, the ſepulchres of kings.* And in particular he calls another near the lake of *Mœris, the* [c] *ſepulchre of Imandes.* To which alſo the writings of the *Arabians* are conſonant, who make the three greater the monuments of *Saurid, Hougib,* and *Fazfarinoun.* And the *Sabæans* the firſt of them, the ſepulchre of *Seth,* the ſecond of *Hermes,* the third of *Sab,* from whom they ſuppoſe themſelves denominated *Sabæans,* as we formerly mentioned. And if none of theſe authorities were extant, yet the tomb found in the greateſt Pyramid to this day of *Cheops,* as *Herodotus* names him, or *Chemmis,* according to *Diodorus,* puts it out of controverſy. Which may farther be confirmed by the teſtimony of *Ibn Abd Alhokm* an *Arabian,* where he diſcourſes of the wonders of *Ægypt,* who relates that after *Almamon* the calif of *Babylon,* had cauſed this Pyramid to be open'd [about eight hundred years ſince,] [d] *they found in it towards the top a chamber, with an hollow ſtone, in which there was a ſtatue like a man, and within it a man, upon whom was a breaſt-plate of gold ſet with jewels, upon this breaſt-plate was a ſword of ineſtimable price, and at his head a carbuncle of the bigneſs of an egg, ſhining like the light of the day, and upon him were characters writ with a pen, which no man underſtood.*

Note, *In* Mr. Greaves's *edition of this work, printed at* London, Anno 1646. *the* Arabick *is cited at large, to which the curious reader may have recourſe.*

But why the Ægyptian kings ſhould have been at ſo vaſt an expence in the building of theſe Pyramids, is an enquiry of an higher nature. [e] *Ariſtotle* judges them to have been the works of tyranny: And *Pliny* conjectures, that they built them, partly out of oſtentation, and partly out of ſtate-policy, by keeping the people in employment, to divert them from mutinies and rebellions. [f] *Regum pecuniæ otioſa, ac ſtulta oſtentatio. Quippe cum faciendi eas cauſa a pleriſque tradatur, ne pecuniam ſucceſſoribus, aut æmulis inſidiantibus præberent, aut ne plebs eſſet otioſa.*

But the true reaſon depends upon higher and more weighty conſiderations; though I acknowledge theſe alledged by *Pliny* might be ſecondary motives. And this ſprang from the theology of the *Ægyptians,* who, as *Servius* ſhews in his comment upon theſe words of [g] *Virgil,* deſcribing the funeral of *Polydorus,*

——Animamque ſepulchro
Condimus.——

believed, that *as long as the body endured, ſo long the ſoul continued with it,* which alſo was the opinion of the [h] Stoicks. [i] *Hence the* Ægyptians *ſkilful in wiſdom, do keep their dead imbalmed ſo much the longer, to the end that the ſoul may for a long while continue, and be obnoxious to the body, leſt it ſhould quickly paſs to another. The Romans did the contrary, burning their dead, that the ſoul might ſuddenly return into the generality, that is, into its own nature.* Wherefore that the body might not, either by putrefaction be reduced to duſt, out of which it was firſt formed, or by fire be converted into aſhes, (as the manner of the *Græcians* and *Romans* was) they invented curious compoſitions, beſides the intombing them in ſtately reconditories, hereby endeavouring to preſerve them from rottenneſs, and to make them eternal. [k] *Nec cremare, aut fodere fas putant, verùm arte medicatos intra penetralia collocant,* ſaith *Pomponius Mela:* And *Herodotus* gives the reaſon why they did neither burn nor bury. For diſcourſing, in his third book, of the cruelty of *Cambyſes,* and of his commanding that the body of

[a] Τῶν δὲ βασιλέων τῶν κατασκευασάντων αὐτὰς ἑαυτοῖς τάφους συνέβη μηδέτερον αὐτῶν ταῖς πυραμίσιν ἐνταφῆναι. Diod. Sic. lib. 1.

[b] Τετταράκοντα δ' ἀπὸ τῆς πόλεως σταδίους προελθόντι ὀρεινή τις ὀφρύς ἐστιν, ἐφ' ᾗ πολλαὶ μὲν πυραμίδες εἰσὶ τάφοι τῶν βασιλέων. Strab. lib. 17.

[c] Ἰμάνδης δ' ὄνομα ὁ ταφείς. Ibid.

[d] G. Almec. Hiſt. Arab. ex Edit. Erp. [e] Ariſt. l. 3. Polit. [f] Plin. l. 26. c. 12.

[g] Æneid. lib. 3. [h] *Stoici medium ſequentes, tam diu animam durare dicunt, quam diu durat & corpus.* Serv. Com. in lib. 3. Æneid. [i] *Unde Ægypti periti ſapientiæ condita diutius reſervant cadavera, ſcilicet ut anima multo tempore perduret, & corpori ſit obnoxia, ne cito ad aliud tranſeat. Romani contra faciebant comburentes cadavera, ut ſtatim anima in generalitatem, id eſt, in ſuam naturam rediret.* Serv. Com. in lib. 3. Æneid. [k] Pompon. Mel. l. 1. c. 9.

GREAVES *Amasis*, an Ægyptian king, should be taken out of his sepulchre, whipt, and used with all contumely, he reports, that after all he bid it to be burnt, [m] *commanding that which was not holy. For the Persians imagine the fire to be a god, and neither of them are accustomed to burn the dead body. The Persians for the reason before alledged, because they conceive it unfitting for a god to devour the carcass of a man; and the Ægyptians, because they are persuaded the fire is a living creature, devouring all things that it receives, and after it is satisfied with food, dies with that which it hath devoured. Nor is it their custom of giving the dead body* [n] *to beasts, but of imbalming* (or salting) *it, not only for this reason, but that it may not be consumed with worms.* The term used by *Herodotus* ταριχεύειν, *of salting or imbalming* the dead, is also used by [o] *Baruch* and by [p] *Plato*, and by [q] *Lucian* in his discourse *de luctu*, treating of the several sorts of burial practised by several nations. [r] *The Grecian doth burn* [the dead] *the Persian bury, the Indian doth anoint with the fat of swine, the Scythian eats, and the Ægyptian* ταριχεύει, *embalms*, (or powders.) Which manner also is alluded to by *Antoninus* under the word τάριχος, [s] *that which the other day was excrementitious matter, within few days shall either be* τάριχος, *an imbalmed body, or meer ashes:* In the one expressing the custom of the *Ægyptians*, in the other of the *Romans*; where doctor [t] *Casaubone*, the learned son of a learned father, hath rightly corrected the errors of those who render τάριχος *to be a certain sort of fish*. By this means then salting the body, and imbalming it, (the manner of both we shall describe out of *Herodotus* and *Diodorus*,) the soul was obliged (according to the belief of the *Ægyptians*) to abide with the body, and the body came to be as durable as marble. Insomuch as *Plato*, who lived in *Ægypt* with *Eudoxus* no less than XIII years, as [u] *Strabo* witnesseth, brings it for an argument in his *Phædon* to prove the immortality of the soul, by the long duration of these bodies. Which surely would have been more conclusive with him, could he have imagined that to these times, that is, till CIↃ CIↃ years after him, they should have continued so solid and intire, as to this day we find many of them. Wherefore [x] St. *Augustin* truly affirms, that the *Ægyptians alone believe the resurrection, because they carefully preserve their dead corpses. For they have a custom of drying up the bodies, and rendering them as durable as brass; these* [in their language] *they call Gabbares.* Whence the gloss of *Isidore*, *Gabbares mortuorum*, in *Vulcanius*, his edition; or as [y] *Spondanus* reads *Gabbares mortuorum condita corpora*.

The manner how the *Ægyptians* prepared and imbalmed these bodies, is very copiously, and by what I observed, very faithfully described by *Herodotus* and *Diodorus*, and therefore I shall put down their own words: *Their mourning*, saith, [z] *Herodotus*, *and manner of burial are in this kind: When any man of quality of the family is dead, all the women besmear their heads and faces with dirt, then leaving the body with their kindred, they go lamenting up and down the city with their kinsfolks, their apparel being girt about them, and their breasts naked. On the other side, the men having likewise their cloaths girt about them, beat themselves. These things being done, they carry it to be* [a] *imbalmed. For this there are some appointed, that profess the art; these, when the body is brought to*

[m] Herodot. lib. 3. Ἐντελλόμενος οὐκ ὅσια. Πέρσαι γὰρ θεὸν νομίζουσι εἶναι τὸ πῦρ, &c.

[n] This barbarous custom is still practised in the *East-Indies*; as *Teixeira* (who from his own travels, and the writings of *Emir Cond*, a *Persian*, hath given us the best light of those countries) truly informs us. Wherefore, we may give credit to that of *Tully*: *Magorum mos est non humare corpora suorum, nisi à feris sint antea laniata. In Hyrcania plebs publicos alit canes, optimates domesticos, (Nobile autem genus canum illud scimus esse,) sed pro sua quisque facultate parat, à quibus lanietur, eamque optimam illi esse censent sepulturam.* Tusc. q. l. 1. [o] Baruch. vi. 71. [p] Plat. Phædon. [q] Lucian de Luct.

[r] Ὁ μὲν Ἕλλην ἔκαυσεν, ὁ δὲ Πέρσης ἔθαψεν, ὁ δὲ Ἰνδὸς ὑάλῳ περιχρίει, ὁ δὲ Σκύθης κατεσθίει, ταριχεύει δὲ ὁ Αἰγύπτιος.

[s] M. Aurel. Anton. lib. 4. Ἐχθὲς μὲν μυξάριον, αὔριον δὲ τάριχος ἢ τέφρα. [t] Casaub. ann. in lib. 4. M. Aurel. Anton. [u] Strabo, lib. 17. [x] *Ægyptii verò soli credunt resurrectionem, quia diligenter curant cadavera mortuorum, morem enim habent siccare corpora, & quasi ænea reddere, Gabbaras ea vocant.* Aug. Serm. 120. De diversis. [y] Spondanus de Cœmet. sacris, lib. 1. par. in c. 5.

[z] Herodotus, lib. 2. Θρῆνοι δὲ καὶ ταφαὶ σφέων εἰσὶ αἵδε, &c.

[a] Amongst these imbalmed bodies are found *Ægyptian* idols, *Omni-genumque Deûm monstra, & latrator Anubis*, to use *Virgil*'s expression, (*Æn.* 8.) Some of these are in great, some in little portraictures, formed either with potters earth baked, or else of stone, or metal, or wood, or the like; in all which kinds I have bought some. One of them for the rarity of the matter, and for the illustration of the scriptures deserves to be here mentioned; being cut out of a *magnes*, in the form and bigness of the κάνθαρος, or *scarabæus*; which as * *Plutarch* testifies, was worshipped by the *Ægyptians*, and was by military men ingraven as an emblem on their seals. To which sort of idols, it may be *Moses* alluded, when speaking of the gods of *Ægypt* he terms גלולים *gillulim*, *stercoreos deos*, † as the original is rendred by *Junius*, and *Tremellius*; for such places are the unsavoury dwellings of the *scarabæus*. That which is remarkable of it in nature is this, that the stone, though probably two thousand years since taken out of its natural bed, the rock, yet still retains its attractive and magnetical virtue.

* De If. & Osir. τοῖς δὲ μαχίμοις κάνθαρος ἦν γλυφὴ σφραγῖδος. † Deut. xxix. 17. *Vidistis abominandos & stercoreos deos illorum.*

them,

GREAVES

them, shew to the bringers of it certain patterns of dead bodies in wood, like it in painting. One of these they say is accurately made, (which I think it not lawful to name,) they shew a second inferior to it, and of an easier price, and a third cheaper than the former. Which being seen, they ask of them according to what pattern they will have the dead body prepared? When they have agreed upon the price, they depart thence; those that remain, carefully imbalm the body in this manner: First of all they draw out the brain with a crooked iron by the nostrils, which being taken out, they infuse [b] *medicaments. Then with a sharp Æthiopick stone they cut it about the bowels, and take out all the guts: these purged and washed with wine made of palms, they again wash with sweet odours beaten; next filling up the* [c] *belly with pure mirrhe beaten, and cassia, and other odours, except frankincense, they sew it up again; having done this, they salt it with nitre, hiding it seventy days, (for longer it is not lawful to salt it;) seventy days being ended, after they have washed the body, binding it with fillets, (or* [d] *ribbands,) and wrapping it in a shrowd of silk linen, they smear it with gum, which the Ægyptians often use instead of glue. The kindred receiving it thence, make* [e] *a coffin of wood, in the similitude of a man, in which they put the dead body; and being thus inclosed, they place it in a reconditory in the house, setting it upright against the wall. In this manner with great expences they prepare the funerals of their dead. But those who avoiding too great expences desire a mediocrity, prepare them in this manner. They take a clyster with the juice of cedar, with which they fill the belly by the fundament, neither cutting it, nor taking it out, and salt it so many days, as we mentioned before. In the last of which they take out that* (clyster) *of cedar out of the belly, which before they injected. This hath such efficacy, that it carries out with it the whole paunch and entrails corrupted. The nitre consumes the flesh, and there is only left the skin and bones of the dead body. When they have done this, they restore*

[b] Having caused the head of one of the richer sort of these imbalmed bodies to be opened, in the hollow of the skull I found the quantity of two pounds of these medicaments; which had the consistence, blackness, and smell of a kind of *bitumen*, or pitch, and by the heat of the sun waxed soft. This infusion could not well have been made any other way, than as *Herodotus* here intimates, by the nostrils. The tongue of this imbalmed body being weighed by me, was less than seven grains *English*. So light was that member, which St. *James* calls *a world of mischief*, James iii. 6.

[c] *Plutarch* writes, that they first exposed the belly, being opened, to the sun, casting the bowels into the river (*Nilus*,) *tanquam inquinamentum corporis*: this being done, they filled up the belly, and the hollow of the breast with unguents and odours, as it is manifest by those which I have seen.

[d] These ribbands, by what I observed, were of linen, which was also the habit of the *Ægyptian* priests. For *Herodotus, lib.* 2. writes, that it was prophane for the *Ægyptians* either to be buried in woollen garments, or to use them in their temples: and *Plutarch de Iside & Osiride* expresly tells us, that *the priests of* Isis *used linen vestments, and were shaved; Suetonius in Orthone,* (*lib.* 7.) *sacra etiam Isidis sæpe linteâ religiosâque veste propalam celebravit.* And therefore the goddess *Isis* is called in *Ovid* (2 *Amor. Elen.* 2.) Linigera.

Nec tu Linigeram fieri quid possit ad Isim,
Quæsieris. ———

Of these Ribbands I have seen some so strong and perfect, as if they had been newly made. With these they bound and swathed the dead body, beginning with the head, and ending with the feet: Over these again, they wound others so often upon one another, that there could not be much less than a thousand ells upon one body.

[e] These coffins are fashioned in the similitude of a man, or rather resembling one of those imbalmed bodies; which, as we described before, are bound with ribbands, and wrapped in a shroud of linen. For as in those there is the shape of a head, with a kind of painted vizard, or face fastened to it, but no appearance without of the arms and legs: so it is with these coffins; the top of them hath the shape of the head of a man, with a face painted on it resembling a woman, the residue being one continued trunk: at the end of this trunk is a *pedestal*, somewhat broad; upon which it stood upright in the reconditory, as *Herodotus* here mentions. Some of these coffins are handsomely painted without, with several hieroglyphicks. Opening two of them, I found within, over the body, divers scroles fastened to the linen shrowd. These were painted with sacred characters, for the colours very lively, and fresh; amongst which, were in a larger size the pictures of men or women, some headed like hawks, some like dogs, and sometimes dogs in shards standing alone. These scroles either ran down the belly and sides, or else were placed upon the knees and legs. On the feet was a linen cover, (and so were all the scroles before-mentioned of *linen*,) painted with hieroglyphicks, and fashioned like to a high slipper. The breast had a kind of breast-plate covering it, made with folds of linen cut scolopwise, richly painted and gilt. In the midst of the bend at the top of it, was the face of a woman with her arms expanded; on each side of them, at the two outmost ends, the head of an hawk fairly gilt, by which they represented the Divine Nature, according to *Plutarch* (in his book *de Iside & Osiride*,) as by a serpent with the tail in his mouth, the revolution of the year was resembled; in which kind also I have seen fair sculptures in gemms, found at *Alexandria*: and as by the sign of the cross they did denote *vitam æternam*, in *Ruffinus*'s expression. Of these crosses I have seen several amongst their hieroglyphicks; some painted, and some engraven in this manner ✠, and some others amongst their mummies formed of stone (or baked earth) in this figure.

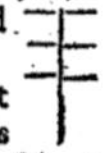

At *Rome*, on the statue of *Osiris*, it is engraven thus: T. which may serve for confirmation of what *Socrates* and *Sozomen* relate; that at *Alexandria*, the temple of *Serapis* or *Osiris* (for † *Plutarch* judges *Serapis* and *Osiris* to be one and the same,) being by the command of *Theodosius* demolished, they found characters resembling *crosses* cut in stone; *these, in the interpretation of the wise men of Ægypt, signified,* ζωὴν ἐπερχομένην, *vitam venturam*: which discovery, as the same authors report, occasioned the conversion to Christianity of some of the *Gentiles*. *Socr. hist. eccles. lib.* 5. *cap.* 17. *Sozomen. hist. eccles. lib.* 7. *cap.* 15.

† Ἀμφοῖν δὲ ἑνὸς Θεοῦ καὶ μιᾶς δυνάμεως ἡγούμενος. Plut de If. & Osir.

the

GREAVES *the body to the kindred, doing nothing more. The third manner of preparing the dead, is of them which are of meaner fortune: With lotions they wash the belly, and dry it with salt seventy days, then they deliver it to be carried away.*

Diodorus Siculus[f], as his manner is, more distinctly and clearly with some remarkable circumstances, expresseth the same thing. *If any one die amongst the Ægyptians, all his kindred and friends casting dirt upon their heads, go lamenting about the city, till such time as the body is buried. In the mean time, they abstain from baths and wine, and all delicate meat, neither do they wear costly apparel: The manner of their burial is three-fold. The one is very costly, the second less, the third very mean. In the first, they say there is spent a talent of silver, in the second twenty* minæ, *in the last there is very little expence. Those who take care to dress the body are artizans receiving this skill from their ancestors. These shewing a bill to the kindred of the dead, of the expences upon each kind of burial, ask them in what manner they will have the body to be prepared. When they have agreed upon it, they deliver the body to such as are usually appointed to this office. First, he which is called the scribe, laying it upon the ground, describes about the bowels on the left side, how much is to be cut away. Then he which is called the cutter, taking an Æthiopick stone, and cutting away as much of the flesh as the law commands, presently flies away as fast as he can; they which are present, running after him, and casting stones at him, and cursing him,* (hereby) *turning all the execration upon him. For whosoever doth offer violence, or wound, or do any kind of injury to a body of the same nature with himself, they think him worthy of hatred. But those which are called the imbalmers, they esteem them worthy of honour and respect. For they are familiar with their priests, and they go into the temples, as holy men without any prohibition. As soon as they meet about the dressing of the dissected body, one thrusting his hand by the wound of the dead body into his entrails, takes out all the bowels within, besides the heart and kidneys; another cleanses all the entrails washing them with wine made of palms, and with odours. Lastly, the whole body being carefully anointed with the juice of cedar, and other things for above thirty days, and afterwards with myrrhe and cinnamon, and such other things, which have power not only to keep it for a long time, but also to give a sweet smell, they deliver it to the kindred. This being thus finished, every member of the body is kept so intire, that upon the brows and* [g] *eye-lids, the hairs remain, and the whole shape of the body* (continues) *unchanged, the image of the countenance may be known. Hence many of the Ægyptians keeping the bodies of their ancestors in magnificent houses, do see so expresly the faces of them dead many ages before they were born, that beholding the bigness of each of them, and the dimensions of their bodies, and the lineaments of their faces, it affords them wonderful content of mind, no otherwise than as if they were now living with them.* Thus far *Diodorus*. By which description of his, and that of *Herodotus*, we see the truth of what [h] *Tully* writes: *The Ægyptians imbalm their dead, and keep them at home: Amongst themselves above ground*, saith *Sextus Empericus*; And [i] *intra penetralia* in *Pomponius Mela*'s expression: And in *lectulis*, according to *Athanasius* in the life of *Antony*. *Lucian* adds farther in his tract *de luctu*. [k] *They bring the dried body (I speak what I have seen,) as a guest to their feasts, and invitations, and oftentimes one necessitous of money is supplied, by giving his brother or his father in pledge.* The former custom is intimated by *Silius* [l] *Italicus*, speaking of the several manners of burial practised in divers nations.

> *Ægyptia tellus*
> *Claudit odorato post funus stantia saxo,*
> *Corpora, & à mensis exanguem haud separat umbram.*

The latter is confirmed by *Diodorus Siculus*[m]. *They have a custom of depositing for a pledge the bodies of their dead parents. It is the greatest ignominy that may be not to redeem them; and if they do it not, they themselves are deprived of burial.* And therefore says he immediately before, *Such as for any crime or debt, are hindred from being buried, are kept at home without a coffin; whom afterwards their posterity growing rich, discharging their debts, and paying money in compensation of their crimes, honourably bury; for the Ægyptians glory, that their parents and ancestors were buried with honour.*

This manner of the *Ægyptians* imbalming, we find also practised by *Joseph* upon his father *Jacob* in *Ægypt:* And if we will

[f] Diod. Sic. lib. 1. [g] I find in the travels of monsieur *de Breves*, embassador at *Constantinople*, that at his being in *Ægypt* about forty years since, they saw some of these imbalmed bodies, with hairs remaining on their heads, and with beards; which I easily believe. *Nous en vismes aucuns la teste & les pieds descouverts (à cause que les dites bandes estorent pourries,) qui avoient encore les chevaux, la barbe & les ongles.* Les voyages de M. de Breves. [h] *Condiunt Ægyptii mortuos, & eos domi servant.* Tuscul. qu. lib. 1.

[i] Lib. 1. cap. 9. [k] Οὗτος μέντοι ὁ (λέγω δὲ ἰδών) ξηράνας τὸν νεκρὸν, σύνδειπνον καὶ συμπότην ἐποιήσατο, πολλάκις δὲ καὶ δεομένῳ χρημάτων ἀνδρὶ Αἰγυπτίῳ ἔλυσε τὴν ἀπορίαν ἐνέχυρον ἢ ὁ ἀδελφὸς ἢ ὁ πατὴρ γενόμενος ἐν καιρῷ. Luc. an. περὶ πένθους. [l] Lib. 3. Punicorum. [m] Diodor. Sic. l. 1.

believe

believe *Tacitus*, [n] *the Hebrews* (in general) *learned from the Ægyptians rather to bury their dead than to burn them.* Where [o] *Spondanus* instead of *condere cadavera*, reads *condire*, as if it had been their custom of powdering or imbalming their dead. Wash them and anoint them we know they did, by what was done to our *Saviour* and to the *widow Dorcas*; and long before it was in use amongst the Gentiles, as well as Jews, as appears by the funeral of *Patroclus* in [p] *Homer*, and of *Missenus* the *Trojan* in [q] *Virgil.*

Corpusque lavant frigentis, & ungunt.

And of *Tarquinius* the *Roman* in *Ennius:*

Tarquinii corpus bona fœmina lavit, & unxit.

But certainly the *Ægyptian* manner of imbalming, which we have described out of *Herodotus* and *Diodorus*, was not received by them; or if it were, [r] *Martha* the sister of *Lazarus*, needed not to have fear'd, that after four days the body should have stunk. [s] They which infer out of the funeral of *Asa*, king of *Judah*, that it was the custom of the *Jews* as well as *Ægyptians*, have very little probability for their assertion. [t] We read, that *they buried him in his own sepulchre, which he had made for himself in the city of David, and laid him in the bed, which was filled with sweet odours, and divers kinds of spices prepared by the apothecaries art; and they made a very great burning for him.* This very great burning is so contrary to the practice of the *Ægyptians*, to whom it was an abomination, as appears by the authorities before cited of *Herodotus* and *Mela*, besides the little affinity of filling the bed with sweet odours, and the *Ægyptians* filling the body and the place of the entrails with sweet odours, according both to *Herodotus* and *Diodorus*, that we shall not need to enlarge our selves in any other confutation. But as for that of *Jacob* and *Joseph*, the father and the son both living and dying in *Ægypt*, the text is clear, they were imbalmed after the fashion of the *Ægyptians*. [v] *And Joseph commanded his servants the physicians to imbalm his father, and the physicians imbalmed Israel, and forty days were fulfilled for him (for so are fulfilled the days of those which are imbalmed;) and the Ægyptians mourned for him threescore and ten days.* In the same chapter we read, [u] *So Joseph died being an hundred and ten years old, and they imbalm'd him, and he was put in a coffin in Ægypt.* Both which places are very consonant to the traditions of *Herodotus* and *Diodorus*, and *may serve to shew what necessity there is of having oft-times recourse to the learning of the heathen*, for the illustration of the scriptures. *Forty days were fulfilled for the imbalming of Jacob:* This [w] *Diodorus* tells us was their custom, *They anointed the dead body with the juice of cedar, and other things for above thirty days, and afterward with myrrhe and cinnamon, and the like*; which might make up the residue of the forty days: *And the Ægyptians mourned for him threescore and ten days.* This time out of *Herodotus* may be collected to have been from the first day of the death of the person, till the body was returned by the physicians after seventy days perfectly imbalmed. The text says, *And Joseph was put in a coffin*; which is very livelily represented by [x] *Herodotus. The kindred receiving the dead body from the imbalmers, make a coffin of wood in the similitude of a man, in which they put it.* This coffin then, as it is probable, of *Joseph*, was of wood, and not *marmorea theca*, as *Cajetan* imagines, the former being the custom of the *Ægyptians*. Besides, that this was much easier and fitter to be carried by the *Israelites* into *Canaan*, marching on foot, and for ought we read destitute of waggons and other carriages.

The [y] *tradition of the ancient Hebrews* in their commentaries, is very probable and consonant to it. *They carried in the desert two arks, the one of God, the other of Joseph; that the ark of the covenant, this the ark* (or coffin) *in which they carried Joseph's bones out of Ægypt.* This coffin (if it be lawful for me to conjecture after the revolution of three thousand years,) I conceive to have been of sycomore, (a great tree very plentifully growing in *Ægypt*,) of which sort there are many found in the mummies, very fair, entire, and free from corruption to this day. Though I know the *Arabians* and *Persians* have a different tradition, that his coffin was of glass. [z] *They put his blessed body, after they*

[n] *Judæos ab Ægyptiis didicisse, condere cadavera, potiùs quàm cremare.* Tacit. histor. lib. 5.

[o] Spondan. lib. 1. part 1. cap. 5. *de cæmeteriis sacris.*

[p] Καὶ τότε δὴ λουσάν τε, καὶ ἤλειψαν λιπ' ἐλαίῳ. Iliad. lib. 19. [q] Æneid. lib. 6. [r] John xi. 39.

[s] *Transtulerunt Israelitæ hunc ritum ex Ægypto secum in Cananæam, quo deinceps in sepulturis principum & regum usi dicuntur in historia Asiæ.* 2 Paral. vi. & alibi. D. Paræi. Com. in Gen. l. 2. [t] 2 Chron. xvi. 14.

[v] Gen. l. 2, 3. [u] Gen. l. 26.

[w] Diod. Sic. lib. 1. Καθόλε ϛ πᾶν τὸ σῶμα τὸ μὲν πρῶτον κεδρίᾳ καὶ τισὶν ἄλλοις ἐπιμελείαις ἀξιοῦσιν ἐφ' ἡμέρας πλείους τῶν τριάκοντα, ἔπειτα σμύρνῃ καὶ κινναμώμῳ, &c. [x] Herod. lib. 2..

[y] *Veteres Hebræi commentati sunt duas fuisse arcas, unam incedentes in deserto, alteram Divinitatis, alteram Josephi; illam scilicet arcam fœderis, hanc verò loculos quibus Josephi ossa ex Ægypto asportabantur in regionem Chanaan.* Perer. Com. in l. cap. Genes.

[z] *Note,* In Mr. *Greaves*'s edition of this work, printed at *London, anno* 1646, the *Arabick* is cited at large, to which the curious reader may have recourse.

GREAVES *had washed it, into a coffin of glass. and buried it in the channel of the river Nilus,* saith *Emir Cond*, a *Persian*.

That phrase of *Joseph*, where he takes an oath of the children of *Israel*, [a] *Ye shall carry up my bones from hence*, surely is a *synecdoche*, or figurative speech. And so is that in *Exodus: And* [b] *Moses took the bones of Joseph with him; for he had straitly sworn the children of Israel, saying,* GOD *will surely visit you, and ye shall carry up my bones away hence with you:* for his body being boweled, and then imbalmed, after the manner of the *Ægyptians*, not only the bones, but the skin, the flesh, and all besides the entrails, (which according to [c] *Plutarch*, were thrown into the river,) would have continued perfect and intire, a much longer space than from his death to their migration out of *Ægypt*.

Having thus by art found out ways to make the body durable, whereby the soul might continue with it, as we shewed before, which else would have been at liberty to have passed *into some other body*, [d] this also being the opinion of the *Ægyptians, from whom Pythagoras borrowed his* μετεμψύχωσις, or transanimation, (the which made him to forbid his disciples the eating of flesh, *Ne forte bubulam quis de aliquo proavo suo obsonaret*, as *Tertullian* wittily speaks;) the next care of the *Ægyptians* was to provide conditories, which might be as lasting as the body, and in which it might continue safe from the injury of time and men. That occasioned the ancient kings of *Thebes* in *Ægypt* to build those, which [e] *Diodorus* thus describes: *There are, they say, the wonderful sepulchres of the ancient kings, which in magnificence exceeds the imitation of posterity. Of these in the sacred commentaries, forty seven are mentioned; but in the time of Ptolemæus Lagi, there remained but* XVII. *Many of them at our being in Ægypt, in the hundred and eightieth olympiad, were decayed; neither are these things alone reported by the Ægyptians, out of the sacred books, but by many also of the Græcians, who in the time of Ptolemæus Lagi went to Thebes, and having compiled histories, (amongst whom is Hecatæus,) agree with our relations.* And this might occasion also those others recorded by *Strabo*, which he calls ἑρμαῖα, or *mercuriales tumulos*, seen by him near *Siene*, in the upper parts of *Ægypt*, very strange and memorable, [f] *Passing in a chariot from Siene to Philæ, over a very even plain, about an hundred stadia, all the way almost, of both sides, we saw in many places mercurial tombs; a great stone, smooth, and almost spherical, of that black and hard marble out of which mortars are made, placed upon a greater stone, and on the top of this another, some of them lying by themselves; the greatest of them was no less than twelve feet diameter, all of them greater than the half of this.* Many ages after, when the regal throne was removed from *Thebes* to *Memphis*, the same religion and opinion continuing amongst the Ægyptians, *that so long as the body indured, so long the soul continued with it,* not as quickning and animating it, but as an attendant or guardian, and as it were unwilling to leave her former habitation. It is not to be doubted, this incited the kings there, together with their private ambition, and thirst after glory, to be at so vast expences in the building of these *Pyramids*; and the *Ægyptians* of lower quality, to spare for no cost, in cutting those *hypogæa*, those caves or dormitories in the *Lybian* desarts, which by the Christians now adays are called the *mummies*. *Diodorus Siculus* excellently expresses their opinion and belief in this particular, together with their extreme cost of building sepulchres, in these words: [g] *The Ægyptians make small account of the time of this life being limited, but that which after death is joined with a glorious memory of virtue they highly value: They call the houses of the living, inns, because for a short space we inhabit these: But the sepulchres of the dead they name eternal mansions, because they continue with the gods for an infinite space. Wherefore in the structures of their houses they are little solicitous, but in exquisitely adorning their sepulchres they think no cost sufficient.*

Now why the *Ægyptians* did build their sepulchres often in the form of Pyramids, (for they were not always of this figure, as appears by those ἑρμαῖα, or *mercuriales tumuli*, before cited out of *Strabo*, which were spherical; and by those *hypogæa*, or caves still extant in the rocks of the desart,) *Pierius* in his hieroglyphicks, or rather the *Anonymous Author* at the end of him, gives several philosophical reasons: [h] *By a Pyramid*, saith he, *the antient Ægyptians*

[a] Gen. l. 25. [b] Exod. xiii. 19.

[c] Plutar. 7. sapient. convivio. [d] Πρῶτοι δὲ καὶ τὸν δὲ τὸν λόγον Αἰγύπτιοι εἰσὶ οἱ εἰπόντες, ὡς ἀνθρώπου ψυχὴ ἀθάνατός ἐστι, τοῦ σώματος δὲ καταφθίνοντος, ἐς ἄλλο ζῶον αἰεὶ γινόμενον ἐσδύεται. Herod. lib. 2.

[e] Diod. Sic. lib. 1. Εἶναι δὲ φασὶ καὶ τάφους ἐνταῦθα τῶν ἀρχαίων βασιλέων θαυμαστοὺς, &c.

[f] Strabo. lib. 17. Ἤλθομεν δ' εἰς Φιλὰς ἐκ Συήνης ἀπήνῃ δι' ὁμαλοῦ σφόδρα πεδίου σταδίους ὅμου τι ἑκατόν. Παρ' ὅλην δὲ τὴν ὁδὸν ἦν ἰδεῖν ἑκατέρωθεν πολλαχοῦ ὥσπερ ἑρμαῖα, &c.

[g] Diod. Sic. lib. 1. Οἱ μὲν γὰρ ἐγχώριοι τὸν μὲν ἐν τῷ ζῆν χρόνον εὐτελῆ παντελῶς εἶναι νομίζουσι, τὸν δὲ μετὰ τὴν τελευτὴν δι' ἀρετὴν μνημονευθησόμενον, περὶ πλείστου ποιοῦνται. Καὶ τὰς μὲν τῶν ζώντων οἰκήσεις καταλύσεις ὀνομάζουσιν, &c.

[h] Ex eruditi cujusd. l. 2. sub finem Hierogl. Pierii. *Per pyramidem veteres (Ægyptii) rerum naturam, & substantiam illam informem formas recipientem significare voluerunt, quòd ut pyramis à puncto, & summo fastigio*

tians expressed the nature of things, and that informed substance receiving all forms. Because as a Pyramid having its beginning from a point at the top, is by degrees dilated on all parts; so the nature of all things proceeding from one fountain and beginning, which is indivisible, namely from God, the chief workmaster; afterwards receives several forms, and is diffused into various kinds and species, all which it conjoins to that beginning and point, from whence every thing issues and flows. There may also be given another reason for this, taken from astronomy: For the Ægyptians were excellent astronomers, yea, the first inventors of it; these [dividing the Zodiack, and all things under it, into twelve signs,] *will have each sign to be a kind of Pyramid, the basis of which shall be in the heaven; (for the heaven is the foundation of astronomy,) and the point of it shall be in the centre of the earth; seeing therefore in these Pyramids all things are made, and that the coming of the sun, which is as it were a point in respect of those signs, is the cause of the production of natural things, and its departure the cause of their corruption, it seems very fitly that by a Pyramid, nature the parent of all things, may be expressed. Also the same Ægyptians under the form of a Pyramid, shadowed out the soul of man, making under huge Pyramids the magnificent sepulchres of their kings and heroes, to testifie that the soul was still existent, notwithstanding the body were dissolved and corrupted, the which should generate and produce another body for it self, when it should seem good to the first agent, (that is, the circle of thirty six thousand years being transacted:) Like as a Pyramid (as it is known to geometricians,) the top of it standing fixed, and the base being moved about, describes a circle, and the whole body of it a cone; so that the circle expresses that space of years, and the cone that body which in that space is produced. For it was the opinion of the Ægyptians, that in the revolution of thirty six thousand years, all things should be restored to their former state; Plato witnesseth, that he received it from them; who seems also to me in his Timæus, to attest this thing, that is, that our soul hath the form of a Pyramid, which (soul) according to the same Plato, is of a fiery nature, and adhereth to the body as a Pyramid doth to the basis, or as fire doth to the fuel.* Thus far the *Anonymous Author* in *Pierius*: Most of which reasons of his are but pretty fancies, without any solid proof from good authors. For he might as well say, that the *Ægyptians* were excellent geometricians, as well as astronomers, (as they were very skillful in both,) and that they made these *Pyramids*, to express the first and most simple of mathematical bodies; or else being excellent arithmeticians, to represent the mysteries of pyramidal numbers; or being well seen in opticks, to shadow out the manner of vision, and the emission of rays from luminous bodies, as also the *effluvium* of the *species intentionales* from the object, all which are supposed to be pyramidal. But this were to play with truth, and to indulge too much to fancy. Wherefore I conceive the reason why they made these sepulchres in the figure of a Pyramid, was, either as apprehending this to be the most permanent form of structure, as in truth it is; (for by reason of the contracting and lessening of it at the top, it is neither overpressed with its own weight; nor his so subject to the sinking in of rain as other buildings:) or hereby they intended to represent some of their gods. For anciently the Gentiles expressed them, either by columns fashioned like cones, or else by quadrilateral obelisks, the *Ægyptian* manner; in which latter kind, I have seen many standing very intire, some of them plain, and some with hieroglyphicks inscribed. Now such obelisks are but lesser models of the Pyramids, as the Pyramids are but greater kinds of obelisks. The first institution of them, as [i] *Pliny* informs us, was by *Mitres* an *Ægyptian* king, whom [k] *Isidore* terms *Mesphres*; both of them affirming him to have consecrated them *solis numini*, to the deity of the sun. Which deity [l] *Diodorus* relates the *Ægyptians* to have worshipped under the name of *Osiris*, as they did the moon by the goddess *Isis*, whom the *Libyans* bordering on the *Ægyptians*, termed *Urania*, and the *Phœnicians Astroarches*, according to [m] *Herodian*: (And therefore as *Isis Cornigera*, in which portraicture I have observed her statue at *Alexandria* to be formed,) did represent the horns of the moon,

tigio incipiens, paulatim in omnes partes dilatatur, sic rerum omnium natura ab unico principio & fonte, qui dividi non potest, nempè à Deo summo opifice profecta, varias deinde formas suscipit, & in varia genera atque species diffunditur, omniaque apici illi & puncto conjungit, à quo omnia manant & fluunt. Verùm & alia hujus rei ratio nempè astronomia reddi potest, &c.

[i] *Trabes ex eo fecere reges quodam certamine, obeliscos vocantes solis numini sacratos. Radiorum ejus argumentum in effigie est; & ita significabatur nomine Ægyptio. Primus omnium id instituit Mitres, qui in solis urbe regnabat, somnio jussus.* Plin. lib. 36. cap. 8.

[k] *Obeliscum Mesphres rex Ægypti primus fecisse fertur —— qui post cæcitatem viso recepto, duos obeliscos soli consecravit.* Isid. lib. 18. cap. 31.

[l] Ὑπολαβεῖν εἶναι δύο θεοὺς ἀϊδίους τε καὶ πρώτους, τόντε ἥλιον, καὶ τὴν σελήνην, ὧν τὸν μὲν Ὄσιριν τὴν δὲ Ἶσιν ὀνομάσαι. Diod. Sic. lib. 1.

[m] Λίβυες μὲν οὖν αὐτὴν Οὐρανίαν καλοῦσι, Φοίνικες δὲ Ἀστροάρχην ὀνομάζουσι, σελήνην εἶναι θέλοντες. Herodian. lib. 5.

or

GREAVES or *luna falcata*; so these quadrilatteral Pyramids, or obelisks, might not unfitly resemble the rays of the sun, or their god *Osiris*: A god denominated, as [n] *Plutarch* testifies, from *Os*, signifying in the *Ægyptian* language, *many*, and *Iri eyes*. For which reason, both [o] *Diodorus* and *Plutarch*, term *Osyris* in *Greek* πολυόφθαλμον, *many eyes*, or *many rays*; the which emitted, as the opticks demonstrate, in pyramidal or conical forms, might not unaptly by the Gentiles be represented in either figure. Hence the *Phœnicians*, next neighbours to the *Ægyptians*, and probably first imitators of this their idolatry, worshipped the sun, whom they named *Elæagabalus*, or as the ancient coins render him, *Alegabalus*, and some inscriptions *Heliogabalus*, an idol, in the similitude of a cone. [p] *Herodian (l. 5.) The Phœnicians worship the sun, calling him in their language Elæagabalus; to whom there is erected a very spacious temple, adorned with gold, plenty of silver, and precious stones. It is not only worshipped by the natives, but likewise the great men, and kings of the Barbarians every year, with a kind of emulation, send honourable presents to the god. There is no statue, as among the Greeks and Romans, which polished by hand, may express the image of the god. But there is a certain great stone circular below, and ending with a sharpness above, in the figure of a cone, of black colour. They report it to have fallen from heaven, and to be the image of the sun.* This idolatry by commerce with the *Ægyptians* and *Phœnicians*, came afterward to be communicated to the *Grecians*, and other nations; and from these, what at the first institution was proper to the sun, came by superstition to be apply'd to their other gods. Thus [q] *Tacitus (lib. II. hist.)* at *Cyprus* in the temple of *Venus*, at *Paphos*, *The image of the goddess is not of human shape, but a figure rising continually round, from a larger bottom to a small top in conical fashion; the reason thereof is not known.* Though what *Tacitus* rendreth *metæ modo exurgens*, or conical, *Maximus Tyrius* termeth pyramidal. [r] *In Paphos, Venus hath the chiefest honour; howbeit, her image you can liken to nothing so well as to a white Pyramid.* In like manner we find in [s] *Clemens Alexandrinus*, that *Calithoe* the priestess of *Juno*, decked *the column of the goddess* with crowns and garlands; that is, saith [t] *Joseph Scaliger, the image of the goddess with crowns and garlands; for at that time the statues of the gods were* κίονες πυραμοειδεῖς, *pyramidal columns*, or obelisks. And Ἀπόλλων ἀγυιεὺς, was nothing else with the *Grecians* but κίων εἰς ὀξὺ λήγων, *a column ending in a point*, as [v] *Suidas* witnesseth: *which kind of columns some make proper to Apollo, others to Bacchus, and others to them both.* In *Pausanias* also we read, that in the city *Corinth*, *Jupiter, Melichius, and Diana sirnamed Patroa, were made with little or no art: Melichius being represented by a Pyramid, and Diana by a column.* Whence not improbably the same [x] *Pausanias*, in his *Corinthiacis*, conjectures, this manner of representation of the gods, to have been the first and most ancient among the *Grecians*. But *Clemens Alexandrinus*, deriving the beginning of it much higher, imagines it to have been the first kind of idolatry in the world, (and therefore well agreeing with the antiquity of the *Ægyptians*:) [y] *Before the exact art of making statues was found out, the ancients erecting columns*, [pyramidal or conical columns,] *worshipped these as the images of God.*

This practice of the *Ægyptians*, I mean of erecting Pyramids for sepulchres, was but rarely imitated by other nations; tho' *Servius* seems to make it frequent in his comment upon these verses of *Virgil*:

> ——*Fuit ingens monte sub alto*
> *Regis Dercenni, terreno exaggere bustum*
> *Antiqui Laurentis, opacaque ilice tectum.*

[z] *With the ancients* (saith *Servius*) *noble men were buried, either under mountains, or*

[n] Τὸν γὰρ βασιλέα καὶ κύριον Ὄσιριν ὀφθαλμῷ καὶ σκήπτρῳ γράφουσιν· ἔνιοι δὲ καὶ τοὔνομα διερμηνεύουσι πολυόφθαλμον, ὡς τὸ μὲν Ὄς τὸ πολὺ, τὸ δὲ Ἶρι τὸν ὀφθαλμὸν Αἰγυπτίᾳ γλώττῃ φράζοντες. Plut. de Isid. & Osir.

[o] Εἶναι τὸν μὲν Ὄσιριν πολυόφθαλμον, εἰκότως, πάντῃ γὰρ ἐπιβάλλοντα τὰς ἀκτῖνας, ὥσπερ ὀφθαλμοῖς πολλοῖς βλέπειν ἅπασαν γῆν καὶ θάλασσαν. Diod. lib. 1.

[p] Τοῦτον [τὸν ἥλιον] οἱ ἐπιχώριοι σέβουσι, τῇ Φοινίκων φωνῇ Ἐλαιαγάβαλον καλοῦντες, νεὼς δὲ αὐτῷ μέγιστος, &c. Λίθος δέ τις ἐστὶ μέγιστος, κάτωθεν περιφερὴς, λήγων εἰς ὀξύτητα. κωνοειδὲς αὐτῷ σχῆμα, μέλαινά τε ἡ χροιά, &c. Herodian. lib. 5.

[q] *Simulacrum Deæ non effigie humanâ, continuus orbis latiore initio tenuem in ambitum metæ modo exurgens: & ratio in obscuro.* Tacit. lib. 2. histor.

[r] Παφίοις ἡ μὲν Ἀφροδίτη τὰς τιμὰς ἔχει, τὸ δὲ ἄγαλμα οὐκ ἂν εἰκάσαις ἄλλῳ τῷ ἢ πυραμίδι λευκῇ. Max. Tyr. διαλέξ. λή.

[s] Clem. Alexandr. lib. 1. Stromatum ex Phoronidis auctore. [t] Scaliger in Eusebii chronicon.

[v] Ἀπόλλων] Ἀγυιεὺς δέ ἐστι κίων εἰς ὀξὺ λήγων. Οἱ ἱστᾶσι πρὸ τῶν θυρῶν ἰδίους δέ φασιν αὐτοὺς εἶναι Ἀπόλλωνος, οἱ δὲ Διονύσου, οἱ δὲ ἀμφοῖν. Suidas.

[x] Ἐστὶ δὲ Ζεὺς Μειλίχιος, καὶ Ἄρτεμις ὀνομαζομένη πατρῴα, σὺν τέχνῃ πεποιημένη οὐδεμιᾷ· Πυραμίδι δὲ ὁ Μειλίχιος, ἡ δὲ κίονι ἐστὶν εἰκασμένη. Pausan. Corinthiaca.

[y] Πρὶν γὰρ ἂν ἀκριβωθῆναι τῶν ἀγαλμάτων σχέσεις κίονας ἱστάντες οἱ παλαιοὶ ἔσεβον τούτους, ὡς ἀφιδρύματα τοῦ Θεοῦ. Clem. Alex. lib. 1. Stromatum.

[z] *Apud majores, nobiles aut sub montibus, aut in montibus sepeliebantur; unde natum est, ut supra cadavera, aut Pyramides fierent, aut ingentes collocarentur columnæ.* Serv. in Virgil.

4 in

in mountains; *whence the custom came, that over the dead, either Pyramids were made or huge columns erected.* In imitation of the latter custom, it may be [a] *Absalom* erected his pillar; and *Pausanias* describing the manner of burial amongst the ancient nation of the *Sicyonians*, tells us, [b] *that they covered the body with earth, and raised pillars over it.* But for the former of the Pyramids, I find none out of *Ægypt* accounted miraculous,, unless it be the sepulchre of *Porsena* king of *Hetruria*, (with which I shall conclude, described by *Pliny* out of *Varro*; being more to be admired for the number and contrivance of the Pyramids, than for any excessive magnitude. [c] *We shall use M.* Varro's *own words in the description of it.*

He was buried, saith he, *without the city Clusium, in which place he left a monument of square stone. Each side of it is three hundred feet broad, and fifty feet high. Within the square basis there is an inextricable labyrinth, whither whoso adventures without a clue can find no passage out. Upon this square there stand five Pyramids, four in the angles, and one in the middle; in the bottom they are broad seventy five feet, and high an hundred and fifty. They are pointed in such a manner, that at the top there is one brass circle, and covering for them all, from which there hangs bells fastened to chains: These being moved by the wind, give a sound afar off, as at Dodona it has formerly been. Upon this circle there are four other Pyramids, each of them an hundred feet high. Above which, upon one plain, there are five Pyramids, the altitude of which* Varro *was ashamed to add. The Hetruscan fables report that it was as much as that of the whole work. With so vain a madness he sought glory by an expence useful to no man; wasting besides the wealth of his kingdom, that in the end the commendation of the artificer should be the greatest.*

Porsena's Tomb at Clusium in Italy Consisting of many Pyramids

[a] 2 Sam. xviii. 18.

[b] Pausaniæ Corinth. sive lib. 2. Αὐτοὶ δὲ Σικυώνιοι τὰ πολλὰ ἐοικότι τρόπῳ θάπτουσι· τὸ μὲν σῶμα γῇ κρύπτουσιν λίθου δὲ ἐποικοδομήσαντες κρηπῖδα, κίονας ἐφιστᾶσι.

[c] Plin. l. 36. c. 13. *Utemur ipsius M. Varronis in expositione ejus verbis. Sepultus est, inquit, sub urbe Clusio, in quo loco monumentum reliquit lapide quadrato, singula latera pedum lata tricenûm, alta quinquagenûm: inque basi quadratâ intus labyrinthum inextricabilem: quo siquis improperet sine glomere lini, exitum invenire nequeat. Supra id quadratum Pyramides stant quinque, quatuor in angulis, & in medio una; in imo latæ pedum septuagenûm quinûm, aliæ centum quinquagenûm: ita fastigiatæ, ut in summo orbis æneus, & petasus unus omnibus sit impositus, ex quo pendeant excepta catenis tintinnabula, quæ vento agitata longè sonitus referant, ut Dodonæ olim factum. Supra quem orbem quatuor Pyramides insuper singulæ extant altæ pedum centenûm. Supra quas uno solo quinque Pyramides, quarum altitudinem Varronem puduit adjicere. Fabulæ Hetruscæ tradunt eandem fuisse quàm totius operis: adeò vesana dementia quæsisse gloriam, impendio nulli profuturo. Præterea fatigâsse regni vires, ut tamen laus major artificio esset.* Plin. l. 36. c. 13.

A Description of the PYRAMIDS *in* ÆGYPT, *as I found them in the* CIↃ XL VIII *Year of the* Hegira, *or in the Years* CIↃ IↃ CXXXVIII, *and* CIↃ IↃ CXXXIX *of our* LORD, *after the* Dionysian *Account.*

GREAVES. HAVING discovered the founders of these Pyramids, and the time in which they were erected, and lastly, the end for which these monuments were built: next, in the method we proposed, the *sciography* of them is to be set down: where, we shall begin with the dimensions of their figure without, and then we shall examine their several spaces and partitions within.

A Description of the first and fairest PYRAMID.

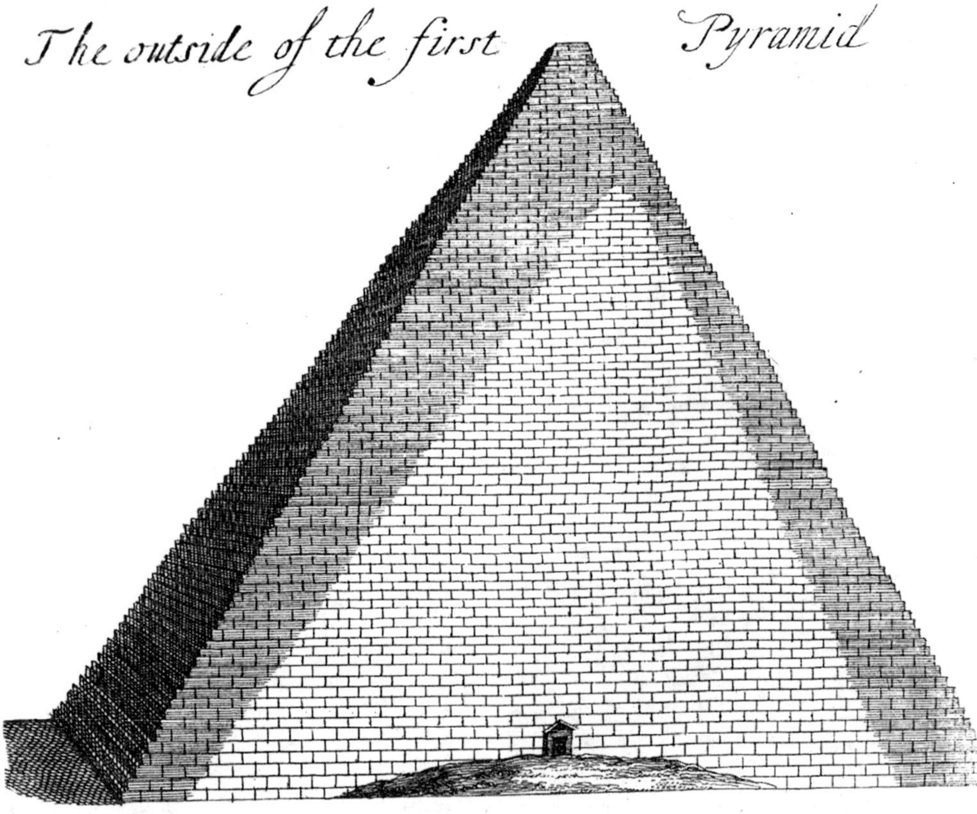

THE first and fairest of the three greater Pyramids, is situated on the top of a rocky hill in the sandy desert of *Libya*, about a quarter of a mile distant to the west, from the plains of *Ægypt:* above which the rock riseth an hundred feet or better, with a gentle and easy ascent. Upon this advantageous rise, and upon this solid foundation the Pyramid is erected; the height of the situation adding to the beauty of the work, and the solidity of the rock giving the superstructure a permanent and stable support. Each side of the Pyramid, computing it according to [d] *Herodotus*, contains in length IↃ CCC *Grecian* feet; and in [e] *Diodorus Siculus*'s account

[d] Herodot. lib. 2.

[e] Diod. l. 1. Ἡ μὲν γὰρ μεγίστη τετράπλευρος οὖσα τῷ σχήματι, τὴν ἐπὶ τῆς βάσεως πλευρὰν ἑκάστην ἔχει πλέθρων ἑπτά.

count ↀ CC: [f] *Strabo* reckons it less than a furlong, that is, less than ↀC *Grecian* feeet, or six hundred twenty five *Roman*; and [g] *Pliny* equals it to ↀ CCC LXXXIII. That of *Diodorus Siculus* in my judgment comes nearest to the truth[h], and may serve in some kind to confirm those proportions, which in another discourse I have assigned to the *Grecian* measures. For measuring the north-side of it, at the *basis*, by an exquisite *radius* of ten feet in length, taking two several stations, as mathematicians use to do, when any obstacle hinders their approach, I found it to be six hundred ninety three feet, according to the *English* standard; which quantity is somewhat less than that of *Diodorus*. The rest of the sides were examined by a line, for want of an even level, and a convenient distance to place my instruments, both which the *area* on the former side afforded.

The altitude of this pyramid was long since measured by *Thales Milesius*, who, according to [i] *Tatianus Assyrius*, lived about the fiftieth olympiad: but his observation is no where by the antients expressed. Only [k] *Pliny* tells us of a course proposed by him, how it might be found, and that is by observing such an hour, when the shadow of the body is equal to its height: A way at the best, by reason of the faintness, and scattering of the extremity of the shadow, in so great an altitude, uncertain and subject to error. And yet [l] *Diogenes Laertius* in the life of *Thales*, hath the same story from the authority of *Hieronymus*. *Hieronymus* reports, *that he measured the Pyramids by their shadow, marking when they are of an equal quantity.* Wherefore I shall pass by his, and give my own observations. The altitude is something defective of the latitude; though in [m] *Strabo*'s computation it exceeds; but [n] *Diodorus* rightly acknowledges it to be less; which, if we measure by its perpendicular, is four hundred ninety nine feet; but if we take it as the Pyramid ascends inclining (as all such figures do,) then is it equal, in respect of the lines subtending the several angles, to the latitude of the *basis*, that is, to six hundred ninety three feet. With reference to this great altitude [o] *Statius* calls them,

GREAVES

—— *audacia saxa*
Pyramidum ——

And [p] *Tacitus*, *Instar montium eductæ Pyramides.*

[q] *Julius Solinus* goes farther yet: *The Pyramids are sharp pointed towers in Ægypt, exceeding all height which may be made by hand.* [r] *Ammianus Marcellinus* in his expression ascends as high: *The Pyramids are towers erected alltogether, exceeding the height which may be made by man; in the bottom they are broadest, ending in sharp points atop; which figure is therefore by geometricians called pyramidal, because in the similitude of fire it is sharpened into a cone, as we speak.* [s] *Propertius* with the liberty of a poet, in an hyperbole, flies higher yet:

Pyramidum sumptus ad sidera ducti.

And the [t] *Greek Epigrammatist* in a transcendent expression, is no way short of him.

Πυραμίδες δ᾽ ἔτι νῦν Νειλώϊδες ἄστρα μέτωπαι,
Κυδῶσι Χρυσέις ἄστρασι πλιάδων.

What excessive heights these fancied to themselves, or borrowed from the relations of others, I shall not now examine: This I am certain of, that the shaft or spire of *Paul*'s in *London*, before it was casually burnt, being as much, or somewhat more than the altitude of the tower now standing, did exceed the height of this Pyramid. For [u] *Camden* describes it in his *Elizabetha*, to be in a perpendicular five hundred and twenty feet from the ground: And in his [w] *Britannia*, to have been somewhat more, ↀ XXXIV feet; whereof the tower CCLX, and the Pyramid on the top CCLXXIV. See *Godw. de præsul.* 229.

If we imagine upon the sides of the *basis*, which is perfectly square, four equila-

[f] Strabo, l. 17. [g] Plin. l. 36. c. 12. *Amplissima octo jugera obtinent soli, quatuor angulorum paribus intervallis, per octingentos octoginta tres pedes, singulorum laterum.*

[h] For the exact dimensions of this Pyramid, see miscellaneous observations upon authors antient and modern. Pag. 119, & *seq.* [i] Tatiani Orat. contra Græcos.

[k] Plin. 36. c. 12. *Mensuram altitudinis earum, omniumquê similium deprehendere invenit Thales Milesius, umbram metiendo, quâ horâ par esse corpori solet.*

[l] Diog. Laert. in vitâ Thaletis, l. 1. Ὁ δὲ Ἱερώνυμος, καὶ ἐκμετρῆσαι, φησὶν αὐτὸν τὰς πυραμίδας, ἐκ τῆς σκιᾶς παρατηρήσαντα ὅτε ἡμῖν ἰσομεγέθεις εἰσί.

[m] Strabo, lib. 17. Ἐστὶ γὰρ σταδιαῖα τὸ ὕψος. Whereas the breadth he reckons less than a stadium.

[n] Diodor. lib. 1. Τὸ δὲ ὕψος ἔχει πλείω τῶν ἓξ πλέθρων. But to the breadth he assigns seven plethra.

[o] Stat. l. 5. Sylv. 3. [p] Tacit. Annal. l. 2. [q] *Pyramides sunt turres in Ægypto, fastigiatæ ultra excelsitatem omnem, quæ manu fieri potest.* Jul. Solin. Polyh. c. 45. [r] Ammian. Marcell. l. 21.

[s] Propertius, l. 3. Eleg. 1. [t] Græc. Epigram. l. 4. Francofurti 1600. cum Annot. Brodæi.

[u] *Pyramis pulcherrima cathedralis ecclesiæ S. Pauli, quæ singulari urbis ornamento in suspiciendam edita altitudinem DXX scilicet pedes à solo & CCLX à turre quadratâ, cui imposita erat è materiâ ligneâ plumbo vestita, de cœlo propè fastigium tacta deflagravit.* Camdeni Elizabetha. [w] Camd. Brit. in Middlesex.

GREAVES teral triangles mutually inclining, till they all meet on high as it were in a point, (for so the top seems to them which stand below,) then shall we have a true notion, of the just dimension and figure of this Pyramid; the perimeter of each triangle comprehending two thousand seventy nine feet, (besides the latitude of a little plain or flat on the top,) and the perimeter of the basis two thousand seven hundred seventy two feet. Whereby the whole area of the basis (to proportion it to our measures,) contains four hundred eighty thousand two hundred forty nine square feet, or eleven English acres of ground, and 1089 of 43560 parts of an acre. A proportion so monstrous, that if the ancients did not attest as much, and some of them describe it to be more, this age would hardly be induced to give credit to it. But *Herodotus* describing each side to contain eight hundred feet, the *area* must of necessity be greater than that by me assigned, the sum amounting to six hundred and forty thousand; or computing it as *Diodorus Siculus* doth, the *area* will comprehend four hundred and ninety thousand feet: And in the calculation of *Pliny*, if we shall square eight hundred eighty three, (which is the number allotted by him to the measure of each side,) the product seven hundred seventy nine thousand six hundred eighty nine, will much exceed both that of *Herodotus* and this of *Diodorus*. Tho' certainly, *Pliny* is much mistaken in assigning the measure of the side to be eight hundred eighty three feet, and the basis of the Pyramid to be but eight *jugera*, or Roman acres. For if we take the Roman *jugerum* to contain in length two hundred and forty feet, and in breadth one hundred and twenty, as may be evidently proved out of [x] *Varro*, and is expresly affirmed by [y] *Quintilian*, then will the superficies or whole extension of the *jugerum* be equal to twenty eight thousand eight hundred Roman feet; with which, if we divide seven hundred seventy nine thousand six hundred eighty nine, the result will be twenty seven Roman *jugera*, and 2089 of 28800 parts of an acre. Wherefore, if we take those numbers eight hundred eighty three of *Pliny* to be true, then I suppose he writ twenty eight *jugera* instead of eight, or else in his proportion of the side to the area of the basis, he hath err'd.

The ascent to the top of the Pyramid is contrived in this manner: from all the sides without we ascend by degrees; the lowermost degree is near four feet in height, and three in breadth; this runs about the Pyramid in a level; and at the first, when the stones were intire, which are now somewhat decayed, made on every side of it a long but narrow walk. The second degree is like the first, each stone amounting to almost four feet in height, and three in breadth; it retires inward from the first near three feet, and thus runs about the Pyramid in a level, as the former. In the same manner is the third row placed upon the second, and so in order the rest, like so many stairs rising one above another to the top. Which ends not in a point, as mathematical Pyramids do, but in a little flat or square. Of this, *Herodotus* hath no where left us the dimensions: But [z] *Henricus Stephanus*, an able and deserving man, in his comment hath supplied it for him. For he makes it to be eight *orgyiæ*. Where if we take the *orgyia* as both [a] *Hesychius* and [b] *Suidas* do, for the distance between the hands extended at length, that is, for the fathom or six feet, then should it be forty eight feet in breadth at the top. But the truth is, *Stephanus* in this particular, whilst he corrects the errors of *Valla*'s interpretation, is to be corrected himself. For that latitude which *Herodotus* assigns to the admirable bridge below, (of which there is nothing now remaining,) he hath carried up, by a mistake to the top of the Pyramid. [c] *Diodorus Siculus* comes nearer to the truth, who describes it to be but nine feet. [d] *Pliny* makes the breadth at the top to be twenty five feet. *Altitudo* (I would rather read it *latitudo*,) *à cacumine pedes* XXV. By my measure it is XIII feet, and 280 of 1000 parts of the English foot. Upon this flat, if we assent to the opinion of [e] *Proclus*, it may be supposed that the Ægyptian priests made their observations in astronomy; and that from hence, or near this place, they first discovered, by the rising of *Sirius*, their *annus* κυνικὸς, or *canicularis*, as also their *periodus Sothiaca*, or *annus magnus* κυνικὸς, *or annus Heliacus*, or *annus Dei*, as it is termed by [f] *Censorinus*, consisting of 1460 sidereal years; in which space their *thoth vagum*, and *fixum*, came to have the same beginning: That the priests might near these Pyramids, make their observati-

[x] *Jugerum quadratos duos actus habet. Actus quadratus qui & latus est pedes* CXX, *& longus totidem. Is modius ac mina appellatur.* Varro de Re R. l. 1. c. 10.

[y] *Jugeri mensuram* CCXL *longitudinis pedes esse dimidiique in latitudinem patere non ferè quisquam est qui ignoret*. Quintil. l. 1. c. 10. [z] Hen. Steph. in 2 lib. Herodoti.

[a] Ὀργυιαὶ ἡ τῶν ἀμφοτέρων χειρῶν ἔκτασις. Hesych. [b] Ὀργυιαὶ τὸ μεταξὺ τῶν ἰδίων χειρῶν. Suid.

[c] Diodor. l. 1. [d] Plin. l. 36. c. 12. [e] Procl. Com. l. 1. in Timæum Platonis.

[f] Censorin. de die natali. *Quem Græci* κυνικὸν, *Latine canicularem vocamus. Hic annus etiam heliacus à quibusdam dicitur, & ab aliis,* ὁ θεοῦ ἐνιαυτὸς.

4 ons

ons I no way question; this rising of the hill being, in my judgment, as fit a place as any in *Ægypt* for such a design; and so much the fitter by the vicinity of *Memphis*. But that these Pyramids were designed for observatories, (whereas by the testimonies of the ancients I have proved before, that they were intended for sepulchres,) is no way to be credited upon the single authority of *Proclus*. Neither can I apprehend to what purpose the priests with so much difficulty should ascend so high, when below with more ease, and as much certainty, they might from their own lodgings hewn in the rocks, upon which the Pyramids are erected, make the same observations. For seeing all *Ægypt* is but as it were one continued plain, they might from these cliffs have, over the plains of *Ægypt*, as free and open a prospect of the heavens, as from the tops of the Pyramids themselves. And therefore *Tully* writes more truly: [g] *Ægyptii, aut Babylonii, in camporum patentium æquoribus habitantes, cùm ex terrâ nihil emineret, quod contemplationi cæli officere posset, omnem curam in siderum cognitione posuerunt.* The top of this Pyramid is covered not with [h] one or [i] three massy stones, as some have imagined, but with nine, besides two which are wanting at the angles: The degrees by which we ascend up, (as I observed in measuring many of them,) are not all of an equal depth, for some are near four feet, others want of three, and these the higher we ascend, do so much the more diminish: Neither is the breadth of them alike; the difference in this kind, being as far as I could conjecture, proportionable to their depth. And therefore a right line extended from any part of the basis without to the top, will equally touch the outward angle of every degree. Of these it was impossible for me to take an exact measure, since in such a revolution of time, if the inner parts of the Pyramid have not lost any thing of their first perfection, as being not exposed to the injury of the [k] *air and fall of rains*; yet the outward parts, that is, these degrees or rows of stone, have been much wasted and impaired by both. And therefore they cannot conveniently now be ascended, but either at the south-side, or at the east-angle, on the north: They are well stiled by *Herodotus*, Βωμίδες, that is, little altars: For in the form of altars they rise one above another to the top. And these are all made of massy and polished stones, hewen according to *Herodotus*, and *Diodorus*, out of the *Arabian* mountains, which bound the upper part of *Ægypt*, or that above the *delta* on the east, as the *Lybian* mountains terminate it on the west, being so vast, that the breadth and depth of every step, is one single and entire stone. The relation of [l] *Herodotus*,

[g] Cicer. de Divin. l. 1. [h] Les voyages de Seign. Villamont. [i] Sand's *travels*.

[k] The air of *Ægypt* is confessed by the antients to be often full of vapours. Which appears both by the great dews, that happen after the deluge of *Nilus* for several months; as also in that I have discovered at *Alexandria*, in the winter time, several obscure stars in the constellation of *Ursa major*, not visible in *England*; the which could not be discerned, were there not a greater refraction at that place than with us, and consequently a greater condensation of the *medium*, or air, as the opticks demonstrate. But I cannot sufficiently wonder at the antients, who generally deny the fall of rain in *Ægypt*. *Plato*, in his *Timæus*, speaking of *Ægypt*, where he had lived many years, writes thus: Κατὰ δὲ τὴν χώραν οὔτε τότε οὔτε ἄλλοτε, ἄνωθεν ἐπὶ τὰς ἀρούρας ὕδωρ ἐπιῤῥεῖ. *Pomponius Mela* in express terms relates, that *Ægypt* is *terra expers imbrium, mirè tamen fertilis.* Whereas for two months, namely *December* and *January*, I have not known it rain so constantly and with so much violence at *London*, as I found it do at *Alexandria*, the winds continuing north north-west; which caused me to keep a diary as well of the weather, as I did of my observations in astronomy: And not only there, but also at *Grand Cairo*, my very noble and worthy friend, sir *William Paston*, at the same time, observed, that there fell much rain. And so likewise about the end of *March* following, being at the *mummies*, somewhat beyond the Pyramids, to the south, there fell a gentle rain for almost a whole day: But it may be the antients mean the upper parts of *Ægypt* beyond *Thebes*, about *Siene*, and near the *Catadupa*, or cataracts of *Nilus*, and not the lower parts; where I have been told by the *Ægyptians*, that it seldom rains. And therefore *Seneca* (*lib.* 4. *Natur. Quæst.*) seems to have writ true, *In eâ parte quæ in Æthiopiam vergit* (speaking of *Ægypt*) *aut nulli imbres sunt, aut rari.* But where he after says, *Alexandria nives non cadunt*, it is false: For at my being there in *January*, at night it snowed. However, farther to the south than *Ægypt*, between the tropicks, and near the line, in *Habassia*, or *Æthiopia*, every year, for many weeks, there falls store of rain, as the *Habassines* themselves at *Grand Cairo* relate. Which may be confirmed by *Josephus Acosta. lib.* 2. *de naturâ orbis novi*, where he observes in *Peru*, and some other places (lying in the same parallel with those of *Æthiopia*) that they have abundance of rains. This then is the true cause of the inundation of *Nilus* in the summer time, being then highest, when other rivers are lowest; and not those which are alledged by *Herodotus*, *Diodorus*, *Plutarch*, *Aristides*, *Heliodorus*, and others: Who are extremely troubled to give a reason of the inundation, imputing it either to the peculiar nature of the river, or to the obstruction of the mouth of it by the *Etesiæ*; or to the melting of snows in *Æthiopia*, (which I believe seldom fall in those hot countries, where the natives, by reason of the extream heats, are all black; and where, if we credit *Seneca*, *argentum replumbatur*, *silver is melted*, by the scorching heats) or to some such other reasons of little weight. In *Diodorus* I find *Agatharchides Cnidius*, to give almost the same reason assigned by me: But those times gave little credit to his assertion. Yet *Diodorus* seems to assent to it, (*Diod. lib.* 1.) *Agatharchides Cnidius hath come nearest to the truth; for he saith: Every year in the mountains about* Æthiopia, *there are continual rains from the summer solstice, to the autumnal equinox, which cause the inundation.* The time of this is accounted generally so certain, that I have seen the *Ægyptian* astronomers to put it down many years before, in their Ephemerides: *That such a day of such a month, the* Nilus *begins to rise.*

and

GREAVES and [m] *Pomponius Mela*, is more admirable, who make *the least stone in this Pyramid to be thirty feet*. And this I can grant in some, yet surely it cannot be admitted in all, unless we interpret their words, that the least stone is thirty square, or to speak more properly, thirty cubical feet; which dimension, or a much greater, in the exterior ones, I can without any difficulty admit. The number of these steps is not mentioned by the ancients, and that caused me, and two that were with me, to be the more diligent in computing them, because by modern writers, and some of those too of repute, they are described with much diversity and contrariety. The degrees, saith [n] *Bellonius*, are about two hundred and fifty, each of them single contains in height forty five digits, at the top it is two paces broad. For this I take to be the meaning of what *Clusius* renders thus: *A basi autem ad cacumen ipsius supputationem facientes, comperimus circiter* CCL *gradus, singuli altitudinem habent* V *solearum calcei* IX *pollicum longitudines, in fastigio duos passus habet.* Where I conceive his *passus* is in the same sense to be understood here above, as not long before he explains himself in describing the *basis* below, which in his account is CCCXXIV *passus paululum extensis cruribus.* [o] *Albertus Lewenstainius* reckons the steps to be two hundred and sixty, each of them a foot and a half in depth. *Johannes Helfricus* counts them to be two hundred and thirty. [p] *Sebastius Serlius*, upon a relation of *Grimano, the patriarch of* Aquileia, *and afterwards cardinal*, (who in his travels in *Ægypt* measured these degrees) computes them to be two hundred and ten; and the height of every step to be equally three palms and an half. It would be but lost labour, to mention the different and repugnant relations of several others: That which by experience, and by a diligent calculation, I, and two others found, is this, that the number of degrees from the bottom to the top, is two hundred and seven; tho' one of them in descending reckoned two hundred and eight.

Such as please, may give credit to those fabulous traditions of [q] some, that a *Turkish* archer standing at the top, cannot shoot beyond the bottom, but that the arrow will necessarily fall upon these steps. If the *Turkish* bow (which by those figures that I have seen in ancient monuments, is the same with that of the *Parthians*, so dreadful to the *Romans*) be but as swift, and strong, as the *English*; as surely it is much more, if we consider with what incredible force some of them will pierce a plank of six inches in thickness, (I speak what I have seen) it will not seem strange, that they should carry twelve score in length; which distance is beyond the *basis* of this Pyramid.

The same credit is to be given to those reports of the ancients, that this *Pyramid*, and the rest, cast no shadows. [r] *Solinus* writes expresly, *Mensuram umbrarum egressæ nullas habent umbras.* And [s] *Ausonius:*

> —*Quadro cui in fastigia cono*
> *Surgit & ipsa suas consumit Pyramis umbras.*

[t] *Ammianus Marcellinus* hath almost the same relation, *umbras quoque mechanicâ ratione consumit.* Lastly, [u] *Cassiodorus* confirms the same, *Pyramides in Ægypto, quarum in suo statu se umbra consumens, ultra constructionis spatia nullâ parte respicitur.* All which in the winter season I can in no sort admit to be true: For at that time I have seen them cast a shadow at noon. And if I had not seen it, yet reason, and the art of measuring altitudes by shadows, and on the contrary, of knowing the length of shadows by altitudes, doth necessarily infer as much. Besides how could *Thales Milesius*, above two thousand years since, have taken their height by shadows, according to *Pliny*, and *Laertius*, as we mentioned before, if so be these *Pyramids* have no shadows at all? To reconcile the difference, we may imagine, *Solinus, Ausonius, Marcellinus*, and *Cassiodorus*, mean in the summer-time; or which is nearer the truth, that almost for three quarters of the year, they have no shadows: And this I grant to be true at midnight.

[l] Ουδεὶς τῶν λίθων τριήκοντα ποδῶν ἐλάσσων. Herod. l. 2. [m] *Pyramides tricenûm pedum lapidibus, exstructæ.* Pomp. Mel. l. 1. c. 9. [n] Bellonius, lib. 2. observ. c. 42. [o] *Albertus Lewenstainius gradus ad cacumen numerat* CCLX. *singulos sesquipedali altitudine, Johannes Helfricus* CCXXX. *Raderus in Martial. Epigr. Barbara Piramidum sileat miracula Memphis*, &c. [p] *Il numero de pezzidalla basa fino alla sommità sono da* CCX, *è sono turtid' una altezza talmente che l' altezza di tutta la massa è quanto lasua basa.* Sebast. Serl. lib. 3. delle Antichità.

[q] Bellon. Observ. lib. 2. cap. 42. & alii. *Peritissimus atque validissimus sagittarius in ejus fastigio existens, atque sagittam in aerem emittens, tam validè eam ejaculari non poterit, ut extra molis basim decidat, sed in ipsos gradus cadet, adeo vastæ magnitudinis, uti diximus, est hæc moles.* Bellon.

[r] Jul. Solin. Polyh. c. 45. [s] Auson. Edyllio 3. [t] Ammian. Marcel. lib. 22. [u] Cassiodor. Var. 7. Formula 15.

A Des-

A Description of the Inside of the first PYRAMID.

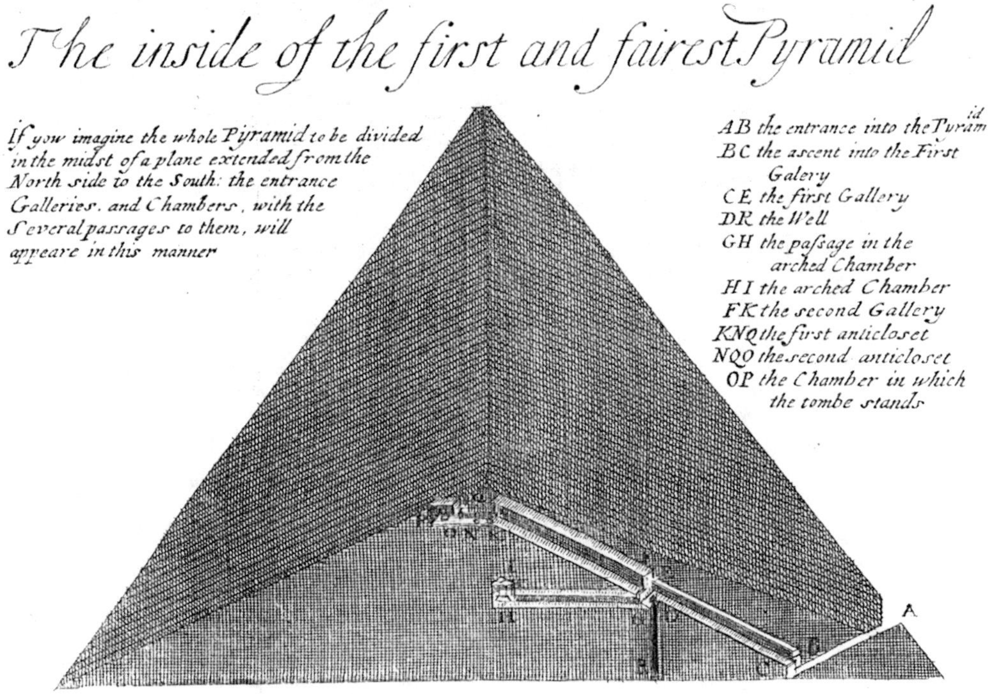

HAving finished the description of the greater *Pyramid*, with the figure, and dimensions of it, as they present themselves to the view without: I shall now look inwards, and lead the reader into several spaces, and partitions within: of which, if the ancients have been silent, we must chiefly impute it to a reverend and awful regard, mixed with superstition, in not presuming to enter those chambers of death, which religion, and devotion, had consecrated to the rest, and quiet of the dead. Wherefore [a] *Herodotus* mentions no more, but only in general, that *some secret vaults are hewn in the rock under the Pyramid. Diodorus Siculus* is silent; though both enlarge themselves in other particulars less necessary. [b] *Strabo* also is very concise, whose whole description both of this, and of the second *Pyramid*, is included in this short expression: *Forty stadia from the city* (Memphis,) *there is a certain brow of an hill, in which are many Pyramids, the sepulchres of kings: Three of them are memorable. Two of these are accounted amongst the seven miracles of the world; each of these are a furlong in height: The figure is quadrilateral, the altitude somewhat exceeds each side, and the one is somewhat bigger than the other. On high, as it were, in the midst between the sides, there is a stone that may be removed, which being taken out, there is an oblique* (or shelving) *entrance* (for so I render that which by him is termed *σύριγξ σκολία*) *leading to the tomb*, [c] *Pliny* expresses nothing within, but only *a well* (which is still extant) *of eighty six cubits in depth*; in which he probably imagines, by some secret aquæduct, the water of the river *Nilus* to be brought. *Aristides*, in his oration, entituled, Αἰγύπτιος, upon a misinformation of the *Ægyptian* priests, makes the foundation of the structure to have descended as far below, as the altitude ascends above. Of which I see no necessity, seeing all of them are founded upon rocks. His words are these: [d] *Now as with admiration we behold the tops of the Pyramids, but that which is as much more under ground opposite to it, we are ignorant of, (I speak what I have received from* GREAVES

[a] Herodot. lib. 2. [b] Strabo, lib. 17. [c] Plin. l. 36. c. 12.

[d] Νῦν δ' ὥσπερ τῶν πυραμίδων τὰς μὲν κορυφὰς ὁρῶντες ἐκπληττόμεθα τὸ δ' ἀντίπαλον καὶ ὑπὸ γῆς ἕτερον τοσοῦτον ἠγνόηται (λέγω δ' αὐτῶν ἱερέων ἤκουον) &c. Aristid. λόγος Αἰγύπτιος.

the

GREAVES *the priests.*) And this is that which hath been delivered to us by the antients; which I was unwilling to pretermit, more out of reverence of antiquity, than out of any special satisfaction. The *Arabian* writers, especially such as have purposely treated of the wonders of *Ægypt*, have given us a more full description of what is within this *Pyramid:* But that hath been mixed with so many fictions of their own, that the truth hath been darkned, and almost quite extinguished by them. I shall put down that which is confessed by them, to be the most probable relation, as is reported by *Ibn Abd Alhokm*, whose words out of the *Arabick* are these: *The greatest part of chronologers agree, that he which built the Pyramids, was,* Saurid Ibn Salhouk, *king of* Ægypt, *who lived three hundred years before the flood. The occasion of this was, because he saw in his sleep, that the whole earth was turned over with the inhabitants of it, the men lying upon their faces, and the stars falling down, and striking one another, with a terrible noise; and being troubled, he concealed it. After this he saw the fixed stars falling to the earth, in the similitude of white fowl, and they snatched up men, carrying them between two great mountains; and these mountains closed upon them, and the shining stars were made dark. Awaking with great fear, he assembled the chief priests of all the provinces of* Ægypt, *an hundred and thirty priests, the chief of them was called* Aclimum: *Relating the whole matter to them, they took the altitude of the stars, and making their prognostication, foretold of a deluge. The king said, Will it come to our country? They answered, Yea, and will destroy it. And there remained a certain number of years for to come, and he commanded in the mean space to build the Pyramids, and a vault to be made, into which the river* Nilus *entring, should run into the countries of the* West, *and into the land* Al-Said; *and he filled them with* [e] telesmes, *and with strange things, and with riches, and treasures, and the like. He ingraved in them all things that were told him by wise men, as also all profound sciences, the names of* [f] alakakirs, *the uses and hurts of them. The science of astrology, and of arithmetick, and of geometry, and of physick. All this may be interpreted by him that knows their characters, and language. After he had given order for this building, they cut out vast columns and wonderful stones. They fetch massy stones from the* Æthiopians, *and made with these the foundation of the three Pyramids, fastning them together with lead and iron. They built the gates of them forty cubits under ground, and they made the height of the Pyramids one hundred royal cubits, which are fifty of ours in these times; he also made each side of them an hundred royal cubits. The beginning of this building was in a fortunate horoscope. After that he had finished it, he covered it with coloured satten, from the top to the bottom; and he appointed a solemn festival, at which were present all the inhabitants of his kingdom. Then he built in the western Pyramid thirty treasures, filled with store of riches, and utensils, and with signatures made of precious stones, and with instruments of iron, and vessels of earth, and with arms which rust not, and with glass which might be bended, and yet not broken, and with strange spells, and with several kinds of* alakakirs, *single and double, and with deadly poisons, and with other things besides. He made also in the east Pyramid, divers cœlestial spheres and stars, and what they severally operate, in their aspects, and the perfumes which are to be used to them, and the books which treat of these matters. He also put in the coloured Pyramid, the commentaries of the priests, in chests of black marble, and with every priest a book, in which were the wonders of his profession, and of his actions, and of his nature, and what was done in his time, and what is, and what shall be, from the beginning of time, to the end of it. He placed in every Pyramid a treasurer: The treasurer of the westerly Pyramid was a statue of marble-stone, standing upright with a lance, and upon his head a serpent wreathed. He that came near it, and stood still, the serpent bit him of one side, and wreathing round about his throat, and killing him, returned to his place. He made the treasurer of the east Pyramid, an idol of black agate, his eyes open and shining, sitting upon a throne with a lance; when any looked upon him, he heard of one side of him a voice, which took away his sense, so that he fell prostrate upon his face, and ceased not till he*

[e] *Telesmes*] The word used by the *Arabians* is derived from the *Greek*, ἀποτέλεσμα, by an *aphæresis* of ἀπὸ. By the like *aphæresis*, together with an *epenthesis*, the *Arabians* call him *Bochtanassar*, whom *Ptolemy* names *Nabonassar:* as by an *aphæresis*, and *syncope*, the *Turks* call *Constantinople*, *Stanpol*, or *Istanbol*; from whence some of our writers term it *Stambol*; tho' the *Arabians* more fully express it by *Costantiniya*, and *Buzantiya*; that is, *Constantinopolis*, and *Byzantium*. The various significations of τελέσματα, and ἀποτελέσματα, see in Mr. *Selden*'s learned discourse, *de diis Syris*; and in *Scaliger*'s annotations, *in apotelesmaticum Manilii*. That which the *Arabians* commonly mean by *telesmes*, are certain *sigilla*, or *amuleta*, made under such and such an aspect, or configuration of the stars and planets, with several characters accordingly inscribed.

[f] *Alakakir*] Amongst other significations, is the name of a precious stone; and therefore in *Abulfeda* it is joined with *yacut*, a *ruby*. I imagine it here to signify some magical spell, which it may be was engraven in this stone.

died. He made the treasurer of the coloured Pyramid a statue of stone, (called) Albut, *sitting: he which looked towards it was drawn by the statue, till he stuck to it and could not be separated from it, till such time as he died. The* Coptites *write in their books, that there is an inscription engraven upon them, the exposition of which in* Arabick *is this: I king* Saurid *built the Pyramids in such and such a time, and finished them in six years: he that comes after me, and says that he is equal to me, let him destroy them in six hundred years; and yet it is known, that it is easier to pluck down, than to build up. I also covered them, when I had finished them, with satten; and let him cover them with mats. After that,* Almamon *the calif entered* Ægypt, *and saw the Pyramids: He desired to know what was within, and therefore would have them opened: They told him, It could not possibly be done: He replied, I will have it certainly done. And that hole was opened for him, which stands open to this day, with fire and vinegar. Two smiths prepared and sharpened the iron, and engines, which they forced in, and there was a great expence in the opening of it: The thickness of the wall was found to be twenty cubits; and when they came to the end of the wall, behind the place they had digged, there was an ewer* (or pot) *of green emerald; in it were a thousand dinars very weighty, every dinar was an ounce of our ounces: they wondered at it, but knew not the meaning of it. Then* Almamon *said, Cast up the account, how much hath been spent in making the entrance: they cast it up, and lo it was the same sum which they found, it neither exceeded, nor was defective. Within they found a square well, in the square of it there were doors, every door opened into an house* (or vault) *in which there were dead bodies wrapped up in linen. They found towards the top of the Pyramid, a chamber, in which there was an hollow stone: in it was a statue of stone like a man, and within it a man, upon whom was a breast-plate of gold, set with jewels, upon his breast was a sword of invaluable price, and at his head a carbuncle of the bigness of an egg, shining like the light of the day, and upon him were characters written with a pen, no man knows what they signify. After* Almamon *had opened it, men entred into it for many years, and descended by the slippery passage, which is in it; and some of them came out safe, and others died.* Thus far the *Arabians*; which traditions of theirs, are little better than a *romance*; and therefore leaving these, I shall give a more true and particular description, out of mine own experience, and observations.

On the north-side ascending thirty eight feet, upon an artificial bank of earth, there is a square and narrow passage leading into the Pyramid, thorough the mouth of which (being equi-distant from the two sides of the Pyramid) we enter, as it were, down the steep of an hill declining with an angle of twenty six degrees. The breadth of this entrance is exactly three feet, and four hundred sixty three parts of one thousand of the *English* foot: The length of it beginning from the first declivity, which is some ten palms without, to the utmost extremity of the neck, or straight within, where it contracts it self almost nine feet continued, with scarce half the depth it had at the first entrance (tho' it keep still the same breadth) is ninety two feet and an half. The structure of it hath been the labour of an exquisite hand, as appears by the smoothness and evenness of the work, and by the close knitting of the joints. A property long since observed, and commended by [g] *Diodorus*, to have run thorough the fabrick of the whole body of this Pyramid. Having passed with tapers in our hands this narrow straight, tho' with some difficulty, (for at the farther end of it we must creep upon our bellies) we land in a place somewhat larger, and of a pretty height, but lying incomposed; having been dug away, either by the curiosity, or avarice of some, in hopes to discover an hidden treasure; or rather by the command of *Almamon*, the deservedly renowned calif of *Babylon*. By whomsoever it were, it is not worth the enquiry, nor doth the place merit describing, but that I was unwilling to pretermit any thing: Being only an habitation for bats, and those so ugly, and of so large a size, (exceeding a foot in length) that I have not elsewhere seen the like. The length of this obscure and broken space, containeth eighty nine feet, the breadth and height is various, and not worth consideration. On the left hand of this, adjoining to that narrow entrance thorough which we passed, we climb up a steep and massy stone, eight or nine feet in height, where we immediately enter upon the lower end of the first gallery. The pavement of this rises with a gentle acclivity, consisting of smooth and polished marble, and were not smeared with filth, appearing of a white and alabaster colour: The sides and roof, as *Titus Livinius Burretinus*, a *Venetian*, an ingenious young man, who accompanied me thither, observ'd, was of impolished stone, not so hard and compact as that on the pavement, but more soft and tender: The breadth almost five feet, and about the same quantity the height, if he have not mistaken. He likewise discovered some irregularity in the breadth, it opening a little wider in some

GREAVES

[g] Diodor. Sic. lib. 8.

GREAVES places than in others; but this inequality could not be discerned by the eye, but only by measuring it with a careful hand: By my observation with a line, this gallery contained in length an hundred and ten feet. At the end of this begins the second gallery; a very stately piece of work, and not inferiour, either in respect of the curiosity of art, or richness of materials, to the most sumptuous aud magnificent buildings. It is divided from the former by a wall, through which stooping, we passed in a square hole, much about the same bigness, as that by which we entred into the Pyramid, but of no considerable length. This narrow passage lieth level, not rising with an acclivity, as doth the pavement below, and roof above, of both these galleries. At the end of it, on the right hand, is the well, mentioned by *Pliny*; the which is circular, and not square, as the *Arabian* writers describe: the diameter of it exceeds three feet, the sides are lin'd with white marble, and the descent into it is by fastning the hands and feet in little open spaces cut in the sides within, opposite, and answerable to one another in a perpendicular. In the same manner are almost all the wells and passages into the cisterns at *Alexandria* contrived, without stairs or windings, but only with inlets, and square holes on each side within; by which using the feet and hands, one may with ease descend. Many of these cisterns are with open and double arches, the lowermost arch being supported by a row of speckled and *Thebaick* marble pillars, upon the top of which stands a second row, bearing the upper and higher arch: The walls within are covered with a sort of plaister, for the colour white; but of so durable a substance, that neither by time, nor by the water, it is yet corrupted and impaired. But I return from the cisterns and wells there, to this in the Pyramid; *which in* [h] Pliny'*s calculation, is eighty six cubits in depth*; and it may be was the passage to those secret vaults mentioned, but not described by *Herodotus*, that were hewn out of the rock, over which this Pyramid is erected. By my measure, sounding it with a line, it contains twenty feet in depth. The reason of the difference between *Pliny*'s observation and mine, I suppose to be this, that since his time it hath almost been

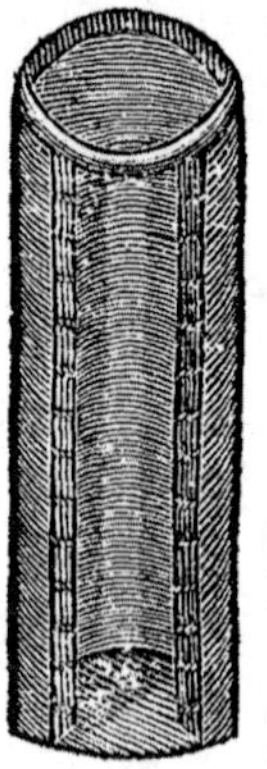

dammed up, and choaked with rubbish, which I plainly discover'd at the bottom, by throwing down some combustible matter set on fire. Leaving the well, and going on strait upon a level, the distance of fifteen feet, we entred another square passage, opening against the former, and of the same bigness. The stones are very massy, and exquisitely jointed, I know not whether of that glistering and speckled marble, I mentioned in the columns of the cisterns at *Alexandria*. This leadeth (running in length upon a level an hundred and ten feet) into an arched vault, or little chamber; which by reason it was of a grave-like smell, and half full of rubbish, occasioned my lesser stay. This chamber stands east and west; the length of it is less than twenty feet, the breadth about seventeen, and the height less than fifteen. The walls are intire, and plaistered over with lime, the roof is covered with large smooth stones, not lying flat but shelving, and meeting above in a kind of arch, or rather an angle. On the east-side of this room, in the middle of it, there seems to have been a passage leading to some other place. Whether this way the priests went into the hollow of that huge *Sphinx*, as *Strabo* and [i] *Pliny* term it, or *androsphinx*, as *Herodotus* calls such kinds, (being by *Pliny*'s calculation CII feet in compass about the head, in height LXII, in length CXLIII: And by my observation made of one intire stone) which stands not far distant without the Pyramid, south-east of it, or into any other private retirement, I cannot determine; and it may be too this served for no such purpose, but rather as a *Theca* or *Nichio*, as the *Italians* speak, wherein some idol might be placed; or else for a piece of ornament (for it is made of polished stone) in the architecture of those times, which ours may no more understand, than they do the reason of the rest of those strange proportions, that appear in the passages and inner-rooms of this Pyramid. Returning back the same way we came, as soon as we are out of this narrow and square passage, we climb over it, and going straight on, in the trace of the second gallery, upon a shelving pavement (like that of the first) rising with an angle of twenty six degrees, we at length came to another partition. The length of the gallery, from the well below to this partition above, is an hundred fifty and four feet; but if we measure the pavement of the floor, it is somewhat less, by reason of a little vacuity (some fifteen feet in length) as we described before, between the well and the square hole we climbed over. And here to reassume some part of

[h] *In Pyramide maximâ est intus puteus* LXXXVI *cubitorum, flumen illo admissum arbitrantur.* Plin. l. 36. cap. 12. [i] Plin. l. 36. cap. 12.

that

GREAVES

that which hath been ſpoken, if we conſider the narrow entrance at the mouth of the Pyramid by which we deſcend; and the length of the firſt and ſecond galleries by which we aſcend, all of them lying as it were in the ſame continu'd line, and leading to the middle of the Pyramid, we may eaſily apprehend a reaſon of that ſtrange ecchoe within, of four or five voices, mentioned by [k] *Plutarch in his fourth book, De placitis Philoſophorum:* Or rather of a long continued ſound; as I found by experience, diſcharging a muſket at the entrance. For the ſound being ſhut in, and carried in thoſe cloſe and ſmooth paſſages, like as in ſo many pipes or trunks, finding no iſſue out, reflects upon it ſelf, and cauſes a confuſed noiſe and circulation of the air, which by degrees vaniſhes, as the motion of it ceaſes. This gallery, or *corridore*, (or whatſoever elſe I may call it) is built of white and poliſhed marble, the which is very evenly cut in ſpacious ſquares, or tables. Of ſuch materials as is the pavement, ſuch is the roof, and ſuch are the ſide walls, that flank it: The coagmentation, or knitting of joints, is ſo cloſe, that they are ſcarce diſcernible to the eye; and that which adds a grace to the whole ſtructure, tho' it makes the paſſage the more ſlippery and difficult, is the acclivity and riſing of the aſcent. The height of this gallery is twenty ſix feet, the breadth is ſix feet, and eight hundred ſeventy parts of the foot divided into a thouſand, of which three feet, and four hundred thirty ſix of a thouſand parts of a foot, are to be allowed for the way in the midſt; which is ſet and bounded on both ſides with two banks (like benches) of ſleek and poliſhed ſtone; each of theſe hath one foot ſeven hundred ſeventeen of a thouſand parts of a foot in breadth, and as much in depth. Upon the top of theſe benches near the angle, where they cloſe, and join with the wall, are little ſpaces cut in right angled parallel figures, ſet on each ſide oppoſite to one another; intended, no queſtion, for ſome other end than ornament. In the caſting and ranging of the marbles in both the ſide-walls, there is one piece of architecture, in my judgment, very graceful; and that is, that all the courſes, or ranges, which are but ſeven (ſo great are thoſe ſtones) do ſet and flag over one another about three inches; the bottom of the uppermoſt courſe over-ſetting the higher part of the ſecond, and the lower part of this overflagging the top of the third, and ſo in order the reſt, as they deſcend. Which will better be conceived by the repreſentation of it to the eye in this figure, than by any other deſcription.

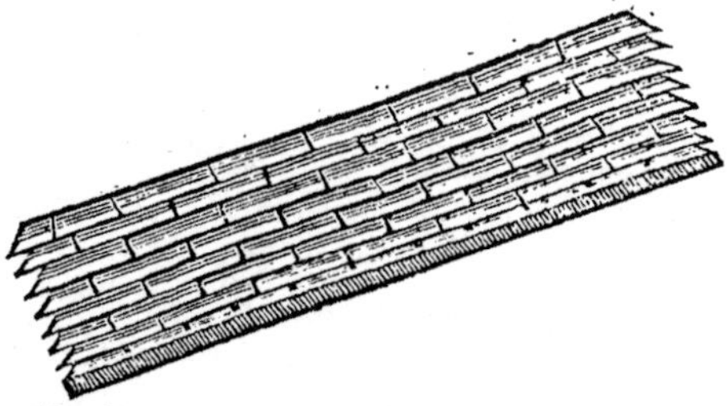

Having paſſed this gallery, we enter another ſquare hole, of the ſame dimenſions with the former, which brings us into two *anticamerette*, as the *Italians* would call them, or *anti-cloſets*, (give me leave in ſo unuſual a ſtructure to frame ſome [l] unuſual terms) lined with a rich and ſpeckled kind of *Thebaick* marble. The firſt of theſe hath the dimenſions almoſt equal to the ſecond: The ſecond is thus proportioned, the *area* is level, the figure of it is oblong, the one ſide containing ſeven feet, the other three and an half, the height is ten feet. On the eaſt and weſt ſides, within two feet and half of the top, which is ſomewhat larger than the bottom, are three cavities, or little ſeats, in this manner: 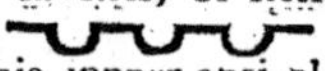

This innner anti-cloſet is ſeparated from the former, by a ſtone of red ſpeckled marble, which hangs in two mortices (like the leaf of a ſluice) between two walls. more than three feet above the pavement, and wanting two of the roof. Out of this cloſet we enter another ſquare hole, over which are five lines cut parallel, and perpendicular in this manner:

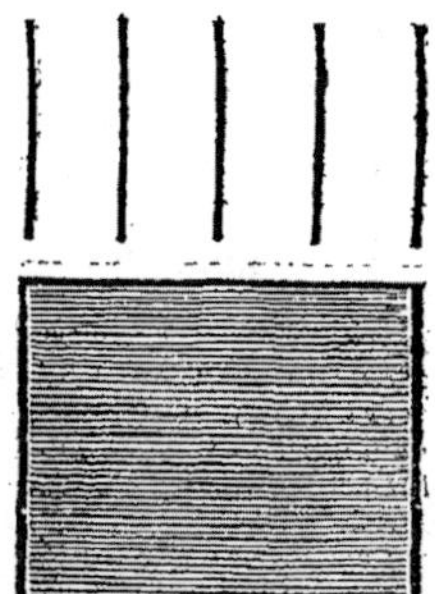

Beſides theſe, I have not obſerved any other ſculptures, or engravings, in the whole Pyramid: and therefore it may juſtly be wondered, whence the *Arabians* borrowed thoſe traditions I before related,

[k] Ἐν γοῦν ταῖς κατὰ Αἴγυπτον πυραμίσιν ἔνδον φωνὴ μία ῥαγνυμένη τέτταρας ἢ καὶ πέντε ἤχους ἀπεργάζεται. Plut. lib. 4. de philoſ. plac. cap. 20.

[l] *Sunt enim rebus novis, nova ponenda nomina.* Cicero, lib. 1. de naturâ deorum.

that

GREAVES *that all ſciences are inſcribed within in hieroglyphicks:* and as juſtly it may be queſtioned, upon what authority *Dio*, or his epitomizer *Xiphilinus*, reports, that *Cornelius Gallus* (whom [m] *Strabo* more truly names *Ælius Gallus*, with whom he travelled into *Ægypt*, as a friend and companion) [n] *engraved in the Pyramids his victories*, unleſs we underſtand ſome other Pyramids not now exiſtent. This ſquare paſſage is of the ſame wideneſs and dimenſions as the reſt, and is in length near nine feet, (being all of *Thebaick* marble, moſt exquiſitely cut) which lands us at the north end of a very ſumptuous and well-proportioned room. The diſtance from the end of the ſecond gallery to this entry, running upon the ſame level, is twenty four feet. This rich and ſpacious chamber, in which art may ſeem to have contended with nature, the curious work being not inferior to the rich materials, ſtands as it were in the heart and centre of the Pyramid, equi-diſtant from all the ſides, and almoſt in the middle between the *baſis* and the top. The floor, the ſides, the roof of it, are all made of vaſt and exquiſite tables of *Thebaick* marble, which if they were not veiled and obſcured by the ſteam of tapers, would appear gliſtering and ſhining. From the top of it deſcending to the bottom, there are but ſix ranges of ſtone, all which being reſpectively ſized to an equal height, very gracefully in one and the ſame altitude, run round the room. The ſtones which cover this place, are of a ſtrange and ſtupendious length, like ſo many huge beams lying flat, and traverſing the room, and withal ſupporting that infinite maſs and weight of the Pyramid above. Of theſe there are nine, which cover the roof; two of them are leſs by half in breadth than the reſt; the one at the eaſt end, the other at the weſt. The length of this [o] chamber on the ſouth ſide, moſt accurately taken at the joint, or line, where the firſt and ſecond row of ſtones meet, is thirty four *Engliſh* feet, and three hundred and eighty parts of the foot divided into a thouſand (that is, thirty four feet, and three hundred and eighty of a thouſand parts of a foot.) The breadth of the weſt ſide at the joint, or line, where the firſt and ſecond row of ſtones meet, is ſeventeen feet, and an hundred and ninety parts of the foot divided into a thouſand (that is, ſeventeen feet, and a hundred and ninety of a thouſand parts of a foot.) The height is nineteen feet and an half.

Within this glorious room (for ſo I may juſtly call it) as within ſome conſecrated oratory, ſtands the monument of *Cheops*, or *Chemmis*, of one piece of marble, hollow within, and uncovered at the top, and ſounding like a bell. Which I mention not as any rarity, either in nature, or in art (for I have obſerved the like ſound, in other tombs of [p] marble cut hollow like this) but becauſe I find modern authors to take notice of it as a wonder. Some write, that the body hath been removed hence; whereas [q] *Diodorus* hath left above ſixteen hundred years ſince, a memorable paſſage concerning *Chemmis* the builder of this Pyramid, and *Cephren*, the founder of the next adjoining. *Altho'* (ſaith he) *theſe kings intended theſe for their ſepulchres, yet it happened that neither of them were buried there: For the people being exaſperated againſt them, by reaſon of the toilſomneſs of theſe works, and for their cruelty and oppreſſion, threatned to tear in pieces their dead bodies, and with ignominy to throw them out of their ſepulchres: Wherefore both of them dying, commanded their friends privately to bury them, in an obſcure place.* This monument, in reſpect of the nature and quality of the ſtone, is the ſame with which the whole room is lined; as by breaking a little fragment of it, I plainly diſcovered, being a ſpeckled kind of marble, with black, and white, and red ſpots, as it were equally mixed, which ſome writers call *Thebaick* marble: tho' I conceive it to be that ſort of porphyry which [r] *Pliny* calls *leucoſtictos*, and de-

[m] Strabo, lib. 17. [n] Xiphil. in Cæſ. Aug. *Τὰ ἔργα ὅσα ἐπεποιήκει, ἐς πυραμίδας ἐσέγραψε.*

[o] Theſe proportions of the chamber, and thoſe which follow, of the length and breadth of the hollow part of the tomb, were taken by me with as much exactneſs as it was poſſible to do; which I did ſo much the more diligently, as judging this to be the fitteſt place for the fixing of meaſures for poſterity. A thing which hath been much deſired by learned men, but the manner how it might be exactly done, hath been thought of by none. I am of opinion, that as this Pyramid has ſtood three thouſand years almoſt, and is no whit decayed within, ſo it may continue many thouſand years longer: and therefore that after-times meaſuring theſe places by me aſſigned, may hereby not only find out the juſt dimenſions of the *Engliſh* foot, but alſo the feet of ſeveral nations in theſe times; which in my travels abroad I have taken from the originals, and have compared them at home with the *Engliſh* ſtandard. Had ſome of the antient mathematicians thought of this way, theſe times would not have been ſo much perplexed, in diſcovering *the meaſures of the Hebrews, Babylonians, Ægyptians, Greeks, and other nations.* Such parts as the *Engliſh* foot contains a 1000, the *Roman* foot, on *Coſſutius* monument (commonly called by writers, *Pes Colatianus*) contains 967. The *Paris* foot 1068. The *Spaniſh* foot 920. The *Venetian* foot 1062. The *Rhinland* foot, or that of *Snellius*, 1033. The *Bracio* at *Florence* 1913. The *Bracio* at *Naples* 2100. The *Derab* at *Cairo* 1824. The greater *Turkiſh Pike* at *Conſtantinople* 2200.

[p] As appears by a fair and antient monument brought from *Smyrna*, to my very worthy friend *Edward Rolt*, Eſq; which ſtands in his park at *Woolwich*. [q] Diod. Sic. lib. 1. *Τῶν δὲ βασιλέων τῶν κατασκευασάντων αὐτὰς ἑαυτοῖς τάφους, συνέβη μηδέτερον αὐτῶν ταῖς πυραμίσιν ἐνταφῆναι,* &c. [r] Plin. lib. 36. cap. 7.

ſcribes thus: *Rubet porphyrites in eadem Ægypto ex eo candidis intervenientibus punctis leucoſtictos appellatur. Quantiſlibet molibus cædendis ſufficiunt lapidicinæ.* Of this kind of marble there was, and ſtill is, an infinite quantity of columns in *Ægypt*. But a *Venetian*, a man very curious, who accompanied me thither, imagined that this ſort of marble came from mount [f] *Sina*, where he had lived among the rocks; which he affirmed to be ſpeckled with party-colours of black and white, and red, like this: and to confirm his aſſertion, he alledg'd, that he had ſeen a great column, left imperfect amongſt the cliffs, almoſt as big as that huge and *admirable* [t] Corinthian *pillar, ſtanding to the ſouth of* Alexandria; which, by my meaſure, is near four times as big as any of thoſe vaſt *Corinthian* pillars, in the *Porticus* before the *Pantheon* at *Rome*; all which are of the ſame coloured marble with this monument, and ſo are all the obeliſks with hieroglyphicks, both in *Rome* and *Alexandria.* Which opinion of his doth well correſpond with the tradition of *Ariſtides*, who reports, that *in* Arabia *there is a quarry of excellent porphyry.* The figure of this tomb without, is like an altar, or more nearly to expreſs it, like two cubes finely ſet together, and hollowed within, it is cut ſmooth and plain, without any ſculpture and engraving, or any relevy and emboſſment. The exterior ſuperficies of it contains in length ſeven feet, three inches, and an half. [u] *Bellonius* makes it twelve feet, and [x] monſieur *de Breves* nine; but both of them have exceeded. In depth it is three feet, three inches, and three quarters, and is the ſame in breadth. The hollow part within, is in length on the weſt-ſide, ſix feet, and four hundred and eight parts of the *Engliſh* foot divided into a thouſand parts (that [y] is ſix feet, and four hundred and eighty eight of the thouſand parts of a foot) in breadth, at the north-end, two feet, and two hundred and eighteen parts of the foot divided into a thouſand parts (that [z] is, two feet, and two hundred and eighteen of a thouſand parts of a foot.) The depth is two feet, and eight hundred and ſixty of the thouſand parts of the *Engliſh* foot. A narrow ſpace, yet large enough to contain a moſt potent and dreadful monarch, being dead, to whom living, all *Ægypt* was too ſtreight and narrow a circuit. By theſe dimenſions, and by ſuch other obſervations as have been taken by me from ſeveral embalmed bodies in *Ægypt*, we may conclude, that there is no decay in nature; (*tho' the queſtion is as old as* [a] Homer) but that the men of this age are of the ſame ſtature they were near three thouſand years ago; notwithſtanding St. [b] *Auguſtin*, and others, are of a different opinion. *Quis jam ævo iſto non minor ſuis parentibus naſcitur?* Is the complaint of *Solinus* above fifteen hundred years ſince. And yet in thoſe *cryptæ ſepulchrales*, at *Rome*, of the primitive Chriſtians, reſembling cities under ground: admired anciently by St. *Hierom*, and very faithfully of late deſcribed by *Boſius*, in his *Roma ſubterranea*, (for I took ſo much pains for

GREAVES

[f] Which may alſo be confirmed by *Bellonius*'s obſervations; who deſcribing the rock, out of which, upon *Moſes* ſtriking it, there guſhed out waters, makes it to be ſuch a ſpeckled kind of Thebaick marble: *Eſt une groſſe pierre maſſive droicte de miſme grain & de la couleur, qu' eſt la pierre Thebaique.*

[t] The compaſs of the *Scapus* of this column at *Alexandria*, near the *Torus*, is XXIV *Engliſh* feet: the compaſs of the *Scapus* of thoſe at *Rome*, is XV *Engliſh* feet, and three inches. By theſe proportions, and by thoſe rules which are expreſſed in *Vetruvius*, and in other books of architecture, the ingenious reader may compute the true dimenſions of thoſe before the *Pantheon*, and of this at *Alexandria*; being, in my calculation, the moſt magnificent column that ever was made, of one entire ſtone.

[u] *Pervenitur in elegans cubiculum quadrangulum ſex paſſus longum, & quatuor latum, quatuor verò vel* VI *orgyiis altum, in quo marmor nigrum ſolidum in ciſtæ formam exciſum invenimus* XII *pedes longum,* V *altum, & totidem latum, ſine operculo.* Bellon. Obſer. lib. 2. cap. 42.

[x] *Les voyages de monſieur de Breves.*

[y] 6 Feet $\frac{488}{1000}$

[z] 2 Feet $\frac{218}{1000}$ In the reiteration of theſe numbers, if any ſhall be offended, either with the novelty or tediouſneſs of expreſſing them ſo often, I muſt juſtify my ſelf by the example of *Vlug Beg*, nephew to *Tamurlanc* the great, (for ſo is his name, and not *Tamerlane*) and emperor of the *Moguls*, or *Tatars*, (whom we term amiſs the *Tartars*.) For I find in his aſtronomical tables (the moſt accurate of any in the eaſt) made about CC years ſince, the ſame courſe obſerved by him, when he writes of the *Grecian*, *Arabian*, *Perſian*, and *Gelalean epocha's*; as alſo of thoſe of *Catæa* and *Turkiſtan*. He expreſſeth the numbers at large, as I have done, then in figures, ſuch as we call *Arabian*, becauſe we firſt learned theſe from them; but the *Arabians* themſelves fetch them higher, acknowledging that they received this uſeful invention from the *Indians*; and therefore, from their authors, they name them *Indian figures*. Laſtly, he renders them again in particular tables, which manner I judge worthy the imitation, in all ſuch numbers as are *radical*, and of more than ordinary uſe. For if they be only twice expreſſed, if any difference ſhall happen by the neglect of ſcribes, or printers, it may often ſo fall out, that we ſhall not know which to make choice of; whereas if they be thrice expreſſed, it will be a rare chance but that two of them will agree; which two we may generally preſume to be the truth.

[a] *Jam verò ante annos propè mille, vates ille Homerus non ceſſavit minora corpora mortalium quam priſca conqueri.* Plin.

Nam genus hoc vivo jam decreſcebat Homero.
Terra malos homines nunc educat atque puſillos. Juven. Sat. 15.

[b] Auguſt. de civ. Dei. l. 15. cap. 9.

GREAVES my own satisfaction, as to enter those wonderful grots, and compare his descriptions) I find the bodies entombed, some of them being as ancient as *Solinus* himself, no way to exceed the proportions of our times.

It may be justly questioned how this monument of *Cheops* could be brought hither, seeing it is an impossibility that by those narrow passages, before described, it should have entered. Wherefore we must imagine that by some *machina* it was raised and conveyed up without, before this oratory or chamber was finished, and the roof closed. The position of it is thus: it stands exactly in the meridian north and south, and is, as it were, equidistant from all sides of the chamber, except the east, from whence it is doubly remoter than from the west. Under it I found a little hollow space to have been dug away, and a large stone in the pavement removed, at the angle next adjoining to it: which [c] *Sands* erroneously imagines to be a passage into some other compartiment: dug away, no doubt, by the avarice of some, who might not improbably conjecture an hidden treasure to be reposited there. An expenceful prodigality, out of superstition used by the ancients, and with the same blind devotion taken up, and *continued to this day in the* East-Indies. And yet it seems by *Josephus*'s relation, that by the wisest king, in a time as clear and unclouded as any, it was put in practice, who thus describes the funeral of king *David:* [d] *His son Solomon buried him magnificently in Hierusalem, who, besides the usual solemnities at the funerals of kings, brought into his monument very great riches, the multitude of which we may easily collect by that which shall be spoken. For thirteen hundred years after, Hyrcanus the high-priest being besieged by Antiochus, surnamed Pius, the son of Demetrius, and being willing to give money to raise the siege, and to lead away his army, not knowing where to procure it, he opened one of the vaults of the sepulchre of David, and took thence three thousand talents; part whereof being given to Antiochus, he freed himself from the danger of the siege, as we have elsewhere declared. And again, after many years, king Herod opened another vault, took out a great quantity of money; yet neither of them came to the coffins of the kings; for they were with much art hid under ground, that they might not be found by such as entered into the sepulchre.*

The ingenious reader will excuse my curiosity, if before I conclude my description of this Pyramid, I pretermit not any thing within, of how light a consequence soever. This made me take notice of two inlets, or spaces, in the south and north sides of this chamber, just opposite to one another; that on the north was in breadth seven hundred of a thousand parts the *English* foot, in depth four hundred of a thousand parts; evenly cut, and running in a straight line six feet, and farther, into the thickness of the wall. That on the south is larger, and somewhat round, not so long as the former, by the blackness within, it seems to have been a receptacle for the burning of lamps. *T. Livius Burretinus*, would gladly have believed, that it had been an hearth for one of those eternal lamps, such as have been found in *Tulliola*'s tomb in *Italy*; and, if [e] *Camden* be not misinformed, in *England*, in the *cryptoporticus* of *Fl. Valerius Constantius*, father to *Constantine* the great, dedicated to the urns and ashes of the dead; but I imagine the invention not to be so ancient as this Pyramid. However, certainly a noble invention; and therefore pity it is it should have been smothered by the negligence of writers, as with a damp. How much better might *Pliny*, if he knew the composition of it, have described it, than he hath done the *linum asbestinum*, a sort of linen spun out of the veins, as some suppose, of the *Caristian*, or *Cyprian* stone? (which in my travels I have often seen:) tho' *Salmasius* [f], with more probability, contends the true *asbestinum* to be the *linum vivum*, or *linum Indicum*; in the folds and wreaths of which, they enclosed the dead body of the prince; (for, saith [g] *Pliny*, *Regum Indæ funebres tunicæ:* and no wonder, seeing not long after he adds, *Æquat pretia excellentium margaritarum*) committing it to the fire and flames till it were consumed to ashes: while in the same flames this shrowd of linen, as if it had only been bathed and washed (to allude to his expression) by the fire, became more white and refined. Surely a rare and commendable piece of skill, which [h] *Pancirollus* justly reckons among the *deperdita*; but infinitely inferior, either in respect of art or use, unto the former. And thus I have finished my description of all the inner parts of this Pyramid: in which I could neither borrow light to conduct me from the ancients; nor receive any manuduction from the uncertain informations of modern travellers, in those dark and hidden paths. We are now come abroad into the light and sun, where I found my janizary, and

[c] *Sands*'s travels. [d] Jos. lib. 7. ant. Judaic. cap. 12. Ἔθαψε δ' αὐτὸν, ὁ παῖς Σολομὼν ἐν Ἱεροσολύμοις διαπρεπῶς, τοῖς τ' ἄλλοις οἷς περὶ κηδείαν νομίζεται βασιλικὴν ἅπασι, καὶ αὐτῷ πλοῦτον πολὺν καὶ ἄφθονον συγκηδεύσας, &c.

[e] Camden Brit. ubi agit de Brigantibus. [f] Salmasii exercit. Plinian.

[g] Plin. lib. 18. cap. 1. [h] Pancirol. Titl. 4. rerum deperditarum.

GREAVES

an *English* captain, a little impatient to have waited above [1] three hours without, in expectation of my return, who imagined what they understood not, to be an *impertinent* and *vain curiosity*.

[1] That I and my company should have continued so many hours in the Pyramid, and live (whereas we found no inconvenience) was much wondered at by Dr. *Harvey*, his majesty's learned physician: for, said he, seeing we never breathe the same air twice, but still new air is requisite to a new respiration, (the *succus alibilis* of it being spent in every expiration) it could not be but by long breathing we should have spent the aliment of that small stock of air within, and have been stifled: unless there were some secret tunnels conveying it to the top of the Pyramid, whereby it might pass out, and make way for fresh air to come in, at the entrance below. To which I returned him this answer: That it might be doubted whether the same numerical air could not be breathed more than once; and whether the *succus*, and aliment of it, could be spent in one single respiration: Seeing those *urinatores*, or divers under water, for spunges in the *Mediterranean* sea, and those for pearls in the *sinus Arabicus*, and *Persicus*, continuing above half an hour under water, must needs often breathe in and out the same air. He gave me an ingenious answer, That they did it by help of spunges filled with oil, which still corrected and fed this air; the which oil being once evaporated, they were able to continue no longer, but must ascend up, or die. An experiment most certain and true. Wherefore I gave him this second answer: That the fuliginous air we breathed out in the Pyramid, might pass thorough those galleries we came up, and so thorough the straight neck, or entrance, leading into the Pyramid, and by the same fresh air might enter in, and come up to us. Which I illustrated with this similitude: As at the streights of *Gibraltar*, the sea is reported by some to enter in on *Europe* side, and to pass out on *Africa* side; so in this streight passage, being not much above three feet broad, on the one side air might pass out, and at the other side fresh air might enter in. And this might no more mix with the former air, than the *Rhodanus*, as *Pomponius Mela*, and some others report, passing through the *lacus Lemanus*, or lake of *Geneva*, doth mix and incorporate with the water of the lake. For as for any *tubuli*, to let out the fuliginous air at the top of the Pyramid, none could be discovered within, or without. He replied, They might be so small, as that they could not easily be discerned, and yet might be sufficient to make way for the air, being a thin and subtile body. To which I answered, That the less they were the sooner they would be obstructed with those tempests of sands, to which these deserts are frequently exposed: and therefore the narrow entrance into the Pyramid, is often so choaked up with drifts of sand, that there is no entrance into it: wherefore we hire *Moors* to remove them, and open the passage, before we can enter into the Pyramid, with which he rested satisfied. But I could not so easily be satisfied with that received opinion, That at the streights of *Gibraltar*, the sea enters in at the one side, and at the same time passes out at the other. For besides that, in twice passing those streights I could observe no such thing, but only an inlet, without any outlet of the sea: I enquired of a captain of a ship, being captain of one of the six that I was then in company with, and an understanding man, who had often passed that way with the pirates of *Algier*, whether ever he observed any outlet of the sea on *Africa* side? He answered, No. Being asked, Why then the pirates went out into the *Atlantick* sea on *Africa* side, if it were not, as the opinion is, to make use of the current? He answered, It was rather to secure themselves from being surprised by the Christians, who had near the mouth of the streights the port of *Gibraltar*, on the other side, to harbour in. Wherefore, when I consider with my self the great draught of waters that enter at this streight, and the swift current of waters which pass out of the *Pontus Euxinus*, by the *Bosphorus Thracius*, into the *Mediterranean* sea, (both which I have seen) besides the many rivers that fall into it, and have no visible passage out: I cannot conceive, but that the *Mediterranean* sea, or *Urinal* (as the *Arabians* call it, from its figure) must long since have been filled up, and swelling higher, have drowned the plains of *Ægypt*; which it hath never done. Wherefore I imagine it to be no absurdity in philosophy, to say that the earth is tubulous, and that there is a large passage under ground, from one sea to another. Which being granted, we may easily thence apprehend the reason why the *Mediterranean* sea rises no higher, notwithstanding the fall into it of so many waters; and also know the reason why the *Caspian* sea, tho' it hath not, in appearance, any commerce with other seas, continues salt, (*for so it is, whatsoever* Policletus, *in* Strabo, *says to the contrary*) and swells not over its banks, notwithstanding the fall of the great river *Volga*, and of others, into it. That which gave me occasion of entring into the speculation was this: In the longitude of eleven degrees, and latitude of forty one degrees, having borrowed the tackling of six ships, and in a calm day sounded with a plummet of almost twenty pounds weight, carefully steering the boat, and keeping the plummet in a just perpendicular, at a thousand forty five *English* fathoms; that is, at above an *English* mile and a quarter in depth, I could find no land, or bottom.

A De-

A Description of the Second PYRAMID.

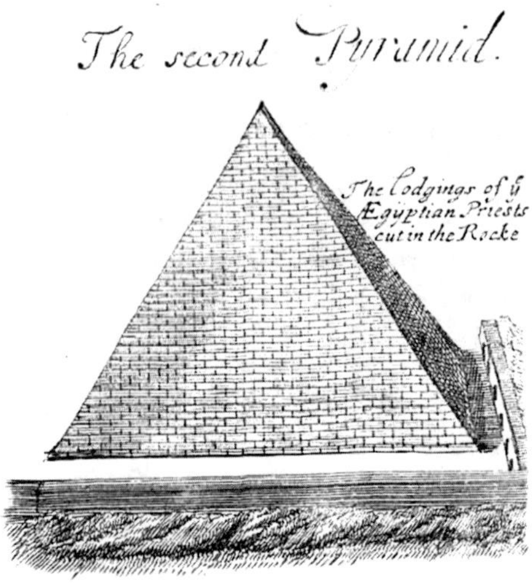

GREAVES FROM the first Pyramid we went to the second, being scarce distant the flight of an arrow. By the way I observed, on the west-side of the first, the ruins of a pile of building, all of square and polished stone; such as [a] *Pliny* calls *basaltes*, and describes to be, *ferrei coloris, & duritiæ: of an iron colour and hardness:* formerly, it may be, some habitation of the priests, or some monument of the dead. To the right hand of this, tending to the south, stands this second Pyramid; of which, besides the miracle, the ancient and modern writers have delivered little. [b] *Herodotus* relates, that *Cephren*, in imitation of his brother *Cheops*, built this; but that he fell short in respect of the magnitude. *For* (saith he) *we have measured them.* It were to be wished for fuller satisfaction of the reader, he had expressed the quantity, and also the manner how he took his measure. He adds, *It hath no subterraneous structures, neither is the* Nilus *by a channel derived into it, as in the former.* [c] *Diodorus* somewhat more particularly describes it thus: That *for the architecture it is like unto the former, but much inferior to it in respect of magnitude; each side of the basis contains a* stadium *in length.* The same measure, by [d] *Strabo*, is assigned to the altitude: *Each of these,* [discoursing of the first and second Pyramids] *is a furlong in height.* That is, to comment on their words, of *Grecian* feet six hundred, of *Roman* six hundred twenty five: So that by the computation of *Diodorus*, each side should want an hundred *Grecian* feet of the former Pyramid. [e] *Pliny* makes the difference to be greater, for assigning eight hundred eighty three feet to the former, he allows to the side of the basis of this, but seven hundred thirty seven. By my observation, the stones are of colour white, nothing so great and vast as those of the first and fairest Pyramid; the sides rise not with degrees like that, but are all of them plain and smooth; the whole fabrick (except where it is opposed to the south) seeming very entire, free from any deformed ruptures or breaches. The height of it, taken by as deliberate a conjecture as I could make (which it was easy to do by reason of the nearness of this, and the former, being both upon the same plain) is not inferior to it; and therefore *Strabo* hath rightly judged them to be equal. The sides also of the *basis* of both are alike; as, besides the authority of [f] *Strabo*, the *Venetian* doctor assured me, who measured it with a line. There is no entry leading into it, and therefore what may be within, whether such spaces and compartiments, as I observed in the former, or whether different, or none, I must leave to the conjecture of travellers, and to the discovery of after-times.

This Pyramid is bounded on the north and west-sides, with two very stately and elaborate pieces; which I do not so much admire, as that by all writers they have been pretermitted about thirty feet in depth, and more than a thousand and four hundred in length, out of the hard rock, these buildings have been cut in a perpendicular, and squared by the chissel, as I suppose, for lodgings of the priests. They run along at a convenient distance, parallel to the two sides we mentioned of this Pyramid, meeting in a right angle, and making a very fair and graceful prospect. The entrance into them is by square openings, hewn out of the rock, much of the same bigness with those I described in the first Pyramid. Whether these where symbolical (as the theology of the *Ægyptians* consisted much in mysterious figures) and the depressure and lowness of these, were to teach the priests humility; and the squareness and evenness of them, an uniform and re-

[a] Plin. l. 35. cap. 7. [b] Herodot. lib. 2. [c] Diodor. Sic. lib. 1. Τῇ μὲν, κατὰ τὴν τέχνην χειρουργίᾳ παραπλησίαν τῇ προειρημένῃ, τῷ δὲ μεγέθει πολὺ λειπομένην ὡς ἂν τῆς ἐν τῇ βάσει πλευρᾶς ἑκάστης οὔσης σταδιαίας.
[d] Εἰσὶ γὰρ σταδιαῖαι τὸ ὕψος. Strabo, lib. 17. [e] Plin. l. 36. cap. 12. *Alterius intervalla singula per quatuor angulos pares* ıɔcc xxxvii [pedes] *comprehendunt.* [f] Strabo, l. 7.

gular

gular deportment in their actions, I leave to ſuch as have written of their hieroglyphicks to determine. The hollow ſpace within, of them all, is ſomewhat like to a ſquare and well proportioned chamber, covered, and arched above with the natural rock: In moſt of which (as I remember) there was a paſſage opening into ſome other compartiment, which the rubbiſh and darkneſs hindred me from viewing. On the north-ſide without, I obſerved a line, and only one, engraven with ſacred and *Ægyptian* characters, ſuch as are mentioned by [g] *Herodotus*, and [h] *Diodorus*, to have been uſed by the prieſts, and were different from the vulgar characters in civil affairs: In which former kind [i] *Juſtin Martyr* makes *Moſes* to have been ſkilful; as the ſcripture ſhews him to have been [k] *learned in all the wiſdom of the Ægyptians*. Theſe ran not downwards, as the *Chineſe* in our times write, but were continued in a ſtreight line, as we uſed to write: And are to be read (if any underſtand thoſe myſterious ſculptures) by proceeding from the right hand to the left, and as it were imitating the motion and courſe of the planets. For ſo [l] *Herodotus* expreſly informs us, That *the* Grecians *write and caſt account, going from the left hand to the right; the* Ægyptians *from the right hand to the left.* And this is that which in an obſcure expreſſion is alſo intimated by [m] *Pomponius Mela: [Ægyptii] ſuis literis perverſe utuntur.* A manner practiſed by the *Hebrews*, *Chaldæans*, and *Syrians*, to this day: And not unlikely to have been borrowed by them from the *Ægyptians*; to whom the *Chaldæans* alſo ow'd their firſt ſkill in aſtrology, as the *Grecians* did their knowledge in geometry; the former being atteſted by [n] *Diodorus*, and the latter confeſſed by [o] *Proclus*, and other *Grecians*. And ſurely in imitation of theſe, or of the *Jews*, the *Arabians* neighbouring upon both, have taken up this manner of writing, and continued it to our times; communicating it alſo by their conqueſts, to the *Perſians* and *Turks*.

GREAVES

[g] Herodot. lib. 2. [h] Παιδεύουσι δὲ τοὺς υἱοὺς οἱ μὲν ἱερεῖς γράμματα διττά. Τά τε ἱερὰ καλούμενα, καὶ κοινοτέραν ἔχοντα τὴν μάθησιν. Diod. l. 1. [i] Ὢν ὁ προφήτης εἰ καὶ τὴν εἴδησιν εἶχεν, ἀλλ' οὐκ ἔτι καὶ τὴν χρῆσιν, &c. Juſt. Martyr. Quæſt. & Reſp. ad Orthodoxos. [k] Acts vii. 22.
[l] Γράμματα γράφουσι καὶ λογίζονται ψήφοισι, Ἕλληνες μὲν ἀπὸ τῶν ἀριστερῶν ἐπὶ τὰ δεξιὰ φέροντες τὴν χεῖρα. Αἰγύπτιοι δὲ, ἀπὸ τῶν δεξιῶν ἐπὶ τὰ ἀριστερά. Herodot. lib. 2. [m] Pompon. Mel. l. 1. c. 9.
[n] Diodor. Sic. l. 1. [o] 2 Lib. commen. Procli, in 1 lib. Eucl.

A Deſcription of the Third PYRAMID.

THE third Pyramid ſtands diſtant from the ſecond about a furlong, upon an advantageous height, and riſing of the rock, whereby afar off it ſeems equal to the former; tho' the whole pile is much leſs, and lower. The time was ſo much ſpent with my other obſervations, that I could not take ſo exact a view as I deſired, and the work deſerved; yet I took ſo much of both, as to be able to confute the errors of others. But before I perform this, I ſhall relate what the ancients, and ſome one or two of our beſt writers, which have travelled thither, have delivered concerning this. [a] *Herodotus* diſcourſing of it, tells us, that *(Mycerinus) left a Pyramid much leſs than that of his father, wanting of all ſides (for it is quadrangular) twenty feet: it is three hundred feet on every ſide, being to the middle of it built with* Æthiopick *marble.* [b] *Diodorus Siculus* is ſomewhat larger and clearer. *Every ſide of the baſis (*Mycerinus*) cauſed to be made three hundred feet in length, he raiſed the walls fifteen ſtories, with black ſtone, like* Thebaick *marble; the reſt of it he finiſhed with ſuch materials as the other Pyramids are built. This work, altho' it is exceeded by the reſt in magnitude, yet for the ſtructure, art, and magnificence of the marble, it very far excels them. In the ſide towards the north,* Mycerinus, *the name of the founder is engraven.* To *Dio-*

[a] Herodot. lib. 2. Πυραμίδα δὲ καὶ οὗτος ἀπελίπετο πολλὸν ἐλάσσω τοῦ πατρὸς, εἴκοσι ποδῶν καταδέουσαν, κώλου ἑκάστου τριῶν πλέθρων, ἐούσης τετραγώνου, λίθου δὲ ἐς τὸ ἥμισυ Αἰθιοπικοῦ. [b] Diodor. Sic. l. 1.

GREAVES *dorus* I shall adjoin the testimony of [c] *Strabo: Farther, upon a higher rise of the hill, is the third (Pyramid) much less than the two former, but built with a greater expence: For almost from the foundation of it to the middle, it consists of black stone, with which they make mortars, brought from the remotest mountains of* Æthiopia, *which being hard, and not easy to be wrought, hath made the work the more costly.* [d] *Pliny* also, not as a spectator, and eye-witness, as the former, but as an historian writes thus: *The third (Pyramid) is less than the former we mentioned, but much more beautiful: it is erected with* Æthiopick *marble, and is three hundred sixty three feet between the angles.* And this is all that hath been preserved of the ancients concerning this Pyramid. Amongst modern writers, none deserve to be placed before *Bellonius*, or rather *P. Gillius:* For [e] *Thuanus* makes the other to have been a *plagiarius*, and to have published in his own name the observations of *P. Gillius:* a man very curious and inquisitive after truth, as appears by his *topography of Constantinople*, and his *Bosphorus Thracius*, to whom *Bellonius* served as an *amanuensis. The third* [f] *Pyramid is much less than the former two, but it is a third part greater than that which is at* Rome, *near the* mons Testaceus, *as you pass to St.* Paul's *in the* Ostian *way. It is still perfect, and no more corrupted than as if it had been newly built: For it is made of a kind of marble, called* basaltes, *or* Æthiopick *marble, harder than iron it self.*

It will be in vain to repeat the traditions and descriptions of several others: All which, by a kind of confederacy, agree in the same tale for the substance, only differing in some circumstances. So that I shrewdly suspect, that *Diodorus* hath borrowed most of his relation from *Herodotus*; and *Strabo* and *Pliny* from *Diodorus*, or from them both; and the more learned moderns from them all: For else how can it be imagined, they should so constantly agree in that, which if my eyes, and [g] memory, extreamly fail me not, is most evidently false? And therefore I have a strong jealousy, that they never came near this third Pyramid; but that they did, as I have observed all travellers, in my time, in *Ægypt* to do, fill themselves so full, and as it were so surfeit with the sight of the greater and fairer Pyramid, that they had no appetite to be spectators of the rest; where they should only see the same miracle (for the Pyramids are all of the same figure) the farther they went, decreasing and presented in a less form: Or if they did view this, it was *quasi per transennam*; very perfunctorily, and slightly; and that through a false and coloured glass; for they have mistaken both in the quality of the stone, and colour of the Pyramid. I begin with [h] *Herodotus*, who by a notable piece of forgetfulness, if it be not a σφάλμα in the copies, makes the dimensions of each of the sides, in the *basis* of this, to be three hundred feet, and yet to want but twenty of the first Pyramid, to which he assigned before eight hundred feet, an impossibility in arithmetick: And therefore it will be no presumption to correct the place, and instead of ἐείκοσι ποδῶν καταδέουσαι, to write πεντεκοσίων ποδῶν καταδέουσαι. I know not how to palliate or excuse his other error, where he makes this Pyramid to be built as far as to the middle of it, with *Æthiopick* marble. If this sort of marble be *ferrei coloris*, as it is described by [i] *Pliny*, and granted by [k] *Diodorus* and [l] *Strabo*, both of these expressing the colour to be black, and the latter bringing it from the remotest mountains of *Æthiopia*, where the marble hath the same tincture and colour with the inhabitants; then can this relation of *Herodotus* no way be admitted: For the whole Pyramid seems to be of clear and white stone, somewhat choicer and brighter, than that in either of the two other Pyramids. And therefore I wonder that *Diodorus, Strabo*, and *Pliny*; and amongst latter authors, *Bellonius, Gillius*, and several others, should have all followed *Herodotus*; when with a little pains and circumspection, they might have reformed his and their own error. It may perhaps be alledged in their defence, that they mean, the buildings within are erected with black and *Æthiopick* marble: And yet if this be granted, since there is no entrance leading into this, no more than is into the second Pyramid, what may be within, depends upon the incertainty of tradition or conjecture, both which are very fallible. Though it cannot be denied, but close by, on the east-side of it, there are the ruins of a pile of building, with a sad and dusky colour, much like that we described in passing to the second Pyramid, which might be the ground and occasion

[c] Strabo, l. 17. Geog. [d] Plin. l. 36. c. 12. *Tertia minor prædictis, sed multò spectatior, Æthiopicis lapidibus assurgit* CCCLXIII *pedibus inter angulos.* [e] Thuan. hist. l. 16. [f] Bellon. observ. l. 2. c. 44. *Tertia Pyramis duabus superioribus longè minor, tertia est autem parte major, ea quæ apud Testaceum montem est Romæ, qua ad D. Pauli eundum est, itinere Ostiensi. Adhuc integra est, necmagis rimis corrupta, quàm si jam recens exstructa esset. Marmoris enim genere constat, quod Basaltes nuncupatur, vel lapis Æthiopicus, ipso ferro duriore.* [g] I have since conferred with an *English* captain, who having been four times at *Alexandria*, and as often at the Pyramids, assures me that I am not mistaken. [h] Herodot. lib. 2. [i] Plin. l. 36. c. 7. [k] Diodor. l. 1. [l] Strabo, l. 7. Geog.

of

of this error. I cannot excuse the antients, but *Bellonius*, or *Gillius*, (for it is no matter which of them owns the relation, when both of them have erred) are far more inexcusable: Because it might have been expected from them, what [m] *Livy* supposes, *Novi semper scriptores, aut in rebus certius aliquid allaturos se, aut scribendi arte rudem vetustatem superaturos credunt.* Whereas these on the contrary, have depraved what hath been in this particular, with truth delivered by the ancients. For whereas *Herodotus*, and *Diodorus*, equal the side of the *basis* to three hundred feet, and *Pliny* extends it to three hundred sixty three, they only make it a third part greater than the Pyramid at *Rome*, of *C. Cestius*, near the *mons Testaceus:* So that either they have much enlarged that at *Rome*, or shrunk and contracted this. For the Pyramid at *Rome*, exactly measured on that side which stands within the city, is compleatly seventy eight feet *English* in breadth; to which if we add a third part of it, the result will be an hundred and four; which should be equal to this *Ægyptian* Pyramid, in the notion and acceptation of *Bellonius*. An unpardonable oversight, no less than two hundred feet, in a very little more than three hundred. For so much, besides the authority of *Herodotus*, and *Diodorus*, before cited, I take the side of this Pyramid to be, and the altitude to have much the same proportion.

I would gladly have seen in this, the name of *Mycerinus*, the founder of it, engraven, as [n] *Diodorus* mentions: Or that other inscription in the first, whereof *Herodotus* procured the interpretation: But both have been defaced by time. His words are these: [o] *In the Pyramid there are* Ægyptian *characters inscribed, which shew how much was expended upon the workmen, in radishes, onions, and garlick; which an interpreter (as I well remember) said, was the sum of a thousand and six hundred talents of silver; which if it be so, how much is it credible was spent in iron, and in meat, and in clothes for the labourers?* Hereby I might have known what to determine of the ancient *Ægyptian* letters: I mean not the sacred ones (for those were all symbolical, expressing the abstractest notions of the mind, by visible similitudes of [p] birds and beasts, or by representations of some other familiar objects) but those used in civil affairs. By such sculptures, which I have seen in gems found at *Alexandria*, and amongst the Mummies, I can no way subscribe to the assertion of *Kircherus*, tho' an able man, who in his *Prodromus Coptus*, contends, that the present *Ægyptian* or *Coptite* character (which certainly is only a corruption and distortion of the *Greek*) is the same with that of the ancient *Ægyptians*. But surely the *Ægyptian* character is of a much higher descent: And if we believe [q] *Tacitus* (whose opinion is very probable) they were the first inventors of letters; tho' some ascribe the honour of this invention to the *Phœnicians*.

[m] T. Liv. lib. 1. [n] Diodor. l. 1. [o] Herodot. l. 2. Σεσήμανται δὲ διὰ γραμμάτων Αἰγυπτίων ἐν τῇ πυραμίδι, ὅσα ἔς τε συρμαίην, καὶ κρόμμυα, καὶ σκόροδα ἀναισιμώθη τοῖσι ἐργαζομένοισι, καὶ ὡς ἐμὲ εὖ μεμνῆσθαι τὰ ὁ ἑρμηνεύς μοι ἐπιλεγόμενος τὰ γράμματα ἔφη, ἑξακόσια καὶ χίλια τάλαντα ἀργυρίου τετελέσθαι, &c.

[p] *Phœnices primi, famæ si creditur, ausi,*
Mansuram rudibus vocem signare figuris.
Nondum flumineas Memphis contexere biblos.
Noverat, & saxis tantùm volucresque feræque.
Sculptaque servabant magicas animalia linguas.
Lucan. lib. 3.

[q] *Primi per figuras animalium Ægyptii sensus mentis effingebant: Et antiquissima monumenta memoriæ humanæ impressa saxis cernuntur: Et literarum semet inventores perhibent. Inde Phœnicas, quia mari præpollebant, intulisse Græciæ, gloriamque adeptos, tanquam repererunt, quæ acceperant.* Tacit. 2. lib. annal.

Of the rest of the PYRAMIDS *in the* Lybian *Desart.*

I Have done with these three Pyramids, each of them being very remarkable, and the two first reckoned amongst the miracles of the world. The rest in the *Libyan* desart lying scattered here and there, are (excepting one of them) but lesser copies, and as it were models of these: And therefore I shall neither much trouble my self, nor the reader, with the description of them. Tho' to speak the truth, did not the three first standing so near together, obscure the lustre of the rest, which lie far scattered, some of them were very considerable. And therefore I cannot but tax the omission of the ancients, and the inadvertency of all modern writers and travellers, who with too much supineness have neglected the description of one of them; which in my judgment is as worthy of memory, and as near a miracle, as any of those three which I have mentioned. And this stands from these south and by west, at twenty miles distance, more within the sandy desart, upon a rocky level like these, and not far from the village whence we enter the *Mummies*. This, as the *Venetian* doctor assured me, and as I could judge by conjecture at a distance, hath the same dimensions that the first and fairest of these; hath graduations, or ascents without, and of the same colour like that, (but more decay'd, especially at the top) and an entrance

GREAVES trance into it on the north-side, which is barred up within; and therefore whatsoever is spoken of the first, in respect of the exterior figure, is appliable to this section. [a] *Bellonius* extremely exceeds in his computation of the number of them, who thus writes: *Above an hundred others are seen dispersed up and down in that plain.* I could not discover twenty. And long since, *Ibn Almatoug*, in his book of the miracles of *Ægypt*, reckons them to be but XVIII. *There are in the west-side no more famous buildings than the Pyramids, the number of them is* XVIII. *Of these, there are three in that part which is opposite to* Fostat (*or* [b] Cairo.)

[a] *Plusquàm centum per eam planiciem hinc indè sparsæ conspiciuntur.* Bellon. l. 2. c. 44.

[b] That *Fostat*, *Metza*, and *Cahira*, (or as we usually term it, *Cairo*) are three distinct names, as it were of one and the same city, appears by the *Geographia Nubiensis*, and *Abulfeda*, in *Arabick*: tho' *Abulfeda* more particularly describes *Alkabira* to be on the north-side of *Fostat*, and *Fostat* to be seated upon the river *Nilus*.

In what manner the PYRAMIDS *were built.*

WE had ended our discourse of the Pyramids, but that I find one scruple touched upon by *Herodotus*, *Diodorus*, and *Pliny*, which is worth the discussion, as a point of some concernment in architecture: And that is, in what manner these Pyramids were built, and with what art and contrivance the stones, especially those vast ones in the first, were conveyed up. [a] *Herodotus* who first raised the doubt, gives this solution: *They carried up the rest of the stones with little engines made of wood, raising them from the ground upon the first row, When the stone was lodged upon this row. it was put into another engine, standing upon the first step, from thence it was conveyed to the second row by another. For so many rows, and orders of steps as there were, so many engines were there: Or else they removed the engine which was one, and easy to be carried to every particular row as often as they moved a stone. We will relate that which is spoken of either part. Therefore those in the Pyramid were first made, which were the highest, then by degrees the rest; last of all those which are nearest to the ground, and are the lowest.* The first part of this solution of *Herodotus* is full of difficulty. How in erecting and placing of so many *machinæ*, charged with such massy stones, and those continually passing over the lower degrees, could it be avoided, but that they must either unsettle them, or endanger the breaking of some portions of them; which mutilations would have been like scars, in the face of so magnificent a building? His second answer is the founder; but I conceive the text to be imperfect. [b] *Diodorus* hath another fancy: *The stones* (saith he) *at a great distance off were prepared in* Arabia: *And they report, that by the help of* aggeres (*engines not being then invented*) *the work was erected. And that which begets the greatest admiration is, that so vast a structure was perfected in that place, which is all about replenished with sand, where there appears not any relicks, either of the* aggeres, *or of the hewing and polishing of the stones. So that it seems not piecemeal by the industry of men, but all together, and at once, the whole pile as it were, by some god, was erected in the midst of the sands. Some of the* Ægyptians *relate wonders of it, and endeavour to obtrude I know not what fables; namely, that these* aggeres *consisting of salt and nitre, were dissolved by letting in the river, which wholly consumed them without the labour of hands, leaving this structure* (entire.) *But the truth of the business is not so, but that those multitudes of men, which were employed in raising the* aggeres, *carried them away unto their former places. For, as they report, three hundred and sixty thousand men were employed in these offices, and the whole work was scarce finished in the space of twenty years.* *Pliny* partly agrees with him, and partly gives another answer. *The question is, by what means the cement was conveyed up to such a height,* (he rather might have questioned, how those vast stones were conveyed up) *some say, that banks of nitre and salt were made up, as the work rose, which being finished, they were washed away*

[a] Ἤειρον τοὺς ἐπὶ λοίπους λίθους μηχανῆσι ξύλων βραχέων πεποιημένῃσι, &c. Herod. l. 2.

[b] Λέγεται δὲ τῶν μὲν λίθων ἐκ τῆς Ἀραβίας ἀπὸ πολλοῦ διαστήματος κομισθῆναι, τὴν δὲ κατασκευὴν διὰ χωμάτων γενέσθαι, μήπω τῶν μηχανῶν εὑρημένων κατὰ ἐκείνους τοὺς χρόνους. Καὶ τὸ θαυμασιώτατον, τὸ τηλικοῦτον ἔργον κατασκευασμένον καὶ τοῦ περιέχοντος τόπου παντὸς ἀμμώδους ὄντος, οὐδὲν ἴχνος οὔτε τοῦ χώματος, οὔτε τῆς τῶν λίθων ξεστουργίας καὶ λαξεύσεως ἀπολείπεται, ὥστε δοκεῖν μὴ κατὰ ὀλίγον ὑπ᾽ ἀνθρώπων ἐργασίας, ἀλλὰ συλλήβδην καὶ ὁμοῦ ὥσπερ ὑπὸ θεοῦ τινὸς τὸ κατασκεύασμα τεθῆναι πᾶν εἰς τὴν περιέχουσαν ἄμμον. Ἐπιχειροῦσι δέ τινες τῶν Αἰγυπτίων τερατολογεῖν καὶ μυθοποιεῖν ὑπὲρ τούτων, λέγοντες ὡς ἐξ ἁλῶν καὶ νίτρου τῶν χωμάτων γεγονότων, ἐπαφεθεὶς ὁ ποταμὸς ἔτηξεν, καὶ διέλυσεν, αὐτὰ καὶ παντελῶς ἠφάνισεν, ἄνευ τῆς χειροποιήτου πραγματείας· οὐ μὴν καὶ τἀληθὲς οὕτως ἔχει, διὰ δὲ τῆς πολυχειρίας τῆς τὰ χώματα βαλούσης πάλιν τὸ πᾶν ἔργον εἰς τὴν προϋπάρχουσαν ἀποκατεστάθη τάξιν. Τριάκοντα μὲν γὰρ καὶ ἓξ μυριάδες ἀνδρῶν ὥς φασι, ταῖς τῶν ἔργων λειτουργίαις προσήδρευσαν, τὸ δὲ πᾶν κατασκεύασμα τέλος ἔσχε μόγις ἐτῶν εἴκοσι. Diodor. Biblioth. Histor. lib. 1. *Quæstionum summa est quanam ratione in tantam altitudinem, subvecta sint cementa. Alii enim nitro ac sale adaggeratis cum crescente opere ac peracto, fluminis irrigatione dilutis: alii lateribus è luto factis extructos pontes, peracto opere in privatas domos distributos. Nilum enim non putant rigare potuisse multò humiliorem.* Plin. l. 36. c. 12.

by

by the river (Nilus.) *Others imagine, that bridges were made with brick: Which, the work being ended, were distributed into private houses. For they conceive, that the* Nilus *being much lower, could not come to wash them* (away.) If I may assume the liberty of a traveller, I imagine, that they were erected, neither as *Herodotus* describes, nor as *Diodorus* reports, nor as *Pliny* relates; but that first they made a large and spacious [c] tower in the midst, reaching to the top; to the sides of this tower, I conceive, the rest of the building to have been applied, piece after piece, like so many buttresses, or supporters, still lessening in height, till at last, they came to the lowermost degree. A difficult piece of building, taken in the best and easiest projection: And therefore it is no wonder, if it were not often imitated by the ancients, and no where expressed or commended, by the great master of architecture *Vitruvius*. Yet surely, if we judge of things by the events, and if we reflect upon the intention of monuments, which are raised by the living to perpetuate the memory of the dead, then is this as commendable a way as any. And therefore we see at *Rome*, that tho' by the revolution of so many ages, the *Mausolæum of Augustus* be almost decayed, and the *Septizonium of Severus* be utterly lost, both intended for lasting and stately sepulchres; yet *the Pyramid of* C. Cæstius *stands fair, and almost entire:* Which is no more to be compared, either for the vastness of the stones, or the whole bulk and fabrick of it, with these, than are the limbs and body of a dwarf, to the dimensions of a giant, or some large *Colossus*.

I have done with the work, but the artizans deserve not to be pretermitted; concerning whom, the observation of [d] *Diodorus* is as true, as it is boldly delivered by him. *It is confessed, that these works* (speaking of the Pyramids) *far excel the rest in* Ægypt, *not only in the massiness of the structures, and in the expences, but also in the industry (and skill) of the artificers. The* Ægyptians *think the architects are more to be admired than the kings who were at the expence: For they by their abilities and study, these by their wealth received by inheritance, and by the labours of others erected them.*

[c] Admitting this supposition, we may easily apprehend, how those huge stones might, by engines, be raised in a perpendicular, as the work rose, with less difficulty and expence, than either in a slope or traverse line, upon banks of nitre, or bridges of brick, according to the traditions of *Diodorus* and *Pliny*: Both which must have been of a stupendious and almost incredible height. *Suetonius in Augusto. Spartianus in Severo.*

[d] Diodor. Sic. l. 1. Ὁμολογεῖται δὲ ταῦτα τὰ ἔργα πολὺ προέχειν τῶν κατὰ Αἴγυπτον οὐ μόνον τῷ βάρει τῶν κατασκευασμάτων καὶ ταῖς δαπάναις, ἀλλὰ καὶ τῇ πολυτεχνίᾳ τῶν ἐργασαμένων. καὶ φασὶ δεῖν θαυμάζειν μᾶλλον τοὺς ἀρχιτέκτονας τῶν ἔργων ἢ τοὺς βασιλεῖς τοὺς παρασχομένους τὰς εἰς ταῦτα χορηγίας. τοὺς μὲν γὰρ ταῖς ἰδίαις ψυχαῖς καὶ ταῖς φιλοτιμίαις, τοὺς δὲ τῷ κληρονομηθέντι πλούτῳ καὶ ταῖς ἀλλοτρίαις κακίαις ἐπὶ τέλος ἀγαγεῖν τὴν προαίρεσιν.

The CONCLUSION.

AND thus much of the *sciography*, or of the artificial and *architectonical* part: I shall shut up all with one observation in nature, for the recreation of the reader, recited by *Strabo*, in these words: [a] *We ought not to omit one of the strange things seen by us at the Pyramids: Some heaps of stone, being fragments hewn off, lie before the Pyramids; amongst these are found little stones, some in the similitude and bigness of lentils, some as of grains of barley, which appear half unscaled: They report these are some relicks of the provisions which were given to the workmen, and have been petrified; which seems probable enough.*

These, if there were ever any such, are either consumed by time, or scattered by the winds, or buried with those tempests of sand, to which the desarts are perpetually exposed: But *Diodorus*, who not long preceded him, was not so curious as to deliver this relation. And were not *Strabo* a writer of much gravity and judgment, I should suspect that these petrified grains (tho' I know such petrefactions to be no impossibility in nature: For I have seen, at *Venice*, the bones and flesh of a man, and the whole head, except the teeth, entirely transmuted into stone: And at *Rome*, clear conduit-water, by long standing in aquæducts, hath been turned into perfect alabaster) are like those loaves of bread, which are reported to be found by the *Red Sea*, converted into stone, and by the inhabitants supposed to be some of the bread the *Israelites* left behind them, when they passed over for fear of *Pharaoh*. They are sold at *Grand Cairo*, handsomely made up, in the manner of the bread of these times; which is enough to discover the imposture. For

[a] Ἓν δέ τι τῶν ὁραθέντων ὑφ' ἡμῶν ἐν ταῖς πυραμίσι παραδόξων οὐκ ἄξιον παραλιπεῖν. Ἐκ γὰρ τῆς λατύπης σωροί τινες πρὸ τῶν πυραμίδων κεῖνται, ἐν τούτοις δ' εὑρίσκεται, ψήγματα καὶ τύπῳ καὶ μεγέθει φακοειδῆ ἐνίοις δὲ, καὶ ὡς ἂν πτίσμα ἡμιλεπίστων ὑποτρέχει φασὶ δ' ἀπολιθωθῆναι λείψανα τῆς τῶν ἐργαζομένων τροφῆς οὐκ ἀπέοικε δέ. Strabo. l. 17. Geog.

GREAVES the scripture makes them to have been unleavened cakes: [b] *They baked unleavened cakes of the dough which they brought forth out of Ægypt.* Or else *Strabo*'s relation may be like the tradition of the rising of dead mens bones every [c] year, in *Ægypt:* A thing superstitiously believed by the Christians; and by the priests, either out of ignorance, or policy, maintained as an argument of the resurrection. The possibility and truth of it, *Metrophanes, the patriarch of Alexandria,* thought (but very illogically) might be proved out of the prophet Esay, [d] *And they shall go forth, and look upon the carcases of the men that have transgressed against me, for their worm shall not die, neither shall their fire be quenched; and they shall be an abhorring unto all flesh.*

But I have digressed too far. The confutation of these, and the description of the *Mummies*, or of the rest of the *Ægyptian* sepulchres (for from thence comes the matter of this their supposed resurrection) and that infinite mass, and variety of hieroglyphicks, which I have either seen there, or bought, or transcribed elsewhere, may be the [e] *argument* of another discourse.

[b] Exod. xii. 39.

[c] *Sands* in his travels writes, *that they are seen to rise on* Good-Friday. A *Frenchman*, at *Grand Cairo*, who had been present at the resurrection, shewed me an arm which he brought from thence; the flesh shrivelled, and dried like that of the Mummies. He observed the miracle to have been always behind him; once casually looking back, he discovered some bones carried privately by an *Ægyptian*, under his vest, whereby he understood the mystery.

[d] Esay lxvi. 24.

[e] An argument intended by me, and for which I made a collection of several antiquities in my travels abroad; but these (and would only these!) have unfortunately perished at home, amidst the sad distractions of the time.

A

A

DISCOURSE

OF THE

ROMAN FOOT

AND

DENARIUS:

From whence, as from two Principles, the

MEASURES and WEIGHTS

Used by the ANCIENTS, may be deduced.

By JOHN GREAVES, *Professor of Astronomy in the University of* Oxford.

Σπουδαστέον ὅπως ὁρισθῶσι καλῶς αἱ ἀρχαί, μεγάλην γὰρ ἔχουσι ῥοπὴν πρὸς ἑπόμενα.

Una fides, pondus, mensura, moneta sit una,
Et status illæsus totius orbis erit.

Budelius de monetis.

To his truly noble and learned FRIEND,

JOHN SELDEN, Esq;

Burgess of the University of OXFORD,

In the Honourable HOUSE of COMMONS.

SIR,

THAT I should present you, who have so honourably deserved of antiquity, and of your country; and, if I may add mine own obligations, in particular of me, with so small a retribution as a Roman foot, *and* denarius, *may seem more proportionable to mine abilities, than to the eminency of your place and worth. But you, who, to the honour of your profession, have joined the wisdom of the ancients, and justly have merited this elogy,*

——— Anglorum gloria gentis
Seldenus.

An elogy long since given you by a man, who is deservedly esteemed, πολλῶν ἀντάξιος ἄλλων, *the learned* Hugo Grotius; *you are best able to judge of what importance these two are, in the discovery of the weights and measures used by the ancients.*

And first, for measures, the אמה *or* cubit of the sanctuary, *in the* scriptures, Josephus, *and the* Rabbins: *The* Αἰγύπτιος, *and* Βαβυλώνιος πῆχυς, *in* Herodotus *(the former equal to that of* Samos: *The latter mis-rendered by* Pliny *and* Solinus, pes Babylonius:) *The* Παρασάγγης Περσικὸς, *in* Herodotus, *containing* XXX. στάδια, *in* Strabo, *sometimes* LX. *sometimes* XL, *and sometimes* XXX. (*but in* Hesychius, ὁ παρασάγγης ἔχει μίλια τέτταρα; *and in* Abulfeda, *three miles: With whom, and with the* Persians, *to this day it is called the* * farsach) *the* σχοῖνος Αἰγύπτιος *in* Herodotus, Artemidorus, *and* Strabo: *The* ποὺς βασιλικὸς, καὶ Φιλεταίρειος, *in* Hero: *The* pes Ptolemaicus *and* Drusianus, *in* Hyginus: *Besides infinite others depending upon the proportions of some of these: I say, these cannot, after the destruction of those ancient monarchies and republicks, any other way be restored, than from such monuments, as, by divine Providence, have escaped the hands of ruin, and continued to these later ages. For were it not that the* pes Romanus, *or* monetalis, *as* Hyginus *terms it, were still extant in* Rome, *on the monuments of* Cossutius, *and of* Tit. Statilius Vol. Aper *(for those two columns, the one with the inscription* ΠΟΔ. Θ. *mentioned by* Marlianus *and* Philander: *The other with* ΠΟΔ. IB. *seen by the same* Philander, *are both lost) we might utterly despair of knowing the measures of the* Hebrews, Babylonians, Persians, Ægyptians, Grecians, Romans, *and of all others described in classical authors; who could not transmit to posterity the individual measures themselves, but only the proportions they respectively had to one another: which proportions being pure habitudes, cannot, as mathematicians observe, be reduced to the measures of these times, unless either some of the ἀποκείμενα themselves were existent; or else exact copies taken from the originals were derived to us.*

In like manner it is for weights, the מנה *the* ככר *the* שקל, *or* σίκλος *of the* Hebrews, *or* סלעא *of the* Chaldeans, *which* Aruck *renders by four* זוזים zuzim; *that is, four* denarii (*from whence the* Persian σίγλος, *in* Xenophon, *and* Hesychius, *may have received its denomination: the* τάλαντον Βαβυλώνιον, *containing seven thousand* Attick *drachms; the* τάλαντον Αἰγιναῖον *ten thousand; the* τάλαντον Σύρον *fifteen hundred; the* τάλαντον Ἀττικὸν *six thousand, all mentioned by* Julius Pollux; *the* talentum Ægyptium, *in* Varro, *containing eighty* pondo, *or pounds; the* talentum Euboicum *in* Festus *four thousand* denarii: *these, with infinite others, both* mensuræ *and* pondera, *whether considered as* medica, *or* georgica, *or* veterinaria, *cannot in our times be restored, but only by such weights of the ancients as are still extant; that is, either by the* denarius *of the* Romans, *or* δραχμὴ *of the* Grecians, *or by the* congius *of* Vespatian, *or by the* libræ, *and* unciæ Romanæ, *and the like, that have been preserved by antiquaries.*

Seeing therefore the denarius *is of as great moment for the discovery of weights, as the* Roman *foot for the knowledge of measures, I have taken these two, as two irrefragable principles, from whence the rest used by the ancients may be deduced. And because the* denarius *may be considered in a double respect, either as* nummus, *or as* pondus: *The first acceptation conducing to the valuation of coins, the second to the certainty of weights: It was*

* The *farsach,* with the ancients and moderns, contains three miles. *Abulf. Geog. MS.*

therefore

therefore necessary that both the weight, and valuation of the denarius, *should be exactly known. To which purpose, in* Italy, *I examined with a balance (the scale of which the eightieth part of a grain would sensibly turn) many hundred fair* denarii, *both* consulares *and* cæsarei, *as also* quinarii, *or* victoriati *in silver; several* aurei *of the former and later emperors; besides the original standard of the* congius, *placed by* Vespatian *in the Capitol; and many* unciæ, *and* libræ, *in brass. From whence I collected the weight of the* denarius, consularis, *and* cæsareus; *that to be the seventh part of the* Roman *ounce, as* Celsus, Scribonius Largus, *and* Pliny, *rightly describe; and this to be sometimes the eighth part, and sometimes the seventh, but most frequently in a middle proportion betwixt eight and seven, till* Severus's *and* Gordianus's *times; under whom, and the succeeding emperors, it recovered the weight of the* denarius consularis; *but lost much of its fineness by the mixture of allay.*

With these denarii, *for the greater certainty, I compared such* Grecian *coins (especially* Athenian*) as I had either seen in choice cabinets, or bought of mine own; and those were* χρυσοῖ, *or* στάτῆρες, *absolutely taken; which, as* Julius Pollux, *and* Hesychius, *out of* Polemarchus *testify, weighed two drachms: The* τετράδραχμα, *or* τέτραχμα, *or* στάτῆρες ἀργυρεῖς, *four drachms: The* δραχμαὶ, *the* τελώβολα, *or as* Pollux *names them, the* ἡμίδραχμα, *with several others.*

By which comparison I first discovered, that howsoever the Romans, *as* Pliny, *and* A. Gellius *expresly;* Valerius, *and* Suetonius, *by way of consequence, equal the* denarius *to the* drachma: *And tho' the* Greeks, *as* Strabo, Cleopatra, Plutarch, Galen, Dio, *and many more, equal the* drachma *to the* denarius, *speaking in a popular estimation, and as they vulgarly passed in way of commerce; yet if we shall put on the resolution of him in the comedy,*

> Oculatæ nostræ sunt manus, credunt quod vident:

We may evidently discern in the scale, the drachma Attica *to be heavier than the* denarius: *And therefore all such writers of the ancients, as equal them, if we speak strictly of weight, and not of estimation, have been deceived; and consequently, all modern writers following their traditions, in discourses* de ponderibus, & de re nummariâ *have erred.*

But because it is not probable, that the ancients, both Greeks *and* Romans, *should be deceived in their own coins, and in their own times; it occasioned me by observing the practice abroad of the* κολλυβισαὶ *in exchanges, with whom the same specifical coins, in different states, pass with different estimations, to think of some means how I might reconcile the traditions of the* Greeks *and* Romans, *concerning the weight and valuation of the* drachma Attica *and* denarius; *notwithstanding the difference in the ballance, of such as are now found at* Athens, *and at* Rome.

And this drew from me that discourse which I have inserted at the end of this book: Of some directions to be observed in comparing the valuations of coins: *Which may serve, not only to reconcile the* Greek *and* Roman *writers, but especially the traditions of* Philo, Josephus, Epiphanius, *St.* Hierom, *and* Hesychius; *who make the* Hebrew שקל *shekel, equal to the* Attick *tetradrachm, whereas in the scale, which is the best judge of this controversie, I find them manifestly unequal; the* Hebrew, *or* Samaritan *shekel, being much less than the* Attick *tetradrachm.*

But it may be questioned, Why after the labours of Portius, Budæus, Alciatus, Agricola, Montanus, Mariana, Budelius, Alcasar, Villalpandus, Jo. Scaliger, Capellus, Snellius, *and of many other eminent men who have writ, either* deditâ operâ, *or* ἐν παρόδῳ, de ponderibus & mensuris, *I should undertake any thing of this nature? My answer is, that observing in them so great a variety, and contradiction of opinions, I was willing to use mine own judgment, how mean soever, in giving my self private satisfaction. And tho' I intended this work as a* πάρεργον *to other employments; yet having, by the advantage of travelling in foreign parts, perused in* Italy, Greece, *and* Ægypt, *more antiquities than I think any of them abovenamed single, I thought it would not be unacceptable, if I did, as it is the manner of travellers, publish at home, such observations and discoveries as I made abroad. The which I humbly dedicate to you, as out of a desire to express my gratitude for many noble favours, So out of an assurance, that if they receive your approbation, I need not to fear the censure of others.*

Your most obliged friend, and humble servant,

JOHN GREAVES.

Of the Roman *FOOT.*

GREAVES

THAT the foot was the most received and usual measure amongst the *Romans*, as the cubit amongst the *Jews*, is a thing not controverted by any: for [a] *Polybius* describing their *scutum*, makes it *in breadth over the bend, two* [Roman] *feet and a half, and in length four feet: Or if it be of a greater sort, a palm more is to be added to this measure.* And not long after, expressing the manner of their castrametation, or encamping, he [b] writes: That *as often as a place is designed for the camp, the* prætorium (or general's lodging) *takes up that part, which is fittest for prospect and direction. Setting therefore up the standard, where they intend to fix the* prætorium, *they so measure out the square about a standard that each side may be distant from it an hundred feet, and the whole area contain four jugera.* In like manner [c] *Cæsar*, in the description of his bridge over the *Rhine*, makes the binders, or transversary beams, to be *bipedales*. [d] *Tully* also judges the quantity of the apparent diameter of the sun to be *pedalis*. And not to produce more authorities, [d] *Suetonius* relates, That *Augustus presented before the people of* Rome, Lucius, *a young gentleman, well descended, only for to shew that he was less than two feet in height, seventeen pounds in weight, and of an immense voice.* But concerning the precise quantity of this foot, there is not any one thing after which learned men have more enquired, or in which they do less agree: For *Budæus* equals it to the *Paris* foot; *Latinus Latinius, Maffæus, Ursinus*, and others, deduce it from an ancient monument in the Vatican of *T. Statilius Vol. Aper. Portius Vicentinus, Philander, Georgius Agricola, Ghetaldus, Donatus*, and several others, contend the foot on *Cossutius* monument in *Rome*, to be the true *Roman* foot: *Marlianus* describes it out of a porphyry column, with this inscription, ΠΟΔ. Θ: *Lucas Pætus* defines it from some brass feet found amongst the *rudera* in *Rome*: *Villalpandus* derives it from the measure of the *congius*, placed by *Vespatian* in the Capitol (the original standard being still extant:) *Willebrordus Snellius* equals it to the *pes Rhinlandicus*; and several others have had several fancies and conjectures. In such a variety and incertainty of opinions, we have no more solid foundation of our inquiry, than either to have recourse to the writings of the ancients; or else to such other monuments of antiquity, as having escaped the injury and calamity of time, have continued intire to this present age.

And first for the ancients: [f] *Vitruvius* in his third book of architecture, gives this description of the *Roman* foot: *E cubito cùm dempti sunt palmi duo, relinquitur pes quatuor palmorum. Palmus autem habet quatuor digitos, ita efficitur uti pes habeat* XVI *digitos, & totidem asses æreos denarius.* [g] *Columella* shews, that it was the basis and foundation to all their other measures: *Modus omnis areæ pedali mensurâ comprehenditur, qui digitorum est* XVI. *Pes multiplicatus in passus, & actus, & climata, & jugera, & stadia, centuriasque, mox etiam in majora spatia procedit. Passus pedes habet* V. [h] *Frontinus* more clearly and distinctly expresseth the several parts and divisions of it. *Pes habet palmos* IV. *uncias* XII. *digitos* XVI. *Palmus habet digitos* IV. *uncias* III. *Sextans, quæ eadem dodrans appellatur, habet palmos* III. *uncias* IX. *digitos* XII. From which authority of *Frontinus*, and the place before cited of *Vitruvius*, we may collect some analogy to have been observed in the proportions of the *Roman* foot, and of the *Roman* coins: For as the *denarius* contain'd XVI *asses*, so the foot contained XVI *digitos:* And as the *assis* was divided in XII *uncias*, so likewise the foot was divided in XII *uncias*; and therefore the *dodrans* is used by *Frontinus*, and the *semuncia* and *sicilicus* by *Pliny*, for proportionable parts of the *Roman* foot; as the same are used by other classical authors for proportionable parts of the *Roman assis*, and *uncia*. From which analogy, the *pes Romanus*, I suppose, is termed by [i] *Hyginus*, *pes monetalis.* Likewise in the ancient law of the XII tables (which *Tully* calls the fountains of the civil law) the *sestertius pes* hath the same proportion with the *sestertius* in coins: For as the *sestertius*, according to [k] *Arruntius*, was *olim dupondius & semis*, anciently *two pounds of brass and a half*; so the *sestertius pes* was two feet and a half. [l] *Volusius Mætianus*, "*Sestertius duos asses & semissem,* "*quasi semis tertius*; *Græca figura* ἕβδομον "ἡμιτάλαντον. *Nam sex talenta & semi-*"*talentum eo verbo significantur. Lex etiam* "XII *tabularum argumento est, in qua* "*duo pedes & semissis, sestertius pes vocatur.* But to return to *Frontinus*, who farther

[a] Polyb. l. 6. [b] Polyb. *ibid.* Τιθείσης δὲ τῆς σημαίας, ᾗ μέλλουσι πηγνύναι ταύτην, διαμετρεῖται πέριξ τῆς σημαίας τετράγωνος τόπος. Ὥς τε πάσας τὰς πλευρὰς ἑκατὸν ἀπέχειν πόδας τῆς σημαίας, &c. [c] Cæs. Com. lib. 4.
[d] Cic. l. 2. Acad. quæst. [e] Suetonius in Augusto. *Adolescentulum Lucium honestè natum exhibuit, tantùm ut ostenderet, quòd erat bipedali minor, librarum* XVII, *ac vocis immensæ.* [f] Vitruvius, lib. 3.
[g] Columella, l. 5. de R. Rust. [h] Frontin. de limitibus agrorum.
[i] Hygin. de limit. constit. [k] Arruntius ex editione Gotafredi. [l] Vol. Mæt. de assis distrib.

discoursing

discoursing of the *Roman* foot, gives a distinction of three sorts of feet: and those were first, *pes porrectus*; next, *pes constratus*, or as [m] *Agricola* reads it, *contractus*; and lastly, *pes quadratus*. The first was the measure of longitudes, the other two of superficies. There were, writes [n] *Frontinus*, *In pede porrecto semipedes duo, in pede constrato semipedes quatuor, in pede quadrato semipedes octo*. Which words of his are to be thus explicated; the *pes porrectus* was the *Roman* foot extended in length, and therefore there were in it *semipedes duo*: the *pes constratus*, was the square of the *semipes*, and therefore the perimeter of it contained *semipedes quatuor*; or, which is all one, two entire *Roman* feet: the *pes quadratus*, was the square of the *Roman* foot; wherefore of necessity there must be four feet in the perimeter, or in *Frontinus*'s expression, eight *semipedes*. The same [o] author likewise in his book *de aquæductibus*, describing the digit and *uncia* of this, (*Est autem digitus*, (says he) *ut convenit, sexta decima pars pedis, uncia duodecima*) useth a distinction of digits, as he did of feet before, not mentioned by any other author, *Quemadmodum autem inter unciam, & digitum diversitas, ita & ipsius digiti simplex observatio non est, nam alius vocatur quadratus, alius rotundus. Quadratus tribus quartis decimis suis rotundo major: rotundus tribus undecimis suis quadrato minor est*. The proportions here assigned by him to the *digitus quadratus*, and *rotundus*, are the same which [p] *Archimedes* long before used: and those are, that a circle hath the same proportion to the square of the diameter, that XI. hath to XIV. *Hero* also, discoursing of several sorts of measures, informs us thus concerning the foot: Ὁ μὲν δάκτυλος, μέτρόν ἐστι σμικρότατον. ἡ δὲ δοχμὴ ἐστὶ δακτύλων δ´, ὅπερ μέτρον καὶ δακτυλοδόχμη παλαιστή τε καὶ δῶρον καλεῖται. ἡ δὲ λιχὰς ἐστι δακτύλων ι´, τὸ δὲ ὀρθόδωρον ια´, ἡ δὲ σπιθαμὴ ιβ´, ὁ δὲ ποὺς δοχμῶν δ´, ἤτοι δακτύλων ις´, ἡ δὲ πυγμὴ δακτύλων ιη´, ὁ δὲ πυγὼν κ´, ὁ δὲ πῆχυς κδ´, ἤτοι δοχμῶν ς´, ἡ δὲ ὀργυιὰ πηχέων δ´, ἤτοι ποδῶν ς´. *The digit is the least measure, the palm consists of* IV *digits, and is called dactylodochme, and palaiste, and doron. The lichas is ten digits, the orthodoron eleven, the span* XII. *The foot hath* IV *palms, or* XVI *digits, the pygme* XVIII *digits, the pygon* XX, *the cubit* XXIV, *or* VI *palms, the orgyia* IV *cubits, or* VI *feet*. Most of which measures the *Romans* borrowed from the *Greeks*; as on the contrary, the *Greeks* borrowed the ἰούγερον, and μίλιον, from the *Roman jugerum* and *milliare*. The same *Hero* describes another sort of foot used in *Italy*: Ὁ δὲ Ἰταλικὸς ποὺς δακτύλους ἔχει τρεῖς καὶ δέκα καὶ τρίτον. *The Italian foot contains thirteen digits, and one third*. Whence [q] *Salmasius* concludes, that the *Romans* used one sort of foot in *Rome*, consisting of XVI *digits*; and in some parts of *Italy* another, being but XIII digits, and one third. Which might be granted, did not [r] *Hyginus*, who is much ancienter, in his tract, *de Limitibus constituendis*, contradict it. His words are these: *Item dicitur in Germaniâ in Tungris pes Drusianus, qui habet monetalem, & sescunciam, ita ut ubicunque extra fines, legesque Romanorum, id est, ut solicitiùs proferam, ubicunque extra Italiam aliquid agitatur inquirendum; & de hâc ipsâ conditione diligenter præmoneo, ne quid sit, quod præteriisse videamur*. Where speaking immediately before of the *pes Romanus*, or as he also calls it, the *pes Monetalis*, by which he measures and defines the *limites*, he gives us this caution, That out of *Italy* (for in *Italy* he supposes one measure to be generally received) we are to observe the quantity of the foot, or measure of the country. And for this reason, to avoid ambiguity, he assigns the proportions of the *pes Drusianus*, at *Tongeren* in *Germany*, to be a *sescuncia*, more than the *pes monetalis* used at *Rome*, and in *Italy*. And so in another part about *Cyrene*, which *Ptolemy* gave to the *Romans*: [s] *Pes eorum qui Ptolemaicus appellatur habet monetalem pedem, & semunciam*. But to omit the *pes Ptolemaicus*, (for our inquiry is only of the *Roman* foot) I cannot but wonder at the mistake of [t] *Joseph Scaliger*, concerning the *Pes Drusianus*, and *Romanus*, who thus writes: *Pes igitur ille Drusianus major est Romana sescunciâ, fuit enim* XXII *digitorum, quantorum* XVI *est pes Romanus*. If it were but a *sescuncia*, greater than the *Roman* foot, as *Hyginus*, and he also make it, how can it possibly be XXII *digitorum*? Or how can he excuse his words, which immediately follow? *Ex quo colligimus pedem Drusianum omnino esse eum, qui hodie in Galliâ, & Belgio in usu est, qui profectò major est* VI *digitis, quantorum* XVI *est pes, qui Romæ in hortis Angeli Colotii sculptus in saxo visitur. Eum enim nos cum pede Gallicano comparantes, id verissimum esse deprehendimus*. Neither is the error of some others much less, in making the *pes Monetalis*, or *Romanus*, and *pes Regius Philetærius*, to be equal. Because the *Roman* foot consisted of XVI digits, as *Frontinus* writes, and the *pes Philetærius* of as many, as [u] *Hero* shews: Ὁ ποὺς ὁ μὲν βασιλικὸς, καὶ φιλεταίριος λεγόμενος ἔχει παλαιστὰς δ´, δακτύλους ις´. There-

GREAVES

[m] Agricola de mensuris quibus intervalla metimur.
[n] Frontinus de limitibus agrorum.
[o] Frontinus de aquæductibus.
[p] Archim. de circ. dimens. prop. 2.
[q] Salmasii Exercit. Plinianæ, p. 684.
[r] Hyginus de limit. constit.
[s] Hyginus ibid.
[t] Jos. Scaliger. de re nummaria.
[u] Hero in Isagoge.

fore

GREAVES fore both these are equal. The error is in supposing all digits to be alike; and therefore the same number of digits being in both, that both are equal. By the same argument we may conclude the *Roman* foot, and *Arabian* foot, and the derah, or cubit of these, to be equal to the cubit, or *sesquipes* of the *Romans*; seeing [x] *Abulfeda*, an *Arabian* geographer, defines the derah to consist of XXIV digits, and so many also did the *Roman sesquipes* contain. But the observation of [y] *Rhemnius Fannius* in this particular, is much better; which he applies to weights, and we may by analogy assign to measures.

> *Semina sex alii siliquis latitantia curvis*
> *Attribuunt scripulo, lentes veraciter octo,*
> *Aut totidem speltas, numerant, tristésve lupinos*
> *Bis duo; sed si par generatim his pondus inesset,*
> *Servarent eadem diversæ pondera gentes:*
> *Nunc variant. Etenim cuncta non fœdere certo*
> *Naturæ, sed lege valent, hominúmque repertis.*

But to return to the *Roman* foot: Lastly, We may alledge, [z] *Isidorus Hispalensis. Palmus autem, quatuor habet digitos, pes* XVI *digitos, passus pedes quinque, pertica passus duos, id est decem pedes.* And this is that which I find delivered by such of the ancients as are extant. Out of which bare and naked descriptions, it is as impossible to recover the *Roman* foot, as it is for mathematicians, to take either the distance, or altitude of places, by the proportions of triangles alone, or by tables of signs and tangents, without having some certain and positive measure given, which must be the foundation of their inquiry. All that can be collected by these descriptions, is this, that we may know into how many parts the *Romans* usually divided their feet; and all these divisions I have seen in some ancient ones. But suppose there were no *Roman* foot extant; how by XVI digits, or by IV palms, or by XII *unciæ*, (which is the most uncertain of all; seeing whatsoever hath quantity, how great or small soever it is, may be divided in XII *uncias*) could it be precisely restored? For if that of [a] *Protagoras* be true, as well in measures, as in intellectual notions, that man is πάντων χρημάτων μέτρον: Whence [b] *Vitruvius* observes, that the *Latins* denominated most of their measures, as *their digit, palm, foot, and cubit,* from the parts and members of a man: Who shall be that perfect and square man, from whom we may take the pattern of these measures? Or if there be any such, how shall we know him? Or how shall we be certain the ancients ever made choice of any such? Unless, as some fancy, that the cubit of the sanctuary was taken from the cubit of *Adam*, he being created in an excellent state of perfection: So we shall imagine these digits, and palms, to have been taken from some particular man of compleater lineaments than others. On the other side, if this foot may be restored by digits, and palms of any man at pleasure, since there is such a difference in the proportions of men, that it is as difficult to find two of the same dimensions, as two that have the same likeness of faces, how will it be possible, out of such a diversity, to produce a certain positive measure, consisting in an indivisibility, not as a point doth in respect of parts, but in an indivisibility of application, as all originals and standards should do? The *Arabians* to avoid this difficulty, shew us a more certain way, as they suppose, how to make this commensural digit, and consequently the foot: and that is by the breadth of six barley-corns laid one contiguous to another: for thus [c] *Muhammed Ibn Mesoud*, in his book, entituled in *Persian*, *Gehandanish*, relates: *That in the time of* Almamon (the learned calif of *Babylon*) *by the elevation of the pole of the Æquator, they measured the quantity of a degree upon the globe of the earth, and found it to be fifty six miles, and two thirds of a mile: every mile containing four thousand cubits, and each cubit twenty four digits, and every digit six barley-corns.* The same proportions are assigned in the *geographia Nubiensis*, printed in *Arabick* at *Rome*: *the cubit is twenty four digits; and every digit is six barley-corns.* But this is as uncertain as the former, and is built upon a supposition, that all such are of the same dimension: whereas those of one country differ much from those of another; and those of the same country (as I have made trial in *Ægypt*, more out of curiosity, than as hoping this way to give my self satisfaction) are not all of the same bigness: And not only so, but in the self same ear, there is a sensible difference as experience doth shew. And yet *Snellius*, a man much to be commended for his abilities in the mathematicks, and to be blamed for his supine negligence, both in his measure of the magnitude of the earth, and in his dimensions of the *Roman* foot, upon these slight and weak principles, deduces the *A-*

[x] Abulfedæ Geogr. Arab. MS. [y] Rhemnii Fannii Fragmentum. [z] Isid. Hispal. l. 15. c. 15.
[a] Protagoras apud Aristot. l. 13. c. 5. Metaphys. Πάντων εἶναι χρημάτων μέτρον τὸν ἄνθρωπον.
[b] *Nec minus mensurarum rationes, quæ in omnibus videntur necessariæ esse, ex corporis membris collegerunt: uti digitum, palmum, pedem, cubitum,* Vitruv. l. 3. c. 1. [c] *Muhammid Ibn Mesoud's Gebandanish.*

rabian

rabian foot, [d] *This containing ninety six grains, such as his* Roman *foot* (for none besides himself will own it) *contains* ninety. Wherefore some other *Arabians*, to mend the matter, limit the breadth of one of them, [e] *by six hairs of a camel, evenly joined one by another:* By which invention their derah being almost answerable to the *Roman sesquibes*, or cubit, shall consist of twenty four digits, and every digit of six barley-corns, and every barley-corn of six hairs of a camel. So that in conclusion the hair of a camel shall be the *minimum* in respect of measures. But this invention, however at the first it may seem somewhat subtile (for we are come now almost as low as atoms) is least of all to be approved. For tho' the supposition were true, that all hairs are of a like bigness in all camels, whereas they are different in one and the same; yet this objection is unanswerable, that seeing hairs are not perfectly round tho' the sense judges them so, but angular, and that with some inequality, as magnifying-glasses plainly demonstrate, it will be very difficult so to size them together, that they shall always take up the same breadth: And if they do not, little errors committed in such small bodies, tho' at the first insensible, will infinitely increase and multiply, in the measuring of great distances, to which these are supposed the foundation. And therefore I cannot but approve the council of [f] *Villalpandus*, who advised such as will examine measures and weights, to begin with the greater, and not with the lesser. And that there is reason for his assertion, may be made evident, especially in weights, to such as shall make an experiment. For admit there were a standard of ten thousand grains, and another of one grain, it will be easy, by a continual subdivision of the former, with a good balance, to produce a weight equal to the standard of one grain: Yea, tho' at the beginning some little error had been committed, which after many divisions will vanish, and become imperceptible. Whereas on the contrary, the most curious man alive, with the exactest scale that the industry of the most skilful artizan can invent, shall never be able out of the standard of one grain, to produce a weight equal to the weight of ten thousand grains, but that there shall be a sensible and apparent difference; yea, tho' he had that excellent scale mentioned by [g] *Capellus* at *Sedan*, which would sensibly be turned with the four hundredth part of a grain. The like difference as we find in weights, we may conceive by analogy to be in measures, when they shall be made out of such little parts as hairs, barley-corns, digits, and the like. And therefore I cannot but disapprove the ordinary course of most geographers, whether *Greeks*, *Latins*, or *Arabians*, that from such nice beginnings measure out a degree upon earth, and consequently the magnitude of this globe. On the contrary, the enterprize of [h] *Snellius*, in his *Eratosthenes Batavus*, and of our countryman [i] *M. Wright*, hath been more commendable: Who by the space of a degree on earth, (or which were better of many degrees) have endeavoured to fix measures with more exactness and certainty for posterity. But of this argument I shall have occasion to speak hereafter. And therefore to return to the business in hand.

Since the *Roman* foot cannot be recover'd by hairs, grains, digits, palms, and such like physical bodies, which being of a various and indeterminate magnitude, cannot give, unless by accident, the commensuration of that which ought to be precisely limited and determinated; some relinquishing the former way as erroneous, have endeavoured with much ingeniousness, by weights to find out the *Roman* foot: For there is the same analogy between measures and weights, as between continued and discrete quantities: And as mathematicians by numbers demonstrate, or rather illustrate the affections of lines, superfices, and geometrical bodies: So by weights, measuring some physical bodies, especially such as are liquid, in cubical vessels, (which are easiest commensurable) we may render the exact quantity of the *Roman* foot, and by consequence of all their other measures. And therefore [k] *Lucas Pætus*, and [l] *Villalpandus*, have attempted with probable reasons to discover the *Roman* foot, the one by the *Sextarius*, the other by the *Roman Congius*. For the *sextarius* being the sixth part of the *congius*, and the *congius* containing x *libræ*, or pounds, as it is manifest by that exquisite standard in *Rome*, with this inscription:

[d] Snellius in Eratosth. Batav. l. 2. cap. 2. [e] *Aly Kushgy*, who assisted *Ulug Beg* in compiling his astronomical tables in *Persian* (tables the most exact of any in the *East*) limits their breadth by six hairs of an horse. *Every digit is six barley-corns laid evenly together, and the breadth of every barley-corn is six hairs of an horse's tail.* Instit. Astron. Aly Cushgy, MS. [f] Villalpandus de apparatu urbis ac templi, par. 2. l. 3. c. 25. *Atque in universum illud unum monitos velim eos omnes, qui mensurarum ac ponderum cognoscendorum desiderio tenentur, ne à minimis incipiant examinare majora: nam vel minimus quisque error sæpius multiplicatus in magnum adducit errorum cumulum.* [g] Capellus de pond. & nummis, lib. 1. [h] Snell. in Eratosth. Bat. l. 2.
[i] *Wright* of the errors of navigation. [k] Luc. Pætus, l. 3. de mensur. & pond. Rom.
[l] Villalpandus de appar. urbis ac templi, par. 2. l. 3. c. 25.

GREAVES

IMP. CAESARE

VESPAS. VI

T. CAES. AVG. F. IIII cos

MENSVRÆ

EXACTAE IN

CAPITOLIO

P X [a]

[a] P X signifies *pondo decem.*

Again, the *congius* being the eighth part of the *amphora*, or *quadrantal*, filled with water or wine, as by the testimonies of [m] *Dioscorides*, [n] *Sex Pompeius*, and of an ancient anonymous *Greek* author, translated by *Alciat*, it doth appear: If therefore a vessel be made of a cubical figure, which may receive VIII *congii*, or XLVIII *sextarii*, or LXXXIV pounds of water or of wine, out of the sides of this cube, by [o] *Rhemnius Fannius* his description, or rather by *Sextus Pompeius*, who is ancienter, will the *Roman* foot be deduced. For both these write (neither is it as yet contradicted by any man) that the longitude of one of the sides of the *amphora* (being a cube) is answerable to the *Roman* foot. And here our enquiry would be at an end (supposing the authorities of *Festus* and *Fannius* to be unquestionable) were there not farther some objections, which cannot easily be removed. And those are first, a supposition that we have the true *Roman libra* (for by this we are to find the *congius*, admitting there were none extant, as by the *congius*, the *amphora*, or *quadrantal*) a thing of as great difficulty as the foot it self. And besides, if this were obtained, yet we cannot have an absolute certainty, that water, or wine, shall in all places alike ponderate; by reason of the different gravity which is observed in natural bodies, tho' they be homogeneous, and of a like substance. Wherefore laying aside all such speculations, as being far from that accurateness which is required, there is no other possible means left for this discovery, but to have recourse to such monuments of antiquity, as have escaped the injury and calamity of time; which is our next, and second enquiry.

And here it will not be amiss to see what learned men, who not long preceded our age have observed out of ancient monuments, concerning the *Roman* foot: And then to relate what course I took to give my self private satisfaction; which, I hope, will be also satisfactory to others. *Philander* in his commentaries upon *Vitruvius*, being one of the first that had seen, and diligently perused many ancient measures in *Rome* (whereas *Portius*, *Agricola*, *Glareanus*, and some others received them upon trust) gives us so much the more certain information. His words are these: [p] *Veruntamen quoniam non statim ex cujuscunque pollicibus, aut digitis, quis fuerit apud antiquos Romanus pes sciri potest, facturum me studiosis rem gratam putavi, si ad marginem libri semipedem apponerem, dimensum ex antiquo pede, in marmore, quod est in hortis Angeli Colotii Romæ sculpto, cujus etiam, nisi me fallit memoria, meminit Leonardus Porcius lib. de Sestertio. Eum enim pedem, nos cæteris qui circumferuntur, prætulimus, quòd conveniret cum eo, quem sculptum invenimus in alio marmoreo epitaphio T. Statilii Vol. Apri mensoris ædificiorum, quod operâ Jacobi Meleghini summi Pont. architecti ex janiculo non ita pridem refossum, in Vaticanum hortum translatum est. Quamvis jacentem in basilicâ apostolorum columnam ex porphyrite, cum his Græcis in calce literis* ΠΟΔ. Θ. *id est pedum novem, nos cum dimensi essemus, deprehenderimus non respondere nostro eum, quo usus fuerat ejus columnæ artifex, sed nostro esse majorem duobus scrupulis & besse, id est unciæ parte nonâ. Ut argumentum aliquod esse possit pedis Græci fuisse modulo scapum columnæ factum; quod facilius conjicere potuissem, si integra esset alia ex eodem lapide columna, quam in viâ latâ est conspicere jacentem, his in calce literis* ΠΟΔ. ΙΒ. *insignitam. Verùm quando stadium Herodoto, l. 2. Heroni, Suidæ, cæteris Græcis sit sexcentorum pedum; Plinio, Columellæ, cæteris Latinis sexcentorum viginti quinque nostrorum, necesse est Romanum à Græco semunciâ superari.* Thus far *Philander*. Not long after him, *Lucas Pætus*, having examined the foot on *T. Statilius tomb*, and that other of *Cossutius*, together with several ancient ones in brass, found amongst the *rudera* at *Rome*, concludes that the [q] true *Roman* foot, *Dictis duobus marmoreis comparatus, septima unciæ parte, sive unciæ scripulis tribus, & duabus scripuli sextulis, & sextulæ semisse brevior est.* Much about the same time I find in *Ciaconius*, out of *Latinus Latinius*, another experiment to have been made, by many eminent men together at *Rome*. *Superioribus autem annis* (saith [r] he) *Ant. Augustinus, qui postmodum fuit archiepiscopus Tarraconensis, Jo. Baptista Sighicellus episcopus Faventinus, P. Octavius, Pacatus, Achilles Maffæus, Achilles Statius, Benedictus Ægius, Fulvius Ursinus, Latinus Latinius,*

[m] Fragmenta Dioscoridis. [n] Sext. Pomp. Fest. de verb. signif. [o] Rhemn. Fann. Fragment.
[p] Philander in lib. 3. c. 3. Vitruvii. [q] Luc. Pætus, l. 1. de antiq. Rom. & Græc. intervall. mensuris.
[r] Ciaconius è Lat. Latinii observationibus de pede Rom.

cùm

cùm veram pedis Rom. quantitatem ſtatuere vellent, plures ejuſd. pedis menſuras ſimul contulerunt, & earum octo cum antiquiſſima dicti pedis forma, quæ in baſi quadam in hortis Vaticanis extat, adamuſſim convenire videntes, ex hoc pede quadrato vas confecerunt, quod etiam nunc octoginta aquæ, vel vini libras, quibus publicè ſignatis civitas utitur, omnino capere invenerunt, & cum octo congiis antiquis ita congruere, ut neque minus quidquam, neque amplius inter utraque eſſet. Quo experimento evidentiſſimè cognoverunt, & libras noſtri temporis cum antiquis Romanis eſſe eaſdem, cùm congii antiqui vas ſub Veſpaſiano Imp. ſignatum decem libras contineret, quot etiam noſtri temporis libras capit; & hunc eſſe juſtum pedem Romanum, cùm ex ejus modulo perfectum quadrantal octoginta libras contineat, quæ cum congii antiqui libris ad momentum reſpondent. Notwithſtanding theſe obſervations, *Villalpandus*, knowing how neceſſary it was to have the true dimenſions of the *Roman* foot, to find out the proportions of the *Hebrew* cubit, made new experiments: And after examination of the meaſures and weights at *Rome*, he thus concludes: [s] *Sed iis omnibus tam variis, aliiſque multis ſententiis prætermiſſis, in hac una conquieſcimus, ut arbitremur unum Farneſianum congium poſſe omnes antiquas Romanorum, atque aliarum gentium menſuras, omnidque pondera priſtinæ integritati reſtituere.* And in another place, *Quapropter aliis omnibus conjecturis, argumentationibus, æreis pedibus, marmoreis dimenſionibus, aut ſculpturis, quaſi maris fluctibus prætermiſſis, in hac una pedis longitudine, quaſi in portu conquieſcere jam tandem decrevimus.* Yet *Snellius* in his *Eratoſthenes Batavus* could not reſt ſatisfied with this foot of *Villalpandus*, how exquiſite ſoever he imagines it: For he had a mind to diſcover it nearer home; making the *Rhinland* foot equal to the *Roman*. The proof of this aſſertion is taken from an ancient *Roman armamentarium*, or fort, near the ſea, not far from *Leiden*, which by the natives is called, *Het huys te Briten*: And is ſuppoſed by *Ortelius* to have been built by *Claudius Cæſar*, in his intended voyage for *Britain*, of which [t] *Suetonius*, and *Dio*, make mention: *Sive in commodiorem legionum, cohortiumque tranſvectionem, ſive quo milites hibernarent* (ſaith Ortelius.) *Arcis ipſius fundamenta*, (according to [u] *Snellius*) *quadrata ſunt forma, & quaquaverſum ducentis quadraginta Rhinlandicis pedibus patent. Ut vel hinc Romanæ menſuræ veſtigia quàm planiſſimè agnoſcas. Nam ipſius podiſmus duorum Romanorum jugerum magnitudinem complectitur. Jugeri enim menſuram ducentos & quadraginta longitudinis pedes eſſe, non eſt ferè quiſquam qui ignoret, inquit Quintilianus, l. 1. cap. X. Varro de re ruſtica libro 1. cap. X. Jugerum quod quadratos duos actus habet. Actus quadratus, qui & latus eſt pedes 120 & longus totidem. Is modius, ac mina Latina appellatur, ut mihi planè dubium non videatur, eos hic Romanæ menſuræ modum ſecutos, hujus ſtructuræ podiſmum ita comprehendiſſe ſecundum jugeri menſuram, ut duo jugera, vel actus quatuor contineret. Frontinus de limitibus. Hi duo fundi juncti jugerum definiunt, deinde hæc duo jugera juncta in unum quadratum agrum efficiunt, quòd ſint omnes actus bini: Ut ſingula ideò latera ducentos & quadraginta pedes in longum patêre neceſſe ſit. Atqui totidem pedibus Rhinlandicis ſingula latera exporrigi Geodætarum experientia confirmat. Unde efficitur Romanum antiquum pedem noſtro Rhinlandico planè æquari.*

After theſe experiments of ſo many able and learned men, and thoſe too taken from ancient monuments, it may ſeem ſtrange, that we ſhould not be able as yet to define the true quantity of the *Roman* foot. For this I can aſſign no other reaſons than theſe: Firſt that thoſe which have deſcribed it, have either not exactly, and with ſuch diligence as was requiſite, performed it; or elſe, if they have been circumſpect in this kind, they have omitted to compare it with the ſtandards for meaſures of other nations. On the contrary thoſe which have compared it with the preſent ſtandards, never took it from the ancient monuments, and originals, which are at *Rome*, but only from ſome draughts, or ſchemes delineated in books. Now how uncertain a way this is, doth appear by [x] *Villalpandus*, who thus writes: *Ego dum hæc ſcriberem, hunc Colotianum pedem circino expendi, & in annotationibus Guil. Philandri ſolertiſſimi viri, & apud Georgium Agricolam, & apud Lucam Pætum, & Staniſlaum Orſepſium, & nullum potui reperire alteri æqualem, imo verò neque ejuſdem pedis aſſignatas ſimiles partes.* The ſame have I obſerved in thoſe *Roman* feet deſcribed by *Portius*, *Agricola*, *Philander*, *Pætus*, *Ciaconius*, and *Villalpandus* himſelf, that they differ one from another. And not only ſo, but thoſe of the ſame author, in the ſame impreſſion, are likewiſe different. Which laſt muſt ariſe, either by the diverſe extention of the paper in the preſs, when it is moiſt, or by the unequal contraction of it, when it grows dry, or by ſome other accident, in the beating and binding. So that tho' it were granted, that ſo many learned men had found out what we enquire after, the *Roman* foot; yet it is im-

[s] Villalpandi apparatus urbis ac templi, par. 2. l. 3. c. 25. [t] Suetonius in Claudio. Dio Hiſt. Rom. l. 60. [u] Snell. in Eratoſth. Bat. l. 2. c. 2. [x] Villalpan. de apparatu urbis ac templi, par. 2. l. 3. c. 25.

possible out of those schemes and draughts delivered in their books, for the reason before specified, to attain an absolute certainty. But [y] *Snellius* shews us a remedy of this difficulty, which, in my opinion, is as vain as his *Roman* foot, (seeing by his supposition all paper must shrink alike, be it thick or thin) and that is, to allow one part in sixty for the shrinking of the paper. *For so much* (saith he) *do typographers observe, that letters contract themselves, when they are taken off wet from the types.*

Wherefore having received small satisfaction from the writings of the ancients, and not much better from the imperfect designations of the *Roman* foot, by modern authors, I proposed to my self in my travels abroad, these ways, which no reasonable man but must approve of. And those were, First, to examine as many ancient measures and monuments, in *Italy*, and other parts, as it was possible. And, Secondly, To compare these with as many standards, and originals, as I could procure the sight of. And last of all, to transmit both these, and them, to posterity, I exactly measured some of the most lasting monuments of the ancients. To this purpose, in the year 1639, I went into *Italy*, to view, as the other antiquities of the *Romans*, so especially those of weights and measures; and to take them with as much exactness as it was possible, I carried instruments with me made by the best artizans.

Where my first enquiry was after that monument of *T. Statilius Vol. Aper*, in the *Vatican* gardens, from whence [z] *Philander* took the dimensions of the *Roman* foot, as others have since borrowed it from him. In the copying out of this upon an *English* foot in brass, divided into 2000 parts, I spent at least two hours, (which I mention, to shew with what diligence I proceeded in this, and the rest) so often comparing the several divisions, and digits of it, respectively one with another, that I think more circumspection could not have been used; by which I plainly discovered the rudeness and insufficiency of that foot. For besides that the length of it is somewhat too much, (whatsoever [a] *Latinius* out of an observation made by *Ant. Augustinus, Sighicellus, Pacatus, Maffæus, Statius, Ægius* and *Fulvius Ursinus*, pretend to the contrary) there is never a digit that is precisely answerable to one another. Howsoever it contains 1944 such parts, as the *English* foot contains 2000.

My next search was for the foot on the monument of *Cossutius*, *in hortis Colotianis*, from whence it hath since received its denomination, (tho' it be now removed) being termed by writers, *pes Colotianus.* This foot I took with great care, as it did well deserve, being very fair and perfect: Afterwards collating it with that *Roman* foot, which *Lucas Pætus* caused to be engraved in the Capitol, in a white marble stone, I found them exactly to agree; and therefore I did wonder, why he should condemn this with his pen (for he makes some [b] objections against it) which notwithstanding he hath erected with his hands (as appears by the inscription in the Capitol, CURANTE LU: PAETO.) It may be, upon second thoughts, he afterward privately retracted his error, which he was not willing to publish to the world. Now this of *Cossutius* is 1934 such parts, as the *English* foot contains 2000.

Next I sought after that porphyry column mentioned by [c] *Marlianus*, as also by [d] *Philander*, and others, with this inscription, ΠΟΔ. Θ. For if the length of that column were assigned according to the proportion of the *Greek* foot, then would the *Roman* foot be thence deduced; this (as I shall elsewhere shew) containing 24 such parts, as that contained 25: Or if it were made according to the *Roman* foot; as the *Grecians* after their subjection to the *Roman* empire, often used the same measures that the *Romans* did, then had I my desire. But the column being defaced or lost my labour was in vain: And it seems [e] *Pætus* about LXX years before made the same enquiry with as little satisfaction.

I should be too tedious in describing the several feet which I have perused in brass, found amongst the *rudera* at *Rome*, and carefully preserved by antiquaries: Of most of which *Peireskius* hath given a good character, in some letters of his, which I have seen in the hands of *Buchardus*, a learned man, not yet printed; [f] who thus writes: *I cannot sufficiently wonder at the inequality which I have found in the divisions by digits, and inches, of the ancient* Roman *feet; which seem to me to have been made for fashion-sake,* & dicis causâ *(as lamps that are found in tombs incapable of oil) more to express the mystery and profession of those that were to use them, than to regulate the measures of any thing besides them.*

Besides these, I examined the ancient structures of the *Romans*, hoping by collating one with another, to deduce the

[y] *Pars sexagesima typorum & formarum longitudini excussis decedit, quemadmodum à diligentibus & peritis typographis sciscitando edoctus sum.* Snell. in Eratosth. Batavo. l. 2. c. 1.

[z] Philander in l. 3. c. 3. Vitruvii.

[a] Ciaconius è Latino Latinio.

[b] Luc. Pætus l. 1. de Antiq. Rom. & Græc. intervall. mensuris.

[c] Marlianus de Antiq. urbis.

[d] Philander in lib. 3. c. 3. Vitruvii.

[e] Luc. Pætus l. 1. de. Antiq. Rom. & Græc. interval. mensuris.

[f] Ex Epistolis Peireskii MSS.

dimension

dimension of their foot. For I presumed, that those excellent architects, before they began their work, must necessarily propose some models to themselves, according to the proportion of which, they meant to raise their fabricks: Which proportions could not be assigned, but in the parts of some common and received quantity; and this in probability was the *Roman* foot; being a measure generally used, and by publick authority prescribed. Upon which grounds I measured *the stones in the foundation of the Capitol,* Domitian'*s, or rather* Vespatian'*s amphitheatre, the triumphal arks of* Titus *and* Severus, *together with that of* Constantine *the great, and above all that exquisite temple of the* Pantheon, built by *Agrippa*, I know not whether with more cost or art: Concerning which [x] *Sebastianus Serlius* is of opinion, *That if all rules of architecture were lost, they might be revived out of this monument alone.* And in truth, this place gave me more satisfaction than any other: For most of the white marble stones on the pavement, contained exactly three of those *Roman* feet on *Cossutius*'s monument, and the lesser stones in porphyry contained one and an half.

But yet I thought this not sufficient, unless I went to *Terracina*, which is the ancient *Anxur*, and LIII miles distant from *Rome:* Having read in [y] *Andreas Schottus*, out of *Pighius*'s *Hercules Prodicius*, that near the sea by the *Via Appia*, in the height of a white rock, whence that of [z] *Horace*,

Impositum saxis latè candentibus Anxur,

There are described the *Roman decempedæ*. And indeed the place is very memorable, for the whiteness, altitude, and hardness of the rock, which notwithstanding is cut away perpendicularly, on the side towards the *Tyrrhene* sea, above an hundred and twenty feet in depth, to make passage for the *Appian* way; and at the space of every *decempeda*, these characters X XX XXX *&c.* (being almost *cubitales)* are fairly engraven, in a continued order, descending to CXX. Measuring below the distance between CXX and CX, it amounted to IX *English* feet, and $\frac{1284}{2000}$ of a foot, computing it from the [a] line engraven above CXX, to the line next under CX. The rest I examined with my eyes, by often comparing the distance between CXX and CX, whether it were equal to that between CX and C, and this again (ascending upwards) to that between C and XC; which manner, though it be uncertain and conjectural, and far from that exactness I used in all others, yet it was the best means I could then put in practice; and I am confident, that whosoever shall measure those spaces, shall find a manifest inequality. To which opinion I am rather induced, because measuring there, in several places, the breadth of the *Appian* way, cut out of the same rock, I found a difference sometimes of one or two inches, or more. It being in one place XIII *English* feet, and $\frac{1622}{2000}$ of a foot; in another, XIII feet and $\frac{1882}{2000}$; in a third XIII and $\frac{1271}{2000}$. Whereby I concluded, that the ancients, in making that way, had not respect to a mathematical point, (as it was not necessary) but only that if any difference were, it should not be sensible. And such differences have I observed in the white *Corinthian* pillars, in the *Pantheon* beforementioned, of above an inch or two, in the circuit of the *Scapus* near the *Torus:* which inequality, seeing no eye could discover, the masters of that exquisite work did justly contemn. Whereas the porphyry stones, and those of white marble, on the pavement, are sized so even, and so exactly to the proportions of the *Roman* foot, that nothing can be more accurate. And this the nature of the work required; for the temple being round, (which hath occasioned the *Italians* vulgarly to call it the *Rotundo)* the circle within could not so exquisitely have been filled up, if there had not been a special care taken in observing the true dimensions in every particular stone. But to return to the rock at *Anxur:* The spaces between those characters, to an eye that shall be intentively fixed upon them, will be apparently different. So that I concur in opinion with [b] *Schottus*, that those figures were placed there, *to give notice to posterity, how much of the rock had been removed, to make passage for the* Appian *way*; and not for any memorial of the *Roman* measures.

Having measured those places in the *Appian* way at *Terracina*, I made trial of at least XX others between *Terracina* and *Naples*, without any great satisfaction; and therefore, partly the incertainty that I found there, and partly the danger of thieves, discouraged me from measuring the *Roman milliare*; a work conceived to be of great use, for the discovery of the *Roman* foot. Seeing the *miliare* containing *mille passus*, as the very name imports, and every *passus* consisting of five feet, as [c] *Columella*, and [d] *Isidorus* expresly tell us; here therefore would be five thousand feet

[x] Sebast. Serl. delle Antichita. [y] Andr. Schot. Ititinerar. [z] Horat. l. 1. Serm. Sat. 5.

[a] See at the end of this book the figure of these characters, as they are cut in the rock at *Anxur*, with lines encompassing them. [b] Schotti Itiner. [c] Columella de re rust. l. 5.

[d] Isidorus, l. 15. c. 15. Origin.

GREAVES to help us to one, could there be but found out a perfect *Roman* mile. And this I imagined might probably be discovered amongst those many *vestigia* of *Roman* ways, which to this day are frequently seen in *Italy*. Wherefore conferring with *Gasparo Berti*, a man curious and judicious, (as appears by his ichnography of *Roma subterranea* in *Bosius*) as also with *Lucas Holstenius*, a learned companion of *Cluverius*, in those honourable travels of his, for the restauration of the ancient geography: they both informed me that there are still in the *Appian* way, where it passes over the *Pomptinæ Paludes*, several *columnæ*, or *lapides milliarii*, standing; whereby the *Romans* divided and distinguished their miles; and which occasioned those phrases, *ad primum, ad quartum, ad centesimum lapidem*, and the like. And these, it may be, at the first were ordinary stones, till *C. Gracchus* caused columns to be erected in their places: Διαμετρήσας κατὰ μίλιον ὁδὸν πᾶσαν (τὸ δὲ μίλιον ὀκτὼ σταδίων ὀλίγον ἀποδεῖ) κίονας λιθίνους σημεῖα τοῦ μέτρου κατέστησεν. *He measured out,* saith [e] *Plutarch, by miles, all the ways, the mile containing little less than eight* stadia, *and placed columns of stone to design the measure.* The thing was of that ornament and use, as that it was afterwards taken up, and continued by the *Roman* emperors; as appears by these inscriptions, which are fairly engraven on the first column, found amongst the ruins in the *Appian* way, and from thence lately removed into the Capitol, by order of the [f] Senate and people of *Rome.*

I

IMP. CAESAR
VESPASIANVS. AVG
PONTIF. MAXIM
TRIB. POTESTAT. VII
IMP. XVII P. P. CENSOR
COS. VII DESIGN. VIII

Below this, on the end of the Scapus.

IMP. NERVA. CAESAR
AVGVSTVS. PONTIFEX
MAXIMVS. TRIBVNICIA
POTESTATE. COS. III PATER
PATRIAE REFECIT

Below this, on the basis of the same pillar.

IMP. CAESARI. DIVI
TRAIANI. PARTHICI. F.
DIVI. NERVAE NEPOTI
TRAIANO. HADRIANO
AVG. PONTIF. MAXIM
TRIB. POTEST. II COS. II
VIATORES. QVI. IPSI. ET. COS. ET
PR. CETERISQVE. MAGISTRATIB.
APPARENT. ET. H. V.

To these I shall also add the inscription of another *columna milliaria*, not extant in *Gruterus*, or any other, that I know, which I have seen at *Terracina*; the column being exactly of the same magnitude with the former, but wanting by the injury of time, a basis below, and a globe of nigh three feet diameter on the top, serving instead of a capital, both which the former hath.

X.[g]

IMP. CAESAR.
DIVI. NERVAE
FILIVS. NERVA
TRAIANVS. AVG
GERMANICVS
DACICVS
PONTIF. MAX
TRIB. POT XIIII
IMP. VI COS. V P. P
XVIIII SILICE. SVA. PECVNIA
STRAVIT

LIII

If

[e] Plutarchus in Gracchis.

[f] S. P. Q. R.
COLVMNAM MILIARIAM
PRIMI. AB. VRBE. LAPIDIS. INDICEM
AB. IMPP. VESPASIANO. ET. NERVA
RESTITVTAM
DE. RVINIS. SVBVRBANIS. VIAE. APPIAE.
IN. CAPITOLIVM. TRANSTVLIT

[g] The figure X signifies the distance of *Terracina* from the next city, or town, in the way to *Rome*: And that was *ad Medias*: A place so called, either because it was *ad Medias Paludes*, or else because it was in the mid-way, almost between *Terracina* and *Appii Forum*: For it was X miles from *Terracina*, and IX from *Appii Forum*; as appears by the *itinerarium Hierosolymitanum* in *Berbius*.

2 Appii

If therefore two such columns were found entire, (as I am informed there are four or five in the *decennovium*, standing in a continued order) the distance between two such being exactly measured, would much conduce to the discovery of the *Roman* foot. Upon which supposition I had almost resolved to have gone thither, as I did to other places, with no other intention, but only to have been a spectator of those columns, and to have trusted to mine own hands, in taking their distances. But upon a more deliberate examination of the business, I perceived that this enquiry did depend upon a very nice supposition: for if the *decempedatores*, or *curatores viarum*, proceeded not with extreme caution, and aimed almost at a mathematical point, in designing the just space of each particular mile (which in a work of that length is not probable; where the inequality of many feet could not be discerned by the eye, and might be admitted without any blemish. For in [h] *Varro's* judgment, *Sensus nullus quod abest mille passus sentire potest)* it could not be, but the same differences, or somewhat like, must have crept in with them, which have been observed amongst us, in our measured and statute miles; out of which it would be a vain attempt exactly to demonstrate the *English* foot. The neglect of which circumspection, amongst some other reasons that may be assigned, I take to be one, of the diversities which astronomers found in that memorable observation, made in the plains of *Singiar*, or *Sinar*, by the command of *Almamon* the renowned califf of *Babylon*, about eight hundred years since, in proportioning the magnitude of a degree upon earth. For having taken the altitude of the pole at two several stations, differing a degree in the heavens, they measured the distance between these stations on earth, going on in the same meridian; where [i] *some of them*, says *Abulfeda*, *found it to be fifty six miles, and two thirds*; *others fifty six*, *without any fraction*. If therefore the *Roman decempedatores*, or *geodætæ*, used not more circumspection than the *Babylonian* astronomers (which is not likely) there can be no trust given to their miles, and less trust to the foot that shall be deduced from thence.

Wherefore to come to a conclusion; having made enquiry more ways than it may be any man hath done, and I think with as much caution and exactness as any, it will be necessary after all, to shew amongst so many feet, as are taken to be *Roman*, which I conceive to be the most genuine and true. And though in such an uncertainty and scarcity of ancient monuments, and in such a diversity of opinions, among modern writers, it may seem too great presumption, positively to define the magnitude of the *Roman* foot; yet having had the opportunity to have perused in this kind, more antiquities than any that have preceded, I may with the more confidence conclude, that the *pes Colotianus*, in my judgment, is the true *Roman* foot; and that for these reasons.

For first, It most exactly agrees with some very ancient and perfect *Roman* feet in brass, found long since amongst the *ru-*

Appii Forum
Ad Medias IX.
Taracina X.

The figure LIII below, signifies the distance of *Terracina* from *Rome*: which distance may be further proved out of *Appian*, in his third book of the civil wars, speaking of *Augustus*: Ὄντι αὐτῷ περὶ Ταρρακίνας ἀπὸ τετρακοσίων τῆς Ῥώμης σταδίων. *Being about* Tarracina, *which is distant* CCCC stadia *from* Rome. The *stadia* reduced to miles, if we allow VII *Greek stadia* and an half to a *Roman* mile, as *Suidas* doth, will make up LIII miles, and one third part of a mile; that is, two *stadia* and a half over and above. Which fraction *Appian* neglects; and therefore uses the round number CCCC *stadia*, for LIII miles.

The figure XVIIII signifies the *decennovium*, or way passing over the fens, between *Appii Forum* and *Terracina*: so denominated, because it contained nineteen miles in length: which may also be proved out of *Procopius*, where he speaks of the δεκαεννεάσιον. This way was paved by *Trajan*, as the inscription shews, and I think first of all by him. Long after it was repaired by *Theodoricus*, according to another inscription that I have seen at *Terracina*, of which *Gruterus* and *Cluverius* also make mention; where, omitting the titles of *Theodoricus*, in the marble we find these words engraven:

DECENNOVII. VIAE. APPIAE. ID. EST. A. TRIP
VSQVE. TERRACENAM. ITER. ET. LOCA. QVAE
CONFLVENTIBVS. AB. VTRAQVE. PARTE. PALVDVM
PER. OMNES. RETRO. PRINCIPVM. INVNDAVERANT
VSVI. PVBLICO. ET. SECVRITATI. VIANTIVM
RESTITVIT. . . . . PER
PLVRIMOS. QVI. ANTE. NON. ERANT. ALBEOS
. . . . DEDVCTA. IN. MARE. AQVA

By this number XVIIII signifying the *decennovium*, and by the *itinerarium Hierosolymitanum*, we may safely correct the *itinerarium Antonini*, in which *Terracina* is placed but XVIII miles distant from *Appii Forum*. And from hence likewise we may certainly know, how far the Christians went to meet St. *Paul*, and that was XXXIV miles. For so much was *Appii Forum* distant from *Rome*, if we subduct XVIIII out of LIII; whereas the itineraries of *Bertius* edition make it more.

[h] Varro de L. L. lib. 5. [i] Abulf. Geogr. Arab. MS.

dera

dera at *Rome*; eſpecially with that excellent one (as I remember) of *F. Urſinus*, a learned antiquary. Tho' I cannot deny but that I have ſeen two ancient feet in braſs different from this; the one of *Gualdus*, a very fair one, wanting two parts and a half, of ſuch as this contains a thouſand, a ſmall and inconſiderable difference. The ſecond of *Gottiſridus*, a gentleman of honourable quality, (to whom I ſtand obliged for the free donation of ſeveral antiquities) which exceeds it by eight parts; but this laſt hath been made by a very rude and unſkilful hand.

Next, the proportions of almoſt all the white marble ſtones, as alſo of thoſe leſſer in porphyry, in the pavement of that admirable temple of the *Pantheon*, are either compleatly three of theſe feet, or one and a half; which, it is not probable, and in a ſtructure of ſo much art, ſhould have been the work of chance. Add to this the dimenſions of ſeveral ſtones in the foundation of the capitol, in *Titus* and *Severus*, triumphal arches, correſponding either to the whole foot, or conjointly to the whole, and ſome *uncia*, or digits of it.

Thirdly, The inſcription on the ſame monument where this foot is found, of the *circinus*, the *libella*, the *norma*, and the like, plainly ſhew, that theſe were intended to expreſs *Coſſutius*'s profeſſion, (whom [k] *Pœtus* imagines to have been a *ſculptor*) and this being intended, I ſee no reaſon why the *Roman* foot ſhould have been cut in ſo fair a relevy, either too ſhort, or too long; when the ſame hand, and the ſame pains, might have made it exact. It is true, that the foot upon *Statilius*'s tomb, is 1944 ſuch parts. as this is but 1934; whereof the *Engliſh* foot taken by me from the iron yard, or ſtandard of three feet, in *Guild-Hall* in *London*, contains 2000: But how rudely, in reſpect of digits, that foot of *Statilius* is deſcribed, I have before diſcovered. And therefore I wonder that [l] *Philander* in his commentaries upon *Vitruvius*, ſhould in a matter of ſuch high concernment in architecture, proceed with ſo much inadvertency, affirming that between this of *Statilius*, and that of *Coſſutius*, there is no difference. And if he a mathematician hath thus erred, (tho' commonly men verſed in thoſe ſciences take not up things at too cheap a rate, without due examination) what opinion may we conceive of another obſervation, made at the ſame moment, by [m] *Ant. Auguſtianus*, *Jo. Baptiſta Sighicellus*, *P. Octavius Pacatus*, *Achilles Maffæus*, *Achilles Statius*, *Benedictus Ægius*, *Fulvius Urſinus*, *Latinus Latinius*, with as many ancient feet as there were men preſent? I ſhrewdly ſuſpect they ſlubbered over their obſervation, as not regarding in nineteen hundred parts and better, the ſmall exceſs or defect of ten parts; or not rightly apprehending what might be the conſequences of ſuch an error, how little ſoever, in meaſuring the vaſt magnitude of the terreſtrial globe, or of the celeſtial bodies.

Laſtly, Beſides the authorities of *Portius Vicentinus*, *Georgius Agricola*, *Glareanus*, *Ghetaldus*, *Donatus*, and of many other learned and judicious men, who approve of this *pes Colotianus*, (tho' bare authority is the worſt, becauſe the weakeſt kind of argument) that excellent *congius* of *Veſpaſian*, now extant in *Rome*, ſo highly and ſo juſtly magnified by [n] *Villalpandus*, may likewiſe ſerve to confirm, if not totally my aſſertion, yet thus far, that I have not exceeded in aſſigning the true longitude: For by the clear evidences of [o] *Dioſcorides*, and of an *anonymous author* before cited, eight *congii* are the juſt meaſure of the *Roman amphora*, or *quadrantal*; and again by as many teſtimonies of [p] *Sextus Pompeius*, and [q] *Rhemnius Fannius*, each of the ſides of the *amphora* is equal in longitude to the *Roman* foot. Wherefore having procured by ſpecial favour the *congius* of *Veſpaſian*, I took the meaſure of it with [r] *milium* (being next to water, very proper for ſuch a work) carefully prepared and cleanſed, which being done with much diligence I cauſed a cube to be made anſwerable to the true dimenſion of the *pes Colotianus*; filling up the capacity of which, and often reiterating the ſame experiment, I found continually the exceſs of about half a *congius* to remain, and that an *amphora* made by the *pes Colotianus*, would contain but VII *congii*, and about an half. And therefore I cannot ſufficiently wonder at the obſervation [ſ] of *Ant. Aguſtianus*, *Pacatus*, *Maffæus*, *Statinius*, *Urſinus*, and others, with a cube of that foot which is deſcribed on *Statilius*'s monument: who affirm the *quadrantal* of this exactly to contain eight of theſe *congii* of *Veſpaſian*: Whereas upon due examination I confidently affirm, that they have erred. And therefore [t] *Villal-*

[k] Luc. Pætus, lib. 1. de antiq. Rom. & Græc. interval. menſuris. [l] Philander in l. 3. c. 3. Vitruvii. [m] Ciaconius è Latini Latinii obſerv. de pede Rom. [n] Villalpandus, l. 2. diſp. 2. c. 11. de apparatu urbis ac templi. [o] Fragmenta Dioſcoridis. [p] Sext. Pomp. Feſtus de verb. ſignif. [q] Rhemn. Fann. carm. fragm. [r] It had been better to have made my experiment with water, and then to have weighed it with an exact balance: but becauſe no balances are found in *Rome* ſo exact as with us, I was fain to meaſure it with *milium*. [ſ] Ciaconius è Latini Latinii obſervationibus de pede Rom. *Cum veram pedis Rom. quantitatem ſtatuere vellent ejuſd. pedis menſuras ſimul contulerunt, & earum octo cum antiquiſſima dicti pedis forma, quæ in baſi quadam in hortis Vaticanis exſtat, adamuſſim convenire videntes, ex hoc pede quadrato vas confecerunt*, &c. Vide ſupra. [t] Villalp. de apparatu urbis ac templi, par. 2. l. 3. c. 25.

pandus

pandus, in this particular, with more judgment and ingenuity hath published his observations, concerning the measure, and precise weight of *Vespasian*'s *congius*, than any other whatsoever. Altho' I cannot be induced to assent to that deduction, which he infers of the *Roman* foot, (from the side of a *quadrantal* containing eight of these *congii*) relying upon the authorities of *Festus* and *Fannius*, against so many evidences produced to the contrary. Wherefore as he is singular in his opinion (for there is not one author of credit which follows his assertion) so is his foot as singular, there being not one of at least ten ancient ones, in the hands of several antiquaries (besides those inscribed on two monuments in *Rome*) which arrive to the proportions of his, by XXVII parts in two thousand. As for those other fancies of his (for they are no better) of describing also the *Roman* foot, by the altitude of *Vespasian*'s *congius*, and assigning the [u] *latus cubicum* of the *modius*, the *semicongius*, the *sextarius*, and *hemina*, from certain parallel circles circumscribed about it, (which certainly, as the scheme of the *congius* it self, drawn by me to the full proportion, shews, were delineated without any farther intention than for ornament) I do not think them worth the computation.

And therefore it will be much better, to give some solution to those authorities of *Sextus Pompeius*, and *Rhemnius Fannius*, alledged by him. For the objection which may be raised thence is very material: How the *pes Colotianus* can be the true *Roman* foot, since it is confessed by me, that it doth not precisely answer to the sides of a *quadrantal*, or cube, containing eight of those *congii* of *Vespasian*, or XLVIII *sextarii*? Whereas on the contrary, *Festus* expresly writes, that the *quadrantal* was the square (he means the cube) of the *Roman* foot. [x] *Quadrantal vocabant antiqui, quam ex Græco amphoram dicunt, quod vas pedis quadrati, octo & quadraginta capit sextarios.* And [y] *Fannius* confirms the same.

Pes longo spatio, latóque notetur in anglo,
Angulus ut par sit, quem claudit linea triplex.
Quatuor ex quadris medium cingatur inane:
Amphora fit cubus: Quam ne violare liceret,
Sacravere Jovi Tarpeio in monte Quirites.

We might elevate their authorities by saying, these are only the testimonies of two grammarians, better versed in disputes of words, than critical in measures, which more properly are the speculation of mathematicians: And therefore if *Vitruvius* had affirmed it, much more credit might have been given. But we shall rather say, they wrote what was vulgarly, and commonly, upon tradition, believed, that the length of one of the sides of the *amphora* was equal to the *Roman* foot: Not that it was precisely and exactly equal, but that of any known measure whatsoever then extant, this came the nearest to it, as indeed it doth; yea, so near, that if at this day the *amphora*, and *Roman* foot, were in use amongst us, many a writer that had never been so curious as diligently to compare them, would not be scrupulous to affirm as much. Which may appear by the practice of *Ant. Augustinus*, *Pacatus*, *Maffæus*, *Statius*, *Ursinus*, and of several other learned men, not long before our times: Who tho' they purposely made it their inquiry to discover the true *Roman* weights and measures, and therefore made special use of this *congius* of *Vespasian*, yet have no less erred, as we shewed before, in the dimension of the *amphora*, than both *Festus* and *Fannius* have done. Neither will this answer seem improbable concerning measures, if we shall examine a place or two concerning coins, in which the ancients, and those too of the better sort of authors, have in the very same manner erred. For [z] *Livy* writing that *Marcellus* gave to *L. Bantius*, (or *Bandius*) 1Ↄ *bigati*, that is *denarii* (so called, because the *biga* was ordinarily stamped upon the reverse of the *denarius*:) [a] *Plutarch* describing the same gift, renders it by 1Ↄ many *drachmæ*, the *Grecian* manner of computation; not that the *drachma*, in the exact and intrinsical valuation, was equal then to the *denarius*, or the *denarius* to the *drachma* (as we shall shew in the ensuing discourse) but that in the vulgar and popular estimation, the one passed for the other, being both not much different in their weight, as well as valuation. [b] Likewise *Dio* informs us, that *Octavius* promised the *Veteran* soldiers 1Ↄ *drachmæ* a man: Whereas [c] *Cicero* expressing the same thing to *Atticus*, terms them 1Ↄ *denarii*. And *Suetonius* writes, that *Cæsar*, by testament, gave to each of the common people, *sestertia trecenta*, that is, LXXV *denarios*; which [d] *Plutarch*, both in the life of *Brutus*, and of *Antonius*, renders δραχμὰς ἑβδομήκοντα πέντε, *seventy five drachms*. In the like manner we may say, that *Festus* and *Fannius* have described the *amphora* by the *Roman* foot; not as if this were the exact measure of it, but as being the most known and nearest proportion, in which, without falling into fractions, it might evenly and roundly be expressed.

And thus have we finished our enquiry after the *Roman* foot: Our next labour should be to compare it with the present standards, and originals, for measures of divers nations. For which I must refer the reader to this ensuing table.

[u] *Vides etiam latus cubicum, modii, semicongii, sextarii, heminæ*, &c. Villalp. ibidem.
[x] Sext. Pomp. Festus de verb. signif. [y] Rhemn. Fannii carmina de pond. & mensuris.
[z] Livius, l. 23. [a] Plutarchus in Marcello. [b] Dio, l. 45. in Cæsare Octav.
[c] Cicero, l. 16. 5 ep. ad Atticum. [d] Plut. in Bruto. Idem in Antonio.

 The

SEMIPES ROM.

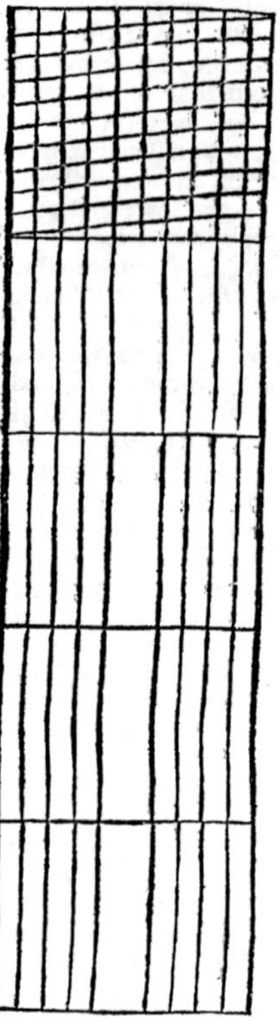

The Roman *FOOT compared with the measures of divers Nations.*

SUCH Parts as the *Roman* foot, or that on the monument of *Cossutius* in *Rome*, contains	1000	
The foot on the monument of *Statilius* in *Rome*, contains	1005	[illegible]
The foot of *Villalpandus*, deduced from the *Congius* of *Vespasian*, contains	1019	65
The ancient *Greek* foot, being in proportion to the ancient *Roman* foot, as XXV to XXIV, contains	1041	67
The *English* foot	1034	13
The *Paris* foot	1104	45
The *Venetian* foot	1201	65
The *Rhinland* foot, or that of *Snellius*	1068	25
The *derah*, or cubit, at *Cairo* in *Ægypt*	1886	25
The *Persian arish*	3306	10
The greater *Turkish* pike, at *Constantinople*	2275	08
The lesser *Turkish* pike, at *Constantinople*, is in proportion to the greater, as 31 to 32		
The *braccio* at *Florence*	1978	28
The *braccio*, for woollen, at *Siena*	1284	38
The *braccio*, for linen, at *Siena*	2041	37
The *braccio* at *Naples*	2171	66
The *canna* at *Naples*	7114	79
The *vara* at *Almaria*, and at *Gibraltar*, in *Spain*	2854	19
Il palmo di Architetti, at *Rome*; whereof X make the *canna di Architetti*	756	98
Il palmo del braccio di Mercantia, & di tessito di tela, at *Rome*; this and the former are both engraven in a white marble-stone in the Capitol, with this inscription, *Curante Lu. Pæto*	719	24
The *Genoa* palm	842	81
The *Antwerp* ell	2360	91
The *Amsterdam* ell	2345	40
The *Leyden* ell	2337	13

The English *FOOT, taken from the Iron-Standard at* Guild-Hall *in* London, *and compared with the Standards for Measures of divers Nations.*

SUCH parts as the *English* foot contains	1000
The *Roman* foot, or that on the monument of *Cossutius* in *Rome*, contains	967
The foot on the monument of *Statilius* in *Rome*, contains	972
The foot of *Villalpandus*, deduced from the *congius* of *Vespasian*, contains	986
The *Greek* foot	1007 22/100
The *Paris* foot	1068
The *Venetian* foot	1162
The *Rhinland* foot, or that of *Snellius*	1033
The *derah*, or cubit, at *Cairo* in *Ægypt*	1824
The *Persian arish*	3197
The greater *Turkish pike*, at *Constantinople*	2200
The lesser *Turkish pike* at *Constantinople*, is in proportion to the greater, as 31 to 32	
The *braccio* at *Florence*	1913
The *braccio* for woollen, at *Siena*	1242
The *braccio* for linen, at *Siena*	1974
The *braccio* at *Naples*	2100
The *canna* at *Naples*	6880
The *vera* at *Almaria*, and at *Gibraltar* in *Spain*	2760
Il palmo di Architetti, at *Rome*; whereof X make the *canna di Architetti*	732
Il palmo del Braccio di Mercantia, & di tessito di Tela, at *Rome*; this and the former are both engraven in a white marble-stone in the Capitol, with this inscription, *Curante Lu. Pæto*	695 1/2
The *Genoa* palm	815
The *Antwerp* ell	2283
The *Amsterdam* ell	2268
The *Leyden* ell	2260

This table I made by the standards, the former by proportion.

Of

Of the DENARIUS.

AS I have made for meaſures, the *Roman* foot the foundation of my enquiry, and therefore have handled it in the precedent treatiſe: So for finding out of weights, I ſhall take the *denarius* as an undeniable principle, from whence thoſe of the ancients, by a neceſſary conſequence may be inferred. For as the unity is in reſpect of numbers, or the *ſeſtertius* in diſcourſes *de re nummariâ*; ſo is the *denarius* for weights, a fit riſe, or beginning, from whence the reſt may be deduced. Not but that it were better (as I gave the caution before) if we abſolutely conſider the exacteſt ways of diſcovering weights, to begin with the greater, and by them to find out the leſs, than by the leſs to produce the greater; but if we look upon the condition of times, and conſider the means that are left after ſo many revolutions and changes of the *Roman* empire, it will be ſafer to alter our method. For to this day there are many thouſand *denarii* left and amongſt theſe ſome ſo perfect and entire, as if they had been but newly brought from the mint; whereas of the *Roman libræ*, and ounces, there are but few extant, if compared with theſe. *Lipſius*, and *Gruterius*, in their inſcriptions mention ſome, and *Pætus* ſome others, beſides ſuch as I have ſeen in the hands of antiquaries, and many of mine own: Moſt of which differ from one another, either as having been conſumed by ruſt and time, or it may alſo be by the men that then lived, for their advantage leſſened: A thing too often practiſed amongſt us. Wherefore I think it more convenient by the *denarius* to deduce the proof and evidence of theſe, than by the diverſity and uncertainty of theſe to conclude the *denarius*: And yet if ſome of the beſt and faireſt of them ſhall agree with this, I ſhall think my ſelf ſo much the more aſſured.

Now ſeeing the *denarius* may be conſidered in a double reſpect, either as *nummus*, or as *pondus*: In the firſt acception, the valuation of it in civil affairs is remarkable, in the latter, the gravity and ponderouſneſs: I ſhall ſpeak no farther of the former, than as it may conduce in ſome ſort to illuſtrate the latter. The *denarius* was a ſilver coin in uſe amongſt the *Romans*, paſſing at the firſt inſtitution for *dena æra*, or ten *aſſes*. And ſo [a] *Vitruvius* expreſly writes, *Noſtri autem primò decem fecerunt antiquum numerum, & in denario denos æreos aſſes conſtituerunt.* The ſame thing is atteſted by [b] *Voluſius Metianus*. *Denarius primò aſſes decem valebat, unde & nomen traxit.* [c] *Pliny*, beſides a confirmation of the ſame valuation, aſſigns alſo the time in which it was firſt ſtamped. *Argentum ſignatum eſt anno urbis* [d] *quingenteſimo octogeſimo quinto, Q. Fabio conſule, quinque annis ante primum bellum Punicum, & placuit denarius pro decem libris æris:* That is, for ten *aſſes*. For the *aſſes* both then, and under the firſt conſuls, were *librales*. *Dionyſius Halicarnaſſeus*, Ἦν ἢ ἀσσάριον, χάλκεον νόμισμα, βάρος λιτραῖον. The *aſſis* was a braſs coin, *weighing a pound.* Where by the way, it is worth the obſervation, the ſtrange, and in mine opinion, the unadviſed proportion, betwixt the braſs and ſilver moneys of thoſe times: That ten pounds of braſs ſhould be but anſwerable to the eighty fourth part (for ſo much, or near it, was the *denarius*) of a pound of ſilver; or to ſpeak more clearly, that one pound in ſilver ſhould be equal in valuation to eight hundred forty pounds in braſs. Neither can there be any excuſe of that error, unleſs this, that there was then an infinite plenty of the one, and as great a ſcarcity of the other. However it were, the ſame proportion is teſtified by *Varro*, who farther adds; that the *Romans* took the firſt uſe and invention of the *denarius*, from the *Sicilians*: [e] *In argento nummi, id à ſiculis, denarii quòd denos æris valebant.* And according to this valuation the *denarius* had an impreſs upon it of the figure X, denoting the *decuſſis*, or number of the *aſſes*, as *Valerius Probus* witneſſes, and ſometimes this character X̶; both which I have ſeen, and can ſhew, in ſeveral ancient ones. This latter by the ignorance of ſcribes formerly in *MSS.* and of our printers of late, in the edition of *Celſus*, and of *Scribonius Largus*, is repreſented by an aſteriſk *; and by a worſe error in the ſame authors, the figure X expreſſing the *denarius*, as a *pondus*, is confounded with the figure X expreſſing a number. From this figure on the *denarius*, or *decuſſis*, [f] *Vitruvius* calls the interſections of lines, *decuſſes*, and *decuſſationes*. And [g] *Columella* uſeth the phraſe *in ſtellam decuſſari*, when lines meet diamond-wiſe, or lozenge-like, as theſe in the character X or X̶. Neither did the *de-*

GREAVES

[a] Vitruv. l. 3. c. 1. [b] Vol. Metianus de aſſis diſtributione. [c] Plinius, l. 33. c. 3.
[d] Budæus, l. 5. *de aſſe*, corrects theſe numbers by *Livy* (l. 30.) and reads them 478.
[e] Varro, l. 4. de ling. Lat. [f] Vitruv. l. 10. [g] Columella, l. 5.

narius

GREAVES *narius* long pass at the valuation of ten *asses*, nor the *asses* which before, and then were *librales*, continue at one stay; but with the exigencies of the *Roman* state, the rate of the *denarius* rose, and the weight of the *asses* fell; that is in effect, both the silver and the brass monies came to be augmented in their estimation. For by a publick edict of *Fabius Maximus* the dictator, the common wealth being hardly pressed upon by *Hannibal*, the *denarius* came to be priced at XVI *asses*, and the *asses* which were then *sextantarii*, or the sixth part of the *Roman* pound, (for in the first *Punick* war, by reason of the excessive expences of the state, they first fell from being *librales*, to be *sextantarii*) came now in the second *Punick* war to be *unciales*. The whole progress and manner of this alteration, is by none so well and fully expressed as by [h] *Pliny*, and therefore I shall a little insist upon his words: *Silver*, says he, *came to be coined in the five hundred eighty fifth year of this city*, Q. Fabius *being consul, five years before the first* Punick *war, and then the* denarius *passed for* X *pounds of brass, the* quinarius *for* V, *the* sestertius *for* II *pounds and an half. The weight of the* assis *in brass was diminished in the first* Punick *war, the common-wealth not being able to support the expences, and then it was decreed, that the* asses *should be coined* sextantario pondere: That is, with the weight of the sixth part of a pound, or two ounces, whereas before they were *librales*. Tho' *Alciatus* here, upon a very gross mistake, contends, that they were then coined *dextantario pondere*, and not *sextantario*; but yet that they were called *asses sextantarii*, because the *sextans*, or sixth part of an ounce was wanting: whereas [i] *Festus* expresly writes: *Grave æs dictum à pondere, quia deni asses singuli pondo libræ efficiebant denarium ab hoc ipso numero dictum: Sed bello Punico populus Romanus pressus ære alieno, ex singulis assibus libralibus senos fecit, qui tantundem valerent.* And these words of *Pliny*, which immediately follow those before recited, put it out of controversy. [k] *Whereby*, says he, *five parts were gained, and the debts* (*of the common-wealth*) *discharged.* I would gladly see by what arithmetick *Alciatus* can demonstrate, that the common-wealth shall gain five parts, making the *asses sextantarii*, in his sense; whereas on the contrary, taking them in this interpretation (as both [l] *Agricola*, and [m] *Villalpandus* do) it is a thing most evident. For the whole pound, or *asses*, before consisting of XII ounces, being now reduced to two ounces, and these two passing at as high a rate in the valuation of things vendible, as the whole *libra* did, it is plain, that the common-wealth by this diminution of weight, keeping the same constant tenure of the estimation of the *asses*, gain'd ten parts in twelve, that is, five in six; and not one in six, as *Alciatus* would have it. But to omit this digression, and to return to [n] *Pliny*: *Afterwards being oppressed by* Hannibal, *under* Q. Fabius Maximus *the dictator, the* asses *were made* unciales, *and the* denarius *passed for* XVI asses, *the* quinarius *for* VIII, *and the* sestertius *for* IV. *And hereby the common-wealth gained half, yet in the pay of the militia, the* denarius *was always accounted for* X asses. *The impress of the silver* [that is of the *denarius*] *were the* bigæ, *and* quadrigæ; *from whence they are called* bigati, *and* quadrigati. *Not long after, by the* lex Papiria, *the* asses *came to be* semunciales. Livius Drusus, *tribune of the people, mixed an eighth part of brass with the silver.* Thus far *Pliny*. Out of which words it is most evident (omitting many passages of his worth our consideration) that as the *denarius* at the first institution passed for X *asses*, so afterwards it was valued at XVI. And *Vitruvius* gives a reason, why next to X, they made choice of XVI, rather than of XII or any other proportion: [o] *Quoniam animadverterunt utrosque numeros esse perfectos, & sex, & decem, utrosque in unum conjecerunt, & fecerunt perfectissimum decussissexi*, where [p] *Budæus* reads *decussissexis*: But [q] *Villalpandus decussi sex*, that it may the better, as he imagines, answer to the *Greek*, δέκα ἕξ. [r] *Hujus autem rei*, saith *Vitruvius*, *autorem invenerunt pedem. E cubito enim cùm dempti sint palmi duo, relinquitur pes quatuor palmorum, palmus autem habet quatuor digitos, ita efficitur uti pes habeat sexdecim digitos, & totidem asses æreos denarius.* [s] *Metianus* also purposely treating of this argument, after that he had related that

[h] *Argentum signatum est anno urbis* ɪↄɪ.XXXV. *Q. Fabio. Cos. quinque annis ante primum bellum Punicum. Et placuit denarius pro X libris æris, quinarius pro quinque, sestertium pro dupondio, ac semisse. Libræ autem pondus æris imminutum bello Punico primo, cum impensis resp. non sufficeret, constitutumque ut asses sextantario pondere ferirentur.* Plin. lib. 33. c. 3.

[i] Sext. Pompeius Fest. de verb. signif.

[k] Plin. l. 33. c. 3. Ita quinque partes factæ lucri dissolutumque æs alienum.

[l] Agricola, lib. 2. de pondere & temperat. monetarum.

[m] Villalp. de appar. urbis ac templi, par. 2. l. 2. disp. cap. 9.

[n] *Postea Hannibale urgente, Q. Fabio Maximo dictatore, asses unciales facti: placuitque denarium* XVI *assibus permutari, quinarium octonis, sestertium quaternis: ita resp. dimidium lucrata est. In militari tamen stipendio semper denarius pro X assibus datus. Nota argenti fuere bigæ atque quadrigæ, & inde bigati, quadrigatique dicti. Mox lege Papiria semunciales asses facti, Livius Drusus in tribunatu plebis octavam partem æris argento miscuit.* Plin. l. 33. c. 3.

[o] Vitruv. l. 3. c. 1.

[p] Budæus, l. 5. de asse.

[q] Villalp. de apparatu urbis ac templi.

[r] Vitruv. l. 3. c. 1.

[s] Vol. Metianus de assis distrib.

the

the *denarius*, at the first institution, was valued at X *asses*, adds, *now it is worth* XVI. And not to cite more authorities, the impress or stamp of XVI, as well as of X, found upon several *denarii*, and seen both by [t] *Antonius Augustinus*, (a man very accurate in coins, as appears by his dialogues) and by *Villalpandus*, besides one with the inscription of *C. Titinius*, with the same character, mentioned by *Fulvius Ursinus*, and [u] *Dalechampius* puts it out of controversy. And this valuation of the *denarius*, as it is more than probable, continued from the first institution of it in the second *Punick* war, without any interruption, to *Justinian*'s time, and it is likely longer; since there is no proof out of any ancient author, nor any character on any ancient *denarius* found to the contrary. As for those authorities which are alledged, and pressed by *Budæus*, and *Alciatus*, of *Varro*, *Apuleius*, *Arruntius*, and *Pompeius*, affirming that after the second *Punick* war, the *denarius* contained X *asses*, the *quinarius*, or *victoriatus* V, the *sestertius* II and a half: We may give a true and easy solution, that these writers expressed the valuation of them, as they were in their first original and beginning, with reflection to their primitive denomination: In which respect the *treviri monetales*, or officers of the mint, usually imprinted on the *denarius* the character X, rather than XVI; the former being the impress of its first institution, and the latter of its after valuation. And so in like manner may those citations be answered by *Plutarch*, *Dionysius*, and others, produced by some learned men to strengthen their assertion, that the *denarius* after the second *Punick* war returned to its first estimation. Which thing could not have been effected, without extreme loss and prejudice to particular men, in their private fortunes and estates; which the justice and wisdom of the *Roman* senate, under the consuls, was not likely to have introduced, or the people to have admitted.

To conclude, the *denarius*, as it is evident by many irrefragable authorities before alledged, in the highest valuation passed for XVI *asses*; and according to that proportion, the *quinarius*, or *victoriatus* for VIII, the *sestertius* for IV: But in the lowest valuation, or first institution, it passed for X *asses*: And then the proportion of the *quinarius* was V, of the *sestertius* II *asses* and a half, and therefore was thus marked IIS, or thus HS, as the *quinarius* had this character V, and also this X, as it is to be seen in a *victoriatus* of mine own (besides several others) with the face and inscription of *M. Cato*. By which coin that place may not unfitly be explained, which troubled [x] *Budæus*, why the *ordo decussatus*, and *ordo quincuncialis*, signify in the ranking of trees the same thing, altho' the *quinarius*, or *quincunx*, give the denomination to one, and the *denarius*, or *decussis*, to the other. The reason is, because the *quinarius* had the character X imprinted on it, as well as the *denarius*, or *decussis*. Besides in [y] *Temporarius*, we find the *quincunx* to be thus ⁻₋⁻ represented, as the *uncia* thus — so that five of these *unciæ* making the *quincunx*, and these five being ranged like the figure X (the character of the *decussis*) it is no wonder if the *ordo decussatus*, and *quincuncialis*, were taken for the same.

That the *denarius* should have passed at any other rate between XVI and X *asses*, as there is no coin extant to prove it, so there is no express authority to conclude it. Tho' some infer out of [z] *Polybius*, that it was valued also at XII *asses*: Because he defines the ἡμιαστάριον, or *semissis*, to be τέταρτον μέρος ὀβολοῦ, *the fourth part of the Attick obolus*; and VI *oboli* being in the δραχμὴ, to which *drachma* they suppose the *denarius* equal, therefore there must be XXIV *semisses*, or XII *asses* in the *denarius*. But with much better reason we may hence infer, that the *drachma* was somewhat bigger than the *denarius*, as we shall prove in this ensuing discourse; and therefore *Polybius* allows XII *asses* to it: Whereas, if it had been precisely equal to the *denarius*, he would have valued it at X, or else XVI of the lesser sort of *asses*. So that sir *H. Savile*, a man of exquisite judgment and learning, in his discourse at the end of *Tacitus*, justly blames *Hottoman* for altering the text of *Polybius*, and is himself to be censured, as also [a] *Lypsius*, in inferring thence that the *denarius* contained XII *asses*.

The several parts of the *denarius*, excepting the *quinarius* and *sestertius*, of both which I have spoken before, are all comprized in this description of [b] *Varro*, with which I shall conclude: *Nummi denarii decima libella, quòd libram pondo as valebat, & erat ex argento parva; sembella quòd sit libellæ dimidium quòd semis assis. Teruncius à tribus unciis sembellæ quod valet dimidium, & est quarta pars sicut quadrans assis.* By which proportions it appears, that the *libella* was the tenth part of the *denarius*, when it was current at X *asses*, the *sembella* the XXth, the *teruncius* the XLth. And thus much of the *denarius* as it is *nummus*.

[t] Anton. August. Dialogo I.
[u] Dalechampius in. Plin. l. 33. c. 3.
[x] Budæus, l. I. de asse.
[y] Cod. MS. Temporarii.
[z] Polyb. l. 2.
[a] Lypsius Elector. c. 2.
[b] Varro, l. 4. de ling. Lat.

GREAVES

The second, and our principal consideration of the *denarius*, is, as it is *pondus*, in which acception it will be necessary to premise a second distinction; that the *denarius* was either [z] *consularis*, or *cæsareus*. The *consularis* was that which was made under the government of the city by the consuls, the *cæsareus* under the *Cæsars*: The *consularis*, (I mean the *consularis* after the second *Punick* war, and under the later consuls) contained precisely the seventh part of the *Roman* ounce, as the other did the eighth part, or somewhat near it.

First that the *denarius consularis* of the later consuls, was the seventh part of the *Roman* ounce: This shall be our principal enquiry, because it is more evident of the two, and will give us the best light to discover the true weight of the *denarius*, in the notion and acception of the ancients, both *Greeks* and *Latins*. It is most apparent both by several fair coins which I have perused of the later consuls, as also by *Cornelius Celsus*, who lived in the beginning of the *Roman* emperors, before there happened a general diminution of the *denarius*, that it was then the seventh part of the ounce, who thus writes, [a] *Sed & antea sciri volo in uncia pondus denariorum esse septem.* The same proportion is also expressed by [b] *Scribonius Largus*, who lived not long after *Celsus*, as some imagine, his words are these: *Erit autem nota denarii unius pro Græca drachma; æquè enim in libra denarii octoginta quatuor apud nos, quot drachmæ apud Græcos incurrunt.* [c] *Pliny* also confirms the same. *Miscuit denario triumvir Antonius ferrum, alii* (he means under the emperors) *è pondere subtrahunt, cùm sit justum octoginta quatuor è libris signari.* Out of which words of his, and of *Scribonius Largus*, it will by a necessary consequence be inferr'd, that the true weight of the *denarius consularis* is the seventh part of an ounce. For if we multiply twelve, the number of the ounces in the *Roman libra* (as by all it is confess'd) by seven the number of the *denarii*, of which the ounce then consisted, the sum will be LXXXIV *denarii*; and so many, say *Scribonius* and *Pliny*, ought justly to be in the *Roman* pound. And these are the only clear and positive authorities that are to be found in classical authors; most of the writings of the ancients, *de ponderibus & mensuris*, having long since been lost; or else those few fragments that are left, of *Cleopatra, Dioscorides*, and of others, are so corrupted, that little truth with any certainty can be collected. From whence it will by way of corollary follow, that if either the *denarius consularis* be given, the *Roman* ounce, and *libra*, in the same proportion will necessarily be thence deduced; or if the *Roman* ounce, and *libra* be given, the *denarius* will as necessarily be concluded.

But before we farther treat of this argument, we shall endeavour also to demonstrate the *denarius*, by the *drachma Attica*. For *Scribonius* seems, and so do other ancients, to make them equal. And therefore *Pliny* writes: [d] *Drachma Attica denarii argentei habet pondus:* Whereas the *drachma Æginea* was much larger, this containing X such *oboli* as the *Attick* contained VI, and therefore the *Athenians* in hatred of the *Ægenians*, called it παχεῖαν δραχμὴν, as [e] *Pollux* testifies. And here as we considered the *denarius*, as *nummus*, and as *pondus*; so likewise must we take the *drachma Attica*, as *nummus*, and as *pondus*: In the prosecution of both which, relatively to the *denarius*, I shall insist so much the longer, because it is an argument that hath scarce at all, or very perfunctorily been handled. The *drachma*, as *nummus*, was a silver coin in use amongst the *Athenians*, (for I intend only to speak of the *drachma Attica*, for the same reason that [f] *Pliny* doth, *Ferè enim Atticâ observatione utuntur medici*) and so it was the measure of things vendible, as all coins are: And as *pondus*, so was it the measure of their gravity and weight. Now the *drachma*, as *nummus*, passed in the estimation of the best authors, both *Greek* and *Latin*, at the same rate and valuation as the *denarius* did. And therefore, as often as the *Latins* are to express the *Greek drachma*, they render it by the *denarius*; and on the contrary, the *Greeks* the *denarius* by the *drachma*. Thus what [g] *Tully* renders by the *denarius*, *Dio* in his forty fifth book expresseth by the *drachma*. Their words, both speaking of *Augustus*, are these, *Veteranos quique Casilini, & Calatiæ sunt* (as *Tully* relates) *perduxit ad suam sententiam, nec mirum, quingenos denarios dat.* Καὶ ἔδωκεν εὐθὺς τότε, saith [h] *Dio*, κατὰ πεντακοσίας δραχμάς. In like manner [i] *Pliny*

[z] The *consularis* again may be considered, either in the time of the former, or of the latter consuls: That of the former consuls, at the first institution of it by *Q. Fabius*, five years before the first *Punick* war, *Peireskius* not improbably imagines to have been the sixth part of the *Roman* ounce: And *Agricola* by comparing it with the *talentum Atticum*, which *Varro* values at 15000 *Sestertii* and with the *tetradrachme*, which *Livy* (*lib.* 34.) estimates, *Trium fere denariorum*; as also upon the authority of the *Scholiast of Nicander*, who equals the *denarius* to a drachme and an half, as *Priscian* doth to a drachme and a third part; I say, *Agricola* assigns it to almost the same proportion with *Peireskius*. But because I have seen no *denarii consulares* of so great antiquity, and these authorities may perchance admit other constructions, I shall leave this opinion as only probable, and follow what is more certain and demonstrative, of the later consuls.

[a] Celsus, l. 5. c. 17.

[b] Scrib. Largus in præfatione.

[c] Plinius, l. 33. c. 9.

[d] Plinius, l. 21. c. 34.

[e] Jul. Pol. l. 9. c. 6.

[f] Plinius, l. 21. c. 34.

[g] Cicer. 16. l. 5. Ep. ad Attic.

[h] Dio, l. 45.

[i] Plinius, l. 1. 27.

writes,

writes, *Venisse murem ducentis nummis*, (that is, *denariis*; for *nummus* absolutely put is often, tho' not always, taken for the *denarius*, as on the contrary the *denarius* is taken for *nummus* in *Hesychius*, [k] δηνάριον τὸ νόμισμα, ἢ εἶδος ἀργυρίου.) *Casilinum obsidente Annibale, eumque qui vendiderat fame interisse, emptorem vixisse annales tradunt.* The same thing [l] *Valerius Maximus* reports in his seventh book, and sixth chapter, and [m] *Strabo* in his fifth book; the former writing that it was sold for 200 *denarii*, and the latter that it was bought for 200 *drachmæ*. To these authorities I shall adjoin [n] *Cleopatra*, Τὸ Ἰταλικὸν δηνάριον ἔχει δραχμὴν α'. *The* Italian denarius *containeth one* drachma: And [o] *A. Gellius*, *Lais* μυρίας δραχμὰς ἢ τάλαντον *poposcit, hoc facit nummi nostratis, denariûm decem millia.*

These two thus passing the one for the other, being also at the first institution much of the same fineness in respect of silver, it must necessarily be admitted, either that they were exactly the same for weight, which is our next enquiry, or else that they were not much different. For in comparing of foreign coins, the κολλυβισαὶ, or *nummularii*, in ancient times, must have taken the same course, which our most knowing bankers do practise now. First, to respect the pureness and fineness of the coins, whether they be alike *for the intrinsick*; and next, whether they have the same weight; and if they differ in either, or both of these, according to those differences to proportion their exchanges. Those other accidental causes of the rising and falling of exchanges of moneys, since they are meerly contingent, depending upon the necessities either of times, or places, or persons, I purposely pretermit, as not so proper and essential to our enquiry. As *for the extrinsick of coins*, by which I mean the outward form, or character, and inscription of the prince, or state, tho' this may raise the valuation of them in those countries, which are subject to the prince, or state, and lessen them in those which are out of their dominions; yet this can produce no remarkable difference, more than what is usually assigned by the masters of the mint, for the waste in coining, and for the labour of the work.

With these cautions, if we shall examine the *Attick drachma*, and by such writings of the ancients, or by such coins as are extant, enquire their true weight, we shall come to such a preciseness as may be hoped for in a work of this nature. [p] *Suidas* tells us in the general, Δραχμὴ δὲ ὁλκὴ νομίσματος ἀργυροῦ. *The* drachma *is the weight of the silver money.* And [q] *Hesychius* more particularly informs us: Δραχμὴ τὸ ὄγδοον τῆς οὐγγίας· *The* drachma *is the eighth part of the ounce.* And [r] *Fannius* yet more distinctly writes:

In scrupulis ternis drachmam, quo pondere doctis
Argenti facilis signatur pondus Athenis.

To which we may add [f] *Cleopatra*, Ἡ δραχμὴ ἔχει γράμματα γ'. ὀβολοὺς ς'. θέρμους θ'. κεράτια ιη'. χαλκοὺς μη'. *The* drachme *hath three* scruples, *six* oboli, *nine* lupini, *eighteen* siliquæ, *forty eight* æreola. The [t] *Scholiast of Nicander* also makes the δίδραχμον to be τὸ τέταρτον τῆς οὐγγίας, *The fourth part of the* [Attick] *ounce.* In the same proportion are we to take those other silver *Athenian* coins mentioned by [u] *Julius Pollux*, namely, the τρίδραχμον, which consisted of three drachmes, the τετράδραχμον, or τέτραχμον, which by a syncope is the same with the τετράδραχμον, containing four drachmes, or the half ounce. Τέτραχμον, τετράδραχμον, saith [x] *Hesychius*; tho' [y] *Ammonius* puts a distinction between them, τέτραχμον μὲν γὰρ ἐστι τὸ νόμισμα, τετράδραχμον δὲ τὸ τεσσάρων δραχμῶν [ἄξιον.] This the *Greeks* also called στατὴρ, as [z] *Cleopatra*, and [a] *Epiphanius* witness, Ὁ στατὴρ, in *Cleopatra*, ἄγει λ' δ'. καλοῦσι δὲ αὐτὸν τετράδραχμον: *The stater weighs four drachms, this they call the tetradrachme.* And this also may most clearly be collected out of [b] St. *Matthew*, where seeing the original expresseth it more fully than our translation, I shall recite the words as they are in *Greek*: Ἐλθόντων δὲ αὐτῶν εἰς Καπερναοὺμ, προσῆλθον οἱ τὰ δίδραχμα λαμβάνοντες τῷ Πέτρῳ, καὶ εἶπον, ὁ διδάσκαλος ὑμῶν οὐ τελεῖ τὰ δίδραχμα; which the vulgar renders thus: *Et cum venissent Capernaum, accesserunt qui didrachma accipiebant, ad Petrum, & dixerunt ei, Magister vester non solvit didrachma?* And our translation thus: *And when they were come to Capernaum, they that received tribute-money, came to Peter, and said, Doth not your master pay tribute?* In the twenty seventh verse of the same chapter, our Saviour answers: Ἵνα μὴ σκανδαλίζωμεν αὐτοὺς, πορευθεὶς εἰς τὴν θάλασσαν βάλε ἄγκιστρον, καὶ τὸν ἀναβαίνοντα πρῶτον ἰχθὺν ἆρον, καὶ ἀνοίξας τὸ στόμα αὐτοῦ εὑρήσεις στατῆρα. ἐκεῖνον λαβὼν δὸς αὐτοῖς ἀντὶ ἐμοῦ καὶ σοῦ. *Notwithstanding, lest we should offend them, go thou to the sea, and cast an hook, and take up the fish that first cometh up: And*

[k] Hesychius in voce δηνάριον. [l] Valer. Max. l. 7. c. 6. [m] Strabo, l. 5. Geogr. [n] Fragmenta Cleopatræ. [o] A. Gellius l. 1. c. 8. Noct. Att. [p] Suidas in voce δραχμή. [q] Hesychius in voce δραχμή. [r] Rhemn. Fann. [f] Fragmenta Cleopatræ. [t] Scholiastes Nicandri. [u] Jul. Poll. l. 9. c. 6. [x] Hesychius in voce τέτραχμον. [y] Ammonius περὶ ὁμοίων καὶ διαφόρων λέξεων. [z] Fragmenta Cleopatræ. [a] Epiphanius, περὶ σταθμῶν. [b] Mat. c. xvii. v. 24.

when

GREAVES *when thou hast opened his mouth, thou shalt find a piece of money: That take, and give unto them for me, and thee.* This, which our translation calls *tribute-money*, in the twenty fourth verse, is called in the original δίδραχμον, or *two drachmes*; and so much was paid by the pole, according to [c] *Josephus*, for each particular person. Our Saviour therefore paying for himself, and St. *Peter*, in the twenty seventh verse, bids him to give a *stater*; that is, a τετράδραχμον, or four drachmes; namely the double to the δίδραχμον, which our translation renders too generally by *a piece of money:* But the [d] *Persian* translation interprets it distinctly by four drachmes: *Thou shalt find four drachmes in it; that take, and give for thee, and me.*

With this *Attick tetradrachme*, or silver *stater*, the *Hebrew* and *Samaritan* שקל *Shekel*, that is, *Sicle*, did also agree. For if we give credit to *Josephus*, who in [e] *Scaliger's* esteem is, *diligentissimus* καὶ φιλαληθέστατος *omnium scriptorum*, we shall find them to be the same. [f] Ὁ δὲ σίκλος νόμισμα ἑβραίων ὤν, Ἀττικὰς δέχεται δραχμὰς τέσσαρας. *The sicle is a sort of money amongst the* Hebrews, *that contains four* Attick drachmes. The same proportion is evidently collected out of [g] *Philo*, where for L shekels mentioned in the law, he renders CC drachmes, and for XXX an CXX. [h] *Hesychius* likewise testifies as much, Σίκλος τετράδραχμον Ἀττικόν, *The sicle is* [in valuation] *the* Attick tetradrachme: And [i] St. *Hierome* the ablest of the fathers in the Jewish antiquities, [k] *Siclus, id est stater, habet quatuor drachmas Atticas.*

These testimonies are so positive, and from so good authors (to which also I might adjoin [l] *Epiphanius* in his book περὶ σαθμῶν, did I not conceive him to be full of errors in that discourse) that I cannot sufficiently wonder at that strange opinion of [m] *Grsepsius*, and some others, introduced out of affection of novelty, of a double shekel, the one sacred, equal to the tetradrachme, the other profane, weighing the didrachme: That used in the sanctuary, this in civil commerce, without any solid foundation in the writ, or without any probability of reason, that in any wise state, the prince and people should have one sort of coin, and the priests should have another: And that this of the sanctuary should be in a double proportion to the other; and yet that both should concur in the same name. It is true there is often mention in the [n] scriptures of the *weights of the sanctuary*, not as if these were different from what were used vulgarly in the city; but because the standards, and originals, the rules of commutative justice, and therefore of an high and sacred use, were kept (as it is more probable) in the sanctuary; for God himself makes this one of the priest's offices, [o] *ut sint super omne pondus atque mensuram.* And it is no wonder that God, who so much hated a [p] *false balance*, and a *false measure*, should commit the charge of these to the priests, as things most holy; since the heathens themselves out of a reverent estimation of them, placed them in their temples, as appears by that inscription of the *congius* of *Vespasian* before alledged, and now extant in *Rome*, and by these verses of [q] *Fannius*, treating of the *Roman* measures:

Amphora fit cubus, quam, ne violare liceret.
Sacravere Jovi Tarpeio in monte Quirites.

And afterwards in the times of Christianity, they were kept in churches, as it is to be seen in the [r] *authenticks of Justinian*; where he commands that the weights and

[c] Josephus l. 7. Bell. Jud. c. 27. [d] Evangelia Pers. MSS. Eruditissimi viri D. Pocockii.

[e] Scal. προλεγόμ. in libr. de Emend. Temp. [f] Josephus l. 3. Antiq. Judaic. [g] Philo de decalogo. [h] Hesychius in voce Σίκλος. [i] Hieronym. in *Ezek.* iii. [k] Such sicles, I conceive, were those τριάκοντα ἀργύρια, *the* XXX *pieces of silver*, which were given to *Judas*, as the reward of his treason. *Eusebius* relating the story expresly, terms them *silver staters*, which an *Hebrew* would have termed either silver shekels, or absolutely כסף *Cesef:* This in scripture phrase being frequently put for the shekel, and therefore the *Syriack* translation of the new testament reads it כספא: Whence *Tremellius* hath this annotation: *Observant Hebræi, ubicunque in scripturis argenteorum fit mentio, non expressâ numismatis argentei specie, intelligi siclum sanctuarii æquivalentem quatuor denariis.* Some modern writers imagine them to have been but XXX *denarii*; but *Baronius* contends that they were, *vel librarum argenti* XXX, *vel aureorum coronatorum trecentorum.* And *Arias Montanus*, that they were either XXX *libræ*, or XXX *talenta*. The most probable opinion is, that this sum was neither so great as *Baronius* and *Montanus* make it, nor yet so little as some moderns would have it, but between both, and that is XXX shekels. *M. Casaubone* in his exercitations upon *Baronius*, hath a probable conjecture to strengthen this assertion: *Non enim temere factum videtur, quòd filius Dei qui sese exinanivit, assumptâ servi formâ,* Phil. ii. 7. *Triginta argenteis venderetur, sicut lege Dei mancipia totidem siclis æstimantur.* Exod. xxi. 32. *& apud Josephum, lib.* 4. *c.* 8. *Facit hoc quoque non parum ad Domini abjectionem declarandum, quando caput ejus tam parvi æstimatum est.* A small price I confess, XXX shekels being less than XV of our ordinary crowns. But *Hierome* upon St. *Matthew* thought it to be as little, who thus writes, as M. *Casaubone* renders him, *Infelicem Judam non cogitasse quanti precii rem venderet. Sed Christum mundi salvatorem, Dei filium, ceu vile aliquod mancipium minimo pretio addixisse.* Now the price of a servant we find in *Exodus* to have been thirty shekels. [l] Epiphanius περὶ σαθμῶν. [m] Grsepsius de multiplici siclo & talento.

[n] And all thy estimation shall be according to the shekel of the sanctuary. *Levit.* xxvii. 25. *Vet. vulg. siclo sanctuarii ponderabitur.* [o] 1 Paral. xxiii. 29. [p] Prov. xi. 1. item c. xx. ver. 10, 23.

[q] Rhemn. Fann. carmina de pond. & mensuris. [r] Authentic. collat, 9. de collatoribus tit. 11. novel. 128. c. 15.

measures

measures should be kept, *in sacratissimâ cujusvis civitatis ecclesiâ*. As for these allegations taken out of the interpretation of the LXX, whereby *Grsepsius*, and others, go about to prove a double shekel, they are well, and solidly, in my judgment, answered by [s] *Villalpandus*, and others to whom I shall refer the judicious reader: For I intend not here to speak of the *Hebrew* shekel, or *Attick* drachme, more than what may serve to illustrate the *denarius*.

Seeing therefore, as we have proved, that the *Attick drachma* was equal in the notion and acception of the ancients, to the *denarius:* If therefore an entire, either *Attick* Δραχμὴ, or Δίδραχμον, or Τετράδραχμον, were found, we might thence conclude the *denarius*. Again, since the *Hebrew* shekel hath likewise been demonstrated to be equal to the *Attick* Τετράδραχμον, and this *Attick* Τετράδραχμον to four *denarii*, by the common and received [t] axiom of geometricians, we may conclude, that the *Hebrew* shekel was also equal to four *denarii*; that is, that four *Roman denarii*, the *Attick* Τετράδραχμον, and the *Hebrew* שקל were all respectively equal to one another. If therefore an *Hebrew* shekel, fair and entire, were found, we might as necessarily thence infer the *denarius*, as by the Τετράδραχμον.

We shall endeavour by both these to enquire out the truth, and first by the *Attick tetradrachmes* in silver: Because of these I have seen and weighed many, some of them very fair and perfect, and found at many several places, as *Athens*, *Constantinople*, *Tenedos*, and other parts; where the art of counterfeiting coins is not as yet crept in, and where it is to little purpose to practise it: Seeing in those places there are few so curious as to buy them, or that will give a greater valuation than what they are worth in the *intrinsick*. Wherefore having in *Italy*, and elsewhere, perused many hundred *denarii consulares*, I find by a frequent and exact trial, the best of them to amount to LXII grains *English*, such as I have carefully taken from the standards of the troy, or silver weights, kept in the tower in *London*, and in goldsmiths-hall, and in the university of *Oxford:* On the other side weighing many *Attick tetradrachmes*, with the image of *Pallas* on the forepart, and of the *noctua* on the reverse: I find the best of these to be CCLXVIII grains; that is, each particular drachme LXVII grains.

And that no man may doubt whether these were true *Athenian tetradrachmes*, we are to observe, that the ancients used several impresses on their coins, by which they might be known and distinguished. GREAVES And therefore *argentum signatum*, in the description of *Quintius* his triumph over *Philip*, is by [u] *Livy* opposed to *argentum infectum*, which [x] *Pollux* terms ἄσημον, as [y] *Tully* calls the former sort, *Factum atque signatum*, and the [z] *Greeks*, ἐπίσημον. Thus the *denarius* had the impress of the *biga*, or *quadriga*, as *Pliny* informs us: And therefore [a] *Livy* uses the word *bigati* for *denarii*, and [b] *Pliny* both *bigati* and *quadrigati*. The brass coins of the *Romans* were thus marked: [c] *Nota æris fuit ex alterâ parte Janus geminus, ex alterâ rostrum navis, in triente vero & quadrante rates.* The *Persians* stamped on the reverse an [d] archer: Which occasioned that conceit of *Agesilaus*, mentioned by [e] *Plutarch*, *That the king of* Persia *had beaten him back with ten thousand archers*; when with so much money he had corrupted the *Grecians*. The *Carthaginians* on the one side signed the face of a woman, (I suppose in memory of queen *Dido*) on the reverse the head of an horse, or in *Virgil*'s expression, [f] *Caput acris æqui*, both which I have seen. The *Peloponnesians* had the impress of a tortoise on their money, whence that witty *Greek* proverb took its original: [g] Τὰν ἀρετὰν, καὶ τὰν σοφίαν νικῶντι χελῶναι. The money at *Tenedos* had on the one side a double hatchet, and on the other side two heads, one of a man, and another of a woman, arising from the same stem, or neck, in memory of a law made by the king of that island (whom [h] *Heraclides* names Τέννης, placing him ancienter than the *Trojan* war,) that a man and a woman, taken in adultery, should have their heads struck off with an hatchet. In which kind I met with two very rare and ancient coins in silver, at *Constantinople*, both made with a very fair relevy, and both agreeing in the same image and inscription; the one weighed less than the *Attick tetradrachme*, the other wanted somewhat of the *drachme*. And because the coin hath not, I think, been seen by any antiquary, and the history is remarkable, I shall here express the figure of the fairest of these.

[s] Villal. de appar. urbis ac templi, par. 2. lib. 2. disp. 4. c. 28. Item par. 2. l. 2. disp. 4.
[t] *Quæ eidem æqualia, sunt æqualia inter se.* Eucl. ax. 1. l. 1. [u] Livius, l. 34. [x] Jul. Poll. l. 9. c. 6. [y] Cicer. 6. Verr. [z] Jul. Poll. l. 9. c. 6. [a] Liv. l. 34. [b] Plinius, l. 33. c. 3. [c] Plin. ib. [d] Plutarchus in Artaxerxe. Τὸ τῆς Περσικὸν νόμισμα τοξότην ἐπίσημον εἶχεν. [e] Plut. Agesil. [f] Virg. 1. Æneid. [g] Jul. Poll. l. 9. c. 6. [h] Heraclides, περὶ πολιτειῶν.

GREAVES

And the history I shall relate out of [b] *Heraclides:* Νόμον δέ τινά φασι τ̃ βασιλέα Τέννην διαθέσθαι, εἴτις λάβοι μοιχὸν ἀποκτείνειν τȣ̃τον πελέκει, ἁλόντ☉ δὲ τȣ̃ υἱȣ̃ αὐτȣ̃, καὶ τȣ̃ λαβόντ☉ ἐρομένȣ τ̃ βασιλέα τί χρὴ ποιεῖν, ἀποκρίνασθαι τῷ νόμῳ χρῆσθαι· καὶ διὰ τȣ̃το τȣ̃ νομίσματ☉ αὐτȣ̃ ἐπὶ θάτερα πέλεκυς κεχάρακται, ἐπὶ θάτερα δὲ ἐξ ἑνὸς αὐχέν☉ πρόσωπον ἀνδρὸς καὶ γυναικός. καὶ ἐκ τȣ́τȣ λέγεται ἐπὶ τ̃ ἀποτόμων, τὸ ἀποκεκόφθαι Τενεδίῳ πελέκει. *They say king* Tennes *made a law, That if one took another in adultery, he should kill him with an hatchet. His son being found so, and he that took him, asking the king, What he should do? He answered him, Execute the law: and for this reason on one side of his money there was an hatchet imprinted; on the other, the face of a man and of a woman, arising out of one neck. From hence it is said of severe actions, to be cut with a* Tenedian *hatchet.* For which exemplary justice those of *Tenedos*, as it is probable, deified king *Tenes.* [c] *Tully* writes, *Tenedii Tenem* [*Deum appellant*]: And again, *Tenem apud Tenedios putant esse sanctissimum Deum, ac eorum urbem condidisse.* Where his name is truer writ than in *Heraclides:* for the coin hath only a single *N*, and so hath [d] *Eustathius.*

The money of *Chios*, as *Julius Pollux* witnesses, had the effigies, or resemblance of *Homer*; no doubt in honour of his memory; though [e] *Herodotus* relates, that whilst he was living he found at first but cold entertainment in that island. *Theseus* the tenth king of the *Athenians* signed his money with the impress of an ox: hence that proverb, Βȣ̃ς ἐπὶ γλώσσῃ βέβηκεν. This, as [f] *Julius Pollux* testifies, was the δίδραχμον: Who farther adds, Τὸ δὲ παλαιὸν τȣ̃το ἦν Ἀθηναίοις νόμισμα, καὶ ἐκαλεῖτο βȣ̃ς ὅτι βȣ̃ν εἶχεν ἐντετυπωμένον. εἰδέναι δ' αὐτὸ καὶ Ὅμηρον νομίζȣσιν εἰπόντα, ἑκατόμβοι ἐννεαβοίων, καὶ μὲν κἂν τοῖς Δράκοντ☉ νόμοις ἐστὶν ἀποτίνειν δεκάβοιον, καὶ ἐν τῇ παρὰ Δηλίας θεωρίᾳ τ̃ κήρυκα κηρύττειν φασὶν ὁπότε δωρεάν τινι ἐδίδοτο, ὅτι δοθήσονται αὐτῷ τοσȣ̃τοι βόες, καὶ δίδοσθαι καθ' ἕκαστον βȣ̃ν δύο δραχμὰς Ἀττικάς. *This was an ancient coin amongst the* Athenians, *and was called* βȣ̃ς, *because it had the figure of an ox instamped. They imagine that* Homer *knew this, when he said, nine hecatombs of oxen; and also in the laws of* Draco, *it is to pay the mulct of ten oxen. And they say, that at the solemn shew at* Delos, *the crier, when any gift is to be given, cries so many oxen shall be given, and for every ox so many* Attick didrachmes *are given.* The same [g] author writes, that the *Attick tetradrachme* was stamped with the face of *Minerva*; and he might have added, with the *noctua* on the reverse. This [h] *Eubulus* pleasantly calls Παλλάδ☉ πῶλον, *Minervæ pullum.* The διώβολον had the face of *Jupiter*, it may be it is an error in *Pollux* for *Pallas*, and on the other side the *noctua.* The τετρώβολον had on the one side *Jupiter*, according to [i] *Pollux*, (I conceive it to be a mistake for *Pallas*, or *Minerva*) on the other side two *noctuæ*, because it was the double to the διώβολον. From the *diobolum*, [k] *Plautus* uses the term *diobolaris servorum sordidulorum, scorta diobolaria*, which [l] *Festus* interprets thus, *meretrices diobolares appellatas, ex eo quod duobus obolis ducerentur.* To which I may adjoin, out of such ancient coins as I have seen, that the *triobolum* (whence that phrase of [m] *Plautus, homo trioboli*, and of the *Greeks*, ἄξι☉ τριωβόλȣ) which by [n] *Pollux* is called the ἡμίδραχμον, had the face of *Pallas* on the one side, and the *noctua* on the other; and so likewise had the *obolus* and *drachma* of such as I perused; and all of them on the reverse the inscription ΑΘΕ. And I think I may safely add, that on such coins as we find the *noctua*, with a deep relevy, we may conclude them to be *Athenian* coins. [o] *Plutarch* is of the same opinion in the life of *Lysander*, where he discourses of *Gylippus*, a commander as famous for defeating the *Athenians* in *Sicily*, as infamous for stealing the silver consigned to him by *Lysander*, for the city *Sparta.* *When he arrived*, saith *Plutarch*, *at* Sparta, *he hid the silver that he had stollen, under the tiles of his house, and delivered into the hands of the* Ephori *the bags, shewing them the seals* [entire:] *which being opened, and the money told, they found the sums to disagree from the labels; wherewith being troubled, a servant of* Gylippus, *in obscure terms, intimated to them, That under the tiles of his master's house, there were hid many* noctuæ, *or owls;* ἦν γὰρ (ὡς ἔοικε) τὸ χάραγμα τȣ̃ πλείςȣ τότε νομίσματ☉, διὰ τȣ̀ς Ἀθηναίȣς γλαῦκες. *For the greatest part (as it seems) of the money then had the stamp of the* noctua, *by reason of the* Athenians: who not long before, as *Thucydides*, and the best historians of those times shew, were the richest and most flourishing state amongst the *Grecians.*

Having therefore had the opportunity to have bought, or else the favour to have weigh'd many fair and perfect *tetradrachmes*, found at remote places, with the *Pallas galeata* on the one side, and the *noctua*, with the inscription ΑΘΕ on the reverse, where Ε being placed for Η, proves the antiquity of them. (For the *Atticks* at the first used not Η, but only Ε, for both Ε and Η) I find by the best of these (to re-

[b] Heraclides περὶ πολιτειῶν. [c] Cicer. l. 3. de naturâ deorum. [d] Eustathii παρεκβολαὶ εἰς τὴν ῥαψῳδ. [e] Herodot. in vita Homeri. [f] Jul. Poll. l. 9. c. 6. [g] Ibid. [h] In anchise. [i] Jul. Poll. l. 9. c. 6. [k] Plautus in Pœnulo. [l] Sextus Pompeius Festus de verb. signif. [m] Plautus in Pœnulo. [n] Jul. Poll. 9. c. 6. [o] Plutarchus in Lysandro.

assume

assume what I said before) that the *Attick tetradrachme* is two hundred sixty eight grains, and the *drachme* is sixty seven of our Troy, or *English* standard. Which may farther be confirmed by an *Attick drachme* of mine own, found in the *Black Sea*, with this inscription, ΑΘΕ ΤΙΝΑΡΝΙΚΑ ΑΡΧΕ; and by a [o] τελώβολον, or *semidrachme*, bought by me at *Alexandria*; that weighing near sixty six grains, and this thirty and better: the face of *Minerva*, either by use or time, being a little diminished in both; but yet so little, that they cannot have lost above two or three grains of their primitive weight. And as this single *Attick drachme* of mine is much to be valued by antiquaries for the weight, and therefore was desired by the learned *Peireskius*: So is the inscription, ΤΙΝΑΡΝΙΚΑ ΑΡΧΕ, no less worth consideration, for the explication of a place in [p] *Livy*; who describing the naval triumph of *L. Æmilius*, writes thus: *Pecunia translata nequaquam tanta pro specie regii triumphi. Tetracina Attica* CCXXXIII *millia. Cistophori* CCCXXII *mil.* Where [q] *Budæus*, and *Rhodiginus*, instead of *tetracina*, read *tetradrachma*. *Tetracinum enim quid sit, nemo ut arbitror novit*, saith *Budæus*. I would rather read it, as the coin doth, *Tinarnika*; this having almost the same letters with *tetracina*, which by the scribes, I suppose, have been inverted. Neither is there any reason, why *Livy* might not as well mention in this triumph, *Attica tinarnica*, as *tetradrachma*; these being the fourth part of the *tetradrachme*, and therefore better agreeing with his description: *Pecunia translata nequaquam tanta pro specie regii triumphi*: and also better agreeing with the *cistophori* he here mentions: a sort of coin about half of these *Attica tinarnica*, whereas the *tetradrachma* were eight times as great. For [r] *Festus* expressing the *talentum Euboicum*, renders it by 7500 *cistophori*, and by 4000 *denarii*, that is CIↃ *tetradrachmes*. *Euboicum talentum nummo Græco septem millium & quingentorum cistophorum est: nostro quatuor millium denariorum.*

And as these testimonies above alledged are beyond all exceptions, so the *gold coins of the* Grecians, which I have examined, do most evidently prove this proportion assigned to the *Attick drachme*. Which that we may the better understand, we are to observe what proportion the valuation of the gold of those times had to the silver; and next, what proportion it had in respect of weight.

For the first, [s] *Julius Pollux*, in very perspicuous terms, puts it down: Τὸ δὲ χρυσίον, ὅτι τοῦ ἀργυρίου δεκαπλάσιον ἦν, σαφῶς ἄν τις ἐκ τῆς Μενάνδρου παρακαταθήκης μάθοι. *That the gold was in the tenfold proportion to the silver, one may evidently learn out of* Menander's paracatathece. [t] The *scholiast* of *Aristophanes* implies as much: Εἰσὶ μὲν χρυσοῖ στατῆρες οἱ Δαρεικοί· ἐδύνατο δὲ ἕκαστος αὐτῶν, ὅπερ ὁ παρὰ τοῖς Ἀττικοῖς ὀνομαζόμενος χρυσοῦς, οὐκ ἀπὸ Δαρείου τοῦ Ξέρξου πατρὸς ἀλλ᾽ ἀφ᾽ ἑτέρου τινὸς παλαιοτέρου βασιλέως ὠνομάσθησαν. Λέγουσι δέ τινες δύνασθαι τὸν Δαρεικὸν δραχμὰς ἀργυρίου εἴκοσιν· ὡς τοὺς πέντε Δαρεικοὺς δύνασθαι μνᾶν ἀργυρίου. *The* daricks *are golden* staters, *each of them is worth as much as that which is named by the* Atticks *the* χρυσοῦς. *They are called so not from* Darius *the father of* Xerxes, *but from another king more ancient than he. Some say that the* darick *is valued at* xx drachms *of silver, so that* v. daricks *are worth a* mina *of silver*. For the *Attick* μνᾶ, or *mina*, containeth an hundred *drachmes* in weight, as it is very clear out of [u] *Pliny*, [x] *Pollux*, and others. *Mna* (saith *Pliny*) *quam nostri minam vocant, pendet drachmas Atticas centum*. And *Pollux*, Ἡ μνᾶ δὲ παρ᾽ Ἀθηναίοις ἑκατὸν εἶχε δραχμὰς Ἀττικάς: *The* mina *with the* Athenians *containeth an hundred* Attick drachmes, and the Χρυσοῦς Δαρεικὸς, or Στατὴρ Χρυσοῦς of *Darius*, consisting of two *drachmes* in weight, as we shall presently prove, it will necessarily follow, that the proportion of the δραχμὴ χρυσίου, was to the δραχμὴ ἀργυρίου, *in decuplá ratione*: and therefore, that five *daricks*, or ten *drachmes* of gold, were equal in valuation to an hundred *drachmes* in silver, that is, to the μνᾶ. The same proportion may be collected out of [y] *Polybius*, when the *Romans* upon a sum of money to be received, concluded a peace with the *Ætolians*, Ἀντὶ τρίτου μέρους τοῦ ἀργυρίου χρυσίου, χρυσίον ἐὰν βούλωνται διδόντες τῶν δέκα μνῶν ἀργυρίου, χρυσίου μνᾶν. Which words [z] *Livy* renders thus: *Pro argento si aurum dare mallent, dare convenit, dum pro argenteis decem aureus unus valeret*. This being granted, as certainly of necessity it must, I would correct that place of [a] *Hesychius* concerning the δραχμὴ χρυσίου, and read it thus: Δραχμὴ δὲ χρυσίου ὁλκὴ νομισμάτιον εἰς ἀργυρίου λόγον δραχμῶν ι, and not διδραχμῶν ι. as it is in the printed copies. And by this

[o] I have since perused a fair *Athenian* Τριώβολον, of my very worthy and learned friend, *John Marsham*, Esq; weighing completely thirty three grains *English*. As also another of sir *Tho. Roe's*, together with an Ὀβολὸς of his, weighing eleven grains. [p] Livius, l. 37. [q] Bud. l. 2. de asse. Rhodigin. lect. antiq. l. 10. c. 2. [r] Sextus Pompeius Festus de verb. signif. [s] Jul. Poll. l. 9. c. 3. [t] Scholiastes Aristophanis. [u] Plinius, l. 21. c. 34. [x] Jul. Poll. l. 9. c. 3. [y] Polybii ἐκλογαὶ περὶ πρεσβειῶν, c. 28. Ex Biblioth. Fulvii Ursini. Antv. 1582. [z] Livius, l. 31. Παρὰ δὲ τοῖς Ἕλλησιν κ᾽ δραχμῶν τὸ χρυσοῦν ἀλλάττεται νόμισμα. Zonaras. [a] Hesychius in voce δραχμή.

GREAVES this of *Hesychius* I would supply the defect of [b] *Suidas, who writes*: Δραχμὴ δὲ ὁλκὴ νομίσματος εἰς ἀργυρίου δραχμὰς ἰ. and make it thus, Δραχμὴ δὲ χρυσίου ὁλκὴ νομίσματος εἰς ἀργυρίου λόγον δραχμὰς ἰ. For without the addition of χρυσίου, and λόγον, there is no sense: and I believe *Suidas* took these very words out of *Hesychius*.

Having thus found the proportion that the δραχμὴ χρυσίου had to the silver, our next enquiry is, how many of the *drachmes* in weight the χρυσοῦς, or χρυσοῦς στατὴρ, or *aureus* contained. [c] *Julius Pollux* gives us in this particular the best, and most positive information of any, ὁ δὲ χρυσοῦς στατὴρ δύο εἶχε δραχμὰς Ἀττικάς. *The golden* stater [or aureus,] *contains two* Attick drachmes. The same is confirmed by [d] *Hesychius*: Πολέμαρχος φησὶ δύνασθαι τὸν χρυσοῦν παρὰ τοῖς Ἀττικοῖς δραχμὰς δύο· τὴν δὲ τοῦ χρυσοῦ δραχμὴν νομίσματος ἀργυρίου, δραχμὰς δέκα. Polemarchus *says, that the* aureus *amongst the* Athenians *contains two* drachmes, *and that the* drachme *of gold is worth ten* drachmes *of silver*. And to this of *Pollux* and *Hesychius*, all the *aurei* of the ancient *Grecians*, which have passed through my hands, do very well correspond. Now these *aurei*, as they had several impresses upon them, so had they several names, by which they are distinguished. For they were either Ἀττικοὶ, or Δαρεικοὶ, or Φιλίππειοι, or Ἀλεξάνδρειοι, or the like; all which we may prove by *Xenophon*, [e] *Harpocratio*, the *scholiast of Aristophanes*, and others, to have been equal unto two *Attick drachmes*, and therefore respectively equal to one another. Neither is this much to be wondered at, that the *Grecians* and *Persians*, though at enmity amongst themselves, yet should agree in the *aurei*; seeing that in our times the *Venetian chequeen*, the *Barbary ducat*, the *Ægyptian* and *Turkish sherif*, are almost all of the same pureness in respect of the gold, and not differing above a grain in the weight. Which difference we may also allow to those of the ancients, without any prejudice to our enquiry. Concerning these *aurei*, or golden *staters*, the observation of [f] *Julius Pollux* is worth our consideration: Καὶ οἱ μὲν Δαρεικοὶ ἐκαλοῦντο στατῆρες, οἱ δὲ Φιλίππειοι οἱ δὲ Ἀλεξάνδρειοι, χρυσοῖ πάντες ὄντες, καὶ εἰ μὲν χρυσοῦς εἴποις προσακούεται ὁ στατὴρ, εἰ δὲ στατὴρ εἴποις οὐ πάντως ὁ χρυσοῦς. *Of the* staters *some were denominated from* Darius, *some from* Philip, *some from* Alexander, *and were all of gold. And when you say the* aureus, *the* stater *is understood; but if you say the* stater, *the* aureus *is not always meant*. And this is most true; for the χρυσοῦς, or *aureus*, (I speak not here of the *aureus Romanus*, this being somewhat less than these mentioned by *Pollux*) did always imply the στατὴρ, but the στατὴρ did not always infer the *aureus*: the *stater* being more general, signifying as well the *argenteus*, as the *aureus*, and that was double to this; the *stater argenteus* being four *drachmes*, as we proved before, and therefore the same with the *tetradrachme*, and the *aureus* two *drachmes*, and therefore equal in weight to the *didrachme*. Wherefore every *aureus* was rightly called a *stater*, but every *stater* could not rightly be called an *aureus*.

From these *aurei* then, or χρυσοῖ στατῆρες, we may deduce the silver *Attick drachme*, if we either had the Δαρεικοὶ, some of which to this day are found in *Persia*, or if we had the Φιλίππειοι, or the Ἀλεξάνδρειοι. To pass by the Δαρεικοὶ, because I have not perused any of them, and to speak only of the Φιλίππειοι and Ἀλεξάνδρειοι, of which there are many extant.

Concerning the Φιλίππειοι [g] *Snellius* writes thus: *Philippi nummum unicum, & Alexandri Macedonum, solertissimus veterum nummorum æstimator Nicolaus Rockoxius possidet, utrumque eodem pondere granorum* 179. Now CLXXIX grains of gold in *Holland*, such as *Snellius* used, are answerable to an hundred thirty four grains *English* and an half. Near which proportion I have observed two others, with the inscription ΦΙΛΙΠΠΟΥ, excepting only a grain or two.

As for the Ἀλεξάνδρειοι, I find the weight of one of the fairest for impression, and character, I think, in the world, which I bought at *Alexandria*, with the image and inscription ΑΛΕΞΑΝΔΡΟΥ, to be exactly of *English* grains 133½, and another at *Constantinople* 133, and in the same proportion several others. With which comparing one of mine honoured and learned friend, *John Marsham*, Esq; I find his a grain defective: and weighing since some others, out of that choice and rare Κειμήλιον of ancient coins, collected by the noble sir *Simonds D'Ewes*, knight baronet, I observed two of his to exceed 133 grains by half a grain.

Wherefore I may conclude (allowing only half a grain for so much wanting by time, or by the mint) from the *aureus* being double to the *Attick drachme*, that it hath been rightly assigned by me to be LXVII grains: and from this with those limitations above mentioned, I may conclude the *denarius consularis* (which is our princi-

[b] Suidas in voce δραχμή. [c] Jul. Poll. l. 4. c. 24. [d] Hesychius in voce χρυσοῦς.

[e] Λέγουσι δὲ τινες δύνασθαι τὸν Δαρεικὸν ἀργυρᾶς δραχμὰς κ' (as *Jos. Scaliger* rightly corrected the printed copies, which render it ή or ὀκτὼ) ὡς τοὺς πέντε Δαρεικοὺς δύνασθαι μνᾶν ἀργυρίου. Harpocr. Τρισχίλιοι Δαρεικοὶ Xenophonti sunt δέκα τάλαντα. Talentum autem 600 drachmæ. Ergo Δαρεικὸς sunt 20 drachmæ. Scal. de re num.

[f] Jul. Poll. l. 9. c. 6. [g] Snellius de re nummaria.

pal

pal enquiry) seeing [h] *Galen*, *l.* 8. *c.* 3. *de compositione medicam.* According to the *Latin* manner of division, speaking of an antidote prescribed by *Asclepiades*, whereof the *dosis* was to be one *drachme*, or *denarius*, writes thus: Ἡγοῦμαι δὲ λέγειν αὐτὸν δραχμὴν ἀργυρᾶν, καὶ γὰρ οὕτω σχεδὸν ἅπασι τοῖς νεωτέροις ἰατροῖς ἔθος ὀνομάζειν. ἄλλο δὲ νοεῖν ἡμᾶς οὐδὲν ἡ τοῦ πράγματος φύσις ἀναγκάζει. πρόδηλον δ' ὅτι δραχμὴν λεγομένην νῦν ἐν τοῖς τοιούτοις ἅπαντες, ὅπερ Ῥωμαῖοι δηνάριον ὀνομάζουσιν. *I suppose, that he means the silver drachme, for so all the later physicians are wont to call it; neither will the nature of the thing suffer us to understand any other. And it is manifest, that in such things as we all now name the* drachme, *the* Romans *name the* denarius.

The *denarius* also, as we proved before out of *Philo*, *Josephus*, St. *Hierom*, and *Hesychius*, may be inferred by the *Hebrew* or *Samaritan* shekel: the shekel, by the joint testimony of all of them, being equal in valuation to the *Attick stater Argenteus*, or *tetradrachme*, and the *Attick tetradrachme*, as we have shewed, to four *denarii consulares*: If therefore an *Hebrew* or *Samaritan* shekel in silver, fair, and not impaired, were found, we might by this as well discover the *denarius*, as by the *tetradrachme*, or the *aureus*. And here I must confess I have not seen so many perfect and entire, with the *Samaritan* characters, which certainly are the best and truest, (for those with the later characters, invented, as some suppose, by *Esdras*, are most of them counterfeit, as to give my self satisfaction. For tho' I have perused that of *Arias Montanus*, now in the university of *Oxford*, which he describes in his tract *De Siclo*, and from whence he deduces the proportion of the *Hebrew* shekel; yet to speak the truth, there is no trust to be given to it: Not but that the coin is very ancient, and the inscription upon it in *Samaritan* characters well made; but the sides of it have been so filed away, that it hath very much lost of the true weight: For I find it to be scarce the weight of twenty-pence of our *English* standard. Whereas *Montanus*, if he made his observation exactly, equals it to almost four *Spanish rials*, or to four *Roman julio's*; both which exceed two of our *English* shillings. So that till such time as I may procure out of the east, (whither I have often sent) some perfect shekels, I must be content to take up the relations of others. And here I shall begin with *Moses Nehemani Gerundensis*, a jew, a learned expositor of the *Pentateuch*; who, as *Arias Montanus* tells us, flourished in *Catalonia* above 400 years since. His words, as *Montanus* hath delivered them in his tract *de siclo*, are these: [i] *In comment. Exod.* xxxix. *Multis verbis differens significabat se non facile ad Salomonis Jarrhæi, qui ante illum in Galliâ scripserat, sententiam de siclo accedere; cum Salomon affirmasset, Siclum esse dimidiam argenti unciam. Postea jam absoluto in omnem legem commentariorum opere, idem Moses Gerundensis capite ad eam rem propriè addito, sicli æstimationem à Salomone illo indicatam, re ipsâ doctus, ingenuè, & apertè, ut viros doctos, & veri inveniendi, atque docendi cupidos decet, comprobavit. Narrat autem se eo anno, quo illa scriberet, in Palæstinam ex Hispaniâ sacrorum locorum visendi causa navi delatum Acconam, quam nunc Jachan vocant, devenisse; ibidemque sibi ab incolis ostensum fuisse nummum argenteum antiquissimum, expressis tamen signis & literis conspicuum; in cujus altero latere forma esset vasculi illius, quod manna plenum in sacra arca ad sæculorum monumentum, Dei jussu, & Mosis procuratione fuerat repositum: Et in altero ramus ille admirabilis, quem in fasciculum virgularum plurimarum Aaronis nomine illatum (cùm illius sacerdotali dignitati ab æmulis quibusdam obtrectaretur) postera die populus omnis florentem, amygdalàque explicantem vidit; inscriptiones etiam fuisse in eodem nummo Samaritanis characteribus, quæ olim communes totius Israelis literæ fuerant, ante discessionem decem tribuum à duabus, lingua planè Hebraica, quarum exemplum ex altera parte erat* SEKEL ISRAEL, *quod Latinè sonat siclus Israelis: Ex altera verò* JERUSALEM KEDESSAH, *hoc est Jerusalem sancta: Qui nummus antiquitatem cùm primis magnam probabat, utpote cujus nomine Israelis, eo tempore quo omnes* XII *tribus communi concordia Israelis nomen obtinebant; quoque Hierosolyma ipsis omnibus regia urbs, sanctaque erat; eademque communis omnibus & religionis, & publicæ rei, & monetæ, atque literarum ratio, quæ postea discessione facta, alia atque alia utrique parti fuit. Namque Judæi, ut omnes ferè scriptores asserunt, ne cum schismaticis Israelitis ullo sacrorum usu communicarent, eam literarum formam, quæ nunc etiam in usu est, hoc est quadratam, mutatis valde alterius prioris figuris, adinvenêre. Affirmat præterea idem Gerundensis, nummum illum, qui siclus inscribebatur, sibi in statera pensum dimidiæ argenti unciæ pondus reddidisse, ostensam quoque alteram monetam dimidiato pondere minorem, iisdem omnino vasis & rami figuris quæ tamen non* SEKEL, *sed* HASZI SEKEL, *hoc est dimidius siclus diceretur, probare itaq; sibi vel maximè Salomonis Jarrhæi de sicli pondere, & valore, sententiam.* Thus

GREAVES

[h] Galenus, l. 8. de composit medicam.

[i] Arias Montanus de Siclo, in libro qui inscribitur Thubal Kain, sive de mensuris.

far *Gerundensis*: who if he had expressed with what half ounce he had compared his shekel, or if *Montanus* had done it for him, they had given the judicious reader better satisfaction. But this, I suppose, by a probable conjecture, may be supplied, in saying, that he living in *Catalonia*, weighed it with the *Catalonian*, or *Spanish* half ounce; which [k] *Villalpandus*, and [l] *Ciaconius*, both of them *Spaniards*, make equal to the half ounce now used at *Rome*; that is, to two shillings three pence farthing; *q.* of our money. This conjecture of mine will exceeding well confirm those many observations of *Villalpandus*, a man in this kind very curious, which he made of several ancient shekels in silver, who thus writes: [m] *Igitur ante aliquot annos appendimus siclum unum apud F. Ursinum & postmodum eos omnes, quos præcedenti capite percensuimus, atque comperimus singulos argenti siclos ex æquo semunciæ Romanæ antiquæ respondere; ita ut ne minimum quidem hordei aut frumenti granulum, huic, vel illi lanci addi potuerit, quin in eam examen propenderet. Nec mirum cuiquam videri debet, antiquissimos nummos suo pristino ponderi nunc respondere, neque ullam argenti partem vetustate consumptam tot sæculis fuisse. Nam singulari Dei beneficio nobis contigit, tot integros appendere potuisse siclos. Id quod nummi ipsi integri vetustatem maximè præ se ferentes, literæ expressæ, extantésque, argenti color, atque alia id genus multa facile probant.* With these observations of *Villalpandus*, I find the weight of a very fair *Samaritan* shekel, of *the truly noble and learned Mr.* Selden, to agree: To whom I stand obliged for this favour as he doth for the coin, *to the honourable antiquary, Sir* Robert Cotton. To these testimonies, tho' (it may be) sufficient of themselves, I shall add [n] one more, for farther illustration of the weight of the *Hebrew*, or *Samaritan* shekel, and that is of an ancient, and fair one, in silver, amongst his majesty's coins, perused by *the most reverend primate of* Ireland, *a man of exquisite learning and judgment*, who hath often assured me, that it weighs two shillings five pence of the *English* standard; which proportion, excepting some few grains, in which it doth exceed, does well correspond with those of *Villalpandus*. And this may farther be confirmed out of the *Talmud*, [o] כל כסף האמורה בתורה כסף צורי ושל דברו הכם כסף מדינה *Argentum omne cujus in lege fit mentio, intelligitur argentum Tyrium (ponderis & bonitatis ut in urbe Tyri:* As [p] *Schlinder* interprets it) *sed Rabbinorum argentum intelligitur argentum commune provinciale.* Taking therefore the *silver money of* Judea, as the *Talmud* doth, to be equal to the *Tyrian*, and that of *Carthage* to be equal to that of *Tyre*: As it is very probable that the *Carthaginians*, being a plantation of the *Tyrians*, might observe their proportions in coins, as well as their customs in religion, we may by these discover the shekel to be much about the same weight that hath been assigned: For [q] *Ant. Augustinus*, describing in his dialogues the weight of two fair *Carthaginian* coins in silver, writes, *that they are each of them somewhat more than four drachms*: that is, as he elsewhere explains himself, a little more than half the *Roman* ounce. If therefore we shall adhere to the observation of *Gerundensis*, made four hundred years since, or to these later of *Villalpandus*, and others; or to this conjecture of mine, the *Hebrew* shekel, and half the present *Roman* ounce, are either both the same, or else very near in proportion.

And this may easily be granted; but if it be, how will four *denarii consulares*, four *Attick drachmes*, and the *Hebrew shekel*, be reciprocally equal one to another, as they should be by those several testimonies before alledged? Whereas, by many hundred *denarii consulares*, tried by an exact ballance, I find the best of these to contain LXII grains *English*, and the *Attick drachme* LXVII. And the fourth part of the *shekel* to be but LVI grains $\frac{1}{4}$, if we admit of *Gerundensis*, and *Villalpandus*'s observations. Which notwithstanding, according to *Philo*, *Josephus*, St. *Hierom*, *Epiphanius*, and *Hesychius*, should be equal to the *Attick drachme*; and the *Attick drachme*, by the testimonies of the ancients, should be likewise equal to the *denarius*. For the solution of this objection I answer: First, That the *denarius*, and *Attick drachme*, being distinct coins of different states, and not much unequal in the true weight, it is no wonder, especially in *Italy*, and in the *Roman* dominions, that they should pass one for another: no more than that the *Spanish rials*, in our sea-towns in *England*, should pass for testars; or the quarters of the dollar be exchanged for our shillings: whereas the *rial* in the intrinsical valuation, is better than our testar by four grains, and somewhat more; and the quarter of the dollar is better than our shilling by more than eight grains, or a penny; but because they

[k] *Eædem omnino sunt unciæ, quibus olim Romani Hispanique utuntur*, &c. Villalp. de appar urb. ac templi, par. 2. l. 3. c. 20. [l] Ciaconius de ponderibus, pag. 45. [m] Villalpan. de app. urbis ac templi, par. 2. l. 5. disp. 4. c. 28. [n] We may also insert the observation of *Anton. August. dialogo* 2. *Ne ho uno* [*siclo*] *che è d' argento, & è di peso di quattro dramme conforme à quello che dice San Girolamo sopra Ezechielle*: Where by four drachms he means half the *Roman* ounce. [o] Kiddushf. 11.
[p] Schindlerus in Pentaglotto. [q] Ant. August. Dialog. 6.

want

want the valuation character, and impression of our princes, which I call the *extrinsick of coin*, therefore doth the *Spanish* money fall from its true value with us, and so would ours do in *Spain*. By the same analogy must we conceive the *Attick drachmes*, tho' in the intrinsick they were somewhat better worth than the *denarius*, yet for want of the extrinsick, to have lost in *Italy*, and thereby to have become equal in valuation to the *denarius*. And this seems to be implied by [r] *Volusius Metianus: Victoriatus enim nunc tantundem valet, quantum quinarius olim. At peregrinus nummus loco mercis, ut nunc tetradrachmum, & drachma habebatur.* Which words of his *loco mercis*, plainly shew they made some gain of the *tetradrachmum*, and *drachma*: As our merchants, and goldsmiths do of the *Spanish rials*, and quarters of a dollar. Which they could not do, if they were precisely equal, but must rather be losers in the melting or new coining of them. And therefore all [s] modern writers that have treated of this argument, some of them making the *drachma* less than the *denarius*, others equal, but none greater, have been deceived by a double paralogism, in standing too nicely upon the bare words of the ancients, without carefully examining the things themselves. First, In making the *denarius*, and *Attick drachme* precisely equal, because all ancient authors generally express the *Attick drachme* by the *denarius*, or the *denarius* by the *drachme*; either because in ordinary commerce, and in vulgar estimation, they passed one for another, in the *Roman* state; or else if any were so curious to observe their difference, as surely the κολλυβιςαὶ were, yet by reason of their nearness, and to avoid fractions, and having no other names of coins that were precisely equal, whereby to render them, therefore all *Greek* and *Latin* authors, mutually used one for the other. And, secondly, Because some writers, (as *Dioscorides* and *Cleopatra*) affirm, that the *Roman* ounce contained eight *drachmes*, therefore modern authors infer, that the *denarius*, being equal to the *drachme*, and eight *drachmes* being in the *Roman* ounce (as so many were in the *Attick*) that therefore there are eight *denarii* in the *Roman*, and consequently that the *Roman* and *Attick* ounces are equal. Whereas *Celsus*, *Scribonius Largus*, and *Pliny*, as we shewed before, expresly write, that the *Roman* ounce contained in their time, which was after *Dioscorides*, seven *denarii*. And being natural *Romans*, and purposely mentioning the proportion of the *denarius* to the ounce, thereby the better to regulate their *doses* in physick, it is not probable but they must better have known it than the *Grecians*. Besides, who with any certainty can collect out of these imperfect fragments of *Dioscorides* and *Cleopatra* (for those tracts of theirs, *de ponderibus* are no better) whether at the first they wrote in that manner, as they are now printed? Or if they did, why might not they endeavour to introduce into the *Roman* ounce, in imitation of the *Attick*, that manner of division, which is now generally received in our times, of making the ounce, of what kind soever it be, to contain eight *drachmes*. And surely this of eight being a *compound number*, as arithmeticians use to speak, was much fitter than seven, used by the *Romans*, which being *a prime number*, is therefore incapable of any other division. And then for to conclude, that because the *Attick* ounce had eight *drachmes*, and the *Roman* as many, that therefore their ounces are equal, is all one as to conclude, that the *Paris* and *English* ounces are equal, because the *French* as well as we (and so do all physicians of all countries that I know) divide their ounce by eight *drachmes*. And thus, I suppose, I have sufficiently answered the first part of the objection, concerning the *denarius*, and the *Attick drachme*: that if we respect the vulgar and popular estimation, in which sense classical authors understood them (for they could not well otherwise render them, than as they were current) so were they equal; but if we respect the intrinsical valuation, which depends upon the weight, especially when coins are of a like fineness, so were they unequal: the *Attic drachme* being, of our money, eight pence farthing *q.* and the *denarius consularis* seven pence half-peny farthing; allowing for the standard [t] VIII *English* grains to the silver peny.

[r] *Vol. Metianus de assis distributione.* These words of *Metianus* I find in a *MS* of *Temporarius*, thus corrected: *Victoriatus enim nunc tantundem valet quantum quinarius. Olim ut peregrinus nummus loco mercis, ut nunc tetradrachmum, & drachma habebatur.* Whether it be by conjecture, or that he found it in some ancient *MS*. I know not, but the emendation I cannot but approve.

[s] *Budæus drachmam putat ejusdem ponderis esse cum denario: Onuphrius vero inter utrumque statuit rationem sesquitertiam, Agricoli sesquiseptimam, ut Panvinio tres denarii quatuor drachmas, Agricolæ verò septem denarii octo drachmas efficiant. Capel de pond. & nummis, l. 1.* LXXXIV *denarii, quæ est libra Romana, sunt æquales* XCVI *drachmis, quæ est libra Italica, & medica.* Scal. de re nummaria.

[t] These proportions, with those before, and those which follow, are taken from the *English* standard at five shillings the ounce (as it was formerly coined) to avoid fractions: that is, eight grains to the silver penny: whereas in these times it is five shillings, two pence. Not that the ounce is encreased, for this is always constant and fixed; but that for reasons of state, our silver coins are diminished, and consequently contain fewer grains. And this diminution must necessarily be, as often as other nations, with whom we have commerce, rebate in the proportions of their coins; or else we must be content to be losers.

Neither

Neither do I know any authority, that either expreſly, or by a true and logical conſequence, can be produced out of claſſical authors, to infringe this aſſertion of mine, unleſs it be one in *Fannius*, which being a fragment is the leſs to be valued: and another in *Livy*, who thus writes, *lib.* XXXIV. in his deſcription of the triumph of *Quintius: ſignati argenti octoginta quatuor millia fuere Atticorum, tetradrachmum vocant; trium ferè denariorum in ſingulis argenti eſt pondus.* Which words of his occaſioned [v] *Georgius Agricola*, not knowing how to anſwer them, to bring in a diſtinction of three ſorts of *denarii:* the *gravis* weighing an *Attic drachme* and an half, the *mediocris* one and a ſeventh part, the *levis* moſt commonly one; without any clear proof or evidence in any ancient author, and directly contrary to all ancient coins of the *Atticks* and *Romans* which I have ſeen: of which error he would not have been guilty (for there is no man that hath writ either *de ponderibus & menſuris*, or *de re metallica*, more ſolidly and judiciouſly than he) if he had been ſo happy as to have peruſed many entire *Grecian aurei* and *tetradrachmes*, or elſe to have examin'd a greater and more ſelect quantity of *Roman* coins. To ſatisfy my ſelf concerning that place of *Livy*, I had recourſe to our MSS. here (and I could wiſh I had done the like in *Italy*) and theſe I find to agree with the printed copies; tho' the coins, which are much ancienter than any MSS. conſtantly diſagree. Wherefore if it be not a miſtake in *Livy* himſelf, which I am not apt to believe in ſo grave an author, I would correct the copies by the coins, and inſtead of III *fere denariorum*, make it thus, IV *fere denariorum.* Where the figure V being reſolved into two lines, and left a little open at the bottom, might eaſily be taken by the ſcribe for the figure II. And this I do certainly [w] believe is the true ground of that error, wherewith ſo many of late hath been perplexed. However it were, it is as ancient as *Priſcian*, or *Pſeudo-Priſcian* (as Capellus ſtiles him) who, in his tract *De ponderibus*, reads thoſe words of *Livy* in the ſame manner, *Trium ferè denariorum.*

As for the *denarius aureus*, a name I think not known to the ancients, which *Salmaſius* and others collect out of [x] *Livy, De fœdere Ætolico. Pro argento ſi aurum dare mallent, dare convenit, dum pro argenteis decem aureus unus valeret.* I ſee no ſolid foundation for that opinion; all that can be collected thence is, that the gold then was *in decupla ratione* to the ſilver, which I have proved before. And whereas [y] *Plautus* hath his *denaria Philippea,*

Nummi octingenti aurei in marſupio inſuerunt,
Præterea centum denaria Philippea.

This is a metaphorical or comical expreſſion of him, and no certain ſort of coin; which he pleaſantly calls *denarii*, becauſe half the χρυσοῖ Φιλίππειοι were equal in weight to the *drachma*, and ſo alſo was the *Roman denarius* ſuppoſed to be.

Nor are we to take the κῆνσος, which is thrice mentioned by St. *Matthew*, and once by St. *Mark*, for the *denarius*, as ſome have done: no, nor for any other ſort of coin: for it is preciſely the *Latin* word *cenſus*; that is, ὁ φόρος, *tributum*, and ſo it is rendered by St. *Luke*, ἔξεστι Καίσαρι φόρον δοῦναι, ἢ οὔ; where St. *Matthew* and St. *Mark* have it, ἔξεστι δοῦναι κῆνσον Καίσαρι ἢ οὔ; tho' *Heſychius* and *Moſcopulus*, both upon an error, interpret it a ſort of coin. *Heſychius*, κῆνσος εἶδος νομίσματος ἐπικεφάλαιον, or νομίσματος ἐπικεφαλαίου, as M. *Caſaubone* corrects it: and *Moſcopulus*, κῆνσος νόμισμα δραχμῆς ἰσοστάσιον, *the* cenſus *is a coin equal in weight to the* drachme: that is, in the notion of the *Greeks*, equal to the *denarius.* The error of theſe two *Greek* grammarians, is a miſunderſtanding the propriety of the *Latin* word *cenſus:* and that occaſioned them to take κῆνσος, and νόμισμα τοῦ κήνσου, for the ſame. But the evangeliſt *Matthew* puts a manifeſt difference between κῆνσος *tributum*, and νόμισμα, the money that was paid for tribute. Ἐπιδείξατέ μοι τὸ νόμισμα τοῦ κήνσου, writes St. *Matthew*, *Shew me the money of the tribute:* or as our new tranſlation renders it, *Shew me the tribute-money.* And the three evangeliſts, *Matthew*, *Mark*, and *Luke*, immediately after expreſly term this money the δηνάριον. Οἱ δὲ προσήνεγκαν αὐτῷ δηνάριον: *and they brought unto him a penny.* Which being a *Roman* coin, and current amongſt the *Jews*, being then in ſubjection to the *Romans*, it is more than probable that they paid their tribute to *Cæſar*, in the ſame ſpecies of money that was uſed by *Cæſar*; and not with any new or peculiar ſort of coin, according to *Baronius* (which M. *Caſaubone* hath juſtly

[v] *G. Agricolæ reſponſio ad Alciatum de pond. & menſuris. Argentei Romanorum denarii triplices ſunt: Graves, qui pendunt drachmam Atticam cum dimidia: Mediocres, qui drachmam & ſeptimam ejus partem: Leves, qui plerunque drachmam.*

[w] If this anſwer be not ſatisfactory, we may ſay, as ſome have done, that *Livy*, *Fannius*, and the *ſcholiaſt of Nicander*, ſpeak of the *denarii* of the former conſuls immediately ſucceeding *Q. Fabius.* For there being but ſix of thoſe in the ounce, (as they ſuppoſe) the *denarius* will be greater than the *drachma*, as it will be leſs when ſeven were coined, under the later conſuls, which is our aſſertion.

[x] Livius, l. 38. [y] Plautus in Rudente.

confuted) but with the ordinary current money of *Rome*, and that was the *denarius*.

Our next solution should be of the *shekel*. how it could be equal to the *tetradrachme*, and consequently to four *denarii*, when by the constant weight of the best *Hebrew*, or *Samaritan shekels* extant, we find them to be much less. And here I am a little unsatisfied, how to reconcile the coins to *Philo*, *Josephus*, *Epiphanius*, St. *Hierom*, and *Hesychius*: or else, if we admit of the coins (as I know no just exceptions against them) how to excuse these authors of too supine negligence in comparing them, if so be they ever were so curious as to collate them with the *Attick tetradrachmes*. For if we shall say, that the silver *stater*, or *Attick tetradrachme* was a foreign coin, in respect of the rep. of the *Jews*, and therefore that in *Judea* it might somewhat fall from its true valuation, we shall say no more than what reason and experience confirm. But then that the *tetradrachme* should sink so low as to lose four-pence-half-peny, if we take the *reverend primate*'s observation before-mentioned; or which is more, six-pence *q.* if we follow that of *Gerundensis* and *Villalpandus*, or *those of mine*, upon two shillings nine pence half-peny, for so much was the *tetradrachme* of our money, it may seem too great a diminution; especially the *Attick* money being as pure, and fine, as that of the shekel; and therefore no goldsmith amongst the *Jews*, but would have given a greater rate only to melt it, and turn it into bullion. Yet on the other side, when I consider the practice of the money-changers amongst the *Jews* at this day, which it may be was as bad in *Philo*'s and *Josephus*'s time, and might occasion our Saviour not long before to whip them out of the temple, *which they by their extortions had made a den of thieves*; who now make it a trade at *Alexandria*, and elsewhere, in changing *Spanish* dollars into [z] *madines*, (or the small silver money current in *Ægypt*) to gain one or two *madines* upon every dollar, notwithstanding the *Spanish* money is as frequent, and as well known in *Turky*, as their own. I can the better imagine they might make the same advantage, or a little more, upon the *Attick tetradrachmes*: Which it may be also were not permitted, being contrary to their law, to pass so generally with them, as the *Spanish* money now doth (by reason of the image of *Pallas*, and the *Noctua* instamped:) or if they were permitted, yet they might not be so common, and so well known: and therefore upon strangers in *Judea*, in giving them current money for that which was foreign, they would gain so much the more. So that *Philo*, and *Josephus*, when they equal the *shekel* to the *tetradrachme*, may have taken it upon the relation and practice of these money-changers, and not upon any experiment of their own. The same answer may serve for *Epiphanius*, St. *Hierom*, and *Hesychius*: tho' it may be these borrowed their descriptions from *Philo* or *Josephus*, who long preceded them: and being *Jews*, and living in the time when the state of the *Jews* was in being; whereas these did not, their authority is the more to be credited. And thus have we finished our enquiry of the *denarius consularis*, by comparing it with the *Attick drachmes*, and the *Hebrew shekels*. GREAVES

ON CONGII VESPASIANI IN PALATIO FARNESIANO ROMÆ.

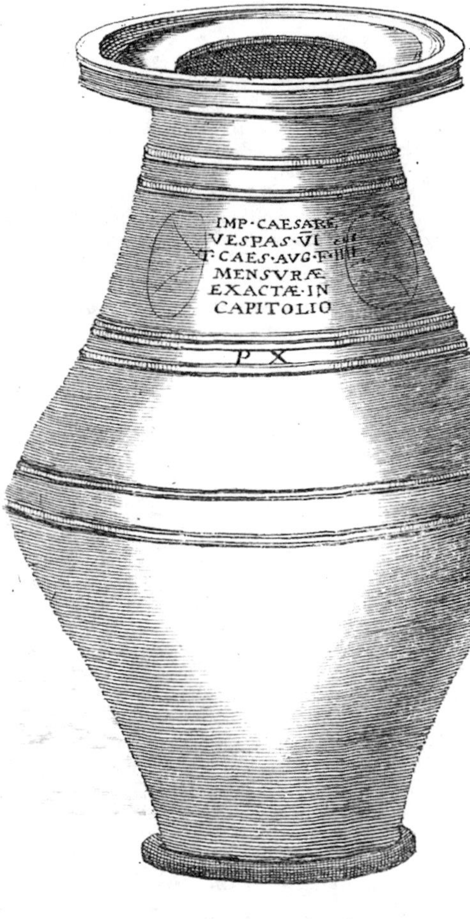

[z] At my being in *Ægypt*, thirty fives *madines* passed for a dollar: *Sands* in his travels writes forty.

GREAVES

The last and best way to discover the true weight of it, is by the *congius Romanus*, whereof by a special providence, as [a] *Pætus*, and *Villalpandus*, have well observed, the original standard of *Vespasian* is still extant in *Rome*. This, as the superscription upon it, XP demonstrates, contains the weight of ten *Roman* pounds, and is equal (by the joint confession of all authors treating this argument) to six *sextarii*. Again, the *sextarius*, as [b] *Galen* writes, Ἔχει μίαν λίτραν καὶ ἡμίσειαν καὶ ἕκτον, ὡς εἶναι τὰς πάσας οὐγγίας κʹ. *Contains one pound and an half, and a sixth part, so that it hath in all twenty ounces.* Or as [c] *Oribasius*, physician to *Julian* the apostate, informs us, is equal to the *Roman* pound, and eight ounces. Ἰταλικὸν κεράμιον ἔχει ξέστας μηʹ. ξέστης λίτραν μίαν, καὶ οὐγγίας ηʹ. *The* Italian amphora *contains forty eight* sextarii, *and the* sextarius *one pound and eight ounces.* The capacity therefore of this *congius* being fill'd up with six *sextarii*, of some certain sort of liquors, (for it is *liquorum mensura*) will give us ten *Roman* pounds, and consequently their ounces and *denarii*. The only difficulty is, with what sort of liquor we must measure it: for all liquors are not of the same gravity. And this is well cleared by [d] *Rhemnius Fannius*, and others.

Illud præterea tecum cohibere memento,
Finitum pondus varios servare liquores.
Nam libræ, ut memorant, bessem sextarius addet,
Seu puros pendas latices, seu dona Lyæi.

The *sextarius*, saith *Fannius*, contains one pound and eight ounces, whether we weigh clear water, or wine: where by wine, according to [e] *Agricola*, is to be understood, *vinum fulvum*, such as the *Greeks* call κιῤῥόν. Rather, I imagine, that wine, which *Galen* calls λευκὸν, καὶ ὀλιγόφορον. The *sextarius* then being one pound eight ounces of clear water, or pure wine, and six *sextarii* being in the *congius*, it is most evident that the *congius* contains ten pounds of water, or of wine. This also appears by a *plebiscitum* of the two *Silii*, *Publius*, and *Marius*, which is to be seen in the best copies of [f] *Sextus Pompeius*.

The same is confirmed by [g] *Dioscorides*; who for farther certainty, mentions with what sort of water we should measure it: and that is with rain [h]-water, which he makes to be the most infallible of all: Ὁ χοῦς τελέσι τὸ κόγγιον ἔχει λι. ιʹ. τὸ ἡμικόγγιον ἔχει λι. εʹ. ὁ ξέστης ἔχει λίτραν μίαν γο. ηʹ, &c. ὁ αὐτὸς δὲ σταθμός ἐστι καὶ ὕδατος καὶ ὄξους. Φασὶ δὲ τοῦ ὀμβρίου ὕδατος πληρωθεῖσαν ἀψευδέστατον εἶναι τὸν σταθμὸν, ἄγειν δὲ ὁλκὰς ψκ τὸν χοῦν. *The* chus, (*that is, the* congius,) *contains ten pounds*; *the* semicongius *five*; *the* sextarius *one pound and eight ounces*, &c. *The weight of water, and of vinegar is the same. They say, that if it be filled up with rain-water, the weight will be most certain.* [i] *The* congius *weighs seven hundred and twenty drachmes.* An *anonymous Greek author*, falsly reputed to be *Galen*, in the edition at *Venice*, confirms the same, [k] Παρὰ δὲ τοῖς Ἰταλοῖς διέγνωκε ὁ χοῦς μέτρῳ μὲν ἔχων ξ ϛ. κοτύλας ιβ. σταθμὸν δὲ ὕδατος ὀμβρίου, ὅπερ ἐστιν ἀψευδέστατον, δραχ-

[a] Pætus, l. 3. de antiq. liquid. arid. que mens. Villalp. de appar. urbis ac templi, par. 2. l. 3. c. 25.
[b] Galen, l. 1. de compos. medicam.
[c] Oribasius, l. 2. ad Eustathium filium.
[d] Rhemn. Fan. carmina de pond. & mens.
[e] Agricola, l. 3. de ponder. rerum.
[f] Sextus Pomp. de verb. signif. VTI. QVADRANTAL. VINI. OCTOGINTA PONDO. SIET
CONGIVS. VINI. DECEM. IS. SIET
SEX. SEXTARII. CONGIVS. SIET. VINI
DVO. DE. QVINQVAGINTA. SEXTARII
QVADRANTAL. SIET. VINI.
SEXTARIVS. ÆQVVS. ÆQVO. CVM. LIBRARIO. SIET

[g] Fragmenta Dioscoridis.

[h] The proportion that rain-water hath to fountain-water, is as 1000000 to 1007522, and the proportion that it hath to water distilled, is as 1000000 to 997065, as it hath been observed by *Snellius in Eratosth. Bat. l. 2. c. 5. Est in æquali mole ratio aquæ pluviæ ad distillatam, quemadmodum* 1000000 *ad* 997065; *pluviæ autem ad putealem ut* 1000000 *ad* 1007522.

[i] This authority of *Dioscorides*, with that other citation following out of an *anonymous Greek author*, strongly proves my assertion, that the *drachma Attica* was more ponderous than the *denarius consularis*. For there being eighty four of these *denarii* in the *Roman* pound, as we have elsewhere proved, and ten *Roman* pounds in the *congius*, it is most evident there are ɪↄↄcccxʟ. *denarii* in the whole *congius*. Again, ɪↄↄccxx *drachms* by the testimonies of *Dioscorides*, and this *anonymous* writer being equal to the *congius*, and the *congius* being equal to ɪↄↄcccxʟ *denarii*, therefore ɪↄↄccxx *drachmes* are equal to ɪↄↄcccxʟ *denarii*, and therefore of necessity every particular *drachme* of these, must be greater than each particular *denarius*. And tho', according to my assertion, the *congius* containeth some few *drachmes* more than are by them assigned; yet that difference, seeing it might many ways happen, as I afterwards shew in the like experiments of *Villalpandus*, and *Gassendus*, it cannot any way overthrow my conclusion: for the *drachmes* are still fewer than the *denarii consulares*, and therefore greater; which was the thing intended to be proved. And this may farther be confirmed, in that both *Cleopatra*, and this *anonymous* author, make also the ξέστης, or *sextarius* (being the sixth part of the *congius*) to contain an hundred twenty *drachmes* of fountain-water. Whereby it appears there is no error committed in the former numbers: Ὁ ξέστης μέτρῳ μὲν ἔχει κοτύλας βʹ σταθμῷ δὲ λʹ ρκ. The *sextarius*, saith *Cleopatra*, *contains in measure two* cotyls, *but in weight an hundred and twenty* drachmes. And the *anonymous* writer, Ἔχει δὲ ὁ ξέστης σταθμῷ δραχμὰς ρκ. *The* sextarius *contains in weight an hundred and twenty* drachmes.

[k] Anonymus Græc.

μὰς

μιᾶς ψκ: *Amongst* [t]*he* Romans *is found the* congius, *containing in measure six* sextarii (*that is*) XII cotylæ: *but in weight of rain-water, which is most infallible*, IↃCCXX drachmes. And whereas [l] *Dioscorides* elsewhere writes: Τὸ κόγϊιον ἔχει λίτρας θ. τὸ ἡμικόγϊιον λ. δ'. S. ὁ ξέςης ἔχει λ'. ά. S. *The* congius *hath nine pounds*; *the* semicongius *four and a half*; *the* sextarius *one and an half*: there is no repugnancy between this and his former assertion. For here he speaks of the *congius* filled with oil, and before of the same *congius* filled with water, or wine: and that this should be but nine pounds, whereas the former is ten, is no more repugnant to reason, than it is to nature, that oil should be lighter than water or wine: which [m] *Ghetaldus*, in his *Archimedes promotus*, hath demonstrated the most accurately of any man, to be in the proportion that 1 is to 1 $\frac{1}{11}$ in respect of water, and as 1 is to 1 $\frac{4}{55}$ in respect of wine; which is almost the same with *Dioscorides*. The not observing this difference of weight, arising from the different gravity of several liquors, in vessels of one and the same capacity, is that which hath occasioned much uncertainty and confusion, in modern writers. And therefore we shall for farther perspicuity insert that distinction, which is often inculcated by [n] *Galen*, that the *Romans* used two sorts of ounces and pounds: and those were either ςαθμικαὶ, or μετρικαὶ, *ponderal* or *mensural*; the one had respect solely to the gravity, the other to the *moles*, and gravity conjointly; the former were always certain and fixed, consisting of solid matter; the latter were *vasa* (frequently, ἐν κέϱασι) being receptacles and measures of liquid substances: and therefore the *libræ*, and *unciæ mensurales*, in these were greater or less, according as the liquor to be measured was heavier or lighter. Whence [o] *Galen* blames physicians for not expressing this difference: Διὸ γϱάφειν ἐχϱῆν ἐπιμελέςεϱον ἐν τ͂ φαϱμακίτισι βίϐλοις τὺς ἰατϱὺς ὁποίας τινὰς κελεύυσι βάλλεσθαι τὰς ὐγγίας ἢ τὰς λίτϱας τ͂ ὑγϱῶν φαϱμάκων, πότεϱον τὰς μετϱικὰς, ἢ τὰς ςαθμικάς. And he gives the reason of it. [p] Αἱ μὲν γὰϱ ςαθμικαὶ τὸ βάϱος κϱίνυσι τ͂ σωμάτων, αἱ δὲ μετϱικαὶ τ͂ ὄγκον. *For the* ponderal *examine the weight of bodies, but the* mensural *the moles*. But to return to the *congius*, and by it to our discovery of the *denarius*. The water then must be natural, either of some fountain, or of rain. For if it be artificial, such as are made by distillations, whether by a strong reverberation, or by a gentle, in an alembeck; these having somewhat of the property of fire, will be lighter than the natural, as [q] *Agricola* and others observe. I shall produce two observations of the *congius*, with fountain-water, made by two very eminent and able men, *Villalpandus*, and *Gassendus*, the one at *Rome*, with the *Roman* weights, from the [r] original *congius* itself; the other at *Aix*, with the *Paris* weights, from a model, or copy of that at *Rome*, procured by *Peireskius*. And here to compare the *denarius consularis* with their observations, it is necessary to have exactly both the *Roman* and *Paris* weights. The former, with as much accurateness as it was possible, were taken in *Rome*: the other were sent me by monsieur *Hardy*, *a learned man of honourable quality in Paris*, who compared them with the standard. To begin with that of *Villalpandus*, who gives us a large description, with how much caution and circumspection, and with how exquisite a balance he twice made his experiment, whereby he discovered the weight of it in

[l] Fragmenta Dioscoridis.

[m] Ghetaldus in Archim. promoto.

[n] Galenus, l. 1. & 6. de comp. medicam. secundum genera.

[o] Lib. 6.

[p] Ibid. lib. 1.

[q] *Perinde verò ut vinum hoc factitium omni nativo est levius, sic aquæ ferè omnes, quæ ignis calore rebus quibuseunque excoctis distillarint, quas ob id distillatas appellant, cæteris aquis leviores sunt.* Agricola, l. 3. de pondere rerum.

[r] This *congius* I had weighed, if I could have procured a ballance of such exactness, as was fitting for such a work. The want of which occasioned *Villalpandus* to suspect the observation of *Pætus*; though *Pætus* writes thus of himself. *Plenum, cùm justissimâ trutinâ, quâ hodie Romæ utimur cùm appendissem* [congium,] *inveni aquam, quâ eum compleveram, libras nostri temporis novem, uncias sex semis efficere, quibus uncias quinque drachmas quatuor, scripulum unum, & grana* XIV (*quæ amplius sunt in his nostris, quam in antiquis libris computando eum congium libras decem*) *& ultra scripulum unum, & grana* XIV (*de quibus nullam rationem habendam esse judicavi*) *ex antiquis libris prædictis pendere inveni.* But *Villalpandus* trying it long after *Pætus*, with more care, and with a ballance made of purpose, found it to be exactly ten such pounds as are now used in *Rome*. All that I could do was to fill the capacity of it with *milium* well cleansed, and to compare it with the *English* measures taken from the standards. *It contained of our measures for wine three quarts, one pint, and one eighth part of a pint. Of our corn, or dry measures, three quarts, and about one sixth part of a pint.* At my being in *Italy*, there was found amongst the ruins at *Rome* a *semicongius* in brass, of the same figure with this of *Vespasian*'s, the sides much consumed by rust. This I also measured, and found it to be the half of *Vespasian*'s *congius*. From this measure of the *congius* we may rightly apprehend how vast that draught was of *Novellus Torquatus*, who drank three of these *congii* at once: from whence he was called *Novellus Tricongius*. The story is recited by *Pliny*, (l. 14. c. 22.) *Apud nos cognomen etiam Novellus Torquatus Mediolanensis ad proconsulatum usque è præturâ honoribus gestis, tribus congiis* (*unde & nomen illi fuit*) *epotis uno impetu, spectante miraculi gratiâ Tiberio principe in senecta jam severo, atque etiam aliàs sævo, sed ipsâ juventâ ad merum pronior fuerat.* In the same chapter *Pliny* likewise discourses thus of *Cicero*, son to that famous orator: *Tergilla Ciceronem Marci filium binos congios simul baurire solitum ipsi objicit, Marcoque Agrippæ à temulento scyphum impactum.*

water

GREAVES water to be exactly anſwerable to ten ſuch pounds as are now uſed in *Rome*: whence he concludes, [f] *Conſtanter aſſerimus antiquam Romanorum libram, unciam, ac pondera, tot ætatum ſucceſſione, ac Romani imperii perturbationibus minimè immutata fuiſſe, ſed eadem per manus tradita uſque ad noſtra tempora perduraſſe.* This *Roman* pound of his reduced to the *Engliſh* ſtandard for ſilver, or *Troy* weight, with which I have faithfully collated it, is 5256 grains *Engliſh*, ſuch as the *Troy* pound is 5760; the whole *congius* therefore conſiſting of ten pounds, will be 52560 *Engliſh* grains. The other obſervation is related by [t] *Gaſſendus*, in his excellent diſcourſe *De vitâ Peireſkii*: *Ut paucis ergo res dicatur, cautiones adhibuimus eaſdem, quas Lucas Pætus, & Villalpandus, dum vas ipſum, ad ſummum collum puteali aquâ opplevimus, expendimus, vaſis pondus ſubduximus. Deprehendimus autem aquam, quæ Romano pondere eſſe debuit decem librarum, ſeu unciarum centum viginti, eſſe pondere Pariſienſi (quale nempe Pariſiis exploratum, miſſumque eſt) librarum ſeptem, minus unciæ quadrante: Seu unciarum centum undecim, & quadrantum unciæ trium. Deinde ex hac proportione collegimus unciam Romanam continere grana quingenta, & triginta ſex, qualium quingenta, & ſeptuaginta ſex in Pariſienſi continentur: unde & illis in drachmas collectis, obvenere cuilibet drachmæ grana ſexaginta ſeptem: idque proinde cenſuimus pondus denarii Cæſarei, quem dictum eſt fuiſſe* [u] *drachmalem.* Now the *Paris* ounce ſent to me by monſieur *Hardy*, containing four hundred ſeventy two grains *Engliſh*, and an half; and the *congius*, according to *Gaſſendus*, of the *Paris* ounces 111 $\frac{1}{2}$, the complete weight of the *congius*, in grains, will be 52801 $\frac{1}{3}$. Which ſum exceeds that of *Villalpandus* by 241 $\frac{7}{8}$; that is, by more than half a *Roman* ounce. This difference (tho' it is not great) between theſe two obſervations of theirs, might ariſe, either from the unequal ſwelling of the water in the *congius*; or from the different gravity of fountain-water at *Rome*, and at *Aix*; or from ſome inequality of the model and original; or from defect in the *jugum*, or beam of the balance, which if it were not made by a very ſkilful hand, by the preſſure of ſo great a weight, would ſuffer ſome alteration. Which way ſoever it was, either by ſome, or all of theſe, the difference cannot prejudice my concluſion a compleat grain; which no reaſonable man but will allow, either for coining, or for waſte: for if I divide 52560, the number of grains in the *congius*, according to *Villalpandus*, by IↃCCCCXL the number of the *denarii* in ten pounds, the ſum will be LXII $\frac{4}{7}$. Or if we ſhall follow *Gaſſendus*, though I ſhould rather prefer *Villalpandus*, becauſe he took his immediately from the original, then will the weight of the *denarius conſularis* be LXII $\frac{361}{430}$. The fraction in both without any convenience may be omitted. And this proportion of the weight of the *denarius conſularis*, if it were neceſſary, I could farther prove by ſome of the *aurei conſulares*, which often were double in weight to the *denarii*, as the χρυσοῖ Ἀττικοὶ were double to the δραχμαὶ Ἀργυραῖ; as alſo by ſeveral *quinarii* in ſilver (which are the half of the *denarii*) by a very ancient and perfect [x] *ſemuncia*, by a *quadrans* and *triens*, all of them in braſs of mine own, and by ſeveral other weights examined abroad. One of them I cannot pretermit, being near five *Roman* pounds, and very remarkable for this inſcription: EX. AUCTORITATE. Q. JUNI. RUSTICI. PR. VR. but the weight of it is a little defective; part of the *ſilex* (as many of the ancient *Roman* weights that I have ſeen, were [y] *ex ſilice*, which is as hard or harder than marble) being broken away, elſe the reſt is very entire and well poliſhed. But I conceive, that by thoſe former ways I have ſo irrefragably demonſtrated the true ponderouſneſs of the *denarius conſularis*, that it would be thought ſuperfluous, or a vain oſtentation, to endeavour any farther to prove it. Wherefore inſtead of that I ſhall handle the *denarius cæſareus*, which is our ſecond enquiry.

The *denarius cæſareus*, was that which was made under the government of the *Cæſars*. And this inſtead of the face and inſcription *ROMA*, with the character X

[f] Villalpandus, l. 2. diſp. 2. c. 11. de apparatu urbis ac templi. [t] Gaſſendus in vitâ Peireskii.

[u] The inference of *Gaſſendus* I eaſily grant, that the *denarius*, under ſome of the *Cæſars*, was *drachmalis*; that is, the eighth part of the *Roman* ounce. But neither was it always ſo under the *Cæſars*, nor if it had been ſo, will it therefore follow that it was *drachmalis*, or the eighth part in reſpect of the *Attick* ounce. Seeing the *Athenian* ounce was greater than the *Roman*, as we have before proved; and therefore the *denarius conſularis*, which was the ſeventh part of the *Roman* ounce, was ſcarce the eighth part of the *Attick*. Wherefore he muſt ſee how he can make it good, where he brings *Peireskius*, in the ſecond book of his life, thus diſcourſing: ——*Denarium, cùm tempore regum pependiſſet trientem unciæ, ſub antiquâ tamen rep. pependiſſe ſolum ſextantem, ſub recentiore partem ſeptimam, ſub primis Cæſaribus octavam, ſeu drachmam (Atticæ nempe drachmæ æqualem.)*

[x] Of theſe *Roman ſemunciæ*, I have bought and ſeen ſeveral in braſs. Beſides one, which I owe to *my very worthy and learned friend, doctor* Ent.

[y] *Pætus, l. 1. de antiq. Rom. & Græc interv. menſuris*, makes mention of a *libra Romana* in braſs, procured by *Fulvius Urſinus*, of ſingular rarity: *In cujus ſupremâ planitie argenteis literis hæc erat nota I, & in circumferentiâ hæ aliæ EX. AVG. D. CAES.* but this I had not the happineſs to ſee in *Italy*.

or X on the fore-part, and the impreſs of the *biga*, or *quadriga* on the reverſe, (in which kind moſt of the *denarii conſulares* were ſtamped) had on the reverſe ſeveral impreſſes, and on the other ſide the image or reſemblance of the emperor: which occaſioned our Saviour to aſk the queſtion, when a δηνάριον, or *Roman* penny was ſhewed to him, [a] *Whoſe is this image and ſuperſcription? They ſay unto him, Cæſar's.* This *denarius Cæſareus*, if we reſpect ſome definitive quantity and weight, was as various and uncertain as the *denarius conſularis* of the later conſuls was conſtant and fixt; being under the firſt emperors, ſometimes more, ſometimes leſs, as the reaſons and exigencies of the ſtate did require, or the profuſeneſs and prodigality of thoſe times. Yet this uncertainty (as far as I have obſerved) was limited within ſome certain and determinate bounds: the *denarius Cæſareus* never exceeding the ſeventh part of the *Roman* ounce, and never being leſs than the eighth part, but often in a middle proportion between both, and that with much inequality. And this made [a] *Villalpandus*, after many experiments at *Rome*, to conclude, that out of the *denarii* nothing concerning the *Roman* weights could be determined. Tho' *Portius*, *Agricola*, *Ciaconius*, *Snellius*, and ſeveral others, before and after him, are of a contrary opinion. And it may be, if *Villalpandus* had diſtinguiſhed between the difference of times, and in them of the different coins, and conſidered thoſe of the conſuls, diſtinctly from thoſe of the *Cæſars*, and thoſe of the former *Cæſars* from thoſe of the later, he would have reformed his judgment: for it plainly appears, upon examination, that the diminution of their weight was an invention introduced after *Antonius* the *Triumvir*'s time, whereas before the *denarius* was fix'd. *Miſcuit*, ſaith [b] *Pliny*, *denario triumvir Antonius ferrum, alii è pondere ſubtrahunt* (his meaning is under the emperors, to *Veſpaſian*'s, or his own time) *cùm ſit juſtum octoginta quatuor è libris ſignari.* Where he ſays very well in ſpeaking ſo generally, *alii è pondere ſubtrahunt*, without preciſely limiting the proportion. For this, as we obſerved, was very various and undeterminate: ſo that whereas the juſt number of the *denarii*, according to the practice of the later conſuls, ſhould be eighty four in the *Roman* pound, we find by the weight of the beſt of them under the former *Cæſars*, that they coined ſometimes eighty ſix, eighty eight, *&c.* till at laſt there came to be ninety ſix *denarii* in the *Roman* pound, that is, eight in the ounce. And this, by a very neceſſary conſequence, may be inferred out of another place of *Pliny*, if we take for granted what ſome learned moderns confeſs, and the gold and ſilver coins found to this day, of the later conſuls, and firſt emperors, ſtrongly prove, that as the *Atticks* made their χρυσοῦς, or *aureus* double in weight to the δραχμὴ ἀργυρᾶ: ſo did the *Romans* make their *aureus* double in weight to the *denarius*. Which proportion they might borrow from the *Athenians*, and other *Grecians*, who, as [c] *Arias Montanus* imagines, firſt received it from the practice of the *Hebrews*: or rather, as I ſuppoſe, from the *Phœnicians*, and theſe from the *Hebrews*. From whenceſoever it came, it is not much material in our enquiry: that which we may ſafely conclude from thence is this; that the gold being in reſpect of weight, double to the ſilver, the *aureus Romanus* falling in its weight, the *denarius* likewiſe of neceſſity muſt fall: elſe could they not have continued *in duplâ ratione.* Now in what manner the *aureus* was firſt coined, and how afterwards it loſt of its primitive weight, [d] *Pliny* informs us: *aureus nummus, poſt annum* LXII *percuſſus eſt, quam argenteus, ita ut ſcrupulum valeret ſeſtertiis vicenis, quod efficit in libras ratione ſeſtertiorum, qui tunc erant, ſeſtertios* ƆƆCCCC. *Poſt hæc placuit* XL. M. *ſignari ex auri libris: paulatimque principes imminuere pondus, imminuiſſe vero ad* XLV. M. For this teſtimony, and the former, we are to thank *Pliny*, ſeeing there is neither *Greek* nor *Latin* author extant, from his time to *Theodoſius*, that gives us any certainty, what to conclude concerning the ancient coins. And therefore ſince this later is of great conſequence, but ſomewhat corrupted, I compared it with the *MSS.* in the *Vatican* and *Florentine* libraries, and with a fair one in *Baliol*-college, which renders the later part of it thus: *Poſtea placuit* X. XL. *ſignari ex auri libris, paulatimque principes imminuere pondus, imminuiſſe verò ad* XLVIII. Where for XLVIII, [e] *Villalpandus* corrects, or rather corrupts the text in writing XLV. But *Agricola*, and [f] *Snellius* read it by conjecture thus: *Poſt hæc placuit* XLII *ſignari ex auri libris, paulatimque principes imminuere pondus, minutiſſimè verò ad* XLVIII. And [g] *Snellius* gives a reaſon of it in his *Eratoſthenes Batavus. Nam ita argentei denarii, & aurei nummi eadem manet analogia, pondere ſubduplo, ut quamdiu octoginta quatuor argentei è libra, & è ſingulis unciis ſeptem cudebantur, tam diu quoque aurei duo & quadraginta libram implerent, poſtquam vero argentei num-*

[a] Mat. xxii. 20. [a] Villalp. de appar. urbis ac templi, par. 2. lib. 2. diſp. 2. c. 13.
[b] Plin. l. 33. c. 9. [c] *Arias Montanus* in *Thubal Cain, ſive de menſuris.* [d] Plinius, l. 3. c. 33.
[e] Villalpan. de app. urbis ac templi, par. 2. l. 2. diſp. 2. c. 12. [f] Snell. in Eratoſth. Batav. l. 2. c. 5. [g] Ibid.

GREAVES *mi pondus imminutum est: ut sex & nonaginta in libram constituerentur, tum quoque duo de quinquaginta aurei, pondere tanto leviore, in singulis libris cudi cœperunt.* Which conjecture seems not altogether improbable, if we respect the later consuls, and first *Cæsars*, in whose times we find the *aurei* to have been double to the *denarii Cæsarei*; but surely long before *Justinian*, the *aurei*, or as they were then also called the *solidi*, lost that proportion to the silver, and kept it only to the *semisses aurei*, to which they were double, as they were in a treble proportion to the *tremisses*.

Wherefore instead of these conjectures (which have been the bane of many a good author) of *Agricola*, *Villalpandus*, and *Snellius*, I would read the later part of those words of *Pliny*, as the *MSS*. do, till I can see some concluding reason, or good authority of ancient authors to the contrary, for I do not see why the *Romans* at the first might not coin forty *aurei* out of the *libra*, as well as forty silver *teruncii* out of the *denarius*: which [h] *Varro* assures us they did. And who knows whether at the first making of their gold coins, which was sixty two years according to *Pliny*, after the first coining of silver, they endeavoured to keep them in *duplâ ratione*, in respect of weight: which graceful manner they might afterwards introduce by commerce with the *Grecians*.

And here, e'er I proceed any farther in my enquiry after the *denarius Cæsareus*, I cannot but complain, either of the negligence of former times, or unhappiness of ours; in that not one author extant mentions the true weight of the *denarii*, under the *Cæsars*. [i] *Xiphilinus* relates in his epitome of *Dio*, how *Antoninus Caracalla* corrupted and abased the coins; but makes no mention of the weight. Τῷ οὖν Ἀντωνίνῳ, τἆτε ἄλλα καὶ τὸ νόμισμα κίβδηλον ἦν, τόδε ἀργύρειον καὶ τὸ χρυσίον, ὃ παρεῖχεν ἡμῖν, τὸ μὲν ἐκ μολίβδου καταργυρούμενον, τὸ δὲ καὶ ἐκ χαλκοῦ καταχρυσούμενον ἐσκευάζετο. *To* Antoninus, *as other things, so also his money was adulterated: for the silver and gold, which he gave us, the one was prepared of lead silvered over, and the other of brass gilt.* [k] *Suidas* also speaking of the *monetarii* writes thus: Μονητάριοι οἱ περὶ τὸ νόμισμα τεχνῖται, οἱ ἐπὶ Αὐρελιανοῦ διέφθειραν τὸ νόμισμα, καὶ τὸν ἴδιον ἄρχοντα Φιλικήσιμον ἀνελόντες ἐμφύλιον ἐγείρουσι πόλεμον, οὓς μόλις Αὐρηλιανὸς χειρωσάμενος ὑπερβαλλούσῃ κολάσεων ὠμότητι κατειργάσατο. *The* monetarii *are artizans employed in the making of money. These, in* Aurelian's *time, corrupted the money; and, having slain their governor* Felicissimus, *raised a civil war; whom* Aurelianus *with much difficulty conquering, put to death with exquisite torments.* And many good laws were made by several emperors, against adulterating and corrupting of coins: and those executed with much severity, even in the time of Christianity: for we find under the emperor *Constantine*, that such as offended in this kind, were not only put to death, but to a cruel and bitter death by fire. *L. OMNES SOLIDI. C. THEOD. SIQUIS SOLIDI CIRCULUM EXTERIOREM INCIDERIT, VEL ADULTERATUM IN VENDENDO SUBJECERIT. Omnes solidi, in quibus nostri vultus, ac veneratio una est, uno pretio æstimandi sunt, atque vendendi, quanquam diversa formæ mensura sit: quod siquis aliter fecerit, aut capite puniri debet, aut flammis tradi, vel aliâ pœnâ mortiferâ. Quod ille etiam patietur, qui mensuram circuli exterioris adraserit, ut ponderis minuat quantitatem, vel figuratum solidum, adulteriâ imitatione, in vendendo subjecerit.* In *Constantius*'s time the same punishment was inflicted. *L. PRÆMIO. C. THEOD. DE FALSA MONETA. Præmio accusatoribus proposito, quicunque solidorum adulter potuerit reperiri, vel à quoquam fuerit publicatus, illico omni dilatione submotâ flammarum exustionibus mancipetur.* And afterwards under *Valentinianus*, *Theodosius*, and *Arcadius*, they were accounted, and suffered as *rei læsæ majestatis*. *L. FALSÆ MONETÆ. COD. EODEM. Falsæ monetæ rei, quos vulgò paracharactas vocant, majestatis crimine tenentur obnoxii.* But no where is it mentioned concerning the *denarii* and *quinarii*, which were the silver coins in common use, how much should be their weight. Wherefore in such a silence of ancient authors, we have no more solid and sure foundation of our enquiry, than either by our selves to examine the weight of the fairest coins under the emperors; or else to relate what others long before our time have observed. *Antonius Augustinus* in general informs us, when coins were at their highest perfection, and how they began to decline with the *Roman* empire: as commonly when money comes to be abased, and that the mint, like the pulse, beats too slowly and irregularly, it is an evident symptom of some distempers in the bowels of a state. [l] *The medals of all times* (saith he)

[h] Varro, l. 4. de ling. Lat. [i] Xiphilinus in Anton. Caracalla. [k] Suidas in voce Μονητάριοι *sive* Μονητάριοι.

[l] *Le medaglie di tutti i temi* [*sono degne da esser osservate degli Artifeci*] *comminciando de Alessandro magno, nell' età del quale principalmente fiorirono, per fin al tempo dell Imperador Gallieno, nell quale caddero affatto insieme con l' imperio. Da indi poi in fina Giustiniano si trovano bon medaglie di tutti gli Imperadori ma con notabil perdita della pulitezza, & perfetione antica. Quelpoi che habbiamo duppo Giustiniano, è tanto cativo*

he) [*are worthy to be observed by artizans*] *beginning from* Alexander *the great, in whose time they principally flourished, till the emperor* Gallienus, *when they chiefly fell together with the empire. From thence to the end of* Justinian, *there are found good medals of all the emperors, but with a notable diminution of their politeness and ancient perfection. Those which we have after* Justinian *are insufferably bad. The fault by all men is assigned to the* Huns, *and* Vandals, *and* Alanes, *and* Goths, *and* Longobards, *and to other barbarous and savage nations, who conquered the greatest part of* Europe. *Erizzo*, who lived almost an hundred years since, a very diligent man in the *Roman* coins, but it is to be wished that he had used more judgment in the explication of them, more particularly informs us. [m] *Having compared the weight of those sorts of money, which are equal in weight to the* Roman denarius, *with the medals of silver, which have the heads of the* Roman *emperors imprinted, I have found them not a little different, so that as it were all those medals weigh less than the* denarius. *And having also weighed those medals which have the effigies of the* Cæsars, *I have continually found them different amongst themselves in weight.* This uncertainty so troubled *Villalpandus*, after many experiments made at *Rome*, that he knew not what to determine. And it seems [n] *Blondus* long before conceived it impossible: *Hæc omnia qualia per singulas ætates fuerint, ex amussim ostendere, non magis difficile, quàm impossibile fuerit, non solùm quia obscuris & nostrâ ætate ignotis verbis sunt à majoribus tradita, sed quia omnis ferè ætas suam habuit cudendi varietatem, & formam.* Wherefore, for farther satisfaction of the reader, I shall relate some observations of mine own: especially those of the twelve first *Cæsars*, which I took, with many others, by an accurate balance, from such choice cabinets in *Italy*. And first, I shall begin with the gold coins: for seeing the *aurei* under the former *Cæsars* were *in duplâ ratione* to the *denarii*, therefore the weight of those being known, we cannot be ignorant of the weight of the *denarii Cæsarei*. Besides, they are not subject to be consumed by time and rust, but only *ex intertrimento*, and therefore we may the safelier give credit to them. And lastly, because the difference, tho' but of a grain, is of some consideration in gold, the masters of the mint use to be the more circumspect about them: whereas in silver coins, since it is hardly worth the pains to stand precisely upon the excess or defect of every grain, therefore there are few of these so exact, but either exceed or want in the very mint, one or two grains, and sometimes more.

The Weight of some AUREI *under the first twelve* CÆSARS.

	Eng. Grains.
* C. CAES. COS. III	123 $\frac{2}{11}$
* *A second, on the reverse*, A. HIRTIVS. PR.	122 $\frac{1}{4}$
* *A third*	124 $\frac{1}{4}$
AVGVSTVS. CAESAR. III. VIR	119 $\frac{1}{2}$
A second, on the reverse, OB CIVES SERVATOS	119 $\frac{4}{5}$
* *A third, on the reverse*, DIVOS. AVG. DIVI. F.	119
TIBERIVS	118 $\frac{1}{4}$
* *A second, on the forepart*, TI. CAESAR. DIVI. AVG. F. AVGVSTVS. *On the reverse, a temple*	117 $\frac{1}{2}$
CALIGVLA	
CLAVDIVS, *on the reverse* S. P. Q. R. OB. CIVES SERVATOS	117
A second	117 $\frac{1}{2}$
A third	118 $\frac{1}{2}$
* NERO, *on the reverse*, SALVS	116
* *A second, on the reverse*, JVPPITER. CVSTOS	113 $\frac{1}{2}$
* *A third, on the reverse*, CONCORDIA. AVGVSTA	113
GALBA, *on the reverse*, CONCORDIA. PROVINCIARVM	115
OTHO, *on the reverse*, SECVRITAS S. P. Q. R.	108 $\frac{1}{4}$
VITELLIVS, *on the reverse*, LIBERTAS RESTITVTA	112 $\frac{1}{4}$
VESPASIANUS, *on the reverse*, PACI AVGVSTI	111
* *A second, on the reverse*, COS. III TR. POT.	114 $\frac{1}{4}$
A third, on the reverse, PONT. MAX. TR. P. COS. VI	111
* *A fourth, on the reverse*, PACI. AVGVSTI	108 $\frac{1}{4}$
A fifth, on the reverse, PACI. AVGVSTI	110
* T. VESPASIANVS, *on the reverse*, ANNONA AVG	109 $\frac{1}{4}$
* DOMITIANNS. COS. II.	113
* *A second*, DOMITIANVS. COS. VI. CAESAR. AVG. F. *on the reverse*, IVVENTVTIS. PRINCEPS	122 $\frac{1}{4}$

cattivo che non si può sofferire. Et se ne dà quasi da ognuno la colpa à gli Unni, à i Vandali, à gli Alani, à i Goti, à i Longobardi, & ad altre barbare, & fiere nationi, che signoreggiarono gran parte d' Europa. Ant. August. dialog. 1.

[m] *Havendo io tali monete le quali sono del peso di un denario Rom pareggiate di peso alle medaglie di argento, che hanno scolpite le teste de i Principi Romani, le ho ritrovate differenti non poco del peso, si che quelle medaglie pesano quasi tutte meno del denario; & havendo ancora pesate quelle medaglie che hanno scolpita la effigie de i Cæsari, le ho sempre ritrovate differenti fra loro nel peso.* Erizzo.

[n] Blond. l. 5. de Roma triumph.

2

These

These *aurei* were selected by me out of several others, as the fairest and entirest; and amongst these to such as I have prefixed an asterisk, they are such as seemed so perfect, that I could make no just objections against them. By these it appears that [r] *Pliny* speaking of the gold coins, rightly informs us: *Paulatimque principes imminuere pondus, imminuisse vero ad* XLVIII. *That by degrees the emperors lessened the weight* [of the *aurei*] *to the forty eighth part of the* Roman *pound*; that is, to the fourth part of the ounce. For this is the lowest weight, that I find, till *Heliogabalus*'s time, who coined new sorts of *aurei*, different from what had been the constant practice of the *Roman* state: some of which were the fifthtieth part of the *libra Romana*, and others again so massy, that they were *centeni*, or *bilibres*; which not long after were altered and abolished by *Alexander Severus*. The manner is expressed by [s] *Ælius Lampridius*, in the life of *Alexander Severus*: *Formas binarias, ternarias, & quaternarias, & denarias etiam, atque amplius, usque ad bilibres quoque & centenas, quas Heliogabalus invenerat, resolvi præcepit, nec in usu cujusquam versari: atque ex eo his materiæ nomen inditum est, cum diceret plus largiendi hanc esse imperatori causam, si cum multos solidos minores dare posset, dans decem vel amplius una forma, triginta, & quinquaginta, & centum dare cogeretur.* Under the same *Alexander Severus* began the *semisses aureorum*, and *tremisses* to be coined, which had not formerly been in use. The *semisses* were answerable in weight to the *denarii Cæsarei*, when they were least, that is, ninety six in the *Roman* pound; though *Agricola*, *Villalpandus*, and others, upon a mistake, equal them then to the *drachma Attica*. [t] *Ælius Lampridius* writing of *Alexander Severus*, plainly expresses, that in his time they began. *Tumque primum semisses aureorum formati sunt, tunc etiam, cum ad tertiam partem aurei vectigal decidisset, tremisses, dicente Alexandro etiam quartarios futuros, quod minus non posset.* Afterwards *Constantine*, *Constantius*, *Julian*, and other succeeding emperors, lessened the weight of the *aurei*, whereby there came to be seventy two in the *Roman* pound, so that each of them weighed the *sextula*, or four *scrupula*. That the *aurei* of *Constantine*'s time were sixty two in the *Roman* pound, is most evident out of the *codex Theodosianus*, where they are also absolutely called *solidi*, without the addition of *aurei*. [u] *L. SIQVIS. C. THEOD. DE PONDERATORIBVS, ET AVRI INLATIONE. Siquis solidos appendere voluerit auri cocti, septem solidos quaternorum scrupulorum, nostris vultibus figuratos, adpendat pro singulis unciis.* XIV. *vero pro duabus, juxta hanc formam omnem summam debiti inlaturus, eadem ratione servanda, etsi materiam quis inferat, ut solidos dedisse videatur.* [x] *Pancirollus*, in his *Thesaurus variarum lectionum utriusque juris*, reads VI *solidos*, instead of VII, and XII instead of XIV. And that it must necessarily be so, besides that the *solidi* of *Constantine* now extant prove as much, may be collected out of the proportion of weight which is here assigned by *Constantine* himself to the *solidi*, and that is four scruples, or the *sextula*. For the *solidus* containing four scruples, and the ounce containing twenty four scruples, there will therefore be six *solidi* in the ounce: again, the pound consisting of twelve ounces, and the ounce of six *solidi*, the whole pound therefore will consist of seventy two *solidi*. These *aurei* by *Justinian*, in like manner, are termed *solidi*. *L. QUOTIESCVNQVE. C. DE SVSCEPTORIBVS, PRÆPOSITIS, ET ARCARIIS.* Where he also defines the same weight. [y] *Quotiescunque certa summa solidorum pro tituli qualitate debetur, & auri massa transmittitur,* [z] *in* LXXII. *solidos libra feratur accepta.* The same thing is implicity confirmed by *Isidorus*, (*l.* XVI. *Orig. c.* 24.) *Solidus alio nomine sextula dicitur, quod iis sex uncia compleatur. Hunc ut diximus, vulgus aureum solidum vocat, cujus tertiam partem ideo dixerunt tremissem, quod solidum faciat ter missus.* Where [a] *Agricola*, I imagine, truly finds fault with him for calling the *solidus*, *sextula*; tho' the proportion he assigns is right; that is, that the *solidus* was the sixth part of the *Roman* ounce, and contained ἑξαγίȣ σαθμὸν, *the weight of the sextula*, as it is attested by [b] *Zonaras*: or, which is all one, that seventy two *solidi* were made out of a *Roman* pound, as *Justinian* before expresly assigned: and as infinite store of the *solidi*,

[r] Plin. l. 33. c. 3. [s] Lampridius in Alex. Severo. [t] Lampridius in Alex. Severo.
[u] Codex Theodos. l. 1. de ponderatoribus. [x] Gui. Pancirolli thesaur. var. lect. utr. juris.
[y] Cod. lib. 10. tit. 70. in rescripto Valentiniani & Valentis Impp.
[z] This excellent place very hardly escaped *Haloander*'s emendation, who had a great mind to have played the critick, and to have altered it. For he thus writes, *In vestuto codice in rasam membranam hæc ita reposita sunt, ut certum sit alteram, & fortasse genuinam lectionem sublatam, & legendum, duodequinquegintà, aut certe quinquaginta.* A goodly consequence, because the parchment was scraped, and the first writing altered, therefore the true reading must be expunged, and a false one put in: whereas he might with more candour aud ingenuity have concluded the contrary, that the false one was expunged by the scribe, and the true one inserted. For who uses in copying of *MSS.* to scrape any thing out of the *apographum*, but only when by collating it he finds it to be different from the original?
[a] Agricola, l. 2. de pond. & temperat. monetarum. [b] Zonar. l. 3.

or

or *aurei*, from *Constantine* to *Focas*, which I have weighed, manifestly prove.

In the same place of [a] *Isidorus* we may collect the reason why the *aureus* was called *solidus*. After that, the *semisses*, and *tremisses aurei* were coined, the *aureus* was called *solidus*, because nothing was wanting to it. *Solidum enim antiqui integrum dicebant, & totum:* in which sense the *solidus* was also taken for the *libra* or *assis*; that is, as the *assis* is taken for the whole, according to that usual phrase of *civilians*, *ex asse hæres*, when one is heir to the whole inheritance: so the *solidus* was taken for the whole *assis*. [b] *Volusius Metianus: Prima divisio solidi, id est libræ quod as vocatur, in duas partes dimidias deducitur. From hence* (saith [c] *Salmasius*) *the* Romans *called that the* solidus aureus, *when it had the same weight in gold, which the* solidus, *that is, the* assis *had in respect of brass, that is, two drachmes.* Though I rather suppose that the *aureus* was called *solidus*, first of all in *Severus*'s time, not for containing two *denarii* in weight, (which *Salmasius* calls *drachmes*) for so it always did under the later consuls, and first emperors, but because the *aureus* was then first divided into two parts, that is, into the *semisses* and *tremisses*, and so relatively to these the whole *aureus* was rightly called *solidus*. Of the same opinion is [d] *Agricola: Quos aureos, cum respectum ad semisses & tremisses haberent, tunc primo dixerunt solidos, quod semisses ex dimidia eorum parte, tremisses ex tertia constarent.*

The *semissis* and *tremissis* of the other emperors, at some distance after *Severus*, came to be less in the same proportion, as the *aurei* were lessened. For the *aurei* of *Severus* were double to the *denarii Cæsarei*, and therefore but forty eight in the pound, and not fifty, as *Heliogabalus* made, whose error *Severus* corrected. But when the later emperors made seventy two *aurei* out of the *Roman* pound, the *semisses* came also to be diminished, and were half of these new *aurei*, and not of the former, and the *tremisses* the third part. And here the *aurei* lost that proportion which they kept before, of being double to the *denarii*. Of these *tremisses* is *Justinian* to be understood, *L. FORTISS. MILITIBUS. COD. DE MILITARI VESTE. Fortissimis militibus nostris per Illyricum non binos tremisses pro singulis clamydibus, sed singulos solidos dare præcipimus.* And this may be farther proved by a fair [e] *tremissis* in gold of mine own of *Justinian*, with the inscription D. N. JUSTINIANUS, weighing twenty one grains *English*, and therefore wanting only three grains ½, which it may have lost by time: otherwise it would be exactly the 216th part of the *Roman* pound; that is, the third part of the *aureus*, or *solidus* of those times: whereas if it had been coined to the proportion of the *aureus*, when there were forty eight in the pound, it should have weighed 36 grains ½, so that it must have lost 15 ½, a difference so great in a piece of gold so fair, and withal of so small a quantity, altogether improbable. And therefore this coin alone, if no more were extant, would confute their opinion, who maintain that the *tremissis* of *Justinian* differed not from the *tremissis* of *Severus*, and consequently the *aurei* of them both, better than the reasons produced by [f] *Covarruvias* to the contrary have done.

GREAVES

[a] Isidorus, l. 16. orig. c. 24. [b] Vol. Metianus de assis distrib. [c] *Hinc & solidum aureum dixere Romani, ubi idem pondus habere cœpi in auro, quod solidus, id est, as haberet in ære, duarum nempe drachmarum.* Salmas. de modo Usur. [d] Agricola, l. 2. de pond. & temp. monetarum.

[e] I have since perused another *Tremissis* in gold, a very fair one, with this inscription, D. N. JUSTINUS. P. F. AUG. weighing twenty two grains, and better; which formerly belonged to the learned geographer, *Ortelius*. Besides a third, of *Majorianus*, with CONOB superscribed (which signifies, *Constantinopolitanum Obrizum*, or *Constantinopoli Obsignatum*) weighing likewise twenty two grains. And a fourth, of *Justinian*, weighing twenty three. [f] Covarruvias, tom. 1. c. 3. paragr. 1, & 2. de vet. aureis, & argenteis nummis.

The Weight of some of the fairest AUREI *of the* Roman *Emperors, from* Nerva *to* Heraclius.

On the fore-part of the AUREI *are these characters:*	*On the reverse, these:*	Eng. Grains.
IMP. NERVA. CAES. AVG. P. M. TR. P. II. COS. IIII. P. P.	FIDES. EXERCITVS	111½
IMP. TRAIANVS. AUG. GER. DAC. P. M. TR. P. COS. VI. P. P.	DIVVS. PATER. TRAIANI	110½
IMP. CAESAR. TRAIAN. HADRIANVS. AVG.	COS. II. P. M. TR. P. P. AVG	121⅜
ANTONINVS. AVG. PIVS. P. P. TR. P. XII.	COS. IIII	119⅛

		Eng. Grains.
GREAVES. ANTONINVS. AVG. ARMENIACVS.	P. M. TR. P. XVIII. IMP. II. COS. III. *in scuto victoriæ.* VIC. AVG.	$118\frac{1}{8}$
IMP. CAES. L. AVREL. VERVS. AVG.	CONCORDIAE. AVGVSTOR. TR. P. II. COS. II.	$117\frac{1}{4}$
L. VERVS. AVG. ARM. PARTHI. MAX.	TR. P. V. IMP. III. COS. II	$113\frac{1}{8}$
M. COMM. ANT. P. FEL. AVG. P. P.	IOVI VLTORI	114
SEVER. P. AVG. P. M. TR. P. X. COS. III	FELICITAS. SAECVLI	$114\frac{1}{2}$
IMP. M. ANT. GORDIANVS. AFR. AVG	CAESAR. M. ANT. GORDIANVS. AFR. AVG	114
Trebonianus Gallus.	P. M. T. R. P. IIII. COS. II. P. P	$75\frac{1}{4}$
Gallienus.	P. M. TR. P. III. COS. P. P	$74\frac{1}{2}$
IMP. PROBVS. P. F. AVG	VICTORIOSO. SEMPER	106
IMP. C. CARINVS. P. F. AVG.	SPES. AVGG	$72\frac{1}{2}$
DIOCLETIANVS. P. F. AVG.	IOVI. CONSERVAT. AVGG	$77\frac{1}{2}$
MAXIMIANVS.	VIRTVS. MILITVM T.	$74\frac{1}{4}$
CONSTANTINVS. MAX. AVG	SECVRITAS. REIPVBLICAE *Infra* T. R.	$70\frac{1}{2}$
CONSTANTINVS. P. F. AVG	VIRTVS. AVGVSTI. N	68
CONSTANTIVS	GLORIA. REIPVBLICAE. VOT XXX. MVLTIS. XXXX. *infra* SNNS	70
IM. CAE. MAGNENTIVS. AVG	VICTORIA AVGG. LIB. ROMANOR *Infra* TR	$70\frac{1}{4}$
FL. CL. IVLIANVS. P. F. AVG	VOT. X. MVLT. XX. *infra* ANT	$68\frac{1}{4}$
D. N. IOVIANVS. P. F. PERP. AVG	SECVRITAS. REIPVBLICAE VOT. V. MVLT. X. *infra* COS. P	68
D. N. VALENS. P. F. AVG	RESTITVTOR. REIP. *infra* ANTO	$68\frac{1}{4}$
D. N. VALENTINIANVS. P. F. AVG	RESTITVTOR. REIPVBLICAE	$69\frac{1}{4}$
A second		69
D. N. GRATIANVS. P. F. AVG	VICTORIAE. AVGG. *infra* TROES	69
A second		$68\frac{1}{4}$
D. N. THEODOSIVS. P. F. AVG.	VICTORIA. AVGG. *infra* CON	68
A second		$69\frac{1}{4}$
D. N. ARCADIVS. P. F. AVG	NOVA. SPES. REIPVBLICAE *Intra Corollam* XX. XXX. *Infra* CONOB	$67\frac{1}{2}$
A second		68
D. N. HONORIVS. P. F. AVG.	VICTORIA. AVGGG *Statua, cui inscripit.* R. V. *Infra* CONOB	$69\frac{1}{4}$
A second		$69\frac{1}{4}$
A third, D. N. HONORIVS. P. F. AVG	VICTORIA. AVGGG. N. D. *infra* CONOB	$68\frac{1}{4}$
D. N. THEODOSIVS, P. F. AVG	IMP. XXXXII. COS. XVII. P. F. *infra* CONOB.	$69\frac{1}{2}$
D. N. PLA. VALENTINIANVS	VICTORIA. AVGGG. *infra* CONOB	68
D. N. VALENTINIANVS. AVG.	VICTORIA. AVGGG. *infra* CONOB	$69\frac{1}{4}$
D. N. VALENTINIANVS. P. F. AVG.	VICTORIA. AVGG. *infra* TROES	68
D. N. IVL. NEPOS. P. F. AVG	VICTORIA. AVGGG. A. *infra* CONOB	$69\frac{1}{4}$
D. N. ANASTASIVS. P. F. AVG	VICTORIA. AVGGG. *infra* CONOB	$68\frac{1}{2}$
D. N. IVSTINIANVS. P. F. AVG	VICTORIA AVGGG. A. *infra* CONOB	69
D. N. FOCAS. PERP. AVG	VICTORIA. AVGGG. *infra* CONOB	$68\frac{1}{4}$
D. N. FOCAS. PERP. AVG	VICTORIA. AVG. *infra* CONOB	$69\frac{1}{2}$
HERACLIVS		$69\frac{1}{2}$
A second		$69\frac{1}{2}$

And

GREAVES

And thus much of the *aurei* under the former and later emperors, as they serve to illustrate and prove the weight of the *denarii Cæsarei*, which is our next and principal enquiry.

The *denarii* under the *Cæsars* were almost as various and unconstant as the *aurei*, sometimes more, sometimes less; and if they had not been so, they could not have kept that proportion to the *aurei* of the former emperors, which we assigned. From *Augustus*'s time to *Vespasian*, as I find by examining many of them, they continually almost decreased, till from being the seventh part of the *Roman* ounce, they came now to be the eighth part: and therefore ninety six were coined out of the *Roman libra*, whereas before under the consuls eighty four. From *Vespasian* to *Alex. Severus*, as far as I have observed, the silver continued at a kind of stay in respect of weight, excepting only such coins, as upon some extraordinary occasion, both then, and in the first emperor's time, were stamped either in honour of the prince, or of the empress, and *Augusta Familia*, or else in memory of some eminent action. These last, most usually, were equal to the *denarii consulares*, and many of them had these characters, *E. X. S. C.* or else *S. P. Q. R.* Under *Severus* and *Gordianus*, the *denarii* began to recover their primitive weight, and came to be equal to the *denarii consulares*, the half of which also were exactly the *quinarii*; and so continued during the succeeding emperors, till *Justinian*, with little diminution, but most commonly with a notable abasement and mixture of allay. After *Justinian* there happened such a deluge of barbarous nations, which overflowed the greatest part of *Europe*, that not only the coins, but even the liberal arts and sciences, began with the majesty of the empire to decline from their first lustre and perfection.

Wherefore I shall not speak of the μιλιαρήσιον, or μιλιαρίσιον, a sort of silver coin in use before, and after *Justinian* which some collect out of [a] *Cedrenus* to have been the eighth part of the ounce, and therefore equal to the *denarius* in the lowest valuation; tho' [b] *Suidas* renders, μιλιαρήσιον τὸ τοῦ νομίσματος δέκατον, and the *Scholiastes Basilic. eclog.* 723. δωδέκατον, and to contain twenty four φόλλεις. But I shall not positively determine either the weight of this, or of the κεράτιον, or *siliqua* in silver, both coined when the imperial seat was translated to *Byzantium*, unless I had examined some of the fairest of them. And for the same reason I shall not define the *Hebrew denarius*, mentioned by *Elias* the *Thisbite*, in the word דינר and by [c] *Moses Gerundensis* upon *Exodus*, and by the *Chaldee paraphrase*, 2 *Reg.* v. 5. which I imagine to have been no other than the *Roman denarius*, used by the *Jews*: neither shall I determine the *Arabian dinar*, and *derham*; the former of which the Rabbins call דינרא ערבאי used by *Rhasis*, *Avicen*, *Mesue*, and by several other *Arabians*, both physicians and historians. All that can certainly be concluded is this, that by the *dinar*, when we speak of a coin, is meant sometime the *denarius*, and sometime the *aureus*: but when we speak of a weight, always the *aureus* is understood; as by the *derham*, the δραχμή, or silver drachme. But surely the quality of the thing is different from the name: the silver drachme of the *Arabians*, as it is generally now used in the *Mahometan dominions* in the *East*, consisting of XLVII 4/5 grains *English*, (as I have found by weighing many of them) which is much less than either the *drachma Attica*, or the *denarius Consularis*; and somewhat less than the *denarius Cæsareus*. And yet it is not improbable but that this may have continued with them without any diminution, for six or seven hundred years to our times, as well as the *Roman* pound and ounce have continued entire sixteen hundred years and better. But to omit any farther prosecution of the *dinar* and *derham* of the *Arabians*, which may hereafter more fully be discussed, when we shall handle their measures and weights, and to go on with our discourse of the *Roman denarius*. After the breaking in of so many barbarous nations, as of a torrent, into the *Roman* empire, the *denarius* began generally to be disused; every one almost of these, as an argument of their sovereignty and conquests, making new coins of their own: or else such as continued the former, either by allays so abased the fineness, and valuation of the coins, or by several diminutions so impaired the weight, that the *denarius* totally fell, and at last almost vanished into nothing. Neither will this seem strange, if we shall consider, that the like alteration, in respect of weight, hath happened by the revolution of a less time, in our own coins. I shall instance in our *denarius* or penny, which in *Ethelred*'s time, that is, a little more than 100 years since, was the twentieth part of the Troy, or silver ounce: as [d] M. *Lambard*, in his *Saxon* Glossary observes, and as by experience I have found (and the same proportion was anciently observed, by the [e] *French*, in their *denier*.)

[a] Cedrenus in histor. compend. [b] Suidas in voce μιλιαρήσιον. [c] P. 72. col. 4.
[d] Lambardi Glossarium Cantabrig. 1644. [e] *In appendice libri de limit. agrorum: Juxta Gallos vigessima pars unciæ denarius est, & XII denarii solidum reddunt.*

GREAVES This proportion continued ſucceſſively to *Edward* the firſt, in whoſe time we find the weight of the *denarius* by [f] ſtatute to be thus defined: *Per ordinationes totius regni Angliæ denarius Angliæ, qui vocatur Sterlingus, rotundus, ſine tonſura, ponderabit* XXXII *grana frumenti in medio ſpicæ, &* XX *denarii faciunt unciam, &* XII *unciæ faciunt libram.* Under [g] *Edward* the third it came firſt to be diminiſhed to the twenty ſixth part of the Troy ounce; and under [h] *Henry* the ſixth it fell to the two and thirtieth; in [i] *Edward* the fourth's time it came to be the fortieth; under [k] *Henry* the eighth at firſt it was the fortieth, then the forty fifth. Afterward ſixty pence were coined out of the ounce in the ſecond year of [l] queen *Elizabeth*; and during her reign ſixty two: which proportion is obſerved in theſe times. So that it is evident that *Ethelred*'s penny was bigger than three of ours. And after times may ſee this of ours, as well as the *Roman denarius*, to be quite diminiſhed, and brought to nothing. For if either our own exigencies, or the exigencies of foreign ſtates with whom we have commerce, cauſe us or them (as occaſions will never be wanting) to alter the proportions of the gold and ſilver coins, either in reſpect of weight, or in reſpect of purity, or laſtly, in reſpect of the valuation the gold bears to ſilver; by all, or ſome of theſe cauſes, there will inevitably happen ſuch a diminution of the penny (and proportionably of our other coins) that at length it will not be worth the coining. But I leave this ſpeculation to ſuch, whom it doth more nearly concern. And certainly it is a conſideration not of the leaſt importance; money being as the ſinews and ſtrength of a ſtate, ſo the life and ſoul of commerce: and if thoſe advantages which one country may make upon another, in the myſtery of exchanges, and valuation of coins, be not throughly diſcovered, and prevented, by ſuch as ſit at the helm of the ſtate, it may fare with them after much commerce, as with ſome bodies after much food, that inſtead of growing full, and fat, they may pine away, and fall into an irrecoverable conſumption. But I return to the *Roman denarius*, which we have brought ſo low, that there is nothing now left of it, but only the name; and that alſo ſuffered an [m] alteration: for the later *Greeks* inſtead of the δηνάριον, called it the δηνέριον: and both *Greeks* and *Latins*, and ſometimes the *Arabians*, took it not in the ſame ſenſe, as it paſſed for in the firſt inſtitution; that is, for a ſilver coin, worth in valuation ten or ſixteen *aſſes*, but for any ſort of coin whatſoever. And therefore [n] *Meurſius*'s obſervation, in his *Gloſſarium Græco-Barbarum*, is worth our conſideration. *Poſtea* δινέριον *dixerunt ævo corruptiore, & generaliter pro quavis pecunia. Sicut Itali denaro. Galli denier. Hiſpani dinero. Anonymus de bello ſacro.*

Δινέρια ἔχετε πολλὰ, δῶτε τὰ ταβερνάρῃ,
Επάρετε πολλοὺ κρασὶ ϗ πίνετε μετ' αὐτοῦς.

Whence the learned [o] *Joſ. Scaliger* rightly obſerves, that, *Ultimis temporibus denarii pro exigua ſtipe uſurpati ſunt, ut hodie in Gallia. Imperator Aurelianus: Philippeos minutulos quinquagenos, æris denarios centum. Eos Vopiſcus in Bonoſo ſeſtertios æris vocat. Macrobius de nummo ratito loquens, qui erat æreus:* Ita fuiſſe ſignatum hodieque intelligitur in aleæ luſu, cum pueri denarios in ſublime jactantes, capita, aut navia luſu teſte vetuſtatis exclamant. *In Evangelio ſecundum Marcum* xii. λεπτὰ δύο ὅ ἐςι κοδράντης. *Hilarius, duos denarios viduæ inopis Deo acceptiores. Luc.* x. ἐκβαλὼν δύο δηνάρια, *Ambroſius, duo æra. Vetuſtiſſimus eſt igitur denarii uſus,* ἀντὶ τοῦ χαλκισμοῦ, *vel ſtipe.* Thus far *Scaliger*.

Such an uncertainty being then, as we have mentioned, both of the *aurei* and *denarii*, under the firſt *Cæſars*, in whoſe times the pureſt coins, and the beſt wits moſt flouriſhed, and ſuch an abaſement and impureneſs of the ſilver under the later emperors, no reaſonable man can imagine, that either the ancient grammarians, poets, orators, hiſtorians, or eſpecially phyſicians, whom it did moſt concern to be preciſe, and moſt of which lived under the former emperors, did ever allude to the weight of the *denarius Cæſareus*, but rather to the *Conſularis*. And to this only, and to no other, did the *Attick drachme* mentioned by *Dioſcorides*, *Cleopatra*, *Galen*, *Julius Pollus*, *Oribaſius*, and the reſt of the *Greek* authors correſpond. And thus have we finiſhed our diſcourſe concerning the *denarius*, in the notion and acception of the ancients, both *Greeks* and *Latins*.

Our next labour ſhould be to compare it with the ſtandards for weights of divers nations uſed in theſe times: for which I had recourſe to the publick *Zygoſtatæ*, and *Ponderatores*, in my travels abroad; and for my obſervations I muſt refer the reader to this enſuing table.

[f] Stat. 31. Edov. 1. [g] Stat. 9. Edov. 3. [h] Stat. 2. Hen. 6. [i] Stat. 5. Ed. 4.
[k] Stat. 36. Hen. 8. [l] Stat. 2. Eliz.

[m] In the ſame manner the *ſolidus*, or *aureus*, as it loſt its valuation, ſo ſuffered an alteration in the *Greek* name: for inſtead of χρυσοῦς, we find the gloſſes to render it χρύσινος. *Gloſſæ*, χρύσινος *ſolidus:* and in the ſame gloſſes we read δινάρια interpreted *biniones*, and δηνάριον *ſeſtertium*, and δηνάριον λευκὸν *aſprum*.

[n] Meurſii Gloſſarium Græco. Barbar. in voce δηνάριον. [o] Scalig. de re num.

A Table

GREAVES

*A TABLE of the gold and silver** *Weights of several Nations: Taken from their Standards, and compared with the* Denarius.

	Eng. Grains.
SUCH parts, or grains of the *English* standard for gold and silver (or of the *Troy* weight) as the *denarius Consularis* containeth sixty two, according to the weight of the best coins, or according to the weight of the *congius* of *Vespasian*	$62\frac{4}{7}$
The ancient and modern *Roman* ounce containeth	438
The ancient and modern *Roman* pound, consisting of twelve ounces, containeth	5256
The *Troy* pound, or *English* standard of gold and silver, consisting of twelve ounces, containeth	5760
The *Troy*, or *English* ounce, (to which five shillings two pence of our money, in these times are equal) containeth	480
The *Paris* pound, or standard for gold and silver, of sixteen ounces	7560
The *Paris* ounce	$472\frac{1}{2}$
The *Spanish* pound, or standard, for gold and silver, of sixteen ounces, taken by me at *Gibraltar*	7090
Another weigh'd by me at *Gibraltar*	7085
The *Spanish* pound in *Villalpandus*, is (I know not by what error) but	7035
The *Spanish* ounce at *Gibraltar* (the pound consisting of 7090 grains *English*	$443\frac{1}{2}$
The *Venetian* pound, or standard, for gold and silver, of twelve ounces	5528
The *Venetian* ounce	$460\frac{2}{3}$
The *Neapolitan* pound, or standard, for gold and silver, of twelve ounces	4950
The *Neapolitan* ounce	$412\frac{1}{2}$
The pound, or standard, for gold and silver, of twelve ounces, at *Florence*, *Pisa*, and *Leghorne*	5286
The ounce at *Florence*, *Pisa*, and *Leghorne*	$440\frac{1}{2}$
The pound, or standard, at *Siena*, for gold and silver, of twelve ounces	5178
The ounce at *Siena*	$431\frac{1}{2}$
The ounce at *Genoa*, for gold and silver	$405\frac{1}{2}$
The *Turkish okeh*, or *oke*, at *Constantinople*, consisting of four hundred silver drams	19128
The silver dram generally used in the *Great Turk*'s dominions: as also in *Persia*, and in the *Mogul*'s countries, if I be not misinformed	$47\frac{4}{5}\frac{1}{10}$
The *Turkish sultani*, or *Ægyptian sherif*, being a gold coin, with which the *Barbary* and *Venetian chequeen*, and *Norimberg* ducat, within a grain more or less, agree	$53\frac{1}{2}$
The *ratel*, or *rotulo*, for gold and silver of a hundred forty four drams at *Cairo*	$6886\frac{2}{25}$
The *ratel*, or *rotulo*, for silk of seven hundred and twenty drams at *Damascus* (with which I suppose they there formerly weighed their gold and silver; because most countries use the same weights for silks, gold, and silver	$34430\frac{2}{5}$

* The weights (excepting *the rotulo of Damascus*) were diligently compared with the originals and standards; in like manner as I examined the measures above described. In both which, if any shall find some little difference from some originals, as five or six grains in the *English* pound, and it may be one or two parts of a thousand in the *English* foot, different from *the standards in the Exchequer, or the Tower, or at Winchester*, or some other place, it is not much to be wondered: for I have found as great differences in collating the *English* standards themselves: and have heard *Gasparo Berti* (one of the exactest men in this kind that I have known) to complain of the same diversity at *Rome*. And tho' it be a shame, that in any well-governed kingdom, or common-wealth, the standards, which are the rules of *commutative justice*, should be unequal, and therefore unjust; yet unless more art and circumspection be used, than hitherto hath been put in practice, it is impossible but such inequalities will creep in.

But this observation of mine, by some, may be thought too nice and curious. That which follows, I am certain, is as necessary, as the preservation of the life of many a man. And that is, that some physicians erroneously imagine the *granum auri* to be alike in all nations. And therefore *Fernelius*, a very able man (who, I think, was the first author of that opinion) writes thus: (*Fern. l. 4. c. 6. Method. medendi*) *Granum, cui tanquam basi reliqua innituntur pondera, ratum constansque esse decet; neque id granum esse hordei, neque tritici, neque ciceris, neque frugis ullius, aut leguminis, quod nullius par sit ubique gentium pondus. At vero nummarium minutum, quod aurifabri granum appellant, & Latinè momentum dici potest, omnibus mundi nationibus unum idemque est, & stabile, quod auri sacra fames, & opum furiosa libido, inviolatè & incorruptè servat, idque signis & exemplaribus undique identidem collatis.* Indeed it was an useful fancy of his to think of some common measure, in which all nations might concur; tho' it is more to be wished for, than ever to be expected. But that asseveration of his, *Inviolatè, & incorruptè servat, idque signis & exemplaribus undique identidem collatis*, from a man of such rare abilities, I cannot but extremely wonder at: for if we shall go no farther to confute his assertion, than to compare our *grana aurei* with those of *Paris*, which *Fernelius* used, we shall find ours much bigger; XXIX *English* grains almost equalling XXXVI of *Paris*. Or if we shall compare the *Spanish grana aurei*, with his, we shall find those much less; XXXVI *Spanish* grains weighing but XXVIII and a half of his at *Paris*. The like could I demonstrate in those of other countries. By which dangerous and notable error, for want either of due care, or an exact balance, we may conceive that whatsoever also is delivered by the ancients, in the like nature, is not presently without due examination to be credited.

In this table I judged it much fitter to compare the *denarius* with the standards for gold and silver of several nations, than with their gold and silver coins now current. Because the pounds and ounces of the standard continue alway the same; whereas the gold and silver coins being cut in several proportions, according to the exigencies of the state, admit of several alterations and diminutions.

The CONCLUSION.

GREAVES

IT was my intention from the *pes Rom.* and *denarius*, together with the *congius of Vespasian*, to have deduced the other weights and measures, used by the *Romans*; and from those of the *Romans*, by such testimonies as are upon record in the writings of the ancients, to have inferred those of the *Hebrews*, *Babylonians*, *Ægyptians*, *Grecians*, *and of other nations.* A work, I confess, intricate and full of difficulties; wherein I could expect neither to give my self, nor others satisfaction, without first laying some sure and solid principles for the *basis* and foundation. Therefore that occasioned me to insist the more largely in the prosecution of the *pes Rom.* and *denarius*, and to examine all the ways I could possibly imagine, for the evident proof and confirmation of them. What in this kind I have done, and with how much truth and diligence, I leave to the impartial test of after-times, the rest at more leisure may be perfected. Yet these following observations, as a *coronis* to the whole work, I thought would not be unacceptable, if by way of anticipation I communicated them to the world: And those are how the originals and standards of weights and measures, notwithstanding the revolutions and vicissitudes of empires, may be perpetuated to posterity. Amongst several ways, which I have thought of, I know none more certain and unquestionable, than to compare them with some remarkable and lasting monuments, in remote countries, that have stood unimpaired for many hundred years, and are like to continue as many more. In which kind I made choice of the *first and most easterly of the three great pyramids in* Ægypt; *of the basis of that admirable* Corinthian *pillar*, erected (as I suppose) by one of the *Ptolemys, a quarter of a mile distant to the south from* Alexandria, being one vast and entire marble-stone: *of the rock at Terracina* or *Anxur*, where it adjoins to the *Via Appia*, and almost touches the *Tyrrhene* sea: *of the gate or entrance into the Pantheon*, or temple of *Agrippa*, dedicated by him to all the gods, and by the Christians to all saints: *of the Porta Sancta*, in that new and exquisite structure of St. *Peter's church in Rome.* If the like had been attempted by some of the ancient mathematicians, our times would have been freed from much uncertainty, in discovering the weights and measures of the *Greeks* and *Latines*.

The first and most easterly of the three great pyramids in *Ægypt*, hath on the north-side a square descent, when you are enter'd a little past the mouth of it, there is a joint, or line, made by the meeting of two smooth and polished stones over your head, which are parallel to those under your feet, the breadth at that joint, or line, is three feet and $\frac{462}{1000}$ of the *English* foot.

Within the pyramid, and about the midst of it, there is a fair room, or chamber, the top of which is flat, and covered with nine massy stones; in it there stands a hollow tomb of one entire marble-stone: the length of the south-side of this room at the joint, or line, where the first and second rows of stone meet, is thirty four feet $\frac{380}{1000}$.

The breadth of the west-side of the same room at the joint or line, where the first and second row of stones meet, is seventeen feet $\frac{190}{1000}$.

The hollow or inner part of the marble tomb, near the top, on the west side of it, is in length six feet $\frac{488}{1000}$.

The hollow, or inner part of the marble tomb, near the top of it, on the north side, is in breadth two feet $\frac{218}{1000}$.

The basis of the vast *Corinthian* pillar, about a quarter of a mile from *Alexandria* to the south, on the west-side of the pillar at *a b*, is in breadth twelve feet $\frac{312}{1000}$. At *c d* it is fourteen feet $\frac{412}{1000}$.

The rock at *Terracina*, or *Anxur*, near the *Via Appia*, close by the *Tyrrhene* sea, hath these figures, besides several others in the same perpendicular, very deeply engraven.

The uppermost line *b c*, over the figures CXX, in the innermost, and deepest part of the engraving, is in length four *English* feet, and $\frac{702}{1000}$.

The

The lowermost line *d a* in the innermost, and deepest part of the engraving, is in length four feet $\frac{622}{1000}$.

The stately gate or entrance into the *Pantheon*, or temple, built by *Agrippa* in *Rome*, the jambs, and top and bottom of it, being all of one entire marble-stone, is in breadth between the jambs, or sides, some three inches above the bottom, and some nine inches within, nineteen feet $\frac{682}{1000}$.

The *Porta Sancta*, on the right-hand of the frontispiece of St. *Peter*'s church in *Rome*, is in breadth on the pavement, or threshold, between the jambs or sides of the entrance, eleven feet $\frac{222}{1000}$.

The great gate, or entrance, which is the middlemost of the five in the frontispiece of St. *Peter*'s church in *Rome*, the doors of which are covered with leaves of brass, with very fair and exquisite figures, is in breadth, on the pavement, or threshold, between the jambs, or sides of it, eleven feet $\frac{248}{1000}$.

The measures being fixed, we may likewise fix the weights in this manner; by making a vessel of a cubical figure, answerable to the proportion of any one of these feet, or palms, or braces, which are described in the table at the end of the first treatise. This cubical vessel being filled with clear fountain-water, we are to weigh it with an exact ballance, and to express the weight of it by some one of those weights, which we have placed in a table at the end of the second treatise. The side of this cube being known, and the weight of it in water defined, the rest of the weights in the second table, by way of consequence, by those proportions which we have assigned, may be discovered. Thus for example: the *Roman* foot described by *Villalpandus*, is nine hundred eighty six parts, such as the *English* foot contains a thousand: this being cubed (saith he) weighs of fountain-water eighty *Roman* pounds. If therefore there be given nine hundred eighty six parts of a thousand of the *English* foot, the cube of this will give us eighty *Roman* pounds in fountain-water; and consequently the other measures will be discovered by those proportions we have assigned to them, in respect of the *Roman* pound. Again, eighty *Roman* pounds of water being given, if we reduce this into a cubical body, the side of it will give the *Roman* foot described by *Villalpandus*: and consequently the other measures may be deduced by those proportions we have given them in a peculiar table. Whereby it appears, that as *by measures* weights may be preserved, so on the contrary, *by weights* measures may be restored.

GREAVES

Some Directions to be observed in comparing the Valuations of COINS.

IN comparing the valuations either of ancient coins with modern, or of modern one with another, we are to consider: first, the *intrinsick* of them, and then the *extrinsick*: the intrinsick is either the *fineness* of the coin, in respect of metal, or the *gravity* in respect of weight. The extrinsick I term, first, the *character* imprinted on the coin. And, secondly, the *valuation* enjoined by the prince, or state: by which character and valuation, what *originally* and *materially* was but common metal, or plate, comes now *legally* and *formally* to be current money. With these limitations, if we shall compare ancient coins with modern, and modern one with another, it will be no difficult matter to proportion out their several respective valuations; and withal to reconcile the seeming repugnancies, either of ancient coins now found, differing from the traditions of ancient authors, or the traditions of ancient authors differing among themselves.

I shall first give an instance of modern coins compared with modern, in our *English* money compared with that of *Spain*, as being most familiar to us; the application of which will by analogy serve for all other distinct states and times, using distinct coins.

In comparing therefore *English money with Spanish* money in *England*, or *Spanish money with English* in *Spain*, we are thus to proceed: First, We are to examine whether they be of a like fineness for the *intrinsick*; if they be, then an ounce of *English* money, and an ounce of *Spanish* (supposing the weight of the ounce to be alike) will be of like value in any other country out of *England* and *Spain*; where neither are current, but only considered as so much metal, or plate. Secondly, We are to consider the *extrinsick*, that is, the form and stamp of the coin, with the valuation of it by the injunction of the prince of either state; and here that which before was *equal*, comes now to be *unequal*: for an ounce of *English* money in *England* comes to be more worth than an ounce of *Spanish* money in *England*; because this wants the character, stamp, and valuation of our princes, whereby it is current: and for the same reason will an ounce of *English* money be less in valuation than the ounce of *Spanish* money in *Spain*, supposing (as I said) the ounce in both countries to be exactly one and the same.

The same analogy will be, if we compare ancient coins, as those of the *Hebrews*, *Greeks*, and *Romans*, with our *modern coins*.

We

GREAVES We are first to consider the *intrinsick* of them, whether they be of a like weight and fineness for the metal with ours: and this is the *natural or physical consideration.* From whence we may conclude, that if, for example, so many *Attick tetradrachmes* do equal in pureness and weight, so many of our *English* shillings, newly brought from the mint, or so many of our *Troy or silver ounces*, taken from the standard, then are they to be balanced with these in the acception of them as plate; and a silversmith, abstracting from the *extrinsick*, that were to melt them both, would give a like value for them both. But if we, secondly, look upon them with the image and character of the state, and in the notion of money, which is *the politick consideration*, then that which before in the *trutinâ*, and scale, was equal, in the *foro*, and in commerce, comes to be unequal: and an ounce of *English* money shall pass for more than an ounce in *Attick tetradrachmes*, with reference to the expences of the mint, and to the civil valuation, depending upon a mandate, or law, enacted by the prince.

In like manner will it be, if we compare ancient coins with ancient, made in different states, as it is in comparing ancient coins with modern.

Upon these grounds of reason it will follow, that whereas the *Roman* authors make the *denarius consularis* to be equal to the *drachma Attica*, and the *Greeks* equal the *drachma Attica* to the *denarius consularis*, that both say true; and yet both of them, if we speak strictly and exactly, may be deceived. For the *denarius consularis* examined by *the balance, which is the best judge of the intrinsick*, (I speak of the *intrinsick in respect of weight*, and not the *intrinsick in respect of fineness*, that being best discovered by the *scale*, and this by the *test*: which last, for the more clearness of my discourse, I suppose in all these coins to be alike.) I say, the *denarius consularis* is found by me, contrary to the opinion of all modern writers, to be lighter than the *drachma Attica*: and therefore to speak strictly, and precisely, cannot be equal to it in the *intrinsick*. But again, if we look upon the *extrinsick* of the *drachma Attica*, and *denarius consularis*, that having the stamp of *Athens*, and this of *Rome*, here reason must be our balance, and not the *trutina*. For the *Athenian* coin being a foreigner, and not current in *Italy*, in the way of exchange and commerce, will lose of its primitive valuation it had at *Athens*, and for want of the *extrinsick* of the *Roman* stamp, necessarily rebate in the *intrinsick*. And therefore both *Greeks* and *Romans* writing in *Italy*, might truly say, that the *denarius consularis*, and *drachma Attica*, were equal, that is, speaking in *civil commerce*, and *popular estimation*: altho' they were unequal *in the intrinsick* and *natural valuation*.

But if we shall change the scene, and carry the *denarius consularis* to *Athens*, the case will be quite altered. For the *denarius* being a stranger, and the *drachma Attica* a denizon, that cannot have the same privileges with this: and therefore the *extrinsick* of the *denarius* being there of no use, and the *intrinsick* in respect of weight falling short of the *drachma*, it must necessarily be much less in valuation at *Athens* than the *drachma*: and I think no advised *Athenian*, writing in *Attica*, would make them equal, I am certain no *nummularius* would.

The same may be said of the *Hebrew shekel*, and the *Attick tetradrachme*, and of all other coins of distinct states, mention'd in classical authors. Thus *Philo* and *Josephus*, in *Judea*, both truly equal the *shekel* to the *Attick tetradrachme*, that is in way of *commerce*; tho' the *shekel* be unequal, and less than the *tetradrachme*, (as I have found by examining many of them) in a just notion of weight. The reason is evident by what hath been expressed before: for in *Judea* the *extrinsick* makes amends for what the *shekel* wants in the *intrinsick*; and on the contrary, what the *tetradrachme* exceeds in the *intrinsick*, is diminished for want of the *extrinsick*, till at length in a popular estimation they come to be equal. But the quite contrary would happen, in the transportation of *shekels* from *Jerusalem* to *Athens*. Here the *shekel* would necessarily fall from its primitive valuation, and the *tetradrachme*, being considered now no longer as a foreigner, would recover what it lost in *Judea*, and consequently rise above the *Hebrew shekel*; as having a double advantage in the *extrinsick* from the state, and in the *intrinsick* from its weight.

But what need we to go so far for examples, when as we instanced before, we have them nearer home? The *Spanish* quarters of the *dollar*, or *double rials*, pass ordinarily in our sea-towns but for *shillings*, (whereas they are worth in the *intrinsick* thirteen pence farthing) and our *shillings* pass in *Spain* scarce for a *rial* and an half. For theirs wanting in *England* our *extrinsick*, and ours in *Spain* wanting their *extrinsick*, must respectively rise and fall in their valuation.

AN

ACCOUNT

OF

COCHIN-CHINA.

In TWO PARTS.

The FIRST Treats
Of the TEMPORAL STATE *of that Kingdom.*

The SECOND,
Of what concerns the SPIRITUAL.

Written in ITALIAN,
By the R. F. *CHRISTOPHER BORRI*, a *Milaneze*, of the SOCIETY of JESUS, who was one of the First MISSIONERS in that Kingdom.

To the READER.

THIS account is so short, it requires not much preface, or to say the truth, any at all; a little time sufficing the curious to inform himself of the value and contents of it. Who the author was appears by the title, and what the cause of his going into that kingdom, his profession and only business being to preach Christianity to the infidels: he lived five years among them, and learn'd their language to perfection; and therefore his relation is not like those of travellers, who just pass through a country; or merchants, that touch at ports upon the business of trade, and consequently deliver very fabulous accounts, either to make their travels the more surprizing, or for want of knowing better, taking things upon hear-say, and not understanding their language to get certain information. This father on the contrary frequently conversing with all sorts of people, and having a settled residence there for years, had the opportunity of knowing what he writ. He gives the description of the kingdom, a considerable part whereof he travell'd over: he speaks of its product, which he had the benefit of for sustenance and cloathing: he tells us the temper and seasons of the air, which he several times felt: he relates the inundations which he often saw: he gives an account of their sects, which he learn'd from their priests, or omsays, *whom he converted to Christianity: he sets down the power and government of the kingdom which he could be no stranger to, being familiar with several men in great authority: and to conclude, he particularizes how far the christian faith has been there propagated; which he well knows, as having been himself a labourer in the vineyard for the first five years; and after that, receiving it from those that succeeded him. In fine, the relation is curious, tho' short, and seems to carry all the air of truth imaginable, besides the general approbation it has always received in all parts, which is the greatest commendation that can be given it.*

AN

ACCOUNT

OF

COCHIN-CHINA.

The FIRST PART.

OF THE

Temporal State of the Kingdom of *Cochin-China.*

CHAP. I.

Of the Name, Situation, and Extent of this Kingdom.

BORRI.

Name of *Cochin-China.*

COchin-China, so call'd by the *Portugueses*, is by the natives call'd *Anam*, signifying a western country, because it lies west of *China*; for which same reason the *Japoneses* in their language give it the name of *Cochi*, signifying the same as *Anam*, in the *Cochi-Chinese* Language. But the *Portugueses* having by means of the *Japoneses* been admitted to trade in *Anam*, of the *Japonese* word *Cochi*, and this other word *China*, compounded the name *Cochin-China*, applying it to this kingdom, as if they call'd it *Cochin* of *China*, the better to distinguish it from *Cochin* the city in *India*, inhabited by the *Portugueses*; and the reason why in the maps of the world we generally find *Cochin-China* set down under the denomination of *Cauchin-China*, or *Cauchina*, or the like, is no other but the corruption of the right name, or that the authors of those maps would signify, that this kingdom was the beginning of *China*.

Its bounds

This kingdom on the south borders upon that of *Chiampà*, in 11 degrees of north latitude, on the north somewhat inclining east-ward with *Tunchim*, on the east is the *Chinese* sea, and on the west north west the kingdom of *Lais*.

Extent.

As to its extent, I shall here speak only of *Cochin-China*, which is part of the great kingdom of *Tunchim*, usurp'd by a king who was grandfather to him now reigning in *Cochin-China*, who rebell'd against the great king of *Tunchim*: for as yet the *Portugueses* have traded only in this province; and here only the fathers of the society have been conversant, in order to introduce Christianity: yet at the end of this account, I shall discourse concerning some particulars of *Tunchim*, where our fathers got footing since my return into *Europe*.

Cochin-China extends above a hundred leagues along the sea, reckoning from the kingdom of *Chiampà*, in the aforesaid 11 degrees of north latitude, to the gulf of *Ainam*, in the latitude of 17 degrees, or thereabouts, where the king of *Tunchim*'s dominions begin. The breadth is not much, being about twenty miles, all the country plain, shut up on the one side by the sea, and on the other by a ridge of mountains inhabited by the *Kemois*, which signifies a savage people; for tho' they are *Cochin-Chineses*, yet they no way acknowledge or submit to the king, keeping in the fastnesses of the uncouth mountains, bordering on the kingdom of *Lais*.

Division.

Cochin-China is divided into five provinces, the first bordering on *Tunchim*, where this king resides, is call'd *Sinuvà*; the second *Cachiam*, here the prince, the king's son resides and governs; the third, *Quamguya*; the fourth *Quignin*, by the *Portugueses* call'd *Pullucambi*; and the fifth confining on *Chiampà*, is *Renran*.

CHAP.

CHAP. II.

Of the Climate, and Nature of the Country of Cochin-China.

Great heat of *India.*

THO' this kingdom, as has been ſaid, lies between 11 and 17 degrees of north latitude; hence it follows of courſe, that the country is rather hot than cold, and yet it is not ſo hot as *India*, tho' it be in the ſame latitude, and within the torrid zone. The cauſe of the difference is, becauſe in *India* there is no diſtinction of the four ſeaſons of the year, ſo that the ſummer laſts there nine months without intermiſſion, without ſeeing ſo much as a cloud either day or night, and therefore the air is continually, as it were, inflamed with the great reflection of the ſun-beams. The other three months are call'd winter, not becauſe there is any want of heat, but becauſe at that time it generally rains day and night; and tho' to appearance, ſuch continual rains ſhould naturally cool the air, yet they falling in the three months of *May*, *June*, and *July*, when the ſun is in its greateſt elevation, and in the *zenith* of *India*, and no winds blowing but what are hot, the air continues ſo inflam'd, that ſometimes the heat is more intenſe than in ſummer, when for the moſt part there are pleaſant winds blowing from the ſea, which cool the ground, wherewith, if Almighty GOD did not relieve thoſe countries, they would be uninhabitable.

Four ſeaſons in *Cochin-China.*

But *Cochin-China* enjoying the diſtinction of the four ſeaſons, tho' not in ſo perfect a manner as *Europe*, is much more temperate: for tho' its ſummer, which comprehends the three months of *May*, *June*, and *July*, be violent hot; becauſe it lies within the torrid zone, and becauſe the ſun is then in its zenith, yet in *September*, *October*, and *November*, the autumn ſeaſon, the heat ceaſes, and the air becomes very temperate by reaſon of the continual rains, which at this time uſually fall upon the mountains of the *Kemois*, whence the waters running down in abundance do ſo flood the kingdom, that meeting with the ſea, they ſeem to be all of a piece. Theſe inundations during theſe three months, for the moſt part happen once a fortnight, and laſt three days at a time. They ſerve not only to cool the air, but to fertilize the earth, making it fruitful and abounding in all things, but particularly in rice, which is the moſt common and univerſal food of all the kingdom. During the other three winter months, which are *December*, *January*, and *February*, there are cold northerly winds, bringing cool rains, and ſo ſufficiently diſtinguiſhing the winter from other ſeaſons. To conclude, in *March*, *April*, and *May*, the effects of ſpring appear, all things being green and bloſſoming.

BORRI.

Notable inundations.

Now ſince we have ſpoke of theſe inundations, I will not conclude this chapter without firſt obſerving ſome curioſities that occur on occaſion of them.

The firſt is, That all men in general wiſh for them, not only that they may cool the air, but much more for the fertilizing of the earth: for which reaſon as ſoon as they appear, all the people are ſo pleas'd and joyful, that they expreſs it by viſiting, feaſting, and preſenting one another, all of them crying, and often repeating, *Daden Lut*, *Daden Lut*; that is, the inundation is come, it is here: and this is done by perſons of all degrees, even to the king himſelf.

A pleaſant law.

And in regard the inundations often come ſo unexpectedly, that very often when they do not think of it at night, they find themſelves the next morning ſurrounded with water; ſo that they cannot go out of their houſes, throughout the whole kingdom, as has been ſaid: hence it is that abundance of cattle are drowned, for want of time to retire to the mountains, or higher grounds. For this reaſon there is a pleaſant ſort of law throughout the kingdom; which is, that if oxen, goats, ſwine, or other beaſts, are drowned, the owner loſes them, and they belong to him that firſt takes them: which cauſes much ſport and jollity; becauſe when the *Lut* happens, they all go out in boats, to ſeek the drowned cattle; upon which they afterwards feaſt and treat one another.

Beneficial ſport.

Nor are the younger ſort without their paſtime; for there being in thoſe fields of rice, an infinite number of rats, their neſts filling with water, they are forced to ſwim out, and get upon the trees to ſave themſelves: and it is pleaſant to ſee the boughs loaded with rats, like fruit hanging on them. Then do the boys run out in their boats, ſtriving to out-do one another, in ſhaking the trees, that the rats may fall and be drowned: which childiſh paſtime is wonderful beneficial to the country, delivering it from thoſe miſchievous creatures, that otherwiſe, by degrees, would devour all the harveſt.

Markets and fairs on the water.

In ſhort, the *Lut* cauſes another conſiderable advantage: which is, that it affords every body the opportunity of furniſhing his houſe with all neceſſaries, becauſe the country being all navigable, during theſe three days, commodities are very eaſily convey'd from one city to another, and therefore then are held the greateſt fairs and markets,

BORRI. kets, and with greater concourse of people than at any other time in the year. Then also it is, that they lay in provision of wood to burn and build, bringing it from the mountains in boats; which to this purpose come into the streets, and into the very houses, built for this purpose upon high pillars, that water may have free passage, the people living during that time in the upper floors; to which it were a wonder if the *Lut* should ever rise, they being built according to the situation of the place, to such a height as they know by long experience, is sufficiently above the waters.

CHAP. III.

Of the Fruitfulness of the Country.

IT is an easy matter to conceive the fertility of *Cochin-China*, by the advantages accruing from the *Lut*; yet we will mention some other particulars relating to it. The *Lut* leaves the land so fruitful, that rice is gathered three times a year, in such great plenty and abundance, that there is no body will work for gain; all persons having enough to live on plentifully.

Rice.

Oranges.

There are great quantities of fruit of several sorts, all the year about; and they are the same with those in *India*, *Cochin-China* being within the same climate. But to come to particulars; the oranges there are bigger than ours in *Europe*, and very full; the rind of them is thin, tender, and so well tasted, that it is eaten with the juice, which has a pleasant relish like limons in *Italy*.

Banana's.

There is a sort of fruit which the *Portugueses* call *banana's*, and others *Indian* figs; tho', in my judgment, the name of a fig is neither proper to those in *India*, nor in *Cochin-China*, because neither the tree nor fruit has any resemblance with our figs, the tree being like that we call *Indian Wheat*, but higher, and the leaves so long and broad, that two of them would serve to wrap a man in quite round, and from head to feet. Hence some have taken occasion to say, that this was the tree in paradise, with the leaves whereof *Adam* cover'd himself. This tree at the top produces a cluster of twenty, thirty, or forty of these *banana's* together; and each of them is in shape, length, and thickness, of an indifferent citron in *Italy*. Before the fruit is ripe, the rind is green; but afterwards yellow, as the citrons are. There is no need of a knife to pare this fruit, for the rind comes off as we shell beans. This fruit has a most fragrant smell; the pith or flesh of it is yellow, and firm, like that of a *bergamot* pear, when full ripe, that melts in the mouth. By this it appears to be no way like our fig, except in the taste and sweetness. There is another sort of them, which is only eaten roasted, and with wine: the stem dies every year, when it has produc'd the fruit, and leaves a young sprout at the foot, which grows up against the next year. That which in *Italy* they call an *Indian* fig, is nothing like the plant, or fruit of this *banana*, we now speak of; nor is this which we have in *Italy* call'd an *Indian* fig, in those parts. This fruit is common throughout all *India*. There is another sort in *Cochin-China*, that is not found in *China*, nor *India*: it is as big as the largest citrons we have in *Italy*; so that one of them is enough to satisfy a man. These are nourishing, very white within, and full of black round seeds, which chew'd together with the white substance, are of a delicious taste, and a good medicine against the flux.

There is another fruit in *Cochin-China*, which I have not seen in any other country of *India*; and this they call *Can*: the outward form and nature of the rind is like our pomegranate; but within it contains a substance almost liquid, which is taken out, and eaten with a spoon; the taste is aromatick, and the colour like that of a ripe medlar.

Can.

They have another peculiar to the country, that grows, and is like our cherries, but tastes like raisins, and is call'd *gnoo*.

Gnoo.

There are also melons, but not so good as ours in *Europe*; nor are they eaten without sugar or honey. The water-melons are large and delicate.

Melons.

There is a fruit they call *giacca*, which is common to the other parts of *India*, but much larger in *Cochin-China*: It grows on a tree as high as the walnut, or chesnut, and has much longer prickles than the *jubeb*. It is as big as a very large pompion in *Italy*, so that one of them is a man's load. The out-rine is like that of a pine-apple, but soft and tender within. This fruit is full of certain yellow round kernels, like a small piece of coin, that is round and flat; and in the middle of every one of them, is a stone that is thrown away. There are two sorts of this fruit; one in *Portuguese* is call'd *giacca barca*: the stone of this is thrown away, and the pulp is stiff; they do not take out the stone of the other; nor is the pulp hard, but soft as glue: both these in taste somewhat resemble that delicious fruit called the *durion*, whereof we shall speak next.

Giacca.

This *durion* is one of the most delicious fruits in the world, and only found in *Malaca*,

Durion.

laca, *Borneo*, and the adjacent iſlands. The tree differs little from the *giacca* laſt mentioned, and the fruit it ſelf is like it without, and that reſembles the pine-apple, even in the hardneſs of the rind. The meat within is very white about the bone, to which it ſticks like glue, and taſtes very like our *mangiare bianco* (a dainty among the *Italians*.) This meat and liquor is divided into ten or twelve little apartments, in each of which the fleſh and moiſture is about its ſtone, which is as big as a large cheſnut. And it is to be obſerv'd, that when they break open the ſhell of this fruit, there comes from it an ill ſcent, like that of a rotten onion, all the ſubſtance within remaining of a moſt ſweet and unexpreſſible ſavour, whereupon I will relate what happened in my preſence: a prelate arrived at *Malacca*, and one there opened a *durion* before him to give him a taſte; the prelate was ſo offended at that nauſeous ſmell that came from it when broke, that he would not taſte it by any means. Being afterwards ſet down to dinner, they gave the reſt of the company *mangiare bianco*; but on this prelate's plate they laid the white ſubſtance of this fruit, which is ſo like the *mangiare bianco*, that he could not diſtinguiſh the difference by the ſight. The prelate taſted it, and thought it ſo much more delicious than uſual, that he ask'd, what cook dreſs'd it ſo rarely? Then he that had invited him to dinner, ſmiling, told him, It was no other cook but God himſelf, who had produc'd that fruit, which was the very *durion* he would not taſte. The prelate was ſo aſtoniſh'd, that he thought he could never eat enough; and they ſo dear, that even at *Malacca*, where they grow, they ſometimes coſt a crown apiece.

Ananas. *Cochin-China* abounds in another ſort of fruit, by the *Portugueſes* call'd *ananas*; which tho' it be common to all *India*, and *Brazile*, yet becauſe I have not found it well deſcrib'd by thoſe that have writ of it, I would not paſs it by. This fruit does not grow on a tree, nor from a ſeed, but on a ſtalk, like our artichokes, and the ſtem and leaves are much like thoſe of the thiſtle or artichoke. The fruit is like a cilinder, a ſpan long, and ſo thick that it requires both hands to graſp it. The pulp within is cloſe, and like a radiſh, the rind ſomewhat hard, ſcaly like a fiſh. When ripe, it is yellow both within and without, is par'd with a knife, and eaten raw, the taſte of it an eager ſweet, and as ſoft as a full-ripe *bergamot*-pear.

Areca. There is beſides, in *Cochin-China*, a fruit peculiar to that country, which the *Portugueſes* call *areca*. The trunk of it is as ſtrait as a palm-tree, hollow within, and produces leaves like thoſe of the palm, only at the top among theſe leaves, there grow ſome ſmall boughs, which bear the fruit in ſhape and bigneſs like a walnut, green without juſt as the nut is; within it is white and hard like a cheſnut, and has no taſte at all. This fruit is not eaten alone, but is wrapp'd up in leaves of *betle*, well known in *India*, which are like our ivy-leaves in *Europe*, and the plant it ſelf clings to trees like the ivy. Theſe leaves are cut in pieces, and in them they wrap a bit of *areca*, each of them making four or five morſels; and with the *areca* they put ſome lime, which is not there made of ſtone, as in *Europe*, but of oiſter-ſhells; and as among us there are cooks and caterers, &c. ſo in *Cochin-China* there is one in every family, whoſe buſineſs is to wrap up theſe morſels of *areca* in *betle*, and theſe perſons being women, are call'd *Betleres*. They fill their boxes with theſe morſels, and chew them all day, not only when they are at home, but when they are walking, or talking, at all times, and in all places, never ſwallowing, but ſpitting them out when they are well chew'd, retaining nothing but the reliſh and vertue of it, which wonderfully comforts the ſtomach. Theſe morſels are ſo much in uſe, that when one of them goes to make a viſit, he carries a box full of them, and preſently preſents ſome of the party viſited, who claps it into his mouth; and before the viſitor departs, he that is viſited ſends to his *Betler*-woman for a box of the ſame, and preſents it to the viſitor, to return his kindneſs; and theſe morſels muſt be ſtill making. And there is ſo much of this *areca* us'd, that the greateſt revenues of that country come from the fields of it, as among us of olive-gardens, and the like.

BORRI.

Tobacco is alſo u'd there, but not ſo much as *betle*. The country alſo abounds in all ſorts of pumpions and ſugar canes. The *European* fruits are not yet come thither; but I believe grapes and figs would take very well. Our herbs, as lettice, endive, colworts, and the like, come up well in *Cochin-China*, as they do throughout all *India*: But they grow into leaf, without producing any ſeed, ſo that it muſt be ſtill ſupplied out of *Europe*. Other growth.

There is alſo great plenty of fleſh, by reaſon of the great multitude not only of tame cattle, as cows, goats, ſwine, buffaloes, and the like; but of wild, ſuch as deer, much bigger than thoſe of *Europe*, wild boars, &c. and of hens both tame and wild, of which ſort the fields are full, turtles, pigeons, ducks, geeſe, and cranes, which are ſavory enough; and in ſhort, other ſorts, which we have not in *Europe*. Cattle and fowl.

Their fiſhery is very great, and fiſh ſo delicious, that tho' I have travell'd ſo many Fiſh.

BORRI. countries, I do not think I have met with any to compare to that of *Cochin-China*. And the country, as was said before, lying all along upon the sea, there are so many boats go out a fishing, and they bring in so much fish to all ports of the kingdom, that it is really very remarkable to see the long rows of people continually carrying fish from the shore to the mountains; which is duly done every day, for four hours before sun-rising. And tho' generally among the *Cochin-Chineses*, fish is more valu'd than flesh, yet the main reason why they apply themselves so much to fishing, is to furnish themselves with a kind of sauce, which they call *balachiam*, which is made of salt fish macerated and steeped in water. This is a sharp liquor, not unlike mustard, whereof every body lays in such store, that they fill barrels and tubs of it, as many in *Europe* lay in their stocks of wine. This of it self is no food, but serves to sharpen the appetite to the rice, which they cannot eat without it. For this reason, tho' rice be the general and most common sustenance in *Cochin-China*, there must be vast quantities of *balachiam*, without which it is not eaten, and consequently there is continual fishing. There is no less plenty of shell-fish, oisters, and other product of the sea, especially of one sort, which they call *cameron*. (I suppose this to be the *Portuguese* word *camerano*, signifying shrimps, or prawns.)

Balachiam

Besides all this, providence has furnish'd them with a sort of food so rare and delicate, that in my opinion it may be compar'd to the *manna*, wherewith the chosen people of GOD were fed in the desart. This is so peculiar to *Cochin-China*, that it is no where else to be found: and I will give an account of what I know of it by experience, and not by hear-say, having seen and eaten of it several times.

Wonderful nests.

In this country there is found a small bird like a swallow, which fastens its nest to the rocks, the sea-waves break against. This little creature with its beak, takes up some of the foam of the sea, and mixing it with a certain moisture it draws from its own stomach, makes a sort of slime, or bituminous substance, which serves to build its nest, which when dry and hardened, remains transparent, and of a colour between green and yellow. The country people gather these nests, and being soften'd in water, they serve to season meat, whether fish, flesh, herbs, or any sort whatsoever; and give every thing so different a relish, and so proper to it, as if they had been season'd with pepper, cinnamon, cloves, and the richest spice; this nest alone being enough to season all sorts of provisions, without salt, oil, bacon, or any other addition; and therefore I said I thought it like manna, which had in it the taste of all the most delicious meats; saving that this is the work of a small bird, and that was made by GOD's angels. And such great store of them is found, that I my self saw ten small boats loaden with nests, taken among the rocks, in not above a mile's distance. But they being so precious a commodity, only the king deals in them, they being all kept for him; and his greatest vent is to the king of *China*, who values them at a great rate.

They eat no sort of white meats, looking upon it as a sin to milk the cows, or other creatures: and the reason they give for this nicety, is, that milk was by nature appointed for sustenance of the young ones: as if the owner of the young ones could not dispose of their sustenance. They eat some things which we loath, and count venomous, as camelions, which are here somewhat bigger than those that are sometimes brought dry'd up into *Italy*, out of other countries. I saw a friend buy some ty'd together in a cluster, and lay them upon the live coals, which having burn'd the string, they walk'd about gently, as they used to do till they felt the heat of the fire; which being of a violent cold nature, they resisted a-while, but were at last broil'd: my friend took them up, and scraping off the burn'd skin with a knife, the flesh remain'd extraordinary white; then he bruis'd and boil'd them in a certain sort of sauce like butter, and then eat them as a great dainty, inviting me to bear him company: but I had enough with the sight of it.

Camelions eaten.

Cochin-China abounds in all other things necessary for the support of human life; and in the first place for cloathing: there is such plenty of silk, that the peasants and mechanicks generally wear it; so that I was often pleas'd to see men and women at their labour, carrying stone, earth, lime, or the like, without the least fear of tearing or spoiling the rich cloaths they had on. Nor will they wonder at it, who shall know, that the mulberry-trees, whose leaves feed the silk-worms, grow in vast plains, as hemp does among us, and run up as fast; so that in a few months the said worms appear upon them, and feed in the open air, spinning their thread at the proper time, and winding their bottoms in such plenty, that the *Cochin-Chineses* have not only enough for their own uses, but they furnish *Japan*, and send it into the kingdom of *Lais*, whence it afterwards spreads as far as *Tibet*; this silk being not so fine and soft, but stronger and more substantial than that of *China*.

All wear silk.

The structures the *Cochin-Chineses* use of wood, are nothing inferior to those of any other part of the world; for without falsifying,

Buildings.

falsifying, this country has the best timber in the universe, in the opinion of all that have been there to this time. Among the variety and multitude of their trees, there are two that most usually serve for building, and are so incorruptible, that they do not decay in the least, either under ground, or under water; and they are so solid and heavy, that they do not swim upon the water, and a log of them serves instead of an anchor to a ship. One of them is black, but not so as ebony; the other is red, and both of them, when the bark is taken off are so smooth and slick, that they scarce need any plaining. These trees are call'd *tin*; and they would not deviate much from the truth, who should say, they were that incorruptible wood, which *Solomon* made use of for building the temple: for we know the scripture gives them a name much like this, calling them *ligna thyina*. The mountains of *Cochin-China* are all full of these trees, all strait, of such a prodigious height, that they seem to touch the clouds, and so thick that two men cannot fathom them. Of this timber the *Cochin-Chineses* build their houses, every man being free to cut down as many as he pleases.

Incorruptible trees call'd *tin*.

The houses.

The whole fabrick of their houses rests upon high, solid, and well settled pillars, between which they place boards to remove at pleasure; either to exchange them for cane-lattices, which they weave neatly, to let in the air in hot weather; or to leave a free passage for the water and boats, at the time of the inundation, as we observ'd above. They have also a thousand curious inventions, and ingenious contrivances to set off their houses, with carving, and other works on wood, which are a very great ornament.

Aquila, and *calamba*, odoriferous wood.

Since we have begun to talk of the trees, before we proceed upon any other matter, I will here mention something of a sort of wood, accounted the richest commodity that can be carried out of *Cochin-China* to other parts; which is the most famous wood called *aquila*, or eagles-wood, and *calamba*; which are the same thing as to the tree, but differ in their value and vertue. Of these trees, which are thick and high enough, the *Kemois* mountains are very full; if the wood be cut off a young tree, it proves *aquila*, or eagle-wood, and this there is most plenty of, every one cutting as much as he can: but when the wood is of an old tree, that proves *calamba*; which were very hard to be found, had not nature it self provided for it, causing these same trees to grow on the tops of unaccessible mountains, where growing old without being expos'd to destruction, some boughs of them now and then drop down, breaking off either for want of moisture, or through age, and are therefore found rotten and worm-eaten, infinitely exceeding the common *aquila*, or eagle-wood, in vertue and sweet scent; and this is the so highly valu'd and famous *calamba*. The *aquila* is sold by any body, but the *calamba* belongs only to the king, because of the high value of its perfume and vertue. And to say the truth, it is so sweet where they gather it, that some pieces being presented me, for a trial, I buried them above a yard and a half under ground, and yet they discovered themselves by their fragrancy. The *calamba*, where taken, is worth five ducats a pound; but in the port of *Cochin-China*, where the trade is, it bears a much greater price, and is not sold under sixteen ducats a pound. In *Japan* it is worth two hundred ducats a pound; but if there be a piece big enough for a man to lay his head on like a pillow, the *Japoneses* will give after the rate of three or four hundred ducats a pound: the reason of it is, because they instead of a soft down-pillow, when they sleep, lay their head on some hard thing, and generally it is a piece of wood, which every one according to his ability endeavours to have of as great value as can; and a piece of *calamba* is look'd upon as a pillow fit for none but a king, or some great lord. Yet the *aquila*, tho' of less price and esteem than the *calamba*, is so considerable, that one ship's load of it, enriches any merchant for ever: and the best advantage the king can allow the governor of *Malacca*, is to grant him one voyage of *aquila*; because the *Brachmans* and *Banians* of *India*, using to burn their dead with this sweet wood, the consumption of it is continually very great.

Great wealth of *Cochin-China*.

To conclude, *Cochin-China* abounds in rich mines of the most precious metals, especially of gold: and to reduce to a few words, what might be said more at large of the plenty of this country, I will conclude with that which the *European* merchants trading thither commonly say of it; which is, that in some measure the wealth of *Cochin-China* is greater than that of *China* it self; and we all know how rich that country is in all respects.

I ought in this place to say something of the beasts, whereof we before observ'd there was great variety and numbers in *Cochin-China*: but that I may not dilate too much, I will only treat of the elephants and abadas, or rhinocero's, chiefly found here; of which many curious things may be said, which perhaps very many have not heard of.

CHAP.

CHAP. IV.

Of the Elephants and Abadas, or Rhinocero's.

Borri.

THERE are abundance of elephants in the woods of *Cochin-China*, which they make no uſe of, becauſe they know not how to take, or tame them: therefore they bring them tame and well taught from *Cambogia*, a neighbouring kingdom. Theſe are twice as big as thoſe of *India*, the round print of their feet they leave behind them, is not leſs than half a yard diameter; the two teeth ſtriking out of the mouth, whereof ivory is made, are very often four yards and a half long; that is, thoſe of the males, for thoſe of the females are much ſhorter; by which it is eaſy to compute, how much thoſe elephants of *Cochin-China* are bigger than thoſe ſhewn about in *Europe*, whoſe teeth are not above three quarters of a yard long. The elephants live many years; and I asking, how old one might be? The driver of it told me, It was ſixty years old before it came from *Cambogia*, and had lived forty in *Cochin-China*: and having my ſelf ſeveral times travell'd upon elephants in that kingdom, I can relate many things that will ſeem ſtrange, but yet are very true.

Elephants their age.

They carry by land and water.

An elephant generally carries thirteen or fourteen perſons, who are thus diſpos'd of: as we lay a ſaddle on a horſe, ſo they clap a certain machine upon the elephant, which is like a coach, wherein there are four ſeats; it is faſtned with chains under the elephant's belly, as a horſe's ſaddle is girt. The coach has two doors on the ſides, where ſix perſons ſit, three on a ſide; and another behind, where there are two more; and laſtly, the *nayre*, who ſupplies the place of a choachman, ſits over the elephant's head, and guides him. Nor have I travell'd in this manner by land only, but very often by ſea too, croſſing arms of it above a mile over: and it was wonderful to any body that knew it not before, to ſee ſuch a vaſt great lump of fleſh ſwimming under ſuch a weight, ſo that it look'd like a boat rowing. True it is, the beaſt groan'd under the toil, occaſion'd by the unreaſonable bulk of its own body, and the difficulty of breathing; and therefore to eaſe it ſelf in that pain, it ſuck'd in water with the trunk, and ſpouted it out ſo high, that it look'd like ſome great whale gliding along the ocean.

They help up paſſengers.

For the ſame reaſon of its mighty corpulency it finds much difficulty in ſtooping down; and this being abſolutely neceſſary for the conveniency of paſſengers to get up to, or down from the coach, he does it not but when commanded by the *nayre*; and if when he is kneeling, any one ſtops but never ſo little, upon ceremony, or any other account, he riſes up, not having patience to continue in that poſture, it is ſo painful.

Nor is it leſs worderful to behold, how at the *nayre*'s command, he makes, as it were, a ladder of his limbs, for the greater conveniency of thoſe that are to get up into the coach: the firſt ſtep is his foot, which is high enough; for the ſecond, he turns out the firſt joint above the ſame foot, diſtant enough from the other; for the third, he bends his knee; for the fourth, his hip-bone, ſticking out to that purpoſe; and from whence, he that gets up, lays hold of a chain faſtned to the coach it ſelf, where he ſeats himſelf.

How they ſleep.

By this it plainly appears, how much they are miſtaken, who ſay and write, that the elephant can neither kneel nor bow down; and that the only way to take him, is to cut the tree he leans againſt to ſleep: for that falling together with the falſe ſupport, and not being able to riſe, he becomes a certain prey to him that lies in wait: which is all a fable, tho' it be true that he lies not down to ſleep, that being an uneaſy poſture to him, as has been ſaid, but ſleeps always ſtanding, with a continual agitation of his head.

Their vaſt ſtrength.

Upon occaſion of war or battle, they take off the roof of the coach, whence, as it were from a tower, the ſoldiers fight with muſkets, arrows, and ſometimes a ſmall piece of cannon, the elephant being ſtrong enough to carry it, his ſtrength being anſwerable to all the reſt: and I have ſeen one my ſelf, that would carry vaſt weights upon his trunk; and another that lifted up a great piece of cannon with it; and another, who by himſelf launch'd ten galliots one after another, taking hold of them very dexterouſly with his teeth, and ſhoving them into the ſea. I have ſeen others pull up large trees with as much eaſe we do a cabbage, or a lettice: with the ſame eaſe they throw down houſes, levelling whole ſtreets when they are commanded, either to do harm to an enemy in war, or to ſtop the fury of the flames upon occaſion of any fire.

The trunk

The trunk's length is proportionable to the height of the reſt of his body, ſo that he can take up any thing off the ground without ſtooping. It is made of abundance of ſmall ſinews knit together, which makes it ſo pliable, that he can take up the leaſt thing, and yet ſo ſtrong and firm as we have ſhewn.

All the body is covered with a rough ash-colour skin. An elephant's usual day's journey is twelve leagues, and his motion has the same effect upon those that are not used to it, as that of a ship has at sea.

Great sense of the elephant.

I shall say nothing more wonderful concerning the elephant's docility, or aptness to learn, than what is generally reported; by which it will appear, there was reason to say, *No beast was more sensible than the elephant*: for it does such things as seem to be the acts of prudence and understanding. In the first place, though the *nayre* makes use of a certain instrument of iron a yard long, which has a hook at one end, wherewith he strikes and punces him, that he may be watchful, and mind what he bids him do, yet for the most part, he governs him only by words: by which it appears he understands the language very well; and some of them understand three or four that are very different, according to the several countries they have lived in. Thus he that I travelled on, seemed to understand the language of *Cambogia*, whence he came, and that of *Cochin-China*, where he was. And who would not admire to hear the *nayre* discourse with his elephant, tell him the way and road he is to take, what place he is to pass by, what inn they are to lie at, what they shall there find to eat; and in short, give him an exact account of all that is to be done during the journey? and to see the elephant perform what he expects from him, as regularly as any man of good sense could do: insomuch, that when the elephant seems to have understood what place he was to go to, he takes the shortest cut to it, without minding the beaten road, rivers, woods, or mountains, but goes on, not doubting to overcome all difficulties, as in effect he does: for if any rivers be in the way, he either fords or swims them; if woods, he breaks the boughs of the trees, pulls them up whole, or cuts them with a sharp iron like a scithe, which to this purpose is fastened to the fore-part of the top of the coach, wherewith upon occasion having first laid hold of the boughs, he cuts them with his trunk, and makes himself way, cutting through the thickest forest, where it is easily known to have been an elephant that made the way: and all this he does with great ease and expedition, in obedience to the *nayre*.

The elephant understands what is said.

One only thing disturbs this creature, and puts it to great pain; which is, when a thorn, or such like thing, runs into the bottom of his foot, which is extraordinary soft and tender, and therefore he treads very cautiously, when he goes thro' places where there may be danger of such an accident. I went a journey once with seven or eight elephants in a company, and heard the *nayres*, every one warn his own beast, to look out carefully where he set his feet: for they were to pass over a sandy place about a mile in length, where thorns grew up among the sand; upon this intimation all the elephants held down their heads, and looking out, as it were, for some small thing that is lost, they walk'd that mile very cautiously, step by step; till being told there was no more to fear, they lifted up their heads, going on as they had done at first. Being come at night to the inn, the *nayres* sent the elephants to the wood to feed, without taking the coach off their backs; and I asking, why they did not take it down: They answered, That the elephants fed on the boughs of trees, and therefore they left the coach on their backs, that they might cut them with that iron we said was before it. The next day being come where there was no wood, every *nayre* carried a large bundle of green boughs for his elephant. I took particular satisfaction to observe one, who more nimbly than the rest, laying hold of those boughs with his trunk, barked them with his teeth, and then eat them up as quick, and with as good a gust, as we would a fig, or any other sort of fruit. Discoursing the next day with my fellow-travellers, who were about twenty, I told them, how much I was pleased to see that elephant eat the boughs so cleverly. Then the *nayre*, by order of the elephant's master, called him by his name, which was *Gnin*, he being at some distance, but presently lifted up his head to give ear to what was said to him. *Remember*, said the *nayre*, *that father, the passenger that looked upon you yesterday, when you was eating; take such a bough as one of them was, and come before him, as you did yesterday*. No sooner had the *nayre* spoke the words, but the elephant came before me with a bough in his trunk, singling me out among all the company, shew'd it me, bark'd, and eat it; then inclining himself very low, he went away, as it were, laughing, making signs of joy and satisfaction; leaving me full of astonishment, to see that a beast should be so apt to understand, and do what it was commanded. Yet the elephant is obedient to none but the *nayre*, or his master; and he will only endure to see them get upon him: for if he should see any other person mount, there were danger that he would throw down the coach with his trunk, and kill him: and therefore when any body is to get up, the *nayre* generally covers his eyes with his ears, which are very large and ill shap'd.

How they are corrected.

If at any time the elephant does not obey so readily as he should, the *nayre* beats him cruelly on the middle of his forehead, standing

Borri. standing himself all the while upright on his head: One time when I was upon him, with several others, the *nayre* beat him, as has been said, and every stroke he gave him, it looked as if we should have been all thrown down headlong. Generally they give him six or seven strokes on the middle of the forehead; but with such force, that the elephant quakes and yet bears all patiently. There is only one time when he obeys neither the *nayre*, nor any other body; which is when on a sudden he is inflamed with lust: for then, being quite besides himself, he bears with no body, but lays hold of the coach with all that are in it, killing, destroying, and beating every thing to pieces. But the *nayre* by certain signs discovers it a little before it comes, and getting down speedily with all the passengers, unloads him, taking down the coach, and leaves him alone in some by-place, till that fury be over: after which, being sensible of his error, and as it were ashamed of himself, he goes with his head low to receive the blows that are to be given him, thinking he has deserved them.

Now useless in war. Formerly the elephants were of great use in war, and those armies were formidable that carried great troops of them into the field; but since the *Portugueses* found out the way of using artificial fireworks to them, they are rather hurtful than otherwise: for not being able to endure those sparks of fire which get into their eyes, they betake themselves to flight, breaking their own armies, killing and confounding all that stands in their way.

The Rhinoceros. The tame elephant fights with only two creatures, which are the wild elephant, and the abada, or rhinoceros; the latter it overcomes, by the first is generally conquered. The rhinoceros is a beast of shape between a horse and an ox, but as big as one of the smallest elephants, covered all over with scales, as it were so many plates of armour. He has but one horn in the middle of the forehead, which is straight and pyramidal, and his feet and hoofs are like those of an ox. When I was at *Nuocmon*, a city in the province of *Pulucambi*, the governor went out to hunt a *rhinoceros*, that was in a wood near our dwelling place. He had with him above an hundred men, some a foot, and some a horseback, and eight or ten elephants. The rhinoceros came out of the wood, and seeing so many enemies, was so far from giving any tokens of fear, that it furiously encountred them all; who opened and making a lane, let the rhinoceros run through: It came to the rear, where the governor was a top of his elephant, waiting to kill it: the elephant endeavours to lay hold with his trunk, but could not by reason of the rhinoceros's swiftness and leaping, that striving to wound the elephant with its horn. The governor knowing it could receive no hurt, by reason of the scales, unless they struck it on the side, waited till leaping it laid open the naked place, and casting a dart, dexterously struck it through from side to side, with great applause and satisfaction of all the multitude of spectators; who without any more to do, laid it upon a great pile of wood, setting fire to it, leaped and danc'd about, whilst the scales were burning, and flesh roasting, cutting pieces as it roasted, and eating them. Of the entrails, that is the heart, liver, and brain, they made a more dainty dish, and gave it to the governor, who was upon a rising ground, diverting himself with their merriment. I being present obtained the hoofs of the governor; which are looked upon to have the same quality and vertue, as the claws of the great beast (or the hoof of the elk) and so the horn is good against poison, as is the unicorn's.

CHAP. V.

Of the Qualities, Customs, and Manners of the Cochin-Chineses; *of their way of Living, their Habit and Cures.*

Colour and disposition of body of the Cochin-Chineses. THE *Cochin-Chineses* are in colour like the *Chineses*; that is, inclined to an olive-colour: I mean those that are nearest the sea; for those up the inland, as far as *Tonchin*, are as white as the *Europeans*. The shape of their faces is exactly like the *Chineses*, with flat noses, little eyes, but of an indifferent stature, not so small as the *Japoneses*, nor so tall as the *Chineses*. Yet they are stronger and more active than either of them, and braver than the *Chineses*, but are out-done by the *Japoneses* in one thing, which is the contempt of life in dangers and battles; the *Japoneses* seeming to make no account of life, nor to apprehend the least fear of death.

Their civility. The *Cochin-Chineses* are naturally the most courteous and affable of all the *Eastern* nations; and tho' on the one side they value themselves much upon their valour, yet on the other they look upon it as a great shame, to suffer themselves to be transported with passion. And whereas all the other *Eastern* nations, looking upon the *Europeans* as a profane people, do naturally abhor them, and therefore fly from us when first we come among them: in *Cochin-China* it falls out just contrary; for they

they strive who shall be nearest us, ask a thousand questions, invite us to eat with them, and in short use all manner of courtesy with much familiarity and respect. So it happened to me and my companions when we first came there, being, as it were, among friends of an old standing. This is a very good disposition to facilitate the preaching of the gospel.

Liberality This loving and easy disposition is the cause of much concord among them, they all treating one another as familiarly as if they were brothers or of the same family, tho' they have never known or seen one another before; and it would be look'd upon as a most vile action, if one man eating any thing, tho' never so little, should not share with all about him, giving every one a bit. They are also naturally kind and free-hearted to the poor, to whom it is customary among them never to deny an alms, when asked; and it would be reputed a great fault to deny it, as if it were due to them. Thus it happened, that some strangers escaping from a shipwreck in a port in *Cochin-China*, and not knowing the language to make known their want, but learning only this word *doii*, which signifies, *I am hungry:* when the natives saw strangers at their doors, crying out *doii*, as if the greatest misfortune in the world had befallen them, every one strove to be before another in giving them to eat; so that in a short time they gathered so much provision, that a ship being afterwards given them by the king to return to their country, they took such an affection to that country, where they found all things for their sustenance at such easy rate, that not a man of them would go away; so that the captain of the ship was forced to drive them aboard with many blows and cuts, which he effectually did, loading the ship with the rice they had gathered only by going about, crying, *I am hungry.*

But as ready as the *Cochin-Chineses* are to give, so are they as apt, if not more, to ask any thing they see, so that as soon as ever they cast their eye on any thing that is new to them, and curious, they say, *Schin Mocaii*; that is, *Give me one of these things:* and it is such a rudeness to refuse them, tho' the thing be rare and precious, that whosoever should do it, would be ever after looked upon as a vile person; so that a man must either hide, or be ready to give what he shews. A *Portuguese* merchant disliking this uncommon custom, as not used to it, resolved, since every one asked of him whatsoever he saw, to do the same with them: accordingly he came to a poor fisherman's boat, and laying hold of a pannier full of fish, in the country language; said to him, *Schin Mocaii*, the honest man made no answer, but gave him all the pannier as it was, for him to carry home, as he did, admiring the liberality of the *Cochin-Chineses*; but taking compassion on the poor fisherman, he afterwards paid him the full value of it. BORRI.

The manner of breeding and civility the *Cochin-Chineses* use, is more or less the same with that of the *Chineses*, always punctually observing all niceties; we know these latter observe between superiors and inferiors, equals, and the respect due to ancient persons, ever preferring the eldest, of what degree soever, and giving them preference before the younger. Wherefore some of those gentlemen coming often a visiting to our house, tho' the interpreter told them, that a father we had there somewhat elder than the rest, was not our superior: yet they could never be brought to pay their respect to the young superior, before the old man. In every house, tho' never so poor, the *Cochin-Chineses* have three sorts of seats; the first and meanest, is a mat upon the bare floor, on which persons of equal quality sit, as those that are of the same family. The next is, a low stool, covered with a very fine mat; which is for persons of better account. The third, is a couch about three quarters of a yard high, on which only the lords and governors of places sit, or persons dedicated to the divine service, and on this they always make our fathers sit. Their breeding.

This good nature and civility of the *Cochin-Chineses*, makes them so courteous to strangers, whom they allow to live according to their own laws, and to wear what cloaths they please; and so they praise their customs, and admire their doctrine, frankly preferring them before their own; quite contrary to the *Chineses*, who despise all but their own customs and doctrine.

Fashion of clothes. As for their habit, we have before observed, that it is the general custom in *Cochin-China* to wear silk; it only remains to speak of the fashion of their clothes. To begin with the women; I think the modestest garb of all *India*; for even in the hottest weather, they suffer no part of the body to be uncovered: they wear five or six petticoats one over another, all of several colours; the first reaches to the ground, which they trail along the ground with such gravity and state, that the tips of their toes are not seen: the second is half a span shorter than the first: the third shorter than that; and so one over another; so that all the several colours appear: and this is the womens habit from the waste downwards, for on their bodies they wear doublets checkered, of several colours; over all they have a veil; but so thin, that tho' it covers them, yet it is transparent, and shews all their gaiety with

BORRI. with modesty, and makes a beauteous majestick appearance. Their hair is loose, spreading over their shoulders, so long that it reaches to the ground, and the longer the greater beauty it is reckon'd. On their head they wear such a broad cap, that it covers all their faces, so that they cannot see above four or five paces before them; and these caps are interwoven with silk and gold, according to the quality of the person. The women when met, are not obliged to any other return of civility, but to lift up the brims of their caps, so much, as their face may be seen. The men, instead of breeches, swath themselves with a whole piece of stuff, putting on over them five or six long and large gowns all of fine silk, and of several colours, with wide sleeves, like those of the monks of the order of St. *Benedict*; and these gowns, from the waste downwards, are all slashed curiously, so that as a man moves, he makes a shew of all those several colours together, and if any wind blows to lift them up, they look like peacocks with their fine feathers spread abroad.

Hair and nails never cut. They let their hair grow as the women do, down to their heels, and wear the same sort of hats, or broad caps. Those who have any beard, and they are but few, never cut it; being in this like the *Chineses*, as they are in suffering the nails of their hands to grow, which the people of note never pare; this being a mark of distinction between them and the commonalty, who always keep them short, for the conveniency of their trades; whereas the gentry have them so long, that they cannot grasp any small thing in their hands. Nor can they approve of our fashion of cutting our hair and nails; being of opinion, that they were given by nature, as an ornament to man: so that some discourse arising once concerning hair, they started an objection, which was not so easy to answer at sight, saying: *If the Saviour of the world, whom in your actions you profess your selves to imitate, wore his hair long, after the manner of the* Nazarites, *as you your selves do affirm, and shew by your pictures; why do not you do so too?* Adding, *That our Saviour's wearing long hair, demonstrated it to be the better fashion.* But at last they were satisfy'd with the answer we made, that this imitation did not consist in the outward dress.

The scholars. The scholars and doctors are somewhat more gravely clad, without so many colours and slashes, and therefore cover all their gowns with one of black damask. They also wear a thing like a stole about their necks, and a blew silk maniple on their arms, covering their heads with caps made after the manner of mitres.

Both men and women carry fans in their hands, rather for ornament than use, and they are not unlike to those the women in *Europe* use. For mourning, as we *Europeans* use black, they wear white. They never uncover their heads in saluting, that being looked upon as an uncivil action. Wherein they agree with the *Chineses*, among whom that custom is reputed so unmannerly, that to comply with them in this particular, the fathers of the society were forced to obtain leave of pope *Paul* the fifth, to celebrate the holy sacrifice of the mass covered. In short, the *Cochin-Chineses* wear neither shoes nor stockings, only saving their feet with leather soles fastened across the toes with silk, like sandals; nor do they think it indecent to go quite barefoot; and though going shod or unshod, they are apt to dirty their feet, they value it not, there being in every house at the door of the chief room, a large pan of clean water, in which they wash their feet, leaving those soles or sandals they use there, to take them again when they go away, because they cannot then dirt their feet, all the floors being covered with mats.

The *Cochin-Chineses* not being so fond of their own customs, as to despise those of strangers, as the *Chineses* do, our fathers in those parts have no occasion to change their habit, wherein they differ but little from the generality of all *India*. They wear a thin cotton cassock, which they call *Ebingon*, and is generally blew, without any cloak, or other upper-garment. They have no shoes, neither after the *European*, nor country fashion; the first they cannot get, because there is no body knows how to make them; and the latter they cannot endure, because of the pain it is to any body that is not used to it, to have his toes spread at a distance from one another, by reason of the buttons that fasten them on, and therefore they choose as the less evil, to go quite barefoot, tho' it exposes them to continual pains in the bowels, especially at first, by reason of the dampness of the country, and their not being used to it. True it is, that in time nature complies, and the skin grows so hard, that it is no pain to walk upon stones or briars. When I returned to *Macao*, I could not endure shoes, thinking them a weight and encumbrance to my feet.

The chief sustenance of the *Cochin-Chineses* is rice; and it is wonderful, that tho' the country abounds in flesh, fowl, fish, and fruit, of so many several sorts, yet when they eat, they first fill their belly with rice, and then taste of other things, as it were for *fashion*-sake. They make more account of rice than we do of bread, and that it may not clog them, they eat it alone without any seasoning of salt, sugar, Their diet.

gar,

gar, oil, or butter, but boiled in so much water as will keep it from burning to, so that the grain remains whole, only soften'd and moisten'd. For this very reason that the rice is not seasoned, it is the easier of digestion, and therefore they that live upon rice, as they do in the *East*, commonly eat it at least four times a day, and a great quantity of it to support nature. The *Cochin-Chineses* eat sitting cross-legged on the ground, with a round table before them breast-high, with mouldings, or adorned with silver or gold, according to the people's quality or wealth. It is not very large; because the custom is for every man to have one to himself; so that at a feast, as many guests as there are, so many tables are provided, and the same is done when they dine privately; only, sometimes man and wife, or father and son, will make a shift with the same table. They neither use knives nor forks; of the first they have no need, because every thing is brought up from the kitchen cut into small bits; the place of the last is supplied by two little sticks, wherewith they neatly and very readily take up any thing; nor have they any need of napkins, for they never foul their hands, nor touch any thing with them.

Their treats. There are frequent invitations among neighbours, and at these entertainments they provide other sorts of dishes than what we have hitherto spoke of; for they make no account of rice, supposing every man has enough of that at home; and tho' he that treats be never so poor, he does not come off with credit, unless every guest's table be served with at least an hundred dishes; and it being the custom to invite all their friends, kindred and neighbours, there is no feast where there is less than thirty, forty, fifty, sometimes a hundred, and even two hundred guests: I was once my self at a solemn entertainment, at which no less than two thousand were feasted, and therefore these banquets must be made in the country, that there may be room for so many tables. Nor must any body admire that the tables being small, they be furnished with a hundred dishes at least; for upon these occasions they very curiously make frames of sugar-canes on the table, on which they dispose of the said dishes; and there must be in them all the varieties of meat the country produces, as well flesh as fish, and butcher's meat as fowl, wild and tame creatures, with all sorts of fruit the season affords; for if but one were wanting, it would be a great fault in the entertainer, and they would not count it a feast. The men of quality that are invited eat first, being waited on by their chief servants. When the masters have tasted of all they like best, these same principal servants take their places, and eat, being waited on by the inferior sort: then these succeed in their places; and because all of them are not able to consume such plenty, and according to custom all the dishes must be emptied; when these are satisfied, then the very meanest servants of every great man come in, and do not only eat their belly full, but put up all the fragments in bags they carry for that purpose, and carry them home, where they merrily divide it among the boys, and other mean fry, and so the feast ends. BORRI.

Their drink. *Cochin-China* produces no grapes, and therefore instead of wine they drink a liquor distilled from rice, which tastes like brandy, and resembles it in colour and harshness, spirit and briskness, and they have such plenty of it, that all people in general drink as much as they will of it, and are as drunk as people are among us with wine. Graver persons mix that liquor with some other water distilled from *calamba*; which gives it a delicious smell, and is a delicate composition.

Between meals they drink hot water, wherein they boil the root of an herb they call *chia*, from which the liquor takes name. It is cordial, and helps to dispel humours from the stomach, and advance digestion. The *Japoneses* and *Chineses* use such a sort of drink, only that in *China*, instead of the root, they boil the leaves of the herb; and in *Japan*, a powder made of the same leaves; but the effect is the same, and they all call it *chia*.

Amidst this great plenty of meat, and abundance of provisions, it is incredible how much hunger and thirst we *Europeans* endure; not so much for want of food, as because we are not used to that diet, nature finding a very great miss of bread and wine: and I believe the *Cochin-Chineses* would be in the same condition, should they come into *Europe*, where they would be deprived of their usual sustenance of rice, tho' they had plenty of other delicate provisions. To this purpose I will not omit to relate what happened to us with a governor of *Cochin-China*, he being a friend of ours, was invited by us to eat at our house; and the more to shew our affection, we endeavoured to have several dishes dressed for him after the *European* manner. He sat down to table, and when we expected he should acknowledge our kindness, commend the cookery, and thank us for the rarity, because we had been at much trouble about it: when he had tasted them all, he could not eat of any one, though out of civility he strove against his stomach; and we were forced to dress more meat after the country-fashion, the best we could, whereof he afterwards eat very savourily, to

BORRI. to his own and our satisfaction. Yet providence does not neglect a thousand ways to support those that undergo these hardships for the preaching of the gospel, finding means, even in this world, to requite what they suffer for the sake of GOD, as happens in this particular of food, as was before said of going bare-foot; for by degrees nature grows familiar with it, and comes to be so habituated to the custom of the country, that it looks strange when to return to its first ways. This happened to me, who when I returned from thence, coveted nothing but the rice of *Cochin-China*, which I thought satisfied me more than any other thing.

Physicians As for physicians, and their way of practice, there are abundance of doctors, not only *Portugueses*, but natives; and it often is experimentally known, that the country physicians easily cure several diseases, which the *European* physicians know not what to do with: so it sometimes happens, that after our physicians have given over a patient, they call one of the country, and he cures him.

Way of practice. The physicians of the country use this sort of practice: being come to the patient's bed-side, they stay a little to settle themselves after the motion of coming; then they feel the pulse for a long while together, very attentively, and with much consideration; after which they usually say, You have such a distemper; and if incurable, they honestly say, I have no cure for this disease: which is a sign the patient will die. If they find the disease curable, they say, I have a medicine that will cure him; and I will do it in so many days. Then they agree what they are to have if they cure the sick man, bargaining the best they can, and sometimes they draw up writings to bind the contract. After this the physician himself prepares the medicine, without the help of an apothecary; for which reason there are none in the country: and this they do, that they may not discover the secret of the art they work; and because they will not trust another to put together the ingredient they prescribe. If the patient recovers within the time appointed, as generally happens, he pays the price agreed on; if he miscarries, the physician loses his labour and medicines.

Medicines The medicines they give are not like ours, which cause a loathing, and are laxative; but theirs are palatable as their broths, and nourishing without any other sustenance, which makes them give the patient several doses in a day, as we give broth at so many hours interval; and these do not alter the course of nature, but only help the usual operations of nature dispersing the peccant humours, without wracking the patient.

I remember a passage worth the relating in this place: a *Portuguese* falling sick, sent for the *European* physicians; who having used their endeavours, gave him over. When they were gone, a physician of the country was called; who undertook to cure him in so many days, strictly enjoining him, whilst he was under his hands, to have a care of having to do with women upon pain of certain death, from which the vertue of his medicine could not deliver him. They agreed upon the price, and the physician undertook to cure him in thirty days. The patient took the medicines prescribed him, and in a few days found himself so well recovered, that he was not afraid to transgress the physician's injunction; who coming to visit him, by the alteration of his pulse discovered the sick man's incontinency, and bid him prepare to die, because there was no cure for him; but that he should pay him his money, since it was none of his fault that he must die. The case was try'd; the sick man was adjudged to pay: and so he died. A notable story.

Bleeding is also used, but not so much as in *Europe*, nor is it done with a steel lancet; but they have abundance of goose-quills, in which they fix some bits of fine porcelane, made sharp, and shaped like the teeth of a saw, some bigger, some less, of several sizes. When they are to let blood, they apply one of these quills to the vein, proportionable to the bigness of it, and giving it a fillip with the finger, open the vein, only so much of the porcelane entring as is requisite: and what is most wonderful, when they have drawn the blood, they use no fillet or binding to stop it; but wetting their thumb with spittle they press the orifice, so that the flesh returning to the place whence it was parted, the blood is stopt, and runs out no more: which I suppose to proceed from the manner of opening the vein, as it were sawing it with that porcelane full of teeth, and therefore it closes again the easier. Bleeding.

There are also surgeons, who have some wonderful secrets, whereof I will give but two instances; one practised upon my self, the other upon one of our brothers, my companion: I happened to fall from a very high place, with my breast against the corner of a stone, whereupon I presently began to spit blood, and had a wound in my breast outwardly. We applied some medicines after our *European* manner, but to no purpose. A surgeon of the country came and took a quantity of a certain herb like that we call mercury, and making it into a plaister, laid it on my breast; then he caused some of that herb to be boiled for me to drink, and made me eat the Surgeons. Great Cures.

the ſame herb raw: and thus in a few days perfectly cured me. I, to make another experiment, cauſed the leg of a hen to be broke in ſeveral places, and making a plaiſter as he had done of the ſame herb, bound it upon the broken leg, and in a few days it was whole and ſound.

A ſcorpion bit a brother of ours, my companion, in the neck; and in that kingdom the bite of a ſcorpion is mortal. All his throat ſwelled immediately, and we were about giving him extreme unction. A ſurgeon was ſent for, who immediately ſet a pot of rice a boiling in nothing but fair water, then clapping the pot to the brother's feet, covered him and it cloſe with cloths, that the ſteam might not go out, and as ſoon as the ſaid ſteam and hot ſmoke of the rice came up to the place where the bite was, the brother felt the pain aſſwage, the ſwelling in his throat fell, and he remained as ſound as if nothing had ailed him. BORRI.

Many other inſtances might be added, but I ſhall only ſay, that the medicines in thoſe parts have a greater virtue than when they come to us; and particularly I can affirm, that I brought with me a ſmall caſk of *rhubarb*, which was extraordinary good there, and when I came into *Europe*, having ſpent two years by the way, I found it ſo changed, that I ſcarce knew it my ſelf, ſo that thoſe medicines loſe much of their virtue in bringing from thoſe countries to our parts.

CHAP. VI.

Of the Civil and Political Government of the Cochin-Chineſes.

I Will give a brief account of as much as may ſuffice for the reader's information; for it would be too tedious, and from the purpoſe of this my ſhort relation, to diſcourſe of every thing in particular. The government of *Cochin-China*, in general, is a medium betwixt thoſe of *China* and *Japan:* for whereas the *Japoneſes* make leſs account of learning than military knowledge: and on the contrary, the *Chineſes* attribute all to learning, taking little notice of warlike affairs. The *Cochin-Chineſes* following the example of neither, equally encourage learning, and ſkill in war, according as occaſion offers, ſometimes preferring the ſoldier, and ſometimes the ſcholar, and ſo repulſing them as appears moſt convenient.

Learning. In *Cochin-China* there are ſeveral univerſities, in which there are profeſſors, ſcholars, and degrees conferred by way of examination, in the ſame manner as is practiſed in *China*, the ſame ſciences being taught, and the ſame books and authors read; that is, *Zinſu*, or *Confucius*, as the *Portugueſes* call them; which are authors of ſuch profound learning, and in ſuch eſteem and reputation among them, as *Ariſtotle* is among us, being much ancienter than he. Theſe books of theirs are full of erudition, of ſtories, of grave ſentences, of proverbs, and ſuch like things, for the directing a civil life, as are *Seneca*, *Cato*, and *Cicero*, among us; and they ſpend many years in learning the true ſenſe of the phraſes, words, characters, and hieroglyphicks, they are writ in; but that they moſt value is moral philoſophy, or ethicks, œconomy, and policy. It is comical to ſee and hear them, when they are ſtudying, read and repeat their leſſons in ſuch a tone as if they were ſinging, which they do to uſe themſelves to it, and give every word its proper accents, which are many, every one expreſſing a ſeveral thing: and therefore one would think, that to converſe with them, a man muſt underſtand the grounds of muſick.

The language they generally ſpeak, is different from that they read and teach in at the ſchools, and which their books are writ in: as among us the vulgar language differs from the *Latin* uſed in the ſchools. Wherein they differ from the *Chineſes*, who, if they are learned, or noble, always uſe the ſame language, which they call of *mandarines*; that is, of doctors, judges, and governors, and the characters they uſe in writing and printing their books, are above eight thouſand, all differing from one another. And for this reaſon the fathers of the ſociety ſpend eight, and even ten years, in ſtudying the *Chineſe* books, before they can be maſters, and go abroad to converſe with them. But the *Cochin-Chineſes* have reduced the characters to three thouſand, which they generally make uſe of: and theſe are enough to expreſs themſelves in their harangues, letters, petitions, memorials, and ſuch things which do not belong to printed books; for thoſe of neceſſity muſt be in *Chineſe* characters. The *Japoneſes* have been more ingenious, who tho' in all that belongs to books, whether written or printed, they agree with the *Chineſes*; yet for common uſes have found out forty eight letters, wherewith they expreſs whatſoever they pleaſe, as well as we do with our alphabet: and yet the *Chineſe* characters are in ſuch eſteem even among the *Japoneſes*, that theſe forty eight letters, notwithſtanding the uſe they are of above the

others,

BORRI.

others, are contemned in comparison of them; insomuch, that in scorn they call them women's letters.

The ingenious invention of printing was found out in *China*, and *Cochin-China*, long before it was in *Europe:* but not in such perfection: for they do not compose joining letters and characters, but with a graver, penknife, or such instrument, cut and carve the characters upon a stone as they will have them in their books: on this board so carved they lay their paper, and print it off, as we in *Europe* do copper-plates, or the like.

Besides these books of morals, they have others, which contain things they account sacred; as for instance: the creation and beginning of the world: of the rational souls of demons: of idols, and of their several sects. These books are called *Sayc Kim*, to distinguish them from the profane, which they call *Sayc Chiu*. Of the doctrine of their sacred books, we shall treat in the second part of this account, where the subject will be more suitable.

The language.

Tho' the language of the *Cochin-Chineses* be in one respect like that of the *Chineses*, both of them using all monasyllables, delivered in several tones and accents; yet they utterly differ in the word it self, the *Cochin-Chineses* being more full of vowels, and consequently softer and sweeter, more copious in tones and accents, and therefore more harmonious. The language of *Cochin-China* is, in my opinion, the easiest of any, for those that have a musical ear, to take the tones and accents; for it has no variety by way of conjunction of verbs, or declination of nouns, but one and the same word, with the addition of an adverb, or pronoun, signifies the present, the preterit, and future tenses, the singular number, and the plural; and in fine, serves for all moods, tenses, and persons, and the diversity of numbers and cases. For instance: This word, *To have*, which in the *Chinese* language is *Co*, by only adding a pronoun, serves all occasions, saying, *I have*, *Thou have*, *He have*; the name of the person making that diversity, which we express by altering the termination, thus, *I have*, *Thou hast*, *He has*. In the same manner they make the several tenses; saying, for the present, *I now have*; for the preterit, *I heretofore have*; and for the future, *I hereafter have:* And so without ever altering the word *Co*; by which it appears how easily this language may be learned: as it happened to me, who in six months understood so much, that I could discourse, and even hear their confessions, tho' not so perfectly, for it requires at least four years to be a master. [*This variety of moods and tenses, appears better by the* Latin, *or other languages, than in* English, *where we use much the same method, as he represents in* Cochin-China; *our variations the same, being but few, as to instance in the same word,* I have, You have, We have, They have, I shall have, May we have: *and so in this, and many others.*]

Rewards for military men.

But to return to our relation: I was saying, that the *Cochin-Chineses* reward not only the learned with dignities, employments, and revenues; but that they make great account of good soldiers, in which particular they act differently from us; for instead of assigning brave commanders, some land, earldom, or marquisate, as a reward of their valour, they allot him such a number of people, and vassals, belonging to the king himself, who whatsoever part of the kingdom they live in, are obliged to own him as their lord, to whom they have been assigned by the king, being bound upon all occasions to serve him with their weapons, and to pay him all those duties they before paid to the king himself; and therefore, as we say, such a one is lord, earl, or marquess of such a place; they say, such a one is a man of fifty, such a one of a thousand men, to such a one the king has added three thousand, to such a one two thousand; their dignity, wealth, and grandeur increasing by the addition of many vassals. We shall speak of the wars of this kingdom in the next chapter.

Trials at law.

It remains that we say somewhat worth being known of the civil government. In the first they govern rather after a military manner, than by judges, counsellors, and lawyers, and their formalities, the vice-roys and governors of provinces performing that function; for every day they give publick audience for four hours daily, in a large court within their own palace, two hours in the morning, and two after dinner. Hither all suits and complaints are brought, and the vice-roy, or governor, sitting on a tribunal raised like a balcony, hears every man in his turn; and these governors being generally men of sound judgment, capacity, and experience, they easily discover the truth of the matter by the questions they put, and much more by the common consent of the stander-by, which is gathered by the applause they give the plaintiff, or defendant, and accordingly they immediately, without delay, give judgment with a loud voice, which is immediately executed without any demur, or appeal, whether the sentence be death, banishment, whipping, or fine, every crime being punish'd as the law appoints.

False witnesses, how punished.

The crimes generally try'd and severely punished are many, but they are particularly rigid against false witnesses, thieves, and adulterers. The first of these being convicted

convicted of having given false evidence, are themselves indispensably condemned, as if they themselves had committed the crime they accuse others of. And if the crime they alledged deserved death, they are sentenced to die: and experience teaches, that this way of trial is very proper to find out the truth.

Thieves. Thieves, if the theft be considerable, are beheaded; if small, as for example, a hen, for the first offence they have a finger cut off, for the second another finger, for the third an ear, and for the fourth the head.

Adulterers. Adulterers, both men and women, indifferently are cast to the elephants to be killed, which is done thus: They lead the criminal out into the field, where in the presence of an infinite number of people flocking together, he is set in the middle with his hands and feet bound, near an elephant, to whom the condemned person's sentence is read, that he may execute every part of it orderly; first that he lay hold of, grasp, and hold him fast with his trunk, and so hold him in the air, shewing him to all the company; then that he toss him up, and catch him upon the points of his teeth, that his own weight may strike them through him; that then he dash him against the ground; and lastly, that he bruise and crush him to pieces with his feet: All which is exactly performed by the elephant, to the great terror and amazement of the spectators, who are taught by this punishment, at another man's cost, what fidelity is due between married persons.

Since we are upon this point of matrimony, it will not be from the purpose to deliver some farther particulars concerning it, before we conclude this chapter. The *Cochin-Chineses*, tho' heathens, never use to contract matrimony within those degrees forbid by the laws of God and nature, nor within the first degree of the collateral line of brothers and sisters. In other degrees matrimony is lawful to every man with only one woman; tho' rich men use to have many concubines, under pretence of grandeur and generosity, looking upon it as covetousness, not to have as many as every man's income will conveniently maintain; and these are called second, third, fourth, and fifth wives, and so on, according to every one's rank, all which wait upon the first, which is accounted, and really is the true wife, whose business it is to chuse the others for her husband. But these marriages of theirs are not indissoluble, the laws of *Cochin-China* allowing of divorces, but not at the will of either party, it being first requisite, that the person suing for it, convict the other of many offences; which being made out, it is lawful to dissolve the first marriage, and marry again. The husbands bring the portion, and leave their own houses to go to the wife's; upon whose fortunes they live, the women managing all the houshold-affairs, and governing the family whilst the husband lives idle at home, hardly knowing what there is in the house, satisfied that they have meat and clothes. Borri. Matrimony.

CHAP. VII.

Of the Power of the King of Cochin-China, *and of the Wars he has in his Kingdom.*

Their skill in cannon and small arms. I Took notice at the beginning of this account, that *Cochin-China* was a province of the great kingdom of *Tonchin*, usurp'd by the grandfather of the king now reigning; who being made governor of it, rebelled against the said king of *Tonchin*; to which he was not a little encouraged, by having in a short time got together a great many pieces of cannon of the wrecks of several *Portuguese* and *Dutch* ships, cast away upon those rocks, which being taken up by the country people, there are above sixty of the biggest, at this time, to be seen in the king's palace. The *Cochin-Chineses* are now become so expert in managing artillery, that they perform it better than the *Europeans*, practising continually to shoot at a mark, with such success, that being proud of their skill, as soon as any *European* ship arrives in their ports, the king's gunners challenge ours, who being sensible that they cannot stand in competition with them, as near as they can, avoid this trial of skill, being convinced by experience, that they will hit any thing as exactly with a cannon, as another shall do with a firelock; which they are also very expert at, often drawing out into the field to exercise. Another great encouragement to rebellion, was, his having above a hundred gallies, which rendring him formidable by sea, and the artillery by land, he easily compass'd his designs against the king of *Tonchin*. Besides, by reason of the constant trade in *Japan*, there were in *Cochin-China* abundance of *Catana's*, which are scymitars made in *Japan*, and excellently temper'd: And all the country abounding in horses, which tho' small, are handsome and mettlesome, Gallies, scymitars, and horses.

tlesome, on which they fight, casting darts, and daily exercise themselves.

King's power.

The power of this king is so great, that whensoever he pleases, he can bring 80000 fighting men into the field, and yet is always in fear of the king of *Tonchin*, whose power is four times as great; to whom, for quietness sake, he, by agreement, pays a tribute, of all such things as his kingdom affords, and are useful for that of *Tonchin*, particularly of gold, silver, and rice; furnishing, besides all this, plank and timber for building of gallies. And for the same reason he was about entring into a league with the fugitive son of the late king, who lorded it in the utmost province of *Tonchin*, which borders upon *China*, that in case he succeeded, and became master of *Tonchin*, *Cochin-China* might remain free from all tribute and acknowledgment.

For the better understanding hereof, it is to be observed, that when I was in *Cochin-China*, that kingdom was in the possession not of the precedent king, but the tutor or governor of that son, who made his escape from the said governor to save his life. The said prince lived like a fugitive, in the farthest province adjoining to *China*; where being known to be what he was, that is the late king's son, he was received by that people as their sovereign lord, and by his good government he had so strengthened himself, that his tutor already declared king of *Tonchin*, was much afraid, seeing him grow so great, lest he should agree with the king of *Cochin-China*, who is of the opposite side, to catch him between them, and expel him his unjust possession. He therefore every year form'd a considerable army to destroy the aforesaid prince; but always to no purpose, because the army being of necessity to march five or six days, through a country where there is no other water to drink, but that of some rivers coming from the enemies country; the army always found it poison'd by the prince's party, with a sort of herb, the effect whereof was such, that it destroyed both men and horses; which obliged him always to retire after much trouble and expence cast away.

Wars in Cochin-China.

The military discipline, and art of war in *Cochin-China*, is almost the same as in *Europe*, the same form being observed in drawing up, fighting, and retiring. This king has generally war in three parts of his kingdom: First, he is always upon his defence against the king of *Tonchin*, who as has been said continually threatens and assaults his frontiers, and therefore the king of *Cochin-China* has his residence in *Sinuua*, the extreme part of his dominions, the better to oppose him, and march his forces towards the confines of *Tonchin*, which is a powerful province, and generally under experienced and martial governours.

The next is a sort of civil war, raised by two of his own brothers, who aiming to be equal in command and power, not satisfied with what has been allotted them, have rebelled against him, and craving succours from *Tonchin*, gave him perpetual trouble. Whilst I lived in those parts, they having got some pieces of cannon, which they carried upon elephants, fortified themselves so well upon the frontiers, that the king's army marching against them, was in the first engagement routed with the loss of 3000 men; but coming to a second battle, the king's brothers lost all they had gained before, being both made prisoners; and they had both immediately lost their lives, had not his majesty's natural clemency and brotherly affection prevailed, and taken place of his anger, so far as to spare their lives, yet so as to keep them prisoners.

The third place where he has continual war, is on the west-side, and utmost bound of his kingdom called *Renran*, against the king of *Chiampá*; whose efforts being weaker, are sufficiently repulsed by the troops of that same province, and the governor.

He is also in continual motion, and making warlike preparations to assist the king of *Cambogia*, who has married his bastard daughter, sending him succours of gallies, and men, against the king of *Siam*; and therefore the arms of *Cochin-China*, and their valour, is famous and renowned, as well by sea as by land.

The gallies.

At sea they fight in gallies, as has been said, each of which carries cannon, and is mann'd with musketeers: Nor will it seem strange, that the king of *Cochin-China* has an hundred, or more, gallies in a readiness, when the method of furnishing them is known. It is therefore to be observed, that the *Cochin-Chineses* do not use to have a crew of criminals, or other slaves, to row in their gallies; but when they are to go out to fight, or for any other purpose, the way to man them immediately is this: A great number of officers, and commissaries, go out privately, and scouring on a sudden all together throughout the whole kingdom, with the king's authority, press all they find fit for the oar, conducting them all together to the gallies, unless they be exempted by birth, or any other privilege. Nor is this method so troublesome as it appears at first sight; for in the first place they are well used and paid aboard the gallies; and besides, their wives and children are fed and provided with all things necessary,

ceſſary, according to their condition, all the while they are from their houſes. Nor do they only ſerve at the oar, but upon occaſion lay hold of their weapons, and behave themſelves bravely; for which purpoſe every one has his muſket, darts, and ſcymitar allotted him; and the *Cochin-Chineſes* being of an undaunted ſpirit, and brave, they give good tokens of their valour, either rowing to join their enemies, or with their arms when joined. Their gallies are ſomewhat leſs, but particularly narrower than ours, but ſo neat, and ſo well adorned with gold and ſilver, that they afford a glorious ſight. Chiefly the ſtem, which they account the moſt honourable poſt, is all over gold, there the captain and perſons of chief note have their ſtation: and the reaſon they give for it is, that it being the captain's duty to be the firſt upon any danger, it is fit he ſhould be in the propereſt part of the gally for that purpoſe. BORRI.

Among other ſorts of defenſive arms they uſe in war, they have certain oval, hollow targets, ſo long that they cover a man quite, and ſo light, that they can manage them without any trouble. The cities of this kingdom have a great advantage in the manner of their houſes, which being all of wood upon pillars of timber, as has been ſaid before when the enemy comes ſo ſtrong, that they perceive they cannot oppoſe him, every man flies to the mountain with what he has, firing the houſes, ſo that the enemy finds nothing but the ruins left by the flames, and having no place to fortify himſelf, nor any thing to ſubſiſt on, is forced to retire back to his own country, and the inhabitants returning to the ſame place in a ſhort time, with great eaſe rebuild their houſes.

CHAP. VIII.

Of the Trade and Ports of Cochin-China.

Trade of *Cochin-China.*

THE great plenty *Cochin-China* affords of all things neceſſary for the ſupport of human life, as has been ſaid before, is the cauſe that the people have no curioſity, or inclination to go into other kingdoms to trade; and therefore they never go ſo far to ſea, as to loſe ſight of their beloved ſhore; yet they are very ready to admit of ſtrangers, and are very well pleaſed they ſhould come not only from the neighbouring countries, but from the remoteſt parts to trade with them. Nor do they need to uſe any art for this purpoſe, ſtrangers being ſufficiently allured by the fruitfulneſs of the country, and the great wealth which abounds there; and therefore they reſort thither not only from *Tonchin*, *Cambogia*, *Chincheos*, and other neighbouring places, but from the remoteſt, as *China*, *Macao*, *Japan*, *Manila*, and *Malacca*, all of them carrying ſilver to *Cochin-China*, to carry away the commodities of the country, which are not bought, but exchanged for plate, which is here put off as a commodity, being ſometimes worth more, and ſometimes leſs, according as there is more or leſs plenty of it, as is uſual with ſilk and other goods.

All the coin they uſe is of braſs, and of the ſame value, like a *quatrine*, 500 of which make a crown. Theſe pieces are quite round, with the king's arms and enſign ſtamped on them, and every one of them has a hole through the middle, which ſerves to ſtring them by thouſands, and every thouſand is worth two crowns.

Rich trade of the *Chineſes* and *Japoneſes.*

The *Chineſes* and *Japoneſes*, drive the chief trade of *Cochin-China*; which is managed at a fair held yearly at one of the ports of this kingdom, and laſting about four months. The *Chineſes*, in their veſſels they call *junks*, bring the value of four or five millions in plate; and the *Japoneſes*, in their ſhips called *ſommes*, an infinite quantity of very fine ſilk, and other commodities of their country. The king has a vaſt revenue from this fair by cuſtoms, and impoſt, and all the whole country receives great profit. The *Cochin-Chineſes* applying themſelves very little to arts, becauſe plenty makes them lazy; and being ſoon taken with the curioſities of other countries it comes to paſs, that they put a great value upon, and buy at great rates, many things, which to others are of very ſmall worth; as for inſtance, combs, needles, bracelets, and pendants of glaſs, and ſuch-like womens tackling. I remember a *Portugueſe*, who bringing into *Cochin-China* from *Macao*, a box full of needles, which could not be worth above thirty ducats, made above a thouſand of it, ſelling that for ſixpence in *Cochin-China*, which had not coſt him above a farthing at *Macao*. In ſhort, they out-bid one another, in buying any thing that is very new and ſtrange without ſparing for price. They are very fond of our hats, of caps, of girdles, ſhirts, and all other ſorts of garments we wear, becauſe they are quite different from theirs; but above all, they put a great value upon coral.

As for their ports, it is wonderful that in a coaſt little more than an hundred leagues in length, there ſhould be above ſixty moſt convenient landing-places; which is Sea-ports.

Borri. is ſo, becauſe there are many large arms of the ſea. But the principal port, to which all ſtrangers reſort, and where the afore-mentioned fair is kept, is that of the province of *Cacchian*; which has two mouths, or inlets from the ſea, the one called *Pulluchiampello*, and the other of *Turon*, being at firſt three or four leagues diſtant from one another, but running in ſeven or eight leagues like two great rivers, at laſt join in one, where the veſſels that come in both ways meet. Here the king of *Cochin-China* aſſigned the *Chineſes*, and *Japoneſes*, a convenient ſpot of ground, to build a city for the benefit of the fair. This city is called *Faifó*, and is ſo large, that we may ſay they are two, one of *Chineſes*, the other of *Japoneſes*; for they are divided from one another, each having their diſtinct governor, and the *Chineſes* living according to the laws of *China*, as the *Japoneſes* do according to thoſe of *Japan*.

All nations admitted to trade. And becauſe, as we ſaid before, the king of *Cochin-China* gave free admittance to all nations whatſoever, the *Dutch* reſorted thither with all ſorts of commodities. Hereupon the *Portugueſes* of *Macao* reſolved to ſend an embaſſador to the king, to demand in their name, that the *Dutch*, as mortal enemies to their nation, ſhould be excluded all *Cochin-China*. One captain *Ferdinand de Coſta*, a man well known for his valour, was appointed to go upon this embaſſy; which he delivered and was favourably heard, with aſſurances of obtaining his demands. Neverthelefs, whilſt he was yet at that court, there arrived a *Dutch* ſhip, and coming to an anchor in the port, ſome of them landed with much mirth and jollity, and preſently went with rich preſents to the king: He accepted of them very graciouſly, and granted them the uſual liberty of trading freely in his kingdom. *Acoſta* hearing of it, went preſently to the king, and complaining, That his majeſty did not keep his word with him, in a *Portugueſe* bravado gave a ſtamp on the ground to ſhew his reſentment. The king and all the courtiers were pleaſed at his paſſion, and bidding him have patience, and expect the event, for he ſhould find he had no cauſe to complain, diſmiſſed him. In the mean while he ordered all the *Dutch* to go aſhore, and land all their goods againſt the fair at *Turon*, as the *Portugueſes* did; which they perform'd: But as they were going upon the river in boats, they were on a ſudden aſſaulted by the gallies, which deſtroyed moſt of them. The king remained maſter of their goods; and to juſtify this action, alledged, that he very well knew the *Dutch*, as notorious pirates, who infeſted all the ſeas, were worthy of ſeverer puniſhment; and therefore, by proclamation, forbid any of them ever reſorting to his country: and it was actually found, that thoſe very men had robbed ſome veſſels of *Cochin-China*, and therefore took this juſt revenge; admitting the *Portugueſes* as good and ſincere friends: Who not long after ſent another embaſſador from *Macao*, to obtain of the king a confirmation of the aforeſaid edict, at the inſtance of *Acoſta*, alledging as a motive, the danger that the *Dutch*, in time, might cunningly poſſeſs themſelves of ſome part of *Cochin-China*, as they had done in other parts of *India*. But the new embaſſador was adviſed by knowing men of that country, not to mention any ſuch thing to the king, becauſe that very thing would be a motive to him to grant the *Dutch* a free trade, and invite all *Holland* to come over; he pretended to be afraid of no nation in the world; quite contrary to the king of *China*, who being afraid of every body, forbids all ſtrangers trading in his kingdom; and therefore the embaſſador muſt urge other motives to obtain his deſire.

Dutch baniſhed.

The king of *Cochin-China* has always ſhewn himſelf a great friend to the *Portugueſes* that trade in that kingdom, and has ſeveral times offered them three or four leagues of the fruitfulleſt country about the port of *Turon*, that they may build a city there with all ſorts of conveniences, as the *Chineſes*, and *Japoneſes*, have done. And were it allowed me to give his catholick majeſty my opinion in this point, I ſhould ſay, he ought, by all means, to command the *Portugueſes* to accept of the kind offer made them, and to build a good city there as ſoon as poſſible; which would be a refuge, and brave defence, for all the ſhips that paſs by towards *China*: For here a fleet might be kept in readineſs againſt the *Dutch*, that ſail to *China* and *Japan*, who of neceſſity muſt paſs through the middle of the bay, that lies between the coaſt of this kingdom, in the provinces of *Ranran*, and *Pulucambi*, and the rocks of *Puluſiſi*. *Portugueſes* favour'd in *Cochin-China*.

This is what ſmall matter I thought I could, with truth, give an account of, concerning the temporal ſtate of *Cochin-China*, according to the knowledge I could gain in ſome years I reſided there; as will farther appear in the ſecond part of this relation.

The End of the Firſt Part.

The

The Second PART.

TREATING Of the SPIRITUAL STATE of *Cochin-China.*

CHAP. I.

Of the first entring of the Fathers of the Society of JESUS into that Kingdom: And of the two Churches built at Turon *and* Cacchian.

The jesuits the first that taught Christianity in *Cochin-China.*

BEFORE the fathers of the society of JESUS went into *Cochin-China*, it was the custom of the *Portugueses* trading thither, to carry thither with them from *Malacca*, and *Macao*, and the *Spaniards* from *Manila*, some chaplains, to say mass and administer the sacraments to them, during their stay there, which generally was three or four months in a year. These chaplains having no other obligation but only to serve the *Portugueses*, never thought of promoting the spiritual welfare of the natives of that country, not applying themselves to learn their language, nor using any other means to communicate the light of the gospel to them. And yet there was one of these who had the face to publish in *Spain*, in a book call'd, *The Voyage of the World*; that he had catechis'd and baptis'd the infanta or princess of *Cochin-China*, and a great many of her ladies: whereas never infanta, nor any other person of all that royal family, till this time, has shewn any inclination to become Christian, notwithstanding we fathers go every year to visit the king, and discourse with all the great men of the court; and yet the infanta has not given any token of being a Christian, or so much as knowing what a Christian is. And it may well be discern'd, how falsly he talks in this point, by the other fables he adds in the same book, concerning that infanta; as that she would have marry'd the said chaplain, and the like. We know of none but some fathers of the order of St. *Francis*, that went from *Manila*, and one of St. *Augustine*, from *Macao* to *Cochin-China*, merely for the conversion of those souls. But they meeting with no success, by reason of the many several difficulties that occur, they return'd to their countries: Providence so ordering it, which had design'd that land to be cultivated by the sons of the holy patriarch *Ignatius*, which was done as follows.

BORRI.

Manner of their going thither.

Certain *Portuguese* merchants acquainted the superiors of the society of JESUS at *Macao*, with the great advantages that might be gain'd, to advance the glory of GOD in *Cochin-China*, if there were undaunted and zealous labourers sent thither; and particularly one captain earnestly pres-sed the father provincial, not to abandon a kingdom so capable of being instructed in the holy faith. The proposal seem'd to the father very agreeable to the spirit of our vocation, and therefore without demurring upon the execution of it, he made choice for this enterprize of F. *Francis Buzome*, who had been professor of divinity at *Macao*, by birth a *Genoese*, but educated in the kingdom of *Naples*, where he was admitted into the society, and whence he set out for *India*: together with F. *James Caravalho*, a *Portuguese*, who from *Cochin-China* was to attempt to go over to *Japan*, as he did. This was he, who being put into a pool of cold water in the dead of winter, and expos'd to the wind and snow, gave up his life for the sake of his Redeemer, freezing leisurely to death. F. *Caravalho* being gone, F. *Buzome* was left alone in *Cochin-China*, with only a lay-brother to attend him: being zealously inflam'd with the desire of saving souls, he us'd all possible means for their conversion, and to this purpose began his mission at *Turon*. But as yet he knew not the language, nor could he find any interpreter that knew any more *Portugueze* than what was requisite for buying and selling, and some words or phrases, which the interpreters of the chaplains of ships, who were there before the fathers of the society, made use of to ask the *Cochin-Chineses*, Whether they would be Christians? After this manner they

Mistaken conversions.

BORRI.

they had made some, but such as might rather be accounted so by name than by profession; for they did not so much as understand what the name of a Christian meant: and this by reason of the phrase the interpreters us'd to ask them, Whether they would be Christians: for the words they made use of, signify'd nothing more, than that they would become *Portuguese*; which F. *Francis Buzome* found out by this following accident: a play was acted in the publick market-place, at which the father saw one in the habit of a *Portuguese*, brought in by way of ridicule, with a great belly so artificially made, that a boy was hid in it; the player, before the audience, turn'd him out of his belly, and ask'd him, Whether he would go into the belly of the *Portuguese?* Using these words, *Con gnoo muon bau tlom laom Hoalaom chiam?* That is, *Little boy, will you go into the belly of the* Portuguese, *or not?* The boy answer'd, *He would:* and then he put him in again, often repeating the same thing to divert the spectators. The father observing, that the phrase the player so often repeated, *Muon bau tlom laom Hoalaom chiam*, was the same the interpreters us'd, when they ask'd any one, Whether he would be a Christian? Presently conceiv'd the mistake the *Cochin-Chineses* were under; who thought, that to become a Christian was only to cease being a *Cochin-Chinese*, and become a *Portuguese*; which to make sport was express'd in the play, by making the boy go into the belly of him that acted the *Portuguese*. The father took care, that so pernicious an error should spread no farther, teaching those already baptis'd their duty, and instructing those that were newly converted, what it was to be baptis'd and become a Christian, taking particular care that the interpreters should be well inform'd in this particular, that they might afterwards serve faithfully in teaching of others; changing the abovemention'd phrase into this, *Muon bau dau christiam chiam?* That is, *Will you enter into the christian law, or no?* His great diligence and charity was so successful, that within a few days he began to reap the fruit of his labours, as well by the reformation of those who before were Christians only in name, as the conversion of many more. Nor was the fame of his charity and zeal for the gaining of souls confin'd to *Turon*, his usual place of residence, but spread abroad into other places; he labouring in all places to instruct, convert, and dispose the people to receive baptism with such fervour, and so great a concourse about him, that in a short time those new Christians built a very large church at *Turon*, in which the most holy sacrifice of the mass was publickly celebrated, and the christian doctrine preach'd and taught, by means of the interpreters, then well instructed; all persons being very much taken with F. *Francis Buzome:* who besides his being a person of great knowledge and virtue, entirely gain'd the affections of those heathens, by his great meekness and affability, insomuch that they all flock'd after him. This particularly happened at *Cacchiam*, the city where the king resides, six or seven leagues from *Turon*, up the river.

Churches erected.

Here F. *Buzome* made so great an impression, that a place was presently allotted him for a church, which was built in a very short time, every body contributing to the expence, and to the work, according to their power. Besides, he had a good house assign'd him, fit for to make a residence of fathers, who were to go thither in time to instruct that people in matters of faith: all which was done with the assistance of a most noble lady, who was converted, and in baptism took the name of *Joanna*. She not only undertook the foundation of the house and church, but erected several altars and places of prayer in her own house, never ceasing to bless and praise GOD for the mercy shewn her, in enlightening and drawing her to the faith. All this his divine majesty brought to pass in the space of a year, through the means of his servant, F. *Francis Buzome*; whose fame being spread as far as *Macao*, the following year our father provincial thought fit to send him another father, that was younger, with a *Japonese* brother, that learning the language, he might afterwards preach without standing in need of an interpreter. This was F. *Francis de Pina*, a *Portuguese*, who had learn'd divinity under F. *Francis Buzome*. And tho' this second year the increase was not answerable to that of the first, as to the conversion of souls, yet the advantage was much greater in the sufferings of a cruel persecution, rais'd by the enemy that sow'd the tares, who could not endure to see the divine seed grow up so prosperously in those parts, and endeavour'd to choke it; as shall be shewn in the next chapter.

CHAP.

CHAP. II.

Of the Persecution the New Church of Cochin-China *endur'd, at its first Institution: and how I was sent thither to be assisting to it, by my Superiors.*

Cause of the persecution.

THE persecution against the fathers took its beginning from an accident at first sight ridiculous, and of no moment, which afterwards gave them much cause to lament. That year there happened an universal barrenness throughout the whole kingdom, for want of the usual inundation in autumn; which, as was said in the first part, is so necessary for bringing up the rice, the chief support of life in that country. Hereupon their priests, whom they call *omsaiis*, held a great council, to find out the cause why their idols were so angry with all their kingdom, that seeing the people starve to death about the fields, yet they were not the least mov'd to compassion for so great a calamity. It was there unanimously agreed, that there was nothing new in the kingdom, so opposite to the worship of the idols, as the admitting of strangers freely to preach up a law there, that utterly contradicted the honour given to those Idols; and that they being justly provok'd at it, reveng'd themselves by denying them their desired rain.

The fathers banish'd.

This being agreed on as a most undoubted truth, according to their ignorance, they presently went in a tumultuous manner to the king, and press that the preachers of the new law may be banish'd all the kingdom, that being the only means to appease the wrath of their gods. The wise king laugh'd at their project, knowing it to be a foolish notion of those priests, and made little account of it, having a great esteem for the fathers, and a kindness for the *Portuguese*. Yet this favour of the king avail'd them but little to oppose the fury of the ministers of Satan; for they so stirr'd up the people to press that the preachers of the gospel might be expell'd the kingdom, that the king, not able to resist without danger of a mutiny, sent for the fathers, and with much concern told them, He was sensible of the folly of the people, and ignorance of the priests; but that it was not prudence to withstand a multitude, so eagerly bent upon such an affair as that was, which was designed for the removing so general a calamity; and therefore they must depart his kingdom as soon as possible. The fathers having heard these words with tears in their eyes, seeing themselves oblig'd to forsake those new and tender plants of Christianity, yet ever submitting to the will of God, went away to embark; but being got aboard, in obedience to the king's command, they could never get out of the harbour, because at that time a sort of contrary winds, which usually hold three or four months, had begun to blow, which by the *Portugueses* are call'd *Moncao*, or general winds. The *Cochin-Chineses* observing it, would not allow them to return into the city, but oblig'd them to remain upon the shore depriv'd of all human comfort, and expos'd to the burning heat of the sun, which in those parts is very violent. It was a great satisfaction to them in the midst of their sufferings, to see the constancy of some of those new Christians, who never forsook their masters, following, accompanying, and relieving them the best they could, becoming voluntary companions in their sufferings. F. *Buzome* had here a new trial of his virtue; for the uneasiness of this uncomfortable life, in a few days, caus'd an imposthume to break out in his breast, from which abundance of corruption ran, and was a mighty weakening to him.

An hypocrite priest of the idols detected and punish'd.

The infernal fiend, not satisfied to have brought the preachers of the gospel to this miserable condition, made yet farther efforts to discredit their doctrine, and catholick religion, making use to this purpose of one of those *omsaiis*, who living a solitary life, was therefore in great reputation of sanctity. This man coming one day from his hermitage, publickly boasted, That by his prayers he would cause the idols immediately to send rain: and without more to do, went away follow'd by an innumerable multitude to the top of a mountain, where he began to call upon his devils, and striking the earth three times with his foot, the sky was presently clouded, and there fell a shower of rain; which tho' not sufficient to supply the want, yet was enough to give a reputation to that minister of hell, and to discredit our holy faith, every one saying, They had not yet seen the foreign priests obtain so much by their prayers of the great God, whose servants they profess'd themselves. This accident troubled the fathers more than the misery they liv'd in: but Providence comforted them by the means of the lady *Joanna* above-mention'd. She, as it were, with a prophetick spirit, bid them not be concern'd at any thing that had happened; for in a little time God would make the hypocrisy of that *omsaii*, and the vanity of his idols, known to all men, by destroying the reputation he had gain'd till then; all which was verified to a tittle soon after. For the fame of his

sanctity

BORRI. sanctity being spread abroad upon account of the rain, and coming to the king's ear, he presently sent for him, and gave him an apartment in the palace. There he fell in love with one of the king's concubines, and found no difficulty to compass his design; but the matter being known, tho' in *Cochin-China* this be accounted a most heinous crime, and it be death to have to do with a woman the king has once touch'd; yet they could not proceed to execution against him, as being a person sacred among them, but according to the form appointed by their laws. The king therefore gave the sentence, That the *omsaii* should vanish; but that he should neither go east, west, north, nor south, nor through any part whatsoever of his kingdom. This decree being publish'd, was immediately executed in such manner, that the *omsaii* vanish'd with great shame, and was never more seen in the kingdom, nor out of it.

The church burnt.

But the devil being enraged, vented his fury against GOD's servants, stirring up the people to fire the church in *Turon*, to the grief of the fathers, who beheld all from the shore without hopes of redress.

The author in *Cochin-China.*

In the mean while the news of the fathers misfortune was spread all about the neighbouring countries, and even as far as *Macao*, which was a great trouble to the fathers of that college, who pitying their brethren, resolv'd to send them some relief by a *Portuguese* vessel that was ready to sail to *Cochin-China*; and the fathers judg'd the business might succeed the better, if two fathers going in it, one had the name of chaplain of the ship, to return in it; and that the *Cochin-Chineses* might have no cause to complain, or be incens'd, he that remain'd was to go disguis'd: F. *Peter Marques*, a *Portuguse*, was appointed chaplain; and I had the good fortune to be his companion, obedience so ordering it: for tho' I had been destin'd for *China* by our father general, I freely and affectionately embraced the opportunity of dedicating my self to GOD in the mission of *Cochin-China*, and for the comfort of those afflicted fathers, seeing my self quite shut out of *China*, by reason of the persecution rais'd there. I set out from *Macao* in the habit of a slave, and soon arrived in *Cochin-China* upon my birth day, which was very near opening the way for me to a blessed life; but it pleas'd Providence to order matters otherwise, either because my sins made me unworthy of such a mercy, or for other causes only known to GOD: as the vessel was entring the harbour, upon which there were abundance of the country people, there happened, I know not how, a quarrel between two *Portugueses*, and one of them falling down for dead, the other leap'd into the sea to escape the wounded man's friends and companions, who would have kill'd him. He swam a-while, but being tir'd, drew towards the ship again, to save himself from sinking, and endeavouring to catch hold could not, because they were ready above with half-pikes, javelins, and swords, to wound him. I seeing him in that distress, endeavour'd to relieve him; and tho' I was in a servile habit, ran among them, and calling out to one, and pulling another, took such pains that I appeas'd them. The *Cochin-Chineses* who were aboard the Ship, seeing the *Portugueses* pacified at the sight of a slave, began presently to suspect the matter; and knowing by experience, that the *Portugueses*, when in a passion, are not so easily quell'd, unless religious men interpose, said to one another, This man is certainly no slave, as his habit seems to suggest; and being no merchant, as the rest are, he is certainly one of their religious men, that endeavours, contrary to the king's command, to be conceal'd in our country, but we will discover him to the king himself, that he may be punish'd as he deserves. Immediately they flock'd about me, and tho' I did not understand their language, yet I plainly perceiv'd they had all a jealousy of me; and notwithstanding all my endeavours not to discover my self, I could not prevent their sending advice to court. When I had satisfy'd my self as to this point, believing I was certainly a dead man, I resolv'd to die as what I was: accordingly I put on my habit of the society, a surplice over it, and a stole about my neck; and in that habit I began publickly to preach the faith of Christ by means of the interpreter; then erecting an altar on the shore, I said mass, and gave the communion to the *Portugueses* that were present, standing ready for whatsoever it should please GOD to appoint: But it pleas'd him not that I should then shed my blood for him. Whilst my cause was in hand, it rain'd so abundantly day and night, without ever ceasing, that every man apply'd himself to tilling of the ground, and sowing of rice, and perhaps reflecting that they had obtain'd that at my arrival, which they had so long wish'd for, looking upon it as a good omen; and concluding it was not the fault of the fathers that they had wanted rain, they repented them of all they had done against us, and never gave us any farther trouble, but suffer'd us to live freely throughout the kingdom.

Charity of *Japonese* Christians

Matters being thus pacified, I resolved to go look out F. *Buzome*, and his companion, since I was gone thither to that end; and whilst I was endeavouring to hear some news of him, the report of my arrival being spread about the city, that lady *Joanna*

Joanna above-mentioned found me out. By her I understood that F. *Francis de Pina*, with the *Japonese* brother, had been privately conveyed by *Japonese* Christians to the city *Faifó*, all people certainly concluding that the fathers were then got out of the kingdom. Upon this information, F. *Peter Marques*, who knew the language of *Japan* very well, would have us go to *Faifó*, where we found F. *Francis de Pina*, who was there hid, but very well used by those good *Japonese* Christians, to whom he privately administred the sacraments. We received incredible joy in meeting: for besides the general charity of religion, we had been companions, and great friends, in the college of *Macao*; and the kindness of the *Japoneses* was extraordinary, for they treated us during a fortnight very splendidly, with great demonstrations of affection and joy.

Here I also understood how, through GOD's special providence, F. *Buzome* was also safe in the kingdom, as if GOD had particularly defended him for the good of that mission, where whilst he was upon the strand amidst so many afflictions, and with that impostume in his breast, the governor of *Pulucambi* came to *Turon*; who seeing that man so ill used, that he looked like a walking ghost, being moved to compassion asked who he was, and what misfortune had brought him to that miserable condition. He was told all that had happened; and that the want of rain being laid to his and his companion's charge, he had been banished by the king's order. The governor was not a little amazed, and laughed to think that this should be attributed to a poor religious man, which could no way depend of him; therefore he ordered him to be taken from that open shore, and carry'd into one of his gallies, in which he carry'd him to his province, entertained him in his own house, had him looked after by the most skilful physicians in that city, and made his own children attend him during a whole year; for so long his sickness lasted: all men admiring that a heathen should behave himself so charitably towards a stranger utterly unknown to him only out of mere natural compassion.

Thus we were four priests of the society in *Cochin-China*: F. *Buzome*, at *Pulucambi*, one hundred fifty miles from the port of *Turon*; F. *Peter Marques* remained at *Faifó*, as superior, and to serve the *Japoneses*; keeping F. *Francis de Pina* for his companion: and I returned to *Turon*, there to serve the *Portugueses*, to say mass, preach to them, and hear their confessions, and learning at the same time the language of *Cochin-China*, endeavoured, with the assistance of the interpreters, to persuade some of those heathens to be baptized; and above all, to encourage and confirm those that were already baptized. Soon after my first coming, their happened a mean accident worthy to be known: I was called to make a dying infant a Christian; I did so, and soon after it gave up the ghost. I was concerned, not knowing where to bury it, which made me think of fixing a burying-place for all the Christians that should die for the future. To this purpose I ordered a mast of a ship that was cast by, to be taken, and a stately cross to be made of it: which done, I invited all the *Portugueses*, and sailors, to help to carry it to the appointed place, I attending with my surplice and stole. Whilst the hole was digging to erect the holy cross, a company of armed men came out from the neighbourhood, who with their muskets threatned to kill me; which I perceiving, caus'd the interpreter to endeavour to know of them, what it was they would be at? And was told, they would not have that cross erected there, because they feared the devils would infest their houses. I answer'd, It would be quite contrary; because the cross had such a virtue, that it put the devil to flight. With this they were so well pleased, that laying down their arms, they all ran to help: and thus the cross was set up to the general satisfaction of all parties, and the burial-place fixed. Soon after the governor of *Pulucambi* came thither, and brought F. *Buzome* with him; and we met all four fathers of the society, to our unspeakable joy at *Falfó*, together with two lay-brothers, one a *Portuguese*, and the other a *Japonese*. After a charitable reception, we consulted together about the most proper means of promoting that mission. It was unanimously agreed, that F. *Peter Marques* should stay at *Falfó* with the *Japonese* brother, because he was a good preacher; and the other three, with the *Portuguese* brother, should follow the governor of *Pulucambi*, who earnestly desired it; which was accordingly done, as shall be here related.

BORRI.

CHAP. V.

The Governor of Pulucambi *introduces the Fathers of the Society into his Province, building them a House and Church.*

BORRI.

F. *Francis Buzome*, F. *Francis de Pina*, and I, set out from *Faifó*, for *Pulucambi*, with the governor of that province; who all the way treated us with inexpressible courtesie and kindness, always lodging us near himself, and behaving himself in such manner, that there being no human motives to incline him so to do, it plainly appeared to be the work of Providence.

Great goodness of the governor of *Pulucambi*

He appointed a galley only to carry us and our interpreters, not suffering so much as our baggage to be put aboard it, but ordered another boat for it. In this easie manner we travelled twelve large days journey, putting into a port morning and evening, and all the ports being near great towns or cities of the province of *Quanghia*, in which province the governor had as much power as in his own at *Pulucambi*; all people ran to pay their respects and acknowledgments, bringing him rich presents, the first of which always fell to our share, he himself so ordering it, every one admiring to see us so honoured; which gained us much esteem and reputation among those people, that being the design of the governor: and this was much forwarded by the great account he made of our intercession, when any criminal was to be punished: for we no sooner opened our mouths, but we obtained all we desired; by which means we not only gained the reputation of being great with the governor, but of having compassion and kindness for those people, who therefore loved and respected us. Besides, during the whole voyage, he treated us as if we had been some great lords, contriving sports and pastimes in all parts, causing the gallies sometimes to represent a sea-fight, sometimes to row for rewards. Nor did there a day pass but he came aboard our galley to visit us, seeming much pleased with our conversation, especially when we discoursed of religion and our holy faith. In this manner we came to the province of *Pulucambi*, thro' which we had still some days journey to make, before we arrived at the governor's palace, who for our greater diversion would have us travel by land. To this purpose he ordered seven elephants to be provided; and the more to honour us, would have one for each, causing an hundred men, some on horseback, and some a foot, to attend us: and the journey being for recreation, we spent eight days in it, being royally entertained wheresoever we came; but particularly in the house of a sister of his, we had a most splendid entertainment, not only for the variety and number of dishes, but much more for the rarity of the dressing, all things being dressed after the *European* manner, tho' neither the governor, nor any of the family were to taste of them.

His grandeur, and affection to the fathers.

Being at length come to the governor's palace, all the entertainments and dainties of the journey concluded in such a reception as he used to make for kings and great princes, treating us for eight days together in most splendid manner, making us sit in his royal throne, and eating with us himself in publick, with his wife and children, to the great astonishment of all that city, where it was unanimously affirmed, such a reception had never been seen, unless it were for some royal person: and this was the cause of the report generally spread throughout the kingdom, that we were a king's sons, and were come thither about matter of great concern; which being known by the governor, he was mightily pleased; and before the chiefest men of the court he publickly said, *It is very true, that the fathers were the sons of a king, for they were angels, come thither, not for any want or necessity of their own, being provided with all things in their own countries, but only out of pure zeal to save their souls:* And therefore he advised them, *to give ear to the fathers, and observe the law they would preach to them, learn the doctrine they taught, and receive the faith they delivered: for* (said he) *I have often discoursed and conversed with these men, and plainly perceive by the doctrine they teach, that there is no true law but theirs, nor no way but that they shew, which leads to eternal salvation. But take heed what you do; for unless you learn that true doctrine, which I, your chief, bring to you by means of these fathers, your neglect and infidelity will be punished eternally in hell.* Thus spoke that lord, becoming a preacher of the gospel, tho' himself a heathen; all men being the more amazed and astonished at it, because of the great conceit they had of his wisdom.

The fathers settled.

After the first eight days, we gave him to understand, that we would rather go live in the city, the better to promote the preaching of the gospel, which we could not so well attend in the palace, because it was three miles from the city, in an open field, according to the custom of the country. The governor would not have parted with

with us, because of the great affection he had for us, but preferring the publick good before his own satisfaction, he immediately ordered there should be a very convenient house provided in the city *Nuoecman:* and moreover told us, we might see above a hundred houses that were about his palace, and take our choice of the convenientest of them, to make a church of it; and acquainting him with it, he would provide all that was necessary. We returned him thanks for so many favours bestowed on us during our journey, and those we still received. Having taking our leaves for the present, we mounted the elephants again, and with a great attendance went away to the city *Nuoecman,* which extends it self five miles in length, and half a mile in breadth, where we were by the governor's order received with extraordinary honour. He not being able to endure to be so far from us, came the next day to visit us, to know whether the house we had given us was convenient; and told us, he knew that we being strangers, could not have money and other necessaries, but that he took upon him to provide every thing; and immediately ordered a good sum to be paid us monthly, and every day flesh, fish, and rice to be sent in for us, our interpreters, and all the servants of the house: and not so satisfied, he frequently sent us so many presents, that they alone were sufficient to furnish us plentifully with all things. The more to honour and credit us among all men, he one day gave publick audience in the court of our house, in the manner as we said above was practised in *Cochin-China.* Here several criminals were tryed, every one receiving sentence according to his crime; among the rest, two were condemned to be shot to death with arrows, and whilst they were bound we undertook to beg their pardon; which was immediately granted, and he ordered them to be discharged, publickly protesting, he would not have done it at the request of any other, but to these holy men, who teach the true way for the salvation of souls, (said he) I can deny nothing; and I am my self impatient to be rid of those impediments that obstruct my being baptized, and receiving their holy faith; which is what you all ought to do, if you desire to oblige me.

A rare way of building a church.

Then turning to us, he again desired we would appoint the place for the church, that he might give orders for its speedy fitting up. We shew'd him a place that seem'd convenient enough, and he approving of it, went away to his palace. Before three days were over, news was brought us, that the church was coming: we went out with great joy, and no less curiosity, to see how a church should come, which tho' we knew was to be made of timber, as had been agreed, yet it could not choose but be a great pile, according to the space it must fill, standing upon great pillars. On a sudden, in the field, we spied above a thousand men, all loaded with materials for this fabrick. Every pillar was carried by thirty lusty men; others carried the beams, others the planks, others the capitals, others the bases; some one thing, some another, and so all of them went in order to our house, filling all the court, which was very large, to our unspeakable joy and satisfaction. One only thing displeased us, that we had not provisions enough in the house, to give so great a multitude a small entertainment; for tho' they were paid by the governor, yet it looked like ill-breeding to send them away without some refreshment: but we were soon eased of this trouble; seeing every one sit down upon the piece he brought, being obliged to keep and deliver it, and take out of his wallet, his pot with flesh, fish, and rice, and lighting a fire, fall to cooking very quietly, without asking any thing. When they had eaten, the architect came, and taking out a line, view'd the ground, mark'd out the distances, and calling those that carried the pillars, fixed them in their places; this done, he called for the other parts, one after another, that every man might give an account of what he brought, and go his way: and thus all things proceeding very regularly, and every man labouring his best, all that great pile was set up in one day; yet either through over-much haste, or the negligence of the architect, it proved somewhat awry, and leaning to one side; which being made known to the governor, he presently commanded the architect, upon pain of cutting off his legs, to call all the workmen he had need of, and mend it. The architect obey'd, and taking the church to pieces with a like number of workmen, rebuilt it in a very short time very compleatly. And we blessed GOD, for that a time when Christians were so lukewarm, it had pleased him to stir up a heathen so zealously to build a church, in honour of his Divine Majesty.

And to shew how affectionately the governor looked to our affairs, I will give one particular instance, and so end this chapter. In the months of *June, July,* and *August,* the south-west winds generally reign in *Cochin-China,* which causes such an extraordinary heat, that the houses are perfectly parch'd and dried up; and being all of wood, the least spark of fire, that through negligence or other accident falls upon them, immediately takes, as it would

BORRI. would do in tinder; and therefore during those months, there are generally great fires throughout the kingdom; for when it has taken hold of one house, the flame soon catches hold of those that lie the way the wind blows, and miserably consumes them. To deliver us from this danger, our house being in the middle of the city, and to make it farther appear what esteem the governor made of us, he put out an edict, commanding, that the tops of all the houses that lay south-west of us, should be taken off; and there were so many of them, that they extended at least two miles; which he did to the end, that if any of them took fire, it might be the easier to prevent its passing forward to ours: and this was readily performed by them all, by reason of the great respect they bore us.

CHAP. IV.

Of the Governor of Pulucambi's *Death.*

OUR affairs advanced very prosperously in this city, and it was now the time, when the Divine Providence was, according to its usual method, to give us a taste of sufferings, wherewith GOD frequently tries his servants; and so we ever see he gives such a mixture of prosperity and adversity, that they neither be depressed by the one, nor puffed up by the other: and as the primitive church was founded by the holy apostles upon these two pillars of prosperity and tribulation, even so it pleased the Almighty, that the new church of *Cochin-China* should be established by his apostolical ministers. The first beginnings of this mission were very successful, as has been seen in the first chapter of this second part; but very soon after ensued that terrible persecution for want of rain, which had like to have ruined all. Afterwards, with the favour of the governor of *Pulucambi*, the storms seemed to be blown off, and the budding vine seemed to promise abundance of fruit: but it pleased him that disposes of all things, that the governor of *Pulucambi*'s death, like a violent north-wind, almost destroyed all in the bud. This misfortune happen'd as follows: the governor went out one day a hunting on his elephant, very well pleased, and the sport drawing him on, he made no reflection that he rode all day over a scorching plain, where the heat pierced his head in such manner, that at night he fell into a burning fever; upon notice whereof, we hasted to the palace to visit, or rather to baptize him, if we found him in imminent danger. He kept us with him two days, we still pressing him to be baptised, as he had often said he would; to which he always answered, he was ordering his affairs for that purpose, but came to no conclusion. The third day he lost his senses, GOD so permitting, for causes only known to himself; and perhaps that vain honour he ever passionately coveted, was the reward of the good turns he did us: in fine, he began to rave, and so continued three days, till overcome by the violence of the distemper, he died without baptism.

The governor's death.

Any man may guess how much we were concerned at this accident, seeing ourselves forsaken in a strange country, and destitute of all human help; but it chiefly grieved us, that a person so well disposed, and through whose means we had conceived hopes, that the faith might spread throughout the whole kingdom, should die so in our hands without baptism. Abundance of their rites and superstitious ceremonies were performed at this governor's death, at which we were present till the last. It would be endless to relate them all, and therefore I will set down two or three, by which the others used by those gentiles upon such occasions may be guessed at. First, whilst he lay in his agony, there was a multitude of armed men, who did not cease to cut and make thrusts in the air with their scimitars, cast darts and fire muskets in the rooms of the palace; but particularly two, that stood on each side of the dying man, were continually striking the air about his mouth with their scimitars, and both these and the others being asked, why they did so, told us, they frighted the devils, that they might not hurt the governor's soul, as it was departing his body. These superstitious ceremonies made us pity their ignorance, but not fear any harm to our selves, as followed when the governor was dead: for we had much cause to fear being expelled that province of *Pulucambi*, and perhaps all the kingdom, with the loss of all we had acquired towards settling Christianity, and perhaps worse. It is the custom when any great person dies, for all the *omsaiis*, or priests of the country, to meet together, in order to find out not the natural, but the superstitious cause of his death; and being agreed upon what it may be, immediately that thing to which it is attributed, is ordered to be burnt, whether it be a house, garment, man or beast. Accordingly all the *omsaiis* being assembled in a great hall, they began to argue this point: we

Heathen ceremonies at the governor's death.

we who were present, remembring the persecution for want of rain, there being at that time nothing extraordinary in the province, but the governor's kind reception to us, and his assigning a house, and building a church in the city, with such extraordinary tokens of affection for our holy law; did not at all question, but that these things being represented to them, they would lay the death of that lord to our charge, and consequently would order us all to be burnt alive, together with our house and church, and all our goods. Therefore we stood in a corner of the hall, recommending our selves to GOD, and preparing our selves for whatsoever his Divine Majesty should suffer to be decreed against us; when one of the *omsaiis*, who was the eldest of them, and as it were their dean, standing-up, said with a loud voice, that, in his opinion, the only cause of the governor's death, was the falling of a beam some days since in the new palace; and he was the more apt to believe it, because all the distemper was in his head, as appeared by his raving; an evident sign, as he said, of the stroke he had received in his head by the aforesaid beam: all which he meant metaphorically, and in a superstitious sense, and therefore it pleased the other *omsaiis*, who all unanimously agreed in the same sentiment: and so rising without more to do, they went and set fire to that palace, which was all reduced to ashes, whilst we gave thanks to GOD for having escaped so manifest a danger.

Sorcery to discover the state of the soul departed.

This done, some other *omsaiis*, who profess necromancy, came to the governor's palace, to perform another superstitious ceremony, according to the custom of the country. The kindred of the party deceased looking upon it as a great blessing, that any body inspired by an evil spirit, should speak concering the state of the soul departed; and to this purpose those wizard *omsaiis* were called, of whom they all earnestly beg that devilish favour, he that obtains it being much envyed by the rest. These conjurers made their circles, and used several charms both in words and actions, that the devil might enter into some one of the governor's kindred, who were there in a suppliant posture, but all in vain. At last a sister of the governor's, for whom he had an extraordinary kindness, came in, and begging the same favour, immediately gave manifest signs that she was possest: for being decrepid, by reason of her great age, and not able to go alone, she began, to the astonishment of the spectators, to skip as nimbly as if she had been a young girl, and the stick she threw from her hung in the air, all the while the devil was in her body, during which time talking in a raving manner, and doing many disorderly actions, she uttered several extravagancies about the state and place her brother's soul was in; and concluding her mad discourse, the devil leaving her, she fell down as if she had been dead, remaining so spent for the space of eight days, that she could not stir for meer weakness, all the kindred and friends flocking to visit her, and congratulate her happiness, in that she had been chosen among all the relations for an action (as they thought it) so glorious and honourable for the dead man.

Heathen canonization.

At length they began to order the funeral of this lord; and as in the catholick church it is the custom to honour the memory of men renowned for sanctity of life, by a solemn canonization; so in *Cochin-China*, the devil always mimicking holy things, the more to delude the people, it is customary to honour the death of those who have been universally reputed just men, and upright in their actions, and adorned with moral virtues, with great solemnity and magnificence, canonizing them, if we may so call it, after their manner, by eternizing their memory, and giving them immortal veneration. For this reason, the governor of *Pulucambi*, who by all men, not only in his own province, but throughout all the kingdom was, for his extraordinary natural parts, reputed a man of great wisdom, and incomparable prudence, his government being adorned with singular justice and integrity, together with an unusual inclination and affection for all needy persons, was judged not to require a doleful sad funeral pomp, as was due to others; but on the contrary, all demonstrations of joy and grandeur, which might declare him worthy of religious honours, and to be added to the number of their gods. This being decreed, they all endeavoured to lay aside their mourning and sorrow, and to express all pleasure and satisfaction; and to this purpose all the governor's kindred, for the space of eight days, sumptuously treated all the people, during which time, they did nothing from morning till night, but eat and drink, sing, dance, and play upon musical and warlike instruments.

The governor's funeral.

After the eight days, the body was carry'd in a silver coffin gilt, under a canopy, to the city where he was born, called *Chifu*, three days journey distant, attended by a multitude of all sorts of people, dancing and rejoicing, leaving the palace where he died utterly disinhabited, that it might run to ruin, and no sign of it remaining; so the memory of the governor's death might be lost in perpetual oblivion, he still remaining alive with perpetual praise and veneration in the hearts

BORRI. hearts and mouths of all men. Being come to a spacious plain without *Chifu*, they all fell to work upon a palace, twice as magnificent and sumptuous as that the governor died in; and to make a greater shew of the dead man's wealth, they built as many gallies as he used to keep, upon wheels, for them to run upon dry land. In the same manner they made wooden elephants and horses, and all other moveables used when the governor went abroad when alive, without sparing any cost. In the midst of the palace they erected a stately temple, with a fine altar, on which they placed the coffin covered, and hid with such curious workmanship, that the hieroglyphicks, carving, and painting, greatly move those gentiles to respect. For three days continually they performed several sacrifices and ceromonies, by the ministry of five or six hundred *omsaiis*, all clad in white, who spent the time in singing and sacrificing, offering wine, oxen, and buffaloes, in great numbers, the publick entertainments continuing these three days, for above two thousand men of note, every one having his table to himself, according to custom, and each of them covered with above two hundred dishes. At the end of these three days they set fire to all that pile, burning the palace and temple, with all the perfumes and furniture, only saving the coffin with the body, which was afterwards buried, and privately removed to twelve several graves, that the people being always in doubt where it had been left, that uncertainty might increase the honour of the new idol, they adoring it in all those places where they thought the bones might be. Thus the solemnity ended for that time, till some months after, that is, in the seventh moon, according to their computation of time, it was repeated in the same manner as it had been performed at first; a few months after it was done a third time, and so from time to time for three years, all the revenues assigned the governor of that province by the king, being spent upon this solemnity for those three years, and therefore no other governor was appointed during that time, they being persuaded that the dead man's soul, which was placed among the gods, would continue in the government for those three years. However, his own son was appointed his deputy-governor, or lieutenant.

The fathers questioned concerning the governor's soul. We three fathers of the society then in that province, were present at most of this solemnity; and tho' we did not attend at their superstitious ceremonies, yet to avoid being thought ungrateful and unmannerly, we were forced to accept of some invitations, in one of which we were forewarned we should be asked where the governor's soul was; assuring us, that if we said it was in hell, we should presently be cut to pieces. We were a little after publickly asked the question, and answered, That no man could be saved without baptism; but that through the mercy of GOD, and earnest desire to be baptized sufficing, where better cannot be; if the governor, at last, had such a desire, as it was likely he had, because of the affection he bore our faith, as we said above, and that he would have asked it, but that the violence of his distemper hindred, therefore it might be believed he was saved, and not damned.

This answer, tho' new and unexpected, in some measure satisfy'd them, in token whereof they offer'd us some whole buffaloes, some boiled, some roasted, which had been sacrificed to their new idol, the dead governor; but we refusing them, saying, Our law forbid us to eat of that flesh so defiled by their sacrifice: instead of the dead sacrificed buffaloes, they ordered others alive to be given us; the governor's kindred afterwards sending us elephants, that we might return on them to *Pulucambi*, with as much honour as when the governor was living.

These were the last favours we received in virtue of the governor of *Pulucambi*'s favour; and therefore returning home, we were left like fatherless children, forsaken by all the world. Now no body minded us, the allowance of rice for our maintenance failed, and we having but twenty crowns must in a few days have been reduced to great misery and want; and if any one fell sick, we durst not call any body to breath a vein, because we had not wherewithal to pay for it; and tho' there were among them people very ready to supply the needy, especially with sustenance, as was said above, yet it was not convenient for us to ask any thing, lest we should lose all the advantage we made, as to the conversion of souls, because they would have said, we went not thither to preach the law of JESUS CHRIST, but to supply our wants under the protection of the governor. No body now came to our house, that first shew of authority ceasing, and tho' we had learned the language of the country, yet they made no account of the words of three poor men, left in the midst of infinite idolaters, and despised our doctrines, as an invention of our own, carried thither to oppose the ancient sects and tenets. The fathers in distress.

Three years pass'd after this manner, and yet we were not so much troubled at our own wants, which GOD knows were very great, as to see every day less hopes of promoting the service of GOD among those

those pagans, having during those three years converted but very few, and that with unspeakable labour and toil. Things being in this posture, in some measure desperate, we being inclinable to believe the time was not yet come, when it would please GOD to enlighten the darkness of those people, either because our sins obstructed it, or for some other hidden judgments of GOD. But when our human frailty shewed it self most diffident of divine assistance, even then, the more to confound us, the GOD of mercy shewed the wonderful effects of his divine omnipotency, that the noble undertaking of converting souls might be wholly attributed to him, we then owning we had no power to proceed in it, and that we might know experimentally, that *neither he who waters, nor he who plants, does any thing; but it is* GOD *that gives the increase*; as will appear in the following chapter.

CHAP. V.

How God made way for the Conversion of the Province of Pulucambi, *by means of the noblest Persons in it.*

The fathers disperse.

WE having nothing to maintain us at *Pulucambi*, and converting no body, dispersed our selves into several parts: F. *Francis de Pina* went to live at *Faifó*, a *Japonese* city, as has been said, with a design to serve those Christians, whose pastor he had been before, and to live upon their alms. He being well skilled in the language of *Cochin-China*, and talking it naturally, never ceased there to preach our holy faith. F. *Francis Buzome* went away for *Turon*, carrying along with him the best interpreter we had, to endeavour to obtain some alms of the *Portugueses* there, that might at least maintain us two in *Pulucambi*, in our house at *Nuoecman*, till some supply came from *Macao*.

Conversion of a great lady.

Thus was I left in *Pulucambi*, solitary and disconsolate, without any hopes of the conversion of those gentiles. When one day being at home, far from any such thought, I saw a number of elephants before our door, with many ladies, and a large retinue of gentlemen, after whom followed a great lady, and principal matron, most richly clad, and adorned with abundance of rich jewels, according to the country fashion. I was much surprized at the unusual spectacle, and majesty of the lady, and in suspence, not imagining what might be the design of the new visit. Going out at last to receive her, I understood she was wife to the embassador the king of *Cochin-China* was sending to the king of *Cambogia*, which embassador was a native of *Nuoecman*, where we dwelt, and next the governor the chief man in that city, who was then at the court of *Sinuá*, treating with that king upon the subject of his embassy. After the usual ceremonies and compliments, according to the custom of the country, the lady being unwilling to lose time upon matters that were not to her purpose, *Let us come* (said she) *to the business I aim at; I have been fully informed, father, of your coming into this our country and province, and of the occasion of your coming; I see the holy and unblemished life you lead, I know you preach and teach the true* GOD; *and being satisfied that this is most agreeable to reason, am persuaded that there is no true law but yours, nor other* GOD *but yours, nor any way to life everlasting, but that you teach; and therefore my coming to your house, is for no other intent, but earnestly to beg of you, that bathing me in your holy water, you will add me to the number of Christians; this is the utmost of my wishes and desires.* In the first place I commended her good and holy resolution, exhorting her to return thanks to GOD for so signal a mercy bestowed on her, in calling her to the knowledge of his holy law, there being nothing in this world to be valued equal to the soul's salvation. Next I made my excuse for not complying out of hand with her pious and reasonable request; because, altho' I had some knowledge of the *Cochin-Chinese* language, yet it was not enough to instruct her in the lofty mysteries of our christian religion; and therefore I advised her excellency to wait for F. *Buzome*, who in a few days was to return from *Turon*, having with him an excellent interpreter, by whose means she would be instructed as she ought to be to her own satisfaction, and obtain the end of her holy desires. *The great fire* (replied she) *that inflames my heart, will not allow of such a long delay; and the more, for that my husband is hourly expected from court, with whom I am soon to embark for the kingdom of* Cambogia, *where the dangers of the sea being frequent, a storm may happen to rise, where dying, I may perish for ever.* She added, that it was enough if I discoursed of matters divine, as I did of other things; for she should understand all I said. These visible tokens of her resolution obliging me to it, I began the best I could to inform her in several matters and principles of our holy faith. Soon after it pleased GOD, F. *Buzome* returned, and seeing this good success, gave infinite thanks to

Borri. to God. The lady was much pleased with the arrival of the interpreter, whom she had so earnestly expected; with whose assistance, and her continual application, study, and attention at catechizing, which was done for two hours before and two hours after dinner, in a fortnight's time she became perfect in the christian doctrine. Above all, what made the greatest impression on her heart, was the knowledge of Jesus Christ, true God, made man, and humbled for the sake of man; and therefore in some measure to imitate our Saviour's great humility, she for the future came to our house, which was a good mile from hers, not only without the state and elephants she used before, but bare-footed, in dirt, and upon stones, obliging her gentlemen and ladies, by her example, to imitate her devotion.

Twenty six baptized.

In our spiritual discourses, and exposition upon the catechism, when we came to make mention of hell, describe its torments, represent the greatness, eternity, and variety of torments there suffered, the horrible company of devils, the darkness of those infernal dungeons, and uninhabitable dens; and lastly, the torture of fire: both she and her ladies were so terrified, that having by themselves, all night, considered upon what they had heard, they came again the next day to tell us, they would all be Christians, to avoid that everlasting misery: But we telling them it was impossible, they being servants, and consequently concubines to the embassador, according to the custom of the country, as has been mentioned in the first treatise, the embassador's lady answered, *That impediment does not concern me.* *It is so,* said we, *for your excellency is your husband's only wife, and has not to do with other men, and therefore may freely be baptized.* At these words, lifting up her hands to heaven, she gave such tokens of joy, as if she had been besides her self, tho' she had never been truly so much her self, as when she shewed such signs of joy, for that which ought to be the only cause of all our satisfaction. Her women on the other side, seeing themselves excluded the way of salvation, cried out aloud, they would forbear being the embassador's concubines, since it obstructed their baptism, and was the way to damnation. The lady seconded their good purposes, taking upon her to deliver them from that sin, and get every one of them a husband. All lets and impediments being removed by these promises of the lady, and firm purposes of the women, one day, which was the joyfullest I ever saw in my life, the embassador's lady richly apparelled, and dressed with jewels, and nobly attended to our church by gentlemen, was baptized, with twenty five of her women, and as chief of them called *Ursula*, to the glory of Jesus Christ, who by means of these few women, opened a way to the conversions made by our mission in *Cochin-China*.

Zeal of the converts.

After they were baptized, we went in procession to the palace of the embassador's lady *Ursula*, where there was an oratory, in which she used before to perform her superstitious devotions to an idol. When we came in, we first sprinkled the house with holy water, and then the lady, and her women, couragiously laid hold of the idol, and throwing it violently against the ground, beat it to peices, trampling on it; in whose place we set up a fine picture of our Saviour, which those new devout Christians falling down, devoutly worshipped, owning themselves his most humble and devout slaves. Then we put about their necks some *Agnus Dei's*, crosses, medals, and relicks, which they valued above the gold chains, and strings of pearls they were adorned with. Having obtained this victory over the devil, after saying the litany, and other prayers in the oratory, now blessed, F. *Buzome*, and I, returned home with that satisfaction and thanksgiving that every man may imagine. The embassador's lady, and her women, came after this, every day duly to mass, catechize, and other spiritual exercises, with great tokens of fervour, and christian piety.

The lady's carriage to her husband.

At this time the embassador, husband to the lady *Ursula*, came from court, to depart in a short time upon his embassy to the king of *Cambogia*. *It is the* custom of that country, when the head of the family comes from afar off, for the wife, children, and rest of the family, to go out at least a mile upon the way to meet him. The lady *Ursula* failed to perform this ceremony, being then retired in her oratory. The husband wondring at it, and suspecting she might be hindred by sickness, asked what was become of her; but understanding she was well, admired it the more, till coming to the gate of his palace, and missing the usual reception, he began to mistrust she was angry with him. At length he went up, and into the oratory, where he found his lady and her maids, with *Agnus Dei's*, and relicks about their necks, beads in their hands, and other christian signs, praying before the image of our Saviour. The embassador was astonished at this sight, and his lady directing her discourse to him, bid him not admire that she had forbore the usual compliments to him, because she was raised to a higher pitch of honour than he was, both she and her women being children of the

true

true GOD, and Saviour of the world, JESUS CHRIST, whose picture she shewed him, saying, he ought to adore him, if he would be equal to them in dignity. The embassador moved by his lady's words, and the beauty of the picture, with tears in his eyes fell down and adored, then standing up, he turned to his wife and women, saying, *How is it possible you should be Christians? Have you a mind to leave me? Do not you know that the law the fathers preach forbids polygamy? Therefore you must either find another dwelling-place, or I leave this to you, and seek out another house.* His lady answered, *Neither need you depart, nor we leave you, for there will be a remedy for all things:* Wisely concealing for the present, the prohibition of plurality of wives, to avoid that difficulty which would have bred a disturbance. The embassador took heart at these words, and conceiving, as yet, that he need not be obliged to leave his women; thus piously imposed upon, he said, he would be a Christian too, and follow the good example set him by his wife, and her women.

The next morning betimes the embassador came to our house, to tell us, that since we had made his wife a Christian, he had a mind to embrace the same religion, if we thought it practicable. Very practicable, said we, full of joy and satisfaction at so grateful a question: For in case he were resolved, we would in a short time instruct him sufficiently to be baptized. He was pleased, and because the affairs of his embassy took up the day, so that he had not leisure to be instructed: upon his request we agreed to go to his house at night, where we began to catechize him, continuing it for twenty nights, four or five hours at a time, informing him in the mysteries of our holy faith, from the creation of the world, till the redemption of man, the glory of heaven, and pains of hell. It was no small matter for so great a person, and so full of business, to lose his sleep to hear the word of GOD; and he gave himself to them with great application, asking many very ingenious questions, which shewed his great wit. In all our discourses, our whole aim was to imprint the truth of our holy law in the heart of this noble-man, and make it agreeable to reason, that being made sensible of the great importance of salvation, and the terror of the pains of hell, and being well inclined to, and convinced of the certainty of our religion, he might afterwards make less difficulty in the main point concerning polygamy, which was the only thing he stuck at, and which we till then had designedly forbore to speak of. Having gone so far towards the embassador's

The embassador instructed

conversion, we began to expound upon the commandments, where we informed him, that among Christians it was unlawful to have many wives.

BORRI.

This proposition was so unexpected, that like fire that has water thrown on it, the embassador presently cooled, and taking leave of us, said, this was a matter of great consequence, and therefore required time to come to a resolution. This answer was so displeasing and grievous to us, that returning home we spent that night in prayer and mortification, praying to GOD with all the fervour we could, that he would be pleased to put a happy conclusion to the work he had so well begun. Next morning one of the most learned *omsaiis* in the city came to us from the embassador, to examine the reasons for the prohibition of polygamy. Among other objections, this man made one, in his opinion, of the greatest force; which was, Why plurality of wives should be forbid, since generation and children were a work of perfection, and so agreeable to nature, chiefly when a man had a barren wife, as was the embassador's case, and might not have another to get heirs upon. We wanted not answers according to our divinity, but perceiving they were not satisfactory to them because they were not used to our theological notions, we at last added a reason out of scripture, whereof the embassador had before some knowledge from us, and it pleased GOD, this made an impression on his heart, and absolutely convinced him. This was putting of him in mind, that GOD being so just, and the law he had prescribed so agreeable to natural reason, as he himself had owned, he ought without doubt to obey in this point, since GOD himself commanded it; and this so much the more, in regard that GOD creating man, intimated the same to him, when there was most occasion for propagating human race, and yet he gave *Adam* but one wife, whereas he could as easily have given him many more, that man might multiply the faster. This reason, I say, fully satisfied the embassador, yet finding it difficult to observe the precept, as being a thing he was much addicted to: *Is there no remedy*, said he, *or dispensation from the pope, or any other means, tho' never so difficult, to have this point remitted?* We told him, it was in vain to seek any redress whatsoever in this case; and therefore, if he desired to be saved, he must dismiss the other women, and stick to his wife. Then the embassador lifting up his eyes and hands to heaven, as it were struggling with himself, and press'd on by truth, with a generous resolution said, *If then multiplicity of wives be incon-*

Convinced about polygamy.

BORRI. *sistent with my salvation, let them all go in the name of* GOD; *for it is pity to lose an eternity of glory, for a transitory delight.* Then turning to his concubines, who were present with his wife, he discharged them all: but perceiving they laughed at his discharge, as a thing that would never stand good; to shew he was in earnest, he ordered his wife to pay them all off immediately, and let not one of them stay in his palace that night. After which turning again to the fathers, *Behold*, said he, *I have readily performed all you commanded me.* Having obtained our desires, we went home to give thanks to Almighty GOD.

His conversion. But the devil found out a way still to make opposition, making use of the lady *Ursula*'s womanish temper; for she had not the heart to turn away those women she had bred up from their infancy in her house, and loved them as if they were her own children. Therefore some strife arising between the man and his wife, he pressing to have them gone, and she opposing, the embassador dissatisfied, came to us to justify himself, and desire to be baptized, since the impediment was removed, he being willing the women should depart his house. We were about going to work, perceiving he spoke rationally, and particularly because he resolved they should not continue in his house as his concubines, but as his lady's servants. But the good man making a stand as if he were thinking, at last said he had a scruple to propose: *Since, according to what you fathers have taught me,* said he, GOD *sees into the heart of man, and cannot be deceived, tho' I desire to forsake and send away the women, yet whilst they continue in the house, I plainly see, either my ancient habit, or frailty of nature will easily cause me to fall again into sin; therefore methinks I do not proceed with due sincerity in this affair.* We perceiving, by the embassador's discreet and christian discourse, he foresaw the danger of being in the immediate occasion of sin, studied some proper means to remove so considerable an impediment; but nothing occurring for the present he himself being very earnest upon the business, proposed a method, which we stuck to as the best of all others: *Fathers*, said he, *the safest way I can think of is that you as their directors powerfully persuade the christian women that were my concubines, (for the heathens I will infallibly make my wife turn away) that in case through frailty I should be under any temptation they resist me resolutely; and forasmuch as I bear a great respect to, and stand in awe of our Saviour's picture placed in the oratory, if the women lie in that place, I will rather be torn to pieces than have any thing to do with them in the presence of that great Lord; and they being thus secured against me, till there be an opportunity of marrying them, it will be known abroad, that they are not kept in the house as my concubines, but only as servants to my only wife* Ursula, *and the people will be sensible I do not act contrary to the law of* GOD. This method was so well approved of, that the day after it was put in execution, the embassador was baptized in great state, attended by drums, fifes and other instruments, and he himself clad in rich apparel. With him were baptized twenty other gentlemen, his best friends, and he had the name of our holy patriarch *Ignatius* given him. After which, taking his wife *Ursula* by the hand, she renewed the old contract of matrimony as a sacrament of the church. The joy they all conceived at their baptism, and new marriage, was unspeakable.

It now remained that the embassador should depart on his embassy for *Cambogia*; and he ordered, that the ship which was to carry him, should have a cross in its colours, and the picture of the glorious father S. *Ignatius* his protector, causing all the jacks and pennants to express the religion he professed. Embarking with all his gentlemen and christian women, he had a prosperous voyage from *Nuoecman* to *Cambogia*. When the squadron appeared, being well known to the people of *Cambogia* to be the embassador's, they were all astonished, seeing christian colours set up; and therefore they imagined that the king of *Cochin-China*, instead of the ordinary embassador, had sent some extraordinary *Portuguese* Christian; but their doubt was soon cleared, seeing the usual embassador land with a cross and medals on his breast, among the gold chains and jewels. This sight on the one hand, moved the *Portuguese* and *Japonese* Christians, who reside there on account of trade, to give shouts of joy, and bless GOD for this new off-spring *Cochin-China* had produced; and on the other, the heathens could not believe that the embassador, who before was observed to be excessively lascivious, should embrace the christian religion, which forbids all immodesty. But the grace of the holy Ghost soon appeared to strengthen human frailty; for tho' the embassador at his palace in *Cambogia*, had double the number of concubines, as generally used to attend his wife, he ordered them to be all dismissed; nor did he ever lift up his eyes to look at them, which made his fame spread abroad, as of a man of singular sanctity and virtue; and being reputed a man of great knowledge, his example moved many of the most learned persons of *Pulucambi* to be baptized.

CHAP.

CHAP. VI.

How God open'd another way to Christianity, through the means of the learned People among the Heathens.

Means for the conversion of the *Cochin-Chineses.*

GOD's infinite mercy, and his ardent desires for the salvation of mankind, finds out divers means suitable to the several conditions of persons, which are as it were so many ways to direct and lead them to that end for which they were created. Thus we see he himself in person called upon his people, and complying with the inclination of the persons, invited the wise men by means of the star; *Denis* the *Areopagite* the astronomer, by the prodigy of the wonderful eclipse; S. *Augustine* by the knowledge of the true light and law, and the confusion and obscurity of former errors; and in fine, he calls the ignorant multitude, by the means of prodigies, wonders and miracles. So it fell out in the new church of *Cochin-China*; for when his divine majesty had by himself convinced some of the principal persons, as has been shewn, next he call'd not only the learned and wise philosophers and mathematicians, by means of some eclipses, as shall be shewn in this chapter, but also the *omsaiis* or priests, who were hardened in the errors of their heathen sects, to the knowledge of the true religion, as the following chapter will make appear. And lastly, in the next to that we shall set down, how he opened the way of salvation to the people by means of several prodigies and miracles.

Astrology in great esteem.

Now to come to the manner of converting the wise and learned *Cochin-Chineses*, reputed excellent mathematicians, by means of the eclipse. For the better understanding of what we are to say, it is requisite in the first place to be acquainted with a custom they have in this kingdom, relating to the science of astrology, but particularly of eclipses; for they make such a great account of it, that they have large halls where it is taught in their university; and there are special allowances assign'd the astrologers; as for instance, Lands which pay them a tribute or stipend. The king has his peculiar astrologers, and so has the prince his son, who use all their art to set down eclipses exactly. But wanting the reformation of the calendar, and other matters, relating to the motion of the sun and moon which we have, they commit some mistakes in the calculation of the moons and eclipses, wherein they generally err two or three hours, and sometimes, tho' not so often, a whole day; tho' generally they are right as to the material part of the eclipse. Every time they hit right, the king rewards them with a certain quantity of land; and so when they mistake, that same quantity is taken from them.

BORRI.

Superstitions concerning eclipses.

The reason why they make such account of fortelling the eclipse, is because of the many superstitions at that time us'd towards the sun and moon, for which they prepare themselves in very solemn manner: for the king being told the day and hour a month before the eclipse happens, sends orders throught all the provinces of the kingdom, for the learned and common sort to be in a readiness that day. When the time is come, all the lords in every province meet with their governors, commanders and gentry, and people with their proper officers in every city and liberty. The greatest assembly is at court, where the principal men of the kingdom are, who all go out with colours and arms. First goes the king cloath'd in mourning, and after him all the court, who lifting up their eyes to the sun or moon, as the eclipse comes on them, make several obeisances and adorations, speaking some words of compassion for the pain those planets endure; for they look upon the eclipse to be no other, but that the dragon swallows up the sun or moon; and therefore, as we say, the moon is all or half eclips'd; so they say, *Da an nua, Da an het*; that is, the dragon has eaten half, now he eats all.

Their astrological terms and ours alike.

Which way of expression, tho' it be nothing to the purpose, yet it shews that they assign the same ground for the eclipse originally that we do, which is cutting of the eclíptick, that is the sun's circle and the line of the course of the moon, in those two points which we call the dragon's head and tail, as astronomers well know: whence it follows, that the very same doctrine, and the same terms and names of the dragon, are common both to us and them, and so they give names like ours to the signs of the zodiack, such as *Aries*, *Taurus*, *Gemini*, &c. And thus in process of time the people have invented fabulous causes of the eclipse, instead of the true, saying that the sun and moon, when eclipsed are drown'd by the dragon; whereas, at that time they are really in the head or tail of the astronomical dragon.

Now to return to the compassion they have for those suffering planets; when the adoration is over, they begin first at the king's palace, and then throughout all the city to fire muskets and cannon, ring bells, sound trumpets, beat drums, and play upon other instruments, even to clattering.

BORRI. ing of the kettles, and other utensils of the kitchen in all houses: and this is done, to the end the dragon may be frighted with the great noise, and not proceed to eat any more, but vomit up what he has already eaten of the sun or moon.

Conversions by means of an eclipse. When we were inform'd of this custom, the first eclipse that happened was one of the moon, in the year 1620. on the ninth of *December*, at eleven at night. I was then in the city *Nuoecman*, in the province of *Pulucambi*, where there was the commander of the ward we liv'd in, whose son was become a Christian; tho' the father, as proud of his own learning, despis'd not only our religion but our knowledge; and we earnestly desir'd his conversion, hoping that if he receiv'd the catholick faith, his example would induce those of his ward or quarter to do the same. This man came once to visit us before the eclipse of the moon happened, and in discourse we happened to talk of it, he positively affirming there would be no such eclipse: and tho' we demonstrated it to him, according to our calculation, and shew'd him the figure of it in our books, yet he would never believe it; alledging among other arguments for his obstinacy, that if any such eclipse were like to be, the king would doubtless have sent him notice a month before, according to the custom of the kingdom, whereas there wanted but eight days of the time by us appointed; wherefore he having no such advice, it was a certain sign that there would be no such eclipse. He persisting obstinately in his opinion, would needs lay a wager of a *Cabaia*, which is a silk gown. We agreed to it upon condition, that if we lost we were to give him such a garment; but if we won, instead of paying the gown, he was to come to us for eight days together, to hear the catechize and mysteries of our faith expounded. He reply'd, he would not only do so, but the very moment he saw the eclipse would become a Christian: for he said, if our doctrine was so certain and infallible in such hidden and heavenly things as eclipses are, and theirs so erroneous, there was no doubt but our religion and knowledge of the true GOD was no less assured and safe, and theirs false. The day of the eclipse being come, the aforesaid gentleman with a great many scholars came to our house at night, bringing them as witnesses of the event. But because the eclipse was to be at eleven at night, I went to say my office, turning up the hour glass in the mean while. An hour before the time these men came several times, calling upon me by way of derision to see the eclipse, thinking I had not withdrawn to say my office, but had hid my self for shame that there would be no eclipse. Yet they could not but admire at my assurance in answering them, that the hour was not yet come, till the glass was run out, which they gaz'd at, as if it had been some wonderful thing. Then going out, I shew'd them that the circle of the moon on that side the eclipse began, was not so perfect as it should be, and soon after all the moon being darkened, they perceiv'd the truth of my prediction. The commander and all of them being astonish'd, presently sent to give notice of it to all the ward, and spread the news of the eclipse throughout the city, that every man might go out to make the usual noise in favour of the moon; giving out every where, that there were no such men as the fathers, whose doctrine and books could not choose but be true, since they had so exactly foretold the eclipse, which their learned men had taken no notice of; and therefore in performance of his promise, the commander with all his family became Christians, as did many more of his ward, with some of the most learned men in the city, and other men of note.

Such another accident happened at the same time, tho' among people of greater quality, and in a more eminent place. Tho' the king's astrologers had not foreseen this eclipse, yet those belonging to the prince at *Cacciam*, being more studious and intelligent, foretold it; but with a gross mistake as to time: for it was not of an hour or two, as is usual, but of a whole day, giving out that the full moon, and consequently the eclipse would be a day sooner than it was. F. *Francis de Pina*, who was then at court, had given notice of it to a courtier who was very great with the prince, being his *omgne*; that is, in the nature of master of the ceremonies. The father told him, That since the eclipse was not to fall out as their astrologers said, but as F. *Christopher Borri* affirm'd, the following night, he should give the prince his master notice of it. But the *omgne* not giving entire credit to the father, would not do that duty of his office at that time. The hour appointed by the astrologers being come, and the prince having notice of it, he went out with his whole court, according to custom, to see and help the moon, that as they said was to be eclips'd; but finding he was deceiv'd, and growing angry with his mathematicians for their mistake, he order'd they should forfeit the revenue of a town, according to the custom before-mention'd. Hence the *omgne* took occasion to acquaint the prince that the *European* father had, before this happened, told him the eclipse would be the night following. The prince was mightily pleas'd that the fathers should hit right,

The fathers foretel the eclipse truer than the *Cochin-Chinese* astrologers.

right, where his mathematicians had miscarry'd.

The *omgne* repair'd immediately to the father, to know the precise time of the eclipse; who having shew'd him that it was to be exactly at eleven the following night, he still continu'd doubtful of the truth of the matter, and therefore would not wake the prince till he saw the beginning of the eclipse. Then he ran to rouze him, and he coming out with some of his courtiers, perform'd the usual ceremonies and adorations to the moon. Yet he would not make the matter publickly known, for fear of utterly discrediting their books and mathematicians, tho' all men conceiv'd a great opinion of our doctrine, and particularly the *omgne*, who from that time forwards for a whole month came to hear the catechising, diligently learning all that belongs to our holy faith. However he was not baptiz'd, wanting resolution to overcome the difficulty of the multiplicity of women, as the embassador *Ignatius* had done before. He forbore not nevertheless publickly with much fervour to declare our doctrine and law were true, and all others false, and said he would certainly die a Christian, which mov'd many others to desire to be baptis'd.

An eclipse of the sun mistaken.

Having talk'd of the eclipse of the moon, we will conclude with another of the sun, which happened on the 22d of *May*, 1621, which the king's astrologers foretold was to last two hours; but having conceiv'd a great opinion of us as to this particular, for their own greater security, they came to ask our opinions concerning it. I told them it was true there would be an eclipse of the sun, the figure whereof I shew'd in our *ephemerides*; but I purposely forbore to let them know, that it would not be seen in *Cochin-China*, by reason of the moon's parallax to the sun. Now they know not what the parallax is, which is the cause they are often deceiv'd, not finding the just time by their books and calculations. This I did, that their error being observ'd, our knowledge might appear the more: I therefore demanded time to find out the precise time, saying in general terms, it was requisite to measure heaven by the earth, to discover whether that eclipse would be visible in their country; and I delay'd the answer so long, till the time of making known the eclipse being come, the astrologers satisfy'd that our book agreed with their opinion, without farther reflection, concluded the eclipse was most certain, and advis'd the king to publish it after the usual manner. When the astrologers had spread their false prediction throughout the kingdom, I gave it out that the eclipse would not be seen at all in *Cochin-China*. This assertion of ours was carry'd to the prince, who being doubtful in the matter, sent his mathematicians to me to ask my opinion, and argue the point. This dispute had no other effect on them, but only to increase their doubt, and hold the prince in suspense, whether he ought to send his orders throughout the kingdom, as the king his father had done, or publish the contrary; for on the one hand it wrought upon him to see that both their books and ours granted the eclipse, wherefore he thought it would be a dishonour to him, in case it happened not to have sent the usual advice; and on the other side, he had a great opinion of us on account of the antecedent eclipse of the moon. Hereupon sending to consult me again, I answer'd, that having calculated the eclipse very exactly, I found it could not possibly be visible in his kingdom; and therefore he need not take any care to send advice about the country, for I would be answerable for his and his astrologers reputation, against the king and his mathematicians. He at last rely'd upon my words, and took no care to give notice in his liberty of the eclipse, the whole court and king's astrologers admiring at it; and they enquiring into the cause of the prince's neglect, were answer'd, that he had better mathematicians in his court than the king his father: by which they understood that some of our fathers being there, he forsook the opinion of the natives for theirs. However the publication they had made being irrevokable, the usual preparations were made against the day of the eclipse, till the hour being come they experimentally perceiv'd their error. The day was clear and not a cloud to be seen, and tho' it was the month of *May*, when the sun is there in the zenith, and the time of the day about three in the afternoon when the heat is violent, yet the king did not omit to go out with his courtiers, enduring all the burning sun for a long time; but finding himself impos'd upon, and being much incens'd, as well by reason of the great heat he endur'd, as at the ignorance of his methematicians, who had put him to that trouble without any reason, he reprimanded them severely. They alledg'd for their excuse, that there would be an eclipse infallibly, but that they had made a day's mistake as to the conjunction of the moon, and therefore it would be seen the next day at that same hour. The king submitted to his astrologers, and coming out the next day at the same hour, suffer'd the same inconveniency of heat, to the great shame of his astrologers, who escap'd not unpunish'd; for he not only took away their revenues, but order'd they should kneel a whole day in the court of the palace, bare-headed expos'd to the heat

BORRI.

Borri. heat of the sun, and to the scorn of all the courtiers. To return to the prince who had got the better in this point, he writ to his father in a jesting manner, That tho' he was his son, he had out-done him as to the eclipse, and had more learned men at his court.

It is not to be imagin'd how much reputation this accident gain'd us among the learned, insomuch that even the king's and prince's mathematicians came to us, earnestly begging we would receive them for our scholars; and upon this account the fame of the fathers was every where so great, that not only our knowledge in astronomy, but our religion was extoll'd above their own, they arguing from the heavenly bodies to things above the heavens, as I said before.

CHAP. VII.

How God open'd another way to Christianity, by means of the Omsaiis, *or Heathen Priests.*

Conversion of a heathen priest.

GOD in his infinite wisdom foreknowing of how great consequence it would be for the conversion of those heathens, that some of their priests or *omsaiis* should be converted, because of the great authority they have among all the people, it pleas'd his Divine Majesty to open even this way to his holy faith. An *omsaii* whose name was *Ly*, liv'd near to our house, and had the charge of an idol temple, and being a neighbour had frequent opportunities of conversing with us, and of coming to some knowledge of our rules, actions, and course of life. This pleas'd him so well, that proceeding still farther, he would needs be inform'd as to the law of God, whereof we gave him a full account; and coming to discourse of the resurrection of our Lord, shewing him how he rose again, that he and all men might rise again the last day, he was so pleas'd at it, that being inspir'd by God, he ask'd to be baptis'd, which was accordingly granted to him and all his family upon Christmas night, which he spent on his knees in prayer with floods of tears, uttering these words, *Tuii ciam biet*; that is, I knew not, as if he would have said, Forgive me my God, for till now I knew you not. Then continuing some time very still, as it were contemplating, he repeated the same words, making a sweet harmony to the new born infant. After baptism he took such an affection for us, that he resolv'd to come to us with all his family, that he might live under our rule; but being inform'd that could not be, because he was marry'd, he concluded to live nearer to our house, that he might regulate his actions by the sound of our bell, even to saying the long litany in his oratory, at the time we use to say it every day, according to the custom of the society. And it is remarkable, that observing me at a certain hour us'd to say our beads walking, he would walk at the same time, to the amazement of his countrymen, who look upon walking as a strange and ridiculous action, because they never going a step but what is about business, or to some diversion, look'd upon our action of walking as idle, because we went to a place to no other end but to return; so that the people flock'd to see us walk, and admiring the strangeness of it said, *Omsaii di lay*; that is, the father goes and come, goes and comes. Yet their gazing did not make *omsaii Ly* leave his custom, which tended to nothing but to be like us in all points. He had but one wife, and had lived about thirty years, which was his age, so strictly up to the law of nature, that he had never, as he said, to that time, knowingly deviated in any matter of consequence from what was just and upright; and his adoring of idols was because he thought it contrary to reason not to adore them. This shews how true that doctrine of divines is, to wit, that God never fails to have baptism administred, either by the hands of men, as this was, or the ministry of angels, to a heathen who lives a good moral life, according to the dictates of reason, and law of nature. This *omsaii Ly* wholly devoted himself to the service of God, and after providing for the maintenance of his family, all he and they could earn was bestow'd upon our church, taking special care of its neatness and decency, and of adorning the altars.

A notable moral heathen.

Nor was this all God requir'd of this his belov'd servant; for he so inflam'd his heart, that he applied himself to preach the faith of Christ publickly, making the mystery of the resurrection the usual subject of his discourse, whereby he attracted and converted abundance, not only of the common sort, but several *omsaiis*; for tho' he was none of the most learned, yet his fervour so well supply'd that defect, that among those who came to desire baptism, there was one of the most learned and famous men in the kingdom, whose authority, he himself proving the falsity of the heathen sects, immediately increas'd the harvest of the church. This man therefore

Other converts.

fore took upon him to oppose the other gentiles, easily confuting them, as being well acquainted with the grounds they went upon; herein very much easing our fathers, who not being so well acquainted with their sects, could not so well oppose them.

Several sorts of *omsaiis.* And in truth there was need of such a help; for there is such variety of *omsaiis* in that country, that it looks as if the devil had endeavoured among those gentiles, to represent the beauty and variety of religious orders instituted by holy men in the catholick church, their several habits answering their several professions; for some are clad in white, others in black, others in blue, and other colours; some living in community, some like curates, chaplains, canons, and prebends; others profess poverty, living upon alms; others exercise the works of mercy, ministring to the sick, either natural physick, or magick charms, without receiving any reward; others undertaking some pious work, as building of bridges, or other such things for the publick good, or erecting of temples, and going about the kingdom, begging alms to this purpose, even as far as the kingdom of *Tonchin*; others teach the doctrine of their religion, who being very rich, have publick schools, as universal masters. There are also some *omsaiis* who profess the farriers trade, compassionately cure elephants, oxen, and horses, without asking any reward, being satisfy'd with any thing that is freely given them. Lastly, Others look to the monasteries of women, who live in community, and admit of no man among them but the *omsaii* who looks to them, and they are all his wives. BORRI.

The temples. There are vast temples with beautiful towers and steeples, nor is there any town, tho' never so little, without a temple to worship its idols, which are generally very large statues, with abundance of gold and silver shut up in their breasts or bellies, where no body dares to touch it, till extream necessity obliges some thief to gut the idol, without regard to so great a sacrilege as that is accounted among them; and what is very remarkable, they have chaplets and strings of beads about their necks, and make so many processions that they outdo the Christians in praying to their false gods. There are also among them some persons resembling abbots, bishops, and arch-bishops, and they use gilt staves, not unlike our crosiers, insomuch that if any man come newly into that country, he might easily be persuaded there had been Christians there in former times; so near has the devil endeavoured to imitate us. This will give us an opportunity of adding here a chapter of the sects in *Cochin-China*, to give some light how we may draw that people out of such darkness, and bring them into the light of the gospel.

CHAP. VIII.

A short Account of the Sects in Cochin-China.

THE end of all sects is either the god they adore, or the glory and happiness they expect, some believing the immortality of the soul, others concluding that all ends when the body dies. Upon these two principles the eastern nations build all their sects; all which took their origin from a great metaphysician of the kingdom of *Siam*, whose name was *Xaca*, much ancienter than *Aristotle*, and nothing inferior to him in capacity, and the knowledge of natural things. The sharpness of this man's wit raising him to consider the nature and fabrick of the world, reflecting on the beginning and end of all things, and particularly of human nature, the chief lady of this worldly palace; he once went up to the top of a mountain, and there attentively observing the moon, which rising in the darkness of the night, gently raised it self above the horizon to be hid again the next day in the same darkness, and the sun getting up in the morning to set again at night, he concluded that as well moral as physical and natural things were nothing, came of nothing, and ended in nothing. Therefore returning home, he writ several books and large volumes upon this subject, calling them, *Of nothing*; wherein he taught that the things of this world, by reason of the duration and measure of time, are nothing: for tho' they had a being, said he, yet they would be nothing, nothing at present, and nothing in the time to come, for the present being but a moment, was the same as nothing.

The philosopher *Xaca.*

His opinion, that all this world is nothing. His second argument he grounded on the composition of things; let us instance, said he, in a rope, the which not being naturally distinguished from its parts, inasmuch as they give its being and composition, so it appears that the rope as a rope is nothing; for as a rope it is no distinct thing from the threads it is compos'd of, and the threads themselves are no distinct thing from the hemp they are made of, and the hemp has no other being but the elements, whereof its substance consists: so that resolving all things after this manner into the elements, and those to a sort of *materia prima*, and meer *potentia*,

 which

Borri. which is therefore actually nothing, he at last proved, that as well the heavenly things, as those under heaven, were truly nothing.

So of all moral things. In the same manner did he argue as to moral things: that the natural happiness of man did not consist in a positive concurrence of all that is good, which he looked upon as impossible, but rather in being free from all that is evil, and therefore said, it was no other thing but to have no disease, pain, trouble, or the like; and for a man to have such power over his passions, as not to be sensible of affection or aversion, to honour or disgrace, want or plenty, riches or poverty, life or death, and that herein consisted true beatitude. Whence he inferred, that all these things being nothing, they took their origin as it were from a cause not efficient but material, from a principle which in truth was nothing, but an eternal, infinite, immense, immutable, almighty, and to conclude, a God that was nothing, and the origin of this nothing.

The world how made. As a prelude or introduction to his sect, this philosopher gave some account of the making of the world under two metaphors. The one was, that the world came out of an egg, which stretched out so vastly, that the heavens were made of the shell; the air, fire, and water, of the white; and of the yolk, the earth and all earthly things. The other metaphor he took from the body of a vast great man, whom they call *Banco*, whom he would call *Microcosm*, saying that the mass of the world came from him, his scull extending to form the heavens, his two eyes making the sun and moon, his flesh the earth, his bones the mountains, his hair plants and trees, and his belly the sea, and thus applying all the limbs and parts of man's body, to the fabrick and ornament of the world; he added, that the other men spread about all the world, were made of this great man's lice.

Another doctrine of the same philosopher. Having estabished this doctrine of nothing, he gathered some scholars, by whose means he spread it throughout all the east. But the *Chineses* who knew that a sect which reduced all things to nothing, was hurtful to the government, would not hearken to it, nor allow there was no punishment for wicked men, or that the happiness of the good should be reduced only to the being free from sufferings in this world, and the authority of the *Chineses* being so great, others following their example, rejected his doctrine. *Xaca* dissatisfied that he was disappointed of followers, changed his mind, and retiring writ several other great books; teaching that there was a real origin of all things, a Lord of heaven, hell, immortality, and transmigration of souls from one body to another, better or worse, according to the merits or demerits of the person; tho' they do not forget to assign a sort of heaven and hell for the souls departed, expressing the whole metaphorically under the names of things corporeal, and of the joys and sufferings of this world.

The sect that believes all to be nothing. This second doctrine being made publick, the *Chineses* received it, and above others the *bonzis*, who are generally the meanest and most inconsiderable people in *Japan*, who being zealous for their spiritual advantage admitted this doctrine, and preserved it in twelve several sorts of sects all differing from one another, tho' that which is most followed and esteemed, is the opinion and sect that believes all to be nothing, which they call *gensiu*. These sometimes go abroad into a field to hear a sermon, that is a discourse of bliss made by a *bonzo*, who treats of no other subject, but to persuade his congregation, that human bliss is nothing, and that he is happy who values not whether he has children or no children, whether he is rich or poor, sick or well, and the like; and the *bonzo* preaches this doctrine with such strength of argument, and vehemency, that the audience being fully bent upon the contempt of all things, which in themselves they look upon as nothing, suffering themselves to be in a manner transported, they express their satisfaction and happiness in this manner, that is often crying out with a loud voice, *xin*, *xin*, *xin*; that is, nothing, nothing, nothing, accompanying their voices with certain bits of boards they clap between the fingers of one hand striking them together with the other (as boys play on their snappers) and with this noise they are quite besides themselves as if they were drunk, and then they say they have done an act of bliss. The *Japoneses* and others making so great account of this opinion of nothing, was the cause that when *Xaca* the author of it was come to his last, calling together his disciples, he protested to them upon the word of a dying man, that in the many years he had lived and study'd, he had found nothing so true, nor any opinion so well grounded, as was the sect of nothing; and tho' his second doctrine seemed to differ from it, yet they must look upon it as no contradiction or recantation, but rather a proof and confirmation of the first, tho' not in plain terms, yet by way of metaphors and parables, which might all be apply'd to the opinion of nothing, as would plainly appear by his books.

Errors of the Cochin-Chineses. But it is time to return to our *Cochin-Chineses*, who not receiving this most foolish and vain doctrine, which denying the substantial

ſtantial form, reduces all things to nothing, they generally throughout all the kingdom hold the immortality of the ſoul, and conſequently the eternal rewards for the juſt, and puniſhments for the wicked, yet mixing a thouſand errors with theſe truths. The firſt of which is, that they do not diſtinguiſh between the immortal ſoul and the demons, calling both by one and the ſame name *Maa*, and attributing to them both, the ſame practice of doing miſchief to the living. The ſecond is, that they aſſign one of the rewards of the ſoul to be tranſmigration from one body to another, more worthy, nobler, and in greater dignity; as from one of the common ſort to a king, or great lord. The third, that the ſouls of the dead ſtand in need of ſuſtenance and corporal food, and therefore at certain times in the year according to their cuſtom, the children make plentiful entertainments for their dead parents, men for their wives, and friends for their acquaintance departed, expecting a long time for the dead gueſt to come and ſit down at table to eat. We one day confuted theſe errors with arguments which the philoſopers call *à priori*, and therefore told them that the ſoul was a ſpirit, and had no mouth or other material part to eat, and therefore they were deceived to think they could feed. And then *à poſteriori*, for in caſe they did eat, then the diſhes would not be as full after they had done as they were before. They laughed at theſe arguments, ſaying, theſe fathers know nothing; and to ſolve both difficulties, anſwered, that meat conſiſted of two parts, one the ſubſtance, the other the accidents of quantity, quality, ſmell, taſte, and the like. The immaterial ſouls of the dead, ſaid they, taking only the ſubſtance of the meat, which being immaterial, was proper ſuſtenance for the incorporeal ſpirit, left only the accidents in the diſhes, as they appear to our corporal eyes, to which purpoſe the dead had no need of corporeal parts as we ſaid. Any wiſe man may by this falſe anſwer diſcover the acuteneſs of the *Cochin-Chineſe* philoſophers, tho' they abſolutely err as to the reality of the argument. BORRI.

They alſo err in reſpect to the ſouls themſelves, adoring thoſe of men who were looked upon as holy in this world, adding them to the number of their idols, whereof their temples are full, placing them orderly according to their ſeveral degrees, in rows along the ſides of the temples, the leaſt firſt, and ſo bigger and bigger, till the laſt are extraordinary large. But the high altar being the moſt honourable place in the temple, is purpoſely kept empty, behind which is a vacant dark ſpace, to expreſs that he whom they adore as GOD, and on whom the pagods, who like us were viſible and corporeal men, is inviſible, wherein they think the greateſt honour conſiſts. Such a multitude of idols, by them accounted gods, giving us occaſion to endeavour to demonſtrate to them, that there can be but one only GOD: They anſwered, they agreed to it, ſuppoſing thoſe that were placed along the ſides of the temples, were not they that had created heaven and earth, but holy men whom they honoured, as we do the holy apoſtles, martyrs, and confeſſors, with the ſame diſtinction of greater and leſſer ſanctity, as we aſſign among our ſaints. And therefore to corroborate their aſſertion they added, that the vacant dark place about the high altar, was the proper place of the Creator of heaven and earth, who being inviſible, and quite remote from our ſenſes, could not be repreſented by viſible images of idols, but that under that vacuity and darkneſs the due adoration was to be given him as to a thing incomprehenſible, uſing the interceſſion of the idols, that they may obtain favours and bleſſings of him. And altho' according to what has been hitherto ſaid, they ſeem to have an efficient and intellectual cauſe for GOD, yet upon mature examination of the matter and their books, we find that they certainly adore a predominant element.

CHAP. IX.

How God opened another Way to the Converſion of the meaner ſort by miraculous Means.

Frequent apparitions of devils.

IT remains that we ſhew how GOD acting conformably to the mean vulgar people of *Cochin-China*, who were uſed to ſee phantoms, viſions, and apparitions, the devil often appearing to them, was pleaſed to ſhew ſome miracles, to the end that declining in their opinion of diabolical prodigies, they might own the only Lord and ſingular worker of true wonders. The devils appear ſo frequently among thoſe heathens, that not to ſpeak of the oracles they deliver by the mouth of idols, which are in great eſteem among the wretched gentiles, they walk about the cities ſo familiarly in human ſhapes, that they are not at all feared but admitted into company, and this is carried ſo far, that there are abundance of *Incubi* and *Succubi*. And

Incubi and *Succubi*.

BORRI. among great people those husbands account themselves happy, who know their wives have such familiars; for generally they have to do with none but married women, publickly boasting that they are worthy to mix with a nature so much above their own as is the devils. It happened in my time, that a woman of great quality, mother to two sons who were Christians, envyed by her neighbours not so much for her beauty, as for her dishonest familiarity with the devil, positively refusing to become a Christian, came to die in labour, and by the assistance of the devil brought forth two eggs: Now it being held as most certain among them, that the devil her *Incubus* was god of the rivers, they did not bury the body in a cave, building a chapel over it as is the usual custom, but carrying it in solemn procession to a river cast it into the deep, together with the two eggs, saying, let her go to the lord of the river, since she was worthy to have to do with him when living. Among the common sort this filthiness is not esteemed an honour, but they rather account it a grievous distemper when their women are thus molested by the devil, as we should their being possest. These women therefore understanding that the religion of the fathers was altogether opposite to the devil, they imagined they might have some medicine against this distemper, calling holy things, as the water of baptism, *Agnus Deis*, and the like, medicines, and therefore came to our house to beg such medicines; and by the grace of GOD all those that carried away with them any bit of *Agnus Dei*, were never more molested by the devil, yet with this difference, that those who were not Christians saw the *Incubus* come to the bed's-side, but had not power to lay hold on, or touch their persons, whereas the Christians perceived that he could not come near the chamber-door, which occasioned several to be baptized.

Other monstrous visions.

Tho' these *Incubus* devils appearing in human shapes, do no harm to the body, yet sometimes there are others that appear in horrid and frightful shapes, and the *Cochin-Chineses*, who have often seen, describe them after the same manner as we paint them, for example, with a cock's face, a long tail, a bat's wings, a hideous look, bloody flaming eyes; and when they appear in such shapes, they are much feared, being then generally hurtful to men, sometimes carrying them up to the tops of houses to cast them down headlong. We once heard a wonderful noise of people in our street, crying out very loud, *Maqui Maco*, that is, the devil in a monstrous shape; whereupon some gentiles came running to desire us, that since we had weapons against those evil spirits, we would go relieve those distressed people who were infested by them. Having recommended our selves to GOD, and arm'd our selves with crosses, *Agnus Deis* and relicks, we went two of us to the place where the devil was, and came so near, that we only wanted turning of a corner to be upon him, when he suddenly vanished, leaving three prints of feet upon the pavement, which I saw, and were above two spans long, with the marks of a cock's talons and spurs. Some attributed the devil's flying to the virtue of the holy cross and relicks we carried with us.

Good visions.

These frightful apparitions GOD has made use of to attract many to his holy faith, yet not denying them good visions, as will appear by the following accidents, which happened before me in that kingdom. The first was, that as we were one day in our own house, we saw a procession of a vast multitude of people in a field making towards us, whither when they came, being asked what they would have, they answered, that a most beautiful lady came from their land through the air, on a throne of bright clouds, who bid them go to that city, where they should find the fathers, who would shew them the sure way to bliss, and the knowledge of the true GOD of heaven. This made us give thanks to the blessed Virgin, whose this great benefit was owned to be, and having catechised and baptised the people sent them home well pleased.

The second was at another time, F. *Francis Buzome* and I returning homeward together, such a multitude of people came to another place, who having paid us very much respect, told F. *Francis Buzome*, they were come to him to teach them what he had promised them the night before when he was in their town. The father was astonished at their demand, having never been in the place they spoke of; but examining into the matter, I found that GOD of his infinite mercy had caused some angel in the father's shape, or in a dream had given those people some knowledge of our holy faith. The fame of these miracles being spread abroad, such numbers of people were converted, that the church given us by the governor was too little, and we were forced to build one larger, his wife, children, and kindred, with many other Christians contributing towards it.

CHAP.

CHAP. X.

Of the Churches and Christans of Faifo, Turon, and Cacchiam.

What the fathers did at *Faifo.*

F. *Francis de Pina* being gone to *Faifo*, a city of the *Japoneses*, as was said before, he there joined F. *Peter Marques*, and they did great service in that city. The last of them, who was master of the *Japonese* tongue, in a short time reformed some of those Christians who were become libertines, and kept women, and converted many pagans. The other who understood the language of *Cochin-China* made many Christians, and having convinced some *bonzos* and *omsaiis*, by that means drew over many more to the holy faith; so that between *Japoneses* and *Cochin-Chineses*, that church for number and religious observance might compare with many in *Europe*, such was their piety, zeal, frequenting of the sacraments, and other godly works. The church of *Turon*, which we said in the second chapter of this book, the heathens burnt down during the first persecution, was by GOD's permission rebuilt by means of the fathers of the society, who gained many Christians in that city.

At *Turon.*

At *Cacchiam.*

Abundance of people were likewise converted to our faith at *Cacchiam*; which good work was much forwarded by the *Omgne*, who on account of the father's fortelling the eclipse so certainly, as was before observed, publickly affirmed, there was no other true religion but that the fathers taught. This was the state of affairs there, when I came away out of that country for *Europe*, which was in the year 1622. BORRI.

Afterwards by the annual letters sent me by those fathers, my companions left there cultivating that vineyard, I understood that there were still about a thousand converted and baptized in a year, and that Christianity flourished more than ever it had done at *Cacchiam* particularly. But now of late they write, that the king had forbid any more becoming Christians, and threatned to expel the fathers out of the kingdom, and this because the *Portuguese* trade failed. Yet it pleased GOD this persecution went no farther, the king being satisfied, provided one of the fathers went away to *Macao*, to endeavour to persuade the *Portugueses* to continue the trade, as it seems was afterwards done; so that things are now quiet, and the fathers continue gaining new Christians as they did at first.

CHAP. XI.

Of the Kingdom of Tunchim.

WHEN the superiors of *Macao* sent me into *Cochin-China*, they told me, they did not absolutely design I should continue in that mission, but only to learn the language, that I might afterwards discover the kingdom of *Tunchim*. For this reason during those five years I dwelt there, I almost made it my business to enquire into, and get certain information of the affairs of that kingdom, the language being the same, as formerly it was but one kingdom. I will therefore say as much of it as any way concerns *Cochin-China*, which has some dependance upon *Tunchim*, and this according to the accounts given me by natives of *Tunchim*, who came to the province of *Pulucambi*, where I resided most part of my time; the rest I will leave to the news we shall receive from our fathers, who are there still making further discoveries.

A description of *Tunchim.*

This kingdom, besides *Cochin-China* which belongs to it, contains four other provinces, all extending equally in length and breadth. In the very center of them is the royal city of *Tunchim*, from which all the kingdom takes name, there the court is kept, and the king resides, being encompassed on all sides by those four provinces, composing a square four times as big as *Cochin-China*. On the east-side of this kingdom is the gulf of *Ainam*, into which falls a great and navigable river that runs down eighteen leagues from the city *Tunchim*, and *Japonese* ships call'd *Jonks* go up it. This river generally overflows twice a year, in *June* and *November*, drowning almost half the city, but it lasts not long. On the south are the frontiers of *Sinuva*, the court of *Cochin-China*, as has been observed already. On the north of it is *China*, without the defence of a wall, the trade and commerce between the *Chineses* and *Tunchineses* being so mutual and constant, that it will not allow of walls and gates shut, as they are against other foreigners. This is the reason that induces the fathers of our society to attempt the entrance into *China* that way, knowing they shall not on this side meet with all those impediments that strangers meet with throughout all the rest of the kingdom, and more especially about *Canton*. Lastly, on the west it borders on the kingdom of *Lai*,

BORRI. *Lai*, into which F. *Alexander Rhodes* of *Avignon* made his way thro' *Cochin-China*; and this kingdom, I am of opinion, cannot but border upon that of *Tibet*, newly discovered; which I am apt to believe, as well by reason of the extent and length of the land of *Tibet* and borders of *Lai*, because by the greatness and compass of these two kingdoms, it seems impossible that any other land should lie betwixt them; as also much more on account of what the same fathers who were there relate of *Tibet*, who report that the farthest province of *Tibet* eastward borders upon, and trades with a people, who sell them raw silk and fine dishes, like those of *China*, and such like commodities, which we know *Tunchim* abounds in, and sell them to the *Laiis*.

The government. As to the government of this kingdom it is hereditary, and ruled as follows: The supreme regal dignity resides in one they call *Buna*; but he of himself does nothing at all, all things being left to his favourite, whom they call *Chiuua*, whose power is so absolute both in peace and war, that he is come by degrees to own no superior; the *Buna* remaining in his royal palace, quite cut off from all management of the publick affairs, satisfied with an exteriour respect due to him as a sort of sacred person, and with the authority of making laws, and confirming all edicts. When the *Chiuua* dies, he always endeavours to have his son succeed him in the government; but for the most part it falls out that the tutors of those sons aspiring themselves to that dignity, endeavour to murder them, and by that means possess themselves of the dignity of *Chiuua*.

Power. The *Chiuua*'s power is so great, that suitable to the bigness of the kingdom, he is able to bring into the field three or four times the number of men as the king of *Cochin-China*, whose army as was said above amounts to 80000 men. Nor is it any difficult matter for the *Chiuua*, as often as he pleases, to raise 300000 armed men or more, because the prime lords of his kingdom, such as among us, dukes, marquesses, and earls, are oblig'd in time of war to furnish them at their own expence. The *Buna*'s strength is not above 40000 men for his guard. Yet he is always own'd as superiour to the *Chiuua* of *Tunchim*, by the king of *Cochin-China*, and by that other *Chiuua*, we observ'd in the first book to be fled into the province bordering upon *China*, tho' these are continually at war against one another; and the king of *Lais* bordering upon *Tunchim*, pays him a certain tribute.

Therefore when we say this crown is hereditary, it is to be understood only in reference to the *buna* whose children always succeed, the royal race being continued in his family. This is as much as I thought fit briefly to say of the kingdom of *Tunchim*, from what I could learn of it till my return into *Europe*. Succession

Since then I have been inform'd, that F. *Julian Baldinotte*, an *Italian* born at *Pistoria* in *Tuscany*, was sent into that kingdom to make some way for the gospel, and arriv'd from *Macao* at the city *Tunchim*, after a month's sail. As for what the said father found in that country, what pass'd between the king and him, the solemnity of his reception, and the first foundation he laid for Christianity, I refer the reader to the account given lately by that father himself; and we are still expecting fresh advices from the other fathers, as F. *Peter Marques* a *Portuguese*, and F. *Alexander Rhodes* of *Avignon*, who we said before had been in *Cochin-China* and are there still gaining Christians. We therefore hope both these kingdoms of *Tunchim* and *Cochin-China*, will soon be united to the flock of the church, acknowledging and giving the due obedience to the universal pastor and vicar of CHRIST our LORD on earth.

The CONCLUSION.

IT is not possible but that such as have least inclination to the discovery of the world, and are most affected to their own countries and homes, must be excited by this short account to desire to see not only the variety but the truth of such strange things, which tho' they be not supernatural, may yet be term'd miracles of nature. Such are those I have said I saw in *Cochin-China*, a land as to its climate and seasons of the year habitable, by reason of the fruitfulness of its soil abounding in provisions, fruit, birds, and beasts, and the sea, in choice and delicious fish; and most healthy, because of the excellent temper of the air, insomuch that those people do not yet know what the plague is. It is rich in gold, silver, silk, *Calambá*, and other things of great value, fit for trade by reason of the ports and resort of all nations: peaceable, because of their loving, generous, and sweet disposition: and lastly secure, not only by the valour and bravery of the *Cochin-Chineses* accounted such by other countries, and their store of arms, and skill in managing them; but even by nature, which has shut it in on the one side by the sea, and on the other by the rocky *Alps*, and uncouth mountains of the *Kemois*. This is that part of the earth call'd *Cochin-China*, which

BORRI. which wants nothing to make it a part of heaven, but that GOD should send thither a great many of his angels, so S. *John Chrysostom* calls apostolical men, and preachers of the gospel. How easily would the faith be spread abroad in this kingdom of *Cochin-China*, where there are not those difficulties which we fathers of the society dispers'd about the *East*, do meet with in other countries; for there is no need here of being disguis'd or conceal'd, these people admitting of all strangers in their kingdom, and being well pleas'd that every one should live in his own religion. Nor is it necessary before preaching to spend many years in studying their letters and hieroglyphicks, as the fathers in *China* do, for here it is enough to learn the language, which as has been said is so easie, that a man may preach in a year. The people are not shy, nor do they shun strangers, as is practis'd in other eastern nations, but make much of them, affect their persons, prize their commodities, and commend their doctrine.

They do not lie under that great impediment for the receiving the grace of the gospel, that is, the sin of sodomy, and others contrary to nature, which is frequent in all the other eastern countries, the very name whereof the *Cochin-Chineses* naturally abhor. In short, these people may very easily be taught the principal mysteries of our holy faith, they, as we have shewn, in a manner adoring but one only GOD, accounting the idols as inferior saints, allowing the immortality of the soul, eternal punishments for the wicked, and bliss for the just, using temples, sacrifices, processions; so that changing the objects, it would be easie to introduce the worship. That there will be no difficulty in making out the mystery of the holy eucharist may appear by the distinction they make between the accidents and substance of the meat they provide for the dead, as has been said above in this second book. All these things inflame the minds of the children of the society, who tho' recluse and shut up in the colleges and provinces of *Europe*, have an ardent desire to convert the world. And tho' many of them put it in practice with the assistance of the holy see apostolick, which with a fatherly care relieves the mission of *Japan*; as also by his catholick majesty king *Philip*, and his council of the *Indies*, who so frequently with incredible bounty supply the *East* and *West-Indies* with ministers of the gospel, yet it is impossible that these two great pillars which support other mighty weights, and bear almost all the world on their shoulders, can sufficiently supply all that daily occurs and is discover'd. I therefore trust in GOD, that his Divine Providence will rouze up some generous soul, inflam'd with the zeal of GOD's honour, to send and maintain some evangelical ministers, who satisfy'd with a religious and poor sustenance, may convey the food of the gospel not only throughout *Cochin-China*, but unto the great kingdom of *Tunchim*, founding a church and christian flock that may compare with the most renowned in the world.

F I N I S.

FISH MARKET of BA

V. II.

Betwixt p. 270. 271.

Betwixt P. 268. 269.

Betwixt pag. 6, 7.

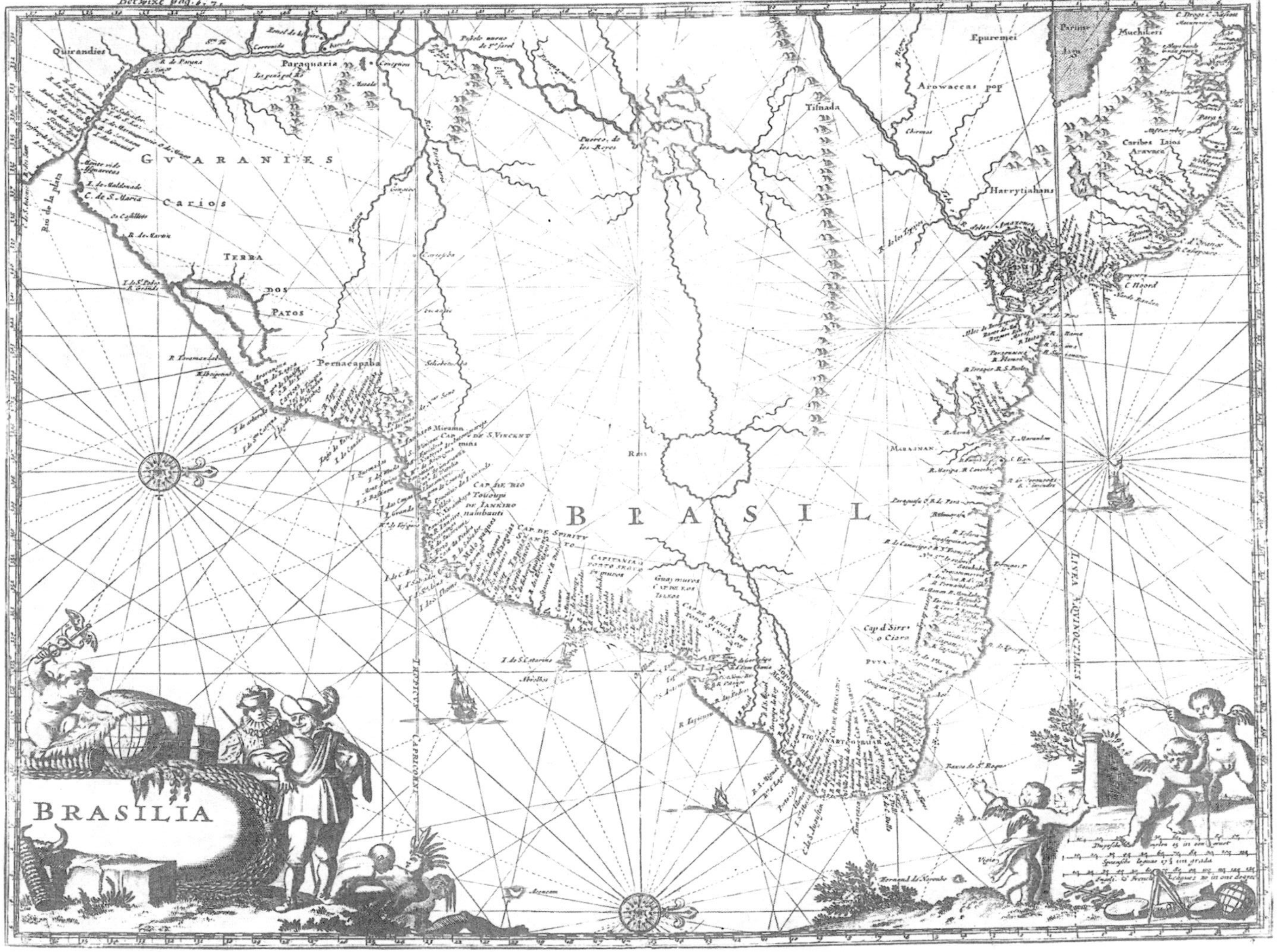

Sugar reeds
Sugar reeds
The Tree and Fruit of Kaschou
Papayen
Indigo
Brasil Pepper
Fruit of Kaschou
Fruit of Paklas

St. ANTHONY

St. VINCENT

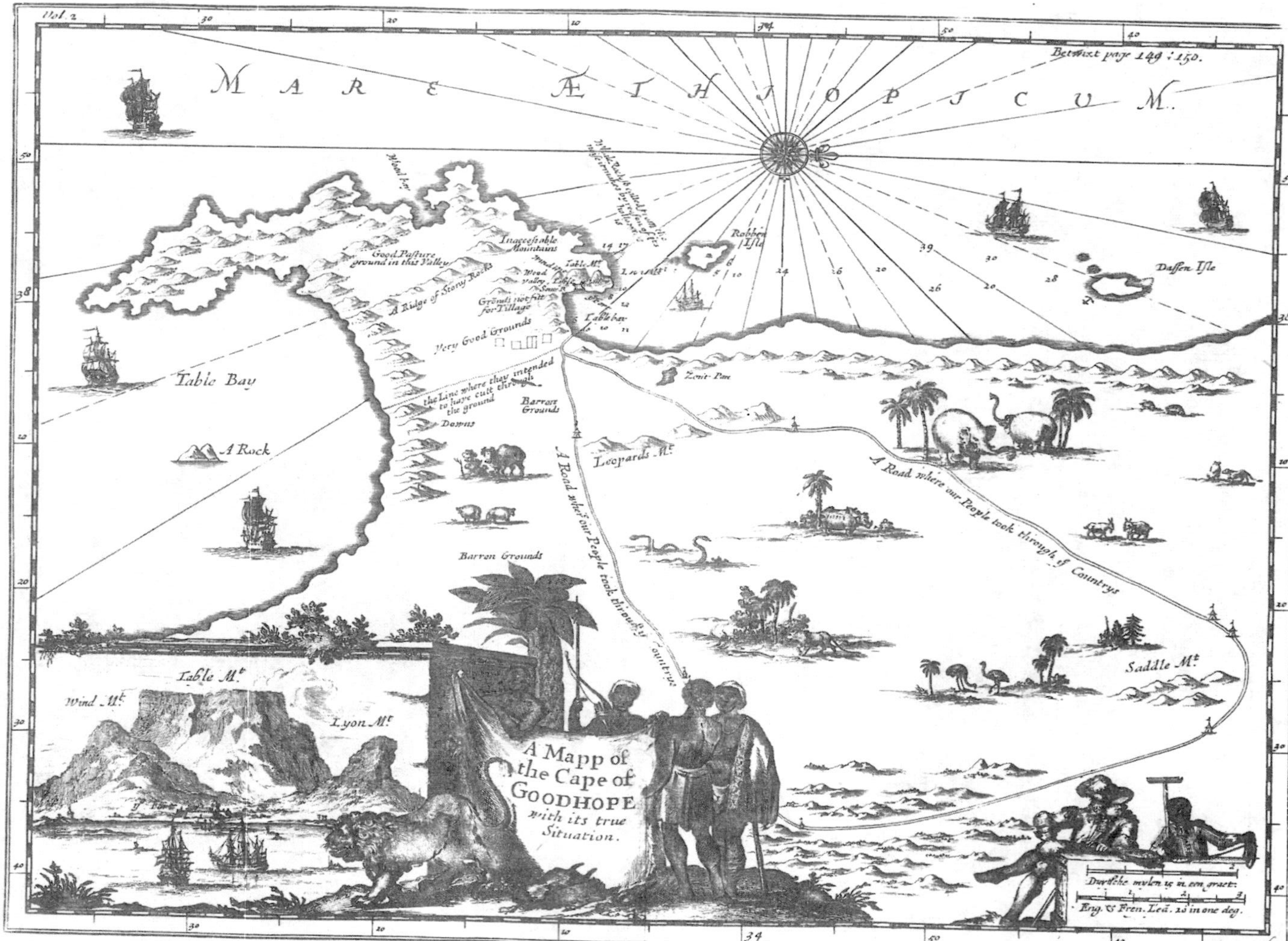
Vol. 2
Betwixt page 149 : 150.
MARE ÆTHIOPICUM.
Good Pasture ground in that Valley
Inaccessable Mountains
Table Mt.
A Ridge of Stony Rocks
Grounds not fit for Tillage
Very Good Grounds
Robben Isle
Dassen Isle
Table Bay
A Rock
the Line where they intended to have cutt through the ground
Barren Grounds
Downs
Zout-Pan
Leopards Mt.
A Road where our People took through ye Countrys
Barron Grounds
Saddle Mt.
Table Mt.
Wind Mt.
Lyon Mt.
A Mapp of the Cape of GOODHOPE with its true Situation.
Dutsche mylen 15 in een graet.
Eng. & Fren. Lea. 20 in one deg.

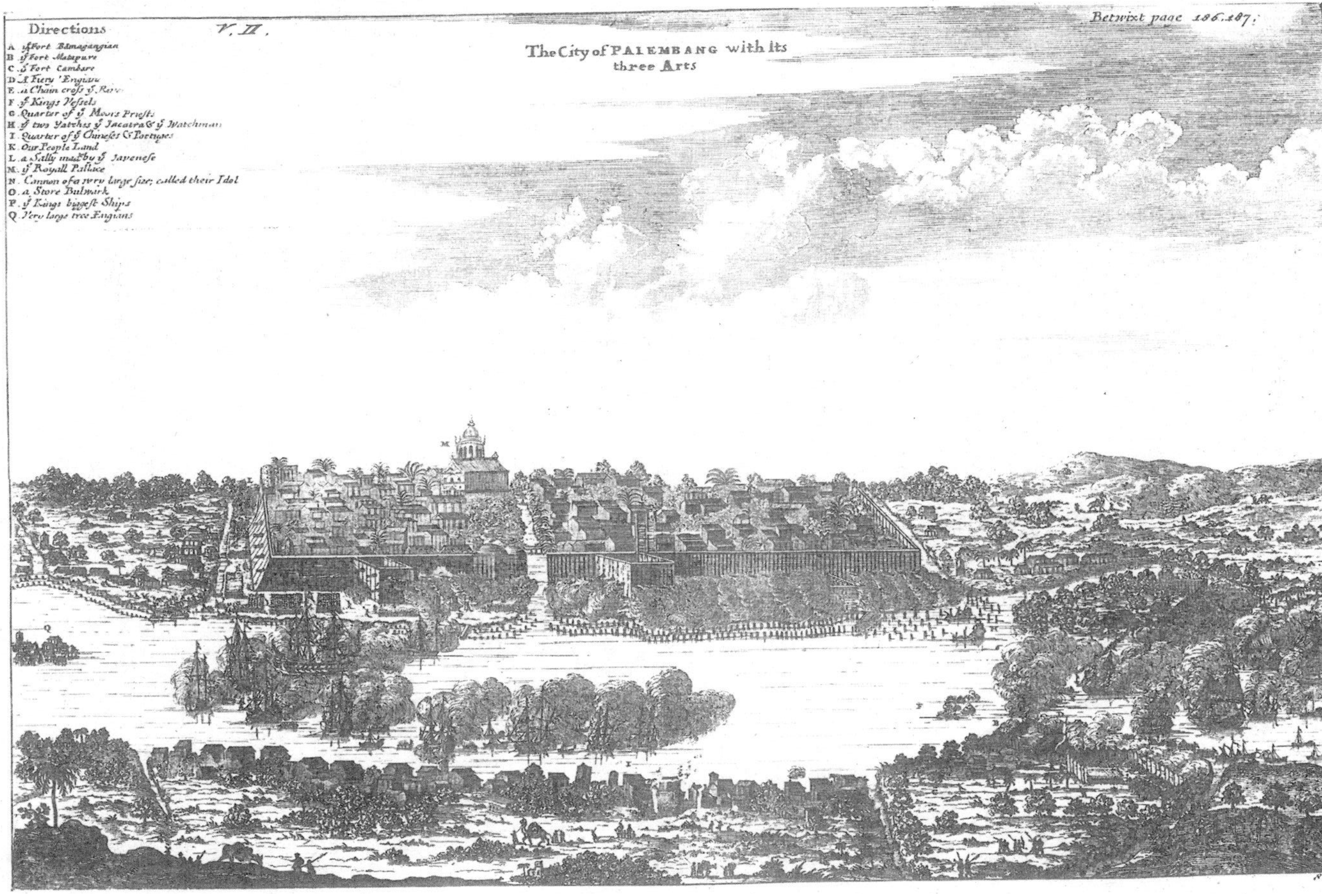
Directions
V. II.
Betwixt page 186.187.
The City of PALEMBANG with its three Arts
A. yᵉ Fort Bamagangian
B. yᵉ Fort Matapure
C. yᵉ Fort Cambare
D. A Fiery Engian
E. a Chain cross yᵉ Rive
F. yᵉ Kings Vessels
G. Quarter of yᵉ Moors Priests
H. yᵉ two Yatches yᵉ Jacatra & yᵉ Watchman
I. Quarter of yᵉ Chineses & Portuges
K. Our People Land
L. a Sally madᵉ by yᵉ Javenese
M. yᵉ Royall Pallace
N. Cannon of a very large size; called their Idol
O. a Store Bulwark
P. yᵉ Kings biggest Ships
Q. Very large tree Engians

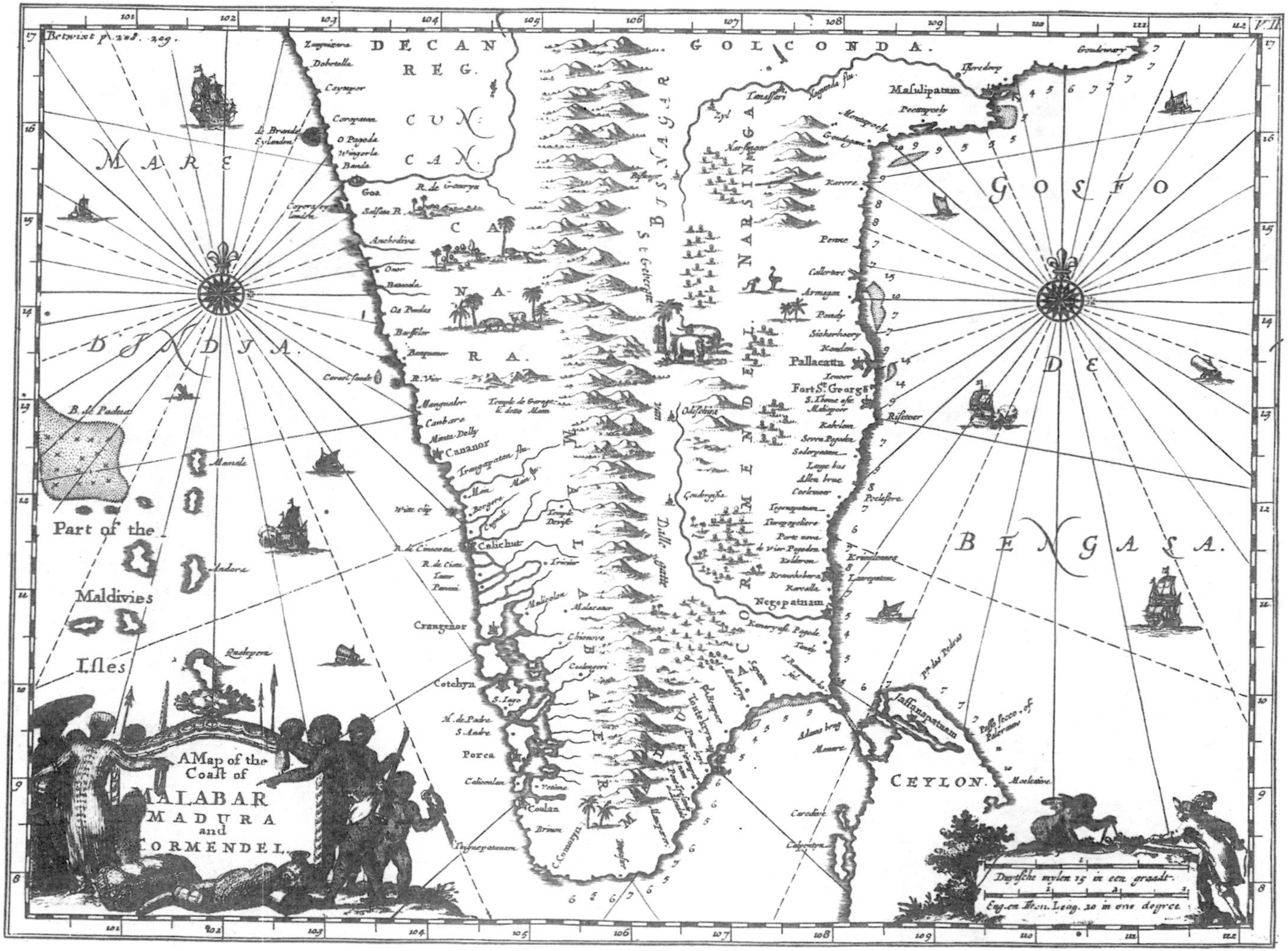
A Map of the Coast of MALABAR MADURA and CORMENDEL
Betwixt p. 248. 249.
DECAN REG.
CUNCAN
GOLCONDA.
BISNAGAR
NARSINGA
CANARA
MALABAR
MARE
DINDIA
GOLFO DE BENGALA.
CEYLON.
Part of the Maldivies Isles
Masulipatam
Goa
Calichut
Cotchyn
Cananor
Pallacatta
Fort St. Georg
Negepatnam
Jaffanapatnam
Crangenor
Porca
Coulan
Dutysche mylen 15 in een graadt.
Eng. en Fran. Leag. 20 in one degree.

V. II

Betwixt Pag. 213.214.

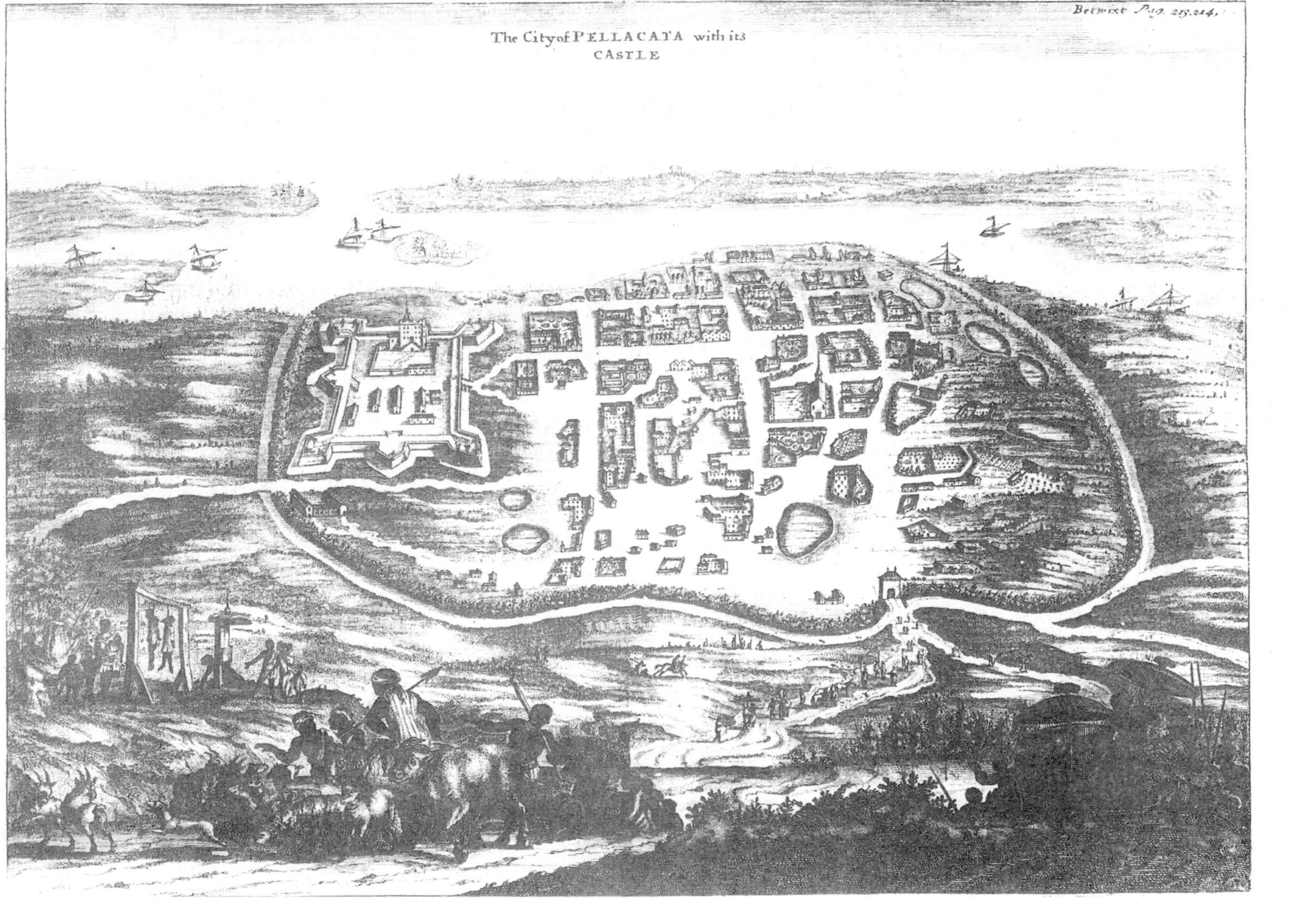

Betwixt p. 220. 221. V. II.

12.

V. II.

A Branch with Cocoa Nuts

Betwixt pag. 260. 261.

Betwixt p. 204. 265

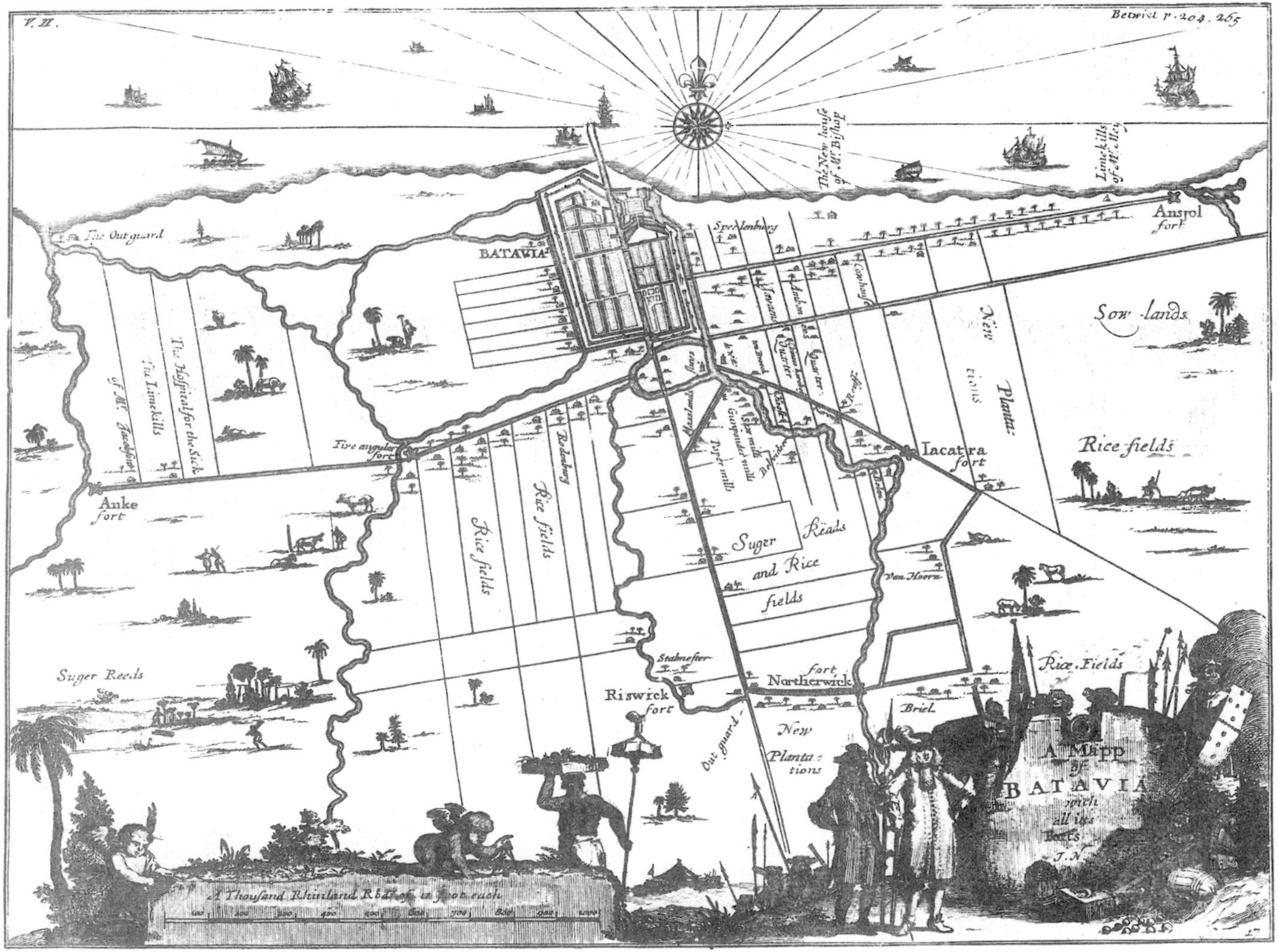

17

V. II

Betwixt pag. 206. 207

V. II.

18

Betwixt page 266. 267.

Betwixt p. 260. 207

Betwixt p. 268, 269.

GOVERNOURS HOUSE
WITHIN THE CASTLE

V. II. Betwixt pag. 288, 289.

20

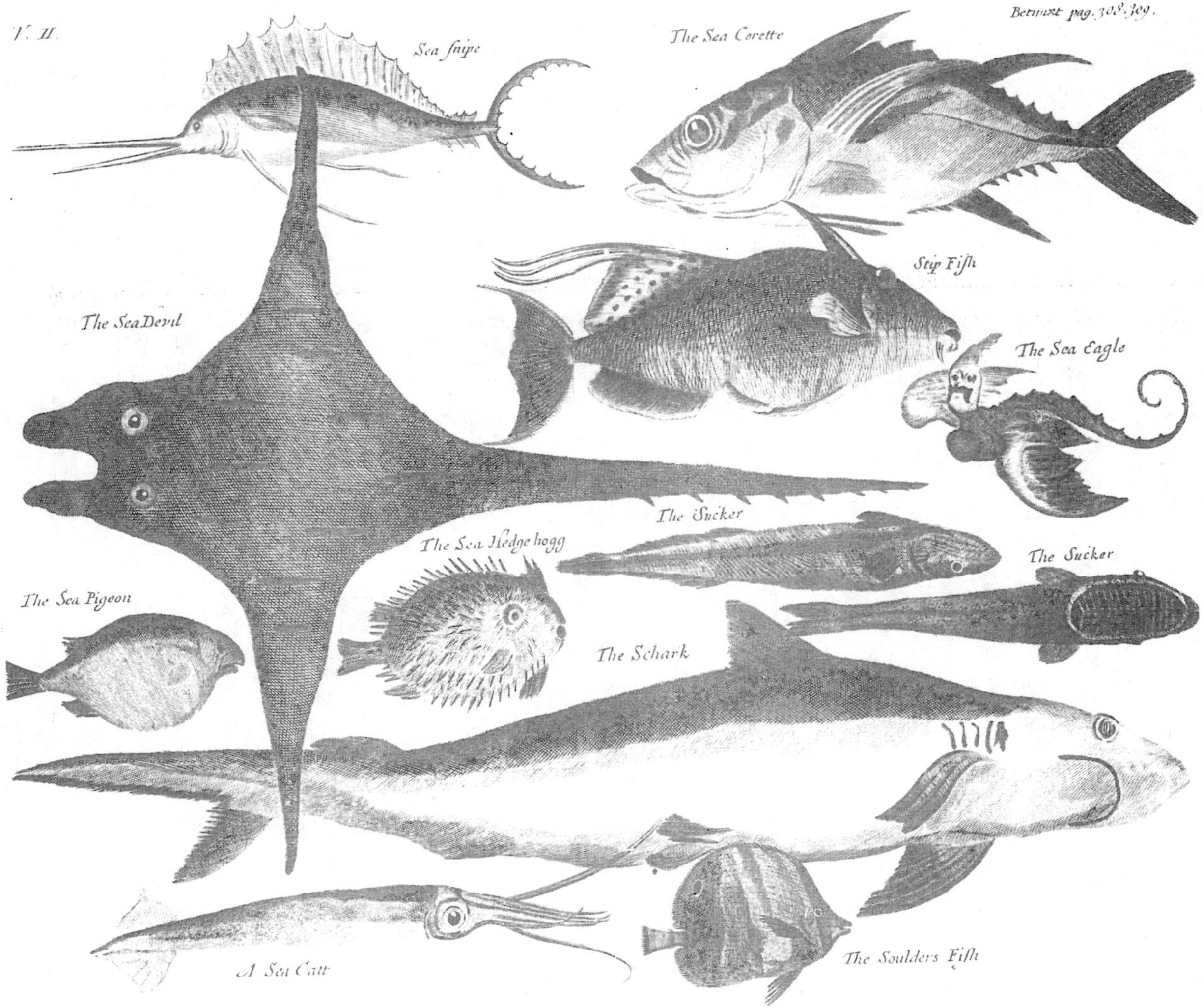
V. II.
Betwixt pag. 308, 309.
Sea snipe
The Sea Corette
Stip Fish
The Sea Devil
The Sea Eagle
The Sucker
The Sucker
The Sea Hedge hogg
The Sea Pigeon
The Schark
A Sea Catt
The Soulders Fish

V. II. Betwixt Pag. 286. 287.

Sagou Tree
Huntsmans Tree
Blimbing
Dogs Tongue
Pepper Tree
Durions
Sagou Fruit
Blimbing Fruit

Betwixt pag. 304. 305.

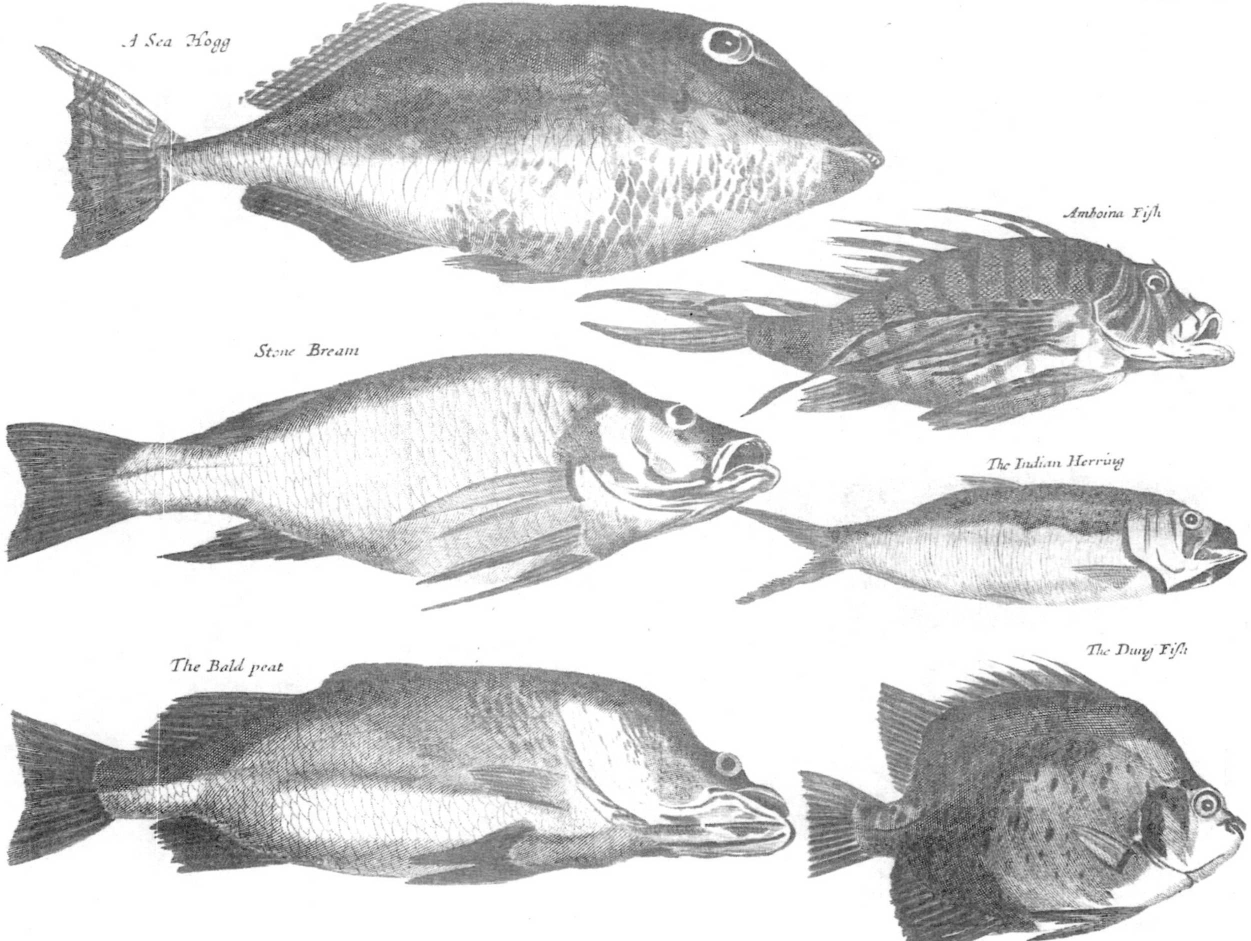

40

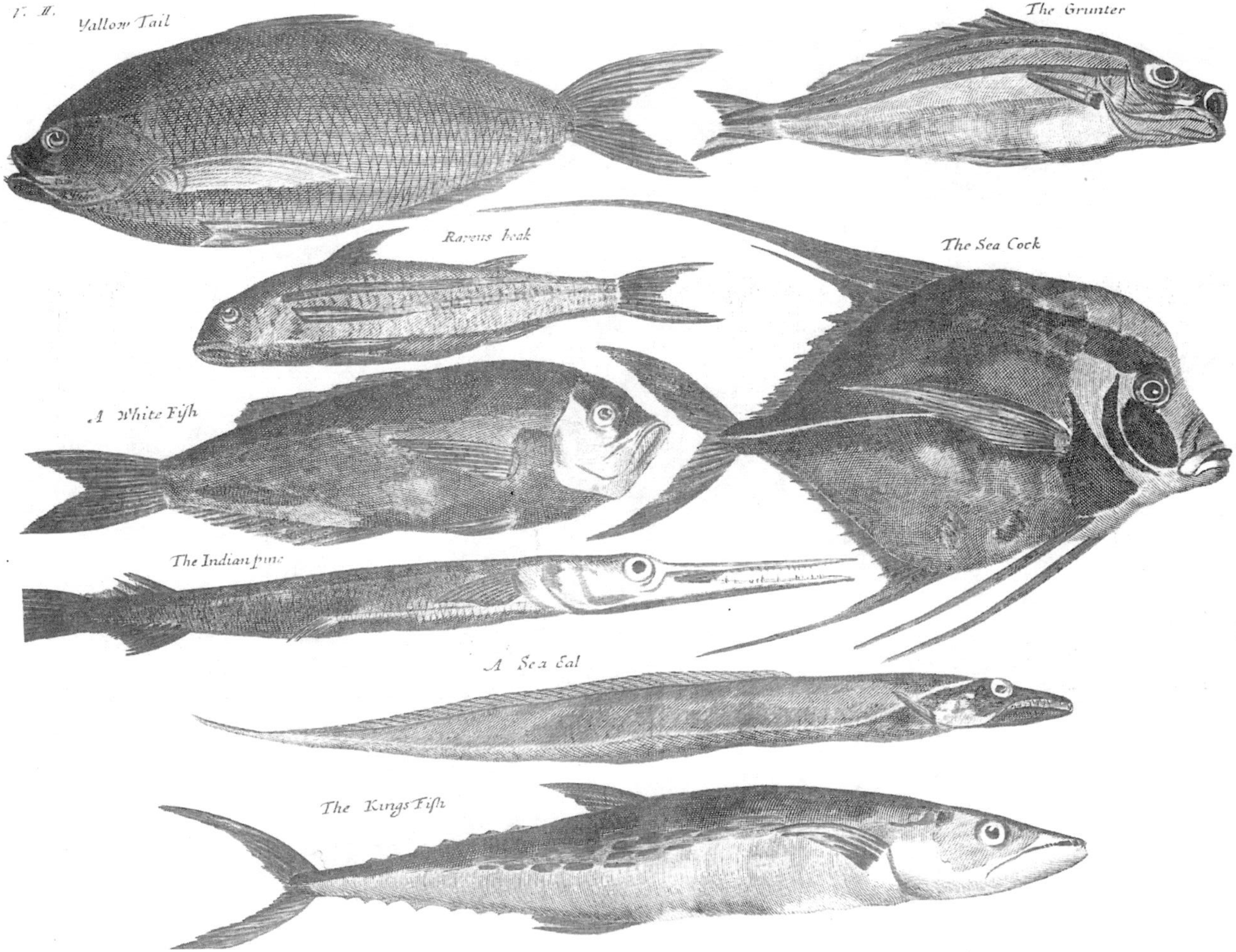
V. II.
Yallow Tail
The Grunter
Raven's beak
The Sea Cock
A White Fish
The Indian pipe
A Sea Eal
The Kings Fish

 Betwixt pag. 306.307.

Betwixt pag. 310 311

V. II.

N°

A Mestice Woman

Betwixt p. 214, 215. V. II.

Negros Playing upon Kalabasses

THE INDEX TO THE Second Volume.

A.

B.

Index *to the* Second Volume.

Columbus

Index *to the* Second *Volume.*

Dutch

Index to the Second Volume.

Index *to the Second Volume.*

Indian

Magnus

N.